D1244777

The Librarian's Guide to Public Records

The Complete State, County & Courthouse Locator

2000 Edition

©2000 by BRB Publications Inc
1971 East Fifth Street, Suite 101
Tempe, AZ 85281
(800) 929-3811
www.brbpub.com

The Librarian's Guide to Public Records
The Complete State, County, & Courthouse Locator
2000 Edition

©2000 by BRB Publications Inc.
1971 East Fifth Street, Suite 101
Tempe, AZ 85281
(800) 929-3811

ISBN 1-889150-56-7
Cover Design by Robin Fox & Associates
Edited by Michael L. Sankey, James R. Flowers Jr., and Peter J. Weber

Cataloging-in-Publication Data

The librarian's guide to public records : the
   complete state, county, and courthouse locator /
      [edited by Michael L. Sankey & James R. Flowers,
      Jr.]. -- 2000 [4th] ed.

      p. ; cm. -- (Public record research library)

      ISBN: 1-889150-56-7

      1. Public records--United States--Information
   services--Directories. I. Sankey, Michael L.,
   1949- II. Flowers, James Robert, 1973-
   III. Series.

   JK468.P76L53 2000   352'.387'02573
                      QBI99-1838

Contents

Introduction

Complex and Mysterious?

> *The words "Public Records" often convey a complex, almost mysterious source of information that is perceived as difficult to access, hard to decipher and likely to be of interest only to private investigators and reporters. This view could not be further from the truth!*
>
> *Indeed, the use of current public records is one of the fundamental pillars of our democratic society.*

The Information Trail

Have you ever—

- applied for a job?
- purchased a home or a vehicle?
- applied for a credit card?
- looked into your "family tree?"
- or renewed your driver's license?

If so, YOU have become part of the "public record information paper trail!"

Modern society has become extremely dependent on information. Information is, indeed, the life load of most business and personal interaction. Government and private industry require record keeping to regulate, license and hire/fire. Individuals need public information for managing personal affairs and meeting one's responsibilities as citizens. Nearly all individuals and entities create a **trail of information** that is a **history of daily life**.

You could say that the trail starts with a birth certificate, a Social Security Number or articles of incorporation. The trail extends past the death certificate or record of dissolution into, virtually, infinite time. These many records—some accessible, some accessible with restrictions, and some inaccessible—create and embellish an identity.

Your Access to Over 20,000 Government Agencies

Herein, we will examine these paper trails that begin or maintained at the federal, state, county, and in certain instances, the city & town level. The *Librarian's Guide* is especially useful for these applications:

Background Searching and Investigation

Pre-Employment Verification and Tenant Background Checking

Locating People

Locating Assets

Legal Research

The Librarian's Guide to Public Records reveals where records are kept, outlines the access requirements and gives searching hints, tells which agencies are online. Over 20,000 government agencies are profiled so you can explore the depths of the public record industry.

Public records are meant to be used for the benefit of society. As a member of the public, you or someone in authority is entitled to review the public records held and established by government agencies. Whether you are a business owner, a reporter, an investigator, or even a father trying to check on your daughter's first date, you can access public records to meet your needs.

Equipped with the information contained in these pages, you can find the facts, gain access to the information you need and even track your own "information trail!"

Special Note From the Editors

The Librarian's Guide to Public Records represents thousands of hours of research right up to the day of printing.

For those of you who need to know more or need to have this information constantly updated, we recommend three expanded versions of this product. *The Public Records Research System* (PRRS) is available on CD-ROM and is updated quarterly. The looseleaf version (2,400 pages) of PRRS is updated every six months. Also, there is an annual compendium called *The Sourcebook to Public Record Information*. BRB Publications is 100% devoted to the understanding of public records.

How This Book is Organized

General Layout

The *Librarian's Guide* is organized into three Sections--

♦ Introduction, including the Public Record Primer

♦ Individual State Chapters

♦ Additional Information (free Internet sites, private vendors, and useful government web sites).

The Public Record Primer

The purpose of this section is to assist the reader in knowing *how to search* and *where categories of records can be found.* An important part of this section is the discussion of privacy issues including public information vs. personal information and how records enter the public domain.

The Primer contains many searching hints and is an excellent overall source of information that will especially help those not familiar with searching government records.

The State Chapters

The individual state chapters in the *Librarian's Guide* have been compiled into an easy to use format. Six sub-chapters or directories are presented in this order:

1. State Public Record Agencies

2. Federal Courts (US District and Bankruptcy)

3. County Courts

4. County Recorder Offices

Public Records Unveiled

Definition of Public Records

The strict **definition** of **public records** is—

> *"Those records maintained by government agencies that are open without restriction to public inspection, either by statute or by tradition."*

If access to a record that is held by a government agency is restricted in some way, then it is not a public record.

Accessibility Paradox

Adding to the mystique of government records is the accessibility paradox. For example, in some states a specific category of records is severely restricted, and therefore those records are not "public," while the very same category of records may be 100% open in other states. Among these categories are criminal histories, vehicle ownership records and worker's compensation records.

At times, you will see the following box printed on pages throughout the *Librarian's Guide*. We are not trying to fill up space. As your public record searching takes you from state-to-state, this is the one important adage to keep in mind.

> "Just because records are maintained in a certain way in your state or county, do not assume that any other county or state does things the same way you are used to."

Public vs. Private vs. Personal

Before reading further, let's define types of records held by government or by private industry. Of course, not all information about a company or individual is public. The boundaries between public and private information are not well understood, and continually undergo intense scrutiny. The following is an introduction to the subject from a viewpoint of a professional record searcher.

Public Record

Public records are records of **incidents** or **actions** filed or recorded with a government agency for the purpose of notifying others about the matter—the "public." The **deed** to your house recorded at the county recorder's office is a public record—it is a legal requirement that you record it with the county recorder. Anyone requiring details about your property may review or copy the documents.

Public Information

Your **telephone listing** in the phone book is public information; that is, you freely furnished the information to ease the flow of commercial and private communications.

Personal Information

Any information about a person or business that the person or business might consider private and confidential in nature, such as your **Social Security Number**, is personal information. Such information will remain private to a limited extent unless it is disclosed to some outside entity that could make it public. **Personal information may be found in either public records or in public information.**

How Personal Information Enters the Public Domain

Many people confuse the three categories above, lump them into one and wonder how "big brother" accumulated so much information about them. Therefore, these distinctions are important. The reality is that **much of this information is given willingly**.

Actually, there are two ways that personal information can enter the public domain—statutory and voluntary. In a **voluntary** transaction, you **share** personal information of your own free will. In a **statutory** transaction, you **disclose** personal information because the law requires you to.

The confusion of terms used today feeds the increasing conflict between privacy advocates and commercial interests. This, in turn, is driving legislation towards more and more **restrictions** on the **dissemination of personal information**—the same personal information which, in fact, is willingly shared by most people and companies in order to participate in our market economy.

Where Public Records are Held

There are two places you can find public records—

♦   at a government agency

♦   within the database of a private company

Government agencies keep or maintain records in a variety of ways. While many state agencies and highly populated county agencies are computerized, many still use microfiche, microfilm, and paper storage of files and indexes. Agencies that have converted to computer will not necessarily place complete file records on their system; they are more apt to include only an index, pointer or summary data to the files.

Private enterprises develop their databases in one of two ways: they buy the records in bulk from government agencies; or they send personnel to the agencies and compile this information by using a copy machine or keying information into a laptop computer. The database is then available for internal use or for resale purposes. An example of such a company is *Superior Information* (800 848-0489). Superior maintains a very comprehensive database of civil judgments, tax liens, Uniform Commercial Code filings and bankruptcy data for the Mid-Atlantic States.

The Common Methods Used to Access Public Records

The following is a look at the various methods available to access public records.

Visit in Person

This is easy if you live close by. Many courthouses and recorders offices have free access terminals open to the public. Certain records, such as corporate or UCC records are generally found at the Secretary of State, can be viewed or pulled for free, but will incur a fee for copies. Other records may require special paperwork like a signed release or fingerprints before the agency will respond to a request. A signed release is a common requirement for accessing motor vehicle and criminal records.

Mail, Fax, or Telephone

Although some agencies permit phone or fax requests, the majority of agencies prefer mail requests. Some agencies consider fax requesting an expedited service that incurs higher fees. Agencies that permit telephone requests may merely answer "Yes" or "No" to questions such as "Does John Doe have a boat registered in his name?" We have indicated when telephone and fax requesting is available, as well as the extent of the service.

Online and the Internet

Commercial online access of public records is much more prevalent at the state level compared to the county level. Many agencies, such as DMVs, make the information available to pre-approved, high volume, ongoing accounts. Typically these commercial accounts involve fees and a specified, minimum amount of usage.

The Internet may serve as an alternative dial-up entry to the commercial accounts described above. Also, there is a definite trend of certain agencies posting public record data on the Internet for free. Three examples are the Secretary of State offices (whose records include corporation, UCC and tax liens) the county/city tax assessor offices (whose records reveal property ownership) and the federal court systems (whose case includes bankruptcy, civil and criminal proceedings). Usually this information is limited to name indexes and summary data, rather than complete file information. In addition, there are a growing number of occupational licensing agencies posting their membership lists on the net (although addresses and phone numbers of the licensed individuals typically are not listed).

Also, the Internet is a good place to find *general* information about government agencies. Many web sites enable one to download, read and/or print current forms, policies and regulations.

Hire Someone Else

As mentioned above, one place to access public records is from a private company. The companies must comply with state and federal laws, so if the government agency will not a release a record, chances are a private company will not either. There are a variety of types of companies that can be hired to perform record searches. An excellent source to find the right vendor for a particular need is www.publicrecordsources.com.

Bulk or Database Purchases

Many agencies offer programs to purchase all or parts of their database for statistical or commercial purposes. The restrictions vary widely from state to state even within the same record type or category. Typically, records are available (to those who qualify) in the following media types; magnetic tape, disk, paper printouts, labels, disks, microfiche and/or microfilm. Throughout the state chapters, we have indicated where these bulk purchases are available, to whom, and for what purposes as well as the costs involved.

Using the Freedom of Information Act and Other Acts

The Federal Freedom of Information Act has bearing on state, county or local government agencies. These agencies are subject to that state's individual act. The record categories profiled in this book virtually have no need for the use of such an act. However, if you are trying to obtain records from agencies beyond the scope of this book, there are many useful Internet sites that will give you the information you need to complete such a request. We can recommend these sites:

www.epic.org/open_gov/rights.html

http://spj.org/foia

Public Record & Public Information Categories

The following descriptions of the record categories fall into our definitions of either "public records" or "public information."

In considering these definitions, keep the following points in mind:

◆ Very little government record information is truly open to the public. Even presumably harmless information is subject to restrictions somewhere in the US. Likewise items that you believe should be highly confidential are probably considered "public information" in one or more states.

◆ Just because your state or county has certain rules, regulations and practices regarding the accessibility and content of public records does not mean that any other state or county follows the same rules.

Business Records

Corporation Records (found at the state level)

Checking to see if a corporation is incorporated is considered a **"status check."** The information that results from a status check typically includes the date of incorporation, status, type, registered agent and, sometimes, officers or directors. This is a good way to find the start of a paper trail and/or to find affiliates of the subject of your search. Some states permit status checks over the telephone.

If available, articles of incorporation (or amendments to them) as well as copies of annual reports may also provide useful information about a business or business owner. However, corporate records may *not* be a good source for a business address because most states allow corporations to use a registered agent as their address for service of process.

Partnership Records (found at the state level)

Some state statutes require registration of certain kinds of partnerships at the state level. Sometimes, these partner names and addresses may be available from the same office that handles corporation records. Some states have a department created specifically to administer limited partnerships and the records associated with them. These filings provide a wealth of information about other partners. Such information can be used to uncover other businesses that may be registered as well.

Limited Liability Companies (found at state level)

A newer form of business entity, that looks like a corporation but has the favorable tax characteristics of a partnership, is known as the Limited Liability Company (LLC). An LLC is legal in most every state. An offspring of this, which some states now permit, is the Limited Liability Partnership (LLP).

Trademark & Trade Name (found at state and county levels)

States will not let two entities use the same (or close to the same) name or trademark, as such they must be registered. Furthermore, "trade names" and "trademarks" are relative terms. A trademark may be known as a "service mark." Trade names may be referred to as "fictitious names," "assumed names," or "DBAs."

Typically, the agency that oversees corporation records usually maintains the files for trademarks and/or trade names. Most states will allow verbal status checks of names or worded marks. Some states will administer "fictitious names" at the state level while county agencies administer "trade names," or vice versa.

Sales Tax Registrations (found at state level)

Any individual or firm that sells applicable goods or services to the end user of the product or service, is required to register with the appropriate state agency. Such registration is necessary to collect applicable sales tax on the goods and services, and to ensure remittance of those taxes to the state.

45 states collect some sort of sales tax on a variety of goods and services. Of these, 38 will at the very least confirm that a tax permit exists. Each sales tax registrant is given a special state tax permit number, which may be called by various names, including tax ID number or seller's permit number. These numbers are not to be confused with the federal employer identification number.

SEC & Other Financial Data

The Securities and Exchange Commission is the public repository for information about publicly held companies, which are required to share their material facts with existing and prospective stockholders.

Private companies, on the other hand, are not subject to public scrutiny, so their financial information is public information only to the extent that the company itself decides to disclose information.

Lien and Security Interest Records

Uniform Commercial Code (found at state and county or city levels)

All 50 states and the District of Columbia have passed a version of the model Uniform Commercial Code (UCC). Article 9 of this code covers security interests in personal property. As such, UCC filings are used in financing transactions such as equipment loans, leases, inventory loans, and accounts receivable financing. The Code allows other possible lenders to be notified that certain assets belonging to a debtor are being used to secure a loan or lease. *Therefore, examining UCC filings is one way to find bank accounts, security interests, financiers, and assets.*

Of the 7.5 million new UCC financing statements filed annually, 2.5 million are filed at the state level; 5 million are filed at the local level within the states. Although there are significant variations among state statutes, the state level is usually a good starting place to uncover liens filed against an individual or business.

Tax Liens (found at state and county or city levels)

The federal government and every state have some sort of taxes, such as those associated with sales, income, withholding, unemployment, and/or personal property. When these taxes go unpaid, the appropriate state agency can file a lien on the real or personal property of the subject. *Normally, the state agency that maintains UCC records also maintains tax liens.*

Individuals vs. Businesses

Tax liens filed against individuals are frequently maintained at separate locations from those liens filed against businesses. For example, a large number of states require liens filed against businesses to be filed at a central state location (i.e., Secretary of State's office) and liens against individuals to be filed at the county level (i.e., Recorder, Register of Deeds, Clerk of Court, etc.).

State vs. Federal Liens

Liens for a company may not all be filed in the same location. A federal tax lien will not necessarily be recorded at the same location/jurisdiction as a lien filed by the state.. This holds true for both individual liens and as well as business liens filed against personal property. Typically, state tax liens on personal property will be found where UCCs are filed. *Tax liens on real property will be found where real property deeds are recorded*, with few exceptions. Unsatisfied state and federal tax liens may be renewed if prescribed by individual state statutes. However, once satisfied, the time the record will remain in the repository before removal varies by jurisdiction.

Real Estate and Tax Assessor (found at county and local levels)

Traditionally, real estate records are public so that everyone can know who owns what property. Liens on real estate must be public so a buyer knows all the facts. The county (or parish) recorder's office is the source. However, many private companies purchase entire county record databases and create their own database for commercial purposes.

This category of public record is perhaps the fastest growing in regards to becoming free over the Internet. We have indicated all the recorder offices that offer **name queries;** many more offer location searches (using maps and parcel numbers to locate an address).

Bankruptcies (found at federal court level)

This entails case information about people and businesses that have filed for protection under the bankruptcy laws of the United States. Only federal courts handle bankruptcy cases. Some private companies compile databases with names and dates. Many types of financial records maintained by government agencies are considered public records; bankruptcy records, unlike some other court records, are in this class of fully open court records.

Important Individual Records

Criminal Records (found at state level, county courts, and federal courts)

Every state has a central repository of major misdemeanor, felony arrest records and convictions. States submit criminal record activity to the National Crime Information Center (which is not open to the public). Of those states that *will* release records to the public, many require fingerprints or signed release forms. The information that *could be* disclosed on the report includes the arrest record, criminal charges, fines, sentencing and incarceration information.

Not all states open their criminal records to the public. In this case, the best places to search for criminal record activity is at the city or county level with the county or district court clerk. Many of these searches can be done with a phone call.

Litigation and Civil Judgments (found at county, local, and federal courts)

Actions under federal laws are found at US District Courts. Actions under state laws are found within the state court system at the county level. Municipalities also have courts. Litigation and judgment information is often collected by commercial database vendors. For more information, please refer to the **Searching County Court Records** chapter.

Motor Vehicle Records

Driver History Records (found at state level; on occasion, at county level)
The retrieval industry often refers to driving records as "MVRs." Typical information on an MVR might include full name, address, Social Security Number, physical description and date of birth as well as the actual driving history. Also, the license type, restrictions and/or endorsements can provide background data on an individual.

In recent years there have been major changes regarding the release of motor vehicle data to the public. This is the result of the Driver's Privacy Protection Act (DPPA). Thus, some states differentiate between casual requesters and permissible users; some states only release to permissible users. If a driver has "opted-out" in a state that allows for such a thing, that driver's personal information will not be released to a casual requester. In some states, personal information is never released, even if the requester is classified as permissible.

Ironically, as states are moving towards making data readily available electronically, they are also closing the door to many users. Pay particular attention to the restriction requirements mentioned in this category throughout this publication. Also, we strongly urge those interested in further information about either driver or vehicle records to obtain BRB Publication's *The MVR Book*.

Vehicle & Vessel Ownership, Registration, VINs, Titles, and Liens (found at state and, on occasion, at county level)

State repositories of vehicle/vessel registration and ownership records encompass a wide range of publicly accessible data. Generally, you submit a name to uncover vehicle(s) owned, or you submit vehicle information to learn a name and address. The laws and policies passed to comply with the DPPA vary widely from state to state with regard to the release of these records for investigative purposes. Nonetheless, state vehicle and owner databases can be an excellent source for asset and lien data, commercial mailing lists (when permissible) and vehicle recall uses.

Vehicle and vessel records may not be held by the same state agency that maintains driver records. It is important to note that if the DMV maintains the records, the access policies fall under the same DPPA provisions as vehicle records. In those 36 states where the DMV is not involved (and thus, compliance with DPPA is not a factor) restrictions to access are not nearly as strict.

Some states do not issue titles (only registrations), others require a title if a vessel is a certain length or propelled by a certain size motor or by sail. All states require some form of registration.

Accident Reports (found at state level or local level)

The State Police or Department of Public Safety usually maintains accident reports. For the purposes of this publication, "accident records" are those that are prepared by the investigating officer. Copies of a *citizen's* accident report are not usually available to the public and are not mentioned here. Typical information found on a state accident report includes drivers' addresses and license numbers as well as a description of the incident. Accidents investigated by local officials and accidents where the damage does not exceed the state reporting limit, are not available from state agencies.

Occupational Licensing & Business Registration (found at state boards)

Occupational licenses and business registrations contain a plethora of information readily available from various state agencies. A common reason to call these agencies is to corroborate professional or industry credentials. Often, a telephone call to the agency may secure an address and phone number.

GED Records (found at state level)

By contacting the state offices that oversee GED Records, one can verify whether someone truly received GED certificate for the high school education equivalency. These records are useful for pre-employment screening or background checking purposes. Most states will verify over the phone the existence of a GED certificate. Many even offer copies of transcripts free-of-charge. When doing a record search, you must know the name of the student at the time of the test and a general idea of the year and test location. GED Records are *not* very useful when trying to locate an individual.

Hunting & Fishing Licenses (found at state, county and local levels)

We have singled out one type of state license that merits a closer look. When trying to locate an individual, state hunting and fishing license information can be very informative. Currently 37 states maintain a central repository of fishing and/or hunting license records that may be accessed in some capacity by the public. Although some of these record repositories are literally "in boxes in the basement," more and more are becoming computerized.

Effects of Cooperative State-Federal Program on Hunting/Fishing License Databases

In 1992, the US Fish and Wildlife Service implemented a Migratory Bird Harvest Information Program which will change state hunting licensing procedures. Under this cooperative program, which will help biologists better manage the Nation's migratory bird populations, hunters will provide their names and addresses when buying state licenses to hunt migratory birds. The states must provide the name and address information to the US Fish and Wildlife Service on a timely basis. In 1997, 23 states participated in the program. All states except Hawaii are scheduled to participate in 1998. Each state will have several options for how they provide the US Fish and Wildlife Service with the names and address of their hunters.

The policy of the Service is to use the names and addresses only for conducting hunter surveys. All records of hunters' names and addresses will be deleted after the surveys, and no permanent record would be maintained.

However, since the states collect these names and addresses under state authority, the state may decide not to delete the information. Therefore, as more states begin to maintain new automated record repositories, the possible release of these records, by the states, for investigative or search purposes will depend on individual "state sunshine laws." For more information about the program, contact the Office of Migratory Bird Management in Laurel, MD at 301-497-5980.

Workers' Compensation Records (found at state level)

Researching at state workers' compensation boards is generally limited to determining if an employee has filed a claim and/or obtaining copies of the claim records themselves. With the passage of the Americans with Disabilities Act (ADA) in the early 1990s, pre-employment screening using information from workers' compensation boards has been virtually eliminated. However, *a review of workers' compensation histories may be conducted after a conditional job offer has been made* and when medical information is reviewed. The legality of performing this review is subject to individual state statutes, which vary widely.

Voter Registration (found at state and county levels)

Every state has a central election agency or commission, and most have a central repository of voter information. The degree or level of accessibility to these records varies widely from state to state. Over half of the states will sell portions of the registered voter database, but only ten states permit individual searching by name. Most states only allow access for political purposes such as "Get Out the Vote" campaigns or compilation of campaign contribution lists.

Voting Registration Records are a good place to find addresses and voting history. Nearly every state blocks the release of Social Security Numbers and telephone numbers found on these records.

Vital Records: Birth, Death, Marriage, and Divorce Records (found at state and county levels)

Copies of vital record certificates are needed for a variety of reasons—social security, jobs, passports, family history, litigation, lost heir searching, proof of identity, etc. Most states understand the urgency of these requests, and many offer an expedited service. *A number of states will even take requests over the phone if you use a credit card.* Searchers must also be aware that in many instances certain vital records are *not* kept at the state level. The searcher must then turn to city and county record repositories to find the information needed.

Most states offer expedited fax ordering, requiring the use of a credit card, through the services of an outside vendor known as VitalChek. This independent company maintains individual fax lines at each state office they service. Whether it is behind the scenes or not, ordering vital records by fax typically involves VitalChek in some manner.

Older vital records may be found in the state archives. Another source of historical vital record information is The Family History Library of the Mormon Church (located at 35 North West Temple, Salt Lake City 84150). They have millions of microfilmed records from church and civil registers from all over the world.

Additional Information Sources Worth Mentioning

State Legislation and Regulations

Telephone numbers, costs and procedures for obtaining copies of passed and pending bills are listed under the heading "Legislation." Many states now offer Internet access (all www addresses are listed) to the text of bills. Notwithstanding federal guidelines, the state legislatures and legislators control the policies and provisions for the release of state held information. Every year there is a multitude of bills introduced in state legislatures that would, if passed, create major changes in the access and retrieval of records and personal information. —

Laws and regulations at all levels of government. The state legislative branches make this information available, although older records are harder to find. Some private companies market regulatory books and CD-ROMs.

Education and Employment

Information about an individual's schooling, training, education, and jobs is important to any employer. Learning institutions maintain their own records of attendance, completion and degree/certification granted. Employers will confirm certain information about former employees. This is an example of private information that becomes public by voluntary disclosure. As part of your credit record, this information would be considered restricted. If, however, you disclose this information to Who's Who, or to a credit card company, it becomes public information.

Environmental

Information about hazards to the environment is critical. There is little tradition and less law regarding how open or restricted information is at the state and local (recorder's office) levels. Most information on hazardous materials, soil composition, even OSHA inspection reports is public record.

Medical

Medical record Information about an individual's medical status and history are summarized in various repositories which are accessible only to authorized insurance and other private company employees. Medical information is neither public information nor closed record. Like credit information, it is not meant to be shared with anyone, unless you give authorization. Each branch maintains its own records. Much of this, such as years of service and rank, is open public record. However, some details in the file of an individual may be subject to restrictions on access—approval by the subject may be required

Social Security Numbers

There is a persistent myth that a Social Security Number is private information. The truth is individuals gave up the privacy of that number by writing it on a voter registration form, using it a driver's license number, or any of a myriad of other voluntary disclosures made over the years. It is probable that a good researcher can find the Social Security Number of anyone (along with at least an approximate birth date) with ease.

Addresses & Phone Numbers

This is basic locator information about a person or organization and is a category of information that may be obtained from both government and private sources. Even though you have an unlisted telephone number, anyone can still find you if you have listed your number on, for example, a voter registration card or magazine subscription form. The most elementary of public information categories, addresses and telephone numbers are no longer considered unrestricted information by some people.

Credit Information

These are records derived from financial transactions of people or businesses. **Private companies maintain this information; government only regulates access.** Certain credit information about individuals is restricted by law, such as the Fair Credit Reporting Act, at the federal level and by even more restrictive laws in many states. Credit information about businesses is not restricted by law and is fully open to anyone who requests (pays for) it.

Searching for
State Public Records

The previous chapter includes a wealth of knowledge about the various types of public records found at the state level. The introduction to the State Agencies in the body of *Librarian's Guide* is a good place to start, if you have questions not answered in the individual profiles.

We have included some general information here and chosen not to be redundant and repeat what is printed elsewhere, but offer further suggestions and information.

Other State Offices That May Be Helpful

Governor's Office

The office of the Governor is a good place to start if you are looking for an obscure agency, phone number or address. We have found that typically the person who answers the phone will point you in the right direction if he or she cannot answer your question.

Attorney General's Office

If you are looking for a non-profit organization, the Attorney General's Office may be able to help you out.

State Archives

The state archives contain an abundance of historical documents and records, especially useful to those interested in genealogy.

State Court Administrator

The court administrator oversees the state court system, which is also known as the county court system. This office can inform you of the structure of that system (i.e. the courts of general and limited jurisdiction and the types of cases they handle). The state judicial web site is a good place to find opinions of state supreme court and appeals court opinions.

There are five state court administration offices that oversee a statewide online access system to court records. These are commercial systems and fees are involved.

State Restrictions Table

The next two pages present a helpful State Public Record Restrictions Table. This quick guide indicates if records are truly open, and if not, the level of restriction.

The Table also indicates if special forms are needed prior to doing a search.

State Agency Public Record Restrictions Table

Codes

O	Open to Public
R	Some Access Restrictions (Requesters Screened)
N/A	Not Available to the Public
F	Special Form Needed
S	Severe Access Restrictions (Signed Authorization, etc.)
L	Available only at Local Level

State	Criminal Records	UCC Records	Worker's Comp	Driving Record [2]	Vehicle Records	Vessel Records	Voter Reg. [3]
Alabama	S	O,F	S	R	S	O	L
Alaska	R	O,F	R	S	R	N/A	L
Arizona	R	O,F	S	S	S	R	L
Arkansas	S	O,F	O	S	R	O	L
California	N/A,L	O,F	R	S	S	S	L
Colorado	O	O,F	S	R	R	O	O
Connecticut	O	O,F	S	S	S	O	L
Delaware	S	O,F	S	R	R	R	O
Dist. of Columbia	S,F	O,F	S	S	S	S	O
Florida	O	O,F	S	R	R	R	L
Georgia	S	L,F₁	S	S	S	O	O
Hawaii	O	O,F	S	R	N/A	R	L
Idaho	S	O,F	S	R	R	S	L
Illinois	S,F	O,F	O	S	R	O	L
Indiana	R,F	O,F	S	R	R	R	L
Iowa	O	O,F	O	R	R	L	O
Kansas	O,F	O,F	R	R	R	R	L
Kentucky	R	O,F	R	R	R	O	O
Louisiana	S	L,F₁	R	R	R	O	L
Maine	O	O,F	R	R	R	O	L
Maryland	S	O,F	O	R	R	O	L
Massachusetts	R,F	O,F	R	R	R	O	L
Michigan	O	O,F	R	R	R	R	L
Minnesota	R	O,F	S	R	R	O	L
Mississippi	N/A,L	O,F	R	R	R	O	L
Missouri	O	O,F	R	R	R	R	L

State	Criminal Records	UCC Records	Worker's Comp	Driving Record [2]	Vehicle Records	Vessel Records	Voter Reg.[3]
Montana	O	O,F	R	R	R	R	O
Nebraska	O	O,F	R	R	R	L	L
Nevada	S	O,F	S	R	R	O	L
New Hampshire	S	O,F	S	R	S	S	L
New Jersey	R	O,F	O,F	S	S	S	L
New Mexico	S	O,F	S	S	S	S	L
New York	L	O,F	S	R	R	R	L
North Carolina	N/A,L	O,F	R	R	R	O	L
North Dakota	S	O,F	S	R	R,F	O	L
Ohio	S,F	O,F	O	R	R	O	O&L
Oklahoma	O	O,F	O	R	O	R	O&L
Oregon	O	O,F	S	R	R	O	L
Pennsylvania	R,F	O,F	S	S	S	N/A	L
Rhode Island	S,L	O,F	S	R	S	R	L
South Carolina	O	O,F	S	R	R	O	O
South Dakota	S,F	O,F	S	R	R	R	L
Tennessee	N/A,L	O,F	S	R	R	O	L
Texas	O	O,F	S,F	R	R	R	L
Utah	N/A,L	O,F	S	R	R	R	L
Vermont	N/A,L	O,F	S	R	R	R	L
Virginia	S,F	O,F	R	S	S	R	L
Washington	O	O,F	S	S	S	S	L
West Virginia	S,F	O,F	S	R	R	R	L
Wisconsin	O	O,F	S	R	R	O	L
Wyoming	S,F	O,F	S	R	R	O	L

[1] = Georgia and Louisiana UCCs are filed locally, but a state central index is available.

[2] = This category, Driving, indicates restriction codes based on the assumption the requester is the general public. In general, these records are open ("O") to employers and their agents.

[3] = This category, Voter Registration, indicates most record searching requires going to the local county or municipality. However, many state election agencies will sell customized voter lists statewide or for multiple counties.

Searching
Federal Court Records

Every Federal Court in the United States has converted to a computerized index.

Federal Court Structure

The Federal Court system includes three levels of courts, plus some special courts, described as follows—

Supreme Court of the United States

The Supreme Court of the United States is the court of last resort in the United States. It is located in Washington, DC, where it hears appeals from the United States Courts of Appeals and from the highest courts of each state.

United States Court of Appeals

The United States Court of Appeals consists of thirteen appellate courts which hear appeals of verdicts from the courts of general jurisdiction. They are designated as follows:

The Federal Circuit Court of Appeals hears appeals from the US Claims Court and the US Court of International Trade. It is located in Washington, DC.

The District of Columbia Circuit Court of Appeals hears appeals from the district courts in Washington, DC as well as from the Tax Court.

Eleven geographic **Courts of Appeals**—each of these appeal courts covers a designated number of states and territories. The chart on the pages xix-xx lists the circuit numbers (1 through 11) and location of the Court of Appeals for each state.

United States District Courts

The United States District Courts are the courts of general jurisdiction, or trial courts, and are subdivided into two categories—

The District Courts are courts of general jurisdiction, or trial courts, for federal matters, excluding bankruptcy. Essentially, this means they hear cases involving federal law and cases where there is diversity of citizenship. Both **civil** and **criminal** cases come before these courts.

The Bankruptcy Courts generally follow the same geographic boundaries as the US District Courts. There is at least one bankruptcy court for each state; within a state there may be one or more judicial districts and within a judicial district there may be more than one location (division) where the courts hear cases. While civil lawsuits may be filed in either state or federal courts depending upon the applicable law, all bankruptcy actions are filed with the US Bankruptcy Courts.

Special Courts/Separate Courts

The Special Courts/Separate Courts have been created to hear cases or appeals for certain areas of litigation demanding special expertise. Examples include the US Tax Court, the Court of International Trade and the US Claims Court.

How Federal Trial Courts are Organized

At the federal level, all cases involve federal or US constitutional law or interstate commerce. The task of locating the right court is seemingly simplified by the nature of the federal system—

♦   All court locations are based upon the plaintiff's county of domicile.

♦   All civil and criminal cases go to the US District Courts.

♦   All bankruptcy cases go to the US Bankruptcy Courts.

However, a plaintiff or defendant may have cases in any of the 500 court locations, so it is really not all that simple to find them.

There is at least one District and one Bankruptcy Court in each state. In many states there is more than one court, often divided further into judicial districts— e.g., the State of New York consists of four judicial districts, the Northern, Southern, Eastern and Western. Further, many judicial districts contain more than one court location (usually called a division).

The Bankruptcy Courts generally use the same hearing locations as the District Courts. If court locations differ, the usual variance is to have fewer Bankruptcy Court locations.

Case Numbering

When a case is filed with a federal court, a case number is assigned. This is the primary indexing method. Therefore, in searching for case records, you will need to know or find the applicable case number. If you have the number in good form already, your search should be fast and reasonably inexpensive.

You should be aware that case numbering procedures are not consistent throughout the Federal Court system: one judicial district may assign numbers by district while another may assign numbers by location (division) within the judicial district or by judge. Remember that case numbers appearing in legal text citations may not be adequate for searching unless they appear in the proper form for the particular court.

All the basic civil case information that is entered onto docket sheets, and into computerized systems like PACER (see on next page), starts with standard form JS-44, the Civil Cover Sheet, or the equivalent.

Docket Sheet

As in the state court system, information from cover sheets, and from documents filed as a case goes forward, is recorded on the **docket sheet**, which then contains the case history from initial filing to its current status. While docket sheets differ somewhat in format, the basic information contained on a docket sheet is consistent from court to court. As noted earlier in the state court section, all docket sheets contain:

♦   Name of court, including location (division) and the judge assigned;

♦   Case number and case name;

♦   Names of all plaintiffs and defendants/debtors;

♦   Names and addresses of attorneys for the plaintiff or debtor;

♦   Nature and cause (e.g., US civil statute) of action;

♦   Listing of documents filed in the case, including docket entry number, the date and a short description (e.g., 12-2-92, #1, Complaint).

Assignment of Cases

Traditionally, cases were assigned within a district by county. Although this is still true in most states, the introduction of computer systems to track dockets has led to a more flexible approach to case assignment, as is the case in Minnesota and Connecticut. Rather than blindly assigning all cases from a county to one judge, their districts are using random numbers and other logical methods to balance caseloads among their judges.

This trend may appear to confuse the case search process. Actually, the only problem that the searcher may face is to figure out where the case records themselves are located. Finding cases has become significantly easier with the wide availability of PACER from remote access and on-site terminals in each court location with the same district-wide information base.

Computerization

Traditionally, cases were assigned within a district by county. Although this is still true in most states, the introduction of computer systems to track dockets has led to a more flexible approach to case assignment, as is the case in Minnesota and Connecticut. Rather than blindly assigning all cases from a county to one judge, their districts are using random numbers and other logical methods to balance caseloads among their judges.

This trend may appear to confuse the case search process. Actually, the only problem that the searcher may face is to figure out where the case records themselves are located. Finding cases has become significantly easier with the wide availability of PACER from remote access and on-site terminals in each court location with the same district-wide information base.

Computerized Indexes are Available

Computerized courts generally index each case record by the names of some or all the parties to the case—the plaintiffs and defendants (debtors and creditors in Bankruptcy Court) as well as by case number. Therefore, when you search by name you will first receive a listing of all cases in which the name appears, both as plaintiff and defendant.

Electronic Access to Federal Courts

Numerous programs have been developed for electronic access to Federal Court records. In recent years the Administrative Office of the United States Courts in Washington, DC has developed three innovative public access programs: VCIS, PACER, and ABBS. The most useful program for online searching is PACER.

PACER

PACER, the acronym for **P**ublic **A**ccess to **E**lectronic **C**ourt **R**ecords, provides docket information online for open cases at **all US Bankruptcy courts** and **most US District courts**. Cases for the US Court of Federal Claims are also available. The user fee is $.60 per minute. Each court controls its own computer system and case information database; therefore, there are some variations among jurisdictions as to the information offered.

A continuing problem with PACER is that each court determines when records will be purged and how records will be indexed, leaving you to guess how a name is spelled or abbreviated and how much information about closed cases your search will uncover. A PACER search for anything but open cases **cannot** take the place of a full seven-year search of the federal court records available by written request from the court itself or through a local document retrieval company. Many districts report that they have closed records back a number of years, but at the same time indicate they purge docket items every six months.

Sign-up and technical support is handled at the PACER Service Center in San Antonio, Texas (800) 676-6856. You can sign up for all or multiple districts at once. In many judicial districts, when you sign up for PACER access, you will receive a PACER Primer that has been customized for each district. The primer contains a summary of how to access PACER, how to select cases, how to read case numbers and docket sheets, some searching tips, who to call for problem resolution, and district specific program variations.

The most impressive change in Federal Courts record access is the expansion of the PACER System. It covers all 190 Bankruptcy Court Districts and all but 8 of the 300 Civil/Criminal Court Districts.

Before Accessing PACER, search the "national" US Party/Case Index

It is no longer necessary to call each court in every state and district to determine where a debtor has filed bankruptcy, or if someone is a defendant in Federal litigation. National and regional searches of district and bankruptcy filings can be made with one call (via modem) to the US Party/Case Index.

The **US Party/Case Index** is a national index for U.S. district, bankruptcy, and appellate courts. This index allows searches to determine whether or not a party is involved in federal litigation almost anywhere in the nation.

The US Party/Case Index provides the capability to perform national or regional searches on party name and Social Security Number in the bankruptcy index, party name and nature of suit in the civil index, and party name in the criminal and appellate indices.

The search will provide a list of case numbers, filing locations and filing dates for those cases matching the search criteria. If you need more information about the case, you must obtain it from the court directly or through that court's individual PACER system.

You may access the US Party/Case Index through the Internet or via dialup connection. The web site is http://pacer.uspci.uscourts.gov. The toll free modem number is (800) 974-8896. The local number is (210) 301-6499 if you reside in the San Antonio calling area. You will need to emulate a vt100 terminal with N/8/1 as the settings.

In accordance with Judicial Conference policy, most courts charge a $.60 per minute access fee for this service. Persons desiring to use this service must first register with the PACER Service Center at 1-800 676-6856. For more information on the U.S. Party/Case Index, please contact the PACER Service Center at 1-800-676-6856.

ECF

Electronic Case Files (ECF) is a prototype system that focuses on the filing of cases electronically. This service initially introduced in January 1996 enables participating attorneys and litigants to electronically submit pleadings and corresponding docket entries to the court via the Internet thereby eliminating substantial paper handling and processing time. ECF permits any interested parties to instantaneously access the entire official case docket and documents on the Internet of selective civil and bankruptcy cases within these jurisdictions.

It is important to note, that when you search ECF you are ONLY searching cases that have been filed electronically. You must still conduct a search using PACER if you want to know if a case exists.

The following courts utilize ECF, see their profiles for more information:

Arizona (Bankruptcy)	California (Bankruptcy – Southern)
Georgia (Bankruptcy – Northern)	Missouri (District – Western)
New York (Bankruptcy – Southern)	New York (District – Eastern)
Ohio (District – Northern)	Oregon (District)
Virginia (Bankruptcy – Eastern)	

Although, all of the above courts offer filing electronically, not all of them offer searching of those same files. Arizona does not allow searching at this time. In addition, both California and Virginia have additional systems in place.

PACER-Net

PACER-Net is a new system that offers access to PACER through the Internet. You must have a PACER id and password in order to access PACER-Net. PACER-Net is currently available for free, but there are plans to make it a fee-based system. The following courts offer PACER-Net (for more information see the profiles for the individual courts):

California (Bankruptcy – Southern)   Texas (Bankruptcy – Northern)

Texas (District – Northern)

RACER

RACER stands for Remote Access to Court Electronic Records. Accessed through the Internet, RACER offers access to the same records as PACER. At present, searching RACER is free, but there are plans to make it a fee-based system. The following courts offer RACER access (for more information see the profiles for the individual courts):

Idaho (Bankruptcy)   Idaho (District)

Nevada (Bankruptcy)

webPACER

webPACER is a system that has replaced the traditional PACER system for the Central District of California. At this time, it is only being offered for that district. According to court employees, there are plans to make webPACER more widespread, and possibly, the dominant online system.

One must have a PACER id and password to use the system, and the .60 per minute charge applies.

Although, webPACER includes "web" in its name, it is still very much a dial-up system. One must have special software (in addition to a compatible Internet browser application), and one must use access numbers. For access information, see the profiles for the courts in the Central District of California.

Miscellaneous Online Systems

Many courts have developed their own online systems. The Bankruptcy Courts for the Eastern District of Virginia have an elaborate system accessible for free and available on their web site. In addition to RACER, Idaho's Bankruptcy and District Courts have additional searching options available on their web site. Likewise, the Southern District Court of New York offers CourtWeb, which provides information to the public on selected recent rulings of those judges who have elected to make information available in electronic form.

VCIS

Another system worth mentioning is **VCIS** (Voice Case Information System). Nearly all of the US Bankruptcy Court judicial districts provide **VCIS**, a means of accessing information regarding open bankruptcy cases by merely using a touch-tone telephone. There is no charge. Individual names are entered last name first with as much of the first name as you wish to include. For example, Carl R. Ernst could be entered as ERNSTC or ERNSTCARL. Do not enter the middle initial. Business names are entered as they are written, without blanks. BRB Publications has books available with all the VCIS numbers listed (800-929-3811).

The VCIS System, like the PACER System, has become pervasive and now covers open cases for all but 18 US Bankruptcy Court locations.

The remaining US Bankruptcy Courts without VCIS are the **Northern District of Alabama (all four divisions), Montgomery Division (Middle District-AL), Yuma Division (AZ), Tampa Division (Middle District-FL), Northern District of Florida (both divisions), Southern District of Georgia (both divisions), Honolulu Division (HI), Tulsa Division (Northern District-OK), Middle District of Pennsylvania (both divisions), and the Western District of Virginia (all three divisions).**

A survey conducted in 1999 indicated that none of these districts has plans to implement VCIS.

A Few Searching Hints

VCIS should *only* be used to locate information about open cases. Do not attempt to use VCIS as a substitute for a PACER search.

Since this publication includes the counties of jurisdiction for each court, the list of counties in each Court's profile is a good starting point for determining where case records may or may not be found.

Before performing a general PACER search to determine whether cases exist under a particular plaintiff, debtor, or defendant name, first be certain to review that Court's profile, which will show the earliest dates of case records available on the PACER. Also, searchers need to be sure that the Court's case index includes all cases, open and closed, for that particular period. Be aware that some courts purge older, closed cases after a period of time, making such a PACER search incomplete. (Wherever known, this publication indicates within the court profiles the purge timeframe for PACER records. Times vary from court to court and state to state.)

Experience shows that court personnel are typically not aware of — nor concerned about — the types of searches this publication's readers do. Court personnel often focus on only open cases, whereas a searcher may want to know as much about closed cases as open ones. Thus, court personnel are sometimes fuzzy in answering questions about how far back case records go on PACER, and whether closed cases have been purged. If you are looking for cases older than a year or two, there is no substitute for a real, on-site search performed by the court itself or by a local search expert (if the court allows full access to its indexes).

Courts are more willing to give out information by telephone because most courts have converted from the old card index system to fully computerized indexes, which are easily accessible, while on the phone.

Federal Records Centers and the National Archives

After a federal case is closed, the documents are held by Federal Courts themselves for a number of years, then stored at a designated Federal Records Center (FRC). After 20 to 30 years, the records are then transferred from the FRC to the regional archives offices of the National Archives and Records Administration (NARA). The length of time between a case being closed and its being moved to an FRC varies by district. Each court has its own transfer cycle and determines access procedures, even after they have been sent to the FRC.

When case records are sent to an FRC, the boxes of records are assigned accession, location and box numbers. These numbers, which are called case locator information, **must be obtained from the originating court in order to retrieve documents from the FRC.** Some courts will provide such information over the phone, but others require a written request. For some districts, the data is available on PACER. The Federal Records Center for is as follows:

State	Circuit	Appeals Court	Federal Records Center
AK	9	San Francisco, CA	Anchorage (Some temporary in Seattle)
AL	11	Atlanta, GA	Atlanta
AR	8	St. Louis, MO	Fort Worth
AZ	9	San Francisco, CA	Los Angeles
CA	9	San Francisco, CA	Los Angeles (Central & Southern) San Francisco (Eastern & Northern)
CO	10	Denver, CO	Denver
CT	2	New York, NY	Boston
DC		Washington, DC	Washington, DC
DE	3	Philadelphia, PA	Philadelphia
FL	11	Atlanta, GA	Atlanta
GA	11	Atlanta, GA	Atlanta
GU	9	San Francisco, CA	San Francisco
HI	9	San Francisco, CA	San Francisco
IA	8	St. Louis, MO	Kansas City, MO
ID	9	San Francisco, CA	Seattle
IL	7	Chicago, IL	Chicago
IN	7	Chicago, IL	Chicago
KS	10	Denver, CO	Kansas City, MO
KY	6	Cincinnati, OH	Atlanta
LA	5	New Orleans, LA	Fort Worth
MA	1	Boston, MA	Boston
MD	4	Richmond, VA	Philadelphia

State	Circuit	Appeals Court	Federal Records Center
ME	1	Boston, MA	Boston
MI	6	Cincinnati, OH	Chicago
MN	8	St. Louis, MO	Chicago
MO	8	St. Louis, MO	Kansas City, MO
MS	5	New Orleans, LA	Atlanta
MT	9	San Francisco, CA	Denver
NC	4	Richmond, VA	Atlanta
ND	8	St. Louis, MO	Denver
NE	8	St. Louis, MO	Kansas City, MO
NH	1	Boston, MA	Boston
NJ	3	Philadelphia, PA	New York
NM	10	Denver, CO	Denver
NV	9	San Francisco, CA	Los Angeles (Clark County) San Francisco (Other counties)
NY	2	New York, NY	New York
OH	6	Cincinnati, OH	Chicago, Dayton (Some bankruptcy)
OK	10	Denver, CO	Fort Worth
OR	9	San Francisco, CA	Seattle
PA	3	Philadelphia, PA	Philadelphia
PR	1	Boston, MA	New York
RI	1	Boston, MA	Boston
SC	4	Richmond, VA	Atlanta
SD	8	St. Louis, MO	Denver
TN	6	Cincinnati, OH	Atlanta
TX	5	New Orleans, LA	Fort Worth
UT	10	Denver, CO	Denver
VA	4	Richmond, VA	Philadelphia
VI	3	Philadelphia, PA	New York
VT	2	New York, NY	Boston
WA	9	San Francisco, CA	Seattle
WI	7	Chicago, IL	Chicago
WV	4	Richmond, VA	Philadelphia
WY	10	Denver, CO	Denver

GU is Guam, PR is Puerto Rico, and VI is the Virgin Islands.

According to some odd logic, the following Federal Records Centers are located somewhere else:

Atlanta—East Point, GA; Boston—Waltham, MA; Los Angeles—Laguna Niguel, CA; New York—Bayonne, NJ; San Francisco—San Bruno, CA

Searching Other Federal Records Online

EDGAR

EDGAR, the Electronic Data Gathering Analysis, and Retrieval system was established by the Securities and exchange Commission (SEC) to allow companies to make required filing to the SEC by direct transmission. As of May 6, 1996, all public domestic companies are required to make their filings on EDGAR, except for filings made to the Commission's regional offices and those filings made on paper due to a hardship exemption.

EDGAR is an extensive repository of US corporation information and it is available online.

What is Found on EDGAR?

Companies must file the following reports with the SEC:

◆   10-K, an annual financial report, which includes audited year-end financial statements.

◆   10-Q, a quarterly report, unaudited.

◆   8K - a report detailing significant or unscheduled corporate changes or events.

◆   Securities offering and trading registrations and the final prospectus.

The list above is not conclusive. There are other miscellaneous reports filed, including those dealing with security holdings by institutions and insiders. Access to these documents provides a wealth on information.

How to Access EDGAR Online

EDGAR is searchable online at: www.sec.gov/edgarhp.htm. LEXIS/NEXIS (see page 393) acts as the data wholesaler or distributor on behalf of the government. LEXIS/NEXIS sells data to information retailers, including it's own NEXIS service.

There is an additional number of companies found in the Company Information Category Index (see page 299) that may very well offer online access to EDGAR. Many of these companies have compiled data prior to May 1996 and offer proprietary databases of SEC and other company documents.

Aviation Records

The Federal Aviation Association (FAA) is the US government agency with the responsibility of all matters related to the safety of civil aviation. The FAA, among other functions, provides the system that registers aircraft, and documents showing title or interest in aircraft. Their web site, at www.faa.gov, is the ultimate source of aviation records, airports and facilities, safety regulations, and civil research and engineering.

The Aircraft Owners and Pilots Association is the largest organization of its kind with a 340,000 members. Their web site is www.aopa.org and is an excellent source of information regarding the aviation industry.

Two other excellent sources are *Jane's World Airlines* at www.janes.com and the Insured Aircraft Title Service at 800-654-4882 or its web site at www.insured.aircraft.com

Military Records

This topic is so broad that there can be a book written about it, and in fact there is! *The Armed Forces Locator Directory* from MIE Publishing (800-937-2133) is an excellent source. The reference covers every conceivable topic regarding military records.

The Privacy Act of 1974 (5 U.S.C. 552a) and the Department of Defense directives require a written request, signed and dated, to access military personnel records. For further details, visit the NPRC site listed below.

Military Internet Sources

There are a number of great Internet sites that provide valuable information on obtaining military and military personnel records as follows:

www.nara.gov/regional/mpr.html This is the National Personnel Records Center (NPRC), maintained by the National Archives and Records Administration. This site is full of useful information and links.

www.army.mil	The official site of the US Army
www.af.mil	The official site of the US Air Force
www.navy.mil	The official site of the US Navy

`www.usmc.mil`   The official site of the US Marine Corps

`www.ngb.dtic.mil`   The official site of the National Guard

`www.uscg.mil`   The official site of the US Coast Guard

Searching
County Court Records

Using the County Court Records Sections

The County Court Records sections detail more than 6,4000 major courts that have jurisdiction over significant criminal and civil cases under state law.

Included in *The Librarian's Guide to Public Records* are all state felony courts, larger claim civil courts, and probate courts in the United States. Since most courts have jurisdiction over a number of categories of cases, we also profile thousands of courts that hear misdemeanor, eviction, and small claims court cases. In addition, each County Court Records Chapter begins with an introduction that summarizes where other major categories of court cases—DUI, preliminary hearings, and juvenile cases—can be found.

The term "County Courts," as used in this publication, refers to those courts of original jurisdiction (trial courts) within each state's court system that handle...

- **Felonies** -- Generally defined as crimes punishable by one year or more of jail time

- **Civil Actions** -- For money damages greater than usually $3,000 or more.

- **Probate** -- Estate matters

- **Misdemeanors** -- Generally defined as minor infractions with a fine or minimal jail time

- **Evictions** -- Landlord/tenant actions

- **Small Claims** -- Actions for minor money damages, usually $3,000 or less

Useful Applications

The Librarian's Guide is especially useful for four kinds of applications—

General litigation searching/background searching... Combined with the *Federal Court section*, you have complete coverage of all important courts in the United States.

Employment background checking... Included is full coverage of local criminal courts at the felony level, and many misdemeanor courts as well.

Tenant background checking... Courts where landlord/tenant cases are filed are included in the state introduction charts, and most of the courts handling such cases are profiled.

Assets searching... The probate courts have records of wills and estate matters that can be used to determine assets, related parties, and useful addresses.

Some Court Basics

Before trudging into a courthouse and demanding to view a document, you should first be aware of some basic court procedures. Whether the case is filed in a state, municipal, or federal court, each case follows a similar process.

A **civil case** usually commences when a plaintiff files a complaint with a court against defendants. The defendants respond to the complaint with an answer. After this initial round, there may be literally hundreds of activities before the court issues a judgment. These activities can include revised complaints and their answers, motions of various kinds, discovery proceedings (including depositions) to establish the documentation and facts involved in the case. All of these activities are listed on a **docket sheet**, which may be a piece of paper or a computerized index.

Once the court issues a judgment, either party may appeal the ruling to an appellate division or court. In the case of a money judgment, the winning side can usually file it as a judgment lien with the county recorder. Appellate divisions usually deal only with legal issues and not the facts of the case.

In a **criminal case**, the plaintiff is a government jurisdiction. The Government brings the action against the defendant for violation of one or more of its statutes.

In a **bankruptcy case,** which can be heard only in a federal courts, there is neither defendant nor plaintiff. Instead, the debtor files voluntarily for bankruptcy protection against creditors, or the creditors file against the debtor in order to force the debtor into involuntary bankruptcy.

Types of Litigation in Trial Courts

Criminal

Criminal cases are categorized as *felonies* or *misdemeanors*. A general rule, used in this publication, makes this distinction: usually a felony involves a jail term of one year or more, whereas a misdemeanor may only involve a monetary *fine*.

Civil

Civil cases are categorized as *tort*, *contract*, and *real property* rights. Torts can include *automobile accidents*, *medical malpractice*, and *product liability* cases. Actions for small money damages, typically under $3,000, are known as *small claims*.

Other

Other types of cases that frequently are handled by separate courts or specialized divisions of courts include *juvenile*, *probate* (wills and estates), and *domestic relations*.

Reading the Court Profiles

Basic Information

The 3,139 US counties (and where applicable—parishes, towns, cities, etc.) are listed in alphabetical order, within each state. When a county has more than one court profiled, the courts appear in order beginning with the court of general jurisdiction, then proceeding down to more limited jurisdictions. If a level of court has divisions, civil courts are listed before criminal courts. Where more than one court of the same type is located in a county, they are listed in alphabetical order by the name of the city where they are located.

Additional information for each court includes whether the court accepts searches by phone (1,320 do accept some type of telephone request), whether the office's records are accessible by modem.

Furthermore, to maximize your search possibilities, online system availability for each state, if any, is summarized in the state introductions.

Major Variations

Do not assume that the structure of the court system in another state is anything like your own. In one state, the Circuit Court may be the highest trial court whereas in another it is a limited jurisdiction court. Examples are: (1) New York, where the Supreme Court is not very "supreme," and the downstate court structure varies from upstate; and (2) Tennessee, where circuit courts are in districts.

Access

The number of courts that no longer conduct name searches has risen to 1,150 from 766 in 1996. For these, you must hire a local retriever, directly or through a search company, to search for you. It should be noted that usually these courts still take specific document copy requests by mail. Because of long mail turnaround times and court fees, local retrievers are frequently used even when the court will honor a request by mail. A court's entry indicates if it is one of the many to offer a public access terminal, free of charge, to view case documents or indexes.

Note: in many instances two types of courts (e.g., circuit and district) are combined. When phoning or writing these courts, we recommend that your request specifically state in your request that you want both courts included in the search.

Special Notes

Where two or more courts divide jurisdiction of a county, a profile for each court is given. Often a city is specified to help you determine which court to access.

State Court Structure

The secret to determining where a state court case is located is to understand how the court system is structured in that particular state. The general structure of all state court systems has four parts:

Appellate courts   Limited jurisdiction trial courts

Intermediate appellate courts   General jurisdiction trial courts

The two highest levels, appellate and intermediate appellate courts, only hear cases on appeal from the trial courts. Opinions of these appellate courts are of interest primarily to attorneys seeking legal precedents for new cases.

General jurisdiction trial courts usually handle a full range of civil and criminal litigation. These courts usually handle felonies and larger civil cases.

Limited jurisdiction trial courts come in two varieties. First, many limited jurisdiction courts handle smaller civil claims (usually $10,000 or less), misdemeanors, and pretrial hearing for felonies. Second, some of these courts, sometimes called special jurisdiction courts, are limited to one type of litigation, for example the Court of Claims in New York, which only handles liability cases against the state.

Some states, for instance Iowa, have consolidated their general and limited jurisdiction court structure into one combined court system. In other states there may be a further distinction between state-supported courts and municipal courts. In New York, for example, nearly 1,300 Municipal Justice Courts handle local ordinance and traffic violations, including DWI.

Generalizations should not be made about where specific types of cases are handled in the various states. Misdemeanors, probate, landlord/tenant (eviction), domestic relations, and juvenile cases may be handled in either or both the general and limited jurisdiction courts. To help you locate the correct court to perform your search in, this publication specifically lists the types of cases handled by each court.

How Courts Maintain Records

Case Numbering

When a case is filed, it is assigned a case number. This is the primary indexing method in every court. Therefore, in searching for case records, you will need to know—or find—the applicable case number. If you have the number in good form already, your search should be fast and reasonably inexpensive.

You should be aware that case numbering procedures are not consistent throughout a state court system. One district may assign numbers by district while another may assign numbers by location (division) within the district, or by judge. Remember: case numbers appearing in legal text citations may not be adequate for searching unless they appear in the proper form for the particular court in which you are searching.

All basic civil case information is entered onto docket sheets.

Docket Sheet

Information from cover sheets and from documents filed as a case goes forward is recorded on the docket sheet. The docket sheet then contains an outline of the case history from initial filing to its current status. While docket sheets differ somewhat in format, the basic information contained on a docket sheet is consistent from court to court. All docket sheets contain:

- ♦ Name of court, including location (division) and the judge assigned;

- ♦ Case number and case name;

- ♦ Names of all plaintiffs and defendants/debtors;

- ♦ Names and addresses of attorneys for the plaintiff or debtor;

- ♦ Nature and cause (e.g., statute) of action.

Computerization

Most courts are computerized, which means that the docket sheet data is entered into a computer system. Within a state or judicial district, the courts *may* be linked together via a single computer system.

Docket sheets from cases closed before the advent of computerization may not be in the computer system. For pre-computer cases, most courts keep summary case information on microfilm, microfiche, or index cards.

Case documents are not generally available on computer because courts are still experimenting with and developing electronic filing and imaging of court documents. Generally, documents are only available to be copied by contacting the court where the case records are located.

Performing the County Search

How you search depends on what information you have, what you are looking for, and the time frame you are dealing with. Whichever access method you decide to use, before you begin, you must gather as much of the required, essential information as you can, and be prepared to be as specific as possible in your search request.

Ways to Obtain Records

Here are five ways you can access information from government agencies and courts: Please note this chapter is applicable for both **court records** and **recorder office records**.

Telephone

While the amount of information agencies and courts will release over the telephone varies, this is an inexpensive way to begin a search. Today's widespread computerization of records allows agency/court personnel nearly immediate access to more readily available data. This book contains the phone numbers for every court profiled. However, the trend is towards fewer courts providing information via telephone.

Mail

Many courts and state agencies will conduct a search based upon a written request. Generally, you can call first to see if the agency has the record you are seeking and what the fee will be. Always be sure to be specific in your written request, and include a self-addressed stamped envelope for quicker service.

In Person

If you are near the court or agency where you want to search, you can visit the location yourself. Personnel are usually available to assist you. Many courts now have public access computer terminals for viewing case information within their districts. We recommend that you take the opportunity to visit the nearest court or recorder's office for another reason: by seeing how the office is physically organized and by chatting with personnel, you will get "a feel" for what is involved in searching a similar agency elsewhere.

Online

You will find online access is more readily available at the federal court level and certain state agencies than can be found at the county court level. We have indicated in the State Introductions where online access is available statewide. In the court profiles, we indicate if online access is available for that particular court. Keep in mine these are primarily commercial fee-based systems.

The trend to access information on the Internet is slowing coming to the state court systems. Internet site addresses are indicated for those courts that have a site with some substance. There are two states that have a free statewide access URL (CT and NM).

Provider or Retriever Firm

Hiring a service company that knows the local court(s) in its area is frequently the only way to access remote locations effectively. Among these are national companies that cover all courts, and local companies that cover courts in their geographic vicinity.

Fees, Charges, and Usage

Public records are not necessarily free of charge, certainly not if they are maintained by private industry. Remember that **public records are records of incidents or transactions**. These incidents can be civil or criminal court actions, recordings, filings or occurrences such as speeding tickets or accidents. **It costs money** (time, salaries, supplies, etc.) **to record and track these events**. Common charges found at the government level include copy fees (to make copies of the document), search fees (for clerical personnel to search for the record), and certification fees (to certify that a document as being accurate and coming from the particular agency). Fees can vary from $.10 per page for copies to a $15.00 search fee for court personnel to do the actual look-up. Some government agencies will allow you to walk in and view records at no charge. Fewer will release information over the phone for no fee.

If a private enterprise is in the business of maintaining a public records database, it generally does so to offer these records for resale. Typical clients include financial institutions, the legal industry, the insurance industry, and pre-employment screening firms among others. Usually, records are sold via online access or on a CD-ROM.

Also, there are a number of public record search firms—companies that will do a name search—for a fee. These companies do not warehouse the records, but search on demand for a specific name.

Private companies usually offer different price levels based on volume of usage, while government agencies have one price per category, regardless of the amount of requests.

A Few Words About Searching Public Records Online

No, you will not find an abundance of public records on the Internet. The availability of online public records is not as widespread as one might think. According to studies conducted by the *Public Record Research Library*, only *15% of public records can be found online*. Nonetheless, more than 200 private companies offer online access to proprietary database(s) of public record information.

A key to purchasing public records online direct from a government agency is the frequency of usage. Many agencies require a minimum amount of requests per month or per session. Certainly, it does not make economic sense to spend a lot of money for programming and set-up fees if you will be ordering fewer than five records a month. You would be better off to do the search by more conventional methods—in-person, via mail, fax, or by hiring a vendor. Going online direct to the source is not always the least expensive way to go!

Searching Recording Office Records

Combined, the Recording Offices section for each state chapter contains 4,265 local recording offices where Uniform Commercial Code and real estate records are maintained.

The Lowdown on Recorded Documents

Documents filed and record at local county, parish, city or town offices represent some of the best opportunities to gain access to open public records. If you are lucky enough to live in close proximity, you can visit your local office and, for free, view records. Recorded documents are also one of the most available types of public records that can be viewed or obtain via online and through the Internet.

Real Estate

As mentioned previously, real estate records are public so that everyone can know who owns what property. Liens on real estate must be public so a buyer knows all the facts. The county (or parish or city) recorder's office is the source. Also, access is also available form many private companies that purchase entire county record databases and create their own database for commercial purposes.

Uniform Commercial Code (UCC)

UCC filings are to personal property what mortgages are to real estate property. UCCs are in the category of financial records that must be fully open to public scrutiny so that other potential lenders are on notice about which assets of the borrower have been pledged as collateral.

Special Categories of Collateral

Real Estate Related UCC Collateral

A specific purpose of lien statutes under both the UCC and real estate laws is to put a buyer or potential secured creditor on notice that someone has a prior security interest in real or personal property. UCC financing statements are to personal property what mortgages or deeds of trust are to real property.

One problem addressed by the UCC is that certain types of property have the characteristics of both real and personal property. In those instances, it is necessary to have a way to provide lien notice to two different categories of interested parties: those who deal with the real estate aspect of the property and those who deal with the "personal" aspect of the property.

In general, our definition of real estate related UCC collateral is any property that in one form is attached to land, but that in another form is not attached. For the sake of simplicity, we can define the characteristics of two broad types of property that meet this definition:

>*Property that is initially attached to real property, but then is separated.*
>Three specific types of collateral have this characteristic: *minerals* (including oil and gas), *timber*, and *crops*. These things are grown on or extracted from land. While they are on or in the ground they are thought of as real property, but once they are harvested or extracted they become personal property. Some states have a separate central filing system for crops.

>*Property that is initially personal property, but then is attached to land, generally called fixtures.*
>Equipment such as telephone systems or heavy industrial equipment permanently affixed to a building are examples of fixtures. It is important to realize that what is a fixture, like beauty, is in the eye of the beholder, since it is a vague concept at best.

UCC financing statements applicable to real estate related collateral must be filed where the real estate and mortgage records are kept, which is generally at the county level—except in Connecticut, Rhode Island and Vermont, where the Town/City Clerk maintains these records. The chart gives the titles of the local official who maintains these records.

Consumer Goods

Among the state to state variations, some states require filing where real estate is filed for certain consumer goods.

Equipment Used in Farming Operations

33 states require only local filing for equipment used in farming operations.

Searching Note

If you are looking for information on subjects that might have these types of filings against them, a search of county records may be revealing even if you would normally search only at the state level.

More Details About UCC Records

Uniform Commercial Code financing statements and changes to them may be filed at two or three government agencies in each state, depending upon the type of collateral involved in the transaction. Each state's UCC statute contains variations on a nationally recommended Model Act. Each variation is explained below. The charts appear at the end of this chapter.

33 Central Filing States

Central filing states are those where most types of personal property collateral require filing of a UCC financing statement only at a central filing location within that state.

5 Statewide Database States

Minnesota and **Wisconsin** are central filing states with a difference: UCC financing statements filed at the county level are also entered into a statewide database. In **North Dakota** UCC financing statements may be filed at either the state or county level, and all filings are entered into a statewide database. In **Louisiana**, **Nebraska**, and **Georgia**, UCC financing statements may be filed with **any** county (parish). In each of these six states the records are entered into a central, statewide database that is available (except in Georgia) for searching in each county, as well as at the state agency (no state agency in Louisiana or Georgia).

8 Dual Filing States

The usual definition of a dual filing state is one in which financing statements containing collateral such as inventory, equipment or receivables *must* be filed in *both* a central filing office, usually with the Secretary of State, and in a local (county) office where the collateral or business is located. The three states below are also dual filing states, with a difference.

3 Triple Filing States

The systems in three states, MA, NH, and PA, can be described as triple filing because the real estate portion of the filings goes to an office separate from the UCC filing office. In Massachusetts and New Hampshire, UCC filings go to the town/city while real estate filings go to the county. In Pennsylvania, county government is separated into the Prothonotary for UCC filings and the Recorder for real estate filings.

Some counties in other states do have separate addresses for real estate recording, but this is usually just a matter of local departmentalization.

2 Local Filing States

Kentucky and Wyoming are the only *local filing only* states as of January 1, 1995. In both these states a few filings are also found at the state level. In both states, filings for out of state debtors go to the Secretary of State, and in Wyoming filings for Wyoming debtor accounts receivable and farm products require dual filing.

The UCC Locator Chart

This handy chart will tell you at a glance where UCC and real estate records are filed on a state-by-state basis.

State	Most Personal Property		All Real Property
	Central Filing Office	Local Filing Office	Filing Office
AK	Department of Natural Resources		District Recorder
AL	Secretary of State		Judge of Probate
AR	Secretary of State	and Circuit Clerk	Circuit Clerk
AZ	Secretary of State		County Recorder
CA	Secretary of State		County Recorder
CO	Secretary of State	or any County Recorder (as of July 1, 1996)	County Clerk & Recorder
CT	Secretary of State		Town/City Clerk
DC	County Recorder		County Recorder
DE	Secretary of State		County Recorder
FL	Secretary of State		Clerk of Circuit Court
GA	None	Clerk Superior Court	Clerk of Superior Court
HI	Bureau of Conveyances		Bureau of Conveyances
IA	Secretary of State		County Recorder
ID	Secretary of State		County Recorder
IL	Secretary of State		County Recorder
IN	Secretary of State		County Recorder
KS	Secretary of State		Register
KY	Secretary of State (Out of state only)	County Clerk	County Clerk
LA	None	Clerk of Court	Clerk of Court
MA	Secretary of the Commonwealth	and Town/City Clerk	Register of Deeds
MD	Department of Assessments & Taxation	and Clerk of Circuit Court (until 7/1/95)	Clerk of Circuit Court
ME	Secretary of State		County Register
MI	Secretary of State		County Register
MN	Secretary of State or Recorder		County Recorder
MO	Secretary of State	and County Recorder	County Recorder
MS	Secretary of State	and Chancery Clerk	Chancery Clerk
MT	Secretary of State		Clerk & Recorder

| State | Most Personal Property | | All Real Property |
	Central Filing Office	Local Filing Office	Filing Office
NC	Secretary of State	and Register of Deeds	Register of Deeds
ND	Secretary of State or County Register		County Register
NE	Secretary of State (Out of state only)	County Clerk	County Register
NH	Secretary of State	and Town/City Clerk	County Register
NJ	Secretary of State		County Clerk/Register
NM	Secretary of State		County Clerk
NV	Secretary of State		County Recorder
NY	Secretary of State	and County Clerk (Register)	County Clerk (Register)
OH	Secretary of State	and County Recorder	County Recorder
OK	Oklahoma County Clerk		County Clerk
OR	Secretary of State		County Clerk
PA	Department of State	and Prothonotary	County Recorder
RI	Secretary of State		County Clerk & Recorder
SC	Secretary of State		County Register/Clerk
SD	Secretary of State		County Register
TN	Secretary of State		County Register
TX	Secretary of State		County Clerk
UT	Division of Corporations & Commercial Code		County Recorder
VA	Corporation Commission	and Clerk of Circuit Court	Clerk of Circuit Court
VT	Secretary of State	and Town/City Clerk (until 7/1/95)	Town/City Clerk
WA	Department of Licensing		County Auditor
WI	Dept. of Financial Institutions		County Register
WV	Secretary of State		County Clerk
WY	Secretary of State (Out of state and A/R only)	County Clerk	County Clerk

Alabama

Attorney General's Office
11 S. Union Street
Montgomery, AL 36130
334-242-7300
Fax: 334-242-7458
www.ago.state.al.us

Governor's Office
600 Dexter Ave, #N-104
Montgomery, AL 36130
334-242-7100
Fax: 334-353-0004
www.governor.state.al.us

State Archives
Reference Room, PO Box 300100
Montgomery, AL 36130-0100
334-242-4435
Fax: 334-240-3433
www.archives.state.al.us

Capital:	Montgomery
	Montgomery County
Time Zone:	CST
Number of Counties:	67
Population:	4,319,154
Web Site:	www.state.al.us

Search Unclaimed Property Online
http://209.41.95.201/search.asp

State Agencies

Criminal Records
Alabama Department of Public Safety, A.B.I., Identification Unit, PO Box 1511, Montgomery, AL 36192 (502 Washington St, Montgomery, AL 36104); 334-242-4244; Fax: 334-242-4270; 8AM-5PM. Access by: mail, online.

Corporation Records
Limited Partnership Records
Limited Liability Company Records
Limited Liability Partnerships
Trade Names
Trademarks/Servicemarks
Secretary of State, Corporations Division, PO Box 5616, Montgomery, AL 36103-5616 (11 S Union St, Ste 207, Montgomery, AL 36104); 334-242-5324, 334-242-5325 Trademarks; Fax: 334-240-3138; 8AM-5PM. Access by: mail, online. www.sos.state.al.us

Uniform Commercial Code
Federal Tax Liens
State Tax Liens
UCC Division, Secretary of State, PO Box 5616, Montgomery, AL 36103-5616 (11 South Union St, Suite 207, Montgomery, AL 36104); 334-242-5231; 8AM-5PM. Access by: mail, online. www.sos.state.al.us

Sales Tax Registrations
Restricted access.
According to state law 40-2A-10, this agency is unable to release any information about tax registrations.
Alabama Department of Revenue, Sales, Use and Business Tax Division, 4303 Gordon Persons Bldg, 50 N Ripley St, Montgomery, AL 36104; 334-242-1490; Fax: 334-242-8916; 8AM-5PM
www.ador.state.al.us

Workers' Compensation Records

Department of Industrial Relations, Disclosure Unit, 649 Monroe Street, Rm. 276, Montgomery, AL 36131; 334-242-8980; Fax: 334-261-2304; 8AM-4:30PM.

Birth Certificates

Center for Health Statistics, Record Services Division, PO Box 5625, Montgomery, AL 36103-5625 (RSA Tower Suite 1150, 201 Monroe St, Montgomery, AL 36104); 334-206-5418; Fax: 334-262-9563; 8AM-5PM. Access by: mail, phone, in person. www.alapubhealth.org

Death Records

Center for Health Statistics, Record Services Division, PO Box 5625, Montgomery, AL 36103-5625; 334-206-5418; Fax: 334-262-9563; 8AM-5PM. Access by: mail, phone, in person. www.alapubhealth.org

Marriage Certificates

Center for Health Statistics, Record Services Division, PO Box 5625, Montgomery, AL 36103-5625; 334-206-5418; Fax: 334-262-9563; 8AM-5PM. Access by: mail, phone, in person. www.alapubhealth.org

Divorce Records

Center for Health Statistics, Record Services Division, PO Box 5625, Montgomery, AL 36103-5625; 334-206-5418; Fax: 334-206-2659; 8AM-5PM. Access by: mail, phone, in person. www.alapubhealth.org

Vehicle Ownership
Vehicle Identification

Motor Vehicle Division, Title Section, PO Box 327640, Montgomery, AL 36132-7640 (50 North Ripley St, Montgomery, AL 36140); 334-242-9000; Fax: 334-242-0312; 8AM-5PM. Access by: mail.

Accident Reports

Alabama Department of Public Safety, Accident Records, PO Box 1471, Montgomery, AL 36102-1471 (500 Dexter Ave, Montgomery, AL 36104); 334-242-4241; 8AM-5PM. Access by: mail, phone, in person.

Driver Records

Department of Public Safety, Driver Records-License Division, PO Box 1471, Montgomery, AL 36102-1471 (500 Dexter Ave, Montgomery, AL 36104); 334-242-4400; Fax: 334-242-4639;

8AM-5PM. Access by: mail, online. www.ador.state.al.us/motorvehicle/MVD-MAIN.html

Boat & Vessel Ownership
Boat & Vessel Registration

Dept of Conservation & Natural Resources, Records, PO Box 301451, Montgomery, AL 36130 (64 N Union St, Montgomery, AL 36104); 334-242-3673; Fax: 334-242-0336; 8AM-5PM. www.dcnr.state.al.us

Legislation-Current/Pending
Legislation-Passed

Alabama Legislature, State House, 11 S Union St, Montgomery, AL 36130-4600; 334-242-7826 Senate, 334-242-7637 House; Fax: 334-242-8819; 8:30AM-4:30PM. Access by: mail, phone, in person, online. www.legislature.state.al.us

Voter Registration
Restricted access.

Individual name requests must be done at the county level, there are no restrictions. The SSN is not released. Bulk requests can be ordered from this office for data from 55 of 69 counties. Call for fees and breakdowns of customized requests.

Alabama State House, Voter Registration, 11 S Union, Rm 216, Montgomery, AL 36130; 334-242-4337; Fax: 334-242-2940; 8AM-5PM

GED Certificates

State Dept of Education, GED Testing Office, PO Box 302101, Montgomery, AL 36130-2101 (Gordon Persons Bldg Rm 5345, 50 N Ripley St, Montgomery, AL 36104); 334-242-8181 Main Number; Fax: 334-242-2236; 8AM-5PM. Access by:, phone, in person.

Hunting License Information
Fishing License Information
Records not available from state agency.

They do not have a central database. They only track the number of licenses issued to the issuing agent, not to the individual.

County Courts & Recording Offices

About the Courts...

About the Recording Offices...

Administration

Director of Courts   334-242-0300
300 Dexter Ave   Fax: 334-242-2099
Montgomery, AL 36104
www.alacourt.org

Court Structure

The Circuit are the courts of general jurisdiction and the District Courts have limited jurisdiction in civil matters. These courts are combined in all but eight larger counties. Barbour, Cof-fee, Jefferson, St. Clair, Talladega, and Tallapoosa Counties have two court locations within the county.

Jefferson County (Birmingham), Madison (Huntsville), Marshall, and Tuscaloosa Counties have separate criminal divisions for Circuit and/or District Courts. Misdemeanors committed with felonies are tried with the felony. The Circuit Courts are appeals courts for misdemeanors.

District Courts can receive guilty pleas in felony cases.

All counties have separate probate courts. Probate court telephone numbers are generally included with the Circuit or District Court entry although the court location may be different.

Searching Hints

Although in most counties Circuit and District courts are combined, each index may be separate. Therefore, when you request a search of both courts, be sure to state that the search is to cover "both the Circuit and District Court records." Several offices do not perform searches. Some offices do not have public access computer terminals.

Online Access

Remote, online computer access is available through the Remote Access system of the State Judicial Information System (SJIS). Remote Access is designed to provide "off-site" users with a means to retrieve basic case information and to allow a user access to any criminal, civil, or traffic record in the state. The system is available 24 hours per day. There is a $150 setup fee, and the monthly charge is $50 for unlimited access Call Cheryl Lenoir (334-242-0300 for add'l information. The Alabama legal information web site offers commercial access to appellate opinions. For more information, go to http://alalinc.net.

Organization

67 counties, 71 recording offices. The recording officer is Judge of Probate. Four counties have two recording offices—Barbour, Coffee, Jefferson, and St. Clair. See the notes under each county regarding how to determine which office is appropriate to search. The entire state is in the Central Time Zone (CST).

UCC Records

Financing statements are filed at the state level, except for consumer goods, farm collateral and real estate related collateral, which are filed with the county Judge of Probate. Only one-third of counties will perform UCC searches. Use search request form UCC-11. Search fees vary from $5.00 to $12.00 per debtor name. Copies usually cost $1.00 per page.

Lien Records

Federal and state tax liens on personal property of businesses are filed with the Secretary of State. Other federal and state tax liens are filed with the county Judge of Probate. Counties do not perform separate tax lien searches although the liens are usually filed in the same index with UCC financing statements.

Real Estate Records

Most counties do not perform real estate searches. Copy fees vary. Certification fees vary. Tax records are located at the Assessor's Office.

County Courts & Recording Offices

Autauga

Real Estate Recording—Autauga County Judge of Probate, 176 W. 5th St. Prattville, AL 36067. Fax: 334-361-3740. 8:30AM-5PM.

Felony, Misdemeanor, Civil, Eviction, Small Claims—Circuit & District Court, 134 N Court St, #114, Prattville, AL 36067-3049. 334-775-3203. 8AM-5PM. Access by: mail, phone, in person, online.

Probate—Probate Court, 176 W 5th, Prattville, AL 36067. 334-774-5003, Fax: 334-361-3740. 8:30AM-5PM. Access by: mail, in person.

Baldwin

Real Estate Recording—Baldwin County Judge of Probate, 1 Courthouse Square, Bay Minette, AL 36507. 352-754-4201, Fax: 334-580-2563. 8AM-4:30PM.

Felony, Misdemeanor, Civil, Eviction, Small Claims—Circuit & District Court, PO Box 1149, Bay Minette, AL 36507. 352-793-0211. 8AM-4:30PM. Access by: in person, online.

Probate—Probate Court, PO Box 1258, Bay Minette, AL 36507. 352-793-0215. 8AM-4:30PM. Access by: mail, phone, in person.

Barbour

Real Estate Recording—Barbour County Judge of Probate, Court Square, Clayton, AL 36016. 352-374-3605, Fax: 334-775-1126. 8AM-5PM.

Barbour County Judge of Probate, 303 E. Broad St. Room 101, Eufaula, AL 36027. Fax: 334-687-0921. 8AM-5PM.

Felony, Misdemeanor, Civil, Eviction, Small Claims, Probate—Circuit & District Court-Clayton Division, PO Box 219, Clayton, AL 36016. 352-374-3611, Fax: 334-775-8366. 8AM-5PM. Access by: mail, in person, online. Special note: Probate court is separate from this court, and can be contacted at the telephone number above.

Misdemeanor, Civil, Eviction, Small Claims, Probate—Circuit & District Court-Eufaula Division, 303 E Broad St, Rm 201, Eufaula, AL 36027. 336-372-8949, Fax: 334-687-1599. 8AM-4:30PM. Access by: in person, online. Special note: Probate court is separate from this court, and can be contacted at the telephone number above.

Bibb

Real Estate Recording—Bibb County Judge of Probate, Courthouse, Room 100, 455 Walnut St, Centerville, AL 35042. 205-927-3340, Fax: 205-926-1131. 8AM-5PM.

Felony, Misdemeanor, Civil, Eviction, Small Claims, Probate—Circuit & District Court, Bibb County Courthouse, Centreville, AL 35042. 205-926-3114. 8AM-5PM. Access by: mail, in person, online. Special note: Probate court is separate from this court, and can be contacted at the telephone number above.

Blount

Real Estate Recording—Blount County Judge of Probate, 220 2nd Avenue East, Oneonta, AL 35121. 205-625-4117. 8AM-4PM M-W & F; 8AM-Noon Th & Sat.

Felony, Misdemeanor, Civil, Eviction, Small Claims—Circuit & District Court, 220 2nd Ave East Room 208, Oneonta, AL 35121. 205-625-4153. 8AM-5PM. Access by: mail, in person, online.

Probate—Probate Court, 220 2nd Ave E, Oneonta, AL 35121. 205-625-4191, Fax: 205-625-4206. 8AM-4PM M,T,W,F 8AM-Noon Th,Sat. Access by: mail, phone, in person.

Bullock

Real Estate Recording—Bullock County Judge of Probate, 217 North Prairie, Courthouse, Union Springs, AL 36089. Fax: 334-738-3839. 8AM-4:30PM.

Felony, Misdemeanor, Civil, Eviction, Small Claims, Probate—Circuit & District Court, PO Box 230, Union Springs, AL 36089. 336-593-2416, Fax: 334-738-2282. 8AM-4:30PM. Access by: mail, fax, in person, online. Special note: Probate court is separate from this court, and can be contacted at the telephone number above.

Butler

Real Estate Recording—Butler County Judge of Probate, 700 Court Square, Greenville, AL 36037. Fax: 334-382-5489. 8AM-4PM M,T,Th,F; 8AM-Noon W.

Felony, Misdemeanor, Civil, Eviction, Small Claims, Probate—Circuit & District Court, PO Box 236, Greenville, AL 36037. 334-775-8366. 8AM-4PM. Access by: mail, in person, online. Special note: Probate court is separate from this court, and can be contacted at the telephone number above.

Calhoun

Real Estate Recording—Calhoun County Judge of Probate, 1702 Noble Street, Suite 102, Anniston, AL 36201. Fax: 256-231-1728. 8AM-4:30PM.

Felony, Civil Actions Over $10,000—Circuit Court, 25 W 11th St, Anniston, AL 36201. 256-760-5726, Fax: 256-231-1826. 8AM-4:30PM. Access by: in person, online.

Misdemeanor, Civil Actions Under $10,000, Eviction, Small Claims—District Court, 25 W 11th St, Box 9, Anniston, AL 36201. 203-977-4185, Fax: 205-231-1826. 8AM-4:30PM. Access by: in person, online.

Probate—Probate Court, 1702 Noble St, #102, Anniston, AL 36201. 205-233-6406.

Chambers

Real Estate Recording—Chambers County Judge of Probate, Courthouse, Lafayette, AL 36862. Fax: 334-864-4394. 8AM-4:30PM.

Felony, Misdemeanor, Civil, Eviction, Small Claims, Probate—Circuit & District Court, Chambers County Courthouse, Lafayette, AL 36862. 352-620-3904. 8AM-4:30PM. Access by: mail, in person, online. Special note: Probate court is separate from this court, and can be contacted at the telephone number above.

Cherokee

Real Estate Recording—Cherokee County Judge of Probate, Main Street, Centre, AL 35960. Fax: 256-927-6949. 8AM-4PM M-F; 8AM-Noon Sat.

Felony, Misdemeanor, Civil, Eviction, Small Claims—Circuit & District Court, 100 Main St, Rm 203, Centre, AL 35960-1532. 205-927-3363. 8AM-4:30PM. Access by: mail, in person, online.

Probate—Probate Court, 100 Main St, Rm 204, Centre, AL 35960. 205-932-4617, Fax: 205-927-6949. 8AM-4PM M-F, 8AM-Noon Sat. Access by: mail, in person.

Chilton

Real Estate Recording—Chilton County Judge of Probate, 500 2nd Avenue North, Clanton, AL 35045. Fax: 205-280-7204. 8AM-4PM.

Felony, Misdemeanor, Civil, Eviction, Small Claims, Probate—Circuit & District Court, PO Box 1946, Clanton, AL 35046. 205-755-4275. 8AM-5PM. Access by: in person, online. Special note: Probate court is separate from this court, and can be contacted at the telephone number above.

Choctaw

Real Estate Recording—Choctaw County Judge of Probate, 117 South Mulberry, Courthouse, Butler, AL 36904. 205-459-2155, Fax: 205-459-4666. 8AM-4:30PM.

Felony, Misdemeanor, Civil, Eviction, Small Claims, Probate—Circuit & District Court, Choctaw County Courthouse,

Ste 10, Butler, AL 36904. 205-386-8518. 8AM-4:30PM. Access by: mail, in person, online. Special note: Probate court is separate from this court, and can be contacted at the telephone number above.

Clarke

Real Estate Recording—Clarke County Judge of Probate, 117 Court Street, Courthouse, Grove Hill, AL 36451. 334-690-8520, Fax: 334-275-8517. 8AM-5PM.

Felony, Misdemeanor, Civil, Eviction, Small Claims, Probate—Circuit & District Court, PO Box 921, Grove Hill, AL 36451. 334-687-1513. 8AM-5PM. Access by: mail, in person, online. Special note: Probate court is separate from this court, and can be contacted at the telephone number above.

Clay

Real Estate Recording—Clay County Judge of Probate, Courthouse Square, Ashland, AL 36251. Fax: 256-354-2197. 8AM-4:30PM.

Felony, Misdemeanor, Civil, Eviction, Small Claims, Probate—Circuit & District Court, PO Box 816, Ashland, AL 36251. 205-349-3870. 8AM-4:30PM. Access by: in person, online. Special note: Probate court is separate from this court, and can be reached at the telephone number given above.

Cleburne

Real Estate Recording—Cleburne County Judge of Probate, 120 Vickery Street, Room 101, Heflin, AL 36264. 205-459-2411, Fax: 256-463-2257. 8AM-5PM.

Felony, Misdemeanor, Civil, Eviction, Small Claims, Probate—Circuit & District Court, 120 Vickery St Room 202, Heflin, AL 36264. 262-335-4324, Fax: 256-463-2257. 8AM-4:30PM. Access by: mail, phone, in person, online. Special note: Probate court is separate from this court, and can be contacted at the telephone number above.

Coffee

Real Estate Recording—Coffee County Judge of Probate, 230-P North Court Avenue, Elba, AL 36323. Fax: 334-897-2028. 8AM-4:30PM.

Coffee County Judge of Probate, 301 E. Grubbs, Enterprise, AL 36330. Fax: 334-347-2095. 8AM-4:30PM.

Felony, Misdemeanor, Civil, Eviction, Small Claims—Circuit & District Court-Enterprise Division, PO Box 1294, Enterprise, AL 36331. 334-743-2283. 8AM-4:30PM. Access by: mail, in person, online.

Felony, Misdemeanor, Civil, Eviction, Small Claims, Probate—Circuit & District Court-Elba Division, 230 M Court Ave, Elba, AL 36323. 352-754-4190. 8AM-4:30PM. Access by: mail, in person, online.

Probate—Enterprise Division-Probate, PO Box 311247, Enterprise, AL 36331. 334-749-7141, Fax: 334-347-2095. 8AM-4:30PM. Access by: mail, phone, in person.

Colbert

Real Estate Recording—Colbert County Judge of Probate, Probate Judge, 201 Main St. Tuscumbia, AL 35674. Fax: 256-386-8547. 8AM-4:30PM.

Felony, Civil Actions Over $10,000, Probate—Circuit Court, Colbert County Courthouse, Tuscumbia, AL 35674. 205-384-7276. 8AM-4:30PM. Access by: in person, online. Special note: Probate court is separate from this court, and can be contacted at the telephone number above.

Misdemeanor, Civil Actions Under $10,000, Eviction, Small Claims—District Court, Colbert County Courthouse, Tuscumbia, AL 35674. 205-386-8512. 7:30AM-4:30PM. Access by: in person, online.

Conecuh

Real Estate Recording—Conecuh County Judge of Probate, Jackson Street, Court Square, Evergreen, AL 36401. Fax: 334-578-7002. 8AM-4PM.

Felony, Misdemeanor, Civil, Eviction, Small Claims, Probate—Circuit & District Court, PO Box 107, Evergreen, AL 36401. 334-874-2519. 8AM-4:30PM. Access by: mail, in person,

online. Special note: Probate court is separate from this court, and can be contacted at the telephone number above.

Coosa

Real Estate Recording—Coosa County Judge of Probate, Highway 231 and 22, Courthouse, Rockford, AL 35136. Fax: 256-377-2524. 8AM-4PM.

Felony, Misdemeanor, Civil, Eviction, Small Claims, Probate—Circuit & District Court, PO Box 98, Rockford, AL 35136. 205-372-3598. 8AM-4:30PM. Access by: in person, online. Special note: Probate court is separate from this court, and can be contacted at the telephone number above.

Covington

Real Estate Recording—Covington County Judge of Probate, 1 Court Square, Andalusia, AL 36420. Fax: 334-428-2536. 8AM-5PM.

Felony, Misdemeanor, Civil, Eviction, Small Claims, Probate—Circuit & District Court, Covington County Courthouse, Andalusia, AL 36420. 334-832-1260. 8AM-5PM. Access by: in person, online. Special note: Probate court is separate from this court, and can be contacted at the telephone number above.

Crenshaw

Real Estate Recording—Crenshaw County Judge of Probate, 29 S. Glenwood Avenue, Luverne, AL 36049. Fax: 334-335-3616. 8AM-4:30PM.

Felony, Misdemeanor, Civil, Eviction, Small Claims, Probate—Circuit & District Court, PO Box 167, Luverne, AL 36049. 334-738-2280, Fax: 334-335-2076. 8AM-4:30PM. Access by: mail, in person, online. Special note: Probate court is separate from this court, and can be contacted at the telephone number above.

Cullman

Real Estate Recording—Cullman County Judge of Probate, 200 2nd Avenue SW, Courthouse, Cullman, AL 35055. Fax: 256-775-4813. 8AM-4:30PM.

Felony, Civil Actions Over $10,000, Probate—Circuit Court, Cullman County Courthouse, Rm 303, 500 2nd Ave SW, Cullman, AL 35055. 205-775-4654. 8AM-4:30PM. Access by: mail, in person, online.

Misdemeanor, Civil Actions Under $10,000, Eviction, Small Claims—District Court, 500 2nd Ave SW, Courthouse Rm 211, Cullman, AL 35055-4197. 205-739-3530. 8AM-4:30PM. Access by: mail, in person, online.

Dale

Real Estate Recording—Dale County Judge of Probate, Courthouse, Ozark, AL 36360. Fax: 334-774-0468. 8AM-5PM.

Felony, Misdemeanor, Civil, Eviction, Small Claims, Probate—Circuit & District Court, PO Box 1350, Ozark, AL 36361. 336-761-2250. 8AM-4:30PM. Access by: in person, online. Special note: Probate court is separate from this court, and can be contacted at the telephone number above.

Dallas

Real Estate Recording—Dallas County Judge of Probate, 105 Lauderdale Street, Selma, AL 36701. 352-637-9400. 8:30AM-4:30PM.

Felony, Civil Actions Over $10,000, Probate—Circuit Court, PO Box 1158, Selma, AL 36702. 352-742-4100. 8AM-5PM. Access by: mail, phone, in person, online. Special note: Probate court is separate from this court, and can be contacted at the telephone number above.

Misdemeanor, Civil Actions Under $10,000, Eviction, Small Claims—District Court, PO Box 1158, Selma, AL 36702. 352-742-9808. 8AM-5PM. Access by: in person, online.

De Kalb

Real Estate Recording—De Kalb County Judge of Probate, 300 Grand South West, Courthouse, Suite 100, Fort Payne, AL 35967. 262-636-3137, Fax: 256-845-8514. 7:45AM-4:15PM.

Felony, Misdemeanor, Civil, Eviction, Small Claims, Probate—Circuit & District Court, PO Box 681149, Fort Payne, AL 35968. 205-845-8525. 8AM-4PM. Access by: mail, phone, in person, online. Special note: Probate court is separate from this court, and can be contacted at the telephone number above.

Elmore

Real Estate Recording—Elmore County Judge of Probate, 200 Commerce Street, Wetumpka, AL 36092. 334-867-0305, Fax: 334-567-1144. 8AM-4:30PM.

Civil, Probate—Circuit & District Court-Civil Division, PO Box 310, Wetumpka, AL 36092. 334-847-2239, Fax: 334-567-5957. 8AM-4:30PM. Access by: in person, online. Special note: Probate court is separate from this court, and can be contacted at the telephone number above.

Felony, Misdemeanor—Criminal Circuit Court, PO Box 310, 8935 US Hwy 233, Wetumpka, AL 36092. 334-864-4348, Fax: 334-567-5957. 8AM-4:30PM. Access by: in person, online.

Escambia

Real Estate Recording—Escambia County Judge of Probate, 318 Belleville Avenue, Room 205, Brewton, AL 36426. Fax: 334-867-0284. 8AM-4PM.

Felony, Misdemeanor, Civil, Eviction, Small Claims, Probate—Circuit & District Court, PO Box 856, Brewton, AL 36427. 352-637-9400, Fax: 334-867-0275. 8AM-4:30PM. Access by: mail, in person, online. Special note: Probate court is separate from this court, and can be contacted at the telephone number above.

Etowah

Real Estate Recording—Etowah County Judge of Probate, 800 Forrest Avenue, Courthouse, Gadsden, AL 35901. Fax: 256-546-1149. 8AM-5PM.

Felony, Misdemeanor, Civil, Eviction, Small Claims, Probate—Circuit & District Court, PO Box 798, Gadsden, AL 35902. 205-532-3389. 8AM-5PM. Access by: mail, in person, online. Special note: Probate court is separate from this court, and can be contacted at the telephone number above.

Fayette

Real Estate Recording—Fayette County Judge of Probate, 113 Temple Avenue North, Courthouse, Fayette, AL 35555. Fax: 205-932-7600. 8AM-4PM.

Felony, Misdemeanor, Civil, Eviction, Small Claims, Probate—Circuit & District Court, PO Box 206, Fayette, AL 35555. 205-974-2432. 8AM-4:30PM. Access by: in person, online. Special note: Probate court is separate from this court, and can be contacted at the telephone number above.

Franklin

Real Estate Recording—Franklin County Judge of Probate, 410 North Jackson Street, Russellville, AL 35653. 256-845-8520, Fax: 256-332-8855. 8AM-5PM; 8AM-Noon Sat.

Felony, Misdemeanor, Civil, Eviction, Small Claims, Probate—Circuit & District Court, PO Box 160, Russellville, AL 35653. 262-284-8260. 8AM-4:30PM. Access by: mail, in person, online.

Geneva

Real Estate Recording—Geneva County Judge of Probate, Courthouse, 200 N. Commerce St. Geneva, AL 36340. Fax: 334-684-5602. 8AM-5PM.

Felony, Misdemeanor, Civil, Eviction, Small Claims, Probate—Circuit & District Court, PO Box 86, Geneva, AL 36340. 336-342-8700, Fax: 334-684-5605. 8AM-5PM. Access by: mail, in person, online. Special note: Probate court is separate from this court, and can be contacted at the telephone number above.

Greene

Real Estate Recording—Greene County Judge of Probate, 400 Morrow Ave. Greene County Courthouse, Eutaw, AL 35462. Fax: 205-372-0499. 8AM-4PM.

Felony, Misdemeanor, Civil, Eviction, Small Claims, Probate—Circuit & District Court, PO Box 307, Eutaw, AL 35462. 205-367-2050. 8AM-4PM. Access by: mail, in person, online. Special note: Probate court is separate from this court, and can be contacted at the telephone number above.

Hale

Real Estate Recording—Hale County Judge of Probate, 1001 Main Street, Courthouse, Greensboro, AL 36744. 334-874-2526, Fax: 334-624-8725. 8AM-4PM.

Felony, Misdemeanor, Civil, Eviction, Small Claims, Probate—Circuit & District Court, Hale County Courthouse, Rm 8, Greensboro, AL 36744. 334-897-2954. 8AM-5PM. Access by: mail, in person, online. Special note: Probate court is separate from this court, and can be contacted at the telephone number above.

Henry

Real Estate Recording—Henry County Judge of Probate, Suite A, 101 West Court Square, Abbeville, AL 36310. Fax: 334-585-3610. 8AM-4:30PM.

Felony, Misdemeanor, Civil, Eviction, Small Claims, Probate—Circuit & District Court, 101 W Court St, Suite J, Abbeville, AL 36310-2135. 334-874-2523, Fax: 334-585-5006. 8AM-4:30PM. Access by: mail, in person, online. Special note: Probate court is separate from this court, and can be contacted at the telephone number above.

Houston

Real Estate Recording—Houston County Judge of Probate, 462 North Oates, 2nd Floor, Dothan, AL 36303. Fax: 334-677-4733. 8AM-4:30PM.

Felony, Misdemeanor, Civil, Eviction, Small Claims, Probate—Circuit & District Court, PO Drawer 6406, Dothan, AL 36302. 334-937-0282. 7:30AM-4:30PM. Access by: mail, in person, online. Special note: Probate court is separate from this court, and can be contacted at the telephone number above.

Jackson

Real Estate Recording—Jackson County Judge of Probate, Courthouse Square, Courthouse, Scottsboro, AL 35768. Fax: 256-574-9318. 8AM-4:30PM.

Felony, Misdemeanor, Civil, Eviction, Small Claims, Probate—Circuit & District Court, PO Box 397, Scottsboro, AL 35768. 262-335-4341, Fax: 256-574-6575. 8AM-4:30PM. Access by: mail, in person, online. Special note: Probate court is separate from this court, and can be contacted at the telephone number above.

Jefferson

Real Estate Recording—Jefferson County Judge of Probate, 716 North 21st Street, Courthouse, Birmingham, AL 35203. 205-325-5355, Fax: 205-325-1437. 8AM-4:45PM.

Jefferson County Judge of Probate, 1801 3rd Ave. Bessemer, AL 35020. 8AM-4:45PM.

Felony, Civil Actions Over $10,000—Bessemer Division-Circuit Court, Rm 606, Courthouse Annex, Bessemer, AL 35020. 205-463-2873. 8AM-5PM. Access by: in person, online.

Misdemeanor, Civil Actions Under $10,000, Eviction, Small Claims—Bessemer Division-District Court, Rm 506, Courthouse Annex, Bessemer, AL 35020. 205-481-4165. 8AM-5PM. Access by: in person, online.

Civil Actions Over $10,000 (Over $5,000 if jury trial)—Birmingham Division-Civil Circuit Court, 716 N 21st St, Rm 400, Birmingham, AL 35263. 205-325-5331. 8AM-5PM. Access by: mail, phone, in person, online.

Felony—Birmingham Division-Criminal Circuit Court, 801 N 21st St, Rm 506, Birmingham, AL 35263. 205-236-8231. 8AM-4:55PM. Access by: in person, online.

Civil Actions Under $10,000, Eviction, Small Claims—Birmingham Division-Civil District Court, 716 N 21st St, Rm 500, Birmingham, AL 35263. 205-325-5309. 8AM-5PM. Access by: mail, phone, in person, online.

Misdemeanor—Birmingham Division-Criminal District Court, 801 21st St, Rm 207, Birmingham, AL 35263. 205-325-5285. 8AM-5PM. Access by: mail, in person, online.

Probate—Probate Court, 716 N 21st St, Birmingham, AL 35263. 205-325-5372, Fax: 205-325-4885. 8AM-4:45PM. Access by: in person.

Lamar

Real Estate Recording—Lamar County Judge of Probate, 44690 Hwy 17, Vernon, AL 35592. 205-695-7151, Fax: 205-695-9253. 8AM-5PM M,T,Th,F; 8AM-Noon W,Sat.

Felony, Misdemeanor, Civil, Eviction, Small Claims, Probate—Circuit & District Court, PO Box 434, Vernon, AL 35592. 205-695-7193, Fax: 205-695-7427. 8AM-5PM. Access by: mail, in person, online. Special note: Probate court is separate from this court, and can be contacted at the telephone number above.

Lauderdale

Real Estate Recording—Lauderdale County Judge of Probate, 200 South Court Street, Florence, AL 35630. 8AM-5PM.

Felony, Civil Actions Over $10,000, Probate—Circuit Court, PO Box 795, Florence, AL 35631. 205-760-5710. 8AM-Noon, 1-5PM. Access by: in person, online. Special note: Probate court is separate from this court, and can be contacted at the telephone number above.

Misdemeanor, Civil Actions Under $10,000, Eviction, Small Claims—District Court, PO Box 776, Florence, AL 35631. 262-548-7468, Fax: 256-760-5727. 8AM-Noon, 1-5PM. Access by: mail, in person, online.

Lawrence

Real Estate Recording—Lawrence County Judge of Probate, 14330 Court Street, Suite 102, Moulton, AL 35650. Fax: 256-974-3188. 8AM-4PM.

Felony, Misdemeanor, Civil, Eviction, Small Claims, Probate—Circuit & District Court, PO Box 265, Moulton, AL 35650. 206-296-0133. 8AM-5PM. Access by: in person, online. Special note: Probate court is separate from this court, and can be contacted at the telephone number above.

Lee

Real Estate Recording—Lee County Judge of Probate, 215 South 9th, Opelika, AL 36803. 8:30AM-4:30PM.

Felony, Misdemeanor, Civil, Eviction, Small Claims, Probate—Circuit & District Court, 2311 Gateway Dr, Rm 104, Opelika, AL 36801. 336-694-4171, Fax: 334-749-5886. 8:30AM-4:30PM. Access by: mail, phone, in person, online. Special note: Probate court is separate from this court, and can be contacted at the telephone number above.

Limestone

Real Estate Recording—Limestone County Judge of Probate, Courthouse, 2nd Floor, Athens, AL 35611. Fax: 256-233-6474. 8AM-4:30PM.

Felony, Misdemeanor, Civil, Eviction, Small Claims, Probate—Circuit & District Court, PO Box 964, Athens, AL 35612. 205-231-1850. 8AM-4:30PM. Access by: mail, in person, online. Special note: Probate court is separate from this court, and can be contacted at the telephone number above.

Lowndes

Real Estate Recording—Lowndes County Judge of Probate, Courthouse, 1 Washington St. Hayneville, AL 36040. Fax: 334-548-5398. 8AM-4:30PM.

Felony, Misdemeanor, Civil, Eviction, Small Claims, Probate—Circuit & District Court, PO Box 876, Hayneville, AL 36040. 334-832-4950. 8AM-4:30PM. Access by: mail, phone, in person, online. Special note: Probate court is separate from this court, and can be contacted at the telephone number above.

Macon

Real Estate Recording—Macon County Judge of Probate, 101 E. Northside St. Suite 101, Tuskegee, AL 36083. Fax: 334-724-2512. 8:30AM-4:30PM.

Felony, Misdemeanor, Civil, Eviction, Small Claims, Probate—Circuit & District Court, PO Box 830723, Tuskegee, AL 36083. 336-570-6867. 8AM-4:30PM. Access by: mail, in person, online. Special note: Probate court is separate from this court, and can be contacted at the telephone number above.

Madison

Real Estate Recording—Madison County Judge of Probate, 100 Northside Square, Room 101, Huntsville, AL 35801. Fax: 256-532-6977. 8:30AM-5PM.

Civil Actions Over $10,000, Probate—Civil Circuit Court, 100 N Side Square, Courthouse, Huntsville, AL 35801. 205-489-5533. 8AM-5PM. Access by: in person, online. Special note: Probate court is separate from this court, and can be contacted at the telephone number above.

Felony—Criminal Circuit Court, 100 N Side Square, Courthouse, Huntsville, AL 35801-4820. 205-532-3381. 8AM-5PM. Access by: in person, online.

Misdemeanor, Civil Actions Under $10,000, Eviction, Small Claims—District Court, 100 N Side Square, Rm 822 Courthouse, Huntsville, AL 35801. Fax: 205-532-3768. 8AM-5PM. Access by: in person, online.

Marengo

Real Estate Recording—Marengo County Judge of Probate, 101 East Coats Avenue, Courthouse, Linden, AL 36748. Fax: 334-295-2254. 8AM-4:30PM.

Felony, Misdemeanor, Civil, Eviction, Small Claims, Probate—Circuit & District Court, PO Box 566, Linden, AL 36748. 334-690-8786. 8AM-4:30PM. Access by: mail, in person, online.

Marion

Real Estate Recording—Marion County Judge of Probate, Military St, Hamilton, AL 35570. 205-921-7451, Fax: 205-921-5109. 8AM-Noon, 1-5PM.

Felony, Misdemeanor, Civil, Eviction, Small Claims, Probate—Circuit & District Court, PO Box 1595, Hamilton, AL 35570. 205-926-3103. 8AM-5PM. Access by: mail, in person, online. Special note: Probate court is separate from this court, and can be contacted at the telephone number above.

Marshall

Real Estate Recording—Marshall County Judge of Probate, 425 Gunter Avenue, Guntersville, AL 35976. 262-335-4334, Fax: 256-571-7732. 8AM-4:30PM.

Felony, Misdemeanor, Civil, Eviction, Small Claims—Circuit & District Court-Albertville Division, 200 W Main, Albertville, AL 35950. 205-878-4522. 8AM-4:30PM. Access by: mail, in person, online.

Civil Actions Over $10,000, Small Claims, Probate—Civil Circuit Court-Guntersville Division, PO Box 248, Guntersville, AL 35976. 205-549-5437. 8AM-4:30PM. Access by: mail, in person, online. Special note: Probate court is separate from this court, and can be contacted at the telephone number above.

Felony—Criminal Circuit Court-Guntersville Division, 425 Gunter Ave, PO Box 248, Guntersville, AL 35976. 205-571-7791. 8AM-4:30PM. Access by: mail, in person, online.

Mobile

Real Estate Recording—Mobile County Judge of Probate, 101 Government Street, Mobile, AL 36602. Fax: 334-690-4939. 8AM-5PM.

Felony, Civil Actions Over $10,000—Circuit Court, 205 Government St #C-936, Mobile, AL 36644-2936. 336-570-6865. 8AM-5PM. Access by: in person, online.

Misdemeanor, Civil Actions Under $10,000, Eviction, Small Claims, Probate—District Court, State of Alabama, Mobile County, 205 Government St, Mobile, AL 36644. 336-386-8131, Fax: 334-690-4840. 8AM-5PM. Access by: mail, phone, fax, in person, online. Special note: Probate court is a separate court, and can be reached at the telephone number given above.

Monroe

Real Estate Recording—Monroe County Judge of Probate, South Alabama Avenue, Courthouse Square, Monroeville, AL 36460. 8AM-5PM M,T,W,F; 8AM-Noon Th.

Felony, Misdemeanor, Civil, Eviction, Small Claims, Probate—Circuit & District Court, County Courthouse,

Monroeville, AL 36460. 336-679-8838. 8AM-5PM. Access by: mail, in person, online. Special note: Probate court is separate from this court, and can be contacted at the telephone number above.

Montgomery

Real Estate Recording—Montgomery County Judge of Probate, Room 206, 100 South Lawrence, Montgomery, AL 36104. 8AM-5PM.

Felony, Civil Actions Over $10,000, Probate—Circuit Court, PO Box 1667, Montgomery, AL 36102-1667. 352-463-3170. 8AM-5PM. Access by: mail, in person, online. Special note: Probate court is separate from this court, and can be contacted at the telephone number above.

Misdemeanor, Civil Actions Under $10,000, Eviction, Small Claims—District Court, PO Box 1667, Montgomery, AL 36102. 352-498-1200. 8AM-5PM. Access by: mail, in person, online.

Morgan

Real Estate Recording—Morgan County Judge of Probate, 302 Lee Street, Decatur, AL 35601. 8AM-4:30PM.

Felony, Civil Actions Over $10,000, Probate—Circuit Court, PO Box 668, Decatur, AL 35602. 262-284-8409. 8AM-4:30PM. Access by: in person, online. Special note: Probate court is separate from this court, and can be contacted at the telephone number above.

Misdemeanor, Civil Actions Under $10,000, Eviction, Small Claims—District Court, PO Box 668, Decatur, AL 35602. 262-284-8370. 8:30AM-4:30PM. Access by: in person, online.

Perry

Real Estate Recording—Perry County Judge of Probate, Washington Street, Courthouse, Marion, AL 36756. Fax: 334-683-2201. 8AM-4:30PM.

Felony, Misdemeanor, Civil, Eviction, Small Claims, Probate—Circuit & District Court, PO Box 505, Marion, AL 36756. 336-246-5641. 8AM-4:30PM. Access by: mail, in person, online. Special note: Probate court is separate from this court, and can be contacted at the telephone number above.

Pickens

Real Estate Recording—Pickens County Judge of Probate, Court Square, Probate Building, Carrollton, AL 35447. Fax: 205-367-2011. 8AM-4PM.

Felony, Misdemeanor, Civil, Eviction, Small Claims, Probate—Circuit & District Court, PO Box 418, Carrollton, AL 35447. 205-362-4175. 8AM-4:30PM. Access by: mail, in person, online.

Pike

Real Estate Recording—Pike County Judge of Probate, Church Street, Courthouse, Troy, AL 36081. Fax: 334-566-8585. 8AM-5PM.

Felony, Misdemeanor, Civil, Eviction, Small Claims, Probate—Circuit & District Court, PO Box 948, Troy, AL 36081. 334-847-2208. 8AM-5PM. Access by: mail, in person, online. Special note: Probate court is separate from this court, and can be contacted at the telephone number above.

Randolph

Real Estate Recording—Randolph County Judge of Probate, Courthouse, 1 Main St. Wedowee, AL 36278. Fax: 256-357-9053. 8AM-5PM.

Felony, Misdemeanor, Civil, Eviction, Small Claims, Probate—Circuit & District Court, PO Box 328, Wedowee, AL 36278. 205-354-7926. 8AM-Noon, 1-5PM. Access by: in person, online. Special note: Probate court is separate from this court, and can be contacted at the telephone number above.

Russell

Real Estate Recording—Russell County Judge of Probate, 501 14th Street, Phenix City, AL 36867. Fax: 334-298-7979. 8:30AM-5PM.

Felony, Misdemeanor, Civil, Eviction, Small Claims, Probate—Circuit & District Court, PO Box 518, Phenix City, AL 36868. 334-724-2614, Fax: 334-297-6250. 8:30AM-4:30PM. Access

by: mail, in person, online. Special note: Probate court is separate from this court, and can be contacted at the telephone number above.

Shelby

Real Estate Recording—Shelby County Judge of Probate, Main Street, Columbiana, AL 35051. Fax: 205-669-3714. 8AM-4:30PM.

Felony, Misdemeanor, Civil, Eviction, Small Claims, Probate—Circuit & District Court, PO Box 1810, Columbiana, AL 35051. 205-669-3760. 8AM-4:30PM. Access by: in person, online. Special note: Probate court is separate from this court, and can be contacted at the telephone number above.

St. Clair

Real Estate Recording—St. Clair County Judge of Probate, Administrative Building, 5th Avenue, Ashville, AL 35953. Fax: 205-594-2110. 8AM-5PM.

St. Clair Judge of Probate, Courthouse, Suite 212, 1815 Cogswell Ave. Pell City, AL 35125. Fax: 205-884-1182. 8AM-5PM.

Felony, Misdemeanor, Civil, Eviction, Small Claims, Probate—Circuit & District Court-Ashville Division, PO Box 1569, Ashville, AL 35953. 205-594-2184. 8AM-5PM. Access by: mail, in person, online. Special note: Probate court is separate from this court, and can be contacted at the telephone number above.

Circuit & District Court-Pell City Division, 1815 Cogswell Ave, Pell City, AL 35125. 205-329-8123. 8AM-5PM. Access by: mail, in person, online. Special note: Probate court is separate from this court, and can be contacted at the telephone number above.

Sumter

Real Estate Recording—Sumter County Judge of Probate, Courthouse Square, Livingston, AL 35470. 205-652-2731, Fax: 205-652-6206. 8AM-4PM.

Felony, Misdemeanor, Civil, Eviction, Small Claims, Probate—Circuit & District Court, PO Box 936, Livingston, AL 35470. 205-652-2291. 8AM-4:30PM. Access by: mail, in person, online. Special note: Probate court is separate from this court, but can be contacted at the telephone number above.

Talladega

Real Estate Recording—Talladega County Judge of Probate, Courthouse, Talladega, AL 35161. Fax: 256-761-2128. 8AM-5PM.

Felony, Misdemeanor, Civil, Eviction, Small Claims—Circuit & District Court-Northern Division, PO 6137, Talladega, AL 35161. 262-548-7576. 8AM-5PM. Access by: in person, online.

Misdemeanor, Civil Actions Under $10,000, Eviction, Small Claims—District Court-Southern Division, PO Box 183, Sylacauga, AL 35150. 256-761-2102. 7:30AM-4:30AM. Access by: mail, in person, online.

Probate—Probate Court, PO Box 737, Talladega, AL 35161. 205-357-4551.

Tallapoosa

Real Estate Recording—Tallapoosa County Judge of Probate, Courthouse, Room 126, 125 N. Broadnax St. Dadeville, AL 36853. Fax: 256-825-1604. 8AM-5PM.

Felony, Misdemeanor, Civil, Eviction, Small Claims—Circuit & District Court-Western Division, PO Box 189, Alexander City, AL 35011. 205-325-5420. 8AM-5PM. Access by: mail, in person, online.

Felony, Misdemeanor, Civil, Eviction, Small Claims, Probate—Circuit & District Court-Eastern Division, Tallapoosa County Courthouse, Dadeville, AL 36853. 205-825-1098. 8AM-5PM. Access by: mail, in person, online. Special note: Probate court is separate from this court, and can be contacted at the telephone number above.

Tuscaloosa

Real Estate Recording—Tuscaloosa County Judge of Probate, 714 Greensboro Avenue, Tuscaloosa, AL 35401. 8:30AM-5PM.

Civil Actions Over $10,000, Probate—Civil Circuit Court, 714 Greensboro Ave, Tuscaloosa, AL 35401. 205-338-2511. 8:30AM-5PM. Access by: in person, online. Special note: Probate court is separate from this court, and can be contacted at the telephone number above.

Felony—Criminal Circuit Court, 714 Greensboro Ave, Tuscaloosa, AL 35401. 205-349-3870. 8AM-5PM. Access by: mail, in person, online.

Civil Actions Under $10,000, Eviction, Small Claims—District Court-Civil Division, PO Box 2883, Tuscaloosa, AL 35403. 205-349-3870. 8:30AM-5PM. Access by: mail, phone, in person, online.

Misdemeanor—District Court-Criminal Division, PO Box 1687, Tuscaloosa, AL 35403. 205-349-3870. 8:30AM-5PM. Access by: mail, phone, in person, online.

Walker

Real Estate Recording—Walker County Judge of Probate, 1803 3rd Ave. S.W. Courthouse Room 102, Jasper, AL 35502. 205-384-7268, Fax: 205-384-7005. 8AM-4PM.

Felony, Misdemeanor, Civil, Eviction, Small Claims, Probate—Circuit & District Court, PO Box 749, Jasper, AL 35502. 205-377-4988, Fax: 205-384-7271. 8AM-4:30PM. Access by: in person, online. Special note: Probate court is separate from this court, and can be contacted at PO Box 502 or at 205-384-7281.

Washington

Real Estate Recording—Washington County Judge of Probate, 1 Court Street, Chatom, AL 36518. 352-521-4482, Fax: 334-847-3677. 8AM-4:30PM.

Felony, Misdemeanor, Civil, Eviction, Small Claims, Probate—Circuit & District Court, PO Box 548, Chatom, AL 36518. 352-521-4491. 8AM-4:30PM. Access by: in person, online.

Wilcox

Real Estate Recording—Wilcox County Judge of Probate, 100 Broad Street, Courthouse, Camden, AL 36726. 334-937-9561, Fax: 334-682-9484. 8-11:30AM,Noon-4:30PM.

Felony, Misdemeanor, Civil, Eviction, Small Claims, Probate—Circuit & District Court, PO Box 656, Camden, AL 36726. 334-937-0370. 8AM-Noon, 1-5PM. Access by: in person, online. Special note: Probate court is separate from this court, and can be contacted at the telephone number above.

Winston

Real Estate Recording—Winston County Judge of Probate, Main Street, Courthouse, Double Springs, AL 35553. Fax: 205-489-5135. 8AM-4:30PM (8AM-Noon 1st Sat of every month).

Felony, Misdemeanor, Civil, Eviction, Small Claims, Probate—Circuit & District Court, PO Box 309, Double Springs, AL 35553. 205-481-4187. 8AM-4:30PM. Access by: in person, online. Special note: Probate court is separate from this court, and can be contacted at the telephone number above.

Federal Courts

US District Court

Middle District of Alabama

Dothan Division c/o Montgomery Division, PO Box 711, Montgomery, AL 36101334-223-7308 Counties: Coffee, Dale, Geneva, Henry, Houston. www.almd.uscourts.gov

Montgomery Division Records Search, PO Box 711, Montgomery, AL 36101-0711334-223-7308 Counties: Autauga, Barbour, Bullock, Butler, Chilton, Coosa, Covington, Crenshaw, Elmore, Lowndes, Montgomery, Pike. www.almd.uscourts.gov

Opelika Division c/o Montgomery Division, PO Box 711, Montgomery, AL 36101334-223-7308 Counties: Chambers, Lee, Macon, Randolph, Russell, Tallapoosa. www.almd.uscourts.gov

Northern District of Alabama

Birmingham Division Room 140, US Courthouse, 1729 5th Ave N, Birmingham, AL 35203205-731-1700 Counties: Bibb, Blount, Calhoun, Clay, Cleburne, Greene, Jefferson, Pickens, Shelby, Sumter, Talladega, Tuscaloosa. www.alnd.uscourts.gov

Florence Division PO Box 776, Florence, AL 35630205-760-5815, Civil Docket Phone: 205-760-5722, Criminal Docket Phone: 205-760-5725 Fax: 205-760-5727 Counties: Colbert, Franklin, Lauderdale. www.alnd.uscourts.gov

Gadsden Division c/o Birmingham Division, Room 140, US Courthouse, 1729 5th Ave N, Birmingham, AL 35203205-731-1700 Counties: Cherokee, De Kalb, Etowah, Marshall, St. Clair. www.alnd.uscourts.gov

Huntsville Division Clerk's Office, US Post Office & Courthouse, 101 Holmes Ave NE, Huntsville, AL 35801205-534-6495 Counties: Cullman, Jackson, Lawrence, Limestone, Madison, Morgan. www.alnd.uscourts.gov

Jasper Division c/o Birmingham Division, Room 140, US Courthouse, 1729 5th Ave N, Birmingham, AL 35203205-731-1700 Counties: Fayette, Lamar, Marion, Walker, Winston. www.alnd.uscourts.gov

Southern District of Alabama

Mobile Division Clerk, 113 St Joseph St, Mobile, AL 36602334-690-2371 Counties: Baldwin, Choctaw, Clarke, Conecuh, Escambia, Mobile, Monroe, Washington.

Selma Division c/o Mobile Division, 113 St Joseph St, Mobile, AL 36602334-690-2371, Civil Docket Phone: 334-690-2371, Criminal Docket Phone: 334-690-2371 Counties: Dallas, Hale, Marengo, Perry, Wilcox.

US Bankruptcy Court

Middle District of Alabama

Montgomery Division PO Box 1248, Montgomery, AL 36102-1248334-206-6300 Fax: 334-206-6374 Counties: Autauga, Barbour, Bullock, Butler, Chambers, Chilton, Coffee, Coosa, Covington, Crenshaw, Dale, Elmore, Geneva, Henry, Houston, Lee, Lowndes, Macon, Montgomery, Pike, Randolph, Russell, Tallapoosa. www.almb.uscourts.gov

Northern District of Alabama

Anniston Division Room 103, 12th & Noble Sts, Anniston, AL 36201256-237-5631 Fax: 205-237-6547 Counties: Calhoun, Cherokee, Clay, Cleburne, De Kalb, Etowah, Marshall, St. Clair, Talladega.

Birmingham Division Room 120, 1800 5th Ave N, Birmingham, AL 35203205-714-3830 Counties: Blount, Jefferson, Shelby.

Decatur Division PO Box 1289, Decatur, AL 35602256-353-2817 Fax: 205-350-7334 Counties: Colbert, Cullman, Franklin, Jackson, Lauderdale, Lawrence, Limestone, Madison, Morgan. The part of Winston County North of Double Springs is handled by this division..

Tuscaloosa Division PO Box 3226, Tuscaloosa, AL 35403205-752-0426, Record Room: 205-752-0426 Fax: 205-752-6468 Counties: Bibb, Fayette, Greene, Lamar, Marion, Pickens, Sumter, Tuscaloosa, Walker, Winston. The part of Winston County North of Double Springs is handled by Decatur Division.

Southern District of Alabama

Mobile Division Clerk, 201 St. Louis St, Mobile, AL 36602334-441-5391 Fax: 334-441-6286 Counties: Baldwin, Choctaw, Clarke, Conecuh, Dallas, Escambia, Hale, Marengo, Mobile, Monroe, Perry, Washington, Wilcox. www.alsb.uscourts.gov

Attorney General's Office

PO Box 110300   907-465-3600
Juneau, AK 99811-0300   Fax: 907-465-2075
www.law.state.ak.us

Governor's Office

PO Box 110001   907-465-3500
Juneau, AK 99811-0001   Fax: 907-465-3532
www.gov.state.ak.us/

State Archives

141 Willoughby Ave   907-465-2270
Juneau, AK 99801-1720   Fax: 907-465-2465
www.eed.state.ak.us//am/archives

Capital:	Juneau
	Juneau Borough
Time Zone:	AK (Alaska Standard Time)*

* Alaska's Aleutian Islands are Hawaii Standard Time)

Number of Counties:	23
Population:	609,311
Web Site:	www.state.ak.us

Search Unclaimed Property Online

http://www.revenue.state.ak.us/iea/property/ucpsrch.htm

State Agencies

Criminal Records

Department of Public Safety, Records and Identification, 5700 E Tudor Rd, Anchorage, AK 99507; 907-269-5765; Fax: 907-269-5091; 8AM-4:30PM. Access by: mail.

Corporation Records
Trademarks/Servicemarks
Fictitious Name
Assumed Name
Limited Partnership Records
Limited Liability Company Records

Corporation Section, Department of Commerce, PO Box 110808, Juneau, AK 99811-0808 (150 Third Street Rm 217, Juneau, AK 99801); 907-465-2530; Fax: 907-465-3257; 8AM-5PM. Access by: mail, phone, in person. www.dced.state.ak.us/bsc/bsc.htm

Uniform Commercial Code

UCC Central File Systems Office, Department of Natural Resources, 3601 C St, Suite 1140A, Anchorage, AK 99503-5947; 907-269-8899; 7:30AM-3:30PM. Access by: mail.

Federal Tax Liens
State Tax Liens

Records not available from state agency.

All tax liens are filed at local District Recorder Offices.

Workers' Compensation Records

Workers' Compensation, PO Box 25512, Juneau, AK 99802 (1111 W Eighth St, Room 307, Juneau, AK 99802); 907-465-2790; Fax: 907-465-2797; 8AM-4:30PM. Access by:, online. www.labor.state.ak.us/wc/wc.htm

Birth Certificates

Department of Health & Social Services, Bureau of Vital Statistics, PO Box 110675, Juneau, AK 99811-0675 (350 Main, Room 114, Juneau, AK 99811); 907-465-3391; Fax: 907-465-3618; 8AM-4:30PM. Access by: mail, phone, in person.

Death Records

Department of Health & Social Services, Bureau of Vital Statistics, PO Box 110675, Juneau, AK 99811-0675; 907-465-3391; Fax: 907-465-3618; 8AM-4:30PM. Access by: mail, phone, in person.

Marriage Certificates

Department of Health & Social Services, Bureau of Vital Statistics, PO Box 110675, Juneau, AK 99811-0675; 907-465-3391; Fax: 907-465-3618; 8AM-4:30PM. Access by: mail, phone, in person.

Divorce Records

Department of Health & Social Services, Bureau of Vital Statistics, PO Box 110675, Juneau, AK 99811-0675; 907-465-3391; Fax: 907-465-3618; 8AM-4:30PM. Access by: mail, phone, in person.

Accident Reports

Department of Public Safety, Driver Services, PO Box 20020, Juneau, AK 99802-0020 (450 Whittier, Room 105, Juneau, AK 99801); 907-465-4335; Fax: 907-463-5860; 8AM-5PM. Access by: mail.

Driver Records

Division of Motor Vehicles, Driver's Records, PO Box 20020, Juneau, AK 99802-0020 (450 Whitter St, Room 105, Juneau, AK 99802); 907-465-4335 Motor Vehicle Reports Desk; Fax: 907-463-5860; 8AM-5PM. Access by: mail, online. www.state.ak.us/dmv

Vehicle Ownership
Vehicle Identification

Division of Motor Vehicles, Research, 2150 E Dowling Rd, Anchorage, AK 99507; 907-269-5551; 8AM-5PM. Access by: mail.

Boat & Vessel Ownership
Boat & Vessel Registration

Records not available from state agency.

Alaska is not a title state. All boat registrations are done through the US Coast Guard. Call (970) 463-2200 to do a search. Liens are filed with the Department of Natural Resources at (907) 762-2104.

Legislation-Current/Pending
Legislation-Passed

Alaska State Legislature, State Capitol, 130 Seward St, Suite 313, Juneau, AK 99801-1182; 907-465-4648; Fax: 907-465-2864; 8AM-5PM. Access by: mail, phone, in person, online. www.legis.state.ak.us

Voter Registration

Division of Elections, PO Box 110017, Juneau, AK 99811-0017 (Court Plaza Building, 4th Floor, 240 Main Street, Juneau, AK 99801); 907-465-4611; 8AM-4:30PM. Access by: mail. www.gov.state.ak.us/ltgov/elections/homepage.html

GED Certificates

Department of Education, EPS/AVE, 801 W 10th Street, #200, Juneau, AK 99801-1894; 907-465-4685; Fax: 907-465-3240; 7:30AM-3:30PM.
www.educ.state.ak.us/TLS/AVE/ged.html

Hunting License Information
Fishing License Information

Department of Fish & Game, Licensing Section, PO Box 25525, Juneau, AK 99802-5525 (1255 W 8th St, Juneau, AK 99802); 907-465-2376; Fax: 907-465-2440; 8AM-5PM. Access by: mail, phone, fax, in person. state.ak.us/local/akpages/fishgame/admin/license/license.htm

County Courts & Recording Offices

About the Courts...

Administration

Office of the Administrative Director   907-264-0547
303 K St   Fax: 907-264-0881
Anchorage, AK 99501
www.alaska.net/~akctlib/homepage.htm

Court Structure

Alaska is not organized into counties, but rather into 15 boroughs (3 unified home rule municipalities that are combination borough and city, and 12 boroughs) and 12 home rule cities, which do not directly coincide with the 4 Judicial Districts into which the judicial system is divided, that is, judicial boundaries cross borough boundaries. We have listed the courts by their borough or home rule city in keeping with the format of this book. You should search through the city court location names to determine the correct court for your search. Probate is handled by the Superior Courts.

Searching Hints

Documents may not be filed by fax in any Alaska court location without prior authorization of a judge.

The fees established by court rules for Alaska courts are: Search Fee - $15.00 per hour or fraction thereof; certification Fee - $5.00 per document and $2.00 per additional copy of the document; copy Fee - $.25 per page.

Magistrate Courts vary widely in how records are maintained and in the hours of opera-tion (some are open only a few hours per week)

Online Access

There is no internal or external online statewide judicial computer system available.

About the Recording Offices...

Organization

23 boroughs, 34 recording offices. Recording is done by districts, which overlay the borough system. The recording officer is District Recorder. The entire state except the Aleutian Islands is in the Alaska Time Zone (AK).

UCC Records

Financing statements are filed at the state level, except for consumer goods, farm collateral and real estate related collateral, which are filed with the District Recorder. All districts will perform UCC searches at $5.00 per debtor name for information and $15.00 with copies. Use search request form UCC-11. Copies ordered separately usually cost $2.00 per financing statement.

Lien Records

All state and federal tax liens are filed with the District Recorder. Districts do not perform separate tax lien searches.

Real Estate Records

Districts do not perform real estate searches. Certification fees are usually $5.00 per document. Copies usually cost $1.25 for the first page, $.25 per additional page.

County Courts & Recording Offices

Aleutian Islands

Real Estate Recording—Aleutian Islands District Recorder, 3601 C Street, Suite 1140, Anchorage, AK 99503. 8AM-3:30PM.

Misdemeanor, Civil Actions Under $5,000, Small Claims—Sand Point Magistrate Court (3rd District), c/o/ Joanne Gilson, PO Box 127, Valdez, AK 99696-0127. 907-835-2638. Access by: mail, in person. Special note: Court closed.

St Paul Island Magistrate Court (3rd District), c/o Joanne Gilson, PO Box 127, Valdez, AK 99696-0127. 907-835-2638. Access by: mail, in person. Special note: Court is closed at press time. Cases are currently being handled out of the Seward Court.

Unalaska Magistrate Court (3rd District), Box 245, Unalaska, AK 99685-0245. 907-581-1266, Fax: 907-581-2809. 8:30AM-4:30PM. Access by: mail, in person.

Anchorage

Real Estate Recording—Anchorage District Recorder, 3601 C Street, Suite 1140, Anchorage, AK 99503. 8AM-3:30PM.

Felony, Misdemeanor, Civil, Eviction, Small Claims, Probate—Superior & District Court (3rd District), 825 West 4th, Anchorage, AK 99501-2004. 907-264-0444, Fax: 907-264-0873. 8AM-4:30PM. Access by: mail, phone, fax, in person.

Barrow

Real Estate Recording—Barrow District Recorder, 1648 S. Cushman St. #201, Fairbanks, AK 99701. 8:30AM-4PM.

Bethel

Real Estate Recording—Bethel District Recorder, 204 Chief Eddie Hoffman Highway, City Office Building, Bethel, AK 99559. 907-543-2298. 9:15AM-Noon, 1-3:15PM.

Kuskokwim District Recorder, 204 Chief Eddie Hoffman Highway, City Office Building, Bethel, AK 99559. 9:15AM-Noon, 1-3:15PM.

Felony, Misdemeanor, Civil, Eviction, Small Claims, Probate—Superior & District Court (4th District), Box 130, Bethel, AK 99559-0130. 907-543-2298, Fax: 907-543-4419. 8AM-4:30PM. Access by: mail, phone, in person.

Misdemeanor, Civil Actions Under $7,500, Small Claims—Aniak District Court (4th District), PO Box 147, Aniak, AK 99557-0147. 907-675-4325, Fax: 907-675-4278. 8AM-4:30PM. Access by: mail, in person.

Misdemeanor, Civil Actions Under $5,000, Small Claims—Quinhagak Magistrate Court (4th District), c/o Bethel Clerk, PO Box 130, Bethel, AK 99559-0130. 907-543-2298. Access by: mail, in person.

Bristol Bay

Real Estate Recording—Bristol Bay District Recorder, 3601 C Street, Suite 1140, Anchorage, AK 99503. 8AM-3:30PM.

Misdemeanor, Civil Actions Under $5,000, Small Claims—Naknek Magistrate Court (3rd District), Box 229, Naknek, AK 99633-0229. 907-246-6151, Fax: 907-246-7418. 8:30AM-4:30PM. Access by: mail, in person.

Cape Nome

Real Estate Recording—Cape Nome District Recorder, Front Street, 3rd Floor, Old Federal Building, Nome, AK 99762. 8AM-12:30PM.

Chitina

Real Estate Recording—Chitina District Recorder, Mile 115 Richardson Hwy, ATHNA Bldg. Glennallen, AK 99588. 8:30AM-4PM.

Cordova

Real Estate Recording—Cordova District Recorder, 3601 C Street, Suite 1140, Anchorage, AK 99503. 8AM-3:30PM.

Denali

Misdemeanor, Civil Actions Under $5,000, Small Claims—Healy Magistrate Court (4th District), Box 298, Healy, AK 99743-0298. 907-683-2213, Fax: 907-683-1383. 8AM-4:30PM. Access by: mail, in person.

Dillingham

Felony, Misdemeanor, Small Claims—Dillingham Superior Court (3rd District), Box 909, Dillingham, AK 99576-0909. 907-842-5215, Fax: 907-842-5746. 8AM-4:30PM. Access by: mail, in person.

Fairbanks

Real Estate Recording—Fairbanks District Recorder, 1648 S. Cushman St. #201, Fairbanks, AK 99701. 8:30AM-4PM.

Felony, Misdemeanor, Civil, Eviction, Small Claims, Probate—Superior & District Court (4th District), 604 Barnette St, Fairbanks, AK 99701. 907-452-9265, Fax: 907-452-9342. 8AM-4:30PM. Access by: mail, in person.

Fort Gibbon

Real Estate Recording—Fort Gibbon District Recorder, 1648 S. Cushman St. #201, Fairbanks, AK 99701. 8:30AM-4PM.

Haines

Real Estate Recording—Haines District Recorder, 400 Willoughby, 3rd Floor, Juneau, AK 99801. 8:30AM-4PM.

Misdemeanor, Civil Actions Under $50,000, Small Claims—District Court (1st District), Box 169, Haines, AK 99827. 907-766-2801, Fax: 907-766-3148. 8AM-4:30PM. Access by: mail, phone, fax, in person.

Homer

Real Estate Recording—Homer District Recorder, 195 E. Bunnell Ave. Suite A, Homer, AK 99603. 8:30AM-11:30AM, 12:30-4PM.

Iliamna

Real Estate Recording—Iliamna District Recorder, 3601 C Street, Suite 1140, Anchorage, AK 99503. 8AM-3:30PM.

Juneau

Real Estate Recording—Juneau District Recorder, 400 Willoughby, 3rd Floor, Juneau, AK 99801. 8:30AM-4PM.

Felony, Misdemeanor, Civil, Eviction, Small Claims, Probate—Superior & District Court (1st District), Dimond Courthouse, PO Box 114100, Juneau, AK 99811-4100. 907-463-4700, Fax: 907-463-3788. 8AM-4:30PM. Access by: mail, in person.

Kenai

Real Estate Recording—Kenai District Recorder, 120 Trading Bay Road, Suite 230, Kenai, AK 99611. 8:30AM-4PM.

Felony, Misdemeanor, Civil, Eviction, Small Claims, Probate—Superior & District Court (3rd District), 125 Trading Bay Dr, Ste 100, Kenai, AK 99611. 907-283-3110, Fax: 907-283-8535. 8AM-4:30PM. Access by: mail, in person.

Misdemeanor, Civil Actions Under $50,000, Small Claims—District Court (3rd District), 3670 Lake St, Ste 400, Homer, AK 99603-7686. 907-235-8171, Fax: 907-235-4257. 8AM-4:30PM. Access by: mail, phone, in person.

Misdemeanor, Civil Actions Under $5,000, Small Claims—Seward Magistrate Court (3rd District), Box 1929, Seward, AK 99664-1929. 907-224-3075, Fax: 907-227-7192. 8AM-4:30PM. Access by: mail, fax, in person.

Ketchikan

Real Estate Recording—Ketchikan District Recorder, 415 Main Street, Room 320, Ketchikan, AK 99901. 8:30AM-4PM.

Felony, Misdemeanor, Civil, Eviction, Small Claims, Probate—Superior & District Court (1st District), 415 Main, Rm 400, Ketchikan, AK 99901-6399. 907-225-3195, Fax: 907-225-7849. 8AM-4:30PM. Access by: mail, in person.

Kodiak

Real Estate Recording—Kodiak District Recorder, 204 Mission Road, Room 16, Kodiak, AK 99615. 8:30AM-Noon, 1-4PM.

Kodiak Island

Felony, Misdemeanor, Civil, Eviction, Small Claims, Probate—Superior & District Court (3rd District), 204 Mission Road, Rm 10, Kodiak, AK 99615-7312. 907-486-1600, Fax: 907-486-1660. 8AM-4:30PM M,T,Th,F; 9AM-4:30PM W. Access by: mail, in person.

Kotzebue

Real Estate Recording—Kotzebue District Recorder, 1648 S. Cushman St. #201, Fairbanks, AK 99701. 8:30AM-4PM.

Kvichak

Real Estate Recording—Kvichak District Recorder, 3601 C Street, Suite 1140, Anchorage, AK 99503. 8AM-3:30PM.

Manley Hot Springs

Real Estate Recording—Manley Hot Springs District Recorder, 1648 S. Cushman St. #201, Fairbanks, AK 99701. 8:30AM-4PM.

Matanuska-Susitna

Felony, Misdemeanor, Civil, Eviction, Small Claims, Probate—Superior & District Court (3rd District), 435 S Denali, Palmer, AK 99645-6437. 907-746-8109, Fax: 907-746-4151. 8AM-4:30PM. Access by: mail, in person.

Mount McKinley

Real Estate Recording—Mount McKinley District Recorder, 1648 S. Cushman St. #201, Fairbanks, AK 99701. 8:30AM-4PM.

Nenana

Real Estate Recording—Nenana District Recorder, 1648 S. Cushman St. #201, Fairbanks, AK 99701. 8:30AM-4PM.

Nome

Felony, Misdemeanor, Civil, Eviction, Small Claims, Probate—Superior & District Court (2nd District), Box 1110, Nome, AK 99762-1110. 907-443-5216, Fax: 907-443-2192. 8AM-4:30PM. Access by: mail, fax, in person.

Misdemeanor, Civil Actions Under $5,000, Small Claims—Gambell Magistrate Court (2nd District), Box 48, Gambell, AK 99742-0048. 907-985-5133, Fax: 907-985-5133. 8AM-11:30AM. Access by: mail, phone, fax, in person. Special note: At press time court is vacant. Refer to Superior Court in Nome for records.

Unalakleet Magistrate Court (2nd District), Box 250, Unalakleet, AK 99684-0250. 907-624-3015, Fax: 907-624-3118. 8AM-1:30PM. Access by: mail, in person.

North Slope

Felony, Misdemeanor, Civil, Eviction, Small Claims, Probate—Superior & District Court (2nd District), Box 270, Barrow, AK 99723-0270. 907-852-4800, Fax: 907-852-4804. 8AM-4:30PM. Access by: mail, phone, in person.

Northwest Arctic

Felony, Misdemeanor, Civil, Eviction, Small Claims, Probate—Superior & District Court (2nd District), Box 317, Kotzebue, AK 99752-0317. 907-442-3208, Fax: 907-442-3974. 8AM-4:30PM. Access by: mail, fax, in person.

Misdemeanor, Civil Actions Under $5,000, Small Claims—Ambler Magistrate Court (2nd District), Box 86028, Ambler, AK 99786. 907-445-2137, Fax: 907-445-2136. 9AM-2PM. Access by: mail, in person.

Kiana Magistrate Court (2nd District), Box 170, Kiana, AK 99749-0170. 907-475-2167, Fax: 907-475-2169. 10AM-3PM M,W,F. Access by: mail, in person. Special note: Court is temporarily vacant, call 907-442-3208 for records.

Nulato

Real Estate Recording—Nulato District Recorder, 1648 S. Cushman St. #201, Fairbanks, AK 99701. 8:30AM-4PM.

Palmer

Real Estate Recording—Palmer District Recorder, 836 South Colony Way, Palmer, AK 99645. 8:30AM-4PM.

Petersburg

Real Estate Recording—Petersburg District Recorder, 415 Main Street, Room 320, Ketchikan, AK 99901. 8:30AM-Noon, 1-4PM.

Prince of Wales-Outer Ketchikan

Misdemeanor, Civil Actions Under $5,000, Small Claims—Craig Magistrate Court (1st District), Box 646, Craig, AK 99921. 907-826-3316, Fax: 907-826-3904. 8AM-4:30PM. Access by: mail, phone, in person.

Rampart

Real Estate Recording—Rampart District Recorder, 1648 S. Cushman St. #201, Fairbanks, AK 99701. 8:30AM-4PM.

Seldovia

Real Estate Recording—Seldovia District Recorder, 195 E. Bunnell Ave. Suite A, Homer, AK 99603. 8:30-11:30AM, 12:30-4PM.

Seward

Real Estate Recording—Seward District Recorder, 5th & Adams, Municipal Building Room 208, Seward, AK 99664. 8:30AM-4PM.

Sitka

Real Estate Recording—Sitka District Recorder, 210C Lake Street, Sitka, AK 99835. 8:30AM-Noon, 1-4PM M-Th.

Felony, Misdemeanor, Civil, Eviction, Small Claims, Probate—Superior & District Court (1st District), 304 Lake St, Rm 203, Sitka, AK 99835-7759. 907-747-3291, Fax: 907-747-6690. 8AM-4:30PM. Access by: mail, phone, fax, in person.

Skagway

Real Estate Recording—Skagway District Recorder, 400 Willoughby, 3rd Floor, Juneau, AK 99801. 8:30AM-4PM.

Skagway-Yakutat-Angoon

Misdemeanor, Civil Actions Under $50,000, Small Claims—Hoonah District Court (1st District), PO Box 430, Hoonah, AK 99829-0430. 907-945-3668, Fax: 907-945-3637. 8AM-Noon, 1-4:30PM. Access by: mail, in person.

Misdemeanor, Civil Actions Under $5,000, Small Claims—Angoon Magistrate Court (1st District), Box 202, Angoon, AK 99820. 907-788-3229, Fax: 907-788-3108. 11AM-2PM. Access by: mail, in person.

Pelican Magistrate Court (1st District), Box 36, Pelican, AK 99832-0036. Access by: mail, phone, fax, in person. Special note: This court closed permanently on 12/31/99. All records are at the Sitka court.

Misdemeanor, Civil Actions Under $7,500, Small Claims—Skagway Magistrate Court (1st District), Box 495, Skagway, AK 99840-0495. 907-983-2368, Fax: 907-983-3800. 9AM-Noon, 1-4:30PM M; 8AM-Noon, 1-4:30PM T-F. Access by: mail, in person. Special note: Hours will vary from summer to winter.

Yakutat Magistrate Court (1st District), Box 426, Yakutat, AK 99689-0426. 907-784-3274, Fax: 907-784-3257. 9AM-3:30PM. Access by: mail, phone, fax, in person.

Southeast Fairbanks

Misdemeanor, Civil Actions Under $7,500, Small Claims—Delta Junction Magistrate Court (4th District), Box 401, Delta Junction, AK 99737-0401. 907-895-4211, Fax: 907-895-4204. 8AM-Noon, 1-4:30PM. Access by: mail, in person.

Tok Magistrate Court (4th District), Box 187, Tok, AK 99780-0187. 907-883-5171, Fax: 907-883-4367. 8AM-4:30PM. Access by: mail, in person.

Talkeetna

Real Estate Recording—Talkeetna District Recorder, 836 South Colony Way, Palmer, AK 99645. 8:30AM-4PM.

Valdez

Real Estate Recording—Valdez District Recorder, 213 Meals Avenue, Courthouse, Valdez, AK 99686. 8:30AM-Noon, 1-4PM.

Valdez-Cordova

Felony, Misdemeanor, Civil, Eviction, Small Claims, Probate—Superior & District Court (3rd District), Box 127, Valdez, AK 99686-0127. 907-835-2266, Fax: 907-835-3764. 8AM-4:30PM. Access by: mail, fax, in person.

Felony, Misdemeanor, Civil, Small Claims, Probate—Cordova Court (3rd District), Box 898, Cordova, AK 99574-0898. 907-424-3378, Fax: 907-424-7581. 8AM-4:30PM. Access by: mail, phone, fax, in person.

Misdemeanor, Civil Actions Under $10,000, Small Claims—Glennallen District Court (3rd District), Box 86, Glennallen, AK 99588-0086. 907-822-3405, Fax: 907-822-3601. 8AM-4:30PM. Access by: mail, in person.

Misdemeanor, Civil Actions Under $5,000, Small Claims—Whittier Magistrate Court (3rd District), c/o Karla Utter, 825 W 4th Ave, Anchorage, AK 99500-2004. 907-264-0456. Access by: mail, in person. Special note: Court closed.

Wade Hampton

Misdemeanor, Civil Actions Under $5,000, Small Claims—Chevak Magistrate Court (2nd District), Box 238, Chevak, AK 99563-0238. 907-858-7231, Fax: 907-858-7232. 9AM-3:30PM. Access by: mail, in person.

Emmonak Magistrate Court (2nd District), Box 176, Emmonak, AK 99581-0176. 907-949-1748, Fax: 907-949-1535. 8AM-4:30PM. Access by: mail, phone, fax, in person.

Misdemeanor, Civil Actions Under $7,500, Small Claims—St Mary's Magistrate Court (2nd District), Box 269, St Mary's, AK 99658-0183. 907-438-2912, Fax: 907-438-2819. 8AM-4:30PM. Access by: mail, phone, fax, in person.

Wrangell

Real Estate Recording—Wrangell District Recorder, 415 Main Street, Room 320, Ketchikan, AK 99901. 8:30AM-Noon, 1-4PM.

Wrangell-Petersburg

Felony, Misdemeanor, Civil, Eviction, Small Claims, Probate—Superior & District Court (1st District), Box 1009, Petersburg, AK 99833-1009. 907-772-3824, Fax: 907-772-3018. 8AM-4:30PM. Access by: mail, phone, fax, in person.

Superior & District Court (1st District), Box 869, Wrangell, AK 99929-0869. 907-874-2311, Fax: 907-874-3509. 8AM-4:30PM. Access by: mail, phone, fax, in person.

Misdemeanor, Civil Actions Under $7,500, Small Claims—Kake Magistrate Court (1st District), Box 100, Kake, AK 99830-0100. 907-785-3651, Fax: 907-785-3152. 8AM-Noon. Access by: mail, in person.

Yukon-Koyukuk

Misdemeanor, Civil Actions Under $5,000, Small Claims—Fort Yukon Magistrate Court (4th District), Box 211, Fort Yukon, AK 99740-0211. 907-662-2336, Fax: 907-662-2824. 9:30AM-3PM. Access by: mail, in person.

Galena Magistrate Court (4th District), Box 167, Galena, AK 99741-0167. 907-656-1322, Fax: 907-656-1546. 8AM-4:30PM. Access by: mail, in person.

McGrath Magistrate Court (4th District), Box 167, Galena, AK 99741-0167. 907-656-1322, Fax: 907-656-1546. 8:30AM-4:30PM. Access by: mail, in person.

Nenana Magistrate Court (4th District), Box 449, Nenana, AK 99760-0449. 907-832-5430, Fax: 907-832-5841. 8:30AM-4PM. Access by: mail, in person.

Tanana Magistrate Court (4th District), Box 449, Nenana, AK 99777. 907-366-7243, Fax: 907-832-5841. Th-F 2nd full week ea month. Access by: mail, in person.

Federal Courts

US District Court

Anchorage Division Box 4, 222 W 7th Ave, Anchorage, AK 99513-7564907-271-5568, Civil Docket Phone: 907-271-5574, Criminal Docket Phone: 907-271-5661 Counties: Aleutian Islands-East, Aleutian Islands-West, Anchorage Borough, Bristol Bay Borough, Kenai Peninsula Borough, Kodiak Island Borough, Matanuska-Susitna Borough, Valdez-Cordova. www.akd.uscourts.gov
Fairbanks Division Room 332, 101 12th Ave, Fairbanks, AK 99701907-451-5791 Counties: Bethel, Fairbanks North Star Borough, North Slope Borough, Northwest Arctic Borough, Southeast Fairbanks, Wade Hampton, Yukon-Koyukuk. www.akd.uscourts.gov

Juneau Division PO Box 020349, Juneau, AK 99802-0349907-586-7458 Counties: Haines Borough, Juneau Borough, Prince of Wales-Outer Ketchikan, Sitka Borough, Skagway-Hoonah-Angoon, Wrangell-Petersburg. www.akd.uscourts.gov
Ketchikan Division 648 Mission St, Room 507, Ketchikan, AK 99901907-247-7576 Counties: Ketchikan Gateway Borough. www.akd.uscourts.gov
Nome Division PO Box 1110, Nome, AK 99762907-443-5216 Fax: 907-443-2192 Counties: Nome. www.akd.uscourts.gov

US Bankruptcy Court

Anchorage Division Historic Courthouse, Suite 138, 605 W 4th Ave, Anchorage, AK 99501-2296907-271-2655 Counties: All boroughs and districts in Alaska. www.akb.uscourts.gov

Attorney General's Office
1275 W Washington   602-542-5025
Phoenix, AZ 85007   Fax: 602-542-4085
www.attorney general.state.az.us

Governor's Office
State Capitol, W Wing, 1700 W Washington   602-542-4331
Phoenix, AZ 85007   Fax: 602-542-7601
www.governor.state.az.us/

State Archives
1700 W Washington, Room 342   602-542-4159
Phoenix, AZ 85007   Fax: 602-542-4402
www.dlapr.lib.az.us/archives/index.htm

Capital:	Phoenix
	Maricopa County
Time Zone:	MST
Number of Counties:	15
Population:	4,554,966
Web Site:	www.state.az.us

Search Unclaimed Property Online
There is no Internet-based search for unclaimed property for this state.

State Agencies

Criminal Records
Department of Public Safety, Criminal History Records Unit, PO Box 6638, Phoenix, AZ 85005-6638 (2102 W Encanto, Phoenix, AZ 85005); 602-223-2223; 8AM-5PM. Access by: mail.

Corporation Records
Limited Liability Company Records
Corporation Commission, 1300 W Washington, Phoenix, AZ 85007; 602-542-3026 Status, 602-542-3285 Annual Reports; Fax: 602-542-3414; 8AM-5PM. Access by: mail, phone, in person, online. www.cc.state.az.us

Trademarks/Servicemarks
Trade Names
Limited Partnership Records
Secretary of State, Trademarks/Tradenames/Limited Partnership Division, 1700 W Washington, 7th Floor, Phoenix, AZ 85007; 602-542-6187; Fax: 602-542-7386; 8AM-5PM. Access by: mail, phone, in person.

Sales Tax Registrations
Revenue Department, Taxpayer Assistance, 1600 W Monroe, Phoenix, AZ 85007; 602-542-4656; Fax: 602-542-4772; 8AM-5PM. Access by: mail, phone, in person. www.state.az.us/dor

Uniform Commercial Code
Federal Tax Liens
State Tax Liens
UCC Division, Secretary of State, State Capitol, West Wing, 7th Floor, Phoenix, AZ 85007; 602-542-6178; Fax: 602-542-7386; 8AM - 5PM. Access by: mail, online. www.sosaz.com

Fictitious Name
Assumed Name
Records not available from state agency.

Records are found at the county level.

Workers' Compensation Records

State Compensation Fund, 3031 N Second St, Phoenix, AZ 85012; 602-631-2000; Fax: 602-631-2213; 8AM-5PM. Access by: mail.

Birth Certificates

Department of Health Services, Vital Records Section, PO Box 3887, Phoenix, AZ 85030 (2727 W Glendale Ave, Phoenix, AZ 85051); 602-255-3260; Fax: 602-249-3040; 8AM-5PM (counter closes at 4:30 PM). Access by: mail.

Death Records

Department of Health Services, Vital Records Section, PO Box 3887, Phoenix, AZ 85030; 602-255-3260; Fax: 602-249-3040; 8AM-5PM (counter closes at 4:30 PM). Access by: mail.

Marriage Certificates
Divorce Records

Records not available from state agency.

These records are not available from the state, they must be requested from the county or court of issue.

Accident Reports

Department of Public Safety, Accident Reports, PO Box 6638, Phoenix, AZ 85005 (2102 W Encanto, 1st Floor, Phoenix, AZ 85005); 602-223-2236; 8AM-5PM. Access by: mail.

Driver Records

Motor Vehicle Division, Record Services Section, PO Box 2100, Mail Drop 539M, Phoenix, AZ 85001-2100 (Customer Records Services, 1801 W Jefferson, Rm 111, Phoenix, AZ 85007); 602-255-0072; 8AM-5PM. Access by: mail, online. www.dot.state.az.us/MVD/mvd.htm

Vehicle Ownership
Vehicle Identification

Motor Vehicle Division, Record Services Section, PO Box 2100, Mail Drop 504M, Phoenix, AZ 85001-2100 (Customer Records Services, 1801 W Jefferson, Rm 111, Phoenix, AZ 85007); 602-255-8359; 8AM-5PM. Access by: mail, online. www.dot.state.az.us/MVD/mvd.htm

Boat & Vessel Ownership
Boat & Vessel Registration

Game & Fish Dept, 2222 W Greenway Rd, Phoenix, AZ 85023-4399; 602-942-3000; Fax: 602-789-3729; 8AM-5PM M-F. www.gf.state.az.us

Legislation-Current/Pending
Legislation-Passed

Arizona Legislature, State Senate - Room 203, 1700 W Washington, Phoenix, AZ 85007 (Senate Wing or, House Wing, Phoenix, AZ 85007); 602-542-3559 Senate Information, 602-542-4221 House Information, 602-542-3429 Senate Fax, 602-542-4099 House Fax; 8AM-5PM. Access by: mail, online. www.azleg.state.az.us

Voter Registration

Records not available from state agency.

Records are maintained at the county recorder offices. Records are permitted to be sold in bulk only for political related purposes; however, counties can confirm and release names and addresses on a single inquiry basis.

GED Certificates

Department of Education, GED Testing, 1535 W Jefferson, Phoenix, AZ 85007; 602-542-5802; Fax: 602-542-1161; 8AM-5PM.

Hunting License Information
Fishing License Information

Game & Fish Department, Information & Licensing Division, 2221 W Greenway Rd, Phoenix, AZ 85023-4399; 602-942-3000; Fax: 602-789-3924; 8AM-5PM. www.azgfd.com

County Courts & Recording Offices

About the Courts...

Administration

Administrative Office of the Courts,
Arizona Supreme Court Bldg   602-542-9301
1501 W Washington
Phoenix, AZ 85007
www.supreme.state.az.us

Court Structure

The Superior is the court of general jurisdiction. Justice, and Municipal courts generally have separate jurisdiction over case types as indicated in the text. Most courts will search their records by plaintiff or defendant. Estate cases are handled by Superior Court. Fees are the same as for civil and criminal case searching.

Searching Hints

Public access to all Maricopa County court case indexes is available at a central location - 1 W Madison Ave in Phoenix. Copies, however, must be obtained from the court where the case is heard.

Many offices do not perform searches due to personnel and/or budget constraints. As computerization of record offices increases across the state, more record offices are providing public access computer terminals.

Fees across all jurisdictions, as established by the Arizona Supreme Court and State Legislature, are as follows as of January 1, 1998: Search - Superior Court: $18.00 per name; lower courts: $17.00 per name; Certification - Superior Court: $18.00 per document; lower courts: $17.00 per document; Copies - $.50 per page. Courts may choose to charge no fees.

Online Access

A system called ACAP (Arizona Court Automation Project) is implemented in over 100 courts. Mohave County is not a part of ACAP. ACAP is, fundamentally, a case and cash management information processing system. When fully implemented ACAP will provide all participating courts access to all records on the system. Current plans call for public availability later in 2000.

The Maricopa and Pima county courts maintain their own systems, but will also, under current planning, be part of ACAP. These two counties provide limited remote access capability. For current ACAP information, you may call 602-542-9300.

About the Recording Offices...

Organization

15 counties, 16 recording offices. The Navajo Nation is profiled here. The recording officer is County Recorder. Recordings are usually placed in a Grantor/Grantee index. The entire state is in the Mountain Time Zone (MST), and does not change to daylight savings time.

UCC Records

Financing statements are filed at the state level, except for consumer goods, farm collateral, and real estate related collateral, which are filed with the County Recorder. All counties will perform UCC searches. Use search request form UCC-3. Search fees are generally $10.00 per debtor name. Copies usually cost $1.00 per page.

Lien Records

Federal and state tax liens on personal property of businesses are filed with the Secretary of State. Other federal and state tax liens are filed with the County Recorder. Counties do not perform separate tax lien searches.

Real Estate Records

Counties do not perform real estate searches. Copy fees are usually $1.00 per page. Certification fees are usually $3.00 per document.

County Courts & Recording Offices

Apache

Real Estate Recording—Apache County Recorder, 75 West Cleveland, St. Johns, AZ 85936. 520-337-4364, Fax: 520-337-2003. 8AM-5PM.

Felony, Civil Actions Over $5,000, Probate—Superior Court, PO Box 365, St John's, AZ 85936. 520-337-4364, Fax: 520-337-2771. 8AM-5PM. Access by: mail, in person.

Misdemeanor, Civil Actions Under $5,000, Eviction, Small Claims—Chinle Justice Court, PO Box 888, Chinle, AZ 86503. 520-674-5922, Fax: 520-674-5926. 8AM-5PM. Access by: mail, phone, fax, in person.

Puerco Justice Court, PO Box 610, Sanders, AZ 86512. 520-688-2954. 8AM-Noon, 1-5PM. Access by: mail, in person.

Round Valley Justice Court, PO Box 1356, Springerville, AZ 85938. 520-333-4613, Fax: 520-333-5761. 8AM-Noon, 1-5PM. Access by: mail, phone, fax, in person.

St John's Justice Court, PO Box 308, St John's, AZ 85936. 520-337-4364, Fax: 520-337-2683. 8AM-5PM. Access by: mail, in person.

Cochise

Real Estate Recording—Cochise County Recorder, Cochise County Administrative Building, 4 Ledge Ave. Bisbee, AZ 85603. Fax: 520-432-9274. 8AM-5PM.

Felony, Civil Actions Over $5,000, Probate—Cochise County Superior Court, PO Box CK, Bisbee, AZ 85603. 520-432-9364, Fax: 520-432-4850. 8AM-5PM. Access by: mail, phone, fax, in person. www.apltwo.ct.state.az.us/cochise

Misdemeanor, Civil Actions Under $5,000, Eviction, Small Claims—Benson Justice Court, PO Box 2167, Benson, AZ 85602. 520-586-2247, Fax: 520-586-9647. 8AM-5PM. Access by: mail, fax, in person.

Bisbee Justice Court, 207 N Judd Dr, PO Box 1893, Bisbee, AZ 85603. 520-432-9542, Fax: 520-432-9594. 8AM-5PM. Access by: mail, fax, in person.

Bowie Justice Court, PO Box 317, Bowie, AZ 85605. 520-847-2303, Fax: 520-847-2242. 8AM-5PM. Access by: mail, phone, fax, in person.

Douglas Justice Court, 661 G Ave, Douglas, AZ 85607. 520-364-3561, Fax: 520-364-3684. 8AM-5PM. Access by: mail, fax, in person.

Sierra Vista Justice Court, 4001 E Foothills Dr, Sierra Vista, AZ 85635. 520-452-4980, Fax: 520-452-4986. 8AM-5PM. Access by: mail, fax, in person.

Willcox Justice Court, 450 S Haskell, Willcox, AZ 85643. 520-384-2105, Fax: 520-384-4305. 8AM-5PM. Access by: mail, fax, in person.

Coconino

Real Estate Recording—Coconino County Recorder, 100 E. Birch, Flagstaff, AZ 86001. Fax: 520-779-6739. 8AM-5PM.

Felony, Civil Actions Over $5,000, Probate—Superior Court, 100 E Birch St, Flagstaff, AZ 86001. 520-779-6535. 8AM-5PM. Access by: mail, in person.

Misdemeanor, Civil Actions Under $5,000, Eviction, Small Claims—Flagstaff Justice Court, 100 E Birch Ave, Flagstaff, AZ 86001. 520-779-6806. 8AM-5PM. Access by: mail, in person.

Fredonia Justice Court, 100 N Main, Fredonia, AZ 86022. 520-643-7472, Fax: 520-643-7491. 8AM-5PM. Access by: mail, in person.

Page Justice Court, PO Box 1565, Page, AZ 86040. 520-645-8871, Fax: 520-645-1869. 8AM-5PM. Access by: mail, in person.

Williams Justice Court, 117 W Route 66 #180, Williams, AZ 86046. 520-635-2691. 8AM-5PM. Access by: mail, in person.

Gila

Real Estate Recording—Gila County Recorder, 1400 East Ash Street, Globe, AZ 85501. Fax: 520-425-9270. 8AM-5PM.

Felony, Civil Actions Over $5,000, Probate—Superior Court, 1400 E Ash, Globe, AZ 85501. 520-425-3231. 8AM-5PM. Access by: mail, in person.

Misdemeanor, Civil Actions Under $5,000, Eviction, Small Claims—Globe Justice Court, 1400 E Ash, Globe, AZ 85501. 520-425-3231, Fax: 520-425-4773. 8AM-5PM. Access by: mail, in person.

Hayden-Winkleman Justice Court, PO Box 680, Winkelman, AZ 85292. 520-356-7638. 8AM-5PM. Access by: mail, in person.

Miami Justice Court, 1400 E Ash St, Globe, AZ 85501-1414. 520-425-3231. 8AM-5PM. Access by: mail, in person.

Payson Justice Court, 714 S Beeline Hwy #103, Payson, AZ 85541. 520-474-5267, Fax: 520-474-6214. 8AM-5PM. Access by: mail, phone, fax, in person.

Pine Justice Court, 714 S Beeline Hwy #S-103, Payson, AZ 85541-5371. 520-476-3525, Fax: 520-476-3128. 8AM-5PM. Access by: mail, in person.

Graham

Real Estate Recording—Graham County Recorder, 921 Thatcher Blvd. Safford, AZ 85546. Fax: 520-428-5951. 8AM-5PM.

Felony, Civil Actions Over $5,000, Probate—Superior Court, 800 Main St, Safford, AZ 85546-3803. 520-428-3100, Fax: 520-428-0061. 8AM-5PM. Access by: mail, phone, fax, in person.

Misdemeanor, Civil Actions Under $5,000, Eviction, Small Claims—Pima Justice Court Precinct #2, PO Box 1159, 136 W Center St, Pima, AZ 85543. 520-485-2771, Fax: 520-485-9961. 8AM-5PM. Access by: mail, fax, in person.

Safford Justice Court, 800 W Main St, Safford, AZ 85546. 520-428-1210. 8AM-5PM. Access by: mail, in person.

Greenlee

Real Estate Recording—Greenlee County Recorder, 5th & Leonard, Clifton, AZ 85533. Fax: 520-865-4417. 8AM-5PM.

Felony, Civil Actions Over $5,000, Probate—Superior Court, PO Box 1027, Clifton, AZ 85533. 520-865-4108, Fax: 520-865-4665. 8AM-5PM. Access by: mail, in person.

Misdemeanor, Civil Actions Under $5,000, Eviction, Small Claims—Justice Court Precinct #1, PO Box 517, Clifton, AZ 85533. 520-865-4312, Fax: 520-865-4417. 9AM-5PM. Access by: mail, in person.

Justice Court Precinct #2, PO Box 208, Duncan, AZ 85534. 520-359-2536, Fax: 520-359-2079. 9AM-5PM. Access by: mail, in person.

La Paz

Real Estate Recording—La Paz County Recorder, Suite 201, 1112 Joshua Ave. Parker, AZ 85344. Fax: 520-669-5638. 8AM-5PM.

Felony, Civil Actions Over $5,000, Probate—Superior Court, 1316 Kofa Ave, Suite 607, Parker, AZ 85344. 520-669-6131, Fax: 520-669-2186. 8AM-5PM. Access by: mail, in person.

Misdemeanor, Civil Actions Under $5,000, Eviction, Small Claims—Parker Justice Court, 1105 Arizona Ave, Parker, AZ 85344. 520-669-2504, Fax: 520-669-2915. 8AM-5PM. Access by: in person.

Quartzsite Justice Court, PO Box 580, Quartzsite, AZ 85346. 520-927-6313, Fax: 520-927-4842. 8AM-5PM. Access by: mail, phone, in person.

Salome Justice Court, PO Box 661, Salome, AZ 85348. 520-859-3871, Fax: 520-859-3709. 8AM-5PM. Access by: mail, in person.

Maricopa

Real Estate Recording—Maricopa County Recorder, 111 South 3rd Avenue, Phoenix, AZ 85003. Fax: 602-506-3069. 8AM-5PM.

Felony, Civil Actions Over $5,000, Probate—Superior Court, 201 W Jefferson, Phoenix, AZ 85003. 602-506-3360, Fax: 602-506-

7619. 8AM-5PM. Access by: mail, fax, in person, online. www.supcourt.maricopa.gov

Misdemeanor, Civil Actions Under $5,000, Eviction, Small Claims—Buckeye Justice Court, 100 N Apache Rd, Buckeye, AZ 85326. 623-386-4289, Fax: 623-386-5796. 8AM-5PM. Access by: mail, in person.

Central Phoenix Justice Court, 1 W Madison St, Phoenix, AZ 85003. 602-506-1168, Fax: 602-506-1948. 8AM-5PM. Access by: mail, in person.

Chandler Justice Court, 2051 W Warner Rd, Chandler, AZ 85224. 602-963-6691, Fax: 602-786-6210. 8AM-5PM. Access by: mail, in person.

East Mesa Justice Court, 4811 E Julep #128, Mesa, AZ 85205. 480-985-0188, Fax: 480-396-6327. 7AM-5PM. Access by: mail, in person.

East Phoenix Justice Court #1, 1 W Madison St #1, Phoenix, AZ 85003. 602-506-3577, Fax: 602-506-1840. 8AM-5PM. Access by: mail, in person.

East Phoenix Justice Court #2, 4109 N 12th St, Phoenix, AZ 85014. 602-266-3741, Fax: 602-277-9442. 8AM-4:30PM. Access by: mail, in person.

Gila Bend Justice Court, PO Box 648, Gila Bend, AZ 85337. 520-683-2651, Fax: 520-683-6412. 8AM-5PM. Access by: mail, phone, fax, in person.

Glendale Justice Court, 6830 N 57th Dr, Glendale, AZ 85301. 602-939-9477, Fax: 602-842-2260. 8AM-5PM. Access by: mail, in person.

Maryvale Justice Court, 4622 W Indian School Rd Bldg D, Phoenix, AZ 85031. 602-245-0432, Fax: 602-245-1216. 8AM-5PM. Access by: mail, in person.

North Mesa Justice Court, 1837 S Mesa Dr #A-201, Mesa, AZ 85210. 602-926-9731, Fax: 602-926-7763. 8AM-5PM. Access by: in person.

Northeast Phoenix Justice Court, 10255 N 32nd St, Phoenix, AZ 85028. 602-506-3731, Fax: 602-953-2315. 8AM-5PM. Access by: mail, phone, fax, in person.

Northwest Phoenix Justice Court, 11601 N 19th Ave, Phoenix, AZ 85029. 602-395-0293, Fax: 602-678-4508. 8AM-5PM. Access by: mail, in person.

Peoria Justice Court, 7420 W Cactus Rd, Peoria, AZ 85381. 602-979-3234, Fax: 602-979-1194. 8AM-5PM. Access by: mail, phone, fax, in person.

Scottsdale Justice Court, 3700 N 75th St, Scottsdale, AZ 85251. 602-947-7569, Fax: 602-946-4284. 8AM-5PM. Access by: mail, phone, in person.

South Mesa/Gilbert Justice Court, 1837 S Mesa Dr #B103, Mesa, AZ 85210. 602-926-3051, Fax: 602-545-1638. 8AM-5PM. Access by: mail, in person.

South Phoenix Justice Court, 217 E Olympic Dr, Phoenix, AZ 85040. 602-243-0318, Fax: 602-243-6389. 8AM-5PM. Access by: mail, in person.

Tempe Justice Court, 1845 E Broadway #8, Tempe, AZ 85282. 602-967-8856, Fax: 602-921-7413. 8AM-5PM. Access by: mail, in person.

Tolleson Justice Court, 9550 W Van Buren #6, Tolleson, AZ 85353. 623-936-1449, Fax: 623-936-4859. 8AM-5PM. Access by: mail, in person.

West Mesa Justice Court, 2050 W University Dr, Mesa, AZ 85201. 602-964-2958, Fax: 602-969-1098. 8AM-5PM. Access by: in person.

West Phoenix Justice Court, 527 W McDowell, Phoenix, AZ 85003. 602-256-0292, Fax: 602-256-7959. 8AM-5PM. Access by: mail, phone, in person.

Wickenburg Justice Court, 155 N Tegner, Suite D, Wickenburg, AZ 85390. 602-684-2401. 8AM-5PM. Access by: mail, in person.

Mohave

Real Estate Recording—Mohave County Recorder, 315 Oak Street, Kingman, AZ 86401. 8AM-5PM.

Felony, Civil Actions Over $5,000, Probate—Superior Court, PO Box 7000, Kingman, AZ 86402-7000. 520-753-0713, Fax: 520-753-0781. 8AM-5PM. Access by: mail, phone, fax, in person.

Misdemeanor, Civil Actions Under $5,000, Eviction, Small Claims—Bullhead City Justice Court, 2225 Trane Rd, Bullhead City, AZ 86442. 520-758-0709, Fax: 520-758-2644. 8AM-5PM. Access by: mail, phone, in person.

Kingman Justice Court, 401 E Spring St, PO Box 29, Kingman, AZ 86401-0029. 520-753-0710, Fax: 520-753-7840. 8AM-5PM. Access by: mail, phone, fax, in person.

Lake Havasu City Justice Court, 2001 College Dr Suite 148, Lake Havasu City, AZ 86403. 520-453-0705, Fax: 520-680-0193. 8AM-5PM. Access by: mail, fax, in person.

Moccasin Justice Court, HC65 PO 90, Moccasin, AZ 86022. 520-643-7104, Fax: 520-643-6206. 8AM-5PM. Access by: mail, in person.

Navajo

Real Estate Recording—Navajo County Recorder, 100 East Carter Dr, Courthouse, Holbrook, AZ 86025. Fax: 520-524-4308. 8AM-5PM.

Felony, Civil Actions Over $5,000, Probate—Superior Court, PO Box 668, Holbrook, AZ 86025. 520-524-4188, Fax: 520-524-4261. 8AM-5PM. Access by: mail, fax, in person.

Misdemeanor, Civil Actions Under $5,000, Eviction, Small Claims—Holbrook Justice Court, PO Box 668, Holbrook, AZ 86025. 520-524-4229, Fax: 520-524-4230. 8AM-5PM. Access by: mail, in person.

Kayenta Justice Court, Box 38, Kayenta, AZ 86033. 520-697-3522, Fax: 520-697-3528. 8AM-Noon,1-5PM. Access by: mail, in person.

Pinetop-Lakeside Justice Court, Box 2020, Lakeside, AZ 85929. 520-368-6200, Fax: 520-368-8674. 8AM-5PM. Access by: mail, fax, in person.

Show Low Justice Court, PO Box 3085, Show Low, AZ 85902-3085. 520-532-6030, Fax: 520-532-6035. 8AM-5PM. Access by: mail, fax, in person.

Snowflake Justice Court, 73 West First South St, Snowflake, AZ 85937. 520-536-4141, Fax: 520-536-3511. 8AM-5PM. Access by: mail, phone, fax, in person.

Winslow Justice Court, Box 808, Winslow, AZ 86047. 520-289-6840, Fax: 520-289-2197. 8AM-5PM. Access by: mail, fax, in person.

Navajo Nation

Real Estate Recording—Business Regulatory Department, State Road 264 West, Window Rock, AZ 86515. Fax: 520-871-7381. 8AM-Noon, 1-5PM.

Pima

Real Estate Recording—Pima County Recorder, 115 North Church Avenue, Tucson, AZ 85701. Fax: 520-623-1785. 8AM-5PM.

Felony, Civil Actions Over $5,000, Probate—Superior Court, 110 W Congress, Tucson, AZ 85701. 520-740-3240, Fax: 520-798-3531. 8AM-5PM. Access by: mail, in person. Special note: Address correspondence to attention of civil or criminal section. www.sc.co.pima.az.us

Misdemeanor, Civil Actions Under $5,000, Eviction, Small Claims—Ajo Justice Court, 111 La Mina, Ajo, AZ 85321. 520-387-7684. 8AM-5PM. Access by: mail, in person.

Green Valley Justice Court, 601 N LaCanada, Green Valley, AZ 85614. 520-648-0658, Fax: 520-648-2235. 8AM-5PM. Access by: mail, in person.

Pima County Consolidated Justice Court, 115 Church Ave, Tucson, AZ 85701. 520-882-0044, Fax: 520-884-0346. 8AM-5PM. Access by: mail, fax, in person, online. www.jp.co.pima.az.us

Pinal

Real Estate Recording—Pinal County Recorder, 383 N Main St, Florence, AZ 85232. Fax: 520-868-7170. 8AM-5PM.

Felony, Civil Actions Over $5,000, Probate—Superior Court, PO Box 2730, Florence, AZ 85232-2730. 520-868-6296, Fax: 520-868-6252. 8AM-5PM. Access by: mail, phone, in person.

Misdemeanor, Civil Actions Under $5,000, Eviction, Small Claims—Apache Junction Justice Court, 575 N Idaho, Suite 200,

Apache Junction, AZ 85219. 480-982-2921, Fax: 480-982-9472. 8AM-Noon, 1-5PM. Access by: mail, fax, in person.

Casa Grande Justice Court, Precinct #2, 820 E Cottonwood Lane, Bldg B, Casa Grande, AZ 85222. 520-836-5471, Fax: 520-868-7404. 8AM-5PM. Access by: mail, in person.

Eloy Justice Court, PO Box 586, Eloy, AZ 85231. 520-466-9221, Fax: 520-466-4473. 8AM-Noon, 1-5PM. Access by: mail, fax, in person.

Florence Justice Court, PO Box 1818, Florence, AZ 85232. 520-868-6578, Fax: 520-868-6510. 8AM-5PM. Access by: mail, in person.

Mammoth Justice Court, PO Box 117, Mammoth, AZ 85618. 520-487-2262, Fax: 520-487-2585. 8AM-5PM. Access by: mail, in person.

Maricopa Justice Court, PO Box 201, Maricopa, AZ 85239. 520-568-2451, Fax: 520-568-2924. 8AM-4PM. Access by: mail, fax, in person.

Oracle Justice Court, PO Box 3924, Oracle, AZ 85623. 520-896-9250, Fax: 520-896-2867. 8AM-5PM. Access by: mail, in person.

Superior/Kearny Justice Court, 60 E Main St, Superior, AZ 85273. 520-689-5871, Fax: 520-689-2369. 8AM-Noon, 1-5PM. Access by: mail, in person.

Santa Cruz

Real Estate Recording—Santa Cruz County Recorder, 2150 N. Congress, County Complex, Nogales, AZ 85621. Fax: 520-761-7938. 8AM-5PM.

Felony, Civil Actions Over $5,000, Probate—Superior Court, PO Box 1265, Nogales, AZ 85628. 520-761-7808, Fax: 520-761-7857. 8AM-5PM. Access by: mail, phone, in person.

Misdemeanor, Civil Actions Under $5,000, Eviction, Small Claims—East Santa Cruz County Justice Court-Precinct #2, PO Box 100, Patagonia, AZ 85624. 520-455-5796, Fax: 520-455-5517. 8:30AM-5PM. Access by: mail, in person.

Santa Cruz Justice Court, PO Box 1150, Nogales, AZ 85628. 520-761-7853, Fax: 520-761-7929. 8AM-5PM. Access by: mail, phone, fax, in person.

Yavapai

Real Estate Recording—Yavapai County Recorder, 1015 Fair St, Room 228, Prescott, AZ 86305. 520-771-3233, Fax: 520-771-3258. 8AM-5PM.

Felony, Civil Actions Over $5,000, Probate—Superior Court, Yavapai County Courthouse, Prescott, AZ 86301. 520-771-3313, Fax: 520-771-3111. 8AM-5PM. Access by: mail, fax, in person.

Misdemeanor, Civil Actions Under $5,000, Eviction, Small Claims—Bagdad Justice Court, PO Box 243, Bagdad, AZ 86321. 520-633-2141, Fax: 520-633-4451. 8AM-4PM M,W,TH 8AM-5PM T. Access by: mail, in person.

Bagdad-Yarnell Justice Court, PO Box 65, Yarnell, AZ 85362. 520-427-3318, Fax: 520-771-3362. 8AM-5PM. Access by: mail, in person.

Mayer Justice Court, PO Box 245, Mayer, AZ 86333. 520-771-3355. 8AM-5PM. Access by: mail, in person.

Prescott Justice Court, Yavapai County Courthouse, PO Box 2059, Prescott, AZ 86302. 520-771-3300, Fax: 520-771-3302. 8AM-5PM. Access by: mail, fax, in person.

Seligman Justice Court, PO Box 56, Seligman, AZ 86337-0056. 520-422-3281, Fax: 520-422-3282. 8AM-5PM. Access by: mail, phone, fax, in person.

Verde Valley Justice Court, 260 W Hwy Suite 101, Camp Verde, AZ 86322. 520-567-7715, Fax: 520-567-7750. 8AM-5PM. Access by: mail, in person.

Yuma

Real Estate Recording—Yuma County Recorder, 198 S. Main St, Yuma, AZ 85364. 8AM-5PM.

Felony, Civil Actions Over $5,000, Probate—Superior Court, 168 S 2nd Ave, Yuma, AZ 85364. 520-329-2164, Fax: 520-329-2007. 8AM-5PM. Access by: mail, fax, in person.

Misdemeanor, Civil Actions Under $5,000, Eviction, Small Claims—Somerton Justice Court, PO Box 458, Somerton, AZ 85350. 520-627-2722, Fax: 520-627-1076. 8AM-5PM. Access by: mail, phone, fax, in person.

Wellton Justice Court, PO Box 384, Wellton, AZ 85356. 520-785-3321, Fax: 520-785-4933. 8AM-5PM. Access by: mail, phone, fax, in person.

Yuma Justice Court, 168 S 2nd Ave, Yuma, AZ 85364. 520-329-2180, Fax: 520-329-2005. 8AM-5PM. Access by: mail, in person.

Federal Courts

US District Court

Phoenix Division Room 1400, 230 N 1st Ave, Phoenix, AZ 85025-0093602-514-7101, Civil Docket Phone: 602-514-7102, Criminal Docket Phone: 602-514-7103 Counties: Gila, La Paz, Maricopa, Pinal, Yuma. Some Yuma cases handled by San Diego Division of the Southern District of California. www.azd.uscourts.gov

Prescott Division c/o Phoenix Division, Room 1400, 230 N 1st Ave, Phoenix, AZ 85025-0093602-514-7101 Counties: Apache, Coconino, Mohave, Navajo, Yavapai. www.azd.uscourts.gov

Tucson Division Room 202, 44 E Broadway Blvd, Tucson, AZ 85701-1711520-620-7200 Fax: 520-620-7199 Counties: Cochise, Graham, Greelee, Pima, Santa Cruz. The Globe Division was closed effective January 1994, and all case records for that division are now found here. www.azd.uscourts.gov

US Bankruptcy Court

Phoenix Division PO Box 34151, Phoenix, AZ 85067-4151602-640-5800 Counties: Apache, Coconino, Maricopa, Navajo, Yavapai. www.azb.uscourts.gov

Tucson Division Suite 8112, 110 S Church Ave, Tucson, AZ 85701-1608520-620-7500 Counties: Cochise, Gila, Graham, Greenlee, Pima, Pinal, Santa Cruz. www.azb.uscourts.gov

Yuma Division Suite D, 325 W 19th St, Yuma, AZ 85364520-783-2288 Counties: La Paz, Mohave, Yuma. www.azb.uscourts.gov

Governor's Office

600 Dexter Ave #N104
Montgomery, AL 36130
www.governor.state.al.us

334-242-7100
Fax 334-242-4541

Attorney General's Office

State House
11 S. Union Street
Montgomery, AL 36130
www.ago.state.al.us

334-242-7300
Fax 334-242-7458
8AM-5PM

State Archives

Archives & History Dept
Reference Room,
PO Box 300100
Montgomery, AL 36130-0100
www.asc.edu/archives/agis.html

334-242-4435
Fax 334-240-3433
8AM-5PM T-F
9AM-5PM SA

Capital:	Little Rock
	Pulaski County
Time Zone:	CST
Number of Counties:	75
Population:	2,522,819
Web Site:	www.state.ar.us

Search Unclaimed Property Online

www.state.ar.us/auditor/unclprop

State Agencies

Criminal Records

Arkansas State Police, Identification Bureau, #1 State Police Plaza Dr, Little Rock, AR 72209; 501-618-8500; Fax: 501-618-8404; 8AM-5PM. Access by: mail.

Corporation Records
Fictitious Name
Limited Liability Company Records
Limited Partnerships

Secretary of State, Corporation Department-Aegon Bldg, 501 Woodlane, Rm 310, Little Rock, AR 72201-1094; 501-682-3409; Fax: 501-682-3437; 8AM-4:30PM. Access by: mail, phone, in person, online. sosweb.state.ar.us/corps/incorp

Trademarks/Servicemarks

Secretary of State, Trademarks Section, 501 Woodlane, #301, Little Rock, AR 72201; 501-682-3405; Fax: 501-682-3437; 8AM-5PM. Access by: mail, phone, in person, online. www.sosweb.state.ar.us/corps/trademk

Sales Tax Registrations

Finance & Administration Department, Sales & Use Tax Office, PO Box 1272, Little Rock, AR 72203; 501-682-7104; Fax: 501-682-7900; 8AM-4:30PM. Access by: mail, phone, in person. www.state.ar.us/revenue/eta/sales/salesuseta x.html

Uniform Commercial Code
Federal Tax Liens

UCC Division, Secretary of State, State Capitol Bldg, Room 25, Little Rock, AR 72201-1094; 501-682-5078; Fax: 501-682-3500; 8AM-5PM. Access by: mail. www.sosweb.state.ar/us/ucc.htm

State Tax Liens

Records not available from state agency.

Records are at the county level.

Workers' Compensation Records

Workers Compensation Department, 4th & Spring Streets, PO Box 950, Little Rock, AR 72203-0950; 501-682-3930; Fax: 501-682-6761; 8AM-4:30PM. Access by: mail. www.awcc.state.ar.us

Birth Certificates

Arkansas Department of Health, Division of Vital Records, 4815 W Markham St, Slot 44, Little Rock, AR 72205; 501-661-2134, 501-661-2336 Message Number, 506-661-2726 Credit Card Line; Fax: 501-663-2832; 8AM-4:30PM. Access by: mail, phone, in person.

Death Records

Arkansas Department of Health, Division of Vital Records, 4815 W Markham St, Slot 44, Little Rock, AR 72205; 501-661-2134, 501-661-2336 Message number, 501-661-2726 Credit Card Line; Fax: 501-663-2832; 8AM-4:30PM. Access by: mail, phone, in person.

Marriage Certificates

Arkansas Department of Health, Division of Vital Records, 4815 W Markham St, Slot 44, Little Rock, AR 72205; 501-661-2134, 501-661-2336 Message Number, 501-661-2726 Credit Card Line; Fax: 501-663-2832; 8AM-4:30PM. Access by: mail, phone, in person.

Divorce Records

Arkansas Department of Health, Department of Vital Records, 4815 W Markham St, Slot 44, Little Rock, AR 72205; 501-661-2134, 501-661-2336 Message Number, 501-661-2726 Credit Card Line; Fax: 501-663-2832; 8AM-4:30PM. Access by: mail, phone, in person.

Accident Reports

Arkansas State Police, Accident Records Section, #1 State Police Plaza Drive, Little Rock, AR 72209; 501-618-8130; 8AM-5PM. Access by: mail.

Driver Records

Department of Driver Services, Driving Records Division, PO Box 1272, Room 1130, Little Rock, AR 72203 (7th & Wolfe Sts, Ledbetter Bldg, Room 127, Little Rock, AR 72202); 501-682-7207; Fax: 501-682-2075; 8AM-4:30PM. Access by: mail, online. www.state.ar.us

Vehicle Ownership
Vehicle Identification

Office of Motor Vehicles, MV Title Records, PO Box 1272, Room 106, Little Rock, AR 72203 (7th and Wolfe Sts, Ledbetter Bldg, Room 106, Little Rock, AR 72201); 501-682-4692; 8AM-4:30PM. Access by: mail, phone, in person. www.state.ar.us

Boat & Vessel Ownership
Boat & Vessel Registration

Office of Motor Vehicles, Boat Registration, PO Box 1272, Little Rock, AR 72203; 501-682-4692; 8AM-4:30PM. Access by: mail.

Legislation-Current/Pending
Legislation-Passed

Elections Department, State Capitol, Room 026, Little Rock, AR 72201; 501-682-5070; Fax: 501-682-3408; 8AM-5PM. Access by: mail, fax, online. www.arkleg.state.ar.us

Voter Registration

Restricted access.
The state will sell the voter database for voting or election purposes. All individual search requests must be at the local County Clerk's office. The SSN will not be released.
Secretary of State, Voter Services, State Capitol, Room 026, Little Rock, AR 72201; 501-682-3526; Fax: 501-682-3548; 8AM-5PM
www.sosweb.state.ar.us/elect.html

GED Certificates

GED Testing, Dept of Workforce Education, Three Capitol Mall, Ste 200D, Little Rock, AR 72201-1083; 501-682-1978 Main Number; Fax: 501-682-1982;. www.state.ar.us/ged

Hunting License Information
Fishing License Information

Game & Fish Commission, Two Natural Resource Dr, Little Rock, AR 72205; 501-223-6341; Fax: 501-223-6425; 8AM-4:30PM. Access by: mail. www.agfc.state.ar.us

County Courts & Recording Offices

About the Courts...

Administration

Administrative Office of Courts   501-682-9400
625 Marshall St, Justice Bldg   Fax: 501-682-9410
Little Rock, AR 72201
http://courts.state.ar.us/

Court Structure

28 Circuit Courts are the courts of general jurisdiction and can be combined with the County Courts. County Courts are, fundamentally, administrative courts dealing with county fiscal issues. Probate is handled by the Chancery and Probate Courts, or by County Clerk in some counties. Civil limit raised to $5000 as of 8/2/97.

Searching Hints

Most courts that allow written search requests require an SASE. Fees vary widely across jurisdictions as do prepayment requirements.

Online Access

There is a very limited internal online computer system at the Administrative Office of Courts.

About the Recording Offices...

Organization

75 counties, 85 recording offices. The recording officer is the Clerk of Circuit Court, who is Ex Officio Recorder. Ten counties have two recording offices - Arkansas, Carroll, Clay, Craighead, Franklin, Logan, Mississippi, Prairie, Sebastian, and Yell. See the notes under each county for how to determine which office is appropriate to search. The entire state is in the Central Time Zone (CST).

UCC Records

This is a dual filing state. Financing statements are filed at the state level and with the Circuit Clerk, except for consumer goods, farm and real estate related collateral, which are filed only with the Circuit Clerk. Most counties will perform UCC searches. Use search request form UCC-11. Search fees are usually $10.00 per debtor name. Copy fees vary.

Lien Records

Federal tax liens on personal property of businesses are filed with the Secretary of State. Other federal and all state tax liens are filed with the Circuit Clerk. Many counties will perform separate tax lien searches. Search fees are usually $6.00 per name.

Real Estate Records

Most counties do not perform real estate searches. Copy fees and certification fees vary.

County Courts & Recording Offices

Arkansas

Real Estate Recording—Arkansas County Circuit Clerk, 302 South College, Stuttgart, AR 72160. Fax: 870-673-3869. 8AM-Noon,1-5PM.

Arkansas County Circuit Clerk, 101 Court Square, De Witt, AR 72042. 501-946-4210, Fax: 870-946-1394. 8AM-Noon,1-5PM.

Felony, Civil Actions Over $5,000, Probate—Circuit and Chancery Courts-Northern District, PO Box 719, Stuttgart, AR 72160. 870-673-2056, Fax: 870-673-3869. 8AM-5PM. Access by: mail, fax, in person. Special note: The court reports it is not bonded to search Civil or Chancery records.

Circuit and Chancery Courts-Southern District, 101 Courthouse Sq, De Witt, AR 72042. 870-946-4219, Fax: 870-946-1394. 8AM-5PM. Access by: mail, fax, in person.

Misdemeanor, Civil Actions Under $5,000, Eviction, Small Claims—Municipal Court, PO Box 819, Stuttgart, AR 72160. 870-673-7951, Fax: 870-673-6522. 8AM-5PM. Access by: mail, phone, in person.

Ashley

Real Estate Recording—Ashley County Circuit Clerk, Jefferson Street, Courthouse, Hamburg, AR 71646. 501-853-2010, Fax: 870-853-2005. 8AM-4:30PM.

Felony, Civil Actions Over $5,000, Probate—Circuit and Chancery Courts, Ashley County Courthouse, 205 E Jefferson, Hamburg, AR 71646. 870-853-2030, Fax: 870-853-2005. 8AM-4:30PM. Access by: mail, in person.

Misdemeanor, Civil Actions Under $5,000, Eviction, Small Claims—Municipal Court, PO Box 558 City Hall, Hamburg, AR 71646. 870-853-8326, Fax: 870-853-8134. 7AM-4PM. Access by: mail, phone, in person.

Baxter

Real Estate Recording—Baxter County Circuit Clerk, Courthouse Square, 1 East 7th Street, Mountain Home, AR 72653. 501-425-3444, Fax: 870-425-5105. 8AM-4:30PM.

Felony, Civil Actions Over $5,000, Probate—Circuit and Chancery Courts, 1 E 7th St Courthouse Square, Mountain Home, AR 72653. 870-425-3475, Fax: 870-424-5105. 8AM-4:30PM. Access by: mail, fax, in person.

Misdemeanor, Civil Actions Under $5,000, Eviction, Small Claims—Municipal Court, 720 S Hickory, Mountain Home, AR 72653. 870-425-3140, Fax: 870-425-9290. 8AM-4:30PM. Access by: mail, phone, fax, in person.

Benton

Real Estate Recording—Benton County Circuit Clerk, 215 East Central Street, Suite 6, Bentonville, AR 72712. 501-271-1037, Fax: 501-271-5719. 8AM-4:30PM.

Felony, Civil Actions Over $5,000, Probate—Circuit and Chancery Courts, 102 NE "A" St, Bentonville, AR 72712. 501-271-1015, Fax: 501-271-5719. 8AM-4:30PM. Access by: mail, phone, in person.

Misdemeanor, Civil Actions Under $5,000, Small Claims—Municipal Court, 117 W Central, Bentonville, AR 72712. 501-271-3120, Fax: 501-271-3134. 8AM-4:30PM. Access by: mail, phone, fax, in person.

Boone

Real Estate Recording—Boone County Circuit Clerk, Courthouse, Suite 200, 100 N. Main, Harrison, AR 72601. 501-741-6646, Fax: 870-741-4335. 8AM-4:30PM.

Felony, Civil Actions Over $5,000, Probate—Circuit and Chancery Courts, 100 N Main St, Harrison, AR 72601. 870-741-5560, Fax: 870-741-4335. 8AM-4:30PM. Access by: in person.

Misdemeanor, Civil Actions Under $5,000, Eviction, Small Claims—Municipal Court, PO Box 968, Harrison, AR 72602. 870-741-2788, Fax: 870-741-4329. 8:30AM-4PM. Access by: mail, phone, fax, in person.

Bradley

Real Estate Recording—Bradley County Circuit Clerk, 101 E. Cedar Street, Courthouse, Warren, AR 71671. Fax: 870-226-8401. 8AM-4:30PM.

Felony, Civil Actions Over $5,000, Probate—Circuit and Chancery Courts, Bradley County Courthouse - Records, 101 E Cedar, Warren, AR 71671. 870-226-2272, Fax: 870-226-8401. 8AM-4:30PM. Access by: mail, in person.

Misdemeanor, Civil Actions Under $5,000, Eviction, Small Claims—Municipal Court, PO Box 352, Warren, AR 71671. 870-226-2567, Fax: 870-226-2567. 8AM-5PM. Access by: mail, fax, in person.

Calhoun

Real Estate Recording—Calhoun County Circuit Clerk, Main Street, Courthouse, Hampton, AR 71744. 501-798-2827, Fax: 870-798-2428. 8AM-4:30.

Felony, Civil Actions Over $5,000, Probate—Circuit and County Courts, PO Box 1175, Hampton, AR 71744. 870-798-2517. 8:30AM-4:30PM. Access by: mail, in person.

Misdemeanor, Civil Actions Under $5,000, Eviction, Small Claims—Municipal Court, PO Box 864, Hampton, AR 71744. 870-798-2165. 8:30AM-4:30PM. Access by: mail, in person.

Carroll

Real Estate Recording—Carroll County Circuit Clerk, 210 West Church, Berryville, AR 72616. 501-423-3189, Fax: 870-423-4796. 8:30AM-4:30PM.

Carroll County Circuit Clerk, Courthouse, 2nd Floor, 44 S. Main, Eureka Springs, AR 72632. 8:30AM-4:30PM.

Felony, Civil Actions Over $5,000, Eviction, Probate—Berryville Circuit and Chancery Courts, Berryville Circuit Court, PO Box 71, Berryville, AR 72616. 870-423-2422, Fax: 870-423-3866. 8:30AM-4:30PM. Access by: mail, phone, fax, in person.

Eureka Springs Circuit, County and Chancery Courts, 44 S Main, PO Box 109, Eureka Springs, AR 72632. 501-253-8646. 8:30AM-4:30PM. Access by: mail, phone, in person.

Misdemeanor, Civil Actions Under $5,000, Small Claims—Municipal Court, 103 S Springs, Berryville, AR 72616. 870-423-6247, Fax: 870-423-7069. 8AM-4:30PM. Access by: mail, fax, in person.

Municipal Court, Courthouse, 44 S Main, Eureka Springs, AR 72632. 501-253-8574, Fax: 501-253-6967. 8AM-5PM. Access by: mail, in person. www.cityofeureka.springs.org

Chicot

Real Estate Recording—Chicot County Circuit Clerk, Courthouse, 108 Main St. Lake Village, AR 71653. 501-265-8040, Fax: 870-265-8012. 8AM-4:30PM.

Felony, Civil Actions Over $5,000, Probate—Circuit and Chancery Courts, County Courthouse, Lake Village, AR 71653. 870-265-8010, Fax: 870-265-5102. 8AM-4:30PM. Access by: mail, in person.

Misdemeanor, Civil Actions Under $5,000, Eviction, Small Claims—Municipal Court, PO Box 832, Lake Village, AR 71653. 870-265-3283. 9AM-5PM. Access by: mail, in person.

Clark

Real Estate Recording—Clark County Circuit Clerk, Courthouse Square, Arkadelphia, AR 71923. 501-246-2211. 8:30AM-4:30PM.

Felony, Civil Actions Over $5,000, Probate—Circuit and Chancery Courts, PO Box 576, Arkadelphia, AR 71923. 870-246-4281. 8:30AM-4:30PM. Access by: mail, in person.

Misdemeanor, Civil Actions Under $5,000, Eviction, Small Claims—Municipal Court, PO Box 449, Arkadelphia, AR 71923. 870-246-9552. 8:30AM-4:30PM. Access by: mail, phone, in person.

Clay

Real Estate Recording—Clay County Circuit Clerk, Courthouse, Piggott, AR 72454. Fax: 870-598-2524. 8AM-Noon,1-4:30PM.

Clay County Circuit Clerk, 800 West Second Street, Corning, AR 72422. 501-855-3011, Fax: 870-857-3271. 8AM-Noon, 1PM-4:30PM.

Felony, Civil Actions Over $5,000, Probate—Corning Circuit and County Courts, Courthouse, Corning, AR 72422. 870-857-3271, Fax: 870-857-3271. 8AM-4:30PM. Access by: mail, in person.

Piggott Circuit and County Courts, PO Box 29, Piggott, AR 72454. 870-598-2524, Fax: 870-598-2524. 8AM-4:30PM. Access by: mail, in person.

Misdemeanor, Civil Actions Under $5,000, Eviction, Small Claims—Municipal Court, 121 W Main, Piggott, AR 72454. 870-598-2265, Fax: 870-598-3272. 8AM-4:30PM. Access by: mail, fax, in person.

Cleburne

Real Estate Recording—Cleburne County Circuit Clerk, 301 West Main Street, Heber Springs, AR 72543. 501-362-8124, Fax: 501-362-4650. 8:30AM-4:30PM.

Felony, Civil Actions Over $5,000, Probate, Eviction—Circuit and County Courts, PO Box 543, Heber Springs, AR 72543. 870-362-8149, Fax: 870-362-4650. 8:30AM-4:30PM. Access by: mail, phone, in person.

Misdemeanor, Civil Actions Under $5,000, Small Claims—Municipal Court, 102 E Main, Heber Springs, AR 72543. 501-362-6585, Fax: 501-362-4614. 8:30AM-4:30PM. Access by: mail, phone, in person.

Cleveland

Real Estate Recording—Cleveland County Circuit Clerk, Courthouse, 20 Magnolia, Rison, AR 71665. 501-325-6681, Fax: 870-325-6144. 8AM-4:30PM.

Felony, Civil Actions Over $5,000, Probate—Circuit and County Courts, PO Box 368, Rison, AR 71665. 870-325-6921, Fax: 870-325-6144. 8AM-4:30PM. Access by: in person.

Misdemeanor, Civil Actions Under $5,000, Eviction, Small Claims—Rison Municipal Court, PO Box 405, City Hall, Rison, AR 71665. 870-325-7382, Fax: 870-325-6152. 8AM-4PM. Access by: mail, phone, in person.

Columbia

Real Estate Recording—Columbia County Circuit Clerk, Courthouse, Magnolia, AR 71753. 501-235-3704, Fax: 870-235-3778. 8AM-4:30PM.

Felony, Civil Actions Over $5,000, Probate—Circuit and County Courts, 1 Court Square Ste 6, PO Box 327, Magnolia, AR 71753-3595. 870-235-3700, Fax: 870-235-3786. 8AM-4:30PM. Access by: mail, in person.

Misdemeanor, Civil Actions Under $5,000, Eviction, Small Claims—Magnolia Municipal Court, PO Box 1126, Magnolia, AR 71753. 870-234-7312. 8AM-5PM. Access by: mail, in person.

Conway

Real Estate Recording—Conway County Circuit Clerk, 115 S. Moose Street, County Courthouse - Room 206, Morrilton, AR 72110. 501-354-9623, Fax: 501-354-9612. 8AM-5PM.

Felony, Civil Actions Over $5,000, Probate—Circuit and Chancery Courts, Conway County Courthouse, Rm 206, Morrilton, AR 72110. 501-354-9617, Fax: 501-354-9612. 8AM-5PM. Access by: mail, phone, in person.

Misdemeanor, Civil Actions Under $5,000, Eviction, Small Claims—Municipal Court, PO Box 127,Conway County Courthouse, Morrilton, AR 72110. 501-354-9615, Fax: 501-354-9601. 8AM-4:30PM. Access by: mail, phone, fax, in person.

Craighead

Real Estate Recording—Craighead County Circuit Clerk, 405 Court Street, Lake City, AR 72437. Fax: 870-237-8174. 8AM-Noon, 1-5PM.

Craighead County Circuit Clerk, 511 S. Main, Jonesboro, AR 72401. 501-933-4540, Fax: 870-933-4534. 8AM-5PM.

Felony, Civil Actions Over $5,000, Probate—Jonesboro Circuit and Chancery Courts, PO Box 120, Jonesboro, AR 72403. 870-933-4530, Fax: 870-933-4534. 8AM-5PM. Access by: mail, fax, in person.

Lake City Circuit and County Courts, PO Box 537, Lake City, AR 72437. 870-237-4342, Fax: 870-237-8174. 8AM-5PM. Access by: mail, phone, in person.

Misdemeanor, Civil Actions Under $5,000, Eviction, Small Claims—Municipal Court, 410 W Washington, Jonesboro, AR 72401. 870-933-4509, Fax: 870-933-4582. 8AM-5PM. Access by: mail, phone, fax, in person.

Crawford

Real Estate Recording—Linda Howard, Circuit/Chancery Clerk, 300 Main, Courthouse Room 22, Van Buren, AR 72956. 501-474-6641. 8AM-5PM.

Felony, Civil Actions Over $5,000, Probate—Circuit and Chancery Courts, County Courthouse, 300 Main St, Rm 22, Van Buren, AR 72956. 501-474-1821, Fax: 501-471-0622. 8AM-5PM. Access by: mail, in person.

Misdemeanor, Civil Actions Under $5,000, Eviction, Small Claims—Municipal Court, 1003 Broadway, Van Buren, AR 72956. 501-474-1671, Fax: 501-471-5005. 8AM-5PM. Access by: mail, in person.

Crittenden

Real Estate Recording—Crittenden County Circuit Clerk, 100 Court St. Marion, AR 72364. Fax: 870-739-3072. 8AM-4:30PM.

Felony, Civil Actions Over $5,000, Probate—Circuit and County Courts, PO Box 70, Marion, AR 72364. 870-739-3248. 8AM-4:30PM. Access by: mail, in person.

Misdemeanor, Civil Actions Under $5,000, Eviction, Small Claims—Municipal Court, 100 Court St, West Memphis, AR 72301. 870-732-7560, Fax: 870-732-7538. 8AM-5PM. Access by: mail, phone, in person.

Cross

Real Estate Recording—Cross County Circuit Clerk, 705 East Union, Room 9, Wynne, AR 72396. 501-238-5720, Fax: 870-238-5739. 8AM-4PM.

Felony, Civil Actions Over $5,000, Probate—Circuit and County Courts, County Courthouse, Wynne, AR 72396. 870-238-5720, Fax: 870-238-5739. 8AM-4PM. Access by: mail, in person.

Misdemeanor, Civil Actions Under $5,000, Eviction, Small Claims—Municipal Court, 205 Mississippi St, Wynne, AR 72396. 870-238-9171, Fax: 870-238-3930. 8AM-4PM. Access by: mail, in person.

Dallas

Real Estate Recording—Dallas County Circuit Clerk, Courthouse, 206 West 3rd St, Fordyce, AR 71742. 870-352-7983, Fax: 870-352-7179. 8:30AM-4:30PM.

Felony, Civil Actions Over $5,000, Probate—Circuit and County Courts, Dallas County Courthouse, Fordyce, AR 71742. 870-352-2307, Fax: 870-352-7179. 8:30AM-4:30PM. Access by: mail, fax, in person.

Misdemeanor, Civil Actions Under $5,000, Eviction, Small Claims—Municipal Court, Dallas County Courthouse, Fordyce, AR 71742. 870-352-2332, Fax: 870-352-3414. 8AM-4PM. Access by: mail, phone, in person.

Desha

Real Estate Recording—Desha County Circuit Clerk, Robert Moore Drive, Arkansas City Courthouse, Arkansas City, AR 71630. 501-877-2353, Fax: 870-877-3407. 8AM-4PM.

Felony, Civil Actions Over $5,000, Probate—Circuit and Chancery Courts, PO Box 309, Arkansas City, AR 71630. 870-877-2411, Fax: 870-877-2531. 8AM-4PM. Access by: mail, fax, in person.

Misdemeanor, Civil Actions Under $5,000, Eviction, Small Claims—Dumas Municipal Court, PO Box 157, Dumas, AR 71639-0157. 870-382-6972, Fax: 870-382-1106. 8AM-4:30PM. Access by: mail, fax, in person.

Drew

Real Estate Recording—Drew County Circuit Clerk, 210 South Main, Monticello, AR 71655. 501-460-6225, Fax: 870-460-6246. 8AM-4:30PM.

Felony, Civil Actions Over $5,000, Probate—Circuit and County Courts, 210 S Main, Monticello, AR 71655. 870-460-6250, Fax: 870-460-6246. 8AM-4:30PM. Access by: mail, phone, in person.

Misdemeanor, Civil Actions Under $5,000, Eviction, Small Claims—Municipal Court, PO Box 505, Monticello, AR 71655. 870-367-4420, Fax: 870-367-4405. 8:30AM-5PM. Access by: mail, fax, in person.

Faulkner

Real Estate Recording—Faulkner County Circuit Clerk, 801 Locust Street, Courthouse, Conway, AR 72032. 501-450-4902, Fax: 501-450-4948. 8AM-4:30PM.

Felony, Civil Actions Over $5,000, Probate—Circuit and Chancery Courts, PO Box 9, Conway, AR 72033. 501-450-4911, Fax: 501-450-4948. 8AM-4:30PM. Access by: mail, phone, fax, in person.

Misdemeanor, Civil Actions Under $5,000, Eviction, Small Claims—Municipal Court, 810 Parkway, Conway, AR 72032. 501-450-6112, Fax: 501-450-6184. 8AM-4:30PM. Access by: mail, phone, in person.

Franklin

Real Estate Recording—Franklin County Circuit Clerk, 460 East Main Street, Charleston, AR 72933. 8AM-Noon, 12:30-4:30PM.

Franklin County Circuit Clerk, 211 West Commercial, Ozark, AR 72949. Fax: 501-667-5174. 8AM-4:30PM.

Felony, Civil Actions Over $5,000, Probate—Charleston Circuit and Chancery Courts, PO Box 387, Charleston, AR 72933. 501-965-7332. 8AM-4:30PM. Access by: mail, in person.

Ozark Circuit and Chancery Courts, PO Box 1112, 211 W Commercial, Ozark, AR 72949. 501-667-3818, Fax: 501-667-5174. 8AM-4:30PM. Access by: mail, fax, in person.

Misdemeanor, Civil Actions Under $5,000, Eviction, Small Claims—Municipal Court, PO Box 426, Charleston, AR 72933. 501-965-7455, Fax: 501-965-2231. 8AM-5PM. Access by: mail, in person.

Fulton

Real Estate Recording—Fulton County Circuit Clerk, Court Square Courthouse, Salem, AR 72576. 501-895-3522, Fax: 870-895-3362. 8AM-4:30PM.

Felony, Civil Actions Over $5,000, Probate—Circuit and Chancery Courts, PO Box 485, Salem, AR 72576. 870-895-3310, Fax: 870-865-3362. 8AM-4:30PM. Access by: mail, phone, in person.

Misdemeanor, Civil Actions Under $5,000, Eviction, Small Claims—Municipal Court, PO Box 928, Salem, AR 72576. 870-895-4136, Fax: 870-895-4114. 8AM-4:30PM. Access by: mail, phone, fax, in person.

Garland

Real Estate Recording—Garland County Circuit Clerk, Courthouse - Room 207, Quachita and Hawthorn Streets, Hot Springs, AR 71901. 501-622-3710. 8AM-5PM.

Felony, Civil Actions Over $5,000, Probate—Circuit and Chancery Courts, Garland County Courthouse, 501 Ouachita Ave, Room 207, Hot Springs, AR 71901. 501-622-3630, Fax: 501-624-, 0665. 8AM-5PM. Access by: mail, phone, in person.

Misdemeanor, Civil Actions Under $5,000, Eviction, Small Claims—Municipal Court, PO Box 700, Hot Springs, AR 71902. 501-321-6765, Fax: 501-321-6764. 8AM-5PM. Access by: mail, phone, fax, in person.

Grant

Real Estate Recording—Grant County Circuit Clerk, Courthouse, 101 W. Center, Room 106, Sheridan, AR 72150. 501-942-4315, Fax: 870-942-3564. 8AM-4:30PM.

Felony, Civil Actions Over $5,000, Probate—Circuit and County Courts, Grant County Courthouse, 101 W Center, Rm 106, Sheridan, AR 72150. 870-942-2631, Fax: 870-942-3564. 8AM-4:30PM. Access by: in person.

Misdemeanor, Civil Actions Under $5,000, Eviction, Small Claims—Municipal Court, PO Box 603, Sheridan, AR 72150. 870-942-3464. 8AM-4:30PM. Access by: mail, phone, in person.

Greene

Real Estate Recording—Greene County Circuit Clerk, 320 W. Court St. Room 124, Paragould, AR 72450. Fax: 870-239-3550. 8:30AM-4:30PM.

Felony, Civil Actions Over $5,000, Probate—Circuit and County Courts, 320 W Court #124, Paragould, AR 72450. 870-239-6330, Fax: 870-239-3550. 8AM-4:30PM. Access by: mail, fax, in person.

Misdemeanor, Civil Actions Under $5,000, Eviction, Small Claims—Municipal Court, 320 W Court, Rm 227, Paragould, AR 72450. 870-239-7507, Fax: 870-239-7506. 8AM-4:30PM. Access by: mail, in person.

Hempstead

Real Estate Recording—Hempstead County Circuit Clerk, Fourth & Washington Streets, Courthouse, Hope, AR 71801. 501-777-4103, Fax: 870-777-7827. 8AM-4PM.

Felony, Civil Actions Over $5,000, Probate—Circuit and Chancery Courts, PO Box 1420, Hope, AR 71802. 870-777-2384, Fax: 870-777-7814. 8AM-4PM. Access by: mail, phone, fax, in person. Special note: Probate is handled by the County Clerk at same address.

Misdemeanor, Civil Actions Under $5,000, Eviction, Small Claims—Municipal Court, PO Box 1420, Hope, AR 71802-1420. 870-777-2525, Fax: 870-777-7830. 8AM-4:30PM. Access by: mail, in person.

Hot Spring

Real Estate Recording—Hot Spring County Circuit Clerk, 200 Locust Street, Courthouse, Malvern, AR 72104. 501-332-7211. 8AM-4:30PM.

Felony, Civil Actions Over $5,000, Probate—Circuit and Chancery Court, 200 Locust St, PO Box 1200, Malvern, AR 72104. 501-332-2281. 8:00AM-4:30PM. Access by: mail, in person.

Misdemeanor, Civil Actions Under $5,000, Eviction, Small Claims—Malvern Municipal Court, 305 Locust St, Rm 201, Malvern, AR 72104. 501-332-3144, Fax: 501-332-7607. 8AM-4:30PM. Access by: in person.

Howard

Real Estate Recording—Howard County Circuit Clerk, 421 North Main Street, Room 7, Nashville, AR 71852. 8AM-4:30PM.

Felony, Civil Actions Over $5,000, Probate—Circuit and County Courts, 421 N Main, Rm 7, Nashville, AR 71852. 870-845-7506. 8AM-4:30PM. Access by: mail, phone, in person. Special note: Probate is handled by the County Clerk at this address.

Misdemeanor, Civil Actions Under $5,000, Eviction, Small Claims—Municipal Court, 426 N Main, Suite #7, Nashville, AR 71852-2009. 870-845-7522, Fax: 870-845-3705. 8AM-4:30PM. Access by: mail, phone, fax, in person.

Independence

Real Estate Recording—Independence County Circuit Clerk, 192 Main Street, Batesville, AR 72501. Fax: 870-793-8888. 8AM-4:30PM.

Felony, Civil Actions Over $5,000, Probate—Circuit and County Courts, Main and Broad St, Batesville, AR 72501. 870-793-8833, Fax: 870-793-8888. 8AM-4:30PM. Access by: mail, phone, in person.

Misdemeanor, Civil Actions Under $5,000, Eviction, Small Claims—Municipal Court, 368 E Main, Batesville, AR 72501. 870-793-8817, Fax: 870-793-8875. 8AM-4:30PM. Access by: mail, phone, in person.

Izard

Real Estate Recording—Izard County Circuit Clerk, Main and Lunen Streets, Courthouse, Melbourne, AR 72556. 870-368-4394, Fax: 870-368-4748. 8:30AM-4:30PM.

Felony, Civil Actions Over $5,000, Probate—Circuit and County Courts, PO Box 95, Melbourne, AR 72556. 870-368-4316, Fax: 870-368-4748. 8:30AM-4:30PM. Access by: mail, in person.

Misdemeanor, Civil Actions Under $5,000, Eviction, Small Claims—Municipal Court, PO Box 337, Melbourne, AR 72556. 870-368-4390, Fax: 870-368-5042. 8:30AM-4:30PM. Access by: mail, phone, in person.

Jackson

Real Estate Recording—Jackson County Circuit Clerk, Courthouse, Main Street, Newport, AR 72112. 501-523-7401.

Felony, Civil Actions Over $5,000, Probate—Circuit and Chancery Courts, Jackson County Courthouse, 208 Main St, Newport, AR 72112. 870-523-7423, Fax: 870-523-7404. 8AM-4:30PM. Access by: in person.

Misdemeanor, Civil Actions Under $5,000, Eviction, Small Claims—Municipal Court, 615 3rd St, Newport, AR 72112. 870-523-9555, Fax: 870-523-4365. 8AM-4:30PM. Access by: mail, phone, fax, in person.

Jefferson

Real Estate Recording—Jefferson County Circuit Clerk, Main & Barraque, Room 101, Pine Bluff, AR 71601. 501-541-5302. 8:30AM-5PM.

Felony, Civil Actions Over $5,000, Probate—Circuit and Chancery Courts, PO Box 7433, Pine Bluff, AR 71611. 8:30PM-5PM. Access by: in person.

Misdemeanor, Civil Actions Under $5,000, Eviction, Small Claims—Municipal Court, 200 E 8th, Pine Bluff, AR 71601. 870-543-1860. 8AM-5PM. Access by: mail, in person.

Johnson

Real Estate Recording—Johnson County Circuit Clerk, Main Street, Courthouse, Clarksville, AR 72830. 501-754-3056, Fax: 501-754-4235. 8AM-4:30PM.

Felony, Civil Actions Over $5,000, Probate—Circuit Court, PO Box 217, Clarksville, AR 72830. 501-754-2977. 8AM-4:30PM. Access by: mail, fax, in person. Special note: Probate is handled by County Clerk, PO Box 57.

Misdemeanor, Civil Actions Under $5,000, Eviction, Small Claims—Municipal Court, PO Box 581, Clarksville, AR 72830. 501-754-8533, Fax: 501-754-6014. 8AM-4PM. Access by: mail, phone, in person.

Lafayette

Real Estate Recording—Lafayette County Circuit Clerk, 3 Courthouse Square, Third & Spruce, Lewisville, AR 71845. 501-921-4755. 8AM-4:30PM.

Felony, Civil Actions Over $5,000, Probate—Circuit and Chancery Courts, #3 Courthouse Square, Lewisville, AR 71845. 870-921-4878, Fax: 870-926-4505. 8AM-4:30PM. Access by: in person.

Misdemeanor, Civil Actions Under $5,000, Eviction, Small Claims—Municipal Court, 110 E Fourth St, #1, Lewisville, AR 71845. 870-921-5555, Fax: 870-921-4256. 8AM-4:30PM. Access by: mail, phone, in person.

Lawrence

Real Estate Recording—Lawrence County Circuit Clerk, Main Street, Walnut Ridge, AR 72476. 501-886-1116. 8AM-4:30PM.

Felony, Civil Actions Over $5,000, Probate—Circuit and Chancery Courts, PO Box 581, Walnut Ridge, AR 72476. 870-886-1112, Fax: 870-886-1117. 8AM-4:30PM. Access by: mail, phone, in person.

Misdemeanor, Civil Actions Under $5,000, Eviction, Small Claims—Municipal Court, 201 SW 2nd, Walnut Ridge, AR 72476. 870-886-3905. 8AM-4:30PM. Access by: mail, phone, in person.

Lee

Real Estate Recording—Lee County Circuit Clerk, 15 East Chestnut Street, Courthouse, Marianna, AR 72360. 501-295-5296, Fax: 501-295-7766. 8:30AM-4:30PM.

Felony, Civil Actions Over $5,000, Probate—Circuit and Chancery Courts, 15 E Chestnut, Marianna, AR 72360. 870-295-7710, Fax: 870-295-7766. 8:30AM-4:30PM. Access by: mail, in person.

Misdemeanor, Civil Actions Under $5,000, Eviction, Small Claims—Municipal Court, 15 East Chestnut, Marianna, AR 72360. 870-295-3813, Fax: 870-295-9419. 8AM-Noon; 1-5PM. Access by: mail, in person.

Lincoln

Real Estate Recording—Lincoln County Circuit Clerk, 300 South Drew St, Star City, AR 71667. 501-628-4816, Fax: 870-628-5546. 8AM-5PM.

Felony, Civil Actions Over $5,000, Probate—Circuit and County Courts, Courthouse, 300 S Drew, Star City, AR 71667. 870-628-3154, Fax: 870-628-5546. 8AM-5PM. Access by: mail, in person.

Misdemeanor, Civil Actions Under $5,000, Eviction, Small Claims—Municipal Court, 300 S Drew, Star City, AR 71667. 870-628-4904, Fax: 870-628-4385. 8AM-4:30PM. Access by: mail, in person.

Little River

Real Estate Recording—Little River County Circuit Clerk, 351 North Second, Ashdown, AR 71822. Fax: 870-898-7207. 8:30AM-4:30PM.

Felony, Civil Actions Over $5,000, Probate—Circuit and County Courts, PO Box 575, Ashdown, AR 71822. 870-898-7211, Fax: 870-898-7207. 8:30AM-4:30PM. Access by: mail, phone, fax, in person.

Misdemeanor, Civil Actions Under $5,000, Eviction, Small Claims—Municipal Court, 351 N 2nd St, Ashdown, AR 71822. 870-898-7230. 8:30AM-4:30PM. Access by: mail, in person.

Logan

Real Estate Recording—Logan County Circuit Clerk, Courthouse, Paris, AR 72855. 501-963-2038, Fax: 501-963-3304. 8AM-Noon 1-4:30PM.

Logan County Circuit Clerk, Courthouse, 366 N Broadway #2, Booneville, AR 72927. 501-675-5131, Fax: 501-675-0577. 8AM-Noon, 1-4:30PM.

Felony, Civil Actions Over $5,000, Probate—Circuit and Chancery Courts, Courthouse, 25 W Walnut, Paris, AR 72855. 501-963-2164, Fax: 501-963-3304. 8AM-4:30PM. Access by: mail, fax, in person.

Misdemeanor, Civil Actions Under $5,000, Eviction, Small Claims—Paris Municipal Court, Paris Courthouse, Paris, AR 72855. 501-963-3792, Fax: 501-963-2590. 8:30AM-4:30PM. Access by: mail, phone, fax, in person.

Lonoke

Real Estate Recording—Lonoke County Circuit Clerk, Courthouse, Lonoke, AR 72086. 8AM-4:30PM.

Felony, Civil Actions Over $5,000, Probate—Circuit and Chancery Courts, PO Box 231 Attn: Circuit Clerk, Lonoke, AR 72086. 501-676-2316. 8AM-4:30PM. Access by: mail, in person.

Misdemeanor, Civil Actions Under $5,000, Eviction, Small Claims—Municipal Court, 107 W 2nd St, Lonoke, AR 72086-2701. 501-676-3585, Fax: 501-676-2500. 8AM-4:30PM. Access by: mail, in person.

Madison

Real Estate Recording—Madison County Circuit Clerk, Main Street, Courthouse, Huntsville, AR 72740. 501-738-6514, Fax: 501-738-1544. 8AM-4:30PM.

Felony, Civil Actions Over $5,000, Probate—Circuit and Chancery Courts, PO Box 416, Huntsville, AR 72740. 501-738-2215, Fax: 501-738-1544. 8AM-4:30PM. Access by: in person.

Misdemeanor, Civil Actions Under $5,000, Eviction, Small Claims—Municipal Court, PO Box 549, Huntsville, AR 72740. 501-738-2911, Fax: 501-738-6846. 8AM-4:30PM. Access by: mail, phone, in person.

Marion

Real Estate Recording—Marion County Circuit Clerk, Hwy 62, Courthouse, Yellville, AR 72687. 501-449-6253, Fax: 870-449-4979. 8AM-4:30PM.

Felony, Civil Actions Over $5,000, Eviction, Probate—Circuit and County Courts, PO Box 385, Yellville, AR 72687. 870-449-6226, Fax: 870-449-4979. 8AM-4:30PM. Access by: mail, in person.

Misdemeanor, Civil Actions Under $5,000, Small Claims—Municipal Court, PO Box 301, Yellville, AR 72687. 870-449-6030. 8AM-4:30PM. Access by: mail, in person.

Miller

Real Estate Recording—Miller County Circuit Clerk, County Courthouse-Suite 109, 412 Laurel St. Texarkana, AR 71854. 501-772-0003, Fax: 870-772-5293. 8AM-4:30PM.

Felony, Civil Actions Over $5,000, Probate—Circuit and County Courts, 412 Laurel St Rm 109, Texarkana, AR 71854. 870-774-4501, Fax: 870-772-5293. 8AM-4:30PM. Access by: mail, phone, in person.

Misdemeanor, Civil Actions Under $5,000, Eviction, Small Claims—Municipal Court, 400 Laurel Suite 101, Texarkana, AR 71854. 870-772-2780, Fax: 870-773-3595. 8AM-4:30PM. Access by: mail, in person.

Mississippi

Real Estate Recording—Mississippi County Circuit Clerk, 2nd & Walnut Street, Blytheville, AR 72315. 501-762-2152, Fax: 870-762-8148. 9AM-4:30PM.

Mississippi County Circuit Clerk, Courthouse, Osceola, AR 72370. 501-762-2152, Fax: 870-563-2543. 9AM-4:30PM.

Felony, Civil Actions Over $5,000, Probate—Blytheville Circuit and Chancery Courts, PO Box 1498, Blytheville, AR 72316. 870-762-2332, Fax: 870-763-0150. 9AM-4:30PM. Access by: mail, phone, fax, in person.

Osceola Circuit and Chancery Courts, County Courthouse, PO Box 471, Osceola, AR 72370. 870-563-6471. 9AM-4:30PM. Access by: mail, phone, in person.

Misdemeanor, Civil Actions Under $5,000, Eviction, Small Claims—Blytheville Municipal Court, City Hall, 2nd & Walnut, Blytheville, AR 72315. 870-763-7513, Fax: 870-762-0443. 8AM-5PM. Access by: mail, phone, fax, in person.

Osceola Municipal Court, 297 W Keiser, Osceola, AR 72370. 870-563-1303, Fax: 870-563-5657. 9AM-4:30PM. Access by: in person.

Monroe

Real Estate Recording—Monroe County Circuit Clerk, 123 Madison Street, Clarendon, AR 72029. 501-747-3722, Fax: 870-747-3710. 8AM-4:30PM.

Felony, Civil Actions Over $5,000, Probate—Circuit and Chancery Courts, 123 Madison St, Courthouse, Clarendon, AR 72029. 870-747-3615, Fax: 870-747-3710. 8AM-4:30PM. Access by: mail, fax, in person.

Misdemeanor, Civil Actions Under $5,000, Eviction, Small Claims—Municipal Court, Courthouse, 270 Madison St, Clarendon, AR 72029. 870-747-5200, Fax: 870-747-3903. 8AM-5PM. Access by: mail, in person.

Montgomery

Real Estate Recording—Montgomery County Circuit Clerk, 105 Hwy 270 East, Mount Ida, AR 71957. 501-867-3411, Fax: 870-867-4354. 8AM-4:30PM.

Felony, Civil Actions Over $5,000, Probate—Circuit and County Courts, PO Box 369, Courthouse, Mount Ida, AR 71957. 870-867-3521, Fax: 870-867-2177. 8AM-4:30PM. Access by: mail, phone, fax, in person.

Misdemeanor, Civil Actions Under $5,000, Eviction, Small Claims—Municipal Court, PO Box 548, Mount Ida, AR 71957. 870-867-2221, Fax: 870-867-4354. 8AM-4:30PM M-Th, other days hours may vary. Access by: mail, phone, fax, in person.

Nevada

Real Estate Recording—Nevada County Circuit Clerk, 215 East Second Street, Prescott, AR 71857. 501-887-2811, Fax: 870-887-5795. 8AM-5PM.

Felony, Civil Actions Over $5,000, Probate—Circuit and Chancery Courts, PO Box 204, Prescott, AR 71857. 870-887-2511, Fax: 870-887-5795. 8AM-5PM. Access by: mail, phone, fax, in person.

Misdemeanor, Civil Actions Under $5,000, Eviction, Small Claims—Municipal Court, PO Box 22, Prescott, AR 71857. 870-887-6016, Fax: 870-887-5795. 8AM-5PM. Access by: mail, in person.

Newton

Real Estate Recording—Newton County Circuit Clerk, Courthouse Street, Jasper, AR 72641. 501-446-2936. 8AM-4:30PM.

Felony, Civil Actions Over $5,000, Probate—Circuit and Chancery Courts, PO Box 410, Jasper, AR 72641. 870-446-5125, Fax: 870-446-2106. 8AM-4:30PM. Access by: mail, in person.

Misdemeanor, Civil Actions Under $5,000, Eviction, Small Claims—Municipal Court, PO Box 550, Jasper, AR 72641. 870-446-5335, Fax: 870-446-2234. 8AM-4:30PM. Access by: mail, in person.

Ouachita

Real Estate Recording—Ouachita County Circuit Clerk, 145 Jefferson Street, Camden, AR 71701. Fax: 870-837-2252. 8AM-4:30PM.

Felony, Civil Actions Over $5,000, Probate—Circuit and Chancery Courts, PO Box 667, Camden, AR 71701. 870-837-2230, Fax: 870-837-2252. 8AM-4:30PM. Access by: mail, in person.

Misdemeanor, Civil Actions Under $5,000, Eviction, Small Claims—Municipal Court, 213 Madison St, Camden, AR 71701. 870-836-0331, Fax: 870-836-3369. 8AM-4:30PM. Access by: mail, in person.

Perry

Real Estate Recording—Perry County Circuit Clerk, Main Street, Courthouse Square, Perryville, AR 72126. 501-889-2710, Fax: 501-889-5759. 8AM-4:30PM.

Felony, Civil Actions Over $5,000, Probate—Circuit and Chancery Courts, PO Box 358, Perryville, AR 72126. 501-889-5126, Fax: 501-889-5759. 8AM-4:30PM. Access by: in person.

Misdemeanor, Civil Actions Under $5,000, Eviction, Small Claims—Municipal Court, PO Box 186, Perryville, AR 72126. 501-889-5296, Fax: 501-889-5835. 8AM-4:30PM. Access by: mail, in person.

Phillips

Real Estate Recording—Phillips County Circuit Clerk, Courthouse, Suite 206, 620 Cherry St. Helena, AR 72342. 501-338-5510, Fax: 870-338-5513. 8AM-4:30PM.

Felony, Civil Actions Over $5,000, Probate—Circuit and Chancery Courts, Courthouse, 620 Cherry St Suite 206, Helena, AR 72342. 870-338-5515, Fax: 870-338-5513. 8AM-4:30PM. Access by: mail, in person.

Misdemeanor, Civil Actions Under $5,000, Eviction, Small Claims—Municipal Court, 226 Perry, Helena, AR 72342. 870-338-

8825, Fax: 870-338-9832. 8AM-4:30PM. Access by: mail, phone, in person.

Pike

Real Estate Recording—Pike County Circuit Clerk, Courthouse Square, Murfreesboro, AR 71958. 501-285-2422, Fax: 870-285-3281. 8AM-4:30PM.

Felony, Civil Actions Over $5,000, Probate—Circuit and Chancery Courts, PO Box 219, Murfreesboro, AR 71958. 870-285-2231, Fax: 870-285-3281. 8AM-4:30PM. Access by: mail, fax, in person.

Misdemeanor, Civil Actions Under $5,000, Eviction, Small Claims—Municipal Court, PO Box 197, Murfreesboro, AR 71958. 870-285-3865. 8AM-4:30PM. Access by: mail, fax, in person.

Poinsett

Real Estate Recording—Poinsett County Circuit Clerk, 401 Market Street, Courthouse, Harrisburg, AR 72432. 501-578-4405, Fax: 870-578-2441. 8:30AM-4:30PM.

Felony, Civil Actions Over $5,000, Probate—Circuit and Chancery Courts, PO Box 46, Harrisburg, AR 72432. 870-578-4420, Fax: 870-578-2441. 8:30AM-4:30PM. Access by: mail, in person.

Misdemeanor, Civil Actions Under $5,000, Eviction, Small Claims—Municipal Court, 202 East St, Harrisburg, AR 72432. 870-578-4110. 8AM-4:30PM. Access by: mail, in person.

Polk

Real Estate Recording—Polk County Circuit Clerk, 507 Church, Courthouse, Mena, AR 71953. 501-394-8150. 8AM-4:30PM.

Felony, Civil Actions Over $5,000, Probate—Circuit and Chancery Courts, 507 Church St, Mena, AR 71953. 501-394-8100. 8AM-4:30PM. Access by: mail, in person. Special note: Probate is handled separately from the court.

Misdemeanor, Civil Actions Under $5,000, Eviction, Small Claims—Municipal Court, 507 Church St, Mena, AR 71953. 501-394-3271, Fax: 501-394-6199. 8AM-4:30PM. Access by: in person.

Pope

Real Estate Recording—Pope County Circuit Clerk, 100 West Main, 3rd Floor, County Courthouse, Russellville, AR 72801. 501-968-7016. 8AM-5PM.

Felony, Civil Actions Over $5,000, Probate—Circuit and Chancery Courts, 100 W Main, Russellville, AR 72801. 501-968-7499. 8AM-5PM. Access by: in person. Special note: This court will not do record searches; a local retriever must be hired.

Misdemeanor, Civil Actions Under $5,000, Eviction, Small Claims—Municipal Court, 205 S Commerce, Russellville, AR 72801. 501-968-1393, Fax: 501-968-4166. 8:30AM-5PM. Access by: mail, in person.

Prairie

Real Estate Recording—Prairie County Circuit Clerk, 200 Court Square, Des Arc, AR 72040. 501-256-4137, Fax: 870-256-4434. 8AM-4:30PM.

Prairie County Circuit Clerk, 200 Court Square, Corner of Prairie & Magnolia, De Valls Bluff, AR 72041. 501-998-4786, Fax: 870-998-2314. 8AM-Noon, 1-4:30PM.

Felony, Civil Actions Over $5,000, Probate—Circuit and Chancery Courts-Southern District, PO Box 283, De Valls Bluff, AR 72041. 870-998-2314, Fax: 870-998-2314. 8AM-4:30PM. Access by: mail, phone, fax, in person.

Circuit and County Courts-Northern District, PO Box 1011, Des Arc, AR 72040. 870-256-4434, Fax: 870-256-4434. 8AM-4:30PM. Access by: mail, phone, in person.

Misdemeanor, Civil Actions Under $5,000, Eviction, Small Claims—Municipal Court, PO Box 389, Des Arc, AR 72040. 870-256-3011, Fax: 870-256-4612. 8AM-5PM. Access by: mail, in person.

Pulaski

Real Estate Recording—Pulaski County Circuit Clerk, Room S216, 401 W. Markham St. Little Rock, AR 72201. 501-340-8345, Fax: 501-340-8420. 8:30AM-4:30PM.

Felony, Civil Actions Over $5,000, Probate—Circuit and Chancery Courts, Courthouse, Rm 200, 401 W Marcom St, Ste 102, Little Rock, AR 72201. 501-340-8431, Fax: 501-340-8420. 8:30AM-4:30PM. Access by: mail, in person.

Misdemeanor, Civil Actions Under $5,000, Eviction, Small Claims—Municipal Court, 3001 W Roosevelt, Little Rock, AR 72204. 501-340-6824, Fax: 501-340-6899. 8AM-4:30PM. Access by: mail, fax, in person.

Randolph

Real Estate Recording—Randolph County Circuit Clerk, 107 W. Broadway, Pocahontas, AR 72455. 501-892-5238, Fax: 870-892-8794. 8AM-4:30PM.

Felony, Civil Actions Over $5,000, Probate—Circuit and Chancery Courts, 107 West Broadway, Pocahontas, AR 72455. 870-892-5522, Fax: 870-892-8794. 8AM-4:30PM. Access by: mail, in person.

Misdemeanor, Civil Actions Under $5,000, Eviction, Small Claims—Municipal Court, PO Box 896, Pocahontas, AR 72455. 870-892-4033, Fax: 870-892-4293. 7:30AM-4:30PM. Access by: mail, fax, in person.

Saline

Real Estate Recording—Saline County Circuit Clerk, 200 N. Main St. Courthouse, Benton, AR 72015. 501-776-5633, Fax: 501-303-5675. 8AM-4:30PM.

Felony, Civil Actions Over $5,000, Probate—Circuit and Chancery Courts, PO Box 1560, Benton, AR 72018. 501-303-5615, Fax: 501-303-5675. 8AM-4:30PM. Access by: in person.

Misdemeanor, Civil Actions Under $5,000, Eviction, Small Claims—Municipal Court, 1605 Edison Ave, Benton, AR 72015. 501-303-5670, Fax: 501-776-5696. 8AM-4:30PM. Access by: mail, phone, fax, in person.

Scott

Real Estate Recording—Scott County Circuit Clerk, 100 W. First, Courthouse, Waldron, AR 72958. 501-637-2780, Fax: 501-637-4199. 8AM-4:30PM.

Felony, Civil Actions Over $5,000, Probate—Circuit and Chancery Courts, PO Box 2165, Waldron, AR 72958. 870-637-2642. 8AM-4:30PM. Access by: mail, in person.

Misdemeanor, Civil Actions Under $5,000, Eviction, Small Claims—Municipal Court, 100 W 1st St #15, Waldron, AR 72958. 501-637-4694. 8AM-4:30PM. Access by: mail, in person.

Searcy

Real Estate Recording—Searcy County Circuit Clerk, Courthouse, Town Square, Marshall, AR 72650. 501-448-5050. 8AM-4:30PM.

Felony, Civil Actions Over $5,000, Probate—Circuit and Chancery Courts, PO Box 935, Marshall, AR 72650. 870-448-3807. 8AM-4:30PM. Access by: mail, in person.

Misdemeanor, Civil Actions Under $5,000, Eviction, Small Claims—Municipal Court, General Delivery, PO Box 837, Marshall, AR 72650. 870-448-5411. 9AM-5PM. Access by: mail, phone, in person.

Sebastian

Real Estate Recording—Sebastian County Circuit Clerk, 40 S. 4th St. Fort Smith, AR 72901. Fax: 501-784-1580. 8AM-5PM.

Sebastian County Circuit Clerk, Town Square, Courthouse, Greenwood, AR 72936. Fax: 501-996-6885. 8AM-5PM.

Felony, Civil Actions Over $5,000, Probate—Circuit Court-Greenwood Division, PO Box 310, County Courthouse, Greenwood, AR 72936. 501-996-4175, Fax: 501-996-6885. 8AM-5PM. Access by: mail, in person.

Circuit Court-Fort Smith, 35 S 6th St, PO Box 1179, Fort Smith, AR 72902. 501-782-1046. 8AM-5PM. Access by: mail, in person.

Misdemeanor, Civil Actions Under $5,000, Eviction, Small Claims—Municipal Court, Courthouse, 35 S 6th St, Fort Smith, AR 72901. 501-784-2420, Fax: 501-784-2438. 8:30AM-5PM. Access by: mail, fax, in person.

Sevier

Real Estate Recording—Sevier County Circuit Clerk, 115 North 3rd Street, De Queen, AR 71832. 501-642-2358, Fax: 870-642-9638. 8AM-4:30PM.

Felony, Civil Actions Over $5,000, Probate—Circuit Court, 115 N 3rd, Courthouse, De Queen, AR 71832. 870-584-3055, Fax: 870-642-9638. 8AM-4:30PM. Access by: mail, in person.

Misdemeanor, Civil Actions Under $5,000, Eviction, Small Claims—Municipal Court, 115 N 3rd, De Queen, AR 71832. 870-584-7311. 8AM-4:30PM. Access by: mail, phone, in person.

Sharp

Real Estate Recording—Sharp County Circuit Clerk, Highway 167 North, Courthouse, Ash Flat, AR 72513. 501-994-7347, Fax: 870-994-7712. 8AM-4PM.

Felony, Civil Actions Over $5,000, Probate—Circuit and County Courts, PO Box 307, Ash Flat, AR 72513. 870-994-7361, Fax: 870-994-7712. 8AM-4PM. Access by: mail, fax, in person.

Misdemeanor, Civil Actions Under $5,000, Eviction, Small Claims—Municipal Court, PO Box 2, Ash Flat, AR 72513. 870-994-2745, Fax: 870-994-7901. 8AM-4PM. Access by: mail, in person.

St. Francis

Real Estate Recording—St. Francis County Circuit Clerk, 313 South Izard Street, Forrest City, AR 72335. 501-261-1705, Fax: 870-261-1725. 8AM-4:30PM.

Felony, Civil Actions Over $5,000, Probate—Circuit and County Courts, PO Box 1775, Forrest City, AR 72335. 870-261-1715, Fax: 870-261-1723. 8AM-4:30PM. Access by: mail, fax, in person.

Misdemeanor, Civil Actions Under $5,000, Eviction, Small Claims—Municipal Court, 615 East Cross, Forrest City, AR 72335. 870-261-1410, Fax: 870-261-1411. 8AM-4:30PM. Access by: mail, in person.

Stone

Real Estate Recording—Stone County Circuit Clerk, Courthouse, HC 71 Box 1, Mountain View, AR 72560. 501-269-8426, Fax: 870-269-2303. 8AM-4:30PM.

Felony, Civil Actions Over $5,000, Probate—Circuit and Chancery Courts, HC71 Box 1, Mountain View, AR 72560. 870-269-3271, Fax: 870-269-2303. 8AM-4:30PM. Access by: in person.

Misdemeanor, Civil Actions Under $5,000, Eviction, Small Claims—Municipal Court, HC 71 Box 4, Mountain View, AR 72560. 870-269-3465. 8AM-4:30PM. Access by: mail, phone, in person.

Union

Real Estate Recording—Union County Circuit Clerk, 101 North Washington, Courthouse - Room 201, El Dorado, AR 71730. 501-864-1928. 8:30AM-5PM.

Felony, Civil Actions Over $5,000, Probate—Circuit and Chancery Courts, PO Box 1626, El Dorado, AR 71730. 870-864-1940. 8:30AM-5PM. Access by: mail, in person.

Misdemeanor, Civil Actions Under $5,000, Eviction, Small Claims—Municipal Court, 101 N Washington, Suite 203, El Dorado, AR 71730. 870-864-1950, Fax: 870-864-1955. 8:30AM-5PM. Access by: mail, fax, in person.

Van Buren

Real Estate Recording—Van Buren County Circuit Clerk, Courthouse, Main & Griggs, Clinton, AR 72031. Fax: 501-745-7400. 8AM-5PM.

Felony, Civil Actions Over $5,000, Probate—Circuit and County Courts, Route 6 Box 254-9, Clinton, AR 72031. 501-745-4140. 8AM-5PM. Access by: mail, in person.

Misdemeanor, Civil Actions Under $5,000, Eviction, Small Claims—Municipal Court, PO Box 181, Clinton, AR 72031. 501-745-8894. 8:30AM-4:30PM. Access by: mail, in person.

Washington

Real Estate Recording—Washington County Circuit Clerk, Courthouse, 280 N. College, Suite 302, Fayetteville, AR 72701. 501-444-1526, Fax: 501-444-1537. 8AM-4:30PM.

Felony, Civil Actions Over $5,000, Probate—Circuit and Chancery Courts, 280 N College, Fayetteville, AR 72701. 501-444-1542, Fax: 501-444-1537. 8AM-4:30PM. Access by: mail, fax, in person.

Misdemeanor, Civil Actions Under $5,000, Small Claims—Municipal Court, 100B W Rock, Fayetteville, AR 72701. 501-587-3596, Fax: 501-444-3480. 8AM-5PM. Access by: mail, phone, fax, in person.

White

Real Estate Recording—White County Circuit Clerk, White County Courthouse, Spring St./East Entrance/Courthouse Sq. Searcy, AR 72143. 501-279-6206. 8AM-4:30PM.

Felony, Civil Actions Over $5,000, Probate—Circuit and Chancery Courts, 301 W Arch, Searcy, AR 72143. 501-279-6223, Fax: 501-279-6218. 8AM-4:30PM. Access by: mail, phone, in person.

Misdemeanor, Civil Actions Under $5,000, Small Claims—Municipal Court, 311 N Gum, Searcy, AR 72143. 501-268-7622, Fax: 501-279-1043. 8:30AM-4:30PM. Access by: mail, phone, in person.

Woodruff

Real Estate Recording—Woodruff County Circuit Clerk, 500 North Third Street, Augusta, AR 72006. 501-347-5416. 8AM-4PM.

Felony, Civil Actions Over $5,000, Probate—Circuit and County Courts, PO Box 492, Augusta, AR 72006. 870-347-2391, Fax: 870-347-2915. 8AM-4PM. Access by: mail, phone, in person. Special note: Probate is handled by the County Clerk.

Misdemeanor, Civil Actions Under $5,000, Eviction, Small Claims—Municipal Court, PO Box 381, Augusta, AR 72006. 870-347-2790, Fax: 870-347-2436. 8:30AM-5PM. Access by: mail, fax, in person.

Yell

Real Estate Recording—Yell County Circuit Clerk, East 5th & Main, Danville, AR 72833. Fax: 501-495-3495. 8AM-4PM.

Yell County Circuit Clerk, Union Street, Courthouse, Dardanelle, AR 72834. Fax: 501-229-1130. 8AM-4PM.

Felony, Civil Actions Over $5,000, Probate—Danville Circuit and County Courts, PO Box 219, Danville, AR 72833. 501-495-2414, Fax: 501-495-3495. 8AM-4PM. Access by: mail, in person.

Dardanelle Circuit and County Courts, County Courthouse, PO Box 457, Dardanelle, AR 72834. 501-229-4404. 8AM-4PM. Access by: mail, in person.

Misdemeanor, Civil Actions Under $5,000, Eviction, Small Claims—Municipal Court, Courthouse, Dardanelle, AR 72834. 501-229-1389. 8AM-4PM. Access by: mail, in person.

Federal Courts

US District Court

Eastern District of Arkansas

Batesville Division c/o Little Rock Division, PO Box 869, Little Rock, AR 72201501-324-5351 Counties: Cleburne, Fulton, Independence, Izard, Jackson, Sharp, Stone. www.are.uscourts.gov

Helena Division c/o Little Rock Division, PO Box 869, Little Rock, AR 72203501-324-5351 Counties: Cross, Lee, Monroe, Phillips, St. Francis, Woodruff. www.are.uscourts.gov

Jonesboro Division PO Box 7080, Jonesboro, AR 72403870-972-4610 Fax: 870-972-4612 Counties: Clay, Craighead, Crittenden, Greene, Lawrence, Mississippi, Poinsett, Randolph. www.are.uscourts.gov

Little Rock Division Room 402, 600 W Capitol, Little Rock, AR 72201501-324-5351 Counties: Conway, Faulkner, Lonoke, Perry, Pope, Prairie, Pulaski, Saline, Van Buren, White, Yell. www.are.uscourts.gov

Pine Bluff Division PO Box 8307, Pine Bluff, AR 71611-8307870-536-1190 Fax: 870-536-6330 Counties: Arkansas, Chicot, Cleveland, Dallas, Desha, Drew, Grant, Jefferson, Lincoln. www.are.uscourts.gov

Western District of Arkansas

El Dorado Division PO Box 1566, El Dorado, AR 71731870-862-1202 Counties: Ashley, Bradley, Calhoun, Columbia, Ouachita, Union. www.arwd.uscourts.gov

Fayetteville Division PO Box 6420, Fayetteville, AR 72702501-521-6980 Fax: 501-575-0774 Counties: Benton, Madison, Washington. www.arwd.uscourts.gov

Fort Smith Division PO Box 1523, Fort Smith, AR 72902501-783-6833 Fax: 501-783-6308 Counties: Crawford, Franklin, Johnson, Logan, Polk, Scott, Sebastian. www.arwd.uscourts.gov

Harrison Division c/o Fayetteville Division, PO Box 6420, Fayetteville, AR 72702501-521-6980 Fax: 501-575-0774 Counties: Baxter, Boone, Carroll, Marion, Newton, Searcy. www.arwd.uscourts.gov

Hot Springs Division PO Drawer I, Hot Springs, AR 71902501-623-6411 Counties: Clark, Garland, Hot Springs, Montgomery, Pike. www.arwd.uscourts.gov

Texarkana Division PO Box 2746, Texarkana, AR 75504501-773-3381 Counties: Hempstead, Howard, Lafayette, Little River, Miller, Nevada, Sevier. www.arwd.uscourts.gov

US Bankruptcy Court

Eastern District of Arkansas

Little Rock Division PO Drawer 3777, Little Rock, AR 72203501-918-5500 Fax: 501-918-5520 Counties: Same counties as included in Eastern District of Arkansas, plus the counties included in the Western District divisions of El Dorado, Hot Springs and Texarkana. All bankruptcy cases in Arkansas prior to mid-1993 were heard here.

Western District of Arkansas

Fayetteville Division PO Box 3097, Fayetteville, AR 72702-3097501-582-9800 Fax: 501-582-9825 Counties: Same counties as included in the Western District of Arkansas except that counties included in the divisions of El Dorado, Hots Springs and Texarkana are heard in Little Rock.

California

Attorney General's Office
PO Box 944255   916-445-9555
Sacramento, CA 94244-2550   Fax: 916-324-5205
caag.state.ca.us

Governor's Office
State Capitol, 1st Floor   916-445-2841
Sacramento, CA 95814   Fax: 916-445-4633
www.ca.gov/s/governor

State Archives
1020 "O" St   916-653-7715
Sacramento, CA 95814   Fax: 916-653-7134
www.ss.ca.gov/archives/archives

Capital: Sacramento
Sacramento County

Time Zone: PST

Number of Counties: 58

Population: 32,268,301

Web Site: www.state.ca.us

Search Unclaimed Property Online

http://scoweb.sco.ca.gov/
scoucp/inquiry/index.htm

State Agencies

Criminal Records
Restricted access.
The CA Penal Code does authorize certain categories of businesses (childcare, elderly, handicapped workers, etc.) to receive limited criminal background information. Call to determine if your request is authorized and they will send request form.
Department of Justice, PO Box 903417, Sacramento, CA 94203-4170 (4949 Broadway, Sacramento, CA 95820) (4949 Broadway, Sacramento, CA 95820); 916-227-3460; 8AM-5PM

Corporation Records
Limited Liability Company Records
Limited Partnerships
Secretary of State, Information Retrieval Unit, 1500 11th Street, Sacramento, CA 95814; 916-657-5448, 916-653-3794 LLCs, 916-653-3365 LPs; 8AM-4:30PM. Access by: mail, phone, in person, online.

Sales Tax Registrations
Board of Equalization, Account Analysis and Control, PO Box 942879, Sacramento, CA 94279-0029; 916-445-6362, 800-400-7115 In California Only; Fax: 916-324-4433; 8AM-5PM. Access by: mail, phone, in person. www.boe.ca.gov

Trademarks/Servicemarks
Limited Partnership Records
Secretary of State, Trademark Unit, 1500 11th Street, Rm 345, Sacramento, CA 95814; 916-653-4984; 8AM-5PM. Access by: mail, phone, in person.

Uniform Commercial Code
Federal Tax Liens
State Tax Liens
UCC Division, Secretary of State, PO Box 942835, Sacramento, CA 94235-0001 (1500 11th St, 2nd Fl, Sacramento, CA 95814); 916-653-3516; 8AM-5PM. Access by: mail, online. www.ss.ca.gov

Assumed Name
Fictitious Name
Records not available from state agency.
Records are found at the county level.

Workers' Compensation Records

Division of Workers' Compensation, Headquarters, PO Box 420603, San Francisco, CA 94142 (455 Golden Gate Ave, 9th Fl, San Francisco, CA 94102); 415-703-4600; Fax: 415-703-4717; 8AM-5PM. Access by: mail.

Birth Certificates

State Department of Health Svcs, Office of Vital Records, 304 S Street, Sacramento, CA 95814; 916-445-2684 Recording, 916-445-1719 Attendant; Fax: 800-858-5553; 8AM-4:30PM. Access by: mail. www.dhs.ca.gov/chs

Death Records

State Department of Health Svcs, Office of Vital Records, 304 S Street, Sacramento, CA 95814; 916-445-2684, 916-445-1719 Attendant; Fax: 800-858-5553; 8AM-4:30PM. Access by: mail. www.dhs.ca.gov/chs

Marriage Certificates

State Department of Health Svcs, Office of Vital Records, 304 S Street, Sacramento, CA 95814; 916-445-2684, 916-445-1719 Attendant; Fax: 800-858-5553; 8AM-4:30PM. Access by: mail. www.dhs.ca.gov/chs

Divorce Records

State Department of Health Svcs, Office of Vital Records, 304 S Street, Sacramento, CA 95814; 916-445-2684, 916-445-1719 Attendant; Fax: 800-858-5553; 8AM-4:30PM. Access by: mail. www.dhs.gov/chs

Driver Records

Department of Motor Vehicles, Information Services, PO Box 944247, Mail Station G199, Sacramento, CA 94244-2470 (Bldg East-First Floor, 2415 First Ave, Sacramento, CA 95818); 916-657-8098, 916-657-5564; 8AM-5PM. Access by: mail, phone, in person, online.

Vehicle Ownership
Vehicle Identification
Boat & Vessel Ownership
Boat & Vessel Registration

Department of Motor Vehicle, Public Contact Unit, PO Box 944247, Sacramento, CA 94244-2470 (Bldg East-First Floor, 2415 First Ave, Sacramento, CA 95818); 916-657-8098 Walk-in/Mail-in Phone, 916-657-7914 Commercial Accounts, 916-657-6739 Vessel Registration; Fax: 916-657-9041; 8AM-5PM. Access by: mail, phone, in person, online.

Accident Reports

Records not available from state agency.

Most accident reports are held by the California Highway Patrol or local law enforcement agency that filed the report. There are 115 area offices of the California Highway Patrol. Fees vary.

Legislation-Current/Pending
Legislation-Passed

California State Legislature, State Capitol, Room B-32 (Legislative Bill Room), Sacramento, CA 95814;, 916-445-2323 Current/Pending Bills, 916-653-7715 State Archives; 8AM-5PM. Access by: mail, phone, in person, online. www.leginfo.ca.gov

Voter Registration

Restricted access.

Individual verification must be done at the local level. Records are not open and cannot be viewed. The state will sell all or portions of the statewide database for political or pre-approved purposes. Call (916) 653-6224 for details.

Secretary of State, Elections Division, 1500 11th Street, Sacramento, CA 95814; 916-657-2166; Fax: 916-653-3214; 8AM-5PM

GED Certificates

Dept of Education, State GED Office, PO Box 710273, Sacramento, CA 94244-0273; 800-331-6316 Main Number;.

Hunting License Information
Fishing License Information

Restricted access.

Department of Fish & Game, License & Revenue Branch, 3211 "S" St, Sacramento, CA 95816; 916-227-2244; Fax: 916-227-2261; 8AM-5PM
www.dfg.ca.gov

County Courts & Recording Offices

About the Courts...

About the Recording Offices...

Administration

Administrative Office of Courts	415-865-1200
455 Golden Gate Ave	Fax: 415-865-4205
San Francisco, CA 94102	
www.courtinfo.ca.gov	

Court Structure

As of September 1995, all justice courts were eliminated and converted to municipal courts. Operations, judges, and records became part of the municipal court system.

In July 1998, the judges in individual counties were given the opportunity to vote on unification of superior and municipal courts within their respective counties. As of late 1999, 54 of 58 counties had voted to unify these courts. Court that were formally Municipal Courts are now known as Limited Jurisdiction Superior Courts. In some counties, superior and municipal courts were combined into one superior court. Many counties are facing difficult challenges as they merge which, in turn, create hardships for record searchers.

It is important to note that Municipal Courts may try minor felonies not included under our felony definition.

Searching Hints

If there is more than one court of a type within a county, where the case is tried and where the record is held depends on how a citation is written, where the infraction occurred, or where the filer chose to file the case.

Some courts now require signed releases from the subject in order to perform crimi-nal searches, and will no longer allow the public to conduct such searches.

Personal checks are acceptable by state law.

Although fees are set by statute, courts interpret them differently. For example, the search fee is supposed to be $5.00 per name per year searched, but many courts charge only $5.00 per name. Certification fee is now $6.00 per document.

Online Access

There is no statewide online computer access available, internal or external. However, a number of counties have developed their own online access sytems and may allow access to their internal case management systems by county residents. Also, the web site contains a lot of useful information about the state court system.

Organization

58 counties, 58 recording offices. The recording officer is County Recorder. Recordings are usually located in a Grantor/Grantee or General index. The entire state is in the Pacific Time Zone (PST).

UCC Records

Financing statements are filed at the state level, except for consumer goods, crops, and real estate related collateral, which are filed only with the County Recorder. All counties will perform UCC searches. Use search request form UCC-11. Search fees are usually $15.00 per debtor name. Copy costs vary.

Lien Records

Federal and state tax liens on personal property of businesses are filed with the Secretary of State. Other federal and state tax liens are filed with the County Recorder. Some counties will perform separate tax lien searches. Fees vary for this type of search.

Real Estate Records

Most counties do not perform real estate searches. Copy fees and certification fees vary.

County Courts & Recording Offices

Alameda

Real Estate Recording—Alameda County Recorder, 1225 Fallon Street, Courthouse, Room 100, Oakland, CA 94612. 510-272-6800, Fax: 510-272-6382. 8:30AM-4:30PM.

Civil Actions Over $25,000, Probate—Southern Superior Court-Hayward Branch, 24405 Amador St Rm 108, Hayward, CA 94544. 510-670-5060, Fax: 510-783-9456. 8:30AM-4:30PM. Access by: mail, in person. www.co.alameda.ca.us/courts

Alameda County Superior Court Northern Branch-Civil, 1225 Fallon St Rm 109, Oakland, CA 94612. 510-272-6799. 8:30AM-4:30PM. Access by: mail, in person. www.co.alameda.ca.us/courts/superior

Pleasanton Branch-Superior Court, 5672 Stoneridge Dr 2nd Fl, Pleasanton, CA 94588. 925-551-6883. 8:30AM-4:30PM. Access by: mail, in person. www.co.alameda.ca.us/courts

Felony—Superior Court-Criminal, 1225 Fallon St Rm 107, Oakland, CA 94612. 510-272-6777, Fax: 510-272-0796. 8:30AM-5PM. Access by: mail, fax, in person. www.co.alameda.ca.us/courts

Civil Actions Under $25,000, Eviction, Small Claims—Berkeley-Albany Superior Court-Civil Division, 2000 Center St, Room 202, Berkeley, CA 94704. 510-644-6423. 8:30AM-4:30PM. Access by: mail, in person. Special note: Co-extensive with the city limits of Berkeley and Albany. www.co.alameda.ca.us/courts

Misdemeanor—Berkeley-Albany Branch-Criminal Division, 2120 Martin Luther King Jr Way, Berkeley, CA 94704. 510-644-6917, Fax: 510-848-6916. 8:30AM-4:30PM. Access by: mail, in person. Special note: Co-extensive with the city limits of Berkeley and Albany. www.co.alameda.ca.us/courts

Misdemeanor, Civil Actions Under $25,000, Eviction, Small Claims—Alameda Branch-Superior Court, 2233 Shoreline Dr (PO Box 1470), Alameda, CA 94501. 510-268-4208, Fax: 510-523-7964. 8:30AM-4:30PM. Access by: mail, in person. Special note: Co-extensive with the city limits of Alameda only. www.co.alameda.ca.us/courts

Fremont-Newark-Union City Superior Court, 39439 Paseo Padre Pky, Fremont, CA 94538. Fax: 510-795-2349. 8:30AM-5PM. Access by: mail, fax, in person. Special note: Jurisdiction includes Fremont, Newark and Union City. www.co.alameda.ca.us/courts

Livermore-Pleasanton-Dublin Superior Court, 5672 Stoneridge Dr, Pleasanton, CA 94566-8678. Fax: 925-847-0863. 8:30AM-4:30PM. Access by: mail, in person. Special note: Includes the cities of Livermore, Dublin and Pleasanton and all areas east to San Joaquin County line, north of Highway 580 to Contra Costa line. www.co.alameda.ca.us/courts

Oakland Piedmont Superior Court, 661 Washington St, Oakland, CA 94607. Fax: 510-268-7807. 8:30AM-4:30PM. Access by: mail, in person. Special note: Comprises the cities of Oakland, Piedmont and Emeryville. www.co.alameda.ca.us/courts

San Leandro-Hayward Superior Court, 24405 Amador St, Hayward, CA 94544. 510-670-5522, Fax: 510-670-5522. 8:30AM-4:30PM. Access by: mail, fax, in person. Special note: Includes the cities of San Leandro, Hayward and adjoining unincorporated areas of Castro Valley and San Lorenzo. www.co.alameda.ca.us/courts/hayward/index.htm

Alpine

Real Estate Recording—Alpine County Treasurer-Tax-Collector-Recorder, Administration Building, 99 Water St. Markleeville, CA 96120. 530-694-2286, Fax: 530-694-2491. 9AM-Noon,1-4PM.

Felony, Misdemeanor, Civil, Evictions, Small Claims, Probate—Superior Court, PO Box 518, Markleeville, CA 96120. 530-694-2113, Fax: 530-694-2119. 8AM-Noon, 1-5PM. Access by: mail, in person.

Amador

Real Estate Recording—Amador County Recorder, 500 Argonaut Lane, Jackson, CA 95642. 209-239-9188. 8AM-5PM.

Felony, Misdemeanor, Civil, Eviction, Small Claims, Probate—Superior Court, 108 Court St, Jackson, CA 95642. 209-299-4964. 8AM-5PM. Access by: mail, phone, fax, in person.

Butte

Real Estate Recording—Butte County Recorder, 25 County Center Drive, Oroville, CA 95965. 530-538-7576, Fax: 530-538-7975. 9AM-5PM; Recording hours: 9AM-4PM.

Felony, Civil Actions Over $25,000, Probate—Superior Court, One Court St, Oroville, CA 95965. 530-538-7551, Fax: 530-538-2112. 8:30AM-4PM. Access by: mail, fax, in person. Special note: This court physically holds all the files for all courts in the county; however, one can search the countywide computer index at any court. This court includes family law cases. www.courtinfo.ca.gov/trialcourts/butte

Misdemeanor, Civil Actions Under $25,000, Eviction, Small Claims—Chico Branch-Superior Court, 655 Oleander Ave, Chico, CA 95926. 530-891-2716. 8:30AM-4PM. Access by: mail, in person.

Misdemeanor, Eviction, Small Claims—Paradise Branch-Superior Court, 747 Elliott Rd, Paradise, CA 95969. 530-872-6347. 8AM-1PM M-W & F; 8AM-Noon, 1-5PM Th; Phone Hours: 9AM-Noon M-F. Access by: mail, in person.

Gridley Branch-Superior Court, Gridley Courthouse, 239 Sycamore, Gridley, CA 95948. 530-846-5701. 8AM-1PM 2 days a month. Access by: mail, in person. Special note: Open the first "full week" Thursday and 3rd Thursday.

Calaveras

Real Estate Recording—Calaveras County Recorder, Government Center, 891 Mountain Ranch Rd, San Andreas, CA 95249. 209-867-3448. 8AM-4PM.

Civil Actions Over $25,000, Probate—Superior Court Dept One, 891 Mt Ranch Rd, San Andreas, CA 95249. 209-834-3215. 8AM-4PM. Access by: mail, phone, in person.

Misdemeanor, Civil Actions Under $25,000, Eviction, Small Claims—Superior Court Dept Two, 891 Mt Ranch Rd, San Andreas, CA 95249. 209-846-7371, Fax: 209-754-6689. 8AM-4PM. Access by: mail, in person.

Colusa

Real Estate Recording—Colusa County Recorder, 546 Jay Street, Colusa, CA 95932. 530-458-0440, Fax: 530-458-0512. 8:30AM-5PM.

Felony, Civil Actions Over $25,000, Probate—Colusa County Superior Court, 547 Market St, Colusa, CA 95932. 530-458-0507, Fax: 530-458-2230. 8:30AM-5PM. Access by: mail, in person. Special note: Since 1995, the records have been combined for both courts in this county; prior records must be searched at the individual courts.

Misdemeanor, Civil Actions Under $25,000, Eviction, Small Claims—Colusa Limited Branch Superior Court, 532 Oak St, Colusa, CA 95932. 530-458-5149, Fax: 530-458-2904. 8:30AM-Noon, 1-5PM. Access by: mail, in person. Special note: Since 1995, records from both courts in this county have been combined; prior records must be searched at the individual courts.

Contra Costa

Real Estate Recording—Contra Costa County Recorder, 730 Las Juntas, Martinez, CA 94553. 8AM-4PM.

Felony, Civil Actions Over $25,000, Probate—Superior Court, 725 Court St Rm 103, Martinez, CA 94553. 925-646-2950. 8AM-4PM. Access by: mail, in person. www.co.contra-costra.ca.us

Misdemeanor—Martinez Limited Superior Court-Criminal Division, 1010 Ward St, Martinez, CA 94553. 925-646-5415, Fax:

925-646-1079. 9AM-4PM. Access by: mail, in person. Special note: Includes Avon, Clayton, Clyde, Concord, Martinez, Pacheco, Pleasant Hill.

Misdemeanor, Civil Actions Under $25,000, Eviction, Small Claims—Pittsburg Branch-Superior Court, 45 Civic Ave (PO Box 431), Pittsburg, CA 94565-0431. 8AM-4:30PM. Access by: mail, in person. Special note: Includes Antioch, Bethel Island, Bradford Island, Brentwood, Byron, Coney Island, Discovery Bay, Holland Tract, Jersey Island, Knightsen, Oakley, Pittsburg, Quimby Island, Shore Acres, Webb Tract, West Pittsburg, and parts of Clayton.

Richmond Superior Court, 100 37th St Rm 185, Richmond, CA 94805. 8AM-4PM. Access by: mail, in person. Special note: Includes Crockett, El Cerrito, El Sobrante, Hercules, Kensington, North Richmond, Pinole, Point Richmond, Port Costa, Richmond, Rodeo, Rollingwood and San Pablo.

Walnut Creek Branch-Superior Court, 640 Ygnacio Valley Rd (PO Box 5128), Walnut Creek, CA 94596-1128. 925-646-6578. 8:30AM-4:30PM. Access by: mail, phone, in person. Special note: Includes Alamo, Canyon, Danville, Lafayette, Moraga, Orinda, Rheem, San Ramon, St Mary's College, Walnut Creek and Ygnacio Valley. Effective 01/01/99, this court has all civil records formally at the municipal court in Concord.

Del Norte

Real Estate Recording—Del Norte County Recorder, 457 F Street, Crescent City, CA 95531. 707-464-7283. 8AM-Noon,1-5PM.

Felony, Misdemeanor, Civil, Eviction, Small Claims, Probate—Superior Court, 450 "H" St Rm 182, Crescent City, CA 95531. 707-464-7205, Fax: 707-465-4005. 8AM-Noon,1-5PM. Access by: mail, phone, in person.

El Dorado

Real Estate Recording—El Dorado County Recorder, 360 Fair Lane, Placerville, CA 95667. 530-621-5800, Fax: 530-621-2147. 8AM-5PM (No recordings after 4PM).

Civil, Eviction, Probate—South Lake Tahoe Branch-Superior Court-Civil, 1354 Johnson Blvd #2, South Lake Tahoe, CA 96150. 530-573-3075, Fax: 916-544-6532. 8AM-4PM. Access by: mail, phone, in person.

Felony, Civil, Probate—Placerville Branch-Superior Court, 495 Main St, Placerville, CA 95667. 530-621-6426, Fax: 530-622-9774. 8AM-4PM. Access by: mail, in person.

Felony, Misdemeanor—South Lake Tahoe Branch-Superior Court-Criminal, 1354 Johnson Blvd #1, South Lake Tahoe, CA 96150. 530-573-3047, Fax: 530-542-9102. 8AM-4PM. Access by: mail, in person.

Misdemeanor—Cameron Park Branch-Superior Court, 3321 Cameron Park Dr, Cameron Park, CA 95682. 530-621-5867, Fax: 530-672-2413. 8AM-4PM. Access by: mail, in person. Special note: Civil cases handled in Placerville.

Misdemeanor, Small Claims, Traffic—Fairlane Branch-Superior Court, 2850 Fairlane Ct, Placerville, CA 95667. 8AM-4PM. Access by: mail, in person.

Small Claims—South Lake Tahoe Superior Court-Small Claims, 3368 Lake Tahoe Blvd, Suite 100, South Lake Tahoe, CA 96150. 530-573-3442. 8AM-4PM. Access by: mail, in person.

Fresno

Real Estate Recording—Fresno County Recorder, 2281 Tulare St. Room 302 / Hall of Records, Fresno, CA 93721. 559-488-3486, Fax: 559-488-6774. 9AM-4PM.

Felony, Misdemeanor, Civil, Small Claims, Probate—Superior Court, 1100 Van Ness Ave, Fresno, CA 93721. 209-533-5671, Fax: 209-488-1976. 8AM-4PM. Access by: mail, phone, fax, in person. www.fresno.ca.gov/2810/index.htm

Felony, Misdemeanor, Civil Actions Under $25,000, Eviction, Small Claims—Kingsburg Division-Superior Court, 1600 California St, Kingsburg, CA 93631. 559-897-2241, Fax: 559-897-1419. 8AM-Noon, 1-4PM. Access by: mail, in person. www.fresno.ca.gov/2810/kingsburg.htm

Misdemeanor, Civil Actions Under $25,000, Eviction, Small Claims—Caruthers Division-Superior Court, 2215 W Tahoe,

Caruthers, CA 93609. 210-220-2083, Fax: 209-864-5141. 1-4PM M & F; 8AM-Noon W. Access by: mail, in person. www.fresno.ca.gov/2810/caruthers.htm

Clovis Division-Superior Court, 1011 5th St, Clovis, CA 93612. 209-385-7307, Fax: 209-299-2595. 8AM-4PM. Access by: mail, in person. Special note: Includes the city of Clovis and surrounding area. www.fresno.ca.gov/2810/clovis.htm

Coalinga Division-Superior Court, 160 West Elm St, Coalinga, CA 93210. 210-278-5821, Fax: 209-935-5324. 8AM-Noon, 1-4PM. Access by: mail, in person. www.fresno.ca.gov/2810/coalinga

Firebaugh Division-Superior Court, 1325 "O" St, Firebaugh, CA 93622. 209-754-6350, Fax: 209-659-6228. 8AM-4:30 M; 8AM-4PM T-F. Access by: mail, phone, fax, in person. www.fresno.ca.gov/2810/firebaugh

Fowler Division-Superior Court, PO Box 400, Fowler, CA 93625. 209-935-2017, Fax: 209-834-1645. 8AM-4PM. Access by: mail, in person. Special note: This court holds the records for the closed courts in Caruthers and Parlier. www.fresno.ca.gov/2810/fowler.htm

Kerman Division-Superior Court, 719 S Madera Ave, Kerman, CA 93630. 209-966-2621, Fax: 209-846-5751. 8AM-4PM M-F (2-4 for phone calls). Access by: mail, phone, in person. www.fresno.ca.gov/2810/kerman.htm

Parlier Branch-Superior Court, 580 Tulare St, Parlier, CA 93648. 209-754-6310, Fax: 209-646-3222. 8AM-Noon, 1-4PM; Phone: 2-4PM. Access by: mail, in person. www.fresno.ca.gov/2810/parlier.htm

Reedley Division-Superior Court, 815 "G" St, Reedley, CA 93654. 209-659-2011, Fax: 209-637-1534. 8AM-Noon, 1-4PM (2-4 for phone calls). Access by: mail, in person. www.fresno.ca.gov/2810/reedley

Riverdale Branch-Superior Court, 3563 Henson (PO Box 595), Riverdale, CA 93656. 210-220-2231, Fax: 209-867-4250. 8AM-4PM T-F; Phone Hours: 2-4PM. Access by: mail, in person. www.fresno.ca.gov/2810/riverdale.htm

Sanger Division-Superior Court, 619 "N" St, Sanger, CA 93657. 210-220-2546, Fax: 209-875-0002. 8AM-Noon, 1-4PM. Access by: mail, in person. www.fresno.ca.gov/2810/sanger.htm

Selma Division-Superior Court, 2117 Selma St, Selma, CA 93662. 210-257-7972, Fax: 209-896-4465. 8AM-Noon, 1-4PM. Access by: mail, phone, in person. www.fresno.ca.gov/2810/selma.htm

Glenn

Real Estate Recording—Glenn County Recorder, 526 West Sycamore Street, Willows, CA 95988. 530-934-6410, Fax: 530-934-6305. 8AM-5PM.

Felony, Misdemeanor, Civil, Eviction, Small Claims, Probate—Superior Court, 526 W Sycamore, Willows, CA 95988. 530-934-6446, Fax: 530-934-6406. 8AM-5PM. Access by: mail, in person. Special note: Records from the municipal court were combined with this court when the courts were consolidated.

Humboldt

Real Estate Recording—Humboldt County Recorder, 825 Fifth Street, Room 108, Eureka, CA 95501. 707-445-7331, Fax: 707-445-7324. 10AM-5PM.

Felony, Civil, Probate—Superior Court, 421 I St, Eureka, CA 95501-1153. 707-445-7355. 8:30AM-Noon, 1-4PM. Access by: mail, in person. Special note: County wide searching can be done from this court, records computerized for 10 years. The former Eureka, Eel River, and North Humboldt Municipal Court Divisions have been combined with this court.

Misdemeanor, Civil Actions Under $25,000, Eviction, Small Claims—Garberville Branch-Superior Court, 483 Conger St, Garberville, CA 95542. 707-923-2141, Fax: 707-923-3133. 8:30AM-Noon, 1-5PM. Access by: mail, in person.

Klamath/Trinity Branch-Superior Court, PO Box 698, Hoopa, CA 95546. 530-625-4204. 8:30AM-Noon, 1-5PM M-TH. Access by: mail, in person.

Imperial

Real Estate Recording—Imperial County Clerk/Recorder, 940 Main Street, Room 202, El Centro, CA 92243. 760-339-6281. 9AM-4:30PM.

Felony, Misdemeanor, Civil, Eviction, Small Claims, Probate—Imperial Branch-Superior Court, 939 W Main St, El Centro, CA 92243. 760-339-4217, Fax: 760-352-3184. 8AM-4PM. Access by: mail, in person. Special note: All record searching for Imperial county must be done at each location.

Eviction, Small Claims—Winterhaven Branch-Superior Court, PO Box 1087, Winterhaven, CA 92283. 760-572-0354, Fax: 760-572-2683. 8AM-Noon, 1-4PM. Access by: mail, phone, fax, in person. Special note: Misdemeanor and civil records have been moved to the Calexico Municipal Court. Only small claims and traffic records remain here.

Misdemeanor, Civil Actions Under $25,000, Eviction, Small Claims—Brawley Branch-Superior Court, 383 Main St, Brawley, CA 92227. 760-344-0710, Fax: 760-344-9231. 8AM-4PM. Access by: mail, phone, fax, in person. Special note: There is no countywide database in this county.

Calexico Branch-Superior Court, 415 4th St, Calexico, CA 92231. 760-357-3726, Fax: 760-357-6571. 8AM-4PM. Access by: mail, phone, fax, in person. Special note: There is no countywide database in this county.

Inyo

Real Estate Recording—Inyo County Recorder, 168 North Edwards, Independence, CA 93526. 760-878-0333, Fax: 760-872-2712. 9-Noon,1-5PM.

Felony, Civil Actions Over $25,000, Probate—Superior Court, 168 N Edwards St (PO Drawer F), Independence, CA 93526. 760-878-0218. 9AM-5PM. Access by: mail, in person. Special note: There is no central record database, each court in the county has its own records.

Misdemeanor, Civil Actions Under $25,000, Eviction, Small Claims—Bishop Branch-Superior Court, 301 W Line St, Bishop, CA 93514. 760-872-4971. 9AM-Noon, 1-5PM; Phone: 2-5PM. Access by: mail, in person. Special note: There is no countywide database, each court must be searched.

Independence Limited Branch-Superior Court, 168 N Edwards St (PO Box 518), Independence, CA 93526. 760-878-0319, Fax: 760-872-1060. 9AM-Noon, 1-5PM. Access by: mail, in person. Special note: There is no countywide database, each court must be searched.

Kern

Real Estate Recording—Kern County Recorder, 1655 Chester Avenue, Hall of Records, Bakersfield, CA 93301. 661-861-2601, Fax: 661-868-6401. 8AM-5PM; Recording 8AM-2PM; Copy Service 8AM-5PM.

Felony, Civil Actions Over $25,000, Probate—Superior Court, 1415 Truxtun Ave, Bakersfield, CA 93301. 661-861-2621, Fax: 661-634-4999. 8AM-5PM. Access by: in person.

Misdemeanor, Civil Actions Under $25,000, Eviction, Small Claims—Arvin/Lamont Branch-South Kern Municipal Court, 12022 Main St, Lamont, CA 93241. 661-845-3460, Fax: 661-845-9142. 8AM-4PM. Access by: mail, fax, in person.

Bakersfield Municipal Court, 1215 Truxtun Ave, Bakersfield, CA 93301. Fax: 661-861-2005. 8AM-5PM. Access by: mail, fax, in person. Special note: Includes Bakersfield, Oildale, Edison, Glenville, Woody.

Delano/McFarland Branch-North Kern Municipal Court, 1122 Jefferson Sty, Delano, CA 93215. 661-725-8797, Fax: 661-721-1237. 8AM-Noon, 1-4:30PM. Access by: mail, phone, fax, in person. www.co.kern.ca.us

East Kern Municipal Court, 132 E Coso St, Ridgecrest, CA 93555. 760-375-1397, Fax: 760-375-2112. 8AM-4PM M-T, 8AM-5PM F. Access by: mail, in person. Special note: Includes Eastern Kern County, including Edwards Air Force Base, Lake Isabella, Kernville, China Lake NWC, California City, Ridgecrest, Mojave and Tehachapi.

Maricopa/Taft Branch-South Kern Municipal Court, 311 N Lincoln St, Taft, CA 93268. 661-763-2401, Fax: 661-763-2439. 8AM-Noon,1-4PM. Access by: mail, phone, in person.

Mojave Branch-East Kern Municipal Court, 1773 Hwy 58, Mojave, CA 93501. 661-824-2437. 8AM-Noon, 1-4PM M-Th; 8AM-Noon, 1-5PM F. Access by: mail, in person.

River Branch-East Kern Municipal Court, 7046 Lake Isabella Blvd, Lake Isabella, CA 93240. 760-379-3635, Fax: 760-379-4544. 8AM-4PM M-Th 8AM-5PM F. Access by: mail, phone, fax, in person.

Shafter/Wasco Branch-North Kern Municipal Court, 325 Central Valley Hwy, Shafter, CA 93263. 661-746-7500, Fax: 661-746-0545. 8AM-Noon; 1-4PM;. Access by: mail, phone, fax, in person.

Kings

Real Estate Recording—Kings County Clerk Recorder, 1400 West Lacey Blvd. Hanford, CA 93230. 559-582-3211, Fax: 559-582-6639. 8AM-3PM.

Felony, Civil Actions Over $25,000, Probate—Superior Court, 1400 W Lacey Blvd, Hanford, CA 93230. 559-582-3211, Fax: 559-584-0319. 8AM-5PM. Access by: mail, phone, in person.

Misdemeanor, Civil Actions Under $25,000, Eviction, Small Claims—Avenal Division Municipal Court, 501 E Kings St, Avenal, CA 93204. 559-386-5225, Fax: 559-386-9452. 8AM-5PM. Access by: mail, phone, fax, in person.

Corcoran Division-Municipal Court, 1000 Chittenden Ave, Corcoran, CA 93212. 559-992-5193, Fax: 559-992-5933. 8AM-5PM. Access by: mail, fax, in person.

Hanford Division-Municipal Court, 1400 W Lacey Blvd, Hanford, CA 93230. Fax: 559-584-7054. 8AM-5PM. Access by: mail, fax, in person.

Lemoore Division-Municipal Court, 449 "C" St, Lemoore, CA 93245. 559-924-7757, Fax: 559-925-0319. 8AM-5PM. Access by: mail, in person.

Lake

Real Estate Recording—Lake County Recorder, 255 North Forbes, Room 223, Lakeport, CA 95453. 707-263-2236, Fax: 707-263-3703. 9AM-5PM.

Felony, Misdemeanor, Civil, Eviction, Small Claims, Probate—Superior Court, 255 N Forbes St, Lakeport, CA 95453. 707-263-2374, Fax: 707-262-1327. Public hours 8:30AM-4PM. Access by: mail, in person. Special note: This court holds the records for the former Northlake Municipal Court. www.courtinfo.ca.gov/courts/trialcourts/lake

Misdemeanor, Civil Actions Under $25,000, Eviction, Small Claims—South Lake Division-Superior Court, 7000 S Center Dr, Clearlake, CA 95422. 707-994-4859, Fax: 707-994-1625. 8AM-4:30PM; Phone hours 8:30AM-12:30PM. Access by: mail, in person. www.courtinfo.ca.gov/courts/trialcourts/lake

Lassen

Real Estate Recording—Lassen County Recorder, 220 S. Lassen Street, Suite 5, Susanville, CA 96130. 530-251-8220, Fax: 530-257-3480. Public Hours: 10AM-Noon, 1-3PM; Phone Hours: 8AM-Noon, 1-5PM.

Felony, Misdemeanor, Civil, Eviction, Small Claims, Probate—Lassen County Superior Court, 220 S Lassen St, Susanville, CA 96130. 530-251-8189. 9AM-Noon, 1-4PM; Phone hours 9AM-Noon. Access by: mail, phone, in person. Special note: Dept 1 includes probate, civil over $25,000, eviction, small claims; Dept 2 includes all criminal and civil under $25,000.

Los Angeles

Real Estate Recording—Los Angeles County Recorder, Registrar-Recorder/County Clerk, 12400 E. Imperial Highway, Room 1007, Los Angeles, CA 90650. 313-965-5794. 8AM-5PM.

Felony—Superior Court, 210 W Temple St Rm M-6, Los Angeles, CA 90012. 214-653-7131, Fax: 213-617-1224. 8:30AM-4:30PM. Access by: mail, in person. www.co.la.ca.us/courts/superior-auc

Civil Actions Under $25,000, Eviction, Small Claims—Valley Division-Municipal Court-Civil Division, 14400 Delano St, Van Nuys, CA 91401. 818-374-3060. 8:30AM-4:30PM. Access by: mail, in person. Special note: Small Claims and Civil for that part of city known as Sherman Oaks, Van Nuys, Reseda, North

Hollywood, Woodland Hills, Canoga Park, Tarzana, Proter Ranch, Winnetka and Panorama City. www.lamuni.org

Misdemeanor—Valley Division-Municipal Court-Criminal Division, 14400 Erwin St Mall 2nd Fl, Van Nuys, CA 91401. 818-374-2628. 8:30AM-4:30PM. Access by: mail, phone, in person. Special note: Misdemeanors for that part of city known as Sherman Oaks, Van Nuys, Reseda, North Hollywood, Woodland Hills, Canoga Park, Tarzana, Proter Ranch, Winnetka and Panorama City. www.lamuni.org

Civil Actions Under $25,000, Eviction, Small Claims—Los Angeles Municipal Court-Civil, 110 N Grand Ave Rm 426, Los Angeles, CA 90012. 214-653-7421, Fax: 213-621-2701. 8:30AM-4:30PM. Access by: mail, phone, in person. Special note: Co-extensive with the city limits of Los Angeles and includes the City of San Fernando and sections designated as San Pedro, West Los Angeles, Van Nuys, Venice and the unincorporated area of Los Angeles County known as Florence/Firestone. www.lamuni.org

South Bay Municipal Court-Beach Cities Branch, 117 W Torrance Blvd, Redondo Beach, CA 90277-3638. 313-943-2060, Fax: 310-376-4051. 8:15AM-4:30PM. Access by: mail, in person. www.latrialcourts.org

Misdemeanor—Los Angeles Municipal Court-Criminal, 210 W Temple St Rm 5-305, Los Angeles, CA 90012. 214-653-7421. 8:30AM-4:30PM. Access by: mail, phone, in person. Special note: Includes incorporated City of Los Angeles excluding communities of San Pedro, West Los Angeles, Hollywood and San Fernando Valley. www.lamuni.org

Metropolitan Branch-Municipal Court, 1945 S Hill St Rm 200, Los Angeles, CA 90007. 214-653-6166, Fax: 213-741-0132. 8AM-4:30PM. Access by: mail, phone, in person. Special note: Vehicle Code misdemeanor and traffic citations for the incorporated City of Los Angeles excluding the areas known as San Pedro, West Los Angeles and communities of San Fernando Valley and the unincorporated County area more commonly known as Florence. www.lamuni.org

Misdemeanor, Civil Actions Under $25,000, Eviction, Small Claims—Alhambra Municipal Court, 150 W Commonwealth Ave, Alhambra, CA 91801. 626-308-5521. 8AM-4:30PM. Access by: mail, in person. Special note: Includes cities of Alhambra, Monterey Park, San Gabriel, Temple City and the unincorporated County area known as South San Gabriel. Address the specific division (criminal, civil, small claims) in correspondence. www.latrialcourts.org

Antelope Municipal Court, 1040 W Ave J (PO Box 1898 93539), Lancaster, CA 93534. 661-945-6335, Fax: 661-949-8628. 8AM-4:30PM. Access by: mail, in person. Special note: Includes city of Lancaster, City of Palmdale, and unincorporated County territory including Acton, Agua Dulce, Fairmont, Lake Hughes, Llano, Leona Valley, Littlerock, Pearblossom, Quartz Hill, Roosevelt, Green Valley Big Pines, Lake Elizabeth. www.latrialcourts.org

Beverly Hills Municipal Court, 9355 Burton Way, Beverly Hills, CA 90210. 313-382-8603. 8:30AM-4:30PM. Access by: mail, phone, in person. Special note: Includes cities of Beverly Hills and West Hollywood. www.latrialcourts.org

Burbank Municipal Court, 300 E Olive, PO Box 750, Burbank, CA 91503. 818-557-3461. 8AM-4:30PM. Access by: mail, in person. Special note: Co-extensive with the city limits of Burbank. www.courts.org

Citrus Municipal Court, 1427 W Covina Pky, West Covina, CA 91790. Fax: 626-338-7364. 8AM-4:30PM. Access by: mail, in person. Special note: Includes cities of Azusa, Baldwin Park, Covina, Glendora, Industry, Irwindale, Valinda, West Covina and surrounding unincorporated County area. www.co.la.ca.us/courts/citrus

Compton Municipal Court, 200 W Compton Blvd, Compton, CA 90220. 313-928-0535, Fax: 310-763-4984. 8AM-4:30PM. Access by: mail, phone, in person. Special note: Includes cities of Carson, Compton, Lynwood and Paramount and the unincorporated portions of county that surround them. There is a branch in Lynwood (310-357-5200) that handles pretrials only. www.latrialcourts.org

Culver Municipal Court, 4130 Overland Ave, Culver City, CA 90230. 313-277-8200, Fax: 310-836-8345. 8:30AM-4:30PM. Access by: mail, in person. Special note: Includes Culver City and surrounding unincorporated areas including Angelus Vista, portions

of Marina del Rey, View Park and Windsor Hills, all surrounded by the City of Los Angeles, on south bounded by Inglewood. www.latrialcourts.org

Downey Municipal Court, 7500 E Imperial Hwy, Downey, CA 90242. 8AM-4:30PM T-F 12PM-7:30PM M. Access by: mail, in person. Special note: Comprises the cities of Downey, Norwalk and La Mirada. www.latrialcourts.org

East Los Angeles Municipal Court, 214 S Fetterly Ave, Los Angeles, CA 90022. 8AM-4:30PM. Access by: mail, phone, in person. Special note: Includes cities of Montebello and Commerce and adjacent unincorporated territory bordering Monterey Park on the north and Los Angeles on the west. www.lamuni.org

Glendale Municipal Court, 600 E Broadway, Glendale, CA 91206. 818-500-3523, Fax: 818-548-0486. 8AM-4PM. Access by: mail, in person. Special note: Includes cities of Glendale, LaCanada-Flintridge and unincorporated county area known as Montrose, La Crescenta, Verdugo City and Highway Highlands. www.latrialcourts.org

Huntington Park Municipal Court, 6548 Miles Ave, Huntington Park, CA 90255. Fax: 323-589-6769. 8AM-4PM. Access by: mail, phone, in person. Special note: Includes cities of Bell, Bell Gardens, Cudahy, Huntington Park, Maywood and Vernon. www.latrialcourts.org

Inglewood Municipal Court, 1 Regent St Rm 205, Inglewood, CA 90301. 313-842-7819, Fax: 310-674-4862. 8AM-4:30PM. Access by: mail, in person. Special note: Includes cities of Inglewood, Hawthorne, El Segundo, Lennox and adjoining unincorporated area. www.latrialcourts.org

Long Beach Municipal Court, 415 W Ocean Blvd, Long Beach, CA 90801. 562-491-6201, Fax: 562-437-0147. 8:30AM-4:30PM. Access by: mail, fax, in person. Special note: Includes cities of Long Beach and Signal Hill and adjoining unincorporated area. Address requests to civil or criminal division. www.latrialcourts.org

Los Cerritos Municipal Court, 10025 E Flower St, Bellflower, CA 90706. 562-804-8025. 8AM-4:30PM. Access by: mail, in person. Special note: Includes Artesia, Bellflower, Hawaiian Gardens, Lakewood and Cerritos. Specify civil or criminal search request. www.lamuni.org

Malibu Municipal Court, 23525 W Civic Center Way, Malibu, CA 90265. 313-538-8244, Fax: 310-456-7415. 8AM-4:30PM. Access by: mail, in person. Special note: Includes Malibu, Agoura Hills, Calabasas, Westlake Village, Hidden Hills and unincorporated areas known as Topanga and Chatsworth Lake, bounded by Ventura County on the west and north, Pacific Ocean on the south and City of Los Angeles on the east. http://malibu.co.la.ca.us

Newhall Municipal Court, 23747 W Valencia Blvd, Valencia, CA 91355. 661-253-7316, Fax: 661-254-4107. 8:30AM-4:30PM. Access by: mail, in person. Special note: Includes Saugus, Valencia, Santa Clarita and unincorporated area bound by Ventura County line in the west, Kern County line on the north, Agua Dulce on the east, and Glendale and Los Angeles city limits on the south. www.co.la.ca.us/courts/malibu

Pasadena Municipal Court, 200 N Garfield Ave, Pasadena, CA 91101. Fax: 626-577-1310. 8:30AM-4:30PM. Access by: mail, in person. Special note: Includes cities of Pasadena, South Pasadena, San Marino, Sierra Madre and the area of Altadena and East Pasadena. www.co.la.ca.us/courts/pasadena

Pomona Municipal Court, 350 W Mission Blvd, Pomona, CA 91766. 909-620-3201, Fax: 909-622-2305. 8AM-4:30PM; Phone Hours: 8AM-Noon, 2-4PM. Access by: mail, phone, fax, in person. Special note: Includes cities of Pomona, Claremont, La Verne, Walnut, San Dimas and unincorporated area including Diamond Bar. www.co.la.ca.us/courts/pomona

Rio Hondo Municipal Court, 11234 E Valley Blvd, El Monte, CA 91731. Fax: 626-444-9029. 8-5. Access by: mail, phone, in person. Special note: Includes cities of El Monte, South El Monte, La Puente, Rosemead and adjacent unincorporated county area. Phone Hours: 8:15-11:30AM, 1:30-4:30PM. www.latrialcourts.org/riohondo

San Pedro Branch Municipal Court, 505 S Centre St Rm 202, San Pedro, CA 90731. 313-876-7710. 8:30AM-4:30PM (civ, sm claims & criminal); 8AM-4:30PM (traffic). Access by: mail, in person. Special note: Includes San Pedro, Wilmington and a county strip in

Torrance extending up to Western Avenue. Holds records for Catalina Branch. www.lamuni.org

Santa Anita Municipal Court, 300 W Maple Ave, Monrovia, CA 91016. 626-301-4056, Fax: 626-357-7825. 8AM-4:30PM. Access by: mail, in person. Special note: Includes cities of Monrovia, Arcadia, Duarte, Bradbury and unincorporated county territory in surrounding area. www.latrialcourts.org

Santa Monica Municipal Court, 1725 Main St Rm 224, Santa Monica, CA 90401. 8:30AM-4:30PM. Access by: mail, in person. Special note: Includes city of Santa Monica and the unincorporated territory of the Veteran's Administration facilities located at West Los Angeles. www.latrialcourts.org

South Gate Municipal Court, 8640 California Ave, South Gate, CA 90280. Fax: 323-569-4840. 8AM-4PM T-F; 8AM-7PM M traffic. Access by: mail, in person. Special note: Includes city of South Gate, Hollydale and unincorporated area of Walnut Park. www.latrialcourts.org

West Los Angeles Branch-Municipal Court, 1633 Purdue Ave, Los Angeles, CA 90025. 313-386-7900, Fax: 310-312-2902. 8AM-4:30PM. Access by: mail, in person. Special note: Misdemeanors and Felonies for Palms, Mar Vista, Rancho Park, Marina del Rey, Venice, Playa del Rey and Sawtelle. Holds records for Robertson branch. www.lamuni.org

Whittier Municipal Court, 7339 S Painter Ave, Whittier, CA 90602. Noon-8PM M; 8AM-4:30PM T-F. Access by: mail, in person. Special note: Includes cities of Whittier, Santa Fe Springs, Pico Rivera, La Habra Heights plus unincorporated territory in the Whittier area including areas designated as Los Nietos and South Whittier. www.lamuni.org

Misdemeanor, Small Claims—San Fernando Branch-Municipal Court, 900 Third St, San Fernando, CA 91340. 818-898-2401, Fax: 818-837-7910. 8AM-4:30PM. Access by: mail, in person, online. Special note: Includes Granada Hills, Northridge, Chatsworth, Sunland, Tujunga, Pacoima, Mission Hills, Sylmar, Arleta, Lake View Terrace, Sun Valley and City of San Fernando. Civil actions are handled by the Valley Division-Municipal Court. www.lamuni.org

Misdemeanor, Traffic, Eviction, Small Claims—South Bay Municipal Court, 825 Maple Ave, Torrance, CA 90503-5058. 313-343-2590, Fax: 310-222-7277. 8:30AM-4PM. Access by: mail, in person. Special note: Includes cities of Torrance, Gardena, Rolling Hills, Rolling Hills Estates, Manhattan Beach, Lomita, Redondo Beach, Hermosa Beach, Palos Verdes Estates, Rancho Palos Verdes and Lawndale. http://SouthBayMuniCrt.co.la.ca.us

Madera

Real Estate Recording—Madera County Recorder, 209 West Yosemite, Madera, CA 93637. 559-675-7713, Fax: 559-675-7870.

Felony, Civil, Probate—Superior Court, 209 W Yosemite Ave, Madera, CA 93637. 559-675-7995, Fax: 559-675-0701. 8AM-5PM. Access by: mail, in person. Special note: The Superior and Municipal courts in located in the city of Madera have combined into a consolidated court. There is no countywide database of records, each court must be searched.

Civil Actions Under $25,000, Eviction, Small Claims—Borden Division-Superior Court, 14241 Road 28, Madera, CA 93638. 559-675-7996, Fax: 559-673-0542. 8AM-5PM. Access by: mail, fax, in person.

Misdemeanor, Civil Actions Under $25,000, Eviction, Small Claims—Sierra Division-Superior Court, 40601 Road 274, Bass Lake, CA 93604. 559-642-3235, Fax: 559-642-3445. 8AM-5PM. Access by: mail, in person.

Traffic—Chowchilla Division-Superior Court, 141 S 2nd St, Chowchilla, CA 93610. 559-665-4861, Fax: 559-665-3185. 8AM-5PM. Access by: mail, fax, in person.

Marin

Real Estate Recording—Marin County Recorder, 3501 Civic Center Dr. Room 234, San Rafael, CA 94903. 415-499-6145, Fax: 415-499-7893. 9AM-4PM Research & Copies; 9AM-3PM Recording.

Felony, Misdemeanor, Civil, Eviction, Small Claims, Probate—Marin County Superior Court, PO Box 4988, San Rafael,

CA 94913-4988. 415-499-6244. 8:30AM-4PM. Access by: mail, phone, in person. http://marin.org/mc/courts

Mariposa

Real Estate Recording—Mariposa County Recorder, 4982 10th Street, Mariposa, CA 95338. 210-335-2220. 8AM-5PM (Recording Hours 8AM-3:30PM).

Felony, Misdemeanor, Civil, Small Claims, Evictions, Probate—Superior Court, 5088 Bullion St (PO Box 28), Mariposa, CA 95338. 210-334-3686, Fax: 209-742-6860. 8AM-5PM. Access by: mail, phone, fax, in person. Special note: The former municipal court is now knwo as Department 2.

Mendocino

Real Estate Recording—Mendocino County Recorder, 501 Low Gap Rd. Room 1020, Ukiah, CA 95482. 707-463-4388, Fax: 707-463-4257. 8AM-5PM.

Felony, Civil Actions Over $25,000, Probate—Superior Court, State & Perkins Sts (PO Box 996), Ukiah, CA 95482. Fax: 707-468-3459. 8AM-4PM. Access by: mail, in person.

Misdemeanor, Civil Actions Under $25,000, Eviction, Small Claims—Anderson Branch-Superior Court, 14400 Hwy 128 Veteran Bldg, PO Box 336, Boonville, CA 95415. 707-895-3329, Fax: 707-895-2349. 9AM-1PM, 2-5PM M-F, Closed Monday in Summer. Access by: mail, phone, fax, in person.

Arena Branch-Superior Court, 24000 S Hwy 1 (PO Box 153), Point Arena, CA 95468. 707-882-2116. 9AM-Noon, 1-4PM. Access by: mail, in person.

Long Valley Branch-Superior Court, PO Box 157, Leggett, CA 95585. 707-925-6460, Fax: 707-925-6225. 8AM-4PM. Access by: mail, in person.

Round Valley Branch-Superior Court, 76270 Grange St (PO Box 25), Covelo, CA 95428. 707-983-6446, Fax: 707-983-6446. 8:30AM-5PM M-Th. Access by: mail, in person.

Ten Mile Branch-Superior Court, 700 S Franklin St, Fort Bragg, CA 95437. 707-964-3192, Fax: 707-961-2611. 8AM-4PM. Access by: mail, phone, fax, in person.

Willits Branch-Superior Court, 125 E Commercial St Rm 100, Willits, CA 95490. 707-459-7800, Fax: 707-459-7818. 8AM-4PM. Access by: mail, in person.

Merced

Real Estate Recording—Merced County Recorder, 2222 M Street, Merced, CA 95340. 209-468-2133. 8AM-4:30PM.

Felony, Civil Actions Over $25,000, Probate—Merced Superior Court, 2222 "M" St, Merced, CA 95340. 209-468-2355, Fax: 209-725-9223. 8AM-4PM. Access by: mail, in person. Special note: Courier address is 627 West 21st St.

Misdemeanor, Civil Actions Under $25,000, Eviction, Small Claims—4, 5, 7 & 8 Divisions-Superior Court, 670 W 22nd St, Merced, CA 95340. Fax: 209-725-0323. 8AM-4PM M-F (civil); Noon-4PM M-F (civ only). Access by: mail, in person.

Los Banos Branch-Superior Court, 445 "I" St, Los Banos, CA 93635. 209-875-7158, Fax: 209-826-8108. 8AM-4PM. Access by: mail, in person. Special note: This court was combined with the old Dos Palos Municipal Court.

Modoc

Real Estate Recording—Modoc County Recorder, 204 Court Street, Alturas, CA 96101. Fax: 530-233-6666. 8:30AM-Noon, 1-5PM.

Felony, Civil Actions Over $25,000, Probate—Superior Court, 205 S East St, Alturas, CA 96101. 530-233-6515, Fax: 530-233-6500. 8:30AM-5PM. Access by: mail, fax, in person.

Felony, Misdemeanor, Civil, Eviction, Small Claims, Probate—Modoc Municipal Court Division, 205 S East St, Alturas, CA 96101. 530-233-6515, Fax: 530-233-6500. 8:30AM-5PM. Access by: mail, in person.

Mono

Real Estate Recording—Mono County Recorder, Annex 2, Bryant St. Bridgeport, CA 93517. Fax: 760-932-7035. 9AM-5PM.

Felony, Civil, Probate—Superior Court, PO Box 537, Bridgeport, CA 93517. 760-932-5239. 8:30AM-5PM. Access by: mail, in person.

Misdemeanor, Civil Actions Under $25,000, Eviction, Small Claims—Mammoth Lakes Division-Superior Court, PO Box 1037, Mammoth Lakes, CA 93546. 760-932-5203, Fax: 760-932-5305. 9AM-5PM. Access by: mail, in person.

Monterey

Real Estate Recording—Monterey County Recorder, 240 Church Street, Room 305, Salinas, CA 93902. 831-755-5015, Fax: 831-755-5064. 8AM-4PM.

Felony, Civil Actions Over $25,000, Probate—Superior Court-Monterey Branch, 1200 Aguajito Rd, Monterey, CA 93940. 831-647-7730. 8AM-4PM. Access by: mail, in person. Special note: Civil division is on first floor and criminal division is on second floor.

Superior Court-Salinas Branch, 240 Church St Rm 318 PO Box 1819, Salinas, CA 93902. 831-755-5030. 8AM-4PM. Access by: mail, in person.

Misdemeanor, Civil Actions Under $25,000, Eviction, Small Claims—King City Division-Consolidated Trial Court, 250 Franciscan Way PO Box 647, King City, CA 93930. 8AM-5PM; Public Hours: 8AM-4PM. Access by: mail, in person. Special note: Encompasses the cities of King City, Greenfield, Soledad, areas south of King City to the San Luis Obispo County line.

Salinas Division-Consolidated Trial Courts, 240 Church St PO Box 1051, Salinas, CA 93902. 831-755-5050, Fax: 831-755-5483. 8AM-4PM. Access by: mail, fax, in person. Special note: Includes the City of Salinas and North Monterey County including the areas of Castroville, Aromas, Moss Landing, Prunedale, Pajaro Spreckles, Gonzales and north Soledad.

Misdemeanor, Small Claims—Monterey Division-Consolidated Trial Court, 1200 Aguajito Rd PO Box 751, Monterey, CA 93940. Fax: 831-647-7883. 8AM-3PM. Access by: mail, in person. Special note: Encompasses the cities of Monterey, Carmel, Del Rey Oaks, Seaside, Marina, Sand City, Pacific Grove, areas of Big Sur, Carmel Valley and area west of Arroyo Seco.

Napa

Real Estate Recording—Napa County Recorder, 900 Coombs Street, Room 116, Napa, CA 94559. 707-253-4311, Fax: 707-259-8149. 8AM-5PM.

Felony, Misdemeanor, Civil, Eviction, Small Claims—Superior Court, 825 Brown St, PO Box 880, Napa, CA 94559. 707-253-4481, Fax: 707-253-4229. 8AM-5PM. Access by: mail, in person. Special note: The former municipal court was combined with this court.

Nevada

Real Estate Recording—Nevada County Recorder, 950 Maidu Avenue, Nevada City, CA 95959. 530-265-1285, Fax: 530-265-1497. 9AM-4PM.

Civil, Eviction, Small Claims—Superior Court-Civil Division, 201 Church St, Suite 5, Nevada City, CA 95959. 530-265-7230, Fax: 530-265-1606. 8AM-5PM. Access by: mail, phone, fax, in person. Special note: The phone number for Unlimited Civil, Family Law, Probate and Juvenile is 530-265-1293. The phone number for Evictions and Small Claims is 530-265-7230.

Felony, Misdemeanor, Probate—Superior Court, 201 Church St Suite 7, Nevada City, CA 95959. 530-265-1311, Fax: 530-265-1779. 8AM-5PM. Access by: mail, phone, in person.

Misdemeanor, Civil, Eviction, Small Claims—Truckee Branch-Superior Court, 10075 Levon Ave #301, Truckee, CA 96161. Fax: 530-582-7875. 8AM-5PM. Access by: mail, in person.

Orange

Real Estate Recording—Orange County Clerk-Recorder, 12 Civic Center Plaza, Room 101, Santa Ana, CA 92701. 714-834-2682, Fax: 714-834-2675. 8AM-4:30PM.

Civil Actions Over $25,000—Superior Court-Civil, 700 Civic Center Dr W, Santa Ana, CA 92702. 714-834-2208. 9AM-5PM. Access by: mail, in person. Special note: There is no countywide database, all searches must be conducted within each court. www.oc.ca.gov/superior/civil.htm

Felony—Superior Court-Criminal Operations, 700 Civic Center Dr W (PO Box 22024), Santa Ana, CA 92702-2024. 714-834-2266. 8AM-5PM. Access by: mail, in person. www.oc.ca.gov/superior

Civil Actions Under $25,000, Eviction, Small Claims—South Orange County Superior Court-Civil Division, 23141 Moulton Pkwy 2nd Fl, Laguna Hills, CA 92653-1206. 949-472-6964. 8AM-5PM. Access by: mail, in person. www.oc.ca.gov/southcourt

Misdemeanor—South Orange County Superior Court-Criminal Division, 30143 Crown Valley Parkway, Justice Center, Laguna Niguel, CA 92677. 949-249-5113. 8AM-5PM. Access by: mail, in person. www.oc.ca.gov/southcourt

Misdemeanor, Civil Actions Under $25,000, Eviction, Small Claims—Central Orange Superior Court-Limited Jurisdiction, 700 Civic Ctr Dr W (PO Box 1138, 92702), Santa Ana, CA 92701. 714-834-3575, Fax: 714-953-9032. 8AM-4PM. Access by: mail, in person. Special note: Includes cities of Santa Ana, Orange, Tustin and surrounding unincorporated territories including Cowan Heights, El Modena, Tustin Marine Air Base, Lemon Heights, Modjeska, Orange Park Acres, Silverado Canyon and Villa Park. www.oc.ca.gov/superior

Harbor Superior Court, 4601 Jamboree Road #104, Newport Beach, CA 92660-2595. 949-476-4765. 8AM-5PM. Access by: mail, in person. Special note: Includes Balboa Island, Corona Del Mar, Costa Mesa, Newport Beach, Irvine, Santa Ana Heights, John Wayne/Orange Co Airport, Lido Isle and surrounding unincorporated areas. www.oc.ca.gov/superior

North Orange County Superior Court, 1275 N Berkeley Ave, PO Box 5000, Fullerton, CA 92838-0500. 714-773-4555. 7:30AM-4:30PM. Access by: mail, in person. Special note: Includes the cities of Anaheim, Brea, Buena Park, Fullerton, La Habra, La Palma, Placentia, Yorba Linda and surrounding unincorporated area including Anaheim Hills.

West Orange Superior Court, 8141 13th St, Westminster, CA 92683. 714-896-7181, Fax: 714-896-7356. 8AM-4:30PM. Access by: mail, in person. Special note: Includes the cities of Cypress, Fountain Valley, Garden Grove, Huntington Beach, Los Alamitos, Rossmore, Seal Beach, Stanton, Sunset Beach, Surfside, Westminster and adjoining and unincorporated territory. www.oc.ca.gov/superior

Probate—Probate Court, 341 The City Dr, PO Box 14171, Orange, CA 92868. 714-935-6061. 9AM-5PM. Access by: mail, in person.

Placer

Real Estate Recording—Placer County Recorder, 2954 Richardson Dr. Auburn, CA 95603. Fax: 530-886-5687. 8AM-5PM (Recording Hours 9AM-4PM).

Felony, Civil, Eviction, Probate—Superior Court, 101 Maple St, Auburn, CA 95603. 530-889-6550. 8AM-3PM. Access by: mail, in person. www.placer.ca.gov/courts

Misdemeanor—Auburn Branch-Superior Court, 11532 "B" Ave, Auburn, CA 95603. 530-889-7407, Fax: 530-889-7409. 8AM-4PM. Access by: mail, in person. Special note: Includes Auburn, Penryn, Newcastle, Bowman, Colfax, Wilmar, Alta, Dutch Flat, Loomis. Department 3 in Auburn holds hearings on Tuesday and Thursday only. Also includes criminal for Roseville, Rocklin, Lincoln criminal as of 12/8/97. www.placer.ca.gov/courts

Misdemeanor, Civil Actions Under $25,000, Eviction, Small Claims—Colfax Division-Superior Court-Dept 15, 10 Culver St, PO Box 735, Colfax, CA 95713. 916-346-8721. 8AM-4PM. Access by: mail, in person. Special note: Access terminals located at Superior Court in Auburn. www.placer.ca.gov/courts

Foresthill Division-Superior Court-Dept 4, 101 Maple St, Foresthill, CA 95631. 530-367-2302. 8:30AM-Noon,1-4PM Mondays only. Access by: mail, in person. www.placer.ca.gov/courts

Tahoe Division-Superior Court, PO Box 5669, Tahoe City, CA 96145. 530-581-6337, Fax: 530-581-6344. 8AM-4PM. Access by: mail, in person. www.placer.ca.gov/courts

Small Claims—Lincoln Division-Superior Court-Dept 17, 300 Taylor St, Roseville, CA 95678-2628. 916-645-8955, Fax: 916-652-8284. 8AM-Noon, 12:30-4PM F. Access by: mail, phone, in person. Special note: The mailing address is in Roseville, the location is 453 B Street, Lincoln 95648. www.placer.ca.gov/courts

Small Claims, Traffic—Roseville Division-Superior Court, 300 Taylor St, Roseville, CA 95678. 916-783-1600, Fax: 916-783-1690. 8AM-4PM. Access by: mail, in person. www.placer.ca.gov/courts

Plumas

Real Estate Recording—Plumas County Recorder, 520 Main Street, Room 102, Quincy, CA 95971. 530-283-6260, Fax: 530-283-6415. 8AM-5PM.

Civil, Small Claims, Probate—Superior Court-Civil Division, 520 W Main St, Rm 104, Quincy, CA 95971. 530-283-6305, Fax: 530-283-6415. 8AM-5PM. Access by: mail, phone, fax, in person.

Felony, Misdemeanor—Superior Court-Criminal Division, 520 Main St, Rm 117, Quincy, CA 95971. 530-283-6232, Fax: 530-283-6293. 8AM-5PM. Access by: mail, in person.

Civil Actions Under $25,000, Eviction, Small Claims—Chester Branch-Superior Court, 1st & Willow Way (PO Box 722), Chester, CA 96020. 530-258-2646. 8AM-3PM. Access by: mail, phone, in person.

Misdemeanor, Civil Actions Under $25,000, Eviction, Small Claims—Portola Branch-Superior Court, 161 Nevada St (PO Box 1054), Portola, CA 96122. 530-832-4286, Fax: 530-832-4286. 8AM-3PM M,W,F. Access by: mail, phone, fax, in person.

Small Claims—Greenville Branch-Superior Court, 115 Hwy 89 (PO Box 706), Greenville, CA 95947. 530-284-7213. 8AM-5PM. Access by: mail, phone, in person.

Riverside

Real Estate Recording—Riverside County Recorder, 2724 Gateway Dr. Riverside, CA 92507. 909-275-3900, Fax: 909-486-7007. 8AM-4:30PM (Recording Hours 8AM-2PM).

Civil Actions Over $25,000, Probate—Superior Court-Civil Division, 4050 Main St, Riverside, CA 92501. 909-955-1960, Fax: 909-955-1751. 8AM-5PM. Access by: mail, phone, fax, in person. Special note: A county-wide computer network contains indexes for all Riveside courts. www.co.riverside.ca.us/depts/courts

Felony, Misdemeanor—Superior Court-Criminal Division, 4100 Main St, Riverside, CA 92501. 909-955-2300, Fax: 909-955-4007. 7:30AM-5PM. Access by: mail, phone, fax, in person, online. Special note: A county-wide computer network contains indexed cases for all courts in the county. www.co.riverside.ca.us/depts/courts

Civil Actions Under $25,000, Eviction, Small Claims—Three Lakes District-Lake Elsinore Division-Superior Court, 117 S Langstaff, Lake Elsinore, CA 92530. 909-245-3370, Fax: 909-245-3366. 7:30AM-5PM. Access by: mail, phone, fax, in person, online. www.co.riverside.ca.us/depts/courts

Three Lakes District-Temecula Branch-Superior Court, 41002 County Center Dr, Temecula, CA 92591. 909-694-5160, Fax: 909-694-5084. 7:30AM-5PM. Access by: mail, phone, fax, in person, online. www.co.riverside.ca.us/depts/courts

Felony, Misdemeanor, Civil Actions Under $25,000, Eviction, Small Claims—Three Lakes District-Perris Branch-Superior Court, 277 N "D" St. Perris, CA 92370. 909-940-6820, Fax: 909-940-6810. 7:30AM-5PM. Access by: mail, in person, online. Special note: Holds all records for Three Lakes District. Records are for past 10 years. www.co.riverside.ca.us/depts/courts

Misdemeanor, Civil Actions Under $25,000, Eviction, Small Claims—Banning Division-Superior Court, 155 E Hayes St, Banning, CA 92220. Fax: 909-922-7160. 8AM-4PM. Access by: mail, phone, fax, in person, online. Special note: Includes Banning, Cabazon, Highland Springs, Poppet Flatt, Silent Valley, Beaumont, Calimesa, Cherry Valley and Whitewater. www.co.riverside.ca.us/depts/courts

Blythe Division-Superior Court, 265 N Broadway, Blythe, CA 92225. 760-921-7828, Fax: 760-921-7941. 7:30AM-5PM. Access by: mail, phone, fax, in person, online. Special note: Includes Blythe, Ripley. Phone for Family Law is 760-921-7982. www.co.riverside.ca.us/depts/courts

Corona Branch-Superior Court, 505 S Buena Vista Rm 201, Corona, CA 91720. 909-270-5020, Fax: 909-272-5651. 7:30AM-5PM. Access by: mail, fax, in person, online. Special note: Includes

Corona, El Cerrito, Home Gardens, Norco, Santa Ana Canyon. www.co.riverside.ca.us/depts/courts

Hemet Division-Superior Court, 880 N State St, Hemet, CA 92543. 909-766-2321, Fax: 909-766-2317. 7:30AM-4:30PM; Criminal, Civil/SC 8AM-Noon;. Access by: mail, fax, in person, online. Special note: Includes Aguanga, Anza, Gilman Hot Springs, Hemet, Idylwild, Mountain Center, Pine Cove, Redec, Sage, San Jacinto, Sobba Hot Spring, Valle Vista and Winchester. www.co.riverside.ca.us/depts/courts

Indio Division-Superior Court, 46200 Oasis St, Indio, CA 92201. Fax: 760-863-8707. 7:30AM-5PM. Access by: mail, phone, fax, in person, online. Special note: Includes Desert Center, Eagle Mountain, Indio, La Quinta, Coachella, Bermuda Dunes, Mecca, North Shore, Pinyon Pines, Palm Springs, Salton Sea, Oasis, Thermal. Most Palm Springs records are here. www.co.riverside.ca.us/depts/courts

Misdemeanor, Traffic—Palm Springs Division-Superior Court, 3255 Tahkuits Canyon Way, Palm Springs, CA 92262. 760-320-9764, Fax: 760-778-2269. 7:30AM-5PM. Access by: mail, fax, in person, online. Special note: Includes Cathedral City, Palm Springs, Rancho Mirage, Thousand Palms, Indian Wells, Palm Desert, Desert Hot Springs. See also Indio Court. Call to determine which court to search. www.co.riverside.ca.us/depts/courts

Small Claims, Traffic—Moreno Valley Branch-Superior Court, 13800 Heacock Ave Ste D201, Moreno Valley, CA 92553-3338. 909-955-1960, Fax: 909-341-8876. 7:30AM-5PM. Access by: mail, phone, fax, in person, online. www.co.riverside.ca.us/depts/courts

Sacramento

Real Estate Recording—Sacramento County Clerk and Recorder, 600 8th Street, Sacramento, CA 95814. 8AM-3PM.

Felony, Misdemeanor, Civil, Evictions, Small Claims, Probate—Sacramento Superior Court, 720 9th St Rm 102, Sacramento, CA 95814. 916-874-5522, Fax: 916-874-5620. 8:30AM-4:30PM. Access by: mail, phone, fax, in person. Special note: Probate is located at 3342 Power Inn Rd, Sacramento 95826. www.sac.com/courts

Misdemeanor, Civil Actions Under $25,000, Eviction, Small Claims—South Sacramento Superior Court-Elk Grove Branch, 8978 Elk Grove Blvd, Elk Grove, CA 95624-1994. 916-685-9825, Fax: 916-685-4689. 8:30AM-4:30PM. Access by: mail, in person. Special note: Includes southern portion of county with two other branches. This court holds all case records for South Sacramento branches. www.www.saccourt.com

Misdemeanor, Evictions, Small Claims—Walnut Grove Branch-Superior Court, 14177 Market St, PO Box 371, Walnut Grove, CA 95690. 916-776-1416, Fax: 916-776-1624. 8AM-Noon, 1-4:30PM. Access by: mail, fax, in person. www.sna.com/courts

Misdemeanor, Small Claims—Galt Division-Superior Court, 380 Civic Dr, Galt, CA 95632. 209-826-6500, Fax: 209-745-6176. 8:30AM-4:30PM. Access by: mail. www.sna.com/courts

San Benito

Real Estate Recording—San Benito County Recorder, 440 Fifth Street, Room 206, Hollister, CA 95023. Fax: 831-636-2939. 9:30AM-4PM Recording hours; 8AM-5PM Office hours.

Felony, Misdemeanor, Civil, Small Claims, Evictions, Probate—Superior Court, Courthouse, 440 5th St-Rm 205, Hollister, CA 95023. 831-636-4057, Fax: 831-636-2046. 8AM-5PM. Access by: mail, in person.

San Bernardino

Real Estate Recording—San Bernardino County Recorder, 222 W. Hospitality Ln. 1st Floor, San Bernardino, CA 92415. Fax: 909-386-8940. 8AM-5PM.

Felony, Misdemeanor, Civil to $25,000, Eviction, Small Claims—Twin Peaks Branch-Superior Court, 26010 State Hwy 189, PO Box 394, Twin Peaks, CA 92391. 909-336-0620, Fax: 909-337-2101. 8AM-4PM. Access by: mail, in person. www.co-sanbernardino.ca/courts

Felony, Misdemeanor, Civil, Eviction, Small Claims—Barstow Division-Superior Court, 235 E Mountain View,

Barstow, CA 92311. 8AM-4PM. Access by: mail, in person. Special note: Includes the City of Barstow and the unincorporated areas of Yermo, Lenwood, Daggett, Hinkley and Baker.

Joshua Tree Division-Superior Court, 6527 White Feather Rd PO Box 6602, Joshua Tree, CA 92252. 760-366-4100, Fax: 760-366-4156. 8AM-4PM. Access by: mail, in person. Special note: Includes the incorporated area of Twenty-Nine Palms, Yucca Valley and Morongo Valley.

Victorville Division-Superior Court, 14455 Civic Dr, Victorville, CA 92392. Fax: 760-243-8790. 8AM-4PM. Access by: mail, in person. Special note: Includes the Cities of Victorville, Adelanto Hesperia and the unincorporated area of Apple Valley, El Mirage, Helendale, Lucerne Valley, Oro Grande, Phelan, Pinon Hill and Wrightwood.

Felony, Misdemeanor, Civil, Eviction, Small Claims, Probate—Central District-Superior Court, 351 N Arrowhead Ave, San Bernardino, CA 92415. Fax: 909-387-4428. 8AM-4PM. Access by: mail, in person. www.co.san-bernardino.ca.us/ACR

West District-Superior Court, 8303 Haven Ave, Rancho Cucamonga, CA 91730. Fax: 909-945-4154. 8AM-4PM. Access by: mail, phone, fax, in person. Special note: Includes the cities of Montclair, Ontario, Upland, Rancho Cucamonga and surrounding unincorporated area of Mt Baldy.

Misdemeanor, Civil Actions Under $25,000, Eviction, Small Claims—Big Bear Lake Branch-Superior Court, PO Box 2806, Big Bear Lake, CA 92315. 909-866-0150, Fax: 909-866-0160. 8AM-4PM. Access by: mail, in person.

Central Division Branch-Superior Court, 351 N Arrowhead, San Bernardino, CA 92415. 909-885-0139, Fax: 909-387-4428. 8AM-4PM. Access by: mail, in person. Special note: Includes the City of Bernardino, cities of Grand Terrace, Loma Linda, Colton and Highland and the unincorporated area of Del Rosa, Devore, Miscoy, Patton, Verdemont. www.co.san-bernardino.ca.us/courts

Fontana Division-Superior Court, 17780 Arrow Blvd, Fontana, CA 92335. 909-356-3487, Fax: 909-829-4149. 8AM-4PM. Access by: mail, phone, fax, in person. Special note: Includes the Cities of Fontana, Rialto, Crestmore and the unincorporated areas of Lytle Creek Canyon and Bloomington.

Needles Division-Superior Court, 1111 Bailey Ave, Needles, CA 92363. 760-326-9245, Fax: 760-326-9254. 8AM-4PM. Access by: mail, in person.

Redlands District-Superior Court, 216 Brookside Ave, Redlands, CA 92373. Fax: 909-798-8588. 8AM-4PM. Access by: mail, in person. Special note: Includes Cities of Redlands, Yucaipa and the unincorporated areas of Angeles Oaks, Barton Flats, Forest Home and Mentone.

Misdemeanor, Eviction, Small Claims—Chino Division-Superior Court, 13260 Central Ave, Chino, CA 91710. 909-465-5266, Fax: 909-465-5221. 8AM-4PM. Access by: mail, fax, in person. Special note: Includes City of Chino and surrounding unincorporated area. Rancho Cucamonga Courts handles all civil cases since 01/01/99.

San Diego

Real Estate Recording—San Diego Recorder/County Clerk, 1600 Pacific Highway, Room 260, San Diego, CA 92101. 619-236-3121, Fax: 619-557-4155. 8AM-5PM.

Felony, Civil Actions Over $25,000, Probate—Superior Court, PO Box 2724, San Diego, CA 92112-4104. 619-531-3151. 8:30AM-4:30PM. Access by: mail, in person. www.sandiego.courts.ca.gov

Superior Court, Hall of Justice, PO Box 128, San Diego, CA 92112-4104. 8:30AM-4:30PM. Access by: mail, in person. Special note: Specify which division when sending in written record request. www.sandiego.courts.ca.gov/superior

Felony, Misdemeanor, Civil, Small Claims, Eviction, Probate—El Cajon Branch-Superior Court, 250 E Main St, El Cajon, CA 92020. 619-441-4622. 8AM-4:30PM. Access by: mail, in person. Special note: This court now houses the former municipal court records. www.sandiego.courts.ca.gov

Felony, Civil Actions Over $25,000, Probate—North County Branch-Superior Court, 325 S Melrose Dr, Suite 100, Vista, CA 92083-6627. 760-940-4442. 8:30AM-4:30PM. Access by: mail, in person. www.sandiego.courts.ca.gov

South Bay Branch-Superior Court, 500-C 3rd Ave, Chula Vista, CA 91910. Fax: 619-691-4969. 8:30AM-4:30PM M-F (civil) 7:30AM-4:30PM M-F (criminal). Access by: mail, phone, fax, in person. www.sandiego.courts.ca.gov

Misdemeanor, Civil Actions Under $25,000, Eviction, Small Claims—North County Division-Superior Court, 325 S Melrose Dr Ste 120, Vista, CA 92083. 760-940-4644, Fax: 760-940-4976. 8AM-4:30PM. Access by: mail, in person. Special note: Includes Cities of Oceanside, Del Mar, Carlsbad, Solana Beach, Encinitas, Escondido, San Marcos, Vista and unincorporated towns of Del Dios, Olivehain, San Luis Rey, San Pasqual, Rancho Santa Fe, Valley Center, Bonsall, Palomar Mountain, etc. www.sandiego.courts.ca.gov

Ramona (East) Branch-Superior Court, 1428 Montecito Rd, Ramona, CA 92065. 760-738-2435. 8AM-4:30PM. Access by: mail, in person. www.sandiego.courts.ca.gov

San Diego Central Limited-Superior Court, 1409 4th Ave (Civil), 220 W Broadway Rm 2005 (Criminal), San Diego, CA 92101. 8:30AM-4:30PM. Access by: mail, in person. Special note: Co-extensive with the boundaries of the City of San Diego including the precincts of Mission, Miramar and Poway and excluding that portion of the City of San Diego that lies within the boundaries of the South Bay Judicial District. www.sandiego.courts.ca.gov

South Bay Branch-Limited Superior Court, 500C 3rd Ave, Chula Vista, CA 91910. Fax: 619-691-4438. 8AM-4:30PM. Access by: mail, in person. Special note: Includes National City, Chula Vista, Coronado, Imperial Beach and that portion of the City of San Diego lying south of the City of Chula Vista and contiguous unincorporated areas. www.sandiego.courts.ca.gov

Vista Branch-Superior Court, 325 S Melrose Dr #1000, Vista, CA 92083-6627. 8AM-4:30PM. Access by: mail, in person.

Misdemeanor, Traffic—San Marcos Branch-Superior Court, 338 Via Vera Cruz, San Marcos, CA 92069-2693. 760-940-2888, Fax: 760-940-2802. 8:30AM-4PM. Access by: mail, in person. www.sandiego.courts.ca.gov

San Francisco

Real Estate Recording—San Francisco County Assessor-Recorder, City Hall, Room 190, 1 Dr. Carlton E. Goodlet Pl. San Francisco, CA 94102. Fax: 415-554-4179. 8AM-4PM.

Felony—Superior Court-Criminal Division, 850 Bryant St #306, San Francisco, CA 94107/94103. 415-553-1159. 8AM-4:30PM. Access by: mail, fax, in person. www.ci.sf.ca.us/courts

Civil Actions Over $25,000, Probate—Superior Court-Civil Division, 400 McAllister St, Rm 103, San Francisco, CA 94102. 415-551-3802. 8AM-4PM. Access by: mail, in person. www.ci.sf.ca.us/courts

Misdemeanor—Superior Court-Misdemeanor Division, 850 Bryant St Rm 201, San Francisco, CA 94103. 415-553-1665. 8AM-4:30PM. Access by: mail, in person. Special note: Includes all of San Francisco County. www.ci.sf.ca.us/courts

Civil Actions Under $25,000, Eviction, Small Claims—Limited Superior-Civil Division, 400 McAllister St, Rm 103, San Francisco, CA 94107. 415-551-4032, Fax: 415-551-4041. 8AM-4:30PM. Access by: mail, in person. Special note: Includes all of San Francisco County, including former municipal court on Folsom St. www.ci.sf.ca.us/courts

San Joaquin

Real Estate Recording—San Joaquin County Recorder, 24 South Hunter Street, Room 304, Stockton, CA 95202. 209-468-2355, Fax: 209-468-8040. 8AM-5PM.

Civil Actions, Eviction, Small Claims—Superior Court-Civil, 222 E Weber Ave, Rm 303, Stockton, CA 95202-2709. 209-488-3352, Fax: 209-468-0539. 7:30AM-5 M-F (office); 8AM-5PM M-F (phones). Access by: mail, fax, in person. Special note: Includes City of Stockton and suburban area, Farmington and Linden, Delta area and surrounding unincorporated areas. www.stocktonet.com/courts

Felony, Misdemeanor, Probate—Superior Court-Criminal Division, 222 E Weber St Rm 303, Stockton, CA 95202. 209-533-5555. 7:30AM-4:30PM. Access by: mail, in person. www.stocktonet.com/courts

Misdemeanor, Civil Actions Under $25,000, Eviction, Small Claims—Lodi Division-Superior Court, 315 W Elm St (Civil), 230 W Elm St (Criminal), Lodi, CA 95240. 209-385-7531, Fax: 209-368-3157. 8AM-4PM. Access by: mail, in person. Special note: Includes eight mile road to Sacramento County line, towns of Acampo, Clements, Lockeford, Terminous, Thornton, Woodbridge.

Manteca Branch-Superior Court, 315 E Center St, Manteca, CA 95336. 209-333-6753. 8AM-4PM. Access by: mail, phone, in person. Special note: Includes Cities of Manteca, Ripon, Escalon, French Camp, Lathrop and surrounding unincorporated areas.

Tracy Branch-Superior Court, 475 E 10th St, Tracy, CA 95376. Fax: 209-831-5919. 8AM-4PM. Access by: mail, in person. Special note: Includes Cities of Tracy, Banta, portion of Vernalis and surrounding unincorporated area.

San Luis Obispo

Real Estate Recording—San Luis Obispo County Recorder, 1144 Monterey St. Suite C, San Luis Obispo, CA 93408. 8AM-5PM.

Felony, Civil, Eviction, Probate—Superior Court, Government Center, Rm 385, San Luis Obispo, CA 93408. 805-781-5241. 8AM-5PM. Access by: mail, in person. www.callamer.com/~slosc/court1.htm

Misdemeanor, Civil Actions Under $25,000, Eviction, Small Claims—Grover Beach Branch-Superior Court, 214 S 16th St, Grover Beach, CA 93433-2299. 9AM-4PM. Access by: mail, in person. Special note: Includes Nipomo, Grover Beach, Arroyo Grande, Pismo Beach, Ociano, South Coast unincorporated areas.

Paso Robles Branch-Superior Court, 549 10th St, Paso Robles, CA 93446-2593. 805-237-3080. 8:30AM-4PM. Access by: mail, phone, in person. Special note: Includes Atascadero, Templeton, Paso Robles, San Miguel, Shandon, Cholame, areas north and east of the Cuesta Grade.

Misdemeanor, Civil Actions Under $25,000, smal Claims, Evictions—Limited Jursidiction-Superior Court, 1035 Palm St Rm 385, County Government Center, San Luis Obispo, CA 93408-2510. 805-781-5677. 9AM-4PM. Access by: mail, phone, in person. Special note: The San Luis Obispo County Superior Court has jurisdiction over all of San Luis Obispo County, San Luis Obispo, Morro Bay, Avila Beach areas.

San Mateo

Real Estate Recording—San Mateo County Recorder, 400 County Center, 6th Floor, Redwood City, CA 94063. Fax: 650-363-4843. 8AM-5PM.

Felony, Civil Actions Over $25,000, Probate—Superior Court, 400 County Center, Redwood City, CA 94063. 650-363-4711, Fax: 650-363-4914. 8AM-4PM. Access by: mail, in person. www.co.sanmateo.ca.us/sanmateocourts/index.html

Misdemeanor, Civil Actions Under $25,000, Eviction, Small Claims—Limited Jurisdiction Superior Court, 400 County Center, Redwood City, CA 94063. 650-363-4302. 8AM-4PM. Access by: mail, in person. Special note: Includes Atherton, Menlo Park, Portola Valley, Redwood City, San Carlos, Woodside, East Palo Alto and all unincorporated areas including La Honda and the southern coastal area south of Tunitas Creek Road which includes Pescadara and San Gregorio. www.co.sanmateo.ca.us/sanmateocourts/dome.htm

Misdemeanor, Small Claims, Traffic—Northern Branch-Superior Court, 1050 Mission Rd, South San Francisco, CA 94080. 650-877-5773. 8AM-4PM. Access by: mail, in person. Special note: Includes Brisbane, Daly City (including Westlake), Pacifica, San Bruno, South San Francisco, the northern coastal towns and all unincorporated areas in the north end of the county including Colma and Broadmoor. www.co.sanmateo.ca.us/sanmateocourts/index.html

Santa Barbara

Real Estate Recording—Santa Barbara County Recorder, 1100 Anacapa Street, Santa Barbara, CA 93101. 805-568-2490, Fax: 805-568-2266. 8AM-4:30PM.

Felony, Civil Actions Over $25,000, Probate—Superior Court, Box 21107, Santa Barbara, CA 93121. 805-568-2237, Fax: 805-568-2219. 8AM-4:45PM. Access by: mail, phone, fax, in person.

Misdemeanor, Civil Actions Under $25,000, Eviction, Small Claims—Figueroa Division-Superior Court, 118 E Figueroa St, Santa Barbara, CA 93101. 805-568-2735, Fax: 805-568-2847. 7:45AM-4PM. Access by: mail, in person. Special note: Includes the City of Santa Barbara, Goleta and adjacent unincorporated areas, Carpenteria, Montecito. For civil cases prior to 09/01/98, call 805-568-2750.

Lompoc Division-Superior Court, 115 Civic Center Plz, Lompoc, CA 93436. 805-737-7790, Fax: 805-737-7786. 8:30AM-4:55PM. Access by: mail, phone, in person. Special note: Includes Lompoc and adjacent unincorporated areas, including sections of Vandenburg Air Force Base. The Santa Maria and Solvang courts (civil) were consolidated into this court in late 1995.

Santa Maria Division-Superior Court, 312-M East Cook St, Santa Maria, CA 93454-5165. 805-346-7590, Fax: 805-346-7591. 7:30AM-4:30PM. Access by: mail, in person. Special note: Includes Betteravia, Casmalia, Cuyama, Guadalupe, Gary, Los Alamos, New Cuyama, Orcutt, Santa Maria, Sisquoc, Tepusquet and sections of the Vandenburg Air Force Base.

Misdemeanor, Small Claims, Traffic—Solvang Division-Superior Court, 1745 Mission Dr (PO Box 228), Solvang, CA 93464. 805-686-5040, Fax: 805-686-5079. 8AM-4PM. Access by: mail, phone, in person. www.co.santa-barbara.ca.us

Santa Clara

Real Estate Recording—Santa Clara County Recorder, County Government Center, East Wing, 70 West Hedding St. San Jose, CA 95110. Fax: 408-280-1768. 8AM-4:30PM.

Felony, Civil Actions Over $25,000, Probate—Superior Court, 190 W Hedding St, San Jose, CA 95110. 409-348-9203. 8:30AM-4PM. Access by: mail, in person. http://claraweb.co.santa-clara.ca.us/sct

Felony, Misdemeanor—San Jose Facility-Superior Court, 200 W Hedding St, San Jose, CA 95110. 409-348-5141. 8:30AM-4PM. Access by: mail, in person. Special note: Handles cases for San Jose, Milpitas, Santa Clara, Los Gatos and Campbell areas. http://sccsuperiorcourt.org

Felony, Misdemeanor, Civil Actions Under $25,000, Eviction, Small Claims—South County Facility-Superior Court, 12425 Monterey Hwy, San Martin, CA 95046-9590. 8:30AM-4PM. Access by: mail, in person. Special note: Includes the Cities of Gilroy, Morgan Hill, San Martin and surrounding unincorporated areas. Misdemeanor records are centrally housed at the San Jose Facility. http://sccsuperiorcourt.org

Civil Actions Under $25,000, Eviction, Small Claims—Santa Clara Facility-Superior Court, 1095 Homestead Rd, Santa Clara, CA 95050. 409-348-2638. 8:30AM-4PM. Access by: mail, in person. Special note: Part of combined court. Includes the Cities of San Jose, Alviso, Los Gatos, Campbell, Saratoga, Milpitas, Monte Sereno, Santa Clara and surrounding unincorporated areas.

Felony, Misdemeanor—Sunnyvale Facility-Superior Court, 605 W El Camino Real, Sunnyvale, CA 94087. 409-361-4233. 8:30AM-4PM. Access by: mail, in person. Special note: Includes the cities of Sunnyvale and Cupertino. All traffic and small claims are filed at the San Jose Facility.

Felony, Misdemeanor, Small Claims—Palo Alto Facility-Superior Court, 270 Grant Ave, Palo Alto, CA 94306. 650-324-0373. 8:30AM-4PM. Access by: mail, in person. Special note: Includes Palo Alto, Mountain View, Los Altos, Los Altos Hills, Stanford University and the surrounding unincorporated areas. www.sccsuperiorcourt.org

Small Claims—Los Gatos Facility-Superior Court, 14205 Capri Dr, Los Gatos, CA 95032. 409-379-3951. 8:30AM-4PM. Access by: mail, phone, in person. Special note: Includes the towns of Los Gatos and Monte Sereno and the cities of Campbell, Saratoga, and surrounding unincorporated areas as well as San Jose, Milpitas and Santa Clara. http://sccsuperiorcourt.org

Santa Cruz

Real Estate Recording—Santa Cruz County Recorder, 701 Ocean Street, Room 230, Santa Cruz, CA 95060. Fax: 831-454-2445. 8AM-4PM.

Civil, Probate—Superior Court-Civil, 701 Ocean St Rm 110, Santa Cruz, CA 95060. 831-454-2020, Fax: 831-454-2215. 8AM-4PM.

Access by: mail, in person. www.co.santa-cruz.ca.us/crt/courts.htm

Felony, Misdemeanor—Superior Court-Criminal, 701 Ocean St Rm 120, Santa Cruz, CA 95060. 409-361-4128, Fax: 408-454-2215. 8AM-4PM. Access by: mail, phone, in person. www.co.santa-cruz.ca.us/crt/courts.htm

Misdemeanor, Civil Actions Under $25,000, Eviction, Small Claims—Watsonville Division-Superior Court, 1430 Freedom Blvd, Watsonville, CA 95076. 8AM-4PM. Access by: mail, in person. Special note: Includes all of Santa Cruz County. www.co.santa-cruz.ca.us/crt/courts.htm

Shasta

Real Estate Recording—Shasta County Recorder, 1500 Court St. Room 102, Redding, CA 96001. Fax: 530-225-5673. 8AM-5PM.

Felony, Misdemeanor, Civil, Probate—Shasta County Superior Court, 1500 Court St, Redding, CA 96001. 530-246-6789, Fax: 530-225-5564. 8:30AM-Noon,1-4PM. Access by: mail, in person. Special note: Address Room 319 for civil division and Room 219 for criminal division.

Misdemeanor, Civil Actions Under $25,000, Eviction, Small Claims—Anderson Branch-Superior Court, 1925 W Howard St, Anderson, CA 96007. 530-365-2563, Fax: 530-225-5372. 8:30AM-Noon, 1-4PM. Access by: mail, in person.

Misdemeanor, Eviction, Small Claims—Burney Branch-Superior Court, 20509 Shasta St, Burney, CA 96013. 530-335-3571, Fax: 530-225-5684. 8:30AM-Noon, 1-4PM. Access by: mail, in person. Special note: Civil actions handled by Redding Branch since 1992. Prior civil records are maintained here.

Sierra

Real Estate Recording—Sierra County Recorder, 100 Courthouse Square, Downieville, CA 95936. Fax: 530-289-3300. 9AM-Noon,1-4PM.

Felony, Misdemeanor, Civil, Eviction, Small Claims, Probate—Superior Court, PO Box 476 Courthouse Square, Downieville, CA 95936. 530-289-3698, Fax: 530-289-3318. 8AM-Noon, 1-5PM. Access by: mail, phone, fax, in person.

Siskiyou

Real Estate Recording—Siskiyou County Recorder, 311 Fourth Street, Yreka, CA 96097. Fax: 530-842-8077. 8AM-4PM.

Felony, Misdemeanor, Civil, Probate—Superior Court, 311 4th St PO Box 1026, Yreka, CA 96097. 8AM-5PM. Access by: mail, phone, in person.

Civil Actions Under $25,000, Eviction, Small Claims—Dorris Branch-Superior Court, PO Box 828, Dorris, CA 96023. 530-397-3161, Fax: 530-397-3169. 8AM-Noon, 1-4PM. Access by: mail, phone, in person. Special note: All new misdemeanor cases are referred to Southeastern branch in Weed, CA. Only maintains a few criminal records for a year.

Misdemeanor, Civil Actions Under $25,000, Eviction, Small Claims—Southeastern Municipal Court, PO Box 530, Weed, CA 96094. 530-938-2483, Fax: 530-842-0109. 8AM-5PM. Access by: mail, in person. Special note: This court holds misdemeanor records for Dorris/Tulelake branch.

Solano

Real Estate Recording—Solano County Assessor/Recorder, Old Courthouse, 701 Texas St, Fairfield, CA 94533. 8AM-4PM; 8AM-3:30PM Recording hours; Copies 8AM-3PM.

Civil, Eviction, Probate—Solano County Courts-Civil, 600 Union Ave, Fairfield, CA 94533. 707-421-6479, Fax: 707-421-7817. 8AM-4PM. Access by: mail, phone, in person. Special note: The Northern Solano Municipal Court has been combined with the Superior Court.

Felony, Misdemeanor—Solano County Courts-Criminal, 530 Union Ave #200, Fairfield, CA 94533. 707-421-7440, Fax: 707-421-7439. 8AM-4PM. Access by: mail, in person. Special note: The Northern Solano Municipal Court has been combined with the Superior Court.

Misdemeanor, Civil Actions Under $25,000, Eviction, Small Claims—Vallejo Branch-Superior Court, 321 Tuolumne St, Vallejo, CA 94590. Fax: 707-553-5661. 8AM-4PM. Access by: mail, in

person. Special note: Includes Cities of Vallejo and Benicia and the unincorporated area adjacent thereto.

Sonoma

Real Estate Recording—Sonoma County Recorder, 585 Fiscal Drive, Room 103F, Santa Rosa, CA 95403. Fax: 707-527-3905. 8AM-4:30PM.

Felony, Misdemeanor, Probate—Superior Court-Criminal, 600 Administration Dr, Room 105J, Santa Rosa, CA 95403-0281. 707-527-1100. 8AM-4PM. Access by: mail, phone, in person.

Civil, Eviction, Small Claims—Superior Court-Civil Division, 600 Administration Dr, Rm 107J, Santa Rosa, CA 95403. 707-527-1100. 8AM-4PM. Access by: mail, in person.

Stanislaus

Real Estate Recording—Stanislaus County Recorder, 1021 "I" St. Modesto, CA 95354. Fax: 209-525-5207. 8AM-Noon,1-4PM.

Felony, Misdemeanor, Probate—Superior Court-Criminal, 1100 I Street, PO Box 1098, Modesto, CA 95353. 209-632-3942. 8AM-Noon, 1-3PM. Access by: mail, in person. www.co.stanislaus.ca.us/courts

Civil, Eviction, Small Claims—Modesto Division-Superior Court, 1100 "I" St PO Box 828, Modesto, CA 95353. 209-638-3114, Fax: 209-525-4012. 8AM-Noon, 1-4PM. Access by: mail, in person. Special note: Ceres Branch has been closed and records transferred here. www.co.stanislaus.ca.us/courts

Misdemeanor, Civil Actions Under $25,000, Eviction, Small Claims—Turlock Division-Superior Court, 300 Starr Ave, Turlock, CA 95380. 209-646-2815, Fax: 209-664-8009. 8AM-Noon, 1-3PM. Access by: mail, phone, fax, in person.

Sutter

Real Estate Recording—Sutter County Recorder, 433 Second Street, Yuba City, CA 95991. Fax: 530-822-7214. 8AM-5PM.

Civil, Eviction, Small Claims, Probate—Superior Court-Civil Division, 463 2nd St, Rm 211, Yuba City, CA 95991. 530-822-7352, Fax: 530-822-7192. 8AM-5PM. Access by: mail, fax, in person.

Felony, Misdemeanor—Superior Court-Criminal Division, 446 2nd St, Yuba City, CA 95991. 530-822-7360, Fax: 530-822-7159. 8AM-5PM. Access by: mail, fax, in person.

Tehama

Real Estate Recording—Tehama County Recorder, 633 Washington St. Room 11, Red Bluff, CA 96080. Fax: 530-527-1140. 8AM-1PM, 2-4PM.

Civil, Small Claims, Eviction, Probate—Superior Court, PO Box 310, Red Bluff, CA 96080. 530-527-6441. 9AM-4PM. Access by: mail, in person.

Felony, Misdemeanor—Superior Court-Criminal Division, 445 Pine St PO Box 1170, Red Bluff, CA 96080. 530-527-3563, Fax: 530-527-4974. 8AM-4PM. Access by: mail, in person.

Misdemeanor, Civil Actions Under $25,000, Eviction, Small Claims—Corning Branch-Superior Court, 720 Hoag St, Corning, CA 96021. 530-824-4601, Fax: 530-824-6457. 8AM-4PM. Access by: mail, in person.

Trinity

Real Estate Recording—Trinity County Recorder, 101 Court Street, Courthouse, Weaverville, CA 96093. 530-623-1251, Fax: 530-623-3762. 8AM-5PM.

Felony, Misdemeanor, Civil, Eviction, Small Claims, Probate—Superior Court, 101 Court St PO Box 1258, Weaverville, CA 96093. 530-623-1208, Fax: 530-623-3762. 9AM-4PM. Access by: mail, in person.

Tulare

Real Estate Recording—Tulare County Recorder, County Civic Center, Room 103, 221 S. Mooney Blvd. Visalia, CA 93291. 8AM-5PM; (Recording hours 8AM-3PM).

Felony, Civil Actions Over $25,000, Probate—Superior Court, Courthouse Rm 201, Visalia, CA 93291. 559-733-6374, Fax: 559-737-4547. 8AM-5PM. Access by: mail, in person.

Misdemeanor, Civil Actions Under $25,000, Eviction, Small Claims—Dinuba Division-Superior Court, 920 S College, Dinuba, CA 93618. 559-591-5815. 8AM-4PM. Access by: mail, in person. Special note: Includes Dinuba, Cutler, Orosi, Seville, Traver, London, Delf, Orange Cove.

Exeter Division-Superior Court, 125 S "B" St, Exeter, CA 93221. 559-592-2177, Fax: 559-592-3374. 8AM-4PM. Access by: mail, phone, in person. Special note: Includes Exeter, Farmersville, Woodlake and Lindsay.

Porterville Division-Superior Court, 87 E Morton Ave, Porterville, CA 93257. 559-782-4710, Fax: 559-782-4805. 8AM-4PM. Access by: mail, in person. Special note: Includes Porterville, Springville, Camp Nelson, Johnsondale, Terra Bella, Ducor, Richgrove, Poplar and surrounding areas.

Tulare/Pixley Division-Superior Court, 425 E Kern St PO Box 1136, Tulare, CA 93275. 559-685-2556, Fax: 559-685-2663. 8AM-4PM. Access by: mail, in person. Special note: Includes Tulare, Pixley, Tipton, Earlimart, Alpaugh, Allensworth, Woodville, Waukena and surrounding areas.

Visalia Limited Superior Court, County Civic Center, Visalia, CA 93291. 8AM-5PM. Access by: mail, in person. Special note: Includes Visalia and Goshen. Address criminal requests to Room 124 and civil requests to Room 201.

Tuolumne

Real Estate Recording—Tuolumne County Recorder, 2 South Green Street, County Administration Center, Sonora, CA 95370. Fax: 209-533-5613. 8AM-4PM M-Th; 8AM-5PM F.

Felony, Civil Actions Over $25,000, Probate—Superior Court, 2 S Green St, Sonora, CA 95370. 209-558-6000, Fax: 209-533-5618. 8AM-4:30PM. Access by: mail, in person.

Misdemeanor, Civil Actions Under $25,000, Eviction, Small Claims—Sonora Branch - Superior Court, 60 N Washington St, Sonora, CA 95370. 209-558-6000, Fax: 209-533-5581. 8AM-3PM. Access by: mail, phone, fax, in person. Special note: Formerly West Municipal Court, which has been closed.

Ventura

Real Estate Recording—Ventura County Recorder, 800 South Victoria Avenue, Ventura, CA 93009. 805-654-3735, Fax: 805-654-2392. 8AM-4PM.

Felony, Misdemeanor, Civil, Eviction, Small Claims, Probate—East County Superior Court, PO Box 1200, Simi Valley, CA 93062-1200. 805-582-8080. 8AM-5PM. Access by: mail, phone, in person, online. www.ventura.org/courts/vencrts.htm

Ventura Superior Court, 800 S Victoria Ave PO Box 6489, Ventura, CA 93006-6489. 805-662-6620, Fax: 805-650-4032. 8AM-5PM. Access by: mail, phone, in person, online. www.ventura.org/courts/vencrts.htm

Yolo

Real Estate Recording—Yolo County Recorder, 625 Court Street, Room 105, Woodland, CA 95695. 530-666-8625, Fax: 530-666-8109. 8AM-4PM.

Felony, Misdemeanor, Civil, Eviction, Small Claims, Probate—Superior Court, 725 Court St, Woodland, CA 95695. 530-666-8598, Fax: 530-666-8576. 8AM-Noon, 1-4PM. Access by: mail, phone, fax, in person. Special note: Address civil requests to Room 103 and criminal to Room 111. www.yolocourts.com

Yuba

Real Estate Recording—Yuba County Recorder, 935 14th Street, Marysville, CA 95901. Fax: 530-741-6285. 10AM-3PM.

Felony, Misdemeanor, Civil Actions Over $25,000, Probate—Yuba County Superior Court, 215 5th St, Marysville, CA 95901. 530-749-7600, Fax: 530-634-7681. 8:30AM-4:30PM. Access by: mail, fax, in person.

Civil Actions Under $25,000, Eviction, Small Claims—Marysville Civil Limited Superior Court, 215 5th St, Marysville, CA 95901. 530-749-7600, Fax: 530-634-7687. 8:30AM-5PM. Access by: mail, fax, in person.

Federal Courts

US District Court

Central District of California

Los Angeles (Western) Division US Courthouse, Attn: Correspondence, 312 N Spring St, Room G-8, Los Angeles, CA 90012213-894-5261 Counties: Los Angeles, San Luis Obispo, Santa Barbara, Ventura. www.cacd.uscourts.gov
Riverside (Eastern) Division US Courthouse, , PO Box 13000, Riverside, CA 92502-3000909-276-6170 Counties: Riverside, San Bernardino. www.cacd.uscourts.gov
Santa Ana (Southern) Division 751 W Santa Ana Blvd, Room 101, Santa Ana, CA 92701-4599714-836-2468 Counties: Orange. www.cacd.uscourts.gov

Eastern District of California

Fresno Division US Courthouse, Room 5000, 1130 "O" St, Fresno, CA 93721-2201559-498-7483, Record Room: 559-498-7372, Civil Docket Phone: 559-498-7235, Criminal Docket Phone: 559-498-7235 Counties: Fresno, Inyo, Kern, Kings, Madera, Mariposa, Merced, Stanislaus, Tulare, Tuolumne. www.caed.uscourts.gov
Sacramento Division 2546 United States Courthouse, 650 Capitol Mall, Sacramento, CA 95814-4797916-498-5470, Record Room: 916-498-5415 Fax: 916-498-5469 Counties: Alpine, Amador, Butte, Calaveras, Colusa, El Dorado, Glenn, Lassen, Modoc, Mono, Nevada, Placer, Plumas, Sacramento, San Joaquin, Shasta, Sierra, Siskiyou, Solano, Sutter, Tehama, Trinity, Yolo, Yuba. www.caed.uscourts.gov

Northern District of California

San Jose Division Room 2112, 280 S 1st St, San Jose, CA 95113408-535-5364 Counties: Alameda, Contra Costa, Del Norte, Humboldt, Lake, Marin, Mendocino, Monterey, Napa, San Benito, San Francisco, San Mateo, Santa Clara, Santa Cruz, Sonoma. www.cand.uscourts.gov

Southern District of California

San Diego Division Room 4290, 880 Front St, San Diego, CA 92101-8900619-557-5600, Record Room: 619-557-7362 Fax: 619-557-6684 Counties: Imperial, San Diego. Court also handles some cases from Yuma County, AZ. www.casd.uscourts.gov

US Bankruptcy Court

Central District of California

Los Angeles Division 255 E Temple St, , Los Angeles, CA 90012213-894-3118, Record Room: 213-894-7205 Fax: 213-894-1261 Counties: Los Angeles. Certain Los Angeles ZIP Codes are assigned to a new location, San Fernando Valley Division, as of early 1995. www.cacb.uscourts.gov
Riverside Division 3420 12th St #125, Riverside, CA 92501-3819909-774-1000 Counties: Riverside, San Bernardino. www.cacb.uscourts.gov
Riverside Division 3420 12th St #125, Riverside, CA 92501-3819909-774-1000 Counties: Riverside, San Bernardino. www.cacb.uscourts.gov
San Fernando Valley Division 21041 Burbank Blvd, Woodland Hills, CA 91367818-587-2900, Record Room: 818-587-2870 Counties: Certain ZIP Codes in Los Angeles, Ventura and Kern counties: 90263-90265, 90290, 91301-91313, 91316, 91319-91322,

91324-91328, 91330-91331, 91333-91335, 91337, 91340-91346, 91350-91362, 91364-91365, 91367, 91376, 91380-91386, 91392-91396,91400-91413, 91416, 91423, 91426-91427, 91436, 91600-91610, 91614-91618, 93062-93063, 93065, 93093, 93243 (Kern), 93510, 93523 (Kern), 93532, 93534-93536, 93539, 93543-93544, 93550-93553, 93563, 93584, 93586, 93590-93591. www.cacb.uscourts.gov

Santa Ana Division Ronald Reagan Federal Bldg & US Courthouse, 411 W 4th St #2030, Santa Ana, CA 92701-4593714-836-2993, Record Room: 714-836-2898 Counties: Orange. www.cacb.uscourts.gov

Santa Barbara (Northern) Division 1415 State St, Santa Barbara, CA 93101805-884-4800 Counties: San Luis Obispo, Santa Barbara, Ventura. Certain Ventura ZIP Codes are assigned to the new office in San Fernando Valley. www.cacb.uscourts.gov

Eastern District of California

Fresno Division Room 2656, 1130 O Street, Fresno, CA 93721559-498-7217 Counties: Fresno, Inyo, Kern, Kings, Madera, Mariposa, Merced, Tulare. Three Kern ZIP Codes, 93243 and 93523-24, are handled by San Fernando Valley in the Central District. www.caeb.uscourts.gov

Modesto Division PO Box 5276, Modesto, CA 95352209-521-5160 Counties: Calaveras, San Joaquin, Stanislaus, Tuolumne. The following ZIP Codes in San Joaquin County are handled by the Sacramento Division: 95220, 95227, 95234, 95237, 95240-95242, 95253, 95258, and 95686.Mariposa and Merced counties were transferred to the Fresno Division as of January 1, 1995. www.caeb.uscourts.gov

Sacramento Division US Courthouse, 501 I St, Rm 3-200, Sacramento, CA 95814916-498-5525 Counties: Alpine, Amador, Butte, Colusa, El Dorado, Glenn, Lassen, Modoc, Mono, Nevada, Placer, Plumas, Sacramento, Shasta, Sierra, Siskiyou, Solano, Sutter, Tehama, Trinity, Yolo, Yuba. This court also handles the following ZIP Codes in San Joaquin County:95220, 95227, 95234, 95237,

95240-95242, 95253, 95258 and 95686. www.caeb.uscourts.gov

Northern District of California

Oakland Division PO Box 2070, Oakland, CA 94604510-879-3600 Counties: Alameda, Contra Costa. www.canb.uscourts.gov

Oakland Division PO Box 2070, Oakland, CA 94604510-879-3600 Counties: Alameda, Contra Costa. www.canb.uscourts.gov

San Francisco Division PO Box 7341, San Francisco, CA 94120-7341415-268-2300 Counties: San Francisco, San Mateo. www.canb.uscourts.gov

San Francisco Division PO Box 7341, San Francisco, CA 94120-7341415-268-2300 Counties: San Francisco, San Mateo. www.canb.uscourts.gov

San Jose Division Room 3035, 280 S 1st St, San Jose, CA 95113-3099408-535-5118 Counties: Monterey, San Benito, Santa Clara, Santa Cruz. www.canb.uscourts.gov

San Jose Division Room 3035, 280 S 1st St, San Jose, CA 95113-3099408-535-5118 Counties: Monterey, San Benito, Santa Clara, Santa Cruz. www.canb.uscourts.gov

Santa Rosa Division 99 South E St, Santa Rosa, CA 95404707-525-8539 Fax: 707-579-0374 Counties: Del Norte, Humboldt, Lake, Marin, Mendocino, Napa, Sonoma. www.canb.uscourts.gov

Santa Rosa Division 99 South E St, Santa Rosa, CA 95404707-525-8539 Fax: 707-579-0374 Counties: Del Norte, Humboldt, Lake, Marin, Mendocino, Napa, Sonoma. www.canb.uscourts.gov

Southern District of California

San Diego Division Office of the clerk, US Courthouse, 325 West "F" St., San Diego, CA 92101619-557-5620 Counties: Imperial, San Diego. www.casb.uscourts.gov

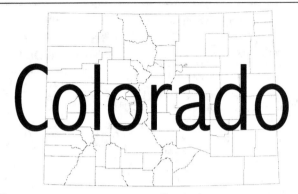

Colorado

Attorney General's Office

1525 Sherman St, 5th Floor   303-866-4500
Denver, CO 80203   Fax: 303-866-5691
www.state.co.us/gov_dir/dol/index.htm

Governor's Office

136 State Capitol Bldg   303-866-2471
Denver, CO 80203-1792   Fax: 303-866-2003
www.state.co.us/gov_dir/governor_office.html

State Archives

1313 Sherman St, Room 1B20   303-866-2055
Denver, CO 80203   Fax: 303-866-2257
www.state.co.us/gov_dir/gss/archives/index.html

Capital:	Denver
	Denver County
Time Zone:	MST
Number of Counties:	63
Population:	3,892,644
Web Site:	www.state.co.us

Search Unclaimed Property Online

There is no Internet-based search for unclaimed property for this state.

State Agencies

Criminal Records

Bureau of Investigation, State Repository, Identification Unit, 690 Kipling St, Suite 3000, Denver, CO 80215; 303-239-4230; Fax: 303-239-0865; 8AM-5PM. Access by: mail, online.

Corporation Records
Trademarks/Servicemarks
Fictitious Name
Limited Liability Company Records
Assumed Name

Secretary of State, Corporation Division, 1560 Broadway, Suite 200, Denver, CO 80202; 303-894-2251 Corporations, 900-555-1717 Status-Name; Fax: 303-894-2242; 8:30AM-5PM. Access by: mail, phone, in person, online. www.state.co.us/gov_dir/sos/index.htm

Sales Tax Registrations

Revenue Department, Taxpayers Services Office, 1375 Sherman St, Denver, CO 80261 (1625 Broadway, Ste 805, Denver, CO 80261); 303-232-2416; Fax: 303-866-3211; 8AM-4:30PM. Access by: mail, phone, in person. www.state.co.us

Uniform Commercial Code
Federal Tax Liens
State Tax Liens

UCC Division, Secretary of State, 1560 Broadway, Suite 200, Denver, CO 80202; 303-894-2200; Fax: 303-894-2242; 8:30AM-5PM. Access by: mail, phone, in person, online. www.state.co.us/gov_dir/sos/index.htm

Workers' Compensation Records

Division of Workers' Compensation, Customer Service, 1515 Arapahoe St, Tower 2, Ste 500, Denver, CO 80202; 303-575-8700; Fax: 303-575-8882; 8AM-5PM. Access by: mail, phone, in person. http://workerscomp.cdle.state.co.us

Birth Certificates

Department of Public Health & Environment, Vital Records Section HSVR-A1, 4300 Cherry Creek Dr S, Denver, CO 80246-1530; 303-756-4464 Recorded Message, 303-692-2224 Credit Card Ordering; Fax: 800-423-1108; 8:30AM-4:30PM. Access by: mail, phone, in person. www.cdphe.state.co.us/hs/certs.html

Death Records

Department of Public Health & Environment, Vital Records Section HSVR-A1, 4300 Cherry Creek Dr S, Denver, CO 80246-1530; 303-756-4464 Recorded Message, 303-692-2224 Credit Card Ordering; Fax: 800-423-1108; 8:30AM-4:30PM. Access by:

mail, phone, in person. www.cdphe.state.co.us/hs/certs.html

Marriage Certificates

Department of Public Health & Environment, Vital Records Section, 4300 Cherry Creek Dr S, Denver, CO 80246-1530; 303-756-4464 Recorded Message, 303-692-2224 Credit Card Ordering; Fax: 800-423-1108; 8:30AM-4:30PM. Access by: mail, phone, in person, online. www.cdphe.state.co.us/hs/certs.html

Divorce Records

Department of Public Health & Environment, Vital Records Section, 4300 Cherry Creek Dr S, Denver, CO 80246-1530; 303-756-4464 Recorded Message, 303-692-2224 Credit Card Ordering; Fax: 800-423-1108; 8:30AM-5PM. Access by: mail, phone, in person, online. www.cdphe.state.co.us/hs/certs.html

Driver Records

Motor Vehicle Division, Driver Services, Denver, CO 80261-0016 (1881 Pierce Street, Lakewood, CO 80261); 303-205-5600; Fax: 303-205-5990; 8AM-5PM. Access by: mail. www.state.co.us/gov_dir/revenue_dir/MV_dir/mv.html

Vehicle Ownership
Vehicle Identification

Department of Motor Vehicles, Driver Support Services, Denver, CO 80261; 303-205-5600; Fax: 303-205-5990; 8AM-5PM. Access by: mail. www.state.co.us/gov_dir/revenue_dir/MV_dir/mv.htm

Accident Reports

Department of Motor Vehicles, Driver Services, Denver, CO 80261-0016; 303-205-5600; 8AM-5PM. Access by: mail.

Boat & Vessel Ownership
Boat & Vessel Registration

Colorado State Parks, Registration, 13787 S Highway 85, Littleton, CO 80125; 303-791-1920; Fax: 303-470-0782; 8AM-5PM. www.dnr.state.co.us/parks

Legislation-Current/Pending
Legislation-Passed

Colorado General Assembly, State Capitol, 200 E Colfax Ave, Denver, CO 80203-1784;, 303-866-3055 Bill Data (during session), 303-866-2358 Archives; 8AM-4:30PM. Access by: mail, phone, in person, online. www.state.co.us/gov_dir/stateleg.html

Voter Registration

Department of State, Elections Department, 1560 Broadway #200, Denver, CO 80202; 303-894-2680; Fax: 303-894-7732; 8:30AM-5PM. www.state.co.us/gov_dir/sos

GED Certificates

Colorado Dept of Education, GED Testing, 201 E Colfax Ave Rm 100, Denver, CO 80203; 303-866-6613;. www.colosys.net/click/ONLINE.html

Hunting License Information
Fishing License Information

Records not available from state agency.

The state attorney general has decided that no information can be given to the public. It is only available to law enforcement officials or to the licensed individual.

County Courts & Recording Offices

About the Courts...

Administration

State Court Administrator
1301 Pennsylvania St, Suite 300
Denver, CO 80203
www.courts.state.co.us

303-861-1111
Fax: 303-837-2340

Court Structure

The District and County Courts have overlapping jurisdiction over civil cases involving less than $10,000. The District and County Courts are combined in most counties. Combined courts usually search both civil or criminal indexes for a single fee, except as indicated in the profiles. Denver is the only county with a separate Probate Court.

Municipal courts only have jurisdiction over traffic, parking, and ordinance violations.

Searching Hints

All state agencies require a self-addressed, stamped envelope (SASE) for return of information.

Co-located with seven district courts are divisions known as Water Courts. The Water Courts are located in Weld, Pueblo, Alamosa, Montrose, Garfield, Routt, and La Platta counties; see the District Court discussion for those counties to determine the jurisdictional area for the Water Court. Water Court records are maintained by the Water Clerk and fees are similar to those for other court records. To retrieve a Water Court record, one must fur-nish the Case Number or the Legal Description (section, township, and range) or the Full Name of the respondent (note that the case number or legal description are preferred).

Online Access

A statewide online computer system is under development in Colorado.

About the Recording Offices...

Organization

63 counties, 63 recording offices. The recording officer is County Clerk and Recorder. The entire state is in the Mountain Time Zone (MST).

UCC Records

Financing statements are filed at the state level, except for consumer goods, farm and real estate related collateral, which are filed with the County Clerk and Recorder. All counties will perform UCC searches. Use search request form UCC-11. Search fees are usually $5.00 per debtor name for the first year and $2.00 for each additional year searched (or $13.00 for a five year search). Copies usually cost $1.25 per page.

Lien Records

Federal and some state tax liens on personal property are filed with the Secretary of State. Other federal and state tax liens are filed with the County Clerk and Recorder. Many counties will perform tax lien searches, usually at the same fees as UCC searches. Copies usually cost $1.25 per page

Real Estate Records

Counties do not perform real estate searches. Copy fees are usually $1.25 per page and certification fees are usually $1.00 per document. Tax records are located in the Assessor's Office.

County Courts & Recording Offices

Adams

Real Estate Recording—Adams County Clerk and Recorder, 450 South 4th Avenue, Administrative Building, Brighton, CO 80601. 304-257-4545, Fax: 303-654-6009. 8AM-4:30PM.

Felony, Civil Actions Over $10,000, Probate—17th District Court, 1100 Judicial Center Drive, Brighton, CO 80601. 304-257-4637, Fax: 303-654-3216. 8AM-5PM. Access by: mail, in person. Special note: The District and County courts have combined, but records are searched separately unless requester asks to search both courts (at no extra fee).

Misdemeanor, Civil Actions Under $10,000, Eviction, Small Claims—County Court, 1100 Judicial Center Drive, Brighton, CO 80601. 304-257-1818. 8AM-5PM. Access by: mail, in person. Special note: The District and County courts have combined, but records are searched separately unless specifically asked to search both courts for no additional fee.

Alamosa

Real Estate Recording—Alamosa County Clerk and Recorder, 402 Edison Street, Alamosa, CO 81101. 719-589-3626, Fax: 719-589-6118. 8AM-4:30PM.

Felony, Civil Actions Over $10,000, Probate—Alamosa Combined Court, 702 4th St, Alamosa, CO 81101. 719-589-4996, Fax: 719-589-4998. 8AM-4:30PM. Access by: mail, in person.

Misdemeanor, Civil Actions Under $10,000, Eviction, Small Claims—Alamosa County Court, 702 4th St, Alamosa, CO 81101. 719-589-4996, Fax: 719-589-4998. 8AM-4:30PM. Access by: mail, in person.

Arapahoe

Real Estate Recording—Arapahoe County Clerk and Recorder, 5334 South Prince Street, Littleton, CO 80120. 304-258-8631, Fax: 303-794-4625. 7AM-4:30PM.

Felony, Civil Actions Over $10,000, Probate—18th District Court, 7325 S Potomac, Englewood, CO 80112. 304-255-9300. 8AM-5PM. Access by: mail, phone, in person.

Misdemeanor, Civil Actions Under $10,000, Eviction, Small Claims—Arapahoe County Court Division B, 15400 E 14th Pl, Aurora, CO 80011. 303-654-6160. 8AM-5PM. Access by: mail, phone, in person.

Littleton County Court Division A, 1790 W Littleton Blvd, Littleton, CO 80120-2060. 304-264-1918. 8AM-5PM. Access by: mail, phone, in person.

Archuleta

Real Estate Recording—Archuleta County Clerk and Recorder, 449 San Juan Street, Pagosa Springs, CO 81147. 970-264-2152, Fax: 970-264-6423. 8AM-4PM.

Felony, Misdemeanor, Civil, Eviction, Small Claims, Probate—6th District & County Courts, PO Box 148, Pagosa Springs, CO 81147. 970-264-2400, Fax: 970-264-2407. 8AM-5PM. Access by: mail, in person.

Baca

Real Estate Recording—Baca County Clerk and Recorder, 741 Main Street, Courthouse, Springfield, CO 81073. 719-523-4262, Fax: 719-523-4881. 8:30AM-4:30PM.

Felony, Misdemeanor, Civil, Eviction, Small Claims, Probate—Baca County District & County Courts, 741 Main St, Springfield, CO 81073. 719-523-4555. 8AM-5PM. Access by: mail, in person.

Bent

Real Estate Recording—Bent County Clerk and Recorder, 725 Carson, Courthouse, Las Animas, CO 81054. 719-456-2211, Fax: 719-456-0375. 8:30AM-4:30PM.

Felony, Misdemeanor, Civil, Eviction, Small Claims, Probate—16th District Court, Bent County Courthouse, 725 Bent, Las Animas, CO 81054. 719-456-1353, Fax: 719-456-0040. 8AM-12, 1-5PM. Access by: mail, in person.

Boulder

Real Estate Recording—Boulder County Clerk and Recorder, 2020 13th Street, Courthouse, Suite 250, Boulder, CO 80302. 8AM-4:30PM.

Felony, Misdemeanor, Civil, Eviction, Small Claims, Probate—20th District & County Courts, 6th & Canyon, PO Box 4249, Boulder, CO 80306. 303-663-7200, Fax: 303-441-4862. 8AM-5PM. Access by: mail, in person.

Chaffee

Real Estate Recording—Chaffee County Clerk and Recorder, 104 Crestone Ave. Salida, CO 81201. 719-539-6808, Fax: 719-539-8588. 8AM-4PM Recording; 8AM-5PM Researching.

Felony, Civil Actions Over $10,000, Probate—11th District Court, PO Box 279, Salida, CO 81201. 719-539-2561, Fax: 719-539-6281. 8AM-5PM. Access by: mail, fax, in person.

Misdemeanor, Civil Actions Under $10,000, Eviction, Small Claims—County Court, PO Box 279, Salida, CO 81201. 719-539-6031, Fax: 719-539-6281. 8AM-5PM. Access by: mail, phone, fax, in person.

Cheyenne

Real Estate Recording—Cheyenne County Clerk and Recorder, 51 South 1st Street, Cheyenne Wells, CO 80810. 719-767-5657, Fax: 719-767-5540. 8AM-4PM.

Felony, Misdemeanor, Civil, Eviction, Small Claims, Probate—15th District & County Courts, PO Box 696, Cheyenne Wells, CO 80810. 719-767-5649. 8AM-4:30PM. Access by: mail, in person.

Clear Creek

Real Estate Recording—Clear Creek County Clerk and Recorder, 405 Argentine, Courthouse, Georgetown, CO 80444. 303-795-4550, Fax: 303-679-2441. 8:30AM-4:30PM.

Felony, Misdemeanor, Civil, Eviction, Small Claims, Probate—5th District & County Courts, PO Box 367, Georgetown, CO 80444. 303-798-4591, Fax: 303-569-3274. 8AM-5PM. Access by: mail, in person.

Conejos

Real Estate Recording—Conejos County Clerk and Recorder, 6683 County Road 13, Conejos, CO 81129. Fax: 719-376-5661. 8AM-4:30PM.

Felony, Misdemeanor, Civil, Eviction, Small Claims, Probate—12th District & County Courts, PO Box 128, Conejos, CO 81129. 719-376-5466, Fax: 719-376-5465. 8AM-4PM. Access by: mail, in person.

Costilla

Real Estate Recording—Costilla County Clerk and Recorder, 354 Main Street, San Luis, CO 81152. Fax: 719-672-3962.

Felony, Misdemeanor, Civil, Eviction, Small Claims, Probate—12th District & County Courts, PO Box 301, San Luis, CO 81152. 719-672-3681, Fax: 719-672-3681. 8AM-Noon, 1-4PM. Access by: mail, in person.

Crowley

Real Estate Recording—Crowley County Clerk and Recorder, 110 W. 6th St. Ordway, CO 81063. 719-267-4624, Fax: 719-267-4608. 8AM-4PM.

Felony, Misdemeanor, Civil, Eviction, Small Claims, Probate—16th District & County Courts, 6th & Main, Ordway, CO 81063. 719-267-4468, Fax: 719-267-3753. 8AM-4:30PM. Access by: mail, in person.

Custer

Real Estate Recording—Custer County Clerk and Recorder, 205 South 6th Street, Westcliffe, CO 81252. Fax: 719-783-2885. 8AM-4PM.

Felony, Misdemeanor, Civil, Eviction, Small Claims, Probate—11th District & County Courts, PO Box 60, Westcliffe, CO 81252. 719-783-2274, Fax: 719-783-9782. 9AM-2PM. Access by: mail, in person.

Delta

Real Estate Recording—Delta County Clerk and Recorder, 501 Palmer Street, Suite 211, Delta, CO 81416. Fax: 970-874-2161. 8:30AM-4:30PM.

Felony, Misdemeanor, Civil, Eviction, Small Claims, Probate—District & County Courts, Delta County, 501 Palmer St Rm 338, Delta, CO 81416. 970-874-4416. 8:30AM-4:30PM. Access by: mail, in person.

Denver

Real Estate Recording—Denver County Clerk and Recorder, 1437 Bannock Street #200, Denver, CO 80202. 304-255-9135, Fax: 303-640-3628. 8AM-4:30PM.

Felony, Civil Actions Over $10,000—2nd District Court, 1437 Bannock, Denver, CO 80202. 8AM-5PM. Access by: mail, in person.

Civil Actions Under $10,000, Eviction, Small Claims—County Court-Civil Division, 1515 Cleveland Pl 4th Floor, Denver, CO 80202. 304-235-2445, Fax: 303-640-4730. 8AM-5PM. Access by: mail, in person.

Misdemeanor—County Court-Criminal Division, 1437 Bannock St Room 111A, Denver, CO 80202. 304-255-9197. 8AM-5PM. Access by: mail, in person.

Probate—Probate Court, 1437 Bannock, Rm 230, Denver, CO 80202. 304-235-0320, Fax: 303-640-1002. 8AM-5PM. Access by: in person. www.cpbar.org/probate.ct/index.htm

Dolores

Real Estate Recording—Dolores County Clerk and Recorder, 409 North Main Street, Dove Creek, CO 81324. 970-677-2386, Fax: 970-677-2815. 8:30AM-4:30PM.

Felony, Misdemeanor, Civil, Eviction, Small Claims, Probate—22nd District & County Courts, PO Box 511, Dove Creek, CO 81324. 970-677-2258. 8AM-5PM M & T; 8AM-Noon W. Access by: mail, phone, in person.

Douglas

Real Estate Recording—Douglas County Clerk and Recorder, 301 Wilcox Street, Castle Rock, CO 80104. Fax: 303-688-3060. 8AM-4:30PM.

Felony, Misdemeanor, Civil, Eviction, Small Claims, Probate—Douglas County Combined Court, 4000 Justice Way #2009, Castle Rock, CO 80104. 304-258-8562. 8AM-5PM. Access by: mail, in person.

Eagle

Real Estate Recording—Eagle County Clerk and Recorder, 500 Broadway, Eagle, CO 81631. Fax: 970-328-8716. 8AM-5PM.

Felony, Misdemeanor, Civil, Eviction, Small Claims, Probate—Eagle Combined Court, PO Box 597, Eagle, CO 81631. 970-328-6373, Fax: 970-328-6328. 8AM-5PM. Access by: in person.

El Paso

Real Estate Recording—El Paso County Clerk and Recorder, 200 South Cascade, Colorado Springs, CO 80903. Fax: 719-520-6230. 7:30AM-5PM.

Felony, Civil Actions Over $10,000, Probate—4th District Court, 20 E Vermijo Rm 105, Colorado Springs, CO 80903. 719-448-7700. 8AM-5PM. Access by: mail, in person.

Felony, Misdemeanor, Civil Actions Under $10,000, Eviction, Small Claims—El Paso Combined Court, 20 E Vermijo, Rm 105, Colorado Springs, CO 80903. 719-448-7599, Fax: 719-448-

7685. 8AM-5PM. Access by: mail, fax, in person. www.gofourth.org

Elbert

Real Estate Recording—Elbert County Clerk and Recorder, 215 Comanche Street, Kiowa, CO 80117. 304-234-3709, Fax: 303-621-3168. 8AM-4:30PM.

Felony, Misdemeanor, Civil, Eviction, Small Claims, Probate—Elbert District & County Courts, PO Box 232, Kiowa, CO 80117. 304-234-3688. 8AM-5PM. Access by: mail, phone, in person.

Fremont

Real Estate Recording—Fremont County Clerk and Recorder, 615 Macon Avenue, Room 100, Canon City, CO 81212. Fax: 719-275-1594. 8:30AM-4:30PM.

Felony, Misdemeanor, Civil, Eviction, Small Claims, Probate—District & County Courts, 615 Macon Rm 204, Canon City, CO 81212. 719-275-7522, Fax: 719-275-2359. 8AM-4PM. Access by: mail, in person.

Garfield

Real Estate Recording—Garfield County Clerk and Recorder, 109 8th Street, Suite 200, Glenwood Springs, CO 81601. Fax: 970-945-7785. 8:30AM-5PM.

Felony, Misdemeanor, Civil, Eviction, Small Claims, Probate—9th District & County Courts, 109 8th St #104, Glenwood Springs, CO 81601. 970-945-5075, Fax: 970-945-8756. 8AM-5PM. Access by: mail, in person. Special note: This court handles cases in the county east of New Castle.

Misdemeanor, Civil Actions Under $10,000, Eviction, Small Claims—County Court-Rifle, 110 E 18th St, Rifle, CO 81650. 970-625-5100, Fax: 970-625-1125. 8AM-5PM. Access by: mail, phone, fax, in person. Special note: This court handles cases in the county from New Castle to the west.

Gilpin

Real Estate Recording—Gilpin County Clerk and Recorder, 203 Eureka Street, Central City, CO 80427. Fax: 303-582-5440. 8AM-5PM.

Felony, Misdemeanor, Civil, Eviction, Small Claims, Probate—1st District & County Courts, 2960 Dory Hill Rd #200, Golden, CO 80403-8768. 304-234-3611, Fax: 303-582-3112. 8AM-5PM. Access by: mail, in person.

Grand

Real Estate Recording—Grand County Clerk and Recorder, 308 Byers Avenue, Hot Sulphur Springs, CO 80451. Fax: 970-725-0100. 8:30AM-5PM.

Felony, Misdemeanor, Civil, Eviction, Small Claims, Probate—14th District & County Courts, PO Box 192, Hot Sulphur Springs, CO 80451. 970-725-3357. 8AM-5PM. Access by: mail, in person.

Gunnison

Real Estate Recording—Gunnison County Clerk and Recorder, 200 East Virginia Avenue, Courthouse, Gunnison, CO 81230. Fax: 970-641-7690. 8AM-5PM.

Felony, Misdemeanor, Civil, Eviction, Small Claims, Probate—7th District & County Courts, 200 E Virginia Ave, Gunnison, CO 81230. 970-641-3500, Fax: 970-641-6876. 8:30AM-4:30PM. Access by: mail, in person.

Hinsdale

Real Estate Recording—Hinsdale County Clerk and Recorder, 317 Henson Street, Lake City, CO 81235. Fax: 970-944-2202. 7AM-5:30PM.

Felony, Misdemeanor, Civil, Eviction, Small Claims, Probate—7th District & County Courts, PO Box 245, Lake City, CO 81235. 970-944-2227, Fax: 970-944-2289. 8:30-Noon MWF (Jun-Aug) 8:30-12:00 TF (Sept-May). Access by: mail, phone, fax, in person.

Huerfano

Real Estate Recording—Huerfano County Clerk and Recorder, Courthouse, Suite 204, 410 Main St. Walsenburg, CO 81089. 719-782-1191, Fax: 719-738-2364. 8AM-4PM.

Felony, Misdemeanor, Civil, Eviction, Small Claims, Probate—3rd District & County Courts, 401 Main St, Suite 304, Walsenburg, CO 81089. 719-738-1040, Fax: 719-738-3113. 8AM-4PM. Access by: mail, in person.

Jackson

Real Estate Recording—Jackson County Clerk and Recorder, 396 LaFever Street, Walden, CO 80480. 970-723-4220. 8AM-5PM.

Felony, Misdemeanor, Civil, Eviction, Small Claims, Probate—8th District & County Courts, PO Box 308, Walden, CO 80480. 970-723-4363. 9AM-1PM. Access by: mail, in person.

Jefferson

Real Estate Recording—Jefferson County Clerk and Recorder, 100 Jefferson County Parkway, #2530, Golden, CO 80419. Fax: 303-271-8180. 8:30AM-4:30PM.

Felony, Misdemeanor, Civil, Eviction, Small Claims, Probate—1st District & County Courts, 100 Jefferson County Parkway, Golden, CO 80401-6002. 303-659-1161, Fax: 303-271-6188. 8AM-5PM. Access by: mail, in person.

Kiowa

Real Estate Recording—Kiowa County Clerk and Recorder, 1305 Goff Street, Eads, CO 81036. Fax: 719-438-5327. 8AM-4:30PM.

Felony, Misdemeanor, Civil, Eviction, Small Claims, Probate—15th District & County Courts, PO Box 353, Eads, CO 81036. 719-438-5558, Fax: 719-438-5300. 8AM-5PM. Access by: mail, phone, fax, in person.

Kit Carson

Real Estate Recording—Kit Carson County Clerk and Recorder, 251 16th Street, Suite 203, Burlington, CO 80807. 719-346-8434, Fax: 719-346-7242. 8AM-4PM.

Felony, Misdemeanor, Civil, Eviction, Small Claims, Probate—13th District & County Courts, PO Box 547, Burlington, CO 80807. 719-346-5524. 8:30AM-Noon, 1:30-5PM. Access by: mail, in person.

La Plata

Real Estate Recording—La Plata County Clerk and Recorder, Courthouse, Room 134, 1060 E. 2nd Ave. Durango, CO 81301. 970-382-6245, Fax: 970-382-6299. 8AM-5PM.

Felony, Civil Actions Over $10,000, Probate—6th District Court, PO Box 3340, Durango, CO 81302-3340. 970-247-2304, Fax: 970-247-4348. 8AM-4PM. Access by: mail, in person.

Misdemeanor, Civil Actions Under $10,000, Eviction, Small Claims—County Court, PO Box 759, Durango, CO 81302. 970-247-2004, Fax: 970-247-4348. 8AM-4PM. Access by: mail, in person.

Lake

Real Estate Recording—Lake County Clerk and Recorder, 505 Harrison Avenue, Leadville, CO 80461. Fax: 719-486-3972. 9AM-5PM.

Felony, Misdemeanor, Civil, Eviction, Small Claims, Probate—Lake County Combined Courts, PO Box 55, Leadville, CO 80461. 719-486-0535. 8AM-Noon, 1-5PM. Access by: mail, in person.

Larimer

Real Estate Recording—Larimer County Clerk and Recorder, 200 West Oak, Fort Collins, CO 80521. 7:30AM-4:30PM.

Felony, Civil Actions Over $10,000, Probate—8th District Court, PO Box 2066, Ft Collins, CO 80522. 970-498-7918, Fax: 970-498-7940. 8AM-5PM. Access by: mail, phone, in person.

Misdemeanor, Civil Actions Under $10,000, Eviction, Small Claims—County Court, PO Box 800, Ft Collins, CO 80522. 970-498-7550, Fax: 970-498-7569. 8AM-5PM. Access by: mail, in person.

Las Animas

Real Estate Recording—Las Animas County Clerk and Recorder, 200 Maple Street, Room 205, Trinidad, CO 81082. 719-846-2295, Fax: 719-846-0333. 8AM-4PM.

Felony, Misdemeanor, Civil, Eviction, Small Claims, Probate—3rd District Court, 200 E 1st St Rm 304, Trinidad, CO 81082. 719-846-3316, Fax: 719-846-9367. 8AM-5PM. Access by: mail, phone, fax, in person.

Lincoln

Real Estate Recording—Lincoln County Clerk and Recorder, 103 3rd Avenue, Hugo, CO 80821. 719-742-2633, Fax: 719-743-2838. 8AM-4PM.

Felony, Misdemeanor, Civil, Eviction, Small Claims, Probate—18th District & County Courts, PO Box 128, Hugo, CO 80821. 719-743-2455. 8AM-4:30PM. Access by: mail, phone, in person.

Logan

Real Estate Recording—Logan County Clerk and Recorder, 315 Main Street, Logan County Courthouse, Sterling, CO 80751. 970-522-2462, Fax: 970-522-4357. 8AM-5PM.

Felony, Civil Actions Over $10,000, Probate—13th District Court, PO Box 71, Sterling, CO 80751. 970-522-6565, Fax: 970-522-6566. 8AM-4PM. Access by: mail, in person.

Misdemeanor, Civil Actions Under $10,000, Eviction, Small Claims—County Court, PO Box 1907, Sterling, CO 80751. 970-522-1572, Fax: 970-522-2875. 8AM-4PM. Access by: mail, phone, in person.

Mesa

Real Estate Recording—Mesa County Clerk and Recorder, 544 Rood Avenue, Grand Junction, CO 81501. Fax: 970-256-1588. 8:30AM-4:30PM.

Felony, Civil Actions Over $10,000, Probate—21st District Court, Mesa County District Court, PO Box 20000, Grand Junction, CO 81502-5032. 970-257-3625, Fax: 970-257-3690. 8AM-5PM. Access by: mail, phone, in person.

Misdemeanor, Civil Actions Under $10,000, Eviction, Small Claims—County Court, PO Box 20000, Grand Junction, CO 81502-5032. 970-257-3640. 8AM-5PM. Access by: mail, in person.

Mineral

Real Estate Recording—Mineral County Clerk and Recorder, 1201 N. Main St. Courthouse, Creede, CO 81130. 719-658-2325, Fax: 719-658-2931. 8AM-4PM.

Felony, Misdemeanor, Civil, Eviction, Small Claims, Probate—12th District & County Courts, PO Box 337, Creede, CO 81130. 719-658-2575, Fax: 719-658-2575. 10AM-3PM. Access by: mail, in person.

Moffat

Real Estate Recording—Moffat County Clerk and Recorder, 221 West Victory Way, Craig, CO 81625. Fax: 970-824-9191. 8AM-4PM.

Felony, Misdemeanor, Civil, Eviction, Small Claims, Probate—Moffat County Combined Court, 221 W Victory Wy, Craig, CO 81625. 970-824-8254. 8AM-5PM. Access by: mail, phone, in person.

Montezuma

Real Estate Recording—Montezuma County Clerk and Recorder, 109 West Main Street, Room 108, Cortez, CO 81321. Fax: 970-564-0215. 8:30AM-4:30PM.

Felony, Civil Actions Over $10,000, Probate—22nd District Court, 109 W Main St, #210, Cortez, CO 81321. 970-565-1111. 8AM-4:30PM. Access by: mail, in person.

Misdemeanor, Civil Actions Under $10,000, Eviction, Small Claims—County Court, 601 N Mildred Rd, Cortez, CO 81321. 970-

565-7580, Fax: 970-565-8798. 8AM-4:30PM. Access by: mail, in person.

Montrose

Real Estate Recording—Montrose County Clerk and Recorder, 320 South First Street, Courthouse, #101, Montrose, CO 81401. Fax: 970-249-0757. 8:30AM-4:30PM.

Felony, Misdemeanor, Civil, Eviction, Small Claims, Probate—7th District & County Courts, 1200 N Grand Ave #A, Montrose, CO 81401-3164. 970-252-4300, Fax: 970-252-4345. 8:30AM-4:30PM. Access by: mail, in person.

Morgan

Real Estate Recording—Morgan County Clerk and Recorder, 231 Ensign Street, Administration Building, Fort Morgan, CO 80701. Fax: 970-867-6485. 8AM-4PM.

Felony, Civil Actions Over $10,000, Probate—13th District Court, PO Box 130, Ft Morgan, CO 80701. 970-542-3435, Fax: 970-542-3436. 8AM-4PM. Access by: mail, fax, in person.

Misdemeanor, Civil Actions Under $10,000, Eviction, Small Claims—County Court, PO Box 695, Ft Morgan, CO 80701. 970-542-3414, Fax: 970-542-3418. 8AM-4PM. Access by: mail, in person.

Otero

Real Estate Recording—Otero County Clerk and Recorder, 3rd & Colorado, Courthouse, La Junta, CO 81050. Fax: 719-383-3090. 8AM-5PM.

Felony, Civil, Probate—16th District Court, Courthouse Rm 207, La Junta, CO 81050. 719-384-4951, Fax: 719-384-4991. 8AM-5PM. Access by: mail, in person.

Misdemeanor, Civil Actions Under $10,000, Eviction, Small Claims—County Court, Courthouse Rm 105, La Junta, CO 81050. 719-384-4721, Fax: 719-384-4991. 8AM-Noon, 1-5PM. Access by: mail, in person.

Ouray

Real Estate Recording—Ouray County Clerk and Recorder, 541 Fourth Street, Ouray, CO 81427. Fax: 970-325-0452. 9AM-5PM.

Felony, Misdemeanor, Civil, Eviction, Small Claims, Probate—7th District & County Courts, PO Box 643, Ouray, CO 81427. 970-325-4405, Fax: 970-325-7364. 8:30AM-Noon, 1-4PM. Access by: mail, in person.

Park

Real Estate Recording—Park County Clerk and Recorder, 501 Main Street, Fairplay, CO 80440. 719-836-2771, Fax: 719-836-4348. 8AM-5PM.

Felony, Misdemeanor, Civil, Eviction, Small Claims, Probate—Park County Combined Courts, PO Box 190, Fairplay, CO 80440. 719-836-2940, Fax: 719-836-2892. 8AM-4PM. Access by: mail, in person.

Phillips

Real Estate Recording—Phillips County Clerk and Recorder, 221 South Interocean, Holyoke, CO 80734. 970-852-2822, Fax: 970-664-3811. 8AM-4:30PM.

Felony, Misdemeanor, Civil, Eviction, Small Claims, Probate—13th District & County Courts, 221 S Interocean, Holyoke, CO 80734. 970-854-3279, Fax: 970-854-3179. 8AM-Noon, 1-4PM. Access by: mail, phone, fax, in person.

Pitkin

Real Estate Recording—Pitkin County Clerk and Recorder, 530 East Main St. #101, Aspen, CO 81611. Fax: 970-920-5196. 8:30AM-4:30PM.

Felony, Misdemeanor, Civil, Eviction, Small Claims, Probate—9th District & County Courts, 506 E Main St, Ste 300, Aspen, CO 81611. 970-925-7635, Fax: 970-925-6349. 8AM-Noon, 1-5PM. Access by: mail, in person.

Prowers

Real Estate Recording—Prowers County Clerk and Recorder, 301 South Main Street, Lamar, CO 81052. Fax: 719-336-5306. 8:30AM-4:30PM.

Felony, Civil Actions Over $10,000, Probate—15th District Court, PO Box 1178, Lamar, CO 81052. 719-336-7424, Fax: 719-336-9757. 8AM-5PM. Access by: mail, fax, in person.

Misdemeanor, Civil Actions Under $10,000, Eviction, Small Claims—County Court, PO Box 525, Lamar, CO 81052. 719-336-7416, Fax: 719-336-9757. 8AM-5PM. Access by: mail, in person.

Pueblo

Real Estate Recording—Pueblo County Clerk and Recorder, 215 West 10th Street, Pueblo, CO 81003. Fax: 719-583-6549. 8AM-4:30PM.

Felony, Misdemeanor, Civil, Eviction, Small Claims, Probate—Combined Courts, 320 West 10th St, Pueblo, CO 81003. 719-583-7055, Fax: 719-583-7126. 8AM-5PM. Access by: mail, in person.

Rio Blanco

Real Estate Recording—Rio Blanco County Clerk and Recorder, 555 Main Street, P.O. Box 1067, Meeker, CO 81641. 970-878-3614. 8AM-5PM.

Felony, Misdemeanor, Civil, Eviction, Small Claims, Probate—9th District & County Courts, 555 Main St Rm 303, PO Box 1150, Meeker, CO 81641. 970-878-5622. 8AM-Noon, 1-5PM. Access by: mail, phone, in person.

Rio Grande

Real Estate Recording—Rio Grande County Clerk and Recorder, Annex Building, 965 6th St. Del Norte, CO 81132. Fax: 719-657-2621. 8AM-4PM.

Felony, Misdemeanor, Civil, Eviction, Small Claims, Probate—12th District & County Courts, 6th & Cherry, PO Box 427, Del Norte, CO 81132. 719-657-3394. 8AM-Noon, 1-4PM. Access by: mail, in person.

Routt

Real Estate Recording—Routt County Clerk and Recorder, 522 Lincoln Avenue, Steamboat Springs, CO 80487. Fax: 970-870-1329. 8AM-4:30PM; Recording Hours: 8AM-4PM.

Felony, Misdemeanor, Civil, Eviction, Small Claims, Probate—Routt Combined Courts, PO Box 773117, Steamboat Springs, CO 80477. 970-879-5020, Fax: 970-879-3531. 8AM-5PM. Access by: mail, in person.

Saguache

Real Estate Recording—Saguache County Clerk and Recorder, 501 4th St. Saguache, CO 81149. 719-655-2656, Fax: 719-655-2635. 8AM-4PM.

Felony, Misdemeanor, Civil, Eviction, Small Claims, Probate—12th District & County Courts, PO Box 164, Saguache, CO 81149. 719-655-2522, Fax: 719-655-2522. 8AM-Noon, 1-5PM. Access by: mail, in person.

San Juan

Real Estate Recording—San Juan County Clerk and Recorder, 15th & Green Street, Silverton, CO 81433. Fax: 970-387-5671. 9AM-5PM.

Felony, Misdemeanor, Civil, Eviction, Small Claims, Probate—6th District & County Courts, PO Box 441, Silverton, CO 81433. 970-387-5790. 8AM-4PM T & TH, 8AM-Noon W. Access by: mail, in person.

San Miguel

Real Estate Recording—San Miguel County Clerk and Recorder, 305 West Colorado Avenue, Telluride, CO 81435. 970-728-4451, Fax: 970-728-4808. 9AM-Noon,1-5PM.

Felony, Misdemeanor, Civil, Eviction, Small Claims, Probate—7th District & County Courts, PO Box 919, Telluride, CO 81435. 970-728-3891, Fax: 970-728-6216. 9AM-Noon, 1PM-4:30PM. Access by: mail, in person.

Sedgwick

Real Estate Recording—Sedgwick County Clerk and Recorder, 315 Cedar St. Courthouse, Julesburg, CO 80737. Fax: 970-474-0954. 8AM-4PM.

Felony, Misdemeanor, Civil, Eviction, Small Claims, Probate—13th District & County Courts, Third & Pine, Julesburg, CO 80737. 970-474-3627, Fax: 970-474-2026. 8AM-1PM. Access by: mail, fax, in person.

Summit

Real Estate Recording—Summit County Clerk and Recorder, 208 East Lincoln, Breckenridge, CO 80424. Fax: 970-453-3540. 8AM-5PM.

Felony, Misdemeanor, Civil, Eviction, Small Claims, Probate—5th District & County Courts, PO Box 185, Breckenridge, CO 80424. 970-453-2272. 8AM-5PM. Access by: in person.

Teller

Real Estate Recording—Teller County Clerk and Recorder, 101 West Bennett Avenue, Cripple Creek, CO 80813. 719-689-2985, Fax: 719-689-3524. 8AM-4:30PM.

Felony, Misdemeanor, Civil, Eviction, Small Claims, Probate—4th District & County Courts, PO Box 997, Cripple Creek, CO 80813. 719-689-2543. 8:30AM-4PM. Access by: mail, in person.

Washington

Real Estate Recording—Washington County Clerk, 150 Ash, Courthouse, Akron, CO 80720. Fax: 970-345-6607. 8AM-4:30PM.

Felony, Misdemeanor, Civil, Eviction, Small Claims, Probate—Washington County Combined Court, PO Box 455, Akron, CO 80720. 970-345-2756, Fax: 970-345-2829. 8AM-Noon, 1-5PM. Access by: mail, phone, in person.

Weld

Real Estate Recording—Weld County Clerk and Recorder, 1402 N. 17th Ave. Greeley, CO 80631. Fax: 970-353-1964. 8:30PM-4:30PM.

Felony, Misdemeanor, Civil, Eviction, Small Claims, Probate—19th District & County Courts, PO Box C, Greeley, CO 80632. 970-351-7300, Fax: 970-356-4356. 8AM-5PM. Access by: mail, phone, fax, in person.

Yuma

Real Estate Recording—Yuma County Clerk and Recorder, Third & Ash, Wray, CO 80758. 8:30AM-4:30PM.

Felony, Misdemeanor, Civil, Eviction, Small Claims, Probate—13th District & County Courts, PO Box 347, Wray, CO 80758. 970-332-4118, Fax: 970-332-4119. 8AM-4PM. Access by: mail, in person.

Federal Courts

US District Court

Denver Division US Courthouse, Room C-145 (Civil) Room C-161 (Criminal), 1929 Stout St, Denver, CO 80294-3589303-844-3433, Civil Docket Phone: 303-844-3434, Criminal Docket Phone: 303-844-2115 Counties: All counties in Colorado.

US Bankruptcy Court

Denver Division US Custom House, Room 114, 721 19th St, Denver, CO 80202-2508303-844-4045, Record Room: 303-844-0235 Counties: All counties in Colorado. www.ck10.uscourts.gov/cobk

Connecticut

Attorney General's Office

55 Elm St   860-808-5318
Hartford, CT 06106   Fax: 860-808-5387
www.cslnet.ctstateu.edu/attygenl

Governor's Office

State Capitol, 210 Capitol Ave, Room 202   860-566-4840
Hartford, CT 06106   Fax: 860-566-4677
www.state.ct.us/governor

State Archives

231 Capitol Ave   860-566-3692
Hartford, CT 06106   Fax: 860-566-2133
www.cslib.org/handg.htm

Capital:	Hartford
	Hartford County
Time Zone:	EST
Number of Counties:	8
Population:	3,269,858
Web Site:	www.state.ct.us

Search Unclaimed Property Online

http://www.state.ct.us/ott/ucp
listing.htm

State Agencies

Criminal Records

Department of Public Safety, Bureau of Identification, PO Box 2794, Middleton, CT 06759-9294 (1111 Country Club Rd, Middleton, CT 06457); 860-685-8480; Fax: 860-685-8361; 8:30AM-4:30PM. Access by: mail. www.state.ct.us/dps

Corporation Records
Limited Partnership Records
Trademarks/Servicemarks
Limited Liability Company Records

Secretary of State, Commercial Recording Division, 30 Trinity St, Hartford, CT 06106; 860-509-6003; Fax: 860-509-6068; 8:30AM-4PM. Access by: mail, phone, in person. www.state.ct.us/sots

Sales Tax Registrations

Department of Revenue, Taxpayer Services Division, 25 Sigourney St, Hartford, CT 06106; 860-297-4880; Fax: 860-297-5714; 8AM-5PM. Access by: mail, phone, fax, in person.

Uniform Commercial Code
Federal Tax Liens
State Tax Liens

UCC Division, Secretary of State, PO Box 150470, Hartford, CT 06115-0470 (30 Trinity St, Hartford, CT 06106); 860-509-6004; Fax: 860-509-6068; 8:30AM-4PM. Access by: mail, online. www.state.ct.us/sots

Workers' Compensation Records

Workers Compensation Commission, 21 Oak Street, Hartford, CT 06106; 860-493-1500; Fax: 860-247-1361; 7:45AM-4:30PM. Access by: mail, phone, in person. http://wcc.state.ct.us

Birth Certificates
Death Records
Marriage Certificates
Divorce Records

Restricted access.
The state is in the process of microfilming all records. You must go to the town/city clerk to obtain copies of records. The web site has a great list of towns and phone numbers.

Department of Public Health, Vital Records Section MS# 11VRS, PO Box 340308, Hartford, CT 06134-0308 (410 Capitol Ave, Hartford, CT 06134) (410 Capitol Ave, Hartford, CT 06134); 860-509-7897, 860-509-8000; Fax: 860-509-7964; 8:30AM-4:30PM M-F
www.state.ct.us/dph

Accident Reports

Department of Public Safety, Reports and Records Section, PO Box 2794, Middletown, CT 06457; 860-685-8250; 8:30AM-4:30PM. Access by: mail.

Driver Records

Department of Motor Vehicles, Copy Records Section, 60 State St, Room 305, Wethersfield, CT 06109-1896; 860-263-5154; 8:30AM-4:30PM T,W,F; 8:30AM-7:30PM TH; 8:30AM-12:30 S. Access by: mail.

Vehicle Ownership
Vehicle Identification

Department of Motor Vehicles, Copy Record Unit, 60 State St, Branch Operations, Wethersfield, CT 06109-1896; 860-263-5154; 8:30AM-4:30PM T,W,F; 8:30AM-7:30 PM TH; 8:30AM-12:30 S. Access by: mail, online. http://dmvct.org

Boat & Vessel Ownership
Boat & Vessel Registration

Department of Motor Vehicles, Boat Registration, 60 State Street, Wethersfield, CT 06161-3032; 860-263-5151; Fax: 860-263-5555; 8-4:30 T,W,F; 8-7:30 Th, 8-12:30 Sat. Access by: mail. http://dmvct.org

Legislation-Current/Pending
Legislation-Passed

Connecticut General Assembly, State Library, 231 Capitol Ave, Bill Room, Hartford, CT 06106; 860-566-5736; Fax: 860-566-2133; 9AM-5PM. Access by: mail, phone, in person, online. www.cga.state.ct.us

Voter Registration

Records not available from state agency.

Records are open at the town level. There are 169 towns.

GED Certificates

Department of Education, GED Records, 25 Industrial Park Rd, Middletown, CT 06457; 860-638-4151, 860-638-4027; Fax: 860-638-4156; 8AM-5PM.

Hunting License Information
Fishing License Information

Department of Environmental Protection, License Division, 79 Elm St, Hartford, CT 06106; 860-424-3105; Fax: 860-424-4072; 9AM-3:30PM. Access by: mail.

County Courts & Recording Offices

About the Courts...

Administration

Chief Court Administrator   860-566-4461
231 Capitol Av   Fax: 860-566-3308
Hartford, CT 06106
www.jud.ct.us

Court Structure

The Superior Court is the sole court of original jurisdiction for all causes of action, except for matters over which the probate courts have jurisdiction as provided by statute. The Geographic Area Courts are actually divisions of the Superior Court given jurisdiction over lesser offenses and actions. The Superior Court has five divisions: Criminal, Civil, Family, Juvenile, and Administrative Appeals

Searching Hints

Some courts do not perform criminal searches, but rather forward search requests to the Department of Public Safety, 1111 Country Club Rd, PO Box 2794, Middletown, CT 06457, 860-685-8480. The search fee is $15.00 per name, plus an additional $10.00 for a list of convictions, if any are found. Use of a special request form is required.

There is a State Record Center, which serves as the repository for criminal and some civil records, in Enfield CT open 9AM-5PM M-F. Case records are sent to the Record Center from 3 months to 5 years after disposition by the courts. These records are then maintained 10 years for misdemeanors and 20+ years for felonies. If a requester is certain that the record is at the Record Center, it is quicker to direct the request there rather than to the original court of record. Only written requests are accepted. Search requirements: full defendant name, docket number, disposition date, and court action. Fee is $5.00 for each docket. Fee payee is Treasurer-State of Connecticut. Direct Requests to: Connecticut Record Center, 111 Phoenix Avenue, Enfield CT 06082, 860-741-3714.

Many clerks state that they will send an extract of a record without copying originals or certification at no charge.

Online Access

There are two online systems available for civil and family records only, statewide. The Internet access, located at www.jud2.state.ct.us/Civil Inquiry/GetParty .asp, is free. The commercial system, which provides direct access to Superior Court records, is available through the Judicial Information Systems. User can access all civil and family records. The system is available from 8AM to 5PM Eastern Time Monday through Friday except on holidays. The fee is $30 per month network charge, $10.00 per use per month user authorization fee, plus a per minute usage fee. For information brochure or subscription information call the CT JIS Office at 860-566-8580. There is currently no online access to criminal records. However, there is a central records repository (see below).

About the Recording Offices...

Organization

8 counties and 170 towns/cities. The recording officer is Town/City Clerk. Counties have no administrative offices. Be careful not to confuse searching in the following towns/cities as equivalent to a county-wide search: Fairfield, Hartford, Litchfield, New Haven, New London, Tolland, and Windham. The entire state is in the Eastern Time Zone (EST).

UCC Records

Financing statements are filed at the state level, except for real estate related collateral, which are filed only with the Town/City Clerk. Towns will not perform UCC searches. Copies usually cost $1.00 per page.

Lien Records

All federal and state tax liens on personal property are filed with the Secretary of State. Federal and state tax liens on real property are filed with the Town/City Clerk. Towns will not perform tax lien searches.

Real Estate Records

Towns do not perform real estate searches. Copy fees are usually $1.00 per page. Certification fees are usually $1.00 per document or per page.

County Courts & Recording Offices

Andover

Real Estate Recording—Andover Town Clerk, Town Office Building, 17 School Road, Andover, CT 6232. Fax: 860-742-7535. 8:30-12,1-4,5-7 M; 8:30-Noon,1-4PM T-Th;8:30-12:30PM F.

Ansonia

Real Estate Recording—Ansonia City Clerk, 253 Main Street, City Hall, Ansonia, CT 6401. 203-734-1277. 8:30AM-4:30PM.

Ashford

Real Estate Recording—Ashford Town Clerk, 25 Pompey Hollow Road, Ashford, CT 6278. Fax: 860-487-2025. 8:30AM-3PM M-W & F; 7-9PM Wed.

Avon

Real Estate Recording—Avon Town Clerk, 60 West Main Street, Avon, CT 6001. Fax: 860-677-8428. 8:30AM-4:30PM (Summer hours: 8AM-4:45PM M-Th; 8AM-12:30PM F).

Barkhamsted

Real Estate Recording—Barkhamsted Town Clerk, Route 318, 67 Ripley Hill Rd. Town Hall, Pleasant Valley, CT 6063. Fax: 860-379-9284. 9AM-4PM (F open until 1PM).

Beacon Falls

Real Estate Recording—Beacon Falls Town Clerk, 10 Maple Avenue, Beacon Falls, CT 6403. Fax: 203-720-1078. 9AM-Noon, 1-4PM.

Berlin

Real Estate Recording—Berlin Town Clerk, 240 Kensington Road, Kensington, CT 6037. Fax: 860-828-7180. M-W, 8:30AM-4:30PM; Th 8:30AM-7PM; F 8:30AM-1PM.

Bethany

Real Estate Recording—Bethany Town Clerk, 40 Peck Road, Bethany, CT 6524. Fax: 203-393-0821. 9:30AM-4:30PM (No copying or recording after 4PM).

Bethel

Real Estate Recording—Bethel Town Clerk, 1 School St. Bethel, CT 6801. Fax: 203-794-8588. 9AM-5PM M-W, F; 9AM-7PM Th.

Bethlehem

Real Estate Recording—Bethlehem Town Clerk, 36 Main St. So. Bethlehem, CT 6751. Fax: 203-266-7670. 9AM-Noon T,W,Th,F,Sat.

Bloomfield

Real Estate Recording—Bloomfield Town Clerk, 800 Bloomfield Avenue, Town Hall, Bloomfield, CT 6002. Fax: 860-769-3597. 9AM-5PM.

Bolton

Real Estate Recording—Bolton Town Clerk, 222 Bolton Center Road, Bolton, CT 6043. 860-649-8066, Fax: 860-643-0021. 9AM-4PM M,W,Th; 9AM-5PM, 6-8PM T; 9AM-3PM F.

Bozrah

Real Estate Recording—Bozrah Town Clerk, 1 River Road, Town Hall, Bozrah, CT 6334. Fax: 860-887-5449. 9AM-4PM T,W; 9AM-6PM Th; 9AM-Noon Fri.

Branford

Real Estate Recording—Branford Town Clerk, 1019 Main Street, Town Hall, Branford, CT 6405. Fax: 203-481-5561. 9AM-4:30PM (9AM-4PM Recording hours).

Bridgeport

Real Estate Recording—Bridgeport Town Clerk, 45 Lyon Terrace, City Hall, Room 124, Bridgeport, CT 6604. 9AM-4:30PM; Recording until 4PM.

Bridgewater

Real Estate Recording—Bridgewater Town Clerk, Main Street, Town Hall, Bridgewater, CT 6752. Fax: 860-350-5944. 8AM-Noon M,W,F; 8AM-5PM T.

Bristol

Real Estate Recording—Bristol City Clerk, 111 North Main Street, City Hall, Bristol, CT 6010. Fax: 860-584-3827. 8:30AM-5PM.

Brookfield

Real Estate Recording—Brookfield Town Clerk, Pocono Road, Town Hall, Brookfield, CT 6804. 8:30AM-4:30PM.

Brooklyn

Real Estate Recording—Brooklyn Town Clerk, 4 Wolf Den Road, Town Hall, Brooklyn, CT 6234. Fax: 860-779-3744. M-W 9AM-4:30PM; Th 9AM-6PM; F 9AM-1PM.

Burlington

Real Estate Recording—Burlington Town Clerk, 200 Spielman Highway, Burlington, CT 6013. Fax: 860-675-9312. 8:30AM-4PM.

Canaan

Real Estate Recording—Canaan Town Clerk, 107 Main Street, Town Hall, Falls Village, CT 6031. Fax: 860-824-4506. 9AM-3PM.

Canterbury

Real Estate Recording—Canterbury Town Clerk, 45 Westminster Road, Town Hall, P.O. Box 27, Canterbury, CT 6331. Fax: 860-546-7805. 9:30AM-4:30PM M-W; 9:30AM-7PM Th; 9:30AM-2PM F.

Canton

Real Estate Recording—Canton Town Clerk, 4 Market Street, Collinsville, CT 6022. 860-693-8712, Fax: 860-693-7840. 8:30AM-4:30PM.

Chaplin

Real Estate Recording—Chaplin Town Clerk, 495 Phoenixville Road, Town Hall, Chaplin, CT 6235. Fax: 860-455-0027. 9AM-3PM M,Th;9AM-3PM, 7-9PM T; 9AM-1PM F.

Cheshire

Real Estate Recording—Cheshire Town Clerk, 84 South Main Street, Town Hall, Cheshire, CT 6410. 8:30AM-4PM (Recording until 3:30PM).

Chester

Real Estate Recording—Chester Town Clerk, 65 Main Street, Chester, CT 6412. Fax: 860-526-0004. 9AM-Noon, 1-4PM M,W,Th; 9AM-Noon, 1-7PM T; 9AM-Noon F.

Clinton

Real Estate Recording—Clinton Town Clerk, 54 East Main Street, Clinton, CT 6413. 9AM-4PM.

Colchester

Real Estate Recording—Colchester Town Clerk, 127 Norwich Avenue, Colchester, CT 6415. Fax: 860-537-0547. 8:30AM-4:30PM M-W & F; 8:30-7PM Th.

Colebrook

Real Estate Recording—Colebrook Town Clerk, 558 Colebrook Road, Rte 183, Town Hall, Colebrook, CT 6021. Fax: 860-379-7215. 10AM-4:30PM.

Columbia

Real Estate Recording—Columbia Town Clerk, 323 Jonathan Trumbull Hwy, Columbia, CT 6237. Fax: 860-228-1952. 8:30AM-3PM M-W; 9AM-7PM Th; 8AM-Noon Fri.

Cornwall

Real Estate Recording—Cornwall Town Clerk, 26 Pine St. Cornwall, CT 6753. 9AM-4PM M-Th.

Coventry

Real Estate Recording—Coventry Town Clerk, 1712 Main Street, Coventry, CT 6238. Fax: 860-742-8911. 8:30AM-4:30PM M-W; 8:30AM-6:30PM Th; 8:30AM-1:30PM F.

Cromwell

Real Estate Recording—Cromwell Town Clerk, 41 West Street, Cromwell, CT 6416. Fax: 860-632-7048. 8:30AM-4PM.

Danbury

Real Estate Recording—Danbury Town Clerk, 155 Deer Hill Avenue, City Hall, Danbury, CT 6810. 203-797-4521. 8:30AM-4:30PM.

Darien

Real Estate Recording—Darien Town Clerk, 2 Renshaw Road, Darien, CT 6820. 203-630-4150. 8:30AM-4:30PM.

Deep River

Real Estate Recording—Deep River Town Clerk, 174 Main Street, Town Hall, Deep River, CT 6417. Fax: 860-526-6023. 9AM-Noon,1-4PM.

Derby

Real Estate Recording—Derby Town Clerk, 35 Fifth Street, Derby, CT 6418. Fax: 203-736-1458. 9AM-5PM.

Durham

Real Estate Recording—Durham Town Clerk, 30 Town House Road, Town Hall, Durham, CT 6422. Fax: 860-349-0547. 9AM-4:30PM.

East Granby

Real Estate Recording—East Granby Town Clerk, 9 Center Street, Town Hall, East Granby, CT 6026. Fax: 860-653-4017. 8:30AM-Noon, 1-4PM M-Th; 8:30am-1PM F.

East Haddam

Real Estate Recording—East Haddam Town Clerk, Goodspeed Plaza, Town Office Building. PO Box K, East Haddam, CT 6423. 9AM-Noon, 1-4PM M,T,W,Th; 9AM-Noon F (T open until 7PM).

East Hampton

Real Estate Recording—East Hampton Town Clerk, 20 East High Street, Town Hall, East Hampton, CT 6424. Fax: 860-267-1027. 8AM-4PM M,W,Th; 8AM-7:30PM T; 8:30AM-12:30PM F.

East Hartford

Real Estate Recording—East Hartford Town Clerk, 740 Main Street, East Hartford, CT 6108. Fax: 860-289-0831. 8:30AM-4:30PM.

East Haven

Real Estate Recording—East Haven Town Clerk, 250 Main Street, East Haven, CT 6512. Fax: 203-468-3372. 8:30AM-4:15PM.

East Lyme

Real Estate Recording—East Lyme Town Clerk, 108 Pennsylvania Avenue, Niantic, CT 6357. Fax: 860-739-6930. 8:30AM-4:30PM.

East Windsor

Real Estate Recording—East Windsor Town Clerk, 11 Rye Street, Town Hall, Broad Brook, CT 6016. 8:30-4:30PM M,T,W; 8:30AM-7:30PM Th; 8:30AM-12:30PM F.

Eastford

Real Estate Recording—Eastford Town Clerk, 16 Westford Road, Eastford, CT 6242. Fax: 860-974-0624. 10AM-Noon, 1-4PM T,W.

Easton

Real Estate Recording—Easton Town Clerk, 225 Center Road, Easton, CT 6612. 203-263-2417, Fax: 203-261-6080. 8:30AM-4:30PM.

Ellington

Real Estate Recording—Ellington Town Clerk, 55 Main Street, PO Box 187, Ellington, CT 6029. Fax: 860-875-0788. 9AM-7PM M; 9AM-4:30PM T-F (Recording ends 15 min prior closing).

Enfield

Real Estate Recording—Enfield Town Clerk, 820 Enfield Street, Enfield, CT 6082. Fax: 860-253-6310. 9AM-5PM.

Essex

Real Estate Recording—Essex Town Clerk, 29 West Avenue, Essex, CT 6426. 9AM-4PM.

Fairfield

Real Estate Recording—Fairfield Town Clerk, 611 Old Post Road, Fairfield, CT 6430. 8:30AM-5PM (8:30AM-4:30PM Memorial Day-Labor Day).

Felony, Civil Actions Over $2,500—Danbury Superior Court, 146 White St, Danbury, CT 06810. 202-879-4800. 9AM-1PM, 2:30-4PM. Access by: mail, in person.

Fairfield Superior Court, 1061 Main St Attn: criminal or civil, Bridgeport, CT 06604. 203-488-0318. 9AM-5PM. Access by: mail, in person.

Stamford-Norwalk Superior Court, 123 Hoyt St, Stamford, CT 06905. 9AM-Noon, 1:30PM-4PM. Access by: mail, phone, in person.

Misdemeanor, Eviction, Small Claims—Geographical Area Court #2, 172 Golden Hill St, Bridgeport, CT 06604. 203-579-6527. 9AM-4PM. Access by: mail, phone, in person.

Geographical Area Court #20, 17 Belden Ave, Norwalk, CT 06850. 203-797-4650. 9AM-5PM. Access by: in person.

Geographical Area Court #3, 146 White St, Danbury, CT 06810. 203-207-8600. 9AM-5PM. Access by: mail, in person.

Probate—Bethel Probate Court, 1 School St, PO Box 144, Bethel, CT 06801. 203-789-7908, Fax: 203-794-8552.

Bridgeport Probate District, 202 State St McLevy Hall, 3rd Floor, Bridgeport, CT 06604. 203-323-2149, Fax: 203-576-7898. 9AM-4PM. Access by: mail, in person.

Brookfield Probate Court, 100 Pocono Rd, PO Box 5192, Brookfield, CT 06804. 203-755-1127. 9AM-2PM and by appointment.

Danbury Probate Court, 155 Deer Hill Ave, Danbury, CT 06810. 203-794-8508, Fax: 203-796-1526. 8:30AM-4:30PM. Access by: mail, in person.

Darien Probate Court, Town Hall, 2 Renshaw Rd, Darien, CT 06820. 203-656-7334, Fax: 203-656-7385. 9AM-12:30PM, 1:30AM-4:30PM M-F, 9AM-12:30PM Fri July-Labor Day.

Fairfield Probate Court, Independence Hall, Fairfield, CT 06430. 203-245-5661, Fax: 203-256-3080. 9AM-5PM M-F, 9AM-4:30PM (July-Aug).

Greenwich Probate Court, PO Box 2540, Greenwich, CT 06836. 203-596-4050, Fax: 203-622-6451. 9AM-4:30PM M-F, 9AM-12PM Fri (July-Aug).

New Canaan Probate Court, PO Box 326, 77 Main St, New Canaan, CT 06840. 203-946-4880, Fax: 203-966-5555. 8:30AM-1PM 2-4:30PM M-F, (8:30AM-Noon Fri July-Aug). Access by: mail, in person.

New Fairfield Probate Court, Town Hall, New Fairfield, CT 06812. 203-294-2100, Fax: 203-312-5612. 9AM-Noon Wed-Thu. Access by: in person.

Newtown Probate Court, Edmond Town Hall, 45 Main St, Newtown, CT 06470. 203-268-6291, Fax: 203-270-4205. 8:30AM-Noon,1-4:30PM. Access by: mail.

Norwalk Probate Court, 125 East Ave, PO Box 2009, Norwalk, CT 06852-2009. 203-846-3237, Fax: 203-854-7817. 9AM-4:30PM M-F (And by appointment). Special note: District includes Town of Wilton.

Redding Probate Court, PO Box 1125, Redding, CT 06875-1125. 203-937-3552, Fax: 203-938-8816. 9AM-1PM. Access by: mail, in person.

Ridgefield Probate Court, Town Hall, 400 Main St, Ridgefield, CT 06877. 203-393-3774, Fax: 203-431-2772. 8:30AM-4:30PM.

Shelton Probate Court, PO Box 127, 40 White St, Shelton, CT 06484. 203-891-2160, Fax: 203-924-8943. 9AM-Noon, 1-4:30PM. Access by: mail, in person.

Sherman Probate Court, Mallory Town Hall, Sherman, CT 06784. 860-355-1821, Fax: 860-350-5041. 9AM-Noon Tue (And by appointment). Access by: mail, in person.

Stamford Probate Court, 888 Washington Blvd, 8th Floor, PO Box 10152, Stamford, CT 06904-2152. 203-315-6007, Fax: 203-964-1830. 9AM-4PM.

Stratford Probate Court, Town Hall, 2725 Main St, Stratford, CT 06615. 203-341-1100, Fax: 203-375-6253. 9:30AM-4:30PM.

Trumbull Probate Court, Town Hall, 5866 Main St, Trumbull, CT 06611-5416. 203-452-5014, Fax: 203-452-5038. 9AM-4:30PM. Access by: mail, in person. Special note: District includes Town of Easton.

Westport Probate Court, Town Hall, 110 Myrtle Ave, Westport, CT 06880. 203-333-4165, Fax: 203-341-1153. 9AM-4:30PM. Special note: District includes Town of Weston.

Farmington

Real Estate Recording—Farmington Town Clerk, 1 Monteith Drive, Farmington, CT 6032. Fax: 860-675-7140. 8:30AM-4:30PM.

Franklin

Real Estate Recording—Franklin Town Clerk, 7 Meeting House Hill Road, Town Hall, North Franklin, CT 6254. 860-642-7352, Fax: 860-642-6606. 8:30AM-3PM M-Th; 6PM-8PM T.

Glastonbury

Real Estate Recording—Glastonbury Town Clerk, 2155 Main Street, Glastonbury, CT 6033. Fax: 860-652-7610. 8AM-4:30PM.

Goshen

Real Estate Recording—Goshen Town Clerk, 42 North Street, Town Office Building, Goshen, CT 6756. 9AM-Noon,1-4PM M-Th; 9AM-1PM F.

Granby

Real Estate Recording—Granby Town Clerk, 15 North Granby Road, Granby, CT 6035. 9AM-Noon,1-4PM.

Greenwich

Real Estate Recording—Greenwich Town Clerk, 101 Field Point Road, Town Hall, Greenwich, CT 6836. 8AM-4PM.

Griswold

Real Estate Recording—Griswold Town Clerk, 32 School Street, Jewett City, CT 6351. Fax: 860-376-7070. 8:30AM-4PM M,T,Th,F; 8:30AM-Noon W.

Groton

Real Estate Recording—Groton Town Clerk, 45 Fort Hill Road, Groton, CT 6340. 8:30AM-4:30PM M-W & F; 9AM-4:30PM Th.

Guilford

Real Estate Recording—Guilford Town Clerk, 31 Park Street, Town Hall, Guilford, CT 6437. 8:30AM-4:30PM.

Haddam

Real Estate Recording—Haddam Town Clerk, 30 Field Park Drive, Town Hall, Haddam, CT 6438. Fax: 860-345-3730. 9AM-4PM M,T,W,; 9AM-7PM Th; 9AM-Noon F.

Hamden

Real Estate Recording—Hamden Town Clerk, 2372 Whitney Avenue, Memorial Town Hall, Hamden, CT 6518. 203-385-4023, Fax: 203-287-2518. 9AM-4PM.

Hampton

Real Estate Recording—Hampton Town Clerk, Town Office Building, 164 Main St. Hampton, CT 6247. Fax: 860-455-0517. 9AM-4PM T,Th; 9AM-Noon Sat.

Hartford

Real Estate Recording—Hartford City Clerk, 550 Main Street, Hartford, CT 6103. 860-543-8530, Fax: 860-722-8041. 8:30AM-4:30 PM.

Felony, Civil Actions Over $2,500—New Britain Superior Court, 20 Franklin Square, New Britain, CT 06051. 9AM-5PM. Access by: mail, in person.

Misdemeanor, Eviction—Geographical Area Court #13, 111 Phoenix, Enfield, CT 06082. 860-741-3727. 9AM-1PM, 2:30-4PM. Access by: in person.

Misdemeanor, Eviction, Small Claims—Geographical Area Court #12, 410 Center St, Manchester, CT 06040. 860-647-1091. 9AM-5PM; Phone Hours: 9AM-4PM. Access by: mail, in person. Special note: Evictions are handled by a special Housing Court, 18 Trinity, Hartford, CT, 860-566-8550.

Geographical Area Court #15, 125 Columbus Blvd, New Britain, CT 06051. 8:15AM-5PM. Access by: mail, in person.

Geographical Area Court #17, 131 N Main St, Bristol, CT 06010. 860-582-8111. 9AM-5PM. Access by: mail, phone, in person.

Civil—Hartford Superior Court-Civil, 95 Washington St, Hartford, CT 06106. 860-548-2700, Fax: 860-548-2711. 9AM-5PM. Access by: mail, in person.

Misdemeanor—Geographical Area Court #14, 101 LaFayette St, Hartford, CT 06106. 860-566-1630. 1PM-2:30PM. Access by: mail, phone, in person.

Geographical Area Court #16, 105 Raymond Rd, West Hartford, CT 06107. 860-236-4551, Fax: 860-236-9311. 9AM-5PM. Access by: mail, in person.

Felony—Hartford Superior Court-Criminal, 101 LaFayette St, Hartford, CT 06106. 860-566-1634. 9AM-5PM. Access by: mail, in person.

Probate—Avon Probate Court, 60 W Main St, Avon, CT 06001-0578. 860-409-4348, Fax: 860-409-4368. 9AM-Noon. Access by: mail, in person.

Berlin Probate Court, 177 Columbus Blvd, PO Box 400, New Britain, CT 06050-0400. 860-826-2696, Fax: 860-826-2695. 9AM-4PM. Access by: mail, in person. Special note: District includes Town of New Britain.

Bloomfield Probate Court, Town Hall, 800 Bloomfield Ave, Bloomfield, CT 06002. 860-769-3548, Fax: 860-769-3598. 9AM-1PM, 2AM-4:30PM.

Bristol Probate Court, 111 N Main St, 3rd Fl, Bristol, CT 06010. 860-584-7650, Fax: 860-584-3818. 9AM-5PM.

Burlington Probate Court, 200 Spielman Highway, Burlington, CT 06013. 860-673-2108, Fax: 860-675-9312. 9AM-1PM Fri.

Canton Probate Court, Town Hall, 4 Market St, PO Box 175, Collinsville, CT 06022. 860-693-7851, Fax: 860-693-7840. 8:30AM-1:30PM Tue-Fri (And by appointment).

East Granby Probate Court, PO Box 542, East Granby, CT 06026. 860-653-3434, Fax: 860-653-7085. 9AM-Noon W-Thu, till 1PM on T.

East Hartford Probate Court, Town Hall, 740 Main St, East Hartford, CT 06108. 860-291-7278, Fax: 860-289-0831. 9AM-4:30PM.

East Windsor Probate Court, Town Hall, 1540 Sullivan Ave, South Windsor, CT 06074. 860-644-2511, Fax: 860-644-3781. 8AM-2PM M-F. Access by: mail, in person. Special note: District includes Town of South Windsor.

Enfield Probate Court, 820 Enfield St, Enfield, CT 06082. 860-253-6305, Fax: 860-253-6357. 9AM-4:30PM.

Farmington Probate Court, One Monteith, Farmington, CT 06032. 860-673-2360. 9AM-4PM.

Glastonbury Probate Court, 2155 Main St, Glastonbury, CT 06033. 860-652-7629. 9:30AM-4:30PM. Access by: mail, in person.

Granby Probate Court, 15 N Granby Rd, Town Hall, Granby, CT 06035. 860-653-8944, Fax: 860-653-4769. 9AM-Noon T,W,F. Access by: mail, in person.

Hartford Probate Court, 10 Prospect St, Hartford, CT 06103. 860-522-1813, Fax: 860-724-1503. 9AM-4PM.

Hartland Probate Court, PO Box 158, West Hartland, CT 06027. 860-653-9710, Fax: 860-738-1003. 10AM-1PM Mon-Fri (And by appointment). Access by: mail, in person.

Manchester Probate Court, 66 Center St, Manchester, CT 06040. 860-647-3227, Fax: 860-647-3236. 8:30AM-12PM 1AM-4:30PM M-F, 6:30PM-8PM Thu (By appointment).

Marlborough Probate Court, PO Box 29, N Main St, Marlborough, CT 06447. 860-295-6200, Fax: 860-295-0317. By appointment. Special note: Hours are 9AM-4:30PM on Mon, 2:30PM-7PM on Tues, and 2PM-4:30PM on Thurs.

Newington Probate Court, 66 Cedar Street, Newington, CT 06111. 860-665-1285, Fax: 860-665-1331. 9AM-4PM. Special note: District includes towns of Rocky Hill, Wethersfield.

Simsbury Probate Court, PO Box 495, 933 Hopmeadow St, Simsbury, CT 06070. 860-658-3200, Fax: 860-658-3206. 9AM-1PM, 2-4:30PM M-F (And by appointment).

Southington Probate Court, 75 Main St, PO Box 165, Southington, CT 06489. 860-276-6253, Fax: 860-628-8669. 8:30AM-Noon, 1-4:30PM. Access by: in person.

Suffield Probate Court, 83 Mountain Rd, PO Box 234, Suffield, CT 06078. 860-668-3835, Fax: 860-668-3029. 9AM-1PM. Access by: mail, in person.

West Hartford Probate Court, 50 S Main St, West Hartford, CT 06107. 860-523-3174, Fax: 860-236-8352. 8:30AM-4:30PM.

Windsor Locks Probate Court, Town Office Bldg, 50 Church St, Windsor Locks, CT 06096. 860-627-1450, Fax: 860-292-1121. 9AM-2PM Mon-Thu.

Windsor Probate Court, PO Box 342, 275 Broad St, Windsor, CT 06095. 860-285-1976, Fax: 860-285-1909. 8:30AM-4:30PM M-Th; 8:30AM-Noon Fri. Access by: mail, in person.

Hartland

Real Estate Recording—Hartland Town Clerk, Town Office Building, 22 South Road, East Hartford, CT 6027. Fax: 860-653-7919. 1-4PM M,T,W (T open 7-8PM).

Harwinton

Real Estate Recording—Harwinton Town Clerk, 100 Bentley Drive, Town Hall, Harwinton, CT 6791. Fax: 860-485-0051. 8:30AM-4PM.

Hebron

Real Estate Recording—Hebron Town Clerk, 15 Gilead Street, Hebron, CT 6248. Fax: 860-228-4859. 8AM-4PM M-W; 8AM-7PM Th; 8AM-12:30PM F.

Kent

Real Estate Recording—Kent Town Clerk, 41 Kent Green Blvd. Town Hall, Kent, CT 6757. 9AM-Noon, 1-4PM.

Killingly

Real Estate Recording—Killingly Town Clerk, 172 Main Street, Danielson, CT 6239. Fax: 860-779-5394. 8:30AM-4:30PM.

Killingworth

Real Estate Recording—Killingworth Town Clerk, 323 Route 81, Killingworth, CT 6419. Fax: 860-663-3305. 9AM-Noon,1-4PM.

Lebanon

Real Estate Recording—Lebanon Town Clerk, 579 Exeter Road, Town Hall, Lebanon, CT 6249. 9AM-4PM M,T,F; 9AM-7PM Th.

Ledyard

Real Estate Recording—Ledyard Town Clerk, 741 Col. Ledyard Highway, Ledyard, CT 6339. 860-464-8740, Fax: 860-464-1126. 8:30AM-4:30PM.

Lisbon

Real Estate Recording—Lisbon Town Clerk, 1 Newent Road, RD 2 Town Hall, Lisbon, CT 6351. 860-376-3400, Fax: 860-376-6545. 9AM-4PM M-Th; 6PM-8PM W; 9AM-2PM F; 9AM-Noon Sat.

Litchfield

Real Estate Recording—Litchfield Town Clerk, 74 West Street, Town Office Building, Litchfield, CT 6759. 9AM-4:30PM.

Felony, Civil Actions Over $2,500—Litchfield Superior Court, PO Box 247, Litchfield, CT 06759. 860-567-0885, Fax: 860-567-4779. 9AM-5PM. Access by: mail, fax, in person.

Misdemeanor, Eviction, Small Claims—Geographical Area Court #18, 80 Doyle Rd (PO Box 667), Bantam, CT 06750. 860-567-3942. 9AM-4PM. Access by: mail, in person.

Probate—Barkhamsted Probate Court, 67 Ripley Hill Rd, PO Box 185, Pleasant Valley, CT 06063-0185. 860-379-8665, Fax: 860-379-9284. 10AM-1PM M-W (And by appointment). Access by: mail, in person.

Canaan Probate Court, Town Hall, 100 Pease St, PO Box 905, Canaan, CT 06018-0905. 860-824-7114, Fax: 860-824-9922. 9AM-1PM M-F (And by appointment).

Cornwall Probate Court, PO Box 157, Town Office Bldg, Cornwall, CT 06753-0157. 860-672-2677, Fax: 860-672-2677. 9AM-4:30PM M-Thu. Access by: mail, in person.

Harwinton Probate Court, Town Hall, 100 Bentley Dr, Harwinton, CT 06791. 860-485-1403, Fax: 860-485-0051. 9AM-14PM Tue-Wed or by appointment.

Kent Probate Court, PO Box 185, Town Hall, Kent, CT 06757. 860-927-3729, Fax: 860-927-1313. 9AM-12PM Tue & Thu (And by appointment). Access by: mail, in person.

Litchfield Probate Court, 74 West St, PO Box 505, Litchfield, CT 06759. 860-567-8065, Fax: 860-567-2538. 9AM-1PM. Access by: mail, in person. Special note: District includes towns of Morris, Warren, and Litchfield.

New Hartford Probate Court, Town Hall, 530 Main St, PO Box 308, New Hartford, CT 06057. 860-379-3254, Fax: 860-379-8560. 9AM-12 T&TH or by appointment.

New Milford Probate Court, 10 Main St, New Milford, CT 06776. 860-355-6029, Fax: 860-355-6002. 9AM-Noon, 1-5PM M-F, 9AM-Noon Fri (July-Aug). Access by: mail, in person. Special note: District includes Town of Bridgewater.

Norfolk Probate Court, PO Box 648, 19 Maple Ave, Norfolk, CT 06058. 860-542-5134, Fax: 860-542-5876. 9AM-12PM Tue & Thu (And by appointment).

Plymouth Probate Court, 80 Main St, Terryville, CT 06786. 860-585-4014. 9AM-1PM.

Roxbury Probate Court, Town Hall, 29 North St, PO Box 203, Roxbury, CT 06783. 860-354-1184, Fax: 860-354-0560. 9AM-3PM T-Th. Access by: mail, in person.

Salisbury Probate Court, Town Hall, 27 Main St, PO Box 525, Salisbury, CT 06068. 860-435-5183, Fax: 860-435-5172. 9Am-12PM M-F (And by appointment).

Connecticut

Sharon Probate Court, PO Box 1177, Sharon, CT 06069. 860-364-5514, Fax: 860-364-5789. 2PM-4PM M-W & F (and by appointment). Access by: in person.

Thomaston Probate Court, PO Box 136, Town Hall Bldg 158 Main St, Thomaston, CT 06787. 860-283-4874, Fax: 860-283-1013. 9AM-Noon M-F (And by appointment). Access by: mail, in person.

Torrington Probate Court, Municipal Bldg, 140 Main St, Torrington, CT 06790. 860-489-2215. 9-12, 1-4:30. Special note: District includes Town of Goshen.

Washington Probate Court, Town Hall, PO Box 295 Washington Depot, Washington Depot, CT 06794. 860-868-7974, Fax: 860-868-9685. 9AM-Noon, 1-3PM M,W,F. Access by: mail, in person.

Watertown Probate Court, 37 DeForest St, PO Box 7, Town Hall, Watertown, CT 06795. 860-945-5237, Fax: 860-945-4741. 9AM-Noon, 1-3PM.

Winchester Probate Court, PO Box 625, 338 Main St, Winsted, CT 06098. 860-379-5576, Fax: 860-738-7053. 9AM-12,1-4PM M-TH, til noon on F. Special note: District includes towns of Colebrook, Winsted.

Woodbury Probate Court, PO Box 84, 281 Main St, South, Woodbury, CT 06798. 203-262-0641, Fax: 203-263-2748. 9AM-Noon, 1-4PM Th. Access by: mail, in person. Special note: District includes Town of Bethlehem.

Lyme

Real Estate Recording—Lyme Town Clerk, 480 Hamburg Rd. Town Hall, Lyme, CT 6371. Fax: 860-434-2989. 9AM-4PM.

Madison

Real Estate Recording—Madison Town Clerk, 8 Campus Dr. Madison, CT 6443. Fax: 203-245-5613. 8:30AM-4PM.

Manchester

Real Estate Recording—Manchester Town Clerk, 41 Center Street, Manchester, CT 6040. 860-647-3023, Fax: 860-647-3029. 8:30AM-5PM.

Mansfield

Real Estate Recording—Mansfield Town Clerk, 4 South Eagleville Road, Mansfield, CT 6268. 8:15AM-4:30PM M-W; 8:15AM-6:30PM Th; 8AM-Noon F.

Marlborough

Real Estate Recording—Marlborough Town Clerk, 26 North Main Street, Marlborough, CT 6447. Fax: 860-295-0317. 8AM-4:30PM M-Th; 8AM-7PM T; 8AM-Noon F.

Meriden

Real Estate Recording—Meriden City Clerk, 142 East Main Street, Meriden, CT 6450. Fax: 203-630-4059. 9AM-7PM M; 9AM-5PM T-F.

Middlebury

Real Estate Recording—Middlebury Town Clerk, Town Hall, 1212 Whittemore Rd. Middlebury, CT 6762. 9AM-Noon,1-5PM.

Middlefield

Real Estate Recording—Middlefield Town Clerk, 393 Jackson Hill Road, Middlefield, CT 6455. Fax: 860-349-7115. 9AM-5PM M; 9AM-4PM T-Th; 9AM-3PM F.

Middlesex

Civil—Middlesex Superior Court-Civil, 1 Court St, 2nd Floor, Middletown, CT 06457-3374. 860-343-6400, Fax: 860-343-6423. 9AM-5PM. Access by: mail, in person.

Felony—Middlesex Superior Court-Criminal, 1 Court St, 1st Flr, Middletown, CT 06457-3348. 860-343-6445. 9AM-5PM. Access by: mail, in person.

Probate—Clinton Probate Court, 50 E Main St, PO Box 130, Clinton, CT 06413-0130. 860-669-6447. 10AM-3PM M-TH. Access by: in person.

Deep River Probate Court, Town Hall, 174 Main St, PO Box 391, Deep River, CT 06417. 860-526-6026. 10AM-12PM, 2PM-4PM Tue & Thu (And by appointment).

East Haddam Probate Court, Godspeed Plaza, PO Box 217, East Haddam, CT 06423. 860-873-5028, Fax: 860-873-5025. 10AM-2PM M-F (And by appointment).

Essex Probate Court, Town Hall, 29 West Ave, Essex, CT 06426. 860-767-4347, Fax: 860-767-8509. 9AM-1PM M-F (And by appointment). Access by: mail, in person.

Haddam Probate Court, 30 Field Park Dr, Haddam, CT 06438. 860-345-8531, Fax: 860-345-3730. 10AM-3PM Tue, Wed, Thu.

Killingworth Probate Court, 323 Route 81, Killingworth, CT 06419. 860-663-2304, Fax: 860-663-3305. 9AM-Noon Mon, Wed, Fri (And by appointment). Access by: mail, in person.

Middletown Probate Court, 94 Court St, Middletown, CT 06457. 860-347-7424. 8:30AM-4:30PM M-F, 6PM-7:40PM Tue (Sept-May). Special note: District includes towns of Cornwall, Durham, Middlefield.

Old Saybrook Probate Court, 263 Main St, #105, Old Saybrook, CT 06475. 860-395-3128, Fax: 860-395-3125. 9AM-1PM M,T,TH,F. Special note: Court is open on Wed. evenings, also.

Portland Probate Court, PO Box 71, 265 Main St, Portland, CT 06480. 860-342-6739, Fax: 860-342-0001. 9AM-12PM.

Saybrook Probate Court, PO Box 628, 65 Main St, Chester, CT 06412. 860-526-0007, Fax: 860-526-0004. 9:30AM-12:30 PM T,Th and by appointment. Special note: District includes Town of Chester.

Westbrook Probate Court, PO Box 676, Westbrook, CT 06498. 860-399-5661, Fax: 860-399-9568. 1-4:30PM. Access by: mail, in person.

Middletown

Real Estate Recording—Middletown Town Clerk, 245 DeKoven Drive, Middletown, CT 6457. 860-344-3438, Fax: 860-344-3591. 8:30AM-4:30PM.

Milford

Real Estate Recording—Milford City Clerk, 70 West River Street, Milford, CT 6460. 8:30AM-5PM.

Monroe

Real Estate Recording—Monroe Town Clerk, 7 Fan Hill Road, Monroe, CT 6468. 203-452-5068, Fax: 203-261-6197. 9AM-5PM.

Montville

Real Estate Recording—Montville Town Clerk, 310 Norwich-New London Tpke. Town Hall, Uncasville, CT 6382. 860-848-0139, Fax: 860-848-1521. 9AM-5PM.

Morris

Real Estate Recording—Morris Town Clerk, 3 East Street, Morris, CT 6763. Fax: 860-567-7432. 9AM-Noon, 1-4PM.

Naugatuck

Real Estate Recording—Naugatuck Town Clerk, Town Hall, 229 Church Street, Naugatuck, CT 6770. 203-720-7046, Fax: 203-720-7099. 8:30AM-4PM.

New Britain

Real Estate Recording—New Britain Town Clerk, 27 W. Main Street, New Britain, CT 6051. 8:15AM-3:45PM M-W & F; 8:15AM-6:45PM Th.

New Canaan

Real Estate Recording—New Canaan Town Clerk, 77 Main Street, Town Hall, New Canaan, CT 6840. 203-924-8462, Fax: 203-966-0309. 8:30AM-4PM.

New Fairfield

Real Estate Recording—New Fairfield Town Clerk, Route 39, Town Hall, New Fairfield, CT 6812. 8:30AM-5PM T-F; 8:30AM-Noon Sat.

New Hartford

Real Estate Recording—New Hartford Town Clerk, 530 Main Street, Town Hall, New Hartford, CT 6057. Fax: 860-379-0940. 9AM-Noon, 12:40-4PM M,T,Th; 9AM-Noon, 1PM-6PM W; 9AM-Noon F.

New Haven

Real Estate Recording—New Haven City Clerk, 200 Orange Street, Room 202, New Haven, CT 6510. Fax: 203-946-6974. 9AM-5PM.

Felony, Civil Actions Over $2,500—Ansonia-Milford Superior Court, 14 W River St (PO Box 210), Milford, CT 06460. 203-874-0674. 9AM-4PM. Access by: mail, in person.

Superior Court, 235 Church St, New Haven, CT 06510. 203-789-7461, Fax: 203-789-6424. 9AM-4PM. Access by: mail, phone, in person. www.jud2.state.ct.us

Waterbury Superior Court, 300 Grand St, Waterbury, CT 06702. 203-579-6560, Fax: 203-596-4032. 9AM-5PM. Access by: mail, phone, fax, in person.

Misdemeanor, Eviction, Small Claims—Geographical Area Court #22, 14 W River St, Milford, CT 06460. 203-854-7737. 1-2:30PM, 4-5PM. Access by: mail, in person.

Geographical Area Court #4, 300 Grand St, Waterbury, CT 06702. 203-596-4023, Fax: 203-596-4057. 9AM-1PM; 2:30-4PM. Access by: mail, phone, in person. Special note: Misdemeanors are at 400 Grand St.

Geographical Area Court #5, 106 Elizabeth St, Derby, CT 06418. 203-734-5920. 9AM-4PM. Access by: mail, in person.

Geographical Area Court #6, 121 Elm St, New Haven, CT 06510. 203-783-3205, Fax: 203-789-6455. 9AM-5PM. Access by: mail, in person.

Geographical Area Court #7, 54 W Main St, Meriden, CT 06450. Fax: 203-238-6322. 9AM-5PM. Access by: mail, phone, in person.

Civil Actions Over $2,500—New Haven Superior Court-Meriden, 54 W Main St, Meriden, CT 06451. 203-207-8600. 9AM-4PM. Access by: mail, in person.

Probate—Bethany Probate Court, Town Hall, 40 Peck Rd, Bethany, CT 06524. 203-389-3414, Fax: 203-393-0821. 9AM-Noon T;TH.

Branford Probate Court, PO Box 638, 1019 Main St, Branford, CT 06405-0638. 203-468-3895, Fax: 203-315-4715. 9AM-Noon, 1-4:30PM. Access by: mail, phone, fax, in person.

Cheshire Probate Court, 84 S Main St, Cheshire, CT 06410-3193. 203-270-4280, Fax: 203-271-6664. 8:30AM-12:30PM, 1:30PM-4PM. Access by: mail, in person. Special note: District includes town of Prospect. On Fridays, they close at 12:30.

Derby Probate Court, 253 main St, Ansonia, CT 06401. 203-729-4571, Fax: 203-734-0922. 9AM-5:30PM M-TH. Special note: District includes towns of Ansonia, Seymour.

East Haven Probate Court, 250 Main St, East Haven, CT 06512. 203-453-8007. 9AM-4PM, except 1PM on Fri.

Guilford Probate Court, Town Hall, Park St, Guilford, CT 06437. 203-452-5433, Fax: 203-453-8017. 9AM-Noon,1-4PM M,T,Th,F; 9AM-Noon W. Access by: mail, in person.

Madison Probate Court, PO Box 205, Town Hall, 8 Campus Dr, Madison, CT 06443. 203-239-5321, Fax: 203-245-5653. 9AM-3PM M-F (And by appointment).

Meriden Probate Court, City Hall, E Main St, Meriden, CT 06450. 203-622-3766, Fax: 203-630-4043. 8:30AM-7PM M; 8:30-4:30 T-F. Access by: in person.

Milford Probate Court, 70 W River St, PO Box 414, Parsons Office Complex, Milford, CT 06460. 203-775-3700, Fax: 203-876-1960. 9AM-5PM. Access by: mail, in person.

Naugatuck Probate Court, Town Hall, 229 Church St, Naugatuck, CT 06770. 203-656-7342. 9AM-4PM. Access by: mail, in person. Special note: District includes Town of Beacon Falls.

New Haven Probate Court, PO Box 905, 200 Orange St, 1st Floor, New Haven, CT 06504. 203-938-2326, Fax: 203-946-5962. 9AM-4PM. Access by: mail.

North Branford Probate Court, PO Box 214, 1599 Foxon Rd, North Branford, CT 06471. 203-312-5627. 9AM-12PM.

North Haven Probate Court, 18 Church St, North Haven, CT 06473. 203-238-6666, Fax: 203-239-1874. 8:30AM-4:30PM M-Th.

Orange Probate Court, 525 Orange Center Rd, Orange, CT 06477. 203-888-2543, Fax: 203-891-2161. 9AM-12PM.

Oxford Probate Court, c/o Town Hall, 486 Oxford Rd, Oxford, CT 06478. 203-888-0581, Fax: 203-888-2136. 7AM-9PM Mon, 1-5PM Tue & Wed, 9AM-5PM, 7-9PM Thu. Access by: mail, in person.

Southbury Probate Court, Townhall Annex, 421 Main St South, PO Box 674, Southbury, CT 06488. 203-256-3041, Fax: 203-264-9310. 9AM-4:30PM M-F (And by appointment). Access by: mail, in person.

Wallingford Probate Court, 45 S Main St, Wallingford, CT 06492. 203-271-6608, Fax: 203-294-2073. 9AM-5PM.

Waterbury Probate Court, 236 Grand St Chase Bldg, Waterbury, CT 06702. 203-735-7438, Fax: 203-597-0824. 9AM-4:45PM MTWF, 9AM-6PM Thu, 9AM-Noon Sat. Special note: District includes towns of Middlebury, Wolcott.

West Haven Probate Court, PO Box 127, 355 Main St, West Haven, CT 06516. 203-927-2340, Fax: 203-937-3556. 9AM-Noon, 1-4PM; closed 2nd Th of the month.

Woodbridge Probate Court, Town Hall, 11 Meetinghouse Ln, Woodbridge, CT 06525. 203-387-2530, Fax: 203-289-3480. 3-7PM M, 9AM-1PM W.

New London

Real Estate Recording—New London City Clerk, 181 State Street, New London, CT 6320. 860-447-5209, Fax: 860-447-1644. 8:30AM-4PM.

Felony, Civil Actions Over $2,500—New London Superior Court, 70 Huntington St, New London, CT 06320. 860-443-5363. 9AM-5PM. Access by: mail, in person.

Misdemeanor, Eviction, Small Claims—Geographical Area Court #10, 112 Broad St, New London, CT 06320. 860-443-8343. 9AM-5PM. Access by: mail, in person.

Geographical Area Court #21, 1 Courthouse Sq, Norwich, CT 06360. 860-889-7338. 1-2:30PM, 4-5PM. Access by: mail, in person. www.jud.state.ct.us

Civil Actions Over $2,500—Norwich Superior Court, 1 Courthouse Square, Norwich, CT 06360. 860-887-3515, Fax: 860-885-0509. 9AM-5PM. Access by: mail, phone, in person.

Probate—Bozrah Probate Court, Town Hall, One River Rd, Bozrah, CT 06334. 860-889-2958, Fax: 860-887-7571. 10AM-1PM M & W or by appointment.

Colchester Probate Court, Town Hall, 127 Norwich Ave, Colchester, CT 06415. 860-537-7290, Fax: 860-537-0547. 12:30PM-4:30PM M,T,Th,F; 9AM-1PM W (And by appointment). Access by: mail, in person.

East Lyme Probate Court, PO Box 519, 108 Pennsylvania Ave, Niantic, CT 06357. 860-739-6931, Fax: 860-739-6930. 8:30AM-12:30PM.

Griswold Probate Court, Town Hall, 32 School St, Jewett City, CT 06351. 860-376-0216, Fax: 860-376-0216. 5PM-12PM M; 1PM-4PM T-F.

Lebanon Probate Court, Town Hall, 579 Exeter Rd, Lebanon, CT 06249. 860-642-7429, Fax: 860-642-7716. 10AM-Noon, 1:30-4PM T; 4-6PM Th; 10AM-Noon F(And by appt).

Ledyard Probate Court, 741 Col Led Hwy, Ledyard, CT 06339. 860-464-8740, Fax: 860-464-1126. 9:30AM-12:30PM M-F (And by appointment). Access by: mail, in person.

Lyme Probate Court, Town Hall, 480 Hamburg Rd, Lyme, CT 06371. 860-434-7733, Fax: 860-434-2989. 9AM-1PM M-F (And by appointment).

Montville Probate Court, 310 Norwich-New London Turnpike, Uncasville, CT 06382. 860-848-9847, Fax: 860-848-4534. 9AM-1PM M,T,Th,F, 9AM-4:30PM W. Access by: mail, in person.

New London Probate Court, 181 Captain's Walk Municipal Bldg, PO Box 148, New London, CT 06320. 860-443-7121, Fax: 860-437-8155. 9AM-4PM. Special note: District includes Town of Waterford.

North Stonington Probate Court, PO Box 204, North Stonington, CT 06359. 860-535-8441, Fax: 860-535-8441. 9AM-Noon M & W; 1-4PM T,Th & F.

Norwich Probate Court, PO Box 38, City Hall, Norwich, CT 06360. 860-887-2160, Fax: 860-887-2401. 9AM-4:30PM. Access by: mail, in person. Special note: District includes Towns of Franklin, Lisbon, Preston, Sprague, Voluntown.

Old Lyme Probate Court, PO Box 273, 52 Lyme St, Old Lyme, CT 06371. 860-434-1406, Fax: 860-434-9283. 9AM-Noon, 1-4PM. Access by: mail, in person.

Salem Probate Court, 270 Hartford Rd, Salem, CT 06420-3809. 860-859-3873, Fax: 860-443-5160. By appointment.

Stonington Probate Court, PO Box 312, 152 Elm St, Stonington, CT 06378. 860-535-5090, Fax: 860-535-0520. 9AM-Noon, 1-4PM. Special note: District includes Town of Mystic.

New Milford

Real Estate Recording—New Milford Town Clerk, 18 Church Street, New Milford, CT 6776. Fax: 860-355-6002. 9AM-5PM.

Newington

Real Estate Recording—Newington Town Clerk, 131 Cedar Street, Newington, CT 6111. 8:30AM-4:30PM.

Newtown

Real Estate Recording—Newtown Town Clerk, 45 Main Street, Newtown, CT 6470. 8AM-4:30PM.

Norfolk

Real Estate Recording—Norfolk Town Clerk, 19 Maple Avenue, Norfolk, CT 6058. 9AM-Noon,1-4PM.

North Branford

Real Estate Recording—North Branford Town Clerk, 1599 Foxon Road, North Branford, CT 6471. 8:30AM-4:30PM.

North Canaan

Real Estate Recording—North Canaan Town Clerk, 100 Pease Street, Town Hall, North Canaan, CT 6018. Fax: 860-824-3139. 9:30AM-Noon, 1-4PM.

North Haven

Real Estate Recording—North Haven Town Clerk, 18 Church Street, Town Hall, North Haven, CT 6473. 8:30AM-4:30PM.

North Stonington

Real Estate Recording—North Stonington Town Clerk, 40 Main Street, North Stonington, CT 6359. 860-535-0793, Fax: 860-535-4554. 9AM-4PM.

Norwalk

Real Estate Recording—Norwalk Town Clerk, 125 East Avenue, City Hall, Norwalk, CT 6851. 8:30AM-5PM.

Norwich

Real Estate Recording—Norwich City Clerk, 100 Broadway, City Hall, Room 214, Norwich, CT 6360. Fax: 860-823-3790. 8:30AM-4:30PM.

Old Lyme

Real Estate Recording—Old Lyme Town Clerk, 52 Lyme Street, Town Hall, Old Lyme, CT 6371. 860-434-5003, Fax: 860-434-9283. 9AM-Noon,1-4PM.

Old Saybrook

Real Estate Recording—Old Saybrook Town Clerk, 302 Main Street, Old Saybrook, CT 6475. 860-395-3132, Fax: 860-395-5014. 8:30AM-4:30PM.

Orange

Real Estate Recording—Orange Town Clerk, Town Hall, 617 Orange Center Rd. Orange, CT 6477. Fax: 203-891-2185. 8:30AM-4:30PM.

Oxford

Real Estate Recording—Oxford Town Clerk, 486 Oxford Road, Oxford, CT 6478. 9AM-5PM M-Th; 7-9PM Mon & Th.

Plainfield

Real Estate Recording—Plainfield Town Clerk, 8 Community Avenue, Town Hall, Plainfield, CT 6374. 8:30AM-4:30PM M,T,W; 8:30AM-6:30PM Th; 8:30AM-1PM F.

Plainville

Real Estate Recording—Plainville Town Clerk, 1 Central Square, Municipal Center, Plainville, CT 6062. 8:30AM-4:30PM.

Plymouth

Real Estate Recording—Plymouth Town Clerk, 80 Main Street, Town Hall, Terryville, CT 6786. Fax: 860-585-4015. 8:30-4:30PM.

Pomfret

Real Estate Recording—Pomfret Town Clerk, 5 Haven Road, Pomfret Center, CT 6259. Fax: 860-974-3950. 9AM-4PM.

Portland

Real Estate Recording—Portland Town Clerk, 265 Main Street, Portland, CT 6480. Fax: 860-342-0001. 9AM-4:30PM.

Preston

Real Estate Recording—Preston Town Clerk, 389 Route 2, Town Hall, Preston, CT 6365. Fax: 860-885-1905. 9AM-Noon, 12:30PM-4:30PM T-F; Th until 7:30.

Prospect

Real Estate Recording—Prospect Town Clerk, 36 Center Street, Prospect, CT 6712. Fax: 203-758-4466. 9AM-4PM.

Putnam

Real Estate Recording—Putnam Town Clerk, 126 Church Street, Putnam, CT 6260. Fax: 860-963-2001. 8:30AM-Noon,1-4:30PM.

Redding

Real Estate Recording—Redding Town Clerk, Route 107, 100 Hill Rd. Town Office Building, Redding, CT 6875. Fax: 203-938-8816. 9AM-4:30PM.

Ridgefield

Real Estate Recording—Ridgefield Town Clerk, 400 Main Street, Ridgefield, CT 6877. Fax: 203-431-2722. 8:30AM-4:30PM.

Rocky Hill

Real Estate Recording—Rocky Hill Town Clerk, 699 Old Main Street, Rocky Hill, CT 6067. 8:30AM-4:30PM.

Roxbury

Real Estate Recording—Roxbury Town Clerk, 29 North St. Roxbury, CT 6783. Fax: 860-354-0560. 9AM-Noon, 1-4PM T & Th; 9AM-Noon F.

Salem

Real Estate Recording—Salem Town Clerk, Town Office Building, 270 Hartford Road, Salem, CT 6420. Fax: 860-859-1184. 8AM-4PM.

Salisbury

Real Estate Recording—Salisbury Town Clerk, 27 Main Street, Town Hall, Salisbury, CT 6068. 860-435-9140, Fax: 860-435-5172. 9AM-4PM.

Scotland

Real Estate Recording—Scotland Town Clerk, 9 Devotion Rd. Town Hall, Scotland, CT 6264. Fax: 860-423-3666. 9AM-3PM M,T,Th,; Noon-8PM W; Closed Friday.

Seymour

Real Estate Recording—Seymour Town Clerk, 1 First Street, Town Hall, Seymour, CT 6483. 203-877-4293. 9AM-5PM (No Recording after 4:15PM).

Sharon

Real Estate Recording—Sharon Town Clerk, 63 Main Street, Town Hall, Sharon, CT 6069. Fax: 860-364-5789. 9:00AM-Noon, 1-4PM.

Shelton

Real Estate Recording—Shelton City Clerk, 54 Hill Street, Shelton, CT 6484. Fax: 203-924-1721. 8AM-5:30PM.

Sherman

Real Estate Recording—Sherman Town Clerk, 9 Route 39 North, Town Hall, Sherman, CT 6784. Fax: 860-350-5041. 9AM-Noon, 1-4PM T,W,Th,F; 9AM-Noon Sat.

Simsbury

Real Estate Recording—Simsbury Town Clerk, 933 Hopmeadow Street, Simsbury, CT 6070. Fax: 860-658-3206. 8:30AM-4:30PM.

Somers

Real Estate Recording—Somers Town Clerk, 600 Main Street, Somers, CT 6071. Fax: 860-763-8228. 8:30AM-4:30PM M-W,F; 8:30AM-7PM Th.

South Windsor

Real Estate Recording—South Windsor Town Clerk, 1540 Sullivan Avenue, South Windsor, CT 6074. Fax: 860-644-3781. 8AM-4:30PM.

Southbury

Real Estate Recording—Southbury Town Clerk, 501 Main Street South, Southbury, CT 6488. Fax: 203-264-9762. 8:30AM-4:30PM.

Southington

Real Estate Recording—Southington Town Clerk, 75 Main Street, Town Office Building, Southington, CT 6489. Fax: 860-628-8669. 8:30AM-4:30PM.

Sprague

Real Estate Recording—Sprague Town Clerk, 1 Main Street, Baltic, CT 6330. Fax: 860-822-3013. 8:30AM-4PM M-F (Th Open Until 6:30PM).

Stafford

Real Estate Recording—Stafford Town Clerk, Warren Memorial Town Hall, 1 Main St. Stafford Springs, CT 6076. 8:15AM-4PM M-W; 8:15AM-6:30PM Th; 8AM-Noon F.

Stamford

Real Estate Recording—Stamford City Clerk, 888 Washington Blvd, Stamford, CT 6901. 203-972-7500, Fax: 203-977-4943. 8:30AM-4:30PM (July,August 8AM-4PM).

Sterling

Real Estate Recording—Sterling Town Clerk, 1114 Plainfield Pike, Oneco, CT 6373. Fax: 860-564-1660. 8:30AM-3:30PM.

Stonington

Real Estate Recording—Stonington Town Clerk, 152 Elm Street, Stonington, CT 6378. Fax: 860-535-1046. 8:30AM-4PM.

Stratford

Real Estate Recording—Stratford Town Clerk, 2725 Main Street, Room 101, Stratford, CT 6497. Fax: 203-385-4108. 8AM-4:30PM.

Suffield

Real Estate Recording—Suffield Town Clerk, 83 Mountain Road, Town Hall, Suffield, CT 6078. Fax: 860-668-3898. 8:30AM-4:30PM; Summer: 8AM-4:30PM M-Th; 8AM-1PM F.

Thomaston

Real Estate Recording—Thomaston Town Clerk, 158 Main Street, Thomaston, CT 6787. 860-283-9678, Fax: 860-283-1013. 9AM-4:30PM.

Thompson

Real Estate Recording—Thompson Town Clerk, 815 Riverside Drive, No. Grosvenor Dale, CT 6255. Fax: 860-923-3836. 9AM-5PM.

Tolland

Real Estate Recording—Tolland Town Clerk, Hicks Memorial Municipal Center, 21 Tolland Green, Tolland, CT 6084. 9AM-4:30PM M,T,W,Th; 9AM-12:30PM F; (Th open 5:30-8:30PM).

Felony—Tolland Superior Court-Criminal Branch, 20 Park St, Vernon, CT 06066. 860-870-3200. 9AM-5PM. Access by: mail, in person. Special note: The address can use either Rockville or Vernon, but the US Posatl Service will sometimes return mail addressed to Rockville.

Civil Actions Over $2,500—Tolland Superior Court-Civil Branch, 69 Brooklyn St, Rockville, CT 06066. 860-875-6294. 9AM-5PM. Access by: mail, in person.

Misdemeanor—Geographical Area Court #19, PO Box 980, 20 Park St, Vernon, CT 06066-0980. 860-870-3200. 9AM-4PM. Access by: mail, in person.

Probate—Andover Probate Court, 222 Bolton Center Rd, Bolton, CT 06043. 860-647-7979, Fax: 860-649-3187. 9AM-4PM M & W; 9AM-3PM F. Access by: mail, in person. Special note: District includes towns of Andover, Bolton and Columbia.

Ashford Probate Court, 20 Pompey Hollow Rd, PO Box 61, Ashford, CT 06278. 860-429-4986. 1AM-3:30PM Thu (and by appointment).

Coventry Probate Court, Town Hall, 1712 Main St, Coventry, CT 06238. 860-742-6791, Fax: 860-742-5570. 9AM-Noon W,Th; 7:30PM-9PM Tue. Access by: mail, in person.

Ellington Probate Court, PO Box 268, 14 Park Place, Rockville, CT 06066. 860-872-0519, Fax: 860-870-5140. 8:30-4:30 M,W,F; 8:30-7PM TH; 8:30-1PM F. Special note: District includes Town of Vernon.

Hebron Probate Court, 15 Gilead Rd, Hebron, CT 06248. 860-228-5971, Fax: 860-228-4859. 8AM-4PM Tu, 4PM-6PM Th.

Mansfield Probate Court, 4 South Eagleville Rd, Storrs, CT 06268. 860-429-3313, Fax: 860-429-6863. 2-5PM T,W; 3-5PM Th or by appointment. Access by: mail, in person.

Somers Probate Court, PO Box 63, Stafford Springs, CT 06076-0063. 860-763-8212, Fax: 860-763-0973. 9AM-1PM Tue & Thu (and by appointment). Special note: The Sommers Probate Court merged with the Stafford Probate Court on 1-6-99.

Stafford Probate Court, PO Box 63, Main St, Stafford Springs, CT 06076. 860-684-3423, Fax: 860-684-7173. 9AM-Noon, 1-4:30PM M; 9AM-Noon Tue-Fri. Special note: District includes towns of Union and Somers.

Tolland Probate Court, 21 Tolland Green, Tolland, CT 06084. 860-871-3640, Fax: 860-871-3641. 9AM-12:30 M,W&F; 5:30-8:30PM Th. Special note: District includes Town of Willington.

Torrington

Real Estate Recording—Torrington City Clerk, 140 Main Street, City Hall, Torrington, CT 6790. Fax: 860-489-2548. 8AM-4:30PM.

Trumbull

Real Estate Recording—Trumbull Town Clerk, 5866 Main Street, Trumbull, CT 6611. 203-431-2776, Fax: 203-452-5038. 9AM-5PM.

Union

Real Estate Recording—Union Town Clerk, 1043 Buckley Highway, Route 171, Union, CT 6076. Fax: 860-684-8830. 9AM-Noon T,Th; 9AM-Noon, 1-3PM W.

Vernon

Real Estate Recording—Vernon Town Clerk, 14 Park Place, Rockville, CT 6066. 8:30AM-4:30PM M-W; 8:30AM-7PM Th; 8:30AM-1PM F.

Voluntown

Real Estate Recording—Voluntown Town Clerk, 115 Main Street, Town Hall, Voluntown, CT 6384. Fax: 860-376-3295. 9AM-2PM; 6-8PM T Evening.

Wallingford

Real Estate Recording—Wallingford Town Clerk, 45 South Main Street, Municipal Building, Room 108, Wallingford, CT 6492. Fax: 203-294-2073. 9AM-5PM.

Warren

Real Estate Recording—Warren Town Clerk, 7 Sackett Hill Road, Town Hall, Warren, CT 6754. Fax: 860-868-0090. 10AM-4PM W,Th; 10AM-Noon M,F.

Washington

Real Estate Recording—Washington Town Clerk, 2 Bryan Plaza, Washington Depot, CT 6794. Fax: 860-868-3103. 9AM-Noon, 1-4:45PM.

Waterbury

Real Estate Recording—Waterbury Town Clerk, 235 Grand Street, City Hall, Waterbury, CT 6702. Fax: 203-574-6887. 8:30AM-4:50PM.

Waterford

Real Estate Recording—Waterford Town Clerk, 15 Rope Ferry Road, Waterford, CT 6385. Fax: 860-437-0352. 8AM-4PM.

Watertown

Real Estate Recording—Watertown Town Clerk, 37 DeForest Street, Watertown, CT 6795. 9AM-5PM.

West Hartford

Real Estate Recording—West Hartford Town Clerk, 50 South Main Street, Room 313 Town Hall Common, West Hartford, CT 6107. Fax: 860-523-3522. 8:30AM-4:30PM.

West Haven

Real Estate Recording—West Haven City Clerk, 355 Main Street, West Haven, CT 6516. Fax: 203-937-3706. 9AM-5PM.

Westbrook

Real Estate Recording—Westbrook Town Clerk, 1163 Boston Post Road, Westbrook, CT 6498. Fax: 860-399-9568. 9AM-4PM M-W & F; 9AM-6PM Th.

Weston

Real Estate Recording—Weston Town Clerk, 56 Norfield Road, Weston, CT 6883. Fax: 203-222-8871. 9AM-4:30PM.

Westport

Real Estate Recording—Westport Town Clerk, 110 Myrtle Avenue, Room 105, Westport, CT 6880. Fax: 203-341-1112. 8:30AM-4:30PM.

Wethersfield

Real Estate Recording—Wethersfield Town Clerk, 505 Silas Deane Highway, Wethersfield, CT 6109. 860-721-2861, Fax: 860-721-2994. 8AM-4:30PM.

Willington

Real Estate Recording—Willington Town Clerk-UCC Recorder, 40 Old Farms Road, Willington, CT 6279. Fax: 860-429-8415. 9AM-2PM (M open 6-8PM).

Wilton

Real Estate Recording—Wilton Town Clerk, 238 Danbury Road, Wilton, CT 6897. Fax: 203-563-0299. 8:30AM-4:30PM, Memorial Day to Labor Day; 9AM-5PM.

Winchester

Real Estate Recording—Winchester Town Clerk, 338 Main Street, Town Hall, Winsted, CT 6098. Fax: 860-738-7053. 8AM-4PM.

Windham

Real Estate Recording—Windham Town Clerk, 979 Main Street, Willimantic, CT 6226. Fax: 860-465-3012. 8AM-5PM M-W; 8AM-7:30PM Th; 8AM-Noon F.

Felony, Civil Actions Over $2,500—Windham Superior Court, 155 Church St, Putnam, CT 06260. 860-928-7749, Fax: 860-928-7076. 9AM-5PM. Access by: mail, phone, in person.

Misdemeanor, Eviction, Small Claims—Geographical Area Court #11, 120 School St #110, Danielson, CT 06239-3024. 860-774-8516, Fax: 860-774-1209. 9AM-4PM. Access by: mail, phone, in person.

Probate—Brooklyn Probate Court, Town Hall, 4 WOlf Den Rd, PO Box 356, Brooklyn, CT 06234-0356. 860-774-5973, Fax: 860-779-3744. 11:30AM-4:30PM T, (And by appointment).

Canterbury Probate Court, 43 Maple Lane, Canterbury, CT 06331. 860-546-9605, Fax: 860-546-9693. 8AM-4:30PM Wed (And by appointment, evenings).

Chaplin Probate Court, c/o Eastford Probate District, PO Box 61, Ashford, CT 06278-0061. 860-974-1885, Fax: 860-974-0624.

Eastford Probate Court, PO Box 61, Ashford, CT 06278-0061. 860-974-1885, Fax: 860-974-0624. 10AM-12PM Wed (And by appointment).

Hampton Probate Court, Town Hall, 164 Main St, Hampton, CT 06247. 860-455-9132. 9:30AM-12PM Thu (And by appointment).

Killingly Probate Court, 172 Main St, Danielson, CT 06239. 860-774-8601, Fax: 860-774-5811. 1-4:30PM. Access by: mail, in person.

Plainfield Probate Court, Town Hall, 8 Community Ave, Plainfield, CT 06374. 860-564-0019, Fax: 860-564-0612. 8:30-3:30PM M-Th; 8:30AM-12PM. Access by: mail, in person.

Pomfret Probate Court, 5 Haven Rd, Pomfret Center, CT 06259. 860-974-0186, Fax: 860-974-3950. 10AM-4PM Tue-Thu (And by appointment).

Putnam Probate Court, Town Hall, 126 Church St, Putnam, CT 06260. 860-963-6868, Fax: 860-963-6814. 9AM-Noon M-Th. Access by: mail, in person.

Sterling Probate Court, 1114 Plainfield Pike, PO Box 157, Oneco, CT 06373. 860-564-8488, Fax: 860-564-1660. 8:30AM-3:30PM.

Thompson Probate Court, 815 Riverside Dr, Town Hall, PO Box 74, North Grosvenordale, CT 06255. 860-923-2203, Fax: 860-923-3836. 9AM-Noon M-F (And by Appointment).

Windham Probate Court, PO Box 34, 979 Main St, Willimantic, CT 06226. 860-465-3049, Fax: 860-465-3012. 9AM-1PM M-Th; 9AM-Noon F. Access by: mail. Special note: District includes Town of Scottland.

Woodstock Probate Court, 415 Route 169, Woodstock, CT 06281. 860-928-2223, Fax: 860-963-7557. 3PM-6PM Wed, 1:30PM-4:30PM Thu (And by appointment). Access by: in person.

Windsor

Real Estate Recording—Windsor Town Clerk, 275 Broad Street, Windsor, CT 6095. Fax: 860-285-1909. 8AM-5PM M,W-F; 8AM-8PM T.

Windsor Locks

Real Estate Recording—Windsor Locks Town Clerk, 50 Church Street, Town Office Building, Windsor Locks, CT 6096. 8AM-4PM M-W; 8AM-6PM Th; 8AM-1PM F.

Wolcott

Real Estate Recording—Wolcott Town Clerk, 10 Kenea Avenue, Town Hall, Wolcott, CT 6716. 9AM-4:30PM (Recording until 4PM).

Woodbridge

Real Estate Recording—Woodbridge Town Clerk, 11 Meetinghouse Lane, Woodbridge, CT 6525. 203-389-3410, Fax: 203-389-3480. 8:30AM-4PM.

Woodbury

Real Estate Recording—Woodbury Town Clerk, 275 Main Street South, Woodbury, CT 6798. Fax: 203-263-4755. 8:30AM-4:30PM (Summer Hours 8AM-4PM).

Woodstock

Real Estate Recording—Woodstock Town Clerk, Town Office Building, 415 Route 169, Woodstock, CT 6281. Fax: 860-963-7557. 8:30AM-4:30PM M,T,Th; 8:30AM-6PM W; 8:30AM-3PM F.

Federal Courts

US District Court

Bridgeport Division Office of the clerk, Room 400, 915 Lafayette Blvd, Bridgeport, CT 06604203-579-5861 Counties: Fairfield (prior to 1993). Since January 1993, cases from any county may be assigned to any of the divisions in the district.
Hartford Division 450 Main St, Hartford, CT 06103860-240-3200 Counties: Hartford, Tolland, Windham (prior to 1993). Since 1993, cases from any county may be assigned to any of the divisions in the district.
New Haven Division 141 Church St, New Haven, CT 06510203-773-2140 Counties: Litchfield, Middlesex, New Haven, New London (prior to 1993). Since 1993, cases from any county may be assigned to any of the divisions in the district.
Waterbury Division c/o New Haven Division, 141 Church St, New Haven, CT 06510203-773-2140 Counties: New Haven (prior to 1993). Since 1993, cases from any county may be assigned to any of the divisions in the districtAfter 1993, this office was closed and all records sent to the Federal Records Facility.

US Bankruptcy Court

Bridgeport Division 915 Lafayette Blvd, Bridgeport, CT 06604203-579-5808, Record Room: 203-579-5808 Counties: Fairfield.
Hartford Division 450 Main St, Hartford, CT 06103860-240-3675 Counties: Hartford, Litchfield, Middlesex, Tolland, Windham.
New Haven Division The Connecticut Financial Center, 157 Church St, 18th Floor, New Haven, CT 06510203-773-2009 Counties: New Haven, New London.

Delaware

Attorney General's Office
820 N French St, 7th floor   302-577-3047
Wilmington, DE 19801   Fax: 302-577-3090
www.state.de.us

Governor's Office
820 N. French St, Carvel State Bldg   302-577-3210
Wilmington, DE 19801   Fax: 302-577-3118
www.state.de.us

State Archives
121 Duke of York St   302-739-5318
Dover, DE 19901   Fax: 302-739-2578
www.state.de.us

Capital: Dover

Kent County

Time Zone: EST

Number of Counties: 3

Population: 731,581

Web Site: www.state.de.us

Search Unclaimed Property Online

http://www.state.de.us/revenue
/escheat/escheat.htm

State Agencies

Criminal Records
Delaware State Police Headquarters, Criminal Records Section, PO Box 430, Dover, DE 19903-0430 (1407 N Dupont Highway, Dover, DE 19930); 302-739-5880; Fax: 302-739-5888; 8AM-4PM. Access by: mail.

Corporation Records
Limited Partnership Records
Trademarks/Servicemarks
Limited Liability Company Records
Assumed Name
Secretary of State, Division of Corporations, PO Box 898, Dover, DE 19903 (John G Townsend Bldg, 401 Federal Street #4, Dover, DE 19901); 302-739-3073; Fax: 302-739-3812; 8AM-4:30PM. Access by: mail, phone, in person. www.state.de.us/corp

Sales Tax Registrations
Finance Department, Revenue Division, PO Box 8911, Wilmington, DE 19899-8911 (Carvel State Office Bldg, 820 N French St, 8th Fl, Wilmington, DE 19801); 302-577-8450; Fax: 302-577-8656; 8AM-4:30PM. Access by: mail, phone, in person. www.state.de.us/govern/agencies/revenue/revenue.htm

Uniform Commercial Code
Federal Tax Liens
UCC Division, Secretary of State, PO Box 793, Dover, DE 19903 (Townsend Bldg, 401 Federal Street, Dover, DE 19901); 302-739-3077; Fax: 302-739-3813; 8:30AM-4:30PM. Access by: mail. www.state.de.us/corp/ucc.htm

State Tax Liens
Records not available from state agency.

Records are at the county level.

Workers' Compensation Records
Labor Department, Industrial Accident Board, 4425 N Market Street, Wilmington, DE 19802; 302-761-8200; Fax: 302-761-6601; 8AM-4:30PM. Access by: mail, phone, in person.

Birth Certificates
Department of Health, Office of Vital Statistics, PO Box 637, Dover, DE 19903 (William Penn & Federal Sts, Jesse Cooper Bldg, Dover, DE 19901); 302-739-4721; 8AM-4:30PM (Counter closes at 4:20 PM). Access by: mail, phone, in person.

Death Records

Department of Health, Office of Vital Statistics, PO Box 637, Dover, DE 19903; 302-739-4721; 8AM-4:30PM. Access by: mail, phone, in person.

Marriage Certificates

Department of Health, Office of Vital Statistics, PO Box 637, Dover, DE 19903; 302-739-4721; 8AM-4:30PM. Access by: mail, phone, in person.

Divorce Records

Records not available from state agency.

Divorce records are found at county of issue. Records prior to 1975 are held by the agency granting the decree and from 1976 are held by the Family Court granting the decree.

Accident Reports

Delaware State Police Traffic Section, Accident Records, PO Box 430, Dover, DE 19903 (1441 N Dupont Hwy, Dover, DE 19903); 302-739-5931; Fax: 302-739-5982; 8AM-4PM. Access by: mail.

Driver Records

Division of Motor Vehicles, Driver Services, PO Box 698, Dover, DE 19903 (303 Transportation Circle, Dover, DE 19901); 302-739-4343; Fax: 302-739-2602; 8AM-4:30PM M-T-TH-F; 12:00PM-8PM W. Access by: mail, online.

Vehicle Ownership
Vehicle Identification

Division of Motor Vehicles, Correspondence Section, PO Box 698, Dover, DE 19903 (303 Transportation Circle, Dover, DE 19901); 302-739-3147; Fax: 302-739-2042; 8:30AM-4:30PM M-T-TH-F; 12-8PM W. Access by: mail, online.

Boat & Vessel Ownership
Boat & Vessel Registration

Dept of Natural Resources & Environmental Control, 89 Kings Highway, Dover, DE 19901; 302-739-4431; Fax: 302-739-6157; 8AM-4:30PM. www.dnrec.state.de.us

Legislation-Current/Pending
Legislation-Passed

Delaware General Assembly, Legislative Avenue, Legislative Hall - D580D, Dover, DE 19903; 302-739-4114, 302-739-5318 Archives for old bills; 8AM-4:30PM. Access by: mail, phone, in person.

Voter Registration

Commissioner of Elections, 32 Lockerman Sq, M-101, Dover, DE 19904; 302-739-4277; 8AM-4:30PM.

GED Certificates

Department of Education, GED Testing, PO Box 1402, Dover, DE 19903; 302-739-3743; Fax: 302-739-2770;. Access by: mail.

Hunting License Information
Fishing License Information

Restricted access.

Records are not on a computerized database, but kept on paper in boxes. Records may be rviewed, but research would be very tedious.

Natural Resources & Environmental Control Dept, Divsion of Fish & Wildlife, 89 Kings Hwy, Dover, DE 19901; 302-739-5296; Fax: 302-739-6157; 8AM-4:30PM Access by: mail, phone, in person.

www.dnrec.state.de.us/fw/fwwel.htm

County Courts & Recording Offices

About the Courts...

Administration

Administrative Office of the Courts   302-577-2480
PO Box 8911   Fax: 302-577-3139
Wilmington, DE 19899
www.state.de.us/dejudic.htm

Court Structure

Superior Courts have jurisdiction over felonies and all drug offenses, the Court of Common Pleas has jurisdiction over all misdemeanors except those involving drug offenses. The Common Pleas courts handle some minor felonies as defined in state statutes. Court of Chancery handles corporation and equity matters as well as probate and estates. Guardianships are handled by the Register of Wills, corporate matters such as equity disputes and injunctions are handled by the Clerk of Chancery.

The Municipal Court of Wilmington merged with the Court of Common Pleas in New Castle in May 1998.

Searching Hints

Effective 1/15/95, the civil case limit of the Justice of the Peace Courts increased from $5,000 to $15,000; the Courts of Common Pleas' limit went from $15,000 to $50,000.

Criminal histories are available with a signed release from the offender at the State Bu-reau of Identification in Dover DE. For information on criminal history retrieval re-quirements, call 302-739-5880.

Online Access

An online system called CLAD, developed by Mead Data Central and the New Castle Superior Court, is currently available in Delaware. CLAD contains only toxic waste, asbestos, and class action cases; however, based on CLAD's success, Delaware may pursue development of online availability of other public records by working in conjunction with private information resource enterprises.

About the Recording Offices...

Organization

Delaware has 3 counties and 3 recording offices. The recording officer is County Recorder in both jurisdictions. Delaware is in the Eastern Time Zone (EST).

UCC Records

Financing statements are filed at the state level, except for real estate related collateral, which are filed only with the County Recorder. All counties perform UCC searches. Copy and certification fees vary.

Lien Records

Federal tax liens on personal property of businesses are filed with the Secretary of State. Other federal and all state tax liens on personal property are filed with the County Recorder. Copy and certification fees vary.

Real Estate Records

Counties do not perform real estate searches.

County Courts & Recording Offices

Kent

Real Estate Recording—Kent County Recorder of Deeds, County Administration Bldg. Room 218, 414 Federal St. Dover, DE 19901. 302-995-8646, Fax: 302-736-2035. 8:30AM-4:30PM.

Civil, Probate—Chancery Court, 38 The Green, Dover, DE 19901. 303-214-4000, Fax: 302-736-2244. 8:30AM-4:30PM. Access by: mail, in person.

Felony, Misdemeanor, Civil Actions Over $50,000—Superior Court, Office of Prothonotary, 38 The Green, Dover, DE 19901. 303-271-6267, Fax: 302-739-6717. 8AM-5PM. Access by: mail, in person.

Misdemeanor, Civil Actions Under $50,000—Court of Common Pleas, 38 The Green, Dover, DE 19901. 303-569-3273, Fax: 302-739-4501. 8:30AM-4:30PM. Access by: mail, in person.

Civil Actions Under $15,000, Eviction, Small Claims—Dover Justice of the Peace, 480 Bank Lane, Dover, DE 19904. 303-441-3750, Fax: 302-739-6797. 8AM-4PM. Access by: mail, in person.

Misdemeanor—Dover Justice of the Peace, 480 Bank Lane, Dover, DE 19903. 303-569-3251, Fax: 302-739-6797. Open 24 hours. Access by: mail, fax, in person.

Harrington Justice of the Peace #6, 17111 South DuPont Hwy, Harrington, DE 19952. 302-736-2242. 8AM-4PM. Access by: mail, in person.

Smyrna Justice of the Peace, 100 Monrovia Ave, Smyrna, DE 19977. 302-995-8640, Fax: 302-653-2888. 8AM-4PM. Access by: mail, phone, in person.

New Castle

Real Estate Recording—New Castle County Recorder of Deeds, 800 French Street, 4th Floor, Wilmington, DE 19801. 302-739-4618, Fax: 302-571-7708. 9AM-4:45PM.

Civil, Probate—Chancery Court, PO Box 8811, Wilmington, DE 19899. 302-739-4554, Fax: 302-571-7751. 8:30AM-5PM. Access by: mail, phone, fax, in person.

Felony, Misdemeanor, Civil Actions Over $50,000—Superior Court, County Courthouse, Prothonotary Office, Wilmington, DE 19801. 302-856-1445, Fax: 302-577-6487. 8:30AM-5PM. Access by: in person.

Misdemeanor, Civil Actions Under $50,000—Court of Common Pleas, 100 N King St, Wilmington, DE 19801-3348. 302-798-5327, Fax: 302-577-2193. 8:30AM-4:30PM. Access by: mail, fax, in person.

Civil Actions Under $15,000, Eviction, Small Claims—Wilmington Justice of the Peace, 212 Greenbank Rd, Wilmington, DE 19808. 303-654-1161, Fax: 302-995-8642. 8:30AM-4:30PM. Access by: in person.

Wilmington Justice of the Peace Court 13, 1010 Concord Ave, Concord Professional Center, Wilmington, DE 19802. 302-855-7842, Fax: 302-577-2526. 8AM-4PM. Access by: mail, phone, fax, in person.

Civil Under$15,000, Misdemeanor, Eviction, Small Claims—Middletown Justice of the Peace Court 9, 5355 Summitt Bridge Rd, Middletown, DE 19709. 302-736-2141. 8AM-4PM. Access by: in person.

Misdemeanor—New Castle Justice of the Peace Court 11, 61 Christiana Rd, New Castle, DE 19720. 302-653-7083, Fax: 302-323-4452. Open 24 hours. Access by: mail, in person.

Wilmington Justice of the Peace, 1301 E 12th St, Wilmington, DE 19809. 302-739-4316. 8:30AM-Midnight. Access by: mail, phone, fax, in person.

Wilmington Justice of the Peace, 130 Hickman Rd #13, Wilmington, DE 19703. 303-582-5323. 8AM-4PM M; 8AM-Midnight T-F; 8AM-4PM Sat. Access by: mail, fax, in person. Special note: Effective 06/01/99, the court assumed DUi and truancy cases. This court was formally located at 716 Phildelphia Pike in Wilmington.

Wilmington Justice of the Peace, 210 Greenbank Rd, Wilmington, DE 19808. 303-649-6355, Fax: 302-995-8642. 8AM-11PM. Access by: mail, fax, in person.

Wilmington Justice of the Peace #20, Public Safety Building, 300 N Walnut Street, Wilmington, DE 19801. 302-856-1447. 8AM-midnight. Access by: in person.

Sussex

Real Estate Recording—Sussex County Recorder of Deeds, Administration Bldg. Lower Level, Georgetown, DE 19947. Fax: 302-855-7787. 8:30AM-4:30PM.

Civil, Probate—Chancery Court, PO Box 424, Georgetown, DE 19947. 303-621-2131. 8:30AM-4:30PM. Access by: mail, phone, in person.

Felony, Misdemeanor, Civil Actions—Superior Court, PO Box 756, Georgetown, DE 19947. 303-640-5555, Fax: 302-856-5739. 8AM-4:30PM. Access by: in person.

Misdemeanor, Civil Actions Under $50,000—Court of Common Pleas, PO Box 426, Georgetown, DE 19947. 303-640-5161, Fax: 302-856-5056. 8:30AM-4:30PM. Access by: mail, phone, fax, in person.

Civil Actions Under $15,000, Eviction, Small Claims—Georgetown Justice of the Peace #17, 17 Shortly Rd, Georgetown, DE 19947. 303-640-2327, Fax: 302-856-5923. 8AM-4PM. Access by: mail, in person.

Seaford Justice of the Peace Court #19, 408 Stein Highway, Seaford, DE 19973. 302-856-5740, Fax: 302-628-2049. 8AM-4PM. Access by: in person.

Misdemeanor—Milford Justice of the Peace #5, 715 S DuPont Highway, Milford, DE 19963. 302-739-3184. 8AM-4PM. Access by: mail, in person. Special note: Some old civil cases also located here.

Georgetown Justice of the Peace 3, 17 Shortly Rd, Georgetown, DE 19947. 303-621-2341. 24 hours daily. Access by: mail, in person.

Justice of the Peace Court 2, 31 Route 24, Rehoboth Beach, DE 19971-9738. 302-934-7268, Fax: 302-645-8842. 8AM-4PM M & Sat; 8AM-Noon T-F. Access by: mail, phone, in person.

Millsboro Justice of the Peace, Rt 113, 553 E DuPont Hwy, Millsboro, DE 19966. 303-640-5911, Fax: 302-934-1414. 8AM-4PM. Access by: mail, phone, fax, in person.

Seaford Justice of the Peace #4, 408 Stein Highway, Seaford, DE 19973. 302-856-5333, Fax: 302-528-2049. 8AM-4PM M & Sat; 8AM-Noon T-F. Access by: in person.

Federal Courts

US District Court

Wilmington Division US Courthouse, Lock Box 18, 844 N King St, Wilmington, DE 19801302-573-6170, Record Room: 302-573-6158 Counties: All counties in Delaware.

US Bankruptcy Court

Wilmington Division 824 Market St, 5th Floor, Marine Midland Plaza, Wilmington, DE 19801302-573-6174 Counties: All counties in Delaware. www.deb.uscourts.gov

District of Columbia

Mayor's Office
One Judiciary Square,
441 4th St NW #1100   202-727-2980
Washington, DC 20001   Fax: 202-727-0505
www.ci.washington.dc.us

State Archives
1300 Naylor Ct NW   202-727-2052
Washington, DC 20001-4225   Fax: 202-727-6076

Time Zone: EST

Population: 528-964

Web Site: www.capcityon-line.com

Search Unclaimed Property Online
http://ww2.dccfo.com/uncl3.htm

District Agencies

Criminal Records
Metropolitan Police Department, Identification and Records Section, 300 Indiana Ave NW, Rm 3055, Washington, DC 20001; 202-727-4302 Police, 202-879-1373 Superior Court; 8AM-5PM. Access by: mail.

Corporation Records
Limited Partnership Records
Limited Liability Company Records
Department of Consumer & Regulatory Affairs, 614 H St, NW, Room 407, Washington, DC 20001; 202-727-7283; 9AM-3PM. Access by: mail, phone, in person. www.dcra.org

Sales Tax Registrations
Office of Tax and Revenue, Audit Division, 941 N. Capitol Street NE, Washington, DC 20002; 202-727-4829; Fax: 202-442-6550; 8:15AM-4:30PM. Access by: mail, phone, in person. www.dccfo.com

Uniform Commercial Code
Federal Tax Liens
State Tax Liens
UCC Recorder, District of Columbia Recorder of Deeds, 515 D Street NW, Washington, DC 20001; 202-727-5381; 8:15AM-4:45PM.

Workers' Compensation Records
Office of Workers Compensation, PO Box 56098 3rd Floor, Washington, DC 20011 (1200 Upshur St NW, Washington, DC 20011); 202-576-6265; Fax: 202-541-3595; 8AM-5PM. Access by: mail, phone, in person.

Birth Certificates
Department of Health, Vital Records Division, 825 North capitol St NE, Washington, DC 20002; 202-442-9009, 202-783-1809 Vital Chek; 8:30AM-3:30PM. Access by: mail.

Divorce Records
Superior Court House, Divorce Records, 500 Indiana Ave, NW, Room 4230, Washington, DC 20001; 202-879-1261; Fax: 202-879-1572; 9AM-4PM. Access by: mail.

Marriage Certificates
Superior Court House, Marriage Bureau, 500 Indiana Ave, NW, Room 4485, Washington, DC 20001; 202-879-4840; Fax: 202-879-1280; 9AM-4PM. Access by: mail. www.dcbar.org/dcsc/fam.html

Death Records
Department of Health, Vital Records Division, 825 North capitol St NE, Washington, DC 20002; 202-442-9009, 202-783-1809 Vital Chek; 8:30AM-3:30PM. Access by: mail.

Accident Reports

Insurance Operations Branch, Accident Report Section, 65 "K" St, NE, Room 2100, 2nd Floor, Washington, DC 20002; 202-727-5986; Fax: 202-727-4601; 8:30AM-3PM. Access by: mail.

Driver Records

Department of Motor Vehicles, Driver Records Division, 301 "C" St, NW, Washington, DC 20001; 202-727-6761; 8:15AM-4PM M-T-TH-F; 8:15AM-7:00PM W. Access by: mail, online. http://dmv.dcgov.org

Vehicle Ownership
Vehicle Identification

Department of Motor Vehicles, Vehicle Control Division, 301 "C" St, NW, Room 1063, Washington, DC 20001; 202-727-4768; 8:15AM-4PM M-T-TH-F; 8:15AM-7PM W. Access by: mail. http://dmv.dcgov.org

Boat & Vessel Ownership
Boat & Vessel Registration

Restricted access.
All vessels regardless of size must be titled and registered. Information is not open to the public. Any emergency requests must be in writing and the agency will use some discretion in release of data for lawful purposes.

Harbor Police, 550 Water St SW, Washington, DC 20024; 202-727-4582;

Legislation-Current/Pending
Legislation-Passed

Council of the District of Columbia, 441 4th Street, Rm 714, Washington, DC 20004; 202-724-8050; Fax: 202-347-3070; 9AM-5:30PM. Access by: mail, phone, in person. dccouncil.washington.dc.us

Voter Registration

Board of Elections, 441 4th St NW, #250, Washington, DC 20001; 202-727-2525; Fax: 202-347-2648; 8:30AM-4:45PM.

GED Certificates

GED Testing Center, 17093 3rd St NE, Rm 201, Washington, DC 20002; 202-576-6308; Fax: 202-576-7899; 8AM-5PM.

Fishing License Information

Restricted access.
Environmental Health Regulation, Fisheries & Wildlife Division, 51 N Street NE - 5th Fl, Washington, DC 20002-3323; 202-535-2266; Fax: 202-535-1373; 8AM-5PM

District Courts & Recording Offices

About the Courts...

Administration

Executive Office
500 Indiana Av NW, Room 1500
Washington, DC 20001
www.dcsc.gov

202-879-1700
Fax: 202-879-4829

Court Structure

The Superior Court in DC is divided into 17 divisions, 4 of which are shown in this book: Criminal, Civil, Family, and Tax-Probate. Probate is handled by the Tax-Probate Division of the Superior Court. Eviction is part of the court's Landlord and Tenant Branch.

Online Access

The Court of Appeals maintains a bulletin board system for various court notices, and can be dialed from computer at 202-626-8863 The Court of Appeals has their own web site at www.dcca.state.state.dc.us.

About the Recording Offices...

Organization

District of Columbia is in the Eastern Time Zone (EST).

UCC Records

Financing statements are filed at the state level, except for real estate related collateral, which are filed only with the Recorder. UCC searches performed for $30.00 per debtor name. Copies cost $2.25 per page.

Lien Records

Federal tax liens on personal property of businesses are filed with the Secretary of State. Other federal and all state tax liens on personal property are filed with the Recorder.

Real Estate Records

The District does not perform real estate searches.

District Courts & Recording Offices

District of Columbia

Real Estate Recording—District of Columbia Recorder of Deeds, 515 D Street NW, Room 203, Washington, DC 20001. 201-881-4777. 8:15AM-4:45PM.

Felony, Misdemeanor—Superior Court-Criminal Division, 500 Indiana Ave NW Room 4001, Washington, DC 20001. 202-879-1133, Fax: 202-638-5352. 8:30AM-5PM. Access by: mail, phone, in person.

Civil Actions Over $5,000—Superior Court-Civil Division, 500 Indiana Ave NW JM 170, Washington, DC 20001. 202-879-1120, Fax: 202-737-0827. 9AM-4PM. Access by: mail, phone, in person.

Civil Actions Under $5,000, Eviction, Small Claims—DC Superior Court-Civil Division-Small Claims Branch, 500 Indiana Ave NW Room JM 260, Washington, DC 20001. 202-727-6055. 8:30AM-4PM M,T,TH,F; 8:30AM-4PM, 6:30-8PM W; 9AM-Noon Sat. Access by: mail, in person.

Probate—Superior Court-Tax/Probate Division, 500 Indiana Ave NW, Washington, DC 20001. 202-879-1373, Fax: 202-393-5849. 9AM-4PM. Access by: mail, in person.

Federal Courts

US District Court

Division US Courthouse, Clerk's Office, Room 1225, 3rd & Constitution Ave NW, Washington, DC 20001202-273-0555, Record Room: 202-273-0520, Civil Docket Phone: 202-273-0564, Criminal Docket Phone: 202-273-0503 Fax: 202-273-0412 Counties: District of Columbia. www.dcd.uscourts.gov

US Bankruptcy Court

Division E Barrett Prettyman Courthouse, Room 4400, 333 Constitution Ave NW, Washington, DC 20001202-273-0042 Counties: District of Columbia.

Florida

Attorney General's Office
The Capitol, PL-01 850-414-3300
Tallahassee, FL 32399-1050 Fax: 850-487-2564
legal.firn.edu

Governor's Office
The Capitol 850-488-4441
Tallahassee, FL 32399-0001 Fax: 850-487-0801
www.flgov.com

State Archives
R A Gray Bldg, 500 S Bronough 850-487-2073
Tallahassee, FL 32399-0250 Fax: 850-488-4894
http://dlis.dos.state.fl.us/barm

Capital: Tallahassee
Leon County

Time Zone: EST*
* Florida's ten western-most counties are CST:
They are: Bay, Calhoun, Escambia, Gulf, Holmes,
Jackson, Okaloosa, Santa Rosa, Walton, Washington.

Number of Counties: 67

Population: 14,653,945

Web Site: www.state.fl.us

Search Unclaimed Property Online
http://up.dbf.state.fl.us/
Isearch.cfm

State Agencies

Criminal Records
Florida Department of Law Enforcement, User Services Bureau, PO Box 1489, Tallahassee, FL 32302 (2331 Phillip Rd, Tallahassee, FL 32308); 850-488-6236; Fax: 850-488-1413; 8AM-5PM. Access by: mail, online.

Corporation Records
Limited Partnership Records
Trademarks/Servicemarks
Assumed Name
Fictitious Names
Division of Corporations, Department of State, PO Box 6327, Tallahassee, FL 32314 (409 E Gaines St, Tallahassee, FL 32399); 850-488-9000 Telephone Inquires, 850-487-6053 Copy Requests, 850-487-6056 Annual Reports; 8AM-5PM. Access by: mail, online. www.dos.state.fl.us

Sales Tax Registrations
Florida Department of Revenue, 5050 W Tennessee St, Tallahassee, FL 32399-0100; 850-487-7000; Fax: 850-488-0024; 8AM-5PM. Access by: mail, phone, in person.

Uniform Commercial Code
Federal Tax Liens
UCC Division, Secretary of State, PO Box 5588, Tallahassee, FL 32314 (409 E Gaines St, Tallahassee, FL 32399); 850-487-6055; Fax: 850-487-6013; 8AM-4:30PM. Access by:, online. www.dos.state.fl.us

State Tax Liens
Records not available from state agency.

These records are filed and found at the county level.

Workers' Compensation Records
Workers Compensation Division, Information Management Unit, Forrest Bldg, 2728 Centerview Dr, Ste 202, Tallahassee, FL 32399; 850-488-3030; Fax: 850-921-0305; 7:30AM-5PM. Access by: mail. www.wc.les.state.fl.us/dwc

Birth Certificates
Department of Health, Office of Vital Statistics, PO Box 210, Jacksonville, FL 32231-0042 (1217 Pearl St, Jacksonville, FL 32202); 904-359-6911; Fax: 904-359-6993; 8AM-5PM. Access by: mail, phone, in person. www.doh.state.fl.us

Death Records

Department of Health, Office of Vital Statistics, PO Box 210, Jacksonville, FL 32231-0042; 904-359-6911; Fax: 904-359-6993; 8AM-5PM. Access by: mail, phone, in person. www.doh.state.fl.us

Marriage Certificates

Department of Health, Office of Vital Statistics, PO Box 210, Jacksonville, FL 32231-0042; 904-359-6911; Fax: 904-359-6993; 8AM-5PM. Access by: mail, phone, in person. www.doh.state.fl.us

Divorce Records

Department of Health, Office of Vital Statistics, PO Box 210, Jacksonville, FL 32231-0042; 904-359-6911; Fax: 904-359-6993; 8AM-5PM. Access by: mail, phone, in person. www.doh.state.fl.us

Accident Reports

Crash Records-Room A325, DHSMV, Neil Kirkman Bldg, 2900 Apalachee Prky, Tallahassee, FL 32399-0538; 850-488-5017; Fax: 850-922-0488; 8AM-4:45PM. Access by: mail.

Driver Records

Department of Highway Safety & Motor Vehicles, Division of Drivers Licenses, PO Box 5775, Tallahassee, FL 32314-5775 (2900 Apalachee Pky, Rm B-239, Neil Kirkman Bldg, Tallahassee, FL 32399); 850-488-0250; Fax: 850-487-7080; 8AM-4:30PM. Access by: mail, online. www.hsmv.state.fl.us

Vehicle Ownership
Vehicle Identification

Division of Motor Vehicles, Information Research Section, Neil Kirkman Bldg, A-126, Tallahassee, FL 32399; 850-488-5665; Fax: 850-488-8983; 8AM-4:30PM. Access by: mail. www.hsmv.state.fl.us

Boat & Vessel Ownership
Boat & Vessel Registration

Dept of Highway Safety, Bureau of Vessels, Titles & Registrations, 2900 Apalachee Parkway, Rm C-214, Tallahassee, FL 32399; 850-488-1195;. www.state.fl.us

Legislation-Current/Pending
Legislation-Passed

Joint Legislative Mgmt Committee, Legislative Information Division, 111 W Madison St, Pepper Bldg, Rm 704, Tallahassee, FL 32399-1400; 850-488-4371, 850-487-5285 Senate Bills, 850-488-7475 House Bills, 850-488-8427 Session Laws; Fax: 850-921-5334; 8AM-5PM. Access by: mail, phone, in person, online. www.leg.state.fl.us

Voter Registration

Restricted access.
All individual searching must be done at the county level. However, the state maintains a central voter file limited to purchase by government agencies and those involved in the political process.
Department of State, Division of Elections, Room 1801, The Capitol, Tallahassee, FL 32399-0250; 850-488-7690; Fax: 850-488-1768; 8AM-5PM
www.election.dos.state.fl.us

GED Certificates

GED Testing Office, 325 W Gaines St Rm 634, Tallahassee, FL 32399; 850-487-1619; 8AM-5PM. Access by:, phone, in person.

Hunting License Information
Fishing License Information

Game & Fresh Water Fish Commission, Revenue & Licensing Division, 620 S Meridian St, Tallahassee, FL 32399-1600; 850-488-3641; Fax: 850-488-3641; 8AM-5PM. Access by: mail. fcn.state.fl.us/gfc/gfchome.html

County Courts & Recording Offices

About the Courts...

Administration

Office of State Courts Administrator,
Supreme Court Bldg   850-922-5082
500 S Duval   Fax: 850-488-0156
Tallahassee, FL 32399-1900
www.flcourts.org/index.html

Court Structure

All counties have combined Circuit and County Courts. The Circuit Court is the court of general jurisdiction.

Searching Hints

All courts have one address and switchboard; however, the divisions within the court(s) are completely separate. Requesters should specify which court and which division, e.g., Circuit Civil, County Civil, etc., the request is directed to, even though some counties will automatically check both with one request.

Fees are set by statute and are as follows: Search Fee - $1.00 per name per year; Certification Fee - $1.00 per document plus copy fee; Copy Fee - $1.00 per certified page; $.15 per non-certified page.

Most courts have very lengthy phone recording systems.

Online Access

There is a statewide, online computer system for internal use only; there is no external access available nor planned currently. A number of courts do offer online access to the public.

About the Recording Offices...

Organization

67 counties, 67 recording offices. The recording officer is Clerk of the Circuit Court. All transactions are recorded in the "Official Record," a grantor/grantee index. Some counties will search by type of transaction while others will return everything on the index. 57 counties are in the Eastern Time Zone (EST) and 10 are in the Central Time Zone (CST).

UCC Records

Financing statements are filed at the state level, except for farm and real estate related collateral. All but a few counties will perform UCC searches. Use search request form UCC-11. Search fees are usually $1.00 per debtor name per year searched and include all lien and real estate transactions on record. Copies usually cost $1.00 per page.

Lien Records

Federal tax liens on personal property of businesses are filed with the Secretary of State. All other federal and state tax liens on personal property are filed with the county Clerk of Circuit Court. Usually tax liens on personal property are filed in the same index with UCC financing statements and real estate transactions. Most counties will perform a tax lien as part of a UCC search. Copies usually cost $1.00 per page.

Real Estate Records

Any name searched in the "Official Records" will usually include all types of liens and property transfers for that name. Most counties will perform searches. In addition to the usual $1.00 per page copy fee, certification of documents usually cost $1.00 per document. Tax records are located at the Property Appraiser Office.

Note that a number of counties make their real estate records available online.

County Courts & Recording Offices

Alachua

Real Estate Recording—Alachua County Clerk of the Circuit Court, 12 S.E. 1st St. County Administration Bldg.-Room 151, Gainesville, FL 32601. 360-378-2171, Fax: 352-491-4649. 8:30AM-5PM.

Felony, Misdemeanor, Civil, Eviction, Small Claims, Probate—Circuit and County Courts, PO Box 600, Gainesville, FL 32602. 360-378-4017, Fax: 352-338-3201. 8:30AM-5PM. Access by: mail, phone, fax, in person, online. www.co.alachua.fl.us/clerk

Baker

Real Estate Recording—Baker County Clerk of the Circuit Court, 339 East MacClenny Avenue, MacClenny, FL 32063. 904-259-3616, Fax: 904-259-4176. 8:30AM-5PM.

Civil, Eviction, Small Claims, Probate—Circuit and County Courts-Civil, 339 E Macclenny Ave, Macclenny, FL 32063. 904-259-3121. 8:30AM-5PM. Access by: mail, in person.

Felony, Misdemeanor—Circuit and County Courts-Criminal, 339 E Macclenny Ave, Macclenny, FL 32063. 904-259-8449, Fax: 904-259-4176. 8:30AM-5PM. Access by: mail, phone, in person.

Bay

Real Estate Recording—Bay County Clerk of the Circuit Court, 300 East 4th Street, Courthouse, Panama City, FL 32401. Fax: 850-747-5199. 8AM-4:30PM.

Civil Actions Over $15,000, Probate—Circuit Court-Civil, PO Box 2269, Panama City, FL 32402. 850-763-9061, Fax: 850-747-5188. 8AM-5PM. Access by: mail, phone, fax, in person.

Felony—Circuit Court-Criminal, PO Box 2269, Panama City, FL 32402. 850-747-5123, Fax: 850-747-5188. 8AM-4:30PM. Access by: mail, fax, in person.

Civil Actions Under $15,000, Eviction, Small Claims—County Court-Civil, PO Box 2269, Panama City, FL 32402. 850-747-5141, Fax: 850-747-5188. 8AM-4:30PM. Access by: mail, phone, fax, in person.

Misdemeanor—County Court-Misdemeanor, PO Box 2269, Panama City, FL 32402. 850-747-5144, Fax: 850-747-5188. 8AM-4:30PM. Access by: mail, phone, fax, in person.

Bradford

Real Estate Recording—Bradford County Clerk of the Circuit Court, 945 North Temple Avenue, Starke, FL 32091. Fax: 904-964-4454. 8AM-5PM.

Felony, Civil Actions Over $15,000, Probate—Circuit Court, PO Drawer B, Starke, FL 32091. 904-964-6280, Fax: 904-964-4454. 8AM-5PM. Access by: mail, phone, in person.

Misdemeanor, Civil Actions Under $15,000, Eviction, Small Claims—County Court, PO Drawer B, Starke, FL 32091. 904-964-6280, Fax: 904-964-4454. 8AM-5PM. Access by: mail, in person.

Brevard

Real Estate Recording—Brevard County Clerk of the Circuit Court, 700 South Park Ave. Building #2, Titusville, FL 32780. Fax: 407-264-5246. 8AM-5PM.

Civil, Eviction, Small Claims, Probate—Circuit and County Courts-Civil, PO Box H, 700 S Park Ave, Titusville, FL 32780. 409-275-2452, Fax: 407-264-5246. 8AM-5PM. Access by: mail, phone, fax, in person, online. www.clerk.co.brevard.fl.us

Felony—Circuit Court-Felony, 700 S Park Ave (PO Box H, 32781-0239), Titusville, FL 32780. 409-277-6200, Fax: 407-264-5395. 8AM-5PM. Access by: mail, phone, fax, in person, online. www.clerk.co.brevard.fl.us

Misdemeanor—County Court-Misdemeanor, 700 S Park Ave (PO Box H, 32781-0239), Titusville, FL 32780. 409-275-9472, Fax: 407-264-5395. 8AM-4:30PM. Access by: mail, phone, fax, in person, online. www.clerk.co.brevard.fl.us

Broward

Real Estate Recording—Broward County Board of County Commissioners, 115 South Andrews Avenue, Room 114, Fort Lauderdale, FL 33301. Fax: 954-357-7267. 8:30AM-4:15PM M,T,Th,F; 8:30AM-3PM W.

Felony, Misdemeanor, Civil, Eviction, Small Claims, Probate—Circuit and County Courts, 201 SE 6th St, Ft Lauderdale, FL 33301. 954-831-5729, Fax: 954-831-7166. 9AM-4PM. Access by: mail, phone, in person, online.

Calhoun

Real Estate Recording—Calhoun County Clerk of the Circuit Court, 425 East Central Avenue, Room 130, Blountstown, FL 32424. 904-674-5636, Fax: 850-674-5553. 8AM-4PM.

Felony, Misdemeanor, Civil, Eviction, Small Claims, Probate—Circuit and County Court, 425 E Central Ave, Blountstown, FL 32424. 850-674-4545, Fax: 850-674-5553. 8AM-4PM. Access by: mail, phone, fax, in person.

Charlotte

Real Estate Recording—Charlotte County Clerk of the Circuit Court, 410 Taylor Rd. Punta Gorda, FL 33950. Fax: 941-637-2172. 8AM-5PM.

Civil, Eviction, Small Claims, Probate (Separate)—Circuit and County Courts-Civil Division, PO Box 1687, Punta Gorda, FL 33951-1687. 941-637-2230, Fax: 941-637-2159. 8AM-5PM. Access by: mail, in person. Special note: Probate is handled by a separate court at the telephone given above.

Felony, Misdemeanor—Circuit and County Courts-Criminal Division, PO Box 1687, Punta Gorda, FL 33951-1687. 941-637-2115, Fax: 941-637-2159. 8AM-5PM. Access by: mail, phone, in person.

Citrus

Real Estate Recording—Citrus County Clerk of the Circuit Court, 110 North Apopka Ave. Room 101, Inverness, FL 34450. Fax: 352-637-9477. 8AM-5PM.

Felony, Civil Actions Over $15,000, Probate—Circuit Court, 110 N Apopka Rm 101, Inverness, FL 34450. 360-427-9670, Fax: 352-637-9413. 8AM-5PM. Access by: mail, phone, fax, in person.

Misdemeanor, Civil Actions Under $15,000, Eviction, Small Claims—County Court, 110 N Apopka, Rm 101, Inverness, FL 34450. 360-417-2373, Fax: 352-637-9413. 8AM-5PM. Access by: mail, phone, fax, in person.

Clay

Real Estate Recording—Clay County Clerk of the Circuit Court, 825 North Orange Avenue, Green Cove Springs, FL 32043. Fax: 904-284-6390. 8:30AM-4:30PM.

Felony, Civil Actions Over $15,000, Probate—Circuit Court, PO Box 698, Green Cove Springs, FL 32043. 904-284-6302, Fax: 904-284-6390. 8:30AM-4:30PM. Access by: mail, in person, online. www.state.fl.us/clayclerk

Misdemeanor, Civil Actions Under $15,000, Eviction, Small Claims—County Court, PO Box 698, Green Cove Springs, FL 32043. 904-284-6316, Fax: 904-284-6390. 8:30AM-4:30PM. Access by: mail, in person, online. www.state.fl.us/clayclerk

Collier

Real Estate Recording—Collier County Clerk of the Circuit Court, 3301 Tamiami Trail East, Administration Bldg. 4th floor, Naples, FL 34112. Fax: 941-774-8003. 8AM-5PM (No recording after 4:30PM).

Felony, Civil Actions Over $15,000, Probate—Circuit Court, PO Box 413044, Naples, FL 34101-3044. 941-732-2646. 8AM-5PM. Access by: mail, in person, online.

Misdemeanor, Civil Actions Under $15,000, Eviction, Small Claims—County Court, PO Box 413044, Naples, FL 34101-3044.

941-732-2646, Fax: 941-774-8020. 8AM-5PM. Access by: mail, in person, online.

Columbia

Real Estate Recording—Columbia County Clerk of the Circuit Court, 145 North Hernando Street, Lake City, FL 32055. Fax: 904-758-1337. 8AM-5PM.

Felony, Misdemeanor, Civil, Eviction, Small Claims, Probate—Circuit and County Courts, PO Drawer 2069, Lake City, FL 32056. 904-758-1353. 8AM-5PM. Access by: mail, in person.

Dade

Real Estate Recording—Dade County Clerk of the Circuit Court, 44 West Flager Street, 8th Floor, Miami, FL 33130. Fax: 305-372-7775. 9AM-4PM.

Civil, Eviction, Small Claims, Probate—Circuit and County Courts-Civil, 73 W Flagler St, Miami, FL 33130. 307-334-2432, Fax: 305-375-5819. 9AM-4PM. Access by: mail, phone, fax, in person.

Felony, Misdemeanor—Circuit and County Courts-Criminal, 1351 NW 12th St, Suite 9000, Miami, FL 33125. 307-332-3239, Fax: 305-548-5526. 9AM-4PM. Access by: mail, phone, fax, in person, online.

De Soto

Real Estate Recording—De Soto County Clerk of the Circuit Court, 115 East Oak Street, Arcadia, FL 33821. Fax: 863-993-4669. 8AM-5PM.

Felony, Misdemeanor, Civil, Eviction, Small Claims, Probate—Circuit and County Courts, PO Box 591, Arcadia, FL 34265. 863-993-4876, Fax: 863-993-4669. 8AM-5PM. Access by: mail, phone, fax, in person. Special note: County Court & Evictions 863-993-4880.

Dixie

Real Estate Recording—Dixie County Clerk of the Circuit Court, Courthouse, 150 NE Cedar St. Cross City, FL 32628. Fax: 352-498-1201. 9AM-Noon,1-5PM.

Felony, Misdemeanor, Civil, Eviction, Small Claims, Probate—Circuit and County Courts, PO Drawer 1206, Cross City, FL 32628-1206. 360-385-9135, Fax: 352-498-1201. 9AM-5PM. Access by: mail, in person.

Duval

Real Estate Recording—Duval County Clerk of the Circuit Court, 330 East Bay Street, Courthouse, Jacksonville, FL 32202. 904-630-2068, Fax: 904-630-2959. 8AM-5PM.

Civil, Eviction, Small Claims, Probate—Circuit and County Courts-Civil Division, 330 E Bay St, Jacksonville, FL 32202. 904-630-2039, Fax: 904-630-7506. 8AM-5PM. Access by: mail, fax, in person, online. www.ci.jax.fl.us/pub/clerk/default.htm

Felony, Misdemeanor—Circuit and County Courts-Criminal Division, 330 E Bay St, Rm M106, Jacksonville, FL 32202. 904-630-2070, Fax: 904-630-7505. 8AM-5PM. Access by: mail, in person, online. www.ci.jax.fl.us/pub/clerk/default.htm

Escambia

Real Estate Recording—Escambia Clerk of Circuit Court, 223 Palafox Place, Old Courthouse, Pensacola, FL 32501. 904-436-5200, Fax: 850-595-3925. 8AM-5PM.

Civil, Eviction, Small Claims, Probate—Circuit and County Courts-Civil Division, 190 Governmental Center, Pensacola, FL 32501. 850-595-4170. 8AM-5PM. Access by: mail, in person.

Felony, Misdemeanor—Circuit and County Courts-Criminal Division, 190 Governmental Center, Pensacola, FL 32501. 850-595-4150, Fax: 850-595-4198. 8AM-5PM. Access by: mail, fax, in person. Special note: Misdemeanor records phone is 850-595-4185.

Flagler

Real Estate Recording—Flagler County Clerk of the Circuit Court, Courthouse, Room 115, 200 E. Moody Blvd. Bunnell, FL 32010. 904-437-7414, Fax: 904-437-7406. 8AM-5PM.

Felony, Misdemeanor, Civil, Eviction, Small Claims, Probate—Circuit and County Courts, PO Box 787, Bunnell, FL 32110. 904-437-7430, Fax: 904-437-7454. 8AM-5PM. Access by: mail, phone, fax, in person.

Franklin

Real Estate Recording—Franklin County Clerk of the Circuit Court, 33 Market Street, Apalachicola, FL 32320. 904-653-8861, Fax: 850-653-2261. 8:30AM-4:30PM.

Felony, Misdemeanor, Civil, Eviction, Small Claims, Probate—Circuit and County Courts, 33 Market St, Suite 203, Apalachicola, FL 32321. 850-653-8862, Fax: 850-653-2261. 8:30AM-4:30PM. Access by: mail, in person.

Gadsden

Real Estate Recording—Gadsden County Clerk of the Circuit Court, 10 East Jefferson Street, Quincy, FL 32351. Fax: 850-875-8612. 8:30AM-5PM.

Civil, Eviction, Small Claims, Probate—Circuit and County Courts-Civil Division, PO Box 1649, Quincy, FL 32353. 850-875-8621, Fax: 850-875-8612. 8:30AM-5PM. Access by: mail, phone, fax, in person.

Felony, Misdemeanor—Circuit and County Courts-Criminal Division, 112 South Adams St, Quincy, FL 32351. 850-875-8609, Fax: 850-875-7625. 8:30AM-5PM. Access by: mail, fax, in person.

Gilchrist

Real Estate Recording—Gilchrist County Clerk of the Circuit Court, Courthouse, 112 S. Main St. Trenton, FL 32693. Fax: 352-463-3166. 8:30AM-5PM.

Felony, Misdemeanor, Civil, Eviction, Small Claims, Probate—Circuit and County Courts, Po Box 37, Trenton, FL 32693. 360-385-9125, Fax: 352-463-3166. 8AM-5PM. Access by: mail, phone, fax, in person.

Glades

Real Estate Recording—Glades County Clerk of the Circuit Court, Highway 27 and 5th Street, 500 Ave. J, Moore Haven, FL 33471. Fax: 863-946-0560. 8AM-5PM.

Felony, Misdemeanor, Civil, Eviction, Small Claims, Probate—Circuit and County Courts, PO Box 10, Moore Haven, FL 33471. 863-946-0113, Fax: 863-946-0560. 8AM-5PM. Access by: mail, phone, in person.

Gulf

Real Estate Recording—Gulf County Clerk of the Circuit Court, 1000 5th Street, Port St. Joe, FL 32456. Fax: 850-229-6174. 9AM-5PM.

Felony, Misdemeanor, Civil, Eviction, Small Claims, Probate—Circuit and County Courts, 1000 5th St, Port St Joe, FL 32456. 850-229-6112, Fax: 850-229-6174. 9AM-5PM. Access by: mail, phone, fax, in person.

Hamilton

Real Estate Recording—Hamilton County Clerk of the Circuit Court, 207 NE 1st Street, Room 106, Jasper, FL 32052. 904-792-1288, Fax: 904-792-3524. 8:30AM-4:30PM.

Felony, Misdemeanor, Civil, Eviction, Small Claims, Probate—Circuit and County Courts, 207 NE 1st St #106, Jasper, FL 32052. 904-792-1288, Fax: 904-792-3524. 8:30AM-4:30PM. Access by: mail, phone, in person.

Hardee

Real Estate Recording—Hardee County Clerk of the Circuit Court, 417 West Main Street, Wauchula, FL 33873. Fax: 863-773-4422. 8:30AM-5PM; 8:30AM-3:15PM Recording hours.

Felony, Misdemeanor, Civil, Eviction, Small Claims, Probate—Circuit and County Courts, PO Drawer 1749, Wauchula,

FL 33873-1749. 863-773-4174, Fax: 863-773-4422. 8:30AM-5PM. Access by: mail, in person.

Hendry

Real Estate Recording—Hendry County Clerk of the Circuit Court, Corner of Highway 80 and 29, Courthouse, La Belle, FL 33935. 941-675-5318, Fax: 941-675-5238. 8:30AM-5PM.

Felony, Misdemeanor, Civil, Eviction, Small Claims, Probate—Circuit and County Courts, PO Box 1760, LaBelle, FL 33975-1760. 863-675-5217, Fax: 863-675-5238. 8:30AM-5PM. Access by: mail, phone, in person.

Hernando

Real Estate Recording—Hernando County Clerk of the Circuit Court, 20 North Main, Room 215, Brooksville, FL 34601. 360-532-7061, Fax: 352-754-4243. 8AM-5PM.

Felony, Misdemeanor, Civil, Eviction, Small Claims, Probate—Circuit and County Courts, 20 N Main St, Brooksville, FL 34601. 360-568-8572, Fax: 352-754-4247. 8AM-5PM. Access by: mail, in person, online. www.co.hernandoo.fl.us/ccc

Highlands

Real Estate Recording—Highlands County Clerk of the Circuit Court, 590 South Commerce Avenue, Sebring, FL 33870. 863-386-6685. 8AM-5PM.

Felony, Misdemeanor, Civil, Eviction, Small Claims, Probate—Circuit and County Courts, 590 S Commerce Ave, Sebring, FL 33870-3867. 863-385-6500, Fax: 863-386-6575. 8AM-4:30PM. Access by: mail, in person.

Hillsborough

Real Estate Recording—Hillsborough County Clerk of the Circuit Court, 419 Pierce Street, Room 114-K, Tampa, FL 33602. Fax: 813-276-2114. 8AM-5PM.

Felony, Misdemeanor, Civil, Eviction, Small Claims, Probate—Circuit and County Courts, 419 Pierce St, Tampa, FL 33602. 813-276-8100, Fax: 813-272-7707. 8AM-5PM. Access by: mail, fax, in person, online.

Holmes

Real Estate Recording—Holmes County Clerk of the Circuit Court, 201 North Oklahoma Street, Bonifay, FL 32425. 904-547-1103, Fax: 850-547-6630. 8AM-4PM.

Felony, Misdemeanor, Civil, Eviction, Small Claims, Probate—Circuit and County Courts, PO Box 397, Bonifay, FL 32425. 850-547-1100, Fax: 850-547-6630. 8AM-4PM. Access by: mail, in person.

Indian River

Real Estate Recording—Indian River County Clerk of the Circuit Court, 2000 16th Ave. Vero Beach, FL 32960. 8:30AM-5PM.

Felony, Misdemeanor, Civil, Eviction, Small Claims, Probate—Circuit and County Courts, PO Box 1028, Vero Beach, FL 32961. 561-770-5185, Fax: 561-770-5008. 8:30AM-5PM. Access by: mail, in person.

Jackson

Real Estate Recording—Jackson County Clerk of the Circuit Court, 4445 East Lafayette Street, Courthouse, Marianna, FL 32446. 904-482-9653, Fax: 850-482-7849. 8AM-4:30PM.

Felony, Misdemeanor, Civil, Eviction, Small Claims, Probate—Circuit and County Courts, PO Box 510, Marianna, FL 32447. 850-482-9552, Fax: 850-482-7849. 8AM-4:30PM. Access by: mail, fax, in person.

Jefferson

Real Estate Recording—Jefferson County Clerk of the Circuit Court, Courthouse, Room 10, Monticello, FL 32344. Fax: 850-342-0222. 8AM-5PM.

Felony, Misdemeanor, Civil, Eviction, Small Claims, Probate—Circuit and County Courts, Jefferson County Courthouse, Rm 10, Monticello, FL 32344. 850-342-0218, Fax: 850-342-0222. 8AM-5PM. Access by: mail, fax, in person.

Lafayette

Real Estate Recording—Lafayette County Clerk of the Circuit Court, Main & Fletcher Streets, Courthouse, Mayo, FL 32066. 904-294-1961, Fax: 904-294-4231. 8AM-5PM.

Felony, Misdemeanor, Civil, Eviction, Small Claims, Probate—Circuit and County Courts, PO Box 88, Mayo, FL 32066. 904-294-1600, Fax: 904-294-4231. 8AM-5PM. Access by: mail, phone, in person.

Lake

Real Estate Recording—Lake County Clerk of the Circuit Court, 550 West Main Street, Tavares, FL 32778. 360-427-9670, Fax: 352-742-4191. 8:30AM-5PM (Recording hours: 8:30AM-4:30PM).

Felony, Misdemeanor, Civil, Eviction, Small Claims, Probate—Circuit and County Courts, 550 W Main St or PO Box 7800, Tavares, FL 32778. 360-427-9670, Fax: 352-742-4166. 8:30AM-5PM. Access by: mail, fax, in person.

Lee

Real Estate Recording—Lee County Clerk of the Circuit Court, 2115 Second Street, Courthouse - 2nd Floor, Fort Myers, FL 33901. 7:45AM-5PM.

Felony, Misdemeanor, Civil, Eviction, Small Claims, Probate—Circuit and County Courts, PO Box 2469, Ft Myers, FL 33902. 941-335-2283. 7:45AM-5PM. Access by: mail, in person, online.

Leon

Real Estate Recording—Leon County Clerk of the Circuit Court, 301 South Monroe Street, Room 123, Tallahassee, FL 32301. Fax: 850-921-1310. 8:30AM-5PM.

Felony, Misdemeanor, Civil, Eviction, Small Claims, Probate—Circuit and County Courts, PO Box 726, Tallahassee, FL 32302. 850-488-7534, Fax: 850-488-8863. 8:30AM-5PM. Access by: mail, in person, online. www.clerk.leon.fl.us

Levy

Real Estate Recording—Levy County Clerk of the Circuit Court, Courthouse, 355 N. Court St. Bronson, FL 32621. 8AM-5PM.

Felony, Misdemeanor, Civil, Eviction, Small Claims, Probate—Circuit and County Courts, PO Box 610, Bronson, FL 32621. 904-486-5100, Fax: 904-486-5166. 8AM-5PM. Access by: mail, in person.

Liberty

Real Estate Recording—Liberty County Clerk of the Circuit Court, Highway 20, Courthouse, Bristol, FL 32321. 904-643-2442, Fax: 850-643-2866. 8AM-5PM.

Felony, Misdemeanor, Civil, Eviction, Small Claims, Probate—Circuit and County Courts, PO Box 399, Bristol, FL 32321. 850-643-2215, Fax: 850-643-2866. 8AM-5PM. Access by: mail, in person.

Madison

Real Estate Recording—Madison County Clerk of the Circuit Court, Courthouse, 101 South Range Street, Room 108, Madison, FL 32340. Fax: 850-973-2059. 8AM-5PM.

Felony, Misdemeanor, Civil, Eviction, Small Claims, Probate—Circuit and County Courts, PO Box 237, Madison, FL 32341. 850-973-1500, Fax: 850-973-2059. 8AM-5PM. Access by: mail, phone, in person.

Manatee

Real Estate Recording—Manatee County Clerk of the Circuit Court, 1115 Manatee Avenue West, Bradenton, FL 34205. Fax: 941-741-4082. 8:30AM-5PM.

Felony, Misdemeanor, Civil, Eviction, Small Claims, Probate—Circuit and County Courts, PO Box 1000, Bradenton, FL 34206. 941-749-1800, Fax: 941-741-4082. 8:30AM-5PM. Access by: mail, phone, in person, online. www.clerkofcourts.com

Marion

Real Estate Recording—Marion County Clerk of the Circuit Court, 110 N.W. First Avenue, Ocala, FL 34475. 8AM-5PM.

Felony, Misdemeanor, Civil, Eviction, Small Claims, Probate—Circuit and County Courts, PO Box 1030, Ocala, FL 34478. 360-417-2333, Fax: 352-620-3300. 8AM-5PM. Access by: mail, fax, in person.

Martin

Real Estate Recording—Martin County Clerk of the Circuit Court, 100 E. Ocean Blvd, 3rd Floor, Stuart, FL 34994. Fax: 561-223-7920. 8AM-5PM.

Felony, Misdemeanor, Civil, Eviction, Small Claims, Probate—Circuit and County Courts, PO Box 9016, Stuart, FL 34995. 561-288-5576, Fax: 561-288-5990. 8AM-5PM. Access by: mail, phone, fax, in person, online.

Monroe

Real Estate Recording—Monroe County Clerk of the Circuit Court, 500 Whitehead Street, Courthouse, Key West, FL 33040. 307-334-2736, Fax: 305-295-3660. 8:30AM-5PM.

Felony, Misdemeanor, Civil, Eviction, Small Claims, Probate—Circuit and County Courts, 500 Whitehead St, Key West, FL 33040. 307-334-3845, Fax: 305-295-3623. 8:30AM-5PM. Access by: mail, in person.

Nassau

Real Estate Recording—Nassau County Clerk of the Circuit Court, 191 Nassau Place, Fernandina, FL 32097. Fax: 904-321-5723. 9AM-5PM (Recording Hours: 9AM-4PM).

Felony, Misdemeanor, Civil, Eviction, Small Claims, Probate—Circuit and County Courts, PO Box 456, Fernandina Beach, FL 32035. 904-321-5700, Fax: 904-321-5723. 9AM-5PM. Access by: mail, phone, fax, in person.

Okaloosa

Real Estate Recording—Okaloosa County Clerk of the Circuit Court, 101 East James Lee Blvd. Crestview, FL 32536. Fax: 850-689-5886. 8AM-5PM.

Felony, Misdemeanor, Civil, Eviction, Small Claims, Probate—Circuit and County Courts, 1250 Eglin Pkwy, Shalimar, FL 32579. 850-651-7200, Fax: 850-651-7230. 8AM-5PM. Access by: mail, in person, online.

Okeechobee

Real Estate Recording—Okeechobee County Clerk of the Circuit Court, 304 N.W. 2nd Street, Room 101, Okeechobee, FL 34972. 8:30AM-5PM.

Felony, Misdemeanor, Civil, Eviction, Small Claims, Probate—Circuit and County Courts, 304 NW 2nd St Rm 101, Okeechobee, FL 34972. 863-763-2131. 8:30AM-5PM. Access by: mail, in person.

Orange

Real Estate Recording—Orange County Comptroller, 401 S. Rosaland Ave. Orlando, FL 32801. 409-327-6814, Fax: 407-836-5120. 7:30AM-4:30PM.

Felony, Misdemeanor, Civil, Eviction, Small Claims, Probate—Circuit and County Courts, 37 N Orange Ave #550, Orlando, FL 32801. 409-327-6804. 8AM-5PM. Access by: mail, in person, online.

Misdemeanor, Civil Actions Under $15,000, Eviction, Small Claims—County Court #3, 475 W Story Rd, Ocoee, FL 34761. 409-283-2162. 8AM-5PM. Access by: mail, in person.

County Court-Apopka Branch, 1111 N Rock Springs Rd, Apopka, FL 32712. 409-336-4670, Fax: 407-889-4146. 8AM-5PM. Access by: mail, fax, in person. Special note: Records maintained at Orlando office.

County Court-NE Orange Division, 450 N Lakemont Ave, Winter Park, FL 32792. 409-283-3054. 8AM-5PM. Access by: mail, phone, in person. www.orangeclerk.org

Osceola

Real Estate Recording—Osceola County Clerk of the Circuit Court, Room 231-C, Dept R, 17 S. Vernon Ave. Kissimmee, FL 34741. Fax: 407-847-0783. 8:30AM-5PM; 8:30AM-4PM Recording hours.

Civil Actions Over $5,000—Circuit Court-Civil, 12 S Vernon Ave, Kissimmee, FL 34741. 409-336-4600. 8:30AM-5PM. Access by: mail, in person.

Felony, Misdemeanor—Circuit and County Courts-Criminal Division, 17 S Vernon Ave, Kissimmee, FL 34741. 409-277-6200. 8:30AM-5PM. Access by: mail, in person.

Eviction, Small Claims—County Court-Civil, 12 S Vernon Ave, Kissimmee, FL 34741. 409-327-6816. 8:30AM-5PM. Access by: mail, in person.

Palm Beach

Real Estate Recording—Palm Beach County Clerk of the Circuit Court, 205 N. Dixie Highway, Room 4.2500, West Palm Beach, FL 33402. 8AM-5PM.

Civil—Circuit Court-Civil Division, PO Box 4667, West Palm Beach, FL 33402. 561-355-2986, Fax: 561-355-4643. 8AM-5PM. Access by: mail, phone, in person.

Felony, Misdemeanor—Circuit and County Courts-Criminal Division, 205 North Dixie, West Palm Beach, FL 33401. 561-355-2519, Fax: 561-355-3802. 8AM-5PM. Access by: mail, phone, fax, in person, online.

Eviction, Small Claims—County Court-Civil Division, PO Box 3406, West Palm Beach, FL 33402. 561-355-2986, Fax: 561-355-4643. 8AM-5PM. Access by: mail, phone, in person.

Probate—County Court-Probate Division, PO Box 4238, West Palm Beach, FL 33402. 561-355-2986, Fax: 561-355-4643. 8AM-5PM. Access by: mail, phone, in person.

Pasco

Real Estate Recording—Pasco County Clerk of the Circuit Court, 38053 Live Oak Ave. Room 205, Dade City, FL 33523. 8:30AM-5PM.

Civil, Eviction, Small Claims, Probate—Circuit and County Courts-Civil Division, 38053 Live Oak Ave, Dade City, FL 33523. 360-385-9150. 8:30AM-5PM. Access by: mail, in person.

Felony, Misdemeanor—Circuit and County Courts-Criminal Division, 38053 Live Oak Ave, Dade City, FL 33523-3894. 360-417-2285. 8:30AM-5PM. Access by: mail, in person, online.

Pinellas

Real Estate Recording—Pinellas County Clerk of the Circuit Court, 315 Court Street, Room 150, Clearwater, FL 33756. Fax: 727-464-4383. 8AM-5PM.

Civil, Eviction, Small Claims, Probate—Circuit and County Courts-Civil Division, 315 Court St, Clearwater, FL 33756. 727-464-3267, Fax: 727-464-4070. 8AM-5PM. Access by: mail, phone, fax, in person.

Felony—Criminal Justice Center, Circuit Criminal Court Records, 14250 49th St N, Clearwater, FL 34622. 727-464-3267, Fax: 727-464-6233. 8AM-5PM. Access by: mail, phone, fax, in person, online.

Misdemeanor—County Court-Criminal Division, 14250 49th St N, Clearwater, FL 34622-2831. 727-464-6800, Fax: 727-464-6072. 8AM-5PM. Access by: mail, in person, online.

Polk

Real Estate Recording—Polk County Clerk of the Circuit Court, 255 N. Broadway, Bartow, FL 33830. Fax: 863-534-4089. 8:30AM-4:30PM.

Civil Actions Over $15,000, Probate—Circuit Court-Civil Division, PO Box 9000, Drawer CC2, Bartow, FL 33831-9000. 863-534-4488, Fax: 863-534-4089. 8AM-5PM. Access by: mail, phone, in person, online.

Felony—Circuit and County Courts-Felony Division, PO Box 9000 Drawer CC9, Bartow, FL 33830. 863-534-4000, Fax: 863-534-4089. 8AM-5PM. Access by: mail, phone, in person, online.

Misdemeanor—Circuit and County Courts-Misdemeanor Division, PO Box 9000 Drawer CC10, Bartow, FL 33830. 863-534-4446, Fax: 863-534-4137. 8AM-5PM. Access by: mail, phone, in person, online.

Civil Actions Under $15,000, Eviction, Small Claims—County Court-Civil Division, PO Box 9000 Drawer CC12, Bartow, FL 33830-9000. 863-534-4556, Fax: 863-534-4089. 8AM-5PM. Access by: mail, phone, in person, online.

Putnam

Real Estate Recording—Putnam County Clerk of the Circuit Court, 518 St. Johns Avenue, Bldg. 1-E, Palatka, FL 32177. Fax: 904-329-0889. 8:30AM-5PM.

Civil, Eviction, Small Claims, Probate—Circuit and County Courts-Civil Division, PO Box 758, Palatka, FL 32178. 904-329-0361, Fax: 904-329-0888. 8:30AM-5PM. Access by: mail, in person.

Felony, Misdemeanor—Circuit and County Courts-Criminal Division, PO Box 758, Palatka, FL 32178. 904-329-0249, Fax: 904-329-0888. 8:30AM-5PM. Access by: mail, phone, fax, in person, online. www.co.putnam.fl.us/clerkofcourt

Santa Rosa

Real Estate Recording—Santa Rosa County Clerk of the Circuit Court, Clerk of Courts Recording Dept, 6865 Caroline Street, Milton, FL 32570. 904-623-0135, Fax: 850-626-7248. 8AM-4:30PM.

Civil, Eviction, Small Claims, Probate—Circuit and County Courts-Civil Division, PO Box 472, Milton, FL 32572. 850-623-0135, Fax: 850-626-7248. 8AM-4:30PM. Access by: mail, fax, in person.

Felony, Misdemeanor—Circuit and County Courts-Criminal Division, PO Box 472, Milton, FL 32572. 850-623-0135, Fax: 850-626-7248. 8AM-4:30PM. Access by: mail, fax, in person.

Sarasota

Real Estate Recording—Sarasota County Clerk of the Circuit Court, 2000 Main Street, Sarasota, FL 34237. 8:30AM-5PM.

Civil, Eviction, Small Claims, Probate—Circuit and County Courts-Civil Division, PO Box 3079, Sarasota, FL 34230. 941-951-5206. 8:30AM-5PM. Access by: mail, in person.

Felony, Misdemeanor—Circuit and County Courts-Criminal, PO Box 3079, Sarasota, FL 34230. 941-362-4066. 8:30AM-5PM. Access by: mail, in person.

Seminole

Real Estate Recording—Seminole County Clerk of the Circuit Court, 301 N. Park Avenue, Room A-132, Sanford, FL 32771. 8AM-4:30PM.

Civil, Eviction, Small Claims, Probate—Circuit and County Courts-Civil Division, PO Drawer C, Sanford, FL 32772-0659. 409-277-6200, Fax: 407-330-7193. 8AM-4:30PM. Access by: mail, in person. www.seminoleclerk.org

Felony, Misdemeanor—Circuit and County Courts-Criminal Division, 301 N Park Ave, Sanford, FL 32771. 409-283-2281. 8AM-4:30PM. Access by: mail, in person.

St. Johns

Real Estate Recording—St. Johns County Clerk of the Circuit Court, 4010 Lewis Speedway, St. Augustine, FL 32095. Fax: 904-823-2294. 8AM-5PM (No Recording after 4:15PM).

Civil, Eviction, Small Claims, Probate—Circuit and County Courts-Civil Division, PO Drawer 300, St Augustine, FL 32085-0300. 904-823-2333, Fax: 904-823-2294. 8AM-5PM. Access by: mail, fax, in person, online.

Felony, Misdemeanor—Circuit and County Courts-Criminal Division, PO Drawer 300, St Augustine, FL 32085-0300. 904-823-2333, Fax: 904-823-2294. 8AM-5PM. Access by: mail, fax, in person, online.

St. Lucie

Real Estate Recording—St. Lucie County Clerk of the Circuit Court, 221 South Indian River Drive, Fort Pierce, FL 34950. Fax: 561-462-1283. 8AM-5PM.

Civil, Eviction, Small Claims, Probate—Circuit and County Courts-Civil Division, PO Drawer 700, Ft Pierce, FL 34954. 561-462-2758, Fax: 561-462-1283. 8AM-5PM. Access by: mail, in person.

Felony, Misdemeanor—Circuit and County Courts-Criminal Division, PO Drawer 700, Ft Pierce, FL 34954. 561-462-6900, Fax: 561-462-6975. 8AM-5PM. Access by: mail, fax, in person.

Sumter

Real Estate Recording—Sumter County Clerk of the Circuit Court, 209 North Florida Street, Room 106, Bushnell, FL 33513. Fax: 352-793-0218. 8:30AM-5PM.

Civil, Eviction, Small Claims, Probate—Circuit and County Courts-Civil Division, 209 N Florida St, Bushnell, FL 33513. 360-577-3060, Fax: 352-793-0218. 8:30AM-5PM. Access by: mail, phone, fax, in person.

Felony, Misdemeanor—Circuit and County Courts-Criminal Division, 209 N Florida St, Bushnell, FL 33513. 360-577-3016, Fax: 352-568-6608. 8:30AM-5PM. Access by: mail, in person.

Suwannee

Real Estate Recording—Suwannee County Clerk of the Circuit Court, 200 South Ohio Avenue, Live Oak, FL 32060. 904-364-3414, Fax: 904-362-0548. 8:30AM-5PM.

Felony, Misdemeanor, Civil, Eviction, Small Claims, Probate—Circuit and County Courts, 200 S Ohio Ave, Live Oak, FL 32060. 904-364-3532, Fax: 904-362-2421. 8AM-5PM. Access by: mail, in person.

Taylor

Real Estate Recording—Taylor County Clerk of the Circuit Court, 108 North Jefferson Street, Perry, FL 32347. Fax: 850-838-3549. 8AM-5PM.

Felony, Misdemeanor, Civil, Eviction, Small Claims, Probate—Circuit and County Courts, PO Box 620, Perry, FL 32347. 850-838-3506, Fax: 850-838-3549. 8AM-5PM. Access by: mail, phone, fax, in person.

Union

Real Estate Recording—Union County Clerk of the Circuit Court, State Road 100, Courthouse Room 103, Lake Butler, FL 32054. 904-496-1026, Fax: 904-496-1718. 8AM-5PM.

Felony, Misdemeanor, Civil, Eviction, Small Claims, Probate—Circuit and County Courts, Courthouse Rm 103, Lake Butler, FL 32054. 904-496-3711, Fax: 904-496-1718. 8AM-5PM. Access by: mail, in person.

Volusia

Real Estate Recording—Volusia County Clerk of the Circuit Court, 235 W. New York Ave. De Land, FL 32720. Fax: 904-740-5104. 8AM-4:30PM.

Civil, Eviction, Small Claims, Probate—Circuit and County Courts-Civil Division, PO Box 43, De Land, FL 32721. 904-736-5915, Fax: 904-822-5711. 8AM-4:30PM. Access by: mail, phone, fax, in person, online.

Felony, Misdemeanor—Circuit and County Courts-Criminal Division, PO Box 43, De Land, FL 32721-0043. 904-736-5915, Fax: 904-822-5711. 8AM-4:30PM. Access by: mail, fax, in person, online.

Wakulla

Real Estate Recording—Wakulla County Clerk of the Circuit Court, Wakulla County Court House, 3056 Crawfordville Hwy, Crawfordville, FL 32327. 904-926-3371, Fax: 850-926-8326. 8AM-4PM.

Felony, Misdemeanor, Civil, Eviction, Small Claims, Probate—Circuit and County Courts, 3056 Crawfordville Hwy, Crawfordville, FL 32327. 850-926-0905, Fax: 850-926-0938. 8AM-5PM. Access by: mail, phone, fax, in person.

Walton

Real Estate Recording—Walton County Clerk of the Circuit Court, 571 US Highway 90 East, Courthouse, De Funiak Springs, FL 32435. 904-892-8121, Fax: 850-892-7551. 8AM-4PM.

Felony, Misdemeanor, Civil, Eviction, Small Claims, Probate—Circuit and County Courts, PO Box 1260, De Funiak Springs, FL 32433. 850-892-8115, Fax: 850-892-7551. 8AM-4:30PM. Access by: mail, fax, in person, online.

Washington

Real Estate Recording—Washington County Clerk of the Circuit Court, 1293 Jackson Avenue, Suite 101, Chipley, FL 32428. 904-638-6205, Fax: 850-638-6297. 8AM-4PM.

Felony, Misdemeanor, Civil, Eviction, Small Claims, Probate—Circuit and County Courts, PO Box 647, Chipley, FL 32428-0647. 850-638-6285, Fax: 850-638-6297. 8AM-4PM. Access by: mail, phone, fax, in person.

Federal Courts

US District Court

Middle District of Florida

Fort Myers Division 2110 First St, Room 2-194, Fort Myers, FL 33901941-461-2000 Counties: Charlotte, Collier, De Soto, Glades, Hendry, Lee.

Jacksonville Division PO Box 53558, Jacksonville, FL 32201904-232-2854 Counties: Baker, Bradford, Clay, Columbia, Duval, Flagler, Hamilton, Nassau, Putnam, St. Johns, Suwannee, Union.

Ocala Division c/o Jacksonville Division, PO Box 53558, Jacksonville, FL 32201904-232-2854 Counties: Citrus, Lake, Marion, Sumter.

Orlando Division Room 218, 80 North Hughey Ave, Orlando, FL 32801407-648-6366 Counties: Brevard, Orange, Osceola, Seminole, Volusia.

Tampa Division Office of the clerk, US Courthouse, Room B-100, 611 N Florida Ave, Tampa, FL 33602813-228-2105, Record Room: 813-228-2105 Counties: Hardee, Hernando, Hillsborough, Manatee, Pasco, Pinellas, Polk, Sarasota.

Northern District of Florida

Gainesville Division 401 SE First Ave, Room 243, Gainesville, FL 32601352-380-2400 Fax: 352-380-2424 Counties: Alachua, Dixie, Gilchrist, Lafayette, Levy. Records for cases prior to July 1996 are maintained at the Tallahassee Division.

Panama City Division c/o Pensacola Division, 1 N Palafox St, #226, Pensacola, FL 32501850-435-8440 Fax: 850-433-5972 Counties: Bay, Calhoun, Gulf, Holmes, Jackson, Washington.

Pensacola Division US Courthouse, 1 N Palafox St, #226, Pensacola, FL 32501850-435-8440 Fax: 850-433-5972 Counties: Escambia, Okaloosa, Santa Rosa, Walton.

Tallahassee Division Suite 122, 110 E Park Ave, Tallahassee, FL 32301850-942-8826 Fax: 850-942-8830 Counties: Franklin, Gadsden, Jefferson, Leon, Liberty, Madison, Taylor, Wakulla.

Southern District of Florida

Fort Lauderdale Division 299 E Broward Blvd, Fort Lauderdale, FL 33301954-769-5400 Counties: Broward.

Fort Pierce Division c/o Miami Division, Room 150, 301 N Miami Ave, Miami, FL 33128305-536-4131 Counties: Highlands, Indian River, Martin, Okeechobee, St. Lucie.

Key West Division c/o Miami Division, Room 150, 301 N Miami Ave, Miami, FL 33128-7788305-536-4131 Counties: Monroe.

Miami Division Room 150, 301 N Miami Ave, Miami, FL 33128-7788305-536-4131 Counties: Dade. www.netside.net/usdcfls

West Palm Beach Division Room 402, 701 Clematis St, West Palm Beach, FL 33401561-803-3400 Counties: Palm Beach.

US Bankruptcy Court

Middle District of Florida

Jacksonville Division PO Box 559, Jacksonville, FL 32201904-232-2852 Counties: Baker, Bradford, Citrus, Clay, Columbia, Duval, Flagler, Hamilton, Marion, Nassau, Putnam, St. Johns, Sumter, Suwannee, Union, Volusia. www.flmb.uscourts.gov

Orlando Division Suite 950, 135 W Central Blvd, Orlando, FL 32801407-648-6365 Counties: Brevard, Lake, Orange, Osceola, Seminole. www.flmb.uscourts.gov

Tampa Division 801 N Florida Ave #727, Tampa, FL 33602813-243-5162 Counties: Charlotte, Collier, De Soto, Glades, Hardee, Hendry, Hernando, Hillsborough, Lee, Manatee, Pasco, Pinellas, Polk, Sarasota. www.flmb.uscourts.gov

Northern District of Florida

Pensacola Division Suite 700, 220 W Garden St, Pensacola, FL 32501904-435-8475 Counties: Escambia, Okaloosa, Santa Rosa, Walton.

Tallahassee Division Room 3120, 227 N Bronough St, Tallahassee, FL 32301-1378850-942-8933 Counties: Alachua, Bay, Calhoun, Dixie, Franklin, Gadsden, Gilchrist, Gulf, Holmes, Jackson, Jefferson, Lafayette, Leon, Levy, Liberty, Madison, Taylor, Wakulla, Washington.

Southern District of Florida

Fort Lauderdale Division 299 E Broward Blvd, Room 310, Fort Lauderdale, FL 33301954-769-5700 Counties: Broward.

Miami Division Room 1517, 51 SW 1st Ave, Miami, FL 33130305-536-5216 Counties: Broward, Dade, Highlands, Indian River, Martin, Monroe, Okeechobee, Palm Beach, St. Lucie. Cases may also be assigned to Fort Lauderdale or to West Palm Beach.

West Palm Beach Division Federal Bldg, Room 202, 701 Clematis St, West Palm Beach, FL 33401561-655-6774 Counties: Any case in the Miami Division may be assigned here.

Georgia

Attorney General's Office
40 Capitol Square SW 404-656-3300
Atlanta, GA 30334-1300 Fax: 404-651-9148
www.ganet.org/ago

Governor's Office
203 State Capitol 404-656-1776
Atlanta, GA 30334 Fax: 404-657-7332
www.gagovernor.org

State Archives
330 Capitol Ave SE 404-656-2393
Atlanta, GA 30334 Fax: 404-657-8427
www.sos.state.ga.us/archives

Capital:	Atlanta
	Fulton County
Time Zone:	EST
Number of Counties:	159
Population:	7,486,242
Web Site:	www.state.ga.us

Search Unclaimed Property Online

http://www.state.ga.us/dor/ptd/ucp

State Agencies

Criminal Records
Georgia Bureau of Investigations, Attn: GCIC, PO Box 370748, Decatur, GA 30037-0748 (3121 Panthersville Rd, Decatur, GA 30037); 404-244-2601; Fax: 404-244-2878; 8AM-4PM. Access by: mail. www.ganet.org/gbi

Corporation Records
Limited Partnership Records
Limited Liability Company Records
Secretary of State, Corporation Division, 2 M L King Dr, Suite 315, W Tower, Atlanta, GA 30334-1530; 404-656-2817; Fax: 404-651-9059; 8AM-5PM. Access by: mail, phone, in person, online. www.sos.state.ga.us/corporations

Trademarks/Servicemarks
Secretary of State, Trademark Division, 2 Martin Luther King, Room 315, W Tower, Atlanta, GA 30334; 404-656-2861; Fax: 404-657-6380; 8AM-5PM. Access by: mail, phone, in person. www.sos.state.ga.us

Sales Tax Registrations
Sales & Use Tax Division, Taxpayer Services Unit, 270 Washington St SW, Atlanta, GA 30334; 404-651-8651; Fax: 404-651-9490; 8AM-4:30PM. Access by:, phone, in person.

Uniform Commercial Code
Superior Court Clerks' Cooperative Authority, 1875 Century Blvd, #100, Atlanta, GA 30345; 404-327-9058; Fax: 404-327-7877; 9AM-5PM. Access by: mail, online. gsccca.org

Federal Tax Liens
State Tax Liens
Records not available from state agency.

All tax liens are filed at the county level.

Workers' Compensation Records
Workers Compensation Board, 270 Peachtree St, Atlanta, GA 30303-1299; 404-656-3875; 8AM-4:30PM. Access by: mail. www.ganet.org/sbwc

Birth Certificates

Department of Human Resources, Vital Records Unit, 47 Trinity Ave, SW, Room 217-H, Atlanta, GA 30334; 404-656-7456, 404-657-7996 Credit Card Line, 404-524-4278 VitalChek Fax; Fax: 404-651-9427; 8AM-4PM. Access by: mail, phone, in person.

Death Records

Department of Human Resources, Vital Records Unit, 47 Trinity Ave, SW, Room 217-H, Atlanta, GA 30334; 404-656-7456, 404-657-7996 Credit Card Line, 404-524-4278 VitalChek Fax; Fax: 404-651-9427; 8AM-4PM. Access by: mail, phone, in person.

Marriage Certificates

Department of Human Resources, Vital Records Unit, 47 Trinity Ave, SW, Room 217-H, Atlanta, GA 30334; 404-656-7456, 404-657-7996 Credit Card Line, 404-524-4278 VitalChek Fax; Fax: 404-651-9427; 8AM-4PM. Access by: mail, phone, in person.

Divorce Records

Department of Human Resources, Vital Records Unit, 47 Trinity Ave, SW, Room 217-H, Atlanta, GA 30334; 404-656-7456, 404-657-7996 Credit Card Line, 404-524-4278 VitalChek Fax; Fax: 404-651-9427; 8AM-4PM. Access by: mail, phone, in person.

Accident Reports

Department of Public Safety, Accident Reporting Section, PO Box 1456, Atlanta, GA 30371 (959 E Confederate Ave, Atlanta, GA 30316); 404-624-7660; Fax: 404-624-7835; 8AM-4:30PM. Access by: mail.

Driver Records

Department of Motor Vehicles, Driver's License Section, MVR Unit, PO Box 1456, Atlanta, GA 30371-2303 (959 E Confederate Ave, Atlanta, GA 30316); 404-624-7479; 8AM-3:30PM. Access by: mail. www.ganet.org/dps

Vehicle Ownership
Vehicle Identification

Department of Revenue, Motor Vehicle Division - Research, PO Box 740381, Atlanta, GA 30374-0381; 404-362-6500; 8AM-4:30PM. Access by: mail. www2.state.ga.us/Departments/DOR/dmv

Boat & Vessel Ownership
Boat & Vessel Registration

Georgia Dept of Natural Resources, 2189 Northlake Parkway Bldg 10 #108, Tucker, GA 30084; 770-414-3338; Fax: 770-414-3344; 8AM-4:30PM.

Legislation-Current/Pending
Legislation-Passed

General Assembly of Georgia, State Capitol, Atlanta, GA 30334; 404-656-5040 Senate, 404-656-5015 House, 404-656-2370 Archives; Fax: 404-656-5043; 8:30AM-4:30PM. Access by: mail, phone, in person, online. www.ganet.org/services/leg

Voter Registration

Secretary of State, Elections Division, 2 Martin Luther King Dr SE, Suite 1104, West Tower, Atlanta, GA 30334; 404-656-2871; Fax: 404-651-9531; 8AM-5PM. Access by: mail. www.sos.state.ga.us/elections

GED Certificates

GED Testing Services, 1800 Century Pl #555, Atlanta, GA 30345; 404-679-1644; 8:30AM-4:30PM M-F.

Hunting License Information
Fishing License Information

Records not available from state agency.

They do not have a central database. You must contact the vendor where the license was purchased.

County Courts & Recording Offices

About the Courts...

Administration

Court Administrator 404-656-5171
244 Washington St SW, Suite 550 Fax: 404-651-6449
Atlanta, GA 30334
www2.state.ga.us/Courts/Supreme

Court Structure

There is a Superior Court in each county, which assumes the role of State Court if the county does not have one.

The Magistrate Court has jurisdiction over one type of misdemeanor related to passing bad checks. This court also issues arrest warrants and sets bond on all felonies.

Online Access

There is no online access available locally or statewide.

About the Recording Offices...

Organization

159 counties, 159 recording offices. The recording officer is Clerk of Superior Court. All transactions are recorded in a "General Execution Docket." The entire state is in the Eastern Time Zone (EST).

UCC Records

Financing statements are filed only with the Clerk of Superior Court in each county. Their system, in effect as of January 1, 1995, merges all new UCC filings into a central statewide database, and allows statewide searching for new filings only from any county office. However, filings prior to that date will remain at the county offices. Only a few counties will perform local UCC searches. Use search request form UCC-11 for local searches. Search fees vary from $2.50 to $25.00 per debtor name. Copies usually cost $.25 per page if you make it and $1.00 per page if the county makes it.

Lien Records

All tax liens on personal property are filed with the county Clerk of Superior Court in a "General Execution Docket" (grantor/grantee) or "Lien Index." Most counties will not perform tax lien searches. Copy fees are the same as for UCC.

Real Estate Records

Most counties will not perform real estate searches. Copy fees are the same as for UCC. Certification fees are usually $2.00 per document - $1.00 for seal and $1.00 for stamp - plus $.50 per page.

County Courts & Recording Offices

Appling

Real Estate Recording—Appling County Clerk of the Superior Court, 110 Tippins St. Baxley, GA 31513. 912-367-8100. 8AM-5PM.

Felony, Misdemeanor, Civil—Superior & State Court, PO Box 269, Baxley, GA 31513. 912-367-8126. 8AM-5PM. Access by: in person.

Civil Actions Under $15,000, Eviction, Small Claims—Magistrate Court, Box 366, Baxley, GA 31513. 912-367-8116, Fax: 912-367-8126. 8:30AM-5PM. Access by: in person.

Probate—Probate Court, Courthouse Square, Baxley, GA 31513. 912-367-8114. 8:30AM-5PM. Access by: mail, in person.

Atkinson

Real Estate Recording—Atkinson County Clerk of the Superior Court, Highway 441 South, Courthouse, Pearson, GA 31642. Fax: 912-422-3429. 8AM-Noon, 1-5PM.

Felony, Misdemeanor, Civil—Superior Court, PO Box 6, South Main, Courthouse Square, Pearson, GA 31642. 912-422-3343, Fax: 912-422-3429. 8AM-Noon, 1-5PM. Access by: in person.

Civil Actions Under $15,000, Eviction, Small Claims—Magistrate Court, PO Box 674, Pearson, GA 31642. 912-422-7158, Fax: 912-422-3429. 9AM-4:30PM. Access by: mail, in person.

Probate—Probate Court, PO Box 855, Pearson, GA 31642. 912-422-3552, Fax: 912-422-3429. 8AM-5PM.

Bacon

Real Estate Recording—Bacon County Clerk of the Superior Court, 301 N. Pierce St. Alma, GA 31510. Fax: 912-632-2757. 9AM-5PM.

Felony, Misdemeanor, Civil—Superior Court, PO Box 376, Alma, GA 31510. 912-632-4915. 9AM-5PM. Access by: mail, in person.

Civil Actions Under $15,000, Eviction, Small Claims—Magistrate Court, Box 389, Alma, GA 31510. 912-632-5961. 9AM-5PM. Access by: mail, in person.

Probate—Probate Court, PO Box 146, Alma, GA 31510. 912-632-7661, Fax: 912-632-2757. 9AM-5PM.

Baker

Real Estate Recording—Baker County Clerk of the Superior Court, Courthouse Way, Newton, GA 31770. 9AM-5PM.

Felony, Misdemeanor, Civil—Superior Court, PO Box 10, Governmental Bldg, Newton, GA 31770. 912-734-3004, Fax: 912-734-8822. 9AM-5PM. Access by: in person.

Civil Actions Under $15,000, Eviction, Small Claims—Magistrate Court, Box 548, Newton, GA 31770. 912-734-3007. 9AM-5PM. Access by: in person.

Probate—Probate Court, PO Box 548, Newton, GA 31770. 912-734-3007, Fax: 912-734-8822. 9AM-5PM M-W & F; 9AM-Noon Th. Access by: in person.

Baldwin

Real Estate Recording—Baldwin County Clerk of the Superior Court, 121 N. Wilkinson St. Suite 209, Milledgeville, GA 31061. 912-434-4791, Fax: 912-445-6320. 8:30AM-5PM.

Felony, Misdemeanor, Civil—Superior & State Court, PO Drawer 987, Milledgeville, GA 31061. 912-445-4007, Fax: 912-445-1404. 8:30AM-5PM. Access by: in person.

Civil Actions Under $15,000, Eviction, Small Claims—Magistrate Court, 121 N Wilkinson St, Suite 107, Milledgeville, GA 31061. 912-453-4446, Fax: 912-445-5918. 8:30AM-5PM. Access by: mail, fax, in person.

Probate—Probate Court, PO Box 964, Milledgeville, GA 31061. 912-453-4807, Fax: 912-453-5178. 8:30AM-5PM.

Banks

Real Estate Recording—Banks County Clerk of the Superior Court, Courthouse, 144 Yonah Homer Rd. Homer, GA 30547. Fax: 706-677-2337. 8AM-5PM.

Felony, Misdemeanor, Civil—Superior Court, PO Box 337, 144 Yorah Homer Road, Homer, GA 30547. 706-677-6240, Fax: 706-677-2337. 8:30AM-5PM. Access by: in person.

Civil Actions Under $15,000, Eviction, Small Claims—Magistrate Court, Box 364, Homer, GA 30547. 706-677-6270, Fax: 706-677-2337. 8:30AM-5PM. Access by: in person.

Probate—Probate Court, PO Box 7, Homer, GA 30547. 706-677-6250, Fax: 706-677-2337. 80AM-5PM. Access by: mail, in person.

Barrow

Real Estate Recording—Barrow County Clerk of the Superior Court, 30 North Broad Street, Winder, GA 30680. 770-307-3106. 8AM-5PM.

Felony, Misdemeanor, Civil—Superior Court, PO Box 1280, Winder, GA 30680. 770-307-3035, Fax: 770-307-3033. 8AM-5PM. Access by: in person.

Civil Actions Under $15,000, Eviction, Small Claims—Magistrate Court, 30 N Broad St, Ste 321, Winder, GA 30680. 770-307-3050. 8AM-5PM. Access by: in person.

Probate—Probate Court, Barrow County Courthouse, 30 N Broad St, Winder, GA 30680. 770-307-3045, Fax: 770-868-1440. 8AM-5PM.

Bartow

Real Estate Recording—Bartow County Clerk of the Superior Court, 135 W. Cherokee Ave. Suite 233, Cartersville, GA 30120. Fax: 770-386-0846. 8AM-5PM.

Felony, Misdemeanor, Civil—Superior Court, 135 W Cherokee #233, Cartersville, GA 30120. 770-387-5025, Fax: 770-386-0846. 8AM-5PM. Access by: in person.

Civil Actions Under $15,000, Eviction, Small Claims—Magistrate Court, 135 W Cherokee Ave #225, Cartersville, GA 30120-3101. 770-387-5070, Fax: 770-387-5073. 7AM-5:30PM. Access by: in person.

Probate—Probate Court, 135 W Cherokee #243A, Cartersville, GA 30120. 678-387-5075, Fax: 678-387-5074. 8AM-5PM.

Ben Hill

Real Estate Recording—Ben Hill County Clerk of the Superior Court, 401 E. Central Ave. Courthouse, Fitzgerald, GA 31750. Fax: 912-426-5487. 8:30AM-5PM.

Felony, Misdemeanor, Civil—Superior Court, PO Box 1104, 401 Central, Fitzgerald, GA 31750. 912-426-5135, Fax: 912-426-5487. 8:30AM-5PM. Access by: in person.

Civil Actions Under $15,000, Eviction, Small Claims—Magistrate Court, Box 1163, Fitzgerald, GA 31750. 912-426-5140, Fax: 912-426-5123. 8:30AM-5:30PM. Access by: mail, phone, fax, in person.

Probate—Probate Court, 401 E Central Ave, Fitzgerald, GA 31750. 912-423-2317, Fax: 912-423-5715. 9AM-5PM.

Berrien

Real Estate Recording—Berrien County Clerk of the Superior Court, 101 E. Marion Ave. #3, Nashville, GA 31639. 912-686-7461. 8AM-5PM.

Felony, Misdemeanor, Civil—Superior Court, 101 E Marion Ave, Ste 3, Nashville, GA 31639. 912-686-5506. 8AM-5PM. Access by: mail, in person.

Civil Actions Under $15,000, Eviction, Small Claims—Magistrate Court, 115 S Davis, Box 267, Nashville, GA 31639. 912-686-7019, Fax: 912-686-6328. 8:30AM-4:30PM. Access by: mail, in person.

Probate—Probate Court, 101 E Marion Ave, Ste 1, Nashville, GA 31639. 912-686-5213, Fax: 912-686-9495. 7AM-5PM Sun-Sat.

Bibb

Real Estate Recording—Bibb County Clerk of the Superior Court, 275 Second Street, Suite 216, Macon, GA 31201. 912-749-6310, Fax: 912-749-6539. 8:30AM-5PM.

Felony, Civil—Superior Court, PO Box 1015, 601 Mulberry St Rm 216, Macon, GA 31202. 912-749-6527. 8:30AM-5PM. Access by: mail, in person.

Misdemeanor, Civil—State Court, PO Box 5086, Macon, GA 31213-7199. 912-749-6676, Fax: 912-748-6326. 8:30AM-5:30PM. Access by: mail, in person.

Civil Actions Under $25,000, Eviction, Small Claims—Civil & Magistrate Court, 601 Mulberry St, Bibb County Courthouse, Macon, GA 31201. 912-749-6495, Fax: 912-722-5861. 8AM-5PM. Access by: in person.

Probate—Probate Court, PO Box 6518, Macon, GA 31208-6518. 912-749-6494, Fax: 912-749-6686. 8AM-5PM. Access by: mail, in person.

Bleckley

Real Estate Recording—Bleckley County Clerk of the Superior Court, Courthouse, Cochran, GA 31014. 912-934-3200, Fax: 912-934-3205. 8:30AM-5PM.

Felony, Misdemeanor, Civil—Superior Court, 306 SE 2nd St, Cochran, GA 31014. 912-934-3210, Fax: 912-934-3205. 8:30AM-5PM. Access by: in person.

Civil Actions Under $15,000, Eviction, Small Claims—Magistrate Court, 101 Eighth St, Cochran, GA 31014. 912-934-3202, Fax: 912-934-3226. 8:30AM-5PM. Access by: in person.

Probate—Probate Court, 306 SE Second St, Cochran, GA 31014. 912-934-3204, Fax: 912-934-3205. 8:30AM-5PM.

Brantley

Real Estate Recording—Brantley County Clerk of the Superior Court, Corner of Brantley & Highway 301, 117 Brantley St. Nahunta, GA 31553. 912-462-5256, Fax: 912-462-5538. 8AM-5PM.

Felony, Misdemeanor, Civil—Superior Court, PO Box 1067, 117 Brantley St, Nahunta, GA 31553. 912-462-5635, Fax: 912-462-6247. 8AM-5PM. Access by: mail, phone, fax, in person.

Civil Actions Under $15,000, Eviction, Small Claims—Magistrate Court, PO Box 998, Nahunta, GA 31553. 912-462-6780, Fax: 912-462-5538. 8AM-4:30PM. Access by: mail, phone, fax, in person.

Probate—Probate Court, PO Box 207, Nahunta, GA 31553. 912-462-5192, Fax: 912-462-5538. 9AM-5PM.

Brooks

Real Estate Recording—Brooks County Clerk of the Superior Court, Screven Street, Courthouse, Quitman, GA 31643. Fax: 912-263-5050. 8AM-5PM.

Felony, Misdemeanor, Civil—Superior Court, PO Box 630, Quitman, GA 31643. 912-263-4747, Fax: 912-263-7559. 8:30AM-5PM. Access by: in person.

Civil Actions Under $15,000, Eviction, Small Claims—Magistrate Court, PO Box 387, Quitman, GA 31643. 912-263-9989, Fax: 912-263-7847. 8AM-5PM. Access by: mail, in person.

Probate—Probate Court, PO Box 665, Quitman, GA 31643. 912-263-5567. 8:30AM-5PM.

Bryan

Real Estate Recording—Bryan County Clerk of the Superior Court, 151 South College Street, Pembroke, GA 31321. Fax: 912-653-3695. 8AM-5PM.

Felony, Misdemeanor, Civil—Superior & State Court, PO Drawer H, Pembroke, GA 31321. 912-653-3872, Fax: 912-653-3695. 8AM-5PM. Access by: mail, in person.

Civil Actions Under $15,000, Eviction, Small Claims—Magistrate Court, Box 927, Pembroke, GA 31321. 912-653-3860, Fax: 912-653-4603. 8AM-5PM. Access by: in person.

Probate—Probate Court, PO Box 418, Pembroke, GA 31321. 912-653-3856, Fax: 912-653-4691. 8AM-12, 1-5PM.

Bulloch

Real Estate Recording—Bulloch County Clerk of the Superior Court, Judicial Annex, 20 Siebald St. Statesboro, GA 30458. 912-764-6285. 8:30AM-5PM.

Felony, Misdemeanor, Civil—Superior & State Court, Judicial Annex Bldg, 20 Siebald St, Statesboro, GA 30458. 912-764-9009. 8:30AM-5PM. Access by: in person.

Civil Actions Under $15,000, Eviction, Small Claims—Magistrate Court, Box 1004, Statesboro, GA 30458. 912-764-6458, Fax: 912-489-6731. 8:30AM-5PM. Access by: in person.

Probate—Probate Court, PO Box 1005, Statesboro, GA 30459. 912-489-8749, Fax: 912-764-8740. 8:30AM-5PM. Access by: mail, in person.

Burke

Real Estate Recording—Burke County Clerk of the Superior Court, 111 East 6th St. Courthouse, Waynesboro, GA 30830. 706-554-2607, Fax: 706-554-7887. 9AM-5PM.

Felony, Misdemeanor, Civil—Superior & State Court, PO Box 803, Waynesboro, GA 30830. 706-554-2279, Fax: 706-554-7887. 9AM-5PM. Access by: in person.

Civil Actions Under $15,000, Eviction, Small Claims—Magistrate Court, Box 401, Waynesboro, GA 30830. 706-554-4281. 9AM-5PM. Access by: in person.

Probate—Probate Court, PO Box 322, Waynesboro, GA 30830. 706-554-3000. 9AM-5PM.

Butts

Real Estate Recording—Butts County Clerk of the Superior Court, 26 Third Street, Jackson, GA 30233. 770-775-8200, Fax: 770-775-8211. 8AM-5PM.

Felony, Misdemeanor, Civil—Superior Court, PO Box 320, 26 3rd St, Jackson, GA 30233. 770-775-8215. 8AM-5PM. Access by: in person.

Civil Actions Under $15,000, Eviction, Small Claims—Magistrate Court, Box 457, Jackson, GA 30233. 678-775-8220, Fax: 678-775-8236. 8AM-5PM. Access by: mail, in person.

Probate—Probate Court, 25 Third Strret, #7, Jackson, GA 30233. 770-775-8204, Fax: 770-775-8211. 8AM-5PM.

Calhoun

Real Estate Recording—Calhoun County Clerk of the Superior Court, Courthouse Square, 111 School Street, Morgan, GA 31766. 912-849-2970, Fax: 912-849-0072. 8AM-5PM.

Felony, Misdemeanor, Civil—Superior Court, PO Box 69, Morgan, GA 31766. 912-849-2715, Fax: 912-849-2971. 8AM-5PM. Access by: mail, in person.

Civil Actions Under $15,000, Eviction, Small Claims—Magistrate Court, Box 87, Morgan, GA 31766. 912-849-2115, Fax: 912-849-2072. 8AM-5PM. Access by: mail, in person.

Probate—Probate Court, PO Box 87, Morgan, GA 31766. 912-849-2115, Fax: 912-849-0099.

Camden

Real Estate Recording—Camden County Clerk of the Superior Court, 200 East 4th St. Courthouse Square, Woodbine, GA 31569. 912-576-5601. 9AM-5PM.

Felony, Misdemeanor, Civil—Superior Court, PO Box 578, 200 E Courthouse Square, Woodbine, GA 31569. 912-576-5601. 9AM-5PM. Access by: in person.

Civil Actions Under $15,000, Eviction, Small Claims—Magistrate Court, Box 386, Woodbine, GA 31569. 912-576-5658, Fax: 912-576-5683. 9AM-5PM. Access by: mail, in person.

Probate—Probate Court, PO Box 818, Woodbine, GA 31569. 912-576-3785, Fax: 912-576-5484. 9AM-Noon, 1-5PM. Access by: mail, in person.

Candler

Real Estate Recording—Candler County Clerk of the Superior Court, 355 South Broad Street, West, Courthouse, Metter, GA 30439. 912-685-5257, Fax: 912-685-2160. 8:30AM-5PM.

Felony, Misdemeanor, Civil—Superior & State Court, PO Draawer 830, Metter, GA 30439. 912-685-5257. 8:30AM-5PM. Access by: in person.

Civil Actions Under $15,000, Eviction, Small Claims—Magistrate Court, Box 682, Metter, GA 30439. 912-685-2888. 9AM-5PM. Access by: mail, in person.

Carroll

Real Estate Recording—Carroll County Clerk of the Superior Court, 311 Newnan Street, Room 203, Carrollton, GA 30117. 770-830-5801, Fax: 770-214-3125. 8AM-5PM.

Felony, Misdemeanor, Civil—Superior & State Court, PO Box 1620, Carrollton, GA 30117. 770-830-5830, Fax: 770-830-5988. 8AM-5PM. Access by: mail, in person.

Civil Actions Under $15,000, Eviction, Small Claims—Magistrate Court, PO Box 338, Carrollton, GA 30117. 770-830-5874, Fax: 770-830-5851. 9AM-5PM. Access by: mail, in person.

Probate—Probate Court, PO Box 338, Rm 204, Carrollton, GA 30117. 770-830-5840, Fax: 770-830-5995. 8AM-5PM. Access by: mail, in person.

Catoosa

Real Estate Recording—Catoosa County Clerk of the Superior Court, 875 Lafayette Street, Courthouse, Ringgold, GA 30736. 706-935-2500. 8:30AM-5PM.

Felony, Misdemeanor, Civil, Eviction, Small Claims—Superior & Magistrate Court, 875 LaFayette St, Ringgold, GA 30736. 706-935-4231. 8:30AM-5PM. Access by: in person.

Probate—Probate Court, Courthouse, Ringgold, GA 30736. 706-935-3511. 9AM-5PM. Access by: in person.

Charlton

Real Estate Recording—Charlton County Clerk of the Superior Court, Courthouse, 100 S. Third St. Folkston, GA 31537. Fax: 912-496-3882. 8AM-5PM.

Felony, Misdemeanor, Civil—Superior Court, Courthouse, Folkston, GA 31537. 912-496-2354. 8:30AM-5PM. Access by: mail, in person.

Civil Actions Under $15,000, Eviction, Small Claims—Magistrate Court, 100 A County St, Folkston, GA 31537. 912-496-2617, Fax: 912-496-2560. 8AM-5PM. Access by: mail, phone, fax, in person.

Probate—Probate Court, 100 S 3rd St, Folkston, GA 31537. 912-496-2230, Fax: 912-496-1156. 8AM-5PM.

Chatham

Real Estate Recording—Chatham County Clerk of the Superior Court, 133 Montgomery Street, Courthouse Rm. 304, Savannah, GA 31401. Fax: 912-652-7380. 8AM-5PM.

Felony, Misdemeanor, Civil—Superior Court, PO Box 10227, 133 Montgomery St, Savannah, GA 31412. 912-652-7197, Fax: 912-652-7380. 8AM-5PM. Access by: mail, in person.

Misdemeanor, Civil—State Court of Chatham County, County Courthouse 133 Montgomery St, Savannah, GA 31401. 912-652-7224, Fax: 912-652-7229. 8AM-5PM. Access by: mail, in person.

Civil Actions Under $15,000, Eviction, Small Claims—Magistrate Court, 133 Montgomery St Room 303, Savannah, GA 31401. 912-652-7188, Fax: 912-652-7550. 8AM-5PM. Access by: mail, phone, in person. www.chathamcourts.org

Probate—Probate Court, 133 Montgomery St, Savannah, GA 31401. 912-652-7264, Fax: 912-652-7262. 8AM-5PM. Access by: mail, in person. www.chathamcourts.org

Chattahoochee

Real Estate Recording—Chattahoochee County Clerk of the Superior Court, Broad Street, Courthouse, Cusseta, GA 31805. Fax: 706-989-0396. 8AM-5PM.

Felony, Misdemeanor, Civil, Eviction, Small Claims—Superior & Magistrate Court, PO Box 120, Cusseta, GA 31805. 706-989-3424, Fax: 706-989-0396. 8AM-5PM. Access by: in person. Special note: Magistrate Court is 706-989-3643.

Probate—Probate Court, PO Box 119, Cusseta, GA 31805. 706-989-3603, Fax: 706-989-2005. 8AM-Noon, 1-5PM.

Chattooga

Real Estate Recording—Chattooga County Clerk of the Superior Court, Commerce Street, Courthouse, Summerville, GA 30747. 706-857-0703. 8:30AM-5PM.

Felony, Misdemeanor, Civil, Eviction, Small Claims—Superior & State Court, PO Box 159, Summerville, GA 30747. 706-857-0706. 8:30AM-5PM. Access by: in person.

Probate—Probate Court, PO Box 467, Summerville, GA 30747. 706-857-0709, Fax: 706-857-0726. 8:30AM-Noon, 1-5PM.

Cherokee

Real Estate Recording—Cherokee County Clerk of the Superior Court, 90 North Street, Suite G-170, Canton, GA 30114. 770-479-0425. 8:30AM-5PM.

Felony, Misdemeanor, Civil—Superior & State Court, 990 North St, Ste G170, Canton, GA 30114. 770-479-0538. 8:30AM-5PM. Access by: in person. Special note: This court location also handles juvenile records.

Civil Actions Under $15,000, Eviction, Small Claims—Magistrate Court, PO Box 255, Canton, GA 30114. 678-479-8516. 8:30AM-5PM. Access by: mail, in person.

Probate—Probate Court, 90 North St, Rm 340, Canton, GA 30114. 770-479-0541, Fax: 770-479-0567. Access by: mail, in person.

Clarke

Real Estate Recording—Athens-Clarke County Clerk of the Superior Court, 325 East Washington Street, Room 100, Athens, GA 30601. 706-613-3320, Fax: 706-613-3189. 8AM-5PM.

Felony, Misdemeanor, Civil—Superior & State Court, PO Box 1805, Athens, GA 30603. 706-613-3190. 8AM-5PM. Access by: in person.

Civil Actions Under $15,000, Eviction, Small Claims—Magistrate Court, 325 E Washington St, Athens, GA 30601. 706-613-3313, Fax: 706-613-3314. 8AM-5PM. Access by: mail, fax, in person.

Probate—Probate Court, 325 E Washington St, Rm 215, Athens, GA 30601. 706-613-3320, Fax: 706-613-3323. 8AM-5PM.

Clay

Real Estate Recording—Clay County Clerk of the Superior Court, 210 Washington Street, Courthouse, Fort Gaines, GA 31751. 912-768-2915, Fax: 912-768-3047. 8AM-4:30PM.

Felony, Misdemeanor, Civil, Eviction—Superior Court, PO Box 550, Ft Gaines, GA 31751. 912-768-2631, Fax: 912-768-3047. 8AM-4:30PM. Access by: in person.

Misdemeanor, Civil Under $45,000, Eviction, Small Claims—Magistrate Court, PO Box 73, Ft Gaines, GA 31751. 912-768-2631, Fax: 912-768-3443. 8AM-4:30PM. Access by: in person.

Probate—Probate Court, PO Box 448, Ft. Gaines, GA 31751. 912-768-2445, Fax: 912-768-2710. 8AM-4:30PM.

Clayton

Real Estate Recording—Clayton County Clerk of the Superior Court, 121 South McDonough Street, Room 202, Jonesboro, GA 30236. 770-477-3285. 8AM-5PM.

Felony, Misdemeanor, Civil—Superior Court, 121 S McDonough St, Jonesboro, GA 30236. 770-477-3405. 8AM-5PM. Access by: mail, in person.

Misdemeanor—State Court, 121 S McDonough St, Jonesboro, GA 30236. 770-477-4522. 8AM-5PM. Access by: in person. www.co.clayton.gaq.us

Civil Actions Under $15,000, Eviction, Small Claims—Magistrate Court, 121 S McDonough St, Jonesboro, GA 30236. 770-477-3443. 8AM-5PM. Access by: mail, in person.

Probate—Probate Court, 121 S McDonough St, Annex 3, Jonesboro, GA 30236-3694. 770-477-3299, Fax: 770-477-3306. 8AM-5PM. Access by: mail, in person.

Clinch

Real Estate Recording—Clinch County Clerk of the Superior Court, Courthouse, Homerville, GA 31634. Fax: 912-487-3083. 8AM-5PM.

Felony, Misdemeanor, Civil—Superior & State Court, PO Box 433, Homerville, GA 31634. 912-487-5854, Fax: 912-489-3083. 8AM-5PM. Access by: mail, in person.

Civil Actions Under $15,000, Eviction, Small Claims—Magistrate Court, 100 Court Square, Homerville, GA 31634. 912-487-2514, Fax: 912-487-3658. 9AM-5PM. Access by: mail, in person.

Probate—Probate Court, PO Box 364, Homerville, GA 31634. 912-487-5523, Fax: 912-487-3083. 9AM-5PM.

Cobb

Real Estate Recording—Cobb County Clerk of the Superior Court, 10 East Park Square, Marietta, GA 30090. 770-528-8600. 8AM-5PM.

Felony, Misdemeanor, Civil—Superior Court, PO Box 3370, Marietta, GA 30061. 770-528-1300, Fax: 770-528-1382. 8AM-5PM. Access by: in person, online. www.clerksuperiorcourt.wl.com

Misdemeanor, Civil, Eviction—State Court-Civil & Criminal Divisions, 12 East Park Square, Marietta, GA 30090-9630. 8AM-5PM. Access by: mail, in person. Special note: A public access terminal will be available by year end. www.mindspring.com/~statecourt/clerks.htm

Civil Actions Under $15,000, Small Claims—Magistrate Court, 32 Waddell St, Marietta, GA 30090-9656. 770-528-8910, Fax: 770-528-8929. 8AM-5PM. Access by: mail, in person. www.cobbmagistratecourt.org

Probate—Probate Court of Cobb County, 32 Waddell St, Marietta, GA 30060. 770-528-1900, Fax: 770-528-1996. 8AM-4:30PM.

Coffee

Real Estate Recording—Coffee County Clerk of the Superior Court, Courthouse, 101 S. Peterson Ave. Douglas, GA 31533. 912-384-4799. 8:30AM-5PM.

Felony, Misdemeanor, Civil—Superior & State Court, 101 S Peterson Ave, Douglas, GA 31533. 912-384-2865. 8:30AM-5PM. Access by: in person.

Civil Actions Under $15,000, Eviction, Small Claims—Magistrate Court, 101 S Peterson Ave, Douglas, GA 31533. 912-384-2983. 8AM-5PM. Access by: mail, in person.

Probate—Probate Court, 109 S Peterson Ave, Douglas, GA 31533. 912-384-5213, Fax: 912-384-0291. 9AM-5PM. Access by: mail, in person.

Colquitt

Real Estate Recording—Colquitt County Clerk of the Superior Court, Governmental Bldg, Room 214, 1220 South Main St. Moultrie, GA 31776. 912-985-5306. 8AM-5PM.

Felony, Misdemeanor, Civil—Superior & State Court, PO Box 2827, Moultrie, GA 31776. 912-985-1324. 8AM-5PM. Access by: in person.

Civil Actions Under $15,000, Eviction, Small Claims—Magistrate Court, PO Box 70, Moultrie, GA 31776. 912-891-7450, Fax: 912-891-7494. 8AM-5PM. Access by: mail, in person.

Probate—Probate Court, PO Box 264, Moultrie, GA 31776-0264. 912-891-7415, Fax: 912-891-7403. 8AM-5PM.

Columbia

Real Estate Recording—Columbia County Clerk of the Superior Court, 1954 Appling Harlem Rd. Appling, GA 30802. Fax: 706-541-4013. 8AM-5PM.

Felony, Misdemeanor, Civil—Superior Court, PO Box 100, Appling, GA 30802. 706-541-1139, Fax: 706-541-4013. 8AM-5PM. Access by: in person.

Civil Actions Under $15,000, Eviction, Small Claims—Magistrate Court, PO Box 777, Evans, GA 30809. 706-868-3316, Fax: 706-868-3314. 8AM-5PM. Access by: mail, phone, in person.

Probate—Probate Court, PO Box 525, Appling, GA 30802. 706-541-1254, Fax: 706-541-4001. 8AM-5PM.

Cook

Real Estate Recording—Cook County Clerk of the Superior Court, 212 North Hutchinson Avenue, Adel, GA 31620. 912-896-3151. 8:30AM-4:30PM.

Felony, Misdemeanor, Civil—Superior Court, 212 N Hutchinson Ave, Adel, GA 31620. 912-896-7717. 8:30AM-4:30PM. Access by: mail, phone, in person.

Civil Actions Under $15,000, Eviction, Small Claims—Magistrate Court, 212 N Hutchinson Ave, Adel, GA 31620. 912-896-3151, Fax: 912-896-7629. 8AM-4:30PM. Access by: mail, in person.

Probate—Probate Court, 212 N Hutchinson Ave, Adel, GA 31620. 912-896-3941. 8:30AM-5PM. Access by: mail, in person.

Coweta

Real Estate Recording—Coweta County Clerk of the Superior Court, Courthouse, First FLoor, 200 Court Square, Newnan, GA 30263. Fax: 770-254-3700. 8AM-5PM.

Felony, Misdemeanor, Civil—Superior & State Court, PO Box 943, Newnan, GA 30264. 770-254-2690, Fax: 770-254-3700. 8:30AM-5PM. Access by: mail, phone, in person.

Civil Actions Under $15,000, Eviction, Small Claims—Magistrate Court, 22-34 E Broad St, Newnan, GA 30263. 678-254-2610, Fax: 678-254-2606. 8AM-5PM. Access by: mail, in person.

Probate—Probate Court, 22 E Broad St, Newnan, GA 30263. 678-254-2640, Fax: 678-254-2648. 8AM-5PM. Access by: mail, in person.

Crawford

Real Estate Recording—Crawford County Clerk of the Superior Court, Courthouse, US Highway 80 & State Highway 42, Roberta, GA 31050. 912-836-3575. 9AM-5PM.

Felony, Misdemeanor, Civil, Eviction, Small Claims—Superior Court, PO Box 1037, Roberta, GA 31058. 912-836-3328. 9AM-5PM. Access by: in person. Special note: Magistrate Court is at PO Box 568, call at 912-836-5804.

Probate—Probate Court, PO Box 1028, Roberta, GA 31078. 912-836-3313. 8:30AM-4:30PM. Access by: mail, in person. Special note: The record search fee is $4.00.

Crisp

Real Estate Recording—Crisp County Clerk of the Superior Court, 210 7th Street South, Courthouse, Cordele, GA 31015. 912-276-2630. 8:30AM-5PM.

Felony, Misdemeanor, Civil Actions Over $5,000—Superior & Juvenile Court, PO Box 747, Cordele, GA 31010-0747. 912-276-2616. 8:30AM-5PM. Access by: mail, in person.

Civil Actions Under $15,000, Eviction, Small Claims—Magistrate Court, 210 S 7th St Room 102, Cordese, GA 31015. 912-276-2618. 8:30AM-5PM. Access by: in person.

Probate—Probate Court, 210 S 7th St, Rm 103, PO Box 26, Cordele, GA 31010-0026. 912-276-2621. 9AM-5PM.

Dade

Real Estate Recording—Dade County Clerk of the Superior Court, Main Street-U.S. Highway 11, Courthouse Sq. Trenton, GA 30752. Fax: 706-657-8284. 8:30AM-5PM.

Felony, Misdemeanor, Civil, Eviction, Small Claims—Superior Court, PO Box 417, Trenton, GA 30752. 706-657-4778. 8:30AM-5PM. Access by: mail, phone, in person.

Probate—Probate Court, PO Box 605, Trenton, GA 30752. 706-657-4414, Fax: 706-657-5116. 8:30AM-5PM. Access by: mail, in person.

Dawson

Real Estate Recording—Dawson County Clerk of the Superior Court, Courthouse, 25 Tucker Ave. Dawsonville, GA 30534. Fax: 706-344-3511. 8AM-5PM.

Felony, Misdemeanor, Civil—Superior Court, PO Box 249, Dawsonville, GA 30534. 706-265-2525, Fax: 706-265-3071. 8AM-5PM. Access by: in person.

Civil Actions Under $15,000, Eviction, Small Claims—Magistrate Court, 367 Hwy 53W, Dawsonville, GA 30534. 706-265-8000. 10AM-8PM M,T; 10AM-2PM W; 8:30AM-5PM F. Access by: mail, in person.

Probate—Probate Court, 25 Tucker Ave #211, Dawsonville, GA 30534. 706-344-3580, Fax: 706-265-2358. 8AM-5PM.

De Kalb

Real Estate Recording—De Kalb County Clerk of the Superior Court, 556 North McDonough Street, Courthouse, Room 208, Decatur, GA 30030. 8:30AM-5PM.

Felony, Misdemeanor, Civil—Superior Court, 556 N McDonough St, Decatur, GA 30030. 405-282-0123, Fax: 404-371-2635. 8:30AM-5PM. Access by: in person.

Misdemeanor, Civil—State Court, 556 N McDonough St, Decatur, GA 30030. 405-276-2360, Fax: 404-371-3064. 8:30AM-5PM. Access by: mail, in person.

Civil Actions Under $15,000, Eviction, Small Claims—Magistrate Court, 556 N McDonough St, Decatur, GA 30030. 678-371-2261. 8:30AM-5PM. Access by: mail, in person.

Probate—Probate Court, 556 N McDonough St, Rm 103, Decatur, GA 30030. 678-371-2601, Fax: 678-371-7055. 8:30AM-4PM.

Decatur

Real Estate Recording—Decatur County Clerk of the Superior Court, 1400 East Shotwell St. Bainbridge, GA 31717. 912-248-3030, Fax: 912-248-3029. 8AM-5PM.

Felony, Misdemeanor, Civil—Superior & State Court, PO Box 336, Bainbridge, GA 31717. 912-248-3025. 9AM-5PM. Access by: in person.

Civil Actions Under $15,000, Eviction, Small Claims—Magistrate Court, 912 Spring Creek Rd Box #3, Bainbridge, GA 31717. 912-248-3014. 9AM-5PM. Access by: mail, in person.

Probate—Probate Court, 112 W Water, PO Box 234, Bainbridge, GA 31718. 912-248-3016. 9AM-5PM. Access by: mail.

Dodge

Real Estate Recording—Dodge County Clerk of the Superior Court, Anson Avenue, Courthouse, Eastman, GA 31023. 912-374-3775. 9AM-Noon,1-5PM.

Felony, Misdemeanor, Civil—Superior Court, PO Drawer 4276, 407 Anson Ave, Eastman, GA 31023. 912-374-2871. 9AM-5PM. Access by: in person.

Civil Actions Under $15,000, Eviction, Small Claims—Magistrate Court, Courthouse Square, Eastman, GA 31023. 912-374-7243. 8:30AM-4:30PM. Access by: in person.

Probate—Probate Court, PO Box 514, Eastman, GA 31023. 912-374-3775, Fax: 912-374-9197. 9AM-Noon, 1-5PM. Access by: mail, in person.

Dooly

Real Estate Recording—Dooly County Clerk of the Superior Court, 104 Second Street, Room 12, Vienna, GA 31092. 912-268-4228, Fax: 912-268-6142. 8:30AM-5PM.

Felony, Misdemeanor, Civil—Superior Court, PO Box 326, Vienna, GA 31092-0326. 912-268-4234, Fax: 912-268-6142. 8:30AM-5PM. Access by: mail, fax, in person.

Civil Actions Under $15,000, Eviction, Small Claims—Magistrate Court, W Union St, Courthouse Annex, Vienna, GA 31092. 912-268-4324. 8AM-Noon, 1-5PM M,W,F. Access by: in person.

Probate—Probate Court, 104 2nd St, Vienna, GA 31092. 912-268-4217, Fax: 912-268-6142. 8AM-5PM M,T,Th,F; 8:30AM-Noon W & Sat or by appointment.

Dougherty

Real Estate Recording—Dougherty County Clerk of the Superior Court, 225 Pine Avenue, Room 126, Albany, GA 31702. 912-431-2130, Fax: 912-431-2850. 8:30AM-5PM.

Felony, Misdemeanor, Civil—Superior & State Court, PO Box 1827, Albany, GA 31703. 912-431-2198. 8:30AM-5PM. Access by: in person, online. www.dougherty.ga.us/dococlk.htm

Civil Actions Under $15,000, Eviction, Small Claims—Magistrate Court, PO Box 1827, Albany, GA 31703. 912-431-3216, Fax: 912-434-2692. 8:30AM-5PM. Access by: mail, fax, in person.

Probate—Probate Court, 225 Pine Ave, PO Box 1827, Albany, GA 31702. 912-431-2102, Fax: 912-434-2694. 8:30AM-5PM. www.dougherty.ga.us

Douglas

Real Estate Recording—Douglas County Clerk of the Superior Court, Douglas County Courthouse, 8700 Hospital Dr. Douglasville, GA 30134. 8AM-5PM.

Felony, Misdemeanor, Civil—Superior Court, Douglas County Courthouse, 8700 Hospital Dr, Douglasville, GA 30134. 770-920-7252. 8AM-5PM. Access by: in person.

Civil Actions Under $15,000, Eviction, Small Claims—Magistrate Court, 8700 Hospital Dr, Douglasville, GA 30134. 770-920-7215. 8AM-5PM. Access by: in person.

Probate—Probate Court, 8700 Hospital Dr, Douglasville, GA 30134. 770-920-7249, Fax: 770-920-7381. 8AM-5PM. Access by: mail, in person.

Early

Real Estate Recording—Early County Clerk of the Superior Court, Courthouse, Court Square, Blakely, GA 31723. 912-723-4024, Fax: 912-723-5246. 8AM-5PM.

Felony, Misdemeanor, Civil—Superior & State Court, PO Box 849, Blakely, GA 31723. 912-723-3033, Fax: 912-723-5246. 8AM-5PM. Access by: in person.

Civil Actions Under $15,000, Eviction, Small Claims—Magistrate Court, Courthouse Square, Blakely, GA 31723. 912-723-5492, Fax: 912-723-5246. 8AM-5PM. Access by: mail, in person.

Probate—Probate Court, Early Courthouse Square, Rm 8, Blakely, GA 31723. 912-723-3454, Fax: 912-723-5246. 8AM-5PM.

Echols

Real Estate Recording—Echols County Clerk of the Superior Court, Courthouse, 110 Highway 94 East, Statenville, GA 31648. 912-559-5253, Fax: 912-559-5792. 8AM-Noon, 1-4:30PM.

Felony, Misdemeanor, Civil—Superior Court, PO Box 213, Statenville, GA 31648. 912-559-5642, Fax: 912-559-5792. 8AM-Noon, 1-4:30PM. Access by: in person.

Civil Actions Under $15,000, Eviction, Small Claims—Magistrate Court, HWY 94 & 129, Statenville, GA 31648. 912-559-7526, Fax: 912-559-5792. 8:30AM-4:30PM. Access by: in person.

Probate—Probate Court, PO Box 118, Statenville, GA 31648. 912-559-7526, Fax: 912-559-7526. 8:30AM-4:30PM. Access by: mail, in person.

Effingham

Real Estate Recording—Effingham County Clerk of the Superior Court, 901 North Pine Street, Courthouse, Springfield, GA 31329. 912-754-6071. 8:30AM-5PM.

Felony, Misdemeanor, Civil—Superior & State Court, PO Box 387, Springfield, GA 31329. 912-754-6071. 8:30AM-5PM. Access by: mail, in person.

Civil Actions Under $15,000, Eviction, Small Claims—Magistrate Court, PO Box 819, Springfield, GA 31329. 912-754-2124, Fax: 912-754-4893. 8:15AM-4:15PM. Access by: mail, in person.

Probate—Probate Court, PO Box 387, Springfield, GA 31329. 912-754-2112, Fax: 912-754-3894. 8:30AM-5PM. Access by: mail, in person.

Elbert

Real Estate Recording—Elbert County Clerk of the Superior Court, Courthouse, Oliver Street, Elberton, GA 30635. Fax: 706-213-7286. 8AM-5PM.

Felony, Misdemeanor, Civil—Superior & State Court, PO Box 619, Elberton, GA 30635. 706-283-2005, Fax: 706-283-2028. 8AM-5PM. Access by: in person.

Civil Actions Under $15,000, Eviction, Small Claims—Magistrate Court, PO Box 763, Elberton, GA 30635. 706-283-2027. 8AM-5PM. Access by: mail, phone, in person.

Probate—Probate Court, Elbert County Courthouse, Elberton, GA 30635. 706-283-2016. 8AM-5PM. Access by: mail, in person.

Emanuel

Real Estate Recording—Emanuel County Clerk of the Superior Court, Court Street, Courthouse, Swainsboro, GA 30401. Fax: 912-237-2173. 8AM-5PM.

Felony, Misdemeanor, Civil—Superior & State Court, PO Box 627, Swainsboro, GA 30401. 912-237-8911, Fax: 912-237-2173. 8AM-5PM. Access by: in person.

Civil Actions Under $15,000, Eviction, Small Claims—Magistrate Court, 107 N Main St, Swainsboro, GA 30401. 912-237-7278. 8AM-5PM. Access by: in person.

Probate—Probate Court, Court St, PO Drawer 70, Swainsboro, GA 30401. 912-237-7091, Fax: 912-237-3651. 8AM-5PM.

Evans

Real Estate Recording—Evans County Clerk of the Superior Court, 123 W. Main Street, Courthouse, Claxton, GA 30417. 912-739-1147, Fax: 912-739-2327. 8AM-5PM.

Felony, Misdemeanor, Civil—Superior & State Court, PO Box 845, Claxton, GA 30417. 912-739-3868, Fax: 912-739-2327. 8AM-5PM. Access by: in person.

Civil Actions Under $15,000, Eviction, Small Claims—Magistrate Court, Courthouse Annex, Rm 7, Freeman St, Claxton, GA 30417. 912-739-3745, Fax: 912-739-3745. 8AM-5PM. Access by: mail, phone, fax, in person.

Probate—Probate Court, County Courthouse, PO Box 852, Claxton, GA 30417. 912-739-4080, Fax: 912-739-4077. 8AM-5PM.

Fannin

Real Estate Recording—Fannin County Clerk of the Superior Court, 420 West Main St. Courthouse, Blue Ridge, GA 30513. 706-632-2645. 9AM-5PM.

Felony, Misdemeanor, Civil—Superior Court, PO Box 1300, 420 W Main St, Blue Ridge, GA 30513. 706-632-2039. 9AM-5PM. Access by: in person.

Civil Actions Under $15,000, Eviction, Small Claims—Magistrate Court, 400 W Main St, #7, Blue Ridge, GA 30513. 706-632-5558, Fax: 706-632-8236. 9AM-5PM. Access by: mail, in person.

Probate—Probate Court, PO Box 245, Blue Ridge, GA 30513. 706-632-3011, Fax: 706-632-8236. 8AM-5PM.

Fayette

Real Estate Recording—Fayette County Clerk of the Superior Court, 145 Johnson Avenue, Fayetteville, GA 30214. 770-461-8611. 8AM-5PM.

Felony, Misdemeanor, Civil—Superior Court, PO Box 130, Fayetteville, GA 30214. 770-461-4703. 8AM-5PM. Access by: in person.

Civil Actions Under $15,000, Eviction, Small Claims—Magistrate Court, 155 S Jeff Davis Dr, Fayetteville, GA 30214. 770-461-2116, Fax: 770-719-2357. 8AM-5PM. Access by: mail, in person.

Probate—Probate Court, 145 Johnson Ave, Fayetteville, GA 30214. 770-461-9555, Fax: 770-460-8685. 8AM-5PM.

Floyd

Real Estate Recording—Floyd County Clerk of the Superior Court, 3 Government Plaza, Suite 103, Rome, GA 30162. 706-291-5148, Fax: 706-233-0035. 8AM-5PM.

Felony, Misdemeanor, Civil—Superior Court, PO Box 1110, #3 Government Plaza #101, Rome, GA 30163. 706-291-5190, Fax: 706-233-0035. 8AM-5PM. Access by: mail, fax, in person.

Civil Actions Under $15,000, Eviction, Small Claims—Magistrate Court, 401 Tribune St, Rm 227, 3 Government Plaza, Rome, GA 30161. 706-291-5250, Fax: 706-291-5269. 9AM-5PM. Access by: mail, phone, fax, in person.

Probate—Probate Court, #3 Government Plaza, Rome, GA 30162. 706-291-5136, Fax: 706-291-5189. 8AM-4:30PM. Access by: mail, in person.

Forsyth

Real Estate Recording—Forsyth County Clerk of the Superior Court, 100 Courthouse Square, Room 010, Cumming, GA 30040. Fax: 770-886-2858. 8:30AM-5PM.

Felony, Misdemeanor, Civil, Eviction, Small Claims—Superior, State & Magistrate Court, 100 Courthouse Square, Rm 010, Cumming, GA 30040. 678-781-2120. 8:30AM-5PM. Access by: in person. www.9thjudicialdistrict~ga.org/bellforsythhp.shtml

Probate—Probate Court, County Courthouse, 100 Courthouse Sq, Rm 150, Cumming, GA 30130. 770-781-2140. 8:30AM-5PM.

Franklin

Real Estate Recording—Franklin County Clerk of the Superior Court, Courthouse Square, 9592 Lavonia Rd. Carnesville, GA 30521. Fax: 706-384-2185. 8AM-5PM.

Felony, Misdemeanor, Civil—Superior Court, PO Box 70, Carnesville, GA 30521. 706-384-2514. 8AM-5PM. Access by: in person.

Civil Actions Under $15,000, Eviction, Small Claims—Magistrate Court, PO Box 467, Carnesville, GA 30521. 706-384-7473, Fax: 706-384-4346. 8AM-5PM. Access by: in person.

Probate—Probate Court, PO Box 207, Carnesville, GA 30521. 706-384-2403. 8AM-4:30PM.

Fulton

Real Estate Recording—Fulton County Clerk of the Superior Court, 136 Pryor Street, Atlanta, GA 30303. 405-321-6402, Fax: 404-730-7993. 8:30AM-5PM.

Felony, Misdemeanor, Civil, Eviction—Superior Court, 136 Pryor St SW, Rm 106, Atlanta, GA 30303. Fax: 404-730-7993. 8:30AM-5PM. Access by: mail, in person.

Misdemeanor, Civil—State Court, TG100 Justice Center Tower, 185 Central Ave SW, Atlanta, GA 30303. 405-286-5128, Fax: 404-730-8141. 8:30AM-5PM. Access by: mail, in person.

Civil Actions Under $15,000, Eviction, Small Claims—Magistrate Court, 185 Central Ave SW, Rm TG700, Atlanta, GA 30303. 405-298-2580, Fax: 404-730-5027. 8:30AM-5PM. Access by: mail, in person.

Probate—Probate Court, 136 Pryor St SW #C230, Atlanta, GA 30303. 405-282-3150, Fax: 404-730-8283. 8:30AM-5PM. Access by: mail, in person.

Gilmer

Real Estate Recording—Gilmer County Clerk of the Superior Court, 1 West Side Square, Courthouse, Box #30, Ellijay, GA 30540. 706-635-4361, Fax: 706-635-1462. 8:30AM-5PM.

Felony, Misdemeanor, Civil—Superior Court, #1 Westside Square, Ellijay, GA 30540. 706-635-4462, Fax: 706-635-1462. 8:30AM-5PM. Access by: mail, in person.

Civil Actions Under $15,000, Eviction, Small Claims—Magistrate Court, #1 Westside Square, Ellijay, GA 30540. 706-635-2515, Fax: 706-635-7756. 8:30AM-5PM. Access by: mail, in person.

Probate—Probate Court, #1 Westside Square, Ellijay, GA 30540. 706-635-4763, Fax: 706-635-4761. 8:30AM-5PM. Access by: mail.

Glascock

Real Estate Recording—Glascock County Clerk of the Superior Court, 62E Main Street, Courthouse, Gibson, GA 30810. 706-598-2671. 8AM-Noon,1-5PM.

Felony, Misdemeanor, Civil—Superior Court, PO Box 231, 62 E Main St, Gibson, GA 30810. 706-598-2084, Fax: 706-598-2577. 8AM-Noon, 1-5PM. Access by: in person.

Civil Actions Under $15,000, Eviction, Small Claims—Magistrate Court, PO Box 201, Gibson, GA 30810. 706-598-2013. 4-8PM T; 9AM-1PM W & Sat. Access by: mail, phone, in person.

Probate—Probate Court, Courthouse, Main St, PO Box 64, Gibson, GA 30810. 706-598-3241. 8AM-Noon, 1-5PM.

Glynn

Real Estate Recording—Glynn County Clerk of the Superior Court, 701 H Street, Brunswick, GA 31520. 912-267-5680, Fax: 912-267-5625. 8:30AM-5PM.

Felony, Misdemeanor, Civil—Superior Court, PO Box 1355, Brunswick, GA 31521. 912-554-7272, Fax: 912-267-5625. 8:30AM-5PM. Access by: mail, phone, in person.

Misdemeanor, Civil—State Court, PO Box 879, Brunswick, GA 31521. 912-267-5674, Fax: 912-261-3849. 9AM-5PM. Access by: in person.

Civil Actions Under $15,000, Eviction, Small Claims—Magistrate Court, 701 H St, Brunswick, GA 31521. 912-267-5650, Fax: 912-267-5677. 8:30AM-5PM. Access by: mail, in person.

Probate—Probate Court, 701 H St, Brunswick, GA 31521. 912-554-7231, Fax: 912-466-8001. 8:30AM-5PM. Access by: mail, in person.

Gordon

Real Estate Recording—Gordon County Clerk Court, Courthouse, Suite 102, 100 Wall St. Calhoun, GA 30701. 706-629-9242, Fax: 706-629-2139. 8:30AM-5PM.

Felony, Misdemeanor, Civil—Superior Court, PO Box 367, Calhoun, GA 30703. 706-629-9533, Fax: 706-625-3310. 8:30AM-5PM. Access by: mail, fax, in person.

Civil Actions Under $15,000, Eviction, Small Claims—Magistrate Court, 100 Wall St, PO Box 1025, Calhoun, GA 30703. 706-629-6818, Fax: 706-602-1751. 8:30AM-5PM. Access by: in person.

Probate—Probate Court, 100 Wall St, PO Box 669, Calhoun, GA 30703. 706-629-7314, Fax: 706-629-4698. 8:30AM-5PM. Access by: mail, in person.

Grady

Real Estate Recording—Grady County Clerk of the Superior Court, 250 North Broad Street, Box 8, Cairo, GA 31728. 912-377-3327. 8:30AM-5PM.

Felony, Misdemeanor, Civil—Superior Court, 250 N Broad St, Box 8, Cairo, GA 31728. 912-377-2912. 8AM-5PM. Access by: in person.

Civil Actions Under $15,000, Eviction, Small Claims—Magistrate Court, 250 N Broad St, Cairo, GA 31728. 912-377-4132, Fax: 912-377-4127. 8AM-5PM. Access by: mail, in person.

Probate—Probate Court, Courthouse, 250 N Broad St, Cairo, GA 31728. 912-377-4621, Fax: 912-377-4127. 8AM-5PM.

Greene

Real Estate Recording—Greene County Clerk of the Superior Court, Courthouse, Suite 109, 113 North Main St. Greensboro, GA 30642. Fax: 706-453-9179. 7:30AM-5PM.

Felony, Misdemeanor, Civil, Eviction, Small Claims—Superior & Juvenile Court, 113 North Main St, #109, Greensboro, GA 30642. 706-453-3340, Fax: 706-453-3341. 8AM-5PM. Access by: in person.

Probate—Probate Court, 113 N Main St #113, Greensboro, GA 30642. 706-453-3346, Fax: 706-453-7649. 8:30AM-5PM. Access by: mail, in person.

Gwinnett

Real Estate Recording—Gwinnett County Clerk of the Superior Court, 75 Langley Drive, Lawrenceville, GA 30045. 770-822-8000. 8AM-5PM.

Felony, Misdemeanor, Civil, Eviction, Small Claims—Superior, State & Magistrate Court, PO Box 880, Lawrenceville, GA 30246. 770-822-8100. 8AM-5PM. Access by: in person.

Probate—Probate Court of Gwinnett County, 75 Langley Dr, Lawrenceville, GA 30045. 770-822-8250, Fax: 770-822-8274. 8:30AM-4:30PM. Access by: mail, in person.

Habersham

Real Estate Recording—Habersham County Clerk of the Superior Court, Highway 115, 555 Monroe St. Unit 35, Clarkesville, GA 30523. Fax: 706-754-8779. 8AM-5PM.

Felony, Misdemeanor, Civil—Superior & State Court, 555 Monroe St, Unit 35, Clarkesville, GA 30523. 706-754-2923. 8:30AM-5PM. Access by: in person.

Civil Actions Under $15,000, Eviction, Small Claims—Magistrate Court, PO Box 580, Clarkesville, GA 30523. 706-754-4871, Fax: 706-839-7093. 8AM-5PM. Access by: in person.

Probate—Probate Court, Habersham County Courthouse, PO Box 625, Clarkesville, GA 30523. 706-754-2013, Fax: 706-754-5093. 8AM-5PM.

Hall

Real Estate Recording—Hall County Clerk of the Superior Court, Courthouse, 111 Spring St. Gainesville, GA 30501. 770-531-6950, Fax: 770-536-0702. 8AM-5PM.

Felony, Misdemeanor, Civil—Superior & State Court, PO Box 1275, Gainesville, GA 30503. 770-531-7025, Fax: 770-531-7070. 8AM-5PM. Access by: in person.

Civil Actions Under $15,000, Eviction, Small Claims—Magistrate Court, PO Box 1435, Gainesville, GA 30503. 770-531-6912, Fax: 770-531-6917. 8AM-5PM. Access by: mail, in person. www.hallcounty.org/clerkct.htm

Probate—Probate Court, Hall County Courthouse, Rm 123, Gainesville, GA 30501. 770-531-6921, Fax: 770-531-4946. 8AM-5PM. Access by: mail, in person. Special note: The search fee is $4.00 per record.

Hancock

Real Estate Recording—Hancock County Clerk of the Superior Court, Courthouse Square, Sparta, GA 31087. Fax: 706-444-6221. 8AM-5PM M-W & F; 9AM-12 Th.

Felony, Misdemeanor, Civil—Superior Court, PO Box 451, Courthouse Square, Sparta, GA 31087. 706-444-6644, Fax: 706-444-6221. 8AM-5PM, 8AM-Noon Th. Access by: mail, in person.

Civil Actions Under $15,000, Eviction, Small Claims—Magistrate Court, 601 Courthouse Square, Sparta, GA 31087. 706-444-6234. 9AM-5PM. Access by: mail, in person.

Probate—Probate Court, 601 Court St, Sparta, GA 31087. 706-444-5343. 8AM-5PM M-W & F; 8AM-Noon Th.

Haralson

Real Estate Recording—Haralson County Clerk of the Superior Court, 4485 State Highway 120 East, Buchanan, GA 30113. 770-646-2022, Fax: 770-646-2035. 8:30AM-5PM.

Felony, Misdemeanor, Civil—Superior Court, Drawer 849, 4485 Georgia Hwy 120, Buchanan, GA 30113. 770-646-2005, Fax: 770-646-2035. 8:30AM-5PM. Access by: mail, in person.

Civil Actions Under $15,000, Eviction, Small Claims—Magistrate Court, PO Box 1040, Buchanan, GA 30113. 678-646-2015. 8:30AM-5PM. Access by: mail, in person.

Probate—Probate Court, PO Box 620, Buchanan, GA 30113. 770-646-2008, Fax: 770-646-3419. 8:30AM-5PM. Access by: mail, in person.

Harris

Real Estate Recording—Harris County Clerk of the Superior Court, Courthouse, 102 College St. Highway 27, Hamilton, GA 31811. Fax: 706-628-7039. 8AM-5PM.

Felony, Misdemeanor, Civil—Superior Court, PO Box 528, Hamilton, GA 31811. 706-628-4944, Fax: 706-628-7039. 8AM-5PM. Access by: in person.

Civil Actions Under $15,000, Eviction, Small Claims—Magistrate Court, PO Box 347, Hamilton, GA 31811. 706-628-4977, Fax: 706-628-4223. 8AM-5PM. Access by: in person.

Probate—Probate Court, PO Box 569, Hamilton, GA 31811. 706-628-5038, Fax: 706-628-4223. 8AM-Noon, 1-5PM. Access by: mail, in person.

Hart

Real Estate Recording—Hart County Clerk of the Superior Court, 185 West Franklin Street, Courthouse Annex, Rm 1, Hartwell, GA 30643. 706-376-2024, Fax: 706-376-1277. 8:30AM-5PM.

Felony, Misdemeanor, Civil—Superior Court, PO Box 386, Hartwell, GA 30643. 706-376-7189, Fax: 706-376-1277. 8:30AM-5PM. Access by: in person.

Civil Actions Under $15,000, Eviction, Small Claims—Magistrate Court, PO Box 698, Hartwell, GA 30643. 706-376-6817, Fax: 706-376-6821. 8:30AM-5PM. Access by: mail, in person.

Probate—Probate Court, PO Box 1159, Hartwell, GA 30643. 706-376-2565, Fax: 706-376-9032. 8:30AM-5PM.

Heard

Real Estate Recording—Heard County Clerk of the Superior Court, Courthouse, 215 E. Court Sq. Franklin, GA 30217. Fax: 706-675-0819.

Felony, Misdemeanor, Civil—Superior Court, PO Box 249, Franklin, GA 30217. 706-675-3301. 8:30AM-5PM. Access by: in person.

Civil Actions Under $15,000, Eviction, Small Claims—Magistrate Court, PO Box 395, Franklin, GA 30217. 706-675-3002, Fax: 706-675-0819. 8:30AM-5PM. Access by: mail, in person.

Probate—Probate Court, PO Box 478, Franklin, GA 30217. 706-675-3353, Fax: 706-675-0819. 8:30AM-5PM. Access by: mail, in person.

Henry

Real Estate Recording—Henry County Clerk of the Superior Court, Courthouse, #1 Courthouse Square, McDonough, GA 30253. 770-954-2470. 8AM-5PM.

Felony, Misdemeanor, Civil—Superior Court, One Courthouse Square, McDonough, GA 30253. 770-954-2121. 8AM-5PM. Access by: in person.

Civil Actions Under $15,000, Eviction, Small Claims—Magistrate Court, 30 Atlanta St, McDonough, GA 30253. 770-954-2111, Fax: 770-957-2144. 8AM-5PM. Access by: mail, phone, in person.

Probate—Probate Court, 20 Lawrenceville St, McDonough, GA 30253. 770-954-2303, Fax: 770-954-2308. 8AM-5PM.

Houston

Real Estate Recording—Houston County Clerk of the Superior Court, 800 Carroll Street, Perry, GA 31069. Fax: 912-987-3252. 8:30AM-5PM.

Felony, Misdemeanor, Civil—Superior Court, 800 Carroll St, Perry, GA 31069. 912-987-2170, Fax: 912-987-3252. 8:30AM-5PM. Access by: mail, phone, fax, in person.

Misdemeanor, Civil—State Court, 202 Carl Vinson Pkwy, Warner Robins, GA 31088. 912-542-2105, Fax: 912-542-2077. 8AM-5PM. Access by: mail, phone, fax, in person.

Probate—Probate Court, PO Box 1801, Perry, GA 31069. 912-987-2770, Fax: 912-988-4511. 8AM-4PM. Access by: mail, in person.

Irwin

Real Estate Recording—Irwin County Clerk of the Superior Court, Courthouse, Suite 105, 301 S. Irwin Avenue, Ocilla, GA 31774. 912-468-5505. 8AM-5PM.

Felony, Misdemeanor, Civil—Superior Court, 301 S Irwin Ave, Suite 105, Ocilla, GA 31774. 912-468-5356. 8:30AM-5PM. Access by: mail, phone, in person.

Civil Actions Under $15,000, Eviction, Small Claims—Magistrate Court, 207 S Irwin Ave Suite 3, Ocilla, GA 31774. 912-468-7671, Fax: 912-468-9672. 8AM-5PM. Access by: mail, in person.

Probate—Probate Court, 301 W 2nd St, PO Box 566, Ocilla, GA 31774. 912-468-5138, Fax: 912-468-7765. 8AM-5PM. Access by: in person.

Jackson

Real Estate Recording—Jackson County Clerk of the Superior Court, Courthouse, 85 Washington Street, Jefferson, GA 30549. Fax: 706-367-2468. 8AM-5PM.

Felony, Misdemeanor, Civil—Superior & State Court, PO Box 7, Jefferson, GA 30549. 706-367-6360, Fax: 706-367-2468. 8AM-5PM. Access by: in person.

Civil Actions Under $15,000, Eviction, Small Claims—Magistrate Court, PO Box 751, Commerce, GA 30529. 706-335-6545, Fax: 706-335-5221. 8AM-5PM. Access by: mail, in person.

Probate—Probate Court, 85 Washington St, Jefferson, GA 30549. 706-367-6367, Fax: 706-367-2468. 8:30AM-5PM. Access by: mail, in person.

Jasper

Real Estate Recording—Jasper County Clerk of the Superior Court, Courthouse, Monticello, GA 31064. 706-468-4900, Fax: 706-468-4946. 8AM-5PM.

Felony, Misdemeanor, Civil—Superior Court, County Courthouse, Monticello, GA 31064. 706-468-4901, Fax: 706-468-4946. 8AM-5PM. Access by: in person.

Civil Actions Under $15,000, Eviction, Small Claims—Magistrate Court, County Courthouse, 123 W Green St, Monticello, GA 31064. 706-468-4909, Fax: 706-468-4928. 8:30AM-4:30PM. Access by: in person.

Probate—Jasper County Probate Court, Jasper County Courthouse, Monticello, GA 31064. 706-468-4903, Fax: 706-468-4926. 8AM-4:30PM. Access by: mail, in person.

Jeff Davis

Real Estate Recording—Jeff Davis County Clerk of the Superior Court, Jeff Davis Street, Courthouse Annex, Hazlehurst, GA 31539. Fax: 912-375-0378. 8AM-5PM.

Felony, Misdemeanor, Civil—Superior & State Court, PO Box 248, Hazlehurst, GA 31539. 912-375-6615, Fax: 912-375-0378. 8AM-5PM. Access by: mail, fax, in person.

Civil Actions Under $15,000, Eviction, Small Claims—Magistrate Court, PO Box 568, Hazlehurst, GA 31539. 912-375-6630, Fax: 912-375-0378. 8AM-5PM. Access by: mail, in person.

Probate—Probate Court, PO Box 13, Hazlehurst, GA 31539. 912-375-6626, Fax: 912-375-0378. 9AM-5PM.

Jefferson

Real Estate Recording—Jefferson County Clerk of the Superior Court, 202 E. Broad Street, Courthouse, Louisville, GA 30434. 912-625-7736, Fax: 912-625-9589. 9AM-5PM.

Felony, Misdemeanor, Civil—Superior & State Court, PO Box 151, Louisville, GA 30434. 912-625-7922, Fax: 912-625-4002. 9AM-5PM. Access by: mail, in person.

Civil Actions Under $15,000, Eviction, Small Claims—Magistrate Court, PO Box 749, Louisville, GA 30434. 912-625-8834. 8AM-5PM. Access by: mail, in person.

Probate—Probate Court, 202 Broad St, PO Box 307, Louisville, GA 30434. 912-625-3258, Fax: 912-625-9589. 9AM-4:30PM.

Jenkins

Real Estate Recording—Jenkins County Clerk of the Superior Court, Harvey Street, Courthouse, Millen, GA 30442. 912-982-4925, Fax: 912-982-1274. 8:30AM-Noon, 1-5PM.

Felony, Misdemeanor, Civil—Superior & State Court, PO Box 659, Millen, GA 30442. 912-982-4683, Fax: 912-982-1274. 8:30AM-5PM. Access by: in person.

Civil Actions Under $15,000, Eviction, Small Claims—Magistrate Court, PO Box 892, Millen, GA 30442. 912-982-5580. 8:30AM-5PM. Access by: mail, in person.

Probate—Probate Court, PO Box 904, Millen, GA 30442. 912-982-5581, Fax: 912-982-2829. 8:30AM-5PM. Access by: mail, in person.

Johnson

Real Estate Recording—Johnson County Clerk of the Superior Court, Courthouse Square, Wrightsville, GA 31096. 912-864-2565, Fax: 912-864-1343. 9AM-5PM.

Felony, Misdemeanor, Civil, Eviction, Small Claims—Superior & Magistrate Court, PO Box 321, Wrightsville, GA 31096. 912-864-3484, Fax: 912-864-1343. 9AM-5PM. Access by: in person.

Probate—Probate Court, 301 S Marcus St, PO Box 264, Wrightsville, GA 31096. 912-864-3316, Fax: 912-864-0745.

Jones

Real Estate Recording—Jones County Clerk of the Superior Court, Jefferson Street, Courthouse, Gray, GA 31032. 912-986-6538. 8:30AM-4:30PM.

Felony, Misdemeanor, Civil—Superior Court, PO Drawer 39, Courthouse Jefferson St, Gray, GA 31032. 912-986-6671. 8:30AM-4:30PM. Access by: in person.

Civil Actions Under $15,000, Eviction, Small Claims—Magistrate Court, PO Box 88, Gray, GA 31032. 912-986-5113, Fax: 912-986-1715. 8:30AM-4:30PM. Access by: in person.

Probate—Probate Court, PO Box 1359, Gray, GA 31032. 912-986-6668, Fax: 912-986-1715. 8:30AM-4:30PM.

Lamar

Real Estate Recording—Lamar County Clerk of the Superior Court, 326 Thomaston Street, Courthouse, Barnesville, GA 30204. 770-358-5162, Fax: 770-358-5149. 8AM-5PM.

Felony, Misdemeanor, Civil—Superior Court, 326 Thomaston St, Barnesville, GA 30204. 770-358-5145, Fax: 770-358-5149. 8AM-5PM. Access by: mail, phone, in person.

Civil Actions Under $15,000, Eviction, Small Claims—Magistrate Court, 121 Roberta Dr, Barnesville, GA 30204. 678-358-5154. 8AM-5PM. Access by: in person.

Probate—Probate Court, 326 Thomaston St, Barnesville, GA 30204. 770-358-5155, Fax: 770-358-5348. 8AM-5PM.

Lanier

Real Estate Recording—Lanier County Clerk of the Superior Court, County Courthouse, 100 Main Street, Lakeland, GA 31635. 912-482-3795, Fax: 912-482-8333. 8AM-Noon,1-5PM.

Felony, Misdemeanor, Civil—Superior Court, County Courthouse, 100 Main St, Lakeland, GA 31635. 912-482-3594, Fax: 912-482-8333. 8AM-Noon, 1-5PM. Access by: in person.

Civil Actions Under $15,000, Eviction, Small Claims—Magistrate Court, County Courthouse, Lakeland, GA 31635. 912-482-2207, Fax: 912-482-8358. 8AM-5PM. Access by: mail, phone, fax, in person.

Probate—Probate Court, County Courthouse, 100 Main St, Lakeland, GA 31635. 912-482-3668, Fax: 912-482-8333. 8AM-5PM.

Laurens

Real Estate Recording—Laurens County Clerk of the Superior Court, Courthouse Square, 101 N. Jefferson St. Dublin, GA 31021. 912-272-6994, Fax: 912-275-2595. 8:30AM-5:30PM.

Felony, Misdemeanor, Civil, Eviction, Small Claims—Superior & Magistrate Court, PO Box 2028, Dublin, GA 31040. 912-272-3210. 8:30AM-5:30PM. Access by: in person.

Probate—Probate Court, PO Box 2098, Dublin, GA 31040. 912-272-2566, Fax: 912-277-2932. 8:30AM-5:30PM. Access by: mail, in person.

Lee

Real Estate Recording—Lee County Clerk of the Superior Court, 100 Leslie Highway, Leesburg, GA 31763. 912-759-6000. 8AM-5PM.

Felony, Misdemeanor, Civil—Superior Court, PO Box 597, Leesburg, GA 31763. 912-759-6018. 8AM-5PM. Access by: mail, in person.

Civil Actions Under $15,000, Eviction, Small Claims—Magistrate Court, PO Box 522, Leesburg, GA 31763. 912-759-6016, Fax: 912-759-3303. 8AM-5PM. Access by: mail, in person.

Probate—Probate Court, 100 Leslie Hwy, PO Box 592, Leesburg, GA 31763. 912-759-6006, Fax: 912-759-6032. 8AM-5PM.

Liberty

Real Estate Recording—Liberty County Clerk of the Superior Court, Courthouse Square, 100 Main St. Hinesville, GA 31313. 912-876-3389, Fax: 912-369-5463. 8AM-5PM.

Felony, Misdemeanor, Civil—Superior & State Court, PO Box 50, Hinesville, GA 31313-0050. 912-876-3625. 8AM-5PM. Access by: mail, phone, fax, in person.

Civil Actions Under $15,000, Eviction, Small Claims—Magistrate Court, PO Box 912, Hinesville, GA 31310. 912-876-2343, Fax: 912-369-5463. 8AM-5PM. Access by: mail, in person. www.libertyco.com

Probate—Probate Court, 112 N Main St, Courthouse Annex Rm 100, PO Box 28, Hinesville, GA 31313. 912-876-3635, Fax: 912-876-3589. 8AM-5PM.

Lincoln

Real Estate Recording—Lincoln County Clerk of the Superior Court, 210 Humphrey Street, Courthouse Room 103, Lincolnton, GA 30817. 706-359-4444. 9AM-Noon, 1PM-5PM.

Felony, Misdemeanor, Civil—Superior Court, PO Box 340, Lincolnton, GA 30817. 706-359-4444. 9AM-5PM. Access by: in person.

Civil Actions Under $15,000, Eviction, Small Claims—Magistrate Court, PO Box 205, Lincolnton, GA 30817. 706-359-5519, Fax: 706-359-5027. 8:30AM-4:30PM. Access by: mail, phone, fax, in person.

Probate—Probate Court, PO Box 340, Lincolnton, GA 30817. 706-359-4444, Fax: 706-359-4729. 9AM-5PM.

Long

Real Estate Recording—Long County Clerk of the Superior Court, Courthouse, MacDonald Street, Ludowici, GA 31316. 912-545-2127. 8:30AM-4:30PM.

Felony, Misdemeanor, Civil—Superior & State Court, PO Box 458, Ludowici, GA 31316. 912-545-2123. 8:30AM-4:30PM. Access by: mail, in person.

Civil Actions Under $15,000, Eviction, Small Claims—Magistrate Court, PO Box 87, Ludowici, GA 31316. 912-545-2315. 8:30AM-4:30PM. Access by: mail, in person.

Probate—Probate Court, McDonald St, PO Box 426, Ludowici, GA 31316. 912-545-2131, Fax: 912-545-2150. 8:30AM-4:30PM. Access by: mail, in person.

Lowndes

Real Estate Recording—Lowndes County Clerk of the Superior Court, 108 E. Central Ave. Valdosta, GA 31601. 912-333-5106, Fax: 912-333-7637. 8AM-5PM.

Felony, Misdemeanor, Civil—Superior & State Court, PO Box 1349, Valdosta, GA 31603. 912-333-5101. 8AM-5PM. Access by: mail, in person.

Civil Actions Under $15,000, Eviction, Small Claims—Magistrate Court, PO Box 1349, Valdosta, GA 31603. 912-333-5110, Fax: 912-333-7616. 9AM-5PM. Access by: mail, in person.

Probate—Probate Court, PO Box 72, Valdosta, GA 31603. 912-333-5103, Fax: 912-333-7646. 8AM-5PM.

Lumpkin

Real Estate Recording—Lumpkin County Clerk of the Superior Court, 99 Courthouse Hill, Suite D, Dahlonega, GA 30533. 706-864-3742, Fax: 706-864-5298. 8AM-5PM.

Felony, Misdemeanor, Civil, Eviction, Small Claims—Superior, Juvenile & Magistrate Court, 99 Courthouse Hill, #D, Dahlonega, GA 30533-0541. 706-864-3736, Fax: 706-864-5298. 8AM-5PM. Access by: in person.

Probate—Probate Court, 99 Courthouse Hill, Suite C, Dahlonega, GA 30533. 706-864-3847, Fax: 706-864-9271. 8:30AM-4:30PM. Access by: mail, in person.

Macon

Real Estate Recording—Macon County Clerk of the Superior Court, 100 Sumter Street, Courthouse, Oglethorpe, GA 31068. 912-472-7031. 8:30AM-5PM.

Felony, Misdemeanor, Civil—Superior Court, PO Box 337, Oglethorpe, GA 31068. 912-472-7661. 8AM-5PM. Access by: mail, in person.

Civil Actions Under $15,000, Eviction, Small Claims—Magistrate Court, PO Box 605, Oglethorpe, GA 31068. 912-472-8509. 8AM-Noon, 1-5PM. Access by: mail, phone, in person.

Probate—Probate Court, PO Box 216, Oglethorpe, GA 31068. 912-472-7685. 8AM-Noon, 1-5PM.

Madison

Real Estate Recording—Madison County Clerk of the Superior Court, Courthouse Square, Hwy 29, Danielsville, GA 30633. 706-795-3351, Fax: 706-795-5668. 8AM-5PM.

Felony, Misdemeanor, Civil—Superior Court, PO Box 247, Danielsville, GA 30633. 706-795-3352, Fax: 706-795-5668. 8AM-5PM. Access by: in person.

Civil Actions Under $15,000, Eviction, Small Claims—Magistrate Court, PO Box 6, Danielsville, GA 30633. 706-795-5679, Fax: 706-795-2228. 8AM-5PM. Access by: mail, fax, in person.

Probate—Probate Court, PO Box 207, Danielsville, GA 30633. 706-795-3354, Fax: 706-795-5933. 8AM-5PM. Access by: mail, in person.

Marion

Real Estate Recording—Marion County Clerk of the Superior Court, Courthouse Square, Broad Street, Buena Vista, GA 31803. Fax: 912-649-2059. 9AM-5PM.

Felony, Misdemeanor, Civil—Superior Court, PO Box 41, Buena Vista, GA 31803. 912-649-7321, Fax: 912-649-2059. 8:30AM-5PM. Access by: in person.

Civil Under $5,000, Eviction, Small Claims, Probate—Magistrate and Probate Court, Courthouse Sq, PO Box 207, Buena Vista, GA 31803. 912-649-5542, Fax: 912-649-2059. 8:30AM-Noon, 1-5PM. Access by: mail, in person.

McDuffie

Real Estate Recording—McDuffie County Clerk of the Superior Court, 337 Main Street, Courthouse, Room 101, Thomson, GA 30824. 706-595-2100, Fax: 706-595-9150. 8AM-5PM.

Felony, Misdemeanor, Civil—Superior Court, PO Box 158, 337 Main St, Thomson, GA 30824. 706-595-2134. 8AM-5PM. Access by: in person.

Civil Actions Under $15,000, Eviction, Small Claims—Magistrate Court, PO Box 252, Thomson, GA 30824. 706-597-2618, Fax: 706-597-4710. 8AM-5PM. Access by: mail, in person.

Probate—Probate Court, PO Box 2028, Thomson, GA 30824. 706-595-2124, Fax: 706-595-4710. 8AM-5PM.

McIntosh

Real Estate Recording—McIntosh County Clerk of the Superior Court, Courthouse, 310 Northway, Darien, GA 31305. 912-437-6627, Fax: 912-437-6673. 8AM-4:30PM.

Felony, Misdemeanor, Civil—Superior & State Court, PO Box 1661, Darien, GA 31305. 912-437-6641, Fax: 912-437-6673. 8AM-4:30PM. Access by: in person.

Civil Actions Under $15,000, Eviction, Small Claims—Magistrate Court, PO Box 459, Darien, GA 31305. 912-437-4888, Fax: 912-437-2768. 8AM-4:30PM. Access by: mail, phone, fax, in person.

Probate—Probate Court, PO Box 453, Darien, GA 31305. 912-437-6636, Fax: 912-437-6635. 8AM-5PM.

Meriwether

Real Estate Recording—Meriwether County Clerk of the Superior Court, 100 Court Square, Meriwether County Courthouse, Greenville, GA 30222. 706-672-4219, Fax: 706-672-1886. 8:30AM-5PM.

Felony, Misdemeanor, Civil—Superior Court, PO Box 160, Greenville, GA 30222. 706-672-4416, Fax: 706-672-1886. 9AM-5PM. Access by: in person.

Civil Actions Under $15,000, Eviction, Small Claims—Magistrate Court, PO Box 702, Greenville, GA 30222. 706-672-1247. 9AM-4:30PM M,T,TH,F/9AM-11:30PM W. Access by: in person.

Probate—Probate Court, PO Box 608, Greenville, GA 30222. 706-672-4952, Fax: 706-672-1886. 8:30AM-5PM. Access by: mail, in person.

Miller

Real Estate Recording—Miller County Clerk of the Superior Court, 155 First Street, Colquitt, GA 31737. 912-758-4101, Fax: 912-758-2229. 8AM-Noon,1-5PM.

Felony, Misdemeanor, Civil—Superior & State Court, PO Box 66, Colquitt, GA 31737. 912-758-4102. 8AM-5PM. Access by: in person.

Civil Actions Under $15,000, Small Claims, Probate—Magistrate & Probate Court, 155 S 1st St, Rm 1, Colquitt, GA 31737. 912-758-4110, Fax: 912-758-9183. 8AM-5PM. Access by: mail, phone, fax, in person.

Probate—Probate Court, 155 S 1st St, Box 1, Colquitt, GA 31737. 912-758-4110, Fax: 912-758-8133. 9AM-5PM. Access by: mail, in person.

Mitchell

Real Estate Recording—Mitchell County Clerk of the Superior Court, Courthouse, 11 Broad St. Camilla, GA 31730. 912-336-2010, Fax: 912-336-2003. 8:30AM-5PM.

Felony, Misdemeanor, Civil—Superior & State Court, PO Box 427, Camilla, GA 31730. 912-336-2022. 8:30AM-5PM. Access by: in person.

Civil Actions Under $15,000, Eviction, Small Claims—Magistrate Court, PO Box 626, Camilla, GA 31730. 912-

336-2077, Fax: 912-336-2039. 8:30AM-5PM. Access by: mail, fax, in person.

Probate—Probate Court, 11 Broad St, PO Box 229, Camilla, GA 31730. 912-336-2016, Fax: 912-336-2004. 8:30AM-5PM.

Monroe

Real Estate Recording—Monroe County Clerk of the Superior Court, 1 Courthouse Square, Forsyth, GA 31029. Fax: 912-994-7053. 8:30AM-4:30PM.

Felony, Misdemeanor, Civil—Superior Court, PO Box 450, 1 Courthouse Square, Forsyth, GA 31029. 912-994-7022, Fax: 912-994-7053. 8:30AM-4:30PM. Access by: mail, in person.

Civil Actions Under $15,000, Eviction, Small Claims—Magistrate Court, PO Box 974, Forsyth, GA 31029. 912-994-7018, Fax: 912-994-7284. 8:30AM-Noon, 1:30-4:30PM. Access by: mail, in person.

Probate—Monroe County Probate Court, Monroe County Courthouse, Rm 2, PO Box 187, Forsyth, GA 31029. 912-994-7036, Fax: 912-994-7054. 8:30AM-4:30PM.

Montgomery

Real Estate Recording—Montgomery County Clerk of the Superior Court, Highway 221 & 56, Courthouse, Mount Vernon, GA 30445. 9AM-5PM.

Felony, Misdemeanor, Civil—Superior Court, PO Box 311, Mt Vernon, GA 30445. 912-583-4401. 8AM-5PM. Access by: in person.

Civil Actions Under $15,000, Eviction, Small Claims—Magistrate Court, PO Box 174, Mt Vernon, GA 30445. 912-583-2170, Fax: 912-583-4343. 8AM-5PM. Access by: in person.

Probate—Probate Court, 400 Railroad Ave, PO Box 302, Mt Vernon, GA 30445. 912-583-2681, Fax: 912-583-4343. 9AM-5PM. Access by: mail.

Morgan

Real Estate Recording—Morgan County Clerk of the Superior Court, 141 East Jefferson Street, Madison, GA 30650.

Felony, Misdemeanor, Civil—Superior Court, PO Box 130, 149 E Jefferson St, Madison, GA 30650. 706-342-3605. 8:30AM-5PM. Access by: in person.

Civil Actions Under $15,000, Eviction, Small Claims—Magistrate Court, Courthouse, Rm 105, Madison, GA 30650. 706-342-3088, Fax: 706-343-0000. 8AM-5PM. Access by: mail, phone, fax, in person.

Probate—Probate Court, Morgan County Courthouse, Madison, GA 30650. 706-342-1373, Fax: 706-342-5085. 8AM-5PM. Access by: mail, in person.

Murray

Real Estate Recording—Murray County Clerk of the Superior Court, 121 N 3rd Avenue, Courthouse, Chatsworth, GA 30705. 706-695-3423. 8:30AM-5PM.

Felony, Misdemeanor, Civil—Superior Court, PO Box 1000, Chatsworth, GA 30705. 706-695-2932. 8:30AM-5PM. Access by: in person.

Civil Actions Under $15,000, Eviction, Small Claims—Magistrate Court, 121 4th Ave, Chatsworth, GA 30705. 706-695-3021, Fax: 706-695-8721. 8AM-Noon, 1-5PM. Access by: mail, phone, in person.

Probate—Murray County Probate Court, 115 Fort St, Chatsworth, GA 30705. 706-695-3812, Fax: 706-517-1340. 8:30AM-5PM.

Muscogee

Real Estate Recording—Muscogee County Clerk of the Superior Court, 100 10th Street, Columbus, GA 31901. 706-571-4800, Fax: 706-653-4359. 8:30AM-5PM.

Felony, Misdemeanor, Civil—Superior & State Court, PO Box 2145, Columbus, GA 31994. 706-653-4351, Fax: 706-653-4359. 8:30AM-5PM. Access by: mail, in person.

Civil Actions Under $15,000, Eviction, Small Claims—Magistrate Court, Box 1340, Columbus, GA 31902. 706-653-4390, Fax: 706-653-4559. 8:30AM-5PM. Access by: mail, in person.

Probate—Probate Court, 100 10th St, PO Box 1340, Columbus, GA 31993. 706-571-4847. 8:30AM-4PM.

Newton

Real Estate Recording—Newton County Clerk of the Superior Court, Newton County Judicial Center, 1132 Usher St. 3rd Floor, Covington, GA 30014. 8AM-5PM.

Felony, Misdemeanor, Civil—Superior Court, 1124 Clark St, Covington, GA 30014. 770-784-2035. 8AM-5PM. Access by: in person.

Civil Actions Under $15,000, Eviction, Small Claims—Magistrate Court, 1132 Usher St, Covington, GA 30209. 678-784-2050, Fax: 678-784-2145. 8AM-5PM. Access by: mail, phone, fax, in person.

Probate—Probate Court, 1132 Usher St, Rm 148, Covington, GA 30014. 678-784-2045, Fax: 678-784-2145. 8AM-5PM.

Oconee

Real Estate Recording—Oconee County Clerk of the Superior Court, 23 N. Main Street, Watkinsville, GA 30677. Fax: 706-769-3948. 8:30AM-5PM.

Felony, Misdemeanor, Civil, Eviction, Small Claims—Superior & Magistrate Courts, PO Box 113, Watkinsville, GA 30677. 706-769-3940, Fax: 706-769-3948. 8AM-5PM. Access by: in person.

Probate—Probate Court, PO Box 54, Watkinsville, GA 30677. 706-769-3936, Fax: 706-769-3934. 8AM-5PM.

Oglethorpe

Real Estate Recording—Oglethorpe County Clerk of the Superior Court, 111 West Main Street, Courthouse, Lexington, GA 30648. Fax: 706-743-5335. 8AM-5PM.

Felony, Misdemeanor, Civil—Superior Court, PO Box 68, Lexington, GA 30648. 706-743-5731, Fax: 706-743-5335. 8AM-5PM. Access by: in person.

Civil Actions Under $15,000, Eviction, Small Claims—Magistrate Court, Box 356, Lexington, GA 30648. 706-743-8321, Fax: 706-743-8321. 8AM-5PM. Access by: mail, in person.

Probate—Probate Court, 111 W. Main St Hwy 78, PO Box 70, Lexington, GA 30648. 706-743-5350, Fax: 706-743-8219. 8AM-5PM.

Paulding

Real Estate Recording—Paulding County Clerk of the Superior Court, 11 Courthouse Sq. Room G-2, Dallas, GA 30132. 8AM-5PM.

Felony, Misdemeanor, Civil—Superior Court, 11 Courthouse Square, Rm G2, Dallas, GA 30132. 770-443-7529. 8AM-5PM. Access by: in person.

Civil Actions Under $15,000, Eviction, Small Claims—Magistrate Court, 11 Courthouse Square, Rm G2, Dallas, GA 30132. 8AM-5PM. Access by: mail, in person.

Probate—Probate Court, 11 Courthouse Square, Rm G2, Dallas, GA 30132. 770-443-7529, Fax: 770-443-7538. 8AM-5PM.

Peach

Real Estate Recording—Peach County Clerk of the Superior Court, 205 West Church Street, Courthouse, Fort Valley, GA 31030. 912-825-2535. 8:30AM-5PM.

Felony, Misdemeanor, Civil—Superior Court, PO Box 389, Ft Valley, GA 31030. 912-825-5331. 8:30AM-5PM. Access by: mail, in person.

Civil Actions Under $15,000, Eviction, Small Claims—Magistrate Court, 700 Spruce St, Bldg A, Ft Valley, GA 31030. 912-825-2060, Fax: 912-825-1893. 8AM-5PM. Access by: mail, in person.

Probate—Probate Court, PO Box 327, Ft Valley, GA 31030. 912-825-2313, Fax: 912-825-2678.

Pickens

Real Estate Recording—Pickens County Clerk of the Superior Court, 52 North Main Street, Courthouse Annex - Suite 102, Jasper, GA 30143. 8AM-5PM.

Felony, Misdemeanor, Civil—Superior Court, 52 N Main St Ste 102, Jasper, GA 30143. 706-692-2014. 8AM-5PM. Access by: in person.

Civil Actions Under $15,000, Eviction, Small Claims—Magistrate Court, 50 N Main St, Jasper, GA 30143. 706-692-3550, Fax: 706-692-2850. 8AM-5PM. Access by: mail, in person.

Probate—Probate Court, 50 N Main St, Suite 3, Jasper, GA 30143. 706-692-2515, Fax: 706-692-2473. 8AM-Noon, 1-5PM.

Pierce

Real Estate Recording—Pierce County Clerk of the Superior Court, Courthouse, Highway 84, Blackshear, GA 31516. 9AM-5PM.

Felony, Misdemeanor, Civil—Superior Court, PO Box 588, Blackshear, GA 31516. 912-449-2020. 9AM-5PM. Access by: in person.

Misdemeanor, Civil—State Court, PO Box 588, Blackshear, GA 31516. 912-449-2020. 9AM-5PM. Access by: in person.

Civil Actions Under $15,000, Eviction, Small Claims—Magistrate Court, 102 Hwy 84 W, Blackshear, GA 31516. 912-449-2027, Fax: 912-449-2024. 9AM-5PM. Access by: in person.

Probate—Probate Court, PO Box 406, Blackshear, GA 31516. 912-449-2029. 9AM-5PM.

Pike

Real Estate Recording—Pike County Clerk of the Superior Court, Highway 18 & Highway 19, Courthouse Square, Zebulon, GA 30295. 8AM-5PM.

Felony, Misdemeanor, Civil—Superior Court, PO Box 10, Zebulon, GA 30295. 770-567-2000. 8AM-5PM. Access by: in person.

Civil Actions Under $15,000, Eviction, Small Claims—Magistrate Court, PO Box 466, Zebulon, GA 30295. 770-567-2004, Fax: 770-567-2032. 8AM-5PM. Access by: mail, phone, fax, in person.

Probate—Probate Court, PO Box 324, Zebulon, GA 30295. 770-567-8734, Fax: 770-567-2006. 9AM-5PM.

Polk

Real Estate Recording—Polk County Clerk of the Superior Court, Courthouse #1, Room 106, 100 Pryor St. Cedartown, GA 30125. 770-749-2108, Fax: 770-749-2148. 9AM-5PM.

Felony, Misdemeanor, Civil—Superior Court, PO Box 948, Cedartown, GA 30125. 770-749-2114, Fax: 770-749-2148. 9AM-5PM. Access by: in person.

Civil Actions Under $15,000, Eviction, Small Claims—Magistrate Court, PO Box 948, Cedartown, GA 30125. 770-749-2130, Fax: 770-749-2117. 9AM-5PM. Access by: mail, in person.

Probate—Polk County Probate Court, Polk County Courthouse, Cedartown, GA 30125. 770-749-2128, Fax: 770-749-2150. 9AM-5PM.

Pulaski

Real Estate Recording—Pulaski County Clerk of the Superior Court, Courthouse, 350 Commerce Street, Hawkinsville, GA 31036. 912-783-2811, Fax: 912-892-3308. 8AM-5PM.

Felony, Misdemeanor, Civil—Superior Court, PO Box 60, Hawkinsville, GA 31036. 912-783-1911, Fax: 912-892-3308. 8AM-5PM. Access by: mail, phone, in person.

Civil Actions Under $15,000, Eviction, Small Claims—Magistrate Court, PO Box 667, Hawkinsville, GA 31036. 912-783-1357, Fax: 912-892-3308. 8AM-5PM. Access by: in person.

Probate—Probate Court, PO Box 156, Hawkinsville, GA 31036. 912-783-2061, Fax: 912-892-3308. 8AM-5PM. Access by: mail, in person.

Putnam

Real Estate Recording—Putnam County Clerk of the Superior Court, Courthouse, 100 S. Jefferson St. Eatonton, GA 31024. 706-485-5441, Fax: 706-485-2515. 8AM-5PM.

Felony, Misdemeanor, Civil—Superior & State Court, County Courthouse, Eatonton, GA 31024. 706-485-4501, Fax: 706-485-2515. 8AM-5PM. Access by: in person.

Civil Actions Under $15,000, Eviction, Small Claims—Magistrate Court, 108 S Madison Ave, Eatonton, GA 31024. 706-485-4306, Fax: 706-485-2527. 8AM-5PM. Access by: mail, in person.

Probate—Putnam County Probate Court, County Courthouse, 100 S Jefferson St, Eatonton, GA 31024. 706-485-5476, Fax: 706-485-2515. 8AM-5PM.

Quitman

Real Estate Recording—Quitman County Clerk of the Superior Court, Main Street, Courthouse, Georgetown, GA 31754. Fax: 912-334-2151. 8AM-Noon, 1-5PM.

Felony, Misdemeanor, Civil—Superior Court, PO Box 307, Georgetown, GA 31754. 912-334-2578. 8AM-Noon, 1-5PM. Access by: mail, in person.

Civil Actions Under $15,000, Eviction, Small Claims—Magistrate Court, PO Box 7, Georgetown, GA 31754. 912-334-2224, Fax: 912-334-2151. 8:30AM-5PM. Access by: mail, in person.

Probate—Probate Court, Courthouse Main St, PO Box 7, Georgetown, GA 31754. 912-334-2224, Fax: 912-334-2151. 8AM-5PM. Access by: mail, in person.

Rabun

Real Estate Recording—Rabun County Clerk of the Superior Court, 25 Courthouse Square # 7, Clayton, GA 30525. 706-782-3813, Fax: 706-782-7588. 8:30AM-5PM.

Felony, Misdemeanor, Civil—Superior Court, 25 Courthouse Sq, Box 7, Clayton, GA 30525. 706-782-3615, Fax: 706-782-7588. 8:30AM-5PM. Access by: in person.

Civil Actions Under $15,000, Eviction, Small Claims—Magistrate Court, 25 Courthouse Sq, Box 7, Clayton, GA 30525. 706-782-3615. 8:30AM-5PM. Access by: mail, in person.

Probate—Probate Court, 25 Courthouse Square, Box 15, Clayton, GA 30525. 706-782-3614, Fax: 706-782-7588. 8:30AM-Noon, 1-5PM. Access by: mail, in person.

Randolph

Real Estate Recording—Randolph County Clerk of the Superior Court, 208 Court Street, Cuthbert, GA 31740. 912-732-2881, Fax: 912-732-5881. 8AM-5PM.

Felony, Misdemeanor, Civil—Superior Court, PO Box 98, Cuthbert, GA 31740. 912-732-2216, Fax: 912-732-5881. 8AM-5PM. Access by: in person.

Civil Actions Under $15,000, Eviction, Small Claims—Magistrate Court, PO Box 6, Cuthbert, GA 31740. 912-732-6182, Fax: 912-732-5781. 9AM-5PM. Access by: mail, in person.

Probate—Probate Court, Court St, PO Box 424, Cuthbert, GA 31740. 912-732-2671, Fax: 912-732-5781. 8AM-5PM.

Richmond

Real Estate Recording—Richmond County Clerk of the Superior Court, 530 Green Street, 5th Floor, Room 503, Augusta, GA 30911. 706-821-2391, Fax: 706-821-2448. 8:30AM-5PM.

Felony, Misdemeanor, Civil—Superior Court, 530 Green St, Augusta, GA 30911. 706-821-2460, Fax: 706-821-2448. 8:30AM-5PM. Access by: mail, phone, in person.

Misdemeanor, Civil—State Court, 401 Walton Way, #218A, Augusta, GA 30911. 706-821-1233. 8:30AM-5PM. Access by: in person.

Civil Actions Under $45,000, Eviction, Small Claims—Civil & Magistrate Court, 530 Greene St, Rm 705, Augusta, GA 30911.

706-821-2370, Fax: 706-821-2381. 8:30AM-5PM. Access by: mail, phone, in person.

Probate—Probate Court, Municipal Bldg Rm 401, 530 Greene St, Augusta, GA 30911. 706-821-2434, Fax: 706-821-2442. 8:30AM-5PM. Access by: mail, in person.

Rockdale

Real Estate Recording—Rockdale County Clerk of the Superior Court, 922 Court Street, Room 203, Conyers, GA 30207. 770-929-4009, Fax: 770-860-0381. 8:15AM-4:45PM.

Felony, Misdemeanor, Civil—Superior Court, PO Box 937, 922 Court St, Conyers, GA 30207. 770-929-4021. 8AM-5PM. Access by: in person.

Misdemeanor, Civil—State Court, PO Box 938, Conyers, GA 30012. 770-929-4019. 8AM-4:45PM. Access by: mail, in person.

Civil Actions Under $15,000, Eviction, Small Claims—Magistrate Court, PO Box 289, Conyers, GA 30012. 770-929-4014, Fax: 770-785-2496. 8:30AM-4:30PM. Access by: mail, in person. Special note: Court also has jurisdiction for bad checks, arrest warrants, preliminary hearings, and county ordinace violations.

Probate—Probate Court, 922 Court St, Rm 107, Conyers, GA 30012. 770-929-4058, Fax: 770-918-6463. 8:30AM-4:30PM.

Schley

Real Estate Recording—Schley County Clerk of the Superior Court, US Highway 19, Courthouse Square, Ellaville, GA 31806. Fax: 912-937-5047. 8AM-Noon,1-5PM.

Felony, Misdemeanor, Civil—Superior Court, PO Box 7, US Hwy 19-Courthouse Square, Ellaville, GA 31806. 912-937-5581, Fax: 912-937-5047. 8AM-Noon,1-5PM. Access by: in person.

Civil Actions Under $15,000, Eviction, Small Claims—Magistrate Court, PO Box 372, Ellaville, GA 31806. 912-937-5581, Fax: 912-937-5047. 8AM-5PM. Access by: mail, in person.

Probate—Probate Court, Hwy 19, PO Box 385, Ellaville, GA 31806. 912-937-5047, Fax: 912-937-2609. 8:30AM-Noon, 1-5PM.

Screven

Real Estate Recording—Screven County Clerk of the Superior Court, 216 Mims Road, Sylvania, GA 30467. Fax: 912-564-2622. 8:30AM-5PM.

Felony, Misdemeanor, Civil—Superior Court, PO Box 156, Sylvania, GA 30467. 912-564-2614, Fax: 912-564-2622. 8:30AM-5PM. Access by: in person.

Misdemeanor, Civil—State Court, PO Box 156, Sylvania, GA 30467. 912-564-2614, Fax: 912-564-2622. 8:30AM-5PM. Access by: in person.

Civil Actions Under $15,000, Eviction, Small Claims—Magistrate Court, PO Box 64, Sylvania, GA 30467. 912-564-7375, Fax: 912-564-5618. 8AM-5PM. Access by: mail, phone, fax, in person.

Probate—Probate Court, 216 Mims Rd, Sylvania, GA 30467. 912-564-2783, Fax: 912-564-2562. 8:30AM-5PM.

Seminole

Real Estate Recording—Seminole County Clerk of the Superior Court, Courthouse, 200 S. Knox St. Donalsonville, GA 31745. Fax: 912-524-8528. 9AM-5PM.

Felony, Misdemeanor, Civil—Superior Court, PO Box 672, Main St, Donalsonville, GA 31745. 912-524-2525, Fax: 912-524-8528. 8AM-5PM. Access by: mail, phone, fax, in person.

Civil Actions Under $15,000, Eviction, Small Claims—Magistrate Court, PO Box 672, Donalsonville, GA 31745. 912-524-5256, Fax: 912-524-8528. 8AM-5PM. Access by: mail, in person.

Probate—Probate Court, Seminole County Courthouse, 2nd St, Donalsonville, GA 31745. 912-524-5256, Fax: 912-524-8528. 9AM-5PM. Access by: mail, in person.

Spalding

Real Estate Recording—Spalding County Clerk of the Superior Court, 132 East Solomon Street, Griffin, GA 30223. 8AM-5PM.

Felony, Misdemeanor, Civil—Superior Court, PO Box 1046, Griffin, GA 30224. 770-467-4745. 8AM-5PM. Access by: mail, in person.

Misdemeanor, Civil—State Court, PO Box 1046, Griffin, GA 30224. 770-467-4745. 8AM-5PM. Access by: mail, in person.

Civil Actions Under $15,000, Eviction, Small Claims—Magistrate Court, 132 E Solomon, Griffin, GA 30223. 770-467-4321, Fax: 770-467-0081. 8AM-5PM. Access by: in person.

Probate—Probate Court, 132 E Solomon St, Griffin, GA 30224. 770-467-4340, Fax: 770-467-4243. 8AM-5PM.

Stephens

Real Estate Recording—Stephens County Clerk of the Superior Court, Stephens County Courthouse, 150 West Doyle St. Toccoa, GA 30577. 8AM-5PM.

Felony, Misdemeanor, Civil—Superior Court, 150 W Doyle St, Toccoa, GA 30577. 706-886-3598. 8AM-5PM. Access by: mail, in person.

Misdemeanor, Civil—State Court, 150 W Doyle St, Toccoa, GA 30577. 706-886-3598. 8AM-5PM. Access by: mail, in person.

Civil Actions Under $15,000, Eviction, Small Claims—Magistrate Court, PO Box 1374, Courthouse Annex Room 303, Toccoa, GA 30577. 706-886-6205, Fax: 706-886-5569. 8AM-5PM. Access by: mail, in person.

Probate—Probate Court, County Courthouse, PO Box 456, Toccoa, GA 30577. 706-886-2828. 8AM-5PM. Access by: mail, in person.

Stewart

Real Estate Recording—Stewart County Clerk of the Superior Court, Main Street, Courthouse, Lumpkin, GA 31815. 8AM-4:30PM.

Felony, Misdemeanor, Civil—Superior Court, PO Box 910, Main St, Lumpkin, GA 31815. 912-838-6220. 8AM-5PM. Access by: in person.

Civil Actions Under $15,000, Eviction, Small Claims—Magistrate Court, PO Box 713, Lumpkin, GA 31815. 912-838-0505. 8AM-5PM. Access by: mail, in person.

Probate—Probate Court, PO Box 876, Lumpkin, GA 31815. 912-838-4394, Fax: 912-838-4394. 8AM-Noon, 1-5PM. Access by: mail, in person.

Sumter

Real Estate Recording—Sumter County Clerk of the Superior Court, Lamar Street, Courthouse, Americus, GA 31709. 9AM-5PM.

Felony, Misdemeanor, Civil—Superior Court, PO Box 333, Americus, GA 31709. 912-924-5626. 9AM-5PM. Access by: in person.

Misdemeanor, Civil—State Court, PO Box 333, Americus, GA 31709. 912-924-5626. 9AM-5PM. Access by: in person.

Civil Actions Under $15,000, Eviction, Small Claims—Magistrate Court, PO Box 563, Americus, GA 31709. 912-924-6699. 9AM-5PM. Access by: mail, in person.

Probate—Probate Court, Courthouse, Lamar St, PO Box 246, Americus, GA 31709. 912-924-7693. 9AM-5PM.

Talbot

Real Estate Recording—Talbot County Clerk of the Superior Court, Monroe Street, Courthouse Square #1, Talbotton, GA 31827. 706-665-3240, Fax: 706-665-8637. 9AM-5PM.

Felony, Misdemeanor, Civil—Superior Court, PO Box 325, Talbotton, GA 31827. 706-665-3239, Fax: 706-665-8199. 9AM-5PM. Access by: in person.

Civil Actions Under $15,000, Eviction, Small Claims—Magistrate Court, PO Box 157, Talbotton, GA 31827. 706-665-3598, Fax: 706-665-8199. 8AM-5PM. Access by: mail, phone, in person.

Probate—Probate Court, Hwy 80, PO Box 157, Talbotton, GA 31827. 706-665-8866, Fax: 706-665-8199. 8AM-5PM. Access by: mail, in person.

Taliaferro

Real Estate Recording—Taliaferro County Clerk of the Superior Court, Monument Street, Courthouse, Crawfordville, GA 30631. 9AM-Noon, 1-5PM.

Felony, Misdemeanor, Civil—Superior Court, PO Box 182, Crawfordville, GA 30631. 706-456-2123. 9AM-5PM. Access by: in person.

Civil Actions Under $15,000, Eviction, Small Claims—Magistrate Court, PO Box 264, Crawfordville, GA 30631. 706-456-2253, Fax: 706-456-2904. 8AM-5PM. Access by: mail, in person.

Probate—Probate Court, PO Box 264, Crawfordville, GA 30631. 706-456-2253, Fax: 706-456-2904. 8:30AM-4:30PM.

Tattnall

Real Estate Recording—Tattnall County Clerk of the Superior Court, 108 Brazell Street, Courthouse, Reidsville, GA 30453. Fax: 912-557-4552. 8AM-4:30PM.

Felony, Misdemeanor, Civil—Superior Court, PO Box 39, Reidsville, GA 30453. 912-557-6716. 8AM-4:30PM. Access by: in person.

Misdemeanor, Civil—State Court, PO Box 39, Reidsville, GA 30453. 912-557-6716, Fax: 912-557-4552. 8AM-4:30PM. Access by: mail, in person.

Civil Actions Under $15,000, Eviction, Small Claims—Magistrate Court, PO Box 513, Reidsville, GA 30453. 912-557-4372, Fax: 912-557-3136. 8AM-4:30PM. Access by: mail, fax, in person.

Probate—Probate Court, PO Box 699, Reidsville, GA 30453. 912-557-6719, Fax: 912-557-3976. 8:30AM-4:30PM. Access by: in person.

Taylor

Real Estate Recording—Taylor County Clerk of the Superior Court, Courthouse Square, Butler, GA 31006. Fax: 912-862-5334. 8AM-5PM.

Felony, Misdemeanor, Civil—Superior Court, PO Box 248, Courthouse Square, Butler, GA 31006. 912-862-5594, Fax: 912-862-5334. 8AM-5PM. Access by: mail, in person.

Civil Actions Under $15,000, Eviction, Small Claims—Magistrate Court, PO Box 536, Butler, GA 31006. 912-862-3357, Fax: 912-862-2871. 8AM-5PM. Access by: in person.

Probate—Probate Court, Courthouse Sq, PO Box 536, Butler, GA 31006. 912-862-3357, Fax: 912-862-5334. 8AM-5PM. Access by: mail, in person.

Telfair

Real Estate Recording—Telfair County Clerk of the Superior Court, Courthouse, Oak Street, McRae, GA 31055. Fax: 912-868-7956. 8:30AM-4:30PM.

Felony, Misdemeanor, Civil—Superior Court, Courthouse, Oak St, McRae, GA 31055. 912-868-6525, Fax: 912-868-7956. 8:30AM-4:30PM. Access by: in person.

Civil Actions Under $15,000, Eviction, Small Claims—Magistrate Court, County Courthouse, McRae, GA 31055. 912-868-6772, Fax: 912-868-7956. 8:30AM-4:30PM. Access by: mail, phone, fax, in person.

Probate—Probate Court, Courthouse Square, Telfair County Courthouse, McRae, GA 31055. 912-868-6038, Fax: 912-868-7956. 8:30AM-Noon, 1-4:30PM.

Terrell

Real Estate Recording—Terrell County Clerk of the Superior Court, 235 Lee Street, Courthouse, Dawson, GA 31742. 912-995-5151. 8:30AM-5PM.

Felony, Misdemeanor, Civil—Superior Court, PO Box 189, 335 E Lee, Dawson, GA 31742. 912-995-2631. 8:30AM-5PM. Access by: in person.

Civil Actions Under $15,000, Eviction, Small Claims—Magistrate Court, PO Box 793, Dawson, GA 31742. 912-995-3757. 8AM-5PM. Access by: mail, in person.

Probate—Probate Court, PO Box 67, Dawson, GA 31742. 912-995-5515, Fax: 912-995-5515.

Thomas

Real Estate Recording—Thomas County Clerk of the Superior Court, 225 North Broad Street, Courthouse, Thomasville, GA 31792. 912-225-4133, Fax: 912-225-4110. 8AM-5PM.

Felony, Misdemeanor, Civil—Superior & State Court, PO Box 1995, Thomasville, GA 31799. 912-225-4108, Fax: 912-225-4110. 8AM-5PM. Access by: in person.

Civil Actions Under $15,000, Eviction, Small Claims—Magistrate Court, PO Box 879, Thomasville, GA 31799. 912-225-3330, Fax: 912-225-3342. 8AM-5PM. Access by: mail, in person.

Probate—Probate Court, (225 N Broad, 31792), PO Box 1582, Thomasville, GA 31799. 912-225-4116, Fax: 912-226-3430. 8AM-5PM. Access by: mail, in person.

Tift

Real Estate Recording—Tift County Clerk of the Superior Court, Corner of Tift Avenue & 2nd Street, Courthouse, Tifton, GA 31794. Fax: 912-386-7807. 9AM-5PM.

Felony, Misdemeanor, Civil—Superior & State Court, PO Box 354, Tifton, GA 31793. 912-386-7810. 8AM-5PM. Access by: in person.

Civil Actions Under $15,000, Eviction, Small Claims—Magistrate Court, PO Box 214, Tifton, GA 31793. 912-386-7907, Fax: 912-386-7978. 8AM-5PM. Access by: mail, in person.

Probate—Probate Court, PO Box 792, Tifton, GA 31793. 912-386-7913, Fax: 912-386-7386. 9AM-5PM.

Toombs

Real Estate Recording—Toombs County Clerk of the Superior Court, 100 Courthouse Square, Lyons, GA 30436. 912-526-8575, Fax: 912-526-1004. 8:30AM-5PM.

Felony, Misdemeanor, Civil—Superior & State Court, PO Drawer 530, Lyons, GA 30436. 912-526-3501, Fax: 912-526-1004. 8:30AM-5PM. Access by: in person.

Civil Actions Under $15,000, Eviction, Small Claims—Magistrate Court, PO Box 1460, Lyons, GA 30436. 912-526-4602, Fax: 912-526-8985. 8:30AM-5PM. Access by: mail, fax, in person.

Probate—Probate Court, Toombs County Courthouse, Lyons, GA 30436. 912-526-8696, Fax: 912-526-1004. 8:30AM-5PM.

Towns

Real Estate Recording—Towns County Clerk of the Superior Court, 48 River St. Courthouse, Suite E, Hiawassee, GA 30546. 8:30AM-4:30PM.

Felony, Misdemeanor, Civil—Superior Court, 48 River St Suite E, Hiawassee, GA 30546. 706-896-2130. 8:30AM-4:30PM. Access by: mail, phone, in person.

Civil Actions Under $15,000, Eviction, Small Claims, Probate—Magistrate Court, 48 River St, Hiawassee, GA 30546. 706-896-3467, Fax: 706-896-1772. 8:30AM-4:30PM. Access by: mail, phone, fax, in person.

Treutlen

Real Estate Recording—Treutlen County Clerk of the Superior Court, 200 Georgia Ave. Soperton, GA 30457. Fax: 912-529-6364. 8AM-5PM.

Felony, Misdemeanor, Civil—Superior & State Court, PO Box 356, Soperton, GA 30457. 912-529-4215. 8AM-5PM. Access by: mail, in person.

Civil Actions Under $15,000, Eviction, Small Claims, Probate—Magistrate Court, 200 W Georgia Ave, Soperton, GA 30457. 912-529-3342, Fax: 912-529-6062. 9AM-12; 1-5PM. Access by: mail, phone, in person.

Troup

Real Estate Recording—Troup County Clerk of the Superior Court, Courthouse, 118 Ridley Avenue, LaGrange, GA 30240. 706-883-1620. 8AM-5PM.

Felony, Misdemeanor, Civil—Superior & State Court, 118 Ridley Ave (PO Box 866, 30241), LaGrange, GA 30240. 706-883-1740. 8AM-5PM. Access by: in person.

Civil Actions Under $15,000, Eviction, Small Claims—Magistrate Court, 119 Ridley Ave, LaGrange, GA 30240. 706-883-1695. 8AM-5PM. Access by: mail, phone, in person.

Probate—Probate Court, 900 Dallis St, LaGrange, GA 30240. 706-883-1690, Fax: 706-812-7933. 8AM-5PM. Access by: mail, in person.

Turner

Real Estate Recording—Turner County Clerk of the Superior Court, 219 East College Avenue, Ashburn, GA 31714. 912-567-3636, Fax: 912-567-0450. 8AM-5PM.

Felony, Misdemeanor, Civil—Superior Court, PO Box 106, 219 E College Ave, Ashburn, GA 31714. 912-567-2011, Fax: 912-567-0450. 8AM-5PM. Access by: mail, phone, in person.

Civil Actions Under $15,000, Eviction, Small Claims—Magistrate Court, 219 E College Ave, Rm 2, Ashburn, GA 31714. 912-567-3155. 9AM-6PM M,T,Th/9AM-4PM F. Access by: mail, in person.

Probate—Probate Court, 219 E College Ave, PO Box 2506, Ashburn, GA 31714. 912-567-2151, Fax: 912-567-0358. 8AM-5PM. Access by: mail, in person.

Twiggs

Real Estate Recording—Twiggs County Clerk of the Superior Court, 109 E. Main St. Jeffersonville, GA 31044. 912-945-3629. 8AM-5PM.

Felony, Misdemeanor, Civil—Superior Court, PO Box 228, Jeffersonville, GA 31044. 912-945-3350. 8AM-5PM. Access by: in person.

Civil Actions Under $15,000, Eviction, Small Claims—Magistrate Court, PO Box 146, Jeffersonville, GA 31044. 912-945-3428, Fax: 912-945-2083. 9AM-5PM. Access by: mail, in person.

Probate—Probate Court, PO Box 307, Jeffersonville, GA 31044. 912-945-3390, Fax: 912-945-6070. 9AM-5PM.

Union

Real Estate Recording—Union County Clerk of the Superior Court, 114 Courthouse Street, Box 5, Blairsville, GA 30512. 706-745-2260, Fax: 706-745-3822. 8AM-5PM.

Felony, Misdemeanor, Civil—Superior Court, 114 Courthouse St, Box 5, Blairsville, GA 30512. 706-745-2611, Fax: 706-745-3822. 8AM-5PM. Access by: mail, phone, fax, in person.

Civil Actions Under $15,000, Eviction, Small Claims, Probate—Magistrate & Probate Court, 114 Courthouse St, Box 8, Blairsville, GA 30512. 706-745-2654, Fax: 706-745-9384. 8AM-4:30PM. Access by: mail, in person.

Upson

Real Estate Recording—Upson County Clerk of the Superior Court, 116 W. Main Street, Courthouse Annex, Thomaston, GA 30286. Fax: 706-647-8999. 8AM-5PM.

Felony, Misdemeanor, Civil—Superior Court, PO Box 469, Thomaston, GA 30286. 706-647-7835, Fax: 706-647-7030. 8AM-5PM. Access by: in person.

Civil Actions Under $15,000, Eviction, Small Claims—Magistrate Court, PO Box 890, Thomaston, GA 30286. 706-647-6891, Fax: 706-647-1248. 8AM-5PM. Access by: mail, in person.

Probate—Probate Court, PO Box 906, Thomaston, GA 30286. 706-647-7015, Fax: 706-646-3341. 8AM-5PM. Access by: mail, in person.

Walker

Real Estate Recording—Walker County Clerk of the Superior Court, South Duke Street, Courthouse, La Fayette, GA 30728. 706-638-2929. 8AM-5PM.

Felony, Misdemeanor, Civil—Superior & State Court, PO Box 448, LaFayette, GA 30728. 706-638-1772. 8AM-5PM. Access by: in person.

Civil Actions Under $15,000, Eviction, Small Claims—Magistrate Court, 102 Napier St, LaFayette, GA 30728. 706-638-1217, Fax: 706-638-1218. 8AM-5PM. Access by: mail, phone, in person.

Probate—Probate Court, PO Box 436, LaFayette, GA 30728. 706-638-2852, Fax: 706-638-2869. 8AM-5PM. Access by: mail, in person.

Walton

Real Estate Recording—Walton County Clerk of the Superior Court, 116 S. Broad St. Judicial Bldg. Monroe, GA 30655. Fax: 770-267-1441. 8:30AM-5PM.

Felony, Misdemeanor, Civil—Superior Court, PO Box 745, Monroe, GA 30655. 770-267-1307, Fax: 770-267-1441. 8:30AM-5PM. Access by: in person.

Civil Actions Under $15,000, Eviction, Small Claims—Magistrate Court, PO Box 1188, Monroe, GA 30655. 770-267-1349, Fax: 770-267-1417. 8:30AM-5PM. Access by: mail, phone, fax, in person.

Probate—Probate Court, 111 E Spring St, PO Box 629, Monroe, GA 30655. 770-267-1345, Fax: 770-267-1417. 8:30AM-5PM. Access by: mail, in person. Special note: This location also has traffic and misdemeanor records.

Ware

Real Estate Recording—Ware County Clerk of the Superior Court, 800 Church Street, Waycross, GA 31501. 912-287-4305. 9AM-5PM.

Felony, Misdemeanor, Civil—Superior & State Court, PO Box 776, Waycross, GA 31502. 912-287-4340. 9AM-5PM. Access by: in person.

Civil Actions Under $15,000, Eviction, Small Claims—Magistrate Court, 201 State St, Rm 102, PO Box 17, Waycross, GA 31501. Fax: 912-287-4377. 9AM-5PM. Access by: mail, in person.

Probate—Probate Court, Ware County Courthouse, Rm 105, Waycross, GA 31501. 912-287-4315, Fax: 912-287-4301. 9AM-5PM. Access by: mail, in person.

Warren

Real Estate Recording—Warren County Clerk of the Superior Court, Community Services Bldg. 100 Warren St. Warrenton, GA 30828. 706-465-2177, Fax: 706-465-0232. 8AM-Noon, 1-5PM.

Felony, Misdemeanor, Civil—Superior Court, PO Box 227, 100 Warren St, Warrenton, GA 30828. 706-465-2262, Fax: 706-465-0232. 8AM-5PM. Access by: in person.

Civil Actions Under $15,000, Eviction, Small Claims—Magistrate Court, PO Box 203, Warrenton, GA 30828. 706-465-3123. 8AM-5PM. Access by: mail, in person.

Probate—Probate Court, 100 E Main St, PO Box 364, Warrenton, GA 30828. 706-465-2227. 8AM-5PM.

Washington

Real Estate Recording—Washington County Clerk of the Superior Court, Courthouse, Sandersville, GA 31082. 9AM-5PM.

Felony, Misdemeanor, Civil—Superior & State Court, PO Box 231, Sandersville, GA 31082. 912-552-3186. 9AM-5PM. Access by: in person.

Civil Actions Under $15,000, Eviction, Small Claims—Magistrate Court, PO Box 1053, Sandersville, GA 31082. 912-552-3591. 9AM-5PM. Access by: in person.

Probate—Probate Court, 132 W Haynes St, PO Box 669, Sandersville, GA 31082. 912-552-3304, Fax: 912-552-7424. 9AM-Noon, 1-5PM. Access by: mail, in person.

Wayne

Real Estate Recording—Wayne County Clerk of the Superior Court, 240 E. Walnut, Courthouse Square, Jesup, GA 31546. 912-427-5900, Fax: 912-427-5939. 8:30AM-5PM.

Felony, Misdemeanor, Civil—Superior & State Court, PO Box 918, Jesup, GA 31545. 912-427-5930, Fax: 912-427-5939. 8:30AM-5PM. Access by: in person.

Civil Actions Under $15,000, Eviction, Small Claims—Magistrate Court, PO Box 27, Jesup, GA 31598. 912-427-5960, Fax: 912-427-5906. 8:30AM-5PM. Access by: mail, in person.

Probate—Probate Court, PO Box 1093, Jesup, GA 31598. 912-427-5940, Fax: 912-427-5944.

Webster

Real Estate Recording—Webster County Clerk of the Superior Court, County Courthouse, U.S. Highway 280, Preston, GA 31824. 8AM-Noon, 12:30PM-4:30PM.

Felony, Misdemeanor, Civil—Superior Court, PO Box 117, Preston, GA 31824. 912-828-3525. 8AM-4:30PM. Access by: in person.

Civil Actions Under $15,000, Eviction, Small Claims—Magistrate Court, PO Box 18, Preston, GA 31824. 912-828-3615, Fax: 912-828-3616. 8:30AM-4:30PM. Access by: mail, fax, in person. Special note: This court will not give out SSNs.

Probate—Probate Court, Hwy 280, PO Box 135, Preston, GA 31824. 912-828-3615. 8AM-Noon, 12:30-4:30PM.

Wheeler

Real Estate Recording—Wheeler County Clerk of the Superior Court, 119 West Pearl St. Alamo, GA 30411. 912-568-7131, Fax: 912-568-7453. 8AM-4PM.

Felony, Misdemeanor, Civil—Superior Court, PO Box 38, Alamo, GA 30411. 912-568-7137. 8AM-4PM. Access by: in person.

Civil Actions Under $15,000, Eviction, Small Claims, Probate—Magistrate & Probate Court, PO Box 477, Alamo, GA 30411. 912-568-7133. 8AM-4PM. Access by: mail, in person.

White

Real Estate Recording—White County Clerk of the Superior Court, 59 South Main Street, Courthouse, Suite B, Cleveland, GA 30528. Fax: 706-865-7749. 8:30AM-5PM.

Felony, Misdemeanor, Civil—Superior Court, 59 S Main St, Ste B, Cleveland, GA 30528. 706-865-2613, Fax: 706-865-7749. 8:30AM-5PM. Access by: in person.

Civil Actions Under $15,000, Eviction, Small Claims—Magistrate Court-Civil Division, 59 S Main St, Ste D, Cleveland, GA 30528. 706-865-6636, Fax: 706-865-7138. 8:30AM-5PM. Access by: in person.

Civil Actions Under $15,000, Misdemeanor, Eviction, Small Claims—Magistrate Court, 59 S Main St, Ste D, Cleveland, GA 30528. 706-865-6636, Fax: 706-865-7738. 8:30AM-5PM. Access by: mail, phone, fax, in person.

Probate—Probate Court, 59 S Main St Ste H, Cleveland, GA 30528. 706-865-4141, Fax: 706-865-1324. 8:30AM-5PM. Access by: mail, in person.

Whitfield

Real Estate Recording—Whitfield County Clerk of the Superior Court, 300 West Crawford Street, Courthouse, Dalton, GA 30722. 706-275-7510, Fax: 706-275-7456. 8AM-5PM.

Felony, Misdemeanor, Civil—Superior Court, PO Box 868, Dalton, GA 30722. 706-275-7450, Fax: 706-275-7456. 8AM-5PM. Access by: in person.

Civil Actions Under $15,000, Eviction, Small Claims—Magistrate Court, 210 N Thorton Ave PO Box 386, Dalton, GA 30722-0386. 706-278-5052, Fax: 706-278-8810. 8AM-5PM M-W, F; 9AM-5PM Th. Access by: mail, in person.

Probate—Probate Court, 301 Crawford St, Dalton, GA 30720. 706-275-7400, Fax: 706-275-7501. 8AM-5PM. Access by: mail, in person.

Wilcox

Real Estate Recording—Wilcox County Clerk of the Superior Court, Courthouse, 103 North Broad St. Abbeville, GA 31001. Fax: 912-467-2000. 9AM-5PM.

Felony, Misdemeanor, Civil, Eviction, Small Claims—Superior & Magistrate Courts, 103 N Broad St, Abbeville, GA 31001. 912-467-2442, Fax: 912-467-2000. 9AM-5PM. Access by: mail, in person.

Probate—Probate Court, 103 N Broad St, Abbeville, GA 31001. 912-467-2220, Fax: 912-467-2000. 9AM-5PM.

Wilkes

Real Estate Recording—Wilkes County Superior Court Clerk, 23 East Court Street, Room 205, Washington, GA 30673. Fax: 706-678-2115. 9AM-5PM.

Felony, Misdemeanor, Civil—Superior Court, 23 E Court St, Rm 205, Washington, GA 30673. 706-678-2423. 9AM-5PM. Access by: mail, fax, in person.

Civil Actions Under $15,000, Eviction, Small Claims—Magistrate Court, 23 E Court St, Rm 427, Washington, GA 30673. 706-678-1881, Fax: 706-678-1865. 8:30AM-5PM. Access by: in person.

Probate—Probate Court, 23 E Court St, Rm 422, Washington, GA 30673. 706-678-2523, Fax: 706-678-1865. 8:30AM-5PM.

Wilkinson

Real Estate Recording—Wilkinson County Clerk of the Superior Court, 100 Main Street, Courthouse, Irwinton, GA 31042. Fax: 912-946-7274. 8AM-5PM.

Felony, Misdemeanor, Civil—Superior Court, PO Box 250, Irwinton, GA 31042. 912-946-2221, Fax: 912-946-3767. 8AM-5PM. Access by: in person.

Civil Actions Under $15,000, Eviction, Small Claims, Probate—Magistrate Court, PO Box 201, Irwinton, GA 31042. 912-946-2222, Fax: 912-946-1497. 8AM-5PM. Access by: mail, in person.

Worth

Real Estate Recording—Worth County Clerk of the Superior Court, 201 North Main Street, Courthouse, Room 13, Sylvester, GA 31791. 912-776-8204. 8AM-5PM.

Felony, Misdemeanor, Civil, Eviction, Small Claims—Superior and State Court, 201 N Main St, Rm 13, Sylvester, GA 31791. 912-776-8205, Fax: 912-776-8232. 8AM-5PM. Access by: in person.

Misdemeanor, Civil Under $45,000, Eviction, Small Claims—Magistrate Court, 201 N Main St, Rm 13, Sylvester, GA 31791. 912-776-8210. 8:30AM-5PM. Access by: in person.

Probate—Probate Court, 201 N Main St, Rm 12, Sylvester, GA 31791. 912-776-8207, Fax: 912-776-8232. 8AM-5PM.

Federal Courts

US District Court

Middle District of Georgia

Albany/Americus Division PO Box 1906, Albany, GA 31702912-430-8432 Fax: 912-430-8538 Counties: Baker, Ben Hill, Calhoun, Crisp, Dougherty, Early, Lee, Miller, Mitchell, Schley, Sumter, Terrell, Turner, Webster, Worth. Ben Hill and Crisp were transfered from the Macon Division as of October 1, 1997. www.gamd.uscourts.gov

Athens Division PO Box 1106, Athens, GA 30603706-227-1094 Fax: 706-546-2190 Counties: Clarke, Elbert, Franklin, Greene, Hart, Madison, Morgan, Oconee, Oglethorpe, Walton. Closed cases before April 1997 are located in the Macon Division. www.gamd.uscourts.gov

Columbus Division PO Box 124, Columbus, GA 31902706-649-7816 Counties: Chattahoochee, Clay, Harris, Marion, Muscogee, Quitman, Randolph, Stewart, Talbot, Taylor. www.gamd.uscourts.gov

Macon Division PO Box 128, Macon, GA 31202-0128912-752-3497 Fax: 912-752-3496 Counties: Baldwin, Ben Hill, Bibb, Bleckley, Butts, Crawford, Crisp, Dooly, Hancock, Houston, Jasper, Jones, Lamar, Macon, Monroe, Peach, Pulaski, Putnam, Twiggs, Upson, Washington, Wilcox, Wilkinson.Athens Division cases closed before April 1997 are also located here. www.gamd.uscourts.gov

Thomasville Division c/o Valdosta Division, PO Box 68, Valdosta, GA 31601912-242-3616 Counties: Brooks, Colquitt, Decatur, Grady, Seminole, Thomas. www.gamd.uscourts.gov

Valdosta Division PO Box 68, Valdosta, GA 31603912-242-3616 Fax: 912-244-9547 Counties: Berrien, Clinch, Cook, Echols, Irwin, Lanier, Lowndes, Tift. www.gamd.uscourts.gov

Northern District of Georgia

Atlanta Division 2211 US Courthouse, 75 Spring St SW, Atlanta, GA 30303-3361404-331-6496, Civil Docket Phone: 404-331-6613, Criminal Docket Phone: 404-331-4227 Counties: Cherokee, Clayton, Cobb, De Kalb, Douglas, Fulton, Gwinnett, Henry, Newton, Rockdale. www.gand.uscourts.gov

Gainesville Division Federal Bldg, Room 201, 121 Spring St SE, Gainesville, GA 30501770-534-5954 Counties: Banks, Barrow, Dawson, Fannin, Forsyth, Gilmer, Habersham, Hall, Jackson, Lumpkin, Pickens, Rabun, Stephens, Towns, Union, White. www.gand.uscourts.gov

Newnan Division PO Box 939, Newnan, GA 30264770-253-8847 Counties: Carroll, Coweta, Fayette, Haralson, Heard, Meriwether, Pike, Spalding, Troup. www.gand.uscourts.gov

Rome Division PO Box 1186, Rome, GA 30162-1186706-291-5629 Counties: Bartow, Catoosa, Chattooga, Dade, Floyd, Gordon, Murray, Paulding, Polk, Walker, Whitfield. www.gand.uscourts.gov

Southern District of Georgia

Augusta Division PO Box 1130, Augusta, GA 30903706-722-2074 Counties: Burke, Columbia, Glascock, Jefferson, Lincoln, McDuffie, Richmond, Taliaferro, Warren, Wilkes.

Brunswick Division PO Box 1636, Brunswick, GA 31521912-265-1758 Counties: Appling, Camden, Glynn, Jeff Davis, Long, McIntosh, Wayne.

Dublin Division c/o Augusta Division, PO Box 1130, Augusta, GA 30903706-722-2074 Counties: Dodge, Johnson, Laurens, Montgomery, Telfair, Treutlen, Wheeler.

Savannah Division PO Box 8286, Savannah, GA 31412912-650-4020 Fax: 912-650-4030 Counties: Bryan, Chatham, Effingham, Liberty.

Statesboro Division c/o Savannah Division, PO Box 8286, Savannah, GA 31412912-650-4020 Counties: Bulloch, Candler, Emanuel, Evans, Jenkins, Screven, Tattnall, Toombs.

Waycross Division c/o Savannah Division, PO Box 8286, Savannah, GA 31412912-650-4020 Counties: Atkinson, Bacon, Brantley, Charlton, Coffee, Pierce, Ware.

US Bankruptcy Court

Middle District of Georgia

Columbus Division PO Box 2147, Columbus, GA 31902706-649-7837 Counties: Berrien, Brooks, Chattahoochee, Clay, Clinch, Colquitt, Cook, Decatur, Echols, Grady, Harris, Irwin, Lanier, Lowndes, Marion, Muscogee, Quitman, Randolph, Seminole, Stewart,Talbot, Taylor, Thomas, Tift. www.gamb.uscourts.gov

Macon Division PO Box 1957, Macon, GA 31202912-752-3506 Fax: 912-752-8157 Counties: Baldwin, Baker, Ben Hill, Bibb, Bleckley, Butts, Calhoun, Clarke, Crawford, Crisp, Dooly, Dougherty, Early, Elbert, Franklin, Greene, Hancock, Hart, Houston, Jasper, Jones, Lamar, Lee, Macon, Madison, Miller, Mitchell, Monroe, Morgan, Oconee, Oglethorpe,Peach, Pulaski, Putnam, Schley, Sumter, Terrell, Turner, Twiggs, Upson, Walton, Washington, Webster, Wilcox, Wilkinson, Worth. www.gamb.uscourts.gov

Northern District of Georgia

Atlanta Division 1340 US Courthouse, 75 Spring St SW, Atlanta, GA 30303-3361404-215-1000 Counties: Cherokee, Clayton, Cobb, De Kalb, Douglas, Fulton, Gwinnett, Henry, Newton, Rockdale. http://ecf.ganb.uscourts.gov

Gainesville Division 121 Spring St SE, Room 203-C, Gainesville, GA 30501770-536-0556 Counties: Banks, Barrow, Dawson, Fannin, Forsyth, Gilmer, Habersham, Hall, Jackson, Lumpkin, Pickens, Rabun, Stephens, Towns, Union, White. http://ecf.ganb.uscourts.gov

Newnan Division Clerk, PO Box 2328, Newnan, GA 30264770-251-5583 Counties: Carroll, Coweta, Fayette, Haralson, Heard, Meriwether, Pike, Spalding, Troup. http://ecf.ganb.uscourts.gov

Rome Division Clerk, 600 E 1st St, Room 339, Rome, GA 30161-3187706-291-5639 Counties: Bartow, Catoosa, Chattooga, Dade, Floyd, Gordon, Murray, Paulding, Polk, Walker, Whitfield. http://ecf.ganb.uscourts.gov

Southern District of Georgia

Augusta Division PO Box 1487, Augusta, GA 30903706-724-2421 Counties: Bulloch, Burke, Candler, Columbia, Dodge, Emanuel, Evans, Glascock, Jefferson, Jenkins, Johnson, Laurens, Lincoln, McDuffie, Montgomery, Richmond, Screven, Taliaferro, Tattnall, Telfair, Toombs, Treutlen, Warren, Wheeler, Wilkes.

Savannah Division PO Box 8347, Savannah, GA 31412912-650-4100, Record Room: 912-650-4107 Counties: Appling, Atkinson, Bacon, Brantley, Bryan, Camden, Charlton, Chatham, Coffee, Effingham, Glynn, Jeff Davis, Liberty, Long, McIntosh, Pierce, Ware, Wayne.

Hawaii

Attorney General's Office
425 Queen St   808-586-1500
Honolulu, HI 96813   Fax: 808-586-1239
www.state.hi.us/ag

Governor's Office
415 S Beretania St   808-586-0034
Honolulu, HI 96813   Fax: 808-586-0006
www.state.hi.us/gov

State Archives
Iolani Palace Grounds   808-586-0329
Honolulu, HI 96813   Fax: 808-586-0330
www.state.hi.us/dags/archives

Capital: Honolulu
Honolulu County

Time Zone: HT (Hawaii Standard Time)

Number of Counties: 4

Population: 1,186,602

Web Site: www.state.hi.us

Search Unclaimed Property Online
There is no Internet-based search for unclaimed property for this state.

State Agencies

Criminal Records
Hawaii Criminal Justice Data Center, Liane Moriyama, Administrator, 465 S King St, Room 101, Honolulu, HI 96813; 808-587-3106; 8AM-4PM. Access by: mail.

Corporation Records
Fictitious Name
Limited Partnership Records
Assumed Name
Trademarks/Servicemarks
Business Registration Division, PO Box 40, Honolulu, HI 96810 (1010 Richard St, 1st Floor, Honolulu, HI 96813); 808-586-2727; Fax: 808-586-2733; 7:45AM-4:30PM. Access by: mail, phone, in person, online. www.businessregistrations.com

Uniform Commercial Code
Federal Tax Liens
State Tax Liens
UCC Division, Bureau of Conveyances, PO Box 2867, Honolulu, HI 96803 (Dept. of Land & Natural Resources, 1151 Punchbowl St, Honolulu, HI 96813); 808-587-0154; Fax: 808-587-0136; 7:45AM-4:30PM. Access by: mail. www.hawaii.gov/dlnr/bc/bc.html

Workers' Compensation Records
Labor & Industrial Relations, Disability Compensation Division, 830 Punchbowl St, Room 209, Honolulu, HI 96813; 808-586-9151; Fax: 808-586-9219; 7:45AM-4:30PM. Access by: mail.

Birth Certificates
State Department of Health, Vital Records Section, PO Box 3378, Honolulu, HI 96801 (1250 Punchbowl St, Room 103, Honolulu, HI 96813); 808-586-4533; Fax: 808-586-4606; 7:45AM-2:30PM. Access by: mail. www.hawaii.gov/health

Death Records

State Department of Health, Vital Records Section, PO Box 3378, Honolulu, HI 96801; 808-586-4533; Fax: 808-586-4606; 7:45AM-2:30PM. Access by: mail.

Marriage Certificates

State Department of Health, Vital Records Section, PO Box 3378, Honolulu, HI 96801; 808-586-4533; Fax: 808-586-4606; 7:45AM-2:30PM. Access by: mail.

Divorce Records

State Department of Health, Vital Records Section, PO Box 3378, Honolulu, HI 96801; 808-586-4533; Fax: 808-586-4606; 7:45AM-2:30PM. Access by: mail.

Driver Records

Traffic Violations Bureau, Abstract Section, 1111 Alakea St, Honolulu, HI 96813; 808-538-5510; 7:45AM-9:00PM. Access by: mail.

Vehicle Ownership
Vehicle Identification

Restricted access.

Accident Reports

Records not available from state agency.

Accident reports are not available from the state. Records are maintained at the county level at the police departments.

Boat & Vessel Ownership
Boat & Vessel Registration

Land & Natural Resources, Division of Boating & Recreation, 333 Queen St Rm 300, Honolulu, HI 96813; 808-587-1963; Fax: 808-587-1977; 7:45AM-4:30PM. Access by: mail.

Legislation-Current/Pending
Legislation-Passed

Hawaii Legislature, 415 S Beretania St, Honolulu, HI 96813; 808-587-0700 Bill # and Location, 808-586-6720 Clerk's Office-Senate, 808-586-6400 Clerk's Office-House, 808-586-0690 State Library; Fax: 808-587-0720; 7AM-6PM. Access by:, phone, in person, online. www.hawaii.gov

Voter Registration

Records not available from state agency.

Voter information is maintained by the County Clerks.

GED Certificates

Department of Education, GED Records, 634 Pensacola, #222, Honolulu, HI 96814; 808-594-0170; Fax: 808-594-0181; 8AM-5PM.

Hunting License Information
Fishing License Information

Records not available from state agency.

Fishing information is kept by the Aquatic Resources Division; Hunting information by the Division of Forestry & Wildlife.

County Courts & Recording Offices

About the Courts...

About the Recording Offices...

Administration

Administrative Director of Courts,
Judicial Branch
417 S King St, PO Box 2560
Honolulu, HI 96813
www.state.hi.us/jud

808-539-4900
Fax: 808-539-4855

Court Structure

The Circuit Court is the court of general jurisdiction. There are 4 circuits in Hawaii: #1, #2, #3, and #5. The 4th Circuit merged with the 3rd Circuit in 1943. There are no records available for minor traffic offenses after 7/1/94.

The District Court handles some minor "felonies" and some civil cases up to $20,000.

Online Access

There is no online access to court records, but most courts offer a public access terminal to search records at the courthouse.

Organization

All UCC financing statements, tax liens, and real estate documents are filed centrally with the Bureau of Conveyances. The entire state is in the Hawaii Time Zone (HT).

County Courts & Recording Offices

Hawaii

Felony, Misdemeanor, Civil Actions Over $5,000, Probate—3rd Circuit Court Legal Documents Section, PO Box 1007, Hilo, HI 96721-1007. 808-961-7404, Fax: 808-961-7416. 7:45AM-4:30PM. Access by: mail, in person.

Misdemeanor, Civil Actions Under $20,000, Eviction, Small Claims—District Court, PO Box 4879, Hilo, HI 96720. 808-961-7470, Fax: 808-961-7447. 7:45AM-4:30PM. Access by: mail, phone, fax, in person.

Honolulu

Felony, Civil Actions Over $5,000, Probate—1st Circuit Court, Legal Documents Branch, 777 Punchbowl St, Honolulu, HI 96813. 808-539-4300, Fax: 808-539-4314. 7:45AM-4:30PM. Access by: mail, in person.

Civil Actions Under $15,000, Eviction, Small Claims—District Court-Civil Division, 1111 Alakea St, 3th Floor Records, Honolulu, HI 96813. 808-538-5151, Fax: 808-538-5232. 7:45AM-4:30PM. Access by: mail, fax, in person.

Misdemeanor—District Court-Criminal Division, 1111 Alakea St, 9th Floor Records, Honolulu, HI 96813. 806-935-6164, Fax: 808-538-5309. 7:45AM-4:30PM. Access by: mail, fax, in person.

Kauai

Felony, Misdemeanor, Civil Actions Over $10,000, Probate—5th Circuit Court, 3059 Umi St Rm #101, Lihue, HI 96766. 808-246-3300, Fax: 808-246-3310. 7:45AM-4:30PM. Access by: mail, in person.

Civil Actions Under $20,000, Eviction, Small Claims—District Court of the 5th Circuit, 4357 Rice St, #101, Lihue, HI 96766. 808-246-3301, Fax: 808-241-7103. 7:45AM-4:30PM. Access by: mail, phone, fax, in person. www.state.hi.us/jud

Misdemeanor—District Court of the 5th Circuit, 3059 Umi St, Room 111, Lihue, HI 96766. 808-246-3330, Fax: 808-246-3353. 7:45AM-4:30PM. Access by: mail, phone, fax, in person.

Maui

Felony, Misdemeanor, Civil Actions Over $5,000, Probate—2nd Circuit Court, 2145 Main St, Wailuku, HI 96793. 808-244-2929, Fax: 808-244-2932. 7:45AM-4:30PM. Access by: mail, in person. Special note: This court also covers the counties of Lanai and Molokai.

Misdemeanor, Civil Actions Under $20,000, Eviction, Small Claims—Lanai District Court, PO Box 630070, Lanai City, HI 96763. 808-565-6447. 8:30AM-12:30PM. Access by: mail, in person.

Molokai District Court, PO Box 284, Kaunakakai, HI 96748. 808-533-5451, Fax: 808-553-3374. 7:45AM-4PM. Access by: mail, in person.

Wailuku District Court, 2145 Main St, Ste 137, Wailuku, HI 96793. 808-244-2800, Fax: 808-244-2849. 7:45AM-4:30PM. Access by: mail, fax, in person.

Federal Courts

US District Court

Honolulu Division 300 Ala Moana Blvd, Rm C-338, Honolulu, HI 96850808-541-1300, Civil Docket Phone: 808-541-1297, Criminal Docket Phone: 808-541-1301 Fax: 808-541-1303 Counties: All counties. www.hid.uscourts.gov

US Bankruptcy Court

Honolulu Division 1132 Bishop St, Suite 250-L, Honolulu, HI 96813808-522-8100 Counties: All counties.

Attorney General's Office

PO Box 83720　　　　　　　　208-334-2400
Boise, ID 83720-0010　　　　　Fax: 208-334-2530
www.state.id.us/ag/homepage.htm

Governor's Office

PO Box 83720　　　　　　　　208-334-2100
Boise, ID 83720-0034　　　　　Fax: 208-334-3454
www.state.id.us/gov/govhmpg.htm

State Archives

450 N 4th Street　　　　　　　208-334-3356
Boise, ID 83702-6027　　　　　Fax: 208-334-3198
www.state.id.us/ishs/index.html

Capital:	Boise
	Ada County

Time Zone:　　　　　　　　　　　　　　MST*

* Idaho's ten northwestern-most counties are PST:
They are: Benewah, Bonner, Boundary, Clearwater,
Idaho, Kootenai, Latah, Lewis, Nez Perce, Shoshone.

Number of Counties:　　　　　　　　　44

Population:　　　　　　　　　1,210,232

Web Site:　　　　　　　www.state.id.us

> Search Unclaimed Property Online
>
> www.state.id.us/tax/
> unclaimed_idaho.htm

State Agencies

Criminal Records

State Repository, Bureau of Criminal Identification, PO Box 700, Meridian, ID 83680-0700 (700 S Stratford Dr, Meridian, ID 83642); 208-884-7130; Fax: 208-884-7193; 8AM-5PM. Access by: mail.

Corporation Records
Limited Partnerships
Trademarks/Servicemarks
Limited Liability Company Records
Fictitious Names
Trade Names

Secretary of State, Corporation Division, PO Box 83720, Boise, ID 83720-0080 (700 W Jefferson, Boise, ID 83720); 208-334-2301; Fax: 208-334-2847; 8AM-5PM. Access by: mail, online. idsos.state.id.us

Sales Tax Registrations

Revenue Operations Division, Records Management, PO Box 36, Boise, ID 83722 (800 Park, Boise, ID 83722); 208-334-7660, 208-334-7792 Records Management; Fax: 208-334-7650; 8AM-5:30PM. Access by: mail, phone, in person. www.state.id.us/tax/index.html

Uniform Commercial Code
Federal Tax Liens

UCC Division, Secretary of State, PO Box 83720, Boise, ID 83720-0080 (700 W Jefferson, Boise, ID 83720); 208-334-3191; Fax: 208-334-2847; 8AM-5PM. Access by: mail, phone, in person, online. www.idsos.state.id.us

Workers' Compensation Records

Industrial Commission of Idaho, Attn: Records Management, PO Box 83720, Boise, ID 83720-0041; 208-334-6000; Fax: 208-334-2321; 8AM-5PM. Access by: mail. www2.state.id.us/iic

Birth Certificates

State Department of Health & Welfare, Center for Vital Statistics & Health Policy, PO Box 83720, Boise, ID 83720-0036 (450 W State St, 1st Floor, Boise, ID 83702); 208-334-5988; Fax: 208-389-9096; 8AM-5PM. Access by: mail, fax. www.state.id.us/dhw

Death Records

State Department of Health, Center for Vital Statistics & Health Policy, PO Box 83720, Boise, ID 83720-0036; 208-334-5988; Fax: 208-389-9096; 8AM-5PM. Access by: mail. www.state.id.us/dhw

Marriage Certificates

State Department of Health, Center for Vital Statistics & Health Policy, PO Box 83720, Boise, ID 83720-0036; 208-334-5988; Fax: 208-389-9096; 8AM-5PM. Access by: mail. www.state.id.us/dhw

Divorce Records

State Department of Health, Center for Vital Statistics & Health Policy, PO Box 83720, Boise, ID 83720-0036; 208-334-5988; Fax: 208-389-9096; 8AM-5PM. Access by: mail. www.state.is.us/dhw

Accident Reports

Idaho Transportation Department, Office of Highway Safety-Accident Records, PO Box 7129, Boise, ID 83707-1129 (3311 W State St, Boise, ID 83707); 208-334-8100; Fax: 208-334-4430; 8AM-12:00PM; 1PM-5PM. Access by: mail, phone, in person.

Driver Records

Idaho Transportation Department, Driver's Services, PO Box 34, Boise, ID 83731-0034 (3311 W State, Boise, ID 83703); 208-334-8736; Fax: 208-334-8739; 8:30AM-5PM. Access by: mail, online. www.state.id.us/itd/dmv.html

Vehicle Ownership
Vehicle Identification

Idaho Transportation Department, Vehicle Services, PO Box 34, Boise, ID 83731-0034 (3311 W State St, Boise, ID 83707); 208-334-8773; Fax: 208-334-8542; 8:30AM-5PM. Access by: mail, online. www.state.id.us/itd/dmv.htm

Boat & Vessel Ownership
Boat & Vessel Registration

Idaho Parks & Recreation, PO Box 83720, Boise, ID 83720-0065 (5657 Warm Springs, Boise, ID 83712); 208-334-4199; Fax: 208-334-3741; 8AM-5PM. www.idoc.state.id.us

Legislation-Current/Pending
Legislation-Passed

Legislature Services Office, Research and Legislation, PO Box 83720, Boise, ID 83720-0054 (700 W Jefferson, Lower Level, East, Boise, ID 83720); 208-334-2475; Fax: 208-334-2125; 8AM-5PM. Access by: mail, phone, in person, online. www.state.id.us/legislat/legislat.html

Voter Registration

Records not available from state agency.

Records are maintained by the County Clerks. The counties will generally release name, address, and voting precinct on individual request.

GED Certificates

Department of Education, GED Testing, PO Box 83720, Boise, ID 83720-0027; 208-332-6980; Fax: 208-332-6878; 8AM-5PM.

Hunting License Information
Fishing License Information

Fish & Game Department, Fish & Game Licenses Division, PO Box 25, Boise, ID 83707-0025 (1075 Park Blvd, Boise, ID 83707); 208-334-3717 License Department, 208-334-3736 Enforcement Office; Fax: 208-334-2114; 8AM-5PM. Access by: mail. www.state.id.us/fishgame/fishgame.html

County Courts & Recording Offices

About the Courts...

About the Recording Offices...

Administration

Administrative Director of Courts,
Supreme Court Building   208-334-2246
451 W State St   Fax: 208-334-2146
Boise, ID 83720
www.idwr.state.id.us/judicial/judicial.html

Court Structure

The District Court oversees felony and most civil cases. Small claims are handled by the Magistrate Division of the District Court. Probate is handled by the Magistrate Division of the District Court.

Searching Hints

A statewide court administrative rule states that record custodians do not have a duty to "compile or summarize information contained in a record, nor ... to create new records for the requesting party." Under this rule, some courts will not perform searches.

Many courts require a signed release for employment record searches.

The following fees are mandated statewide: Search Fee - none; Certification Fee - $1.00 per document plus copy fee; Copy Fee - $1.00 per page. Not all jurisdictions currently follow these guidelines.

Online Access

There is no statewide computer system offering external access. ISTARS is a statewide intra-court/intra-agency system run and managed by the State Supreme Court. All counties are on ISTARS, and all courts provide public access terminals on-site.

Organization

44 counties, 44 recording offices. The recording officer is County Recorder. Many counties utilize a grantor/grantee index containing all transactions recorded with them. 34 counties are in the Mountain Time Zone (MST), and 10 are in the Pacific Time Zone (PST).

UCC Records

Financing statements are filed at the state level except for real estate related filings. All counties will perform UCC searches. Use search request form UCC-4. Search fees are usually $6.00 per debtor name for a listing of filings and $12.00 per debtor name for a listing plus copies at no additional charge. Separately ordered copies usually cost $1.00 per page.

Lien Records

Until 07/01/98, state tax liens were filed at the local county recorder. Now they are filed with the Secretary of State who has all active case files. Federal tax liens on personal property of businesses are filed with the Secretary of State. Other federal tax liens are filed with the county recorder. Some counties will perform a combined tax lien search for $5.00 while others will not perform tax lien searches.

Real Estate Records

Most counties will not perform real estate searches. Certification of copies usually costs $1.00 per document.

County Courts & Recording Offices

Ada

Real Estate Recording—Ada County Clerk and Recorder, 650 Main Street, Boise, ID 83702. 208-374-5402. 8:30AM-4:30PM.

Felony, Misdemeanor, Civil, Eviction, Small Claims, Probate—District & Magistrate Courts-I, 514 W. Jefferson St, Boise, ID 83702-5931. 208-365-4561. 8:30AM-5PM. Access by: mail, in person.

Misdemeanor—Ada County Traffic Court, 7180 Barrister, Boise, ID 83704. 208-354-2239. 8AM-5PM. Access by: mail, in person.

Adams

Real Estate Recording—Adams County Clerk and Recorder, Michigan St. Council, ID 83612. 208-253-4561, Fax: 208-253-4880. 8AM-Noon, 1-5PM.

Felony, Misdemeanor, Civil, Eviction, Small Claims, Probate—District & Magistrate Courts, PO Box 48, Council, ID 83612. 208-265-1433, Fax: 208-253-4880. 8AM-Noon, 1-5PM. Access by: mail, fax, in person.

Bannock

Real Estate Recording—Bannock County Clerk and Recorder, 624 East Center, Courthouse, Room 211, Pocatello, ID 83201. Fax: 208-236-7345. 8AM-5PM.

Felony, Misdemeanor, Civil, Eviction, Small Claims, Probate—District & Magistrate Courts, PO Box 4847, Pocatello, ID 83205. 208-245-2421, Fax: 208-236-7013. 8AM-5PM. Access by: mail, fax, in person.

Bear Lake

Real Estate Recording—Bear Lake County Clerk and Recorder, 7th East Center, Paris, ID 83261. Fax: 208-945-2780. 8:30AM-5PM.

Felony, Misdemeanor, Civil, Eviction, Small Claims, Probate—District & Magistrate Courts, PO Box 190, Paris, ID 83261. 208-983-2801, Fax: 208-945-2780. 8:30AM-5PM. Access by: mail, fax, in person.

Benewah

Real Estate Recording—Benewah County Clerk and Recorder, 701 College, St. Maries, ID 83861. 208-245-3241, Fax: 208-245-3046. 9AM-5PM.

Felony, Misdemeanor, Civil, Eviction, Small Claims, Probate—District & Magistrate Courts, Courthouse, 701 College Ave, St Maries, ID 83861. 208-253-4263, Fax: 208-245-3046. 9AM-5PM. Access by: mail, fax, in person.

Bingham

Real Estate Recording—Bingham County Clerk and Recorder, 501 North Maple #205, Blackfoot, ID 83221. 208-788-5525, Fax: 208-785-4131. 8AM-5PM.

Felony, Misdemeanor, Civil, Eviction, Small Claims, Probate—District & Magistrate Courts, 501 N Maple St, #402, Blackfoot, ID 83221-1700. 208-799-3030, Fax: 208-785-8057. 8AM-Noon, 1-5PM. Access by: mail, phone, fax, in person.

Blaine

Real Estate Recording—Blaine County Clerk and Recorder, Courthouse, Suite 200, 206 1st Ave. South, Hailey, ID 83333. Fax: 208-788-5501. 9AM-5PM.

Felony, Misdemeanor, Civil, Eviction, Small Claims, Probate—District & Magistrate Courts, 201 2nd Ave S #110, Hailey, ID 83333. 208-799-3040, Fax: 208-788-4759. 9AM-5PM. Access by: mail, phone, fax, in person. Special note: The Magistrate Court is in suite #106.

Boise

Real Estate Recording—Boise County Clerk and Recorder, 420 Main, Courthouse, Idaho City, ID 83631. Fax: 208-392-4473. 8AM-5PM.

Felony, Misdemeanor, Civil, Eviction, Small Claims, Probate—District & Magistrate Courts, PO Box 126, Idaho City, ID 83631. 208-454-7354, Fax: 208-392-6712. 8AM-5PM. Access by: mail, fax, in person.

Bonner

Real Estate Recording—Bonner County Clerk and Recorder, 215 South First, Sandpoint, ID 83864. 208-267-5504, Fax: 208-265-1447. 9AM-5PM.

Felony, Misdemeanor, Civil, Eviction, Small Claims, Probate—District & Magistrate Courts, 215 S. First St, Sandpoint, ID 83864. 208-267-3291, Fax: 208-265-1447. 9AM-5PM. Access by: mail, in person.

Bonneville

Real Estate Recording—Bonneville County Clerk and Recorder, 605 North Capital, Idaho Falls, ID 83402. 208-547-4342, Fax: 208-529-1353. 8AM-5PM.

Felony, Misdemeanor, Civil, Eviction, Small Claims, Probate—District & Magistrate Courts, 605 N. Capital, Idaho Falls, ID 83402. 208-547-3726, Fax: 208-529-1300. 8AM-5PM. Access by: mail, in person.

Boundary

Real Estate Recording—Boundary County Clerk and Recorder, 6452 Kootenai, Courthouse, Bonners Ferry, ID 83805. 208-324-8811, Fax: 208-267-7814. 9AM-5PM.

Felony, Misdemeanor, Civil, Eviction, Small Claims, Probate—District and Magistrate Courts, Boundary County Courthouse, PO Box 419, Bonners Ferry, ID 83805. 208-324-8811, Fax: 208-267-7814. 9AM-5PM. Access by: mail, in person.

Butte

Real Estate Recording—Butte County Clerk and Recorder, 248 West Grand, Courthouse, Arco, ID 83213. 208-529-1382, Fax: 208-527-3295. 9AM-5PM.

Felony, Misdemeanor, Civil, Eviction, Small Claims, Probate—District & Magistrate Courts, PO Box 737, Arco, ID 83213. 208-529-1350, Fax: 208-527-3448. 9AM-5PM. Access by: mail, phone, fax, in person.

Camas

Real Estate Recording—Camas County Clerk and Recorder, Corner of Soldier & Willow, Courthouse, Fairfield, ID 83327. Fax: 208-764-2349. 8:30AM-Noon, 1-5PM.

Felony, Misdemeanor, Civil, Eviction, Small Claims, Probate—District & Magistrate Courts, PO Box 430, Fairfield, ID 83327. 208-766-4285, Fax: 208-764-2349. 8:30AM-Noon, 1-5PM. Access by: mail, in person.

Canyon

Real Estate Recording—Canyon County Recorder, 1115 Albany Street, Caldwell, ID 83605. 208-476-5596. 8:30AM-5PM.

Felony, Misdemeanor, Civil, Eviction, Small Claims, Probate—District & Magistrate Courts, 1115 Albany, Caldwell, ID 83605. 8:30AM-5PM. Access by: in person. www.webpak.net/~tca3sec

Caribou

Real Estate Recording—Caribou County Clerk and Recorder, 159 South Main, Soda Springs, ID 83276. 208-549-0324, Fax: 208-547-4759. 9AM-5PM.

Felony, Misdemeanor, Civil, Eviction, Small Claims, Probate—District & Magistrate Courts, 159 S. Main, Soda Springs, ID 83276. 208-549-2092, Fax: 208-547-4759. 9AM-5PM. Access by: mail, phone, fax, in person.

Cassia

Real Estate Recording—Cassia County Clerk and Recorder, 1459 Overland Ave. Room 105, Burley, ID 83318. Fax: 208-878-1003. 8:30AM-5PM.

Felony, Misdemeanor, Civil, Eviction, Small Claims, Probate—District & Magistrate Courts, 1459 Overland, Burley, ID 83318. 208-879-2359, Fax: 208-878-1003. 8:30AM-5PM. Access by: mail, phone, fax, in person. www.safelink.net/ccounty

Clark

Real Estate Recording—Clark County Clerk and Recorder, 320 West Main, Courthouse, Dubois, ID 83423. Fax: 208-374-5609. 9AM-5PM.

Felony, Misdemeanor, Civil, Eviction, Small Claims, Probate—District & Magistrate Courts, PO Box 205, DuBois, ID 83423. 208-382-4293, Fax: 208-374-5609. 9AM-5PM. Access by: mail, fax, in person.

Clearwater

Real Estate Recording—Clearwater County Clerk and Recorder, 150 Michigan Avenue, Courthouse, Orofino, ID 83544. 208-495-1158, Fax: 208-476-9315. 8AM-5PM.

Felony, Misdemeanor, Civil, Eviction, Small Claims, Probate—District & Magistrate Courts, PO Box 586, Orofino, ID 83544. 208-495-2806, Fax: 208-476-5159. 8AM-5PM. Access by: mail, phone, fax, in person.

Custer

Real Estate Recording—Custer County Clerk and Recorder, Main Street, Courthouse, Challis, ID 83226. 208-882-8580, Fax: 208-879-5246. 9AM-5PM.

Felony, Misdemeanor, Civil, Eviction, Small Claims, Probate—District & Magistrate Courts, PO Box 385, Challis, ID 83226. 208-883-2255, Fax: 208-879-5246. 8AM-5PM. Access by: mail, phone, in person.

Elmore

Real Estate Recording—Elmore County Clerk and Recorder, 150 South 4th East, Suite #3, Mountain Home, ID 83647. 208-624-7401, Fax: 208-587-2159. 9AM-5PM.

Felony, Misdemeanor, Civil, Eviction, Small Claims, Probate—District & Magistrate Courts, 150 S 4th East, Ste 5, Mountain Home, ID 83647. 208-624-3361, Fax: 208-587-1320. 9AM-5PM. Access by: mail, fax, in person.

Franklin

Real Estate Recording—Franklin County Clerk and Recorder, 39 West Oneida, Preston, ID 83263. 208-879-2330, Fax: 208-852-1094. 9AM-5PM.

Felony, Misdemeanor, Civil, Eviction, Small Claims, Probate—District & Magistrate Courts, 39 West Oneida, Preston, ID 83263. 208-878-7351, Fax: 208-852-2926. 9AM-5PM. Access by: mail, phone, fax, in person.

Fremont

Real Estate Recording—Fremont County Clerk and Recorder, 151 West 1st N. Room 12, St. Anthony, ID 83445. 208-634-8102, Fax: 208-624-4607. 9AM-5PM.

Felony, Misdemeanor, Civil, Eviction, Small Claims, Probate—District & Magistrate Courts, 151 W 1st North, St Anthony, ID 83445. 208-642-6000, Fax: 208-624-4607. 9AM-5PM. Access by: mail, fax, in person.

Gem

Real Estate Recording—Gem County Clerk and Recorder, 415 East Main, Emmett, ID 83617. Fax: 208-365-6172. 8AM-5PM.

Felony, Misdemeanor, Civil, Eviction, Small Claims, Probate—District & Magistrate Courts, 415 East Main St, Emmett, ID 83617. 208-382-4150, Fax: 208-365-6172. 8AM-5PM. Access by: mail, in person. Special note: Felony and misdemeanor records in different offices; therefore, a search fee is charged for each.

Gooding

Real Estate Recording—Gooding County Clerk and Recorder, 624 Main, Courthouse, Gooding, ID 83330. 9AM-5PM.

Felony, Misdemeanor, Civil, Eviction, Small Claims, Probate—District & Magistrate Courts, PO Box 477, Gooding, ID 83330. 208-937-2341, Fax: 208-934-4408. 8AM-5PM. Access by: in person.

Idaho

Real Estate Recording—Idaho County Clerk and Recorder, 320 W. Main, Room 5, Grangeville, ID 83530. 209-223-6463, Fax: 208-983-1428. 8:30AM-5PM.

Felony, Misdemeanor, Civil, Eviction, Small Claims, Probate—District & Magistrate Courts, 320 West Main, Grangeville, ID 83530. 209-223-6364, Fax: 208-983-2376. 8:30AM-5PM. Access by: mail, phone, fax, in person.

Jefferson

Real Estate Recording—Jefferson County Clerk and Recorder, 134 North Clark, Courthouse, Rigby, ID 83442. 208-756-2815, Fax: 208-745-6636. 9AM-5PM.

Felony, Misdemeanor, Civil, Eviction, Small Claims, Probate—District & Magistrate Courts, PO Box 71, Rigby, ID 83442. 208-752-1266, Fax: 208-745-6636. 9AM-5PM. Access by: mail, fax, in person.

Jerome

Real Estate Recording—Jerome County Clerk and Recorder, 300 North Lincoln, Courthouse, Room 301, Jerome, ID 83338. 208-337-4540, Fax: 208-324-2719. 8:30AM-5PM.

Felony, Misdemeanor, Civil, Eviction, Small Claims, Probate—District & Magistrate Courts, 300 N Lincoln St, Jerome, ID 83338. 208-327-5352, Fax: 208-324-2719. 8:30AM-5PM. Access by: mail, fax, in person.

Kootenai

Real Estate Recording—Kootenai County Clerk and Recorder, 451 Government Way, Coeur d'Alene, ID 83814. 208-785-5005. 9AM-5PM.

Felony, Misdemeanor, Civil, Eviction, Small Claims, Probate—District Court, 324 West Garden Ave PO Box 9000, Coeur d'Alene, ID 83816-9000. 208-785-5005, Fax: 208-664-0639. 9AM-5PM. Access by: mail, fax, in person. www.co.kootenai.id.us

Latah

Real Estate Recording—Latah County Clerk and Recorder, Room 101, 5th and Van Buren, Moscow, ID 83843. 208-886-2173, Fax: 208-883-7203. 8AM-5PM.

Felony, Misdemeanor, Civil, Eviction, Small Claims, Probate—District & Magistrate Courts, PO Box 8068, Moscow, ID 83843. 208-886-7681, Fax: 208-883-2259. 8:30AM-5PM M-W, 8AM-5PM TH,F. Access by: mail, phone, fax, in person.

Lemhi

Real Estate Recording—Lemhi County Clerk and Recorder, 206 Courthouse Drive, Salmon, ID 83467. 208-766-2962, Fax: 208-756-8424. 9AM-5PM.

Felony, Misdemeanor, Civil, Eviction, Small Claims, Probate—District & Magistrate Courts, 206 Courthouse Dr, Salmon, ID 83467. 208-764-2238, Fax: 208-756-8424. 9AM-5PM. Access by: mail, phone, fax, in person.

Lewis

Real Estate Recording—Lewis County Clerk and Recorder, 510 Oak, Courthouse, Nezperce, ID 83543. 208-983-2776. 9AM-5PM.

Felony, Misdemeanor, Civil, Eviction, Small Claims, Probate—District & Magistrate Courts, 510 Oak St (PO Box 39), Nezperce, ID 83543. 208-945-2208, Fax: 208-937-9223. 9AM-5PM. Access by: mail, phone, fax, in person.

Lincoln

Real Estate Recording—Lincoln County Clerk and Recorder, 111 West B Street, Courthouse, Shoshone, ID 83352. 208-937-2251, Fax: 208-886-2707. 8:30AM-5PM.

Felony, Misdemeanor, Civil, Eviction, Small Claims, Probate—District & Magistrate Courts, Drawer A, Shoshone, ID 83352. 208-934-4261, Fax: 208-886-2458. 9AM-5PM. Access by: in person.

Madison

Real Estate Recording—Madison County Clerk and Recorder, 134 East Main, Courthouse Annex Bldg. Rexburg, ID 83440. 208-364-2000, Fax: 208-356-8396. 9AM-5PM.

Felony, Misdemeanor, Civil, Eviction, Small Claims, Probate—District & Magistrate Courts, PO Box 389, Rexburg, ID 83440. 208-364-2233, Fax: 208-356-5425. 9AM-5PM. Access by: mail, in person.

Minidoka

Real Estate Recording—Minidoka County Clerk and Recorder, 715 G Street, Courthouse, Rupert, ID 83350. Fax: 208-436-0737. 8:30AM-5PM.

Felony, Misdemeanor, Civil, Eviction, Small Claims, Probate—District & Magistrate Courts, PO Box 368, Rupert, ID 83350. 208-476-5213, Fax: 208-436-5857. 8:30AM-5PM. Access by: mail, phone, fax, in person.

Nez Perce

Real Estate Recording—Nez Perce County Auditor and Recorder, 1230 Main Street, Room 100, Lewiston, ID 83501. 208-852-0877, Fax: 208-799-3070. 8AM-5PM.

Felony, Misdemeanor, Civil, Eviction, Small Claims, Probate—District Court, PO Box 896, Lewiston, ID 83501. 208-852-1095, Fax: 208-799-3058. 8AM-5PM. Access by: mail, phone, fax, in person.

Oneida

Real Estate Recording—Oneida County Clerk and Recorder, 10 Court Street, Malad, ID 83252. 208-769-4400, Fax: 208-766-2448. 9AM-5PM.

Felony, Misdemeanor, Civil, Eviction, Small Claims, Probate—District & Magistrate Courts, 10 Court St, Malad City, ID 83252. 208-769-4440, Fax: 208-766-2990. 9AM-5PM. Access by: mail, phone, fax, in person.

Owyhee

Real Estate Recording—Owyhee County Clerk and Recorder, Highway 78, Courthouse, Murphy, ID 83650. 208-527-3021, Fax: 208-495-1173. 8:30AM-5PM.

Felony, Misdemeanor, Civil, Eviction, Small Claims, Probate—District & Magistrate Courts-I, Courthouse, Murphy, ID 83650. 208-527-3047, Fax: 208-495-1173. 8:30AM-5PM. Access by: mail, fax, in person.

Misdemeanor, Civil Actions Under $10,000, Eviction, Small Claims—Homedale Magistrate Court, 31 W Wyoming Ave, Homedale, ID 83628-3402. 208-354-2254, Fax: 208-337-3035. 8:30AM-5PM. Access by: in person.

Payette

Real Estate Recording—Payette County Clerk and Recorder, 1130 3rd Avenue North, Courthouse, Payette, ID 83661. Fax: 208-642-6011. 9AM-5PM.

Felony, Misdemeanor, Civil, Eviction, Small Claims, Probate—District & Magistrate Courts, 1130 3rd Ave N, Payette, ID 83661. 208-736-4013, Fax: 208-642-6011. 9AM-5PM. Access by: mail, fax, in person.

Power

Real Estate Recording—Power County Clerk and Recorder, 543 Bannock, American Falls, ID 83211. 208-236-7350, Fax: 208-226-7612. 9AM-5PM.

Felony, Misdemeanor, Civil, Eviction, Small Claims, Probate—District & Magistrate Courts, 543 Bannock Ave, American Falls, ID 83211. 208-226-7614, Fax: 208-226-7612. 9AM-5PM. Access by: mail, phone, fax, in person.

Shoshone

Real Estate Recording—Shoshone County Clerk and Recorder, Courthouse, Suite 120, 700 Bank St. Wallace, ID 83873. Fax: 208-753-2711. 9AM-5PM.

Felony, Misdemeanor, Civil, Eviction, Small Claims, Probate—District & Magistrate Courts, 700 Bank St, Wallace, ID 83873. 208-756-2816, Fax: 208-753-0921. 9AM-5PM. Access by: mail, phone, fax, in person.

Teton

Real Estate Recording—Teton County Clerk and Recorder, 89 North Main #1, Driggs, ID 83422. 208-356-9383, Fax: 208-354-8410. 9AM-5PM.

Felony, Misdemeanor, Civil, Eviction, Small Claims, Probate—District & Magistrate Courts, 89 N Main #1, Driggs, ID 83422. 208-356-6871, Fax: 208-354-8410. 9AM-5PM. Access by: mail, phone, fax, in person. Special note: Address and telephone given above are for District Court. If you wish to access only the Magistrate Court, address to PO Box 770 and call 208-354-2239.

Twin Falls

Real Estate Recording—Twin Falls County Clerk and Recorder, 425 Shoshone Street North, Twin Falls, ID 83301. 208-745-7736, Fax: 208-736-4182. 8AM-5PM.

Felony, Misdemeanor, Civil, Eviction, Small Claims, Probate—District & Magistrate Courts, PO Box 126, Twin Falls, ID 83301. 208-745-9219, Fax: 208-736-4002. 8AM-5PM. Access by: mail, phone, fax, in person.

Valley

Real Estate Recording—Valley County Clerk and Recorder, 219 North Main, Courthouse, Cascade, ID 83611. 208-436-9041, Fax: 208-382-4955. 9AM-5PM.

Felony, Misdemeanor, Civil, Eviction, Small Claims, Probate—District & Magistrate Courts-I, PO Box 650, Cascade, ID 83611. 208-392-4452, Fax: 208-382-3098. 9AM-5PM. Access by: mail, phone, fax, in person.

Misdemeanor, Civil Actions Under $10,000, Eviction, Small Claims—Magistrate Court II, Valley County Courthouse Annex, 550 Deinhard Lane, McCall, ID 83638. 208-736-4008, Fax: 208-634-4040. 9AM-5PM. Access by: mail, phone, fax, in person.

Washington

Real Estate Recording—Washington County Clerk and Recorder, 256 East Court Street, Weiser, ID 83672. 208-587-2133, Fax: 208-549-3925. 8:30AM-5PM.

Felony, Misdemeanor, Civil, Eviction, Small Claims, Probate—District & Magistrate Courts, PO Box 670, Weiser, ID 83672. 208-587-2138, Fax: 208-549-3925. 8:30AM-5PM. Access by: in person.

Federal Courts

US District Court

Boise Division MSC 039, Federal Bldg, 550 W Fort St, Room 400, Boise, ID 83724208-334-1361 Fax: 208-334-9362 Counties: Ada, Adams, Blaine, Boise, Camas, Canyon, Cassia, Elmore, Gem, Gooding, Jerome, Lincoln, Minidoka, Owyhee, Payette, Twin Falls, Valley, Washington. www.id.uscourts.gov

Coeur d' Alene Division c/o Boise Division, MSD 039, Federal Bldg, 550 W Fort St, Room 400, Boise, ID 83724208-334-1361 Counties: Benewah, Bonner, Boundary, Kootenai, Shoshone. www.id.uscourts.gov

Moscow Division c/o Boise Division, Box 039, Federal Bldg, 550 W Fort St, Boise, ID 83724208-334-1361 Counties: Clearwater, Latah, Lewis, Nez Perce. www.id.uscourts.gov

Pocatello Division c/o Boise Division, Box 039, Federal Bldg, 550 W Fort St, Boise, ID 83724208-334-1361 Counties: Bannock, Bear Lake, Bingham, Bonneville, Butte, Caribou, Clark, Custer, Franklin, Fremont, Idaho, Jefferson, Lemhi, Madison, Oneida, Power, Teton. www.id.uscourts.gov

US Bankruptcy Court

Boise Division MSC 042, US Courthouse, 550 W Fort St, Room 400, Boise, ID 83724208-334-1074 Fax: 208-334-9362 Counties: Ada, Adams, Blaine, Boise, Camas, Canyon, Cassia, Elmore, Gem, Gooding, Jerome, Lincoln, Minidoka, Owyhee, Payette, Twin Falls, Valley, Washington. www.id.uscourts.gov

Coeur d' Alene Division 205 N 4th St, 2nd Floor, Coeur d'Alene, ID 83814208-664-4925 Fax: 208-765-0270 Counties: Benewah, Bonner, Boundary, Kootenai, Shoshone. www.id.uscourts.gov

Moscow Division 220 E 5th St, Moscow, ID 83843208-882-7612 Fax: 208-883-1576 Counties: Clearwater, Idaho, Latah, Lewis, Nez Perce. www.id.uscourts.gov

Pocatello Division 250 S 4th Ave, Room 263, Pocatello, ID 83201208-236-6912 Fax: 208-232-9308 Counties: Bannock, Bear Lake, Bingham, Bonneville, Butte, Caribou, Clark, Custer, Franklin, Fremont, Jefferson, Lemhi, Madison, Oneida, Power, Teton. www.id.uscourts.gov

Attorney General's Office
500 S 2nd St
Springfield, IL 62706
217-782-1090
Fax: 217-524-4701
www.ag.state.il.us

Governor's Office
207 Statehouse
Springfield, IL 62706
217-782-0244
Fax: 217-524-4049
www.state.il.us/gov

State Archives
Norton Bldg, Capitol Complex
Springfield, IL 62756
217-782-4682
Fax: 217-524-3930
www.sos.state.il.us/depts/archives/
arc_home.html

Capital:	Springfield
	Sangamon County
Time Zone:	CST
Number of Counties:	102
Population:	11,895,849
Web Site:	www.state.il.us

Search Unclaimed Property Online
There is no Internet-based search for unclaimed property for this state.

State Agencies

Criminal Records
Illinois State Police, Bureau of Identification, 260 N Chicago St, Joliet, IL 60432-4075; 815-740-5164; Fax: 815-740-5193; 8AM-4PM M-F. Access by: mail. www.state.il.us/isp/isphpage.htm

Corporation Records
Limited Partnership Records
Trade Names
Assumed Name
Limited Liability Company Records
Department of Business Services, Corporate Department, Howlett Bldg, 3rd Floor, Copy Section, Springfield, IL 62756 (Corner of 2nd & Edwards Sts, Springfield, IL 62756); 217-782-7880; Fax: 217-782-4528; 8AM-4:30PM. Access by: mail, phone, in person, online. www.sos.state.il.us

Sales Tax Registrations
Revenue Department, Taxpayer Services, PO Box 19001, Springfield, IL 62794-9001 (101 W Jefferson, Springfield, IL 62702); 800-732-8866; Fax: 217-782-4217; 8AM-5PM. Access by: mail, phone, in person.

Uniform Commercial Code
Federal Tax Liens
Secretary of State, UCC Division, 2nd & Edwards St, Howlett Bldg, Room 030, Springfield, IL 62756; 217-782-7518; 8AM-4:30PM. Access by: mail.

State Tax Liens
Records not available from state agency.

All state tax liens are filed at the county.

Workers' Compensation Records

Industrial Commission, 100 W Randolph, 8th Floor, Chicago, IL 60601; 312-814-6611; 8:30AM-5PM. Access by: mail, phone, in person. www.state.il.us/agency/iic

Birth Certificates

State Department of Health, Division of Vital Records, 605 W Jefferson St, Springfield, IL 62702-5097; 217-782-6553; Fax: 217-523-2648; 8AM-5PM M-F. Access by: mail, phone, in person. www.idph.state.il.us/vital/home.htm

Death Records

State Department of Health, Division of Vital Records, 605 W Jefferson St, Springfield, IL 62702-5097; 217-782-6553; Fax: 217-523-2648; 8AM-5PM. Access by: mail, phone, in person.

Marriage Certificates
Divorce Records

Records not available from state agency.

State will verify marriage or divorce from 1962-present, but will not issue certificate. Verification requests must be in writing and there is a fee of $5.00 per event requested. Records of marriage and divorce are found at the county of issue.

Accident Reports

Illinois State Police, Records Bureau, 500 Iles Park Place, Ste 200, Springfield, IL 62718; 217-785-0612; 8AM-5PM. Access by: mail, phone, in person.

Driver Records

Abstract Information Unit, Drivers Services Department, 2701 S Dirksen Prky, Springfield, IL 62723; 217-782-2720; 8AM-4:30PM. Access by: mail. www.sos.state.il.us

Vehicle Ownership
Vehicle Identification

Vehicle Services Department, Vehicle Record Inquiry, 501 S 2nd Street #408, Springfield, IL 62756; 217-782-6992; Fax: 217-524-0122; 8AM-4:30PM. Access by: mail. www.sos.state.il.us

Boat & Vessel Ownership
Boat & Vessel Registration

Department of Natural Resources, 524 S 2nd St, Springfield, IL 62701; 800-382-1696; Fax: 217-782-5016; 8AM-5PM. http://dnr.state.il.us

Legislation-Current/Pending
Legislation-Passed

Illinois General Assembly, State House, House (or Senate) Bills Division, Springfield, IL 62706; 217-782-3944 Bill Status Only, 217-782-7017 Index Div-Older Bills, 217-782-5799 House Bills, 217-782-9778 Senate Bills; Fax: 217-524-6059; 8AM-4:30PM. Access by: mail, phone, in person, online. http://legis.state.il.us

Voter Registration

Restricted access.

The data is not considered public record at the state level and is only available in bulk format to political committees and government agencies. County Clerks control the information at the local level.

Board of Elections, 1020 S Spring, Springfield, IL 62704; 217-782-4141; Fax: 217-782-5959; 8AM-4:30PM www.elections.state.il.us

GED Certificates

Restricted access.

All GED information is kept at the county level. You must contact the county where the test was taken. If you need assistance determining which county, contact the State Board of Education at the number listed here.

State Board of Education, 100 N 1st St, Springfield, IL 62777; 217-782-3370 Main Number;

Hunting License Information
Fishing License Information

Records not available from state agency.

They do not have a central database. The vendors hold license records.

County Courts & Recording Offices

About the Courts...

Administration

Administative Office of Courts	312-793-3250
222 N LaSalle 13th Floor	Fax: 312-793-1335
Chicago, IL 60601	

Court Structure

Illinois is divided into 22 judicial circuits; 3 are single county Cook, Du Page (18th Circuit) and Will (12th Circuit). The other 19 consist of 2 or more contiguous counties. The civil part of Circuit Court in Cook County is divided as follows: civil cases over $30,000 and civil cases under $30,000. The criminal part of Circuit Court in Cook County is divided into a criminal section and a misdemeanor section. The case indexes are maintained in one location. Felony and misdemeanor cases are heard at six locations within Cook County. All felony cases are maintained at one central location; misdemeanor case files are located at each of the hearing locations, as follows:

Felony Division, 2600 S. California, Chicago, IL 60608 (See court profile)

District 2, 5600 Old Orchard Rd, Skokie, IL 60077, 847-470-7500

District 3, 2121 Euclid Ave, Rolling Meadows, IL 60008, 847-818-2700

District 4, 1500 Maybrook Dr, Maywood, IL 60153, 708-865-6047

District 5, 10220 S. 76th Ave, Bridgeview, IL 60455, 708-974-6500

District 6, 16501 S. Kedzie, Markham, IL 60426, 708-210-4230

Probate is handled by the Circuit Court in all counties.

Searching Hints

The search fee is set by statute and has three levels based on the county population. The higher the population, the larger the fee. In most courts, both civil and criminal data is on computer from the same starting date. In most Illinois courts the search fee is charged on a per name per year basis.

Online Access

While there is no statewide public online system available, a number of Illinois Circuit Courts offer online access.

About the Recording Offices...

Organization

102 counties, 103 recording offices. Cook County has separate offices for UCC and real estate recording. The recording officer is Recorder of Deeds. Many counties utilize a grantor/grantee index containing all transactions. The entire state is in the Central Time Zone (CST).

UCC Records

Financing statements are filed at the state level except for real estate related filings. Most counties will perform UCC searches. Use search request form UCC-11. Search fees are usually $10.00 per debtor name/address combination. Copies usually cost $1.00 per page.

Lien Records

Federal tax liens on personal property of businesses are filed with the Secretary of State. Other federal and all state tax liens on personal property are filed with the County Recorder of Deeds. Some counties will perform tax lien searches for $5.00-$10.00 per name (state and federal are separate searches in many of these counties) and $1.00 per page of copy.

Real Estate Records

Most counties will not perform real estate searches. Cost of certified copies varies widely, but many counties charge the same as the cost of recording the document. Tax records are usually located at the Treasurer's Office.

County Courts & Recording Offices

Adams

Real Estate Recording—Adams County Recorder, 507 Vermont Street, Quincy, IL 62306. 217-322-4633. 8:30AM-4:30PM.

Felony, Misdemeanor, Civil, Eviction, Small Claims, Probate—Circuit Court, 521 Vermont St, Quincy, IL 62301. 217-357-2616, Fax: 217-277-2116. 8:30AM-4:30PM. Access by: mail, in person.

Alexander

Real Estate Recording—Alexander County Recorder, 2000 Washington Avenue, Cairo, IL 62914. 618-734-7009, Fax: 618-734-7002. 8AM-Noon, 1-4PM.

Felony, Misdemeanor, Civil, Eviction, Small Claims, Probate—Circuit Court, 2000 Washington Ave, Cairo, IL 62914. 618-734-0107, Fax: 618-734-7003. 8AM-4PM. Access by: mail, fax, in person.

Bond

Real Estate Recording—Bond County Recorder, 203 West College Avenue, Greenville, IL 62246. 618-664-0618, Fax: 618-664-9414. 8AM-4PM.

Felony, Misdemeanor, Civil, Eviction, Small Claims, Probate—Circuit Court, 200 W College Ave, Greenville, IL 62246. 618-664-3208, Fax: 618-664-4676. 8AM-4PM. Access by: mail, in person.

Boone

Real Estate Recording—Boone County Recorder, 601 North Main Street, Suite 202, Belvidere, IL 61008. 815-544-2666, Fax: 815-547-8701. 8:30AM-5PM.

Felony, Misdemeanor, Civil, Eviction, Small Claims, Probate—Circuit Court, 601 N Main, Belvidere, IL 61008. 815-544-0371. 8:30AM-5PM. Access by: mail, in person.

Brown

Real Estate Recording—Brown County Recorder, Courthouse - Room 4, #1 Court Street, Mount Sterling, IL 62353. Fax: 217-773-2233. 8:30AM-4:30PM.

Felony, Misdemeanor, Civil, Eviction, Small Claims, Probate—Circuit Court, County Courthouse, Mt Sterling, IL 62353. 217-854-3211. 8:30AM-4:30PM. Access by: mail, phone, fax, in person.

Bureau

Real Estate Recording—Bureau County Recorder, 700 South Main St. Courthouse, Princeton, IL 61356. 815-875-3241, Fax: 815-879-4803. 8AM-4PM.

Felony, Misdemeanor, Civil, Eviction, Small Claims, Probate—Circuit Court, 700 S Main, Princeton, IL 61356. 815-872-2001, Fax: 815-872-0027. 8AM-4PM. Access by: mail, in person, online.

Calhoun

Real Estate Recording—Calhoun County Clerk and Recorder, County Road, Hardin, IL 62047. 618-576-2421, Fax: 618-576-2895. 8:30AM-4:30PM.

Felony, Misdemeanor, Civil, Eviction, Small Claims, Probate—Circuit Court, PO Box 486, Hardin, IL 62047. 618-576-2451. 8:30AM-4:30PM. Access by: mail, phone, in person.

Carroll

Real Estate Recording—Carroll County Recorder, 301 North Main, Mount Carroll, IL 61053. 815-244-9171, Fax: 815-244-3709. 8:30AM-4:30AM.

Felony, Misdemeanor, Civil, Eviction, Small Claims, Probate—Circuit Court, 301 N Main St, PO Box 32, Mt Carroll, IL 61053. 815-244-0230, Fax: 815-244-3869. 8:30AM-4:30PM. Access by: mail, in person.

Cass

Real Estate Recording—Cass County Recorder, Courthouse, Virginia, IL 62691. 217-732-3761, Fax: 217-452-7219. 8:30AM-4:30PM.

Felony, Misdemeanor, Civil, Eviction, Small Claims, Probate—Circuit Court, PO Box 203, Virginia, IL 62691. 217-728-4622. 8:30AM-4:30PM. Access by: mail, in person.

Champaign

Real Estate Recording—Champaign County Recorder, 1776 E. Washington, Urbana, IL 61802. 217-532-9520, Fax: 217-344-1663. 8AM-4:30PM.

Felony, Misdemeanor, Civil, Eviction, Small Claims, Probate—Circuit Court, 101 E Main, Urbana, IL 61801. Fax: 217-384-3879. 8:30AM-4:30PM. Access by: mail, in person, online.

Christian

Real Estate Recording—Christian County Recorder, Courthouse on the Square, Taylorville, IL 62568. 217-942-3421, Fax: 217-824-5105. 8AM-4PM.

Felony, Misdemeanor, Civil, Eviction, Small Claims, Probate—Circuit Court, PO Box 617, Taylorville, IL 62568. 217-935-2359, Fax: 217-824-5105. 8AM-4PM. Access by: mail, phone, in person.

Clark

Real Estate Recording—Clark County Recorder, Courthouse, Marshall, IL 62441. 218-253-2797. 8AM-4PM.

Felony, Misdemeanor, Civil, Eviction, Small Claims, Probate—Circuit Court, PO Box 187, Marshall, IL 62441. 217-942-5124. 8AM-4PM. Access by: mail, in person.

Clay

Real Estate Recording—Clay County Recorder, County Building Room 106, Louisville, IL 62858. 618-665-3727, Fax: 618-665-3607. 8AM-4PM.

Felony, Misdemeanor, Civil, Eviction, Small Claims, Probate—Circuit Court, PO Box 100, Louisville, IL 62858. 618-665-3523, Fax: 618-665-3543. 8AM-4PM. Access by: mail, fax, in person.

Clinton

Real Estate Recording—Clinton County Recorder, Room 207 (Upstairs), First National Bank Building, Carlyle, IL 62231. 618-594-2464, Fax: 618-594-8715. 8AM-4PM.

Felony, Misdemeanor, Civil, Eviction, Small Claims, Probate—Circuit Court, County Courthouse, PO Box 407, Carlyle, IL 62231. 618-594-2415. 8AM-4PM. Access by: mail, in person.

Coles

Real Estate Recording—Coles County Recorder, 651 Jackson Ave. Room 122, Charleston, IL 61920. 217-431-2534, Fax: 217-348-7337. 8:30AM-4:30PM.

Felony, Misdemeanor, Civil, Eviction, Small Claims, Probate—Circuit Court, PO Box 48, Charleston, IL 61920. 217-431-2631. 8:30AM-4:30PM. Access by: mail, phone, fax, in person.

Cook

Real Estate Recording—, 118 North Clark Street, Room 120, Chicago, IL 60602. Fax: 312-603-5063. 9AM-5PM.

Cook County Recorder, 118 North Clark St. Room 230, Chicago, IL 60602. 313-994-2520, Fax: 312-603-5063.

Felony—Circuit Court-Criminal Division, 2650 S California Ave, Chicago, IL 60608. Fax: 773-869-4444. 9AM-5PM. Access by: mail, in person. Special note: Cases are heard in six district courts within the county and each court has a central index, eventually all case files are maintained here. www.cookcountyclerkofcourt.org

Civil Actions Over $30,000—Circuit Court-Civil, 50 W Washington Rm 601, Chicago, IL 60602. 314-456-3389. 8:30AM-4:30PM. Access by: mail, phone, in person. www.cookcountyclerkofcourt.com

Felony, Civil Action Under $100,000, Eviction, Small Claims—Bridgeview District, 10220 S 76th Ave Rm 121, Bridgeview Court Bldg, Bridgeview, IL 60453. Access by: in person. www.cookcountyclerkofcourt.com

Markham District, 16501 S Kedzie Pkwy Rm119, Markham, IL 60426-5509. Access by: mail, in person. www.cookcountyclerkofcourt.com

Maybrook Division, 1500 S Maybrook Dr, Rm 236, Maywood, IL 60153-2410. 9AM-5PM. Access by: mail, in person. www.cookcountyclerkofcourt.com

Rolling Meadows Division, 2121 Euclid Ave, Rolling Meadows, IL 60008-1566. 8:30AM-4:30PM. Access by: mail, in person. www.cookcountyclerkofcourt.com

Misdemeanor, Civil Action Under $100,000, Eviction, Small Claims—Skokie Division, Skokie Court Bldg Rm 136, 5600 Old Orchard Rd, Skokie, IL 60076-1023. 847-470-7250. 8:30AM-4:30PM. Access by: mail, phone, in person. Special note: Cases are heard in six district courts within the county, all courts have access to the index, but case files are maintained at each of the six district locations. www.cookcountyclerkofcourt.org

Misdemeanor, Civil Actions Under $100,000, Eviction, Small Claims, Probate—Chicago District, 50 W Washington, Chicago, IL 60602. 314-323-8271, Fax: 312-443-4557. 8:30AM-4:30PM. Access by: mail, phone, in person. Special note: Probate is a separate division at the same address. www.cookcountyclerkofcourt.com

Crawford

Real Estate Recording—Crawford County Recorder, Courthouse, 1 Courthouse Square, Robinson, IL 62454. 618-546-1212, Fax: 618-546-0140. 8AM-4PM.

Felony, Misdemeanor, Civil, Eviction, Small Claims, Probate—Circuit Court, PO Box 655, Robinson, IL 62454-0655. 618-544-3512, Fax: 618-546-5628. 8AM-4PM. Access by: mail, fax, in person.

Cumberland

Real Estate Recording—Cumberland County Recorder, 740 Courthouse Square, Toledo, IL 62468. 218-253-4281, Fax: 217-849-2968. 8AM-4PM.

Felony, Misdemeanor, Civil, Eviction, Small Claims, Probate—Circuit Court, PO Box 145, Toledo, IL 62468. 218-262-0100, Fax: 217-849-3183. 8AM-4PM. Access by: mail, phone, in person.

De Kalb

Real Estate Recording—De Kalb County Recorder, 110 East Sycamore Street, Sycamore, IL 60178. 815-895-7112. 8:30AM-4:30PM.

Felony, Misdemeanor, Civil, Eviction, Small Claims, Probate—Circuit Court, 133 W State St, Sycamore, IL 60178. Fax: 815-895-7140. 8:30AM-4:30PM. Access by: mail, in person.

De Witt

Real Estate Recording—De Witt County Recorder, 201 West Washington Street, Clinton, IL 61727. 218-299-5065, Fax: 217-935-4596. 8:30AM-4:30PM.

Felony, Misdemeanor, Civil, Eviction, Small Claims, Probate—Circuit Court, 201 Washington St, Clinton, IL 61727. 218-299-5011, Fax: 217-935-3310. 8:30AM-4:30PM. Access by: mail, in person.

Douglas

Real Estate Recording—Douglas County Recorder, 401 South Center, Second Floor, Tuscola, IL 61953. 217-348-0516, Fax: 217-253-2233. 8:30AM-4:30PM.

Felony, Misdemeanor, Civil, Eviction, Small Claims, Probate—Circuit Court, PO Box 50, Tuscola, IL 61953. 217-348-0501. 8:30AM-4:30PM. Access by: mail, in person.

Du Page

Real Estate Recording—Du Page County Recorder, 421 North County Farm Road, Wheaton, IL 60187. 630-682-7012, Fax: 630-682-7204. 8AM-4:30PM.

Felony, Misdemeanor, Civil, Eviction, Small Claims, Probate—Circuit Court, PO Box 707, Wheaton, IL 60189-0707. Fax: 630-682-7082. 8:30AM-4:30PM. Access by: mail, phone, in person. www.co.dupage.il.us

Edgar

Real Estate Recording—Edgar County Recorder, Courthouse - Room "J", 115 W. Court St. Paris, IL 61944. 217-735-2376, Fax: 217-466-7430. 8AM-4PM.

Felony, Misdemeanor, Civil, Eviction, Small Claims, Probate—Circuit Court, County Courthouse, Paris, IL 61944. 217-742-3368. 8AM-4PM. Access by: mail, in person.

Edwards

Real Estate Recording—Edwards County Recorder, 50 East Main Street, Courthouse, Albion, IL 62806. 618-445-3581, Fax: 618-445-3505. 8AM-4PM.

Felony, Misdemeanor, Civil, Eviction, Small Claims, Probate—Circuit Court, County Courthouse, Albion, IL 62806. 618-445-2016, Fax: 618-445-4943. 8AM-4PM. Access by: mail, in person.

Effingham

Real Estate Recording—Effingham County Clerk and Recorder, 101 North 4th Street, Suite 201, Effingham, IL 62401. 217-424-1454, Fax: 217-342-3577. 8AM-4PM.

Felony, Misdemeanor, Civil, Small Claims, Probate—Circuit Court, 100 E Jefferson, PO Box 586, Effingham, IL 62401. 217-424-1426, Fax: 217-342-6183. 8AM-4PM. Access by: mail, in person.

Fayette

Real Estate Recording—Fayette County Recorder, 221 South 7th Street, Vandalia, IL 62471. 618-283-5022, Fax: 618-283-5004. 8AM-4PM.

Felony, Misdemeanor, Civil, Eviction, Small Claims, Probate—Circuit Court, 221 S 7th St, Vandalia, IL 62471. 618-283-5009. 8AM-4PM. Access by: mail, in person.

Ford

Real Estate Recording—Ford County Recorder, 200 West State Street, Room 101, Paxton, IL 60957. 217-463-6050, Fax: 217-379-3258. 8:30AM-4:30PM.

Felony, Misdemeanor, Civil, Eviction, Small Claims, Probate—Circuit Court, 200 W State St, Paxton, IL 60957. 217-466-7447, Fax: 217-379-3258. 8:30AM-4:30PM. Access by: mail, in person.

Franklin

Real Estate Recording—Franklin County Clerk & Recorder, Courthouse, Benton, IL 62812. 618-438-7311, Fax: 618-439-4119. 8AM-4PM.

Felony, Misdemeanor, Civil, Eviction, Small Claims, Probate—Circuit Court, County Courthouse, Benton, IL 62812. 618-439-2011. 8AM-4PM. Access by: mail, in person.

Fulton

Real Estate Recording—Fulton County Recorder, 100 North Main, Lewistown, IL 61542. 310-312-6547. 8AM-4PM.

Felony, Misdemeanor, Civil, Eviction, Small Claims, Probate—Circuit Court, PO Box 152, Lewistown, IL 61542. 310-288-1227, Fax: 309-547-3674. 8AM-4PM. Access by: mail, in person.

Gallatin

Real Estate Recording—Gallatin County Recorder, West Lincoln Blvd, Shawneetown, IL 62984. 618-269-3022, Fax: 618-269-3343. 8AM-4PM.

Felony, Misdemeanor, Civil, Eviction, Small Claims, Probate—Circuit Court, County Courthouse, Shawneetown, IL 62984. 618-269-3140, Fax: 618-269-4324. 8AM-4PM. Access by: in person.

Greene

Real Estate Recording—Greene County Recorder, 519 North Main Street, Courthouse, Carrollton, IL 62016. 218-384-4281. 8AM-4PM.

Felony, Misdemeanor, Civil, Eviction, Small Claims, Probate—Circuit Court, 519 N Main, County Courthouse, Carrollton, IL 62016. 218-327-2870, Fax: 217-942-6211. 8AM-4PM. Access by: mail, phone, fax, in person.

Grundy

Real Estate Recording—Grundy County Recorder, 111 East Washington Street, Morris, IL 60450. 815-941-3215, Fax: 815-942-2220. 8AM-4:30PM.

Felony, Misdemeanor, Civil, Eviction, Small Claims, Probate—Circuit Court, PO Box 707, Morris, IL 60450. 815-941-3256, Fax: 815-942-2222. 8AM-4:30PM. Access by: mail, in person.

Hamilton

Real Estate Recording—Hamilton County Recorder, Courthouse, Room 2, Mcleansboro, IL 62859. 618-643-3313. 8AM-4:30PM.

Felony, Misdemeanor, Civil, Eviction, Small Claims, Probate—Circuit Court, County Courthouse, McLeansboro, IL 62859. 618-643-3224, Fax: 618-643-3455. 8AM-4:30PM. Access by: mail, in person.

Hancock

Real Estate Recording—Hancock County Recorder, 500 Blk Main Street, Courthouse, 2nd Floor, Carthage, IL 62321. 217-452-7721. 8AM-4PM.

Felony, Misdemeanor, Civil, Eviction, Small Claims, Probate—Circuit Court, PO Box 189, Carthage, IL 62321. 217-452-7225, Fax: 217-357-2231. 8AM-4PM. Access by: mail, in person.

Hardin

Real Estate Recording—Hardin County Recorder, Courthouse, Elizabethtown, IL 62931. 618-287-2053, Fax: 618-287-7833. 8AM-4PM.

Felony, Misdemeanor, Civil, Eviction, Small Claims, Probate—Circuit Court, County Courthouse, Elizabethtown, IL 62931. 618-287-2735, Fax: 618-287-7833. 8AM-4PM. Access by: mail, in person.

Henderson

Real Estate Recording—Henderson County Recorder, 4th & Warren Streets, Oquawka, IL 61469. 313-224-5509, Fax: 309-867-2033. 8AM-4PM.

Felony, Misdemeanor, Civil, Eviction, Small Claims, Probate—Circuit Court, County Courthouse, PO Box 546, Oquawka, IL 61469. 313-224-2921, Fax: 309-867-3207. 8AM-4PM. Access by: mail, phone, in person.

Henry

Real Estate Recording—Henry County Recorder, 100 South Main, Cambridge, IL 61238. 313-277-7480, Fax: 309-937-2796. 8AM-4PM.

Felony, Misdemeanor, Civil, Eviction, Small Claims, Probate—Circuit Court, Henry County Courthouse, PO Box 9, Cambridge, IL 61238. 313-252-0300. 8AM-4:30PM. Access by: mail, in person.

Iroquois

Real Estate Recording—Iroquois County Recorder, 1001 East Grant Street, Watseka, IL 60970. 815-432-6985, Fax: 815-432-6984. 8:30AM-4:30PM.

Felony, Misdemeanor, Civil, Eviction, Small Claims, Probate—Circuit Court, 550 S 10th St, Watseka, IL 60970. 815-432-6950, Fax: 815-432-6953. 8:30AM-4:30PM. Access by: mail, fax, in person.

Jackson

Real Estate Recording—Jackson County Recorder, The Courthouse, 1001 & Walnut, Murphysboro, IL 62966. 618-687-3555. 8AM-4PM.

Felony, Misdemeanor, Civil, Eviction, Small Claims, Probate—Circuit Court, County Courthouse, 1001 Walnut, PO Box 730, Murphysboro, IL 62966. 618-687-7300. 8AM-4PM. Access by: mail, in person.

Jasper

Real Estate Recording—Jasper County Recorder, 100 West Jourdan, Newton, IL 62448. 618-783-3211, Fax: 618-783-4137. 8AM-4:30PM.

Felony, Misdemeanor, Civil, Eviction, Small Claims, Probate—Circuit Court, 100 W Jourdan St, Newton, IL 62448. 618-783-2524. 8AM-4:30PM. Access by: mail, in person.

Jefferson

Real Estate Recording—Jefferson County Recorder, Courthouse, 100 S. 10th St. Room 105, Mount Vernon, IL 62864. 618-244-8011. 8AM-5PM.

Felony, Misdemeanor, Civil, Eviction, Small Claims, Probate—Circuit Court, PO Box 1266, Mt Vernon, IL 62864. 618-244-8008, Fax: 618-244-8029. 8AM-5PM. Access by: mail, phone, fax, in person. www.cookcountyclerkof court.org

Jersey

Real Estate Recording—Jersey County Recorder, 201 West Pearl Street, Courthouse, Jerseyville, IL 62052. 618-498-5571, Fax: 618-498-6128. 8:30AM-4:30PM.

Felony, Misdemeanor, Civil, Eviction, Small Claims, Probate—Circuit Court, 201 W Pearl St, Jerseyville, IL 62052. 618-498-5571, Fax: 618-498-6128. 8:30AM-4:30PM. Access by: mail, in person.

Jo Daviess

Real Estate Recording—Jo Daviess County Recorder, 330 North Bench Street, Galena, IL 61036. 815-777-0355, Fax: 815-777-3688. 8AM-4PM.

Felony, Misdemeanor, Civil, Eviction, Small Claims, Probate—Circuit Court, 330 N Bench St, Galena, IL 61036. 815-777-2295. 8AM-4PM. Access by: mail, fax, in person.

Johnson

Real Estate Recording—Johnson County Recorder, Courthouse Square, Vienna, IL 62995. 618-658-8042, Fax: 618-658-2908. 8AM-Noon,1-4PM.

Felony, Misdemeanor, Civil, Eviction, Small Claims, Probate—Circuit Court, PO Box 517, Vienna, IL 62995. 618-658-4751, Fax: 618-658-2908. 8AM-4PM. Access by: mail, in person.

Kane

Real Estate Recording—Kane County Recorder, 719 South Batavia Avenue, Bldg C, Geneva, IL 60134. 630-232-3565, Fax: 630-232-5945. 8:30AM-4:30PM.

Felony, Misdemeanor, Civil, Eviction, Small Claims, Probate—Circuit Court, PO Box 112, Geneva, IL 60134. 630-232-3413, Fax: 630-208-2172. 8:30AM-4:30PM. Access by: mail, phone, fax, in person.

Kankakee

Real Estate Recording—Kankakee County Recorder, 189 East Court Street, Kankakee, IL 60901. 815-937-2990, Fax: 815-937-3657. 8:30AM-4:30PM.

Felony, Misdemeanor, Civil, Eviction, Small Claims, Probate—Circuit Court, 450 E Court St, County Courthouse, Kankakee, IL 60901. 815-937-2905, Fax: 815-939-8830. 8:30AM-4:30PM. Access by: mail, in person.

Kendall

Real Estate Recording—Kendall County Recorder, 111 West Fox Street, Yorkville, IL 60560. 630-553-4124, Fax: 630-553-4119. 8AM-4:30PM.

Felony, Misdemeanor, Civil, Eviction, Small Claims, Probate—Circuit Court, PO Drawer M, 807 W John St, Yorkville, IL 60560. 630-553-4183. 8AM-4:30PM. Access by: mail, in person.

Knox

Real Estate Recording—Knox County Recorder, County Court House, Galesburg, IL 61401. 309-867-3121, Fax: 309-343-7002. 8:30AM-4:30PM.

Felony, Misdemeanor, Civil, Eviction, Small Claims, Probate—Circuit Court, County Courthouse, Galesburg, IL 61401. 309-837-4889. 8:30AM-4:30PM. Access by: mail, phone, in person.

La Salle

Real Estate Recording—La Salle County Recorder, 707 Etna Road, Government Center Room 269, Ottawa, IL 61350. 815-434-8202, Fax: 815-434-8260. 8AM-4:30PM.

Civil, Eviction, Small Claims, Probate—Circuit Court-Civil Division, PO Box 617, Ottawa, IL 61350-0617. 815-434-8671, Fax: 815-433-9198. 8AM-4:30PM. Access by: mail, fax, in person.

Felony, Misdemeanor—Circuit Court-Criminal Division, 707 Etna Rd, Ottawa, IL 61360. 815-434-8271, Fax: 815-434-8299. 8AM-4:30PM. Access by: mail, fax, in person.

Lake

Real Estate Recording—Lake County Recorder, 18 North County Street, Courthouse - 2nd Floor, Waukegan, IL 60085. 847-360-3610, Fax: 847-625-7200. 8:30AM-5PM.

Felony, Misdemeanor, Civil, Eviction, Small Claims, Probate—Circuit Court, 18 N County St, Waukegan, IL 60085. 847-360-6794. 8:30AM-5PM. Access by: mail, phone, in person.

Lawrence

Real Estate Recording—Lawrence County Recorder, Courthouse, Lawrenceville, IL 62439. 618-943-2016, Fax: 618-943-5205. 9AM-5PM.

Felony, Misdemeanor, Civil, Eviction, Small Claims, Probate—Circuit Court, County Courthouse, Lawrenceville, IL 62439. 618-943-2815, Fax: 618-943-5205. 9AM-5PM. Access by: mail, in person.

Lee

Real Estate Recording—Lee County Recorder, 112 E. Second St. Dixon, IL 61021. 815-288-4477, Fax: 815-288-6492. 8:30AM-4:30PM.

Felony, Misdemeanor, Civil, Eviction, Small Claims, Probate—Circuit Court, PO Box 325, Dixon, IL 61021. 815-284-5234. 8:30AM-4:30PM. Access by: mail, in person.

Livingston

Real Estate Recording—Livingston County Recorder, 112 West Madison, Courthouse, Pontiac, IL 61764. 815-844-5166, Fax: 815-842-1844. 8AM-4:30PM.

Felony, Misdemeanor, Civil, Eviction, Small Claims, Probate—Circuit Court, 112 W Madison St, Box 320, Pontiac, IL 61764. 815-844-2602. 8AM-4:30PM. Access by: mail, in person.

Logan

Real Estate Recording—Logan County Recorder, Courthouse, 601 Broadway Room 20, Lincoln, IL 62656. 217-774-3841, Fax: 217-732-6064. 8:30AM-4:30PM.

Felony, Misdemeanor, Civil, Eviction, Small Claims, Probate—Circuit Court, County Courthouse, Lincoln, IL 62656. 217-774-4212, Fax: 217-732-1231. 8:30AM-4:30PM. Access by: mail, in person.

Macon

Real Estate Recording—Macon County Recorder, 141 S. Main St. Room 201, Decatur, IL 62523. 217-532-9546, Fax: 217-428-2908. 8:30AM-4:30PM.

Felony, Misdemeanor, Civil, Eviction, Small Claims, Probate—Circuit Court, 253 E Wood St, Decatur, IL 62523. 217-632-2333, Fax: 217-424-1350. 8AM-4:30PM. Access by: mail, phone, in person, online. www.court.co.macon.il.us

Macoupin

Real Estate Recording—Macoupin County Recorder, Courthouse, Carlinville, IL 62626. 218-283-6261, Fax: 217-854-8461. 8:30AM-4:30PM.

Felony, Misdemeanor, Civil, Eviction, Small Claims, Probate—Circuit Court, PO Box 197, Carlinville, IL 62626. 218-281-2332, Fax: 217-854-8461. 8:30AM-4:30PM. Access by: mail, in person.

Madison

Real Estate Recording—Madison County Recorder, 157 North Main, Suite 211, Madison County Administration Bldg. Edwardsville, IL 62025. 618-692-6200, Fax: 618-692-9843. 8AM-5PM.

Felony, Misdemeanor, Civil, Eviction, Small Claims, Probate—Circuit Court, 155 N Main St, Edwardsville, IL 62025. 618-692-6240, Fax: 618-692-0676. 8AM-5PM. Access by: mail, in person.

Marion

Real Estate Recording—Marion County Recorder, Marion County Courthouse, 100 East Main St. Room 201, Salem, IL 62881. 618-548-3858, Fax: 618-548-2226. 8AM-4PM.

Felony, Misdemeanor, Civil, Eviction, Small Claims, Probate—Circuit Court, 100 E Main, PO Box 130, Salem, IL 62881. 618-548-3856, Fax: 618-548-2358. 8AM-4PM. Access by: mail, in person.

Marshall

Real Estate Recording—Marshall County Recorder, 122 North Prairie, Lacon, IL 61540. 309-734-8536, Fax: 309-246-3667. 8:30AM-4:30PM.

Felony, Misdemeanor, Civil, Eviction, Small Claims, Probate—Circuit Court, PO Box 328, Lacon, IL 61540-0328. 309-786-4451, Fax: 309-246-2173. 8:30AM-Noon, 1-4:30PM. Access by: mail, in person.

Mason

Real Estate Recording—Mason County Recorder, 100 North Broadway, Havana, IL 62644. 310-202-3181, Fax: 309-543-2085. 8AM-4PM.

Felony, Misdemeanor, Civil, Eviction, Small Claims, Probate—Circuit Court, 125 N Plum, Havana, IL 62644. 310-222-6501, Fax: 309-543-2085. 8AM-4PM. Access by: mail, in person.

Massac

Real Estate Recording—Massac County Recorder, Courthouse, Room 2-A, Superman Square, Metropolis, IL 62960. 618-524-5121, Fax: 618-524-4230. 8AM-4PM.

Felony, Misdemeanor, Civil, Eviction, Small Claims, Probate—Circuit Court, PO Box 152, Metropolis, IL 62960. 618-524-9359, Fax: 618-524-4850. 8AM-Noon, 1-4PM. Access by: mail, in person.

McDonough

Real Estate Recording—McDonough County Recorder, 1 Courthouse Square, Macomb, IL 61455. 312-443-5030, Fax: 309-836-3368. 8AM-4PM.

Felony, Misdemeanor, Civil, Eviction, Small Claims, Probate—Circuit Court, County Courthouse, PO Box 348, Macomb, IL 61455. 313-224-2500, Fax: 309-836-3013. 8AM-4PM. Access by: mail, phone, fax, in person.

McHenry

Real Estate Recording—McHenry County Recorder, 2200 North Seminary Avenue, Room A280, Woodstock, IL 60098. 815-334-2098, Fax: 815-338-9612. 8AM-4:30PM.

Felony, Misdemeanor, Civil, Eviction, Small Claims, Probate—Circuit Court, 2200 N Seminary Ave, Woodstock, IL 60098. 815-334-4307, Fax: 815-338-8583. 8AM-4:30PM. Access by: mail, phone, in person, online. www.co.mchenry.il.us

McLean

Real Estate Recording—McLean County Recorder, 104 West Front Street, Room 708, Bloomington, IL 61701. 313-243-7049, Fax: 309-888-5927. 8AM-4:30PM.

Felony, Misdemeanor, Civil, Eviction, Small Claims, Probate—Circuit Court, PO Box 2420, Bloomington, IL 61702-2420. 8:30AM-4:30PM. Access by: mail, in person.

Menard

Real Estate Recording—Menard County Recorder, Seventh Street, Courthouse, Petersburg, IL 62675. 217-753-6800, Fax: 217-632-4124. 8:30AM-4:30PM.

Felony, Misdemeanor, Civil, Eviction, Small Claims, Probate—Circuit Court, PO Box 466, Petersburg, IL 62675. 217-762-4866. 8:30AM-4:30PM. Access by: mail, in person.

Mercer

Real Estate Recording—Mercer County Recorder, 100 S.E. 3rd Street, 2nd Floor, Aledo, IL 61231. 310-317-1312, Fax: 309-582-7022. 8AM-4PM.

Felony, Misdemeanor, Civil, Eviction, Small Claims, Probate—Circuit Court, PO Box 175, Aledo, IL 61231. 310-419-5121, Fax: 309-582-7121. 8AM-4PM. Access by: mail, phone, fax, in person.

Monroe

Real Estate Recording—Monroe County Recorder, 100 South Main, Courthouse, Waterloo, IL 62298. 618-939-8681, Fax: 618-939-8639. 8AM-4:30PM.

Felony, Misdemeanor, Civil, Eviction, Small Claims, Probate—Circuit Court, 100 S Main St, Waterloo, IL 62298. 618-939-8681, Fax: 618-939-5132. 8AM-4:30PM. Access by: mail, phone, fax, in person.

Montgomery

Real Estate Recording—Montgomery County Recorder, Historic Courthouse, 1 Courthouse Square, Hillsboro, IL 62049. 217-742-5217, Fax: 217-532-9581. 8AM-4PM.

Felony, Misdemeanor, Civil, Eviction, Small Claims, Probate—Circuit Court, County Courthouse, PO Box C, Hillsboro, IL 62049. 217-753-6674. 8AM-4PM. Access by: mail, in person.

Morgan

Real Estate Recording—Morgan County Recorder, 300 West State Street, Courthouse, Jacksonville, IL 62650. 217-342-6844. 8:30AM-4:30PM.

Felony, Misdemeanor, Civil, Eviction, Small Claims, Probate—Circuit Court, 300 W State St, Jacksonville, IL 62650. 217-342-4065, Fax: 217-243-2009. 8:30AM-4:30PM. Access by: mail, in person.

Moultrie

Real Estate Recording—Moultrie County Recorder, Courthouse, Suite 6, 10 S. Main, Sullivan, IL 61951. 217-762-4966, Fax: 217-728-8178. 8:30AM-4:30PM.

Felony, Misdemeanor, Civil, Eviction, Small Claims, Probate—Moultrie County Courthouse, 10 S Main, #7, Sullivan, IL 61951. 217-773-2713. 8:30AM-4:30PM. Access by: mail, in person. www.circuit-clerk.moultrie.il.us

Ogle

Real Estate Recording—Ogle County Recorder, Fourth & Washington Streets, Oregon, IL 61061. 815-732-3201. 8:30AM-4:30PM.

Felony, Misdemeanor, Civil, Eviction, Small Claims, Probate—Circuit Court, PO Box 337, Oregon, IL 61061. 815-732-1130. 8:30AM-4:30PM. Access by: mail, in person.

Peoria

Real Estate Recording—Peoria County Recorder, County Courthouse - Room G04, 324 Main Street, Peoria, IL 61602. 310-519-6014. 9AM-5PM.

Felony, Misdemeanor, Civil, Eviction, Small Claims, Probate—Circuit Court, 324 Main St, Peoria, IL 61602. 310-603-7101, Fax: 309-677-6228. 9AM-5PM. Access by: mail, phone, in person.

Perry

Real Estate Recording—Perry County Recorder, Rt 1 Box 63, Pinckneyville, IL 62274. 618-357-5002, Fax: 618-357-3194. 8AM-4PM.

Felony, Misdemeanor, Civil, Eviction, Small Claims, Probate—Circuit Court, PO Box 219, Pinckneyville, IL 62274. 618-357-6726. 8AM-4PM. Access by: mail, in person.

Piatt

Real Estate Recording—Piatt County Recorder, 101 West Washington, Courthouse, Room 101, Monticello, IL 61856. 217-849-2321, Fax: 217-762-7563. 8:30AM-4:30PM.

Felony, Misdemeanor, Civil, Eviction, Small Claims, Probate—Circuit Court, PO Box 288, Monticello, IL 61856. 217-849-3601, Fax: 217-762-8394. 8:30AM-4:30PM. Access by: mail, phone, fax, in person. www.co.piatt.il.us

Pike

Real Estate Recording—Pike County Recorder, Courthouse, 100 E. Washington St. Pittsfield, IL 62363. 217-357-2624, Fax: 217-285-5820. 8:30AM-4PM.

Felony, Misdemeanor, Civil, Eviction, Small Claims, Probate—Circuit Court, Pike County Courthouse, Pittsfield, IL 62363. 217-379-2532, Fax: 217-285-4726. 8:30AM-4:30PM. Access by: mail, in person.

Pope

Real Estate Recording—Pope County Recorder, Courthouse, Golconda, IL 62938. 618-683-5501, Fax: 618-683-6231. 8AM-Noon, 1-4PM.

Felony, Misdemeanor, Civil, Eviction, Small Claims, Probate—Circuit Court, County Courthouse, Golconda, IL 62938. 618-683-3941, Fax: 618-683-3018. 8AM-4PM. Access by: mail, phone, fax, in person.

Pulaski

Real Estate Recording—Pulaski County Recorder, Corner of 2nd & High, Courthouse, Mound City, IL 62963. 618-748-9322. 8AM-Noon, 1-4PM.

Felony, Misdemeanor, Civil, Eviction, Small Claims, Probate—Circuit Court, PO Box 88, Mound City, IL 62963. 618-748-9300, Fax: 618-748-9338. 8AM-4PM. Access by: mail, in person.

Putnam

Real Estate Recording—Putnam County Recorder, Courthouse, 120 North 4th Street, Hennepin, IL 61327. 815-925-7226, Fax: 815-925-7549. 8AM-Noon, 1-4:30PM.

Felony, Misdemeanor, Civil, Eviction, Small Claims, Probate—Circuit Court, 120 N 4th St, Hennepin, IL 61327. 815-925-7016, Fax: 815-925-7549. 9AM-4PM. Access by: mail, in person.

Randolph

Real Estate Recording—Randolph County Recorder, 1 Taylor Street, Courthouse, Chester, IL 62233. 618-826-3715, Fax: 618-826-3750. 8AM-4:30PM.

Felony, Misdemeanor, Civil, Eviction, Small Claims, Probate—Circuit Court, County Courthouse, Chester, IL 62233. 618-826-5000. 8AM-4PM. Access by: mail, in person.

Richland

Real Estate Recording—Richland County Recorder, 103 West Main, Courthouse, Olney, IL 62450. 618-392-8341, Fax: 618-393-4005. 8AM-4PM.

Felony, Misdemeanor, Civil, Eviction, Small Claims, Probate—Circuit Court, 103 W Main #21, Olney, IL 62450. 618-392-2151, Fax: 618-395-8445. 8AM-4PM. Access by: mail, in person.

Rock Island

Real Estate Recording—Rock Island County Recorder, 210 15th Street, Rock Island, IL 61201. 312-443-5030. 8AM-4:30PM.

Felony, Misdemeanor, Civil, Eviction, Small Claims, Probate—Circuit Court, 210 15th St, PO Box 5230, Rock Island, IL 61204-5230. 312-443-4436, Fax: 309-786-3029. 8AM-4:30PM. Access by: mail, fax, in person, online.

Saline

Real Estate Recording—Saline County Recorder, 10 E. Poplar, Harrisburg, IL 62946. 618-253-6915. 8AM-4PM.

Felony, Misdemeanor, Civil, Eviction, Small Claims, Probate—Circuit Court, County Courthouse, Harrisburg, IL 62946. 618-253-5096, Fax: 618-252-8438. 8AM-4PM. Access by: mail, fax, in person.

Sangamon

Real Estate Recording—Sangamon County Recorder, 200 S. 9th St. Room 211, Springfield, IL 62701. 217-826-8311, Fax: 217-535-3159. 8:30AM-5PM.

Felony, Misdemeanor, Civil, Eviction, Small Claims, Probate—Circuit Court, 200 S Ninth St Rm 405, Springfield, IL 62701. 217-826-2811, Fax: 217-753-6665. 8:30AM-4:30PM. Access by: mail, fax, in person.

Schuyler

Real Estate Recording—Schuyler County Recorder, Courthouse, 102 S. Congress, Rushville, IL 62681. 217-379-2641, Fax: 217-322-6164. 8AM-4PM.

Felony, Misdemeanor, Civil, Eviction, Small Claims, Probate—Circuit Court, PO Box 80, Rushville, IL 62681. 217-384-3734, Fax: 217-322-6164. 8AM-4PM. Access by: mail, in person.

Scott

Real Estate Recording—Scott County Recorder, Courthouse, Winchester, IL 62694. 217-824-4966, Fax: 217-742-5853. 8AM-4PM.

Felony, Misdemeanor, Civil, Eviction, Small Claims, Probate—Circuit Court, 35 E Market St, Winchester, IL 62694. 217-824-4969, Fax: 217-742-5853. 8AM-Noon, 1-4PM. Access by: mail, in person.

Shelby

Real Estate Recording—Shelby County Recorder, Courthouse, 301 E. Main St. Shelbyville, IL 62565. 217-854-3214, Fax: 217-774-5291. 8AM-4PM.

Felony, Misdemeanor, Civil, Eviction, Small Claims, Probate—Circuit Court, County Courthouse, PO Box 469, Shelbyville, IL 62565. 217-935-2195, Fax: 217-774-4190. 8AM-4PM. Access by: mail, phone, in person.

St. Clair

Real Estate Recording—St. Clair County Recorder, #10 Public Square, County Building, Belleville, IL 62220. 618-277-6600. 8:30AM-5PM.

Felony, Misdemeanor, Civil, Eviction, Small Claims, Probate—Circuit Court, 10 Public Square, Belleville, IL 62220-1623. 618-227-6832, Fax: 618-277-1562. 9AM-4PM. Access by: mail, in person.

Stark

Real Estate Recording—Stark County Recorder, 130 West Main, Toulon, IL 61483. 309-786-4451, Fax: 309-286-4039. 8AM-Noon, 12:30-4:30PM.

Felony, Misdemeanor, Civil, Eviction, Small Claims, Probate—Circuit Court, 130 E Main St, Toulon, IL 61483. 309-833-2032. 8AM-4:30PM. Access by: mail, in person.

Stephenson

Real Estate Recording—Stephenson County Recorder, 15 North Galena Ave. Suite 1, Freeport, IL 61032. 815-235-8264. 8:30AM-4:30PM.

Felony, Misdemeanor, Civil, Eviction, Small Claims, Probate—Circuit Court, 15 N Galena Ave, Freeport, IL 61032. 815-235-8266. 8:30AM-4:30PM. Access by: mail, in person.

Tazewell

Real Estate Recording—Tazewell County Recorder, Arcade Bldg. 13 S. Capitol St. Pekin, IL 61554. 309-937-5192, Fax: 309-477-2321. 8:30AM-5PM.

Felony, Misdemeanor, Civil, Small Claims, Probate—Circuit Court, Courthouse, 4th & Court Sts, Pekin, IL 61554. 309-937-3572. 8:30AM-5PM. Access by: mail, in person.

Union

Real Estate Recording—Union County Recorder, 311 West Market, Jonesboro, IL 62952. 618-833-5621, Fax: 618-833-8712. 8AM-4PM.

Felony, Misdemeanor, Civil, Eviction, Small Claims, Probate—Circuit Court, PO Box 360, Jonesboro, IL 62952. 618-833-5913, Fax: 618-833-5223. 8AM-Noon,1-4PM. Access by: mail, in person.

Vermilion

Real Estate Recording—Vermilion County Recorder, 6 North Vermilion Street, Danville, IL 61832. 217-728-4032, Fax: 217-431-7460. 8AM-4:30PM.

Felony, Misdemeanor, Civil, Eviction, Small Claims, Probate—Circuit Court, 7 N Vermilion, Danville, IL 61832. 217-632-2615, Fax: 217-431-2538. 8:30AM-4:30PM. Access by: mail, phone, in person.

Wabash

Real Estate Recording—Wabash County Recorder, 401 Market Street, Mount Carmel, IL 62863. 618-262-5262. 8AM-5PM.

Felony, Misdemeanor, Civil, Eviction, Small Claims, Probate—Circuit Court, PO Box 1057, Mt Carmel, IL 62863. 618-262-5362, Fax: 618-263-4441. 8AM-4PM. Access by: mail, in person.

Warren

Real Estate Recording—Warren County Recorder, Courthouse, 100 W. Broadway, Monmouth, IL 61462. 310-974-2101, Fax: 309-734-7406. 8AM-4:30PM.

Felony, Misdemeanor, Civil, Eviction, Small Claims, Probate—Circuit Court, 100 W Broadway, Monmouth, IL 61462. 310-798-6875. 8AM-4:30PM. Access by: mail, in person.

Washington

Real Estate Recording—Washington County Recorder, County Courthouse, 101 E. St. Louis Street, Nashville, IL 62263. 618-327-3384, Fax: 618-327-3582. 8AM-4PM.

Felony, Misdemeanor, Civil, Eviction, Small Claims, Probate—Circuit Court, 101 E St Louis St, Nashville, IL 62263. 618-327-4800, Fax: 618-327-3583. 8AM-4PM. Access by: mail, in person.

Wayne

Real Estate Recording—Wayne County Recorder, 301 East Main, Fairfield, IL 62837. 618-842-5087, Fax: 618-842-2556. 8AM-4:30PM.

Felony, Misdemeanor, Civil, Eviction, Small Claims, Probate—Circuit Court, County Courthouse, Fairfield, IL 62837. 618-842-7684, Fax: 618-842-2556. 8AM-4:30PM. Access by: mail, in person.

White

Real Estate Recording—White County Recorder, 301 East Main Street, Courthouse, Carmi, IL 62821. 618-382-8122. 8AM-4PM.

Felony, Misdemeanor, Civil, Small Claims, Probate—Circuit Court, PO Box 310, County Courthouse, Carmi, IL 62821. 618-382-2321, Fax: 618-382-2322. 8AM-4PM. Access by: mail, fax, in person.

Whiteside

Real Estate Recording—Whiteside County Recorder, 200 East Knox, Morrison, IL 61270. 815-772-5196. 8:30AM-4:30PM.

Felony, Misdemeanor, Civil, Eviction, Small Claims, Probate—Circuit Court, 200 E Knox St, Morrison, IL 61270-2698. 815-772-5188, Fax: 815-772-5187. 8:30AM-4:30PM. Access by: mail, phone, fax, in person.

Will

Real Estate Recording—Will County Recorder, 302 N. Chicago Street, Joliet, IL 60432. 815-740-4675, Fax: 815-740-4697. 8:30AM-4:30PM.

Felony, Misdemeanor, Civil, Eviction, Small Claims, Probate—Circuit Court, 14 W Jefferson St, Joliet, IL 60432. 815-727-8592, Fax: 815-727-8896. 8:30AM-4:30PM. Access by: mail, fax, in person. www.willcountycircuitcourt.com

Williamson

Real Estate Recording—Williamson County Recorder, 200 West Jefferson, Marion, IL 62959. 618-997-1301, Fax: 618-993-2071. 8AM-4PM.

Felony, Misdemeanor, Civil, Eviction, Small Claims, Probate—Circuit Court, 200 W Jefferson St, Marion, IL 62959. 618-997-1301. 8AM-4:30PM. Access by: mail, in person.

Winnebago

Real Estate Recording—Winnebago County Recorder, 404 Elm St. Room 405, Rockford, IL 61101. 815-987-3010, Fax: 815-961-3261. 8AM-5PM.

Felony, Misdemeanor, Civil, Eviction, Small Claims, Probate—Circuit Court, 400 W State St, Rockford, IL 61101. Fax: 815-987-3012. 8AM-5PM. Access by: mail, phone, in person, online.

Woodford

Real Estate Recording—Woodford County Recorder, 115 North Main, Courthouse, Room 202, Eureka, IL 61530. 309-888-5180. 8AM-5PM.

Felony, Misdemeanor, Civil, Eviction, Small Claims, Probate—Circuit Court, County Courthouse, PO Box 284, 115 N Main, Suite 201, Eureka, IL 61530. 309-867-3121. 8AM-5PM. Access by: mail, in person.

Federal Courts

US District Court

Central District of Illinois

Danville/Urbana Division 201 S Vine, Room 218, Urbana, IL 61801217-373-5830 Counties: Champaign, Coles, Douglas, Edgar, Ford, Iroquois, Kankakee, Macon, Moultrie, Piatt, Vermilion. www.ilcd.uscourts.gov
Peoria Division US District Clerk's Office, 305 Federal Bldg, 100 NE Monroe St, Peoria, IL 61602309-671-7117 Counties: Bureau, Fulton, Hancock, Knox, Livingston, McDonough, McLean, Marshall, Peoria, Putnam, Stark, Tazewell, Woodford. www.ilcd.uscourts.gov
Rock Island Division US District Clerk's Office, Room 40, Post Office Bldg, 211 19th St, Rock Island, IL 61201309-793-5778 Counties: Henderson, Henry, Mercer, Rock Island, Warren. www.ilcd.uscourts.gov
Springfield Division Clerk, 151 US Courthouse, 600 E Monroe, Springfield, IL 62701217-492-4020 Counties: Adams, Brown, Cass, Christian, De Witt, Greene, Logan, Macoupin, Mason, Menard, Montgomery, Morgan, Pike, Sangamon, Schuyler, Scott, Shelby. www.ilcd.uscourts.gov

Northern District of Illinois

Chicago (Eastern) Division 20th Floor, 219 S Dearborn St, Chicago, IL 60604312-435-5698, Record Room: 312-435-5863 Counties: Cook, Du Page, Grundy, Kane, Kendall, Lake, La Salle, Will. www.ilnd.uscourts.gov
Rockford Division Room 211, 211 S Court St, Rockford, IL 61101815-987-4355 Counties: Boone, Carroll, De Kalb, Jo Daviess, Lee, McHenry, Ogle, Stephenson, Whiteside, Winnebago. www.ilnd.uscourts.gov

Southern District of Illinois

Benton Division 301 W Main St, Benton, IL 62812618-438-0671 Counties: Alexander, Clark, Clay, Crawford, Cumberland, Edwards, Effingham, Franklin, Gallatin, Hamilton, Hardin, Jackson, Jasper, Jefferson, Johnson, Lawrence, Massac, Perry, Pope, Pulaski, Richland, Saline, Union, Wabash, Wayne, White, Williamson. Cases mayalso be allocated to the Benton Division. www.ilsb.uscourts.gov
East St Louis Division PO Box 249, East St Louis, IL 62202618-482-9371, Record Room: 618-482-9371 Counties: Bond, Calhoun,

Clinton, Fayette, Jersey, Madison, Marion, Monroe, Randolph, St. Clair, Washington. Cases for these counties may also be allocated to the Benton Division. www.ilsd.uscourts.gov

US Bankruptcy Court

Central District of Illinois

Danville Division 201 N Vermilion #130, Danville, IL 61832-4733217-431-4820 Counties: Champaign, Coles, Douglas, Edgar, Ford, Iroquois, Kankakee, Livingston, Moultrie, Piatt, Vermilion.
Peoria Division 131 Federal Bldg, 100 NE Monroe, Peoria, IL 61602309-671-7035 Counties: Bureau, Fulton, Hancock, Henderson, Henry, Knox, Marshall, McDonough, Mercer, Peoria, Putnam, Rock Island, Stark, Tazewell, Warren, Woodford.
Springfield Division 226 US Courthouse, , Springfield, IL 62701-4551217-492-4551 Fax: 217-492-4560 Counties: Adams, Brown, Cass, Christian, De Witt, Greene, Logan, Macon, Macoupin, Mason, McLean, Menard, Montgomery, Morgan, Pike, Sangamon, Schuyler, Scott, Shelby.

Northern District of Illinois

Chicago (Eastern) Division 219 S Dearborn St, Chicago, IL 60604-1802312-435-5694, Record Room: 312-435-5862 Counties: Cook, Du Page, Grundy, Kane, Kendall, La Salle, Lake, Will. www.ilnb.uscourts.gov
Rockford Division Room 110, 211 S Court St, Rockford, IL 61101815-987-4350 Fax: 815-987-4205 Counties: Boone, Carroll, De Kalb, Jo Daviess, Lee, McHenry, Ogle, Stephenson, Whiteside, Winnebago. www.ilnb.uscourts.gov

Southern District of Illinois

Benton Division 301 W Main, Benton, IL 62812618-435-2200 Counties: Alexander, Edwards, Franklin, Gallatin, Hamilton, Hardin, Jackson, Jefferson, Johnson, Massac, Perry, Pope, Pulaski, Randolph, Saline, Union, Wabash, Washington, Wayne, White, Williamson. www.ilsb.uscourts.gov
East St Louis Division PO Box 309, East St Louis, IL 62202-0309618-482-9400 Counties: Bond, Calhoun, Clark, Clay, Clinton, Crawford, Cumberland, Effingham, Fayette, Jasper, Jersey, Lawrence, Madison, Marion, Monroe, Richland, St. Clair. www.ilsb.uscourts.gov

Indiana

Attorney General's Office

402 W Washington, 5th Fl   317-232-6201
Indianapolis, IN 46204   Fax: 317-232-7979
www.state.in.us/hoosieradvocate/index.html

Governor's Office

206 State House   317-232-4567
Indianapolis, IN 46204   Fax: 317-232-3443
www.state.in.us/gov

State Archives

140 N Senate Ave   317-232-3660
Indianapolis, IN 46204   Fax: 317-233-1085
www.state.in.us/icpr

Capital: Indianapolis
Marion County

Time Zone: EST*
* Indiana's 11 northwestern-most counties are CST:
They are: Gibson, Jasper, Laporte, Lake, Newton, Porter,
Posey, Spencer, Starke, Vanderburgh, Warrick.

Number of Counties: 92

Population: 5,864,108

Web Site: www.state.in.us

Search Unclaimed Property Online
www.state.in.us/serv/ag_ucp

State Agencies

Criminal Records

Indiana State Police, Central Records, IGCN - 100 N Senate Ave
Room 302, Indianapolis, IN 46204-2259; 317-232-8266; 8AM-
4:30PM. Access by: mail. www.state.in.us/isp

Corporation Records
Limited Partnerships
Fictitious Name
Assumed Name
Limited Liability Company Records
Limited Liability Partnerships

Corporation Division, Secretary of State, 302 W Washington St,
Room E018, Indianapolis, IN 46204; 317-232-6576; Fax: 317-
233-3387; 8AM-5:30PM M-F. Access by: mail, phone, in person,
online. www.ai.org/sos

Trademarks/Servicemarks

Secretary of State, Trademark Division, 302 W Washington St,
IGC-East, Room E111, Indianapolis, IN 46204; 317-232-6540;
Fax: 317-233-3675; 8:45AM-4:45PM. Access by: mail, phone, in
person. www.state.in.us/sos

Sales Tax Registrations

Revenue Department, Taxpayer Services, Government Center N,
100 N Senate Ave, Room N248, Indianapolis, IN 46204; 317-
233-4015;   Fax: 317-232-2103;   8:15AM-4:45PM.
www.ai.org/dor

Uniform Commercial Code

UCC Division, Secretary of State, 302 West Washington St,
Room E-018, Indianapolis, IN 46204; 317-233-3984; Fax: 317-
233-3387; 8AM-5:30PM. Access by: mail. www.ai.org/sos

Federal Tax Liens
State Tax Liens

Records not available from state agency.

All tax liens are found at the county level.

Workers' Compensation Records

Workers Compensation Board, 402 W Washington St, Room W196, Indianapolis, IN 46204-2753; 317-232-3808; 8AM-4:30PM. Access by: mail.

Birth Certificates

State Department of Health, Vital Records Office, PO Box 7125, Indianapolis, IN 46206-7125 (2 N. Meridian, Indianapolis, IN 46204);, 317-233-2700; Fax: 317-233-7210; 8:15AM-4:45PM. Access by: mail, phone, in person.

Death Records

State Department of Health, Vital Records Office, PO Box 7125, Indianapolis, IN 46206-7125;, 317-233-2700; Fax: 317-233-7210; 8:15AM-4:45PM. Access by: mail, phone, in person.

Marriage Certificates
Divorce Records

Records not available from state agency.

Marriage and divorce records are found at county of issue. The state tells us that the index can also be found at the Indiana State Library.

Accident Reports

State Police Department, Vehicle Crash Records Sections, Room N301, Indiana Government Center, Indianapolis, IN 46204; 317-232-8286; Fax: 317-232-0652; 8AM-4PM. Access by: mail, phone, in person.

Driver Records

BMV-Driving Records, 100 N Senate Ave, Indiana Government Center North, Room N405, Indianapolis, IN 46204; 317-232-6000 x2; 8:15AM-4:30PM. Access by: mail, online. www.state.in.us/bmv

Vehicle Ownership
Vehicle Identification
Boat & Vessel Ownership
Boat & Vessel Registration

Bureau of Motor Vehicles, Records, 100 N Senate Ave, Room N404, Indianapolis, IN 46204; 317-233-6000; 8:15AM-4:45PM. Access by: mail, online. www.state.in.us/bmv

Legislation-Current/Pending
Legislation-Passed

Legislative Services Agency, State House, 200 W Washington, Room 301, Indianapolis, IN 46204-2789; 317-232-9856; 8:15AM-4:45PM. Access by: mail, phone, in person, online. www.state.in.us

Voter Registration

Restricted access.
The data cannot be purchased for commercial or investigative reasons at the state level. The state will sell the data in bulk format for political purposes at a cost of $5,000. The SSN is not released. In general, the Circuit Court has records locally.
Elections Commission, 300 Washington, Room E-204, Indianapolis, IN 46204-2767; 317-232-3939; Fax: 317-233-6793; 8AM-4:30PM
www.ai.org

GED Certificates

Division of Adult Education, GED Testing, State House Rm 229, Indianapolis, IN 46204-2798; 317-232-0522; Fax: 317-233-0859;. http://ideanet.doe.state.is.us/adulted/adult2.htm

Hunting License Information
Fishing License Information

Records not available from state agency.

They do not have a central database. Vendors keep all records.

County Courts & Recording Offices

About the Courts...

Administration

State Court Administrator   317-232-2542
115 W Washington St Suite 1080   Fax: 317-233-6586
Indianapolis, IN 46204
www.state.in.us/judiciary

Court Structure

There are 90 judical ciicuits with Circuit Courts or Combined Circuit and Superior Courts. In addition, there are 47 City Courts and 25 Town Courts. Note that Small Claims in Marion County are heard at the township and records are maintained at that level. The phone number for the township offices are indicated in Marion County.

Searching Hints

The Circuit Court Clerk/County Clerk in every county is the same individual and is responsible for keeping all county judicial records. However, it is recommended that, when requesting a record, the request indicate which court heard the case (Circuit, Superior, or County).

Many courts are no longer performing searches, especially criminal searches, based on a 7/8/96 statement by the State Board of Accounts.

Certification and copy fees are set by statute as $1.00 per document plus copy fee for certification and $1.00 per page for copies.

Online Access

No online access computer system, internal or external, is available, except for Marion County through CivicNet/Access Indiana Information Network, which is available on the Internet (www.civicnet.net). Account and password are required. No charge for civil court name searches. Fees range from $2.00 to $5.00 for civil case summaries, civil justice name searches, criminal case summaries, and party booking details.

About the Recording Offices...

Organization

92 counties, 92 recording offices. The recording officer is County Recorder (Circuit Clerk for state tax liens on personal property). Many counties utilize a "Miscellaneous Index" for tax and other liens. 81 counties are in the Eastern Time Zone (EST), and 11 are in the Central Time Zone (CST).

UCC Records

Financing statements are filed at the state level except for consumer goods, farm related and real estate related filings. All counties will perform UCC searches. Use search request form UCC-11. Search fees are usually $1.00 per debtor name. Copies usually cost $.50 per page. Most counties also charge $.50 for each financing statement reported on a search.

Lien Records

All federal tax liens on personal property are filed with the County Recorder. State tax liens on personal property are filed with the Circuit Clerk, who is in a different office from the Recorder. Refer to The Sourcebook of County Court Records for information about Indiana Circuit Courts. Most counties will not perform tax lien searches.

Real Estate Records

Most counties will not perform real estate searches. Copies usually cost $1.00 per page, and certification usually costs $5.00 per document.

County Courts & Recording Offices

Adams

Real Estate Recording—Adams County Recorder, Adams County Service Complex, 313 W. Jefferson, Room 240, Decatur, IN 46733. Fax: 219-724-2815. 8AM-4:30PM.

Felony, Misdemeanor, Civil, Eviction, Small Claims, Probate—Circuit & Superior Court, 2nd St Courthouse, Decatur, IN 46733. 219-772-9128, Fax: 219-724-3848. 8AM-4:30PM. Access by: in person.

Allen

Real Estate Recording—Allen County Recorder, 1 East Main Street, City County Building Room 206, Fort Wayne, IN 46802. 219-563-0661. 8AM-4:30PM.

Felony, Misdemeanor, Civil, Eviction, Small Claims, Probate—Circuit & Superior Court, 715 S. Calhoun St. Rm 200 Courthouse, Ft Wayne, IN 46802. 219-563-0661. 8AM-4:30PM. Access by: in person.

Bartholomew

Real Estate Recording—Bartholomew County Recorder, 440 3rd Street, Suite 203, Columbus, IN 47201. 8AM-5PM.

Felony, Misdemeanor, Civil, Eviction, Small Claims, Probate—Circuit & Superior Court, PO Box 924, Columbus, IN 47202-0924. 812-379-1600, Fax: 812-379-1675. 8AM-5PM. Access by: mail, fax, in person.

Benton

Real Estate Recording—Benton County Recorder, 706 East 5th Street, Suite 24, Fowler, IN 47944. 318-368-3055, Fax: 765-884-2013. 8:30AM-4PM.

Felony, Misdemeanor, Civil, Eviction, Small Claims, Probate—Circuit Court, 706 E 5th St, Suite 37, Fowler, IN 47944-1556. 765-884-0930, Fax: 765-884-2013. 8:30AM-4PM. Access by: mail, in person. www.benton

Blackford

Real Estate Recording—Blackford County Recorder, 110 West Washington Street, Courthouse, Hartford City, IN 47348. Fax: 765-348-7222. 8AM-4PM.

Felony, Misdemeanor, Civil, Eviction, Small Claims, Probate—Circuit & County Court, 110 W Washington St, Hartford City, IN 47348. 765-348-1130. 8AM-4PM. Access by: mail, in person.

Boone

Real Estate Recording—Boone County Recorder, 202 Courthouse Square, Lebanon, IN 46052. 318-253-9208. 8AM-4PM.

Felony, Misdemeanor, Civil, Eviction, Small Claims, Probate—Circuit & Superior Court I & II, Rm 212, Courthouse Sq, Lebanon, IN 46052. 765-482-3510. 7AM-4PM. Access by: mail, in person.

Brown

Real Estate Recording—Brown County Recorder, County Office Bldg. 120 Gould St. Nashville, IN 47448. 812-988-5458, Fax: 812-988-5520. 8AM-4PM.

Felony, Misdemeanor, Civil, Eviction, Small Claims, Probate—Circuit Court, Box 85, Nashville, IN 47448. 812-988-5510, Fax: 812-988-5562. 8AM-4PM. Access by: in person.

Carroll

Real Estate Recording—Carroll County Recorder, Court House, 101 West Main St, Delphi, IN 46923. 318-256-5637, Fax: 765-564-2576. 8AM-5PM M,T,Th,F; 8AM-Noon W.

Felony, Misdemeanor, Civil, Eviction, Small Claims, Probate—Circuit & Superior Court, Courthouse, 101 W Main, Delphi, IN 46923. 765-564-4485, Fax: 765-564-6907. 8AM-5PM M,T,Th,F; 8AM-Noon W. Access by: mail, in person.

Cass

Real Estate Recording—Cass County Recorder, 200 Court Park, Logansport, IN 46947. 219-866-4939. 8AM-4PM; F 8AM-5PM.

Felony, Misdemeanor, Civil, Eviction, Small Claims, Probate—Circuit & Superior Court, 200 Court Park, Logansport, IN 46947. 219-866-4941. 8AM-4PM. Access by: mail, in person.

Clark

Real Estate Recording—Clark County Recorder, 501 East Court Avenue, Room 105, Jeffersonville, IN 47130. 812-285-6205. 8AM-5PM.

Felony, Misdemeanor, Civil, Eviction, Small Claims, Probate—Circuit, Superior, & County Court, 501 E Court, Rm 137, Jeffersonville, IN 47130. 812-285-6244. 8:30AM-4:30PM M-F, 8:30-Noon S. Access by: mail, in person.

Clay

Real Estate Recording—Clay County Recorder, Courthouse, Room 111, 609 E National Ave. Brazil, IN 47834. 812-442-1442, Fax: 812-446-5095. 8AM-4PM.

Felony, Misdemeanor, Civil, Eviction, Small Claims, Probate—Circuit & Superior Court, Box 33, Brazil, IN 47834. 812-448-8727. 8AM-4PM. Access by: mail, in person.

Clinton

Real Estate Recording—Clinton County Recorder, 270 Courthouse Square, Frankfort, IN 46041. Fax: 765-659-6391. 8AM-4PM M-Th; 8AM-5PM F.

Felony, Misdemeanor, Civil, Eviction, Small Claims, Probate—Circuit & Superior Court, 265 Courthouse Square, Frankfort, IN 46041. 765-659-6335. 8AM-4PM M-TH,8AM-5PM F. Access by: mail, in person.

Crawford

Real Estate Recording—Crawford County Recorder, Courthouse, PO Box 214, English, IN 47118. 812-338-2651, Fax: 812-338-2507. 8AM-4PM M & F; 8AM-6PM T & Th; Closed W.

Felony, Misdemeanor, Civil, Eviction, Small Claims, Probate—Circuit Court, Box 375, English, IN 47118. 812-338-2565, Fax: 812-338-2507. 8AM-4PM M,F; 8AM-6PM T-Th. Access by: mail, fax, in person.

Daviess

Real Estate Recording—Daviess County Recorder, 200 East Walnut, Courthouse, Washington, IN 47501. 812-254-8677, Fax: 812-254-8697. 8AM-4PM.

Felony, Misdemeanor, Civil, Eviction, Small Claims, Probate—Circuit & Superior Court, PO Box 739, Washington, IN 47501. 812-254-8664, Fax: 812-254-8698. 8AM-4PM. Access by: mail, in person.

Dearborn

Real Estate Recording—Dearborn County Recorder, 215 B West High Street, Lawrenceburg, IN 47025. 812-537-8811. 8:30AM-4:30PM.

Felony, Misdemeanor, Civil, Eviction, Small Claims, Probate—Circuit & County Court, Courthouse, 215 W High St, Lawrenceburg, IN 47025. 812-537-8867, Fax: 812-537-4295. 8:30AM-4:30PM. Access by: mail, in person.

Decatur

Real Estate Recording—Decatur County Recorder, 150 Courthouse Square, Suite 121, Greensburg, IN 47240. 812-663-4190, Fax: 812-663-2242. 8AM-4PM (F open until 5PM).

Felony, Misdemeanor, Civil, Eviction, Small Claims, Probate—Circuit & Superior Court, 150 Courthouse Square, Suite 244, Greensburg, IN 47240. 812-663-8223, Fax: 812-663-7957. 8AM-4PM, 8AM-5PM F. Access by: mail, in person.

DeKalb

Real Estate Recording—DeKalb County Recorder, Courthouse, 1st Floor, 100 S. Main St. Auburn, IN 46706. Fax: 219-925-5126. 8:30AM-4:30PM.

Felony, Misdemeanor, Civil, Eviction, Small Claims, Probate—Circuit & Superior Court, PO Box 230, Auburn, IN 46706. 225-562-7496, Fax: 219-925-5126. 8:30AM-4:30PM. Access by: in person.

Delaware

Real Estate Recording—Delaware County Recorder, 100 West Main Street, Room 209, Muncie, IN 47305. 8:30AM-4:30PM.

Felony, Misdemeanor, Civil, Eviction, Small Claims, Probate—Circuit & Superior Court, Box 1089, Muncie, IN 47308. 318-352-8152, Fax: 317-747-7768. 8:30AM-4:30PM. Access by: mail, phone, fax, in person. www.ecicnet.org/~dcclerk

Dubois

Real Estate Recording—Dubois County Recorder, Room 101, 1 Courthouse Square, Jasper, IN 47546. 812-481-7080, Fax: 812-481-7044. 8AM-4PM.

Felony, Misdemeanor, Civil, Eviction, Small Claims, Probate—Circuit & Superior Court, 1 Courthouse Square, Jasper, IN 47546. 812-481-7070, Fax: 812-481-7030. 8AM-4PM. Access by: in person.

Elkhart

Real Estate Recording—Elkhart County Recorder, 117 North 2nd Street, Room 205, Goshen, IN 46526. 219-726-7007. 8AM-4PM; F 8AM-5PM.

Felony, Misdemeanor, Civil, Eviction, Small Claims, Probate—Circuit, Superior & County Court, Courthouse, 101 N. Main St, Goshen, IN 46526. 219-726-4951, Fax: 219-535-6471. 8AM-4PM M-Th, 8AM-5PM F. Access by: in person.

Fayette

Real Estate Recording—Fayette County Recorder, 401 Central Avenue, Connersville, IN 47331. 765-825-1013. 8:30AM-4PM (8:30AM-5PM F).

Felony, Misdemeanor, Civil, Eviction, Small Claims, Probate—Circuit & Superior Court, PO Box 607, Connersville, IN 47331-0607. 765-825-1813. 8:30AM-4PM M-Th; 8:30AM-5PM F. Access by: in person.

Floyd

Real Estate Recording—Floyd County Recorder, 311 West 1st Street, Room 115, New Albany, IN 47150. 812-948-5477. 8AM-4PM.

Felony, Misdemeanor, Civil, Eviction, Small Claims, Probate—Circuit, Superior, & County Court, Box 1056, City County Bldg, New Albany, IN 47150. 812-948-5414, Fax: 812-948-4711. 8AM-4PM. Access by: mail, in person.

Fountain

Real Estate Recording—Fountain County Recorder, 301 4th Street, Covington, IN 47932. 765-793-4821, Fax: 765-793-5002. 8AM-4PM.

Felony, Misdemeanor, Civil, Eviction, Small Claims, Probate—Circuit Court, Box 183, Covington, IN 47932. 765-793-2192, Fax: 765-793-5002. 8AM-4PM. Access by: mail, in person.

Franklin

Real Estate Recording—Franklin County Recorder, 459 Main Street, Brookville, IN 47012. 765-647-5121. 8:30AM-4PM.

Felony, Misdemeanor, Civil, Eviction, Small Claims, Probate—Circuit Court, 459 Main, Brookville, IN 47012. 765-647-5111, Fax: 765-647-3224. 8:30AM-4PM. Access by: in person.

Fulton

Real Estate Recording—Fulton County Recorder, 815 Main Street, Rochester, IN 46975. 8AM-4PM (F 8AM-5PM).

Felony, Misdemeanor, Civil, Eviction, Small Claims, Probate—Circuit Court, 815 Main St, PO Box 524, Rochester, IN 46975. 219-372-2370, Fax: 219-223-8304. 8AM-4PM M-TH, 8AM-5PM F. Access by: mail, in person.

Gibson

Real Estate Recording—Gibson County Recorder, 101 North Main, Courthouse, Princeton, IN 47670. 812-385-4927. 8AM-4PM.

Felony, Misdemeanor, Civil, Eviction, Small Claims, Probate—Circuit & Superior Court, Courthouse, Princeton, IN 47670. 812-386-8401, Fax: 812-386-5025. 8AM-4PM. Access by: in person.

Grant

Real Estate Recording—Grant County Recorder, 401 South Adams Street, Marion, IN 46953. 318-259-2486. 8AM-4PM.

Felony, Misdemeanor, Civil, Eviction, Small Claims, Probate—Circuit & Superior Court, Courthouse 101 E 4th St, Marion, IN 46952. 765-668-8121, Fax: 765-668-6541. 8AM-4PM. Access by: mail, fax, in person.

Greene

Real Estate Recording—Greene County Recorder, Courthouse, Room 109, Bloomfield, IN 47424. Fax: 812-384-2044. 8AM-4PM.

Felony, Misdemeanor, Civil, Eviction, Small Claims, Probate—Circuit & Superior Court, PO Box 229, Bloomfield, IN 47424. 812-384-8532, Fax: 812-384-8458. 8AM-4PM. Access by: in person.

Hamilton

Real Estate Recording—Hamilton County Recorder, Courthouse, 33 N. 9th St, Suite 309, Noblesville, IN 46060. 318-363-5671, Fax: 317-776-8200. 8AM-4:30PM.

Felony, Misdemeanor, Civil, Eviction, Small Claims, Probate—Circuit & Superior Court, Hamilton Courthouse Square, Suite 106, Noblesville, IN 46060-2233. 318-365-7282, Fax: 317-776-9727. 8AM-4:30PM. Access by: in person.

Hancock

Real Estate Recording—Hancock County Recorder, 9 East Main Street, Courthouse, Room 204, Greenfield, IN 46140. 318-253-7523. 8AM-4PM.

Felony, Misdemeanor, Civil, Eviction, Small Claims, Probate—Circuit & Superior Court, 9 E Main St, Rm 201, Greenfield, IN 46140. 318-251-5130, Fax: 317-462-1163. 8AM-4PM. Access by: mail, phone, in person.

Harrison

Real Estate Recording—Harrison County Recorder, 300 Capitol Avenue, Courthouse, Room 204, Corydon, IN 47112. Fax: 812-738-1153. 8AM-4PM M,T,Th,F; 8AM-Noon W & Sat.

Felony, Misdemeanor, Civil, Eviction, Small Claims, Probate—Circuit & Superior Court, 300 N Capitol, Corydon, IN 47112. 812-738-4289. 8AM-4PM M,T,Th,F; 8AM-Noon W,S. Access by: mail, in person.

Hendricks

Real Estate Recording—Hendricks County Recorder, Courthouse, Danville, IN 46122. 318-281-3343. 8AM-4PM.

Felony, Misdemeanor, Civil, Eviction, Small Claims, Probate—Circuit & Superior Court, PO Box 599, Danville, IN 46122. 318-336-4204, Fax: 317-745-9306. 8AM-4PM. Access by: in person.

Henry

Real Estate Recording—Henry County Recorder, 216 S. 12th St. New Castle, IN 47362. Fax: 765-521-7017. 8AM-4PM (F 8AM-5PM).

Felony, Misdemeanor, Civil, Eviction, Small Claims, Probate—Circuit & Superior Court, PO Box B, New Castle, IN 47362. 765-529-6401. 8AM-4PM. Access by: mail, in person.

Howard

Real Estate Recording—Howard County Recorder, Courthouse, Room 202, 117 N. Main St. Kokomo, IN 46901. 318-233-0150, Fax: 765-456-2259. 8AM-4PM.

Felony, Misdemeanor, Civil, Eviction, Small Claims, Probate—Circuit & Superior Court, PO Box 9004, Kokomo, IN 46904. 765-456-2201, Fax: 765-456-2267. 8AM-4PM. Access by: in person.

Huntington

Real Estate Recording—Huntington County Recorder, 201 N. Jefferson St. Room 101, Huntington, IN 46750. 219-535-6431, Fax: 219-358-4823. 8AM-4:30PM.

Felony, Misdemeanor, Civil, Eviction, Small Claims, Probate—Circuit & Superior Court, Courthouse, Rm 201, Huntington, IN 46750. 219-474-6081. 8AM-4:40PM. Access by: mail, phone, in person.

Jackson

Real Estate Recording—Jackson County Recorder, 101 S. Main - Main Floor, Brownstown, IN 47220. 812-358-6125. 8AM-4:30PM.

Felony, Misdemeanor, Civil, Eviction, Small Claims, Probate—Circuit & Superior Court, PO Box 788, Brownstown, IN 47274. 812-522-9676, Fax: 812-523-6065. 8AM-4:30PM. Access by: mail, fax, in person.

Jasper

Real Estate Recording—Jasper County Recorder, Courthouse, 2nd Floor, 115 W. Washington, Rensselaer, IN 47978. 225-389-3950, Fax: 219-866-4940. 8AM-4PM.

Felony, Misdemeanor, Civil, Eviction, Small Claims, Probate—Circuit Court, 115 W Washington, Rensselaer, IN 47978. 225-473-9866. 8AM-4PM. Access by: mail, in person. Special note: This court also handles juvenile, paternity and adoption.

Felony, Misdemeanor, Civil, Probate—Superior Court I, 115 W Washington St, Rensselaer, IN 47978. 225-389-3276. 8AM-4PM. Access by: mail, in person.

Jay

Real Estate Recording—Jay County Recorder, 120 West Main Street, Portland, IN 47371. 219-866-4922. 8:30AM-4:30PM.

Felony, Misdemeanor, Civil, Eviction, Small Claims, Probate—Circuit & Superior Court, Courthouse, Portland, IN 47371. 219-824-6479. 8:30AM-4:30PM. Access by: mail, in person.

Jefferson

Real Estate Recording—Jefferson County Recorder, Courthouse - Room 104, 300 E. Main St. Madison, IN 47250. 812-265-8910. 8AM-4PM.

Felony, Misdemeanor, Civil, Eviction, Small Claims, Probate—Circuit & Superior Court, Courthouse 300E Main St, Madison, IN 47250. 812-265-8923, Fax: 812-265-8950. 8AM-4PM. Access by: mail, in person.

Jennings

Real Estate Recording—Jennings County Recorder, Courthouse, Vernon, IN 47282. 812-346-8081, Fax: 812-346-4605. 8AM-4PM.

Felony, Misdemeanor, Civil, Eviction, Small Claims, Probate—Circuit Court, Courthouse, PO Box 385, Vernon, IN 47282. 812-346-5977. 8AM-4PM. Access by: mail, in person.

Johnson

Real Estate Recording—Johnson County Recorder, 86 West Court Street, Franklin, IN 46131. 318-263-2123, Fax: 317-736-8066. 8AM-4:30PM.

Felony, Misdemeanor, Civil, Eviction, Small Claims, Probate—Circuit & Superior Court, Courthouse, PO Box 368, Franklin, IN 46131. 318-263-2019, Fax: 317-736-3749. 8AM-4:30PM. Access by: mail, phone, fax, in person.

Knox

Real Estate Recording—Knox County Recorder, Courthouse, 11 N. 7th St. Vincennes, IN 47591. 812-885-2513, Fax: 812-886-2414. 8AM-4PM.

Felony, Misdemeanor, Civil, Eviction, Small Claims, Probate—Circuit & Superior Court, 101 N 7th St, Vincennes, IN 47591. 812-885-2521. 8AM-4PM. Access by: mail, in person.

Kosciusko

Real Estate Recording—Kosciusko County Recorder, 100 West Center Street, Courthouse Room 14, Warsaw, IN 46580. 219-535-6761, Fax: 219-372-2469. 8AM-4:30PM.

Felony, Misdemeanor, Civil, Eviction, Small Claims, Probate—Circuit & Superior Court, 121 N Lake, Warsaw, IN 46580. 219-465-3453. 8AM-4PM. Access by: mail, in person.

La Porte

Real Estate Recording—La Porte County Recorder, 813 Lincolnway, La Porte, IN 46350. 219-474-6081. 8:30AM-5PM (Recording hours 8:30AM-4PM).

Felony, Misdemeanor, Civil, Eviction, Probate—Circuit & Superior Court, 813 Lincolnway, La Porte, IN 46350. 219-465-3470. 8:30AM-5PM. Access by: in person.

LaGrange

Real Estate Recording—LaGrange County Recorder, 114 West Michigan Street, County Office Building PO Box 214, LaGrange, IN 46761. 8AM-4PM M-Th; 8AM-5PM F.

Felony, Misdemeanor, Civil, Eviction, Small Claims, Probate—Circuit & Superior Court, 105 N Detroit St, Courthouse, LaGrange, IN 46761. 219-583-7032. 8AM-4PM M-TH, 8AM-5PM F. Access by: mail, phone, in person.

Lake

Real Estate Recording—Lake County Recorder, 2293 N Main Street, Building A, 2nd Floor, Crown Point, IN 46307. 219-936-8922, Fax: 219-755-3257. 8:30AM-4:30PM.

Felony, Misdemeanor, Civil, Eviction, Small Claims, Probate—Circuit & Superior Court, 2293 N Main St, Courthouse, Crown Point, IN 46307. 219-925-0912. 8:30AM-4:20PM. Access by: mail, in person.

Lawrence

Real Estate Recording—Lawrence County Recorder, Courthouse, Room 21, Bedford, IN 47421. 812-275-2431, Fax: 812-275-4138. 8:30AM-4:30PM.

Felony, Misdemeanor, Civil, Eviction, Small Claims, Probate—Circuit, Superior, & County Court, 31 Courthouse, PO Box 99, Bedford, IN 47421. 812-275-7543, Fax: 812-277-2024. 8:30AM-4:30PM. Access by: in person.

Madison

Real Estate Recording—Madison County Recorder, 16 East 9th Street, Anderson, IN 46016. 765-641-9645. 8AM-4PM.

Felony, Misdemeanor, Civil, Eviction, Small Claims, Probate—Circuit, Superior & County Court, PO Box 1277, Anderson, IN 46015-1277. 765-641-9443, Fax: 765-640-4203. 8AM-4PM. Access by: mail, in person.

Marion

Real Estate Recording—Marion County Recorder, 200 E. Washington, Suite 721, Indianapolis, IN 46204. Fax: 317-327-3942. 8AM-4:30PM.

Felony, Misdemeanor, Civil, Eviction, Small Claims, Probate—Circuit & Superior Court, 200 E Washington St, Indianapolis, IN 46204. 317-776-9629. 8AM-4:30PM. Access by: mail, in person, online. Special note: The Municipal Court of Marion County is housed in the same building, phone is 317-327-4600. They handle civil actions under $25,000 and Class D felony records.

Marshall

Real Estate Recording—Marshall County Recorder, 112 West Jefferson Street, Room 201, Plymouth, IN 46563. 8AM-4PM.

Felony, Misdemeanor, Civil, Eviction, Small Claims, Probate—Circuit & Superior Court, 211 W Madison St, Plymouth, IN 46563. 225-635-3794, Fax: 219-936-8893. 8AM-4PM. Access by: mail, in person.

Martin

Real Estate Recording—Martin County Recorder, Capital Street, Courthouse, Shoals, IN 47581. Fax: 812-247-2756. 8AM-4PM.

Felony, Misdemeanor, Civil, Eviction, Small Claims, Probate—Circuit Court, PO Box 120, Shoals, IN 47581. 812-247-3651, Fax: 812-247-3901. 8AM-4PM. Access by: mail, in person.

Miami

Real Estate Recording—Miami County Recorder, Courthouse, Peru, IN 46970. Fax: 765-472-1412. 8AM-4PM.

Felony, Misdemeanor, Civil, Eviction, Small Claims, Probate—Circuit & Superior Court, PO Box 184, Peru, IN 46970. 765-472-3901, Fax: 765-472-1412. 8AM-4PM. Access by: mail, fax, in person.

Monroe

Real Estate Recording—Monroe County Recorder, Courthouse, Bloomington, IN 47404. 812-333-3530. 8AM-4PM.

Felony, Misdemeanor, Civil, Eviction, Small Claims, Probate—Circuit Court, PO Box 547, Bloomington, IN 47402. 812-349-2600. 8AM-4PM. Access by: mail, in person.

Montgomery

Real Estate Recording—Montgomery County Recorder, 100 East Main Street, Crawfordsville, IN 47933. 317-884-1070, Fax: 765-364-6404. 8AM-4PM.

Felony, Misdemeanor, Civil, Eviction, Small Claims, Probate—Circuit, Superior, & County Court, PO Box 768, Crawfordsville, IN 47933. 765-364-6430, Fax: 765-364-6434. 8:30AM-4:30PM. Access by: mail, phone, fax, in person.

Morgan

Real Estate Recording—Morgan County Recorder, Administration Building, 180 S. Main, Suite 125, Martinsville, IN 46151. 8AM-4PM (8AM-5PM F).

Felony, Misdemeanor, Civil, Eviction, Small Claims, Probate—Circuit, Superior, & County Court, PO Box 1556, Martinsville, IN 46151. 765-342-1025, Fax: 765-342-1111. 8AM-4PM. Access by: in person.

Newton

Real Estate Recording—Newton County Recorder, 201 N. 3rd St. Courthouse - Room 104, Kentland, IN 47951. 219-724-2600. 8AM-4PM.

Felony, Misdemeanor, Civil, Eviction, Small Claims, Probate—Circuit & Superior Court, PO Box 49, Kentland, IN 47951. 219-668-1000. 8AM-4PM. Access by: mail, in person.

Noble

Real Estate Recording—Noble County Recorder, 101 North Orange Street, Courthouse, Room 210, Albion, IN 46701. 219-755-3760, Fax: 219-636-3053. 8AM-4PM.

Felony, Misdemeanor, Civil, Eviction, Small Claims, Probate—Circuit, Superior, & County Court, 101 N Orange St, Albion, IN 46701. 219-759-2501, Fax: 219-636-3053. 8AM-4PM. Access by: mail, fax, in person.

Ohio

Real Estate Recording—Ohio County Recorder, Courthouse, 413 Main St. Rising Sun, IN 47040. Fax: 812-438-4590. 9AM-4PM M,T,Th,F; 9AM-12 Sat; Closed W.

Felony, Misdemeanor, Civil, Eviction, Small Claims, Probate—Circuit & Superior Court, PO Box 185, Rising Sun, IN 47040. 812-438-2610, Fax: 812-438-4590. 9AM-4PM M,T,Th,F 9AM-Noon S. Access by: mail, phone, fax, in person.

Orange

Real Estate Recording—Orange County Recorder, 205 East Main Street, Courthouse, Paoli, IN 47454. 8AM-4PM.

Felony, Misdemeanor, Civil, Eviction, Small Claims, Probate—Circuit & County Court, Courthouse, Court St, Paoli, IN 47454. 812-723-2649. 8AM-4PM. Access by: mail, in person.

Owen

Real Estate Recording—Owen County Recorder, Courthouse, Spencer, IN 47460. 812-829-5011, Fax: 812-829-5004. 8AM-4PM.

Felony, Misdemeanor, Civil, Eviction, Small Claims, Probate—Circuit Court, PO Box 146, Courthouse, Spencer, IN 47460. 812-829-5015, Fax: 812-829-5028. 8AM-4PM. Access by: in person.

Parke

Real Estate Recording—Parke County Recorder, 116 W. High St. Room 102, Rockville, IN 47872. 318-256-6223, Fax: 765-569-4037. 8AM-4PM.

Felony, Misdemeanor, Civil, Eviction, Small Claims, Probate—Circuit Court, 116 W High St, Rm 204, Rockville, IN 47872. 765-569-5132. 8AM-4PM. Access by: in person.

Perry

Real Estate Recording—Perry County Recorder, 2219 Payne St. Room W2, Tell City, IN 47586. 812-547-4816. 8AM-4PM.

Felony, Misdemeanor, Civil, Eviction, Small Claims, Probate—Circuit Court, 2219 Payne St, Courthouse, Tell City, IN 47586. 812-547-3741. 8AM-4PM. Access by: mail, in person.

Pike

Real Estate Recording—Pike County Recorder, Main Street, Courthouse, Petersburg, IN 47567. 812-354-6363, Fax: 812-354-3500. 8AM-4PM.

Felony, Misdemeanor, Civil, Eviction, Small Claims, Probate—Circuit Court, 801 Main St. Courthouse, Petersburg, IN 47567-1298. 812-354-6025, Fax: 812-354-3552. 8AM-4PM. Access by: mail, in person.

Porter

Real Estate Recording—Porter County Recorder, 155 Indiana Ave, Suite 210, Valparaiso, IN 46383. 219-636-2736, Fax: 219-465-3592. 8:30AM-4:30PM.

Felony, Misdemeanor, Civil, Eviction, Small Claims, Probate—Circuit Court, Records Division, Courthouse Suite 217, 16 E Lincolnway, Valparaiso, IN 46383-5659. 219-636-2644, Fax: 219-465-3592. 8:30AM-4:30PM. Access by: mail, in person.

Misdemeanor, Civil, Small Claims, Probate—Superior Court, 3560 Willow Creek Dr, Portage, IN 46368. 219-946-3313. 8:30AM-4:30PM. Access by: mail, in person.

Posey

Real Estate Recording—Posey County Recorder, Coliseum, 123 E. Third, Mount Vernon, IN 47620. 812-838-1316, Fax: 812-838-8563. 8AM-4PM.

Felony, Misdemeanor, Civil, Eviction, Small Claims, Probate—Circuit & Superior Court, PO Box 606, 300 Main St, Mount Vernon, IN 47620-0606. 812-838-1306, Fax: 812-838-1307. 8AM-4PM. Access by: in person.

Pulaski

Real Estate Recording—Pulaski County Recorder, Courthouse - Room 220, 112 E. Main St. Winamac, IN 46996. 225-683-5145. 8AM-4PM.

Felony, Misdemeanor, Civil, Eviction, Small Claims, Probate—Circuit & Superior Court, 112 E Main, Room 230, Winamac, IN 46996. 225-638-9596, Fax: 219-946-4953. 8AM-4PM. Access by: in person.

Putnam

Real Estate Recording—Putnam County Recorder, Courthouse Square, Room 25, Greencastle, IN 46135. 318-259-2424. 8AM-4PM.

Felony, **Misdemeanor, Civil, Eviction, Small Claims, Probate**—Circuit & County Court, PO Box 546, Greencastle, IN 46135. 765-653-2648. 8AM-4PM. Access by: mail, in person.

Randolph

Real Estate Recording—Randolph County Recorder, Courthouse, Room 101, 100 South Main St. Winchester, IN 47394. 765-584-7070. 8AM-4PM.

Felony, Misdemeanor, Civil, Eviction, Small Claims, Probate—Circuit & Superior Court, PO Box 230 Courthouse, Winchester, IN 47394-0230. 765-584-7070, Fax: 765-584-2958. 8AM-4PM. Access by: mail, fax, in person.

Ripley

Real Estate Recording—Ripley County Recorder, Courthouse, 115 N. Main St. Versailles, IN 47042. 812-689-6352. 8AM-4PM.

Felony, Misdemeanor, Civil, Eviction, Small Claims, Probate—Circuit Court, PO BOX 177, Versailles, IN 47042. 812-689-6115. 8AM-4PM. Access by: mail, in person.

Rush

Real Estate Recording—Rush County Recorder, Courthouse, Room 208, Rushville, IN 46173. 765-932-2386. 8AM-4PM.

Felony, Misdemeanor, Civil, Eviction, Small Claims, Probate—Circuit & County Court, PO Box 429, Rushville, IN 46173. 765-932-2086, Fax: 765-932-2357. 8AM-4PM. Access by: in person.

Scott

Real Estate Recording—Scott County Recorder, 1 E. McClain St. Suite 100, Scottsburg, IN 47170. 812-752-8414, Fax: 812-752-7914. 8:30AM-4:30PM.

Felony, Misdemeanor, Civil, Eviction, Small Claims, Probate—Circuit & Superior Court, 1 E McClain Ave, #120, Scottsburg, IN 47170. 812-752-8420, Fax: 812-752-5459. 8:30AM-4:30PM. Access by: in person.

Shelby

Real Estate Recording—Shelby County Recorder, 407 South Harrison, Courthouse, Shelbyville, IN 46176. 318-226-6900, Fax: 317-392-6393. 8AM-4PM.

Felony, Misdemeanor, Civil, Eviction, Small Claims, Probate—Circuit & Superior Court, PO Box 198, Shelbyville, IN 46176. 318-226-6780. 8AM-4PM. Access by: in person.

Spencer

Real Estate Recording—Spencer County Recorder, Courthouse, 200 Main, Rockport, IN 47635. 812-649-4556, Fax: 812-649-6005. 8AM-4PM.

Felony, Misdemeanor, Civil, Eviction, Small Claims, Probate—Circuit Court, PO Box 12, Rockport, IN 47635. 812-649-6027, Fax: 812-649-6030. 8AM-4PM. Access by: in person.

St. Joseph

Real Estate Recording—St. Joseph County Recorder, 227 West Jefferson, Room 321, South Bend, IN 46601. 219-428-7693. 8AM-4:30PM.

Felony, Misdemeanor, Civil, Eviction, Small Claims, Probate—Circuit & Superior Court, 101 South Main St, South Bend, IN 46601. 219-449-7245, Fax: 219-235-9838. 8AM-4:30PM. Access by: mail, in person.

Starke

Real Estate Recording—Starke County Recorder, Courthouse, 53 E. Mound, Knox, IN 46534. 219-946-3632, Fax: 219-772-9178. 8:30AM-4PM.

Felony, Misdemeanor, Civil, Eviction, Small Claims, Probate—Circuit Court, Courthouse, 53 E Washington St, Knox, IN 46534. 225-222-4514. 8:30AM-4PM. Access by: in person.

Steuben

Real Estate Recording—Steuben County Recorder, 317 S. Wayne St. Suite 2F, Angola, IN 46703. Fax: 219-665-8483. 8AM-4:30PM.

Felony, Misdemeanor, Civil, Eviction, Small Claims, Probate—Circuit & Superior Court, Courthouse, 55 S. Public Square, Angola, IN 46703. 219-772-9113. 8AM-4:30PM. Access by: in person.

Sullivan

Real Estate Recording—Sullivan County Recorder, Room 205, 100 Court House Square, Sullivan, IN 47882. Fax: 812-268-0521. 8AM-4PM.

Felony, Misdemeanor, Civil, Eviction, Small Claims, Probate—Circuit & Superior Court, Courthouse, 3rd Fl, PO Box 370, Sullivan, IN 47882-0370. 812-268-4657. 8AM-4PM. Access by: mail, in person.

Switzerland

Real Estate Recording—Switzerland County Recorder, Courthouse, 212 West Main, Vevay, IN 47043. 812-427-3369. 8AM-3:30PM.

Felony, Misdemeanor, Civil, Eviction, Small Claims, Probate—Circuit & Superior Court, Courthouse, Vevay, IN 47043. 812-427-3175, Fax: 812-427-2017. 8:30-3:30PM M-W & F. Access by: mail, in person.

Tippecanoe

Real Estate Recording—Tippecanoe County Recorder, 20 North 3rd Street, Lafayette, IN 47901. Fax: 765-423-9158. 8AM-4:30PM.

Felony, Misdemeanor, Civil, Eviction, Small Claims, Probate—Circuit, Superior, & County Court, PO Box 1665, Lafayette, IN 47902. 765-423-9326, Fax: 765-423-9194. 8AM-4:30PM. Access by: mail, phone, fax, in person.

Tipton

Real Estate Recording—Tipton County Recorder, Courthouse, 101 E. Jefferson St. Tipton, IN 46072. 765-675-2742.

Felony, Misdemeanor, Civil, Eviction, Small Claims, Probate—Circuit Court, Tipton County Courthouse, Tipton, IN 46072. 765-675-2791, Fax: 765-675-7797. 8AM-4PM M-Th, 8AM-5PM F. Access by: in person.

Union

Real Estate Recording—Union County Recorder, 26 West Union Street, Room 106, Liberty, IN 47353. 318-238-1384. 8AM-4PM.

Felony, Misdemeanor, Civil, Eviction, Small Claims, Probate—Circuit Court, 26 W Union St, Liberty, IN 47353. 765-458-6121, Fax: 765-458-5263. 8AM-4PM. Access by: mail, in person.

Vanderburgh

Real Estate Recording—Vanderburgh County Recorder, 231 City-County Admin. Building, 1 NW Martin Luther King, Jr. Blvd. Evansville, IN 47708. 8AM-4:30PM.

Felony, Misdemeanor, Civil, Eviction, Small Claims, Probate—Circuit & Superior Court, PO Box 3356, Evansville, IN 47732-3356. 812-435-5160, Fax: 812-435-5849. 8AM-4:30PM. Access by: in person. www.countyclerk.evansville.net/newhome

Vermillion

Real Estate Recording—Vermillion County Recorder, Courthouse, Room 202, 255 S. Main, Newport, IN 47966. 8AM-4PM.

Felony, Misdemeanor, Civil, Eviction, Small Claims, Probate—Circuit Court, PO Box 8, Newport, IN 47966. 765-492-3500. 8AM-4PM. Access by: in person.

Vigo

Real Estate Recording—Vigo County Recorder, 201 Cherry Street, Terre Haute, IN 47807. Fax: 812-232-2219. 8AM-4PM.

Felony, Misdemeanor, Civil, Eviction, Small Claims, Probate—Circuit, Superior, & County Court, 2nd Fl, Courthouse, PO Box 8449, Terre Haute, IN 47807-8449. 812-462-3211, Fax: 812-640-4203. 8AM-4PM. Access by: mail, in person.

Wabash

Real Estate Recording—Wabash County Recorder, Courthouse, One West Hill St. Wabash, IN 46992. 219-753-7720. 8AM-4PM.

Felony, Misdemeanor, Civil, Eviction, Small Claims, Probate—Circuit & Superior Court, One West Hill St, Wabash, IN 46992. 219-753-7870, Fax: 219-563-3451. 8AM-4PM. Access by: mail, fax, in person.

Warren

Real Estate Recording—Warren County Recorder, 125 N. Monroe, Courthouse - Suite 10, Williamsport, IN 47993. 318-363-5651, Fax: 765-762-7222. 8AM-4PM.

Felony, Misdemeanor, Civil, Eviction, Small Claims, Probate—Circuit Court, Ste 11, 125 N Monroe, Williamsport, IN 47993. 765-762-3510, Fax: 765-762-7222. 8AM-4PM. Access by: mail, fax, in person.

Warrick

Real Estate Recording—Warrick County Recorder, 107 W Locust St. Suite 204, Boonville, IN 47601. Fax: 812-897-6168. 8AM-4PM.

Felony, Misdemeanor, Civil, Eviction, Small Claims, Probate—Circuit & Superior Court, 107 W Locust, Rm 201, Boonville, IN 47601. 812-897-6160. 8AM-4PM. Access by: mail, phone, in person.

Washington

Real Estate Recording—Washington County Recorder, Courthouse, Salem, IN 47167. Fax: 812-883-1933. 8:30AM-4PM (F 8:30AM-6PM).

Felony, Misdemeanor, Civil, Eviction, Small Claims, Probate—Circuit & Superior Court, Courthouse, 99 Public Sq, Salem, IN 47167. 812-883-1634, Fax: 812-883-1933. 8:30AM-4PM M-Th, 8:30AM-6PM F. Access by: mail, in person.

Wayne

Real Estate Recording—Wayne County Recorder, County Administration Bldg. 401 E. Main, Richmond, IN 47374. 765-973-9238, Fax: 765-973-9321. 8:30AM-5PM M; 8:30AM-4:30 PM T-F.

Felony, Misdemeanor, Civil, Eviction, Small Claims, Probate—Circuit & Superior Court, Courthouse, 301 E Main Street, Richmond, IN 47374. 765-973-9200, Fax: 765-973-9490. 8:30AM-5PM M; 8:30AM-4:30PM T-F. Access by: mail, in person. www.co.wayne.in.us/wayneco

Wells

Real Estate Recording—Wells County Recorder, Courthouse - Suite 203, 102 W. Market St. Bluffton, IN 46714. 8AM-4:30PM.

Felony, Misdemeanor, Civil, Eviction, Small Claims, Probate—Circuit & Superior Court, 102 West Market, Rm 201, Bluffton, IN 46714. 225-383-0378. 8AM-4:30PM. Access by: in person.

White

Real Estate Recording—White County Recorder, Corner of Main & Broadway, Courthouse, Monticello, IN 47960. Fax: 219-583-1521. 8AM-4PM.

Felony, Misdemeanor, Civil, Eviction, Small Claims, Probate—Circuit & Superior Court, PO Box 350, Monticello, IN 47960. 219-755-3000, Fax: 219-583-1532. 8AM-4PM. Access by: in person.

Whitley

Real Estate Recording—Whitley County Recorder, Courthouse, 2nd Floor - Room 18, Columbia City, IN 46725. Fax: 219-248-3137. 8AM-4PM (8AM-6PM F).

Felony, Misdemeanor, Civil, Eviction, Small Claims, Probate—Circuit & Superior Court, 101 W Van Buren, Rm 10, Columbia City, IN 46725. 219-463-3442, Fax: 219-248-3137. 8AM-4:30PM. Access by: in person.

Federal Courts

US District Court

Northern District of Indiana

Fort Wayne Division Room 1108, Federal Bldg, 1300 S Harrison St, Fort Wayne, IN 46802 219-424-7360 Counties: Adams, Allen, Blackford, DeKalb, Grant, Huntington, Jay, Lagrange, Noble, Steuben, Wells, Whitley. www.innd.uscourts.gov
Hammond Division Room 101, 507 State St, Hammond, IN 46320 219-937-5235 Counties: Lake, Porter. www.innd.uscourts.gov
Lafayette Division PO Box 1498, Lafayette, IN 47902 765-420-6250 Counties: Benton, Carroll, Jasper, Newton, Tippecanoe, Warren, White. www.innd.uscourts.gov
South Bend Division Room 102, 204 S Main, South Bend, IN 46601 219-246-8000 Fax: 219-246-8002 Counties: Cass, Elkhart, Fulton, Kosciusko, La Porte, Marshall, Miami, Pulaski, St. Joseph, Starke, Wabash. www.innd.uscourts.gov

Southern District of Indiana

Evansville Division 304 Federal Bldg, 101 NW Martin Luther King Blvd, Evansville, IN 47708 812-465-6426, Record Room: 812-465-6427 Fax: 812-465-6428 Counties: Daviess, Dubois, Gibson, Martin, Perry, Pike, Posey, Spencer, Vanderburgh, Warrick. www.insd.uscourts.gov
Indianapolis Division Clerk, Room 105, 46 E Ohio St, Indianapolis, IN 46204 317-229-3700 Fax: 317-229-3959 Counties: Bartholomew, Boone, Brown, Clinton, Decatur, Delaware, Fayette, Fountain, Franklin, Hamilton, Hancock, Hendricks, Henry, Howard, Johnson, Madison, Marion, Monroe, Montgomery, Morgan, Randolph, Rush, Shelby, Tipton, Union, Wayne. www.insd.uscourts.gov
New Albany Division Room 210, 121 W Spring St, New Albany, IN 47150 812-948-5238 Counties: Clark, Crawford, Dearborn, Floyd, Harrison, Jackson, Jefferson, Jennings, Lawrence, Ohio, Orange, Ripley, Scott, Switzerland, Washington. www.insd.uscourts.gov
Terre Haute Division 207 Federal Bldg, 30 N 7th St, Terre Haute, IN 47808 812-234-9484 Counties: Clay, Greene, Knox, Owen, Parke, Putnam, Sullivan, Vermillion, Vigo. www.insd.uscourts.gov

US Bankruptcy Court

Northern District of Indiana

Fort Wayne Division PO Box 2547, Fort Wayne, IN 46801-2547 219-420-5100 Counties: Adams, Allen, Blackford, DeKalb, Grant, Huntington, Jay, Lagrange, Noble, Steuben, Wells, Whitley. www.innb.uscourts.gov
Hammond at Gary Division 221 Federal Bldg, 610 Connecticut St, Gary, IN 46402-2595 219-881-3335 Fax: 219-881-3307 Counties: Lake, Porter. www.innb.uscourts.gov
Hammond at Lafayette Division c/o Fort Wayne Division, PO Box 2547, Fort Wayne, IN 46801-2547 219-420-5100 Counties: Benton, Carroll, Jasper, Newton, Tippecanoe, Warren, White. www.innb.uscourts.gov
South Bend Division PO Box 7003, South Bend, IN 46634-7003 219-236-8247 Fax: 219-236-8886 Counties: Cass, Elkhart, Fulton, Kosciusko, La Porte, Marshall, Miami, Pulaski, St. Joseph, Starke, Wabash. www.innb.uscourts.gov

Southern District of Indiana

Evansville Division 352 Federal Building, 101 NW Martin Luther King Blvd, Evansville, IN 47708812-465-6440 Fax: 812-465-6453 Counties: Daviess, Dubois, Gibson, Martin, Perry, Pike, Posey, Spencer, Vanderburgh, Warrick. www.insb.uscourts.gov
Indianapolis Division 116 US Courthouse, 46 E Ohio St, Indianapolis, IN 46204317-229-3800 Fax: 317-229-3801 Counties: Bartholomew, Boone, Brown, Clinton, Decatur, Delaware, Fayette, Fountain, Franklin, Hamilton, Hancock, Hendricks, Henry, Howard, Johnson, Madison, Marion, Monroe, Montgomery, Morgan, Randolph, Rush, Shelby, Tipton, Union, Wayne. www.insb.uscourts.gov

New Albany Division 110 US Courthouse, 121 W Spring St, New Albany, IN 47150812-948-5254 Fax: 812-948-5262 Counties: Clark, Crawford, Dearborn, Floyd, Harrison, Jackson, Jefferson, Jennings, Lawrence, Ohio, Orange, Ripley, Scott, Switzerland, Washington. www.insb.uscourts.gov
Terre Haute Division 207 Federal Bldg, 30 N 7th St, Terre Haute, IN 47808812-238-1550 Fax: 812-238-1831 Counties: Clay, Greene, Knox, Owen, Parke, Putnam, Sullivan, Vermillion, Vigo. www.insb.uscourts.gov

Attorney General's Office
1305 E Walnut St, 2nd fl   515-281-5164
Des Moines, IA 50319   Fax: 515-281-4209
www.state.ia.us/government/ag/index.html

Governor's Office
State Capitol Bldg   515-281-5211
Des Moines, IA 50319   Fax: 515-281-6611
www.state.ia.us/government/governor/
index.html

State Archives
600 E. Locust   515-281-5111
Des Moines, IA 50319-0290   Fax: 515-282-0502
www.state.ia.us/government/dca

Capital:	Des Moines
	Polk County
Time Zone:	CST
Number of Counties:	99
Population:	2,852,423
Web Site:	www.state.ia.us

Search Unclaimed Property Online

www.treasurer.state.ia.us/
search.html

State Agencies

Criminal Records
Division of Criminal Investigations, Bureau of Identification, Wallace State Office Bldg, Des Moines, IA 50319; 515-281-5138, 515-281-7996; Fax: 515-242-6297; 8AM-4:30PM. Access by: mail. www.state.ia.us/government/dps/dci/crimhist.htm

Corporation Records
Limited Liability Company Records
Fictitious Name
Limited Partnership Records
Assumed Name
Trademarks/Servicemarks
Secretary of State, Corporation Division, 2nd Floor, Hoover Bldg, Des Moines, IA 50319; 515-281-5204, 515-242-6556 Other Fax Line; Fax: 515-242-5953; 8AM-4:30PM. Access by: mail, phone, in person, online. www.sos.state.ia.us

Sales Tax Registrations
Department of Revenue, Taxpayer Services Division, Hoover State Office Bldg, Des Moines, IA 50306-0465; 515-281-3114; Fax: 515-242-6487; 8AM-4PM. Access by: mail, phone, in person. www.state.ia.us/tax

Uniform Commercial Code
Federal Tax Liens
UCC Division, Secretary of State, Hoover Bldg, East 14th & Walnut, Des Moines, IA 50319; 515-281-5204, 515-242-5953 Other Fax Line; Fax: 515-242-6556; 8AM-4:30PM. Access by: mail, phone, in person, online. www.sos.state.ia.us

State Tax Liens
Records not available from state agency.

Records are found at the county recorder's offices.

Workers' Compensation Records
Iowa Work Force Development, Division of Workers' Compensation, 1000 E Grand Ave, Des Moines, IA 50319; 515-

281-5387; Fax: 515-281-6501; 8AM-4:30PM. Access by: mail, phone, in person. www.state.ia.us/iwd/wc

Birth Certificates

Iowa Department of Public Health, Bureau of Vital Records, 321 E 12th St, 4th Floor, Lucas Bldg, Des Moines, IA 50319-0075; 515-281-4944, 515-281-5871 Message Recording; 7AM-4:45PM. Access by: mail, phone, in person. www.idph.state.ia.us

Death Records

Iowa Department of Public Health, Vital Records, 321 E 12th St, 4th Floor, Lucas Bldg, Des Moines, IA 50319-0075; 515-281-4944, 515-281-5871 Message Recording; 7AM-4:45PM. Access by: mail, phone, in person. www.idph.state.ia.us

Marriage Certificates

Iowa Department of Public Health, Vital Records, 321 E 12th St, 4th Floor, Lucas Bldg, Des Moines, IA 50319-0075; 515-281-4944, 515-281-5871 Message Recording; 7AM-4:45PM. Access by: mail, phone, in person. www.idph.state.ia.us

Divorce Records

Records not available from state agency.

Divorce records are found at the county court issuing the decree. In general, records are available from 1880.

Accident Reports

Department of Transportation, Office of Driver Services, Park Fair Mall, 100 Euclid, Des Moines, IA 50313; 515-244-9124, 800-532-1121; Fax: 515-239-1837; 8AM-4:30PM. Access by: mail.

Driver Records

Department of Transportation, Driver Service Records Section, PO Box 9204, Des Moines, IA 50306-9204 (Park Fair Mall, 100 Euclid, Des Moines, IA 50313); 515-244-9124; Fax: 515-237-3152; 8AM-4:30PM. Access by: mail. www.state.ia.us/government/dot

Vehicle Ownership
Vehicle Identification

Department of Transportation, Office of Vehicle Services, PO Box 9278, Des Moines, IA 50306-9278 (Park Fair Mall, 100 Euclid, Des Moines, IA 50313); 515-237-3148, 515-237-3049; Fax: 515-237-3118; 8AM-4:30PM. Access by: mail, phone, in person. www.state.ia.us/government/dot

Boat & Vessel Ownership
Boat & Vessel Registration

Records not available from state agency.

Vessels are registered at the county level.

Legislation-Current/Pending
Legislation-Passed

Iowa General Assembly, Legislative Information Office, State Capitol, Des Moines, IA 50319; 515-281-5129; 8AM-4:30PM. Access by: mail, phone, in person, online. www.legis.state.ia.us

Voter Registration

Secretary of State, Elections Division, Hoover State Office Building, Des Moines, IA 50319--143; 515-281-5760; Fax: 515-242-5953; 8AM-4:30PM. www.sos.state.ia.us

GED Certificates

Department of Education, GED Records, Grimes State Office Building, Des Moines, IA 50319-0146; 515-281-7308, 515-281-3636; Fax: 515-281-6544; 8AM-5PM.

Hunting License Information
Fishing License Information

Department of Natural Resources, Wallace Building, E 9th & Grand Ave, 4th Floor, Des Moines, IA 50319-0034; 515-281-5385; Fax: 515-281-6794; 8AM-4:30PM. Access by: mail, phone, in person. www.state.ia.us

County Courts & Recording Offices

About the Courts...

Administration

State Court Administrator 515-281-5241
State Capitol Fax: 515-242-6164
Des Moines, IA 50319
www.sos.state.ia.us/register/r3/judpage.htm

Court Structure

The District Court is the court of general jurisdiction. Effective 7/1/95, the Small Claims limit was increased to $4000 from $3000.

Vital records are being moved from courts to the County Recorder's office in each county. There is no scheduled completion date for this conversion.

Searching Hints

In most courts, the Certification Fee is $10.00 plus copy fee. Copy Fee is $.50 per page. Many courts do not do searches and recommend either in person searches or use of a rec-ord retriever.

Courts that accept written search requests do require an SASE. Credit cards are not accepted statewide.

Most courts have a public access terminal for access to that court'd records.

Online Access

There is a statewide online computer system called the Iowa Court Information System (ICIS), which is for internal use only. There is no public access system.

About the Recording Offices...

Organization

99 counties, 100 recording offices. The recording officer is County Recorder. Many counties utilize a grantor/grantee index containing all transactions recorded with them. Lee County has two recording offices. See the notes under the county for how to determine which office is appropriate to search. The entire state is in the Central Time Zone (CST).

UCC Records

Financing statements are filed at the state level, except for consumer goods and real estate related filings. All counties will perform UCC searches. Use search request form UCC-11. Search fees are usually $5.00 per debtor name ($6.00 if the standard UCC-11 form is not used). Copies usually cost $1.00 per page.

Lien Records

Federal tax liens on personal property of businesses are filed with the Secretary of State. Other federal and all state tax liens on personal property are filed with the County Recorder. County search practices vary widely, but most provide some sort of tax lien search for $6.00 per name.

Real Estate Records

Most counties are hesitant to perform real estate searches, but some will provide a listing from the grantor/grantee index with the understanding that it is not certified in the sense that a title search is. Certification of copies usually costs $2.00-5.00 per document.

County Courts & Recording Offices

Adair

Real Estate Recording—Adair County Recorder, Courthouse, 400 Public Square, Greenfield, IA 50849. 515-743-2312, Fax: 515-743-2565. 8AM-4:30PM.

Felony, Misdemeanor, Civil, Eviction, Small Claims, Probate—5th District Court, PO Box L, Greenfield, IA 50849. 515-743-2445, Fax: 515-743-2974. 8AM-4:30PM. Access by: in person.

Adams

Real Estate Recording—Adams County Recorder, 500 9th St. Corning, IA 50841. Fax: 515-322-3744. 8:30AM-4:30PM.

Felony, Misdemeanor, Civil, Eviction, Small Claims, Probate—5th District Court, Courthouse, PO Box 484, Corning, IA 50841. 515-322-4711, Fax: 515-322-4523. 8AM-4:30PM. Access by: in person.

Allamakee

Real Estate Recording—Allamakee County Recorder, 110 Allamakee Street, Courthouse, Waukon, IA 52172. 320-564-3231, Fax: 319-568-6419. 8AM-4PM.

Felony, Misdemeanor, Civil, Eviction, Small Claims, Probate—1st District Court, PO Box 248, Waukon, IA 52172. 320-564-3325. 8AM-4:30PM. Access by: in person.

Appanoose

Real Estate Recording—Appanoose County Recorder, Courthouse, Centerville, IA 52544. 515-856-3097.

Felony, Misdemeanor, Civil, Eviction, Small Claims, Probate—8th District Court, PO Box 400, Centerville, IA 52544. 515-856-6101, Fax: 515-856-2282. 8AM-4:30PM. Access by: mail, in person.

Audubon

Real Estate Recording—Audubon County Recorder of Deeds, 318 Leroy St. #7, Audubon, IA 50025. 712-563-2293, Fax: 712-563-4766. 8AM-4:30PM.

Felony, Misdemeanor, Civil, Eviction, Small Claims, Probate—4th District Court, 318 Leroy St #6, Audubon, IA 50025. 712-563-4275, Fax: 712-563-4276. 8AM-4:30PM. Access by: mail, in person.

Benton

Real Estate Recording—Benton County Recorder, Courthouse, Vinton, IA 52349. 320-269-7774, Fax: 319-472-3309. 8AM-4:30PM.

Felony, Misdemeanor, Civil, Eviction, Small Claims, Probate—6th District Court, PO Box 719, Vinton, IA 52349. 320-269-7347, Fax: 319-472-2747. 8AM-4:30PM. Access by: in person.

Black Hawk

Real Estate Recording—Black Hawk County Recorder, 316 East 5th Street, Courthouse, Room 208, Waterloo, IA 50703. 319-462-4341, Fax: 319-833-3170. 8AM-5PM.

Felony, Misdemeanor, Civil, Eviction, Small Claims, Probate—1st District Court, 316 E 5th St, Waterloo, IA 50703. 319-472-2766. 8AM-4:30PM. Access by: in person.

Boone

Real Estate Recording—Boone County Recorder, 201 State Street, Boone, IA 50036. Fax: 515-432-8102. 8AM-4:30PM.

Felony, Misdemeanor, Civil, Eviction, Small Claims, Probate—2nd District Court, 201 State St, Boone, IA 50036. 515-433-0561, Fax: 515-433-0563. 8AM-4:30PM. Access by: in person.

Bremer

Real Estate Recording—Bremer County Recorder, Courthouse, 415 E. Bremer Ave. Waverly, IA 50677. 319-589-4418, Fax: 319-352-0518. 8AM-4:30PM.

Felony, Misdemeanor, Civil, Eviction, Small Claims, Probate—2nd District Court, PO Box 328, Waverly, IA 50677. 319-589-4436, Fax: 319-352-1054. 8AM-4:30PM. Access by: in person.

Buchanan

Real Estate Recording—Buchanan County Recorder, 210 5th Avenue NE, Independence, IA 50644. 319-568-6351, Fax: 319-334-7453. 8AM-4:30PM.

Felony, Misdemeanor, Civil, Eviction, Small Claims, Probate—1st District Court, PO Box 259, Independence, IA 50644. 319-568-3793, Fax: 319-334-7455. 8AM-4:30PM. Access by: mail, in person.

Buena Vista

Real Estate Recording—Buena Vista County Recorder, Courthouse Square, Storm Lake, IA 50588. 712-749-5533, Fax: 712-749-2539. 8AM-4:30PM.

Felony, Misdemeanor, Civil, Eviction, Small Claims, Probate—3rd District Court, PO Box 1186, Storm Lake, IA 50588. 712-749-2546, Fax: 712-749-2700. 8AM-4:30PM. Access by: in person.

Butler

Real Estate Recording—Butler County Recorder, 428 6th Street, Allison, IA 50602. Fax: 319-267-2628. 8AM-4PM.

Felony, Misdemeanor, Civil, Eviction, Small Claims, Probate—2nd District Court, PO Box 307, Allison, IA 50602. 319-462-2477, Fax: 319-267-2487. 8AM-4:30PM. Access by: in person.

Calhoun

Real Estate Recording—Calhoun County Recorder, Courthouse, Rockwell City, IA 50579. 8:30AM-4:30PM.

Felony, Misdemeanor, Civil, Eviction, Small Claims, Probate—2nd District Court, Box 273, Rockwell City, IA 50579. 712-297-8122, Fax: 712-297-8101. 8AM-4:30PM. Access by: in person.

Carroll

Real Estate Recording—Carroll County Recorder of Deeds, 6th & Main, Courthouse, Carroll, IA 51401. 712-792-5503, Fax: 712-792-9493. 8AM-4:30PM.

Felony, Misdemeanor, Civil, Eviction, Small Claims, Probate—2nd District Court, PO Box 867, Carroll, IA 51401. 712-792-4327, Fax: 712-792-4328. 8AM-4:30PM. Access by: in person.

Cass

Real Estate Recording—Cass County Recorder, 5 West 7th, Atlantic, IA 50022. 712-243-5503, Fax: 712-243-4736. 8AM-4:30PM.

Felony, Misdemeanor, Civil, Eviction, Small Claims, Probate—4th District Court, 5 W 7th St, Courthouse, Atlantic, IA 50022. 712-243-2105. 8AM-4:30PM. Access by: in person.

Cedar

Real Estate Recording—Cedar County Recorder, 400 Cedar Street, Courthouse, Tipton, IA 52772. Fax: 319-886-2095. 8AM-4PM.

Felony, Misdemeanor, Civil, Eviction, Small Claims, Probate—7th District Court, PO Box 111, Tipton, IA 52772. 320-679-6400. 8AM-4:30PM. Access by: mail, in person.

Cerro Gordo

Real Estate Recording—Cerro Gordo County Recorder of Deeds, 220 North Washington, Mason City, IA 50401. 515-421-3037, Fax: 515-421-3154. 8AM-4:30PM.

Felony, Misdemeanor, Civil, Eviction, Small Claims, Probate—2nd District Court, 220 W Washington, Mason City, IA 50401. 515-424-6431. 8AM-4:30PM. Access by: in person.

Cherokee

Real Estate Recording—Cherokee County Recorder of Deeds, 520 West Main, Cherokee, IA 51012. 712-225-4670, Fax: 712-225-6708. 8AM-4:30PM.

Felony, Misdemeanor, Civil, Eviction, Small Claims, Probate—3rd District Court, Courthouse Drawer F, Cherokee, IA 51012. 712-225-6744, Fax: 712-225-6747. 8AM-4:30PM. Access by: in person.

Chickasaw

Real Estate Recording—Chickasaw County Recorder, Courthouse, 8 E. Prospect, New Hampton, IA 50659. 515-394-2107, Fax: 515-394-5541. 8:30AM-4:30PM.

Felony, Misdemeanor, Civil, Eviction, Small Claims, Probate—1st District Court, County Courthouse, New Hampton, IA 50659. 515-394-2106, Fax: 515-394-5106. 8AM-4:30PM. Access by: in person.

Clarke

Real Estate Recording—Clarke County Recorder, Courthouse, Osceola, IA 50213. 515-342-3311, Fax: 515-342-3893. 8:30AM-4:30PM.

Felony, Misdemeanor, Civil, Eviction, Small Claims, Probate—5th District Court, Clarke County Courthouse, Osceola, IA 50213. 515-342-6096, Fax: 515-342-2463. 8AM-4:30PM. Access by: mail, in person.

Clay

Real Estate Recording—Clay County Recorder of Deeds, Administration Building, 300 W. 4th St, #3, Spencer, IA 51301. Fax: 712-262-5793. 8AM-4:30PM.

Felony, Misdemeanor, Civil, Eviction, Small Claims, Probate—3rd District Court, Courthouse 215 W 4th St, Spencer, IA 51301. 712-262-4335. 8AM-4:30PM. Access by: in person.

Clayton

Real Estate Recording—Clayton County Recorder, 111 High St. 1st Floor, Elkader, IA 52043. 319-385-0763, Fax: 319-245-2353. 8AM-4:30PM.

Felony, Misdemeanor, Civil, Eviction, Small Claims, Probate—1st District Court, PO Box 418, Clayton County Courthouse, Elkader, IA 52043. 319-398-3411, Fax: 319-245-2825. 8AM-4:30PM. Access by: in person.

Clinton

Real Estate Recording—Clinton County Recorder of Deeds, Clinton County Administration Bldg. 1900 N. 3rd St. Clinton, IA 52732. 319-382-3753. 8AM-4:30PM.

Felony, Misdemeanor, Civil, Eviction, Small Claims, Probate—7th District Court, Courthouse (PO Box 2957), Clinton, IA 52733. 319-382-2469, Fax: 319-243-3655. 8AM-4:30PM. Access by: in person.

Crawford

Real Estate Recording—Crawford County Recorder, 1202 Broadway, Denison, IA 51442. Fax: 712-263-8382. 8AM-4:30PM.

Felony, Misdemeanor, Civil, Eviction, Small Claims, Probate—3rd District Court, 1202 Broadway, Denison, IA 51442. 712-263-2242, Fax: 712-263-5753. 8AM-4:30PM. Access by: in person.

Dallas

Real Estate Recording—Dallas County Recorder, 801 Court Street, Room 203, Adel, IA 50003. 515-993-5804, Fax: 515-933-5790. 8AM-4:30PM.

Felony, Misdemeanor, Civil, Eviction, Small Claims, Probate—5th District Court, 801 Court St, Adel, IA 50003. 515-993-5816, Fax: 515-993-4752. 8AM-4:30PM. Access by: in person.

Davis

Real Estate Recording—Davis County Recorder, Courthouse, Bloomfield, IA 52537. 515-664-2155, Fax: 515-664-3317. 8AM-4PM.

Felony, Misdemeanor, Civil, Eviction, Small Claims, Probate—8th District Court, Davis County Courthouse, Bloomfield, IA 52537. 515-664-2011, Fax: 515-664-2041. 8AM-4:30PM. Access by: in person.

Decatur

Real Estate Recording—Decatur County Recorder, 207 North Main Street, Leon, IA 50144. Fax: 515-446-7159. 8AM-4:30PM.

Felony, Misdemeanor, Civil, Eviction, Small Claims, Probate—5th District Court, 207 N Main St, Leon, IA 50144. 515-446-4331, Fax: 515-446-3759. 8AM-4:30PM. Access by: mail, fax, in person.

Delaware

Real Estate Recording—Delaware County Recorder, Courthouse, 301 East Main, Manchester, IA 52057. 320-693-5230, Fax: 319-927-6423. 8AM-4:30PM.

Felony, Misdemeanor, Civil, Eviction, Small Claims, Probate—District Court, Delaware County Courthouse, PO Box 527, Manchester, IA 52057. 320-693-6234, Fax: 319-927-3074. 8AM-4:30PM. Access by: in person.

Des Moines

Real Estate Recording—Des Moines County Recorder, 513 North Main Street, Burlington, IA 52601. Fax: 319-753-8721. 8AM-4:30PM.

Felony, Misdemeanor, Civil, Eviction, Small Claims, Probate—8th District Court, 513 Main St, PO Box 158, Burlington, IA 52601. 320-656-3620, Fax: 319-753-8253. 8AM-4:30PM. Access by: in person.

Dickinson

Real Estate Recording—Dickinson County Recorder, Corner of Hill and 18th Streets, Courthouse, Spirit Lake, IA 51360. 712-336-1205, Fax: 712-336-2677. 8AM-4:30PM.

Felony, Misdemeanor, Civil, Eviction, Small Claims, Probate—3rd District Court, PO Drawer O N, Spirit Lake, IA 51360. 712-336-1138, Fax: 712-336-4005. 8AM-4:30PM. Access by: in person.

Dubuque

Real Estate Recording—Dubuque County Recorder, Courthouse, 720 Central #9, Dubuque, IA 52001. 320-598-3536, Fax: 319-589-4484. 8:30AM-5PM.

Felony, Misdemeanor, Civil, Eviction, Small Claims, Probate—1st District Court, 720 Central, Dubuque, IA 52001. 320-589-7287. 8AM-4:30PM. Access by: in person.

Emmet

Real Estate Recording—Emmet County Recorder, 609 1st Avenue North, Estherville, IA 51334. 712-362-3824, Fax: 712-362-7454. 8AM-4:30PM.

Felony, Misdemeanor, Civil, Eviction, Small Claims, Probate—3rd District Court, Emmet County, 609 1st Ave N, Estherville, IA 51334. 712-362-3325. 8AM-4:30PM. Access by: in person.

Fayette

Real Estate Recording—Fayette County Recorder, Courthouse, 114 N. Vine St. West Union, IA 52175. 319-927-2845, Fax: 319-422-9201. 8AM-4:30PM.

Felony, Misdemeanor, Civil, Eviction, Small Claims, Probate, Traffic—Fayette County District Court, PO Box 458, West Union, IA 52175. 319-886-2101, Fax: 319-422-3137. 8AM-4:30PM. Access by: in person.

Floyd

Real Estate Recording—Floyd County Recorder, Courthouse, 101 S. Main, Charles City, IA 50616. 515-257-6118, Fax: 515-228-6458. 8AM-4:30PM.

Felony, Misdemeanor, Civil, Eviction, Small Claims, Probate—2nd District Court, 101 S Main St, Charles City, IA 50616. 515-257-6122, Fax: 515-257-6125. 8AM-4:30PM. Access by: in person.

Franklin

Real Estate Recording—Franklin County Recorder, Courthouse, 12 1st Ave NW, Hampton, IA 50441. 515-456-5678, Fax: 515-456-5748. 8AM-4PM.

Felony, Misdemeanor, Civil, Eviction, Small Claims, Probate—2nd Judicial District Court, 12 1st Ave NW, PO Box 28, Hampton, IA 50441. 515-456-5626, Fax: 515-456-5628. 8AM-4:30PM. Access by: in person.

Fremont

Real Estate Recording—Fremont County Recorder, Courthouse, Sidney, IA 51652. 712-374-2031, Fax: 712-374-2826. 8AM-4:30PM.

Felony, Misdemeanor, Civil, Eviction, Small Claims, Probate—4th District Court, PO Box 549, Sidney, IA 51652. 712-374-2232, Fax: 712-374-3330. 8AM-4:30PM. Access by: in person.

Greene

Real Estate Recording—Greene County Recorder, Courthouse, 114 N. Chestnut, Jefferson, IA 50129. 515-386-3716, Fax: 515-386-5274. 8AM-4:30PM.

Felony, Misdemeanor, Civil, Eviction, Small Claims, Probate—2nd District Court, Greene County Courthouse, 114 N Chestnut, Jefferson, IA 50129. 515-386-2516. 8AM-4:30PM. Access by: in person.

Grundy

Real Estate Recording—Grundy County Recorder, 706 G Avenue, Grundy Center, IA 50638. 320-656-3870. 8AM-4:30PM.

Felony, Misdemeanor, Civil, Eviction, Small Claims, Probate—1st District Court, Grundy County Courthouse, 706 G Ave, Grundy Center, IA 50638. 320-679-1951, Fax: 319-824-3447. 8AM-4:30PM. Access by: in person.

Guthrie

Real Estate Recording—Guthrie County Recorder, 200 North 5th, Courthouse, Guthrie Center, IA 50115. 515-747-3414, Fax: 515-747-3346.

Felony, Misdemeanor, Civil, Eviction, Small Claims, Probate—5th District Court, Courthouse, Guthrie Center, IA. 50115. 515-747-3415. 8AM-4:30PM. Access by: in person.

Hamilton

Real Estate Recording—Hamilton County Recorder, 2300 Superior Street, Webster City, IA 50595. 515-832-9542, Fax: 515-833-9525. 8AM-4:30PM.

Felony, Misdemeanor, Civil, Eviction, Small Claims, Probate—2nd District Court, Courthouse PO Box 845, Webster City, IA 50595. 515-832-9600. 8AM-4:30PM. Access by: in person.

Hancock

Real Estate Recording—Hancock County Recorder, 855 State Street, Garner, IA 50438. 515-923-3122, Fax: 515-923-3912. 8AM-4PM.

Felony, Misdemeanor, Civil, Eviction, Small Claims, Probate—2nd District Court, 855 State St, Garner, IA 50438. 515-923-2532, Fax: 515-923-3521. 8AM-4:30PM. Access by: in person.

Hardin

Real Estate Recording—Hardin County Recorder, Courthouse, 1215 Edgington Ave. Eldora, IA 50627. 515-858-3461, Fax: 515-939-8245. 8AM-4:30PM.

Felony, Misdemeanor, Civil, Eviction, Small Claims, Probate—2nd District Court, Courthouse, PO Box 495, Eldora, IA 50627. 515-858-2328, Fax: 515-858-2320. 8AM-4:30PM. Access by: in person.

Harrison

Real Estate Recording—Harrison County Recorder, Courthouse, Logan, IA 51546. 712-644-2750, Fax: 712-644-2643. 8AM-4:30PM.

Felony, Misdemeanor, Civil, Eviction, Small Claims, Probate—District Court, Court House, Logan, IA 51546. 712-644-2665. 8AM-4:30PM. Access by: in person.

Henry

Real Estate Recording—Henry County Recorder, Courthouse, 101 E. Washington, Mount Pleasant, IA 52641. 319-753-8262, Fax: 319-385-0778. 8AM-4:30PM.

Felony, Misdemeanor, Civil, Eviction, Small Claims, Probate—8th District Court, PO Box 176, Mount Pleasant, IA 52641. Fax: 319-385-4144. 8AM-4:30PM. Access by: in person.

Howard

Real Estate Recording—Howard County Recorder, Court House, 137 N. Elm, Cresco, IA 52136. 320-563-4343, Fax: 319-547-2629. 8AM-4:30PM.

Felony, Misdemeanor, Civil, Eviction, Small Claims, Probate—1st District Court, Courthouse, 137 N Elm St, Cresco, IA 52136. 320-523-3680. 8AM-4:30PM. Access by: in person.

Humboldt

Real Estate Recording—Humboldt County Recorder, 203 Main Street, Court House, Dakota City, IA 50529. 515-332-1571, Fax: 515-332-1738. 8AM-4:30PM.

Felony, Misdemeanor, Civil, Eviction, Small Claims, Probate—2nd District Court, Courthouse, Dakota City, IA 50529. 515-332-1806, Fax: 515-332-7100. 8AM-4:30PM. Access by: in person.

Ida

Real Estate Recording—Ida County Recorder, 401 Moorehead, Courthouse, Ida Grove, IA 51445. 712-364-2287, Fax: 712-364-2746. 8AM-4:30PM.

Felony, Misdemeanor, Civil, Eviction, Small Claims, Probate—3rd District Court, Courthouse, 401 Moorehead St, Ida Grove, IA 51445. 712-364-2628, Fax: 712-364-2699. 8AM-4:30PM. Access by: in person.

Iowa

Real Estate Recording—Iowa County Recorder, 901 Court Ave. Marengo, IA 52301. 320-598-3648, Fax: 319-642-5562. 8AM-4:30PM.

Felony, Misdemeanor, Civil, Eviction, Small Claims, Probate—6th District Court, PO Box 266, Marengo, IA 52301. 320-629-5634. 8AM-4:30PM. Access by: in person.

Jackson

Real Estate Recording—Jackson County Recorder, 201 West Platt, Maquoketa, IA 52060. 320-632-0151, Fax: 319-652-6975. 8:30AM-4:30PM.

Felony, Misdemeanor, Civil, Eviction, Small Claims, Probate—7th District Court, 201 West Platt, Maquoketa, IA 52060. 320-629-6781, Fax: 319-652-2708. 8AM-4:30PM. Access by: in person.

Jasper

Real Estate Recording—Jasper County Recorder, Courthouse, Room 205, Newton, IA 50208. 515-792-6115, Fax: 515-791-3680. 8AM-5PM.

Felony, Misdemeanor, Civil, Eviction, Small Claims, Probate—5th District Court, 101 1st Street North, Rm 104, Newton, IA 50208. 515-792-3255, Fax: 515-792-2818. 8AM-4:30PM. Access by: in person.

Jefferson

Real Estate Recording—Jefferson County Recorder, 51 West Briggs, Fairfield, IA 52556. 515-472-2349, Fax: 515-472-6695. 8AM-4:30PM.

Felony, Misdemeanor, Civil, Eviction, Small Claims, Probate—8th District Court, PO Box 984, Fairfield, IA 52556. 515-472-3454, Fax: 515-472-9472. 8AM-4:30PM. Access by: in person.

Johnson

Real Estate Recording—Johnson County Recorder, 913 S. Dubuque Street, Suite 202, Iowa City, IA 52240. 319-642-3914, Fax: 319-339-6181. 8AM-4PM M,W,F; 8AM-5:30PM T,Th.

Felony, Misdemeanor, Civil, Eviction, Small Claims, Probate—6th District Court, PO Box 2510, Iowa City, IA 52244. 319-642-3672, Fax: 319-339-6153. 8AM-4:30PM. Access by: in person.

Jones

Real Estate Recording—Jones County Recorder, Courthouse, Room 116, 500 W. Main, Anamosa, IA 52205. 319-927-4942, Fax: 319-462-5802. 8AM-4PM.

Felony, Misdemeanor, Civil, Eviction, Small Claims, Probate—6th District Court, PO Box 19, Anamosa, IA 52205. 320-231-6206. 8AM-4:30PM. Access by: in person.

Keokuk

Real Estate Recording—Keokuk County Recorder, Courthouse, Sigourney, IA 52591. 515-622-7411, Fax: 515-622-2286. 8AM-4:30PM.

Felony, Misdemeanor, Civil, Eviction, Small Claims, Probate—8th District Court, Courthouse, Sigourney, IA 52591. 515-622-2210, Fax: 515-622-2171. 8AM-4:30PM. Access by: in person.

Kossuth

Real Estate Recording—Kossuth County Recorder, 114 West State, Algona, IA 50511. 515-295-3404, Fax: 515-295-9304. 8AM-4PM.

Felony, Misdemeanor, Civil, Eviction, Small Claims, Probate—3rd District Court, Kossuth County Courthouse, 114 W State St, Algona, IA 50511. 515-295-3240. 8AM-4PM. Access by: in person.

Lee

Real Estate Recording—Lee County Recorder, 25 North 7th, Keokuk, IA 52632. Fax: 319-524-1544. 8:30AM-4:30PM.

Lee County Recorder, 933 Avenue H, Fort Madison, IA 52627. 319-652-4946, Fax: 319-372-7033. 8:30AM-4:30PM.

Felony, Misdemeanor, Civil, Eviction, Small Claims, Probate—8th District Court, PO Box 1443, Ft Madison, IA 52627. 319-652-5649. 8AM-4:30PM. Access by: in person.

Linn

Real Estate Recording—Linn County Recorder, 930 First Street S.W. Cedar Rapids, IA 52404. Fax: 319-362-5329. 8AM-5PM.

Felony, Misdemeanor, Civil, Eviction, Small Claims, Probate—District Court, Linn County Courthouse, PO Box 1468, Cedar Rapids, IA 52406-1468. 319-824-5229, Fax: 319-398-3964. 8AM-4:30PM. Access by: in person.

Louisa

Real Estate Recording—Louisa County Recorder, 117 South Main Street, Wapello, IA 52653. Fax: 319-523-3713. 8AM-4:30PM.

Felony, Misdemeanor, Civil, Eviction, Small Claims, Probate—8th District Court, PO Box 268, Wapello, IA 52653. 320-523-1172, Fax: 319-523-4542. 8AM-4:30PM. Access by: mail, fax, in person.

Lucas

Real Estate Recording—Lucas County Recorder, Courthouse, Chariton, IA 50049. 515-774-5213, Fax: 515-774-2993. 8AM-4PM.

Felony, Misdemeanor, Civil, Eviction, Small Claims, Probate—5th District Court, Courthouse, Chariton, IA 50049. 515-774-4421, Fax: 515-774-8669. 8AM-4:30PM. Access by: in person.

Lyon

Real Estate Recording—Lyon County Recorder, 206 Second Avenue, Courthouse, Rock Rapids, IA 51246. 712-472-3703. 8AM-4:30PM.

Felony, Misdemeanor, Civil, Eviction, Small Claims, Probate—3rd District Court, Courthouse, Rock Rapids, IA 51246. 712-472-2623, Fax: 712-472-2422. 8AM-4:30PM. Access by: in person.

Madison

Real Estate Recording—Madison County Recorder, North John Wayne Drive, Courthouse, Winterset, IA 50273. 515-462-3771, Fax: 515-462-2506. 8AM-4:30PM; 9AM-Noon Last Sat of the month.

Felony, Misdemeanor, Civil, Eviction, Small Claims, Probate—5th District Court, PO Box 152, Winterset, IA 50273. 515-462-4451, Fax: 515-462-9825. 8AM-4:30PM. Access by: in person.

Mahaska

Real Estate Recording—Mahaska County Recorder, Courthouse, Oskaloosa, IA 52577. 515-673-5482. 8AM-4:30PM.

Felony, Misdemeanor, Civil, Eviction, Small Claims, Probate—8th District Court, Courthouse, Oskaloosa, IA 52577. 515-673-7786, Fax: 515-672-1256. 8AM-4:30PM. Access by: in person.

Marion

Real Estate Recording—Marion County Recorder, 214 E. Main St. Knoxville, IA 50138. 515-828-2211, Fax: 515-842-3593. 8AM-4:30PM.

Felony, Misdemeanor, Civil, Eviction, Small Claims, Probate—5th District Court, PO Box 497, Knoxville, IA 50138. 515-828-2207, Fax: 515-828-7580. 8AM-4:30PM. Access by: in person.

Marshall

Real Estate Recording—Marshall County Recorder, Courthouse, 3rd Floor, 1 East Main St. Marshalltown, IA 50158. 515-754-6366, Fax: 515-754-6321. 8AM-4:30PM.

Felony, Misdemeanor, Civil, Eviction, Small Claims, Probate—2nd District Court, Courthouse, Marshalltown, IA 50158. 515-754-6373, Fax: 515-754-6376. 8AM-4:30PM. Access by: in person.

Mills

Real Estate Recording—Mills County Recorder, Courthouse, 418 Sharp St. Glenwood, IA 51534. 712-527-4419. 8AM-4:30PM.

Felony, Misdemeanor, Civil, Eviction, Small Claims, Probate—4th District Court, 418 Sharp St, Courthouse, Glenwood, IA 51534. 712-527-4880, Fax: 712-527-4936. 8AM-4:30PM. Access by: mail, in person.

Mitchell

Real Estate Recording—Mitchell County Recorder, 508 State Street, Osage, IA 50461. 515-732-5861. 8AM-4:30PM.

Felony, Misdemeanor, Civil, Eviction, Small Claims, Probate—2nd District Court, 508 State St, Osage, IA 50461. 515-732-3726, Fax: 515-732-3728. 8AM-4:30PM. Access by: in person.

Monona

Real Estate Recording—Monona County Recorder, 610 Iowa Avenue, Onawa, IA 51040. 712-423-2271, Fax: 712-423-3034. 8AM-4:30PM.

Felony, Misdemeanor, Civil, Eviction, Small Claims, Probate—3rd District Court, PO Box 14, Onawa, IA 51040. 712-423-2491. 8AM-4:30PM. Access by: in person.

Monroe

Real Estate Recording—Monroe County Recorder, Courthouse, 10 Benton Ave. East, Albia, IA 52531. 515-932-5011, Fax: 515-932-2863. 8AM-4PM.

Felony, Misdemeanor, Civil, Eviction, Small Claims, Probate—8th District Court, Courthouse, 10 Benton Ave E, Albia, IA 52531. 515-932-5212, Fax: 515-932-3245. 8AM-4:30PM. Access by: in person.

Montgomery

Real Estate Recording—Montgomery County Recorder, Courthouse, Red Oak, IA 51566. 712-623-2392, Fax: 712-623-2346. 8AM-4:30PM.

Felony, Misdemeanor, Civil, Eviction, Small Claims, Probate—4th District Court, Courthouse, Red Oak, IA 51566. 712-623-4986. 8AM-4:30PM. Access by: in person.

Muscatine

Real Estate Recording—Muscatine County Recorder, 401 East 3rd Street, Courthouse, Muscatine, IA 52761. 319-422-6061, Fax: 319-263-7248. 8AM-4:30PM.

Felony, Misdemeanor, Civil, Eviction, Small Claims, Probate—7th District Court, PO Box 8010, Courthouse, Muscatine, IA 52761. 319-422-5694, Fax: 319-264-3622. 8AM-4:30PM. Access by: in person.

O'Brien

Real Estate Recording—O'Brien County Recorder, Courthouse, Primghar, IA 51245. 712-757-3045, Fax: 712-757-3046. 8AM-4:30PM.

Felony, Misdemeanor, Civil, Eviction, Small Claims, Probate—3rd District Court, Courthouse Criminal Records, Primghar, IA 51245. 712-757-3255, Fax: 712-757-2965. 8AM-4:30PM. Access by: in person. www.obriencounty.com

Osceola

Real Estate Recording—Osceola County Recorder, Courthouse, 300 7th Street, Sibley, IA 51249. 712-754-3217, Fax: 712-754-2872. 8AM-4:30PM.

Felony, Misdemeanor, Civil, Eviction, Small Claims, Probate—3rd District Court, Courthouse Criminal Records, Sibley, IA 51249. 712-754-3595, Fax: 712-754-2480. 8AM-4:30PM. Access by: in person.

Page

Real Estate Recording—Page County Recorder, 112 E. Main St. Courthouse, Clarinda, IA 51632. 712-542-2516, Fax: 712-542-5019. 8AM-4:30PM.

Felony, Misdemeanor, Civil, Eviction, Small Claims, Probate—4th District Court, 112 E Main Box 263, Clarinda, IA 51632. 712-542-3214, Fax: 712-542-5460. 8AM-4:30PM. Access by: in person.

Palo Alto

Real Estate Recording—Palo Alto County Recorder, 1010 Broadway, Emmetsburg, IA 50536. 712-852-3701, Fax: 712-852-3704. 8AM-4PM.

Felony, Misdemeanor, Civil, Eviction, Small Claims, Probate—3rd District Court, PO Box 387, Emmetsburg, IA 50536. 712-852-3603. 8AM-4:30PM. Access by: in person.

Plymouth

Real Estate Recording—Plymouth County Recorder, Courthouse, 215 4th Ave. SE, Le Mars, IA 51031. 712-546-4020. 8AM-5PM.

Felony, Misdemeanor, Civil, Eviction, Small Claims, Probate—3rd District Court, Courthouse 215-4th Ave SE, Le Mars, IA 51031. 712-546-4215. 8AM-4:30PM. Access by: in person.

Pocahontas

Real Estate Recording—Pocahontas County Recorder, 99 Court Square, Pocahontas, IA 50574. 712-335-4334, Fax: 712-335-4502. 8AM-4PM.

Felony, Misdemeanor, Civil, Eviction, Small Claims, Probate—2nd District Court, Courthouse, 99 Court Square, Pocahontas, IA 50574. 712-335-4208, Fax: 712-335-4608. 8AM-4:30PM. Access by: in person.

Polk

Real Estate Recording—Polk County Recorder, 111 Court Avenue, Room 250, County Administration Building, Des Moines, IA 50309. 515-286-3041, Fax: 515-323-5393. 8AM-4:30PM.

Felony, Misdemeanor, Civil, Eviction, Small Claims, Probate—District Court, 500 Mulberry St, Rm 201, Des Moines, IA 50309. 515-286-3772, Fax: 515-286-3172. 8AM-4:30PM. Access by: in person.

Pottawattamie

Real Estate Recording—Pottawattamie County Recorder, 227 South Sixth Street, Council Bluffs, IA 51501. 712-328-5627, Fax: 712-328-4738. 8AM-4PM.

Felony, Misdemeanor, Civil, Eviction, Small Claims, Probate—4th District Court, 227 S 6th St, Council Bluffs, IA 51501. 712-328-5604. 9AM-4:30PM. Access by: in person.

Poweshiek

Real Estate Recording—Poweshiek County Recorder, 302 East Main Street, Montezuma, IA 50171. 515-623-5128, Fax: 515-623-5120. 8AM-4PM.

Felony, Misdemeanor, Civil, Eviction, Small Claims, Probate—8th District Court, PO Box 218, Montezuma, IA 50171. 515-623-5644, Fax: 515-623-5320. 8AM-4:30PM. Access by: in person.

Ringgold

Real Estate Recording—Ringgold County Recorder, Courthouse, Mount Ayr, IA 50854. 515-464-3230, Fax: 515-464-2568. 8AM-4PM.

Felony, Misdemeanor, Civil, Small Claims, Probate—5th District Court, 109 W Madison (PO Box 523), Mount Ayr, IA 50854. 515-464-3234, Fax: 515-464-2478. 8AM-4:30PM. Access by: in person.

Sac

Real Estate Recording—Sac County Recorder, 100 N. West State St. Sac City, IA 50583. 712-662-7411, Fax: 712-662-6298. 8AM-4:30PM.

Felony, Misdemeanor, Civil, Eviction, Small Claims, Probate—2nd District Court, PO Box 368, Sac City, IA 50583. 712-662-7791. 8AM-4:30PM. Access by: in person.

Scott

Real Estate Recording—Scott County Recorder, 416 West 4th Street, Davenport, IA 52801. 319-547-2661, Fax: 319-322-1269. 8AM-4:30PM.

Felony, Misdemeanor, Civil, Eviction, Small Claims, Probate—7th District Court, 416 W 4th St, Davenport, IA 52801. 319-547-3860. 8AM-4:30PM. Access by: in person.

Shelby

Real Estate Recording—Shelby County Recorder, 612 Court Street, Room 201, Harlan, IA 51537. 712-755-5898, Fax: 712-755-2519. 8AM-4:30PM.

Felony, Misdemeanor, Civil, Eviction, Small Claims, Probate—4th District Court, PO Box 431, Harlan, IA 51537. 712-755-5543, Fax: 712-755-2667. 8AM-4:30PM. Access by: mail, in person.

Sioux

Real Estate Recording—Sioux County Recorder, 210 Central Avenue SW, Courthouse, Orange City, IA 51041. 712-737-2229, Fax: 712-737-2537. 8AM-4:30PM.

Felony, Misdemeanor, Civil, Eviction, Small Claims, Probate—3rd District Court, PO Box 47, Courthouse, Orange City, IA 51041. 712-737-2286, Fax: 712-737-8908. 8AM-4:30PM. Access by: in person.

Story

Real Estate Recording—Story County Recorder, 900 6th Street, Courthouse, Nevada, IA 50201. 515-382-6581, Fax: 515-382-7326. 8AM-5PM (No recording after 3:30PM).

Felony, Misdemeanor, Civil, Eviction, Small Claims, Probate—2nd District Court, PO Box 408, Nevada, IA 50201. 515-382-7410. 8AM-4:30PM. Access by: in person.

Tama

Real Estate Recording—Tama County Recorder, High Street, Toledo, IA 52342. 515-484-3141. 8AM-4:30PM.

Felony, Misdemeanor, Civil, Eviction, Small Claims, Probate—6th Judicial District Court, PO Box 306, Toledo, IA 52342. 515-484-3721, Fax: 515-484-6403. 8AM-4:30PM. Access by: in person.

Taylor

Real Estate Recording—Taylor County Recorder, 405 Jefferson St. Courthouse, Bedford, IA 50833. 712-523-2080, Fax: 712-523-2274.

Felony, Misdemeanor, Civil, Eviction, Small Claims, Probate—5th District Court, Courthouse, Bedford, IA 50833. 712-523-2095, Fax: 712-523-2936. 8AM-4:30PM. Access by: in person.

Union

Real Estate Recording—Union County Recorder, 301 North Pine Street, Creston, IA 50801. 515-782-2319, Fax: 515-782-8404. 8:30AM-4:30PM.

Felony, Misdemeanor, Civil, Eviction, Small Claims, Probate—5th District Court, Courthouse, Creston, IA 50801. 515-782-7315, Fax: 515-782-8241. 8AM-4:30PM. Access by: in person.

Van Buren

Real Estate Recording—Van Buren County Recorder, Dodge and Fourth Streets, Keosauqua, IA 52565. 319-523-4541, Fax: 319-293-3828. 8AM-4:30PM.

Felony, Misdemeanor, Civil, Eviction, Small Claims, Probate—8th District Court, Courthouse Criminal Records, Keosauqua, IA 52565. 319-472-5211, Fax: 319-293-3811. 8AM-4:30PM. Access by: in person. Special note: SSNs currently are shown in the public access terminal, but will be maskeed by the end of 1999.

Wapello

Real Estate Recording—Wapello County Recorder, 101 West 4th Street, Ottumwa, IA 52501. 515-683-0040, Fax: 515-683-0019. 8AM-4:30PM.

Felony, Misdemeanor, Civil, Eviction, Small Claims, Probate—8th District Court, 101 W 4th, Ottumwa, IA 52501. 515-683-0060. 8AM-4:30PM. Access by: in person. Special note: SSNs are only maintained on a confidential sheet not available to the public.

Warren

Real Estate Recording—Warren County Recorder, 115 N. Howard, Room 106, Indianola, IA 50125. 515-961-1110. 8AM-4:30PM.

Felony, Misdemeanor, Civil, Eviction, Small Claims, Probate—5th District Court, PO Box 379, Indianola, IA 50125. 515-961-1033, Fax: 515-961-1071. 8AM-4:30PM. Access by: mail, in person.

Washington

Real Estate Recording—Washington County Recorder, 224 West Main St. Washington, IA 52353. 320-632-0325. 8AM-4:30PM.

Felony, Misdemeanor, Civil, Eviction, Small Claims, Probate—8th District Court, PO Box 391, Washington, IA 52353.

320-634-5222, Fax: 319-653-7787. 8AM-4:30PM. Access by: in person.

Wayne

Real Estate Recording—Wayne County Recorder, Junction of Highway 2 and 14, Courthouse, Corydon, IA 50060. 515-872-1676, Fax: 515-872-2843. 8AM-4PM.

Felony, Misdemeanor, Civil, Eviction, Small Claims, Probate—5th District Court, PO Box 424, Corydon, IA 50060. 515-872-2264, Fax: 515-872-2431. 8AM-4:30PM. Access by: in person.

Webster

Real Estate Recording—Webster County Recorder, 701 Central Avenue, Courthouse, Fort Dodge, IA 50501. 515-576-2731, Fax: 515-574-3723. 8AM-4:30PM.

Felony, Misdemeanor, Civil, Eviction, Small Claims, Probate—2nd District Court, 701 Central Ave, Courthouse, Ft Dodge, IA 50501. 515-576-7115. 8AM-4:30PM. Access by: in person.

Winnebago

Real Estate Recording—Winnebago County Recorder, 126 South Clark Street, Courthouse, Forest City, IA 50436. 515-582-2094, Fax: 515-582-2891. 8AM-4:30PM.

Felony, Misdemeanor, Civil, Eviction, Small Claims, Probate—2nd District Court, 126 W Clark, Box 468, Forest City, IA 50436. 515-585-4520, Fax: 515-585-2615. 8AM-4:30PM. Access by: in person.

Winneshiek

Real Estate Recording—Winneshiek County Recorder, 201 West Main Street, Decorah, IA 52101. 319-653-7741, Fax: 319-387-4083. 8AM-4PM.

Felony, Misdemeanor, Civil, Eviction, Small Claims, Probate—1st District Court, 201 W Main St, Decorah, IA 52101. 319-653-7726, Fax: 319-382-0603. 8AM-4:30PM. Access by: in person.

Woodbury

Real Estate Recording—Woodbury County Recorder, 7th & Douglas Street, Courthouse Room 106, Sioux City, IA 51101. Fax: 712-252-4921. 8AM-4:30PM.

Felony, Civil, Eviction, Probate—3rd District Court, 620 Douglas St, Sioux City, IA 51101. 712-279-6616, Fax: 712-279-6021. 7:30AM-4:30PM. Access by: in person.

Misdemeanor, Civil, Eviction, Small Claims—3rd District Court, 407 7th St, Sioux City, IA 51101. 712-279-6624. 8AM-4:30PM. Access by: in person.

Worth

Real Estate Recording—Worth County Recorder, 1000 Central Avenue, Northwood, IA 50459. 515-324-2942, Fax: 515-324-2316. 8AM-4PM.

Felony, Misdemeanor, Civil, Eviction, Small Claims, Probate—2nd District Court, PO Box 243, Northwood, IA 50459. 515-324-2840, Fax: 515-324-2360. 8AM-4:30PM. Access by: in person.

Wright

Real Estate Recording—Wright County Recorder, 115 North Main, Courthouse, Clarion, IA 50525. 515-532-2691. 8AM-4PM.

Felony, Misdemeanor, Civil, Eviction, Small Claims, Probate—2nd District Court, PO Box 306, Clarion, IA 50525. 515-532-3113, Fax: 515-532-2343. 8AM-4:30PM. Access by: in person.

Federal Courts

US District Court

Northern District of Iowa

Cedar Rapids Division Court Clerk, PO Box 74710, Cedar Rapids, IA 52407-4710319-286-2300 Counties: Benton, Cedar, Cerro Gordo, Grundy, Hardin, Iowa, Jones, Linn, Tama. www.iand.uscourts.gov

Dubuque Division c/o Cedar Rapids Division, PO Box 74710, Cedar Rapids, IA 52407-4710319-286-2300 Counties: Allamakee, Black Hawk, Bremer, Buchanan, Chickasaw, Clayton, Delaware, Dubuque, Fayette, Floyd, Howard, Jackson, Mitchell, Winneshiek. www.iand.uscourts.gov

Sioux City Division Room 301, Federal Bldg, 320 6th St, Sioux City, IA 51101712-233-3900 Counties: Buena Vista, Cherokee, Clay, Crawford, Dickinson, Ida, Lyon, Monona, O'Brien, Osceola, Plymouth, Sac, Sioux, Woodbury. www.iand.uscourts.gov

Southern District of Iowa

Council Bluffs Division PO Box 307, Council Bluffs, IA 51502712-328-0283 Fax: 712-328-1241 Counties: Adair, Adams, Audubon, Cass, Clarke, Clinton, Decatur, Fremont, Harrison, Lucas, Mills, Montgomery, Page, Pottawattamie, Ringgold, Shelby, Taylor, Union, Wayne. www.iasd.uscourts.gov

Davenport Division PO Box 256, Davenport, IA 52805, Civil Docket Phone: 319-322-3223, Criminal Docket Phone: 515-284-6248 Fax: 319-322-2962 Counties: Henry, Johnson, Lee, Louisa, Muscatine, Scott, Van Buren, Washington. www.iasd.uscourts.gov

Des Moines (Central) Division PO Box 9344, Des Moines, IA 50306-9344, Civil Docket Phone: 515-284-6447, Criminal Docket Phone: 515-284-6248 Fax: 515-284-6210 Counties: Appanoose, Boone, Dallas, Davis, Des Moines, Greene, Guthrie, Jasper, Jefferson, Keokuk, Madison, Mahaska, Marion, Marshall, Monroe, Polk, Poweshiek, Story, Wapello, Warren. www.iasd.uscourts.gov

US Bankruptcy Court

Northern District of Iowa

Cedar Rapids Division PO Box 74890, Cedar Rapids, IA 52407-4890319-286-2200 Fax: 319-286-2280 Counties: Allamakee, Benton, Black Hawk, Bremer, Buchanan, Buena Vista, Butler, Calhoun, Carroll, Cedar, Cerro Gordo, Cherokee, Chickasaw, Clay, Clayton, Crawford, Delaware, Dickinson, Dubuque, Emmet, Fayette, Floyd, Franklin, Grundy, Hamilton, Hancock, Hardin, Howard, Humboldt, Ida, Iowa, Jackson, Jones, Kossuth, Linn, Lyon, Mitchell, Monona, O'Brien, Osceola, Palo Alto, Plymouth, Pocahontas, Sac, Sioux, Tama, Webster, Winnebago, Winneshiek, Woodbury, Worth, Wright. www.ianb.uscourts.gov

Southern District of Iowa

Des Moines Division PO Box 9264, Des Moines, IA 50306-9264515-284-6230 Fax: 515-284-6404 Counties: Adair, Adams, Appanoose, Audubon, Boone, Cass, Clarke, Clinton, Dallas, Davis, Decatur, Des Moines, Fremont, Greene, Guthrie, Harrison, Henry, Jasper, Jefferson, Johnson, Keokuk, Lee, Louisa, Lucas, Madison, Mahaska, Marion, Marshall, Mills, Monroe,Montgomery, Muscatine, Page, Polk, Pottawattamie, Poweshiek, Ringgold, Scott, Shelby, Story, Taylor, Union, Van Buren, Wapello, Warren, Washington, Wayne.

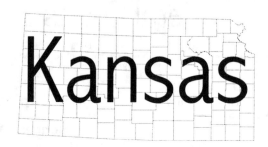

Attorney General's Office

120 SW 10th Ave, 2nd Floor   785-296-2215
Topeka, KS 66612-1597   Fax: 785-296-6296
www.ink.org/public/ksag

Governor's Office

State Capitol Bldg, Room 212S   785-296-3232
Topeka, KS 66612-1590   Fax: 785-296-7973
www.ink.org/public/governor

State Archives

6425 SW 6th Ave   785-272-8681
Topeka, KS 66615-1099   Fax: 785-272-8682
www.kshs.org

Capital:	Topeka
	Shawnee County
Time Zone:	CST*

* Kansas' five western-most counties are MST:
They are: Greeley, Hamilton, Kearny, Sherman, Wallace.

Number of Counties:	105
Population:	2,594,840
Web Site:	www.state.ks.us

Search Unclaimed Property Online

www.treasurer.state.ks.us/
upsearch.htm

State Agencies

Criminal Records

Kansas Bureau of Investigation, Criminal Records Division, 1620 SW Tyler, Attn: NCJRC, Topeka, KS 66612-1837; 785-296-8200; Fax: 785-296-6781; 8AM-5PM. Access by: mail. www.kbi.state.ks.us

Corporation Records
Limited Partnerships
Limited Liability Company Records

Secretary of State, Memorial Hall, 120 SW 10th St, 2nd Floor, Topeka, KS 66612-1594; 785-296-4564; Fax: 785-296-4570; 8AM-5PM. Access by: mail, phone, in person, online. www.kssos.org

Trademarks/Servicemarks

Secretary of State, Trademarks/Servicemarks Division, 120 SW 10th St, 1st floor, Topeka, KS 66612-1594; 785-296-4564; Fax: 785-296-4570; 8AM-5PM. Access by: mail, phone, in person. www.kssos.org

Uniform Commercial Code
Federal Tax Liens

UCC Division, Secretary of State, Memorial Hall, 120 SW 10th, Topeka, KS 66612; 785-296-1849; Fax: 785-296-3659; 8AM-5PM. Access by: mail, phone, in person, online. www.ink.org/public/sos

Sales Tax Registrations

Restricted access.
Sales tax registration information is considered confidential and not public record.
Kansas Department of Revenue, Customer Relations, Docking State Office Bldg, 915 SW Harrison, Topeka, KS 66612-1588; 785-296-0222; Fax: 785-291-3614; 7AM-5PM www.ink.org/public/kdor

Workers' Compensation Records

Human Resources Department, Workers Compensation Division, 800 SW Jackson, Suite 600, Topeka, KS 66612-1227; 785-296-3441, 800-332-0353 Claims Advisor; Fax: 785-296-0025; 8AM-5PM. Access by: mail, phone, in person. www.hr.state.ks.us/wc/html/wc.htm

Birth Certificates

Kansas Department of Health & Environment, Office of Vital Statistics, 900 SW Jackson, Landon State Office Bldg, Topeka, KS 66612-2221; 785-296-1400; Fax: 785-357-4332; 8AM-5PM. Access by: mail, phone, in person. www.kdhe.state.ks.us/vital

Death Records

Kansas State Department of Health & Environment, Office of Vital Statistics, 900 SW Jackson, Landon State Office Bldg, Topeka, KS 66612-2221; 785-296-1400; Fax: 785-357-4332; 8AM-5PM. Access by: mail, phone, in person. www.kdhe.state.ks.us/vital

Marriage Certificates

Kansas State Department of Health & Environment, Office of Vital Statistics, 900 SW Jackson, Landon State Office Bldg, Topeka, KS 66612-2221; 785-296-1400; Fax: 785-357-4332; 8AM-5PM. Access by: mail, phone, in person. www.kdhe.state.ks.us/vital

Divorce Records

Kansas State Department of Health & Environment, Office of Vital Statistics, 900 SW Jackson, Landon State Office Bldg, Topeka, KS 66612-2221; 785-296-1400; Fax: 785-357-4332;. Access by: mail, phone, in person. www.kdhe.state.ks.us/vital

Driver Records
Accident Reports

Department of Revenue, Driver Control Bureau, PO Box 12021, Topeka, KS 66612-2021 (Docking State Office Building, 915 Harrison, 1st Floor, Topeka, KS 66612); 785-296-3671; Fax: 785-296-6851; 8AM-4:45PM. Access by: mail, online.

Vehicle Ownership
Vehicle Identification

Division of Vehicles, Title and Registration Bureau, 915 Harrison, Topeka, KS 66612; 285-296-3621; Fax: 285-296-3852; 7:30AM-4:45PM. Access by: mail, online.

Boat & Vessel Ownership
Boat & Vessel Registration

Kansas Wildlife & Parks Department, Boat Registration, 512 SE 25th Ave, Pratt, KS 67124-8174; 316-672-5911; Fax: 316-672-6020; 8AM-5PM M-F. www.kdwp.state.ks.us

Legislation-Current/Pending
Legislation-Passed

Kansas State Library, Capitol Bldg, 300 SW 10th Ave, Topeka, KS 66612; 785-296-2149; Fax: 785-296-6650; 8AM-5PM. Access by: mail, phone, in person, online. www.ink.org

Voter Registration

Restricted access.
Individual records must be searched at the county level. This agency will sell the database on disk, CD or tape format only for political purposes.
Secretary of State, Department of Elections, 300 SW 10th Street, 2nd Fl, Topeka, KS 66612; 785-296-4564; Fax: 785-291-3051; 8AM-5PM
www.kssos.org

GED Certificates

Board of Education, GED, E 10th Street, Topeka, KS 66612; 785-296-3191; Fax: 785-296-3523;.

Hunting License Information

Dept of Wildlife & Parks, Operations Office, Fish & Wildlife, 512 SE 25th Ave, Pratt, KS 67124-8174; 316-672-5911; Fax: 316-672-6020; 8AM-5PM. Access by: mail. www.kdwp.state.ks.us

Fishing License Information

Records not available from state agency.

County Courts & Recording Offices

About the Courts...

Administration

Judicial Administrator, Kansas Judicial Center   785-296-4873
301 W. 10th St   Fax: 785-296-7076
Topeka, KS 66612
www.law.ukans.edu/kscourts/kscourts.html

Court Structure

The District Court is the court of general jurisdiction. There are 109 courts in 31 districts in 105 counties.

Searching Hints

Five counties - Cowley, Crawford, Labette, Montgomery and Neosho - have two hearing locations, but only one record center, which is the location included in this Sourcebook.

Many Kansas courts do not do criminal record searches and will refer any criminal requests to the Kansas. Bureau of Investigation.

Online Access

Online computer access is available for District Court Records in 4 counties - Johnson, Sedgwick, Shawnee, and Wyandotte - through the Information Network of Kansas (INK) Services. Franklin and Finney counties are to be available in Summer of 2000. There is also a wide range of other state information available through INK. A user can access INK through their Internet site at www.ink.org. The INK subscription fee is $75.00, and the annual renewal fee is $60.00. There is no per minute connect charge, but there is a transaction fee. Drivers License, Title, Registration, Lien, and UCC searches are available by PC through the Internet or through a toll-free number. For additional information or a registration packet, call 800-4-KANSAS (800-452-6727).

About the Recording Offices...

Organization

105 counties, 105 recording offices. The recording officer is Register of Deeds. Many counties utilize a "Miscellaneous Index" for tax and other liens, separate from real estate records. 100 counties are in the Central Time Zone (CST) and 5 are in the Mountain Time Zone (MST).

UCC Records

Financing statements are filed at the state level except for consumer goods and real estate related filings. All counties will perform UCC searches. Use search request form UCC-3. Search fees are usually $8.00 per debtor name. Copies usually cost $1.00 per page.

Lien Records

Federal tax liens on personal property of businesses are filed with the Secretary of State. Other federal tax liens and all state tax liens on personal property are filed with the county Register of Deeds. Most counties automatically include tax liens on personal property with a UCC search. Tax liens on personal property may usually be searched separately for $8.00 per name.

Real Estate Records

Most counties will not perform real estate searches, although some will do as an accommodation with the understanding that they are not "certified." Some counties will also do a search based upon legal description to determine owner. Copy fees vary, and certification fees are usually $1.00 per document. Tax records are located at the Appraiser's Office.

County Courts & Recording Offices

Allen

Real Estate Recording—Allen County Register of Deeds, 1 North Washington, Courthouse, Iola, KS 66749. 316-492-2180, Fax: 316-365-1414. 8AM-5PM.

Felony, Misdemeanor, Civil, Eviction, Small Claims, Probate—District Court, PO Box 630, Iola, KS 66749. 316-532-3461, Fax: 316-365-1429. 8AM-5PM. Access by: mail, fax, in person.

Anderson

Real Estate Recording—Anderson County Register of Deeds, Courthouse, 100 E. 4th Street, Garnett, KS 66032. Fax: 785-448-5621. 8AM-5PM.

Felony, Misdemeanor, Civil, Eviction, Small Claims, Probate—District Court, PO Box 305, Garnett, KS 66032. 785-448-6886, Fax: 785-448-3230. 8AM-5PM. Access by: mail, fax, in person. www.kscourts.org.dstcts/4dstct.htm

Atchison

Real Estate Recording—Atchison County Register of Deeds, 423 North 5th St. Courthouse, Atchison, KS 66002. Fax: 913-367-0227. 8:30AM-5PM.

Felony, Misdemeanor, Civil, Eviction, Small Claims, Probate—District Court, PO Box 408, Atchison, KS 66002. 913-367-7400, Fax: 913-367-1171. 8AM-5PM. Access by: mail, fax, in person.

Barber

Real Estate Recording—Barber County Register of Deeds, 120 East Washington Street, Courthouse, Medicine Lodge, KS 67104. 317-762-3562, Fax: 316-886-5045. 8:30AM-5PM.

Felony, Misdemeanor, Civil, Eviction, Small Claims, Probate—District Court, 118 E Washington, Medicine Lodge, KS 67104. 317-776-9620, Fax: 316-886-5854. 8AM-Noon,1-5PM. Access by: in person.

Barton

Real Estate Recording—Barton County Register of Deeds, Courthouse, #205, 1400 Main St. Great Bend, KS 67530. 317-462-1152, Fax: 316-793-1990. 8AM-5PM.

Felony, Misdemeanor, Civil, Eviction, Small Claims, Probate—District Court, 1400 Main, Rm 306, Great Bend, KS 67530. 317-482-2880, Fax: 316-793-1860. 8AM-5PM. Access by: mail, fax, in person.

Bourbon

Real Estate Recording—Bourbon County Register of Deeds, 210 South National, Fort Scott, KS 66701. 316-330-1070, Fax: 316-223-5241. 8:30AM-4:30PM.

Felony, Misdemeanor, Civil, Eviction, Small Claims, Probate—District Court, PO Box 868, Ft Scott, KS 66701. 316-326-5936, Fax: 316-223-5303. 8:30AM-4:30PM. Access by: mail, fax, in person.

Brown

Real Estate Recording—Brown County Register of Deeds, Courthouse, 601 Oregon, Hiawatha, KS 66434. 913-742-2051, Fax: 785-742-3255. 8AM-5PM.

Felony, Misdemeanor, Civil, Eviction, Small Claims, Probate—District Court, PO Box 417, Hiawatha, KS 66434. 785-742-7481, Fax: 785-742-3506. 8AM-5PM. Access by: mail, phone, fax, in person.

Butler

Real Estate Recording—Butler County Register of Deeds, 205 West Central, Courthouse, Suite 104, El Dorado, KS 67042. 316-376-4292, Fax: 316-321-1011. 8AM-5PM.

Felony, Misdemeanor, Civil, Eviction, Small Claims, Probate—District Court, PO Box 432, El Dorado, KS 67042. 316-376-4413, Fax: 316-321-9486. 8:30AM-5PM. Access by: in person.

Chase

Real Estate Recording—Chase County Register of Deeds, Courthouse Plaza, Cottonwood Falls, KS 66845. 316-365-1415, Fax: 316-273-6617. 8AM-5PM.

Felony, Misdemeanor, Civil, Eviction, Small Claims, Probate—District Court, PO Box 207, Cottonwood Falls, KS 66845. 316-364-8628, Fax: 316-273-6890. 8AM-5PM. Access by: in person.

Chautauqua

Real Estate Recording—Chautauqua County Register of Deeds, 215 North Chautauqua, Courthouse, Sedan, KS 67361. 317-392-6375, Fax: 316-725-5831. 8AM-Noon,1-4PM.

Felony, Misdemeanor, Civil, Eviction, Small Claims, Probate—District Court, 215 N Chautauqua, Sedan, KS 67361. 317-456-2213, Fax: 316-725-3027. 8AM-5PM. Access by: mail, in person.

Cherokee

Real Estate Recording—Cherokee County Register of Deeds, 110 West Maple, Room 121, Courthouse, Columbus, KS 66725. 316-635-2753, Fax: 316-429-1362. 9AM-5PM.

Felony, Misdemeanor, Civil, Eviction, Small Claims, Probate—District Court, PO Box 189, Columbus, KS 66725. 316-659-2442, Fax: 316-429-1130. 8AM-5PM. Access by: in person.

Cheyenne

Real Estate Recording—Cheyenne County Register of Deeds, 212 East Washington, St. Francis, KS 67756. 913-332-8810, Fax: 785-332-8825. 8AM-Noon,1-5PM.

Felony, Misdemeanor, Civil, Eviction, Small Claims, Probate—District Court, PO Box 646, St Francis, KS 67756. 785-332-8850, Fax: 785-332-8851. 8AM-Noon,1-5PM. Access by: mail, in person.

Clark

Real Estate Recording—Clark County Register of Deeds, Courthouse, 913 Highland, Ashland, KS 67831. 316-793-1856, Fax: 316-635-2393. 8:30AM-Noon, 1-4:30PM.

Felony, Misdemeanor, Civil, Eviction, Small Claims, Probate—District Court, PO Box 790, Ashland, KS 67831. 316-795-4533, Fax: 316-635-2155. 8AM-5PM. Access by: mail, in person.

Clay

Real Estate Recording—Clay County Register of Deeds, Courthouse Square, Clay Center, KS 67432. 913-632-3282, Fax: 785-632-2651. 8AM-5PM.

Felony, Misdemeanor, Civil, Eviction, Small Claims, Probate—District Court, PO Box 203, Clay Center, KS 67432. 785-632-3443, Fax: 785-632-2651. 8AM-5PM. Access by: mail, in person.

Cloud

Real Estate Recording—Cloud County Register of Deeds, 811 Washington Street, Concordia, KS 66901. Fax: 785-243-8123. 8AM-4:30PM.

Felony, Misdemeanor, Civil, Eviction, Small Claims, Probate—District Court, 811 Washington, Concordia, KS 66901. 785-243-8124, Fax: 785-243-8188. 8:30AM-5PM. Access by: mail, phone, fax, in person.

Coffey

Real Estate Recording—Coffey County Register of Deeds, Courthouse, Room 205, 110 S. 6th St. Burlington, KS 66839. 316-441-4520. 8AM-5PM.

Felony, Misdemeanor, Civil, Eviction, Small Claims, Probate—District Court, PO Box 330, Burlington, KS 66839. 316-492-2160, Fax: 316-364-8535. 8AM-5PM. Access by: mail, in person. www.kscourts.org/dstcts/4dstct.htm

Comanche

Real Estate Recording—Comanche County Register of Deeds, 201 South New York, Courthouse, Coldwater, KS 67029. 316-723-3317, Fax: 316-582-2390. 9AM-Noon,1-5PM.

Felony, Misdemeanor, Civil, Eviction, Small Claims, Probate—District Court, PO Box 722, Coldwater, KS 67029. 316-723-2681, Fax: 316-582-2603. 8AM-5PM. Access by: mail, fax, in person.

Cowley

Real Estate Recording—Cowley County Register of Deeds, 311 East 9th, Courthouse, Winfield, KS 67156. 316-322-4370, Fax: 316-221-5463. 8AM-Noon,1-5PM.

Felony, Misdemeanor, Civil, Eviction, Small Claims, Probate—Arkansas City District Court, PO Box 1152, Arkansas City, KS 67005. 316-672-4100, Fax: 316-442-7213. 8AM-Noon,1-4PM. Access by: mail, in person. Special note: This court covers the southern part of the county. All felony records are kept at Winfield.

Winfield District Court, PO Box 472, Winfield, KS 67156. 316-326-3371, Fax: 316-221-1097. 8AM-Noon,1-4PM. Access by: mail, fax, in person. Special note: This court covers northern part of county.

Crawford

Real Estate Recording—Crawford County Register of Deeds, Courthouse, 2nd Floor, Girard, KS 66743. Fax: 316-724-8823. 8:30AM-4:30PM.

Felony, Misdemeanor, Civil, Eviction, Small Claims, Probate—Girard District Court, PO Box 69, Girard, KS 66743. 317-392-6320, Fax: 316-724-4987. 8:30AM-4:30PM. Access by: mail, fax, in person. Special note: Records are maintained here for the Pittsburg District Court as well since 8/92. For prior cases, search both courts separately.

Decatur

Real Estate Recording—Decatur County Register of Deeds, Courthouse, 120 E. Hall, Oberlin, KS 67749. 785-475-8103, Fax: 785-475-8150. 8AM-Noon,1-5PM.

Felony, Misdemeanor, Civil, Eviction, Small Claims, Probate—District Court, PO Box 89, Oberlin, KS 67749. 785-475-8107, Fax: 785-475-8170. 8AM-5PM. Access by: in person.

Dickinson

Real Estate Recording—Dickinson County Register of Deeds, First & Buckeye, Courthouse, Abilene, KS 67410. 913-263-3231, Fax: 785-263-1512. 8AM-5PM.

Felony, Misdemeanor, Civil, Eviction, Small Claims, Probate—District Court, PO Box 127, Abilene, KS 67410. 785-263-3142, Fax: 785-263-4407. 8AM-5PM. Access by: mail, in person.

Doniphan

Real Estate Recording—Doniphan County Register of Deeds, Courthouse, 120 E. Chestnut St. Troy, KS 66087. 913-985-3831, Fax: 785-985-3723. 8AM-5PM.

Felony, Misdemeanor, Civil, Eviction, Small Claims, Probate—District Court, PO Box 295, Troy, KS 66087. 785-985-3582, Fax: 785-985-2402. 8AM-5PM. Access by: mail, phone, in person.

Douglas

Real Estate Recording—Douglas County Register of Deeds, 1100 Massachusetts, Courthouse, Lawrence, KS 66044. 913-841-7700, Fax: 785-841-4036. 8AM-5PM.

Felony, Misdemeanor, Civil, Eviction, Small Claims, Probate—District Court, 111 E 11th St Rm 144, Lawrence, KS 66044-2966. 785-841-7700, Fax: 785-832-5174. 8:30AM-4PM. Access by: mail, phone, fax, in person.

Edwards

Real Estate Recording—Edwards County Register of Deeds, 312 Massachusetts, Courthouse, Kinsley, KS 67547. 316-842-5191, Fax: 316-659-2583. 8AM-5PM.

Felony, Misdemeanor, Civil, Eviction, Small Claims, Probate—District Court, PO Box 232, Kinsley, KS 67547. 316-842-3721, Fax: 316-659-2998. 8AM-5PM. Access by: mail, in person.

Elk

Real Estate Recording—Elk County Register of Deeds, Court House, 127 N. Pine, Howard, KS 67349., Fax: 316-374-2771. 8AM-4:30PM.

Felony, Misdemeanor, Civil, Eviction, Small Claims, Probate—District Court, PO Box 306, Howard, KS 67349. 316-544-2484, Fax: 316-374-3531. 8AM-4:30PM. Access by: in person.

Ellis

Real Estate Recording—Ellis County Register of Deeds, 1204 Fort Street, Hays, KS 67601., Fax: 785-628-9451. 8AM-5PM.

Felony, Misdemeanor, Civil, Eviction, Small Claims, Probate—District Court, PO Box 8, Hays, KS 67601. 785-628-9415, Fax: 785-628-8415. 8AM-5PM. Access by: mail, in person.

Ellsworth

Real Estate Recording—Ellsworth County Register of Deeds, 210 N. Kansas, Courthouse, Ellsworth, KS 67439. 913-472-4152, Fax: 785-472-4912. 8AM-Noon,1-5PM.

Felony, Misdemeanor, Civil, Eviction, Small Claims, Probate—District Court, 210 N Kansas, Ellsworth, KS 67439-3118. 785-472-3832, Fax: 785-472-5712. 8AM-5PM. Access by: mail, phone, fax, in person.

Finney

Real Estate Recording—Finney County Register of Deeds, Finney County Administrative Center, 311 North 9th, Garden City, KS 67846. 316-532-5151, Fax: 316-272-3624. 8AM-5PM.

Felony, Misdemeanor, Civil, Eviction, Small Claims, Probate—District Court, PO Box 798, Garden City, KS 67846., Fax: 316-272-3611. 8AM-4:30PM. Access by: in person.

Ford

Real Estate Recording—Ford County Register of Deeds, 100 Gunsmoke, 4th Floor, East Office, Ford County Government Center, Dodge City, KS 67801. 316-331-3040, Fax: 316-227-4699. 9AM-5PM.

Felony, Misdemeanor, Civil, Eviction, Small Claims, Probate—District Court, 101 W Spruce, Dodge City, KS 67801. 316-342-4950, Fax: 316-227-6799. 8AM-5PM. Access by: mail, in person.

Franklin

Real Estate Recording—Franklin County Register of Deeds, 315 South Main, Courthouse, Room 103, Ottawa, KS 66067. 785-242-4201, Fax: 785-229-3419. 8AM-4:30PM.

Felony, Misdemeanor, Civil, Eviction, Small Claims, Probate—District Court, PO Box 637, Ottawa, KS 66067. 785-242-6000, Fax: 785-242-5970. 8AM-5PM. Access by: mail, in person. www.kscourts.org/dstcts/4dstct.htm

Geary

Real Estate Recording—Geary County Register of Deeds, 139 East 8th, County Office Building, Junction City, KS 66441. 913-238-3912, Fax: 785-238-5419. 8:30AM-5PM.

Felony, Misdemeanor, Civil, Eviction, Small Claims, Probate—District Court, PO Box 1147, Junction City, KS 66441. 785-762-5221, Fax: 785-762-4420. 8AM-5PM. Access by: mail, in person.

Gove

Real Estate Recording—Gove County Register of Deeds, 520 Washington Street, Courthouse, Gove, KS 67736. 913-938-2275, Fax: 785-938-4486. 8AM-Noon, 1PM-5PM.

Felony, Misdemeanor, Civil, Eviction, Small Claims, Probate—District Court, PO Box 97, Gove, KS 67736. 785-938-2310, Fax: 785-938-2312. 8AM-Noon, 1-5PM. Access by: mail, fax, in person.

Graham

Real Estate Recording—Graham County Register of Deeds, 410 North Pomeroy, Hill City, KS 67642. 913-674-2331, Fax: 785-421-5463. 8:30AM-5PM.

Felony, Misdemeanor, Civil, Eviction, Small Claims, Probate—District Court, 410 N Pomeroy, Hill City, KS 67642. 785-421-3458, Fax: 785-421-5463. 8AM-5PM. Access by: in person.

Grant

Real Estate Recording—Grant County Register of Deeds, 108 South Glenn, Courthouse, Ulysses, KS 67880. 316-429-2418, Fax: 316-356-5379. 9AM-5PM.

Felony, Misdemeanor, Civil, Eviction, Small Claims, Probate—District Court, 108 S Glenn, Ulysses, KS 67880. 316-421-4120, Fax: 316-353-2131. 8:30AM-5PM. Access by: in person.

Gray

Real Estate Recording—Gray County Register of Deeds, 300 South Main, Courthouse, Cimarron, KS 67835. 317-736-3708, Fax: 316-855-3107. 8AM-5PM.

Felony, Misdemeanor, Civil, Eviction, Small Claims, Probate—District Court, PO Box 487, Cimarron, KS 67835. 317-668-8871, Fax: 316-855-7037. 8AM-5PM. Access by: in person.

Greeley

Real Estate Recording—Greeley County Register of Deeds, 616 Second Street, Courthouse, Tribune, KS 67879. 316-582-2182, Fax: 316-376-2294. 9AM-5PM.

Felony, Misdemeanor, Civil, Eviction, Small Claims, Probate—District Court, PO Box 516, Tribune, KS 67879. 316-549-3295. 9AM-Noon, 1-5PM. Access by: in person.

Greenwood

Real Estate Recording—Greenwood County Register of Deeds, Courthouse, 311 N. Main, Eureka, KS 67045. 316-724-6211, Fax: 316-583-8124. 8AM-5PM.

Felony, Misdemeanor, Civil, Eviction, Small Claims, Probate—District Court, 311 N Main, Eureka, KS 67045. 316-725-3666, Fax: 316-583-6818. 8AM-5PM. Access by: mail, in person.

Hamilton

Real Estate Recording—Hamilton County Register of Deeds, 219 North Main, Courthouse, Syracuse, KS 67878. 316-626-3216, Fax: 316-384-5853. 8AM-Noon, 1-4:30PM.

Felony, Misdemeanor, Civil, Eviction, Small Claims, Probate—District Court, PO Box 745, Syracuse, KS 67878. 316-625-8650, Fax: 316-384-7806. 8AM-5PM. Access by: in person.

Harper

Real Estate Recording—Harper County Register of Deeds, Courthouse, 201 North Jennings, Anthony, KS 67003. 317-653-4510, Fax: 316-842-3455. 8AM-Noon, 1-5PM.

Felony, Misdemeanor, Civil, Eviction, Small Claims, Probate—District Court, PO Box 467, Anthony, KS 67003. 317-569-3437, Fax: 316-842-5937. 8AM-Noon, 1-5PM. Access by: mail, fax, in person.

Harvey

Real Estate Recording—Harvey County Register of Deeds, 8th & Main, Courthouse, Newton, KS 67114. 316-373-3526. 8AM-5PM.

Felony, Misdemeanor, Civil, Eviction, Small Claims, Probate—District Court, PO Box 665, Newton, KS 67114-0665.

316-365-1425, Fax: 316-283-4601. 8AM-5PM. Access by: mail, in person.

Haskell

Real Estate Recording—Haskell County Register of Deeds, 300 S. Inman, Courthouse, Sublette, KS 67877. 316-872-2640. 9AM-Noon,1-5PM.

Felony, Misdemeanor, Civil, Eviction, Small Claims, Probate—District Court, PO Box 146, Sublette, KS 67877. 316-872-7208, Fax: 316-675-8599. 8AM-5PM. Access by: mail, in person.

Hodgeman

Real Estate Recording—Hodgeman County Register of Deeds, Main Street, Courthouse, Jetmore, KS 67854. 316-429-3880, Fax: 316-357-8300.

Felony, Misdemeanor, Civil, Eviction, Small Claims, Probate—District Court, PO Box 187, Jetmore, KS 67854. 316-431-5700, Fax: 316-357-6216. 8:30AM-5PM. Access by: mail, phone, fax, in person.

Jackson

Real Estate Recording—Jackson County Register of Deeds, Courthouse, Room 203, 415 New York, Holton, KS 66436. 913-364-3791, Fax: 785-364-3420. 8AM-4:30PM.

Felony, Misdemeanor, Civil, Eviction, Small Claims, Probate—District Court, PO Box 1026, Holton, KS 66436. 785-364-2191, Fax: 785-364-3804. 8AM-4:30PM. Access by: in person.

Jefferson

Real Estate Recording—Jefferson County Register of Deeds, 310 Jefferson Street, Courthouse, Oskaloosa, KS 66066., Fax: 785-863-2602. 8AM-6:30PM M; 8AM-4PM T-F.

Felony, Misdemeanor, Civil, Eviction, Small Claims, Probate—District Court, PO Box 327, Oskaloosa, KS 66066. 785-863-2461, Fax: 785-863-2369. 8AM-4:30PM. Access by: in person.

Jewell

Real Estate Recording—Jewell County Register of Deeds, 307 North Commercial Street, Courthouse, Mankato, KS 66956. 913-378-4090, Fax: 785-378-4075. 8:30AM-Noon, 1-4:30PM.

Felony, Misdemeanor, Civil, Eviction, Small Claims, Probate—District Court, 307 N Commercial, Mankato, KS 66956. 785-378-4030, Fax: 785-378-4035. 8AM-5PM. Access by: mail, phone, fax, in person.

Johnson

Real Estate Recording—Johnson County Register of Deeds, 111 South Cherry St. Suite 1300, Johnson County Administration Bldg. Olathe, KS 66061. 913-764-8484, Fax: 913-715-2310. 8AM-5PM.

Felony, Misdemeanor, Civil, Eviction, Small Claims, Probate—District Court, 100 N Kansas, Olathe, KS 66061. 913-764-3487, Fax: 913-715-3461. 8:30AM-5PM. Access by: mail, fax, in person.

Kearny

Real Estate Recording—Kearny County Register of Deeds, 304 North Main, Courthouse, Lakin, KS 67860. 316-384-5522, Fax: 316-355-7382. 8AM-5PM.

Felony, Misdemeanor, Civil, Eviction, Small Claims, Probate—District Court, PO Box 64, Lakin, KS 67860. 316-397-2805, Fax: 316-355-7462. 8AM-Noon,1-5PM. Access by: mail, in person.

Kingman

Real Estate Recording—Kingman County Register of Deeds, 130 North Spruce, Kingman, KS 67068. 316-675-2671, Fax: 316-532-2037. 8AM-Noon,1-5PM.

Felony, Misdemeanor, Civil, Eviction, Small Claims, Probate—District Court, PO Box 495, Kingman, KS 67068. 316-694-2938, Fax: 316-532-2952. 8AM-Noon, 1-5PM. Access by: mail, in person.

Kiowa

Real Estate Recording—Kiowa County Register of Deeds, 211 East Florida, Greensburg, KS 67054. 317-327-4600, Fax: 316-723-3234. 8:30AM-Noon, 1-5PM.

Felony, Misdemeanor, Civil, Eviction, Small Claims, Probate—District Court, 211 E Florida, Greensburg, KS 67054. 317-364-6410, Fax: 316-723-2970. 8AM-5PM. Access by: mail, fax, in person.

Labette

Real Estate Recording—Labette County Register of Deeds, Courthouse, 521 Merchant, Oswego, KS 67356., Fax: 316-795-2928. 8:30AM-5PM.

Felony, Misdemeanor, Civil, Eviction, Small Claims, Probate—District Court, 201 South Central, Parsons, KS 67357. 316-635-2745, Fax: 316-421-3633. 8AM-5PM. Access by: mail, in person.

District Court, Courthouse, 517 Merchant, Oswego, KS 67356. 317-564-3446, Fax: 316-795-3056. 8AM-5PM. Access by: mail, in person.

Lane

Real Estate Recording—Lane County Register of Deeds, 144 South Lane, Courthouse, Dighton, KS 67839., Fax: 316-397-5937. 8AM-Noon,1-5PM.

Felony, Misdemeanor, Civil, Eviction, Small Claims, Probate—District Court, PO Box 188, Dighton, KS 67839. 316-626-3265, Fax: 316-397-5526. 8AM-5PM. Access by: mail, phone, in person.

Leavenworth

Real Estate Recording—Leavenworth County Register of Deeds, 300 Walnut, Room 103, Courthouse, Leavenworth, KS 66048. 913-684-0430, Fax: 913-684-0406. 8AM-5PM.

Felony, Misdemeanor, Civil, Eviction, Small Claims, Probate—District Court, 4th & Walnut, Leavenworth, KS 66048. 913-684-0713, Fax: 913-684-0492. 8AM-5PM. Access by: mail, in person.

Lincoln

Real Estate Recording—Lincoln County Register of Deeds, 216 East Lincoln, Lincoln, KS 67455. 913-524-4657, Fax: 785-524-5008. 8AM-Noon,1-5PM.

Felony, Misdemeanor, Civil, Eviction, Small Claims, Probate—District Court, 216 E Lincoln Ave, Lincoln, KS 67455. 785-524-4057, Fax: 785-524-3204. 8AM-12, 1_5PM. Access by: mail, fax, in person.

Linn

Real Estate Recording—Linn County Register of Deeds, Courthouse, 315 Main Street, Mound City, KS 66056. 913-795-2227, Fax: 913-795-2889. 8AM-Noon, 12:30-4:30PM.

Felony, Misdemeanor, Civil, Eviction, Small Claims, Probate—District Court, PO Box 350, Mound City, KS 66056-0350. 913-795-2660, Fax: 913-795-2004. 8AM-5PM. Access by: in person.

Logan

Real Estate Recording—Logan County Register of Deeds, 710 West 2nd Street, Courthouse, Oakley, KS 67748. 913-672-3216, Fax: 785-672-3517. 8AM-Noon,1-5PM.

Felony, Misdemeanor, Civil, Eviction, Small Claims, Probate—District Court, 710 W 2nd St, Oakley, KS 67748. 785-672-3654, Fax: 785-672-3517. 8:30AM-Noon, 1-5PM. Access by: in person.

Lyon

Real Estate Recording—Lyon County Register of Deeds, 402 Commercial Street, Emporia, KS 66801., Fax: 316-342-2652. 8AM-5PM.

Felony, Misdemeanor, Civil, Eviction, Small Claims, Probate—District Court, 402 Commercial St, Emporia, KS 66801. 316-384-5159, Fax: 316-342-8005. 8AM-4PM. Access by: mail, fax, in person.

Marion

Real Estate Recording—Marion County Register of Deeds, Courthouse Square, Marion, KS 66861., Fax: 316-382-3420. 8:30AM-5PM.

Felony, Misdemeanor, Civil, Eviction, Small Claims, Probate—District Court, PO Box 298, Marion, KS 66861. 316-583-8146, Fax: 316-382-2259. 8AM-5PM. Access by: mail, in person.

Marshall

Real Estate Recording—Marshall County Register of Deeds, 1201 Broadway, Courthouse, Marysville, KS 66508. 913-562-5363, Fax: 785-562-5685. 8:30AM-5PM.

Felony, Misdemeanor, Civil, Eviction, Small Claims, Probate—District Court, PO Box 86, Marysville, KS 66508. 785-562-5301, Fax: 785-562-2458. 8AM-5PM; Search hours: 8:30AM-4:30PM. Access by: mail, fax, in person.

McPherson

Real Estate Recording—McPherson County Register of Deeds, 119 North Maple, Courthouse, McPherson, KS 67460. 316-355-6481, Fax: 316-241-1372. 8AM-5PM.

Felony, Misdemeanor, Civil, Eviction, Small Claims, Probate—District Court, PO Box 1106, McPherson, KS 67460. 316-355-6372, Fax: 316-241-1372. 8AM-5PM. Access by: mail, in person.

Meade

Real Estate Recording—Meade County Register of Deeds, 200 North Fowler, Courthouse, Meade, KS 67864. 317-745-9231, Fax: 316-873-8713. 8AM-5PM.

Felony, Misdemeanor, Civil, Eviction, Small Claims, Probate—Meade County District Court, PO Box 623, Meade, KS 67864. 317-747-7726, Fax: 316-873-8759. 8AM-5PM. Access by: mail, in person. Special note: All employment background checks requested by mail, phone, or fax are refered to the KBI (state agency for criminal records).

Miami

Real Estate Recording—Miami County Register of Deeds, 201 S. Pearl St. #101, Paola, KS 66071. 913-294-2353, Fax: 913-294-9515. 8AM-4:30PM.

Felony, Misdemeanor, Civil, Eviction, Small Claims, Probate—District Court, PO Box 187, Paola, KS 66071. 913-294-3326, Fax: 913-294-2535. 8AM-4:30PM. Access by: mail, in person.

Mitchell

Real Estate Recording—Mitchell County Register of Deeds, 111 South Hersey, Courthouse, Beloit, KS 67420. 913-738-3411, Fax: 785-738-5844. 8:30AM-5PM.

Felony, Misdemeanor, Civil, Eviction, Small Claims, Probate—District Court, 115 S Hersey, Beloit, KS 67420. 785-738-3753, Fax: 785-738-4101. 8AM-5PM. Access by: mail, in person.

Montgomery

Real Estate Recording—Montgomery County Register of Deeds, 5th & Main, Courthouse, Independence, KS 67301. 316-383-7707, Fax: 316-331-2619. 8:30AM-5PM.

Felony, Misdemeanor, Civil, Eviction, Small Claims, Probate—Independence District Court, PO Box 768, Independence, KS 67301. 316-383-7302, Fax: 316-331-6120. 8AM-5PM. Access by: mail, fax, in person. Special note: This court covers civil cases for the northern part of the county. It is suggested to search both courts.

Civil, Eviction, Small Claims, Probate—Coffeyville District Court, PO Box 409, Coffeyville, KS 67337. 316-357-6236, Fax: 316-251-2734. 8AM-5PM. Access by: mail, fax, in person. Special note: This court covers civil cases for the southern part of the county, although cases can be filed in either court. It is recommended to search both courts.

Morris

Real Estate Recording—Morris County Register of Deeds, Courthouse, Council Grove, KS 66846. 317-458-6491, Fax: 316-767-6861. 8AM-5PM.

Felony, Misdemeanor, Civil, Eviction, Small Claims, Probate—District Court, County Courthouse, Council Grove, KS 66846. 317-462-1109, Fax: 316-767-6488. 8AM-5PM. Access by: mail, fax, in person.

Morton

Real Estate Recording—Morton County Register of Deeds, 1025 Morton, Courthouse, Elkhart, KS 67950. 316-886-3775, Fax: 316-697-4386. 9AM-5PM.

Felony, Misdemeanor, Civil, Eviction, Small Claims, Probate—District Court, PO Box 825, Elkhart, KS 67950. 316-886-5639, Fax: 316-697-4289. 8AM-Noon, 1-5PM. Access by: mail, in person.

Nemaha

Real Estate Recording—Nemaha County Register of Deeds, 607 Nemaha, Courthouse, Seneca, KS 66538. 913-336-2106, Fax: 785-336-3373. 8AM-4:30PM.

Felony, Misdemeanor, Civil, Eviction, Small Claims, Probate—District Court, PO Box 213, Seneca, KS 66538. 785-336-2146, Fax: 785-336-6450. 8AM-5PM. Access by: mail, phone, in person.

Neosho

Real Estate Recording—Neosho County Register of Deeds, 100 Main, Courthouse, Erie, KS 66733. 316-356-1526, Fax: 316-244-3860. 8AM-4:30PM.

Felony, Misdemeanor, Civil, Eviction, Small Claims, Probate—Chanute District Court, 102 S Lincoln, PO Box 889, Chanute, KS 66720. 316-659-3132, Fax: 316-431-5710. Access by: mail, in person. Special note: This is a branch court of Erie.

Erie District Court, Neosho County Courthouse, PO Box 19, Erie, KS 66733. 316-356-1551, Fax: 316-244-3830. 8AM-4:30PM. Access by: mail, fax, in person. Special note: This is the main court for the county.

Ness

Real Estate Recording—Ness County Register of Deeds, 202 West Sycamore, Courthouse, Ness City, KS 67560., Fax: 785-798-3829. 8AM-Noon, 1PM-5PM.

Felony, Misdemeanor, Civil, Eviction, Small Claims, Probate—District Court, PO Box 445, Ness City, KS 67560. 785-798-3693, Fax: 785-798-3348. 8AM-5PM. Access by: mail, fax, in person.

Norton

Real Estate Recording—Norton County Register of Deeds, Courthouse, Norton, KS 67654. 913-877-5795, Fax: 785-877-5703. 8AM-Noon, 1-5PM.

Felony, Misdemeanor, Civil, Eviction, Small Claims, Probate—District Court, PO Box 70, Norton, KS 67654. 785-877-5720, Fax: 785-877-5722. 8AM-5PM. Access by: mail, in person.

Osage

Real Estate Recording—Osage County Register of Deeds, Courthouse, Lyndon, KS 66451. 913-828-4923, Fax: 785-828-4749. 8AM-5PM.

Felony, Misdemeanor, Civil, Eviction, Small Claims, Probate—District Court, PO Box 549, Lyndon, KS 66451. 785-828-4514, Fax: 785-828-4704. 8AM-Noon,1-5PM. Access by: mail, in person. www.kscourts.org/dstcts/4dstct.htm

Osborne

Real Estate Recording—Osborne County Register of Deeds, Courthouse, 423 W. Main, Osborne, KS 67473. 913-346-2251, Fax: 785-346-5992. 8:30AM-Noon, 1-5PM.

Felony, Misdemeanor, Civil, Eviction, Small Claims, Probate—District Court, 423 W Main, PO Box 160, Osborne, KS 67473. 785-346-5911, Fax: 785-246-5992. 8:30AM-5PM. Access by: in person.

Ottawa

Real Estate Recording—Ottawa County Register of Deeds, Courthouse - Suite 220, 307 N. Concord, Minneapolis, KS 67467. 913-392-3129. 8AM-Noon,1-5PM.

Felony, Misdemeanor, Civil, Eviction, Small Claims, Probate—District Court, 307 N Concord, Minneapolis, KS 67467. 785-392-2917. 8:30AM-5PM. Access by: mail, in person.

Pawnee

Real Estate Recording—Pawnee County Register of Deeds, Courthouse, 2nd Floor, 715 Broadway St. Larned, KS 67550. 316-374-2370, Fax: 316-285-3802. 8:30AM-5PM.

Felony, Misdemeanor, Civil, Eviction, Small Claims, Probate—District Court, PO Box 270, Larned, KS 67550. 316-375-4454, Fax: 316-285-3665. 8AM-5PM. Access by: mail, fax, in person.

Phillips

Real Estate Recording—Phillips County Register of Deeds, Courthouse, 301 State St. Phillipsburg, KS 67661. 913-543-6895. 8AM-5PM.

Felony, Misdemeanor, Civil, Eviction, Small Claims, Probate—District Court, PO Box 564, Phillipsburg, KS 67661. 785-543-6830, Fax: 785-543-6832. 8AM-5PM. Access by: in person.

Pottawatomie

Real Estate Recording—Pottawatomie County Register of Deeds, 207 N. 1st, Westmoreland, KS 66549. 913-457-3681, Fax: 785-457-3577. 8AM-4:30PM.

Felony, Misdemeanor, Civil, Eviction, Small Claims, Probate—District Court, PO Box 129, Westmoreland, KS 66549. 785-457-3392, Fax: 785-457-2107. 8AM-4:30PM. Access by: mail, fax, in person.

Pratt

Real Estate Recording—Pratt County Register of Deeds, 3rd & Ninnescah, Courthouse, Pratt, KS 67124. 316-855-3861. 8AM-Noon,1-5PM.

Felony, Misdemeanor, Civil, Eviction, Small Claims, Probate—District Court, PO Box 984, Pratt, KS 67124. 316-855-3812, Fax: 316-672-2902. 8AM-Noon, 1-5PM. Access by: mail, in person.

Rawlins

Real Estate Recording—Rawlins County Register of Deeds, 607 Main, Courthouse, Atwood, KS 67730. 913-626-3331, Fax: 785-626-9481. 9AM-Noon,1-5PM.

Felony, Misdemeanor, Civil, Eviction, Small Claims, Probate—District Court, PO Box 257, Atwood, KS 67730. 785-626-3465, Fax: 785-626-3350. 9AM-5PM. Access by: mail, fax, in person.

Reno

Real Estate Recording—Reno County Register of Deeds, 206 West First, Hutchinson, KS 67501. 316-873-8740, Fax: 316-694-2944. 8AM-5PM.

Felony, Misdemeanor, Civil, Eviction, Small Claims, Probate—District Court, 206 W 1st, Hutchinson, KS 67501. 316-873-8750, Fax: 316-694-2958. 8AM-Noon, 1-5PM. Access by: mail, in person.

Republic

Real Estate Recording—Republic County Register of Deeds, 1815 M St. Belleville, KS 66935. 785-527-5691, Fax: 785-527-2659. 8AM-5PM.

Felony, Misdemeanor, Civil, Eviction, Small Claims, Probate—District Court, PO Box 8, Belleville, KS 66935. 785-527-5691, Fax: 785-527-2714. 8:30AM-5PM. Access by: mail, in person.

Rice

Real Estate Recording—Rice County Register of Deeds, 101 West Commercial, Lyons, KS 67554. 316-364-5532, Fax: 316-257-3039. 8:30AM-5PM.

Felony, Misdemeanor, Civil, Eviction, Small Claims, Probate—District Court, 101 W Commercial, Lyons, KS 67554. 316-357-6522, Fax: 316-257-3826. 8:30AM-5PM. Access by: mail, fax, in person.

Riley

Real Estate Recording—Riley County Register of Deeds, 110 Courthouse Plaza, 5th & Humboldt Sts. Manhattan, KS 66502., Fax: 785-537-6343. 8AM-5PM.

Felony, Misdemeanor, Civil, Eviction, Small Claims, Probate—District Court, PO Box 158, Manhattan, KS 66505-0158. 785-537-6364. 8:30AM-5PM. Access by: in person. www.co.riley.ks.us/court/default.htm

Rooks

Real Estate Recording—Rooks County Register of Deeds, 115 North Walnut St. Stockton, KS 67669. 913-425-6291. 8AM-Noon,1-5PM.

Felony, Misdemeanor, Civil, Eviction, Small Claims, Probate—District Court, 115 N Walnut, PO Box 532, Stockton, KS 67669. 785-425-6718, Fax: 785-425-6568. 8AM-5PM. Access by: mail, in person.

Rush

Real Estate Recording—Rush County Register of Deeds, 715 Elm, Courthouse, La Crosse, KS 67548. 785-222-3416, Fax: 785-222-3559. 8:30AM-Noon, 1-5PM.

Felony, Misdemeanor, Civil, Eviction, Small Claims, Probate—District Court, PO Box 387, La Crosse, KS 67548. 785-222-2718, Fax: 785-222-2748. 8AM-5PM. Access by: mail, fax, in person.

Russell

Real Estate Recording—Russell County Register of Deeds, 4th & Main, Courthouse, Russell, KS 67665., Fax: 785-483-5725. 8AM-5PM.

Felony, Misdemeanor, Civil, Eviction, Small Claims, Probate—District Court, PO Box 876, Russell, KS 67665. 785-483-5641, Fax: 785-483-2448. 8AM-5PM. Access by: mail, fax, in person.

Saline

Real Estate Recording—Saline County Register of Deeds, 300 West Ash, City County Building, Room 212, Salina, KS 67401. 913-826-6545, Fax: 785-826-6629. 8AM-5PM.

Felony, Misdemeanor, Civil, Eviction, Small Claims, Probate—District Court, PO Box 1756, Salina, KS 67402-1756. 785-826-6617, Fax: 785-826-7319. 8:30AM-4PM. Access by: mail, in person.

Scott

Real Estate Recording—Scott County Register of Deeds, Courthouse, 303 Court St. Scott City, KS 67871. 317-736-3711, Fax: 316-872-7145. 8AM-5PM.

Felony, Misdemeanor, Civil, Eviction, Small Claims, Probate—District Court, 303 Court, Scott City, KS 67871. 317-745-9220. 8AM-Noon, 1-5PM. Access by: mail, in person.

Sedgwick

Real Estate Recording—Sedgwick County Register of Deeds, 525 North Main, 4th Floor/ Room 415, Wichita, KS 67203. 316-625-8610, Fax: 316-383-8066. 8AM-5PM.

Felony, Misdemeanor, Civil, Eviction, Small Claims, Probate—District Court, 525 N Main, Wichita, KS 67203. 316-583-8153, Fax: 316-383-8070. 8AM-5PM. Access by: mail, phone, fax, in person, online.

Seward

Real Estate Recording—Seward County Register of Deeds, 415 North Washington, Courthouse, Suite 105, Liberal, KS 67901. 316-767-6838, Fax: 316-626-5031. 8AM-5PM.

Felony, Misdemeanor, Civil, Eviction, Small Claims, Probate—District Court, 415 N Washington #103, Liberal, KS 67901. 316-793-1827, Fax: 316-626-3302. 8:30AM-5PM. Access by: in person. Special note: Court will do searches on occasion, fee is $10.80 per hour.

Shawnee

Real Estate Recording—Shawnee County Register of Deeds, 200 East 7th Street, Suite 108, Topeka, KS 66603. 913-233-8200, Fax: 785-291-4912. 8AM-4:30PM.

Felony, Misdemeanor, Civil, Eviction, Small Claims, Probate—District Court, 200 E 7th Rm 209, Topeka, KS 66603. 785-233-8200, Fax: 785-291-4911. 8:30AM-5PM. Access by: mail, fax, in person.

Sheridan

Real Estate Recording—Sheridan County Register of Deeds, 925 9th Street, Courthouse, Hoxie, KS 67740. 913-675-3622, Fax: 785-675-3050. 8AM-Noon,1-5PM.

Felony, Misdemeanor, Civil, Eviction, Small Claims, Probate—District Court, PO Box 753, Hoxie, KS 67740. 785-675-3451, Fax: 785-675-2256. 8:30AM-5PM. Access by: mail, phone, fax, in person.

Sherman

Real Estate Recording—Sherman County Register of Deeds, 813 Broadway, Room 104, Goodland, KS 67735. 913-899-4810, Fax: 785-899-4848. 7AM-Noon,1-4PM.

Felony, Misdemeanor, Civil, Eviction, Small Claims, Probate—District Court, 813 Broadway Rm 201, Goodland, KS 67735. 785-899-4850, Fax: 785-899-4858. 8:30AM-5PM. Access by: in person.

Smith

Real Estate Recording—Smith County Register of Deeds, 218 South Grant, Smith Center, KS 66967. 913-282-5170, Fax: 785-282-6257. 8AM-Noon, 1-5PM.

Felony, Misdemeanor, Civil, Eviction, Small Claims, Probate—District Court, PO Box 273, Smith Center, KS 66967. 785-282-5140, Fax: 785-282-5145. 8:30AM-5PM. Access by: mail, in person.

Stafford

Real Estate Recording—Stafford County Register of Deeds, 209 North Broadway, Stafford County Courthouse, St. John, KS 67576. 8AM-Noon,1-5PM.

Felony, Misdemeanor, Civil, Eviction, Small Claims, Probate—District Court, PO Box 365, St John, KS 67576. 316-697-2563, Fax: 316-549-3298. 8AM-5PM. Access by: mail, in person.

Stanton

Real Estate Recording—Stanton County Register of Deeds, 201 North Main, Courthouse, Johnson, KS 67855. 316-672-4118, Fax: 316-492-2688. 8:30AM-Noon, 1-5PM.

Felony, Misdemeanor, Civil, Eviction, Small Claims, Probate—District Court, PO Box 913, Johnson, KS 67855. 316-675-2265, Fax: 316-492-6410. 8AM-5PM. Access by: mail, phone, fax, in person.

Stevens

Real Estate Recording—Stevens County Register of Deeds, 200 East 6th, Hugoton, KS 67951. 316-697-2560, Fax: 316-544-4081. 9AM-5PM.

Felony, Misdemeanor, Civil, Eviction, Small Claims, Probate—District Court, 200 E 6th, Hugoton, KS 67951. 316-694-2956, Fax: 316-544-2528. 8AM-5PM. Access by: mail, in person.

Sumner

Real Estate Recording—Sumner County Register of Deeds, 500 Block North Washington, Suite 103, Wellington, KS 67152. 316-378-4533, Fax: 316-326-8172. 8AM-5PM.

Felony, Misdemeanor, Civil, Eviction, Small Claims, Probate—District Court, PO Box 399, Sumner County Courthouse, Wellington, KS 67152. 316-382-2104, Fax: 316-326-5365. 8AM-Noon, 1-5PM. Access by: mail, in person.

Thomas

Real Estate Recording—Thomas County Register of Deeds, 300 North Court, Colby, KS 67701. 913-462-4520, Fax: 785-462-4512. 8AM-Noon, 1PM-5PM.

Felony, Misdemeanor, Civil, Eviction, Small Claims, Probate—District Court, PO Box 805, Colby, KS 67701. 785-462-4540, Fax: 785-462-2291. 8:30AM-5PM. Access by: mail, in person.

Trego

Real Estate Recording—Trego County Register of Deeds, 216 Main, WaKeeney, KS 67672. 913-743-2001, Fax: 785-743-2461. 8:30AM-5PM.

Felony, Misdemeanor, Civil, Eviction, Small Claims, Probate—District Court, 216 N Main, Wakeeney, KS 67672. 785-743-2148, Fax: 785-743-2726. 8:30AM-5PM. Access by: mail, in person.

Wabaunsee

Real Estate Recording—Wabaunsee County Register of Deeds, 215 Kansas Avenue, Courthouse, Alma, KS 66401., Fax: 785-765-3992. 8AM-4:30PM.

Felony, Misdemeanor, Civil, Eviction, Small Claims, Probate—District Court, Courthouse, Alma, KS 66401. 785-765-2406, Fax: 785-765-2487. 8:30AM-4:30PM. Access by: in person.

Wallace

Real Estate Recording—Wallace County Register of Deeds, 313 North Main, Courthouse, Sharon Springs, KS 67758. 913-852-4281, Fax: 785-852-4783. 8AM-Noon, 1-5PM.

Felony, Misdemeanor, Civil, Eviction, Small Claims, Probate—District Court, PO Box 8, Sharon Springs, KS 67758. 785-852-4289, Fax: 785-852-4271. 8AM-Noon,1-5PM. Access by: mail, in person.

Washington

Real Estate Recording—Washington County Register of Deeds, 214 C Street, Courthouse, Washington, KS 66968. 913-325-2461, Fax: 785-325-2830. 8AM-5PM.

Felony, Misdemeanor, Civil, Eviction, Small Claims, Probate—District Court, Courthouse, 214 C Street, Washington, KS 66968. 785-325-2381, Fax: 785-325-2557. 8AM-Noon,1-5PM. Access by: mail, fax, in person.

Wichita

Real Estate Recording—Wichita County Register of Deeds, Courthouse, 206 S. 4th, Leoti, KS 67861., Fax: 316-375-4350. 8AM-Noon,1-5PM.

Felony, Misdemeanor, Civil, Eviction, Small Claims, Probate—District Court, 206 S 4th St, PO Box 968, Leoti, KS 67861. 316-544-2542, Fax: 316-375-2999. 8AM-5PM. Access by: mail, in person. Special note: The District Court for the Wichita, KS is in Sedgwick County.

Wilson

Real Estate Recording—Wilson County Register of Deeds, Courthouse, Room 106, Fredonia, KS 66736., Fax: 316-378-3841. 8:30AM-5PM.

Felony, Misdemeanor, Civil, Eviction, Small Claims, Probate—District Court, PO Box 246, Fredonia, KS 66736. 316-582-2964, Fax: 316-378-4531. 8:30AM-5PM. Access by: mail, fax, in person.

Woodson

Real Estate Recording—Woodson County Register of Deeds, 105 W. Rutledge, Room 101, Yates Center, KS 66783. 316-767-5614, Fax: 316-625-8670. 8AM-Noon,1-5PM.

Felony, Misdemeanor, Civil, Eviction, Small Claims, Probate—District Court, PO Box 228, Yates Center, KS 66783. 316-725-5870, Fax: 316-625-8674. 8AM-Noon,1-5PM. Access by: mail, fax, in person.

Wyandotte

Real Estate Recording—Wyandotte County Register of Deeds, Courthouse, 710 N. 7th St. Kansas City, KS 66101., Fax: 913-321-3075. 7:30AM-5:30PM.

Felony, Misdemeanor, Civil, Eviction, Small Claims, Probate—District Court, 710 N 7th St, Kansas City, KS 66101., Fax: 913-573-4134. 8AM-5PM. Access by: mail, phone, in person, online.

Federal Courts

US District Court

Kansas City Division Clerk, 500 State Ave, Kansas City, KS 66101913-551-6719 Counties: Atchison, Bourbon, Brown, Cherokee, Crawford, Doniphan, Johnson, Labette, Leavenworth, Linn, Marshall, Miami, Nemaha, Wyandotte. www.ksd.uscourts.gov

Topeka Division Clerk, US District Court, Room 490, 444 SE Quincy, Topeka, KS 66683785-295-2610 Counties: Allen, Anderson, Chase, Clay, Cloud, Coffey, Dickinson, Douglas, Franklin, Geary, Jackson, Jewell, Lincoln, Lyon, Marion, Mitchell, Morris, Neosho, Osage, Ottawa, Pottawatomie, Republic, Riley, Saline, Shawnee, Wabaunsee, Washington, Wilson, Woodson. www.ksd.uscourts.gov

Wichita Division 204 US Courthouse, 401 N Market, Wichita, KS 67202-2096316-269-6491 Counties: All counties in Kansas. Cases may be heard from counties in the other division.

US Bankruptcy Court

Kansas City Division 500 State Ave, Room 161, Kansas City, KS 66101913-551-6732 Counties: Atchison, Bourbon, Brown, Cherokee, Comanche, Crawford, Doniphan, Johnson, Labette, Leavenworth, Linn, Marshall, Miami, Nemaha, Wyandotte. www.ksb.uscourts.gov

Topeka Division 240 Federal Bldg, 444 SE Quincy, Topeka, KS 66683785-295-2750 Counties: Allen, Anderson, Chase, Clay, Cloud, Coffey, Dickinson, Douglas, Franklin, Geary, Jackson, Jewell, Lincoln, Lyon, Marion, Mitchell, Morris, Neosho, Osage, Ottawa, Pottawatomie, Republic, Riley, Saline, Shawnee, Wabaunsee, Washington, Wilson, Woodson. www.ksb.uscourts.gov

Wichita Division 167 US Courthouse, 401 N Market, Wichita, KS 67202316-269-6486 Counties: Barber, Barton, Butler, Chautauqua, Cheyenne, Clark, Comanche, Cowley, Decatur, Edwards, Elk, Ellis, Ellsworth, Finney, Ford, Gove, Graham, Grant, Gray, Greeley, Greenwood, Hamilton, Harper, Harvey, Haskell, Hodgeman, Jefferson, Kearny, Kingman, Kiowa,Lane, Logan, Mcpherson, Meade, Montgomery, Morton, Ness, Norton, Osborne, Pawnee, Phillips, Pratt, Rawlins, Reno, Rice, Rooks, Rush, Russell, Scott, Sedgwick, Seward, Sheridan, Smith, Stafford, Stanton, Stevens, Sumner, Thomas, Trego, Wallace, Wichita. www.ksb.uscourts.gov

Kentucky

Attorney General's Office
700 Capitol Ave # 118   502-696-5300
Frankfort, KY 40601   Fax: 502-573-8317
www.law.state.ky.us

Governor's Office
700 Capitol Ave, Room 100   502-564-2611
Frankfort, KY 40601   Fax: 502-564-2517
www.state.ky.us/agencies/gov/govmenu6.htm

State Archives
300 Coffee Tree Rd   502-564-8300
Frankfort, KY 40601   Fax: 502-564-5773
www.kdla.state.ky.us

Capital: Frankfort
                                        Franklin County

Time Zone: EST*
    Kentucky's forty western-most counties are CST:
    They are: Adair, Allen, Ballard, Barren, Breckinridge,
    Butler, Caldwell, Calloway, Carlisle, Christian, Clinton,
    Crittenden, Cumberland, Daviess, Edmonson, Fulton,
    Graves, Grayson, Hancock, Hart, Henderson, Hickman,
    Hopkins, Livingstone, Logan, Marshall, McCracken,
    McLean, Metcalfe, Monroe, Muhlenberg, Ohio, Russell,
    Simpson, Todd, Trigg, Union, Warren, Wayne, Webster.

Number of Counties: 120

Population: 3,908.124

Web Site: www.state.ky.us

Search Unclaimed Property Online
    http://kydisweb1.state.ky.us/
    treasury/search.htm

State Agencies

Criminal Records
Kentucky State Police, Records Section, 1250 Louisville Rd, Frankfort, KY 40601; 502-227-8713; Fax: 502-227-8734; 8AM-4PM. Access by: mail.

Corporation Records
Limited Partnerships
Assumed Name
Limited Liability Company Records
Secretary of State, Corporate Records, PO Box 718, Frankfort, KY 40602-0718 (700 Capitol Ave, Room 156, Frankfort, KY 40601); 502-564-7330; Fax: 502-564-4075; 8AM-4PM. Access by: mail, phone, in person, online. www.sos.state.ky.us

Sales Tax Registrations

Revenue Cabinet, Tax Compliance Department, Sales Tax Section, Station 53, PO Box 181, Frankfort, KY 40602-0181 (200 Fair Oaks, Bldg 2, Frankfort, KY 40602); 502-564-5170; Fax: 502-564-2041; 8AM-4:30PM. Access by: mail, phone, in person. www.state.ky.us/agencies/revenue/revhome.htm

Trademarks/Servicemarks

Secretary of State, Legal Department, 700 Capitol Ave, Room 86, Frankfort, KY 40601; 502-564-7330; Fax: 502-564-4075; 8AM-4:30PM. Access by: mail. www.sos.state.ky.us

Uniform Commercial Code

UCC Division, Secretary of State, PO Box 718, Frankfort, KY 40602-0718 (State Capitol Bldg, Rm 79, Frankfort, KY 40601); 502-564-2848 x401; Fax: 502-564-4075; 8AM-4:30PM. www.sos.state.ky.us

Federal Tax Liens
State Tax Liens

Records not available from state agency.

All tax liens are at the county level.

Workers' Compensation Records

Kentucky Department of Workers' Claims, Perimeter Park West, 1270 Louisville Rd, Bldg C, Frankfort, KY 40601; 502-564-5550; Fax: 502-564-5732; 8AM-4:30PM. Access by: mail. www.state.ky/us/agencies/labor/wkrclaims.htm

Birth Certificates

Department for Public Health, Vital Statistics, 275 E Main St - IE-A, Frankfort, KY 40621-0001; 502-564-4212; Fax: 502-227-0032; 8AM-4PM. Access by: mail, phone, in person.

Death Records

Department for Public Health, Vital Statistics, 275 E Main St - IE-A, Frankfort, KY 40621-0001; 502-564-4212; Fax: 502-227-0032; 8AM-3PM. Access by: mail, phone, in person.

Marriage Certificates

Department for Public Health, Vital Statistics, 275 E Main St - IE-A, Frankfort, KY 40621-0001; 502-564-4212; Fax: 502-227-0032; 8AM-3PM. Access by: mail, phone, in person.

Divorce Records

Department for Public Health, Vital Statistics, 275 E Main St - IE-A, Frankfort, KY 40621-0001; 502-564-4212; Fax: 502-227-0032; 8AM-3PM. Access by: mail, phone, in person.

Accident Reports

Department of State Police, Records Section, 1250 Louisville Rd, Frankfort, KY 40601; 502-227-8700; Fax: 502-227-8734; 7:30AM-4:30PM. Access by: mail.

Driver Records

Division of Driver Licensing, State Office Bldg, MVRS, 501 High Street, 2nd Floor, Frankfort, KY 40622; 502-564-6800 x2250; Fax: 502-564-5787; 8AM-4:30PM. Access by: mail, online.

Vehicle Ownership
Vehicle Identification

Department of Motor Vehicles, Division of Motor Vehicle Licensing, State Office Bldg, 3rd Floor, Frankfort, KY 40622; 502-564-4076 Title History, 502-564-3298 Other Requests; Fax: 502-564-1686; 8AM-4:30PM. Access by: mail, online. www.kytc.state.ky.us/drlic/drlic.htm

Boat & Vessel Ownership
Boat & Vessel Registration

Division of Motor Vehicle Licensing, Vessel Titles and Registration, State Office Building, 3rd Floor, Frankfort, KY 40622; 502-564-5301; 8AM-5PM. Access by: mail. www.kytc.state.ky.us

Legislation-Current/Pending
Legislation-Passed

Kentucky General Assembly, Legislative Research Commission, 700 Capitol Ave, Room 300, Frankfort, KY 40601; 502-372-7181 Bill Status Only, 502-564-8100 x323 Bill Room, 502-564-8100 LRC Library; Fax: 502-223-5094; 8AM-4:30PM. Access by: mail, phone, in person, online. www.lrc.state.ky.us

Voter Registration

State Board of Elections, 140 Walnut, Frankfort, KY 40601; 502-573-7100; Fax: 502-573-4369; 8AM-4:30PM. www.state.ky.us/agencies/sbe/sbehome.htm

GED Certificates

Adult Education and Literacy, GED Program, Capitol Plaze Tower, 500 Mero St Rm 335, Frankfort, KY 40601; 502-564-5117; Fax: 502-564-5436;. www.state.ky.us/agencies/wforce/welcome.htm

Hunting License Information
Fishing License Information

Fish & Wildlife Resources Department, Division of Administrative Services, 1 Game Farm Rd, Arnold Mitchell Bldg, Frankfort, KY 40601; 502-564-4224; Fax: 502-564-6508; 8AM-4:30PM. Access by: mail. www.state.ky.us/agencies/fw/kdfwr.htm

County Courts & Recording Offices

About the Courts...

Administration

Administrative Office of Courts
100 Mill Creek Park
Frankfort, KY 40601
http://162.114.175.231

502-573-2350
Fax: 502-573-1448

Court Structure

Searching Hints

Until 1978, county judges handled all cases; therefore, in many cases, District and Circuit Court records go back only to 1978. Records prior to that time are archived.

Online Access

A statewide, online computer system called SUSTAIN is available for internal judicial/state agency use only.

About the Recording Offices...

Organization

120 counties, 122 recording offices. The recording officer is County Clerk. Jefferson and Kenton Counties each have two recording offices. See the notes under each county for how to determine which office is appropriate to search. 80 counties are in the Eastern Time Zone (EST) and 40 are in the Central Time Zone (CST)

UCC Records

Financing statements are filed with the County Clerk, except for non-resident debtors, which are filed at the state level. Many counties will not perform UCC searches. Use search request form UCC-11. Search fees are usually $5 per debtor name, and copy fees vary widely.

Lien Records

All federal and state tax liens on personal property are filed with the County Clerk, often in an "Encumbrance Book." Most counties will not perform tax lien searches.

Real Estate Records

Most counties will not perform real estate searches. Copy fees vary. Certification fee is usually $5 per document. Tax records are maintained by the Property Valuation Administrator, designated "Assessor" in this section.

County Courts & Recording Offices

Adair

Real Estate Recording—Adair County Clerk, 424 Public Square, Columbia, KY 42728., Fax: 270-384-4805. 7:30AM-4PM.

Felony, Misdemeanor, Civil, Eviction, Small Claims, Probate—Circuit and District Court, 500 Public Square, Columbia, KY 42728. 270-524-9474, Fax: 270-384-4299. 8AM-4PM. Access by: mail, in person.

Allen

Real Estate Recording—Allen County Clerk, 201 West Main Street, Room 6, Scottsville, KY 42164., Fax: 270-237-9206. 8:30AM-4:30PM, 8:30AM-Noon Sat.

Felony, Misdemeanor, Civil, Eviction, Small Claims, Probate—Circuit and District Court, Box 477, Scottsville, KY 42164. 270-298-3671. 8AM-3:30PM. Access by: in person.

Anderson

Real Estate Recording—Anderson County Clerk, 151 South Main, Lawrenceburg, KY 40342., Fax: 502-839-3043. 8:30AM-5PM M-Th; 8:30AM-6PM F.

Felony, Civil Actions Over $4,000—Circuit Court, Courthouse 151 S Main St, Lawrenceburg, KY 40342. 502-839-3508. 8:30AM-5PM. Access by: in person.

Misdemeanor, Civil Actions Under $4,000, Eviction, Small Claims, Probate—District Court, 151 S Main, Lawrenceburg, KY 40342. 502-839-5445. 8:30AM-5PM M-TH, 8:30AM-6PM F. Access by: mail, in person.

Ballard

Real Estate Recording—Ballard County Clerk, Court Street, Courthouse, Wickliffe, KY 42087. 270-388-7193, Fax: 270-335-3081. 8AM-4PM M-F; 8AM-5:30PM Last Friday of month.

Felony, Misdemeanor, Civil, Eviction, Small Claims, Probate—Circuit and District Court, Box 265, Wickliffe, KY 42087. 270-384-2626, Fax: 270-335-3849. 8AM-4PM. Access by: mail, in person.

Barren

Real Estate Recording—Barren County Clerk, 924 Happy Valley Rd. Suite A, Glasgow, KY 42141., Fax: 270-651-1083. 8AM-4:30AM.

Felony, Misdemeanor, Civil, Eviction, Small Claims, Probate—Circuit and District Court, PO Box 1359, Glasgow, KY 42142-1359., Fax: 270-651-6203. 8AM-4:30PM. Access by: in person.

Bath

Real Estate Recording—Bath County Clerk, Courthouse, 17 Main St. Suite 1, Owingsville, KY 40360., Fax: 606-674-2613. 8AM-4PM; 8AM-Noon Sat.

Felony, Misdemeanor, Civil, Eviction, Small Claims, Probate—Circuit and District Court, Box 558, Owingsville, KY 40360. 606-674-2186, Fax: 606-674-3996. 8AM-4PM. Access by: mail, in person.

Bell

Real Estate Recording—Bell County Clerk, Courthouse Square, Pineville, KY 40977. 606-337-2497, Fax: 606-337-5415. 8AM-4PM M-F; 8AM-Noon Sat.

Felony, Misdemeanor, Civil, Eviction, Small Claims, Probate—Circuit and District Court, Box 306, Pineville, KY 40977. 606-337-2942, Fax: 606-337-8850. 8:30AM-4PM. Access by: mail, phone, in person.

Boone

Real Estate Recording—Boone County Clerk, 2950 East Washington Square, Burlington, KY 41005. 606-334-2150, Fax: 606-334-2193. 8:30AM-4:30PM M, W-F; 8:30AM-6PM T.

Felony, Misdemeanor, Civil, Eviction, Small Claims, Probate—Circuit and District Court, Box 480, Burlington, KY 41005. 606-334-2149, Fax: 606-586-9413. 8:30AM-5:30PM. Access by: mail, in person.

Bourbon

Real Estate Recording—Bourbon County Clerk, Main Street, Courthouse, Paris, KY 40361., Fax: 606-987-5660. 8:30AM-4:30PM M-Th; 8:30AM-6PM F.

Felony, Misdemeanor, Civil, Eviction, Small Claims, Probate—Circuit and District Court, Box 740, Paris, KY 40361. 606-987-2624. 8:30AM-4PM M-TH, 8:30AM-6PM F. Access by: in person.

Boyd

Real Estate Recording—Boyd County Clerk, 2800 Louisa Street, Courthouse, Catlettsburg, KY 41129. 606-739-4242, Fax: 606-739-6357. 8:30AM-4PM Main Office (9AM-4:30PM & 9AM-Noon Sat Branch Office).

Felony, Misdemeanor, Civil, Eviction, Small Claims, Probate—Circuit and District Court, Box 694, Catlettsburg, KY 41129-0694. 606-739-4131, Fax: 606-739-5793. 8:30AM-4PM. Access by: in person.

Boyle

Real Estate Recording—Boyle County Clerk, 321 W. Main St. Room 123, Danville, KY 40422. 606-238-1118, Fax: 606-238-1114. 8:30AM-5PM M; 8:30AM-4PM T-F.

Felony, Civil Actions Over $4,000—Circuit Court, Courthouse, Main St, Danville, KY 40422. 606-236-7442, Fax: 606-238-1114. 8AM-5PM. Access by: mail, phone, in person.

Misdemeanor, Civil Actions Under $4,000, Eviction, Small Claims, Probate—District Court, Courthouse, 3rd Floor, Danville, KY 40422. 606-239-7362, Fax: 606-236-9807. 8AM-4:30PM. Access by: mail, in person.

Bracken

Real Estate Recording—Bracken County Clerk, Courthouse, Brooksville, KY 41004. 606-735-2228, Fax: 606-735-2925. 9AM-4PM M,T,Th,F; 9AM-Noon W,Sat.

Felony, Misdemeanor, Civil, Eviction, Small Claims, Probate—Circuit and District Court, Box 132 Courthouse, Brooksville, KY 41004. 606-735-3328, Fax: 606-735-3900. 9AM-4PM M,T,TH,F, 9AM-Noon W & Sat. Access by: mail, in person.

Breathitt

Real Estate Recording—Breathitt County Clerk, 1137 Main Street, Jackson, KY 41339., Fax: 606-666-3807. 8:30AM-4PM M,T,Th,F; 8:30AM-Noon W; 9AM-Noon Sat.

Felony, Misdemeanor, Civil, Eviction, Small Claims, Probate—Circuit and District Court, 1137 Main St, Jackson, KY 41339. 606-666-5768, Fax: 606-666-4893. 8AM-4PM M,T,TH,F; 8AM-Noon W; 9AM-Noon Sat. Access by: mail, phone, in person.

Breckinridge

Real Estate Recording—Breckinridge County Clerk, Main St. Hardinsburg, KY 40143. 270-932-4024, Fax: 270-756-1569. 8AM-4PM, 8AM-Noon Sat.

Felony, Misdemeanor, Civil, Eviction, Small Claims, Probate—Circuit and District Court, Box 111, Hardinsburg, KY 40143. 270-928-2172, Fax: 270-756-1129. 8AM-4PM. Access by: in person.

Bullitt

Real Estate Recording—Bullitt County Clerk, Courthouse Annex, 149 N. Walnut St. Shepherdsville, KY 40165., Fax: 502-543-9121. 8AM-4PM M,T,W,F; 8AM-6PM Th.

Felony, Misdemeanor, Civil, Eviction, Small Claims, Probate—Circuit and District Court, Box 746, Shephardsville, KY

40165. 502-543-7104, Fax: 502-543-7158. 8AM-4PM. Access by: mail, fax, in person.

Butler

Real Estate Recording—Butler County Clerk, Courthouse, Morgantown, KY 42261., Fax: 270-526-2658. 8AM-4:30PM.

Felony, Misdemeanor, Civil, Eviction, Small Claims, Probate—Circuit and District Court, Box 625, Morgantown, KY 42261. 270-687-7222. 8AM-4PM M-F; 8AM-Noon Sat. Access by: mail, in person.

Caldwell

Real Estate Recording—Caldwell County Clerk, 100 East Market Street, Courthouse - Room 3, Princeton, KY 42445. 270-524-5181, Fax: 270-365-7447. 8AM-4PM.

Felony, Misdemeanor, Civil, Eviction, Small Claims, Probate—Circuit and District Court, 105 West Court Sq, Princeton, KY 42445. 270-522-6270, Fax: 270-365-9171. 8AM-4PM. Access by: fax, in person.

Calloway

Real Estate Recording—Calloway County Clerk, 101 South 5th Street, Murray, KY 42071., Fax: 270-759-9611. 8AM-4:30PM.

Felony, Misdemeanor, Civil, Eviction, Small Claims, Probate—Circuit and District Court, 312 N 4th St, Murray, KY 42071. 270-927-8144, Fax: 270-759-9822. 8AM-4:30PM. Access by: mail, in person.

Campbell

Real Estate Recording—Campbell County Clerk, 4th and York Streets, Courthouse, Newport, KY 41071. 606-292-3838, Fax: 606-292-3887. 8:30AM-6PM M; 8:30AM-4PM T-F; 9AM-Noon Sat.

Felony, Civil Actions Over $4,000—Circuit Court, 330 York St Rm 8, Newport, KY 41071. 606-292-6314, Fax: 606-431-0816. 8:30AM-4PM. Access by: in person.

Misdemeanor, Civil Actions Under $4,000, Eviction, Small Claims, Probate—District Court, 600 Columbia St, Newport, KY 41071-1816. 606-292-6305, Fax: 606-292-6593. 8:30AM-4PM. Access by: mail, in person.

Carlisle

Real Estate Recording—Carlisle County Clerk, West Court Street, Bardwell, KY 42023. 270-746-7400, Fax: 270-628-0191. 8:30AM-4PM.

Felony, Misdemeanor, Civil, Eviction, Small Claims, Probate—Circuit and District Court, Box 337, Bardwell, KY 42023. 270-753-2714, Fax: 270-628-5456. 8AM-4PM. Access by: mail, phone, in person.

Carroll

Real Estate Recording—Carroll County Clerk, 440 Main Street, Court House, Carrollton, KY 41008. 502-732-7007, Fax: 502-732-7007. 8:30AM-4:30PM M,T,Th,F; 8:30AM-Noon W,Sat.

Felony, Misdemeanor, Civil, Eviction, Small Claims, Probate—Circuit and District Court, 802 Clay St, Carrollton, KY 41008. 502-732-4305. 8:30AM-4:30PM. Access by: mail, phone, in person.

Carter

Real Estate Recording—Carter County Clerk, 300 W. Main St. Room 232, Grayson, KY 41143. 606-474-9551, Fax: 606-474-6883. 8:30AM-4PM; 8:30AM-Noon Sat.

Felony, Civil Actions Over $4,000—Circuit Court, 300 W Main St, Rm 308, Grayson, KY 41143. 606-474-5191, Fax: 606-474-8826. 8:30AM-4PM M-F; 9AM-Noon Sat. Access by: mail, in person.

Misdemeanor, Civil Actions Under $4,000, Eviction, Small Claims, Probate—District Court, Courthouse, Rm 203, 300 West Main, Grayson, KY 41143. 606-474-6572, Fax: 606-474-8826. 8:30AM-4PM. Access by: mail, in person.

Casey

Real Estate Recording—Casey County Clerk, 614 Campbellsville St. Liberty, KY 42539., Fax: 606-787-9155. 8AM-4:30PM M-F; 8AM-Noon Sat.

Felony, Misdemeanor, Civil, Eviction, Small Claims, Probate—Circuit and District Court, Box 147, Liberty, KY 42539. 606-787-6510. 8AM-4:30PM M-W, 8AM-4PM TH, 8AM-Noon Sat. Access by: mail, in person.

Christian

Real Estate Recording—Christian County Clerk, 511 South Main, Hopkinsville, KY 42240. 8AM-4:30PM.

Felony, Misdemeanor, Civil, Eviction, Small Claims, Probate—Circuit and District Court, 511 S Main St Rm 301, Hopkinsville, KY 42240-2368. 301-334-1937, Fax: 270-889-6564. 8AM-4:30PM. Access by: mail, in person.

Clark

Real Estate Recording—Clark County Clerk, 34 South Main Street, Winchester, KY 40391. 606-745-0200, Fax: 606-745-4251. 8AM-5PM M; 8AM-4PM T-F.

Felony, Civil Actions Over $4,000—Circuit Court, Box 687, Winchester, KY 40392. 606-737-7264. 8AM-4PM. Access by: mail, in person.

Misdemeanor, Civil Actions Under $4,000, Eviction, Small Claims, Probate—District Court, PO Box 687, Winchester, KY 40392-0687. 606-737-7264. 8AM-4PM. Access by: mail, in person.

Clay

Real Estate Recording—Clay County Clerk, 316 Main Street, Suite 143, Manchester, KY 40962. 606-598-2071, Fax: 606-598-7199. 8AM-4PM; 8AM-Noon Sat.

Felony, Misdemeanor, Civil, Eviction, Small Claims, Probate—Circuit and District Court, 316 Main Street, #108, Manchester, KY 40962. 606-598-3663, Fax: 606-598-4047. 8AM-4PM. Access by: mail, in person.

Clinton

Real Estate Recording—Clinton County Clerk, 212 Washington Street, Courthouse, Albany, KY 42602. 606-387-5234, Fax: 606-387-5258. 8AM-4:30PM; 8AM-Noon Sat.

Felony, Misdemeanor, Civil, Eviction, Small Claims, Probate—Circuit and District Court, Courthouse 2nd Fl, Albany, KY 42602. 606-387-6424, Fax: 606-387-8154. 8AM-4PM M-F; 8AM-Noon Sat. Access by: mail, in person.

Crittenden

Real Estate Recording—Crittenden County Clerk, 107 South Main, Courthouse, Suite 203, Marion, KY 42064., Fax: 270-965-3447. 8AM-4:30PM M,T,Th,F; 8AM-Noon W,Sat.

Felony, Misdemeanor, Civil, Eviction, Small Claims, Probate—Circuit and District Court, 107 S Main, Marion, KY 42064. 301-475-5566. 8AM-4:30PM. Access by: mail, in person.

Cumberland

Real Estate Recording—Cumberland County Clerk, Courthouse - Public Square, Room 6, Burkesville, KY 42717. 301-217-7150, Fax: 270-864-5884. 8AM-4:30PM; 8AM-Noon Sat.

Felony, Misdemeanor, Civil, Eviction, Small Claims, Probate—Circuit and District Court, Box 395, Burkesville, KY 42717. 301-217-1070. 8AM-4PM. Access by: mail, in person.

Daviess

Real Estate Recording—Daviess County Clerk, 212 St. Ann Street, Owensboro, KY 42303. 270-766-5000, Fax: 270-685-2431. 8AM-4PM M-Th; 8AM-6PM F.

Felony, Misdemeanor, Civil, Eviction, Small Claims, Probate—Circuit and District Court, Box 277, Owensboro, KY 42302. 270-824-7502. 8AM-4PM. Access by: in person.

Edmonson

Real Estate Recording—Edmonson County Clerk, 108 Main Street, Community Center, Brownsville, KY 42210., Fax: 270-597-9714. 8AM-5PM M,T,W,F; 8AM-Noon Sat.

Felony, Misdemeanor, Civil, Eviction, Small Claims, Probate—Circuit and District Court, Box 130, Brownsville, KY 42210. 270-726-3107, Fax: 502-597-2884. 8AM-5PM M-W,F; 8AM-Noon Sat. Access by: in person.

Elliott

Real Estate Recording—Elliott County Clerk, Main Street, Courthouse, Sandy Hook, KY 41171. 606-738-5821, Fax: 606-738-4462. 8AM-4PM; 9AM-Noon Sat.

Felony, Misdemeanor, Civil, Eviction, Small Claims, Probate—Circuit and District Court, Box 788, Sandy Hook, KY 41171. 606-738-5238, Fax: 606-738-6962. 8AM-4PM M-F; 9AM-Noon Sat. Access by: mail, phone, in person.

Estill

Real Estate Recording—Estill County Clerk, Courthouse, Irvine, KY 40336., Fax: 606-723-5108. 8AM-4PM M,T,Th,F; 8AM-Noon W,Sat.

Felony, Misdemeanor, Civil, Eviction, Small Claims, Probate—Circuit and District Court, Courthouse 2nd Fl, Irvine, KY 40336. 606-723-3970, Fax: 606-723-1158. 8AM-4PM. Access by: mail, phone, fax, in person.

Fayette

Real Estate Recording—Fayette County Clerk, 162 East Main Street, Lexington, KY 40507. 606-258-3300. 8AM-4:30PM.

Felony, Civil Actions Over $4,000—Circuit Court-Criminal and Civil Divisions, 215 W Main (Civil-Rm 200), Lexington, KY 40507. 8:30AM-4:30PM. Access by: mail, in person.

Misdemeanor, Civil Actions Under $4,000, Eviction, Small Claims, Probate—District Court-Criminal and Civil, 140 N ML King Blvd (Criminal), 136 N ML King Blvd (Civil), Lexington, KY 40507. 8AM-4PM. Access by: mail, in person.

Fleming

Real Estate Recording—Fleming County Clerk, Court Square, Flemingsburg, KY 41041. 606-845-8801, Fax: 606-845-0212. 8:30AM-4:30PM M-F; 8:30AM-Noon Sat.

Felony, Misdemeanor, Civil, Eviction, Small Claims, Probate—Circuit and District Court, Courthouse 100 Court Square, Flemingsburg, KY 41041. 606-845-7011, Fax: 606-849-2400. 8AM-4:30PM M-F, 8:30AM-Noon Sat. Access by: mail, phone, fax, in person.

Floyd

Real Estate Recording—Floyd County Clerk, Courthouse Room 1, 149 S. Central, Prestonsburg, KY 41653., Fax: 606-886-8089. 8AM-4:30PM M,T,W,Th; 8AM-6PM F;9AM-Noon Sat.

Felony, Civil Actions Over $4,000—Circuit Court, 127 S Lake Dr, Prestonsburg, KY 41653-1914. 606-886-3090, Fax: 606-886-9075. 8AM-4PM. Access by: mail, in person.

Misdemeanor, Small Claims—District Court, 127 S Lake Dr, Prestonsburg, KY 41653-1914. 606-886-9114. 8AM-4PM. Access by: mail, phone, in person. Special note: Small cliams can be reached at 606-886-2124.

Franklin

Real Estate Recording—Franklin County Clerk, 315 W. Main Street, Courthouse Annex, Frankfort, KY 40601. 502-875-8747, Fax: 502-875-8718. 8AM-4:30PM.

Felony, Civil Actions Over $4,000—Circuit Court, Box 678, Frankfort, KY 40602. 502-564-8380, Fax: 502-564-8188. 8AM-4:30PM. Access by: mail, fax, in person.

Misdemeanor, Civil Actions Under $4,000, Eviction, Small Claims, Probate—District Court, Box 678, Frankfort, KY 40601. 502-564-7013, Fax: 502-564-8188. 8AM-4:30PM. Access by: mail, in person.

Fulton

Real Estate Recording—Fulton County Clerk, Wellington Street, Johnson Annex, Hickman, KY 42050. 270-273-3966, Fax: 270-236-2522. 8AM-4PM.

Felony, Misdemeanor, Civil, Eviction, Small Claims, Probate—Circuit and District Court, Box 198, Hickman, KY 42050. 270-273-9964, Fax: 270-236-3729. 8:30AM-4PM. Access by: mail, in person.

Gallatin

Real Estate Recording—Gallatin County Clerk, Franklin & Washington, Warsaw, KY 41095., Fax: 606-567-5444. 8AM-6PM M; 8AM-4:40PM T,Th,F; 8AM-Noon Sat.

Felony, Civil Actions Over $4,000—Circuit Court, Box 256, Warsaw, KY 41095. 606-567-5241. 8AM-5PM M,T,Th,F; Closed W. Access by: mail, in person.

Misdemeanor, Civil Actions Under $4,000, Eviction, Small Claims, Probate—District Court, Box 256, Warsaw, KY 41095. 606-567-2388. 8AM-5PM M,T,Th,F; 8AM-Noon Sat. Access by: mail, in person.

Garrard

Real Estate Recording—Garrard County Clerk, Courthouse Building, Lancaster, KY 40444., Fax: 606-792-2010. 8AM-4PM M,T,Th,F; 8AM-Noon W,Sat.

Felony, Misdemeanor, Civil, Eviction, Small Claims, Probate—Circuit and District Court, 7 Public Square, Courthouse Annex, Lancaster, KY 40444. 606-792-6032, Fax: 606-792-6414. 8AM-4PM M,T,TH,F, 8AM-Noon Wed & Sat. Access by: in person.

Grant

Real Estate Recording—Grant County Clerk, Courthouse Basement, Room 15, 101 N. Main St. Williamstown, KY 41097. 606-824-7561, Fax: 606-824-3367. 8:30AM-4PM M-F; 8:30AM-Noon Sat.

Felony, Misdemeanor, Civil, Eviction, Small Claims, Probate—Circuit and District Court, Courthouse 101 N Main, Williamstown, KY 41097. 606-824-4467. 8AM-4PM. Access by: mail, in person.

Graves

Real Estate Recording—Graves County Clerk, Courthouse, Mayfield, KY 42066. 270-335-5776, Fax: 270-247-1274. 8AM-4:30PM M-Th; 8AM-6PM F.

Felony, Misdemeanor, Civil, Eviction, Small Claims, Probate—Circuit and District Court, Courthouse 100 E Broadway, Mayfield, KY 42066. 270-335-5123, Fax: 270-247-8221. 8AM-4:30PM. Access by: in person.

Grayson

Real Estate Recording—Grayson County Clerk, 10 Public Square, Leitchfield, KY 42754. 270-338-4850, Fax: 270-259-9264. 8AM-4PM M,T,W,F; 8AM-Noon Th,Sat.

Felony, Misdemeanor, Civil, Eviction, Small Claims, Probate—Circuit and District Court, 125 E White Oak, Leitchfield, KY 42754. 270-338-0995, Fax: 270-259-9866. 8AM-4PM M-F; 8AM-Noon Sat. Access by: mail, in person.

Green

Real Estate Recording—Green County Clerk, 203 West Court Street, Greensburg, KY 42743. 301-475-4473, Fax: 270-932-6241. 8AM-4PM M-W,F; 8AM-Noon Sat (Closed Th).

Felony, Misdemeanor, Civil, Eviction, Small Claims, Probate—Circuit and District Court, 203 W Court St, Greensburg, KY 42743. 301-475-4530, Fax: 270-932-3635. 8AM-4PM M-W, F; 8AM-12:30PM Sat. Access by: mail, fax, in person.

Greenup

Real Estate Recording—Greenup County Clerk, Main Street, Courthouse, Greenup, KY 41144. 606-473-5350, Fax: 606-473-5354. 9AM-4:30PM M,T,W,F; 9AM-Noon Th,Sat.

Felony, Misdemeanor, Civil, Eviction, Small Claims, Probate—Circuit and District Court, Courthouse Annex, Greenup, KY 41144. 606-473-9869, Fax: 606-473-7388. 9AM-4:30PM M-F. Access by: in person.

Hancock

Real Estate Recording—Hancock County Clerk, 225 Main & Cross St. Courthouse, Hawesville, KY 42348. 301-334-1965, Fax: 270-927-8639. 8AM-4PM M-W,F; 8AM-5:30PM Th.

Felony, Misdemeanor, Civil, Eviction, Small Claims, Probate—Circuit and District Court, Courthouse, PO Box 250,

Hawesville, KY 42348. 301-334-1999, Fax: 270-927-8629. 8AM-4PM M,T,W,F; 8AM-5:30PM Th. Access by: mail, in person.

Hardin

Real Estate Recording—Hardin County Clerk, 14 Public Square, Elizabethtown, KY 42701. 270-932-5631, Fax: 270-769-2682. 8AM-4:30PM.

Felony, Misdemeanor, Civil, Eviction, Small Claims, Probate—Circuit and District Court, Hardin County Justice Center, 120 E Dixie Ave, Elizabethtown, KY 42701. 270-965-4200, Fax: 270-766-5243. 8AM-4:30PM;. Access by: in person.

Harlan

Real Estate Recording—Harlan County Clerk, 210 E. Central St. Suite 205, Harlan, KY 40831. 606-573-4771, Fax: 606-573-0064. 8:30AM-4:30PM M-W & F; 8:30AM-6PM Th.

Felony, Misdemeanor, Civil, Eviction, Small Claims, Probate—Circuit and District Court, Box 190, Harlan, KY 40831. 606-573-2680. 8AM-4:30PM. Access by: in person.

Harrison

Real Estate Recording—Harrison County Clerk, 190 West Pike Street, Cynthiana, KY 41031. 606-234-7136, Fax: 606-234-8049. 9AM-4PM M-Th; 9AM-6PM F; Records Site Hours: 8:30AM-4:30PM.

Felony, Misdemeanor, Civil, Eviction, Small Claims, Probate—Circuit and District Court, Courthouse Box 10, Cynthiana, KY 41031. 606-234-1914. 8:30AM-4:30PM M-F, 9AM-12PM Sat. Access by: mail, in person.

Hart

Real Estate Recording—Hart County Clerk, Main Street, Courthouse, Munfordville, KY 42765. 270-685-8424, Fax: 270-524-0458. 8AM-4PM (8AM-Noon Sat).

Felony, Misdemeanor, Civil, Eviction, Small Claims, Probate—Circuit and District Court, Box 548, Munfordville, KY 42765. 270-653-6195. 8AM-4PM M-F; 8AM-Noon Sat. Access by: in person.

Henderson

Real Estate Recording—Henderson County Clerk, Courthouse, 20 N. Main St. Henderson, KY 42420. 281-341-8685, Fax: 270-826-9677. 8AM-4:30PM M-Th; 8AM-6PM F.

Felony, Civil Actions Over $4,000—Circuit and District Court, PO Box 675, Henderson, KY 42420. 281-341-4515, Fax: 270-827-5932. 8AM-6PM M; 8AM-4:30PM T-F. Access by: in person.

Henry

Real Estate Recording—Henry County Clerk, Courthouse, 30 N. Main, Ste A, New Castle, KY 40050., Fax: 502-845-5708. 8AM-4PM.

Felony, Misdemeanor, Civil, Eviction, Small Claims, Probate—Circuit and District Court, PO Box 359, New Castle, KY 40050. 502-845-7551, Fax: 502-845-6738. 8AM-4:30PM M-F. Access by: in person.

Hickman

Real Estate Recording—Hickman County Clerk, Courthouse, 110 E. Clay, Clinton, KY 42031. 270-765-2350, Fax: 270-653-4248. 8:30AM-4PM.

Felony, Misdemeanor, Civil, Eviction, Small Claims, Probate—Circuit and District Court, 100 Clay St, Clinton, KY 42031. 502-653-3901. 8AM-4PM. Access by: mail, in person.

Hopkins

Real Estate Recording—Hopkins County Clerk, Corner of Main and Center Streets, Courthouse - Room 14, Madisonville, KY 42431. 275-275-3724, Fax: 270-825-7000. 8AM-4PM.

Felony, Misdemeanor, Civil, Eviction, Small Claims, Probate—Circuit and District Court, Courthouse 30 S Main St, Madisonville, KY 42431. 275-275-2221, Fax: 270-824-7051. 8AM-4PM. Access by: in person.

Jackson

Real Estate Recording—Jackson County Clerk, Main Street, Courthouse, McKee, KY 40447. 606-287-8562, Fax: 606-287-4505. 8AM-4PM; 8AM-Noon Sat.

Felony, Civil Actions Over $4,000—Circuit Court, PO Box 84, McKee, KY 40447. 606-287-7783, Fax: 606-287-3277. 8AM-4PM M-F 8AM-Noon Sat. Access by: mail, fax, in person.

Misdemeanor, Civil Actions Under $4,000, Eviction, Small Claims, Probate—District Court, PO Box 84, McKee, KY 40447. 606-287-8651, Fax: 606-287-3277. 8AM-4PM M-F; 8AM-Noon Sat. Access by: mail, fax, in person.

Jefferson

Real Estate Recording—Jefferson County Clerk, 531 Court Place, Room 204A, Louisville, KY 40202., Fax: 502-574-6041. 8AM-4:45PM.

Jefferson County Clerk, 531 Court Place, Room 204A, Louisville, KY 40202., Fax: 502-574-6041. 8AM-4:30PM.

Felony, Misdemeanor, Civil, Eviction, Small Claims, Probate—Circuit and District Court, Hall of Justice 600 W Jefferson St, Louisville, KY 40202. 502-595-3064, Fax: 502-595-4629. 24 HOURS MON-SUN. Access by: mail, phone, in person.

Jessamine

Real Estate Recording—Jessamine County Clerk, 101 North Main Street, Nicholasville, KY 40356. 606-885-4500, Fax: 606-885-5837. 8AM-5PM M; 8AM-4PM T,W,F; 8AM-Noon Th; 9am-Noon Sat.

Felony, Civil Actions Over $4,000—Circuit Court, 101 N Main St, Nicholasville, KY 40356. 606-885-4531. 8AM-4:30PM M-W, F; 8AM-12PM TH. Access by: mail, in person.

Misdemeanor, Civil Actions Under $4,000, Eviction, Small Claims, Probate—District Court, 101 N Main St, Nicholasville, KY 40356. 606-887-1005, Fax: 606-887-0425. 8AM-4:30PM M-W; 8AM-Noon TH; 8AM-4PM F. Access by: mail, in person.

Johnson

Real Estate Recording—Johnson County Clerk, Courthouse, Court St. Paintsville, KY 41240., Fax: 606-789-2559. 8AM-5PM M-Th; 8AM-7PM F; 8:30AM-Noon Sat.

Felony, Misdemeanor, Civil, Eviction, Small Claims, Probate—Circuit and District Court, Box 1405, Paintsville, KY 41240. 606-789-5181, Fax: 606-789-5611. 8AM-4:30PM; 8:30AM-Noon Sat Driver's license only. Access by: mail, phone, in person.

Kenton

Real Estate Recording—Kenton County Clerk, 3rd & Court Streets, Room 102, Covington, KY 41012. 606-491-2800, Fax: 606-491-4515. 8:30AM-4PM M-Th; 8:30AM-6PM F.

Kenton County Clerk, 5272 Madison, Independence, KY 41051. 606-356-4942, Fax: 606-356-9278. 8:30AM-4PM M,T,Th,F; 8:30AM-6PM W.

Felony, Civil Actions Over $4,000—Circuit Court, Box 669, Covington, KY 41012. 606-292-6521, Fax: 606-292-6611. 8AM-5PM. Access by: mail, in person.

Misdemeanor, Civil Actions Under $4,000, Eviction, Small Claims, Probate—District Court, PO Box 669, City Bldg Rm 408, Covington, KY 41012. 606-292-6523, Fax: 606-292-6611. 8AM-4:30PM. Access by: mail, in person.

Knott

Real Estate Recording—Knott County Clerk, Main Street, Courthouse, Hindman, KY 41822. 606-785-5592, Fax: 606-785-0996. 8AM-4PM M,T,W,Th; 8AM-6PM F; 8AM-Noon Sat.

Felony, Misdemeanor, Civil, Eviction, Small Claims, Probate—Circuit and District Court, PO Box 1317, Hindman, KY 41822. 606-785-5021. 8AM-4PM. Access by: mail, fax, in person.

Knox

Real Estate Recording—Knox County Clerk, 401 Court Square, Suite 102, Barbourville, KY 40906., Fax: 606-546-3589. 8:30AM-4PM.

Felony, Misdemeanor, Civil, Eviction, Small Claims, Probate—Circuit and District Court, PO Box 760, Barbourville, KY 40906. 606-546-3075, Fax: 606-546-7949. 8AM-4PM. Access by: mail, in person.

Larue

Real Estate Recording—Larue County Clerk, 209 W. High St. Hodgenville, KY 42748. 270-487-5480, Fax: 270-358-4528. 8AM-4:30PM M,T,Th,F; 8AM-Noon W,Sat.

Felony, Misdemeanor, Civil, Eviction, Small Claims, Probate—Circuit and District Court, Courthouse Annex, Hodgenville, KY 42748. 270-465-6686, Fax: 270-358-3731. 8AM-4PM. Access by: mail, in person.

Laurel

Real Estate Recording—Laurel County Clerk, 101 South Main, Courthouse, London, KY 40741., Fax: 606-864-7369. 8AM-4:30PM; 8:30AM-Noon Sat.

Felony, Misdemeanor, Civil, Eviction, Small Claims, Probate—Circuit and District Court, Box 1798, London, KY 40743-1798. 606-864-2863, Fax: 606-864-8264. 8AM-4PM. Access by: mail, in person.

Lawrence

Real Estate Recording—Lawrence County Clerk, 122 South Main Cross Street, Louisa, KY 41230. 606-638-4102, Fax: 606-638-0638. 8:30AM-4PM; 8:30AM-Noon Sat.

Felony, Misdemeanor, Civil, Eviction, Small Claims, Probate—Circuit and District Court, Courthouse, PO Box 212, Louisa, KY 41230. 606-638-4215, Fax: 606-638-3556. 8:30AM-4:30PM M-F 8:30AM-Noon Sat. Access by: mail, in person.

Lee

Real Estate Recording—Lee County Clerk, Main Street, Courthouse - Room 11, Beattyville, KY 41311. 606-464-4100, Fax: 606-464-4102. 8AM-4PM.

Felony, Misdemeanor, Civil, Eviction, Small Claims, Probate—Circuit and District Court, Box E, Beattyville, KY 41311. 606-464-8400, Fax: 606-464-0144. 8AM-4PM M-F; 8:30AM-11:30AM Sat. Access by: mail, in person.

Leslie

Real Estate Recording—Leslie County Clerk, Main Street, Courthouse, Hyden, KY 41749., Fax: 606-672-4264. 8AM-5PM; 8AM-Noon Sat.

Felony, Misdemeanor, Civil, Eviction, Small Claims, Probate—Circuit and District Court, Box 1750, Hyden, KY 41749. 606-672-2505, Fax: 606-672-5128. 8AM-5PM M; 8AM-4PM T-F; 8AM-Noon Sat. Access by: mail, phone, fax, in person.

Letcher

Real Estate Recording—Letcher County Clerk, 156 Main St. Whitesburg, KY 41858., Fax: 606-632-9282. 8:30AM-4PM; 8:30AM-Noon 1st Sat of month.

Felony, Misdemeanor, Civil, Eviction, Small Claims, Probate—Circuit and District Court, 156 W Main St, #201, Whitesburg, KY 41858. 606-633-7559, Fax: 606-633-5864. 8:30AM-4PM M-F 8:30AM-12PM last Sat of month. Access by: in person.

Lewis

Real Estate Recording—Lewis County Clerk, 514 Second Street, Courthouse, 2nd Floor, Vanceburg, KY 41179. 606-796-2722, Fax: 606-796-6511. 8:30AM-4:30PM M,T,Th,F; 9AM-1PM W; 8:30AM-12:30PM Sat.

Felony, Misdemeanor, Civil, Eviction, Small Claims, Probate—Circuit and District Court, PO Box 70, Vanceburg, KY 41179. 606-796-3053, Fax: 606-796-3030. 8AM-4:30PM M,T,Th,F 8:30-Noon W,Sat. Access by: mail, in person.

Lincoln

Real Estate Recording—Lincoln County Clerk, 102 East Main, Courthouse, Stanford, KY 40484., Fax: 606-365-4572. 8AM-4PM M-F; 9AM-Noon Sat.

Felony, Misdemeanor, Civil, Eviction, Small Claims, Probate—Circuit and District Court, 102 E Main, Stanford, KY 40484. 606-365-2535, Fax: 606-365-3389. 8AM-4PM M-Th; 8AM-5:30PM F. Access by: mail, in person.

Livingston

Real Estate Recording—Livingston County Clerk, 335 Court Street, Courthouse, Smithland, KY 42081., Fax: 270-928-4612. 8AM-4PM; 8AM-6PM M.

Felony, Misdemeanor, Civil, Eviction, Small Claims, Probate—Circuit and District Court, PO Box 160, Smithland, KY 42081. 301-334-8164. 8AM-6PM M 8AM-4PM T-F. Access by: in person.

Logan

Real Estate Recording—Logan County Clerk, 229 W. 3rd St. Russellville, KY 42276. 270-864-2611, Fax: 270-726-4355. 8:30AM-4:30PM.

Felony, Civil Actions Over $4,000—Circuit Court, Box 420, Russellville, KY 42276-0420. 270-864-3444, Fax: 270-726-7893. 8AM-4:30PM M-Th; 8AM-5PM F. Access by: in person.

Misdemeanor, Civil Actions Under $4,000, Eviction, Small Claims, Probate—District Court, Box 420, Russellville, KY 42276. 270-889-6539, Fax: 270-726-7893. 8AM-4:30PM. Access by: in person.

Lyon

Real Estate Recording—Lyon County Clerk, Dale Avenue, Courthouse, Eddyville, KY 42038. 270-526-5631, Fax: 270-388-0634. 8:30AM-4PM.

Felony, Misdemeanor, Civil, Eviction, Small Claims, Probate—Circuit and District Court, Box 565, Eddyville, KY 42038. 270-527-3883. 8AM-4PM. Access by: mail, in person.

Madison

Real Estate Recording—Madison County Clerk, 101 W. Main Street, County Court House, Richmond, KY 40475., Fax: 606-624-8474. 8AM-4PM; 8AM-6PM M.

Felony, Civil Actions Over $4,000—Circuit Court, PO Box 813, Richmond, KY 40476-0813. 606-624-4793. 8AM-4PM. Access by: in person.

Misdemeanor, Civil Actions Under $4,000, Eviction, Small Claims, Probate—District Court, Madison Hall of Justice, 351 West Main St, Richmond, KY 40475. 606-624-4722, Fax: 606-624-4746. 8AM-4PM. Access by: mail, fax, in person.

Magoffin

Real Estate Recording—Magoffin County Clerk, Courthouse, Salyersville, KY 41465. 606-349-2313, Fax: 606-349-2328. 8:30AM-4PM; 8:30AM-Noon Sat.

Felony, Misdemeanor, Civil, Eviction, Small Claims, Probate—Circuit and District Court, Box 147, Salyersville, KY 41465. 606-349-2215, Fax: 606-349-2209. 8AM-4PM. Access by: mail, fax, in person.

Marion

Real Estate Recording—Marion County Clerk, Courthouse, Suite 3, 120 W. Main St. Lebanon, KY 40033. 270-826-2405, Fax: 270-692-9811. 8:30AM-4:30PM; 8:30AM-Noon Sat.

Felony, Misdemeanor, Civil, Eviction, Small Claims, Probate—Circuit and District Court, 120 W Main St, Lebanon, KY 40033. 270-825-2666. 8:30AM-4:30PM M-F; 8:30AM-Noon Sat. Access by: in person.

Marshall

Real Estate Recording—Marshall County Clerk, Courthouse, 1101 Main St. Benton, KY 42025., Fax: 270-527-4738. 8AM-5PM M; 8AM-4:30PM T-F.

Felony, Misdemeanor, Civil, Eviction, Small Claims, Probate—Circuit and District Court, 1101 Main St, Benton, KY 42025. 270-692-2681, Fax: 270-527-5865. 8AM-4:30PM. Access by: mail, phone, fax, in person.

Martin

Real Estate Recording—Martin County Clerk, Main Street, Courthouse, Inez, KY 41224., Fax: 606-298-0143. 8AM-5PM; 8AM-Noon Sat.

Felony, Misdemeanor, Civil, Eviction, Small Claims, Probate—Circuit and District Court, Box 430, Inez, KY 41224. 606-298-3508, Fax: 606-298-4202. 8AM-4:30PM M-TH, 8AM-5:30PM F, 9AM-Noon Sat. Access by: mail, in person.

Mason

Real Estate Recording—Mason County Clerk, West Third Street, Courthouse, Maysville, KY 41056. 606-564-6381, Fax: 606-564-8979. 9AM-5PM; 9AM-Noon Sat.

Felony, Civil Actions Over $4,000—Circuit Court, 27 W 3rd, Maysville, KY 41056. 606-564-4340, Fax: 606-564-0932. 8:30AM-5PM. Access by: in person.

Misdemeanor, Civil Actions Under $4,000, Eviction, Small Claims, Probate—District Court, 221 Court St, Maysville, KY 41056. 606-564-4011, Fax: 606-564-0932. 8:30AM-4:30PM. Access by: in person.

McCracken

Real Estate Recording—McCracken County Clerk, 7th Street between Washington & Clark, Courthouse, Paducah, KY 42001. 270-628-3922, Fax: 270-444-4704. 8:30AM-4:30PM (M open until 5:30PM).

Felony, Civil Actions Over $4,000—Circuit Court, Box 1455, Paducah, KY 42002-1455. 270-726-2167. 8:30AM-5:30PM M, 8:30AM-4:30PM T-F. Access by: mail, in person.

Misdemeanor, Civil Actions Under $4,000, Eviction, Small Claims, Probate—District Court, Box 1436, Paducah, KY 42001. 270-692-3451, Fax: 270-575-7029. 8:30AM-4:30PM. Access by: in person.

McCreary

Real Estate Recording—McCreary County Clerk, Main Street, Courthouse, Whitley City, KY 42653., Fax: 606-376-3898. 8:30AM-4:30PM M-F; 9AM-Noon Sat.

Felony, Misdemeanor, Civil, Eviction, Small Claims, Probate—Circuit and District Court, Box 40, Whitley City, KY 42653. 606-376-5041, Fax: 606-376-8844. 8AM-4:30PM. Access by: mail, in person.

McLean

Real Estate Recording—McLean County Clerk, 210 Main Street, Courthouse, Calhoun, KY 42327. 270-365-6884, Fax: 270-273-5084. 8AM-4:30PM; 9AM-Noon Sat.

Felony, Misdemeanor, Civil, Eviction, Small Claims, Probate—Circuit and District Court, Box 145, Calhoun, KY 42327. 270-358-4400, Fax: 270-273-3791. 8AM-4:30PM M-F; 9AM-Noon Sat. Access by: mail, in person.

Meade

Real Estate Recording—Meade County Clerk, 516 Fairway Drive, Brandenburg, KY 40108., Fax: 270-422-2158. 8AM-4:30PM; 9AM-Noon Sat.

Felony, Misdemeanor, Civil, Eviction, Small Claims, Probate—Circuit and District Court, Courthouse, Brandenburg, KY 40108. 502-422-4961, Fax: 502-422-2147. 8AM-4:30AM. Access by: mail, in person.

Menifee

Real Estate Recording—Menifee County Clerk, Main Street, Courthouse, Frenchburg, KY 40322. 606-768-3514, Fax: 606-768-2144. 8:30AM-4PM M,T,W,F; 8:30-11:30AM Th,Sat.

Felony, Misdemeanor, Civil, Eviction, Small Claims, Probate—Circuit and District Court, Box 172, Frenchburg, KY 40322. 606-768-2461, Fax: 606-768-2462. 8:30AM-4PM. Access by: mail, fax, in person.

Mercer

Real Estate Recording—Mercer County Clerk, 235 S. Main Street, Courthouse Annex, Harrodsburg, KY 40330., Fax: 606-734-6309. 8AM-4:30PM.

Felony, Misdemeanor, Civil, Eviction, Small Claims, Probate—Circuit and District Court, Courthouse, 224 Main St S, Harrodsburg, KY 40330-1696. 606-734-6306, Fax: 606-734-9159. 8AM-4:30PM. Access by: in person.

Metcalfe

Real Estate Recording—Metcalfe County Clerk, 100 E. Stockton St. Suite 1, Edmonton, KY 42129. 502-432-3181, Fax: 270-432-5176. 8AM-4PM.

Felony, Misdemeanor, Civil, Eviction, Small Claims, Probate—Circuit and District Court, Box 485, Edmonton, KY 42129. 270-586-8910, Fax: 270-432-4437. 8AM-4PM. Access by: mail, in person.

Monroe

Real Estate Recording—Monroe County Clerk, Main Street, Courthouse, Tompkinsville, KY 42167. 502-487-5505, Fax: 270-487-5976. 8AM-4:30PM M-F; 8AM-Noon Sat.

Felony, Misdemeanor, Civil, Eviction, Small Claims, Probate—Circuit and District Court, Box 245, Tompkinsville, KY 42167. 270-639-5042, Fax: 270-487-0068. 8AM-5PM. Access by: mail, phone, in person.

Montgomery

Real Estate Recording—Montgomery County Clerk, Court Street, Mount Sterling, KY 40353. 606-498-8703, Fax: 606-498-8729. 8:30AM-4PM; 8:30-6PM F.

Felony, Misdemeanor, Civil, Eviction, Small Claims, Probate—Circuit and District Court, Courthouse One Court St, Mt Sterling, KY 40353. 606-498-5966, Fax: 606-498-9341. 8:30AM-4PM. Access by: mail, in person.

Morgan

Real Estate Recording—Morgan County Clerk, 505 Prestonsburg Street, West Liberty, KY 41472., Fax: 606-743-2111. 8AM-4PM; 8AM-Noon Sat.

Felony, Misdemeanor, Civil, Eviction, Small Claims, Probate—Circuit and District Court, Box 85, West Liberty, KY 41472. 606-743-3763, Fax: 606-743-2633. 8AM-4PM. Access by: mail, in person.

Muhlenberg

Real Estate Recording—Muhlenberg County Clerk, Courthouse, 1st Floor, 100 Court Row, Greenville, KY 42345., Fax: 270-338-1774. 8AM-4PM; 8AM-6PM F.

Felony, Civil Actions Over $4,000—Circuit Court, Box 776, Greenville, KY 42345. 270-389-0800, Fax: 270-338-7482. 8AM-4PM. Access by: in person.

Misdemeanor, Civil Actions Under $4,000, Eviction, Small Claims, Probate—District Court, Box 274, Greenville, KY 42345. 270-388-7231, Fax: 270-338-7482. 8AM-4PM. Access by: mail, in person.

Nelson

Real Estate Recording—Nelson County Clerk, 113 E. Stephen Foster Ave. Bardstown, KY 40004. 502-348-1800, Fax: 502-348-1822. 8:30AM-4:30PM M-F; 8AM-Noon Sat.

Felony, Misdemeanor, Civil, Eviction, Small Claims, Probate—Circuit and District Court, Box 845, Bardstown, KY 40004. 502-348-3648. 8:30AM-4:30PM. Access by: mail, in person.

Nicholas

Real Estate Recording—Nicholas County Clerk, Main Street, Courthouse, Carlisle, KY 40311. 606-289-3725, Fax: 606-289-3709. 8AM-4:30PM; 8-11:30AM Sat.

Felony, Misdemeanor, Civil, Eviction, Small Claims, Probate—Circuit and District Court, PO Box 109, Carlisle, KY 40311. 606-289-2336, Fax: 606-289-6141. 8:30AM-4:30PM M-F. Access by: mail, fax, in person.

Ohio

Real Estate Recording—Ohio County Clerk, 301 South Main Street, Old Courthouse, Hartford, KY 42347., Fax: 270-298-4425. 8AM-4:30PM M-Th; 8AM-6PM F; 8AM-Noon Sat.

Felony, Misdemeanor, Civil, Eviction, Small Claims, Probate—Circuit and District Court, 130 E Washington, Ste 300, Hartford, KY 42347. 270-365-9776, Fax: 270-298-9565. 8:30AM-4:30PM. Access by: in person.

Oldham

Real Estate Recording—Oldham County Clerk, 100 West Jefferson Street, LaGrange, KY 40031., Fax: 502-222-3208. 8:30AM-4PM M-W,F; 8:30AM-6PM Th.

Felony, Misdemeanor, Civil, Eviction, Small Claims, Probate—Circuit and District Court, 100 W Main St, La Grange, KY 40031. 502-222-9837, Fax: 502-222-3047. 8AM-4PM. Access by: in person.

Owen

Real Estate Recording—Owen County Clerk, Courthouse, Madison St. Owenton, KY 40359., Fax: 502-484-1002. 8AM-Noon, 1-4PM M,T,Th,F; 8AM-3PM Sat.

Felony, Misdemeanor, Civil, Eviction, Small Claims, Probate—Circuit and District Court, Box 473, Owenton, KY 40359. 502-484-2232, Fax: 502-484-0625. 8AM-4PM. Access by: mail, fax, in person.

Owsley

Real Estate Recording—Owsley County Clerk, Courthouse, Main St. Booneville, KY 41314. 606-593-6202, Fax: 606-593-5737. 8AM-4PM; 8AM-12 Sat.

Felony, Misdemeanor, Civil, Eviction, Small Claims, Probate—Circuit and District Court, Box 130, Booneville, KY 41314. 606-593-6226, Fax: 606-593-6343. 8AM-4PM M-F, 8AM-Noon Sat. Access by: in person.

Pendleton

Real Estate Recording—Pendleton County Clerk, Courthouse Square, 233 Main St. Room 1, Falmouth, KY 41040. 606-654-4321, Fax: 606-654-5600. 8:30AM-4PM M-F; 8:30AM-Noon Sat.

Felony, Misdemeanor, Civil, Eviction, Small Claims, Probate—Circuit and District Court, PO Box 69, Falmouth, KY 41040. 606-654-3347. 8AM-4PM. Access by: mail, in person.

Perry

Real Estate Recording—Perry County Clerk, Main Street, Courthouse, Hazard, KY 41701. 606-436-1816, Fax: 606-439-0557. 8AM-4PM.

Felony, Civil Actions Over $4,000—Circuit Court, Box 7743, Hazard, KY 41701. 606-435-6000. 8AM-4PM. Access by: mail, phone, in person.

Misdemeanor, Civil Actions Under $4,000, Eviction, Small Claims, Probate—District Court, Box 7733, Hazard, KY 41702. 606-435-6002. 8AM-4PM. Access by: mail, in person.

Pike

Real Estate Recording—Pike County Clerk, 320 Main Street, Pikeville, KY 41501., Fax: 606-432-6222. 8:30AM-4:30PM M,T,W.Th; 8:30AM-6PM F; 8:30AM-Noon Sat.

Felony, Misdemeanor, Civil, Eviction, Small Claims, Probate—Circuit and District Court, PO Box 1002, Pikeville, KY 41501. 606-433-7557, Fax: 606-433-1363. 8AM-4:30PM. Access by: mail, in person.

Powell

Real Estate Recording—Powell County Clerk, 130 Washington Street, Courthouse, Stanton, KY 40380., Fax: 606-663-6406. 9AM-4PM M-W; 9AM-Noon Th; 9AM-4PM F; 9AM-Noon Sat.

Felony, Misdemeanor, Civil, Eviction, Small Claims, Probate—Circuit and District Court, Box 578, Stanton, KY 40380. 606-663-4141, Fax: 606-663-2710. 8AM-4PM M,T,W,F, 8AM-Noon Th & Sat. Access by: mail, in person.

Pulaski

Real Estate Recording—Pulaski County Clerk, Main Street, Somerset, KY 42501. 606-679-1311, Fax: 606-678-0073. 8AM-4:30PM.

Felony, Misdemeanor, Civil, Eviction, Small Claims, Probate—Circuit and District Court, Box 664, Somerset, KY 42502. 606-677-4029, Fax: 606-677-4002. 8AM-4:30PM M-F, 8AM-Noon Sat. Access by: in person.

Robertson

Real Estate Recording—Robertson County Clerk, Courthouse, Mount Olivet, KY 41064. 606-724-5403. 8:30-Noon, 1-4PM M,T,Th,F; 8:30AM-Noon W, Sat.

Felony, Misdemeanor, Civil, Eviction, Small Claims, Probate—Circuit and District Court, PO Box 63, Mt Olivet, KY 41064. 606-724-5993, Fax: 606-724-5721. 8:30AM-4:30PM. Access by: mail, phone, in person.

Rockcastle

Real Estate Recording—Rockcastle County Clerk, Courthouse, Mount Vernon, KY 40456. 606-256-3623, Fax: 606-256-4302. 8:30-4PM; 8;30-Noon Sat.

Felony, Misdemeanor, Civil, Eviction, Small Claims, Probate—Circuit and District Court, Box 750, Mt Vernon, KY 40456. 606-256-2581. 8AM-4PM M-W & F; 8AM-6PM Th; 8:30AM-Noon Sat. Access by: mail, in person.

Rowan

Real Estate Recording—Rowan County Clerk, Courthouse - 2nd Floor, 627 E. Main Street, Morehead, KY 40351. 606-784-4211, Fax: 606-784-2923. 8:30AM-4:30PM M-F; 9AM-Noon Sat.

Felony, Misdemeanor, Civil, Eviction, Small Claims, Probate—Circuit and District Court, 627 E Main, Morehead, KY 40351-1398. 606-784-4574, Fax: 606-784-1899. 8:30AM-4:30PM M-F 8:30AM-12PM SAT. Access by: mail, in person.

Russell

Real Estate Recording—Russell County Clerk, Courthouse, Jamestown, KY 42629. 502-343-2112, Fax: 270-343-4700. 8AM-4PM; 8AM-Noon Sat.

Felony, Misdemeanor, Civil, Eviction, Small Claims, Probate—Circuit and District Court, 410 Monument Square, Suite 203, Jamestown, KY 42629. 270-444-4725, Fax: 270-343-5808. 8AM-4:30PM M-F 8AM-Noon Sat. Access by: in person.

Scott

Real Estate Recording—Scott County Clerk, Courthouse, 101 E. Main St. Georgetown, KY 40324. 502-863-7850, Fax: 502-863-7898. 8:30AM-4:30PM M-Th; 8:30AM-6PM F.

Felony, Misdemeanor, Civil, Eviction, Small Claims, Probate—Circuit and District Court, 119 N Hamilton, Georgetown, KY 40324. 502-863-0474. 8AM-4:30PM. Access by: mail, in person.

Shelby

Real Estate Recording—Shelby County Clerk, 501 Washington, Shelbyville, KY 40065. 502-633-1220, Fax: 502-633-7887. 8:30AM-4:30PM; 8:30AM-Noon Sat.

Felony, Misdemeanor, Civil, Eviction, Small Claims, Probate—Circuit and District Court, 501 Main St, Shelbyville, KY 40065. 502-633-1289, Fax: 502-633-0146. 8:30AM-4:30PM. Access by: mail, fax, in person.

Simpson

Real Estate Recording—Simpson County Clerk, County Annex Building, 103 West Cedar Street, Franklin, KY 42134. 502-586-7184, Fax: 270-586-6464. 8AM-4PM.

Felony, Misdemeanor, Civil, Eviction, Small Claims, Probate—Circuit and District Court, Box 261, Franklin, KY 42135-0261. 270-726-2424, Fax: 270-586-0265. 8AM-4PM. Access by: mail, in person.

Spencer

Real Estate Recording—Spencer County Clerk, Courthouse, 2 W. Main Street, Taylorsville, KY 40071. 502-477-3211, Fax: 502-477-3216. 8AM-4:30PM M-F; 8AM-Noon Sat.

Felony, Misdemeanor, Civil, Eviction, Small Claims, Probate—Circuit and District Court, Box 282, Taylorsville, KY

40071. 502-477-3220, Fax: 502-477-9368. 7:45AM-4PM. Access by: mail, in person.

Taylor

Real Estate Recording—Taylor County Clerk, 203 North Court Street, Suite # 5, Campbellsville, KY 42718. 502-789-1008, Fax: 270-789-1144. 8AM-4:30PM M-Th; 8AM-5PM F.

Felony, Misdemeanor, Civil, Eviction, Small Claims, Probate—Circuit and District Court, 203 N Court Courthouse, Campbellsville, KY 42718. 270-628-5425, Fax: 270-789-4356. 8AM-4:30PM. Access by: mail, in person.

Todd

Real Estate Recording—Todd County Clerk, Washington Street, Courthouse, Elkton, KY 42220. 270-343-2185, Fax: 270-265-2588. 8AM-4:30PM.

Felony, Misdemeanor, Civil, Eviction, Small Claims, Probate—Circuit and District Court, Box 337, Elkton, KY 42220. 270-358-3421, Fax: 270-265-2122. 8AM-4:30PM. Access by: mail, fax, in person.

Trigg

Real Estate Recording—Trigg County Clerk, Courthouse, 41 Main St. Cadiz, KY 42211. 502-522-8459, Fax: 270-522-6662. 8AM-4PM M-Th; 8AM-5PM F.

Felony, Misdemeanor, Civil, Eviction, Small Claims, Probate—Circuit and District Court, Box 673, Cadiz, KY 42211. 270-639-9160. 8AM-4PM M-F 9AM-11:30AM 1st SAT of each month. Access by: in person.

Trimble

Real Estate Recording—Trimble County Clerk, Courthouse, Bedford, KY 40006., Fax: 502-255-7045. 8:30AM-4:30PM M,T,Th,F; 8:30AM-Noon Sat.

Felony, Misdemeanor, Civil, Eviction, Small Claims, Probate—Circuit and District Court, Box 248, Bedford, KY 40006. 502-255-3213, Fax: 502-255-4953. 8AM-4:30PM M,T,Th,F 8AM-Noon Sat. Access by: mail, in person.

Union

Real Estate Recording—Union County Clerk, Main & Morgan Streets, Courthouse, Morganfield, KY 42437., Fax: 270-389-9135. 8AM-4PM.

Felony, Misdemeanor, Civil, Eviction, Small Claims, Probate—Circuit and District Court, Box 59, Morganfield, KY 42437. 270-575-7280, Fax: 270-389-9887. 8AM-4PM (No searches performed on Thursday). Access by: mail, in person.

Warren

Real Estate Recording—Warren County Clerk, 429 East 10th Street, Bowling Green, KY 42101., Fax: 270-843-5319. 8:30AM-4:30PM.

Felony, Misdemeanor, Civil, Eviction, Small Claims, Probate—Circuit and District Court, Box 2170, Bowling Green, KY 42102. 270-927-8101, Fax: 270-842-9316. 8:30AM-4:30PM. Access by: in person.

Washington

Real Estate Recording—Washington County Clerk, Cross Main Annex Building, Springfield, KY 40069., Fax: 606-336-5408. 9AM-4:30PM; 9AM-Noon Sat.

Felony, Misdemeanor, Civil, Eviction, Small Claims, Probate—Circuit and District Court, PO Box 346, Springfield, KY 40069. 606-336-3761, Fax: 606-336-9824. 8:30AM-4:30PM; 8:30-12 on Sat. Access by: mail, in person.

Wayne

Real Estate Recording—Wayne County Clerk, 109 N. Main St. First Floor, Monticello, KY 42633. 606-348-8411, Fax: 606-348-8303. 8AM-4:30PM; 8AM-Noon Sat.

Felony, Misdemeanor, Civil, Eviction, Small Claims, Probate—Circuit and District Court, 109 N Main St, #2, Monticello, KY 42633-1458. 606-348-5841, Fax: 606-348-4225. 8AM-4:30PM M-F; 8AM-Noon Sat. Access by: mail, in person.

Webster

Real Estate Recording—Webster County Clerk, Courthouse, 25 US 41A, Dixon, KY 42409. 270-756-2239, Fax: 270-639-7029. 8AM-4PM M; 8AM-4PM T-F.

Felony, Misdemeanor, Civil, Eviction, Small Claims, Probate—Circuit and District Court, Box 217, Dixon, KY 42409. 270-756-2239, Fax: 270-639-6757. 8AM-4PM. Access by: mail, fax, in person.

Whitley

Real Estate Recording—Whitley County Clerk, Main Street, Courthouse, Room 2, Williamsburg, KY 40769., Fax: 606-549-2790. 8:30AM-4PM; 8:30AM-Noon Sat.

Felony, Misdemeanor, Civil, Eviction, Small Claims, Probate—Corbin Circuit and District Court, 805 S Main St, Corbin, KY 40701. 606-523-1085, Fax: 606-523-2049. 8AM-4PM. Access by: mail, in person.

Williamsburg Circuit and District Court, Box 329, Williamsburg, KY 40769. 606-549-5162. 8AM-4PM. Access by: in person.

Wolfe

Real Estate Recording—Wolfe County Clerk, Courthouse, 1st Floor, 10 Court St. Campton, KY 41301., Fax: 606-668-3492. 8AM-4PM M,T,Th,F; 8AM-Noon W & Sat.

Felony, Misdemeanor, Civil, Eviction, Small Claims, Probate—Circuit and District Court, Box 296, Campton, KY 41301. 606-668-3736, Fax: 606-668-3198. 8:30AM-4:30PM. Access by: mail, in person.

Woodford

Real Estate Recording—Woodford County Clerk, Courthouse - Room 120, 103 S. Main St. Versailles, KY 40383. 606-873-6122, Fax: 606-873-6985. 8AM-4PM M,T,W,Th; 8AM-6PM F.

Felony, Misdemeanor, Civil, Eviction, Small Claims, Probate—Circuit and District Court, 130 Court St, Versailles, KY 40383. 606-873-3711. 8AM-4PM M-Th; 8AM-6PM F. Access by: in person.

Federal Courts

US District Court

Eastern District of Kentucky

Ashland Division Suite 336, 1405 Greenup Ave, Ashland, KY 41101606-329-2465 Counties: Boyd, Carter, Elliott, Greenup, Lawrence, Lewis, Morgan, Rowan.

Covington Division Clerk, PO Box 1073, Covington, KY 41012606-655-3810 Counties: Boone, Bracken, Campbell, Gallatin, Grant, Kenton, Mason, Pendleton, Robertson.

Frankfort Division Room 313, 330 W Broadway, Frankfort, KY 40601502-223-5225 Counties: Anderson, Carroll, Franklin, Henry, Owen, Shelby, Trimble.

Lexington Division PO Box 3074, Lexington, KY 40596-3074606-233-2503, Civil Docket Phone: 606-233-2762, Criminal Docket Phone: 606-233-2503 Counties: Bath, Bourbon, Boyle, Clark, Estill, Fayette, Fleming, Garrard, Harrison, Jessamine, Lee, Lincoln, Madison, Menifee, Mercer, Montgomery, Nicholas, Powell, Scott, Wolfe, Woodford. Lee and Wolfe counties were part of the Pikeville Divisionbefore 10/31/92. Perry became part of Pikeville after 1992.

London Division PO Box 5121, London, KY 40745-5121 606-864-5137 Counties: Bell, Clay, Harlan, Jackson, Knox, Laurel, Leslie, McCreary, Owsley, Pulaski, Rockcastle, Wayne, Whitley.

Pikeville Division Office of the clerk, 203 Federal Bldg, 102 Main St, Pikeville, KY 41501-1144 606-437-6160 Counties: Breathitt, Floyd, Johnson, Knott, Letcher, Magoffin, Martin, Perry, Pike. Lee and Wolfe Counties were part of this division until 10/31/92, when they were moved to the Lexington Division..

Western District of Kentucky

Bowling Green Division US District Court, 241 E Main St, Room 120, Bowling Green, KY 42101-2175 270-781-1110 Counties: Adair, Allen, Barren, Butler, Casey, Clinton, Cumberland, Edmonson, Green, Hart, Logan, Metcalfe, Monroe, Russell, Simpson, Taylor, Todd, Warren. www.kywd.uscourts.gov

Louisville Division Clerk, US District Court, 450 US Courthouse, 601 W Broadway, Louisville, KY 40202 502-582-5156 Fax: 502-582-6302 Counties: Breckinridge, Bullitt, Hardin, Jefferson, Larue, Marion, Meade, Nelson, Oldham, Spencer, Washington. www.kywd.uscourts.gov

Owensboro Division Federal Bldg, Room 126, 423 Frederica St, Owensboro, KY 42301 270-683-0221 Fax: 502-685-4601 Counties: Daviess, Grayson, Hancock, Henderson, Hopkins, McLean, Muhlenberg, Ohio, Union, Webster. www.kywd.uscourts.gov

Paducah Division 127 Federal Building, 501 Broadway, Paducah, KY 42001 270-443-1337 Counties: Ballard, Caldwell, Calloway, Carlisle, Christian, Crittenden, Fulton, Graves, Hickman, Livingston, Lyon, McCracken, Marshall, Trigg. www.kywd.uscourts.gov

US Bankruptcy Court

Eastern District of Kentucky

Lexington Division PO Box 1111, Lexington, KY 40589-1111 606-233-2608 Counties: Anderson, Bath, Bell, Boone, Bourbon, Boyd, Boyle, Bracken, Breathitt, Campbell, Carroll, Carter, Clark, Clay, Elliott, Estill, Fayette, Fleming, Floyd, Franklin, Gallatin, Garrard, Grant, Greenup, Harlan, Harrison, Henry, Jackson, Jessamine, Johnson, Kenton, Knott, Knox, Laurel, Lawrence, Lee, Leslie, Letcher, Lewis, Lincoln, Madison, Magoffin, Martin, Mason, McCreary, Menifee, Mercer, Montgomery, Morgan, Nicholas, Owen, Owsley, Pendleton, Perry, Pike, Powell, Pulaski, Robertson, Rockcastle, Rowan, Scott, Shelby, Trimble, Wayne, Whitley, Wolfe, Woodford. www.kyeb.uscourts.gov

Western District of Kentucky

Louisville Division 546 US Courthouse, 601 W Broadway, Louisville, KY 40202 502-582-5145 Counties: Adair, Allen, Ballard, Barren, Breckinridge, Bullitt, Butler, Caldwell, Calloway, Carlisle, Casey, Christian, Clinton, Crittenden, Cumberland, Daviess, Edmonson, Fulton, Graves, Grayson, Green, Hancock, Hardin, Hart, Henderson, Hickman, Hopkins, Jefferson, Larue, Livingston, Logan, Lyon, Marion, Marshall, McCracken, McLean, Meade, Metcalfe, Monroe, Muhlenberg, Nelson, Ohio, Oldham, Russell, Simpson, Spencer, Taylor, Todd, Trigg, Union, Warren, Washington, Webster.

Louisiana

Attorney General's Office
PO Box 94005
Baton Rouge, LA 70804-9005
www.laag.com/home.cfm

225-342-7013
Fax: 225-342-7335

Governor's Office
PO Box 94004
Baton Rouge, LA 70804-9004
www.gov.state.la.us

225-342-7015
Fax: 225-342-7099

State Archives
3851 Essen Lane
Baton Rouge, LA 70809-2137
www.sec.state.la.us/arch-1.htm

225-922-1000
Fax: 225-922-0433

Capital:	Baton Rouge
	East Baton Rouge Parish
Time Zone:	CST
Number of Parishes:	64
Population:	4,351,769
Web Site:	www.state.la.us

Search Unclaimed Property Online

http://ucp.rev.state.la.us

State Agencies

Criminal Records
State Police, Bureau of Criminal Identification, 265 S Foster, Baton Rouge, LA 70806; 225-925-6095; Fax: 225-925-7005; 8AM-4:30PM. Access by: mail.

Corporation Records
Limited Partnership Records
Limited Liability Company Records
Trademarks/Servicemarks
Commercial Division, Corporation Department, PO Box 94125, Baton Rouge, LA 70804-9125 (3851 Essen Lane, Baton Rouge, LA 70809); 225-925-4704; Fax: 225-925-4726; 8AM-4:30PM. Access by: mail, phone, in person, online. www.sec.state.la.us

Uniform Commercial Code
Secretary of State, UCC Records, PO Box 94125, Baton Rouge, LA 70804-9125; 800-256-3758; Fax: 225-342-5542; 8AM-4:30PM. Access by: mail, online.

Sales Tax Registrations
Restricted access.
This agency will only provide registration information to the registrant itself.
Revenue and Tax Department, Sales Tax Division, PO Box 201, Baton Rouge, LA 70821-0201 (330 N Ardenwwod Blvd, Baton Rouge, LA 70806) (330 N Ardenwwod Blvd, Baton Rouge, LA 70806); 225-925-7356; Fax: 225-925-3860; 8AM-4:30PM
www.rev.state.la.us

Federal Tax Liens
State Tax Liens
Records not available from state agency.
Records are filed with the Clerk of Court at the parish level.

Workers' Compensation Records
Department of Labor, Office of Workers' Compensation, PO Box 94040, Baton Rouge, LA 70804-9040 (LA Department of Labor, Office of Workers' Compensation, Baton Rouge, LA 70802); 225-342-7555; Fax: 225-342-7582; 8AM-5PM. Access by: mail. www.laworks.net

Birth Certificates

Vital Records Registry, PO Box 60630, New Orleans, LA 70160 (325 Loyola Ave Room 102, New Orleans, LA 70112); 504-568-5152, 504-568-5167 For adoptions; Fax: 504-568-5391; 8AM-4PM. Access by: mail. www.dhh.state.la.us/OPH/vrinfo.htm

Death Records

Vital Records Registry, PO Box 60630, New Orleans, LA 70160; 504-568-5152, 504-568-5273 Corrections; Fax: 504-568-5391; 8AM-4PM. Access by: mail. www.dhh.state.la.us/OPH/vrinfo.htm

Marriage Certificates
Divorce Records

Records not available from state agency.

Marriage and divorce records are found at parish of issue. Only Orleans Parish marriage records are available from 1948 on at the VR Registry for a fee of $5.00, same search criteria as others. Include name of bride (maiden), groom and date of marriage.

Accident Reports

Louisiana State Police, Accident Records, PO Box 66614, Baton Rouge, LA 70896 (265 S Foster Blvd, Baton Rouge, LA 70806); 225-925-6388; Fax: 225-925-1898; 8AM-4:30PM. Access by: mail.

Driver Records

Dept of Public Safety and Corrections, Office of Motor Vehicles, PO Box 64886, Baton Rouge, LA 70896 (109 S Foster, Baton Rouge, LA 70806); 225-922-2814, 225-925-6009; Fax: 225-925-6915; 8AM-4:30PM M-F. Access by: mail, online.

Vehicle Ownership
Vehicle Identification

Department of Public Safety & Corrections, Office of Motor Vehicles, PO Box 64884, Baton Rouge, LA 70896 (109 S Foster Dr, Baton Rouge, LA 70806); 225-922-6146, 225-925-7198; Fax: 225-925-3979; 8AM-4PM T-S. Access by: mail, online. www.dps.state.la.us/laomv.html

Boat & Vessel Ownership
Boat & Vessel Registration

Department of Wildlife & Fisheries, PO Box 14796, Baton Rouge, LA 70898 (2000 Quail Road, Baton Rouge, LA 70898); 225-765-2898; Fax: 225-763-5421; 8:15AM-4:15PM. www.wls.state.la.us

Legislation-Current/Pending
Legislation-Passed

Louisiana House (Senate) Representative, State Capitol, 2nd Floor, PO Box 44486, Baton Rouge, LA 70804; 225-342-2456 Information Help Desk, 225-342-2365 Senate Documents (Room 205), 225-342-6458 House Documents (Room 207), 800-256-3793 General Information, In-state; 8AM-5PM. Access by: mail, phone, in person, online. www.legis.state.la.us

Voter Registration

Department of Elections, PO Box 147179, Baton Rouge, LA 70898; 225-925-7885; Fax: 225-925-1841; 8AM-4:30PM.

GED Certificates

Division of Audit Education & Training, PO Box 94064, Baton Rouge, LA 70804-9064; 225-342-0444 Main Number; Fax: 225-219-4439;.

Hunting License Information
Fishing License Information

Wildlife & Fisheries Department, License Division, PO Box 98000, Baton Rouge, LA 70898-9000 (2000 Quail Dr, Baton Rouge, LA 70808); 225-765-2881; Fax: 225-765-2892; 8AM-4:30PM. Access by: mail. wlf.state.la.us

County Courts & Recording Offices

About the Courts...

About the Recording Offices...

Administration

Judicial Administrator, Judicial Council of the Supreme Court 504-5
301 Loyola Av Room 109
New Orleans, LA 70012
www.lasc.org

Court Structure

A District Court Clerk in each Parish holds all the records for that Parish. Each Parish has its own clerk and courthouse.

Online Access

The online computer system, Case Management Information System (CMIS), is operating and development is continuing. It is for internal use only; there is no plan to permit online access to the public. There are a number of Parishes that do offer a means of remote online access to the public.

Organization

64 parishes (not counties), 64 recording offices. The recording officer is the Clerk of Court. Many parishes include tax and other non-UCC liens in their mortgage records. The entire state is in the Central Time Zone (CST).

UCC Records

Financing statements are filed with the Clerk of Court in any parish in the state and are entered onto a statewide computerized database of UCC financing statements available for searching at any parish office. All parishes perform UCC searches for $15.00 per debtor name. Use search request form UCC-11. Cop fees are $.50-1.00 per page.

Lien Records

All federal and state tax liens are filed with the Clerk of Court. Parishes usually file tax liens on personal property in their UCC or mortgage records, and most will perform tax lien searches for varying fees. Some parishes will automatically include tax liens on personal property in a mortgage certificate search.

Real Estate Records

Most parishes will perform a mortgage search. Some will provide a record owner search. Copy and certification fees vary widely.

County Courts & Recording Offices

Acadia

Real Estate Recording—Acadia Parish Clerk of Court, Parkerson Avenue, Court Circle, Crowley, LA 70526. 319-291-2612, Fax: 318-788-1048. 8:30AM-4:30PM.

Felony, Misdemeanor, Civil, Probate—15th District Court, PO Box 922, Crowley, LA 70527. 319-293-3108, Fax: 318-788-1042. 8:30AM-4:30PM. Access by: mail, phone, fax, in person.

Allen

Real Estate Recording—Allen Parish Clerk of Court, Main Street, Courthouse Square, Oberlin, LA 70655., Fax: 318-639-2030. 8AM-4:30PM.

Felony, Misdemeanor, Civil, Probate—33rd District Court, PO Box 248, Oberlin, LA 70655. 318-992-2158, Fax: 318-639-2030. 8AM-4:30PM. Access by: mail, fax, in person.

Ascension

Real Estate Recording—Ascension Parish Clerk of Court, 300 Houmas Street, Donaldsonville, LA 70346., Fax: 225-473-8641. 8:30AM-4:30PM.

Felony, Misdemeanor, Civil, Probate—23rd District Court, PO Box 192, Donaldsonville, LA 70346. 228-435-8258, Fax: 225-473-8641. 8:30AM-4:30PM. Access by: mail, fax, in person.

Assumption

Real Estate Recording—Assumption Parish Clerk of Court, 4809 Highway 1, Courthouse, Napoleonville, LA 70390., Fax: 504-369-2032. 8:30AM-4:30PM.

Felony, Misdemeanor, Civil, Probate—23rd District Court, PO Box 249, Napoleonville, LA 70390. 504-369-6653, Fax: 504-369-2032. 8:30AM-4:30PM. Access by: mail, fax, in person.

Avoyelles

Real Estate Recording—Avoyelles Parish Clerk of Court, East Mark Street, Marksville, LA 71351. 318-437-3680, Fax: 318-253-4614. 8:30AM-4:30PM.

Felony, Misdemeanor, Civil, Probate—12th District Court, PO Box 219, Marksville, LA 71351. 318-437-3550. 8:30AM-4:30PM. Access by: mail, in person.

Beauregard

Real Estate Recording—Beauregard Parish Clerk of Court, 201 West First Street, Courthouse, De Ridder, LA 70634., Fax: 318-462-3916. 8AM-4:30PM.

Felony, Misdemeanor, Civil, Probate—36th District Court, PO Box 100, DeRidder, LA 70634. 318-872-3110, Fax: 318-462-3916. 8AM-4:30PM. Access by: mail, in person.

Bienville

Real Estate Recording—Bienville Parish Clerk of Court, 601 Locust Street, Room 100, Arcadia, LA 71001. 318-574-0655, Fax: 318-263-7426. 8:30AM-4:30PM.

Felony, Misdemeanor, Civil, Probate—2nd District Court, 100 Courthouse Dr, #100, Arcadia, LA 71001. 318-627-3246, Fax: 318-263-7405. 8:30AM-4:30PM. Access by: mail, fax, in person.

Bossier

Real Estate Recording—Bossier Parish Clerk of Court, 200 Burt Blvd, Benton, LA 71006. 8:30AM-4PM.

Felony, Misdemeanor, Civil, Probate—26th District Court, PO Box 430, Benton, LA 71006. 319-372-3405, Fax: 318-965-2713. 8:30AM-4:30PM. Access by: mail, in person, online.

Caddo

Real Estate Recording—Caddo Parish Clerk of Court, 501 Texas Street, Room 103, Shreveport, LA 71101. 318-394-2200, Fax: 318-227-9080. 8:30AM-5PM.

Felony, Misdemeanor, Civil, Probate—1st District Court, 501 Texas St, Rm 103, Shreveport, LA 71101-5408. 318-371-0366, Fax: 318-227-9080. 8:30AM-5PM. Access by: mail, in person.

Calcasieu

Real Estate Recording—Calcasieu Parish Clerk of Court, 1000 Ryan Street, Lake Charles, LA 70601. 318-828-4100, Fax: 318-437-3350. 8:30AM-4:30PM.

Felony, Misdemeanor, Civil, Probate—14th District Court, PO Box 1030, Lake Charles, LA 70602. 318-824-1160, Fax: 318-437-3350. 8:30AM-4:30PM. Access by: mail, fax, in person.

Caldwell

Real Estate Recording—Caldwell Parish Clerk of Court, Main Street, Courthouse, Columbia, LA 71418. 319-243-6210, Fax: 318-649-2037. 8AM-4:30PM.

Felony, Misdemeanor, Civil, Probate—37th District Court, PO Box 1327, Columbia, LA 71418. 319-243-6210, Fax: 318-649-2037. 8AM-4:30PM. Access by: mail, fax, in person. Special note: All record requests must be in writing.

Cameron

Real Estate Recording—Cameron Parish Clerk of Court, 119 Smith Circle, Room 21, Cameron, LA 70631. 319-291-2552, Fax: 318-775-7172. 8:30AM-4:30PM.

Felony, Misdemeanor, Civil, Probate—38th District Court, PO Box 549, Cameron, LA 70631. 319-267-2487, Fax: 318-775-7172. 8:30AM-4:30PM. Access by: mail, fax, in person.

Catahoula

Real Estate Recording—Catahoula Parish Clerk of Court, Courthouse Square, Harrisonburg, LA 71340., Fax: 318-744-5488. 8:30AM-4:30PM.

Felony, Misdemeanor, Civil, Probate—7th District Court, PO Box 198, Harrisonburg, LA 71340. 319-263-6511, Fax: 318-744-5488. 8AM-4:30PM. Access by: mail, in person.

Claiborne

Real Estate Recording—Claiborne Parish Clerk of Court, 512 East Main Street, Homer, LA 71040. 319-334-4340, Fax: 318-927-2345. 8:30AM-4:30PM.

Felony, Misdemeanor, Civil, Probate—2nd District Court, PO Box 330, Homer, LA 71040. 319-352-5040, Fax: 318-927-2345. 8:30AM-4:30PM. Access by: mail, in person.

Concordia

Real Estate Recording—Concordia Parish Clerk of Court, Courthouse, P.O. Box 790, Vidalia, LA 71373. 8:30AM-4:30PM.

Felony, Misdemeanor, Civil, Probate—7th District Court, PO Box 790, Vidalia, LA 71373. 318-639-4351, Fax: 318-336-8217. 8:30AM-4:30PM. Access by: mail, fax, in person.

De Soto

Real Estate Recording—De Soto Parish Clerk of Court, Texas Street, Courthouse Square, Mansfield, LA 71052., Fax: 318-872-4202. 8AM-4:30PM.

Felony, Misdemeanor, Civil, Probate—11th District Court, PO Box 1206, Mansfield, LA 71052. 319-326-8784, Fax: 318-872-4202. 8AM-4:30PM. Access by: mail, in person.

East Baton Rouge

Real Estate Recording—East Baton Rouge Parish Clerk of Court, 222 St. Louis Street, Baton Rouge, LA 70801. 228-435-8220, Fax: 225-389-3392. 7:30AM-5:30PM.

Felony, Misdemeanor, Civil, Probate—19th District Court, PO Box 1991, Baton Rouge, LA 70821. 228-435-8231, Fax: 225-389-3392. 7:30AM-5:30PM. Access by: mail, fax, in person, online.

East Carroll

Real Estate Recording—East Carroll Parish Clerk of Court, 400 First Street, Lake Providence, LA 71254. 318-927-2222. 8:30AM-4:30PM.

Felony, Misdemeanor, Civil, Probate—6th District Court, 400 1st St, Lake Providence, LA 71254. 318-927-9601. 8:30AM-4:30PM. Access by: mail, in person.

East Feliciana

Real Estate Recording—East Feliciana Parish Clerk of Court, 12220 St. Helena Street, Courthouse Square, Clinton, LA 70722., Fax: 225-683-3556. 8AM-4:30PM.

Felony, Misdemeanor, Civil, Probate—20th District Court, PO Box 599, Clinton, LA 70722. 228-467-5573, Fax: 225-683-3556. 8AM-4:30PM. Access by: mail, fax, in person.

Evangeline

Real Estate Recording—Evangeline Parish Clerk of Court, 200 Court Street, Courthouse Bldg. Ville Platte, LA 70586. 318-649-2681. 8AM-4:30PM.

Felony, Misdemeanor, Civil, Probate—13th District Court, PO Drawer 347, Ville Platte, LA 70586. 318-685-4720, Fax: 318-363-5780. 8AM-4:30PM. Access by: mail, in person.

Franklin

Real Estate Recording—Franklin Parish Clerk of Court, 6550 Main Street, Courthouse, Winnsboro, LA 71295., Fax: 318-435-5134. 8:30AM-4:30PM.

Felony, Misdemeanor, Civil, Probate—5th District Court, PO Box 431, Winnsboro, LA 71295. 318-788-8881, Fax: 318-435-5134. 8:30AM-4:30PM. Access by: mail, fax, in person.

Grant

Real Estate Recording—Grant Parish Clerk of Court, 200 Main Street, Colfax, LA 71417., Fax: 318-627-3201. 8:30AM-4:30PM.

Felony, Misdemeanor, Civil, Probate—35th District Court, PO Box 263, Colfax, LA 71417. 318-942-5606. 8:30AM-4:30PM. Access by: mail, phone, in person.

Iberia

Real Estate Recording—Iberia Parish Clerk of Court, 300 Block of Iberia Street, New Iberia, LA 70560. 319-245-1807, Fax: 318-365-0737. 8:30AM-4:30PM.

Felony, Misdemeanor, Civil, Probate—16th District Court, PO Drawer 12010, New Iberia, LA 70562-2010. 318-728-4171, Fax: 318-365-0737. 8:30AM-4:30PM. Access by: mail, phone, fax, in person.

Iberville

Real Estate Recording—Iberville Parish Clerk of Court, 58050 Meriam Street, Plaquemine, LA 70764., Fax: 225-687-5260. 8:30AM-4:30PM.

Felony, Misdemeanor, Civil, Probate—18th District Court, PO Box 423, Plaquemine, LA 70764. 228-769-3080, Fax: 225-687-5260. 8:30AM-4:30PM. Access by: mail, fax, in person.

Jackson

Real Estate Recording—Jackson Parish Clerk of Court, 500 East Court Avenue, Jonesboro, LA 71251. 318-559-2399, Fax: 318-259-5681. 8:30AM-4:30PM.

Felony, Misdemeanor, Civil, Probate—2nd District Court, PO Drawer 730, Jonesboro, LA 71251. 318-559-2000, Fax: 318-259-5681. 8:30AM-4:30PM. Access by: mail, phone, in person.

Jefferson

Real Estate Recording—Jefferson Parish Clerk of Court, 327 Huey P. Long, 2nd Floor, Gretna, LA 70053., Fax: 504-364-3836. 7:30AM-4:30PM.

Jefferson Davis

Real Estate Recording—Jefferson Davis Parish Clerk of Court, 300 State Street, Jennings, LA 70546. 8:30AM-4:30PM.

Felony, Misdemeanor, Civil, Probate—31st District Court, PO Box 799, Jennings, LA 70546. 319-293-3110, Fax: 318-824-1354. 8:30AM-4:30PM. Access by: mail, in person.

La Salle Parish

Real Estate Recording—La Salle Parish Clerk of Court, Courthouse Street, Jena, LA 71342., Fax: 318-992-2157. 8:30AM-4:30PM.

Felony, Misdemeanor, Civil, Probate—28th District Court, PO Drawer 1316, Jena, LA 71342. 319-372-3523, Fax: 318-992-2157. 8:30AM-4:30PM. Access by: mail, phone, in person.

Lafayette

Real Estate Recording—Lafayette Parish Clerk of Court, 800 South Buchanan Street, Lafayette, LA 70501., Fax: 318-269-6392. 8:30AM-4:30PM.

Felony, Misdemeanor, Civil, Probate—15th District Court, PO Box 2009, Lafayette, LA 70502. 318-394-2210, Fax: 318-269-6392. 8:30AM-4:30PM. Access by: mail, phone, in person, online. www.lafayetteparishclerk.com

Lafourche

Real Estate Recording—Lafourche Parish Clerk of Court, 303 West Third, Thibodaux, LA 70301., Fax: 504-447-5800. 8:30AM-4:30PM.

Felony, Misdemeanor, Civil, Probate—17th District Court, PO Box 818, Thibodaux, LA 70302. 504-447-4841, Fax: 504-447-5800. 8:30AM-4:30PM. Access by: mail, fax, in person.

Lincoln

Real Estate Recording—Lincoln Parish Clerk of Court, 100 W. Texas Avenue, Ruston, LA 71270., Fax: 318-255-6004. 8:30AM-4:30PM.

Felony, Misdemeanor, Civil, Probate—3rd District Court, PO Box 924, Ruston, LA 71273-0924. 318-435-5133, Fax: 318-255-6004. 8:30AM-4:30PM. Access by: mail, in person.

Livingston

Real Estate Recording—Livingston Parish Clerk of Court, 20180 Iowa Street, Livingston, LA 70754., Fax: 225-686-1867. 8AM-4:30PM.

Felony, Misdemeanor, Civil, Probate—21st District Court, PO Box 1150, Livingston, LA 70754. 228-769-3025. 8AM-4:30PM. Access by: in person.

Madison

Real Estate Recording—Madison Parish Clerk of Court, 100 North Cedar, Courthouse, Tallulah, LA 71282., Fax: 318-574-3961. 8:30AM-4:30PM.

Felony, Misdemeanor, Civil, Probate—6th District Court, PO Box 1710, Tallulah, LA 71282. 318-932-6741, Fax: 318-574-0656. 8:30AM-4:30PM. Access by: mail, phone, in person.

Morehouse

Real Estate Recording—Morehouse Parish Clerk of Court, 646 School St. Bastrop, LA 71220., Fax: 318-281-3775. 8:30AM-4:30PM.

Felony, Misdemeanor, Civil, Probate—4th District Court, Courthouse, 100 East Madison, Bastrop, LA 71220-3893. 318-628-3515, Fax: 318-281-3775. 8:30AM-4:30PM. Access by: mail, phone, fax, in person.

Natchitoches

Real Estate Recording—Natchitoches Parish Clerk of Court, 200 Church Street, New Courthouse Building-Room 104, Natchitoches, LA 71457., Fax: 318-352-9321. 8:30AM-4:30PM.

Felony, Misdemeanor, Civil, Probate—10th District Court, PO Box 476, Natchitoches, LA 71458. 318-649-2272, Fax: 318-352-9432. 8:15AM-4:30PM. Access by: mail, fax, in person.

Orleans

Real Estate Recording—Orleans Parish Recorder of Mortgages, 421 Loyola Avenue, B-1, Civil Court Building, New Orleans, LA 70112., Fax: 504-592-9192. 9AM-4PM.

Civil Actions Under $20,000, Small Claims—New Orleans City Court, 421 Loyola Ave, Rm 201, New Orleans, LA 70112. 504-592-9155, Fax: 504-592-9281. 8:30AM-4PM. Access by: mail, in person.

Civil, Probate—Civil District Court, 421 Loyola Ave, Rm 402, New Orleans, LA 70112. 504-592-9100, Fax: 504-592-9128. 8AM-5PM. Access by: mail, phone, in person. www.orleanscdc.gov

Felony, Misdemeanor—4th District Court-Criminal Division, 2700 Tulane Ave, Rm 115, New Orleans, LA 70119. 504-827-3520, Fax: 504-827-3385. 8:15AM-3:30PM. Access by: mail, in person.

Ouachita

Real Estate Recording—Ouachita Parish Clerk of Court, 300 St. John, Suite 104, Monroe, LA 71201., Fax: 318-327-1462. 8:30AM-5PM.

Felony, Misdemeanor, Civil, Probate—4th District Court, PO Box 1862, Monroe, LA 71210-1862. 318-628-5824, Fax: 318-327-1462. 8:30AM-5PM. Access by: mail, fax, in person.

Plaquemines

Real Estate Recording—Plaquemines Parish Clerk of Court, 18039 Hwy 15, Courthouse, Pointe a la Hache, LA 70082., Fax: 504-333-9202. 8:30AM-4:30PM.

Felony, Misdemeanor, Civil, Probate—25th District Court, PO Box 129, Pointe A La Hache, LA 70082. 504-333-4377, Fax: 504-333-9202. 8:30AM-4:30PM. Access by: in person.

Pointe Coupee

Real Estate Recording—Pointe Coupee Parish Clerk of Court, 201 East Main, New Roads, LA 70760. 504-638-9556, Fax: 225-638-9590. 8:30AM-4:30PM.

Felony, Misdemeanor, Civil, Probate—18th District Court, PO Box 38, New Roads, LA 70760. 228-467-5404. 8:30AM-4:30PM. Access by: mail, in person.

Rapides

Real Estate Recording—Rapides Parish Clerk of Court, 701 Murray St. Alexandria, LA 71301., Fax: 318-473-4667. 8:30AM-4:30PM.

Felony, Misdemeanor, Civil, Probate—9th District Court, PO Box 952, Alexandria, LA 71309. 318-898-1992, Fax: 318-473-4667. 8:30AM-4:30PM. Access by: mail, in person.

Red River

Real Estate Recording—Red River Parish Clerk of Court, 615 East Carroll Street, Coushatta, LA 71019. 8:30AM-4:30PM.

Felony, Misdemeanor, Civil, Probate—39th District Court, PO Box 485, Coushatta, LA 71019. 319-352-5661. 8:30AM-4:30PM. Access by: mail, in person.

Richland

Real Estate Recording—Richland Parish Clerk of Court, 708 Julia Street, Suite 103, Rayville, LA 71269., Fax: 318-728-7020. 8:30AM-4:30PM.

Felony, Misdemeanor, Civil, Probate—5th District Court, PO Box 119, Rayville, LA 71269. 319-245-2204. 8:30AM-4:30PM. Access by: mail, in person.

Sabine

Real Estate Recording—Sabine Parish Clerk of Court, 400 S Capital Room 102, Many, LA 71449. 318-463-8595, Fax: 318-256-9037. 8AM-4:30PM.

Felony, Misdemeanor, Civil, Probate—11th District Court, PO Box 419, Many, LA 71449. 318-473-8153, Fax: 318-256-9037. 8AM-4:30PM. Access by: mail, fax, in person.

St. Bernard

Real Estate Recording—St. Bernard Parish Clerk of Court, 1101 West St. Bernard Highway, Chalmette, LA 70043. 8:30AM-4:30PM.

Felony, Misdemeanor, Civil, Probate—34th District Court, PO Box 1746, Chalmette, LA 70044. 504-271-3434. 8:30AM-4:30PM. Access by: mail, in person.

St. Charles

Real Estate Recording—St. Charles Parish Clerk of Court, 15045 River Road, Courthouse, Hahnville, LA 70057. 8:30AM-4:30PM.

Felony, Misdemeanor, Civil, Probate—29th District Court, PO Box 424, Hahnville, LA 70057. 504-783-6632, Fax: 504-783-2005. 8:30AM-4:30PM. Access by: mail, in person.

St. Helena

Real Estate Recording—St. Helena Parish Clerk of Court, Courthouse Square, Highway 10, P.O. Box 308, Greensburg, LA 70441. 8:30AM-4:30PM.

Felony, Misdemeanor, Civil, Probate—21st District Court, PO Box 308, Greensburg, LA 70441. 225-686-2216. 8:30AM-4:30PM. Access by: mail, in person.

St. James

Real Estate Recording—St. James Parish Clerk of Court, 5800 LA Highway 44, Courthouse, Convent, LA 70723. 504-562-2300, Fax: 225-562-2383. 8AM-4:30PM.

Felony, Misdemeanor, Civil, Probate—23rd District Court, PO Box 63, Convent, LA 70723. 228-467-4425, Fax: 504-562-2383. 8AM-4:30PM. Access by: mail, in person.

St. John the Baptist

Real Estate Recording—St. John the Baptist Parish Clerk of Court, East 3rd Street & River Road, Edgard, LA 70049. 8:30AM-4:30PM.

Felony, Misdemeanor, Civil, Probate—40th District Court, PO Box 280, Edgard, LA 70049. 504-497-3331. 8:30AM-4:30PM. Access by: mail, in person.

St. Landry

Real Estate Recording—St. Landry Parish Clerk of Court, 100 S. Court St. Opelousas, LA 70570. 319-356-6087, Fax: 318-948-7265. 8AM-4:30PM.

Felony, Misdemeanor, Civil, Probate—27th District Court, PO Box 750, Opelousas, LA 70570. 319-356-6060, Fax: 318-948-1653. 8AM-4:30PM. Access by: mail, in person.

St. Martin

Real Estate Recording—St. Martin Parish Clerk of Court, 415 S. Main Street, Courthouse, St. Martinville, LA 70582. 318-775-5316, Fax: 318-394-7772. 8:30AM-4:30PM.

Felony, Misdemeanor, Civil, Probate—16th District Court, PO Box 308, St. Martinville, LA 70582. 318-775-5718, Fax: 318-394-7772. 8:30AM-4:30PM. Access by: mail, fax, in person.

St. Mary

Real Estate Recording—St. Mary Parish Clerk of Court, 500 Main Street, Courthouse, Franklin, LA 70538., Fax: 318-828-2509. 8:30AM-4:30PM.

Felony, Misdemeanor, Civil, Probate—16th District Court, PO Box 1231, Franklin, LA 70538. 319-326-8621, Fax: 318-828-2509. 8:30AM-4:30PM. Access by: in person.

St. Tammany

Real Estate Recording—St. Tammany Parish Clerk of Court, 510 East Boston Street, Covington, LA 70433. 8:30AM-4:30PM.

Felony, Misdemeanor, Civil, Probate—22nd District Court, PO Box 1090, Covington, LA 70434. 504-898-2430. 8:30AM-4:30PM. Access by: mail, in person. http://stp.pa.st.tammany.la.us/othergov/clerk

Tangipahoa

Real Estate Recording—Tangipahoa Parish Clerk of Court, 110 N. Bay Street, Suite 100, Amite, LA 70422., Fax: 504-748-6503. 8:30AM-4:30PM.

Felony, Misdemeanor, Civil, Probate—21st District Court, PO Box 667, Amite, LA 70422. 504-748-4146, Fax: 504-748-6503. 8:30AM-4:30PM. Access by: mail, phone, fax, in person.

Tensas

Real Estate Recording—Tensas Parish Clerk of Court, Hancock Street, Courthouse, St. Joseph, LA 71366., Fax: 225-222-3443.

Felony, Misdemeanor, Civil, Probate—6th District Court, PO Box 78, St. Joseph, LA 71366. 319-263-7113. 8AM-4:30PM. Access by: in person.

Terrebonne

Real Estate Recording—Terrebonne Parish Clerk of Court, 7856 Main Street, Old Courthouse Building, Houma, LA 70360. 8:30AM-4:30PM.

Felony, Misdemeanor, Civil, Probate—32nd District Court, PO Box 1569, Houma, LA 70361. 504-868-5660. 8:30AM-4:30PM. Access by: mail, in person.

Union

Real Estate Recording—Union Parish Clerk of Court, Courthouse, 100 E. Bayou, Suite 105, Farmerville, LA 71241., Fax: 318-368-3861. 8:30AM-4:30PM.

Felony, Misdemeanor, Civil, Probate—3rd District Court, Courthouse Bldg, 100 E Bayou #105, Farmerville, LA 71241. 318-744-5222, Fax: 318-368-2487. 8:30AM-4:30PM. Access by: mail, in person.

Vermilion

Real Estate Recording—Vermilion Parish Clerk of Court, South State Street, Courthouse, Abbeville, LA 70510., Fax: 318-898-0404. 8:30AM-4:30PM.

Felony, Misdemeanor, Civil, Probate—15th District Court, 100 N. State St, #101, Abbeville, LA 70511-0790. 319-334-2196, Fax: 318-898-0404. 8:30AM-4:30PM. Access by: mail, phone, fax, in person.

Vernon

Real Estate Recording—Vernon Parish Clerk of Court, 201 South Third Street, Leesville, LA 71446., Fax: 318-238-9902. 8AM-4:30PM.

Felony, Misdemeanor, Civil, Probate—30th District Court, PO Box 40, Leesville, LA 71496. 318-428-3281, Fax: 318-238-9902. 8AM-4:30PM. Access by: mail, in person.

Washington

Real Estate Recording—Washington Parish Clerk of Court, Corner of Washington & Main, Franklinton, LA 70438. 8AM-4:30PM.

Felony, Misdemeanor, Civil, Probate—22nd District Court, PO Box 607, Franklinton, LA 70438. 504-839-4663. 8AM-4:30PM. Access by: mail, in person.

Webster

Real Estate Recording—Webster Parish Clerk of Court, 410 Main Street, Courthouse, Minden, LA 71058., Fax: 318-371-0226. 8:30AM-4:30PM.

Felony, Misdemeanor, Civil, Probate—26th District Court, PO Box 370, Minden, LA 71058. 318-766-3921, Fax: 318-371-0226. 8:30AM-4:30PM. Access by: mail, fax, in person.

West Baton Rouge

Real Estate Recording—West Baton Rouge Parish Clerk of Court, 850 8th Street, Port Allen, LA 70767., Fax: 225-383-3694. 8:30AM-4:30PM.

Felony, Misdemeanor, Civil, Probate—18th District Court, PO Box 107, Port Allen, LA 70767. 225-687-5160. 8:30AM-4:30PM. Access by: mail, phone, in person.

West Carroll

Real Estate Recording—West Carroll Parish Clerk of Court, Main Street, Courthouse, Oak Grove, LA 71263. 8:30AM-4:30PM.

Felony, Misdemeanor, Civil, Probate—5th District Court, PO Box 1078, Oak Grove, LA 71263. 318-788-8800. 8:30AM-4:30PM. Access by: mail, in person.

West Feliciana

Real Estate Recording—West Feliciana Parish Clerk of Court, 4789 Prosperity st. Courthouse, St. Francisville, LA 70775., Fax: 225-635-3770. 8:30AM-4:30PM.

Felony, Misdemeanor, Civil, Probate—20th District Court, PO Box 1843, St Francisville, LA 70775. 228-467-5265, Fax: 225-635-3770. 8AM-4:30PM. Access by: mail, in person.

Winn

Real Estate Recording—Winn Parish Clerk of Court, Courthouse, Room 103, 100 Main St. Winnfield, LA 71483. 318-965-2336, Fax: 318-628-2753. 8AM-4:30PM.

Felony, Misdemeanor, Civil, Probate—8th District Court, 100 Main St, Winnfield, LA 71483. 318-948-6516. 8AM-4:30PM. Access by: mail, in person.

Federal Courts

US District Court

Eastern District of Louisiana

New Orleans Division Clerk, Room 151, 500 Camp St, New Orleans, LA 70130504-589-7650 Counties: Assumption Parish, Jefferson Parish, Lafourche Parish, Orleans Parish, Plaquemines Parish, St. Bernard Parish, St. Charles Parish, St. James Parish, St. John the Baptist Parish, St. Tammany Parish, Tangipahoa Parish, Terrebonne Parish, Washington Parish.

Middle District of Louisiana

Baton Rouge Division PO Box 2630, Baton Rouge, LA 70821-2630225-389-3500 Fax: 504-389-3501 Counties: Ascension Parish, East Baton Rouge Parish, East Feliciana Parish, Iberville Parish, Livingston Parish, Pointe Coupee Parish, St. Helena Parish, West Baton Rouge Parish, West Feliciana Parish. www.lamd.uscourts.gov

Western District of Louisiana

Alexandria Division PO Box 1269, Alexandria, LA 71309318-473-7415, Record Room: 318-676-4273, Civil Docket Phone: 318-676-4273, Criminal Docket Phone: 318-676-4272 Fax: 318-473-

7345 Counties: Avoyelles Parish, Catahoula Parish, Concordia Parish, Grant Parish, La Salle Parish, Natchitoches Parish, Rapides Parish, Vernon Parish, Winn Parish.

Lafayette Division Room 113, Federal Bldg, 705 Jefferson St, Lafayette, LA 70501318-262-6613 Counties: Acadia Parish, Evangeline Parish, Iberia Parish, Lafayette Parish, St. Landry Parish, St. Martin Parish, St. Mary Parish, Vermilion Parish.

Lake Charles Division 611 Broad St, Suite 188, Lake Charles, LA 70601318-437-3870 Counties: Allen Parish, Beauregard Parish, Calcasieu Parish, Cameron Parish, Jefferson Davis Parish.

Monroe Division PO Drawer 3087, Monroe, LA 71210318-322-6740 Counties: Caldwell Parish, East Carroll Parish, Franklin Parish, Jackson Parish, Lincoln Parish, Madison Parish, Morehouse Parish, Ouachita Parish, Richland Parish, Tensas Parish, Union Parish, West Carroll Parish..

Shreveport Division US Courthouse, Suite 1167, 300 Fannin St, Shreveport, LA 71101-3083318-676-4273 Counties: Bienville Parish, Bossier Parish, Caddo Parish, Claiborne Parish, De Soto Parish, Red River Parish, Sabine Parish, Webster Parish.

US Bankruptcy Court

Eastern District of Louisiana

New Orleans Division Hale Boggs Federal Bldg, 501 Magazine St, #601, New Orleans, LA 70130504-589-7878 Counties: Assumption Parish, Jefferson Parish, Lafourche Parish, Orleans Parish, Plaquemines Parish, St. Bernard Parish, St. Charles Parish, St. James Parish, St. John the Baptist Parish, St. Tammany Parish, Tangipahoa Parish, Terrebonne Parish, Washington Parish. www.laeb.uscourts.gov

Middle District of Louisiana

Baton Rouge Division Room 119, 707 Florida St, Baton Rouge, LA 70801225-389-0211 Counties: Ascension Parish, East Baton Rouge Parish, East Feliciana Parish, Iberville Parish, Livingston Parish, Pointe Coupee Parish, St. Helena Parish, West Baton Rouge Parish, West Feliciana Parish.

Western District of Louisiana

Alexandria Division Hemenway Bldg, 300 Jackson St, Suite 116, Alexandria, LA 71301-8357318-445-1890 Counties: Avoyelles Parish, Catahoula Parish, Concordia Parish, Grant Parish, La Salle Parish, Natchitoches Parish, Rapides Parish, Vernon Parish, Winn Parish. www.lawb.uscourts.gov

Lafayette-Opelousas Division PO Box J, Opelousas, LA 70571-1909318-948-3451 Fax: 318-948-4426 Counties: Acadia Parish, Evangeline Parish, Iberia Parish, Lafayette Parish, St. Landry Parish, St. Martin Parish, St. Mary Parish, Vermilion Parish. www.lawb.uscourts.gov

Lake Charles Division c/o Lafayette-Opelousas Division, PO Box J, Opelousas, LA 70571-1909318-948-3451 Counties: Allen Parish, Beauregard Parish, Calcasieu Parish, Cameron Parish, Jefferson Davis Parish. www.lawb.uscourts.gov

Monroe Division c/o Shreveport Division, Suite 2201, 300 Fannin St, Shreveport, LA 71101318-676-4267 Counties: Caldwell Parish, East Carroll Parish, Franklin Parish, Jackson Parish, Lincoln Parish, Madison Parish, Morehouse Parish, Ouachita Parish, Richland Parish, Tensas Parish, Union Parish, West Carroll Parish. www.lawb.uscourts.gov

Shreveport Division Suite 2201, 300 Fannin St, Shreveport, LA 71101-3089318-676-4267 Counties: Bienville Parish, Bossier Parish, Caddo Parish, Claiborne Parish, De Soto Parish, Red River Parish, Sabine Parish, Webster Parish. www.lawb.uscourts.gov

Attorney General's Office

6 State House Station   207-626-8800
Augusta, ME 04333   Fax: 207-626-8828
www.state.me.us/ag/homepage

Governor's Office

1 State House Station, Room 236   207-287-3531
Augusta, ME 04333-0001   Fax: 207-287-1034
www.state.me.us

State Archives

84 State House Station   207-287-5790
Augusta, ME 04333-0084   Fax: 207-287-5739
www.state.me.us/sos/arc/general/admin/
mawww001.htm

Capital:	Augusta
	Kennebec County
Time Zone:	EST
Number of Counties:	16
Population:	1,242,051
Web Site:	www.state.me.us

> **Search Unclaimed Property Online**
>
> http://thor.ddp.state.me.us/
> treasurer/plsql/tredev.unclaimed_
> property.search_form

State Agencies

Criminal Records

Maine State Police, State Bureau of Identification, 42 State House Station, Augusta, ME 04333; 207-624-7009; 8AM-5PM. Access by: mail.

Corporation Records
Limited Partnerships
Trademarks/Servicemarks
Assumed Name
Limited Liability Company Records

Secretary of State, Reports & Information Division, 101 State House Station, Augusta, ME 04333-0101; 207-287-4190, 207-287-3676 Main Number; Fax: 207-287-5874; 8AM-5PM. Access by: mail, phone, in person. www.state.me.us/sos/cec/corp/corp.htm

Sales Tax Registrations

Maine Revenue Services, Sales Tax Division, 24 State House Station, Augusta, ME 04333; 207-287-2336; Fax: 207-287-6628; 8AM-4PM. Access by: mail, phone, in person. janus.state.me.us/revenue

Uniform Commercial Code
Federal Tax Liens
State Tax Liens

UCC Filing Section, Secretary of State, 101 State House Station, Augusta, ME 04333-0101 (State Office Bldg, Capitol St, Rm 221, Augusta, ME 04333); 207-287-4177; Fax: 207-287-5874; 8AM-5PM. Access by: mail, phone, in person. www.state.me.us/sos/cec/corp/ucc.htm#fi111

Workers' Compensation Records

Workers Compensation Board, 27 State House Station, Augusta, ME 04333-0027; 207-287-7071; Fax: 207-287-5895; 7:30AM-5PM. Access by: mail, phone, in person. www.state.me.us/wcb

Birth Certificates

Maine Department of Human Services, Vital Records, 11 State House Station, Augusta, ME 04333-0011 (221 State St, Augusta, ME 04333); 207-287-3181, 207-287-3184 Message Phone; Fax: 207-287-1907; 8AM-5PM. Access by: mail, phone, in person.

Death Records

Maine Department of Human Services, Vital Records, 11 State House Station, Augusta, ME 04333-0011; 207-287-3181, 207-287-3184 Message Phone; Fax: 207-287-1907; 8AM-5PM. Access by: mail, phone, in person.

Marriage Certificates

Maine Department of Human Services, Vital Records, 11 State House Station, Augusta, ME 04333-0011; 207-287-3181, 207-287-3184 Message Phone; Fax: 207-287-1907; 8AM-5PM. Access by: mail, phone, in person.

Divorce Records

Maine Department of Human Services, Vital Records, 11 State House Station, Augusta, ME 04333-0011; 207-287-3181, 207-287-3184 Message Phone; Fax: 207-287-1907; 8AM-5PM. Access by: mail, phone, in person.

Accident Reports

Maine State Police, Traffic Division, Station 20, Augusta, ME 04333-0020 (397 Water St, Gardiner, ME 04345); 207-624-8944; Fax: 207-624-8945; 7:30AM-4PM M-F. Access by: mail.

Driver Records

Bureau of Motor Vehicles, Driver License & Control, 29 State House Station, Augusta, ME 04333-0029; 207-287-9005; Fax: 207-287-2592; 8AM-5PM. Access by: mail, online. www.state.me.us/sos/bmv/mbv.htm

Vehicle Ownership
Vehicle Identification

Department of Motor Vehicles, Registration Section, 29 State House Station, Augusta, ME 04333-0029; 207-287-3556; Fax: 207-287-5219; 8AM-5PM M-T,TH-F; 8AM-4PM W. Access by: mail, phone, in person, online. www.state.me.us/sos/bmv/bmv.htm

Boat & Vessel Ownership
Boat & Vessel Registration

Dept of Inland Fisheries & Wildlife, 41 State House Station, Augusta, ME 04333-0041; 207-287-5231; Fax: 207-287-8094; 8AM-5PM M-F. www.state.me.us/ifw

Legislation-Current/Pending
Legislation-Passed

Maine Legislature, 2 State House Station, Legislative Document Room, 3rd Floor, Augusta, ME 04333-0002; 207-287-1692 Bill Status or LD #, 207-287-1408 Document Room; Fax: 207-287-1456; 8AM-5PM. Access by: mail, phone, in person, online. www.state.me.us/legis

Voter Registration

Records not available from state agency.

The data is considered public record in Maine, but can only be accessed at the municipality level.

GED Certificates

Dept of Education, Attn: GED, 23 State House Station, Augusta, ME 04333; 207-287-5890; Fax: 207-287-5894;. http://janus.state.me.us/education

Hunting License Information
Fishing License Information

Inland Fisheries & Wildlife Department, Licensing Division, 284 State St, Augusta, ME 04333; 207-287-5209; Fax: 207-287-8094; 8AM-5PM. Access by: mail, phone, in person. www.state.me.us/ifw

County Courts & Recording Offices

About the Courts...

Administration

State Court Administrator   207-822-0792
PO Box 4820   Fax: 207-822-0781
Portland, ME 04112
www.courts.state.me.us

Court Structure

The Superior Court is the court of general jurisdiction. Circuit Courts may accept civil cases involving claims less than $30,000. District Courts handle some minor "felonies." The small claims limit was raised from $3000 to $4500 as of 7/1/97.

Probate Courts are part of the county court system, not the state system. Even though the Probate Court may be housed with other state courts, it is on a different phone system and calls may not be transferred.

Searching Hints

Many courts will refer written requests for criminal searches to the Maine State Police.

Online Access

Development of a statewide judicial computer system is in progress and will be available statewide sometime in the future. The system will be initially for judicial and law enforcement agencies and will not include public access in the near term. Some counties are online through a private vendor.

About the Recording Offices...

Organization

16 counties, 18 recording offices. The recording officer is County Register of Deeds. Counties maintain a general index of all transactions recorded. Aroostock and Oxford Counties each have two recording offices. There are no county assessors; each town has its own. The entire state is in the Eastern Time Zone (EST).

UCC Records

Financing statements are filed both at the state level, except for real estate related filings, which are filed only with the Register of Deeds. Counties do not perform UCC searches. Copy fees are usually $1.00 per page.

Lien Records

All tax liens on personal property are filed with the Secretary of State. All tax liens on real property are filed with the Register of Deeds.

Real Estate Records

Counties do not usually perform real estate searches, but some will look up a name informally. Copy and certification fees vary widely. Assessor and tax records are located at the town/city level.

County Courts & Recording Offices

Androscoggin

Real Estate Recording—Androscoggin County Register of Deeds, 2 Turner Street, Courthouse, Auburn, ME 4210. 207-794-8512, Fax: 207-784-3163. 8AM-5PM.

Felony, Misdemeanor, Civil Actions Over $30,000—Androscoggin Superior Court, PO Box 3660, Auburn, ME 04212-3660. 207-784-7036. 8AM-4:30PM. Access by: mail, phone, in person.

Misdemeanor, Civil Actions Under $30,000, Eviction, Small Claims—District Court North Androscoggin District 11, 2 Main St, Livermore Falls, ME 04254. 207-941-3040. 8AM-4PM T-Th. Access by: mail, in person.

Lewiston District Court-South #8, PO Box 1345, 85 Park St, Lewiston, ME 04243. 8AM-4PM. Access by: mail, in person.

Waterville District Court-District 7, 18 Colby St, PO Box 397, Waterville, ME 04903. 207-882-6363. 8AM-4PM. Access by: mail, in person.

Probate—Probate Court, 2 Turner St, Auburn, ME 04210. 207-783-5450, Fax: 207-782-5367. 8:30AM-5PM. Access by: mail, in person.

Aroostook

Real Estate Recording—Aroostook County Register of Deeds, 26 Court St. Suite 102, Houlton, ME 4730. 8AM-4:30PM.

Northern Aroostook County Register of Deeds, 13 Hall St. Fort Kent, ME 4743., Fax: 207-834-3138. 8AM-4:30PM.

Felony, Misdemeanor, Civil Actions Over $30,000—Caribou Superior Court, 144 Sweden St, Suite 101, Caribou, ME 04736. 207-532-1502. 8AM-4PM. Access by: mail, in person.

Houlton Superior Court, PO Box 787, Houlton, ME 04730. 207-564-2240. 8AM-4PM. Access by: in person.

Misdemeanor, Civil Actions Under $30,000, Eviction, Small Claims—Caribou District Court-East #1, 144 Sweden St, Caribou, ME 04736. 207-498-8125. 8AM-4PM. Access by: mail, in person.

District Court, PO Box 794 (27 Riverside Dr), Presque Isle, ME 04769. 207-778-3346. 8AM-4PM. Access by: mail, in person.

Fort Kent District Court-District 1, Division of Western Aroostook, PO Box 473, Fort Kent, ME 04743. 207-871-8382. 8AM-4PM. Access by: mail, phone, in person.

Houlton District Court-South #2, PO Box 457, Houlton, ME 04730. 207-532-6563. 8AM-4PM. Access by: mail, phone, in person.

Madawaska District Court-West, PO Box 127, 123 E Main St, Madawaska, ME 04756. 207-743-6671. 8AM-4PM M,T,F. Access by: mail, phone, in person.

Probate—Probate Court, 26 Court St #103, Houlton, ME 04730. 207-532-2147. 8AM-4:30PM. Access by: mail, in person.

Cumberland

Real Estate Recording—Cumberland County Register of Deeds, 142 Federal Street, Portland, ME 4101., Fax: 207-772-4162. 8:30AM-4:30PM.

Civil Actions Over $30,000—Superior Court-Civil, PO Box 287-DTS, Portland, ME 04112. 207-822-4113. 8AM-4:30PM. Access by: mail, phone, in person.

Felony, Misdemeanor—Superior Court-Criminal, PO Box 287, Portland, ME 04112. 207-822-4200. 8AM-4:30PM. Access by: mail, in person.

Civil Actions Under $30,000, Eviction, Small Claims—Portland District Court-South #9-Civil, PO Box 412, 205 Newbury St, Portland, ME 04112. 207-822-4205. 8AM-4:30PM. Access by: mail, in person. Special note: Also see Sagadahoc District Court, which handles cases from the eastern part of Cumberland County.

Misdemeanor—Portland District Court-South #9-Criminal, PO Box 412, Portland, ME 04112. 207-834-5003. 8AM-4:30PM. Access by: mail, in person.

Misdemeanor, Civil Actions Under $30,000, Eviction, Small Claims—Bath District Court-East #6, RR 1, Box 310, Bath, ME 04530. 207-442-0200. 8AM-4PM. Access by: mail, in person.

Bridgton District Court-North #9, 2 Chase Common, Bridgton, ME 04009. 207-667-7141. 8AM-4PM. Access by: phone, in person.

Probate—Probate Court, 142 Federal St, Portland, ME 04101-4196. 207-873-2103. 8:30AM-4:30PM. Access by: mail, in person.

Franklin

Real Estate Recording—Franklin County Register of Deeds, 38 Main Street, Courthouse, Farmington, ME 4938., Fax: 207-778-5899. 8:30AM-4PM.

Felony, Misdemeanor, Civil Actions Over $30,000—Superior Court, 38 Main St, Farmington, ME 04938. 207-778-5888, Fax: 207-778-8261. 8AM-4PM. Access by: phone, in person.

Misdemeanor, Civil Actions Under $30,000, Eviction, Small Claims—District Court #12, 25 Main St, Farmington, ME 04938. 207-782-0281. 8AM-4PM. Access by: in person.

Probate—Probate Court, County Courthouse, 38 Main St, Farmington, ME 04938. 207-778-8200, Fax: 207-778-5899. 8:30AM-4PM.

Hancock

Real Estate Recording—Hancock County Register of Deeds, 50 State Street, Ellsworth, ME 4605., Fax: 207-667-1410. 8:30AM-4PM.

Felony, Misdemeanor, Civil Actions Over $30,000—Superior Court, 60 State St, Ellsworth, ME 04605-1926. 207-667-8434. 8AM-4PM. Access by: mail, in person.

Misdemeanor, Civil Actions Under $30,000, Eviction, Small Claims—Bar Harbor District Court-South #5, 93 Cottage St, Bar Harbor, ME 04609. 207-324-1577. 8AM-4PM. Access by: mail, in person.

Ellsworth District Court-Central #5, 60 State St, Ellsworth, ME 04605. 207-667-7176. 8AM-4PM. Access by: mail, in person.

Probate—Probate Court, 50 State St, Ellsworth, ME 04605. 207-723-4786. 8:30AM-4PM. Access by: mail, in person.

Kennebec

Real Estate Recording—Kennebec County Register of Deeds, 1 Weston Court, 2nd Floor, Augusta, ME 4330., Fax: 207-622-1598. 8AM-4PM.

Felony, Misdemeanor, Civil Actions Over $30,000—Superior Court, 95 State St, Clerk of Court, Augusta, ME 04330. 207-647-3535. 8AM-4PM. Access by: mail, in person.

Misdemeanor, Civil Actions Under $30,000, Eviction, Small Claims—Maine District Court District 7, Division of Southern Kennebec, 145 State St, Augusta, ME 04330-7495. 207-288-3082. 8AM-4PM. Access by: mail, phone, in person.

Probate—Probate Court, 95 State St, Augusta, ME 04330. 207-622-9357, Fax: 207-621-1639. 8AM-4PM. Access by: mail, in person.

Knox

Real Estate Recording—Knox County Register of Deeds, 62 Union Street, Rockland, ME 4841., Fax: 207-594-0446. 8AM-4PM.

Felony, Misdemeanor, Civil Actions Over $30,000—Superior Court, 62 Union St, Rockland, ME 04841-2836. 207-596-2240. 8AM-4PM. Access by: mail, phone, in person.

Misdemeanor, Civil Actions Under $30,000, Eviction, Small Claims—District Court #6, 62 Union St, Rockland, ME 04841. 207-622-7558. 8AM-4PM. Access by: mail, phone, in person.

Probate—Probate Court, 62 Union St, Rockland, ME 04841. 207-594-2576, Fax: 207-594-0443. 8AM-4PM. Access by: mail, in person.

Lincoln

Real Estate Recording—Lincoln County Register of Deeds, 32 High Street, Courthouse, Wiscasset, ME 4578., Fax: 207-882-4061. 8AM-4PM.

Felony, Misdemeanor, Civil Actions Over $30,000—Lincoln County Superior Court, High St, PO Box 249, Wiscasset, ME 04578. 207-897-3800, Fax: 207-882-7741. 8AM-4PM. Access by: mail, in person.

Misdemeanor, Civil Actions Under $30,000, Eviction, Small Claims—District Court #6, 32 High St, PO Box 249, Wiscasset, ME 04578. 207-882-7392, Fax: 207-882-5980. 8AM-4PM. Access by: mail, phone, in person.

Probate—Probate Court, High St, PO Box 249, Wiscasset, ME 04578. 207-882-7517, Fax: 207-882-4061. 8AM-4PM. Access by: mail, in person.

Oxford

Real Estate Recording—Oxford County Register of Deeds, 126 Western Avenue, South Paris, ME 4281., Fax: 207-743-2656. 8AM-4PM.

Felony, Misdemeanor, Civil Actions Over $30,000—Superior Court, Courthouse, 26 Western Ave, PO Box 179, South Paris, ME 04281-0179. 207-743-8942, Fax: 207-743-7346. 8AM-4PM. Access by: mail, in person.

Misdemeanor, Civil Actions Under $30,000, Eviction, Small Claims—Rumford District Court-North #11, Municipal Bldg, 145 Congress St, Rumford, ME 04276. 207-368-5778. 8AM-4PM. Access by: mail, phone, in person.

South Paris District Court-South #11, 26 Western Ave, South Paris, ME 04281. 207-764-2055. 8AM-4PM. Access by: mail, in person.

Probate—Probate Court, 26 Western Ave, PO Box 179, South Paris, ME 04281. 207-743-8936, Fax: 207-743-6671. 8AM-4PM. Access by: mail, in person.

Penobscot

Real Estate Recording—Penobscot County Register of Deeds, 97 Hammond Street, Bangor, ME 4401., Fax: 207-945-4920. 8AM-4:30PM.

Felony, Misdemeanor, Civil Actions Over $30,000—Superior Court, 97 Hammond St, Bangor, ME 04401. 208-226-7611. 8AM-4:30PM. Access by: mail, in person.

Misdemeanor, Civil Actions Under $30,000, Eviction, Small Claims—Bangor District Court, 73 Hammond St, Bangor, ME 04401. 207-942-8769. 8AM-4PM. Access by: mail, in person.

Central District Court-Central #13, 66 Maine St, Lincoln, ME 04457. 207-822-4105. 8AM-4PM. Access by: in person.

Millinocket District Court-North #13, 207 Penobscot Ave, Millinocket, ME 04462. 207-728-4700. 8AM-4PM. Access by: mail, in person.

Newport District Court-West #3, 16 Water St, Newport, ME 04953. 207-442-0200. 8AM-4PM. Access by: mail, in person.

Probate—Probate Court, 97 Hammond St, Bangor, ME 04401-4996. 207-947-0751, Fax: 207-941-8499. 8AM-4:30PM. Access by: mail, in person.

Piscataquis

Real Estate Recording—Piscataquis County Register of Deeds, 51 East Main Street, Dover-Foxcroft, ME 4426., Fax: 207-564-7708. 8:30AM-4PM.

Felony, Misdemeanor, Civil Actions Over $30,000—Superior Court, 51 E Main St, Dover-Foxcroft, ME 04426. 207-594-0427, Fax: 207-564-3363. 8AM-4PM. Access by: mail, in person.

Misdemeanor, Civil Actions Under $30,000, Eviction, Small Claims—District Court #13, 59 E Main St, Dover-Foxcroft, ME 04426. 207-564-2431. 8AM-4PM. Access by: mail, in person.

Probate—Probate Court, 51 E Main St, Dover-Foxcroft, ME 04426. 207-564-8419, Fax: 207-564-3022. 8:30AM-4PM. Access by: mail, in person.

Sagadahoc

Real Estate Recording—Sagadahoc County Register of Deeds, 752 High Street, Bath, ME 4530., Fax: 207-443-8216. 8:30AM-4:30PM.

Felony, Misdemeanor, Civil Actions Over $30,000—Superior Court, 752 High St, PO Box 246, Bath, ME 04530. 207-454-2055. 8AM-4:30PM. Access by: in person.

Misdemeanor, Civil Actions Under $30,000, Eviction, Small Claims—District Court #6, RR 1, Box 310, New Meadows Rd, Bath, ME 04530. 207-443-8218. 8AM-4PM. Access by: mail, in person. Special note: This court handles the eastern part of Cumberland County & all of Sagadahoc County.

Probate—Probate Court, 752 High St, PO Box 246, Bath, ME 04530. 207-443-9733, Fax: 207-443-8217. 8:30AM-4:30PM. Access by: in person.

Somerset

Real Estate Recording—Somerset County Register of Deeds, Corner of Court & High Street, Skowhegan, ME 4976., Fax: 207-474-2793. 8:30AM-4:30PM.

Felony, Misdemeanor, Civil Actions Over $30,000—Superior Court, PO Box 725, Skowhegan, ME 04976. 207-474-9518. 8AM-4PM. Access by: in person.

Misdemeanor, Civil Actions Under $30,000, Eviction, Small Claims—District Court #12, PO Box 525, 88 Water St, Skowhegan, ME 04976. 207-493-3144. 8AM-4PM. Access by: mail, in person.

Probate—Probate Court, Court St, Skowhegan, ME 04976. 207-474-5161. 8:30AM-4:30PM. Access by: mail, in person.

Waldo

Real Estate Recording—Waldo County Register of Deeds, 137 Church Street, Belfast, ME 4915., Fax: 207-338-6360. 8AM-4PM.

Felony, Misdemeanor, Civil Actions Over $30,000—Superior Court, 137 Church St, PO Box 188, Belfast, ME 04915. 207-338-2780, Fax: 207-338-1086. 8AM-4PM. Access by: mail, in person.

Misdemeanor, Civil Actions Under $30,000, Eviction, Small Claims—District Court #5, PO Box 382, 103 Church St, Belfast, ME 04915. 207-363-1230. 8AM-4PM. Access by: mail, in person.

Probate—Probate Court, 172 High St, PO Box 323, Belfast, ME 04915. 207-338-3107, Fax: 207-338-6360. 9AM-4PM. Access by: mail, in person.

Washington

Real Estate Recording—Washington County Register of Deeds, 47 Court Street, Machias, ME 4654., Fax: 207-255-3838. 8AM-4PM.

Felony, Misdemeanor, Civil—Superior Court, Clerk of Court, PO Box 526, Machias, ME 04654. 207-255-6591. 8AM-4PM. Access by: mail, in person.

Misdemeanor, Civil Actions Under $30,000, Eviction, Small Claims—Calais District Court-North #4, 88 South St, Calais, ME 04619. 207-474-3322. 8AM-4PM. Access by: in person.

Maine District Court-4th District, 47 Court St, PO Box 297, Machias, ME 04654. 207-255-3326. 8AM-4PM. Access by: mail, in person.

Probate—Probate Court, PO Box 297, Machias, ME 04654. 207-283-1147. 8AM-4PM.

York

Real Estate Recording—York County Register of Deeds, 45 Kennebunk Rd. Alfred, ME 4002., Fax: 207-324-2886. 8:30AM-4:30PM.

Felony, Misdemeanor, Civil Actions Over $30,000—Superior Court, Clerk of Court, PO Box 160, Alfred, ME 04002. 207-324-6737. 8AM-4:30PM. Access by: in person.

Misdemeanor, Civil Actions Under $30,000, Eviction, Small Claims—Biddeford District Court-East #10, 25 Adams St, Biddeford, ME 04005. 207-287-8075. 8AM-4PM. Access by: in person.

Springvale District Court-West #10, PO Box 95, Butler St, Springvale, ME 04083. 207-338-1940. 8AM-4PM. Access by: mail, in person.

York District Court-South #10, PO Box 770, Chase's Pond Rd, York, ME 03909-0770. 207-364-7171. 8AM-4PM. Access by: in person.

Probate—Probate Court, PO Box 399, 45 Kennebunk Rd, Alfred, ME 04002. 207-324-5122, Fax: 207-324-0163. 8:30AM-4:30PM. Access by: mail, in person.

Federal Courts

US District Court

Bangor Division Court Clerk, PO Box 1007, Bangor, ME 04402-1007207-945-0575 Counties: Aroostook, Franklin, Hancock, Kennebec, Penobscot, Piscataquis, Somerset, Waldo, Washington. www.qwi.net/~uscdcme
Portland Division Court Clerk, 156 Federal St, Portland, ME 04101207-780-3356 Counties: Androscoggin, Cumberland, Knox, Lincoln, Oxford, Sagadahoc, York. www.med.uscourts.gov

US Bankruptcy Court

Bangor Division PO Box 1109, Bangor, ME 04402-1109207-945-0348 Fax: 207-945-0304 Counties: Aroostook, Franklin, Hancock, Kennebec, Knox, Lincoln, Penobscot, Piscataquis, Waldo, Washington. www.meb.uscourts.gov
Portland Division 537 Congress St, Portland, ME 04101207-780-3482 Fax: 207-780-3679 Counties: Androscoggin, Cumberland, Oxford, Sagadahoc, York. www.meb.uscourts.gov

Maryland

Attorney General's Office
200 St Paul Place, 16th Floor   410-576-6300
Baltimore, MD 21202   Fax: 410-576-7003
www.oag.state.md.us

Governor's Office
State House   410-974-3901
Annapolis, MD 21401   Fax: 410-974-3275
www.gov.state.md.us

State Archives
350 Rowe Blvd   410-260-6400
Annapolis, MD 21401   Fax: 410-974-3895
www.mdsa.net

Capital:	Annapolis
	Anne Arundel County
Time Zone:	EST
Number of Counties:	23
Population:	5,094,289
Web Site:	www.mec.state.md.us

Search Unclaimed Property Online
http://in1.comp.state.md.us/ unclaim/default.asp

State Agencies

Criminal Records
Criminal Justice Information System, Public Safety & Correctional Records, PO Box 5743, Pikeville, MD 21282-5743 (6776 Reisterstown Rd, Rm 200, Pikeville, MD 21208); 410-764-4501, 888-795-0011; Fax: 410-974-2169; 8AM-3:30PM. Access by: mail, online.

Corporation Records
Limited Partnerships
Trade Names
Limited Liability Company Records
Fictitious Name
Department of Assessments and Taxation, Corporations Division, 301 W Preston St, Room 809, Baltimore, MD 21201; 410-767-1340, 410-767-1330 Charter Information; Fax: 410-333-7097; 8AM-4:30PM. Access by: mail, phone, in person, online. www.dat.state.md.us/sdatweb/services.html

Sales Tax Registrations
Taxpayer Services, Revenue Administration Division, 301 W Preston St #206, Baltimore, MD 21201; 410-767-1313; Fax: 410-767-1571; 8AM-5PM. Access by: mail, phone, in person. www.comp.state.md.us

Trademarks/Servicemarks
Secretary of State, Trademarks Division, State House, Annapolis, MD 21401; 410-974-5531 x2; Fax: 410-974-5527; 9AM-5PM. Access by: mail. www.sos.state.md.us

Uniform Commercial Code
UCC Division, Department of Assessments & Taxation, 301 West Preston St, Baltimore, MD 21201; 410-767-1340; Fax: 410-333-7097; 8AM-4:30PM. Access by:, online. www.dat.state.md.us/bsfd

Federal Tax Liens
State Tax Liens
Records not available from state agency.

Records are found at the county Circuit Court.

Workers' Compensation Records
Workers Compensation Commission, Six N Liberty St, Baltimore, MD 21201; 410-767-0900; Fax: 410-333-8122; 8AM-4:30PM. Access by: mail, phone, in person, online.

Birth Certificates

Department of Health, Division of Vital Records, 6550 Reisterstown Road, Baltimore, MD 21215; 410-764-3038, 410-764-3069; Fax: 410-358-7381; 8AM-4PM M-F; 3rd Saturday of each month. Access by: mail, phone, in person. www.sos.state.md.us/sos/html/vitalrec.html

Death Records

Department of Health, Division of Vital Records, 6550 Reisterstown Road, Baltimore, MD 21215; 410-764-3038; Fax: 410-358-7381; 8AM-4PM M-F; 3rd Saturday of each month. Access by: mail, phone, in person.

Marriage Certificates

Department of Health, Division of Vital Records, 6550 Reisterstown Road, Baltimore, MD 21215; 410-764-3038; Fax: 410-358-7381; 8AM-4PM M-F; 3rd Saturday of each month. Access by: mail, phone, in person.

Divorce Records

Department of Health, Division of Vital Records, 6550 Reisterstown Road, Baltimore, MD 21215; 410-764-3038; Fax: 410-358-7381; 8AM-4PM M-F; 3rd Saturday of each month. Access by: mail.

Accident Reports

Maryland State Police, Central Records Division, 1711 Belmont Ave, Baltimore, MD 21244; 410-298-3390; Fax: 410-298-3198; 8AM-5PM. Access by: mail.

Driver Records

MVA, Driver Records Unit, 6601 Ritchie Hwy, NE, Glen Burnie, MD 21062; 410-787-7758; 8:15AM-4:30PM. Access by: mail, online. mva.state.md.us

Vehicle Ownership
Vehicle Identification

Department of Motor Vehicles, Vehicle Registration Division, Room 206, 6601 Ritchie Hwy, NE, Glen Burnie, MD 21062; 410-768-7520; Fax: 410-768-7653; 8:15AM-4:30PM. Access by: mail, online. www.mva.state.us

Boat & Vessel Ownership
Boat & Vessel Registration

Dept of Natural Resources, Licensing & Watercraft Division, 580 Taylor Ave, Annapolis, MD 21401; 410-260-8200; 8:30AM-4:30PM. www.dnr.state.md.us

Legislation-Current/Pending
Legislation-Passed

Maryland General Assembly, Dept of Legislative Services, 90 State Circle, Annapolis, MD 21401-1991; 410-946-5400 Bill Status Only, 410-946-5010, 800-492-7122 In-state; Fax: 410-946-5405; 8AM-5PM. Access by: mail, phone, in person, online. http://mlis.state.md.us

Voter Registration

Restricted access.
Records must be viewed or confirmed at the local level. This agency has information for 9 counties and will sell in bulk media format for political purposes only.
State Board of Elections, PO Box 6486, Annapolis, MD 21401-0486; 410-974-3711; Fax: 410-974-2019; 8AM-5PM

GED Certificates

State Department of Education, GED Office, 200 W Baltimore St, Baltimore, MD 21201; 410-767-0538; Fax: 410-333-8435; 8AM-5PM.

Hunting License Information
Fishing License Information

Department of Natural Resources, Licensing & Registration Service, 580 Taylor Ave, Annapolis, MD 21401; 410-260-8200; Fax: 410-260-8217; 8AM-4:30PM. www.dnr.state.md.us

County Courts & Recording Offices

About the Courts...
About the Recording Offices...

Administration

Court Administrator, Administrative Office of the Courts 410-260-1
361 Rowe Blvd, Courts of Appeal Building   Fax: 410-974-2169
Annapolis, MD 21401
www.courts.state.md.us

Court Structure

The Ciruit court is the highest court of record. Effective 10/1/98, the civil judgment limit was increased from $20,000 to $25,000 at the District Court level.

Certain categories of minor felonies are handled by the District Courts. However, all misdemeanors and felonies that require a jury trial are handled by a Circuit Courts.

The Circuit Court handles Probate in Montgomery and Harford counties. In other counties, Probate is handled by the Register of Wills and is a county, not a court, function.

Online Access

An online computer system called the Judicial Information System (JIS) or (SJIS) provides access to civil and criminal case information from the following:

All District Courts

Circuit Court Civil Case Management System

Anne Arundel and Carroll County Circuit Courts

Baltimore City Court

Inquiries may be made to: the District Court traffic system for case information data, calendar information data, court schedule data, or officer schedule data; the District Court criminal system for case information data or calendar caseload data; the District Court civil system for case information data, attorney name and address data; the land records system for land and plat records. The one-time fee for JIS access is $50.00, which must be included with the application, and there is a charge of $.50 per minute for access time. For additional information or to receive a registration packet, write or call Judicial Information Systems, Security Administrator, 2661 Riva Rd., Suite 900, Annapolis, MD 21401, 410-260-1031.

Organization

23 counties and one independent city, 24 recording offices. The recording officer is Clerk of the Circuit Court. Baltimore City has a recording office separate from the county of Baltimore. See the City/County Locator section at the end of this chapter for ZIP Codes that include both the city and the county. The entire state is in the Eastern Time Zone (EST).

UCC Records

This was a dual filing state until July 1995. As of July 1995, all new UCC filings are submitted only to the central filing office. Financing statements are usually filed both at the state level and with the Clerk of Circuit Court, except for consumer goods, farm related and real estate related filings, which will still be filed.

Lien Records

All tax liens are filed with the county Clerk of Circuit Court. Counties will not perform searches.

Real Estate Records

Counties will not perform real estate searches. Copies usually cost $.50 per page, and certification fees $5.00 per document.

County Courts & Recording Offices

Allegany

Real Estate Recording—Allegany County Clerk of the Circuit Court, 30 Washington Street, Cumberland, MD 21502. 302-571-7540, Fax: 301-777-2100. 8AM-4:30PM.

Felony, Misdemeanor, Civil Actions Over $25,000—4th Judicial Circuit Court, 30 Washington St, PO Box 359, Cumberland, MD 21502. 302-429-7740, Fax: 301-777-2100. 8:30AM-4:30PM. Access by: mail, phone, fax, in person.

Misdemeanor, Civil Actions Under $25,000, Eviction, Small Claims—District Court, 3 Pershing St, 2nd Floor, Cumberland, MD 21502. 302-422-5922. 8:30AM-4:30PM. Access by: mail, in person, online.

Probate—Register of Wills, Courthouse 30 Washington St, Cumberland, MD 21502. 301-952-4080. 8AM-4:30PM. Access by: mail, in person. Special note: Toll free in MD is 1-888-724-0148. www.registers.state.md.us/county/allegany.html

Anne Arundel

Real Estate Recording—Anne Arundel County Clerk of the Circuit Court, 7 Church Circle Street, Room 21 21, Annapolis, MD 21401., Fax: 410-222-1087. 8:30AM-4:30PM.

Felony, Misdemeanor, Civil Actions Over $25,000—5th Judicial Circuit Court, Box 71, Annapolis, MD 21404. 410-632-2525. 8:30AM-4:30PM. Access by: mail, phone, in person, online.

Misdemeanor, Civil Actions Under $25,000, Eviction, Small Claims—District Court, 251 Rowe Blvd, #141, Annapolis, MD 21401. 410-651-1555. 8:30AM-4:30PM. Access by: mail, in person, online.

Probate—Register of Wills, 44 Calvert St (PO Box 2368), Annapolis, MD 21404-2368. 410-638-3275, Fax: 410-222-1467. 8:30AM-4PM. Access by: in person. Special note: Wills only, no genealogy searches. www.registers.state.md.us/county/annearundel.htm

Baltimore

Real Estate Recording—Baltimore County Clerk of the Circuit Court, 401 Bosley Ave. County Courts Building, Baltimore, MD 21204., Fax: 410-887-3062. 8:30AM-4:30PM.

Circuit Court for Baltimore City, 100 North Calvert Street, Room 610, Baltimore, MD 21202. 8AM-4:30PM.

Felony, Misdemeanor, Civil Actions Over $25,000—3rd Judicial Circuit Court, 401 Bosley Ave, 2nd Floor, Towson, MD 21204. 410-887-2601. 8:30AM-4:30PM. Access by: in person.

Misdemeanor, Civil Actions Under $25,000, Eviction, Small Claims—District Court, 120 E Chesapeake Ave, Towson, MD 21286-5307. 410-752-5131. 8:30AM-4:30PM. Access by: in person, online.

Probate—Register of Wills, 401 Bosley Ave, Mail Stop 3507, Towson, MD 21204-4403. 410-887-6685, Fax: 410-583-2517. 8AM-4:30PM. Access by: mail, phone, fax, in person. www.registers.state.md.us

Baltimore City

Civil Actions Over $25,000—8th Judicial Circuit Court-Civil Division, 111 N Calvert, Rm 409, Baltimore, MD 21202. 410-758-0414. 8:30AM-4:30PM. Access by: mail, phone, in person.

Felony, Misdemeanor—8th Judicial Circuit Court-Criminal Division, 110 N Calvert Rm 200, Baltimore, MD 21202. 410-758-0585. 8:30AM-4:30PM. Access by: in person, online.

Civil Actions Under $25,000, Eviction, Small Claims—District Court-Civil Division, 501 E Fayette St, Baltimore, MD 21202. 410-878-8900. 8:30AM-4:30PM. Access by: mail, in person.

Misdemeanor—District Court-Criminal Division, 1400 E North Ave, Baltimore, MD 21213. 978-462-4474. 8AM-4:30PM. Access by: mail, in person, online.

Probate—Register of Wills, Courthouse East, 111 N Calvert St, Rm 352, Baltimore, MD 21202. 978-772-2100, Fax: 410-752-3494. 8AM-4:30PM. Access by: mail, in person.

Calvert

Real Estate Recording—Calvert County Clerk of the Circuit Court, 175 Main Street, Courthouse, Prince Frederick, MD 20678. 978-368-7811. 8:30AM-4:30PM.

Felony, Misdemeanor, Civil Actions Over $25,000—7th Judicial Circuit Court, 175 Main St Courthouse, Prince Frederick, MD 20678. 978-356-2681. 8:30AM-4:30PM. Access by: mail, phone, in person.

Misdemeanor, Civil Actions Under $25,000, Eviction, Small Claims—District Court, 200 Duke St Rm 2200, Prince Frederick, MD 20678. 978-373-4151. 8:30AM-4:30PM. Access by: mail, in person, online.

Probate—Register of Wills, 175 Main St Courthouse, Prince Frederick, MD 20678. 978-369-0500, Fax: 410-535-1787. 8:30AM-4:30PM. Access by: mail, phone, in person. www.registers.state.md.us/county/calvert.html

Caroline

Real Estate Recording—Caroline County Clerk of the Circuit Court, Market Street, Courthouse, Denton, MD 21629. 410-778-7466, Fax: 410-479-1142. 8:30AM-4:30PM.

Felony, Misdemeanor, Civil Actions Over $25,000—2nd Judicial Circuit Court, Box 458, Denton, MD 21629. 978-297-0156, Fax: 410-479-1142. 8:30AM-4:30PM. Access by: in person. Special note: Misdemeanor case records held at District Court until appealed, then stored at Circuit Court.

Misdemeanor, Civil Actions Under $25,000, Eviction, Small Claims—District Court, 207 S 3rd St, Denton, MD 21629. 978-345-2111, Fax: 410-479-5808. 8AM-4:30PM. Access by: in person, online.

Probate—Orphan's Court, Caroline County Courthouse, 109 Market St, Rm 108, PO Box 416, Denton, MD 21629. 973-881-4126, Fax: 410-479-4983. 8AM-4:30PM. Access by: mail, in person. www.registers.state.md.us/county/caroline.html

Carroll

Real Estate Recording—Carroll County Clerk of the Circuit Court, 55 North Court Street, Room G8, Westminster, MD 21157., Fax: 410-876-0822. 8:30AM-4:30PM.

Felony, Misdemeanor, Civil Actions Over $25,000—5th Judicial Circuit Court, 55 N Court Street, Westminster, MD 21157. 410-758-5200, Fax: 410-876-0822. 8:30AM-4:30PM. Access by: in person, online.

Misdemeanor, Civil Actions Under $25,000, Eviction, Small Claims—District Court, 55 N Court St, Westminster, MD 21157. 410-758-1773. 8:30AM-4:30PM. Access by: mail, in person, online.

Probate—Register of Wills, 55 N Court St, Rm 104, Westminster, MD 21157. 410-848-2586, Fax: 410-876-0657. 8:30AM-4:30PM. www.registers.state.md.us/county/carroll

Cecil

Real Estate Recording—Cecil County Clerk of the Circuit Court, 129 East Main St. Room 108, Elkton, MD 21921. 410-996-5394. 8:30AM-4:30PM.

Felony, Misdemeanor, Civil Actions Over $25,000—2nd Judicial Circuit Court, 129 E Main St, Rm 108, Elkton, MD 21921. 410-996-5373, Fax: 410-392-6032. 8:30AM-4:30PM. Access by: in person.

Misdemeanor, Civil Actions Under $25,000, Eviction, Small Claims—District Court, 170 E Main St, Elkton, MD 21921. 410-996-0700. 8:30AM-4:30PM. Access by: in person, online.

Probate—Register of Wills, County Courthouse, Rm 307, Elkton, MD 21921. 410-778-1830, Fax: 410-620-3849. 8:30AM-4:30PM. Access by: mail, phone, in person. www.registers.state.md.us/county/cecil.html

Charles

Real Estate Recording—Charles County Clerk of the Circuit Court, 200 Charles Street, Courthouse, La Plata, MD 20646. 301-932-3201. 8:30AM-4:30PM.

Felony, Misdemeanor, Civil Actions Over $25,000—Circuit Court for Charles County, PO Box 970, La Plata, MD 20646. 302-577-2430. 8:30AM-4:30PM. Access by: in person.

Misdemeanor, Civil Actions Under $25,000, Eviction, Small Claims—District Court, PO Box 3070, La Plata, MD 20646. 302-577-2550. 8:30AM-4:30PM. Access by: in person, online.

Probate—Register of Wills, Courthouse, Box 3080, La Plata, MD 20646. 302-577-6470, Fax: 301-932-3349. 8:30AM-4:30PM. Access by: mail, phone, in person. www.registers.state.md/county/charles.html

Dorchester

Real Estate Recording—Dorchester County Clerk of the Circuit Court, 206 High Street, Cambridge, MD 21613. 8:30AM-4:30PM.

Felony, Misdemeanor, Civil Actions Over $25,000—1st Judicial Circuit Court, Box 150, Cambridge, MD 21613. 410-638-3426. 8:30AM-4:30PM. Access by: in person.

Misdemeanor, Civil Actions Under $25,000, Eviction, Small Claims—District Court, Box 547, Cambridge, MD 21613. 410-632-1529. 8:30AM-4:30PM. Access by: in person, online.

Probate—Register of Wills, Box 263, Cambridge, MD 21613. 410-651-0440, Fax: 410-228-4988. 8AM-4:30PM; Public hours 8:30AM-4:30PM. Access by: mail, phone, in person. www.registers.state.md.us/county/dorchester.html

Frederick

Real Estate Recording—Frederick County Clerk of the Circuit Court, 100 West Patrick Street, Frederick, MD 21701. 301-932-3345, Fax: 301-846-2245. 8:30AM-4:30PM.

Felony, Misdemeanor, Civil Actions Over $25,000—6th Judicial Circuit Court, 100 W Patrick St, Frederick, MD 21701. 301-952-3250. 8AM-4:30PM. Access by: in person.

Misdemeanor, Civil Actions Under $25,000, Eviction, Small Claims—District Court, 100 W Patrick St, Frederick, MD 21701. 301-952-3946. 8:30AM-4:30PM. Access by: mail, phone, in person, online.

Probate—Register of Wills, 100 W Patrick St, Frederick, MD 21701. 301-932-3300, Fax: 301-846-0744. 8AM-4:30PM. Access by: mail, phone, in person. www.registers.state.md.us/county/frederick

Garrett

Real Estate Recording—Garrett County Clerk of the Circuit Court, 203 South Fourth Street, Oakland, MD 21550. 301-724-3760, Fax: 301-334-5017. 8:30AM-4:30PM.

Felony, Misdemeanor, Civil Actions Over $25,000—4th Judicial Circuit Court, PO Box 447, Oakland, MD 21550. 301-694-2000, Fax: 301-334-5017. 8:30AM-4:30PM. Access by: mail, in person.

Misdemeanor, Civil Actions Under $25,000, Eviction, Small Claims—District Court, 205 S 3rd St, Oakland, MD 21550. 301-733-8660. 8:30AM-4:30PM. Access by: mail, in person, online.

Probate—Register of Wills, Courthouse, 313 E Alder St, Room 103, Oakland, MD 21550. 301-733-3170, Fax: 301-334-1984. 8AM-4:30PM. Access by: mail, in person. www.registers.state.md.us/county/garrett

Harford

Real Estate Recording—Harford County Clerk of the Circuit Court, 20 West Courtland Street, Bel Air, MD 21014. 8:30AM-4PM.

Felony, Misdemeanor, Civil Actions Over $25,000—3rd Judicial Circuit, 20 W Courtland St, Bel Air, MD 21014. 978-687-7184. 8:30AM-4:30PM. Access by: in person.

Misdemeanor, Civil Actions Under $25,000, Eviction, Small Claims—District Court, 2 S Bond St, Bel Air, MD 21014. 410-838-2300. 8:30AM-4:30PM. Access by: mail, phone, in person, online.

Probate—Register of Wills, 20 W Courtland St, Room 304, Bel Air, MD 21014. 978-632-2373, Fax: 410-893-3177. 8:30AM-4:30PM. Access by: in person. www.registers.state.md.us/county/harford.html

Howard

Real Estate Recording—Howard County Clerk of the Circuit Court, 8360 Court Avenue, Ellicott City, MD 21043. 8:30AM-4:30PM.

Felony, Misdemeanor, Civil Actions Over $25,000—5th Judicial Circuit Court, 8360 Court Ave, Ellicott City, MD 21043. 410-651-1696. 8:30AM-4:30PM. Access by: in person.

Misdemeanor, Civil Actions Under $25,000, Eviction, Small Claims—District Court, 3451 Courthouse Dr, Ellicott City, MD 21043. 410-778-7460. 8:30AM-4:30PM. Access by: mail, in person, online.

Probate—Register of Wills, 8360 Court Ave, Ellicott City, MD 21043. 410-651-2713, Fax: 410-313-3409. 8:30AM-4:30PM. Access by: in person. www.registers.state.md.us/county/howard.html

Kent

Real Estate Recording—Kent County Clerk of the Circuit Court, Courthouse, 103 N. Cross St. Chestertown, MD 21620. 8:30AM-4:30PM.

Felony, Misdemeanor, Civil Actions Over $25,000—2nd Judicial Circuit Court, 103 N Cross St Courthouse, Chestertown, MD 21620. 410-778-7460, Fax: 410-778-7412. 8:30AM-4:30PM. Access by: in person.

Misdemeanor, Civil Actions Under $25,000, Eviction, Small Claims—District Court, 103 N Cross St, Chestertown, MD 21620. 410-778-1830, Fax: 410-778-3474. 8:30AM-4:30PM. Access by: in person, online.

Probate—Register of Wills, 103 N Cross St, Chestertown, MD 21620. 410-778-7466, Fax: 410-778-2466. 8AM-4:30PM. Access by: mail, in person. www.registers.state.md.us/county/kent.html

Montgomery

Real Estate Recording—Montgomery County Clerk of the Circuit Court, 50 Maryland Ave. County Courthouse, Rockville, MD 20850. 301-694-1111, Fax: 301-217-1635. 8:30AM-4:30PM.

Felony, Misdemeanor, Civil Actions Over $25,000—6th Judicial Circuit Court, 50 Maryland Ave, Rockville, MD 20850. 248-691-7440. 8:30AM-4:30PM. Access by: in person.

Misdemeanor, Civil Actions Under $25,000, Eviction, Small Claims—District Court, 8665 Georgia Ave, Silver Spring, MD 20910. 301-791-4740. 8:30AM-4:30PM. Access by: mail, in person, online.

Rockville District Court, 27 Courthouse Square, Rockville, MD 20850. 8:30AM-4:30PM. Access by: mail, in person, online.

Probate—Register of Wills, Maryland Ave, Suite 322, Rockville, MD 20850. 301-694-1972, Fax: 301-217-7306. 8:30AM-4:30PM. Access by: mail, in person. www.co.mo.md.us/judicial

Prince George's

Real Estate Recording—Prince George's County Clerk of the Circuit Court, 14735 Main Street, Upper Marlboro, MD 20772. 302-629-5433.

Felony, Misdemeanor, Civil Actions Over $25,000—7th Judicial Circuit Court, 14735 Main St, Upper Marlboro, MD 20772. 8:30AM-4:30PM. Access by: mail, in person.

Misdemeanor, Civil Actions Under $25,000, Eviction, Small Claims—District Court, 14735 Main St, Rm 173B, Upper Marlboro, MD 20772. 302-645-6163. 8:30AM-4:30PM. Access by: mail, in person, online.

Probate—Register of Wills, PO Box 1729, Upper Marlboro, MD 20773. 302-628-2036, Fax: 301-952-4489. 8:30AM-4:30PM. Access by: mail, in person. www.registers.state.md.us/county/princegeorges.html

Queen Anne's

Real Estate Recording—Queen Anne's County Clerk of the Circuit Court, 100 Court House Square, Centreville, MD 21617. 410-758-0414. 8:30AM-4:30PM.

Felony, Misdemeanor, Civil Actions Over $25,000—2nd Judicial Circuit Court, Courthouse, 100 Courthouse Sq, Centreville, MD 21617. 410-758-1773. 8:30AM-4:30PM. Access by: in person. Special note: Misdemeanor case files at District Court until appealed by jury trial.

Misdemeanor, Civil Actions Under $25,000, Eviction, Small Claims—District Court, 120 Broadway, Centreville, MD 21617. 410-758-5200. 8:30AM-4:30PM. Access by: in person.

Probate—Register of Wills, Liberty Bldg, 107 N Liberty St #220, PO Box 59, Centreville, MD 21617. 410-758-0585, Fax: 410-758-4408. 8AM-4:30PM. Access by: mail, in person. www.registers.state.md.us/county/queenannes.html

Somerset

Real Estate Recording—Somerset County Clerk of the Circuit Court, 30512 Prince William Street, Princess Anne, MD 21853. 978-687-7463, Fax: 410-651-1048. 8:30AM-4:30PM.

Felony, Misdemeanor, Civil Actions Over $25,000—1st Judicial Circuit Court, Box 99, Princess Anne, MD 21853. 978-741-5500, Fax: 410-651-1048. 8AM-4:30PM. Access by: in person.

Misdemeanor, Civil Actions Under $25,000, Eviction, Small Claims—District Court, 11559 Somerset Ave, Princess Anne, MD 21853. 978-744-1167. 8:30AM-4:30PM. Access by: in person, online. Special note: Misdemeanor cases go to Circuit Court if preliminary hearing waived. Records held at court where trial heard.

Probate—Register of Wills, 30512 Prince William St, Princess Anne, MD 21853. 978-744-1020, Fax: 410-651-3873. 8:30AM-4:30PM. Access by: mail, in person. www.registers.state.md.us/county/somerset.html

St. Mary's

Real Estate Recording—St. Mary's County Clerk of the Circuit Court, 41605 Courthouse Dr. Leonardtown, MD 20650. 301-739-3612. 8:30AM-4:30PM.

Felony, Misdemeanor, Civil Actions Over $25,000—7th Judicial Circuit Court, Box 676, Leonardtown, MD 20650. 301-777-5965. 8:30AM-4:30PM. Access by: in person.

Misdemeanor, Civil Actions Under $25,000, Eviction, Small Claims—District Court, Carter State Office Bldg, 23110 Leonard Hall Dr, PO Box 653, Leonardtown, MD 20650. 301-777-2105, Fax: 301-475-4535. 8:30AM-4:30PM. Access by: in person, online.

Probate—Register of Wills, PO Box 602, Leonardtown, MD 20650. 301-777-5922, Fax: 301-475-4968. 8:30AM-4:30PM. Access by: mail, in person.

Talbot

Real Estate Recording—Talbot County Clerk of the Circuit Court, 11 N. Washington Street, Courthouse, Easton, MD 21601., Fax: 410-820-8168. 8:30AM-4:30PM.

Felony, Misdemeanor, Civil Actions Over $25,000—Circuit Court, PO Box 723, Easton, MD 21601. 410-822-2611, Fax: 410-820-8168. 8AM-4:30PM. Access by: in person.

Misdemeanor, Civil Actions Under $25,000, Eviction, Small Claims—District Court, 108 W Dover St, Easton, MD 21601. 410-822-2750, Fax: 410-822-1607. 8AM-4:30PM. Access by: in person, online.

Probate—Register of Wills, PO Box 816, Easton, MD 21601. 410-822-2470, Fax: 410-822-5452. 8AM-4:30PM. Access by: mail, in person. www.registers.state.md.us/county/talbot.html

Washington

Real Estate Recording—Washington County Clerk of the Circuit Court, 95 West Washington Street, Suite 212, Hagerstown, MD 21740. 302-323-4450, Fax: 301-791-1151. 8:30AM-4:30PM.

Felony, Misdemeanor, Civil Actions Over $25,000—Washington County Circuit Court, Box 229, Hagerstown, MD 21741. 302-378-5221, Fax: 301-791-1151. 8:30AM-4:30PM. Access by: in person.

Misdemeanor, Civil Actions Under $25,000, Eviction, Small Claims—District Court, 35 W Washington St, Hagerstown, MD 21740. 302-571-7601. 8:30AM-4:30PM. Access by: mail, in person, online.

Probate—Register of Wills, 95 W Washington, Hagerstown, MD 21740. 302-398-8247, Fax: 301-733-8636. 8:30AM-4:30PM. Access by: mail, in person. www.registers.state.md.us/county/washington.html

Wicomico

Real Estate Recording—Wicomico County Clerk of the Circuit Court, 101 North Division St. Courthouse Room 105, Salisbury, MD 21801. 8:30AM-4:30PM.

Felony, Misdemeanor, Civil Actions Over $25,000—1st Judicial Circuit Court, PO Box 198, Salisbury, MD 21803-0198. 978-453-0201, Fax: 410-548-5150. 8:30AM-4:30PM. Access by: mail, phone, in person.

Misdemeanor, Civil Actions Under $25,000, Eviction, Small Claims—District Court, 201 Baptist St, Salisbury, MD 21801. 978-459-4101. 8:30AM-4:30PM. Access by: in person, online.

Probate—Register of Wills, PO Box 787, Salisbury, MD 21803-0787. 978-462-2652, Fax: 410-334-3440. 8:30AM-4:30PM. Access by: mail, in person. www.registers.state.md.us/county/wicomico.html

Worcester

Real Estate Recording—Worcester County Clerk of the Circuit Court, 1 West Market St. Courthouse Room 104, Snow Hill, MD 21863. 8:30AM-4:30PM.

Felony, Misdemeanor, Civil Actions Over $25,000—1st Judicial Circuit Court, Box 40, Snow Hill, MD 21863. 978-532-3100. 8:30AM-4:30PM. Access by: in person.

Misdemeanor, Civil Actions Under $25,000, Eviction, Small Claims—District Court, 301 Commerce St, Snow Hill, MD 21863-1007. 978-544-8277, Fax: 410-632-2718. 8:30AM-4:30PM. Access by: in person, online.

Probate—Register of Wills, Courthouse, Room 102, One W Market St, Snow Hill, MD 21863-1074. 978-537-3722, Fax: 410-632-5600. 8AM-4:30PM. Access by: mail, in person. www.registers.state.md.us/county/worcester.htm

Federal Courts

US District Court

Baltimore Division Clerk, 4th Floor, Room 4415, 101 W Lombard St, Baltimore, MD 21201410-962-2600 Counties: Allegany, Anne Arundel, Baltimore, City of Baltimore, Caroline, Carroll, Cecil, Dorchester, Frederick, Garrett, Harford, Howard, Kent, Queen Anne's, Somerset, Talbot, Washington, Wicomico, Worcester. www.mdd.uscourts.gov

Greenbelt Division Clerk, Room 240, 6500 Cherrywood Lane, Greenbelt, MD 20770301-344-0660 Counties: Calvert, Charles, Montgomery, Prince George's, St. Mary's. www.mdd.uscourts.gov

US Bankruptcy Court

Baltimore Division 8515 US Courthouse, 101 W Lombard St, Baltimore, MD 21201410-962-2688 Counties: Anne Arundel, Baltimore, City of Baltimore, Caroline, Carroll, Cecil, Dorchester, Harford, Howard, Kent, Queen Anne's, Somerset, Talbot, Wicomico, Worcester.

Rockville Division 6500 Cherrywood Ln, #300, Greenbelt, MD 20770301-344-8018 Counties: Allegany, Calvert, Charles, Frederick, Garrett, Montgomery, Prince George's, St. Mary's, Washington.

Massachusetts

Attorney General's Office

One Ashburton Place, Room 2010   617-727-2200
Boston, MA 02108-1698   Fax: 617-727-5768
www.magnet.state.ma.us/ag

Governor's Office

State House, Room 360   617-727-6250
Boston, MA 02133   Fax: 617-727-9725
www.magnet.state.ma.us/gov/gov.htm

State Archives

220 Morrissey Blvd   617-727-2816
Boston, MA 02125   Fax: 617-288-8429
www.magnet.state.ma.us/sec/arc

Capital:	Boston
	Suffolk County
Time Zone:	EST
Number of Counties:	14
Population:	6,117,520
Web Site:	www.state.ma.us

Search Unclaimed Property Online

www.state.ma.us/scripts/treasury/abp.asp

State Agencies

Criminal Records

Criminal History Systems Board, 200 Arlington Street, #2200, Chelsea, MA 02150; 617-660-4600; Fax: 617-660-4613; 9AM-5PM. Access by: mail.

Corporation Records
Trademarks/Servicemarks
Limited Liability Partnerships
Limited Partnership Records

Secretary of the Commonwealth, Corporation Division, One Ashburton Pl, 17th Floor, Boston, MA 02108; 617-727-9640 Corporations, 617-727-2850 Records, 617-727-8329 Trademarks, 617-727-9440 Forms request line; Fax: 617-742-4538; 8:45AM-5PM. Access by: mail, online. state.ma.us/sec/cor/coridx.htm

Sales Tax Registrations

Revenue Department, Taxpayer Assistance Office, PO Box 7010, Boston, MA 02204 (200 Arlington Street, 4th Floor, Chelsea, MA 02150); 617-887-6100; 8AM-5PM. Access by: mail, phone, in person. www.state.ma.us/dor

Uniform Commercial Code
Federal Tax Liens
State Tax Liens

UCC Division, Secretary of the Commonwealth, One Ashburton Pl, Room 1711, Boston, MA 02108; 617-727-2860; 8:45AM-5PM. Access by: mail, phone, in person, online.

Workers' Compensation Records

Keeper of Records, Department of Industrial Accidents, 600 Washington St, 7th Floor, Boston, MA 02111; 617-727-4900 x301; Fax: 617-727-6477; 8 AM - 4 PM. Access by: mail.

Birth Certificates

Registry of Vital Records and Statistics, 470 Atlantic Ave 2nd Floor, Boston, MA 02210-2224; 617-753-8600, 617-753-8606 Order Line; Fax: 617-423-2038; 8:45AM-4:45PM. Access by: mail, phone, in person.

Death Records

Registry of Vital Records and Statistics, 470 Atlantic Ave 2nd Floor, Boston, MA 02210-2224; 617-753-8600, 617-753-8606 Order Line; Fax: 617-423-2038; 8:45AM-4:45PM. Access by: mail, phone, in person.

Marriage Certificates

Registry of Vital Records and Statistics, 470 Atlantic Ave 2nd Floor, Boston, MA 02210-2224; 617-753-8600, 617-753-8606 Order Line; Fax: 617-423-2038; 8:45AM-4:45PM. Access by: mail, phone, in person.

Divorce Records

Registry of Vital Records and Statistics, 470 Atlantic Ave 2nd Floor, Boston, MA 02210-2224; 617-753-8600, 617-753-8606 Order Line;.

Accident Reports

Accident Records Section, Registry of Motor Vehicles, PO Box 199100, Roxbury, MA 02119-9100; 617-351-9434; Fax: 617-351-9401; 8:45AM-5PM. Access by: mail.

Driver Records-Insurance

Merit Rating Board, Attn: Driving Records, PO Box 199100, Boston, MA 02119-9100; 617-351-4400; Fax: 617-351-9660; 8:45AM-5:00PM. Access by: mail.

Driver Records-Registry

Registry of Motor Vehicles, Driver Control Unit, Box 199100, Roxbury, MA 02119-9100; 617-351-9213 Registry, 617-351-4400 Merit Rating Board; Fax: 617-351-9219; 8AM-4:30PM M-T-W-F; 8AM-7PM TH. Access by: mail, phone, in person. www.state.ma.us/rmv

Vehicle Ownership
Vehicle Identification

Registry of Motor Vehicles, Customer Assistance-Mail List Dept., PO Box 199100, Boston, MA 02119-9100; 617-351-9384; Fax: 617-351-9524; 8AM-4:30PM M-T-W-F; 8AM-7PM TH. Access by: mail, online.

Boat & Vessel Ownership
Boat & Vessel Registration

Massachusetts Environmental Police, 175 Portland St, Boston, MA 02114; 617-727-3900; Fax: 617-727-8897; 8:45AM-5PM.

Legislation-Current/Pending
Legislation-Passed

Massachusetts General Court, State House, Beacon St, Room 428 (Document Room), Boston, MA 02133; 617-722-2860 Document Room; 9AM-5PM. Access by: mail, phone, in person, online. www.state.ma.us/legis.legis.htm

Voter Registration

Records not available from state agency.

Records are maintained at the local city and town level. In general, they are open to the public.

GED Certificates

Massachusetts Dept of Education, GED Processing, 350 Main St, Malden, MA 02148; 781-338-6636;. www.doe.mass.edu/ged

Hunting License Information
Fishing License Information

Division of Fisheries & Wildlife, 100 Cambridge St, Room 1902, Boston, MA 02202; 617-727-3151; Fax: 617-727-7288; 8:45AM-5PM. Access by: mail. www.state.ma.us/dfwele

County Courts & Recording Offices

About the Courts...

Administration

Chief Justice for Administration and Management 617-742-8575
2 Center Plaza, Room 540   Fax: 617-742-0968
Boston, MA 02108
www.state.ma.us/courts/courts.htm

Court Structure

The various court sections are called "Departments." The small claims limit changed in 1993 to $2000 from $1500.

While Superior and District Courts have concurrent jurisdiction in civil cases, the practice is to assign cases less than $25,000 to the District Court and those over $25,000 to Superior Court.

In addition to misdemeanors, the District Courts and Boston Municipal Courts have jurisdiction over certain minor felonies.

There are more than 20 Probate and Family Court locations in MA - one per county plus 2 each in Plymouth and Bristol, a Middlesex satellite in Cambridge and Lawrence.

Online Access

There is no online access computer system, internal or external.

About the Recording Offices...

Organization

14 counties, 312 towns, and 39 cities; 21 recording offices and 365 UCC filing offices. Each town/city profile indicates the county in which the town/city is located. Filing locations vary depending upon the type of document, as noted below. Berkshire and Bristol Counties have three different recording offices; Essex, Middlesex and Worcester Counties each have two separate recording offices. Be careful to distinguish the following names that are identical for both a town/city and a county - Barnstable, Essex, Franklin, Hampden, Nantucket, Norfolk, Plymouth and Worcester. Recording officers are Town/City Clerk (UCC), County Register of Deeds (real estate), and Clerk of US District Court (federal tax liens). The entire state is in the Eastern Time Zone (EST).

UCC Records

This is a dual filing state. Financing statements are usually filed both with the Town/City clerk and at the state level, except for real estate related collateral, which is recorded at the county Register of Deeds. All but twenty recording offices perform searches. Use search request form UCC-11. Search fees are usually $10.00 per debtor name. Copy fees vary widely.

Lien Records

Federal tax liens on personal property were filed with the Town/City Clerks prior to 1970. Since that time, federal tax liens on personal property are filed with the US District Court in Boston as well as with the towns/cities. Following is how to search the central index for federal tax liens - Address:

US District Court (617-223-9152)

Post Office & Courthouse Bldg.

Boston, MA 02109

The federal tax liens are indexed here on a computer system. Searches are available by mail or in person. Do not use the telephone. The court suggests including the Social Security number and/or address of individual names in your search request in order to narrow the results. A mail search costs $15.00 and will take about two weeks. Copies are included. Make your check payable to Clerk, US District Court. You can do the search yourself at no charge on their public computer terminal.

State tax liens on personal property are filed with the Town/City Clerk or Tax Collector. All tax liens against real estate are filed with the county Register of Deeds. Some towns file state tax liens on personal property with the UCC index and include tax liens on personal property automatically with a UCC search. Others will perform a separate state tax lien search, usually for a fee of $10.00 plus $1.00 per page of copies.

Real Estate Records

Real estate records are located at the county level. Each town/city profile indicates the county in which the town/city is located. Counties will not perform searches. Copy fee with certification is usually $.75 per page. Each town also has Assessor/Tax Collector/Treasurer offices from which real estate ownership and tax information is available.

County Courts & Recording Offices

Abington

Real Estate Recording—Abington Town Clerk, 500 Gliniewicz Way, Abington, MA 2351., Fax: 781-982-2138. 8:30AM-4:30PM.

Acton

Real Estate Recording—Acton Town Clerk, 472 Main Street, Town Hall, Acton, MA 1720., Fax: 978-264-9630. 8AM-5PM.

Acushnet

Real Estate Recording—Acushnet Town Clerk, 122 Main Street, Town Hall, Acushnet, MA 2743., Fax: 508-998-0203. 8AM-4PM.

Adams

Real Estate Recording—Adams Town Clerk, 8 Park Street, Adams, MA 1220., Fax: 413-743-8316. 8:30AM-4PM.

Agawam

Real Estate Recording—Agawam Town Hall, 36 Main St. Agawam, MA 1001., Fax: 413-786-9927. 8:30AM-4:30PM.

Alford

Real Estate Recording—Alford Town Clerk, Town Hall, 5 Alford Center Road, Alford, MA 1230., Fax: 413-528-4581. 4:30-7:30PM Th.

Amesbury

Real Estate Recording—Amesbury Town Clerk, 62 Friend Street, Town Hall, Amesbury, MA 1913., Fax: 978-388-8150. 8AM-4PM M-Th; 5PM-8PM Th; 8AM-Noon F.

Amherst

Real Estate Recording—Amherst Town Clerk, Town Hall, 4 Boltwood Ave. Amherst, MA 1002., Fax: 413-256-2504. 8AM-4:30PM.

Andover

Real Estate Recording—Andover Town Clerk, 36 Bartlet Street, Andover, MA 1810., Fax: 978-623-8221. 8:30AM-4:30PM.

Arlington

Real Estate Recording—Arlington Town Clerk, 730 Mass Ave, Town Hall, Arlington, MA 2476. 617-646-1000, Fax: 781-316-3079. 9AM-5PM (8AM-4PM Summer Hours).

Ashburnham

Real Estate Recording—Ashburnham Town Clerk, 32 Main Street, Town Hall, Ashburnham, MA 1430., Fax: 508-827-4105. 9AM-5PM (7-9PM 1st & 3rd Mon of month).

Ashby

Real Estate Recording—Ashby Town Clerk, Town Hall, 895 Main St. Ashby, MA 1431., Fax: 508-386-2490. 9AM-2PM, 6-8PM W.

Ashfield

Real Estate Recording—Ashfield Town Clerk, Town Hall, 412 Main St. Ashfield, MA 1330. 413-628-4441, Fax: 413-628-4588. 1PM-9PM M; 9AM-5PM T.

Ashland

Real Estate Recording—Ashland Town Clerk, 101 Main Street, Town Hall, Ashland, MA 1721., Fax: 508-881-0102. 8:30AM-4:30PM.

Athol

Real Estate Recording—Athol Town Clerk, 584 Main Street, Athol, MA 1331. 508-249-3374. 8AM-5PM M,W,Th; 8AM-8PM T; 8AM-1PM F.

Attleboro

Real Estate Recording—Attleboro City Clerk, 77 Park Street, City Hall, Attleboro, MA 2703. 508-223-2222, Fax: 508-222-3046. 8:30AM-4:30PM.

Auburn

Real Estate Recording—Auburn Town Clerk, 104 Central Street, Auburn, MA 1501. 508-832-7700, Fax: 508-832-6145. 8AM-4PM.

Avon

Real Estate Recording—Avon Town Clerk, Buckley Center, Avon, MA 2322. 508-588-0414, Fax: 508-559-0209. 8:30AM-4:30PM.

Ayer

Real Estate Recording—Ayer Town Clerk, Town Hall, 1 Main St. Ayer, MA 1432. 508-772-8216, Fax: 508-772-8222. 8:30AM-4PM.

Barnstable

Real Estate Recording—Barnstable County Register of Deeds, 3195 Main Street, Route 6A, Barnstable, MA 2630., Fax: 508-362-5065. 8AM-4PM.

Barnstable Town Clerk, 367 Main St. Hyannis, MA 2601. 508-790-6360, Fax: 508-775-3344. 8:30AM-4:30PM.

Felony, Civil Actions Over $25,000—Superior Court, 3195 Main St, PO Box 425, Barnstable, MA 02630. 508-362-2511. 8AM-4:30PM. Access by: mail, in person.

Felony, Misdemeanor, Civil, Eviction, Small Claims—Barnstable Division District Court, Route 6A, PO Box 427, Barnstable, MA 02630. 508-362-2511. 8:30AM-4:30PM. Access by: mail, phone, in person.

Orleans Division District Court, 237 Rock Harbor Rd, Orleans, MA 02653. 508-255-4700. 8:30AM-4:30PM. Access by: in person. Special note: Includes Brewster, Chatham, Dennis, Eastham, Orleans, Truro, Wellfleet, Harwich, and Provincetown.

Probate—Probate and Family Court, PO Box 346, Barnstable, MA 02630. 508-362-2511, Fax: 508-362-3662. 8:30AM-4:30PM. Access by: mail, in person.

Barre

Real Estate Recording—Barre Town Clerk, Town Hall, 2 Exchange St. Barre, MA 1005., Fax: 508-355-5032. 7-9PM M,W; 8AM-Noon, 1-4PM T,Th.

Becket

Real Estate Recording—Becket Town Clerk, Virginia Andrews, 557 Main St. Becket, MA 1223., Fax: 413-623-6036. 9AM-Noon, 1-4PM M & F; 4:30PM-7:30PM W.

Bedford

Real Estate Recording—Bedford Town Clerk, 10 Mudge Way, Town Hall, Bedford, MA 1730. 617-275-8996. 8AM-4PM.

Belchertown

Real Estate Recording—Belchertown Town Clerk, 2 Jabish Street, Belchertown, MA 1007., Fax: 413-323-0411. 8AM-5PM.

Bellingham

Real Estate Recording—Bellingham Town Clerk, #2 Mechanic Street, Town Hall, Bellingham, MA 2019., Fax: 508-966-5804. 8:30AM-4:30PM M,T,W,Th; 8:30AM-1PM F; 6-8PM M Evening.

Belmont

Real Estate Recording—Belmont Town Clerk, 455 Concord Avenue, Town Hall, Belmont, MA 2178. 617-489-8234, Fax: 617-484-6502. 8AM-4PM.

Berkley

Real Estate Recording—Berkley Town Clerk, 1 N. Main Street, Berkley, MA 2779., Fax: 508-822-3511. 9AM-3PM.

Berkshire

Real Estate Recording—Berkshire County Register of Deeds, 334 Main Street, Great Barrington, MA 1230., Fax: 413-528-6878. 8:30AM-4:30PM; Recording hours 8:30AM-4PM.

Berkshire County Register of Deeds, 65 Park Street, Adams, MA 1220., Fax: 413-743-1003. 8:30AM-4:30PM.

Berkshire County Register of Deeds (Middle District), 44 Bank Row, Pittsfield, MA 1201., Fax: 413-448-6025. 8:30AM-4:30PM (No Recording after 3:59PM).

Felony, Civil Actions Over $25,000—Superior Court, 76 East St, Pittsfield, MA 01201. 413-499-7487, Fax: 413-442-9190. 8:30AM-4:30PM. Access by: mail, in person.

Felony, Misdemeanor, Civil, Eviction, Small Claims—North Berkshire Division District Court #28, City Hall, North Adams, MA 01247. 413-663-5339, Fax: 413-664-7209. 8:30AM-4:30PM. Access by: mail, phone, in person. Special note: Handles cases for Clarksburg, Florida, Hancock, New Ashford, North Adams, and Williamstown.

North Berkshire Division District Court #30, 65 Park St, Adams, MA 01220. 413-743-0021, Fax: 413-743-4848. 8AM-4:30PM. Access by: mail, in person. Special note: Handles cases for Adams, Cheshire, Savoy, and Windsor.

Pittsfield Division District Court #27, 24 Wendell Ave, Pittsfield, MA 01201. 413-442-5468, Fax: 413-499-7327. 8:30AM-4:30PM. Access by: mail, phone, in person.

South Berkshire Division District Court, 9 Gilmore Ave, Great Barrington, MA 01230. 413-528-3520, Fax: 413-528-0757. 8AM-4PM. Access by: mail, phone, in person.

Probate—Probate and Family Court, 44 Bank Row, Pittsfield, MA 01201. 413-442-6941, Fax: 413-443-3430. 8:30AM-4PM. Access by: mail, phone, fax, in person.

Berlin

Real Estate Recording—Berlin Town Clerk, 12 Woodward Ave. Berlin, MA 1503., Fax: 978-838-0014. 1-4PM 7-9PM W; 1-4PM Th.

Bernardston

Real Estate Recording—Bernardston Town Clerk, 38 Church Street, Town Hall, Bernardston, MA 1337., Fax: 413-648-9318. 10AM-3PM.

Beverly

Real Estate Recording—Beverly City Clerk, 191 Cabot Street, Beverly, MA 1915. 508-921-6135, Fax: 978-921-8511. 8:30AM-4:30PM M,T,W; 8:30AM-7:30PM Th; 8:30AM-1PM F.

Billerica

Real Estate Recording—Billerica Town Clerk, 365 Boston Road, Town Hall, Billerica, MA 1821., Fax: 508-663-6510. 8:30AM-4PM.

Blackstone

Real Estate Recording—Blackstone Town Clerk, Municipal Center, 15 St. Paul Street, Blackstone, MA 1504., Fax: 508-883-7043. 8AM-3:30PM M,W,Th; 8AM-4:30PM, 5:30-7:30PM T; 8-11:30AM F.

Blandford

Real Estate Recording—Blandford Town Clerk, 28 Blair Rd. Blandford, MA 1008., Fax: 413-848-0908. 6-8PM Mon Evening.

Bolton

Real Estate Recording—Bolton Town Clerk, 663 Main St. Rear Entrance, Bolton, MA 1740., Fax: 978-779-5461. 9AM-1PM T,W,Th; 7-9PM Wed.

Boston

Real Estate Recording—Boston City Clerk, City Hall, Room 601, 1 City Hall Plaza, Boston, MA 2201., Fax: 617-635-4658. 9AM-5PM.

Bourne

Real Estate Recording—Bourne Town Clerk, 24 Perry Avenue, Town Hall, Buzzards Bay, MA 2532., Fax: 508-759-8026. 8:30AM-4:30PM.

Boxborough

Real Estate Recording—Boxborough Town Clerk, 29 Middle Road, Boxborough, MA 1719., Fax: 978-264-3127. 10AM-2PM; Closed T; 7-9PM M; 10AM-1PM Th.

Boxford

Real Estate Recording—Town of Boxford, 28 Middleton Road, Boxford, MA 1921., Fax: 508-887-3546. 8AM-4:30PM M-Th.

Boylston

Real Estate Recording—Boylston Town Clerk, 45 Main Street, Boylston, MA 1505. 508-869-2972, Fax: 508-869-6210. 5-7PM M; 9AM-2PM T-Th.

Braintree

Real Estate Recording—Braintree Town Clerk, 1 JFK Memorial Drive, Braintree, MA 2184., Fax: 781-794-8259. 8:30AM-4:30PM.

Brewster

Real Estate Recording—Brewster Town Clerk, 2198 Main Street, Brewster, MA 2631., Fax: 508-896-8089. 8:30AM-4PM.

Bridgewater

Real Estate Recording—Bridgewater Town Clerk, Town Hall, 64 Central Square, Bridgewater, MA 2324., Fax: 508-697-0941. 8AM-4PM M-Th; 8AM-1PM F.

Brimfield

Real Estate Recording—Brimfield Town Clerk, Town Hall, 21 Main St. Brimfield, MA 1010., Fax: 413-245-4107. 7-8:30PM M; 9-11AM Sat.

Bristol

Real Estate Recording—Bristol County Register of Deeds, 25 North 6th Street, New Bedford, MA 2740. 508-979-1430, Fax: 508-997-4250. 8:30AM-5PM.

Bristol County Register of Deeds, 11 Court Street, Taunton, MA 2780. 508-824-4028, Fax: 508-880-4975. 8:30AM-5PM.

Bristol County Register of Deeds (Fall River District), 441 North Main Street, Fall River, MA 2720., Fax: 508-673-7633. 8:30AM-5PM.

Felony, Civil Actions Over $25,000—Superior Court-Taunton, 9 Court St, Taunton, MA 02780. 508-823-6588. 8AM-4:30PM. Access by: mail, in person.

Felony, Misdemeanor, Civil, Eviction, Small Claims—Attleboro Division District Court 34, Courthouse, 88 N Main St, Attleboro, MA 02703. 508-222-5900, Fax: 508-223-3916. 8:30AM-4:30PM. Access by: mail, phone, in person.

Fall River Division District Court, 45 Rock St, Fall River, MA 02720. 508-679-8161, Fax: 508-675-5477. 8AM-4:30PM. Access by: mail, in person.

New Bedford Division District Court 33, 75 N 6th St, New Bedford, MA 02740. 508-999-9700. 8:30AM-4PM. Access by: mail, in person.

Taunton Division District Court, 15 Court St, Taunton, MA 02780. 508-824-4032, Fax: 508-824-2282. 8AM-4:30PM. Access by: mail, phone, in person.

Probate—New Bedford Probate and Family Court, 505 Pleasant St, New Bedford, MA 02740. 508-999-5249, Fax: 508-991-7421. 8AM-4:30PM. Access by: mail, in person.

Taunton Probate and Family Court, 11 Court St, PO Box 567, Taunton, MA 02780. 508-824-4004, Fax: 508-822-9837. 8AM-4:30PM. Access by: mail, in person.

Brockton

Real Estate Recording—Brockton City Clerk, 45 School Street, Brockton, MA 2401., Fax: 508-580-7104. 8:30AM-4:30PM.

Brookfield

Real Estate Recording—Brookfield Town Clerk, 6 Central St. Brookfield, MA 1506. 508-867-2930, Fax: 508-867-5091. 11AM-2PM, 7-8:30PM T; 9AM-1PM, 7-8PM Th; 9AM-1PM F.

Brookline

Real Estate Recording—Brookline Town Clerk, 333 Washington Street, Town Hall, Brookline, MA 2445., Fax: 617-730-2298. 8AM-5PM M-Th, 8AM-12:30PM F.

Buckland

Real Estate Recording—Buckland Town Clerk, 17 State Street, Buckland, MA 1338., Fax: 413-625-8570. 11AM-4PM T,W,F; 2-7PM Th.

Burlington

Real Estate Recording—Burlington Town Clerk, 29 Center Street, Town Hall, Burlington, MA 1803., Fax: 617-270-1608. 8:30AM-4:30PM.

Cambridge

Real Estate Recording—Cambridge City Clerk, 795 Massachusetts Ave. City Hall, Room 103, Cambridge, MA 2139., Fax: 617-349-4269. 8:30AM-5PM.

Canton

Real Estate Recording—Canton Town Clerk, 801 Washington Street, Memorial Hall, Canton, MA 2021. 617-821-5006, Fax: 781-821-5016. 9AM-5PM.

Carlisle

Real Estate Recording—Carlisle Town Clerk, 22 Bedford Road, Carlisle, MA 1741. 508-369-5557, Fax: 978-371-0594. 9AM-3PM.

Carver

Real Estate Recording—Carver Town Clerk, 108 Main Street, Carver, MA 2330. 508-866-3435, Fax: 508-866-3408. 8AM-4PM M-Th; 8AM-Noon F.

Charlemont

Real Estate Recording—Charlemont Town Clerk, Linda Wagner, 2023 Mohawk Trail, Charlemont, MA 1339., Fax: 413-339-0329. By appointment.

Charlton

Real Estate Recording—Charlton Town Clerk, 37 Main Street, Charlton, MA 1507., Fax: 508-248-2073. 10AM-3PM M-Th; 1st & 3rd Tues of month 6-8PM.

Chatham

Real Estate Recording—Chatham Town Clerk, 549 Main Street, Chatham, MA 2633. 508-945-5108, Fax: 508-945-3550. 8AM-4PM.

Chelmsford

Real Estate Recording—Chelmsford Town Clerk, 50 Billerica Road, Chelmsford, MA 1824., Fax: 978-840-5208. 8:30AM-5PM.

Chelsea

Real Estate Recording—Chelsea City Clerk, 500 Broadway, City Hall Room 209, Chelsea, MA 2150., Fax: 617-889-8367. 8AM-4PM M,W,Th; 8AM-7PM T; 8AM-Noon F.

Cheshire

Real Estate Recording—Cheshire Town Clerk, 80 Church Street, P.O. Box S, Cheshire, MA 1225., Fax: 413-743-0389. 9AM-3PM M,T,W; 9AM-Noon Th.

Chester

Real Estate Recording—Chester Town Clerk, Town Hall, Chester, MA 1011., Fax: 413-354-2268. 7-9PM M.

Chesterfield

Real Estate Recording—Chesterfield Town Clerk, Davenport Bldg. 422 Main Rd. Chesterfield, MA 1012., Fax: 413-296-4394. 7-9PM M or by Appointment.

Chicopee

Real Estate Recording—Chicopee City Clerk, Market Square, City Hall, Chicopee, MA 1013., Fax: 413-594-2057. 8AM-5PM.

Chilmark

Real Estate Recording—Chilmark Town Clerk, Town Hall, 401 Middle Rd. Chilmark, MA 2535., Fax: 508-645-2110. 9AM-Noon (Closed F).

Clarksburg

Real Estate Recording—Clarksburg Town Clerk, 111 River Road, Town Hall, Clarksburg, MA 1247., Fax: 413-664-6575. 9AM-2PM W-F.

Clinton

Real Estate Recording—Clinton Town Clerk, 242 Church Street, Clinton, MA 1510., Fax: 978-895-4130. 8:30AM-4PM.

Cohasset

Real Estate Recording—Cohasset Town Clerk, 41 Highland Avenue, Cohasset, MA 2025., Fax: 781-383-7087. 8:30AM-4:30PM M,T,W; 8:30AM-7PM Th; 8:30AM-1PM F.

Colrain

Real Estate Recording—Colrain Town Clerk, Town Hall, 55 Main Rd. Colrain, MA 1340. 413-624-3454, Fax: 413-624-8852. 9AM-4PM M-Th.

Concord

Real Estate Recording—Concord Town Clerk, 22 Monument Square, Concord, MA 1742., Fax: 978-318-3093. 8:30AM-4:30PM.

Conway

Real Estate Recording—Conway Town Clerk, Town Office Bldg. 32 Main St. Conway, MA 1341. 413-369-4235, Fax: 413-369-4237. 9AM-Noon T,Th,F.

Cummington

Real Estate Recording—Cummington Town Clerk, 585 Berkshire Trail, Cummington, MA 1026., Fax: 413-634-5568. 6-8PM W.

Dalton

Real Estate Recording—Dalton Town Clerk, 462 Main Street, Town Hall, Dalton, MA 1226., Fax: 413-684-6107. 8AM-4PM M-W; 8AM-6PM Th.

Danvers

Real Estate Recording—Danvers Town Clerk, 1 Sylvan Street, Town Hall, Danvers, MA 1923., Fax: 508-777-1025. 8AM-5PM M-W; 8AM-7:30PM Th; 8AM-1:30PM F.

Dartmouth

Real Estate Recording—Dartmouth Town Clerk, 400 Slocum Road, Dartmouth, MA 2747. 508-999-0702, Fax: 508-999-0785. 8:30AM-6:30PM M; 8:30AM-4:30PM T-F.

Dedham

Real Estate Recording—Dedham Town Clerk, 26 Bryant St. Room 207, Dedham, MA 2026., Fax: 781-461-5992. 8:30AM-4:30PM.

Deerfield

Real Estate Recording—Deerfield Town Clerk, 8 Conway St. South Deerfield, MA 1373. 413-665-2130, Fax: 413-665-7275. 9AM-4PM.

Dennis

Real Estate Recording—Dennis Town Clerk, 485 Main Street, Town Hall, South Dennis, MA 2660., Fax: 508-394-8309. 8:30AM-4:30PM.

Dighton

Real Estate Recording—Dighton Town Clerk, 979 Somerset Avenue, Dighton, MA 2715. 508-669-5411, Fax: 508-669-5667. 8:30AM-4PM.

Douglas

Real Estate Recording—Douglas Town Clerk, 29 Depot St. Municipal Center, Douglas, MA 1516., Fax: 508-476-4012. 9AM-Noon, 1-3PM M,W,Th; 9AM-Noon, 1-3PM, 6-8PM T; Closed F.

Dover

Real Estate Recording—Dover Town Clerk, 5 Springdale Avenue, Dover, MA 2030., Fax: 508-785-2341. 9AM-1PM M,W,F; 9AM-4PM T,Th.

Dracut

Real Estate Recording—Dracut Town Clerk, 62 Arlington Street, Room 4, Dracut, MA 1826., Fax: 978-452-7924. 8:30AM-4:30PM.

Dudley

Real Estate Recording—Dudley Town Clerk, Town Hall, 40 Schofield Ave. Dudley, MA 1571., Fax: 508-949-7115. 8AM-6PM Mon; 8AM-4:30PM T & F; 12:30-6PM Th.

Dukes

Real Estate Recording—Dukes County Register of Deeds, Main Street, Courthouse, Edgartown, MA 2539., Fax: 508-627-7821. 8:30AM-4:30PM.

Felony, Civil Actions Over $25,000—Superior Court, PO Box 1267, Edgartown, MA 02539. 508-627-4668, Fax: 508-627-7571. 8AM-4PM. Access by: mail, in person.

Felony, Misdemeanor, Civil, Eviction, Small Claims—Edgartown District Court, Courthouse, 81 Main St, Edgartown, MA 02539-1284. 508-627-3751. 8:30AM-4:30PM. Access by: in person.

Probate—Probate and Family Court, PO Box 237, Edgartown, MA 02539. 508-627-4703, Fax: 508-627-7664. 8:30AM-4:30PM. Access by: mail, in person.

Dunstable

Real Estate Recording—Dunstable Town Clerk, 511 Main St. Dunstable, MA 1827., Fax: 978-649-2205. 8AM-2PM, 7-9PM M; 8AM-2PM T-Th.

Duxbury

Real Estate Recording—Duxbury Town Clerk, 878 Tremont Street, Duxbury, MA 2332. 617-934-6586, Fax: 781-934-9278. 8AM-noon,1-4PM.

East Bridgewater

Real Estate Recording—East Bridgewater Town Clerk, Town Hall, 175 Central St. East Bridgewater, MA 2333., Fax: 508-378-1638. 8:30AM-4:30PM.

East Brookfield

Real Estate Recording—East Brookfield Town Clerk, Town Hall, East Brookfield, MA 1515. 508-867-6769, Fax: 508-867-4190. 7-9PM M; 11AM-1PM F.

East Longmeadow

Real Estate Recording—East Longmeadow Town Clerk, 60 Center Square, East Longmeadow, MA 1028. 413-525-5400, Fax: 413-525-1025. 8AM-4PM.

Eastham

Real Estate Recording—Eastham Town Clerk, 2500 State Highway, Eastham, MA 2642. 8AM-Noon, 1-4PM.

Easthampton

Real Estate Recording—Easthampton Town Clerk, 43 Main Street, Town Hall, Room 1, Easthampton, MA 1027., Fax: 413-529-1488. 8AM-4PM M-F; 7-8PM W.

Easton

Real Estate Recording—Easton Town Clerk, 136 Elm Street, North Easton, MA 2356., Fax: 508-230-2450. 8:30AM-8:30PM M; 8:30AM-4:30PM T,W,Th; 8:30AM-12:30PM F.

Edgartown

Real Estate Recording—Edgartown Town Clerk's Office, 70 Main St. Edgartown, MA 2539. 508-627-6130, Fax: 508-627-6123. 8AM-4PM.

Egremont

Real Estate Recording—Egremont Town Clerk, Route 71, Town Hall, North Egremont/ So. Egremont, MA 1252., Fax: 413-528-5465. 7-9PM T.

Erving

Real Estate Recording—Erving Town Clerk, Town Hall, 12 E. Main St. Erving, MA 1344., Fax: 978-544-5436. 2-5PM, 6-9PM M.

Essex

Real Estate Recording—Essex County Register of Deeds, 381 Common Street, Lawrence, MA 1840. 508-683-2745, Fax: 978-688-4679. 8AM-4:30PM (recording until 4PM.).

Essex County Register of Deeds, 36 Federal Street, Salem, MA 1970., Fax: 978-744-5865. 8AM-4PM.

Essex Town Clerk, Town Hall, Martin St. Essex, MA 1929. 8:30AM-1PM M,W; 1-4PM T & Th; Closed F.

Civil Actions Over $25,000—Superior Court-Lawrence, 43 Appleton Way, Lawrence, MA 01840. 978-687-7463. 8AM-4:30PM. Access by: mail, in person. Special note: Index cards are found in the Salem office (records prior to 1985).

Felony, Civil Actions Over $25,000—Superior Court-Newburyport, 145 High St, Newburyport, MA 01950. 978-462-4474. 8AM-4:30PM. Access by: mail, in person. Special note: All finished criminal record files are in Salem and civil case records Session A in Salem, Session B in Newburyport and Session C & D inr Lawrence.

Superior Court-Salem, 34 Federal St, Salem, MA 01970. 978-741-5500, Fax: 978-741-0691. 8:00AM-4:30PM. Access by: mail, in person.

Felony, Misdemeanor, Civil, Eviction, Small Claims—Haverhill Division District Court, PO Box 1389, Haverhill, MA 01831. 978-373-4151, Fax: 978-521-6886. 8:30AM-4:30PM. Access by: mail, phone, fax, in person.

Ipswich Division District Court, 30 South Main St, PO Box 246, Ipswich, MA 01938. 978-356-2681, Fax: 978-356-4396. 8:30AM-4:30PM. Access by: mail, in person.

Lawrence Division District Court, 381 Common St, Lawrence, MA 01840. 978-687-7184. 8AM-4:30PM. Access by: mail, in person.

Lynn Division District Court, 580 Essex St, Lynn, MA 01901. 617-598-5200. 8AM-4:30PM. Access by: mail, phone, in person.

Newburyport Division District Court 22, 188 State St, Newburyport, MA 01950. 978-462-2652. 8:30AM-4:30PM. Access by: mail, phone, in person.

Peabody Division District Court 86, PO Box 666, Peabody, MA 01960. 978-532-3100. 8:30AM-4:30PM. Access by: mail, phone, in person.

Salem Division District Court 36, 65 Washington St, Salem, MA 01970. 978-744-1167. 8:30AM-4:30PM. Access by: mail, in person.

Probate—Probate and Family Court, 36 Federal St, Salem, MA 01970. 978-744-1020, Fax: 978-741-2957. 8:00AM-4:30PM. Access by: mail, in person.

Everett

Real Estate Recording—Everett City Clerk, City Hall, Room 10, Everett, MA 2149., Fax: 617-387-5770. 8AM-4PM M-F (7-9PM Mon).

Fairhaven

Real Estate Recording—Fairhaven Town Clerk, 40 Center Street, Fairhaven, MA 2719. 508-979-4026, Fax: 508-979-4079. 8:30AM-4:30PM.

Fall River

Real Estate Recording—Fall River City Clerk, One Government Center, Fall River, MA 2722. 508-324-2260, Fax: 508-324-2211. 9AM-5PM (June-October 9AM-4PM).

Falmouth

Real Estate Recording—Falmouth Town Clerk, 59 Town Hall Square, Falmouth, MA 2540., Fax: 508-457-2511. 8AM-4:30PM.

Fitchburg

Real Estate Recording—Fitchburg City Clerk, 718 Main Street, Fitchburg, MA 1420., Fax: 978-345-9595. 8:30AM-4:30PM.

Florida

Real Estate Recording—Florida Town Clerk, Town Hall, 20 South St, Drury, MA 1343. 413-664-6016, Fax: 413-664-8640. By Appointment.

Foxborough

Real Estate Recording—Foxborough Town Clerk, 40 South Street, Foxborough, MA 2035. 508-543-1216, Fax: 508-543-6278. 8:30AM-4PM M,W,Th; 8:30AM-4PM, 5-8PM T; 8:30AM-12:30PM F.

Framingham

Real Estate Recording—Framingham Town Clerk, Memorial Building - Room 105, 150 Concord St. Framingham, MA 1702. 508-620-4866, Fax: 508-620-5910. 8:30AM-8PM M; 8:30AM-5PM T-F.

Franklin

Real Estate Recording—Franklin County Division of Deeds, Court House, 425 Main Street, Greenfield, MA 1301. 413-774-4804, Fax: 413-774-7150. 8:30AM-4:30PM (Recording until 4PM).

Franklin Town Clerk, Municipal Building, 150 Emmons Street, Franklin, MA 2038. 508-520-4950, Fax: 508-520-4903. 8:30AM-4:30PM M,T,Th,F; 8:30AM-7PM W.

Felony, Civil Actions Over $25,000—Superior Court, PO Box 1573, Greenfield, MA 01302. 413-774-5535, Fax: 413-774-4770. 8:30AM-4:30PM. Access by: mail, phone, in person.

Felony, Misdemeanor, Civil, Eviction, Small Claims—Greenfield District Court, 425 Main St, Greenfield, MA 01301. 413-774-5533, Fax: 413-774-5328. 8:30AM-4:30PM. Access by: mail, in person.

Orange Division District Court #42, One Court Square, Orange, MA 01364. 978-544-8277, Fax: 978-544-5204. 8:30AM-4:30PM. Access by: mail, phone, in person.

Probate—Probate and Family Court, PO Box 590, Greenfield, MA 01302. 413-774-7011, Fax: 413-774-3829. 8AM-4:30PM. Access by: mail, in person.

Freetown

Real Estate Recording—Freetown Town Clerk, 3 N. Main Street, Town Hall, Assonet, MA 2702. 508-644-2204, Fax: 508-644-3342. 9AM-4PM.

Gardner

Real Estate Recording—Gardner City Clerk, 95 Pleasant Street, City Hall Room 118, Gardner, MA 1440. 508-630-4016, Fax: 508-630-2520. 8AM-4:30PM; F 8AM-4PM.

Gay Head

Real Estate Recording—Aquinnah Town Clerk, Town Hall, Gay Head, MA 2535., Fax: 508-645-2310. By Appointment.

Georgetown

Real Estate Recording—Georgetown Town Clerk, 1 Library Street, Georgetown, MA 1833. 617-741-0200, Fax: 978-352-5727. 9AM-Noon, 5-8PM M,T; 9AM-Noon W-F.

Gill

Real Estate Recording—Gill Town Clerk, Town Clerk's Office, 325 Main Road, Gill, MA 1376., Fax: 413-863-9347. 9AM-Noon, 2PM-4PM M-W & F; 9AM-Noon Sat.

Gloucester

Real Estate Recording—Gloucester City Clerk, 9 Dale Avenue, Gloucester, MA 1930., Fax: 508-281-8472. 8:30AM-4PM M-W,F Winter; 8:30AM-6:30PM Th; 8:30AM-12:30PM F Memorial Day-Labor Day.

Goshen

Real Estate Recording—Goshen Town Clerk, Town Offices, 40 Main St. Goshen, MA 1032. 413-268-7760, Fax: 413-268-8237. 7-8:30PM Monday.

Gosnold

Real Estate Recording—Gosnold Town Clerk, Town Hall, Gosnold, MA 2713. 508-990-7101, Fax: 508-990-7408. By Appointment.

Grafton

Real Estate Recording—Grafton Town Clerk, Municipal Center, 30 Providence Road, Grafton, MA 1519., Fax: 508-839-4602. 8:30AM-4:30PM (T 8:30AM-7PM).

Granby

Real Estate Recording—Granby Town Clerk, 250 State St. Kellogg Hall, Granby, MA 1033. 413-467-7178, Fax: 413-467-2080. 9AM-3PM M,T,W,Th; 9AM-Noon F; 7-9PM 1st & 3rd M.

Granville

Real Estate Recording—Granville Town Clerk, 707 Main Road, Town Hall, Granville, MA 1034., Fax: 413-357-6002. 9-11AM, 7-9PM M.

Great Barrington

Real Estate Recording—Great Barrington Town Clerk, 334 Main Street, Great Barrington, MA 1230., Fax: 413-528-2290. 8:30AM-4PM.

Greenfield

Real Estate Recording—Greenfield Town Clerk, 14 Court Square, Town Hall, Greenfield, MA 1301., Fax: 413-772-1542. 9AM-5PM.

Groton

Real Estate Recording—Groton Town Clerk, Town Hall, 173 Main St. Groton, MA 1450., Fax: 508-448-2030. 8:30AM-7PM M; 8:30AM-4:30PM T-Th; 9AM-4PM F; 9AM-1PM 1st & 3rd Sat.

Groveland

Real Estate Recording—Groveland Town Clerk, Town Hall, Groveland, MA 1830. 9AM-1PM M,T,Th,F; 9AM-Noon W.

Hadley

Real Estate Recording—Hadley Town Clerk, 100 Middle Street, Hadley, MA 1035. 413-586-3354, Fax: 413-586-5661. 9AM-4PM.

Halifax

Real Estate Recording—Halifax Town Clerk, 499 Plymouth Street, Halifax, MA 2338., Fax: 781-294-7684. 8AM-4PM; 6:30-8:30PM Tues (closed Fri).

Hamilton

Real Estate Recording—Hamilton Town Clerk, 577 Bay Road, Hamilton, MA 1936. 508-468-5575, Fax: 978-468-2682. 8AM-4:30PM (Fri open until Noon); 7-9PM M Evening.

Hampden

Real Estate Recording—Hampden County Register of Deeds, 50 State Street, Hall of Justice, Springfield, MA 1103., Fax: 413-731-8190. 8:30AM-4:30PM; 9AM-4PM(Recording).

Hampden Town Clerk, 625 Main St. Hampden, MA 1036. 413-566-2401, Fax: 413-566-2010. 9AM-1PM M-Th; Closed F.

Felony, Civil Actions Over $25,000—Superior Court, 50 State St, PO Box 559, Springfield, MA 01102-0559. 413-748-8600, Fax: 413-737-1611. 8:30AM-4:30PM. Access by: mail, phone, in person.

Felony, Misdemeanor, Civil, Eviction, Small Claims—Chicopee Division District Court #20, 30 Church St, Chicopee, MA 01020. 413-598-0099, Fax: 413-598-8176. 8AM-4PM. Access by: mail, phone, in person.

Holyoke Division District Court, 20 Court Sq, Holyoke, MA 01041-5075. 413-538-9710, Fax: 413-533-7165. 8:30AM-4:30PM. Access by: mail, phone, in person.

Palmer Division District Court, 235 Sykes St, Palmer, MA 01069. 413-283-8916, Fax: 413-283-6775. 8:30AM-4:30PM. Access by: mail, phone, in person.

Springfield Division District Court, 50 State St, Springfield, MA 01103. 413-748-7613, Fax: 413-747-4841. 8:00AM-4:30PM. Access by: mail, phone, in person.

Westfield Division District Court, 27 Washington St, Westfield, MA 01085. 413-568-8946, Fax: 413-568-4863. 8AM-4PM. Access by: mail, in person.

Probate—Probate and Family Court, 50 State St, Springfield, MA 01103-0559. 413-748-7759, Fax: 413-781-5605. 8AM-4:25PM. Access by: mail, phone, in person.

Hampshire

Real Estate Recording—Hampshire Register of Deeds, 33 King Street, Hall of Records, Northampton, MA 1060., Fax: 413-584-4136. 8:30AM-4:30PM (Recording ends at 4PM).

Felony, Civil Actions Over $25,000—Superior Court, PO Box 1119, Northampton, MA 01061. 413-584-5810, Fax: 413-586-8217. 9AM-4PM. Access by: mail, in person.

Felony, Misdemeanor, Civil, Eviction, Small Claims—Northampton District Court, Courthouse, 15 Gothic St, Northampton, MA 01060. 413-584-7400, Fax: 413-586-1980. 8:30AM-4PM. Access by: mail, phone, fax, in person.

Ware Division District Court, PO Box 300, Ware, MA 01082. 413-967-3301, Fax: 413-967-7986. 8AM-4:30PM. Access by: mail, phone, fax, in person.

Probate—Probate and Family Court, 33 King St, Northampton, MA 01060. 413-586-8500, Fax: 413-584-1132. 9AM-4:30PM. Access by: mail, in person.

Hancock

Real Estate Recording—Hancock Town Clerk, 3650 Hancock Rd. Hancock, MA 1237. 413-738-5211, Fax: 413-738-5310. 7-9PM T; 9AM-Noon Th; 9-11AM 1st Sat of the month.

Hanover

Real Estate Recording—Hanover Town Clerk, 550 Hanover Street, Hanover, MA 2339., Fax: 617-826-5950. 8AM-4PM.

Hanson

Real Estate Recording—Hanson Town Clerk, Town Hall, 542 Liberty St. Hanson, MA 2341., Fax: 781-294-0884. 8AM-5PM M,T,W,Th; 7-9PM Tue.

Hardwick

Real Estate Recording—Hardwick Town Clerk, Myron E. Richardson Building, 307 Main St. Gilbertville, MA 1031., Fax: 413-477-6703. 6:30-8:30PM M; 9AM-Noon Sat.

Harvard

Real Estate Recording—Harvard Town Clerk, Town Hall, 13 Ayer Rd. Harvard, MA 1451. 508-456-4105, Fax: 978-456-4113. 8:30AM-4PM M-Th.

Harwich

Real Estate Recording—Harwich Town Clerk, 732 Main Street, Harwich, MA 2645., Fax: 508-432-5039. 8:30AM-4PM.

Hatfield

Real Estate Recording—Hatfield Town Clerk, 59 Main Street, Hatfield, MA 1038., Fax: 413-347-5029. 8:30AM-4PM (F 8:30AM-12).

Haverhill

Real Estate Recording—Haverhill City Clerk, 4 Summer Street, City Hall, Room 118, Haverhill, MA 1830., Fax: 978-373-8490. 8AM-4PM.

Hawley

Real Estate Recording—Hawley Town Clerk, Town Hall, Hawley, MA 1339. 413-339-5518, Fax: 413-339-4959. 1-5PM Wed.

Heath

Real Estate Recording—Heath Town Clerk, Town Hall, 1 E. Main St. Heath, MA 1346., Fax: 413-337-8542. 9AM-2PM M-Th.

Hingham

Real Estate Recording—Hingham Town Clerk, 7 East Street, Hingham, MA 2043., Fax: 617-740-0239. 8:30AM-4:30PM.

Hinsdale

Real Estate Recording—Hinsdale Town Clerk, Town Hall, P.O. Box 803, Hinsdale, MA 1235. 413-655-2306, Fax: 413-655-8807. 1-3PM, 6:30-8PM W; 12:45-3PM Th.

Holbrook

Real Estate Recording—Holbrook Town Clerk, Town Hall, Holbrook, MA 2343., Fax: 617-767-0705. 8AM-4PM.

Holden

Real Estate Recording—Holden Town Clerk, 1196 Main Street, Town Hall, Holden, MA 1520. 508-829-0235, Fax: 508-829-0252. 8:30AM-4:30PM.

Holland

Real Estate Recording—Holland Town Clerk, Town Hall, Holland, MA 1521., Fax: 413-245-7037. 9AM-Noon, 1-4PM M,W,Th; 9AM-Noon, 1-5PM, 7-8:30PM T.

Holliston

Real Estate Recording—Holliston Town Clerk, 703 Washington Street, Holliston, MA 1746., Fax: 508-429-0684. 8:30AM-4:30PM.

Holyoke

Real Estate Recording—Holyoke City Clerk, City Hall, Holyoke, MA 1040. 413-534-2153, Fax: 413-534-2322. 8:30AM-4:30PM.

Hopedale

Real Estate Recording—Hopedale Town Clerk, Town Hall, 78 Hopedale St. Hopedale, MA 1747., Fax: 508-634-2200. 9AM-2PM M-Th.

Hopkinton

Real Estate Recording—Hopkinton Town Clerk, 18 Main Street, Hopkinton, MA 1748., Fax: 508-497-9702. 8:30AM-4PM.

Hubbardston

Real Estate Recording—Hubbardston Town Clerk, Town Hall, Hubbardston, MA 1452., Fax: 508-928-1402. 2-8PM M; 8AM-4PM T-Th.

Hudson

Real Estate Recording—Hudson Town Clerk, 78 Main Street, Town Hall, Hudson, MA 1749. 8AM-4:30PM.

Hull

Real Estate Recording—Hull Town Clerk, Town Hall, Hull, MA 2045., Fax: 617-925-0224. 8AM-4PM M,T,W; 8:30AM-7:30PM Th; 8AM-Noon F.

Huntington

Real Estate Recording—Huntington Town Clerk, Office of Town Clerk, 50 Searle Rd. Huntington, MA 1050. 413-667-3500, Fax: 413-667-8859. Town Hall: 7-9PM Wed; Home Office Hours: M,T,Th,F eve.

Ipswich

Real Estate Recording—Ipswich Town Clerk, Town Hall, 30 South Main St. Ipswich, MA 1938. 508-356-6601, Fax: 508-356-6616. 8AM-7PM M; 8AM-4PM T,W,Th; 8AM-Noon F.

Kingston

Real Estate Recording—Town of Kingston, 23 Green Street, Town Hall, Kingston, MA 2364., Fax: 781-585-0542. 8:30AM-Noon, 1-4:30PM.

Lakeville

Real Estate Recording—Lakeville Town Clerk, 346 Bedford Street, Lakeville, MA 2347. 508-947-3400, Fax: 508-946-0112. 9AM-4PM.

Lancaster

Real Estate Recording—Lancaster Town Clerk, Town Hall, Box 97, 695 Main St. Lancaster, MA 1523. 508-365-6115. 9AM-4PM M,T,W,Th.

Lanesborough

Real Estate Recording—Lanesborough Town Clerk, 83 North Main Street, Lanesborough, MA 1237., Fax: 413-443-5811. 8AM-1PM.

Lawrence

Real Estate Recording—Lawrence City Clerk, 200 Common Street, Lawrence, MA 1840. 8:30AM-4:30PM.

Lee

Real Estate Recording—Lee Town Clerk, Town Hall, 32 Main St. Lee, MA 1238., Fax: 413-243-5507. 9AM-4PM.

Leicester

Real Estate Recording—Leicester Town Clerk, 3 Washburn Square, Leicester, MA 1524. 508-365-2542, Fax: 508-892-7070. 9AM-4PM.

Lenox

Real Estate Recording—Lenox Town Clerk, 6 Walker Street, Town Hall, Lenox, MA 1240., Fax: 413-637-5518. 9AM-4PM.

Leominster

Real Estate Recording—Leominster City Clerk, 25 West Street, Leominster, MA 1453., Fax: 978-534-7546. 8:30AM-4PM M-W & F; 8:30AM-5:30PM Th.

Leverett

Real Estate Recording—Leverett Town Clerk, Town Hall, 9 Montague Rd. Leverett, MA 1054., Fax: 413-548-9150. 7PM-9PM M; 9AM-Noon W,Th.

Lexington

Real Estate Recording—Lexington Town Clerk, 1625 Massachusetts Avenue, Town Office Building, Lexington, MA 2420., Fax: 781-861-2754. 8:30AM-4:30PM.

Leyden

Real Estate Recording—Leyden Town Clerk, Town Hall, Leyden, MA 1337., Fax: 413-774-4111. 10AM-1PM W-F.

Lincoln

Real Estate Recording—Lincoln Town Clerk, 16 Lincoln Road, Lincoln Center, MA 1773., Fax: 617-259-1677. 8:30AM-4:30PM.

Littleton

Real Estate Recording—Littleton Town Clerk, 37 Shattuck St. Littleton, MA 1460. 508-952-2306, Fax: 508-952-2321. 9AM-3PM M,T,W,F; 9AM-9PM Th.

Longmeadow

Real Estate Recording—Longmeadow Town Clerk, Town Hall, 20 Williams Street, Longmeadow, MA 1106. 413-567-1066, Fax: 413-565-4112. 8:15AM-4:30PM.

Lowell

Real Estate Recording—Lowell City Clerk, City Hall, 375 Merrimack Street, Lowell, MA 1852. 508-970-4224, Fax: 508-970-4162. 8AM-5PM.

Ludlow

Real Estate Recording—Ludlow Town Clerk, 488 Chapin Street, Ludlow, MA 1056. 413-583-5616, Fax: 413-583-5603. 8:30AM-4:30PM.

Lunenburg

Real Estate Recording—Lunenburg Town Clerk, Town Hall, 17 Main Street, Lunenburg, MA 1462., Fax: 978-582-4148. 9AM-5PM M,T,F; 9AM-Noon W; 9AM-6PM Th.

Lynn

Real Estate Recording—Lynn City Clerk, 3 City Hall Square, Lynn, MA 1901., Fax: 781-477-7032. 8:30AM-4PM M,W,Th; 8:30AM-8PM T; 8:30AM-12:30PM F.

Lynnfield

Real Estate Recording—Lynnfield Town Clerk, 55 Summer Street, Lynnfield, MA 1940., Fax: 617-334-0014. 8AM-4:30PM (F 8AM-1PM).

Malden

Real Estate Recording—Malden City Clerk, 200 Pleasant Street, City Hall, Malden, MA 2148., Fax: 718-388-0610. 8AM-4PM M,W,Th; 8AM-7PM T; 8AM-Noon F.

Manchester-by-the-Sea

Real Estate Recording—Manchester-by-the-Sea Town Clerk, Town Hall, Manchester-by-the Sea, MA 1944., Fax: 978-526-2001. 9AM-5PM M-W; 9AM-8PM Th.

Mansfield

Real Estate Recording—Mansfield Town Clerk, Town Hall, 6 Park Row, Mansfield, MA 2048., Fax: 508-261-1083. 8AM-4PM M, T, Th; 8AM-8PM W; 8AM-Noon F.

Marblehead

Real Estate Recording—Marblehead Town Clerk, Abbot Hall, Marblehead, MA 1945. 617-631-1033, Fax: 617-631-8571. 8AM-5PM, M, T, Th; 7:30AM-7:30PM, W; 8AM-1PM F.

Marion

Real Estate Recording—Marion Town Clerk, 2 Spring Street, Marion, MA 2738. 508-748-3505, Fax: 508-748-2845. 8AM-4:30PM M-Th; 8AM-3:30PM F.

Marlborough

Real Estate Recording—Marlborough City Clerk, 140 Main Street, Marlborough, MA 1752., Fax: 508-624-6504. 8:30AM-5PM.

Marshfield

Real Estate Recording—Marshfield Town Clerk, Town Hall, Marshfield, MA 2050., Fax: 781-837-7163. 8:30AM-4:30PM.

Mashpee

Real Estate Recording—Mashpee Town Clerk, Town Hall, 16 Great Neck Rd. N. Mashpee, MA 2649., Fax: 508-539-1403. 9AM-4PM.

Mattapoisett

Real Estate Recording—Mattapoisett Town Clerk, Town Hall, 16 Main St. Mattapoisett, MA 2739. 508-758-4108, Fax: 508-758-3030. 8AM-4PM.

Maynard

Real Estate Recording—Maynard Town Clerk, 195 Main Street, Town Hall, Maynard, MA 1754., Fax: 978-897-8457. 8AM-4PM.

Medfield

Real Estate Recording—Medfield Town Clerk, Town Hall, 459 Main St. Medfield, MA 2052., Fax: 508-359-6182. 8:30AM-4:30PM M-W; 8:30AM-7:30PM Th; 8:30AM-1PM F.

Medford

Real Estate Recording—Medford City Clerk, 85 George P. Hassett Drive, City Clerk, Medford, MA 2155., Fax: 617-391-1895. 8:30AM-4:30PM M,T,Th; 8:30AM-7:30PM W; 8:30AM-12:30PM F.

Medway

Real Estate Recording—Medway Town Clerk, 155 Village St. Medway, MA 2053. 508-533-3205, Fax: 508-533-3207. 8AM-4PM (6-8PM M Evening).

Melrose

Real Estate Recording—Melrose City Clerk, 562 Main Street, City Hall, Melrose, MA 2176. 8AM-4:30PM (July-August:8AM-4:30PM M-Th; 8AM-1PM F).

Mendon

Real Estate Recording—Mendon Town Clerk, 20 Main Street, Mendon, MA 1756., Fax: 508-478-8241. 7:30AM-3PM, 7-9PM M; 7:30AM-3 T-Th; Closed F.

Merrimac

Real Estate Recording—Merrimac Town Clerk, 2 School Street, Merrimac, MA 1860., Fax: 508-346-7832. 9AM-4PM M-Th.

Methuen

Real Estate Recording—Methuen City Clerk, 41 Pleasant St. Room 112, Methuen, MA 1844. 508-794-3205, Fax: 508-794-3215. 8:30AM-7PM 1st Mon of month; 8:30AM-4:30PM T-F.

Middleborough

Real Estate Recording—Middleborough Town Clerk, 20 Centre St. 1st Floor, Middleborough, MA 2346. 508-946-2411, Fax: 508-946-2308. 8:45AM-5PM.

Middlefield

Real Estate Recording—Middlefield Town Clerk, Town Hall, Middlefield, MA 1243., Fax: 413-623-6108. 7PM-9PM; 9AM-Noon Sat.

Middlesex

Real Estate Recording—Middlesex County Division of Deeds, 208 Cambridge Street, East Cambridge, MA 2141. 8AM-4PM.

Middlesex County Division of Deeds, 360 Gorham Street, Lowell, MA 1852., Fax: 978-322-9001. 8:30AM-4:30PM.

Felony, Civil Actions Over $25,000—Superior Court-East Cambridge, 40 Thorndike St, East Cambridge, MA 02141. 617-494-4010. 8:30AM-4:30PM. Access by: mail, in person. Special note: The court is planning to have Internet access to records by the end of 1999.

Superior Court-Lowell, 360 Gorham St, Lowell, MA 01852. 978-453-0201. 8:30AM-4:30PM. Access by: mail, in person.

Felony, Misdemeanor, Civil, Eviction, Small Claims—Ayer Division District Court, 25 E Main St, Ayer, MA 01432. 978-772-2100, Fax: 978-772-5345. 8:30AM-4:30PM. Access by: mail, phone, in person.

Cambridge Division District Court 52, PO Box 338, East Cambridge, MA 02141. 617-494-4310. 8:30AM-4:30PM. Access by: mail, in person.

Concord Division District Court 47, 305 Walden St, Concord, MA 01742. 978-369-0500. 8:30AM-4:30PM. Access by: mail, in person.

Framingham Division District Court, 600 Concord St, Framingham, MA 01701. 508-875-7461. 8:30AM-4:30PM. Access by: mail, in person.

Lowell Division District Court, 41 Hurd St, Lowell, MA 01852. 978-459-4101. 8:30AM-4:30PM. Access by: in person.

Malden Division District Court, 89 Summer, Malden, MA 02148. 617-322-7500, Fax: 617-322-1604. 8:30AM-4:30PM. Access by: mail, phone, in person.

Marlborough Division District Court 21, 45 Williams St, Marlborough, MA 01752. 508-485-3700. 8:30AM-4:30PM. Access by: mail, phone, in person.

Natick Division District Court, 117 E Central, Natick, MA 01760. 508-653-4332. 8:30AM-4:30PM. Access by: mail, phone, in person.

Newton Division District Court, 1309 Washington, West Newton, MA 02165. 617-244-3600, Fax: 617-965-7584. 8:30AM-4:30PM. Access by: mail, phone, fax, in person.

Somerville Division District Court, 175 Fellsway, Somerville, MA 02145. 617-666-8000. 8:30AM-4:30PM. Access by: mail, phone, in person.

Waltham Division District Court 51, 38 Linden St, Waltham, MA 02154. 617-894-4500. 8:30AM-4:30PM. Access by: mail, in person.

Woburn Division District Court 53, 30 Pleasant St, Woburn, MA 01801. 617-935-4000. 8:30AM-4:30PM. Access by: mail, in person.

Probate—Probate and Family Court, 208 Cambridge St, PO Box 410480, East Cambridge, MA 02141-0005. 617-494-4530, Fax: 617-225-0781. 8AM-4PM. Access by: mail, in person.

Middleton

Real Estate Recording—Middleton Town Clerk, Memorial Hall, Middleton, MA 1949. 9AM-4PM M-Th; 9AM-1PM F; 6-8PM T; 9AM-1PM M-F; 6-8PM T July-Aug.

Milford

Real Estate Recording—Milford Town Clerk, 52 Main Street, Milford, MA 1757., Fax: 508-634-2324. 8:30AM-5PM.

Millbury

Real Estate Recording—Millbury Town Clerk, 127 Elm Street, Municipal Office Building, Millbury, MA 1527. 9AM-4PM.

Millis

Real Estate Recording—Millis Town Clerk, 64 Exchange Street, Millis, MA 2054., Fax: 508-376-2941. 8:30AM-4:30PM.

Millville

Real Estate Recording—Millville Town Clerk, Municipal Center, 8 Central St. Millville, MA 1529., Fax: 508-883-2994. M-Th 1PM-5PM; 7-9PM W; 1-4PM F.

Milton

Real Estate Recording—Milton Town Clerk, 525 Canton Avenue, Town Hall, Milton, MA 2186. 617-696-5319. 8:30AM-5PM.

Monroe

Real Estate Recording—Monroe Town Clerk, Town Hall, Monroe, MA 1350. 413-424-4133, Fax: 413-424-5272.

Monson

Real Estate Recording—Monson Town Clerk, 110 Main St. Monson, MA 1057., Fax: 413-267-3726. 9AM-4PM M,Th,F.

Montague

Real Estate Recording—Montague Town Clerk, 1 Avenue A, Turners Falls, MA 1376. 413-863-3207, Fax: 413-863-3224. 8:30AM-4:30PM.

Monterey

Real Estate Recording—Monterey Town Clerk, Town Hall, Monterey, MA 1245. 413-528-1443, Fax: 413-528-9452. 9:30AM-12:30PM Sat, or by appointment.

Montgomery

Real Estate Recording—Montgomery Town Clerk, Town Hall, Montgomery, MA 1085. 413-862-3911, Fax: 413-862-3204. By appointment.

Mt. Washington

Real Estate Recording—Mt. Washington Town Clerk, 118 East St. Mt. Washington, MA 1258. 413-528-4779, Fax: 413-528-2839. 2PM-3PM T for Town Clerk; 8AM-2PM M-F for Town Secretary.

Nahant

Real Estate Recording—Nahant Town Clerk, Town Hall, Nahant, MA 1908., Fax: 781-593-0340. 9AM-Noon.

Nantucket

Real Estate Recording—Nantucket Register of Deeds, 16 Broad Street, Nantucket, MA 2554. 508-228-7265, Fax: 508-325-5331. 8AM-4PM; Recording Hours: 8AM-Noon, 1-3:45PM.

Nantucket Town Clerk, Town & County Building, 16 Broad Street, Nantucket, MA 2554., Fax: 508-325-5313. 8AM-4PM.

Felony, Civil Actions Over $25,000—Superior Court, PO Box 967, Nantucket, MA 02554. 508-228-2559, Fax: 508-228-3725. 8:30AM-4PM. Access by: mail, phone, fax, in person.

Felony, Misdemeanor, Civil, Eviction, Small Claims—Nantucket Division District Court, Broad Street, Nantucket, MA 02554. 508-228-0460. 8AM-4PM. Access by: in person.

Probate—Probate and Family Court, PO Box 1116, Nantucket, MA 02554. 508-228-2669, Fax: 508-228-3662. 8:30AM-4PM. Access by: mail, phone, in person.

Natick

Real Estate Recording—Natick Town Clerk, 13 East Central Street, Natick, MA 1760. 8AM-5PM.

Needham

Real Estate Recording—Needham Town Clerk, 1471 Highland Avenue, Needham, MA 2192., Fax: 617-449-4569. 8:30AM-5PM.

New Ashford

Real Estate Recording—New Ashford Town Clerk, 142 Beach Hill Road, New Ashford, MA 1237., Fax: 413-458-5461. By appointment.

New Bedford

Real Estate Recording—New Bedford City Clerk, 133 William Street, New Bedford, MA 2740. 508-979-1430, Fax: 508-979-1451. 8AM-4PM.

New Braintree

Real Estate Recording—New Braintree Town Clerk, 1750 Hardwick Rd. New Braintree, MA 1531. 413-867-2434, Fax: 508-867-6316. 9AM-5PM M,Th; Noon-5PM F.

New Marlborough

Real Estate Recording—New Marlborough Town Clerk, Town Hall, Mill River-Southfield Rd. Mill River, MA 1244. 413-229-8963, Fax: 413-229-6674. 9AM-2PM.

New Salem

Real Estate Recording—New Salem Town Clerk, Town Hall, 15 S. Main St. New Salem, MA 1355., Fax: 508-544-5775. 6-8PM M; 9-11AM W.

Newbury

Real Estate Recording—Newbury Town Clerk, 25 High Road, Newbury, MA 1951. 508-465-0862, Fax: 508-465-3064. 8AM-3:30PM M,T,W,Th; 8AM-1PM F.

Newburyport

Real Estate Recording—Newburyport City Clerk, 60 Pleasant Street, Newburyport, MA 1950. 508-465-4415, Fax: 978-465-4452. 8AM-4PM M,T,W; 8AM-8PM Th; 8AM-Noon F.

Newton

Real Estate Recording—Newton City Clerk, 1000 Commonwealth Avenue, Newton Center, MA 2159. 617-552-7080, Fax: 617-964-2333. 8:30AM-5PM.

Norfolk

Real Estate Recording—Norfolk County Register of Deeds, 649 High Street, Dedham, MA 2026., Fax: 781-326-4742. 8:30AM-4:45PM.

Norfolk Town Clerk, One Liberty Lane, Norfolk, MA 2056. 508-528-2478, Fax: 508-520-3250. 9AM-4PM.

Felony, Civil Actions Over $25,000—Superior Court, 650 High St, Dedham, MA 02026. 781-326-1600, Fax: 781-326-3871. 8:30AM-4:30PM. Access by: mail, phone, fax, in person.

Felony, Misdemeanor, Civil, Eviction, Small Claims—Brookline Division District Court, 360 Washington St, Brookline, MA 02146. 617-232-4660, Fax: 617-739-0734. 8:30AM-4:30PM. Access by: mail, in person.

Dedham Division District Court, 631 High St, Dedham, MA 02026. 781-329-4777. 8:15AM-4:30PM. Access by: in person.

Quincy Division District Court, One Dennis Ryan Parkway, Quincy, MA 02169. 617-471-1650. 8:30AM-4:30PM. Access by: in person.

Stoughton Division District Court, 1288 Central St, Stoughton, MA 02072. 781-344-2131. 8:30AM-4:30PM. Access by: mail, in person.

Wrentham Division District Court, PO Box 248, Wrentham, MA 02093. 508-384-3106, Fax: 508-384-5052. 8:30AM-4:30PM. Access by: mail, in person.

Probate—Probate and Family Court, 649 High St, PO Box 269, Dedham, MA 02027. 781-326-7200, Fax: 781-326-5575. 8AM-4:30PM. Access by: mail, phone, in person.

North Adams

Real Estate Recording—North Adams City Clerk, 10 Main Street, North Adams, MA 1247. 413-662-3044. 8AM-4:30PM.

North Andover

Real Estate Recording—North Andover Town Clerk, 120 Main Street, North Andover, MA 1845. 508-682-6483, Fax: 508-688-9556. 8:30AM-4:30PM.

North Attleborough

Real Estate Recording—North Attleborough Town Clerk, 43 South Washington Street, North Attleborough, MA 2761., Fax: 508-699-2354. 8AM-4PM (Th 8AM-7PM).

North Brookfield

Real Estate Recording—North Brookfield Town Clerk, 185 No. Main St. North Brookfield, MA 1535., Fax: 508-867-0249. Noon-2:30PM 6PM-8PM T; Noon-2:30PM Th; 9AM-Noon F.

North Reading

Real Estate Recording—North Reading Town Clerk, 235 North Street, North Reading, MA 1864., Fax: 978-664-6048. 8AM-4PM M-Th; 8AM-1PM F.

Northampton

Real Estate Recording—Northampton City Clerk, 210 Main Street, Northampton, MA 1060., Fax: 413-587-1264. 8:30AM-4:30PM.

Northborough

Real Estate Recording—Northborough Town Clerk, 63 Main Street, Northborough, MA 1532. 508-393-5045, Fax: 508-393-6996. 8AM-4PM M,W,F; 8AM-7PM T; 7AM-Noon F.

Northbridge

Real Estate Recording—Northbridge Town Clerk, Town Hall, 7 Main St. Whitinsville, MA 1588. 508-234-5432, Fax: 508-234-7640. 8:30AM-7PM M; 8:30AM-4:30PM T-Th; 8:30AM-1PM F.

Northfield

Real Estate Recording—Northfield Town Clerk, Town Hall, Northfield, MA 1360. 413-498-2901, Fax: 413-498-5115. 2-6PM M; 11AM-3PM, 6-8PM W.

Norton

Real Estate Recording—Norton Town Clerk, 70 East Main Street, Town Hall, Norton, MA 2766. 508-285-0223, Fax: 508-285-0297. 8:30AM-4:30PM M,T,W,F; 8:30AM-8PM Th.

Norwell

Real Estate Recording—Norwell Town Clerk, 345 Main Street, Town Hall, Norwell, MA 2061. 617-659-8072, Fax: 617-659-7795. 8AM-4PM.

Norwood

Real Estate Recording—Norwood Town Clerk, Municipal Building, 566 Washington St. Norwood, MA 2062. 617-762-1260, Fax: 617-762-0954. 8:15AM-4:30PM.

Oak Bluffs

Real Estate Recording—Oak Bluffs Town Clerk, Town Hall, Oak Bluffs, MA 2557., Fax: 508-696-7736. 8:30AM-4PM.

Oakham

Real Estate Recording—Oakham Town Clerk, Town Hall, 2 Coldbrook Rd. Oakham, MA 1068. 508-882-5549, Fax: 508-882-3060. 6-9PM T; 9AM-Noon Th.

Orange

Real Estate Recording—Orange Town Clerk, 6 Prospect Street, Orange, MA 1364. 508-544-1103, Fax: 508-544-1120. 8AM-4PM M-Th; 8AM-1PM F.

Orleans

Real Estate Recording—Orleans Town Clerk, 19 School Road, Orleans, MA 2653., Fax: 508-240-3388. 8:30AM-4:30PM.

Otis

Real Estate Recording—Otis Town Clerk, Town Hall, 1 N. Main St. Otis, MA 1253., Fax: 413-269-0111. 7:30AM-2:30PM M-F; 9AM-Noon Sat.

Oxford

Real Estate Recording—Oxford Town Clerk, 325 Main Street, Oxford, MA 1540. 508-987-6038, Fax: 508-987-6048. 9AM-4:30PM.

Palmer

Real Estate Recording—Palmer Town Clerk, 4417 Main St. Palmer, MA 1079. 413-283-2600, Fax: 413-283-2637. 9AM-4:30PM.

Paxton

Real Estate Recording—Paxton Town Clerk, 697 Pleasant Street, Paxton, MA 1612., Fax: 508-797-0966. 8AM-2PM M-Th.

Peabody

Real Estate Recording—Peabody City Clerk, 24 Lowell Street, City Hall, Peabody, MA 1960., Fax: 978-531-0098. 8:30AM-4PM M-W; 8:30AM-7PM Th; 8:30AM-12:30PM F.

Pelham

Real Estate Recording—Pelham Town Clerk, Rhodes Building, 351 Amherst Rd. Pelham, MA 1002. 9:15AM-1PM.

Pembroke

Real Estate Recording—Pembroke Town Clerk, 100 Center Street, Pembroke, MA 2359. 617-293-3893. 8:30AM-4:30PM.

Pepperell

Real Estate Recording—Pepperell Town Clerk, 1 Main Street, Town Hall, Pepperell, MA 1463. 508-433-0337, Fax: 978-433-0338. 8AM-4:30PM.

Peru

Real Estate Recording—Peru Town Clerk, 63 Middlefield Road, Peru, MA 1235. 413-655-8326, Fax: 413-655-8312. 9:30AM-4:30PM; 6:30PM-8:30PM M.

Petersham

Real Estate Recording—Petersham Town Clerk, Town Hall, 3 South Main St. Petersham, MA 1366., Fax: 508-724-3501. 6-8PM Monday.

Phillipston

Real Estate Recording—Phillipston Town Clerk, 50 The Common, Phillipston, MA 1331., Fax: 978-249-3356. 1-4PM, 5:30-7PM M; 5-7PM W.

Pittsfield

Real Estate Recording—Pittsfield City Clerk, 70 Allen Street, City Hall, Pittsfield, MA 1201. 8:30AM-4PM.

Plainfield

Real Estate Recording—Plainfield Town Clerk, 344 Main Street, Plainfield, MA 1070., Fax: 413-634-5683. 10AM-Noon Sat.

Plainville

Real Estate Recording—Plainville Town Clerk, 142 South Street, Plainville, MA 2762. 508-695-3142, Fax: 508-695-1857. 8AM-4:30PM, 6-9PM M; 8AM-4:30PM T-Th.

Plymouth

Real Estate Recording—Plymouth County Register of Deeds, 7 Russell Street, Plymouth, MA 2360., Fax: 508-830-9280. 8:15AM-4:30PM (Recording 8:30AM-4PM).

Plymouth Town Clerk, 11 Lincoln Street, Plymouth, MA 2360., Fax: 508-830-4062. 8AM-5PM M,W,Th; 8AM-7PM T; 8AM-Noon F.

Felony, Civil Actions Over $25,000—Superior Court-Brockton, 72 Belmont St, Brockton, MA 02401. 508-583-8250. 8:30AM-4:30PM. Access by: mail, in person.

Superior Court-Plymouth, Court St, Plymouth, MA 02360. 508-747-6911. 8:30AM-4:30PM. Access by: mail, phone, in person.

Felony, Misdemeanor, Civil, Eviction, Small Claims—Brockton Division District Court, 155 West Elm St, Brockton, MA 02401. 508-587-8000. 8:30AM-4:30PM. Access by: mail, in person.

Hingham Division District Court, 28 George Washington Blvd, Hingham, MA 02043. 781-749-7000, Fax: 617-740-8390. 8:30AM-4:30PM. Access by: mail, in person.

Plymouth 3rd Division District Court, Courthouse, South Russell St, Plymouth, MA 02360. 508-747-0500. 8:30AM-4:30PM. Access by: mail, in person.

Wareham Division District Court, 2200 Cranberry Hwy, Junction Routes 28 & 58, West Wareham, MA 02576. 508-295-8300, Fax: 508-291-6376. 8:30AM-4:30PM. Access by: mail, phone, in person.

Probate—Probate and Family Court, 11 Russell, PO Box 3640, Plymouth, MA 02361. 508-747-6204, Fax: 508-588-8483. 8:30AM-4PM. Access by: mail, in person.

Plympton

Real Estate Recording—Plympton Town Clerk, Town House, 5 Palmer Rd. Rte 58, Plympton, MA 2367., Fax: 781-582-1505. 9AM-2PM, 7-9PM M; 9AM-2PM T-Th.

Princeton

Real Estate Recording—Princeton Town Clerk, 6 Town Hall Drive, Princeton, MA 1541. 508-464-2105, Fax: 508-464-2106. 8:30AM-12:15PM (M 7-8:30PM).

Provincetown

Real Estate Recording—Provincetown Town Clerk, 260 Commercial Street, Provincetown, MA 2657. 508-487-7015, Fax: 508-487-9560. 8AM-5PM.

Quincy

Real Estate Recording—Quincy City Clerk, 1305 Hancock Street, City Hall, Quincy, MA 2169., Fax: 617-376-1139. 8:30AM-4:30PM.

Randolph

Real Estate Recording—Randolph Town Clerk, 41 S. Main St. Randolph, MA 2368. 8:30AM-4:30PM.

Raynham

Real Estate Recording—Raynham Town Clerk, 53 Orchard Street, Raynham, MA 2767., Fax: 508-823-1812. 8:30AM-4:30PM M-Th; 8:30AM-Noon F.

Reading

Real Estate Recording—Reading Town Clerk, 16 Lowell Street, Reading, MA 1867. 617-942-9032, Fax: 781-942-9070. 8AM-5PM.

Rehoboth

Real Estate Recording—Rehoboth Town Clerk, 148 Peck Street, Rehoboth, MA 2769., Fax: 508-252-5342. 9AM-4PM.

Revere

Real Estate Recording—Revere City Clerk, 281 Broadway, City Hall, Revere, MA 2151. 617-286-8136, Fax: 781-286-8135. 8:15AM-5PM M-Th; 8:15AM-Noon F.

Richmond

Real Estate Recording—Richmond Town Clerk, P.O. Box 81, 1529 State Road, Richmond, MA 1254. 413-698-3355, Fax: 413-698-3272. 9AM-Noon T,Th-Sat.

Rochester

Real Estate Recording—Rochester Town Clerk, Town Hall, 1 Constitution Way, Rochester, MA 2770., Fax: 508-763-4892. 7-9PM M.

Rockland

Real Estate Recording—Rockland Town Clerk, 242 Union Street, Rockland, MA 2370. 8:30AM-4:30PM.

Rockport

Real Estate Recording—Rockport Town Clerk, 34 Broadway, Rockport, MA 1966. 508-546-6648, Fax: 508-546-3562. 8AM-4PM.

Rowe

Real Estate Recording—Rowe Town Clerk, Town Hall, Rowe, MA 1367. 413-339-5520, Fax: 413-339-5316. 9AM-Noon T.

Rowley

Real Estate Recording—Rowley Town Clerk, 139 Main Street 1A Rt. Rowley, MA 1969., Fax: 508-948-2162. By appointment.

Royalston

Real Estate Recording—Royalston Town Clerk, 13 Taft Hill Rd. Royalston, MA 1368., Fax: 508-575-0748. 5-8PM W.

Russell

Real Estate Recording—Russell Town Clerk, Town Hall, Russell, MA 1071., Fax: 413-862-3103. 6-8PM T; 4-6PM F.

Rutland

Real Estate Recording—Rutland Town Clerk, 250 Main Street, Rutland, MA 1543., Fax: 508-886-2929. 7:30AM-4PM M,W,Th; 7:30AM-7PM Th.

Salem

Real Estate Recording—Salem City Clerk, City Hall, 93 Washington, Salem, MA 1970., Fax: 978-740-9209. 8AM-4PM M-W; 8AM-7PM Th; 8AM-4PM F.

Salisbury

Real Estate Recording—Salisbury Town Clerk, 5 Beach Road, Salisbury, MA 1952., Fax: 978-462-4176. 8:30AM-4PM, 7-9PM M; 8:30AM-4PM T-Th; 8:30AM-1PM F.

Sandisfield

Real Estate Recording—Sandisfield Town Clerk, Town Hall, 3 SilverbBrook Rd. Sandisfield, MA 1255., Fax: 413-258-4225. 10AM-2PM, 6-8PM M; 10AM-2PM Th or by Appointment.

Sandwich

Real Estate Recording—Sandwich Town Clerk, 145 Main Street, Sandwich, MA 2563. 508-888-6508, Fax: 508-888-2497. 8:30AM-4:30PM.

Saugus

Real Estate Recording—Saugus Town Clerk, 298 Central Street, Town Hall, Saugus, MA 1906., Fax: 617-231-4109. 8:30AM-8PM M; 8:30AM-5PM T,W,Th; 8:30AM-12:30PM F; Summer hours: 8:30AM-4PM T-Th.

Savoy

Real Estate Recording—Savoy Town Clerk, 720 Main Rd. Savoy, MA 1256., Fax: 413-743-4292. 9-11:30AM.

Scituate

Real Estate Recording—Scituate Town Clerk, Town Hall, 600 C. J. Cushing Way, Scituate, MA 2066., Fax: 617-545-8704. 8:30AM-4:30PM.

Seekonk

Real Estate Recording—Seekonk Town Clerk, 100 Peck Street, Seekonk, MA 2771., Fax: 508-336-0764. 9AM-4:30PM.

Sharon

Real Estate Recording—Sharon Town Clerk, 90 South Main Street, Town Hall, Sharon, MA 2067., Fax: 617-784-1503. 8:30AM-5PM M-W; 8:30AM-8PM Th; 8:30AM-12:30PM F.

Sheffield

Real Estate Recording—Sheffield Town Clerk, 21 Depot Square, Town Hall, Sheffield, MA 1257., Fax: 413-229-7010. 9AM-4PM.

Shelburne

Real Estate Recording—Shelburne Town Clerk, Town Hall, 51 Bridge St. Shelburne, MA 1370. 413-625-0301, Fax: 413-625-0303. 8:30AM-11:30AM T; Noon-8PM Th.

Sherborn

Real Estate Recording—Sherborn Town Clerk, 19 Washington Street, Sherborn, MA 1770., Fax: 508-651-7854. 9AM-1PM M-F.

Shirley

Real Estate Recording—Shirley Town Clerk, Municipal Building, 3 Lancaster Rd. Shirley, MA 1464. 508-425-2604, Fax: 508-425-2602. 8AM-3PM (6-9PM M Evening).

Shrewsbury

Real Estate Recording—Shrewsbury Town Clerk, 100 Maple Ave, Town Hall, Shrewsbury, MA 1545. 508-845-1136, Fax: 508-842-0587. 8AM-4:30PM.

Shutesbury

Real Estate Recording—Shutesbury Town Clerk, Town Hall, 1 Cooleyville Rd. Shutesbury, MA 1072., Fax: 413-259-1107. 9AM-1PM M-Th.

Somerset

Real Estate Recording—Somerset Town Clerk, 140 Wood Street, Somerset, MA 2726., Fax: 508-646-2802. 8:30AM-4PM.

Somerville

Real Estate Recording—Somerville City Clerk's Office, 93 Highland Avenue, Somerville, MA 2143., Fax: 617-625-4239. 8:30AM-4:30PM.

South Hadley

Real Estate Recording—South Hadley Town Clerk, 116 Main Street, South Hadley, MA 1075., Fax: 413-538-7565. 8:30AM-4:30PM.

Southampton

Real Estate Recording—Southampton Town Clerk, Town Hall, 8 East St. Southampton, MA 1073., Fax: 413-529-1006. 8:30AM-4PM M-Th.

Southborough

Real Estate Recording—Southborough Town Clerk, 17 Common Street, Southborough, MA 1772., Fax: 508-480-0161. 9AM-5PM.

Southbridge

Real Estate Recording—Southbridge Town Clerk, 41 Elm Street, Southbridge, MA 1550., Fax: 508-764-5425. 8AM-4PM M-W; 8AM-8PM Th; 8AM-Noon F.

Southwick

Real Estate Recording—Southwick Town Clerk, Town Hall, 11 Depot St. Southwick, MA 1077., Fax: 413-569-5001. 8:30AM-4:30PM.

Spencer

Real Estate Recording—Spencer Town Clerk, 157 Main Street, Town Hall, Spencer, MA 1562., Fax: 508-885-7528. 8AM-4PM, 6-8PM Mon; 8AM-4PM T,Th; 8AM-Noon W.

Springfield

Real Estate Recording—Springfield City Clerk, 36 Court Street, Springfield, MA 1103. 413-787-6130. 9AM-4PM (Th open until 6PM).

Sterling

Real Estate Recording—Sterling Town Clerk, Mary Ellen Butterick Municipal Bldg, 1 Park St. Sterling, MA 1564. 508-422-8111, Fax: 508-422-0289. 8AM-4:30PM M,T,Th,F; 8AM-7PM W.

Stockbridge

Real Estate Recording—Stockbridge Town Clerk, 6 Main St. Stockbridge, MA 1262., Fax: 413-298-4485. 9AM-Noon.

Stoneham

Real Estate Recording—Stoneham Town Clerk, 35 Central Street, Stoneham, MA 2180., Fax: 617-279-2653. 8AM-4PM M,Th; 8AM-7PM T; 1-4PM W; 8AM-Noon F.

Stoughton

Real Estate Recording—Stoughton Town Clerk, 10 Pearl Street, Town Hall, Stoughton, MA 2072. 617-341-1300, Fax: 617-344-5048. 8:30AM-4:30PM M-W; 8:30AM-7PM Th; 8:30AM-1PM F.

Stow

Real Estate Recording—Stow Town Clerk, Town Hall, 380 Great Road, Stow, MA 1775., Fax: 978-897-4534. 9AM-5PM.

Sturbridge

Real Estate Recording—Sturbridge Town Clerk, 308 Main, Sturbridge, MA 1566. 508-347-2509, Fax: 508-347-5886. 8AM-Noon, 1-4PM, 6-8PM M; 8AM-Noon, 1-4PM T-F.

Sudbury

Real Estate Recording—Sudbury Town Clerk, 322 Concord Road, Sudbury, MA 1776., Fax: 978-443-0264. 9AM-5PM.

Suffolk

Real Estate Recording—Suffolk County Register of Deeds, New Chardon Street Courthouse, 24 New Chardon St. Boston, MA 2114., Fax: 617-720-4163. 9AM-4:30PM.

Civil—Superior Court-Civil, Old Courthouse Bldg Rm 117, Boston, MA 02108. 617-725-8235. 8:30AM-5PM. Access by: mail, in person.

Felony—Superior Court-Criminal, New Courthouse, 712 Pemberton, Boston, MA 02108. 617-725-8160, Fax: 617-227-8834. 9AM-5PM. Access by: mail, phone, in person.

Felony, Misdemeanor, Civil, Eviction, Small Claims—Brighton Division District Court Department, 52 Academy Hill Rd, Brighton, MA 02135. 617-782-6521, Fax: 617-254-2127. 8:30AM-4:30PM. Access by: mail, phone, in person.

Charleston Division District Court, 3 City Square, Charleston, MA 02129. 617-242-5400, Fax: 617-242-1677. 8:30AM-4:30PM. Access by: mail, phone, fax, in person.

Chelsea Division District Court, 121 3rd St, Cambridge, MA 02141-1710. 617-252-0960, Fax: 617-621-9743. 8:30AM-4:30PM. Access by: mail, phone, in person.

Dorchester Division District Court, 510 Washington St, Dorchester, MA 02124. 617-288-9500. 8:30AM-4:30PM. Access by: mail, in person.

Roxbury Division District Court, 85 Warren St, Roxbury, MA 02119. 617-427-7000, Fax: 617-541-0286. 8:30AM-5:30PM. Access by: mail, phone, fax, in person.

South Boston Division District Court, 535 East Broadway, South Boston, MA 02127. 617-268-9292, Fax: 617-268-7321. 8:30AM-4:30PM. Access by: in person.

West Roxbury Division District Court, Courthouse, 445 Arborway, Jamaica Plain, MA 02130. 617-522-4710. 8:30AM-4:30PM. Access by: mail, in person.

Misdemeanor, Civil Actions Under $25,000, Eviction, Small Claims—East Boston Division District Court, 37 Meridian St, East Boston, MA 02128. 617-569-7550, Fax: 617-561-4988. 8:30AM-4:30PM. Access by: mail, in person.

Misdemeanor, Civil, Small Claims—Suffolk County Courthouse Boston Municipal Court, Government Center, Boston, MA 02108. 617-725-8000. 8:30AM-4:30PM. Access by: mail, in person.

Probate—Probate and Family Court, 24 New Chardon St, Boston, MA 02114-4703. 617-788-8300, Fax: 617-788-8926. 8:30AM-4:30PM. Access by: mail, in person.

Sunderland

Real Estate Recording—Sunderland Town Clerk, 12 School St. Sunderland, MA 1375. 413-665-1443, Fax: 413-665-1446. 9AM-3PM M-Th.

Sutton

Real Estate Recording—Sutton Town Clerk, Town Hall, 4 Uxbridge Rd. Sutton, MA 1590., Fax: 508-865-8721. 9AM-4PM M,T,W,Th; 7-9PM T; 9AM-Noon F.

Swampscott

Real Estate Recording—Swampscott Town Clerk, Town Hall, 22 Monument Ave. Swampscott, MA 1907., Fax: 617-596-8870. 8:30AM-4:30PM M,W,Th; 8AM-8PM T; 8AM-Noon F.

Swansea

Real Estate Recording—Swansea Town Clerk, 81 Main Street, Town Hall, Swansea, MA 2777. 9AM-4PM M,T,Th,F; 9AM-5PM W.

Taunton

Real Estate Recording—Taunton City Clerk, 15 Summer Street, City Hall, Taunton, MA 2780., Fax: 508-821-1098. 9AM-5PM.

Templeton

Real Estate Recording—Templeton Town Clerk, Town Office Building, 9 Main St. Baldwinville, MA 1436., Fax: 508-939-2125. 8AM-Noon, 1-4 PM M,T,Th,F; 8AM-Noon.

Tewksbury

Real Estate Recording—Tewksbury Town Clerk, 1009 Main Street, Town Hall, Tewksbury, MA 1876. 508-640-4340. 8:30AM-4:30PM.

Tisbury

Real Estate Recording—Tisbury Town Clerk, 51 Spring St. Town Hall, Tisbury, MA 2568., Fax: 508-693-5876. 8:30AM-4:30PM.

Tolland

Real Estate Recording—Tolland Town Clerk, 241 W. Granville Rd. Tolland, MA 1034., Fax: 413-258-4048. 6-7PM First Mon of the Month.

Topsfield

Real Estate Recording—Topsfield Town Clerk, 8 West Common Street, Town Hall, Topsfield, MA 1983., Fax: 978-887-1502. 8:30AM-4PM M-Th (Summer Hours: 8AM-Noon).

Townsend

Real Estate Recording—Townsend Town Clerk, Memorial Hall, 272 Main Street, Townsend, MA 1469., Fax: 508-597-8135. 9AM-4PM M-Th; 9AM-8PM T.

Truro

Real Estate Recording—Truro Town Clerk, Town Hall, 24 Town Hall Rd. Truro, MA 2666., Fax: 508-349-7720. 8AM-4PM.

Tyngsborough

Real Estate Recording—Tyngsborough Town Clerk, 25 Bryants Lane, Tyngsborough, MA 1879. 508-649-2307, Fax: 508-649-2301. 8AM-Noon, 12:30-4PM.

Tyringham

Real Estate Recording—Tyringham Town Clerk, Main Road, Tyringham, MA 1264., Fax: 413-243-4942. 9AM-1PM or By Appointment.

Upton

Real Estate Recording—Upton Town Clerk, 1 Main Street, Upton, MA 1568., Fax: 508-529-1010. 11:30AM-4:30PM.

Uxbridge

Real Estate Recording—Uxbridge Town Clerk, 21 South Main Street, Uxbridge, MA 1569., Fax: 508-278-8605. 9AM-4PM.

Wakefield

Real Estate Recording—Wakefield Town Clerk, 1 Lafayette Street, Town Hall, Wakefield, MA 1880., Fax: 781-246-6266. 9AM-5PM.

Wales

Real Estate Recording—Wales Town Clerk, Town Hall, 3 Hollow Rd. Wales, MA 1081., Fax: 413-245-3261. 9:30AM-Noon M & F; 6:30-8:30PM T.

Walpole

Real Estate Recording—Walpole Town Clerk, 135 School Street, Town Hall, Walpole, MA 2081., Fax: 508-660-7303. 8AM-4PM; M-F; 7-9PM T.

Waltham

Real Estate Recording—Waltham City Clerk, 610 Main Street, Waltham, MA 2452., Fax: 781-894-8414. 8:30AM-4:30PM M,W,F; 8:30AM-1PM T,Th.

Ware

Real Estate Recording—Ware Town Clerk, 126 Main Street, Ware, MA 1082., Fax: 413-967-9600. 8:30AM-Noon, 1-4:30PM.

Wareham

Real Estate Recording—Wareham Town Clerk, 54 Marion Road, Wareham, MA 2571. 508-291-3140, Fax: 508-291-3116. 8:30AM-4:30PM.

Warren

Real Estate Recording—Warren Town Clerk, Shepard Municipal Building, 48 High St. Warren, MA 1083. 413-436-5700, Fax: 413-436-9754. 9AM-3:30PM M-W,F; 5-8PM Th.

Warwick

Real Estate Recording—Warwick Town Clerk, Town Hall, 12 Athol Rd. Warwick, MA 1378., Fax: 978-544-6499. 9AM-3PM M.

Washington

Real Estate Recording—Washington Town Clerk, Town Hall Route 8, GA094, Washington, MA 1223., Fax: 413-623-2116. 7PM-9PM M or by appointment.

Watertown

Real Estate Recording—Watertown Town Clerk, 149 Main Street, Administration Building, Watertown, MA 2472., Fax: 617-972-6403. 8:30AM-5PM.

Wayland

Real Estate Recording—Wayland Town Clerk, 41 Cochituate Road, Wayland, MA 1778., Fax: 508-358-3627. 8:30AM-4:30PM.

Webster

Real Estate Recording—Webster Town Clerk, Main Street, Town Hall, Webster, MA 1570., Fax: 508-949-3888. 8AM-4PM.

Wellesley

Real Estate Recording—Wellesley Town Clerk, 525 Washington Street, Wellesley, MA 2181., Fax: 781-239-1043. 8AM-5PM.

Wellfleet

Real Estate Recording—Wellfleet Town Clerk, 300 Main Street, Wellfleet, MA 2667., Fax: 508-349-0317. 8AM-4PM.

Wendell

Real Estate Recording—Wendell Town Clerk, 270 Wendell Depot Rd. Wendell Depot, MA 1380.

Wenham

Real Estate Recording—Wenham Town Clerk, Town Hall, 138 Main St. Wenham, MA 1984. 508-468-5525, Fax: 508-468-6164. 9AM-4:30PM M,W,Th; 9AM-7PM T; 9AM-1PM F.

West Boylston

Real Estate Recording—West Boylston Town Clerk, 120 Prescott Street, West Boylston, MA 1583. 508-835-6092, Fax: 508-835-4102. 9AM-3:30PM M,T,Th,F; 5-9PM W.

West Bridgewater

Real Estate Recording—West Bridgewater Town Clerk, 65 North Main Street, Town Hall, West Bridgewater, MA 2379., Fax: 508-894-1210. 8AM-Noon, 1-4PM; 1st & 3rd W 7PM-9PM.

West Brookfield

Real Estate Recording—West Brookfield Town Clerk, Town Hall, 2 E. Main, West Brookfield, MA 1585., Fax: 508-867-1401. 9AM-Noon.

West Newbury

Real Estate Recording—West Newbury Town Clerk, Town Office Bldg. 381 Main St. West Newbury, MA 1985., Fax: 978-363-1117. 8AM-4:30PM M-Th; 8AM-Noon F.

West Springfield

Real Estate Recording—West Springfield Town Clerk, 26 Central Street, Town Hall, West Springfield, MA 1089. 8AM-4:30PM.

West Stockbridge

Real Estate Recording—West Stockbridge Town Clerk, 9 Main Street, West Stockbridge, MA 1266. 413-232-0316, Fax: 413-232-0318. 2-8PM M-W; 7AM-Noon F,Sat.

West Tisbury

Real Estate Recording—West Tisbury Town Clerk, Town Hall, West Tisbury, MA 2575., Fax: 508-696-0103. 8:30AM-4:30PM.

Westborough

Real Estate Recording—Westborough Town Clerk, 34 West Main Street, Town Hall, Westborough, MA 1581., Fax: 508-366-3099. 8AM-4:30PM.

Westfield

Real Estate Recording—Westfield City Clerk, 59 Court Street, Westfield, MA 1085., Fax: 413-564-3114. 9AM-5PM.

Westford

Real Estate Recording—Westford Town Clerk, 55 Main Street, Town Hall, Westford, MA 1886., Fax: 508-692-9607. 8AM-4PM.

Westhampton

Real Estate Recording—Westhampton Town Clerk, Town Hall, Westhampton, MA 1027., Fax: 413-527-8655. 7PM-8:30PM M.

Westminster

Real Estate Recording—Westminster Town Clerk, Town Hall, 3 Bacon St. Westminster, MA 1473. 508-874-7403, Fax: 978-874-7411. 8AM-1PM, 2-4:30PM M-Th; 8AM-1PM F.

Weston

Real Estate Recording—Weston Town Clerk, Town House Road, Weston, MA 2493., Fax: 781-891-3697. 8:30AM-5PM.

Westport

Real Estate Recording—Westport Town Clerk, Town Hall, 816 Main Rd. Westport, MA 2790., Fax: 508-636-1147. 8:30AM-Noon, 12:30-4PM.

Westwood

Real Estate Recording—Westwood Town Clerk, 580 High Street, Westwood, MA 2090., Fax: 617-329-8030. 8:30AM-4:30PM M,W,Th; 8:30AM-7PM T; 8:30AM-1PM F.

Weymouth

Real Estate Recording—Weymouth Town Clerk, 75 Middle Street, Town Hall, East Weymouth, MA 2189. 617-335-2000, Fax: 617-335-3283. 8:30AM-4:30PM.

Whately

Real Estate Recording—Whately Town Clerk, 218 Chestnut Plain Rd. Whately, MA 1093., Fax: 413-665-9560. Noon-7PM T; 9AM-1PM Th.

Whitman

Real Estate Recording—Whitman Town Clerk, 54 South Avenue, Whitman, MA 2382., Fax: 617-447-7318. 8AM-4PM M,W,Th; 8AM-7:30PM T.

Wilbraham

Real Estate Recording—Wilbraham Town Clerk, 240 Springfield Street, Wilbraham, MA 1095., Fax: 413-596-2830. 8:30AM-4:30PM.

Williamsburg

Real Estate Recording—Williamsburg Town Clerk, Town Office, 141 Main St. Haydenville, MA 1039., Fax: 413-268-8409. 9AM-2:30PM T; 6-8PM W; 9Am-Noon Th.

Williamstown

Real Estate Recording—Williamstown Town Clerk, 31 North Street, Williamstown, MA 1267., Fax: 413-458-4839. 8:30AM-5PM.

Wilmington

Real Estate Recording—Wilmington Town Clerk, 121 Glen Road, Town Hall, Wilmington, MA 1887. 508-658-3531, Fax: 978-658-3334. 8:30AM-4:30PM.

Winchendon

Real Estate Recording—Winchendon Town Clerk, 109 Front Street, Winchendon, MA 1475. 508-297-0152, Fax: 508-297-1616. 8:30AM-6PM M; 8:30AM-4:30PM T-Th; 8:30AM-Noon F.

Winchester

Real Estate Recording—Winchester Town Clerk, 71 Mount Vernon Street, Town Hall, Winchester, MA 1890. 617-721-7123, Fax: 617-721-1153. 8AM-4PM.

Windsor

Real Estate Recording—Windsor Town Clerk, 3 Hinsdale Rd. Windsor, MA 1270., Fax: 413-684-3806. 5-7PM Monday or by appointment.

Winthrop

Real Estate Recording—Winthrop Town Clerk, Town Hall, Winthrop, MA 2152. 617-846-3226, Fax: 617-846-5458. 8AM-7PM M; 8AM-4PM T-Th; 8AM-Noon F.

Woburn

Real Estate Recording—Woburn City Clerk, 10 Common Street, Woburn, MA 1801. 9AM-4:30PM.

Worcester

Real Estate Recording—Register of Deeds, Courthouse, 84 Elm St. Fitchburg, MA 1420., Fax: 978-345-2865. 8:30AM-4:30PM; Recording Hours 8:30AM-4PM.

Worcester City Clerk, 455 Main Street, City Hall - Room 206, Worcester, MA 1608. 508-799-1077, Fax: 508-799-1194. 8:45AM-4:15PM T,W,Th,F; 8:45AM-5PM M.

Worcester County Register of Deeds (Worcester District), 2 Main Street, Courthouse, Worcester, MA 1608. 508-798-2441, Fax: 508-753-1338. 8:15AM-4:30PM (Recording Hours: 9AM-Noon, 1-4PM).

Felony, Civil Actions Over $25,000—Superior Court, 2 Main St Rm 21, Worcester, MA 01608. 508-770-1899. 8AM-4:30PM. Access by: mail, in person.

Felony, Misdemeanor, Civil, Eviction, Small Claims—Clinton Division District Court, Routes 62 & 70, Boylston St, PO Box 30, Clinton, MA 01510-0030. 978-368-7811, Fax: 978-368-7827. 8:30AM-4:30PM. Access by: mail, in person.

Dudley Division District Court 64, PO Box 100, Dudley, MA 01571. 508-943-7123, Fax: 508-949-0015. 8AM-4:30PM. Access by: mail, phone, in person.

Fitchburg District Court 16, 100 Elm St, Fitchburg, MA 01420. 978-345-2111, Fax: 978-342-2461. 8:30AM-4:30PM. Access by: in person.

Leominster Division District Court, 25 School St, Leominster, MA 01453. 978-537-3722, Fax: 978-537-3970. 8:30AM-4:30PM. Access by: mail, phone, in person.

Milford Division District Court, PO Box 370, Milford, MA 01757. 508-473-1260. 8:30AM-4:30PM. Access by: mail, in person.

Spencer Division District Court, 544 E Main St, East Brookfield, MA 01515-1701. 508-885-6305, Fax: 508-885-7623. 8:30AM-4:30PM. Access by: mail, phone, in person.

Trial Court of the Commonwealth-Gardner Division, 108 Matthews St, PO Box 40, Gardner, MA 01440-0040. 978-632-2373, Fax: 978-630-3902. 8:30AM-4:30PM. Access by: mail, phone, fax, in person.

Uxbridge Division District Court, PO Box 580, Uxbridge, MA 01569. 508-278-2454, Fax: 508-278-2929. 8:30AM-4:30PM. Access by: mail, phone, in person.

Westborough Division District Court, 175 Milk St, Westborough, MA 01581. 508-366-8266, Fax: 508-366-8268. 8AM-4:30PM. Access by: mail, in person.

Winchendon Division District Court, PO Box 309, Winchendon, MA 01475. 978-297-0156, Fax: 978-297-0161. 8:30AM-4:30PM. Access by: mail, phone, in person.

Worcester Division District Court, 50 Harvard St, Worcester, MA 01608. 508-757-8350, Fax: 508-797-0716. 8AM-4:30PM. Access by: mail, in person.

Probate—Probate and Family Court, 2 Main St, Worcester, MA 01608. 508-770-0825, Fax: 508-752-6138. 8AM-4:30PM. Access by: mail, in person.

Worthington

Real Estate Recording—Worthington Town Clerk, Town Hall, Worthington, MA 1098., Fax: 413-238-5579. 9AM-Noon W; 6PM-7PM T.

Wrentham

Real Estate Recording—Wrentham Town Clerk, 79 South Street, Wrentham, MA 2093. 508-384-5413, Fax: 508-384-5415. 8:30AM-7PM M; 8:30AM-4PM T-Th; 8:30AM-1:30PM F.

Yarmouth

Real Estate Recording—Yarmouth Town Clerk, 1146 Route 28, Town Hall, South Yarmouth, MA 2664. 508-398-2231, Fax: 508-398-2365. 8:30AM-4:30PM.

Federal Courts

US District Court

Boston Division Post Office & Courthouse Bldg, 90 Devonshire, Room 700, Boston, MA 02109617-223-9152, Record Room: 617-223-9086 Fax: 617-223-9096 Counties: Barnstable, Bristol, Dukes, Essex, Middlesex, Nantucket, Norfolk, Plymouth, Suffolk.

Springfield Division 1550 Main St, Springfield, MA 01103413-785-0214, Civil Docket Phone: 413-785-0215, Criminal Docket Phone: 413-785-0216 Fax: 413-785-0204 Counties: Berkshire, Franklin, Hampden, Hampshire.

Worcester Division 595 Main St., Room 502, Worcester, MA 01608508-793-0552 Counties: Worcester.

US Bankruptcy Court

Boston Division Room 1101, 10 Causeway, Boston, MA 02222-1074617-565-6051 Fax: 617-565-6087 Counties: Barnstable, Bristol, Dukes, Essex (except towns assigned to Worcester Division), Nantucket, Norfolk (except towns assigned to Worcester Division), Plymouth, Suffolk, and the following towns in Middlesex: Arlington, Belmont, Burlington, Everett,Lexington, Malden, Medford, Melrose, Newton, North Reading, Reading, Stoneham, Wakefield, Waltham, Watertown, Wilmington, Winchester and Woburn. www.mab.uscourts.gov

Worcester Division 595 Main St, Room 211, Worcester, MA 01608508-770-8900 Fax: 508-793-0541 Counties: Berkshire, Franklin, Hampden, Hampshire, Middlesex (except the towns assigned to the Boston Division), Worcester and the following towns: in Essex-Andover, Haverhill, Lawrence, Methuen and North Andover; in Norfolk-Bellingham, Franklin, Medway,Millis and Norfolk. www.mab.uscourts.gov

Michigan

Attorney General's Office

PO Box 30212
Lansing, MI 48909
www.ag.state.mi.us

517-373-1110
Fax: 517-373-3042

Governor's Office

PO Box 30013
Lansing, MI 48909
www.migov.state.mi.us

517-373-3400
Fax: 517-335-6863

State Archives

Michigan Library & Historical Ctr,
717 W Allegan
Lansing, MI 48918-1837
www.sos.state.mi.us/history/archive/archive
.html

517-373-1408
Fax: 517-241-1658

Capital: Lansing
Ingham County

Time Zone: EST*

* Four north-western Michigan counties are CST:
They are: Dickinson, Gogebic, Iron, Menominee.

Number of Counties: 83

Population: 9,773,892

Web Site: www.state.mi.us

Search Unclaimed Property Online

www.mlive.com/news/miou.html

State Agencies

Criminal Records

Michigan State Police, Ident. Section, Criminla Justice Information Center, 7150 Harris Dr, Lansing, MI 48913; 517-322-5531; Fax: 517-322-0635; 8AM-5PM. Access by: mail. www.msp.state.mi.us

Corporation Records
Limited Liability Company Records
Fictitious Name
Limited Partnership Records
Assumed Name

Department of Consumer & Industrial Srvs, Corporation Division, PO Box 30054, Lansing, MI 48909-7554 (6546 Mercantile Way, Lansing, MI 48910); 517-241-6470; Fax: 517-334-8329; 8AM-5PM. Access by: mail, phone, in person. www.cis.state.mi.us/corp

Trademarks/Servicemarks

Department of Consumer & Industry Srvs, Securities Examination Division, PO Box 30054, Lansing, MI 48909 (6546 Mercantile Way, Lansing, MI 48909); 517-334-6302; Fax: 517-

334-7133; 8AM-5PM. Access by:, phone, in person. www.cis.state.mi.us/corp

Uniform Commercial Code
Federal Tax Liens
State Tax Liens

UCC Section, Department of State, PO Box 30197, Lansing, MI 48909-7697 (7064 Crowner Dr, Dimondale, MI 48821); 517-322-1144; Fax: 517-322-5434; 8AM-5PM. Access by: mail, phone, in person.

Sales Tax Registrations

Records not available from state agency.

The agency has recently determined it will not release information to the public nor verify or confirm data.

Workers' Compensation Records

Department of Consumer & Industry Services, Workers Disability Compensation Division, 7150 Harris Dr, Lansing, MI 48909; 517-322-1884; Fax: 517-322-1808; 8AM-5PM. Access by: mail. www.cis.state.mi.us/wkrcomp

Birth Certificates

Department of Community Health, Office of the State Registrar, PO Box 30195, Lansing, MI 48909 (3423 Martin Luther King, Jr Blvd, Lansing, MI 48906); 517-335-8656, 517-335-8666 Certification Unit; Fax: 517-321-5884; 8AM-5PM. Access by: mail.   www.mdch.state.mi.us/pha/osr/ vitframe.htm

Death Records

Department of Health, Office of the State Registrar, PO Box 30195, Lansing, MI 48909; 517-335-8656, 517-335-8666 Certification Unit; Fax: 517-321-5884; 8AM-5PM. Access by: mail. www.mdch.state.mi.us/pha/osr/vitrame.htm

Marriage Certificates

Department of Health, Office of the State Registrar, PO Box 30195, Lansing, MI 48909; 517-335-8656, 517-335-8666 Certification Unit; Fax: 517-321-5884; 8AM-5PM. Access by: mail.
www.mdch.state.mi.us/pha/osr/vitframe.htm

Divorce Records

Department of Health, Office of the State Registrar, PO Box 30195, Lansing, MI 48909; 517-335-8656, 517-335-8666 Certification Unit; Fax: 517-321-5884; 8AM-5PM. Access by: mail.
www.mdch.state.mi.us/pha/osr/vitframe.htm

Accident Reports

Department of State Police, Central Justice Information Center, 7150 Harris Dr, Lansing, MI 48913; 517-322-5509; Fax: 517-323-5350;   8AM-5PM.   Access   by: mail. www.msp.state.mi.us

Driver Records

Department of State Police, Record Look-up Unit, 7064 Crowner Dr, Lansing, MI 48918; 517-322-1624; Fax: 517-322-1181; 8AM-4:45PM. Access by: mail, phone, in person, online. www.sos.state.mi.us/dv

Vehicle Ownership
Vehicle Identification
Boat & Vessel Ownership
Boat & Vessel Registration

Department of State Police, Record Look-up Unit, 7064 Crowner Dr, Lansing, MI 48918; 517-322-1624; Fax: 517-322-1181; 8AM-4:45PM. Access by: mail, phone, in person, online. www.sos.state.mi.us/dv

Legislation-Current/Pending
Legislation-Passed

Michigan Legislature Document Room, State Capitol, PO Box 30036, Lansing, MI 48909 (North Capitol Annex, Lansing, MI 48909); 517-373-0169; 8:30AM-5PM. Access by: mail, phone, in person. www.michiganlegislature.org

Voter Registration

Records not available from state agency.

The city or township keeps all records. In general, the records are open to the public.

GED Certificates

Department of Education, GED Testing, PO Box 30008, Lansing, MI 48909 (608 W Allegan, Lansing, MI 48933); 517-373-1692; Fax: 517-335-3630;   8AM-5PM.   Access   by: mail. www.mde.state.mi.us

Hunting License Information
Fishing License Information

Dept of Natural Resources, License Control, PO Box 30181, Lansing, MI 48909 (530 W Allegan St, Lansing, MI 48933); 517-373-1204; Fax: 517-373-0784; 8AM-5PM. Access by: mail.

County Courts & Recording Offices

About the Courts...

Administration

State Court Administrator   517-373-2222
309 N. Washington Sq, PO Box 30048   Fax: 517-373-2112
Lansing, MI 48909
www.supremecourt.state.mi.us

Court Structure

District Courts and Municipal Courts have jurisdiction over certain minor felonies.

There is a Court of Claims in Lansing which is a function of the 30th Circuit Court with jurisdiction over claims against the state of Michigan.

A Recorder's Court in Detroit was abolished as of October 1, 1997.

As of January 1, 1998, the Family Division of the Circuit Court was created. Domestic relations actions and juvenile cases, including criminal and abuse/neglect, formerly adjudicated in the Probate Court, were transferred to the Family Division of the Circuit Court. Mental health and estate cases continue to be handled by the Probate Courts.

As of January 1, 1998, the limit for civil actions brought in District Court was raised from $10,000 to $25,000. The minimum for civil actions brought in Circuit Court was also raised to $25,000 at that time.

Searching Hints

Court records are considered public except for specific categories: controlled substances, spousal abuse, Holmes youthful trainee, set aside convictions and probation, and sealed records. Courts will, however, affirm that cases exist and provide case numbers.
Some courts will not conduct criminal searches. Rather, they refer requests to the State Police.
Note that costs, search requirements, and procedures vary widely because each jurisdiction may create its own administrative orders.

Online Access

There is a wide range of online computerization of the judicial system from "none" to "fairly complete," but there is no statewide network. Some Michigan courts provide public access terminals in clerk's offices, and some courts are developing off-site electronic filing and searching capability, but none offer remote online to the public.

About the Recording Offices...

Organization

83 counties, 83 recording offices. The recording officer is County Register of Deeds. 79 counties are in the Eastern Time Zone (EST) and 4 are in the Central Time Zone (CST).

UCC Records

Financing statements are filed at the state level except for consumer goods, farm related and real estate related filings. All counties will perform UCC searches. Use search request form UCC-11. Search fees are usually $3.00 per debtor name if federal tax identification number or Social Security number are given, or $6.00 without the number. Copies usually cost $1.00 per page.

Lien Records

Federal and state tax liens on personal property of businesses are filed with the Secretary of State. Other federal and state tax liens are filed with the Register of Deeds. Most counties search each tax lien index separately. Some charge one fee to search both, while others charge a separate fee for each one. When combining a UCC and tax lien search, total fee is usually $9.00 for all three searches. Some counties require tax identification number as well as name to do a search. Copy fees are usually $1.00 per page.

Real Estate Records

Some counties will perform real estate searches. Copies usually cost $1.00 per page. and certification fees vary. Ownership records are located at the Equalization Office, designated "Assessor" in this section. Tax records are located at the Treasurer's Office.

County Courts & Recording Offices

Alcona

Real Estate Recording—Alcona County Register of Deeds, 5th Street, Courthouse, Harrisville, MI 48740. 517-724-5140, Fax: 517-724-5684. 8:30AM-4:30PM.

Felony, Civil Actions Over $25,000—26th Circuit Court, PO Box 308, Harrisville, MI 48740. 517-724-6807, Fax: 517-724-5684. 8:30AM-Noon, 1-4:30PM. Access by: mail, phone, in person.

Misdemeanor, Civil Actions Under $25,000, Eviction, Small Claims—82nd District Court, PO Box 385, Harrisville, MI 48740. 517-724-5313, Fax: 517-724-5397. 8:30AM-4:30PM. Access by: mail, phone, fax, in person.

Probate—Probate Court, PO Box 328, Harrisville, MI 48740. 517-724-6880, Fax: 517-724-6397. 8:30AM-4:30PM. Access by: mail, in person.

Alger

Real Estate Recording—Alger County Register of Deeds, 101 Court Street, Munising, MI 49862. 906-387-4535, Fax: 906-387-2156. 8AM-4PM.

Felony, Civil Actions Over $25,000—11th Circuit Court, 101 Court St, PO Box 538, Munising, MI 49862. 906-387-2076, Fax: 906-387-2156. 8AM-4PM. Access by: mail, phone, fax, in person. www.courts.net/mi/alger.htm

Misdemeanor, Civil Actions Under $25,000, Eviction, Small Claims—93rd District Court, PO Box 186, Munising, MI 49862. 906-387-3879, Fax: 906-387-3289. 8AM-4PM. Access by: mail, phone, fax, in person.

Probate—Alger County Probate Court, 101 Court St, Munising, MI 49862. 906-387-2080, Fax: 906-387-2200. 8AM-Noon, 1-4PM.

Allegan

Real Estate Recording—Allegan County Register of Deeds, 113 Chestnut Street, County Court House, Allegan, MI 49010., Fax: 616-673-0289. 8AM-5PM.

Felony, Civil Actions Over $25,000—48th Circuit Court, 113 Chestnut St, Allegan, MI 49010. 616-673-0300, Fax: 616-673-0298. 8AM-5PM. Access by: mail, in person.

Misdemeanor, Civil Actions Under $25,000, Eviction, Small Claims—57th District Court, 113 Chestnut St, Allegan, MI 49010. 616-673-0400. 8AM-5PM. Access by: mail, in person.

Probate—Probate Court, 2243 33rd StSt, Allegan, MI 49010. 616-673-0250, Fax: 616-673-2200. 8AM-5PM. Access by: mail, in person.

Alpena

Real Estate Recording—Alpena County Register of Deeds, 720 West Chisholm Street, Courthouse, Alpena, MI 49707. 517-356-1751, Fax: 517-356-6559. 8:30AM-4:30PM.

Felony, Civil Actions Over $25,000—26th Circuit Court, 720 West Chisholm, Alpena, MI 49707. 517-356-0115, Fax: 517-356-6559. 8:30AM-4:30PM. Access by: mail, in person.

Misdemeanor, Civil Actions Under $25,000, Eviction, Small Claims—88th District Court, 719 West Chisholm, Alpena, MI 49707. 517-354-3330, Fax: 517-358-9127. 8:30AM-4:30PM. Access by: mail, fax, in person.

Probate—Probate Court, 719 West Chisholm, Alpena, MI 49707. 517-354-8785, Fax: 517-356-3665. 8:30AM-4:30PM. Access by: mail, in person.

Antrim

Real Estate Recording—Antrim County Register of Deeds, 205 East Cayuga Street, Bellaire, MI 49615. 231-592-0799, Fax: 231-533-8317. 8:30AM-5PM.

Felony, Civil Actions Over $25,000—13th Circuit Court, PO Box 520, Bellaire, MI 49615. 231-627-8808, Fax: 231-533-6935. 8:30AM-5PM. Access by: mail, fax, in person.

Misdemeanor, Civil Actions Under $25,000, Eviction, Small Claims—87th District Court, PO Box 597, Bellaire, MI 49615. 231-592-0169, Fax: 231-533-6322. 8AM-4:30PM. Access by: mail, fax, in person.

Probate—Probate Court, PO Box 130, Bellaire, MI 49615. 231-592-0783, Fax: 231-533-6600. 8:30AM-4:30PM. Access by: mail, in person.

Arenac

Real Estate Recording—Arenac County Register of Deeds, 120 Grove Street, Standish, MI 48658. 8:30AM-5PM.

Felony, Civil Actions Over $25,000—34th Circuit Court, 120 N Grove St, PO Box 747, Standish, MI 48658. 517-846-9186, Fax: 517-846-6757. 8:30AM-5PM. Access by: mail, in person.

Misdemeanor, Civil Actions Under $25,000, Eviction, Small Claims—81st District Court, PO Box 129, Standish, MI 48658. 517-846-9538, Fax: 517-846-2008. 8:30AM-5PM. Access by: mail, phone, fax, in person.

Probate—Probate Court, 120 N Grove, PO Box 666, Standish, MI 48658. 517-846-6941, Fax: 517-846-6757. 9AM-5PM.

Baraga

Real Estate Recording—Baraga County Register of Deeds, Courthouse, 16 N. 3rd St. L'Anse, MI 49946. 906-524-7773, Fax: 906-524-6186. 8:30AM-Noon, 1-4:30PM.

Felony, Civil Actions Over $25,000—12th Circuit Court, 16 North 3rd St, L'Anse, MI 49946. 906-524-6183, Fax: 906-524-6186. 8:30AM-4:30PM. Access by: mail, phone, fax, in person.

Misdemeanor, Civil Actions Under $25,000, Eviction, Small Claims—97th District Court, 16 North 3rd St, L'Anse, MI 49946. 906-524-6109, Fax: 906-524-6186. 8:30AM-Noon,1-4:30PM. Access by: mail, in person.

Probate—Probate Court, County Courthouse, 16 N 3rd St, L'Anse, MI 49946. 906-524-6390, Fax: 906-524-6186. 8:30AM-Noon, 1-4:30PM. Access by: mail, in person.

Barry

Real Estate Recording—Barry County Register of Deeds, 220 West State Street, Courthouse, Hastings, MI 49058. 616-948-4818, Fax: 616-948-4820. 8AM-5PM.

Felony, Civil Actions Over $25,000—5th Circuit Court, 220 West State St, Hastings, MI 49058. 616-948-4810, Fax: 616-945-0209. 8AM-5PM. Access by: mail, fax, in person.

Misdemeanor, Civil Actions Under $25,000, Eviction, Small Claims—56B District Court, 220 West Court St, Suite 202, Hastings, MI 49058. 616-948-4835, Fax: 616-948-3314. 8AM-5PM. Access by: mail, phone, fax, in person.

Probate—Probate Court, 220 West Court St, Suite 302, Hastings, MI 49058. 616-948-4842, Fax: 616-948-3322. 8AM-5PM. Access by: mail, in person.

Bay

Real Estate Recording—Bay County Register of Deeds, 515 Center Avenue, Bay City, MI 48708. 517-895-4285, Fax: 517-895-4296. 8AM-5PM (June-September 7:30AM-4PM).

Felony, Civil Actions Over $25,000—18th Circuit Court, 1200 Washington Ave, Bay City, MI 48708. 517-895-2066, Fax: 517-895-4099. 8AM-5PM Winter; 7:30AM-4PM Summer. Access by: mail, phone, fax, in person.

Misdemeanor, Civil Actions Under $25,000, Eviction, Small Claims—74th District Court, 1230 Washington Ave, Bay City, MI 48708. 517-895-4232, Fax: 517-895-4233. 8AM-5PM. Access by: in person.

Probate—Probate Court, 1230 Washington, Ste 715, Bay City, MI 48708. 517-895-4205, Fax: 517-895-4194. 8AM-5PM; Summer hours 7:30AM-4PM. Access by: mail, in person.

Benzie

Real Estate Recording—Benzie County Register of Deeds, 448 Court Place, Beulah, MI 49617. 248-477-5630, Fax: 231-882-0167. 8AM-Noon, 1-5PM.

Felony, Civil Actions Over $25,000—19th Circuit Court, PO Box 398, Beulah, MI 49617. 248-528-0400, Fax: 231-882-5941. 8AM-5PM. Access by: mail, phone, fax, in person.

Misdemeanor, Civil Actions Under $25,000, Eviction, Small Claims—85th District Court, PO Box 398, Beulah, MI 49617. 800-759-5175, Fax: 231-882-0022. 9AM-5PM. Access by: mail, in person.

Probate—Probate Court, PO Box 398, Beulah, MI 49617. 248-544-3300, Fax: 231-882-5987. 8:30AM-Noon, 1-5PM. Access by: mail, in person.

Berrien

Real Estate Recording—Berrien County Register of Deeds, Berrien County Administration Center, 701 Main St. St. Joseph, MI 49085. 616-983-7111, Fax: 616-982-8659. 8:30AM-5PM.

Felony, Civil Actions Over $25,000—2nd Circuit Court, 811 Port St, St Joseph, MI 49085. 616-983-7111, Fax: 616-982-8647. 8:30AM-4PM. Access by: mail, in person.

Misdemeanor, Civil Actions Under $25,000, Eviction, Small Claims—5th District Court, Attn: Records, 811 Port St, St Joseph, MI 49085. 616-983-7111, Fax: 616-982-8643. 8:30AM-4PM. Access by: mail, in person.

Probate—Probate Court, 811 Port St. St Joseph, MI 49085. 616-983-7111, Fax: 616-982-8644. 8:30AM-5PM.

Branch

Real Estate Recording—Branch County Register of Deeds, 31 Division Street, Coldwater, MI 49036. 517-279-8411. 9AM-Noon, 1-5PM.

Felony, Civil Actions Over $25,000—15th Circuit Court, 31 Division St, Coldwater, MI 49036. 517-279-4306, Fax: 517-278-5627. 9AM-5PM. Access by: mail, in person.

Misdemeanor, Civil Actions Under $25,000, Eviction, Small Claims—3A District Court, 31 Division St. Coldwater, MI 49036. 517-279-4308, Fax: 517-278-4333. 8AM-5PM. Access by: mail, phone, in person. www.24thdiscourt.org

Probate—Probate Court, 31 Division St. Coldwater, MI 49036. 517-279-4318, Fax: 517-278-4130. 9AM-Noon, 1-5PM. Access by: mail, in person.

Calhoun

Real Estate Recording—Calhoun County Register of Deeds, 315 West Green Street, Marshall, MI 49068. 616-969-6910, Fax: 616-781-0721. 8AM-5PM.

Felony, Civil Actions Over $25,000—37th Circuit Court, 161 East Michigan, Battle Creek, MI 49014-4066. 616-969-6518. 8AM-5PM. Access by: mail, in person. http://courts.co.calhoun.mi.us

Misdemeanor, Civil Actions Under $25,000, Eviction, Small Claims—10th District Court, 161 E Michigan Ave, Battle Creek, MI 49014. 616-969-6666, Fax: 616-969-6663. 8:30AM-4PM. Access by: mail, fax, in person.

10th District Court-Marshall Branch, 315 West Arlen, Marshall, MI 49068. 616-969-6678, Fax: 616-969-6663. 8:30AM-4PM. Access by: mail, in person.

Probate—Probate Court, Justice Center, 161 E Michigan Ave, Battle Creek, MI 49014. 616-969-6794, Fax: 616-969-6797. 8AM-5PM.

Cass

Real Estate Recording—Cass County Register of Deeds, 120 North Broadway, Suite 123, Cassopolis, MI 49031. 616-445-4468, Fax: 616-445-8978. 8AM-5PM.

Felony, Civil Actions Over $25,000—43rd Circuit Court, 120 North Broadway, File Room, Cassopolis, MI 49031-1398. 616-445-4416, Fax: 616-445-8978. 9AM-12; 1PM-4PM. Access by: mail, fax, in person.

Misdemeanor, Civil Actions Under $25,000, Eviction, Small Claims—4th District Court, 110 North Broadway, Cassopolis, MI 49031. 616-445-4424, Fax: 616-445-4486. 8AM-5PM. Access by: mail, phone, in person.

Probate—Probate Court, 110 North Broadway, Rm 202, Cassopolis, MI 49031. 616-445-4454, Fax: 616-445-4453. 8AM-Noon, 1-5PM. Access by: mail, in person.

Charlevoix

Real Estate Recording—Charlevoix County Register of Deeds, 301 State Street, County Building, Charlevoix, MI 49720. 231-627-8821, Fax: 231-547-7246. 9AM-5PM.

Felony, Civil Actions Over $25,000—33rd Circuit Court, 203 Antrim St, Charlevoix, MI 49720. 231-627-8809, Fax: 231-547-7217. 9AM-5PM. Access by: mail, in person.

Misdemeanor, Civil Actions Under $25,000, Eviction, Small Claims—90th District Court, 301 State St, Court Bldg, Charlevoix, MI 49720. 231-689-7257, Fax: 231-547-7253. 9AM-5PM. Access by: mail, in person.

Probate—Probate Court, 301 State St, County Bldg, Charlevoix, MI 49720. 231-689-7230, Fax: 231-547-7256. 9AM-5PM.

Cheboygan

Real Estate Recording—Cheboygan County Register of Deeds, 870 South Main Street, Cheboygan, MI 49721. 231-724-6250. 9AM-5PM.

Felony, Civil Actions Over $25,000—53rd District Court, PO Box 70, Cheboygan, MI 49721. 231-723-5010. 9AM-5PM. Access by: mail, phone, in person.

Misdemeanor, Civil Actions Under $25,000, Eviction, Small Claims—89th District Court, PO Box 70, Cheboygan, MI 49721. 231-724-6241, Fax: 231-627-8444. 8:30AM-4PM. Access by: mail, phone, fax, in person.

Probate—Probate Court, PO Box 70, Cheboygan, MI 49721. 231-348-1707, Fax: 231-231-8868. 9AM-5PM.

Chippewa

Real Estate Recording—Chippewa County Register of Deeds, Courthouse, 319 Court St. Sault Ste. Marie, MI 49783. 906-635-6308, Fax: 906-635-6855. 8AM-5PM.

Felony, Civil Actions Over $25,000—50th Circuit Court, 319 Court St, Sault Ste Marie, MI 49783. 906-635-6300, Fax: 906-635-6851. 8:30AM-5PM. Access by: mail, in person.

Misdemeanor, Civil Actions Under $25,000, Eviction, Small Claims—91st District Court, 325 Court St, Sault Ste Marie, MI 49783. 906-635-6320, Fax: 906-635-7605. 8AM-4:30PM. Access by: mail, in person.

Probate—Probate Court, 319 Court St. Sault Ste Marie, MI 49783. 906-635-6314, Fax: 906-635-6852. 9AM-5PM. Access by: mail, in person.

Clare

Real Estate Recording—Clare County Register of Deeds, 225 West Main, Harrison, MI 48625. 517-539-7801, Fax: 517-539-6616. 8AM-4:30PM.

Felony, Civil Actions Over $25,000—55th Circuit Court, 225 West Main St, PO Box 438, Harrison, MI 48625. 517-539-7131, Fax: 517-539-6616. 8AM-4:30PM. Access by: mail, in person.

Misdemeanor, Civil Actions Under $25,000, Eviction, Small Claims—80th District Court, 225 W. Main St, Harrison, MI 48625. 517-539-7173, Fax: 517-539-4036. 8AM-4:30PM. Access by: mail, in person.

Probate—Probate Court, 225 W. Main St. PO Box 96, Harrison, MI 48625. 517-539-7109. 8AM-4:30PM. Access by: mail, phone, in person.

Clinton

Real Estate Recording—Clinton County Register of Deeds, 1017 S US 27, Suite B-36, St. Johns, MI 48879. 517-224-5280, Fax: 517-224-5254. 8AM-5PM.

Felony, Civil Actions Over $25,000—29th Circuit Court, PO Box 69, St Johns, MI 48879-0069. 517-224-5140, Fax: 517-224-

5254. 8AM-5PM. Access by: mail, in person. www.clinton-county.org

Misdemeanor, Civil Actions Under $25,000, Eviction, Small Claims—65th District Court, 409 South Whittemore St. St Johns, MI 48879. 517-224-5150, Fax: 517-224-5154. 8AM-5PM. Access by: mail, in person.

Probate—Probate Court, 100 E. State St. St Johns, MI 48879. 517-224-5190, Fax: 517-224-5254. 8AM-Noon, 1-5PM. Access by: mail, in person. www.clinton-county.org

Crawford

Real Estate Recording—Crawford County Register of Deeds, 200 West Michigan, Grayling, MI 49738. 517-348-2841, Fax: 517-344-3223. 8:30AM-4:30PM.

Felony, Civil Actions Over $25,000—46th Circuit Court, 200 West Michigan Ave, Grayling, MI 49738. 517-348-2841, Fax: 517-344-3443. 8:30AM-4:30PM. Access by: mail, in person. www.Circuit46.org

Misdemeanor, Civil Actions Under $25,000, Eviction, Small Claims—83rd District Court, 200 West Michigan Ave. Grayling, MI 49738. 517-348-2841, Fax: 517-348-3290. 8AM-4:30PM. Access by: mail, in person. www.Circuit.org

Probate—Probate Court, 200 NW Michigan Ave. Grayling, MI 49738. 517-348-2841, Fax: 517-348-7582. 8:30AM-4:30PM. Access by: mail, in person. www.Circuit46.org

Delta

Real Estate Recording—Delta County Register of Deeds, 310 Ludington Street, Suite 104, Escanaba, MI 49829. 906-789-5117, Fax: 906-789-5196. 8AM-4PM.

Felony, Civil Actions Over $25,000—47th Circuit Court, 310 Ludington St, Escanaba, MI 49829. 906-789-5105, Fax: 906-789-5196. 8AM-4PM. Access by: mail, in person.

Misdemeanor, Civil Actions Under $25,000, Eviction, Small Claims—94th District Court, 310 Ludington St. Escanaba, MI 49829. 906-789-5106, Fax: 906-789-5196. 8AM-4PM. Access by: mail, in person.

Probate—Probate Court, 310 Ludington St. Escanaba, MI 49829. 906-789-5112, Fax: 906-789-5140. 8AM-Noon, 1-4PM. Access by: mail, in person.

Dickinson

Real Estate Recording—Dickinson County Register of Deeds, 700 Stephenson Avenue, Courthouse, Iron Mountain, MI 49801. 906-774-8130, Fax: 906-774-4660. 8AM-4:30PM.

Felony, Civil Actions Over $25,000—41st Circuit Court, PO Box 609, Iron Mountain, MI 49801. 906-774-0988, Fax: 906-774-4660. 8AM-4:30PM. Access by: mail, in person.

Misdemeanor, Civil Actions Under $25,000, Eviction, Small Claims—95 B District Court, County Courthouse, Iron Mountain, MI 49801. 906-774-0506, Fax: 906-774-3686. 8AM-4:30PM. Access by: mail, in person. Special note: May require a signed release for certain records.

Probate—Probate Court, PO Box 609, Iron Mountain, MI 49801. 906-774-1555, Fax: 906-774-1561. 8AM-4:30PM. Access by: mail, in person.

Eaton

Real Estate Recording—Eaton County Register of Deeds, 1045 Independence Blvd. Room 104, Charlotte, MI 48813. 517-543-7500, Fax: 517-543-7377. 8AM-5PM.

Felony, Civil Actions Over $25,000—56th Circuit Court, 1045 Independence Blvd, Charlotte, MI 48813. 517-543-7500, Fax: 517-543-4475. 8AM-5PM. Access by: mail, phone, fax, in person. www.co.eaton.mi.us/COURTS/COURTS.HTM

Civil Actions Under $25,000, Eviction, Small Claims—56th District Court-Civil Division, 1045 Independence Blvd, Charlotte, MI 48813. 517-543-7500. 8AM-5PM. Access by: mail, in person. www.co.eaton.mi.us/COURTS/COURTS.HTM

Misdemeanor—56th District Court-Criminal, 1045 Independence Blvd, Charlotte, MI 48813. 517-543-7500, Fax: 517-543-7377. 8AM-5PM. Access by: mail, in person. www.co.eaton.mi.us/COURTS/COURTS.HTM

Emmet

Real Estate Recording—Emmet County Register of Deeds, 200 Division, Petoskey, MI 49770. 231-547-7214, Fax: 231-348-0633. 8:30AM-5PM.

Felony, Civil Actions Over $25,000—57th Circuit Court, 200 Division St, Petoskey, MI 49770. 231-547-7227, Fax: 231-348-0633. 8AM-5PM. Access by: mail, in person.

Misdemeanor, Civil Actions Under $25,000, Eviction, Small Claims—90th District Court, 200 Division St. Petoskey, MI 49770. 231-592-0135, Fax: 231-348-0633. 8:30AM-5PM. Access by: mail, fax, in person.

Probate—Probate Court, 200 Division St. Petoskey, MI 49770. 231-547-7202, Fax: 231-348-0672. 8AM-5PM. Access by: mail, in person.

Genesee

Real Estate Recording—Genesee County Register of Deeds, 1101 Beach Street, Administration Building, Flint, MI 48502., Fax: 810-768-7965. 8AM-5PM.

Felony, Civil Actions Over $25,000—7th Circuit Court, 900 South Saginaw, Flint, MI 48502. 810-257-3220. 8AM-5PM. Access by: mail, in person.

Misdemeanor, Civil Actions Under $25,000, Eviction, Small Claims—67th District Court, 630 South Saginaw, Flint, MI 48502. 810-257-3170. 8AM-4PM. Access by: mail, in person.

Probate—Probate Court, 919 Beach St, Flint, MI 48502. 810-257-3528, Fax: 810-257-3299. 8AM-4PM.

Gladwin

Real Estate Recording—Gladwin County Register of Deeds, 401 West Cedar Ave. Ste 7, Gladwin, MI 48624. 517-426-7351. 8:30AM-4:30PM.

Felony, Civil Actions Over $25,000—55th Circuit Court, 401 West Cedar, Gladwin, MI 48624. 517-426-7351, Fax: 417-426-6917. 8:30AM-4:30PM. Access by: mail, fax, in person.

Misdemeanor, Civil Actions Under $25,000, Eviction, Small Claims—80th District Court, 401 West Cedar, Gladwin, MI 48624. 517-426-9207, Fax: 517-426-4281. 8:30AM-4:30PM. Access by: mail, in person.

Probate—Probate Court, 401 West Cedar, Gladwin, MI 48624. 517-426-7451, Fax: 517-426-4281. 8:30AM-4:30PM. Access by: mail, in person.

Gogebic

Real Estate Recording—Gogebic County Register of Deeds, Courthouse, 200 N. Moore St. Bessemer, MI 49911. 906-667-4517, Fax: 906-663-4660. 8:30AM-4:30PM.

Felony, Civil Actions Over $25,000—32nd Circuit Court, 200 North Moore St, Bessemer, MI 49911. 906-663-4518, Fax: 906-663-4660. 8:30AM-4:30PM. Access by: mail, in person.

Misdemeanor, Civil Actions Under $25,000, Eviction, Small Claims—98th District Court, 200 North Moore St, Bessemer, MI 49911. 906-663-4611, Fax: 906-663-4660. 8:30AM-4PM. Access by: mail, in person.

Probate—Probate Court, 200 North Moore St. Bessemer, MI 49911. 906-667-0421, Fax: 906-663-4660. 8:30AM-Noon, 1-4:30PM. Access by: mail, in person.

Grand Traverse

Real Estate Recording—Grand Traverse County Register of Deeds, 400 Boardman Avenue, Traverse City, MI 49684. 248-674-4655, Fax: 231-922-4658. 8AM-5PM (Vault closes at 4:30PM).

Felony, Civil Actions Over $25,000—13th Circuit Court, 328 Washington St, Traverse City, MI 49684. 248-647-1141. 8AM-5PM. Access by: mail, phone, in person.

Misdemeanor, Civil Actions Under $25,000, Eviction, Small Claims—86th District Court, 328 Washington St. Traverse City, MI 49684. 248-546-7780, Fax: 231-922-4454. 8AM-5PM. Access by: mail, phone, in person.

Probate—Probate Court, 400 Boardmen, Traverse City, MI 49684. 248-547-3034, Fax: 231-922-6893. 8AM-5PM. Access by: mail, in person.

Gratiot

Real Estate Recording—Gratiot County Register of Deeds, 214 East Center Street, Ithaca, MI 48847. 517-875-5220. 8:30AM-5PM.

Felony, Civil Actions Over $25,000—29th Circuit Court, 214 East Center St, Ithaca, MI 48847. 517-875-5215. 8:30AM-5PM. Access by: mail, in person.

Misdemeanor, Civil Actions Under $25,000, Eviction, Small Claims—65-B District Court, 245 East Newark St, Ithaca, MI 48847. 517-875-5240, Fax: 517-875-5290. 8AM-4:30PM. Access by: in person.

Probate—Probate Court, PO Box 217, Ithaca, MI 48847. 517-875-5231, Fax: 517-875-3322. 8:30AM-5PM.

Hillsdale

Real Estate Recording—Hillsdale County Register of Deeds, Courthouse, 29 N. Howell, Room 3, Hillsdale, MI 49242. 517-437-4700, Fax: 517-437-3139. 8:30AM-5PM.

Felony, Civil Actions Over $25,000—1st Circuit Court, 29 North Howell, Hillsdale, MI 49242. 517-437-3391. 8:30AM-5PM. Access by: mail, in person.

Misdemeanor, Civil Actions Under $25,000, Eviction, Small Claims—2nd District Court, 49 North Howell, Hillsdale, MI 49242. 517-437-7329, Fax: 517-437-2908. 8AM-4:30PM; 8AM-5PM Traffic. Access by: mail, phone, in person.

Probate—Probate Court, 29 North Howell, Hillsdale, MI 49242. 517-437-4643. 8:30AM-Noon, 1-5PM.

Houghton

Real Estate Recording—Houghton County Register of Deeds, 401 East Houghton Avenue, Houghton, MI 49931. 906-482-0560, Fax: 906-483-0364. 8AM-4:30PM.

Felony, Civil Actions Over $25,000—12th Circuit Court, 401 East Houghton Ave, Houghton, MI 49931. 906-482-5420. 8AM-4:30PM. Access by: mail, in person.

Misdemeanor, Civil Actions Under $25,000, Eviction, Small Claims—97th District Court, 401 East Houghton Ave. Houghton, MI 49931. 906-482-4980, Fax: 906-482-7238. 8AM-4:30PM. Access by: mail, in person.

Probate—Probate Court, 401 East Houghton Ave. Houghton, MI 49931. 906-482-3120, Fax: 906-487-5964. 8AM-4:30PM. Access by: mail, in person.

Huron

Real Estate Recording—Huron County Register of Deeds, 250 East Huron Avenue, Bad Axe, MI 48413. 517-269-9238. 8:30AM-5PM.

Felony, Civil Actions Over $25,000—52nd Circuit Court, 250 East Huron Ave, Bad Axe, MI 48413. 517-269-9942, Fax: 517-269-6152. 8:30AM-5PM. Access by: mail, phone, in person.

Misdemeanor, Civil Actions Under $25,000, Eviction, Small Claims—73rd District Court, 250 East Huron Ave. Bad Axe, MI 48413. 517-269-9987, Fax: 517-269-6167. 8:30AM-5PM. Access by: mail, in person.

Probate—Probate Court, 250 East Huron Ave. Bad Axe, MI 48413. 517-269-9944, Fax: 517-269-0004. 8:30AM-Noon, 1-5PM. Access by: mail, in person.

Ingham

Real Estate Recording—Ingham County Register of Deeds, 341 S. Maple, Jefferson Square, Room 201, Mason, MI 48854. 517-676-7220, Fax: 517-676-7287. 8AM-5PM.

Felony, Civil Actions Over $25,000—30th Circuit Court, 333 South Capital Ave, Ste C, Lansing, MI 48933. 517-483-6500, Fax: 517-483-6501. 9AM-Noon, 1-5PM M,T,Th,F; 8AM-Noon, 1-5PM W. Access by: mail, phone, in person.

Misdemeanor, Civil Actions Under $25,000, Eviction, Small Claims—54 A District Court, 124 West Michigan Ave, Lansing, MI 48933. 517-483-4433, Fax: 517-483-4108. 8AM-4:35PM. Access by: in person. Special note: This court covers the city of Lansing.

54 B District Court, 101 Linden, East Lansing, MI 48823. 517-351-7000, Fax: 517-351-3371. 8AM-4:30PM. Access by: mail, in person. Special note: This court covers the city of East Lansing.

55th District Court, 700 Buhl, Mason, MI 48854. 517-676-8400. 8:30AM-4:30PM. Access by: mail, in person. Special note: This court covers all of Ingham County except for Lansing and East Lansing.

Probate—Ingham County Probate Court, PO Box 176, Mason, MI 48854. 517-676-7276, Fax: 517-676-7344. 8AM-Noon, 1-5PM.

Lansing Probate Court, 303 West Kalamazoo, Lansing, MI 48933. 517-483-6300, Fax: 517-483-6150. 8AM-Noon, 1-5PM. Access by: mail, phone, in person.

Ionia

Real Estate Recording—Ionia County Register of Deeds, 100 Main Street, Courthouse, Ionia, MI 48846. 616-527-5329, Fax: 616-527-5380. 8:30AM-Noon, 1-5PM.

Felony, Civil Actions Over $25,000—8th Circuit Court, 100 Main, Ionia, MI 48846. 616-527-5322, Fax: 616-527-5323. 8:30AM-5PM. Access by: mail, phone, fax, in person.

Misdemeanor, Civil Actions Under $25,000, Eviction, Small Claims—64 A District Court, 101 West Main, Ionia, MI 48846. 616-527-5346, Fax: 616-527-5343. 7:45AM-5:30PM. Access by: mail, fax, in person.

Probate—Probate Court, 100 Main, Ionia, MI 48846. 616-527-5326, Fax: 616-527-5321. 8:30AM-5PM. Access by: mail, in person.

Iosco

Real Estate Recording—Iosco County Register of Deeds, 422 West Lake Street, Tawas City, MI 48763. 517-362-4409, Fax: 517-362-1443. 9AM-5PM.

Felony, Civil Actions Over $25,000—23rd Circuit Court, PO Box 838, Tawas City, MI 48764. 517-362-3497, Fax: 517-362-1444. 9AM-5PM. Access by: mail, phone, in person.

Misdemeanor, Civil Actions Under $25,000, Eviction, Small Claims—81st District Court, PO Box 388, Tawas City, MI 48764. 517-362-4441, Fax: 517-362-3494. 8AM-5PM. Access by: mail, in person.

Probate—Probate Court, PO Box 421, Tawas City, MI 48764. 517-362-3991, Fax: 517-362-1459. 8AM-5PM. Access by: mail, in person.

Iron

Real Estate Recording—Iron County Register of Deeds, 2 South Sixth Street, Courthouse Annex, Suite 11, Crystal Falls, MI 49920. 906-875-3362, Fax: 906-875-4626. 8AM-Noon, 12:30-4PM.

Felony, Civil Actions Over $25,000—41st Circuit Court, 2 South 6th St, Crystal Falls, MI 49920. 906-875-3221, Fax: 906-875-6675. 8AM-4PM. Access by: mail, fax, in person.

Misdemeanor, Civil Actions Under $25,000, Eviction, Small Claims—95 B District Court, 2 South 6th St. Crystal Falls, MI 49920. 906-875-6658, Fax: 906-875-6775. 8AM-4PM. Access by: mail, in person.

Probate—Probate Court, 2 South 6th St, Suite 10, Crystal Falls, MI 49920. 906-875-3121, Fax: 906-875-6775. 8AM-Noon, 12:30-4PM. Access by: mail, in person.

Isabella

Real Estate Recording—Isabella County Register of Deeds, 200 North Main Street, Mt. Pleasant, MI 48858., Fax: 517-773-7431. 8AM-4:30PM.

Felony, Civil Actions Over $25,000—21st Circuit Court, 200 North Main St, Mount Pleasant, MI 48858. 517-772-0911. 8AM-4:30PM. Access by: mail, in person.

Misdemeanor, Civil Actions Under $25,000, Eviction, Small Claims—76th District Court, 200 North Main St. Mount Pleasant, MI 48858. 517-772-0911, Fax: 517-773-2419. 8AM-4:30PM. Access by: mail, in person.

Probate—Probate Court, 200 N Main St, Mount Pleasant, MI 48858. 517-772-0911, Fax: 517-773-2419. 8AM-4:30PM. Access by: mail, in person.

Jackson

Real Estate Recording—Jackson County Register of Deeds, 120 West Michigan Avenue, 11th Floor, Jackson, MI 49201. 517-788-4418, Fax: 517-788-4686. 8AM-5PM.

Felony, Civil Actions Over $25,000—4th Circuit Court, 312 South Jackson St, Jackson, MI 49201. 517-788-4268. 8AM-5PM. Access by: mail, phone, in person.

Misdemeanor, Civil Actions Under $25,000, Eviction, Small Claims—12th District Court, 312 South Jackson St. Jackson, MI 49201. 517-788-4260, Fax: 517-788-4262. 7AM-6PM. Access by: mail, fax, in person. www.d12.com

Probate—Probate Court, 312 S Jackson St, 1st Fl, Jackson, MI 49201. 517-788-4290. 8AM-5PM.

Kalamazoo

Real Estate Recording—Kalamazoo County Register of Deeds, 201 West Kalamazoo Avenue, Kalamazoo, MI 49007. 616-383-8124. 8AM-4:30PM.

Felony, Civil Actions Over $25,000—9th Circuit Court, 227 West Michigan St, Kalamazoo, MI 49007. 616-384-8250. 9AM-4PM. Access by: mail, in person.

Misdemeanor, Civil Actions Under $25,000, Eviction, Small Claims—8th District Court, 227 West Michigan St. Kalamazoo, MI 49007. 616-384-8171, Fax: 616-384-8047. 8:30AM-4PM. Access by: mail, fax, in person. Special note: This court covers the areas in Kalamazoo County not handled by the 9th District Courts.

8th District Court Division 1, 416 S. Rose, Kalamazoo, MI 49007. 616-384-8020, Fax: 616-383-8899. 8AM-4:15PM. Access by: mail, fax, in person. Special note: This court covers city of Kalamazoo.

9th District Court Division 2, 7810 Shaver Rd. Portage, MI 49002. 616-329-4590, Fax: 616-329-4519. 8AM-4:30PM. Access by: mail, in person. Special note: This court covers the city of Portage.

Probate—Probate Court, 227 West Michigan Ave. Kalamazoo, MI 49007. 616-383-8666, Fax: 616-383-8685. 9AM-Noon, 1-5PM M; 8AM-Noon, 1-5PM T-F. Access by: mail, in person.

Kalkaska

Real Estate Recording—Kalkaska County Register of Deeds, 605 North Birch Street, Kalkaska, MI 49646. 231-533-6720, Fax: 231-258-3318. 9AM-5PM.

Felony, Civil Actions Over $25,000—46th Circuit Court, PO Box 10, Kalkaska, MI 49646. 231-533-6681. 9AM-5PM. Access by: mail, in person. www.Circuit46.org

Misdemeanor, Civil Actions Under $25,000, Eviction, Small Claims—87th District Court, PO Box 780, Kalkaska, MI 49646. 231-547-7200, Fax: 231-258-2424. 8AM-4:30PM. Access by: mail, phone, in person. www.Circuit46.org

Probate—Circuit Trial Court-Probate Division, 605 North Birch, PO Box 780, Kalkaska, MI 49646. 231-533-8607, Fax: 231-258-3329. 9AM-Noon, 1-5PM. Access by: mail. www.Circuit46.org

Kent

Real Estate Recording—Kent County Register of Deeds, 300 Monroe Avenue NW, Grand Rapids, MI 49503. 616-336-0762. 8AM-5PM.

Felony, Civil Actions Over $25,000—17th Circuit Court, 333 Monroe Ave NW, Grand Rapids, MI 49503. 616-336-3679, Fax: 616-336-3349. 8AM-5PM. Access by: mail, in person. www.co.kent.mi.us/courts.htm

Misdemeanor, Civil Actions Under $25,000, Eviction, Small Claims—59th District Court-Grandville & Walker, 3181 Wilson Ave SW, Grandville, MI 49418. 616-538-9660, Fax: 616-538-5144. 8:30AM-Noon,1-5PM. Access by: mail, in person.

61st District Court-Grand Rapids, 333 Monroe Ave NW, Grand Rapids, MI 49503., Fax: 616-456-3311. 7:45AM-4:45PM. Access by: mail, in person.

62 A District Court-Wyoming, 2650 De Hoop Ave SW, Wyoming, MI 49509. 616-530-7385, Fax: 616-249-3419. 8AM-5PM. Access by: mail, in person.

62 B District Court-Kentwood, PO Box 8848, Kentwood, MI 49518. 616-698-9310, Fax: 616-698-8199. 8AM-5PM. Access by: mail, fax, in person.

63rd District Court-1st Division, 105 Maple St, Rockford, MI 49341. 616-866-1576, Fax: 616-866-3080. 8AM-5PM. Access by: mail, in person.

Probate—Probate Court, 320 Ottawa NW, Grand Rapids, MI 49503. 616-336-3630, Fax: 616-336-3574. 8:30AM-5PM.

Keweenaw

Real Estate Recording—Keweenaw County Register of Deeds, 4th Street, Courthouse, Eagle River, MI 49924. 906-337-1625, Fax: 906-337-2795. 9AM-4PM.

Felony, Civil Actions Over $25,000—12th Circuit Court, HCI Box 607, Eagle River, MI 49924. 906-337-2229, Fax: 906-337-2795. 9AM-4PM. Access by: mail, in person.

Misdemeanor, Civil Actions Under $25,000, Eviction, Small Claims—97th District Court, HCI Box 607, Eagle River, MI 49924. 906-337-2229, Fax: 906-337-2795. 9AM-4PM. Access by: mail, fax, in person.

Probate—Probate Court, HC1 Box 607, Eagle River, MI 49924. 906-337-1927, Fax: 906-337-2795. 9AM-4PM.

Lake

Real Estate Recording—Lake County Register of Deeds, 800 Tenth Street, Courthouse, Baldwin, MI 49304. 231-839-2169, Fax: 231-745-2241. 8:30AM-Noon, 1-5PM.

Felony, Civil Actions Over $25,000—51st Circuit Court, PO Drawer B, Baldwin, MI 49304. 231-832-6155. 8:30AM-5PM. Access by: mail, in person.

Misdemeanor, Civil Actions Under $25,000, Eviction, Small Claims—Lake County Trial Court, PO Box 1330, Baldwin, MI 49304. 231-832-6124. 8:30AM-5PM. Access by: mail, in person.

Probate—Lake County Trial Court, PO Box 1330, Baldwin, MI 49304. 231-832-6110, Fax: 231-745-2241. 8:30AM-5PM. Access by: mail, in person.

Lapeer

Real Estate Recording—Lapeer County Register of Deeds, 279 North Court Street, Lapeer, MI 48446. 810-667-0239, Fax: 810-667-0293. 8AM-5PM.

Felony, Civil Actions Over $25,000—40th Circuit Court, 255 Clay St, Lapeer, MI 48446. 810-667-0358. 8AM-5PM. Access by: mail, phone, in person.

Misdemeanor, Civil Actions Under $25,000, Eviction, Small Claims—71 A District Court, 255 Clay St. Lapeer, MI 48446. 810-667-0300. 8AM-5PM. Access by: mail, in person.

Probate—Probate Court, 255 Clay St. Lapeer, MI 48446. 810-667-0261, Fax: 810-667-0390. 8AM-5PM. Access by: mail, in person.

Leelanau

Real Estate Recording—Leelanau County Register of Deeds, 301 S. Cedar, Leland, MI 49654. 231-533-6441, Fax: 231-256-8149. 9AM-5PM.

Felony, Civil Actions Over $25,000—13th Circuit Court, PO Box 467, Leland, MI 49654. 231-348-1750, Fax: 231-256-7850. 9AM-5PM. Access by: mail, in person.

Misdemeanor, Civil Actions Under $25,000, Eviction, Small Claims—86th District Court, PO Box 486, Leland, MI 49654. 231-348-1715, Fax: 231-256-8275. 8AM-4PM. Access by: mail, phone, fax, in person.

Probate—Probate Court/Juvenile Division, PO Box 595, Leland, MI 49654. 231-348-1744, Fax: 231-256-9845. 9AM-5PM. Access by: mail, in person.

Lenawee

Real Estate Recording—Lenawee County Register of Deeds, 301 N. Main St. Adrian, MI 49221. 517-264-4554, Fax: 517-264-4543. 8AM-4:30PM.

Felony, Civil Actions Over $25,000—39th Circuit Court, 425 North Main St, Adrian, MI 49221. 517-264-4597. 8AM-4:30PM. Access by: mail, in person.

Misdemeanor, Civil Actions Under $25,000, Eviction, Small Claims—2A District Court, 425 North Main St. Adrian, MI 49221. 517-264-4673, Fax: 517-264-4780. 8AM-4:30PM. Access by: mail, fax, in person.

Probate—Probate Court, 425 North Main St. Adrian, MI 49221. 517-264-4614, Fax: 517-264-4616. 8AM-4:30PM. Access by: mail, in person.

Livingston

Real Estate Recording—Livingston County Register of Deeds, Courthouse, Howell, MI 48843. 517-546-7010, Fax: 517-546-5966. 8AM-5PM.

Felony, Civil Actions Over $25,000—44th Circuit Court, 210 South Highlander Way, Howell, MI 48843. 517-546-9816. 8AM-5PM. Access by: mail, in person. Special note: Juvenile Unit records are at 517-546-1500.

Misdemeanor, Civil Actions Under $25,000, Eviction, Small Claims—53 A District Court, 300 South Highlander Way, Howell, MI 48843. 517-548-1000, Fax: 517-548-9445. 8AM-4:45PM. Access by: mail, in person.

53 B District Court, 224 N First, Brighton, MI 48116., Fax: 810-229-1770. 8AM-4:45PM. Access by: mail, in person.

Probate—Probate Court, 200 East Grand River, Howell, MI 48843. 517-546-3750, Fax: 517-546-3731. 8AM-5PM.

Luce

Real Estate Recording—Luce County Register of Deeds, County Government Building, Newberry, MI 49868., Fax: 906-293-0050. 8AM-4PM.

Felony, Civil Actions Over $25,000—11th Circuit Court, East Court St, Newberry, MI 49868. 906-293-5521, Fax: 906-293-3581. 8AM-4PM. Access by: mail, in person.

Misdemeanor, Civil Actions Under $25,000, Eviction, Small Claims—92nd District Court, 407 W Harrie, Newberry, MI 49868. 906-293-5531, Fax: 906-293-3581. 8AM-4PM. Access by: mail, phone, fax, in person.

Probate—Probate Court, 407 W. Harrie, Newberry, MI 49868. 906-293-5601, Fax: 906-293-3581. 8AM-Noon, 1-4PM. Access by: mail, in person.

Mackinac

Real Estate Recording—Mackinac County Register of Deeds, 100 Marley Street, Saint Ignace, MI 49781. 906-643-7317, Fax: 906-643-7302. 8:30AM-4:30PM.

Felony, Civil Actions Over $25,000—50th Circuit Court, 100 Marley, St Ignace, MI 49781. 906-643-7300, Fax: 906-643-7302. 8:30AM-4:30PM. Access by: mail, in person.

Misdemeanor, Civil Actions Under $25,000, Eviction, Small Claims—92nd District Court, 100 Marley, St Ignace, MI 49781. 906-643-7321, Fax: 906-643-7302. 8:30AM-4:30PM. Access by: mail, in person.

Probate—Probate Court, 100 Marley, St Ignace, MI 49781. 906-643-7303, Fax: 906-643-7302. 8:30AM-Noon, 1-4:30PM. Access by: mail, in person.

Macomb

Real Estate Recording—Macomb County Register of Deeds, 10 North Main, Mt. Clemens, MI 48043., Fax: 810-469-5130. 8:30AM-5PM.

Felony, Civil Actions Over $25,000—16th Circuit Court, 40 N Main St, Mount Clemens, MI 48043. 810-469-5208. 8AM-4:30PM. Access by: mail, in person. www.macomb.lib.mi.us/sabaugh

Misdemeanor, Civil Actions Under $25,000, Eviction, Small Claims—37th District Court-Warren and Center Line, 8300 Common Rd. Warren, MI 48093. 810-574-4928, Fax: 810-547-4932. 8:30AM-4:30PM. Access by: mail, in person.

39th District Court-Roseville and Frasier, 29733 Gratiot Ave, Roseville, MI 48066. 810-773-2010, Fax: 810-774-3310. 8AM-4:30PM. Access by: mail, in person.

40th District Court-St. Clair Shores, 27701 Jefferson, St. Clair Shores, MI 48081. 810-445-5281, Fax: 810-445-4003. 8:30AM-5PM. Access by: mail, in person.

41 A District Court-Shelby, 51660 Van Dyke, Shelby Township, MI 48316. 810-739-7325, Fax: 810-726-4555. 8AM-4:30PM. Access by: mail, in person.

41 A District Court-Sterling Heights, 40111 Dodge Park, Sterling Heights, MI 48313. 810-446-2500. 8:30AM-4:30PM. Access by: mail, in person.

41 B District Court-Clinton, TWP, 40700 Romeo Plank Rd, Clinton Township, MI 48038-2951. 810-286-8010, Fax: 810-228-2555. 8:30AM-4:30PM. Access by: mail, in person.

42nd District Court Division 1, 14713 Thirty-three Mile Rd. Romeo, MI 48065. 810-752-9679, Fax: 810-469-5515. 8:30AM-5PM. Access by: mail, in person.

42nd District Court Division 2 (Lenox, Chesterfield), 36540 Green St, New Baltimore, MI 48047., Fax: 810-469-5516. 8:30AM-5PM. Access by: mail, in person.

Civil Actions Under $25,000, Eviction, Small Claims—41 B District Court-Mt Clemens, 1 Crocker Blvd, Mount Clemens, MI 48043. 810-469-6870, Fax: 810-469-5037. 8AM-4:30PM. Access by: mail, in person.

Probate—Macomb County Probate Court, 21850 Dumham, Mount Clemens, MI 48043-1075. 810-469-5290. 8:30AM-5PM. Access by: mail, in person.

Manistee

Real Estate Recording—Manistee County Register of Deeds, 415 Third Street, Courthouse, Manistee, MI 49660., Fax: 231-723-9069. 8:30AM-Noon, 1-5PM.

Felony, Civil Actions Over $25,000—19th Circuit Court, 415 3rd St, Manistee, MI 49660. 231-745-4622, Fax: 231-723-1492. 8:30AM-Noon, 1-5PM. Access by: mail, in person.

Misdemeanor, Civil Actions Under $25,000, Eviction, Small Claims—85th District Court, 415 3rd St, Manistee, MI 49660. 231-779-9450, Fax: 231-723-1491. 8:30AM-5PM. Access by: mail, fax, in person.

Probate—Probate Court, 415 3rd St, Manistee, MI 49660. 231-745-4614, Fax: 231-723-1492. 8:30AM-Noon, 1-5PM.

Marquette

Real Estate Recording—Marquette County Register of Deeds, 234 West Baraga Avenue, C-105, Marquette, MI 49855. 906-228-1565, Fax: 906-225-8203. 8AM-5PM.

Felony, Civil Actions Over $25,000—25th Circuit Court, 234 W Baraga, Marquette, MI 49855. 906-225-8330, Fax: 906-228-1572. 8AM-5PM. Access by: mail, in person.

Misdemeanor, Civil Actions Under $25,000, Eviction, Small Claims—96th District Court, County Courthouse, Marquette, MI 49855. 906-225-8235, Fax: 906-225-8255. 8:30AM-5PM. Access by: mail, fax, in person.

Probate—Probate Court, 234 W Baraga, Marquette, MI 49855. 906-225-8300, Fax: 906-225-8293. 8AM-5PM. Access by: mail, in person.

Mason

Real Estate Recording—Mason County Register of Deeds, 300 E. Ludington Avenue, Courthouse, Ludington, MI 49431. 231-922-4640, Fax: 231-843-1972. 9AM-5PM.

Felony, Civil Actions Over $25,000—51st Circuit Court, 304 E Ludington Ave, Ludington, MI 49431. 231-922-4580, Fax: 231-843-1972. 9AM-5PM. Access by: mail, phone, in person.

Misdemeanor, Civil Actions Under $25,000, Eviction, Small Claims—79th District Court, County Court, Ludington, MI 49431. 231-882-9671, Fax: 231-845-7779. 8AM-5PM. Access by: mail, fax, in person.

Probate—Probate Court, PO Box 186, Ludington, MI 49431. 231-882-9675, Fax: 231-843-1972. 9AM-Noon, 1-5PM.

Mecosta

Real Estate Recording—Mecosta County Register of Deeds, 400 Elm Street, Big Rapids, MI 49307. 231-689-7270. 8:30AM-5PM.

Felony, Civil Actions Over $25,000—49th Circuit Court, 400 Elm, Big Rapids, MI 49307. 231-723-3261, Fax: 231-592-0193. 8:30AM-5PM. Access by: mail, phone, fax, in person.

Misdemeanor, Civil Actions Under $25,000, Eviction, Small Claims—77th District Court, 400 Elm, Big Rapids, MI 49307. 231-723-3331, Fax: 231-796-2180. 8:30AM-4:30PM. Access by: mail, fax, in person.

Probate—Probate Court, PO Box 820, Big Rapids, MI 49307. 231-689-7269, Fax: 231-592-0191. 8:30AM-5PM.

Menominee

Real Estate Recording—Menominee County Register of Deeds, Courthouse, 839 10th Ave. Menominee, MI 49858. 906-863-5548, Fax: 906-863-8839. 8AM-4:30PM.

Felony, Civil Actions Over $25,000—41st Circuit Court, 839 10th Ave, Menominee, MI 49858. 906-863-9968, Fax: 906-863-8839. 8AM-4:30PM. Access by: mail, in person.

Misdemeanor, Civil Actions Under $25,000, Eviction, Small Claims—95th District Court, 839 10th Ave, Menominee, MI 49858. 906-863-8532, Fax: 906-863-2023. 8AM-4:30PM. Access by: mail, phone, fax, in person.

Probate—Probate Court, 839 10th Ave. Menominee, MI 49858. 906-863-2634, Fax: 906-863-8839. 8AM-4:30PM. Access by: mail, in person.

Midland

Real Estate Recording—Midland County Register of Deeds, 220 West Ellsworth Street, County Services Building, Midland, MI 48640. 517-832-6850, Fax: 517-832-6608. 8AM-5PM.

Felony, Civil Actions Over $25,000—42nd Circuit Court, Courthouse, 301 W Main St, Midland, MI 48640. 517-832-6735, Fax: 517-832-6610. 8AM-5PM. Access by: mail, phone, in person.

Civil Actions Under $25,000, Eviction, Small Claims—75th District Court-Civil Division, 301 W Main St, Midland, MI 48640. 517-832-6701. 8AM-5PM. Access by: mail, in person. Special note: Samal Claims can be reached at 517-832-6717.

Misdemeanor—75th District Court-Criminal Division, 301 W Main St, Midland, MI 48640-5183. 517-832-6702. 8:30AM-4:30PM. Access by: mail, in person.

Probate—Probate Court, 301 W Main St, Midland, MI 48640. 517-832-6880, Fax: 517-832-6607. 8AM-5PM. Access by: mail, in person.

Missaukee

Real Estate Recording—Missaukee County Register of Deeds, 111 S. Canal St. Lake City, MI 49651. 231-873-3977, Fax: 231-839-3684. 9AM-5PM.

Felony, Civil Actions Over $25,000—28th Circuit Court, PO Box 800, Lake City, MI 49651. 231-882-0011, Fax: 231-839-3684. 9AM-5PM. Access by: mail, phone, fax, in person.

Misdemeanor, Civil Actions Under $25,000, Eviction, Small Claims—84th District Court, PO Box 800, Lake City, MI 49651. 231-873-4530. 9AM-5PM. Access by: mail, in person.

Probate—Probate Court, PO Box 800, Lake City, MI 49651. 231-873-3980, Fax: 231-839-5856. 9AM-Noon, 1-5PM. Access by: mail, in person.

Monroe

Real Estate Recording—Monroe County Register of Deeds, 106 East First Street, Monroe, MI 48161. 314-888-2456. 8:30AM-5PM.

Felony, Civil Actions Over $25,000—38th Circuit Court, 106 E 1st St, Monroe, MI 48161. 734-243-7081, Fax: 734-243-7107. 8:30AM-4:30PM. Access by: mail, in person.

Misdemeanor, Civil Actions Under $25,000, Eviction, Small Claims—1st District Court, 106 E 1st St, Monroe, MI 48161. 734-243-7030, Fax: 734-243-7104. 8:30AM-4:45PM. Access by: mail, in person.

Probate—Probate Court, 106 E 1st St, Monroe, MI 48161. 734-243-7018. 8AM-Noon, 1-5PM.

Montcalm

Real Estate Recording—Montcalm County Register of Deeds, 211 West Main Street, Courthouse, Stanton, MI 48888. 517-831-5226, Fax: 517-831-7320. 8AM-Noon, 1-5PM.

Felony, Civil Actions Over $25,000—8th Circuit Court, PO Box 368, Stanton, MI 48888. 517-831-7339, Fax: 517-831-7474. 8AM-5PM. Access by: mail, in person. Special note: The office closes for lunch for one hour.

Misdemeanor, Civil Actions Under $25,000, Eviction, Small Claims—64 B District Court, PO Box 608, Stanton, MI 48888. 517-831-5226, Fax: 517-831-4747. 8AM-5PM. Access by: mail, in person.

Probate—Probate Court, PO Box 309, Stanton, MI 48888. 517-831-7316, Fax: 517-831-7314. 8AM-5PM.

Montmorency

Real Estate Recording—Montmorency County Register of Deeds, 12265 M-32, Courthouse, Atlanta, MI 49709. 517-785-4769, Fax: 517-785-2825. 8:30AM-Noon, 1-4:30PM.

Felony, Civil Actions Over $25,000—26th Circuit Court, PO Box 415, Atlanta, MI 49709. 517-785-4794, Fax: 517-785-2662. 8:30AM-Noon, 1-4:30PM. Access by: mail, phone, fax, in person.

Misdemeanor, Civil Actions Under $25,000, Eviction, Small Claims—88th District Court, County Courthouse, PO Box 789, Atlanta, MI 49709. 517-785-3122, Fax: 517-785-2376. 8:30AM-Noon, 1-4:30PM. Access by: mail, in person.

Probate—Probate Court, PO Box 789, Atlanta, MI 49709-0789. 517-785-4403, Fax: 517-785-2605. Access by: mail, in person.

Muskegon

Real Estate Recording—Muskegon County Register of Deeds, County Building, Muskegon, MI 49442. 231-779-9515, Fax: 231-724-6842. 8AM-5PM; Recording hours: 8AM-4:30PM.

Felony, Civil Actions Over $25,000—14th Circuit Court, County Bldg, 6th Floor, 990 Terrace St, Muskegon, MI 49442. 231-832-6103, Fax: 231-724-6695. 8AM-5PM. Access by: mail, in person.

Misdemeanor, Civil Actions Under $25,000, Eviction, Small Claims—60th District Court, 990 Terrace, 1st Floor, Muskegon, MI 49442. 231-779-9510, Fax: 231-724-3489. 8:30AM-4:45PM. Access by: mail, in person.

Probate—Probate Court, 990 Terrace St, 5th Floor, Muskegon, MI 49442. 231-779-9475, Fax: 231-724-6232. 8AM-5PM.

Newaygo

Real Estate Recording—Newaygo County Register of Deeds, 1087 Newell Street, County Administration Building, White Cloud, MI 49349. 231-724-6261, Fax: 231-689-7205. 8AM-5PM.

Felony, Civil Actions Over $25,000—27th Circuit Court, PO Box 885, White Cloud, MI 49349-0885. 231-745-4614, Fax: 231-689-2120. 8AM-5PM. Access by: mail, fax, in person.

Misdemeanor, Civil Actions Under $25,000, Eviction, Small Claims—78th District Court, 1092 Newell St, White Cloud, MI 49349. 231-724-6447, Fax: 231-689-7258. 8AM-5PM. Access by: mail, fax, in person.

Probate—Probate Court, 1092 Newell, White Cloud, MI 49349. 231-745-4614, Fax: 231-689-7276. 8AM-Noon, 1-5PM. Access by: mail, in person.

Oakland

Real Estate Recording—Oakland County Register of Deeds, 1200 North Telegraph Road, Dept 480, Pontiac, MI 48341. 810-858-0599. 8AM-4:30PM.

Felony, Civil Actions Over $25,000—6th Circuit Court, 1200 N Telegraph Rd, Pontiac, MI 48341. 252-514-4774. 8:30AM-4:30PM. Access by: mail, in person.

Misdemeanor, Civil Actions Under $25,000, Eviction, Small Claims—43rd District Court, 43 E Nine Mile Rd, Hazel Park, MI 48030. 252-232-2010, Fax: 248-546-4088. 8:30AM-5PM. Access by: mail, in person.

44th District Court-Royal Oak, 211 Williams St, Royal Oak, MI 48068. 248-858-0581, Fax: 248-546-6366. 8AM-4:30PM. Access by: mail, in person.

45 A District Court-Berkley, 3338 Coolidge, Berkley, MI 48072. 248-858-0260, Fax: 248-546-2416. 8:30AM-4:30PM. Access by: mail, in person.

45 B District Court, 13600 Oak Park Blvd, Oak Park, MI 48237. 252-357-1365, Fax: 248-691-7158. 9AM-5PM. Access by: mail, in person. Special note: Court covers Huntington Woods, Oak Park, Pleasant Ridge, and Royal Oak Township.

46th District Court, 26000 Evergreen Rd, Southfield, MI 48076. 248-853-5553, Fax: 248-354-5315. 8AM-5PM. Access by: mail, in person.

47th District Court-Farmington, Farmington Hills, 32795 W Ten Mile Rd, Farmington, MI 48336. 248-857-8027, Fax: 248-477-2441. 8:30AM-4:30PM. Access by: mail, in person.

48th District Court, 4280 Telegraph Rd, Bloomfield Hills, MI 48302. 252-257-3261, Fax: 248-647-8955. 8:30AM-4:30PM. Access by: mail, phone, in person.

51st District Court-Waterford, 5100 Civic Center Dr, Waterford, MI 48329. 252-331-4751. 8:30AM-4:45PM. Access by: mail, in person.

52nd District Court-Division 1, 48150 Grand River, Novi, MI 48374. Access by: mail, in person.

52nd District Court-Division 2, 5850 Lorac, PO Box 169, Clarkston, MI 48347-0169., Fax: 248-625-5602. 8:30AM-4:30PM. Access by: mail, phone, fax, in person. Special note: Court covers Sringfield, Holly, Groveland, Brandon, Independence, Clarkston & Ortonville.

52nd District Court-Division 3, 135 Barclay Circle, Rochester Hills, MI 48307. 252-358-7845, Fax: 248-853-3277. 8:15AM-4:45PM. Access by: mail, in person.

52nd District Court-Division 4 (Troy, Clawson), 500 W Big Beaver Rd, Troy, MI 48084. 248-857-8090, Fax: 248-528-3588. 8:30AM-4:45PM. Access by: mail, phone, fax, in person.

Civil Actions Under $25,000, Eviction, Small Claims—50th District Court-Pontiac Civil Division, 70 N Saganaw, Pontiac, MI 48342. 252-473-2950, Fax: 248-857-6028. 8:30AM-5PM. Access by: mail, in person.

Misdemeanor—50th District Court-Pontiac Criminal Division, 70 N Saganaw, Pontiac, MI 48342. 252-426-1505, Fax: 248-857-6028. 8:30AM-5PM. Access by: mail, in person.

Probate—Probate Court, 1200 N Telegraph Rd, Pontiac, MI 48341. 252-482-2323, Fax: 248-452-2016. 8:30AM-5PM. Access by: mail, in person.

Oceana

Real Estate Recording—Oceana County Register of Deeds, 100 State Street, Courthouse, Hart, MI 49420. 240-777-9466. 9AM-5PM.

Felony, Civil Actions Over $25,000—27th Circuit Court, 100 State Street, #M-34, Hart, MI 49420. 231-922-4735. 9AM-Noon,1-5PM. Access by: mail, in person.

Misdemeanor, Civil Actions Under $25,000, Eviction, Small Claims—79th District Court, PO Box 167, Hart, MI 49420. 248-354-9506, Fax: 231-873-5914. 8AM-5PM. Access by: mail, in person.

Probate—Probate Court, County Bldg, 100 S State St, Suite M-34, Hart, MI 49420. 231-922-4710, Fax: 616-873-4177. 9AM-Noon, 1-5PM. Access by: mail, in person.

Ogemaw

Real Estate Recording—Ogemaw County Register of Deeds, 806 West Houghton Ave, Room 104, West Branch, MI 48661. 517-345-0084. 8:30AM-4:30PM.

Felony, Civil Actions Over $25,000—34th Circuit Court, 806 W Houghton, West Branch, MI 48661. 517-345-0215, Fax: 517-345-7223. 8:30AM-4:30PM. Access by: mail, phone, fax, in person.

Misdemeanor, Civil Actions Under $25,000, Eviction, Small Claims—82nd District Court, PO Box 365, West Branch, MI 48661. 517-345-5040, Fax: 517-345-5910. 8:30AM-4:30PM. Access by: mail, fax, in person.

Probate—Probate Court, County Courthouse, Rm 203, 806 W Houghton Ave, West Branch, MI 48661. 517-345-0145, Fax: 517-345-5901. 8:30AM-Noon, 1-4:30PM. Access by: mail, in person.

Ontonagon

Real Estate Recording—Ontonagon County Register of Deeds, 725 Greenland Road, Ontonagon, MI 49953. 906-884-4665, Fax: 906-884-2916. 8:30AM-4:30PM.

Felony, Civil Actions Over $25,000—32nd Circuit Court, 725 Greenland Rd, Ontonagon, MI 49953. 906-884-4255, Fax: 906-884-2916. 8:30AM-4:30PM. Access by: mail, in person.

Misdemeanor, Civil Actions Under $25,000, Eviction, Small Claims—98th District Court, 725 Greenland Rd, Ontonagon, MI 49953. 906-884-2865, Fax: 906-884-2916. 8:30AM-4:30PM. Access by: mail, in person.

Probate—Probate Court, 725 Greenland Rd, Ontonagon, MI 49953. 906-884-4117, Fax: 906-884-2916. 8:30AM-4:30PM.

Osceola

Real Estate Recording—Osceola County Register of Deeds, 301 West Upton Ave. Reed City, MI 49677. 231-845-1445. 9AM-5PM.

Felony, Civil Actions Over $25,000—49th Circuit Court, PO Box 208, Reed City, MI 49677. 231-843-8666, Fax: 231-832-6149. 9AM-5PM. Access by: mail, phone, fax, in person.

Misdemeanor, Civil Actions Under $25,000, Eviction, Small Claims—77th District Court, 410 W Upton, Reed City, MI 49677. 231-873-3666, Fax: 231-832-9190. 8:30AM-4:30PM. Access by: mail, fax, in person.

Probate—Probate Court, 410 W Upton, Reed City, MI 49677. 231-845-8411, Fax: 231-832-9190. 8:30AM-Noon, 1-4:30PM. Access by: in person.

Oscoda

Real Estate Recording—Oscoda County Register of Deeds, 310 Morenci Street, Courthouse, Mio, MI 48647. 517-826-3241, Fax: 517-826-3657. 10AM-4PM.

Felony, Civil Actions Over $25,000—23rd Circuit Court, PO Box 399, Mio, MI 48647. 517-826-1110, Fax: 517-826-3657. 8:30AM-4:30PM. Access by: mail, in person.

Misdemeanor, Civil Actions Under $25,000, Eviction, Small Claims—82nd District Court, PO Box 399, Mio, MI 48647. 517-826-1106. 8:30AM-4:30PM. Access by: mail, in person.

Probate—Probate Court, PO Box 399, Mio, MI 48647. 517-826-1107, Fax: 517-826-1126. 8:30AM-Noon, 1-4:30PM.

Otsego

Real Estate Recording—Otsego County Register of Deeds, 225 West Main St. Room 108, Gaylord, MI 49735. 517-732-6484, Fax: 517-732-1562. 8AM-Noon, 1-4:30PM.

Felony, Civil Actions Over $25,000—46th Circuit Court, 225 Main St, Gaylord, MI 49735. 517-732-6484. 8AM-4:30PM. Access by: mail, phone, in person. www.Circuit46.org

Misdemeanor, Civil Actions Under $25,000, Eviction, Small Claims—87th District Court, 800 Livingston Blvd, #1C, Gaylord, MI 49735. 517-732-6486, Fax: 517-732-5130. 8AM-4:30PM. Access by: mail, in person. www.Circuit46.org

Probate—Probate Court, 225 W Main St, Gaylord, MI 49735. 517-732-6484, Fax: 517-732-1562. 8AM-4:30PM. Access by: in person. Special note: Free record searching online at web site. www.Circuit46.org

Ottawa

Real Estate Recording—Ottawa County Register of Deeds, 414 Washington Avenue, Room 305, Grand Haven, MI 49417. 616-392-3111, Fax: 616-846-8131. 8AM-5PM.

Felony, Civil Actions Over $25,000—20th Circuit Court, 414 Washington Ave, Grand Haven, MI 49417. 616-846-8310, Fax: 616-846-8138. 8AM-5PM. Access by: mail, fax, in person.

Misdemeanor, Civil Actions Under $25,000, Eviction, Small Claims—58th District Court-Grand Haven, 414 Washington Ave, Grand Haven, MI 49417. 616-846-8280, Fax: 616-846-8291. 8AM-5PM. Access by: mail, in person.

58th District Court-Holland, 57 W 8th St, Holland, MI 49423. 616-392-6991, Fax: 616-392-5013. 8AM-5PM. Access by: mail, in person.

58th District Court-Hudsonville, 3100 Port Sheldon, Hudsonville, MI 49426. 616-662-3100, Fax: 616-669-2950. 8AM-5PM. Access by: mail, in person.

Probate—Probate Court, 12120 Fillmore St, West Olive, MI 49460. 616-786-4110, Fax: 616-786-4154. 8AM-5PM. Access by: mail, in person.

Presque Isle

Real Estate Recording—Presque Isle County Register of Deeds, 151 East Huron Street, Rogers City, MI 49779. 517-734-4075, Fax: 517-734-0506. 9AM-5PM.

Felony, Civil Actions Over $25,000—26th Circuit Court, PO Box 110, Rogers City, MI 49779. 517-734-3288, Fax: 517-734-7635. 9AM-5PM. Access by: mail, phone, fax, in person.

Misdemeanor, Civil Actions Under $25,000, Eviction, Small Claims—89th District Court, PO Box 110, Rogers City, MI 49779. 517-734-2411, Fax: 517-734-3400. 8:30AM-4:30PM. Access by: mail, in person.

Probate—Probate Court, PO Box 110, Rogers City, MI 49779. 517-734-3268, Fax: 517-734-4420. 8:30-4:30.

Roscommon

Real Estate Recording—Roscommon County Register of Deeds, 500 Lake Street, Roscommon, MI 48653. 517-275-5823, Fax: 517-275-8640. 8:30AM-4:30PM.

Felony, Civil Actions Over $25,000—34th Circuit Court, PO Box 98, Roscommon, MI 48653. 517-275-1902, Fax: 517-275-0602. 8:30AM-4:30PM. Access by: mail, fax, in person.

Misdemeanor, Civil Actions Under $25,000, Eviction, Small Claims—83rd District Court, PO Box 189, Roscommon, MI 48653. 517-275-5312, Fax: 517-275-6033. 8:30AM-4:30PM. Access by: mail, phone, fax, in person.

Probate—Probate Court, PO Box 607, Roscommon, MI 48653. 517-275-5221, Fax: 517-275-8537. 8:30AM-4:30PM. Access by: mail, in person.

Saginaw

Real Estate Recording—Saginaw County Register of Deeds, 111 South Michigan Avenue, Saginaw, MI 48602. 517-790-5225, Fax: 517-790-5278. 8AM-5PM.

Felony, Civil Actions Over $25,000—10th Circuit Court, 111 S Michigan Ave, Saginaw, MI 48602. 517-790-5544, Fax: 517-790-8254. 8AM-5:00PM. Access by: mail, in person.

Civil Actions Under $25,000, Eviction, Small Claims—70th District Court-Civil Division, 111 S Michigan Ave, Saginaw, MI 48602. 517-790-5380, Fax: 517-790-5589. 8AM-4:45PM. Access by: mail, in person.

Misdemeanor—70th District Court-Criminal Division, 111 S Michigan Ave, Saginaw, MI 48602. 517-790-5385, Fax: 517-790-5589. 8AM-4:45PM. Access by: mail, fax, in person.

Probate—Probate Court, 111 S Michigan St, Saginaw, MI 48602. 517-790-5320, Fax: 517-790-5328. 8AM-5PM. Access by: mail, in person.

Sanilac

Real Estate Recording—Sanilac County Register of Deeds, 60 West Sanilac, Sandusky, MI 48471. 810-648-2127, Fax: 810-648-5461. 8AM-Noon, 1-4:30PM.

Felony, Civil Actions Over $25,000—24th Circuit Court, 60 W Sanilac, Rm 203, Sandusky, MI 48471. 810-648-3212, Fax: 810-648-5466. 8AM-4:30PM. Access by: mail, in person.

Misdemeanor, Civil Actions Under $25,000, Eviction, Small Claims—73rd District Court, 60 W Sanilac, Sandusky, MI 48471. 810-648-3250. 8AM-4:30PM. Access by: mail, in person.

Probate—Probate Court, 60 W Sanilac, Po Box 128, Sandusky, MI 48471. 810-648-3221, Fax: 810-648-2900. 8AM-Noon, 1-4:30PM.

Schoolcraft

Real Estate Recording—Schoolcraft County Register of Deeds, 300 Walnut Street, Room 164, Manistique, MI 49854. 906-341-3622, Fax: 906-341-5680. 8AM-4PM.

Felony, Civil Actions Over $25,000—11th Circuit Court, 300 Walnut St, Rm 164, Manistique, MI 49854. 906-341-3618. 8AM-4PM. Access by: mail, phone, fax, in person.

Misdemeanor, Civil Actions Under $25,000, Eviction, Small Claims—93rd District Court, 300 Walnut St, Rm 135, Manistique, MI 49854. 906-341-3630, Fax: 906-341-8006. 8AM-4PM. Access by: mail, fax, in person.

Probate—Probate Court, 300 Walnut St, Manistique, MI 49854. 906-341-3641. 8AM-Noon, 1-4PM.

Shiawassee

Real Estate Recording—Shiawassee County Register of Deeds, 208 North Shiawassee, Courthouse, Corunna, MI 48817. 517-743-2224, Fax: 517-743-2459. 8AM-5PM.

Felony, Civil Actions Over $25,000—35th Circuit Court, 200 N Shiawassee St, Corunna, MI 48817. 517-743-2302, Fax: 517-743-2241. 8AM-5PM. Access by: mail, phone, fax, in person.

Misdemeanor, Civil Actions Under $25,000, Eviction, Small Claims—66th District Court, 110 E Mack St, Corunna, MI 48817. 517-743-2244. 8AM-5PM. Access by: mail, phone, in person.

Probate—Probate Court, 110 E Mack St, Corunna, MI 48817. 517-743-2211, Fax: 517-743-2349. 8AM-5PM.

St. Clair

Real Estate Recording—St. Clair County Register of Deeds, 201 McMorran Blvd. Room 116, Port Huron, MI 48060. 810-985-2295, Fax: 810-985-4297. 8AM-4:30PM.

Felony, Civil Actions Over $25,000—31st Circuit Court, 201 McMorran Blvd, Port Huron, MI 48060. 810-985-2200, Fax: 810-985-4796. 8AM-4:30PM. Access by: mail, in person.

Misdemeanor, Civil Actions Under $25,000, Eviction, Small Claims—72nd District Court, 201 McMorran Rd, Port Huron, MI 48060. 810-985-2072. 8AM-4:30PM. Access by: mail, in person.

Probate—Probate Court, 201 McMorran Blvd Rm 216, Port Huron, MI 48060. 810-985-2066, Fax: 810-985-2179. 8AM-4:30PM. Access by: mail, in person.

St. Joseph

Real Estate Recording—St. Joseph County Register of Deeds, 125 W. Main, Centreville, MI 49032. 616-467-5581, Fax: 616-467-5628. 9AM-5PM.

Felony, Civil Actions Over $25,000—45th Circuit Court, PO Box 189, Centreville, MI 49032. 616-467-5602, Fax: 616-467-5628. 9AM-5PM. Access by: mail, in person.

Misdemeanor, Civil Actions Under $25,000, Eviction, Small Claims—3-B District Court, PO Box 67, Centreville, MI 49032. 616-467-5627. 8AM-5PM. Access by: mail, phone, fax, in person.

Probate—Probate Court, PO Box 190, Centreville, MI 49032. 616-467-5538, Fax: 616-467-5560. 8AM-5PM. Access by: mail, in person.

Tuscola

Real Estate Recording—Tuscola County Register of Deeds, 440 North State Street, Caro, MI 48723. 517-673-5999, Fax: 517-672-4266. 8AM-Noon, 1-4:30PM.

Felony, Civil Actions Over $25,000—54th Circuit Court, 440 N State St, Caro, MI 48723. 517-672-3780, Fax: 517-672-4266. 8AM-3:30PM. Access by: mail, in person.

Misdemeanor, Civil Actions Under $25,000, Eviction, Small Claims—71 B District Court, 440 N State St. Caro, MI 48723. 517-673-5999, Fax: 517-673-0451. 8AM-4:30PM. Access by: mail, phone, in person.

Probate—Probate Court, 440 N State St, Caro, MI 48723. 517-672-3850, Fax: 517-672-4266. 8AM-Noon, 1-4:30PM. Access by: mail, in person.

Van Buren

Real Estate Recording—Van Buren County Register of Deeds, 212 Paw Paw Street, Paw Paw, MI 49079. 616-657-8228, Fax: 616-657-7573. 8:30AM-5PM.

Felony, Civil Actions Over $25,000—36th Circuit Court, 212 Paw Paw St, Paw Paw, MI 49079. 616-657-8218. 8:30AM-5PM. Access by: mail, in person.

Misdemeanor, Civil Actions Under $25,000, Eviction, Small Claims—7th District Court, 212 Paw Paw St, Paw Paw, MI 49079. 616-657-8222, Fax: 616-657-7573. 9AM-4:30PM. Access by: mail, in person.

7th District Court-West Division, 1007 E Wells, PO Box 311, South Haven, MI 49090. 616-637-5258, Fax: 616-637-9169. 8:30AM-4:30PM. Access by: mail, in person.

Probate—Probate Court, 212 Paw Paw St, Paw Paw, MI 49079. 616-657-8225, Fax: 616-657-7573. 8:30AM-5PM.

Washtenaw

Real Estate Recording—Washtenaw County Register of Deeds, 101 East Huron, Courthouse, Ann Arbor, MI 48107. 315-253-1570. 8:30AM-5PM.

Felony, Civil Actions Over $25,000—22nd Circuit Court, PO Box 8645, Ann Arbor, MI 48107-8645. 734-994-2507. 8:30AM-4:30PM. Access by: mail, in person. www.washtenaw.mi.us/ depts/courts/index.htm

Misdemeanor, Civil Actions Under $25,000, Eviction, Small Claims—14th District Court A-1, 4133 Washtenaw, Ann Arbor, MI 48107-8645. 734-971-6050, Fax: 734-971-5018. 8AM-4:30PM. Access by: mail, in person.

14th District Court A-2, 415 W Michigan Ave, Ypsilanti, MI 48197. 734-484-6690, Fax: 734-484-6697. 8AM-4:30PM. Access by: mail, in person.

14th District Court A-3, 122 S Main St, Chelsea, MI 48118. 734-475-8606, Fax: 734-475-0460. 8AM-4:30PM. Access by: mail, in person.

14th District Court A-4, 122 S Main, Chelsea, MI 48118. 734-475-8606, Fax: 734-475-0460. 8AM-4:30PM M-F (Office), 8AM-3:30PM M-F (Phone). Access by: mail, in person.

Civil Actions Under $25,000, Eviction, Small Claims—14th District Court-B-Civil Division, 7200 S Huron River Dr, Ypsilanti, MI 48197. 734-483-5300, Fax: 734-483-3630. 8AM-5PM. Access by: mail, fax, in person.

Misdemeanor—14th District Court-B-Criminal Division, 7200 S Huron River Dr, Ypsilanti, MI 48197. 734-483-1333, Fax: 734-483-3630. 8AM-5PM. Access by: mail, in person.

Civil Actions Under $25,000, Eviction, Small Claims—15th District Court-Civil Division, 101 E Huron, Box 8650, Ann Arbor, MI 48107. 734-994-2749, Fax: 734-994-2617. 8:30AM-4:30PM. Access by: mail, phone, fax, in person.

Misdemeanor—15th District Court-Criminal Division, 101 E Huron, Box 8650, Ann Arbor, MI 48107-8650. 734-994-2745, Fax: 734-994-2617. 8AM-4:30PM. Access by: mail, phone, in person. Special note: Court no longer handles felonies as of 7/93. Court now has a Unified Trial Court, which is a pilot project. All felonies are now handled through the 22nd Circuit Court.

Probate—Probate Court, PO Box 8645, Ann Arbor, MI 48107. 734-994-2474, Fax: 734-996-3033. 8:30AM-4:30PM.

Wayne

Real Estate Recording—Wayne County Register of Deeds, 400 Monroe, Room 620, Detroit, MI 48226. 314-622-4367, Fax: 313-224-5884. 8AM-4:30PM.

Civil Actions Over $25,000—3rd Circuit Court, 201 County Building, 2 Woodward, Detroit, MI 48226. 314-622-4582. 8AM-4:30PM. Access by: mail, phone, in person.

Felony—Frank Murphy Hall of Justice, 1441 St Antoine, Detroit, MI 48226. 314-622-2062, Fax: 313-224-2786. 8AM-4:30PM. Access by: mail, in person.

Civil Actions Under $25,000, Eviction, Small Claims—36th District Court-Civil (Detroit), 421 Madison Ave, Detroit, MI 48226. 315-253-1271, Fax: 313-965-4059. 8AM-4:30PM. Access by: in person.

Misdemeanor, Civil Actions Under $25,000, Eviction, Small Claims—16th District Court, 15140 Farmington Rd, Livonia, MI 48154-5498. 734-466-2500. 8:30AM-4:30PM. Access by: mail, in person.

17th District Court, 15111 Beech-Daly Rd, Redford, MI 48239. 315-245-0817, Fax: 313-538-3468. 8:30AM-4:15PM. Access by: mail, in person.

18th District Court, 36675 Ford Rd, Westland, MI 48185. 734-595-8720, Fax: 734-595-0160. 8:30AM-4PM M,F; 8:30AM-5:30PM T,W; 8:30AM-6PM Th. Access by: mail, fax, in person.

19th District Court, 16077 Michigan Ave, Dearborn, MI 48126. 315-253-1211, Fax: 313-943-3033. 8AM-4:30PM. Access by: mail, fax, in person.

20th District Court, 6045 Fenton, Dearborn Heights, MI 48127. 314-889-2675, Fax: 313-277-7141. 9AM-5PM. Access by: mail, in person.

21st District Court, 6000 North Middlebelt Rd, Garden City, MI 48135. 734-525-8805, Fax: 734-421-4797. 8:30AM-4:30PM. Access by: mail, in person.

22nd District Court, 27331 S River Park Dr, Inkster, MI 48141. 314-889-3029, Fax: 313-277-8221. 8:30AM-4:30PM. Access by: mail, in person.

23rd District Court, 23511 Goddard Rd, Taylor, MI 48180. 734-374-1328, Fax: 734-374-1303. 8:30AM-4:45PM. Access by: mail, in person.

24th District Court-Allen Park & Melvindale, 6515 Roosevelt, Allen Park, MI 48101-2524. 315-252-8988, Fax: 313-928-1860. 8:30AM-4:30PM. Access by: mail, fax, in person.

25th District Court, 1475 Cleophus, Lincoln Park, MI 48146. 315-232-2548, Fax: 313-382-9361. 9AM-4:30PM. Access by: mail, in person.

26-1 District Court, 10600 W Jefferson, River Rouge, MI 48218. 315-245-2191, Fax: 313-842-5923. 8:30AM-4:30PM. Access by: mail, fax, in person.

26-2 District Court, 3869 W Jefferson, Ecorse, MI 48229. 315-232-4029, Fax: 313-386-4316. 9AM-4PM. Access by: mail, in person.

27-1 District Court, 2015 Biddle Ave, Wyandotte, MI 48192. 734-324-4475, Fax: 734-324-4503. 8:30AM-4:30PM. Access by: mail, in person.

27-2 District Court, 14100 Civic Park Dr, Riverview, MI 48192. 734-281-4204. 8:30AM-4:30PM. Access by: mail, in person.

28th District Court, 14720 Reaume Parkway, Southgate, MI 48195. 734-246-1360, Fax: 734-246-1405. 8:30AM-4:30PM. Access by: mail, fax, in person.

29th District Court, 34808 Sims Ave, Wayne, MI 48184. 734-722-5220, Fax: 734-722-7003. 8AM-4:30PM. Access by: mail, in person.

30th District Court, 28 Gerard Ave, Highland Park, MI 48203. 314-888-3378, Fax: 313-865-1115. 8AM-4:30PM. Access by: mail, in person.

31st District Court, 3401 Evaline Ave, Hamtramck, MI 48212. 315-252-7373, Fax: 313-876-7724. 8AM-4PM. Access by: mail, in person.

33rd District Court, 19000 Van Horn Rd, Woodhaven, MI 48183., Fax: 734-671-0307. 8:30AM-4:30PM. Access by: mail, fax, in person.

34th District Court, 11131 S Wayne Rd, Romulus, MI 48174. 734-941-4462, Fax: 734-941-7530. 8:30AM-4PM. Access by: mail, in person.

35th District Court, 660 Plymouth Rd, Plymouth, MI 48170. 734-459-4740, Fax: 734-454-9303. 8:30AM-4:25PM. Access by: mail, phone, in person.

Misdemeanor, Civil Actions Under $25,000, Small Claims—32 A District Court, 19617 Harper Ave, Harper Woods, MI 48225. 314-889-3090, Fax: 313-343-2594. 8:30AM-4:30PM. Access by: mail, phone, fax, in person.

Wexford

Real Estate Recording—Wexford County Register of Deeds, 437 East Division Street, Cadillac, MI 49601. 231-839-4590, Fax: 231-779-0292. 8:30AM-5PM.

Felony, Civil Actions Over $25,000—28th Circuit Court, PO Box 490, Cadillac, MI 49601. 231-839-2266. 8:30AM-5PM. Access by: mail, phone, in person.

Misdemeanor, Civil Actions Under $25,000, Eviction, Small Claims—84th District Court, 501 S Garfield, Cadillac, MI 49601. 231-843-4130, Fax: 231-779-9485. 8:30AM-5PM. Access by: mail, phone, in person.

Probate—Probate Court, 503 S Garfield, Cadillac, MI 49601. 231-839-4967, Fax: 231-779-9485. 8:30AM-5PM.

Federal Courts

US District Court

Eastern District of Michigan

Ann Arbor Division PO Box 8199, Ann Arbor, MI 48107734-741-2380 Fax: 734-741-2065 Counties: Jackson, Lenawee, Monroe, Oakland, Washtenaw. Civil cases in these counties are assigned randomly to the Detroit, Flint or Port Huron Divisions. Case files are maintained where the case is assigned.

Bay City Division PO Box 913, Bay City, MI 48707517-894-8800 Fax: 517-894-8804 Counties: Alcona, Alpena, Arenac, Bay, Cheboygan, Clare, Crawford, Gladwin, Gratiot, Huron, Iosco, Isabella, Midland, Montmorency, Ogemaw, Oscoda, Otsego, Presque Isle, Roscommon, Saginaw, Tuscola.

Detroit Division 564 Theodore Levin US Courthouse, 231 W Lafayette Blvd, Detroit, MI 48226313-234-5050, Record Room: 313-234-5010 Fax: 313-234-5393 Counties: Macomb, St. Clair, Sanilac, Wayne. Civil cases for these counties are assigned randomly among the Flint, Ann Arbor and Detroit divisions. Port Huron cases may also be assigned here. Case files are kept where the case is assigned..

Flint Division Clerk, Federal Bldg, Room 140, 600 Church St, Flint, MI 48502810-341-7840 Counties: Genesee, Lapeer, Livingston, Shiawassee. This office handles all criminal cases for these counties. Civil cases are assigned randomly among the Detroit, Ann Arbor and Flint divisions.

Port Huron Division c/o Detroit Division, 564 Theodore Levin US Courthouse, 231 W Lafayette Blvd, Detroit, MI 48226313-234-5050 Counties: Cases are assigned out of the Detroit Division.

Western District of Michigan

Grand Rapids Division PO Box 3310, Grand Rapids, MI 49501616-456-2693 Counties: Antrim, Barry, Benzie, Charlevoix, Emmet, Grand Traverse, Ionia, Kalkaska, Kent, Lake, Leelanau, Manistee, Mason, Mecosta, Missaukee, Montcalm, Muskegon, Newaygo, Oceana, Osceola, Ottawa, Wexford. The Lansing and Kalamazoo Divisions also handle casesfrom these counties. www.miw.uscourts.gov

Kalamazoo Division , 123 S Westnedge Ave, Kalamazoo, MI 49007616-349-2922 Counties: Allegan, Berrien, Calhoun, Cass, Kalamazoo, St. Joseph, Van Buren. Also handle cases from the counties in the Grand Rapids Division. www.miw.uscourts.gov

Lansing Division US Post Office & Courthouse Bldg, 315 W Allegan, Rm 101, Lansing, MI 48933517-377-1559 Counties: Branch, Clinton, Eaton, Hillsdale, Ingham. Also handle cases from the counties in the Grand Rapids Division. www.miw.uscourts.gov

Marquette-Northern Division PO Box 909, Marquette, MI 49855906-226-2117 Fax: 906-226-6735 Counties: Alger, Baraga, Chippewa, Delta, Dickinson, Gogebic, Houghton, Iron, Keweenaw, Luce, Mackinac, Marquette, Menominee, Ontonagon, Schoolcraft. www.miw.uscourts.gov

US Bankruptcy Court

Eastern District of Michigan

Bay City Division PO Box 911, Bay City, MI 48707517-894-8840 Counties: Alcona, Alpena, Arenac, Bay, Cheboygan, Clare, Crawford, Gladwin, Gratiot, Huron, Iosco, Isabella, Midland, Montmorency, Ogemaw, Oscoda, Otsego, Presque Isle, Roscommon, Saginaw, Tuscola.

Detroit Division Clerk, 21st Floor, 21 W Fort St, Detroit, MI 48226313-234-0065, Record Room: 313-234-0051 Counties: Jackson, Lenawee, Macomb, Monroe, Oakland, Sanilac, St. Clair, Washtenaw, Wayne.

Flint Division 226 W 2nd St, Flint, MI 48502810-235-4126 Counties: Genesee, Lapeer, Livingston, Shiawassee.

Western District of Michigan

Grand Rapids Division PO Box 3310, Grand Rapids, MI 49501616-456-2693 Fax: 616-456-2919 Counties: Allegan, Antrim, Barry, Benzie, Berrien, Branch, Calhoun, Cass, Charlevoix, Clinton, Eaton, Emmet, Grand Traverse, Hillsdale, Ingham, Ionia, Kalamazoo, Kalkaska, Kent, Lake, Leelanau, Manistee, Mason, Mecosta, Missaukee, Montcalm, Muskegon, Newaygo,Oceana, Osceola, Ottawa, St. Joseph, Van Buren, Wexford. www.miw.uscourts.gov

Marquette Division PO Box 909, Marquette, MI 49855906-226-2117 Fax: 906-226-7388 Counties: Alger, Baraga, Chippewa, Delta, Dickinson, Gogebic, Houghton, Iron, Keweenaw, Luce, Mackinac, Marquette, Menominee, Ontonagon, Schoolcraft. www.miw.uscourts.gov

Minnesota

Attorney General's Office
102 State Capitol
St Paul, MN 55155

651-296-6196
Fax: 651-297-4193

www.ag.state.mn.us/home/mainhi.shtml

Governor's Office
130 State Capitol Bldg,
75 Constitution Ave
St Paul, MN 55155

651-296-3391
Fax: 651-296-0674

www.mainserver.state.mn.us/governor

State Archives
345 Kellogg Blvd West
St Paul, MN 55102-1906

651-296-6126
Fax: 651-297-7436

www.mnhs.org

Capital:	St. Paul
	Ramsey County
Time Zone:	CST
Number of Counties:	87
Population:	4,685,549
Web Site:	www.state.mn.us

Search Unclaimed Property Online

There is no Internet-based search for this state; however, the URL for the agency responsible for unclaimed property is www.commerce.state.mn.us/mainup.htm.

State Agencies

Criminal Records
Bureau of Criminal Apprehension, Records & Identification, 1246 University Ave, St Paul, MN 55104; 651-642-0670; 8:15AM-4PM. Access by: mail. www.dps.state.mn.us/bca

Corporation Records
Limited Liability Company Records
Assumed Name
Trademarks/Servicemarks
Limited Partnerships
Business Records Services, Secretary of State, 180 State Office Bldg, 100 Constitution Ave, St Paul, MN 55155-1299; 651-296-2803 Information, 651-297-9102 Copies; Fax: 651-215-0683; 8AM-4:30PM. Access by: mail, phone, in person, online. www.sos.state.mn.us

Sales Tax Registrations
Minnesota Department of Revenue, Sales & Use Tax Division, 600 N Robert Street MS:6330, St Paul, MN 55146-6330; 651-296-6181; Fax: 651-296-1938; 7:30AM-5PM M-F. Access by: mail, phone, in person. www.taxes.state.mn.us

Uniform Commercial Code
Federal Tax Liens
State Tax Liens
UCC Division, Secretary of State, 180 State Office Bldg, St Paul, MN 55155-1299; 651-296-2803; Fax: 651-297-5844; 8 AM - 4:30 PM. Access by: mail, online. www.sos.state.mn.us

Workers' Compensation Records
Labor & Industry Department, Workers Compensation Division - Records Section, 443 Lafayette Rd -IPC, St Paul, MN 55155; 651-296-6845; Fax: 651-215-0080; 8AM-4:30PM. Access by: mail.

Birth Certificates
Minnesota Department of Health, Vital Records, PO Box 9441, Minneapolis, MN 55440-9441 (717 Delaware St SE, Minneapolis, MN 55414); 612-675-5120; Fax: 612-331-5776; 8AM-4:30PM. Access by: mail, phone, in person. health.state.mn.us

Death Records

Minnesota Department of Health, Section of Vital Records, PO Box 9441, Minneapolis, MN 55440-9441; 612-623-5120; Fax: 612-331-5776; 8AM-4:30PM. Access by: mail, phone, in person.

Marriage Certificates
Divorce Records

Records not available from state agency.

Marriage and divorce records are found at the county level. The Section of Vital Records has an index and they will direct you to the proper county (Marriage since 1958, Divorce since 1970). Call the Section of Vital Records at 651-676-5120.

Accident Reports

Driver & Vehicle Services, Accident Records, 445 Minnesota St, Suite 181, St Paul, MN 55101-5181; 651-296-2060; Fax: 651-282-2360; 8AM-4:30PM. Access by: mail, phone, in person.

Driver Records

Driver & Vehicle Services, Records Section, 445 Minnesota St, #180, St Paul, MN 55101; 651-296-6911; 8AM-4:30PM. Access by: mail, online. www.dps.state.mn.us/dvs

Vehicle Ownership
Vehicle Identification

Driver & Vehicle Services, Records Section, 445 Minnesota St, St Paul, MN 55101; 651-296-6911 General Information; 8AM-4:30PM. Access by: mail, online.

Boat & Vessel Ownership
Boat & Vessel Registration

Department of Natural Resources, License Bureau, 500 Lafayette Rd, St Paul, MN 55155-4026; 651-296-2316; Fax: 651-297-8851; 8AM-4:30PM M-F. www.dnr.state.mn.us

Legislation-Current/Pending
Legislation-Passed

Minnesota Legislature, State Capitol, House-Room 211, Senate-Room 231, St Paul, MN 55155; 651-296-2887 Senate Bills, 651-296-6646 House Bill Status, 651-296-2314 House Bill Copies, 651-296-2146 House Information; Fax: 651-296-1563; 8AM-5PM. Access by: mail, phone, in person, online. www.leg.state.mn.us

Voter Registration

Restricted access.

Records are sold by the state only for political, election, or government purposes and only to MN registered voters. Some counties will honor record requests.

Secretary of State, Elections Division, 180 State Office Bldg, 100 Constitution Ave, St Paul, MN 55155; 651-215-1440; Fax: 651-296-9073; 8AM-4:30PM www.sos.state.mn.us

GED Certificates

Department of Children, Families & Learning, GED Testing, 1500 Highway 36 West, Roseville, MN 55113; 651-582-8445; Fax: 651-582-8496; 7AM-3:30PM. http://cfl.state.mn.us

Hunting License Information
Fishing License Information

Fish & Wildlife Division, DNR Information Center, 500 Lafayette Rd, St Paul, MN 55155-4040; 651-296-6157; Fax: 651-297-3618; 8AM-4:30PM. Access by: mail, phone, in person. www.dnr.state.mn.us

County Courts & Recording Offices

About the Courts...

Administration

State Court Adminstrator, 135 Minn.
Judicial Center   651-296-2474
25 Constitution Ave   Fax: 651-297-5636
St Paul, MN 55155
www.courts.state.mn.us

Court Structure

There are 97 District Courts comprising 10 judicial districts. Effective July 1, 1996, the limit for small claims was raised from $5000 to $7500.

Searching Hints

Statewide certification and copy fees are as follows: Certification Fee: $10.00 per document, Copy Fee: $5.00 per document (not per page).

An exact name is required to search, e.g., a request for "Robert Smith" will not result in finding "Bob Smith." The requester must request both names and pay two search and copy fees.

When a search is permitted by "plaintiff or defendant," most jurisdictions stated that a case is indexed by only the 1st plaintiff or defendant, and a 2nd or 3rd party would not be sufficient to search.

The 3rd, 5th, 8th and 10th Judicial Districts no longer will perform criminal record searches for the public.

Most courts take personal checks. Exceptions are noted.

Online Access

There is an online system in place that allows internal and external access. Some criminal information is available online from St Paul through the Bureau of Criminal Apprehension (BCA), 1246 University Ave, St. Paul, MN 55104. Additional information is available from BCA by calling 651-642-0670.

About the Recording Offices...

Organization

87 counties, 87 recording offices. The recording officer is County Recorder. The entire state is in the Central Time Zone (CST).

UCC Records

Financing statements are filed at the state level except for consumer goods, farm related and real estate related filings. Counties enter all non-real estate filings into a central statewide database which can be accessed from any county office. All counties will perform UCC searches. Use search request form UCC-11. Search fees are usually $15.00 per debtor name if the standard UCC-12 request form is used, or $20.00 if a nonstandard form is used. A UCC search can include tax liens. The search fee usually includes 10 listings or copies. Additional copies usually cost $1.00 per page.

Lien Records

Federal and state tax liens on personal property of businesses are filed with the Secretary of State. Other federal and state tax liens are filed with the County Recorder. A special search form UCC-12 is used for separate tax lien searches. Some counties search each tax lien index separately. Some charge one $15.00 fee to search both indexes, but others charge a separate fee for each index searched. Search and copy fees vary widely.

Real Estate Records

Many Minnesota counties will perform real estate searches, especially short questions over the telephone. Copy fees vary, but do not apply to certified copies. Certification fees are usually $1.00 per page with a minimum of $5.00.

County Courts & Recording Offices

Aitkin

Real Estate Recording—Aitkin County Recorder, 209 Second Street NW, Aitkin, MN 56431. 219-326-6808. 8AM-4:30PM.

Felony, Misdemeanor, Civil, Eviction, Small Claims, Probate—9th Judicial District Court, 209 Second St NW, Aitkin, MN 56431. 219-358-4817, Fax: 218-927-4535. 8AM-4:30PM. Access by: mail, in person.

Anoka

Real Estate Recording—Anoka County Recorder, 2100 3rd Ave. Anoka, MN 55303. 612-323-5400, Fax: 612-323-5421.

Felony, Misdemeanor, Civil, Eviction, Small Claims, Probate—10th Judicial District Court, 325 E Main St, Anoka, MN 55303. 612-422-7350, Fax: 612-422-6919. 8AM-4:30PM. Access by: in person.

Becker

Real Estate Recording—Becker County Recorder, 915 Lake Avenue, Detroit Lakes, MN 56501. 219-326-6808, Fax: 218-846-7323. 8AM-4:30PM.

Felony, Misdemeanor, Civil, Eviction, Small Claims, Probate—7th Judicial District Court, PO Box 787, Detroit Lakes, MN 56502. 219-272-2331, Fax: 218-847-7620. 8AM-4:30PM. Access by: mail, phone, fax, in person.

Beltrami

Real Estate Recording—Beltrami County Recorder, 619 Beltrami Ave. NW, Courthouse, Bemidji, MN 56601. 218-846-7305, Fax: 218-759-4527. 8AM-4:30PM.

Felony, Misdemeanor, Civil, Eviction, Small Claims, Probate—District Court, 619 Beltrami Ave NW, Bemidji, MN 56601. 218-846-7311, Fax: 218-759-4209. 8AM-4:30PM. Access by: mail, in person.

Benton

Real Estate Recording—Benton County Recorder's Office, 531 Dewey Street, Foley, MN 56329. 612-968-6254. 8AM-4:30PM.

Felony, Misdemeanor, Civil, Eviction, Small Claims, Probate—7th Judicial District Court, 615 Highway 23, PO Box 189, Foley, MN 563290189. 330-627-5049, Fax: 320-968-5353. 8AM-4:30PM. Access by: mail, in person.

Big Stone

Real Estate Recording—Big Stone County Recorder, Courthouse, 20 SE 2nd St. Ortonville, MN 56278. 612-839-3445, Fax: 320-839-2308. 8AM-4:30PM.

Felony, Misdemeanor, Civil, Eviction, Small Claims, Probate—8th Judicial District Court, 20 SE 2nd St, Ortonville, MN 56278. 330-448-1726, Fax: 320-839-2537. 8AM-4:30PM. Access by: mail, in person.

Blue Earth

Real Estate Recording—Blue Earth County Recorder, 204 South 5th Street, Mankato, MN 56001. 507-389-8327, Fax: 507-389-8808.

Felony, Misdemeanor, Civil, Eviction, Small Claims, Probate—5th Judicial District Court, 204 S 5th St (PO Box 0347), Mankato, MN 56002-0347. 507-389-8310, Fax: 507-389-8437. 8AM-5PM. Access by: mail, fax, in person.

Brown

Real Estate Recording—Brown County Recorder, 14 South State Street, New Ulm, MN 56073. 507-359-7900, Fax: 507-359-1430. 8AM-5PM.

Felony, Misdemeanor, Civil, Eviction, Small Claims, Probate—5th Judicial District Court, PO Box 248, New Ulm, MN 56073-0248. 507-233-6660, Fax: 507-359-1430. 8AM-5PM. Access by: mail, in person.

Carlton

Real Estate Recording—Carlton County Recorder, Courthouse, 301 Walnut St. Carlton, MN 55718. 218-634-2361, Fax: 218-384-9157. 8AM-4PM.

Felony, Misdemeanor, Civil, Eviction, Small Claims, Probate—6th Judicial District Court, PO Box 190, Carlton, MN 55718. 218-634-1451, Fax: 218-384-9182. 8AM-4PM. Access by: mail, in person.

Carver

Real Estate Recording—Carver County Recorder, Carver County Govt Center, Admin Bldg, 600 East Fourth St, Chaska, MN 55318. 612-361-1980, Fax: 612-361-1931. 8AM-4:30PM.

Felony, Misdemeanor, Civil, Eviction, Small Claims, Probate—1st Judicial District Court, 600 E 4th St, Chaska, MN 55318. 612-361-1420, Fax: 612-361-1491. 8AM-4:30PM. Access by: mail, phone, in person.

Cass

Real Estate Recording—Cass County Recorder, Courthouse, 300 Minnesota Ave. Walker, MN 56484. 218-685-4825, Fax: 218-547-2440. 8AM-4:30PM.

Felony, Misdemeanor, Civil, Eviction, Small Claims, Probate—9th Judicial District Court, 300 Minnesota Ave, PO Box 3000, Walker, MN 56484. 218-694-6130, Fax: 218-547-1904. 8AM-4:30PM. Access by: mail, in person.

Chippewa

Real Estate Recording—Chippewa County Recorder, 629 No. 11th St. Montevideo, MN 56265. 320-762-3882, Fax: 320-269-7168

Felony, Misdemeanor, Civil, Eviction, Small Claims, Probate—8th Judicial District Court, PO Box 697, Montevideo, MN 56265. 320-839-2536, Fax: 320-269-7733. 8AM-4:30PM. Access by: mail, in person.

Chisago

Real Estate Recording—Chisago County Recorder, Government Center, Room/Box 277, 313 N. Main St. Center City, MN 55012., Fax: 651-213-0454. 8AM-4:30PM.

Felony, Misdemeanor, Civil, Eviction, Small Claims, Probate—10th Judicial District Court, 313 N Main St, Rm 358, Center City, MN 55012. 651-257-1300, Fax: 651-257-0359. 8AM-4:30PM. Access by: mail, in person.

Clay

Real Estate Recording—Clay County Recorder, 807 North 11th Street, Courthouse, 2nd Floor, Moorhead, MN 56560. 218-547-3300, Fax: 218-299-7500. 8AM-4:30PM.

Felony, Misdemeanor, Civil, Eviction, Small Claims, Probate—7th Judicial District Court, PO Box 280, Moorhead, MN 56561. 218-547-7200, Fax: 218-299-7307. 8AM-4:30PM. Access by: mail, in person.

Clearwater

Real Estate Recording—Clearwater County Recorder, 213 Main Avenue North, Dept. 207, Bagley, MN 56621. 218-759-4175, Fax: 218-694-6244. 8AM-4:30PM.

Felony, Misdemeanor, Civil, Eviction, Small Claims, Probate—9th Judicial District Court, 213 Main Ave North, Bagley, MN 56621. 218-759-4531, Fax: 218-694-6213. 8AM-4:30PM. Access by: mail, in person.

Cook

Real Estate Recording—Cook County Recorder, Courthouse, 411 W. 2nd St. Grand Marais, MN 55604. 218-643-4972, Fax: 218-387-2610. 8AM-4PM.

Felony, Misdemeanor, Civil, Eviction, Small Claims, Probate—6th Judicial District Court, Po Box 1150, Grand Marais, MN 55604-1150. 218-643-5112, Fax: 218-387-3007. 8AM-4PM. Access by: in person.

Cottonwood

Real Estate Recording—Cottonwood County Recorder, 900 Third Avenue, Courthouse Room 6, Windom, MN 56101. 507-831-1342, Fax: 507-831-3675. 8AM-4:30PM.

Felony, Misdemeanor, Civil, Eviction, Small Claims, Probate—5th Judicial District Court, PO Box 97, Windom, MN 56101. 507-831-4551, Fax: 507-831-1425. 8AM-4:30PM. Access by: mail, in person.

Crow Wing

Real Estate Recording—Crow Wing County Recorder, 326 Laurel Street, Courthouse, Brainerd, MN 56401. 218-935-2251, Fax: 218-825-1808. 8AM-5PM.

Felony, Misdemeanor, Civil, Eviction, Small Claims, Probate—District Court, 326 Laurel St, Brainerd, MN 56401. 219-223-2911, Fax: 218-828-2905. 8AM-5PM. Access by: mail, in person.

Dakota

Real Estate Recording—Dakota County Recorder, 1590 Highway 55, Hastings, MN 55033. 612-438-4360, Fax: 651-438-8176. 8AM-4:30PM.

Felony, Misdemeanor, Civil, Eviction, Small Claims—1st Judicial District Court-Apple Valley, 14955 Galaxie Ave, Apple Valley, MN 55124. 612-891-7256, Fax: 612-891-7285. 8AM-4:30PM. Access by: in person.

Felony, Misdemeanor, Civil, Eviction, Small Claims, Probate—1st Judicial District Court-South St Paul, 125 3rd Ave North, South St Paul, MN 55075. 651-451-1791, Fax: 651-451-3526. 8AM-4:30PM. Access by: in person.

District Court, Judicial Center, 1560 Hwy 55, Hastings, MN 55033. 651-438-8100, Fax: 651-438-8162. 8AM-4:30PM. Access by: in person.

Dodge

Real Estate Recording—Dodge County Recorder, Courthouse, 22 6th St. East, Mantorville, MN 55955. 507-635-6240, Fax: 507-635-6265. 8AM-4:30PM.

Felony, Misdemeanor, Civil, Eviction, Small Claims, Probate—3rd Judicial District Court, PO Box 96, Mantorville, MN 55955. 507-635-6260, Fax: 507-635-6271. 8AM-4:30PM. Access by: mail, fax, in person.

Douglas

Real Estate Recording—Douglas County Recorder, 305 8th Avenue West, Courthouse, Alexandria, MN 56308. 612-762-2381. 8AM-4:30PM.

Felony, Misdemeanor, Civil, Eviction, Small Claims, Probate—7th Judicial District Court, 305 8th Ave West, Alexandria, MN 56308. 330-438-0929, Fax: 320-762-8863. 8AM-4:30PM. Access by: mail, in person.

Faribault

Real Estate Recording—Faribault County Recorder, 415 North Main Street, Blue Earth, MN 56013. 507-526-6260, Fax: 507-526-6227. 8AM-4:30PM.

Felony, Misdemeanor, Civil, Eviction, Small Claims, Probate—5th Judicial District Court, PO Box 130, Blue Earth, MN 56013. 507-526-6273, Fax: 507-526-3054. 8AM-4:30PM. Access by: mail, in person.

Fillmore

Real Estate Recording—Fillmore County Recorder, 101 Fillmore St. Preston, MN 55965. 507-765-3811, Fax: 507-765-4571. 8AM-4:30PM.

Felony, Misdemeanor, Civil, Eviction, Small Claims, Probate—3rd Judicial District Court, 101 Fillmore St, PO Box 436, Preston, MN 55965. 507-765-4483, Fax: 507-765-4571. 8AM-4:30PM. Access by: mail, in person. www.courts.state.mn.us/districts/third/fillmore/index.html

Freeborn

Real Estate Recording—Freeborn County Recorder, 411 South Broadway, Court House, Albert Lea, MN 56007. 507-377-5117, Fax: 507-377-5260. 8AM-5PM.

Felony, Misdemeanor, Civil, Eviction, Small Claims, Probate—3rd Judicial District Court, 411 S Broadway, Albert Lea, MN 56007. 507-377-5153, Fax: 507-377-5262. 8AM-5PM. Access by: mail, in person.

Goodhue

Real Estate Recording—Goodhue County Recorder, 5th & West Avenue, Courthouse, Red Wing, MN 55066. 651-385-3032, Fax: 651-385-3039. 8AM-4:30PM.

Felony, Misdemeanor, Civil, Eviction, Small Claims, Probate—1st Judicial District Court, PO Box 408, Rm 310, Red Wing, MN 55066. 651-385-3051, Fax: 651-385-3065. 8AM-4:30PM. Access by: mail, in person.

Grant

Real Estate Recording—Grant County Recorder, 10th Second Street NE, Courthouse, Elbow Lake, MN 56531., Fax: 218-685-4521.

Felony, Misdemeanor, Civil, Eviction, Small Claims, Probate—8th Judicial District Court, 10 2nd St NE, Elbow Lake, MN 56531. 218-749-7106. 8AM-4PM. Access by: mail, in person.

Hennepin

Real Estate Recording—Hennepin County Recorder, 300 South 6th Street, 8-A Government Center, Minneapolis, MN 55487. 8AM-4:30PM.

Misdemeanor—4th Judicial District Court-Division 4 Southdale Area, 7009 York Ave South, Edina, MN 55435. 612-830-4905, Fax: 612-830-4993. 8AM-4:30PM. Access by: in person. www.co.hennepin.mn.us

Misdemeanor, Eviction, Small Claims—4th Judicial District Court-Division 2 Brookdale Area, 6125 Shingle Creek Pkwy, Brooklyn Center, MN 55430. 612-569-2799, Fax: 612-569-3697. 7:45AM-4:30PM. Access by: mail, in person. www.co.hennepin.mn.us

4th Judicial District Court-Division 3 Ridgedale Area, 12601 Ridgedale Dr, Minnetonka, MN 55305. 612-541-8500, Fax: 612-541-6297. 8AM-4:30PM. Access by: mail, in person. www.co.hennepin.mn.us

Civil—4th Judicial District Court-Division 1, 1251 C Government Center, 300 S 6th St, Minneapolis, MN 55487. 612-348-2611, Fax: 612-348-6099. 8AM-4:30PM. Access by: mail, fax, in person. www.co.hennepin.mn.us/courts/court.htm

Felony, Misdemeanor—4th Judicial District Court-Division 1, 1153 C Government Center, 300 S 6th St, Minneapolis, MN 55487. 612-348-2611, Fax: 612-348-6099. 8AM-4:30PM. Access by: mail, fax, in person. www.co.hennepin.mn.us

Probate—4th Judicial District Court-Division 1, C400 Government Center, 300 S 6th St, Minneapolis, MN 55487. 612-348-3244, Fax: 612-348-5799. 7AM-5PM. Access by: mail, fax, in person.

Houston

Real Estate Recording—Houston County Recorder, 304 South Marshall Street, Caledonia, MN 55921. 507-724-5815, Fax: 507-724-2647. 8:30AM-5PM.

Felony, Misdemeanor, Civil, Eviction, Small Claims, Probate—3rd Judicial District Court, 304 S Marshall, Caledonia, MN 55921. 507-724-5806, Fax: 507-724-5550. 8:30AM-5PM. Access by: mail, fax, in person.

Hubbard

Real Estate Recording—Hubbard County Recorder, Courthouse, Park Rapids, MN 56470. 218-828-3953. 8AM-4:30PM.

Felony, Misdemeanor, Civil, Eviction, Small Claims, Probate—9th Judicial District Court, 301 Court St, Park Rapids, MN 56470. 218-784-7131, Fax: 218-732-0137. 8AM-4:30PM. Access by: mail, in person.

Isanti

Real Estate Recording—Isanti County Recorder, Courthouse, Cambridge, MN 55008. 8AM-4:30PM.

Felony, Misdemeanor, Civil, Eviction, Small Claims, Probate—10th Judicial District Court, 555 18th Ave SW, Cambridge, MN 55008-9386. 612-689-2292, Fax: 612-689-8340. 8AM-4:30PM. Access by: mail, in person.

Itasca

Real Estate Recording—Itasca County Recorder, 123 NE 4th Street, Grand Rapids, MN 55744., Fax: 218-327-0689

Felony, Misdemeanor, Civil, Eviction, Small Claims, Probate—9th Judicial District Court, 123 4th St NE, Grand Rapids, MN 55744-2600. 218-631-7634, Fax: 218-327-2897. 8:30AM-4PM. Access by: mail, in person.

Jackson

Real Estate Recording—Jackson County Recorder, 405 4th St. Jackson, MN 56143. 507-847-2684, Fax: 507-847-4718.

Felony, Misdemeanor, Civil, Eviction, Small Claims, Probate—5th Judicial District Court, PO Box 177, Jackson, MN 56143. 507-847-4400, Fax: 507-847-5433. 8:30AM-4:30PM. Access by: mail, fax, in person.

Kanabec

Real Estate Recording—Kanabec County Recorder, 18 North Vine Street, Mora, MN 55051. 330-385-5151, Fax: 320-679-6431. 8AM-4:30PM.

Felony, Misdemeanor, Civil, Eviction, Small Claims, Probate—10th Judicial District Court, 18 North Vine, Mora, MN 55051. 330-424-5326, Fax: 320-679-6411. 8AM-4PM. Access by: in person.

Kandiyohi

Real Estate Recording—Kandiyohi County Recorder, 400 Benson Ave. SW, Willmar, MN 56201., Fax: 320-231-6284.

Felony, Misdemeanor, Civil, Eviction, Small Claims, Probate—8th Judicial District Court, 505 Becker Ave SW, Willmar, MN 56201. 320-732-7800, Fax: 320-231-6276. 8AM-4:30PM. Access by: mail, in person.

Kittson

Real Estate Recording—Kittson County Recorder, Courthouse, Hallock, MN 56728. 219-235-9635, Fax: 218-843-2020. 8:30AM-4:30PM.

Felony, Misdemeanor, Civil, Eviction, Small Claims, Probate—9th Judicial District Court, PO Box 39, Hallock, MN 56728. 219-248-3102, Fax: 218-843-3634. 8:30AM-4:30PM. Access by: mail, fax, in person.

Koochiching

Real Estate Recording—Koochiching County Recorder, Courthouse, 715 4th St. International Falls, MN 56649., Fax: 218-283-6434. 8AM-5PM.

Felony, Misdemeanor, Civil, Eviction, Small Claims, Probate—9th Judicial District Court, Court House, 715 4th St, International Falls, MN 56649. 218-463-2541, Fax: 218-283-6262. 8AM-5PM. Access by: mail, fax, in person.

Lac qui Parle

Real Estate Recording—Lac qui Parle County Recorder, 600 6th Street, Courthouse, Madison, MN 56256. 330-287-5650.

Felony, Misdemeanor, Civil, Eviction, Small Claims, Probate—8th Judicial District Court, PO Box 36, Madison, MN 56256. 330-287-5590, Fax: 320-598-3915. 8:30AM-4:30PM. Access by: mail, fax, in person.

Lake

Real Estate Recording—Lake County Recorder, 601 Third Avenue, Two Harbors, MN 55616., Fax: 218-834-8365. 8AM-4:30PM.

Felony, Misdemeanor, Civil, Eviction, Small Claims, Probate—6th Judicial District Court, 601 3rd Ave, Two Harbors, MN 55616. 219-235-9531, Fax: 218-834-8397. 8AM-4:30PM. Access by: mail, fax, in person.

Lake of the Woods

Real Estate Recording—Lake of the Woods County Recorder, 206 Southeast Eighth Avenue, Baudette, MN 56623. 218-732-3573, Fax: 218-634-2509. 7:30AM-4PM.

Felony, Misdemeanor, Civil, Eviction, Small Claims, Probate—9th Judicial District Court, PO Box 808, Baudette, MN 56623. 218-726-2380, Fax: 218-634-9444. 7:30AM-4PM. Access by: mail, fax, in person.

Le Sueur

Real Estate Recording—Le Sueur County Recorder, 88 South Park Avenue, Courthouse, Le Center, MN 56057., Fax: 507-357-6375. 8AM-4:30PM.

Felony, Misdemeanor, Civil, Eviction, Small Claims, Probate—1st Judicial District Court, 88 S Park Ave, Le Center, MN 56057. 507-357-2251, Fax: 507-357-6375. 8AM-4:30PM. Access by: mail, fax, in person.

Lincoln

Real Estate Recording—Lincoln County Recorder, 319 North Rebecca, Ivanhoe, MN 56142. 507-694-1550, Fax: 507-694-1198.

Felony, Misdemeanor, Civil, Eviction, Small Claims, Probate—5th Judicial District Court, PO Box 15, Ivanhoe, MN 56142-0015. 507-694-1355, Fax: 507-694-1717. 8:30AM-Noon,1-4:30PM. Access by: mail, fax, in person.

Lyon

Real Estate Recording—Lyon County Recorder, 607 West Main Street, Marshall, MN 56258., Fax: 507-537-6091. 8:30AM-4:30PM.

Felony, Misdemeanor, Civil, Eviction, Small Claims, Probate—5th Judicial District Court, 607 W Main, Marshall, MN 56258. 507-537-6734, Fax: 507-537-6150. 8:30AM-4:30PM. Access by: mail, in person.

Mahnomen

Real Estate Recording—Mahnomen County Recorder, Courthouse, 311 N. Main, Mahnomen, MN 56557., Fax: 218-935-5946. 8AM-4:30PM M-T.

Felony, Misdemeanor, Civil, Eviction, Small Claims, Probate—9th Judicial District Court, PO Box 459, Mahnomen, MN 56557. 219-358-4860, Fax: 218-935-2851. 8AM-4:30PM. Access by: mail, in person.

Marshall

Real Estate Recording—Marshall County Recorder, 208 East Colvin, Warren, MN 56762. 218-834-8330, Fax: 218-745-4343. 8AM-4:30PM.

Felony, Misdemeanor, Civil, Eviction, Small Claims, Probate—9th Judicial District Court, 208 E Colvin, Warren, MN 56762. 218-843-3432, Fax: 218-745-4343. 8AM-4:30PM. Access by: mail, in person.

Martin

Real Estate Recording—Martin County Recorder, 201 Lake Avenue, Courthouse, Fairmont, MN 56031. 507-238-3211, Fax: 507-238-3259. 8AM-5PM.

Felony, Misdemeanor, Civil, Eviction, Small Claims, Probate—5th Judicial District Court, 201 Lake Ave, Rm 304, Fairmont, MN 56031. 507-238-3214, Fax: 507-238-1913. 8:30AM-4:30PM. Access by: mail, in person.

McLeod

Real Estate Recording—McLeod County Recorder, 2391 N. Hennepin Ave. North Complex, Glencoe, MN 55336. 330-533-3643, Fax: 320-864-1295. 8AM-4:30PM.

Felony, Misdemeanor, Civil, Eviction, Small Claims, Probate—1st Judicial District Court, 830 E 11th, Glencoe, MN 55336. 330-627-4886. 8AM-4:30PM. Access by: mail, in person.

Meeker

Real Estate Recording—Meeker County Recorder, 325 North Sibley Avenue, Courthouse, Litchfield, MN 55355. 330-426-3774, Fax: 320-693-5444. 8AM-4:30PM.

Felony, Misdemeanor, Civil, Eviction, Small Claims, Probate—8th Judicial District Court, 325 N Sibley, Litchfield, MN 55355. 330-424-7777, Fax: 320-693-5254. 8AM-4:30PM. Access by: mail, fax, in person.

Mille Lacs

Real Estate Recording—Mille Lacs County Recorder, 635 2nd Street S.E. Milaca, MN 56353., Fax: 320-983-8388. 8AM-4:30PM.

Felony, Misdemeanor, Civil, Eviction, Small Claims, Probate—7th Judicial District Court, Courthouse, Milaca, MN 56353. 330-637-5023, Fax: 320-983-8384. 8AM-4:30PM. Access by: mail, in person.

Morrison

Real Estate Recording—Morrison County Recorder, Administration Building, 213 SE 1st Ave. Little Falls, MN 56345. 330-332-0297, Fax: 320-632-0141. 8AM-4:30PM.

Felony, Misdemeanor, Civil, Eviction, Small Claims, Probate—7th Judicial District Court, 213 SE 1st Ave, Little Falls, MN 56345. 330-335-1596, Fax: 320-632-0340. 8AM-4:30PM. Access by: mail, fax, in person.

Mower

Real Estate Recording—Mower County Recorder, 201 First Street NE, Austin, MN 55912., Fax: 507-437-9471. 8AM-5PM.

Felony, Misdemeanor, Civil, Eviction, Small Claims, Probate—Mower County District Court, 201 1st St NE, Austin, MN 55912. 507-437-9465, Fax: 507-437-9471. 8AM-5PM. Access by: mail, in person.

Murray

Real Estate Recording—Murray County Recorder, 28th & Broadway Avenue, Slayton, MN 56172. 507-836-6148, Fax: 507-836-8904. 8:30AM-Noon, 1-5PM.

Felony, Misdemeanor, Civil, Eviction, Small Claims, Probate—5th Judicial District Court, PO Box 57, Slayton, MN 56172-0057. 507-836-6163, Fax: 507-836-6019. 8AM-5PM. Access by: mail, fax, in person.

Nicollet

Real Estate Recording—Nicollet County Recorder, 501 South Minnesota Avenue, St. Peter, MN 56082. 507-931-6800, Fax: 507-931-9220. 8AM-5PM.

Felony, Misdemeanor, Civil, Eviction, Small Claims, Probate—5th Judicial District Court, PO Box 496, St Peter, MN 56082. 507-931-6800, Fax: 507-931-4278. 8AM-5PM. Access by: mail, in person.

District Court-Branch, PO Box 2055, North Mankato, MN 56002-2055. 507-625-3149, Fax: 507-345-1273. 8AM-5PM. Access by: mail, in person. Special note: Phone number for traffic is 507-625-7795.

Nobles

Real Estate Recording—Nobles County Recorder, 315 10th Street, Nobles County Government Center, Worthington, MN 56187. 507-372-8231, Fax: 507-372-8223. 8AM-4:30PM.

Felony, Misdemeanor, Civil, Eviction, Small Claims, Probate—5th Judicial District Court, PO Box 547, Worthington, MN 56187. 507-372-8263, Fax: 507-372-4994. 8AM-5PM. Access by: mail, in person.

Norman

Real Estate Recording—Norman County Recorder, 16 East 3rd Avenue, Ada, MN 56510. 218-927-7325, Fax: 218-784-2399. 8:30AM-4:30PM.

Felony, Misdemeanor, Civil, Eviction, Small Claims, Probate—9th Judicial District Court, PO Box 272, Ada, MN 56510-0146. 218-927-7350, Fax: 218-784-3110. 8:30AM-4:30PM. Access by: mail, in person.

Olmsted

Real Estate Recording—Olmsted County Recorder, 151 4th St. SE, Rochester, MN 55904., Fax: 507-287-7186. 8AM-5PM.

Felony, Misdemeanor, Civil, Eviction, Small Claims, Probate—Olmsted County District Court, 151 4th St SE, Rochester, MN 55904. 507-285-8210, Fax: 507-285-8996. 8AM-5PM. Access by: mail, in person.

Otter Tail

Real Estate Recording—Otter Tail County Recorder, Junius Avenue, Courthouse, Fergus Falls, MN 56537. 8AM-5PM.

Felony, Misdemeanor, Civil, Eviction, Small Claims, Probate—Otter Tail County District Court, PO Box 417, Fergus Falls, MN 56538-0417. 218-828-3959, Fax: 218-739-4983. 8AM-5PM. Access by: mail, in person.

Pennington

Real Estate Recording—Pennington County Recorder, 1st & Main Street, Courthouse, Thief River Falls, MN 56701. 218-745-4831, Fax: 218-683-7026. 8AM-4:30PM.

Felony, Misdemeanor, Civil, Eviction, Small Claims, Probate—9th Judicial District Court, PO Box 619, Thief River Falls, MN 56701. 218-745-4921, Fax: 218-681-0907. 8AM-4:30PM. Access by: mail, in person.

Pine

Real Estate Recording—Pine County Recorder, Courthouse, 315 Sixth St. Suite 3, Pine City, MN 55063. 330-297-3636, Fax: 320-629-7319. 8AM-4:30PM.

Felony, Misdemeanor, Civil, Eviction, Small Claims, Probate—10th Judicial District Court, 315 6th St, Pine City, MN 55063. 330-297-3586. 8AM-4:30PM. Access by: mail, in person.

Pipestone

Real Estate Recording—Pipestone County Recorder, 416 S. Hiawatha Ave. Pipestone, MN 56164. 507-825-4588, Fax: 507-825-6741. 8AM-4:30PM.

Felony, Misdemeanor, Civil, Eviction, Small Claims, Probate—5th Judicial District Court, 416 S Hiawatha Ave (PO Box 337), Pipestone, MN 56164. 507-825-4550, Fax: 507-825-3256. 8:30AM-4:30PM. Access by: mail, in person.

Polk

Real Estate Recording—Polk County Recorder, 612 Broadway, Courthouse, Suite 213, Crookston, MN 56716., Fax: 218-281-2204.

Felony, Misdemeanor, Civil, Eviction, Small Claims, Probate—9th Judicial District Court, Court Administrator, 612 N Broadway #301, Crookston, MN 56716. 218-463-1215, Fax: 218-281-2204. 8AM-4:30PM. Access by: mail, in person.

Pope

Real Estate Recording—Pope County Recorder, 130 East Minnesota, Glenwood, MN 56334., Fax: 320-634-3087.

Felony, Misdemeanor, Civil, Eviction, Small Claims, Probate—8th Judicial District Court, 130 E Minnesota Ave (PO Box 195), Glenwood, MN 56334. 330-364-4491. 8AM-4:30PM. Access by: mail, in person.

Ramsey

Real Estate Recording—Ramsey County Recorder, 50 West Kellogg Blvd. Suite 812 RCGC-W, St. Paul, MN 55102.

Felony, Misdemeanor, Civil, Probate—2nd Judicial District Court, 15 W Kellogg, St Paul, MN 55101., Fax: 651-266-8278. 8AM-4:30PM. Access by: mail, in person.

Misdemeanor—2nd Judicial District Court-Maplewood Area, 2785 White Bear Ave, Maplewood, MN 55109. 651-777-9111, Fax: 651-777-3970. 8AM-4:30PM. Access by: in person.

2nd Judicial District Court-New Brighton Area, 803 5th Ave NW, New Brighton, MN 55112. 651-636-7101, Fax: 651-635-0722. 8AM-4:30PM. Access by: mail, fax, in person.

Red Lake

Real Estate Recording—Red Lake County Recorder, 124 Main Avenue North, Red Lake Falls, MN 56750. 218-384-4281, Fax: 218-253-4894. 9AM-5PM.

Felony, Misdemeanor, Civil, Eviction, Small Claims, Probate—9th Judicial District Court, PO Box 339, Red Lake Falls, MN 56750. 218-387-2282, Fax: 218-253-4287. 9AM-5PM. Access by: mail, in person.

Redwood

Real Estate Recording—Redwood County Recorder, Courthouse Square, Main Floor, Redwood Falls, MN 56283., Fax: 507-637-4064. 8AM-4:30PM.

Felony, Misdemeanor, Civil, Eviction, Small Claims, Probate—5th Judicial District Court, PO Box 130, Redwood Falls, MN 56283. 507-637-4020, Fax: 507-637-4021. 8AM-4:30PM. Access by: mail, in person.

Renville

Real Estate Recording—Renville County Recorder, 500 East DePue, Olivia, MN 56277. 320-843-2744. 8AM-4:30PM.

Felony, Misdemeanor, Civil, Eviction, Small Claims, Probate—8th Judicial District Court, 500 E DePue Ave, Olivia, MN 56277. 320-864-1203, Fax: 320-523-3689. 8AM-4:30PM. Access by: mail, in person.

Rice

Real Estate Recording—Rice County Recorder, 320 NW 3rd St. Suite 10, Faribault, MN 55021., Fax: 507-332-5999. 8AM-4:30PM.

Felony, Misdemeanor, Civil, Eviction, Small Claims, Probate—3rd Judicial District Court, 218 NW 3rd St, Suite 300, Faribault, MN 55021. 507-332-6107, Fax: 507-332-6199. 8AM-4:30PM. Access by: mail, in person.

Rock

Real Estate Recording—Rock County Recorder, 204 East Brown, Luverne, MN 56156., Fax: 507-283-1343. 8AM-5PM.

Felony, Misdemeanor, Civil, Eviction, Small Claims, Probate—5th Judicial District Court, PO Box 745, Luverne, MN 56156. 507-283-5020, Fax: 507-283-5017. 8AM-5PM. Access by: mail, in person.

Roseau

Real Estate Recording—Roseau County Recorder, 606 5th Ave. SW, Room 170, Roseau, MN 56751. 218-681-4044. 8AM-4:30PM.

Felony, Misdemeanor, Civil, Eviction, Small Claims, Probate—9th Judicial District Court, 606 5th Ave SW Rm 20, Roseau, MN 56751. 218-681-7023, Fax: 218-463-1889. 8AM-4:30PM. Access by: mail, in person.

Scott

Real Estate Recording—Scott County Recorder, 428 South Holmes Street, Shakopee, MN 55379. 612-496-8150, Fax: 612-496-8138. 8AM-4:30PM.

Felony, Misdemeanor, Civil, Eviction, Small Claims, Probate—1st Judicial District Court, Scott County Justice Center, 200 Fourth Ave W, Shakopee, MN 55379. 612-496-8200, Fax: 612-496-8211. 8AM-4:30PM. Access by: mail, in person.

Sherburne

Real Estate Recording—Sherburne County Recorder, 13880 Highway 10, Elk River, MN 55330. 612-438-0575, Fax: 612-241-2995. 8AM-5PM.

Felony, Misdemeanor, Civil, Eviction, Small Claims, Probate—10th Judicial District Court, Sherburne County Government Center, 13880 Hwy #10, Elkriver, MN 55330-4608. 612-241-2800, Fax: 612-241-2816. 8AM-5PM. Access by: mail, in person.

Sibley

Real Estate Recording—Sibley County Recorder, 400 Court Street, Room 26, Gaylord, MN 55334. 507-237-2820, Fax: 507-237-4062. 8AM-5PM.

Felony, Misdemeanor, Civil, Eviction, Small Claims, Probate—1st Judicial District Court, PO Box 867, Gaylord, MN 55334. 507-237-4051, Fax: 507-237-4062. 8AM-5PM. Access by: mail, in person.

St. Louis

Real Estate Recording—St. Louis County Recorder, 100 North 5th Avenue West, Room 101, Duluth, MN 55802. 218-784-2101, Fax: 218-725-5052. 8AM-4:30PM.

Felony, Misdemeanor, Civil, Eviction, Small Claims, Probate—6th Judicial District Court, 100 N 5th Ave W, Rm 320, Duluth, MN 55802-1294., Fax: 218-726-2473. 8AM-4:30PM. Access by: mail, in person. Special note: All three St Louis County courts can access computer records for the county and direct you to the appropriate court to get the physical file.

6th Judicial District Court-Hibbing Branch, 1810 12th Ave East, Hibbing, MN 55746. 218-387-3000, Fax: 218-262-0219. 8AM-4:30PM. Access by: mail, in person. Special note: All three St Louis County courts can access computer records for the county and direct you to the appropriate court for the physical file.

6th Judicial District Court-Virginia Branch, 300 S 5th Ave, Virginia, MN 55792. 218-843-3632, Fax: 218-749-7109. 8AM-4:30PM. Access by: mail, in person. Special note: All three St Louis County courts can access computer records for the county and direct you to the appropriate court for the physical files.

Stearns

Real Estate Recording—Stearns County Recorder, 705 Courthouse Square, Administration Center, Room 131, St. Cloud, MN 56303. 330-364-8811, Fax: 320-656-3916. 8AM-4:30PM.

Felony, Misdemeanor, Civil, Eviction, Probate—Stearns County District Court, PO Box 1168, St Cloud, MN 56302. 330-364-8811, Fax: 320-656-3626. 8AM-4:30PM. Access by: mail, in person.

Steele

Real Estate Recording—Steele County Recorder, 630 Florence Ave. Owatonna, MN 55060. 507-451-8040, Fax: 507-444-7470. 8AM-5PM.

Felony, Misdemeanor, Civil, Eviction, Small Claims, Probate—3rd Judicial District Court, PO Box 487, Owatonna, MN 55060. 507-444-7700, Fax: 507-444-7491. 8AM-5PM. Access by: mail, in person.

Stevens

Real Estate Recording—Stevens County Recorder, 5th & Colorado, Morris, MN 56267. 612-589-7418, Fax: 320-589-2036. 8:30AM-4:30PM (Summer Hours 8AM-4PM).

Felony, Misdemeanor, Civil, Eviction, Small Claims, Probate—8th Judicial District Court, PO Box 530, Morris, MN 56267. 330-287-5450, Fax: 320-589-7288. 8AM-4:30PM (8AM-4PM Summer hours). Access by: mail, in person.

Swift

Real Estate Recording—Swift County Recorder, 301 14th Street North, Benson, MN 56215., Fax: 320-843-2275. 8AM-4:30PM.

Felony, Misdemeanor, Civil, Eviction, Small Claims, Probate—8th Judicial District Court, PO Box 110, Benson, MN 56215. 330-489-3203, Fax: 320-843-4124. 8AM-4:30PM. Access by: mail, phone, in person.

Todd

Real Estate Recording—Todd County Recorder, 215 First Avenue South, Suite 300, Long Prairie, MN 56347. 612-732-4471, Fax: 320-732-4001. 8AM-4:30PM.

Felony, Misdemeanor, Civil, Eviction, Small Claims, Probate—7th Judicial District Court, 221 1st Ave South, Long Prairie, MN 56347. 330-438-0795, Fax: 320-732-2506. 8AM-4:30PM. Access by: mail, in person.

Traverse

Real Estate Recording—Traverse County Recorder, Courthouse, 702 2nd Ave. North, Wheaton, MN 56296. 612-563-4616, Fax: 320-563-4424. 8AM-4:30PM.

Felony, Misdemeanor, Civil, Eviction, Small Claims, Probate—8th Judicial District Court, 702 2nd Ave N (PO Box 867), Wheaton, MN 56296. 320-864-5551, Fax: 320-563-4311. 8AM-Noon, 12:30-4:30PM. Access by: mail, in person.

Wabasha

Real Estate Recording—Wabasha County Recorder, 625 Jefferson Avenue, Wabasha, MN 55981. 651-565-3669, Fax: 651-565-2774. 8AM-4PM.

Felony, Misdemeanor, Civil, Eviction, Small Claims, Probate—3rd Judicial District Court, 625 Jefferson Ave, Wabasha, MN 55981. 651-565-3579, Fax: 651-565-2774. 8AM-4PM. Access by: mail, in person.

Wadena

Real Estate Recording—Wadena County Recorder, 415 South Jefferson, Courthouse, Wadena, MN 56482., Fax: 218-631-7652. 8AM-4:30PM.

Felony, Misdemeanor, Civil, Eviction, Small Claims, Probate—7th Judicial District Court, County Courthouse, 415 South Jefferson St, Wadena, MN 56482. 218-694-6177, Fax: 218-631-7635. 8AM-4:30PM. Access by: mail, in person.

Waseca

Real Estate Recording—Waseca County Recorder, 307 North State Street, Waseca, MN 56093., Fax: 507-835-0633.

Felony, Misdemeanor, Civil, Eviction, Small Claims, Probate—3rd Judicial District Court, 307 N State St, Waseca, MN 56093. 507-835-0540, Fax: 507-835-0633. 8AM-4:30PM. Access by: mail, in person.

Washington

Real Estate Recording—Washington County Recorder, 14900 North 61st Street, P.O. Box 6, Stillwater, MN 55082. 651-430-6175, Fax: 651-430-6753. 8AM-4:30PM.

Felony, Misdemeanor, Civil, Eviction, Small Claims, Probate—10th Judicial District Court, 14949 62nd St North, PO Box 3802, Stillwater, MN 55082-3802. 651-430-6263, Fax: 651-430-6300. 7:30AM-5PM. Access by: mail, in person.

Watonwan

Real Estate Recording—Watonwan County Recorder, Courthouse, St. James, MN 56081. 507-375-1213.

Felony, Misdemeanor, Civil, Eviction, Small Claims, Probate—5th Judicial District Court, PO Box 518, St James, MN 56081. 507-375-1236, Fax: 507-375-5010. 8AM-5PM. Access by: mail, fax, in person.

Wilkin

Real Estate Recording—Wilkin County Recorder, 300 South 5th Street, Courthouse, Breckenridge, MN 56520. 218-739-2271, Fax: 218-643-1617. 8AM-4:30PM.

Felony, Misdemeanor, Civil, Eviction, Small Claims, Probate—8th Judicial District Court, PO Box 219, Breckenridge, MN 56520. 218-732-4348, Fax: 218-643-5733. 8AM-4:30PM. Access by: mail, in person.

Winona

Real Estate Recording—Winona County Recorder, 171 West 3rd Street, Winona, MN 55987. 507-457-6450, Fax: 507-457-6469. 8AM-4:30PM.

Felony, Misdemeanor, Civil, Eviction, Small Claims, Probate—3rd Judicial District Court, 171 West 3rd St, Winona, MN 55987. 507-457-6385, Fax: 507-457-6392. 8AM-4:30PM. Access by: mail, in person.

Wright

Real Estate Recording—Wright County Recorder, 10 2nd Street NW, Room 210, Buffalo, MN 55313. 612-682-7573. 8AM-4:30PM.

Felony, Misdemeanor, Civil, Eviction, Small Claims, Probate—10th Judicial District Court, 10 NW 2nd St, Room 201, Buffalo, MN 55313-1192. 612-682-7539, Fax: 612-682-7300. 8AM-4:30PM. Access by: in person.

Yellow Medicine

Real Estate Recording—Yellow Medicine County Recorder, 415 9th Avenue, Courthouse, Granite Falls, MN 56241. 320-968-5205, Fax: 320-564-3670. 8AM-4PM.

Felony, Misdemeanor, Civil, Eviction, Small Claims, Probate—8th Judicial District Court, 415 9th Ave, Granite Falls, MN 56241. 320-983-8313, Fax: 320-564-4435. 8AM-4PM. Access by: mail, in person.

Federal Courts

US District Court

Duluth Division Clerk's Office, 417 Federal Bldg, Duluth, MN 55802218-529-3500 Fax: 218-720-5622 Counties: Aitkin, Becker*, Beltrami*, Benton, Big Stone*, Carlton, Cass, Clay*, Clearwater*, Cook, Crow Wing, Douglas*, Grant*, Hubbard*, Itasca, Kanabec, Kittson*, Koochiching, Lake, Lake of the Woods*, Mahnomen*, Marshall*, Mille Lacs, Morrison, Norman*, Otter*,Tail, Pennington*, Pine, Polk*, Pope*, Red Lake*, Roseau*, Stearns*, Stevens*, St. Louis, Todd*, Traverse*, Wadena*, Wilkin*. From March 1, 1995, to 1998, cases from the counties marked with an asterisk (*) were heard here.Before and after that period, cases were and are allocated between St. Paul and Minneapolis.

Minneapolis Division Court Clerk, Room 202, 300 S 4th St, Minneapolis, MN 55415612-664-5000 Counties: All counties not covered by the Duluth Division. Cases are allocated between Minneapolis and St Paul.

St Paul Division 708 Federal Bldg, 316 N Robert, St Paul, MN 55101651-290-3212 Fax: 612-290-3817 Counties: All counties not covered by the Duluth Division. Cases are allocated between Minneapolis and St Paul.

US Bankruptcy Court

Duluth Division 416 US Courthouse, 515 W 1st St, Duluth, MN 55802218-720-5253 Counties: Aitkin, Benton, Carlton, Cass, Cook, Crow Wing, Itasca, Kanabec, Koochiching, Lake, Mille Lacs, Morrison, Pine, St. Louis. A petition commencing Chapter 11 or 12 proceedings may initially be filed in any of the four divisons, but may be assigned toanother division. www.mnb.uscourts.gov

Fergus Falls Division 204 US Courthouse, 118 S Mill St, Fergus Falls, MN 56537218-739-4671 Counties: Becker, Beltrami, Big Stone, Clay, Clearwater, Douglas, Grant, Hubbard, Kittson, Lake of the Woods, Mahnomen, Marshall, Norman, Otter Tail, Pennington, Polk, Pope, Red Lake, Roseau, Stearns, Stevens, Todd, Traverse, Wadena, Wilkin. A petition commencingChapter 11 or 12 proceedings may be filed initially in any of the four divisions, but may then be assigned to another division. www.mnb.uscourts.gov

Minneapolis Division 301 US Courthouse, 300 S 4th St, Minneapolis, MN 55415612-664-5200, Record Room: 612-664-5209 Counties: Anoka, Carver, Chippewa, Hennepin, Isanti, Kandiyohi, McLeod, Meeker, Renville, Sherburne, Swift, Wright. Initial petitions for Chapter 11 or 12 may be filed initially at any of the four divisions, but may then be assigned to a judge in another division. www.mnb.uscourts.gov

St Paul Division 200 Federal Bldg, 316 N Robert St, St Paul, MN 55101651-290-3184 Counties: Blue Earth, Brown, Chisago, Cottonwood, Dakota, Dodge, Faribault, Fillmore, Freeborn, Goodhue, Houston, Jackson, Lac qui Parle, Le Sueur, Lincoln, Lyon, Martin, Mower, Murray, Nicollet, Nobles, Olmsted, Pipestone, Ramsey, Redwood, Rice, Rock, Scott,Sibley, Steele, Wabasha, Waseca, Washington, Watonwan, Winona, Yellow Medicine. Cases from Benton, Kanabec, Mille Lacs, Morrison and Pine may also be heard here. A petition commencing Chapter 11 or 12 proceedings may be filed initially with any of thefour divisions, but may then be assigned to another division. www.mnb.uscourts.gov

Mississippi

Attorney General's Office

PO Box 220   601-359-3680
Jackson, MS 39201-0220   Fax: 601-359-3796
www.ago.state.ms.us

Governor's Office

PO Box 139   601-359-3150
Jackson, MS 39205-0139   Fax: 601-359-3741
www.govoff.state.ms.us

State Archives

PO Box 571   601-359-6850
Jackson, MS 39205-0571   Fax: 601-359-6964
www.mdah.state.ms.us

Capital: Jackson
                                 Hinds County

Time Zone: CST

Number of Counties: 82

Population: 2,730,501

Web Site: www.state.ms.us

Search Unclaimed Property Online
www.treasury.state.ms.us/ claim.htm

State Agencies

Criminal Records

Records not available from state agency.

Mississippi does not have a central state repository of criminal records. They suggest that you obtain information at county level.

Corporation Records
Limited Partnership Records
Limited Liability Company Records
Trademarks/Servicemarks

Corporation Commission, Secretary of State, PO Box 136, Jackson, MS 39205-0136 (202 N Congress, Suite 601, Jackson, MS 39201); 601-359-1633, 800-256-3494; Fax: 601-359-1607; 8AM-5PM. Access by: mail, phone, fax, in person, online. www.sos.state.ms.us

Sales Tax Registrations

Revenue Bureau, Sales Tax Division, PO Box 22828, Jackson, MS 39225-2828 (1577 Springridge Rd, Raymond, MS 39154); 601-923-7000; Fax: 601-923-7300; 8AM-5PM. Access by: mail, phone, in person. www.mstc.state.ms.us

Uniform Commercial Code
Federal Tax Liens

UCC Division, Secretary of State, PO Box 136, Jackson, MS 39205-0136 (202 N Congress St, Suite 601, Magnolia Federal Bank Bldg, Jackson, MS 39201); 601-359-1350, 800-256-3494; Fax: 601-359-1607; 8AM-5PM. Access by: mail, phone, in person, online. www.sos.state.ms.us

State Tax Liens

Records not available from state agency.

All state tax liens are filed at the county level.

Workers' Compensation Records

Workers Compensation Commission, PO Box 5300, Jackson, MS 39296-5300 (1428 Lakeland Dr, Jackson, MS 39216); 601-987-4200; 8AM-5PM. Access by: mail. www.mscc.state.ms.us

Birth Certificates

State Department of Health, Vital Statistics & Records, PO Box 1700, Jackson, MS 39215-1700 (2423 N State St, Jackson, MS 39216); 601-576-7960, 601-576-7988; Fax: 601-576-7505; 7:30AM-5PM. Access by: mail, phone, in person. www.msdh.state.ms.us/phs/index.htm

Death Records

State Department of Health, Vital Statistics & Records, PO Box 1700, Jackson, MS 39215-1700; 601-576-7960, 601-576-7988; Fax: 601-576-7505; 7:30AM-5PM. Access by: mail, phone, in person. www.msdh.state.ms.us/phs/index.htm

Marriage Certificates

State Department of Health, Vital Statistics & Records, PO Box 1700, Jackson, MS 39215-1700; 601-576-7960, 601-576-7988; Fax: 601-576-7505; 7:30AM-5PM. Access by: mail, phone, in person. www.msdh.state.ms.us/phs/index.htm

Divorce Records

State Department of Health, Vital Statistics, PO Box 1700, Jackson, MS 39215-1700; 601-576-7960, 601-576-7988; Fax: 601-576-7505; 7:30AM-5PM. Access by: mail, phone, in person. www.msdh.state.ms.us/phs/index.htm

Driver Records

Department of Public Safety, Driver Records, PO Box 958, Jackson, MS 39205 (1900 E Woodrow Wilson, Jackson, MS 39216); 601-987-1274; 8AM-5PM. Access by: mail, online.

Vehicle Ownership
Vehicle Identification

Mississippi State Tax Commission, Registration Department, PO Box 1140, Jackson, MS 39215 (1577 Springridge Rd, Raymond, MS 39154); 601-923-7143; Fax: 601-923-7134; 8AM-5PM. Access by: mail.

Accident Reports

Safety Responsibility, Accident Records, PO Box 958, Jackson, MS 39205 (1900 E Woodrow Wilson, Jackson, MS 39205); 601-987-1278; Fax: 601-987-1261; 8AM-5PM. Access by: mail.

Boat & Vessel Ownership
Boat & Vessel Registration

Wildlife, Fisheries, & Parks Dept, PO Box 451, Jackson, MS 39205; 601-364-2037; Fax: 601-364-2048; 8AM-5PM. www.mdwfp.com

Legislation-Current/Pending
Legislation-Passed

Mississippi Legislature, Documents, PO Box 1018, Jackson, MS 39215 (New Capitol, 3rd Floor, Jackson, MS 39215);, 601-359-3229 Senate, 601-359-3358 House; 8AM-5PM. Access by: mail, phone, in person, online. www.als.state.ms.us

Voter Registration

Records not available from state agency.

Records are open to the public, but must be obtained at the county level. However, MS is going to a statewide system sometime in late 1999 or early 2000.

GED Certificates

State Board for Community & Jr Colleges, GED Office, 3825 Ridgewood Rd, Jackson, MS 39211; 601-982-6338; Fax: 601-982-6363; 8AM-5PM M-F. www.sbcjc.cc.ms.us

Hunting License Information
Fishing License Information

Department of Wildlife, Fisheries & Parks, 2906 N State St, 3rd Floor, Jackson, MS 39205; 601-364-2031 License Division, 601-364-2057 Data Processing Div; Fax: 601-364-2125; 8AM-5PM. Access by: mail, phone, in person. mdwfp.com

County Courts & Recording Offices

About the Courts...

Administration

Court Administrator, Supreme Court   601-359-3697
Box 117   Fax: 601-359-2443
Jackson, MS 39205
www.mssc.state.ms.us

Court Structure

The court of general jurisdiction is the Circuit Court with 70 courts in 22 districts. Justice Courts were first created in 1984, replacing the Justice of the Peace. Prior to 1984, records were kept separately by each Justice of the Peace, so the location of such records today is often unknown. Probate is handled by the Chancery Courts as are property matters.

Searching Hints

A number of Mississippi counties have two Circuit Court Districts. A search of either court in such a county will include the index from the other court.
Full Name is a search requirement for all courts. DOB and SSN are very helpful for differentiating between like-named individuals.

Online Access

A pilot program for a statewide online computer system is in progress, and it is expected to be implemented within the next year. This system is intended for internal use only.

About the Recording Offices...

Organization

82 counties, 92 recording offices. The recording officers are Chancery Clerk and Clerk of Circuit Court (state tax liens). Ten counties have two separate recording offices - Bolivar, Carroll, Chickasaw, Craighead, Harrison, Hinds, Jasper, Jones, Panola, Tallahatchie, and Yalobusha. See the notes under each county for how to determine which office is appropriate to search. The entire state is in the Central Time Zone (CST).

UCC Records

This is a dual filing state. Financing statements are filed both at the state level and with the Chancery Clerk, except for consumer goods, farm related and real estate related filings, which are filed only with the Chancery Clerk. All but one county will perform UCC searches. Use search request form UCC-11. Search fees are usually $5.00 per debtor name. Copy fees vary from $.25 to $2.00 per page.

Lien Records

Federal tax liens on personal property of businesses are filed with the Secretary of State. Federal tax liens on personal property of individuals are filed with the county Chancery Clerk. State tax liens on personal property are filed with the county Clerk of Circuit Court. Refer to The Sourcebook of County Court Records for information about Mississippi Circuit Courts. State tax liens on real property are filed with the Chancery Clerk. Most Chancery Clerk offices will perform a federal tax lien search for a fee of $5.00 per name. Copy fees vary.

Real Estate Records

A few counties will perform real estate searches. Copies usually cost $.50 per page and certification fees $1.00 per document. The Assessor maintains tax records.

County Courts & Recording Offices

Adams

Real Estate Recording—Adams County Clerk of the Chancery Court, 1 Courthouse Square, Natchez, MS 39120., Fax: 601-445-7913. 8AM-5PM.

Felony, Misdemeanor, Civil Actions Over $2,500—Circuit and County Court, PO Box 1224, Natchez, MS 39121. 601-446-6326, Fax: 601-445-7955. 8AM-5PM. Access by: mail, phone, fax, in person.

Misdemeanor, Civil Actions Under $2,500, Eviction, Small Claims—Justice Court, 115 S Wall, Natchez, MS 39120. 601-446-6326, Fax: 601-445-7955. 8AM-5PM. Access by: mail, in person.

Probate—Chancery Court, PO Box 1006, Natchez, MS 39121. 601-446-6684, Fax: 601-445-7913. 8AM-5PM. Access by: mail, in person.

Alcorn

Real Estate Recording—Alcorn County Clerk of the Chancery Court, 501 Waldron Street, Corinth, MS 38834., Fax: 662-286-7706. 8AM-5PM.

Felony, Civil Actions Over $2,500—Circuit Court, PO Box 430 Attn: Circuit Clerk, Corinth, MS 38834. 662-286-7740, Fax: 662-286-5713. 8AM-5PM. Access by: mail, in person.

Misdemeanor, Civil Actions Under $2,500, Eviction, Small Claims—Justice Court, PO Box 226, Corinth, MS 38834. 662-286-7776. 8AM-5PM. Access by: mail, fax, in person.

Probate—Chancery Court, PO Box 69, Corinth, MS 38835-0069. 662-286-7702, Fax: 662-286-7706.

Amite

Real Estate Recording—Amite County Clerk of the Chancery Court, 243 West Main Street, Liberty, MS 39645. 601-657-8932, Fax: 601-657-8288. 8AM-5PM.

Felony, Civil Actions Over $2,500—Circuit Court, PO Box 312, Liberty, MS 39645. 601-657-8932, Fax: 601-657-8288. 8AM-5PM. Access by: mail, fax, in person.

Misdemeanor, Civil Actions Under $2,500, Eviction, Small Claims—Justice Court, PO Box 362, Liberty, MS 39645. 601-657-4527, Fax: 601-657-4527. 8AM-5PM. Access by: mail, in person.

Probate—Chancery Court, PO Box 680, Liberty, MS 39645. 601-657-8022, Fax: 601-657-8288. 8AM-5PM.

Attala

Real Estate Recording—Attala County Clerk of the Chancery Court, Chancery Court Bldg. 230 W. Washington St. Kosciusko, MS 39090., Fax: 662-289-7662. 8AM-5PM.

Felony, Civil Actions Over $2,500—Circuit Court, Courthouse, Kosciusko, MS 39090. 662-289-1471, Fax: 662-289-7666. 8AM-5PM. Access by: mail, phone, fax, in person.

Misdemeanor, Civil Actions Under $2,500, Eviction, Small Claims—Justice Court, Attala County Courthouse, Kosciusko, MS 39090. 662-289-7272. 8AM-5PM. Access by: mail, in person.

Probate—Chancery Court, 230 W. Washington, Kosciusko, MS 39090. 662-289-2921, Fax: 662-289-7662. 8AM-5PM.

Benton

Real Estate Recording—Benton County Clerk of the Chancery Court, Main Street, Courthouse, Ashland, MS 38603., Fax: 662-224-6303. 8AM-5PM.

Felony, Civil Actions Over $2,500—Circuit Court, PO Box 262, Ashland, MS 38603. 662-224-6310, Fax: 662-224-6303. 8AM-5PM. Access by: mail, in person.

Misdemeanor, Civil Actions Under $2,500, Eviction, Small Claims—Justice Court, PO Box 152, Ashland, MS 38603. 662-224-6320, Fax: 662-224-6313. 8AM-5PM. Access by: mail, in person.

Probate—Chancery Court, PO Box 218, Ashland, MS 38603. 662-224-6300, Fax: 662-224-6303. 8AM-5PM. Access by: mail.

Bolivar

Real Estate Recording—Bolivar County Clerk of the Chancery Court, Court Street, Courthouse, Cleveland, MS 38732. 662-843-2071, Fax: 662-846-2940. 8AM-5PM.

Bolivar County Clerk of the Chancery Court, 801 Main Street, Courthouse, Rosedale, MS 38769. 662-843-2531, Fax: 662-759-3467. 8AM-Noon,1-5PM.

Felony, Misdemeanor, Civil—Circuit and County Court-1st District, PO Box 205, Rosedale, MS 38769. 662-759-6521. 8AM-5PM. Access by: mail, in person.

Circuit and County Court-2nd District, PO Box 670, Cleveland, MS 38732. 662-843-2061, Fax: 662-846-2943. 8AM-5PM. Access by: mail, in person.

Misdemeanor, Civil Actions Under $2,500, Eviction, Small Claims—Justice Court, PO Box 1507, Cleveland, MS 38732. 662-843-4008, Fax: 662-846-6783. 8:00AM-5:00PM. Access by: mail, in person.

Probate—Cleveland Chancery Court, PO Box 789, Cleveland, MS 38732. 662-843-2071, Fax: 662-846-5880. 8AM-5PM. Access by: mail, in person.

Rosedale Chancery Court, PO Box 238, Rosedale, MS 38769. 662-759-3762, Fax: 662-759-3467. 8AM-Noon, 1-5PM.

Calhoun

Real Estate Recording—Calhoun County Clerk of the Chancery Court, Courthouse Square, Pittsboro, MS 38951. 662-983-3117, Fax: 662-412-3128. 8AM-5PM.

Felony, Civil Actions Over $2,500—Circuit Court, PO Box 25, Pittsboro, MS 38951. 662-412-3101, Fax: 662-412-3103. 8AM-5PM. Access by: mail, in person.

Misdemeanor, Civil Actions Under $2,500, Eviction, Small Claims—Justice Court, PO Box 7, Pittsboro, MS 38951. 662-412-3134, Fax: 662-412-3143. 8AM-5PM. Access by: in person.

Probate—Chancery Court, PO Box 8, Pittsboro, MS 38951. 662-983-3117, Fax: 662-983-3128. 8AM-5PM.

Carroll

Real Estate Recording—Carroll County Clerk of the Chancery Court, 101 Highway 51, Courthouse, Vaiden, MS 39176., Fax: 662-464-7745. 8AM-5PM.

Carroll County Clerk of the Chancery Court, Courthouse, Carrollton, MS 38917., Fax: 662-237-9642. 8AM-Noon, 1-5PM.

Felony, Civil Actions Over $2,500—Circuit Court, PO Box 6, Vaiden, MS 39176. 662-464-5476, Fax: 662-464-7745. 8AM-5PM. Access by: mail, in person.

Misdemeanor, Civil Actions Under $2,500, Eviction, Small Claims—Justice Court, PO Box 10, Carrollton, MS 38917. 662-237-9285. 8AM-4PM. Access by: mail, in person.

Probate—Chancery Court, PO Box 60, Carrollton, MS 38917. 662-237-9274, Fax: 662-237-9642. 8AM-12; 1-5PM.

Chickasaw

Real Estate Recording—Chickasaw County Clerk of the Chancery Court, Courthouse, Houston, MS 38851. 662-456-3941, Fax: 662-456-5295. 8AM-5PM.

Chickasaw County Clerk of the Chancery Court, 234 Main Street, Room 201, Okolona, MS 38860. 662-456-2513, Fax: 662-447-5024. 8AM-Noon,1-5PM.

Felony, Civil Actions Over $2,500—Circuit Court-1st District, 1 Pinson Sq, Rm 2, Houston, MS 38851. 662-456-2331, Fax: 662-456-5295. 8AM-5PM. Access by: mail, fax, in person.

Circuit Court-2nd District, Courthouse, Okolona, MS 38860. 662-447-2838, Fax: 662-447-5024. 8AM-5PM. Access by: mail, fax, in person.

Misdemeanor, Civil Actions Under $2,500, Eviction, Small Claims—Justice Court, Courthouse, Houston, MS 38851. 662-456-3941, Fax: 662-456-5295. 8AM-5PM. Access by: mail, in person.

Justice Court District 2, 234 W Main, Rm 207, Okolona, MS 38860. 662-447-3402.

Probate—Chancery Court, Courthouse Bldg, 1 Pinson Square, Houston, MS 38851. 662-456-2513, Fax: 662-456-5295.

Chancery Court, 234 W Main, Rm 201, Okolona, MS 38860-1438. 662-447-2092, Fax: 662-447-5024.

Choctaw

Real Estate Recording—Choctaw County Clerk of the Chancery Court, Quinn Street, Ackerman, MS 39735., Fax: 662-285-3444. 8AM-Noon,1-5PM.

Felony, Civil Actions Over $2,500—Circuit Court, PO Box 34, Ackerman, MS 39735. 662-285-6245, Fax: 662-285-3444. 8AM-5PM. Access by: mail, in person.

Misdemeanor, Civil Actions Under $2,500, Eviction, Small Claims—Justice Court, PO Box 357, Ackerman, MS 39735. 662-285-3599, Fax: 662-285-3444. 8AM-5PM. Access by: mail, phone, fax, in person.

Probate—Chancery Court, PO Box 250, Ackerman, MS 39735. 662-285-6329, Fax: 662-285-3444. 8AM-5PM.

Claiborne

Real Estate Recording—Claiborne County Clerk of the Chancery Court, 410 Main Street, Port Gibson, MS 39150. 662-437-4992, Fax: 662-437-3731. 8AM-5PM.

Felony, Civil Actions Over $2,500—Circuit Court, PO Box 549, Port Gibson, MS 39150. 601-437-5841. 8AM-5PM. Access by: mail, in person.

Misdemeanor, Civil Actions Under $2,500, Eviction, Small Claims—Justice Court, PO Box 497, Port Gibson, MS 39150. 601-437-4478. 8AM-5PM. Access by: mail, in person.

Probate—Chancery Court, PO Box 449, Port Gibson, MS 39150. 601-437-4992, Fax: 601-437-3137. 8AM-5PM.

Clarke

Real Estate Recording—Clarke County Clerk of the Chancery Court, Archusa Street, Courthouse, Quitman, MS 39355. 8AM-5PM.

Felony, Civil Actions Over $2,500—Circuit Court, PO Box 216, Quitman, MS 39355. 601-776-3111, Fax: 601-776-1001. 8AM-5PM. Access by: mail, fax, in person.

Misdemeanor, Civil Actions Under $2,500, Eviction, Small Claims—Justice Court, PO Box 4, Quitman, MS 39355. 601-776-5371. 8AM-5PM. Access by: mail, in person.

Probate—Chancery Court, PO Box 689, Quitman, MS 39355. 601-776-2126. 8AM-5PM.

Clay

Real Estate Recording—Clay County Clerk of the Chancery Court, 205 Court Street, West Point, MS 39773. 662-494-2724. 8AM-5PM.

Felony, Civil Actions Over $2,500—Circuit Court, PO Box 364, West Point, MS 39773. 662-494-3384. 8AM-5PM. Access by: mail, in person.

Misdemeanor, Civil Actions Under $2,500, Eviction, Small Claims—Justice Court, PO Box 674, West Point, MS 39773. 662-494-6141, Fax: 662-494-4034. 8AM-5PM. Access by: mail, in person.

Probate—Chancery Court, PO Box 815, West Point, MS 39773. 662-494-3124. 8AM-5PM. Access by: mail, in person.

Coahoma

Real Estate Recording—Coahoma County Clerk of the Chancery Court, 115 First Street, Clarksdale, MS 38614., Fax: 662-624-3029. 8AM-5PM.

Felony, Civil—Circuit and County Court, PO Box 849, Clarksdale, MS 38614-0849. 662-624-3014, Fax: 601-624-3075. 8AM-5PM. Access by: mail, fax, in person.

Misdemeanor, Civil Actions Under $2,500, Eviction, Small Claims—Justice Court, 144 Ritch, Clarksdale, MS 38614. 662-624-3060. 8AM-5PM. Access by: mail, in person.

Probate—Chancery Court, PO Box 98, Clarksdale, MS 38614. 662-624-3000, Fax: 662-624-3029. 8AM-5PM.

Copiah

Real Estate Recording—Copiah County Clerk of the Chancery Court, 100 Caldwell Drive, Courthouse Square, Hazlehurst, MS 39083., Fax: 601-894-3026. 8AM-5PM.

Felony, Civil Actions Over $2,500—Circuit Court, PO Box 467, Hazlehurst, MS 39083. 601-894-1241, Fax: 601-894-3026. 8AM-5PM. Access by: mail, fax, in person.

Misdemeanor, Civil Actions Under $2,500, Eviction, Small Claims—Justice Court, PO Box 798, Hazlehurst, MS 39083. 601-894-3218, Fax: 601-894-1676. 8:00AM-5:00PM. Access by: mail, in person.

Probate—Chancery Court, PO Box 507, Hazlehurst, MS 39083. 601-894-3021, Fax: 601-894-3026. 8AM-5PM.

Covington

Real Estate Recording—Covington County Clerk of the Chancery Court, 101 S. Elm St. Collins, MS 39428., Fax: 601-765-5016. 8AM-5PM.

Felony, Civil Actions Over $2,500—Circuit Court, PO Box 667, Collins, MS 39428. 601-765-6506, Fax: 601-765-1052. 8AM-5PM. Access by: mail, fax, in person.

Misdemeanor, Civil Actions Under $2,500, Eviction, Small Claims—Justice Court, PO Box 665, Collins, MS 39428. 601-765-6581. 8AM-5PM. Access by: mail, in person.

Probate—Chancery Court, PO Box 1679, Collins, MS 39428. 601-765-4242, Fax: 601-765-1052. 8AM-5PM.

De Soto

Real Estate Recording—De Soto County Clerk of the Chancery Court, 2535 Highway 51 South, Courthouse, Room 205, Hernando, MS 38632. 8AM-5PM.

Felony, Misdemeanor, Civil—Circuit and County Court, 2535 Hwy 51 South, Hernando, MS 38632. 662-429-1325. 8AM-5PM. Access by: mail, fax, in person.

Misdemeanor, Civil Actions Under $2,500, Eviction, Small Claims—Justice Court, 8525 Highway 51 North, Southaven, MS 38671. 662-393-5810, Fax: 601-393-5859. 8AM-5PM. Access by: mail, in person.

Probate—Chancery Court, 2535 Hwy 51 South, Hernando, MS 38632. 662-429-1320, Fax: 662-429-1311. 8AM-5PM.

Forrest

Real Estate Recording—Forrest County Clerk of the Chancery Court, 641 Main Street, Chancery Court Building, Hattiesburg, MS 39401., Fax: 601-545-6095. 8AM-5PM.

Felony, Misdemeanor, Civil—Circuit and County Court, PO Box 992, Hattiesburg, MS 39403. 601-582-3213, Fax: 601-545-6093. 8AM-5PM. Access by: mail, phone, in person.

Misdemeanor, Civil Actions Under $2,500, Eviction, Small Claims—Justice Court, 316 Forrest St, Hattiesburg, MS 39401. 601-544-3136. 8AM-5PM. Access by: mail, in person.

Probate—Chancery Court, PO Box 951, Hattiesburg, MS 39403. 601-545-6040. 8AM-5PM.

Franklin

Real Estate Recording—Franklin County Clerk of the Chancery Court, 101 Main Street, Courthouse, Meadville, MS 39653., Fax: 601-384-5864. 8AM-5PM.

Felony, Civil Actions Over $2,500—Circuit Court, PO Box 267, Meadville, MS 39653. 601-384-2320, Fax: 601-384-5864. 8AM-5PM. Access by: mail, in person.

Misdemeanor, Civil Actions Under $2,500, Eviction, Small Claims—Justice Court, PO Box 365, Meadville, MS 39653. 601-384-2002. 8AM-5PM. Access by: mail, in person.

Probate—Chancery Court, PO Box 297, Meadville, MS 39653. 601-384-2330, Fax: 601-384-5864. 8AM-5PM.

George

Real Estate Recording—George County Clerk of the Chancery Court, 355 Cox Street, Lucedale, MS 39452. 601-947-3766. 8AM-5PM; 9AM-Noon Sat.

Felony, Civil Actions Over $2,500—Circuit Court, 355 Cox St, Suite C, Lucedale, MS 39452. 601-947-4881, Fax: 601-947-8804. 8AM-5PM M-F, 9AM-12PM Sat. Access by: mail, fax, in person.

Misdemeanor, Civil Actions Under $2,500, Eviction, Small Claims—Justice Court, 356 A Cox St, Lucedale, MS 39452. 601-947-4834. 8AM-5PM. Access by: mail, in person.

Probate—Chancery Court, 355 Cox St, Suite Cre, Lucedale, MS 39452. 601-947-4881, Fax: 601-947-4812. 8AM-5PM.

Greene

Real Estate Recording—Greene County Clerk of the Chancery Court, Courthouse, Main St. Leakesville, MS 39451. 601-394-2377.

Felony, Civil Actions Over $2,500—Circuit Court, PO Box 310, Leakesville, MS 39451. 601-394-2379, Fax: 601-394-2334. 8AM-5PM M-F. Access by: mail, fax, in person.

Misdemeanor, Civil Actions Under $2,500, Eviction, Small Claims—Justice Court, PO Box 547, Leakesville, MS 39451. 601-394-2347, Fax: 601-394-5939. 8AM-5PM. Access by: mail, in person.

Probate—Chancery Court, PO Box 610, Leakesville, MS 39451. 601-394-2377. 8AM-5PM.

Grenada

Real Estate Recording—Grenada County Clerk of the Chancery Court, 59 Green Street, Courthouse, Grenada, MS 38901. 662-226-1741. 8AM-5PM.

Felony, Civil Actions Over $2,500—Circuit Court, PO Box 1517, Grenada, MS 38902. 662-226-1941, Fax: 662-227-0427. 8AM-5PM. Access by: in person.

Misdemeanor, Civil Actions Under $2,500, Eviction, Small Claims—Justice Court, 16 First St, Grenada, MS 38901. 662-226-3331. 8AM-5PM. Access by: mail, in person.

Probate—Chancery Court, PO Box 1208, Grenada, MS 38902. 662-226-1821, Fax: 662-226-0427. 8AM-5PM.

Hancock

Real Estate Recording—Hancock County Clerk of the Chancery Court, Chancery Clerk's Office, 152 Main St, Bay Saint Louis, MS 39520. 228-865-4040, Fax: 228-467-3159. 8AM-5PM.

Felony, Civil Actions Over $2,500—Circuit Court, PO Box 249 Bay St. Bay St. Louis, MS 39520. 228-865-4092, Fax: 228-467-2779. 8AM-5PM. Access by: mail, in person.

Misdemeanor, Civil Actions Under $2,500, Eviction, Small Claims—Justice Court, 306 Hwy 90, Bay St. Louis, MS 39520. 228-865-4147. 8AM-5PM. Access by: mail, in person.

Probate—Chancery Court, PO Box 429 Bay St. Bay St. Louis, MS 39520. 228-865-4097, Fax: 228-466-5994. 8AM-5PM.

Harrison

Real Estate Recording—Harrison County Chancery Clerk, 730 Washington Loop, Biloxi, MS 39530., Fax: 228-435-8292. 8AM-5PM.

Harrison County Clerk of the Chancery Court, 1801 23rd Avenue, Gulfport, MS 39501. 231-258-3300, Fax: 228-868-1480. 8AM-5PM.

Felony, Civil Actions Over $75,000—Circuit Court-1st District, PO Box 998, Gulfport, MS 39502. 231-258-9031, Fax: 228-865-4099. 8AM-5PM. Access by: mail, in person.

Circuit Court-2nd District, PO Box 235, Biloxi, MS 39533. 228-769-3181, Fax: 228-435-8277. 8AM-5PM. Access by: mail, fax, in person.

Misdemeanor, Civil Actions Under $75,000—County Court-1st District, PO Box 998, Gulfport, MS 39502. 231-258-3330, Fax: 228-865-4099. 8AM-5PM. Access by: mail, in person.

County Court-2nd District, PO Box 235, Biloxi, MS 39533. 228-769-3131, Fax: 228-435-8277. 8AM-5PM. Access by: mail, fax, in person.

Misdemeanor, Civil Actions Under $2,500, Eviction, Small Claims—Justice Court, PO Box 1754, Gulfport, MS 39502., Fax: 228-865-4216. 8AM-5PM. Access by: mail, in person.

Probate—Biloxi Chancery Court, PO Box 544, Biloxi, MS 39533. 228-769-3124, Fax: 228-435-8251. 8AM-Noon, 1-5PM.

Gulfport Chancery Court, PO Drawer CC, Gulfport, MS 39502. 231-258-3310, Fax: 228-865-1646. 8AM-Noon, 1-5PM. Access by: in person.

Hinds

Real Estate Recording—Hinds County Clerk of the Chancery Court, 316 South President Street, Jackson, MS 39201. 601-968-6588, Fax: 601-973-5535. 8AM-5PM.

Hinds County Clerk of the Chancery Court, Main Street, Courthouse Annex, Raymond, MS 39154. 601-857-5574. 8AM-5PM.

Felony, Misdemeanor, Civil—Circuit and County Court-1st District, PO Box 327, Jackson, MS 39205. 601-968-6628. 8AM-5PM. Access by: mail, in person.

Circuit and County Court-2nd District, PO Box 33, Raymond, MS 39154. 601-968-6653. 8AM-Noon, 1-5PM. Access by: mail, in person.

Misdemeanor, Civil Actions Under $2,500, Eviction, Small Claims—Justice Court, 407 E Pascagoula, 3rd floor, PO Box 3490, Jackson, MS 39207. 601-968-6781, Fax: 601-973-5532. 8AM-Noon, 1-5PM. Access by: mail, in person.

Probate—Jackson Chancery Court, PO Box 686, Jackson, MS 39205. 601-968-6540, Fax: 601-873-5554. 8AM-5PM.

Raymond Chancery Court, PO Box 88, Raymond, MS 39154. 601-857-8055, Fax: 601-857-4953. 8AM-5PM. Access by: mail, in person.

Holmes

Real Estate Recording—Holmes County Clerk of the Chancery Court, Courthouse, 2 Court Square, Lexington, MS 39095., Fax: 662-834-3020. 8AM-5PM.

Felony, Civil Actions Over $2,500—Circuit Court, PO Box 718, Lexington, MS 39095. 662-834-2476, Fax: 662-834-3870. 8AM-5PM. Access by: mail, fax, in person.

Misdemeanor, Civil Actions Under $2,500, Eviction, Small Claims—Justice Court, PO Box 99, Lexington, MS 39095. 662-834-4565. 8AM-Noon, 1-5PM. Access by: mail, in person.

Probate—Chancery Court, PO Box 239, Lexington, MS 39095. 662-834-2508, Fax: 662-834-3020. 8AM-5PM. Access by: mail, in person.

Humphreys

Real Estate Recording—Humphreys County Clerk of the Chancery Court, 102 Castleman, Courthouse, Belzoni, MS 39038. 662-247-2552, Fax: 662-247-0101. 8AM-Noon, 1-5PM.

Felony, Civil Actions Over $2,500—Circuit Court, PO Box 696, Belzoni, MS 39038. 662-247-3065, Fax: 662-247-3906. 8AM-5PM. Access by: mail, fax, in person.

Misdemeanor, Civil Actions Under $2,500, Eviction, Small Claims—Justice Court, 102 Castleman St, Belzoni, MS 39038. 662-247-4337, Fax: 662-247-1095. 8AM-Noon, 1-5PM. Access by: mail, in person.

Probate—Chancery Court, PO Box 547, Belzoni, MS 39038. 662-247-1740, Fax: 662-247-1010. 8AM-Noon, 1-5PM.

Issaquena

Real Estate Recording—Issaquena County Clerk of the Chancery Court, 129 Court Street, Mayersville, MS 39113. 662-873-2761, Fax: 662-873-2061. 8AM-Noon,1-5PM.

Felony, Civil Actions Over $2,500—Circuit Court, PO Box 27, Mayersville, MS 39113. 662-873-2761. 8AM-5PM. Access by: mail, in person.

Misdemeanor, Civil Actions Under $2,500, Eviction, Small Claims—Justice Court, PO Box 58, Mayersville, MS 39113. 662-873-6287. 8AM-Noon, 1-5PM. Access by: mail, in person.

Probate—Chancery Court, PO Box 27, Mayersville, MS 39113. 662-873-2761, Fax: 662-873-2061. 8AM-5PM.

Itawamba

Real Estate Recording—Itawamba County Clerk of the Chancery Court, 201 West Main Street, Fulton, MS 38843., Fax: 662-862-3421. 8AM-5PM; 8AM-Noon Sat.

Felony, Civil Actions Over $2,500—Circuit Court, 201 W Main, Fulton, MS 38843. 662-862-3511, Fax: 662-862-4006. 8AM-5PM. Access by: mail, phone, fax, in person.

Misdemeanor, Civil Actions Under $2,500, Eviction, Small Claims—Justice Court, 201 W Main, Fulton, MS 38843. 662-862-4315, Fax: 662-862-5805. 8AM-Noon, 1-5PM. Access by: mail, in person.

Probate—Chancery Court, 201 W Main, Fulton, MS 38843. 662-862-3421, Fax: 662-862-4006. 8AM-5PM M-F; 8AM-Noon Sat. Access by: in person.

Jackson

Real Estate Recording—Jackson County Chancery Clerk, 1710A Market Street, Pascagoula, MS 39567. 231-256-9824, Fax: 228-769-3135. 8AM-5PM.

Felony, Civil—Circuit Court, PO Box 998, Pascagoula, MS 39568-0998. 231-231-8823, Fax: 228-769-3180. 8AM-5PM. Access by: mail, fax, in person.

Misdemeanor, Civil Actions Under $75,000—County Court, PO Box 998, Pascagoula, MS 39568. 231-256-9838. 8AM-5PM. Access by: mail, in person.

Misdemeanor, Civil Actions Under $2,500, Eviction, Small Claims—Justice Court, 5343 Jefferson St, Moss Point, MS 39563. 231-256-8250, Fax: 228-769-3364. 8AM-5PM. Access by: mail, in person.

Probate—Chancery Court, PO Box 998, Pascagoula, MS 39568. 231-256-9803, Fax: 228-769-3397. 8AM-5PM. Access by: mail, in person.

Jasper

Real Estate Recording—Jasper County Clerk of the Chancery Court, Courthouse, 1782 Highway 503, Paulding, MS 39348., Fax: 601-727-4475. 8AM-5PM.

Jasper County Clerk of the Chancery Court, Court Street, Bay Springs, MS 39422., Fax: 601-764-3468. 8AM-5PM.

Felony, Civil Actions Over $2,500—Circuit Court-1st District, PO Box 485, Paulding, MS 39348. 601-727-4941, Fax: 601-727-4475. 8AM-5PM. Access by: mail, fax, in person.

Circuit Court-2nd District, PO Box 447, Bay Springs, MS 39422. 601-764-2245, Fax: 601-764-3078. 8AM-5PM. Access by: mail, in person.

Misdemeanor, Civil Actions Under $2,500, Eviction, Small Claims—Justice Court, PO Box 1054, Bay Springs, MS 39422. 601-764-2065, Fax: 601-764-3402. 8AM-Noon, 1-5PM. Access by: mail, in person.

Probate—Bay Springs Chancery Court, PO Box 1047, Bay Springs, MS 39422. 601-764-3368, Fax: 601-764-3026. 8AM-5PM.

Paulding Chancery Court, PO Box 38, Paulding, MS 39348. 601-727-4941, Fax: 601-727-4475. 8AM-5PM. ᵗ

Jefferson

Real Estate Recording—Jefferson County Clerk of the Chancery Court, 307 Main, Fayette, MS 39069. 601-786-3781, Fax: 601-786-6009. 8AM-5PM.

Felony, Civil Actions Over $2,500—Circuit Court, PO Box 305, Fayette, MS 39069. 601-786-3422, Fax: 601-786-9676. 8AM-5PM. Access by: mail, in person.

Misdemeanor, Civil Actions Under $2,500, Eviction, Small Claims—Justice Court, PO Box 1047, Fayette, MS 39069. 601-786-8594, Fax: 601-786-6017. 8AM-5PM. Access by: mail, phone, fax, in person.

Probate—Chancery Court, PO Box 145, Fayette, MS 39069. 601-786-3021, Fax: 601-786-6009. 8AM-5PM.

Jefferson Davis

Real Estate Recording—Jefferson Davis County Clerk of the Chancery Court, 1025 3rd St. Prentiss, MS 39474. 601-792-4204, Fax: 601-792-2894. 8AM-5PM.

Felony, Civil Actions Over $2,500—Circuit Court, PO Box 1082, Prentiss, MS 39474. 601-792-4231, Fax: 601-792-2849. 8AM-5PM. Access by: mail, fax, in person.

Misdemeanor, Civil Actions Under $2,500, Eviction, Small Claims—Justice Court, PO Box 1407, Prentiss, MS 39474. 601-792-5129. 8AM-Noon, 1-5PM. Access by: mail, in person.

Probate—Chancery Court, PO Box 1137, Prentiss, MS 39474. 601-792-4204, Fax: 601-792-2894. 8AM-5PM. Access by: mail.

Jones

Real Estate Recording—Jones County Clerk of the Chancery Court, Court Street, Jones County Courthouse, Ellisville, MS 39437.

Jones County Clerk of the Chancery Court, 415 North 5th Avenue, Laurel, MS 39441., Fax: 601-428-3602. 8AM-5PM.

Felony, Misdemeanor, Civil—Circuit and County Court-1st District, 101 N. Court St, Ellisville, MS 39437. 601-477-8538. 8AM-5PM. Access by: mail, in person.

Circuit and County Court-2nd District, PO Box 1336, Laurel, MS 39441. 601-425-2556. 8AM-5PM. Access by: mail, in person.

Misdemeanor, Civil Actions Under $2,500, Eviction, Small Claims—Justice Court, PO Box 1997, Laurel, MS 39441. 601-428-3137, Fax: 601-428-0526. 8AM-Noon, 1-5PM. Access by: mail, fax, in person.

Probate—Ellisville Chancery Court, 101-D Court St. Ellisville, MS 39437. 601-477-3307. 8AM-Noon, 1-5PM.

Laurel Chancery Court, PO Box 1468, Laurel, MS 39441. 601-428-0527, Fax: 601-428-3602. 8AM-5PM. Access by: mail.

Kemper

Real Estate Recording—Kemper County Clerk of the Chancery Court, Courthouse Square, De Kalb, MS 39328., Fax: 601-743-2789. 8AM-5PM.

Felony, Civil Actions Over $2,500—Circuit Court, PO Box 130, De Kalb, MS 39328. 601-743-2224, Fax: 601-743-2789. 8AM-5PM. Access by: mail, phone, fax, in person.

Misdemeanor, Civil Actions Under $2,500, Eviction, Small Claims—Justice Court, PO Box 661, De Kalb, MS 39328. 601-743-2793, Fax: 601-743-2789. 8AM-5PM. Access by: mail, in person.

Probate—Chancery Court, PO Box 188, De Kalb, MS 39328. 601-743-2460, Fax: 601-743-2789. 8AM-5PM.

Lafayette

Real Estate Recording—Lafayette County Clerk of the Chancery Court, Courthouse, Oxford, MS 38655. 8AM-5PM.

Felony, Civil Actions Over $2,500—Circuit Court, LaFayette County Courthouse, Oxford, MS 38655. 662-234-4951, Fax: 662-236-0238. 8AM-5PM. Access by: mail, in person.

Misdemeanor, Civil Actions Under $2,500, Eviction, Small Claims—Justice Court, 1219 Monroe, Oxford, MS 38655. 662-234-1545, Fax: 662-238-7990. 8AM-5PM. Access by: mail, in person.

Probate—Chancery Court, PO Box 1240, Oxford, MS 38655. 662-234-2131, Fax: 662-234-5402. 8AM-5PM.

Lamar

Real Estate Recording—Lamar County Clerk of the Chancery Court, 203 Main Street, Purvis, MS 39475., Fax: 601-794-1049. 8AM-5PM.

Felony, Civil Actions Over $2,500—Circuit Court, PO Box 369, Purvis, MS 39475. 601-794-8504, Fax: 601-794-1049. 8AM-5PM. Access by: mail, in person.

Misdemeanor, Civil Actions Under $2,500, Eviction, Small Claims—Justice Court, PO Box 1010, Purvis, MS 39475. 601-794-2950, Fax: 601-794-1076. 8AM-5PM. Access by: mail, fax, in person.

Probate—Chancery Court, PO Box 247, Purvis, MS 39475. 601-794-8504, Fax: 601-794-3903. 8AM-5PM.

Lauderdale

Real Estate Recording—Lauderdale County Clerk of the Chancery Court, 500 Constitution Avenue, Room 105, Meridian, MS 39301. 601-482-4701. 8AM-5PM.

Felony, Civil Actions Over $2,500—Circuit and County Court, PO Box 1005, Meridian, MS 39302-1005. 601-482-9738, Fax: 601-484-3970. 8AM-5PM. Access by: mail, in person. Special note: County Court can be reached at 601-482-9715.

Misdemeanor, Civil Actions Under $2,500, Eviction, Small Claims—Justice Court, PO Box 5126, Meridian, MS 39302. 601-482-9879, Fax: 601-482-9813. 8AM-5PM. Access by: mail, in person.

Probate—Chancery Court, PO Box 1587, Meridian, MS 39302. 601-482-9701, Fax: 601-486-4920. 8AM-Noon, 1-5PM.

Lawrence

Real Estate Recording—Lawrence County Clerk of the Chancery Court, 517 East Broad St. Monticello, MS 39654. 601-587-2211, Fax: 601-587-0750. 8AM-5PM.

Felony, Civil Actions Over $2,500—Circuit Court, PO Box 1249, Monticello, MS 39654. 601-587-4791, Fax: 601-587-0750. 8AM-5PM. Access by: mail, phone, fax, in person.

Misdemeanor, Civil Actions Under $2,500, Eviction, Small Claims—Justice Court, PO Box 903, Monticello, MS 39654. 601-587-7183, Fax: 601-587-0755. 8AM-5PM. Access by: mail, fax, in person.

Probate—Chancery Court, 517 Broad St, Courthouse Sq, PO Box 821, Monticello, MS 39654. 601-587-7162, Fax: 601-587-0750. 8AM-5PM.

Leake

Real Estate Recording—Leake County Clerk of the Chancery Court, Courthouse, Court Square, Carthage, MS 39051. 601-267-7371, Fax: 601-267-6137. 8AM-5PM.

Felony, Civil Actions Over $2,500—Circuit Court, PO Box 67, Carthage, MS 39051. 601-267-8357, Fax: 601-267-8889. 8AM-5PM. Access by: mail, in person.

Misdemeanor, Civil Actions Under $2,500, Eviction, Small Claims—Justice Court, PO Box 69, Carthage, MS 39051. 601-267-5677, Fax: 601-267-6134. 8:00AM-5:00PM. Access by: mail, in person.

Probate—Chancery Court, PO Box 72, Carthage, MS 39051. 601-267-7371, Fax: 601-267-6137. 8AM-5PM.

Lee

Real Estate Recording—Lee County Clerk of the Chancery Court, 200 Jefferson Street, Tupelo, MS 38801. 662-841-9100, Fax: 662-680-6091. 8AM-5PM.

Felony, Civil Actions Over $2,500—Circuit and County Court, Circuit Court-PO Box 762, County Court - PO Box 736, Tupelo, MS 38802. 662-841-9022, Fax: 662-680-6079. 8AM-5PM. Access by: mail, in person.

Misdemeanor, Civil Actions Under $2,500, Eviction, Small Claims—Justice Court, PO Box 108, Tupelo, MS 38802. 662-841-9014, Fax: 662-680-6021. 8AM-5PM. Access by: mail, in person.

Probate—Chancery Court, PO Box 7127, Tupelo, MS 38802. 662-841-9100, Fax: 662-680-6091. 8AM-5PM.

Leflore

Real Estate Recording—Leflore County Clerk of the Chancery Court, 310 West Market, Courthouse, Greenwood, MS 38930., Fax: 662-455-7965. 8AM-5PM.

Felony, Civil Actions Over $2,500—Circuit and County Court, PO Box 1953, Greenwood, MS 38935-1953. 662-453-1041, Fax: 662-455-1278. 8AM-5PM. Access by: mail, fax, in person.

Misdemeanor, Civil Actions Under $2,500, Eviction, Small Claims—Justice Court, PO Box 8056, Greenwood, MS 38935. 662-453-1605. 8AM-5PM. Access by: in person.

Probate—Chancery Court, PO Box 250, Greenwood, MS 38935-0250. 662-453-1041, Fax: 662-455-7959. 8AM-5PM. Access by: mail, in person.

Lincoln

Real Estate Recording—Lincoln County Clerk of the Chancery Court, 300 South First Street, Brookhaven, MS 39601. 601-835-3412. 8AM-5PM.

Felony, Civil Actions Over $2,500—Circuit Court, PO Box 357, Brookhaven, MS 39602. 601-835-3435, Fax: 601-835-3482. 8AM-5PM. Access by: mail, fax, in person.

Misdemeanor, Civil Actions Under $2,500, Eviction, Small Claims—Justice Court, PO Box 767, Brookhaven, MS 39602. 601-835-3474. 8:00AM-5:00PM. Access by: mail, in person.

Probate—Chancery Court, PO Box 555, Brookhaven, MS 39602. 601-835-3412, Fax: 601-835-3423. 8AM-5PM. Access by: mail, in person.

Lowndes

Real Estate Recording—Lowndes County Clerk of the Chancery Court, 515 2nd Avenue North, Courthouse, Columbus, MS 39701. 8AM-5PM.

Felony, Civil—Circuit and County Court, PO Box 31, Columbus, MS 39703. 662-329-5900. 8AM-5PM. Access by: mail, in person.

Misdemeanor, Civil Actions Under $2,500, Eviction, Small Claims—Justice Court, 11 Airline Rd, Columbus, MS 39702. 662-329-5929, Fax: 662-245-4619. 8AM-5PM. Access by: mail, in person.

Probate—Chancery Court, PO Box 684, Columbus, MS 39703. 662-329-5800. 8AM-5PM.

Madison

Real Estate Recording—Madison County Clerk, 146 W. Center St.eet, Courtyard Square, Canton, MS 39046. 8AM-5PM.

Felony, Civil—Circuit and County Court, PO Box 1626, Canton, MS 39046. 601-859-4365, Fax: 601-859-8555. 8AM-5PM. Access by: mail, phone, fax, in person.

Misdemeanor, Civil Actions Under $2,500, Eviction, Small Claims—Justice Court, 175 N Union, Canton, MS 39046. 601-859-6337, Fax: 601-859-5878. 8AM-5PM. Access by: mail, in person.

Probate—Chancery Court, PO Box 404, Canton, MS 39046. 601-859-1177, Fax: 601-859-5875. 8AM-5PM.

Marion

Real Estate Recording—Marion County Clerk of the Chancery Court, 250 Broad Street, Suite 2, Columbia, MS 39429., Fax: 601-736-1232. 8AM-5PM.

Felony, Civil Actions Over $2,500—Circuit Court, 250 Broad St, Suite 1, Columbia, MS 39429. 601-736-8246. 8AM-5PM. Access by: mail, in person.

Misdemeanor, Civil Actions Under $2,500, Eviction, Small Claims—Justice Court, 500 Courthouse Square, Columbia, MS 39429. 601-736-2572, Fax: 601-736-2580. 8AM-5PM. Access by: mail, fax, in person.

Probate—Chancery Court, 250 Broad St, Suite 2, Columbia, MS 39429. 601-736-2691, Fax: 601-736-1232. 8AM-5PM.

Marshall

Real Estate Recording—Marshall County Clerk of the Chancery Court, Court Square, Holly Springs, MS 38635., Fax: 662-252-0004. 8AM-5PM.

Felony, Civil Actions Over $2,500—Circuit Court, PO Box 459, Holly Springs, MS 38635. 662-252-3434, Fax: 662-252-0004. 8AM-5PM. Access by: mail, fax, in person.

Misdemeanor, Civil Actions Under $2,500, Eviction, Small Claims—Justice Court-North and South Districts, PO Box 867, Holly Springs, MS 38635. 662-252-3585. 8AM-5PM. Access by: mail, in person.

Probate—Chancery Court, PO Box 219, Holly Springs, MS 38635. 662-252-4431, Fax: 662-252-0004. 8AM-5PM.

Monroe

Real Estate Recording—Monroe County Clerk of the Chancery Court, 201 West Commerce Street, Aberdeen, MS 39730. 662-369-8143, Fax: 662-369-7928. 8AM-5PM.

Felony, Civil Actions Over $2,500—Circuit Court, PO Box 843, Aberdeen, MS 39730. 662-369-8695, Fax: 662-369-3684. 8AM-5PM. Access by: in person.

Misdemeanor, Civil Actions Under $2,500, Eviction, Small Claims—Justice Court-District 1 & 3, 101 9th St, Amory, MS 38821. 662-256-8493, Fax: 662-256-7876. Access by: in person.

Justice Court-District 2, PO Box F, Aberdeen, MS 39730. 662-369-4971. 8AM-5PM. Access by: mail, in person.

Probate—Chancery Court, PO Box 578, Aberdeen, MS 39730. 662-369-8143, Fax: 662-369-7928. 8AM-5PM.

Montgomery

Real Estate Recording—Montgomery County Clerk of the Chancery Court, 614 Summit Street, Courthouse, Winona, MS 38967., Fax: 662-283-2233. 8AM-5PM.

Felony, Civil Actions Over $2,500—Circuit Court, PO Box 765, Winona, MS 38967. 662-283-4161, Fax: 662-283-2233. 8AM-5PM. Access by: mail, in person.

Misdemeanor, Civil Actions Under $2,500, Eviction, Small Claims—Justice Court, PO Box 229, Winona, MS 38967. 662-283-2290, Fax: 662-283-2233. 8AM-5PM. Access by: mail, in person.

Probate—Chancery Court, PO Box 71, Winona, MS 38967. 662-283-2333, Fax: 662-283-2233. 8AM-5PM.

Neshoba

Real Estate Recording—Neshoba County Clerk of the Chancery Court, 401 Beacon Street, Suite 107, Philadelphia, MS 39350. 8AM-5PM.

Felony, Civil Actions Over $2,500—Circuit Court, 401 E Beacon St Suite 110, Philadelphia, MS 39350. 601-656-4781. 8AM-5PM. Access by: mail, in person.

Misdemeanor, Civil Actions Under $2,500, Eviction, Small Claims—Justice Court, 401 E Beacon St, Philadelphia, MS 39350. 601-656-5361. Access by: in person.

Probate—Chancery Court, 401 Beacon St Suite 107, Philadelphia, MS 39350. 601-656-3581. 8AM-5PM. Access by: in person.

Newton

Real Estate Recording—Newton County Clerk of the Chancery Court, 92 West Broad St. Courthouse, Decatur, MS 39327., Fax: 601-635-3210. 8AM-5PM.

Felony, Civil Actions Over $2,500—Circuit Court, PO Box 447, Decatur, MS 39327. 601-635-2368, Fax: 601-635-3210. 8AM-5PM. Access by: mail, phone, in person.

Misdemeanor, Civil Actions Under $2,500, Eviction, Small Claims—Justice Court, PO Box 69, Decatur, MS 39327. 601-635-2740. 8AM-5PM. Access by: mail, in person.

Probate—Chancery Clerk's Office, PO Box 68, Decatur, MS 39327. 601-635-2367. 8AM-5PM.

Noxubee

Real Estate Recording—Noxubee County Clerk of the Chancery Court, 505 South Jefferson, Macon, MS 39341., Fax: 601-726-2272. 8AM-5PM.

Felony, Civil Actions Over $2,500—Circuit Court, PO Box 431, Macon, MS 39341. 662-726-5737, Fax: 662-726-2938. 8AM-5PM. Access by: mail, in person.

Misdemeanor, Civil Actions Under $2,500, Eviction, Small Claims—Justice Court-North & South Districts, 507 S Jefferson, Macon, MS 39341. 662-726-5834, Fax: 662-726-2938. 8AM-5PM. Access by: mail, in person.

Probate—Chancery Court, PO Box 147, Macon, MS 39341. 662-726-4243, Fax: 662-726-2272. 8AM-5PM.

Oktibbeha

Real Estate Recording—Oktibbeha County Clerk of the Chancery Court, 101 East Main, Courthouse, Starkville, MS 39759. 8AM-5PM.

Felony, Civil Actions Over $2,500—Circuit Court, Courthouse, 101 E Main, Starkville, MS 39759. 662-323-1356. 8AM-5PM. Access by: mail, in person.

Misdemeanor, Civil Actions Under $2,500, Eviction, Small Claims—Justice Court-Districts 1-3, 104 Felix Long Dr, Starkville, MS 39759. 662-324-3032, Fax: 662-338-1060. 8AM-5PM. Access by: mail, phone, fax, in person.

Probate—Chancery Court, Courthouse, 101 E Main, Starkville, MS 39759. 662-323-5834. 8AM-5PM.

Panola

Real Estate Recording—Panola County Clerk of the Chancery Court, 215 S. Pocahontas Street, Sardis, MS 38666. 662-487-6215, Fax: 662-487-3595. 8AM-5PM.

Panola County Clerk of the Chancery Court, 151 Public Square, Batesville, MS 38606. 662-563-6215, Fax: 662-563-8233. 8AM-5PM.

Felony, Civil Actions Over $2,500—Circuit Court-1st District, PO Box 130, Sardis, MS 38666. 662-487-2073, Fax: 662-487-3595. 8AM-5PM. Access by: mail, in person.

Circuit Court-2nd District, PO Box 346, Batesville, MS 38606. 662-563-6210, Fax: 662-487-8233. 8AM-5PM. Access by: mail, phone, fax, in person.

Misdemeanor, Civil Actions Under $2,500, Eviction, Small Claims—Justice Court, PO Box 249, Sardis, MS 38666. 662-487-2080. 8AM-5PM. Access by: mail, in person.

Probate—Panola County Chancery Clerk, 151 Public Square, Batesville, MS 38606. 662-563-6205, Fax: 662-563-8233. 8AM-5PM.

Sardis Chancery Court, PO Box 130, Sardis, MS 38666. 662-487-2070, Fax: 662-487-3595. 8AM-Noon, 1-5PM.

Pearl River

Real Estate Recording—Pearl River County Clerk of the Chancery Court, Courthouse, 200 South Main St. Poplarville, MS 39470. 8AM-5PM.

Felony, Civil Actions Over $2,500—Circuit Court, Courthouse, Poplarville, MS 39470. 601-795-3050, Fax: 601-795-3084. 8AM-5PM. Access by: mail, in person.

Misdemeanor, Civil Actions Under $2,500, Eviction, Small Claims—Justice Court-Northern, Southeastern, and Southwestern Districts, 204 Julia St, Poplarville, MS 39470. 601-795-8018, Fax: 601-795-3063. 8AM-5PM. Access by: mail, in person.

Probate—Chancery Court, PO Box 431, Poplarville, MS 39470. 601-795-2238, Fax: 601-795-3093. 8AM-5PM.

Perry

Real Estate Recording—Perry County Clerk of the Chancery Court, Main Street, New Augusta, MS 39462., Fax: 601-964-8265. 8AM-5PM.

Felony, Civil Actions Over $2,500—Circuit Court, PO Box 198, New Augusta, MS 39462. 601-964-8663, Fax: 601-964-8265. 8AM-5PM. Access by: mail, in person.

Misdemeanor, Civil Actions Under $2,500, Eviction, Small Claims—Justice Court, PO Box 455, New Augusta, MS 39462. 601-964-8366. 8AM-5PM. Access by: mail, in person.

Justice Court-District 1, 5091 Hwy 29, Petal, MS 39465. 601-544-3136. 8AM-5PM. Access by: mail, in person.

Probate—Chancery Court, PO Box 198, New Augusta, MS 39462. 601-964-8398, Fax: 601-964-8265. 8AM-5PM. Access by: mail, in person.

Pike

Real Estate Recording—Pike County Clerk of the Chancery Court, East Bay, Magnolia, MS 39652., Fax: 601-783-2001. 8AM-5PM.

Felony, Misdemeanor, Civil—Circuit and County Court, PO Drawer 31, Magnolia, MS 39652. 601-783-2581, Fax: 601-783-4101. 8AM-5PM. Access by: mail, fax, in person.

Misdemeanor, Civil Actions Under $2,500, Eviction, Small Claims—Justice Court-Divisions 1-3, PO Box 509, Magnolia, MS 39652. 601-783-5333, Fax: 601-783-4181. 8AM-5PM. Access by: mail, in person.

Probate—Chancery Court, PO Box 309, Magnolia, MS 39652. 601-783-3362, Fax: 601-783-4101. 8AM-5PM.

Pontotoc

Real Estate Recording—Pontotoc County Clerk of the Chancery Court, Courthouse, 11 E. Washington St. Pontotoc, MS 38863. 662-489-3904. 8AM-5PM.

Felony, Civil Actions Over $2,500—Circuit Court, PO Box 428, Pontotoc, MS 38863. 662-489-3908. 8AM-5PM. Access by: mail, in person.

Misdemeanor, Civil Actions Under $2,500, Eviction, Small Claims—Justice Court-East & West Districts, 29 E Washington St, Pontotoc, MS 38863-2923. 662-489-3920, Fax: 662-489-3921. 8AM-5PM. Access by: mail, in person.

Probate—Chancery Court, 11 Washington, PO Box 209, Pontotoc, MS 38863. 662-489-3900, Fax: 662-489-3940. 8AM-5PM. Access by: mail, in person.

Prentiss

Real Estate Recording—Prentiss County Clerk of the Chancery Court, 100 North Main Street, Booneville, MS 38829., Fax: 662-728-2007. 8AM-5PM.

Felony, Civil Actions Over $2,500—Circuit Court, 101 N Main St, Booneville, MS 38829. 662-728-4611, Fax: 662-728-2006. 8AM-5PM. Access by: mail, fax, in person.

Misdemeanor, Civil Actions Under $2,500, Eviction, Small Claims—Prentiss County Justice Court, 1901C East Chambers Dr, Booneville, MS 38829. 662-728-8696, Fax: 662-728-2009. 8AM-5PM. Access by: mail, in person.

Probate—Chancery Court, PO Box 477, Booneville, MS 38829. 662-728-8151, Fax: 662-728-2007. 8AM-5PM.

Quitman

Real Estate Recording—Quitman County Clerk of the Chancery Court, Chestnut Street, Courthouse, Marks, MS 38646. 662-326-2661, Fax: 662-326-8004. 8AM-5PM.

Felony, Civil Actions Over $2,500—Circuit Court, Courthouse, Marks, MS 38646. 662-326-8003, Fax: 662-326-8004. 8AM-5PM. Access by: mail, fax, in person.

Misdemeanor, Civil Actions Under $2,500, Eviction, Small Claims—Justice Court-Districts 1 & 2, PO Box 100, Marks, MS 38646. 662-326-2104, Fax: 662-326-2330. 8AM-5PM. Access by: mail, fax, in person.

Probate—Chancery Court, 230 Chestnut St, Marks, MS 38646. 662-326-2661, Fax: 662-326-8004. 8AM-Noon, 1-5PM.

Rankin

Real Estate Recording—Rankin County Chancery Clerk, Suite D, 211 East Government St. Brandon, MS 39042. 601-825-1366, Fax: 601-824-7116. 8AM-5PM.

Felony, Misdemeanor, Civil—Circuit and County Court, PO Drawer 1599, Brandon, MS 39043. 601-825-1466. 8AM-5PM. Access by: mail, in person.

Misdemeanor, Civil Actions Under $2,500, Eviction, Small Claims—Justice Court-Districts 1-4, 110 Paul Truitt Lane, Pearl, MS 39208. 601-939-1885, Fax: 601-939-2320. 8AM-5PM. Access by: mail, in person.

Probate—Chancery Court, 203 Town Sq, PO Box 700, Brandon, MS 39042. 601-825-1649, Fax: 601-824-2450. 8AM-5PM. Access by: in person.

Scott

Real Estate Recording—Scott County Clerk of the Chancery Court, 100 Main Street, Forest, MS 39074., Fax: 601-469-5180.

Felony, Civil Actions Over $2,500—Circuit Court, PO Box 371, Forest, MS 39074. 601-469-3601. 8AM-5PM. Access by: mail, in person.

Misdemeanor, Civil Actions Under $2,500, Eviction, Small Claims—Justice Court, PO Box 371, Forest, MS 39074. 601-469-4555, Fax: 601-469-5193. 8AM-5PM. Access by: mail, in person.

Probate—Chancery Court, 100 Main St, PO Box 630, Forest, MS 39074. 601-469-1922, Fax: 601-469-5180. 8AM-5PM. Access by: mail, in person.

Sharkey

Real Estate Recording—Sharkey County Clerk of the Chancery Court, 400 Locust St.are, Rolling Fork, MS 39159. 662-873-4317, Fax: 662-873-6045. 8AM-Noon,1-5PM.

Felony, Civil Actions Over $2,500—Circuit Court, PO Box 218, Rolling Fork, MS 39159. 662-873-2766, Fax: 662-873-6045. 8AM-Noon, 1-5PM. Access by: mail, in person.

Misdemeanor, Civil Actions Under $2,500, Eviction, Small Claims—Justice Court-East & West Districts, Rolling Fork, MS 39159. 662-873-6140. 8AM-5PM. Access by: mail, in person.

Probate—Chancery Court, 400 Locust St, PO Box 218, Rolling Fork, MS 39159. 662-873-2755, Fax: 662-873-6045. 8AM-Noon,1-5PM. Access by: mail, in person.

Simpson

Real Estate Recording—Simpson County Clerk of the Chancery Court, 111 W Pine Ave. Suite 3, Mendenhall, MS 39114., Fax: 601-847-7004. 8AM-5PM.

Felony, Civil Actions Over $2,500—Circuit Court, PO Box 307, Mendenhall, MS 39114. 601-847-2474, Fax: 601-847-4011. 8AM-5PM. Access by: mail, fax, in person.

Misdemeanor, Civil Actions Under $2,500, Eviction, Small Claims—Justice Court, 159 Court Ave, Mendenhall, MS 39114. 601-847-5848, Fax: 601-847-5856. 8AM-5PM. Access by: mail, fax, in person.

Probate—Chancery Court, Chancery Building, PO Box 367, Mendenhall, MS 39114. 601-847-2626. 8AM-5PM.

Smith

Real Estate Recording—Smith County Clerk of the Chancery Court, Courthouse, 123 Main St. Raleigh, MS 39153. 601-782-9811, Fax: 601-782-4690. 8AM-5PM.

Felony, Civil Actions Over $2,500—Circuit Court, PO Box 517, Raleigh, MS 39153. 601-782-4751, Fax: 601-782-4007. 8AM-5PM. Access by: mail, in person.

Misdemeanor, Civil Actions Under $2,500, Eviction, Small Claims—Justice Court, PO Box 171, Raleigh, MS 39153. 601-782-4334. 8AM-5PM. Access by: mail, in person.

Probate—Chancery Court, 123 Main St, PO Box 39, Raleigh, MS 39153. 601-782-9811. 8AM-Noon, 1-5PM.

Stone

Real Estate Recording—Stone County Clerk of the Chancery Court, 323 Cavers Avenue, Wiggins, MS 39577. 601-928-5266, Fax: 601-928-5248. 8AM-5PM.

Felony, Civil Actions Over $2,500—Circuit Court, Courthouse, 323 Cavers Ave, Wiggins, MS 39577. 601-928-5246, Fax: 601-928-5248. 8AM-5PM. Access by: mail, fax, in person.

Misdemeanor, Civil Actions Under $2,500, Eviction, Small Claims—Justice Court, 231 3rd Street, Wiggins, MS 39577. 601-928-4415, Fax: 601-928-2114. 8AM-5PM. Access by: mail, in person.

Justice Court-West District, 231 3rd St, Wiggins, MS 39577. 601-928-4415. 8AM-5PM. Access by: mail, in person.

Probate—Chancery Court, 323 E Cavers, PO Drawer 7, Wiggins, MS 39577. 601-928-5266, Fax: 601-928-5248. 8AM-5PM. Access by: mail, in person.

Sunflower

Real Estate Recording—Sunflower County Clerk of the Chancery Court, 200 Main St. Indianola, MS 38751., Fax: 662-887-7054. 8AM-5PM.

Felony, Civil Actions Over $2,500—Circuit Court, PO Box 576, Indianola, MS 38751. 662-887-1252, Fax: 662-887-7077. 8AM-5PM. Access by: mail, fax, in person.

Misdemeanor, Civil Actions Under $2,500, Eviction, Small Claims—Justice Court-Northern District, PO Box 52, Ruleville, MS 38771. 662-756-2835. 8AM-Noon, 1-5PM. Access by: mail, in person.

Justice Court-Southern District, PO Box 487, Indianola, MS 38751. 662-887-6921. 8AM-5PM. Access by: mail, in person.

Probate—Chancery Court, 200 Main St, PO Box 988, Indianola, MS 38751. 662-887-4703, Fax: 662-887-7054. 8AM-5PM. Access by: mail, in person.

Tallahatchie

Real Estate Recording—Tallahatchie County Clerk of the Chancery Court, Main Street, Courthouse, Sumner, MS 38957., Fax: 662-375-7252. 8AM-5PM.

Tallahatchie County Clerk of the Chancery Court, Courthouse, Charleston, MS 38921. 8AM-Noon,1-5PM.

Felony, Civil Actions Over $2,500—Charleston Circuit Court, PO Box 86, Charleston, MS 38921. 662-647-8758, Fax: 601-647-8490. 8AM-5PM. Access by: mail, in person.

Misdemeanor, Civil Actions Under $2,500, Eviction, Small Claims—Justice Court, PO Box 155, Sumner, MS 38957. 662-375-9452, Fax: 662-375-8200. 8AM-5PM. Access by: mail, in person.

Probate—Chancery Court, #1 Main St, PO Box 350, Charleston, MS 38921. 662-647-5551, Fax: 662-647-8490. 8AM-5PM.

Chancery Court, PO Box 180, Sumner, MS 38957. 662-375-8731, Fax: 662-375-7252. 8AM-Noon, 1-5PM.

Tate

Real Estate Recording—Tate County Clerk of the Chancery Court, 201 Ward Street, Senatobia, MS 38668., Fax: 601-560-6205.

Felony, Civil Actions Over $2,500—Circuit Court, 201 Ward St, Senatobia, MS 38668. 662-562-5211, Fax: 662-562-7486. 8AM-5PM. Access by: mail, in person.

Misdemeanor, Civil Actions Under $2,500, Eviction, Small Claims—Justice Court, 111 Court St, Senatobia, MS 38668. 662-562-7626. 8AM-5PM. Access by: mail, in person.

Probate—Chancery Court, 201 Ward St, Senatobia, MS 38668. 662-562-5661, Fax: 662-562-7486. 8AM-5PM.

Tippah

Real Estate Recording—Tippah County Clerk of the Chancery Court, Courthouse, Ripley, MS 38663., Fax: 662-837-1030. 8AM-5PM.

Felony, Civil Actions Over $2,500—Circuit Court, Courthouse, Ripley, MS 38663. 662-837-7370, Fax: 662-837-1030. 8AM-5PM. Access by: mail, phone, in person.

Misdemeanor, Civil Actions Under $2,500, Eviction, Small Claims—Justice Court, Justice Court, 205-B Spring Ave, Ripley, MS 38663. 662-837-8842. 8AM-5PM. Access by: mail, in person.

Probate—Chancery Court, PO Box 99, Ripley, MS 38663. 662-837-7374, Fax: 662-837-1030. 8AM-5PM.

Tishomingo

Real Estate Recording—Tishomingo County Clerk of the Chancery Court, 1008 Battleground Dr. Courthouse, Iuka, MS 38852. 662-423-7032, Fax: 662-423-7005. 8AM-5PM.

Felony, Civil Actions Over $2,500—Circuit Court, 1008 Battleground Dr, Iuka, MS 38852. 662-423-7026, Fax: 662-423-1667. 8AM-5PM. Access by: mail, in person.

Misdemeanor, Civil Actions Under $2,500, Eviction, Small Claims—Justice Court-Northern & Southern Districts, 1008 Battleground Drive, Iuka, MS 38852. 662-423-7033. 8AM-5PM. Access by: mail, in person.

Probate—Chancery Court, 1008 Battleground Dr, Iuka, MS 38852. 662-423-7010, Fax: 662-423-7005. 8AM-5PM.

Tunica

Real Estate Recording—Tunica County Clerk of the Chancery Court, Courthouse, Tunica, MS 38676. 662-363-1465. 8AM-Noon, 1-5PM.

Felony, Civil Actions Over $2,500—Circuit Court, PO Box 184, Tunica, MS 38676. 662-363-2842. 8AM-5PM. Access by: mail, in person.

Misdemeanor, Civil Actions Under $2,500, Eviction, Small Claims—Justice Court, 1070 N Court St, Tunica, MS 38676. 662-363-2178, Fax: 662-363-4234. 8AM-5PM. Access by: mail, in person.

Justice Court-Southern District, 5130 Old Moon Landing, Tunica, MS 38676. 662-363-2178. 8AM-5PM. Access by: mail, in person.

Probate—Chancery Court, PO Box 217, Tunica, MS 38676. 662-363-2451, Fax: 662-357-5934. 8AM-Noon, 1-5PM.

Union

Real Estate Recording—Union County Clerk of the Chancery Court, Courthouse, New Albany, MS 38652. 662-534-1973, Fax: 662-534-1907. 8AM-5PM.

Felony, Civil Actions Over $2,500—Circuit Court, PO Box 298, New Albany, MS 38652. 662-534-1910, Fax: 662-534-1961. 8AM-5PM. Access by: mail, fax, in person.

Misdemeanor, Civil Actions Under $2,500, Eviction, Small Claims—Justice Court-East & West Posts, PO Box 27, New Albany, MS 38652. 662-534-1951, Fax: 662-534-1935. 8AM-5PM. Access by: mail, fax, in person.

Probate—Chancery Court, PO Box 847, New Albany, MS 38652. 662-534-1900, Fax: 662-534-1907. 8AM-5PM.

Walthall

Real Estate Recording—Walthall County Clerk of the Chancery Court, 200 Ball Avenue, Tylertown, MS 39667., Fax: 601-876-6026.

Felony, Civil Actions Over $2,500—Circuit Court, 200 Ball Ave, Tylertown, MS 39667. 601-876-5677, Fax: 601-876-6688. 8AM-5PM. Access by: mail, in person.

Misdemeanor, Civil Actions Under $2,500, Eviction, Small Claims—Justice Court-Districts 1 & 2, PO Box 507, Tylertown, MS 39667. 601-876-2311. 8AM-5PM. Access by: mail, in person.

Probate—Chancery Court, 200 Ball Ave, PO Box 351, Tylertown, MS 39667. 601-876-3553, Fax: 601-876-7788. 8AM-5PM.

Warren

Real Estate Recording—Warren County Clerk of the Chancery Court, 1009 Cherry Street, Vicksburg, MS 39180. 601-636-6181, Fax: 601-634-4815. 8AM-5PM.

Felony, Misdemeanor, Civil—Circuit and County Court, PO Box 351, Vicksburg, MS 39181. 601-636-3961, Fax: 601-630-4100. 8AM-5PM. Access by: mail, fax, in person.

Misdemeanor, Civil Actions Under $2,500, Eviction, Small Claims—Justice Court-Northern, Central, and Southern Districts, PO Box 1598, Vicksburg, MS 39181. 601-634-6402. 8AM-5PM. Access by: mail, in person.

Probate—Chancery Court, PO Box 351, Vicksburg, MS 39181. 601-636-4415, Fax: 601-630-8016. 8AM-5PM.

Washington

Real Estate Recording—Washington County Clerk of the Chancery Court, 900 Washington Avenue, Greenville, MS 38701., Fax: 662-334-2725. 8AM-5PM.

Felony, Misdemeanor, Civil—Circuit and County Court, PO Box 1276, Greenville, MS 38702. 662-378-2747, Fax: 662-334-2698. 8AM-5PM. Access by: mail, fax, in person.

Misdemeanor, Civil Actions Under $2,500, Eviction, Small Claims—Justice Court-Districts 1-3, 905 W Alexander, Greenville, MS 38701. 662-332-0633. 8AM-5PM. Access by: mail, in person.

Probate—Chancery Court, PO Box 309, Greenville, MS 38702-0309. 662-332-1595, Fax: 662-334-2725. 8AM-5PM.

Wayne

Real Estate Recording—Wayne County Chancery Clerk, Wayne Co. Courthouse, 609 Azalea Dr. Waynesboro, MS 39367., Fax: 601-735-6224. 8AM-5PM.

Felony, Civil Actions Over $2,500—Circuit Court, PO Box 428, Waynesboro, MS 39367. 601-735-1171, Fax: 601-735-6261. 8AM-5PM. Access by: mail, in person.

Misdemeanor, Civil Actions Under $2,500, Eviction, Small Claims—Justice Court-Posts 1 & 2, 810 Chickasawhay St, Waynesboro, MS 39367. 601-735-3118, Fax: 601-735-6266. Access by: mail, phone, fax, in person.

Probate—Chancery Court, Courthouse, 609 Azalea Dr, Waynesboro, MS 39367. 601-735-2873, Fax: 601-735-6248. 8AM-5PM.

Webster

Real Estate Recording—Webster County Clerk of the Chancery Court, Highway 9 North, Courthouse, Walthall, MS 39771., Fax: 662-258-6657. 8AM-5PM.

Felony, Civil Actions Over $2,500—Circuit Court, PO Box 308, Walthall, MS 39771. 662-258-6287, Fax: 662-258-6657. 8AM-5PM. Access by: mail, fax, in person.

Misdemeanor, Civil Actions Under $2,500, Eviction, Small Claims—Justice Court-Districts 1 & 2, 114 Hwy 9 N, Eupora, MS 39744. 662-258-2590. 8AM-5PM. Access by: mail, in person.

Probate—Chancery Court, PO Box 398, Walthall, MS 39771. 662-258-4131, Fax: 662-258-6657. 8AM-5PM.

Wilkinson

Real Estate Recording—Wilkinson County Clerk of the Chancery Court, 525 Main Street, Woodville, MS 39669. 601-888-4562, Fax: 601-888-6776. 8AM-5PM.

Felony, Civil Actions Over $2,500—Circuit Court, PO Box 327, Woodville, MS 39669. 601-888-6697, Fax: 601-888-6984. 8:00AM-5:00PM. Access by: mail, fax, in person.

Misdemeanor, Civil Actions Under $2,500, Eviction, Small Claims—Justice Court-East & West Districts, PO Box 40, Woodville, MS 39669. 601-888-3538, Fax: 601-888-6776. 8AM-5PM. Access by: mail, in person.

Probate—Chancery Court, PO Box 516, Woodville, MS 39669. 601-888-4381, Fax: 601-888-6776. 8AM-5PM.

Winston

Real Estate Recording—Winston County Clerk of the Chancery Court, South Court Street, Louisville, MS 39339. 662-773-3631, Fax: 662-773-8831. 8AM-5PM.

Felony, Civil Actions Over $2,500—Circuit Court, PO Drawer 785, Louisville, MS 39339. 662-773-3581, Fax: 662-773-8825. 8AM-5PM. Access by: mail, phone, fax, in person.

Misdemeanor, Civil Actions Under $2,500, Eviction, Small Claims—Justice Court, PO Box 327, Louisville, MS 39339. 662-773-6016. 8AM-5PM. Access by: mail, in person.

Probate—Chancery Court, PO Drawer 69, Louisville, MS 39339. 662-773-3631, Fax: 662-773-8825. 8AM-5PM.

Yalobusha

Real Estate Recording—Yalobusha County Chancery Clerk, Courthouse, Coffeeville, MS 38922., Fax: 662-675-8187. 8AM-Noon, 1-5PM.

Yalobusha County Clerk of the Chancery Court, 132 Blackmur Drive, Courthouse, Water Valley, MS 38965., Fax: 601-473-5020. 8AM-Noon,1-5PM.

Felony, Civil Actions Over $2,500—Coffeeville Circuit Court, PO Box 260, Coffeeville, MS 38922. 662-675-8187, Fax: 662-675-8004. 8AM-5PM. Access by: mail, phone, fax, in person.

Water Valley Circuit Court, PO Box 431, Water Valley, MS 38965. 662-473-1341, Fax: 662-473-5020. 8AM-5PM. Access by: mail, fax, in person.

Misdemeanor, Civil Actions Under $2,500, Eviction, Small Claims—Justice Court-District 1, Rt. 3, Box 237, Coffeeville, MS 38922. 662-675-8115. 8AM-5PM. Access by: mail, in person.

Justice Court-Division 2, PO Box 272, Water Valley, MS 38965. 662-473-4502. 8AM-5PM. Access by: mail, in person.

Probate—Chancery Court, PO Box 260, Coffeeville, MS 38922. 662-675-2716, Fax: 662-675-8004. 8AM-Noon, 1-5PM.

Chancery Court, PO Box 664, Water Valley, MS 38965. 662-473-2091, Fax: 662-473-5020. 8AM-5PM.

Yazoo

Real Estate Recording—Yazoo County Clerk of the Chancery Court, 211 East Broadway, Yazoo City, MS 39194. 662-746-2661.

Felony, Misdemeanor, Civil—Circuit and County Court, PO Box 108, Yazoo City, MS 39194. 662-746-1872. 8AM-5PM. Access by: mail, in person.

Misdemeanor, Civil Actions Under $2,500, Eviction, Small Claims—Justice Court-Northern & Southern Districts, PO Box 798, Yazoo City, MS 39194. 662-746-8181. 8AM-5PM. Access by: mail, in person.

Probate—Chancery Court, PO Box 68, Yazoo City, MS 39194. 662-746-2661. 8AM-5PM.

Federal Courts

US District Court

Northern District of Mississippi

Aberdeen-Eastern Division PO Box 704, Aberdeen, MS 39730662-369-4952 Counties: Alcorn, Attala, Chickasaw, Choctaw, Clay, Itawamba, Lee, Lowndes, Monroe, Oktibbeha, Prentiss, Tishomingo, Winston. www.msnd.uscourts.gov

Clarksdale/Delta Division c/o Oxford-Northern Division, PO Box 727, Oxford, MS 38655662-234-1971, Record Room: 662-234-1351 Counties: Bolivar, Coahoma, De Soto, Panola, Quitman, Tallahatchie, Tate, Tunica. www.msnd.uscourts.gov

Greenville Division PO Box 190, Greenville, MS 38702-0190662-335-1651 Fax: 601-332-4292 Counties: Carroll, Humphreys, Leflore, Sunflower, Washington. www.msnd.uscourts.gov

Oxford-Northern Division PO Box 727, Oxford, MS 38655662-234-1971, Record Room: 662-234-1351 Counties: Benton, Calhoun, Grenada, Lafayette, Marshall, Montgomery, Pontotoc, Tippah, Union, Webster, Yalobusha. www.msnd.uscourts.gov

Southern District of Mississippi

Biloxi-Southern Division Room 243, 725 Washington Loop, Biloxi, MS 39530228-432-8623 Fax: 601-436-9632 Counties: George, Hancock, Harrison, Jackson, Pearl River, Stone. www.mssd.uscourts.gov

Hattiesburg Division Suite 200, 701 Main St, Hattiesburg, MS 39401601-583-2433 Counties: Covington, Forrest, Greene, Jefferson Davis, Jones, Lamar, Lawrence, Marion, Perry, Walthall. www.mssd.uscourts.gov

Jackson Division Suite 316, 245 E Capitol St, Jackson, MS 39201601-965-4439 Counties: Amite, Copiah, Franklin, Hinds, Holmes, Leake, Lincoln, Madison, Pike, Rankin, Scott, Simpson, Smith. www.mssd.uscourts.gov

Meridian Division c/o Jackson Division, Suite 316, 245 E Capiton St, Jackson, MS 39201601-965-4439 Counties: Clarke, Jasper, Kemper, Lauderdale, Neshoba, Newton, Noxubee, Wayne. www.mssd.uscourts.gov

Vicksburg Division c/o Jackson Division, Suite 316, 245 E Capitol St, Jackson, MS 39201601-965-4439 Counties: Adams, Claiborne, Issaquena, Jefferson, Sharkey, Warren, Wilkinson, Yazoo. www.mssd.uscourts.gov

US Bankruptcy Court

Northern District of Mississippi

Aberdeen Division PO Drawer 867, Aberdeen, MS 39730-0867662-369-2596, Record Room: 662-369-2596 Counties: Alcorn, Attala, Benton, Bolivar, Calhoun, Carroll, Chickasaw, Choctaw, Clay, Coahoma, De Soto, Grenada, Humphreys, Itawamba, Lafayette, Lee, Leflore, Lowndes, Marshall, Monroe, Montgomery, Oktibbeha, Panola, Pontotoc, Prentiss, Quitman, Sunflower,Tallahatchie, Tate, Tippah, Tishomingo, Tunica, Union, Washington, Webster, Winston, Yalobusha.

Southern District of Mississippi

Biloxi Division Room 117, 725 Washington Loop, Biloxi, MS 39530228-432-5542 Counties: Clarke, Covington, Forrest, George, Greene, Hancock, Harrison, Jackson, Jasper, Jefferson Davis, Jones, Kemper, Lamar, Lauderdale, Lawrence, Marion, Neshoba, Newton, Noxubee, Pearl River, Perry, Stone, Walthall, Wayne.

Jackson Division PO Drawer 2448, Jackson, MS 39225-2448601-965-5301 Counties: Adams, Amite, Claiborne, Copiah, Franklin, Hinds, Holmes, Issaquena, Jefferson, Leake, Lincoln, Madison, Pike, Rankin, Scott, Sharkey, Simpson, Smith, Warren, Wilkinson, Yazoo.

Attorney General's Office
PO Box 899   573-751-3321
Jefferson City, MO 65102   Fax: 573-751-0774
www.ago.state.mo.us/homepg.htm

Governor's Office
PO Box 720   573-751-3222
Jefferson City, MO 65102   Fax: 573-751-1495
www.gov.state.mo.us

State Archives
PO Box 1747   573-751-3280
Jefferson City, MO 65102-1747   Fax: 573-526-7333
mosl.sos.state.mo.us/rec-man/arch.html

Capital:	Jefferson City
	Cole County
Time Zone:	CST
Number of Counties:	114
Population:	5,402,058
Web Site:	www.state.mo.us

Search Unclaimed Property Online

www.sto.state.mo.us/ucp/database/
search.htm

State Agencies

Criminal Records
Missouri State Highway Patrol, Criminal Record & Identification Division, PO Box 568, Jefferson City, MO 65102-0568 (1510 E Elm St, Jefferson City, MO 65102); 573-526-6153; Fax: 573-751-9382; 8AM-5PM. Access by: mail.

Corporation Records
Fictitious Name
Limited Partnership Records
Assumed Name
Trademarks/Servicemarks
Limited Liability Company Records
Secretary of State, Corporation Services, PO Box 778, Jefferson City, MO 65102 (600 W Main, Jefferson City, MO 65101); 573-751-4153; Fax: 573-751-5841; 8AM-5PM. Access by: mail, phone, in person. mosl.sos.state.mo.us

Uniform Commercial Code
UCC Division, Secretary of State, PO Box 1159, Jefferson City, MO 65102 (600 W Main St, Rm 302, Jefferson City, MO 65101); 573-751-2360; Fax: 573-751-5841; 8AM-5PM. Access by: mail, phone, in person.

Federal Tax Liens
State Tax Liens
Records not available from state agency.

All tax liens are filed at the county level.

Sales Tax Registrations
Records not available from state agency.

This agency will neither confirm nor supply any information. They suggest to check at the city level.

Workers' Compensation Records
Labor & Industrial Relations Department, Workers Compensation Division, PO Box 58, Jefferson City, MO 65102-0058 (3315 W Truman Blvd, Jefferson City, MO 65101); 573-751-4231; Fax: 573-751-2012; 8AM-4:30PM. Access by: mail.

Birth Certificates

Department of Health, Bureau of Vital Records, PO Box 570, Jefferson City, MO 65102-0570 (930 Wildwood, Jefferson City, MO 65109); 573-751-6387, 573-751-6400 Message Number; Fax: 573-526-3846; 8AM-5PM M-F. Access by: mail, phone, in person. www.health.state.mo.us

Death Records

Department of Health, Bureau of Vital Records, PO Box 570, Jefferson City, MO 65102-0570; 573-751-6370, 573-751-6400 Message Number; Fax: 573-526-3846; 8AM-5PM M-F. Access by: mail. www.health.state.mo.us

Marriage Certificates
Divorce Records

Department of Health, Bureau of Vital Records, PO Box 570, Jefferson City, MO 65102; 573-751-6382, 573-751-6400 Message Number; Fax: 573-526-3846; 8AM-5PM, M-F. Access by: mail. www.health.state.mo.us

Accident Reports

Missouri Highway Patrol, Traffic Division, PO Box 568, Jefferson City, MO 65102-0568 (1510 E Elm St, Jefferson City, MO 65102); 573-526-6113; Fax: 573-751-9921; 8AM-5PM. Access by: mail. www.mshp.state.mo.us

Driver Records

Department of Revenue, Driver License Bureau, PO Box 200, Jefferson City, MO 65105-0200 (Harry S Truman Bldg, 301 W High St, Room 470, Jefferson City, MO 65105); 573-751-4300; Fax: 573-526-4769; 7:45AM-4:45PM. Access by: mail, phone, in person, online. http://dor.state.mo.us

Vehicle Ownership
Vehicle Identification
Boat & Vessel Ownership
Boat & Vessel Registration

Department of Revenue, Division of Motor Vehicles, PO Box 100, Jefferson City, MO 65105-0100 (Harry S Truman Bldg, 301 W High St, Jefferson City, MO 65105); 573-526-3669; Fax: 573-751-7060; 7:45AM-4:45PM. Access by: mail, phone, in person. http://dor.state.mo.us

Legislation-Current/Pending
Legislation-Passed

Legislative Library, 117A State Capitol, Jefferson City, MO 65101; 573-751-4633 Bill Status Only; 8:30AM-4:30PM. Access by: mail, phone, in person. www.moga.state.mo.us

Voter Registration

Restricted access.
The state neither will permit individual look-ups nor sell the records for commercial purposes. Records are sold in various media formats for political purposes. Individual look-ups can be done at the county level by the County Clerks.
Secretary of State, Division of Elections, PO Box 778, Jefferson City, MO 65102; 573-715-0356; Fax: 573-526-3242; 8AM-5PM mosl.sos.state.mo.us

GED Certificates

GED Office, PO Box 480, Jefferson City, MO 65102; 573-751-3504; 8AM-4:30PM.

Hunting License Information
Fishing License Information

Conservation Department, Fiscal Services, PO Box 180, Jefferson City, MO 65102-0180 (2901 W Truman Blvd, Jefferson City, MO 65102); 573-751-4115; Fax: 573-751-4864; 8AM-Noon; 1PM-5PM. www.state.mo.us/conservation

County Courts & Recording Offices

About the Courts...

Administration

State Court Administrator	573-751-4377
2112 Industrial Dr., PO Box 104480	Fax: 573-751-5540
Jefferson City, MO 65109	
www.osca.state.mo.us	

Court Structure

The Ciircuit Court is the court of general jurisdiction (114 courts in 45 circuits). There are Assouciate Circuit Courts and Combined Courts. Municipal Courts only have jurisdiction over traffic and ordinance violations.

Searching Hints

While the Missouri State Statutes set the Civil Case limit at $25,000 for the Associate Courts, and over $25,000 for the Circuit Courts, a great many Missouri County Courts have adopted their own Local Court Rules regarding civil cases and the monetary limits. Presumably, Local Court's. Rules are setup to allow the county to choose which court - Circuit or Associate - to send a case. This may depend on the court's case load, but generally, the cases are assigned more by "the nature of the case" and less by the monetary amount involved. Often, Local Court Rules are found where both the Circuit and the Associate Court are located in the same building, or share the same offices and perhaps the same phones. A solution for court record searches is to use this source to find a telephone number of a County's Court Clerk, and call to determine the court location of the case.

Online Access

There is limited statewide online internal computer access available on a system called Banner Case Management System. There is legal permission to expand coverage and access using a $7.00 per case fee to be collected, but, there are no implementation plans for the near term.

All Circuit and Associate Circuit Courts will have public access terminals available onsite by the end of 1999.

About the Recording Offices...

Organization

114 counties and one independent city, 115 recording offices. The recording officer is. Recorder of Deeds. The City of St. Louis has its own recording office. See the City/County Locator section at the end of this chapter for ZIP Codes that cover both the city and county of St. Louis. The entire state is in the Central Time Zone (CST).

UCC Records

Missouri is a dual filing state. Financing statements are filed both at the state level and with the Recorder of Deeds, except for consumer goods, farm related and real estate related filings, which are filed only with the Recorder. All but one county will perform UCC searches. Use search request form UCC-11. Search fees are usually $14.00 per debtor name without copies and $28.00 with copies. Copies usually cost $.50 per page.

Lien Records

All federal and state tax liens are filed with the county Recorder of Deeds. They are usually indexed together. Some counties will perform tax lien searches. Search and copy fees vary widely.

Real Estate Records

A few counties will perform real estate searches. Copy and certification fees vary.

County Courts & Recording Offices

Adair

Real Estate Recording—Adair County Recorder of Deeds, Courthouse, 106 W. Washington St. Kirksville, MO 63501., Fax: 660-785-3212. 8:30AM-Noon, 1-4:30PM.

Felony, Misdemeanor, Civil Actions Over $45,000—Circuit Court, PO Box 690, Kirksville, MO 63501. 660-665-2552, Fax: 660-665-3420. 8AM-5PM. Access by: mail, fax, in person.

Misdemeanor, Civil Actions Under $25,000, Eviction, Small Claims, Probate—Associate Circuit Court, Courthouse, Kirksville, MO 63501. 660-665-3877, Fax: 660-785-3222. 8AM-5PM. Access by: mail, phone, fax, in person.

Andrew

Real Estate Recording—Andrew County Recorder of Deeds, Courthouse, Savannah, MO 64485. 816-324-3614, Fax: 816-324-5667. 8AM-5PM.

Felony, Misdemeanor, Civil Actions Over $45,000—Circuit Court, PO Box 208 Division I, Savannah, MO 64485. 816-324-4221, Fax: 816-324-5667. 8AM-5PM. Access by: mail, phone, fax, in person.

Misdemeanor, Civil Actions Under $45,000, Eviction, Small Claims, Probate—Associate Circuit Court, PO Box 49, Savannah, MO 64485. 660-324-3921, Fax: 660-324-5667. 8AM-5PM. Access by: mail, in person.

Atchison

Real Estate Recording—Atchison County Recorder of Deeds, Courthouse, 400 Washington St. Rock Port, MO 64482. 816-744-2800, Fax: 660-744-5705. 8AM-Noon, 1-4:30PM.

Felony, Misdemeanor, Civil Actions Over $25,000—Circuit Court, PO Box 280, Rock Port, MO 64482. 660-744-2707, Fax: 660-744-5705. 8:30AM-4:30PM. Access by: mail, in person.

Misdemeanor, Civil Actions Under $25,000, Eviction, Small Claims, Probate—Associate Division, PO Box 187, Rock Port, MO 64482. 660-744-2700, Fax: 660-744-5705. 8AM-4:30PM. Access by: mail, fax, in person.

Audrain

Real Estate Recording—Audrain County Recorder of Deeds, Room 105, Audrain County Courthouse, 101 N. Jefferson, Mexico, MO 65265., Fax: 573-581-2380. 8AM-5PM.

Felony, Misdemeanor, Civil Actions Over $25,000—Circuit Court, Courthouse, 101 N Jefferson, Mexico, MO 65265. 573-473-5840, Fax: 573-581-3237. 8AM-5PM. Access by: in person.

Misdemeanor, Civil Actions Under $25,000, Eviction, Small Claims, Probate—Associate Circuit Court, Courthouse, 101 N Jefferson, Rm 205, Mexico, MO 65265. 573-473-5850, Fax: 573-581-3237. 8AM-5PM. Access by: mail, in person.

Barry

Real Estate Recording—Barry County Recorder of Deeds, Courthouse, Cassville, MO 65625. 8AM-4PM.

Felony, Misdemeanor, Civil Actions Over $25,000—Circuit Court, Barry County Courthouse, 700 Main, Ste 1, Cassville, MO 65625. 417-847-2361. 8AM-4PM. Access by: mail, in person.

Misdemeanor, Civil Actions Under $25,000, Eviction, Small Claims, Probate—Associate Circuit Court, Barry County Courthouse, Suite H, Cassville, MO 65625. 7:30AM-4PM. Access by: mail, in person.

Barton

Real Estate Recording—Barton County Recorder of Deeds, Courthouse, Room 107, 1004 Gulf, Lamar, MO 64759. 8:30AM-Noon, 12:30-4:30PM.

Felony, Misdemeanor, Civil, Eviction, Small Claims, Probate—Circuit Court, Courthouse, Lamar, MO 64759. 417-682-2444, Fax: 417-682-2960. 8AM-4:30PM. Access by: mail, in person.

Bates

Real Estate Recording—Bates County Recorder of Deeds, Courthouse, 1 N. Delaware, Butler, MO 64730. 816-679-3341. 8:30AM-4:30PM.

Felony, Misdemeanor, Civil Actions Over $25,000—Circuit Court, Bates County Courthouse, Butler, MO 64730. 660-679-5171, Fax: 660-679-4446. 8AM-4:30PM. Access by: mail, in person.

Misdemeanor, Civil Actions Under $25,000, Eviction, Small Claims, Probate—Associate Circuit Court, Courthouse, Butler, MO 64730. 660-679-3311. 8:30AM-4PM. Access by: mail, in person.

Benton

Real Estate Recording—Benton County Recorder of Deeds, Van Buren Street, Courthouse, Warsaw, MO 65355. 816-438-6313, Fax: 660-438-3652. 8:30AM-Noon, 1-4:30PM.

Felony, Misdemeanor, Civil Actions Over $25,000—Circuit Court, PO Box 37, Warsaw, MO 65355. 660-438-7712, Fax: 660-438-5755. 8AM-4:30PM. Access by: in person.

Misdemeanor, Civil Actions Under $25,000, Eviction, Small Claims, Probate—Associate Circuit Court, PO Box 666, Warsaw, MO 65355. 660-438-6231. 8AM-4:30PM. Access by: in person.

Bollinger

Real Estate Recording—Bollinger County Recorder of Deeds, Courthouse, 204 High St. Marble Hill, MO 63764. 573-238-2313, Fax: 573-238-2773. 8AM-4PM M,T,Th,F; 8AM-6PM W; 8Am-Noon 1st&last Sat.

Felony, Misdemeanor, Civil Actions Over $25,000—Circuit Court, PO Box 949, Marble Hill, MO 63764. 573-238-2710, Fax: 573-238-2773. 8AM-4PM. Access by: mail, in person.

Misdemeanor, Civil Actions Under $25,000, Eviction, Small Claims, Probate—Associate Circuit Court, PO Box 1040, Marble Hill, MO 63764-1040. 573-238-2730, Fax: 573-238-4511. 8AM-4PM. Access by: in person.

Boone

Real Estate Recording—Boone County Recorder of Deeds, Boone County Gov't Center, 801 E. Walnut, Rm 132, Columbia, MO 65201. 573-886-4365, Fax: 573-886-4359. 8AM-5PM.

Felony, Misdemeanor, Civil, Eviction, Small Claims, Probate—Circuit Court, 701 E Walnut, Columbia, MO 65201. 573-886-4000, Fax: 573-886-4044. 8AM-5AM. Access by: mail, phone, in person.

Buchanan

Real Estate Recording—Buchanan County Recorder of Deeds, 411 Jules Streets, Courthouse, St. Joseph, MO 64501. 816-271-1432, Fax: 816-271-1582. 8AM-4:30PM.

Felony, Misdemeanor, Civil, Eviction, Small Claims—Circuit Court, 411 Jules St, Rm 331, St Joseph, MO 64501. 816-271-1462, Fax: 816-271-1538. 8AM-5PM. Access by: in person.

Probate—Probate Court, Buchanan County Courthouse, 411 Jules St, Room 333, St Joseph, MO 64501. 816-271-1477, Fax: 816-271-1538. 8AM-5PM.

Butler

Real Estate Recording—Butler County Recorder of Deeds, 100 N. Main Street, Courthouse, Poplar Bluff, MO 63901. 573-686-8085. 8AM-4PM.

Felony, Misdemeanor, Civil Actions Over $45,000—Circuit Court, Courthouse, Poplar Bluff, MO 63901. 573-686-8082, Fax: 573-686-8094. 7:30AM-4PM. Access by: mail, in person.

Misdemeanor, Civil Actions Under $45,000, Eviction, Small Claims, Probate—Associate Circuit Court, Courthouse, Poplar Bluff, MO 63901. 573-686-8087, Fax: 573-686-8093. 7:30AM-4PM. Access by: mail, fax, in person.

Caldwell

Real Estate Recording—Caldwell County Recorder of Deeds, Courthouse, 49 E. Main St. Kingston, MO 64650., Fax: 816-586-2705. 8:30AM-4:30PM.

Felony, Misdemeanor, Civil Actions Over $45,000—Circuit Court, PO Box 86, Kingston, MO 64650. 816-586-2581, Fax: 816-586-2705. 8:30AM-4:30PM. Access by: mail, phone, in person.

Misdemeanor, Civil Actions Under $45,000, Eviction, Small Claims, Probate—Associate Circuit Court, PO Box 5, Kingston, MO 64650. 816-586-2771, Fax: 816-586-2333. 8AM-4:30PM. Access by: in person.

Callaway

Real Estate Recording—Callaway County Recorder of Deeds, 10 East 5th Street, Fulton, MO 65251. 8AM-5PM.

Felony, Misdemeanor, Civil Actions Over $25,000—Circuit Court, 10 E 5th St, Fulton, MO 65251. 573-642-0780, Fax: 573-642-0700. 8AM-5PM. Access by: mail, fax, in person.

Misdemeanor, Civil Actions Under $25,000, Eviction, Small Claims, Probate—Associate Circuit Court, Courthouse, Fulton, MO 65251. 573-642-0777, Fax: 573-642-0700. 8AM-5PM. Access by: mail, in person.

Camden

Real Estate Recording—Camden County Recorder of Deeds, 1 Court Circle, Camdenton, MO 65020. 573-346-4440, Fax: 573-346-5422. 8:30AM-4:30PM.

Felony, Misdemeanor, Civil Actions Over $25,000—Circuit Court, PO Box 930, Camdenton, MO 65020. 573-346-4440, Fax: 573-346-5422. 8:30AM-4:30PM. Access by: mail, in person.

Civil Actions Under $25,000, Eviction, Small Claims, Probate—Associate Circuit Court-Civil Division, PO Box 19, Camdenton, MO 65020. 573-346-4440. 8AM-5PM. Access by: mail, in person.

Misdemeanor—Associate Circuit Court-Criminal Division, PO Box 19, Camdenton, MO 65020. 573-346-4440. 8:00AM-5:00PM. Access by: mail, in person.

Cape Girardeau

Real Estate Recording—Cape Girardeau County Recorder of Deeds, #1 Barton Square, Jackson, MO 63755. 573-243-3720, Fax: 573-243-8124. 8AM-4:30PM.

Civil—Circuit & Associate Circuit Court-Civil Division, 44 N Lorimier, PO Box 2047, Cape Girardeau, MO 63702. 573-335-8253, Fax: 573-335-8295. 8AM-5PM. Access by: mail, in person.

Felony, Misdemeanor—Circuit Court-Criminal Division I & II, 101 Court St, Jackson, MO 63755. 573-243-8446, Fax: 573-243-0787. 8AM-4:30PM. Access by: mail, in person.

Carroll

Real Estate Recording—Carroll County Recorder of Deeds, Courthouse, Carrollton, MO 64633. 816-542-1977, Fax: 660-542-1444. 8:30AM-Noon, 1-4:30PM.

Felony, Misdemeanor, Civil Actions Over $25,000—Circuit Court, PO Box 245, Carrollton, MO 64633. 660-542-1466, Fax: 660-542-1444. 8:30AM-4:30PM. Access by: mail, fax, in person.

Misdemeanor, Civil Actions Under $45,000, Eviction, Small Claims, Probate—Associate Circuit Court, Courthouse, 8 S Main, Suite 1, Carrollton, MO 64633. 660-542-1818, Fax: 660-542-1444. 8:30AM-4:30PM. Access by: mail, in person.

Carter

Real Estate Recording—Carter County Recorder of Deeds, 105 Main Street, Van Buren, MO 63965. 315-253-7748, Fax: 573-323-8577. 8AM-4PM.

Felony, Misdemeanor, Civil Actions Over $45,000—Circuit Court, PO Box 578, Van Buren, MO 63965. 573-323-4513, Fax: 573-323-8577. 8AM-4PM. Access by: mail, phone, in person.

Misdemeanor, Civil Actions Under $45,000, Eviction, Small Claims, Probate—Associate Circuit Court, PO Box 328, Van Buren, MO 63965. 573-323-4344, Fax: 573-323-4344. 8AM-4PM. Access by: mail, phone, fax, in person.

Cass

Real Estate Recording—Cass County Recorder of Deeds, 102 East Wall Street, Cass County Court House, Harrisonville, MO 64701. 816-380-1975, Fax: 816-380-5136. 8AM-4:30PM.

Felony, Misdemeanor, Civil Actions Over $45,000—Circuit Court, 102 E Wall, Harrisonville, MO 64701. 816-380-5100, Fax: 816-380-5798. 8AM-4:30PM. Access by: mail, in person.

Misdemeanor, Civil Actions Under $25,000, Eviction, Small Claims, Probate—Associate Circuit Court, PO Box 384, Harrisonville, MO 64701. 816-380-8100, Fax: 816-380-8195. 8AM-4:30PM. Access by: mail, in person.

Cedar

Real Estate Recording—Cedar County Recorder of Deeds, Courthouse, 103 South St. Stockton, MO 65785. 417-276-4413, Fax: 417-276-5001. 8AM-Noon, 1-4PM.

Felony, Misdemeanor, Civil Actions Over $45,000—Circuit Court, PO Box 665, Stockton, MO 65785. 417-276-6700, Fax: 417-276-5001. 8AM-4:30PM. Access by: mail, in person.

Misdemeanor, Civil Actions Under $45,000, Eviction, Small Claims, Probate—Associate Circuit Court, PO Box 665, Stockton, MO 65785. 417-276-6700, Fax: 417-276-5001. 8AM-4:30PM. Access by: mail, in person.

Chariton

Real Estate Recording—Chariton County Recorder of Deeds, Highway 24 West, Courthouse, Keytesville, MO 65261. 816-288-3789, Fax: 660-288-3602. 8:30AM-Noon, 1-4:30PM.

Felony, Misdemeanor, Civil Actions Over $25,000—Circuit Court, PO Box 112, Keytesville, MO 65261. 660-288-3602, Fax: 660-288-3602. 8:30AM-4:30PM. Access by: mail, fax, in person.

Misdemeanor, Civil Actions Under $25,000, Eviction, Small Claims, Probate—Associate Circuit Court, 306 South Cherry, Keytesville, MO 65261. 660-288-3271, Fax: 660-288-3602. 8AM-4:30PM. Access by: mail, phone, in person.

Christian

Real Estate Recording—Christian County Recorder of Deeds, Church Street, North Side Square, Room 102, Ozark, MO 65721., Fax: 417-581-0391. 8AM-4:30PM.

Felony, Misdemeanor, Civil Actions Over $45,000—Circuit Court, PO Box 278, Ozark, MO 65721. 417-581-6372, Fax: 417-581-0391. 8AM-4:30PM. Access by: mail, in person.

Misdemeanor, Civil Actions Under $45,000, Eviction, Small Claims, Probate—Associate Circuit Court, PO Box 175 (criminal), PO Box 296 (civil), Ozark, MO 65721., Fax: 417-581-0391. 8AM-4:30PM. Access by: mail, phone, in person.

Clark

Real Estate Recording—Clark County Recorder of Deeds, 111 East Court, Courthouse, Kahoka, MO 63445., Fax: 660-727-1051. 8AM-Noon, 1-4PM.

Felony, Misdemeanor, Civil Actions Over $45,000—Circuit Court, 111 E Court, Kahoka, MO 63445. 660-727-3292, Fax: 660-727-1051. 8AM-4PM. Access by: mail, phone, fax, in person.

Misdemeanor, Civil Actions Under $45,000, Eviction, Small Claims, Probate—Associate Circuit Court, 113 W Court, Kahoka, MO 63445. 660-727-3628, Fax: 660-727-2544. 8AM-4PM. Access by: mail, in person.

Clay

Real Estate Recording—Clay County Recorder of Deeds, Courthouse Square, Administration Bldg. Liberty, MO 64068. 816-792-7649. 8AM-4PM.

Felony, Misdemeanor, Civil Actions Over $25,000—Circuit Court, PO Box 218, Liberty, MO 64069-0218. 816-792-7706, Fax: 816-792-7778. 8AM-5PM. Access by: mail, fax, in person.

Misdemeanor, Civil Actions Under $25,000, Eviction, Small Claims, Probate—Associate Circuit Court, PO Box 218, Liberty, MO 64069-0218. 816-792-7706, Fax: 816-792-7778. 8AM-5PM. Access by: mail, in person.

Clinton

Real Estate Recording—Clinton County Recorder of Deeds, 207 North Street, Plattsburg, MO 64477., Fax: 816-539-3893. 8AM-Noon, 1-5PM.

Felony, Misdemeanor, Civil Actions Over $45,000—Circuit Court, PO Box 275, Plattsburg, MO 64477. 816-539-3731, Fax: 816-539-3893. 8AM-5PM. Access by: in person.

Misdemeanor, Civil Actions Under $45,000, Eviction, Small Claims, Probate—Associate Circuit Court, PO Box 383, Plattsburg, MO 64477. 816-539-3755, Fax: 816-539-3893. 8AM-4:30PM. Access by: mail, fax, in person.

Cole

Real Estate Recording—Cole County Recorder of Deeds, 311 East High, Jefferson City, MO 65101. 573-634-9121. 8AM-4:30PM.

Felony, Misdemeanor, Civil Actions Over $25,000—Circuit Court, PO Box 1156, Jefferson City, MO 65102-1156. 573-634-9151, Fax: 573-635-0796. 7AM-4:30PM. Access by: mail, fax, in person.

Misdemeanor, Civil Actions Under $25,000, Eviction, Small Claims, Probate—Associate Circuit Court, PO Box 503, Jefferson City, MO 65102. 573-634-9171, Fax: 573-635-5376. 8AM-4:30PM. Access by: mail, fax, in person.

Cooper

Real Estate Recording—Cooper County Recorder of Deeds, 200 Main Street, Courthouse - Room 26, Boonville, MO 65233., Fax: 660-882-2043. 8:30AM-5PM.

Felony, Misdemeanor, Civil Actions Over $25,000—Circuit Court, 200 Main St, Rm 26, Boonville, MO 65233. 660-882-2232, Fax: 660-882-2043. 8:30AM-5:00PM. Access by: mail, in person.

Misdemeanor, Civil Actions Under $25,000, Eviction, Small Claims, Probate—Associate Circuit Court, 200 Main, Rm 31, Boonville, MO 65233. 660-882-5604, Fax: 660-882-2043. 8:30AM-5PM. Access by: mail, in person.

Crawford

Real Estate Recording—Crawford County Recorder of Deeds, Main Street, Steelville, MO 65565. 573-775-2899, Fax: 573-775-3365. 8AM-4:30PM.

Felony, Misdemeanor, Civil Actions Over $45,000—Circuit Court, PO Box 177, Steelville, MO 65565. 573-775-2866, Fax: 573-775-2452. 8AM-5PM. Access by: mail, in person.

Misdemeanor, Civil Actions Under $25,000, Eviction, Small Claims, Probate—Associate Circuit Court, PO Box B.C. Steelville, MO 65565. 573-775-2149, Fax: 573-775-4010. 8AM-5PM. Access by: mail, phone, fax, in person.

Dade

Real Estate Recording—Dade County Recorder of Deeds, Courthouse, Greenfield, MO 65661. 417-637-2732, Fax: 417-637-5055. 8AM-4PM.

Felony, Misdemeanor, Civil Actions Over $25,000—Circuit Court, Courthouse, Greenfield, MO 65661. 417-637-2271, Fax: 417-637-5055. 8AM-4PM. Access by: mail, in person.

Misdemeanor, Civil Actions Under $45,000, Eviction, Small Claims, Probate—Associate Circuit Court, Courthouse, Greenfield, MO 65661. 417-637-2741, Fax: 417-637-5055. 8AM-4PM. Access by: mail, in person.

Dallas

Real Estate Recording—Dallas County Recorder of Deeds, Courthouse, Room 14, Buffalo, MO 65622., Fax: 417-345-5539. 8AM-Noon,1-4PM.

Felony, Misdemeanor, Civil Actions Over $45,000—Circuit Court, PO Box 373, Buffalo, MO 65622. 417-345-2243, Fax: 417-345-5539. 8AM-4PM. Access by: mail, fax, in person.

Misdemeanor, Civil Actions Under $45,000, Eviction, Small Claims, Probate—Associate Circuit Court, PO Box 1150, Buffalo, MO 65622. 417-345-7641, Fax: 417-345-5358. 8AM-4PM. Access by: mail, in person.

Daviess

Real Estate Recording—Daviess County Recorder of Deeds, Courthouse, 2nd Floor, Gallatin, MO 64640. 816-663-2432, Fax: 660-663-3376. 8AM-Noon, 1-4:30PM.

Felony, Misdemeanor, Civil Actions Over $45,000—Circuit Court, PO Box 337, Gallatin, MO 64640. 660-663-2932, Fax: 660-663-3376. 8AM-4:30PM. Access by: mail, phone, fax, in person.

Misdemeanor, Civil Actions Under $45,000, Eviction, Small Claims, Probate—Associate Circuit Court, Courthouse, Gallatin, MO 64640. 660-663-2532. 8AM-4:30PM. Access by: mail, fax, in person.

De Kalb

Real Estate Recording—De Kalb County Recorder of Deeds, Courthouse, Room 1, 109 W. Main, Maysville, MO 64469. 816-449-5810, Fax: 816-449-2440. 8:30AM-Noon, 1-4:30PM.

Felony, Civil Actions Over $45,000—Circuit Court, PO Box 248, Maysville, MO 64469. 816-449-2602, Fax: 816-449-2440. 8:30AM-4:30PM. Access by: in person.

Misdemeanor, Civil Actions Under $45,000, Eviction, Small Claims, Probate—Associate Circuit Court, PO Box 512, Maysville, MO 64469. 816-449-5400, Fax: 816-449-2440. 8:30AM-4:30PM. Access by: mail, in person.

Dent

Real Estate Recording—Dent County Recorder of Deeds, 112 East 5th Street, Salem, MO 65560. 573-729-8260, Fax: 573-729-9414. 8AM-4:30PM.

Felony, Misdemeanor, Civil Actions Over $45,000—Circuit Court, 112 E 5th St, Salem, MO 65560. 573-729-3931, Fax: 573-729-9414. 8AM-4:30PM. Access by: mail, in person.

Misdemeanor, Civil Actions Under $25,000, Eviction, Small Claims, Probate—Associate Circuit Court, 112 E 5th St, Salem, MO 65560. 573-729-3134, Fax: 573-729-5146. 8AM-4:30PM. Access by: mail, in person.

Douglas

Real Estate Recording—Douglas County Recorder of Deeds, 203 Southeast 2nd Avenue, Ava, MO 65608., Fax: 417-683-3100. 8AM-4:30PM.

Felony, Misdemeanor, Civil Actions Over $45,000—Circuit Court, PO Box 249, Ava, MO 65608. 417-683-4713, Fax: 417-683-3121. 8AM-4:30PM. Access by: mail, phone, in person.

Misdemeanor, Civil Actions Under $45,000, Eviction, Small Claims, Probate—Associate Circuit Court, PO Box 276, Ava, MO 65608. 417-683-2114, Fax: 417-683-3121. 8AM-5PM. Access by: mail, phone, in person.

Dunklin

Real Estate Recording—Dunklin County Recorder of Deeds, Courthouse Square, Room 204, Kennett, MO 63857. 8:30AM-Noon, 1-4:30PM.

Felony, Misdemeanor, Civil Actions Over $45,000—Circuit Court Division I, PO Box 567, Kennett, MO 63857. 315-265-4318, Fax: 314-888-6677. 8:30AM-4:30PM. Access by: mail, phone, fax, in person.

Misdemeanor, Civil Actions Under $25,000, Eviction, Small Claims, Probate—Associate Circuit Court, Courthouse Rm 103, Kennett, MO 63857. 315-265-5890. 8AM-4PM. Access by: mail, in person.

Franklin

Real Estate Recording—Franklin County Recorder of Deeds, 300 East Main St. Room 101, Union, MO 63084. 636-583-6392, Fax: 636-583-6367. 8AM-4:30PM.

Felony, Misdemeanor, Civil Actions Over $45,000—Circuit Court, PO Box 272, Union, MO 63084. 636-583-6300. 8AM-4:30PM. Access by: mail, in person.

Misdemeanor, Civil Actions Under $25,000, Eviction, Small Claims, Probate—Associate Circuit Court, PO Box 526, Union, MO 63084. 636-583-6326. 8AM-4:30PM. Access by: mail, in person.

Gasconade

Real Estate Recording—Gasconade County Recorder of Deeds, 119 E.1st St. Room 6, Hermann, MO 65041. 573-486-2411, Fax: 573-486-3693. 8AM-4:30PM.

Felony, Misdemeanor, Civil Actions Over $45,000—Circuit Court, 119 E 1st St, Rm 6, Hermann, MO 65041-1182. 573-486-2632, Fax: 573-486-3693. 8AM-4:30PM. Access by: mail, phone, fax, in person.

Misdemeanor, Civil Actions Under $25,000, Eviction, Small Claims, Probate—Associate Circuit Court, 119 E. 1st St. Rm 3, Hermann, MO 65041. 573-486-2321, Fax: 573-486-3693. 8AM-4:30PM. Access by: mail, phone, fax, in person.

Gentry

Real Estate Recording—Gentry County Recorder of Deeds, 200 W. Clay, Albany, MO 64402., Fax: 660-726-4102. 8AM-4:30PM.

Felony, Misdemeanor, Civil Actions Over $25,000—Circuit Court, PO Box 27, Albany, MO 64402. 660-726-3618, Fax: 660-726-4102. 8AM-4:30PM. Access by: mail, in person.

Misdemeanor, Civil Actions Under $25,000, Eviction, Small Claims, Probate—Associate Circuit Court, 200 W Clay St, Albany, MO 64402. 660-726-3411, Fax: 660-726-4102. 8AM-4:30PM. Access by: in person.

Greene

Real Estate Recording—Greene County Recorder of Deeds, 940 Boonville, Room 100, Springfield, MO 65802., Fax: 417-868-4807. 8AM-4:30PM.

Felony, Misdemeanor, Civil Actions Over $45,000—Circuit Court, 1010 Boomville, Springfield, MO 65802. 417-868-4074. 7:30AM-5:30AM. Access by: mail, in person.

Misdemeanor, Civil Actions Under $25,000, Eviction, Small Claims, Probate—Associate Circuit Court, 1010 N Boonville, Springfield, MO 65802. 417-868-4110. 8AM-5PM. Access by: mail, phone, in person.

Grundy

Real Estate Recording—Grundy County Recorder of Deeds, Courthouse, 700 Main St. Trenton, MO 64683. 8:30AM-4:30PM.

Felony, Misdemeanor, Civil Actions Over $45,000—Circuit Court, Courthouse, 700 Main St, Trenton, MO 64683. 660-359-6605, Fax: 660-359-6604. 8:30AM-4:30PM. Access by: mail, in person.

Misdemeanor, Civil Actions Under $25,000, Eviction, Small Claims, Probate—Associate Circuit Court, PO Box 26, Trenton, MO 64683. 660-359-6606. 8:30AM-4:30PM. Access by: mail, in person.

Harrison

Real Estate Recording—Harrison County Recorder of Deeds, 1515 Main Street, Courthouse, Bethany, MO 64424. 816-425-6442, Fax: 660-425-3772. 8AM-Noon, 1-4:30PM.

Felony, Misdemeanor, Civil Actions Over $45,000—Circuit Court, PO Box 525, Bethany, MO 64424. 660-425-6425, Fax: 660-425-3772. 8AM-4:30PM. Access by: mail, in person.

Misdemeanor, Civil Actions Under $45,000, Eviction, Small Claims, Probate—Associate Circuit Court, Box 525, Bethany, MO 64424. 660-425-6432, Fax: 660-425-3772. 8AM-5PM. Access by: mail, in person.

Henry

Real Estate Recording—Henry County Recorder of Deeds, 100 W. Franklin #4, Courthouse, Clinton, MO 64735. 816-885-6963, Fax: 660-885-2264. 8:30AM-4:30PM.

Felony, Misdemeanor, Civil Actions Over $45,000—Circuit Court, 100 W Franklin Rm 12, Clinton, MO 64735. 660-885-6963, Fax: 660-885-8247. 8AM-4:30PM. Access by: mail, in person.

Misdemeanor, Civil Actions Under $45,000, Eviction, Small Claims, Probate—Associate Circuit Court, Courthouse, Clinton, MO 64735. 660-885-6963, Fax: 660-885-8456. 8AM-4:30PM. Access by: mail, in person.

Hickory

Real Estate Recording—Hickory County Recorder of Deeds, Courthouse, On the Square, Hermitage, MO 65668. 417-745-6310, Fax: 417-745-6670. 8AM-Noon, 12:30-4:30PM.

Felony, Misdemeanor, Civil Actions Over $45,000—Circuit Court, PO Box 101, Hermitage, MO 65668. 417-745-6421, Fax: 417-745-6670. 8AM-4:30PM. Access by: mail, in person.

Misdemeanor, Civil Actions Under $45,000, Eviction, Small Claims, Probate—Associate Circuit Court, PO Box 75, Hermitage, MO 65668. 417-745-6822, Fax: 417-745-6670. 8AM-4:30PM. Access by: mail, in person.

Holt

Real Estate Recording—Holt County Recorder of Deeds, 100 West Nodaway, Courthouse, Oregon, MO 64473. 816-446-3397. 8:30AM-Noon, 1-4:30PM.

Felony, Misdemeanor, Civil Actions Over $45,000—Circuit Court, PO Box 318, Oregon, MO 64473. 660-446-3301, Fax: 660-446-3328. 8AM-4:30PM. Access by: mail, phone, in person.

Misdemeanor, Civil Actions Under $45,000, Eviction, Small Claims, Probate—Associate Circuit Court, PO Box 173, Oregon, MO 64473. 660-446-3380. 8:30AM-4:30PM. Access by: mail, in person.

Howard

Real Estate Recording—Howard County Recorder of Deeds, 1 Courthouse Square, Fayette, MO 65248. 816-248-2196, Fax: 660-248-1075. 8:30AM-4:30PM.

Felony, Misdemeanor, Civil Actions Over $30,000—Circuit Court, 1 Courthouse Square, Fayette, MO 65248. 660-248-2194, Fax: 660-248-1075. 8:30AM-4:30PM. Access by: in person.

Misdemeanor, Civil Actions Under $45,000, Eviction, Small Claims, Probate—Associate Circuit Court, PO Box 370, Fayette, MO 65248. 660-248-3326, Fax: 660-248-1075. 8:30AM-4:30PM. Access by: in person.

Howell

Real Estate Recording—Howell County Recorder of Deeds, Courthouse, West Plains, MO 65775. 417-256-4261. 8AM-5PM.

Felony, Misdemeanor, Civil Actions Over $45,000—Circuit Court, PO Box 1011, West Plains, MO 65775. 417-256-3741, Fax: 417-256-4650. 8AM-5PM. Access by: mail, phone, fax, in person.

Misdemeanor, Civil Actions Under $45,000, Eviction, Small Claims, Probate—Associate Circuit Court, 222 Courthouse, West Plains, MO 65775. 417-256-4050, Fax: 417-256-5826. 8AM-4:30PM. Access by: mail, in person.

Iron

Real Estate Recording—Iron County Recorder of Deeds, 250 South Main, Ironton, MO 63650. 573-546-7611, Fax: 573-546-2166. 8AM-4:30PM.

Felony, Civil Actions Over $45,000—Circuit Court, PO Box 24, Ironton, MO 63650. 573-546-2811, Fax: 573-546-2166. 8AM-4PM. Access by: in person.

Misdemeanor, Civil Actions Under $45,000, Eviction, Small Claims, Probate—Associate Circuit Court, PO Box 325, Ironton, MO 63650. 573-546-2511, Fax: 573-546-6006. 9AM-4PM. Access by: mail, fax, in person.

Jackson

Real Estate Recording—Jackson County Recorder of Deeds, 415 East 12th Street, Room 104, Kansas City, MO 64106. 816-881-3270, Fax: 816-881-3719. 8AM-5PM.

Civil, Eviction, Small Claims, Probate—Circuit Court-Civil Division, 415 E 12th, Kansas City, MO 64106. 816-881-3926. 8AM-5PM. Access by: in person. Special note: There is a combined computer system with the Independence civil court. www.16thcircuit.org

Independence Circuit Court-Civil Annex, 308 W Kansas, Independence, MO 64050. 816-881-4497, Fax: 816-881-4410. 8AM-5PM. Access by: mail, in person. Special note: This court is on the same computer system as Kansas City for civil cases, but files maintained separately. www.16thcircuit.org

Felony, Misdemeanor—Circuit Court-Criminal Division, 1315 Locust, Kansas City, MO 64106. 816-881-4350, Fax: 816-881-3420. 8AM-5PM. Access by: mail, fax, in person. www.16thcircuit.org

Jasper

Real Estate Recording—Jasper County Recorder of Deeds, 3rd & Main, Room 207, Carthage, MO 64836. 417-358-0448. 8:30AM-4:30PM.

Felony, Misdemeanor, Civil Actions Over $45,000—Circuit Court, Courthouse, Rm 303, Carthage, MO 64836. 417-358-0441, Fax: 417-358-0461. 8:00AM-5:00PM. Access by: mail, fax, in person.

Misdemeanor, Civil Actions Under $45,000, Eviction, Small Claims, Probate—Associate Circuit Court, Courthouse Rm 304, Carthage, MO 64836. 417-358-0450, Fax: 417-358-0460. 8:30AM-4:30PM. Access by: mail, fax, in person.

Jefferson

Real Estate Recording—Jefferson County Recorder of Deeds, 2nd & Maple, Courthouse, Hillsboro, MO 63050. 8:30AM-4:30PM.

Civil Actions Over $25,000—Circuit Court-Civil Division, PO Box 100, Hillsboro, MO 63050. 636-797-5443, Fax: 636-797-5073. 8AM-4:30PM. Access by: mail, phone, fax, in person.

Felony, Misdemeanor—Circuit Court-Criminal Division, PO Box 100, Hillsboro, MO 63050. 636-797-5370, Fax: 636-797-5073. 8AM-4:30PM. Access by: mail, phone, in person.

Civil Under $25,000, Eviction, Small Claims, Probate—Associate Circuit Court, PO Box 100, Hillsboro, MO 63050. 636-789-5362, Fax: 636-789-3804. 8:00AM-4:30PM. Access by: mail, fax, in person.

Johnson

Real Estate Recording—Johnson County Recorder of Deeds, North Holden Street, Courthouse, Warrensburg, MO 64093. 816-747-7411. 8:30AM-4:30PM.

Felony, Civil Actions Over $45,000—Circuit Court, Courthouse, PO Box 436, Warrensburg, MO 64093. 660-747-6331, Fax: 660-747-7927. 8AM-4:30PM. Access by: in person.

Misdemeanor, Civil Actions Under $45,000, Eviction, Small Claims, Probate—Associate Circuit Court, Johnson County Courthouse, Warrensburg, MO 64093. 660-747-2227. 8AM-4:30PM. Access by: mail, in person.

Knox

Real Estate Recording—Knox County Recorder of Deeds, Courthouse, Edina, MO 63537. 816-397-3364, Fax: 660-397-3331. 8:30AM-4PM.

Felony, Misdemeanor, Civil Actions Over $45,000—Circuit Court, PO Box 116, Edina, MO 63537. 660-397-2305, Fax: 660-397-3331. 8:30AM-4PM. Access by: mail, in person.

Misdemeanor, Civil Actions Under $25,000, Eviction, Small Claims, Probate—Associate Circuit Court, PO Box 126, Edina, MO 63537. 660-397-3146, Fax: 660-397-3331. 8:30AM-4PM. Access by: mail, in person.

Laclede

Real Estate Recording—Laclede County Recorder of Deeds, Main Courthouse, 200 North Adams St, Lebanon, MO 65536. 417-532-4741, Fax: 417-532-3852. 8AM-4PM.

Felony, Misdemeanor, Civil Actions Over $45,000—Circuit Court, 200 N Adams St, Lebanon, MO 65536. 417-532-2471, Fax: 417-532-3683. 8AM-4PM. Access by: mail, phone, in person.

Misdemeanor, Civil Actions Under $45,000, Eviction, Small Claims, Probate—Associate Circuit Court, 200 N Adams St, Lebanon, MO 65536. 417-532-9196. 8AM-4PM. Access by: mail, phone, in person.

Lafayette

Real Estate Recording—Lafayette County Recorder of Deeds, 11th & Main, Lexington, MO 64067. 816-259-3711, Fax: 660-259-2918. 8:30AM-4:30PM.

Felony, Misdemeanor, Civil Actions Over $5,000—Circuit Court, PO Box 340, Lexington, MO 64067. 660-259-6101, Fax: 660-259-6148. 8AM-5PM. Access by: mail, in person.

Misdemeanor, Civil Actions Under $25,000, Eviction, Small Claims, Probate—Associate Circuit Court-Division III, PO Box 236, Lexington, MO 64067. 660-259-6151, Fax: 660-259-2884. 8AM-4:30PM. Access by: mail, in person. Special note: Most civil action cases are directed to the Circuit Court, regardless of limits.

Lawrence

Real Estate Recording—Lawrence County Recorder of Deeds, Courthouse on the Square, Mount Vernon, MO 65712. 417-466-2662, Fax: 417-466-4995. 9AM-Noon, 1-5PM.

Felony, Misdemeanor, Civil Actions Over $45,000—Circuit Court, PO Box 488, Mt Vernon, MO 65712. 417-466-2471. 8AM-5PM. Access by: mail, in person.

Misdemeanor, Civil Actions Under $45,000, Eviction, Small Claims, Probate—Associate Circuit Court, 1 Courthouse Sg, Mt Vernon, MO 65712. 417-466-2463. 8:30AM-5PM. Access by: mail, in person.

Lewis

Real Estate Recording—Lewis County Recorder of Deeds, Courthouse, 1 Courthouse Square, Monticello, MO 63457., Fax: 573-767-5378. 8AM-Noon,1-4PM.

Felony, Misdemeanor, Civil Actions Over $25,000—Circuit Court, PO Box 97, Monticello, MO 63457. 573-767-5440, Fax: 573-767-5378. 8AM-Noon,1-4PM. Access by: in person.

Misdemeanor, Civil Actions Under $25,000, Eviction, Small Claims, Probate—Associate Circuit Court, PO Box 36, Monticello, MO 63457. 573-767-5352, Fax: 573-767-5412. 8AM-4:30PM. Access by: mail, fax, in person.

Lincoln

Real Estate Recording—Lincoln County Recorder of Deeds, 201 Main Street, Troy, MO 63379., Fax: 636-528-2665. 8AM-4:30PM.

Felony, Misdemeanor, Civil Actions Over $45,000—Circuit Court, 201 Main St, Troy, MO 63379. 636-528-6300. 8:00AM-4:30PM. Access by: in person.

Misdemeanor, Civil Actions Under $25,000, Eviction, Small Claims, Probate—Associate Circuit Court, 201 Main St, Troy, MO 63379. 636-528-4521. 8AM-4:30PM. Access by: mail, phone, in person.

Linn

Real Estate Recording—Linn County Recorder of Deeds, Courthouse, Room 204, Linneus, MO 64653. 816-895-5410, Fax: 660-895-5533. 9AM-Noon, 1-4:30PM.

Felony, Misdemeanor, Civil Actions Over $45,000—Linn County Circuit Court, PO Box 84, Linneus, MO 64653-0084. 660-895-5212, Fax: 660-895-5277. 8AM-Noon,1-5PM. Access by: mail, fax, in person.

Misdemeanor, Civil Actions Under $25,000, Eviction, Small Claims, Probate—Associate Circuit Court, Box 93, Linneus, MO 64653. 660-895-5419, Fax: 660-895-5533. 8:30AM-4:00PM. Access by: mail, phone, in person.

Livingston

Real Estate Recording—Livingston County Recorder of Deeds, Courthouse, Suite 6, 700 Webster St. Chillicothe, MO 64601. 816-646-3076. 8:30AM-Noon, 1-4:30PM.

Felony, Misdemeanor, Civil Actions Over $45,000—Circuit Court, 700 Webster St, Chillicothe, MO 64601. 660-646-1718, Fax: 660-646-2734. 8:30AM-4:30PM. Access by: in person.

Misdemeanor, Civil Actions Under $25,000, Eviction, Small Claims, Probate—Associate Circuit Court, Livingston County Courthouse, Suite 8, Chillicothe, MO 64601. 660-646-3103, Fax: 660-646-8014. Public hours: 8:30AM-4:30PM; Office hours: 8AM-5PM. Access by: mail, phone, fax, in person.

Macon

Real Estate Recording—Macon County Recorder of Deeds, 101 E. Washington, Bldg 2, Macon, MO 63552. 816-385-2713, Fax: 660-385-4235. 8:30AM-4PM.

Felony, Misdemeanor, Civil Actions Over $45,000—Circuit Court, PO Box 382, Macon, MO 63552. 660-385-4631, Fax: 660-385-4235. 8:30AM-4PM. Access by: mail, fax, in person.

Misdemeanor, Civil Actions Under $45,000, Eviction, Small Claims, Probate—Associate Circuit Court, PO Box 491, Macon, MO 63552. 660-385-3531, Fax: 660-385-3532. 8AM-4:30PM. Access by: mail, phone, fax, in person.

Madison

Real Estate Recording—Madison County Recorder of Deeds, Courthouse, Courtsquare, Fredericktown, MO 63645. 573-783-3325, Fax: 573-783-2715. 8AM-5PM.

Felony, Misdemeanor, Civil Actions Over $45,000—Circuit Court, PO Box 470, Fredericktown, MO 63645-0470. 573-783-2102, Fax: 573-783-2715. 8AM-5PM. Access by: mail, in person.

Misdemeanor, Civil Actions Under $25,000, Small Claims, Probate, Traffic—Associate Circuit Court, PO Box 521, Fredericktown, MO 63645. 573-783-3105, Fax: 573-783-5920. 8AM-5PM. Access by: mail, phone, fax, in person.

Maries

Real Estate Recording—Maries County Recorder of Deeds, Courthouse, 211 Fourth St. Vienna, MO 65582., Fax: 573-422-3269. 8AM-4PM.

Felony, Misdemeanor, Civil Actions Over $2,000—Circuit Court, PO Box 213, Vienna, MO 65582. 573-422-3338, Fax: 573-422-3269. 8AM-4PM. Access by: mail, fax, in person.

Misdemeanor, Civil Actions Under $25,000, Eviction, Small Claims, Probate—Associate Circuit Court, PO Box 490, Vienna, MO 65582. 573-422-3303, Fax: 573-422-3100. 8AM-4PM. Access by: mail, in person. Special note: Most civil cases are directed to the Circuit Court, regardless of limit.

Marion

Real Estate Recording—Marion County Recorder of Deeds, 100 South Main, Palmyra, MO 63461., Fax: 573-769-6012. 8:30AM-5PM.

Felony, Misdemeanor, Civil Actions Over $45,000—Circuit Court, PO Box 392, Palmyra, MO 63461. 573-769-2550, Fax: 573-769-4312. 8AM-5PM. Access by: mail, fax, in person.

Circuit Court (Twps of Miller and Mason only), 906 Broadway, Rm 105, Hannibal, MO 63401. 573-221-0198, Fax: 573-221-9328. 8AM-5PM. Access by: mail, fax, in person.

Misdemeanor, Civil Actions Under $45,000, Eviction, Small Claims, Probate—Hannibal Associate Circuit Court, 906 Broadway, Hannibal, MO 63401. 573-221-0288. 8AM-5PM. Access by: mail, in person.

Palmyra Associate Circuit Court, PO Box 449, Palmyra, MO 63461. 573-769-2318, Fax: 573-769-4558. 8AM-Noon, 1-5PM. Access by: mail, in person.

McDonald

Real Estate Recording—McDonald County Recorder of Deeds, Highway W, Courthouse, Pineville, MO 64856. 417-223-4462, Fax: 417-223-4125. 8AM-4PM.

Felony, Misdemeanor, Civil Actions Over $45,000—Circuit Court, PO Box 157, Pineville, MO 64856. 417-223-7515, Fax: 417-223-4124. 8AM-4:30PM. Access by: in person.

Misdemeanor, Civil Actions Under $25,000, Eviction, Small Claims, Probate—Associate Circuit Court, PO Box 157, Pineville, MO 64856. 417-223-7511, Fax: 417-223-7521. 8:00AM-4:30PM. Access by: mail, fax, in person.

Mercer

Real Estate Recording—Mercer County Recorder of Deeds, Courthouse, Princeton, MO 64673. 816-748-3435, Fax: 660-748-3180. 8:30AM-Noon, 1-4:30PM.

Felony, Misdemeanor, Civil Actions Over $45,000—Circuit Court, Courthouse, 802 East Main, Princeton, MO 64673. 660-748-4335, Fax: 660-748-3180. 8:30AM-4:30PM. Access by: mail, in person.

Misdemeanor, Civil Actions Under $45,000, Eviction, Small Claims, Probate—Associate Circuit Court, Courthouse, Princeton, MO 64673. 660-748-4232, Fax: 660-748-3180. 8:30AM-4:30PM. Access by: mail, in person.

Miller

Real Estate Recording—Miller County Recorder of Deeds, 256 High St. Tuscumbia, MO 65082. 573-369-2214, Fax: 573-369-2910. 8AM-4:30PM.

Felony, Misdemeanor, Civil Actions Over $45,000—Circuit Court, PO Box 11, Tuscumbia, MO 65082. 573-369-2303, Fax: 573-369-2910. 8AM-4:30PM. Access by: mail, phone, fax, in person.

Misdemeanor, Civil Actions Under $25,000, Eviction, Small Claims, Probate—Tuscumbia Associate Circuit Court, Miller County Courthouse Annex, Tuscumbia, MO 65082. 573-369-2330. 8AM-4PM. Access by: mail, in person.

Misdemeanor, Civil Actions Under $45,000, Eviction, Small Claims, Probate—Charleston Associate Circuit Court, PO Box 369, Charleston, MO 63834. 573-683-2146, Fax: 573-649-2284. 8AM-4:30PM. Access by: mail, phone, fax, in person.

Mississippi

Real Estate Recording—Mississippi County Recorder of Deeds, 313 E. Main, East Prairie, MO 63845., Fax: 573-649-2284. 8:30AM-4:30PM.

Felony, Misdemeanor, Civil Actions Over $25,000—Circuit Court, PO Box 369, Charleston, MO 63834. 573-683-2146, Fax: 573-649-2284. 8:30AM-4:30PM. Access by: mail, phone, fax, in person.

Misdemeanor, Civil Actions Under $25,000, Eviction, Small Claims, Probate—Associate Circuit Court, PO Box 369, Charleston, MO 63834. 573-649-3186, Fax: 573-649-2284. 8AM-4:30PM. Access by: mail, phone, fax, in person.

Moniteau

Real Estate Recording—Moniteau County Recorder of Deeds, 200 East Main Street, California, MO 65018., Fax: 573-796-2591. 8AM-4:30PM.

Felony, Misdemeanor, Civil Actions Over $25,000—Circuit Court, 200 E Main, California, MO 65018. 573-796-2071, Fax: 573-796-2591. 8AM-4:30PM. Access by: mail, in person.

Misdemeanor, Civil Actions Under $45,000, Eviction, Small Claims, Probate—Associate Circuit Court, 200 E Main, California, MO 65018. 573-796-2814. 8AM-5PM. Access by: mail, phone, in person.

Monroe

Real Estate Recording—Monroe County Recorder of Deeds, 300 Main Street, Courthouse, Paris, MO 65275. 816-327-4711, Fax: 660-327-5781. 8AM-4:30PM.

Felony, Misdemeanor, Civil Actions Over $45,000—Circuit Court, PO Box 227, Paris, MO 65275. 660-327-5204, Fax: 660-327-5781. 8AM-4:30PM. Access by: mail, fax, in person.

Misdemeanor, Civil Actions Under $45,000, Eviction, Small Claims, Probate—Associate Circuit Court, County Courthouse, 300 N Main, Paris, MO 65275. 660-327-5220, Fax: 660-327-5781. 8AM-4:30PM. Access by: mail, in person.

Montgomery

Real Estate Recording—Montgomery County Recorder of Deeds, 211 East 3rd Street, Montgomery City, MO 63361. 573-564-2319, Fax: 573-564-3914. 8AM-4:30PM.

Felony, Misdemeanor, Civil Actions Over $45,000—Circuit Court, 211 E 3rd, Montgomery City, MO 63361. 573-564-3341, Fax: 573-564-3914. 8AM-4:30PM. Access by: in person.

Misdemeanor, Civil Actions Under $25,000, Eviction, Small Claims, Probate—Associate Circuit Court, 211 E 3rd St, Montgomery City, MO 63361. 573-564-3348. 8:00AM-4:30PM. Access by: in person.

Morgan

Real Estate Recording—Morgan County Recorder of Deeds, 100 Newton Street, Courthouse, Versailles, MO 65084. 573-378-4404, Fax: 573-378-6431. 8:30AM-Noon, 1-4:30PM.

Felony, Misdemeanor, Civil Actions Over $25,000—Circuit Court, 100 E Newton, Versailles, MO 65084. 573-378-4413, Fax: 573-378-2837. 8:30AM-4:30PM. Access by: mail, phone, in person.

Misdemeanor, Civil Actions Under $45,000, Eviction, Small Claims, Probate—Associate Circuit Court, 102 N Monroe, Versailles, MO 65084. 573-378-4235, Fax: 573-378-4670. 8:30AM-5PM. Access by: mail, phone, in person.

New Madrid

Real Estate Recording—New Madrid County Recorder of Deeds, 450 Main Street, New Madrid, MO 63869. 8:30AM-Noon, 1-4:30PM.

Felony, Misdemeanor, Civil Actions Over $45,000—Circuit Court, County Courthouse, New Madrid, MO 63869. 573-748-2228. 8AM-5PM. Access by: mail, in person.

Misdemeanor, Civil Actions Under $45,000, Eviction, Small Claims, Probate—Associate Circuit Court, County Courthouse, New Madrid, MO 63869. 573-748-5556. 8AM-5PM. Access by: mail, in person.

Newton

Real Estate Recording—Newton County Recorder of Deeds, Wood & Main Streets, Neosho, MO 64850. 417-451-8226, Fax: 417-451-8273. 8:30AM-5PM.

Felony, Misdemeanor, Civil Actions Over $45,000—Circuit Court, PO Box 130, Neosho, MO 64850. 417-451-8257, Fax: 417-451-8298. 8:30AM-5PM. Access by: mail, phone, fax, in person.

Misdemeanor, Civil Actions Under $45,000, Eviction, Small Claims, Probate—Associate Circuit Court, PO Box 170, Neosho, MO 64850. 417-451-8212, Fax: 417-451-8272. 8AM-5PM. Access by: mail, phone, in person.

Nodaway

Real Estate Recording—Nodaway County Recorder of Deeds, 305 N. Main, Room 104, Maryville, MO 64468., Fax: 660-582-5282. 8:30AM-Noon, 1-4:30PM.

Felony, Misdemeanor, Civil Actions Over $25,000—Circuit Court, PO Box 218, Maryville, MO 64468. 660-582-5431, Fax: 660-582-5499. 8AM-4:30PM. Access by: mail, fax, in person.

Misdemeanor, Civil Actions Under $45,000, Eviction, Small Claims, Probate—Associate Circuit Court, Courthouse Annex, 303 N Market, Maryville, MO 64468. 660-582-2531, Fax: 660-582-2047. 8AM-4:30PM. Access by: mail, in person.

Oregon

Real Estate Recording—Oregon County Recorder of Deeds, Courthouse, Alton, MO 65606. 417-778-6303, Fax: 417-778-7206. 8AM-4PM.

Felony, Misdemeanor, Civil Actions Over $45,000—Circuit Court, PO Box 406, Alton, MO 65606. 417-778-7460, Fax: 417-778-6641. 8AM-4PM. Access by: mail, phone, fax, in person.

Misdemeanor, Civil Actions Under $45,000, Eviction, Small Claims, Probate—Associate Circuit Court, PO Box 211, Alton, MO 65606. 417-778-7461, Fax: 417-778-6209. 8:00AM-4:00PM. Access by: mail, in person.

Osage

Real Estate Recording—Osage County Recorder of Deeds, Courthouse, 106 E. Main St. Linn, MO 65051. 8AM-4:30PM.

Felony, Misdemeanor, Civil Actions Over $45,000—Circuit Court, PO Box 825, Linn, MO 65051. 573-897-3114. 8AM-4:30PM. Access by: mail, phone, in person.

Misdemeanor, Civil Actions Under $25,000, Eviction, Small Claims, Probate—Associate Circuit Court, PO Box 470, Linn, MO 65051. 573-897-2136, Fax: 573-897-2285. 8AM-4:30PM. Access by: mail, phone, in person.

Ozark

Real Estate Recording—Ozark County Recorder of Deeds, Courthouse, Gainesville, MO 65655. 417-679-3553, Fax: 417-679-4554. 8AM-Noon, 12:30-4:30PM.

Felony, Misdemeanor, Civil Actions Over $45,000—Circuit Court, PO Box 36, Gainesville, MO 65655. 417-679-4232, Fax: 417-679-4554. 8AM-Noon, 1-5PM. Access by: mail, in person.

Misdemeanor, Civil Actions Under $25,000, Eviction, Small Claims, Probate—Associate Circuit Court, PO Box 278, Gainesville, MO 65655. 417-679-4611, Fax: 417-679-2099. 8AM-4:30PM. Access by: mail, fax, in person.

Pemiscot

Real Estate Recording—Pemiscot County Recorder of Deeds, Courthouse, 610 Ward Ave. Caruthersville, MO 63830. 573-333-4171. 8:30AM-4:30PM.

Felony, Misdemeanor, Civil Actions Over $45,000—Circuit Court, County Courthouse, Caruthersville, MO 63830. 573-333-0182. 7:30AM-4:30PM. Access by: in person.

Misdemeanor, Civil Actions Under $45,000, Eviction, Small Claims, Probate—Associate Circuit Court, County Courthouse, PO Drawer 228, Caruthersville, MO 63830. 573-333-2784. 7:30AM-4:30PM. Access by: mail, in person.

Perry

Real Estate Recording—Perry County Recorder of Deeds, 15 West Ste. Marie Street, Suite 1, Perryville, MO 63775. 573-547-4502, Fax: 573-547-2637. 8AM-5PM.

Felony, Misdemeanor, Civil Actions Over $25,000—Circuit Court, 15 W Saint Maries St, Perryville, MO 63775-1399. 573-547-6581, Fax: 573-547-9323. 8AM-5PM. Access by: mail, in person.

Misdemeanor, Civil Actions Under $25,000, Eviction, Small Claims, Probate—Associate Circuit Court, 15 W Saint Maries, Suite 3, Perryville, MO 63775-1399. 573-547-7861, Fax: 573-547-9323. 8AM-5PM. Access by: mail, in person.

Pettis

Real Estate Recording—Pettis County Recorder of Deeds, 415 South Ohio, Sedalia, MO 65301. 816-827-0486, Fax: 660-827-8637. 9AM-4:30PM.

Felony, Misdemeanor, Civil Actions Over $45,000—Circuit Court, PO Box 804, Sedalia, MO 65302-0804. 660-826-0617, Fax: 660-827-8637. 8AM-5PM. Access by: mail, phone, fax, in person.

Misdemeanor, Civil Actions Under $45,000, Eviction, Small Claims—Associate Circuit Court, 415 S Ohio, Sedalia, MO 65301. 660-826-4699, Fax: 660-827-8637. 8:30AM-5PM. Access by: mail, fax, in person.

Probate—Probate Court, 415 S. Ohio, Sedalia, MO 65301. 660-826-0368, Fax: 660-827-8637. 8:30AM-4:30PM.

Phelps

Real Estate Recording—Phelps County Recorder of Deeds, Courthouse, 200 N. Main, Rolla, MO 65401. 573-364-1891, Fax: 573-364-1419. 7:30AM-5PM.

Felony, Misdemeanor, Civil Actions Over $45,000—Circuit Court, 200 N Main St, Rolla, MO 65401. 573-364-1891, Fax: 573-364-1419. 8AM-5PM. Access by: mail, fax, in person.

Misdemeanor, Civil Actions Under $45,000, Eviction, Small Claims—Phelps County Circuit Court Associate Division, 200 N Main, Rolla, MO 65401. 573-364-1891, Fax: 573-364-1419. 8AM-5PM. Access by: mail, fax, in person.

Probate—Phelps County Courthouse, 200 N Main, PO Box 1550, Rolla, MO 65401. 573-364-1891. 8AM-Noon, 1-5PM. Access by: mail, in person.

Pike

Real Estate Recording—Pike County Recorder of Deeds, 115 West Main Street, Bowling Green, MO 63334. 573-324-2102. 9AM-Noon, 1-4:30PM.

Felony, Misdemeanor, Civil Actions Over $45,000—Circuit Court, 115 W Main, Bowling Green, MO 63334. 573-324-3112. 8AM-4:30PM. Access by: mail, in person.

Misdemeanor, Civil Actions Under $25,000, Eviction, Small Claims, Probate—Associate Circuit Court, 115 W Main, Bowling Green, MO 63334. 573-324-5582, Fax: 573-324-6297. 8AM-4:30PM. Access by: mail, in person.

Platte

Real Estate Recording—Platte County Recorder of Deeds, 415 3rd St. Suite 70, Platte City, MO 64079. 816-858-3318, Fax: 816-858-2379. 8AM-5PM.

Felony, Misdemeanor, Civil Actions Over $45,000—Circuit Court, 328 Main St, Box 5CH, Platte City, MO 64079. 816-858-2232, Fax: 816-858-3392. 8AM-5PM. Access by: mail, in person.

Misdemeanor, Civil Actions Under $25,000, Eviction, Small Claims—Associate Circuit Court, 328 Main St, Box 5CH, Platte City, MO 64079. 816-858-2232, Fax: 816-858-3392. 8AM-5PM. Access by: mail, in person.

Probate—Probate Court, 415 Third St, #95, Platte City, MO 64079. 816-858-2232, Fax: 816-858-3392. 8AM-5PM. Access by: mail, in person.

Polk

Real Estate Recording—Polk County Recorder of Deeds, 102 E. Broadway, Courthouse, Bolivar, MO 65613., Fax: 417-326-4194. 8AM-5PM.

Felony, Misdemeanor, Civil Actions Over $45,000—Circuit Court, 102 E Broadway, Rm 14, Bolivar, MO 65613. 417-326-4912, Fax: 417-326-4194. 8AM-5PM. Access by: mail, fax, in person.

Misdemeanor, Civil Actions Under $25,000, Eviction, Small Claims, Probate—Associate Circuit Court, Courthouse, Rm 7, Bolivar, MO 65613. 417-326-4921, Fax: 417-326-5238. 8:00AM-5:00PM. Access by: mail, phone, in person.

Pulaski

Real Estate Recording—Pulaski County Recorder of Deeds, 301 Historic Route 66, Courthouse Suite 202, Waynesville, MO 65583. 573-774-6609, Fax: 573-774-6967. 8AM-4:30PM.

Felony, Misdemeanor, Civil, Eviction, Small Claims—Circuit & Associate Circuit Courts, 301 Historic Rt 66 E, Suite 202, Waynesville, MO 65583. 573-774-6609, Fax: 573-774-6967. 8AM-4:30PM. Access by: mail, fax, in person.

Probate—Probate Court, 301 Historic 66 East, Suite 316, Waynesville, MO 65583. 573-774-4784, Fax: 573-774-6673.

Putnam

Real Estate Recording—Putnam County Recorder of Deeds, Courthouse - Room 202, 1601 W. Main, Unionville, MO 63565., Fax: 660-947-2320. 9AM-Noon,1-5PM.

Felony, Misdemeanor, Civil Actions Over $45,000—Circuit Court, Courthouse Rm 202, Unionville, MO 63565. 660-947-2071, Fax: 660-947-2320. 9:00AM-5:00PM. Access by: mail, in person.

Misdemeanor, Civil Actions Under $45,000, Eviction, Small Claims, Probate—Associate Circuit Court, Courthouse Rm 101, Unionville, MO 63565. 660-947-2117, Fax: 660-947-7348. 9AM-5PM. Access by: mail, in person.

Ralls

Real Estate Recording—Ralls County Recorder of Deeds, Courthouse, 311 S. Main St. New London, MO 63459. 573-985-7151. 8:30AM-Noon, 1-4:30PM.

Felony, Misdemeanor, Civil Actions Over $45,000—Circuit Court, PO Box 444, New London, MO 63459. 573-985-5631. 8:30AM-4:30PM. Access by: mail, in person.

Misdemeanor, Civil Actions Under $25,000, Eviction, Small Claims, Probate—Associate Circuit Court, PO Box 466, New London, MO 63459. 573-985-5641, Fax: 573-985-3446. 8:30AM-4:30PM. Access by: mail, phone, in person.

Randolph

Real Estate Recording—Randolph County Recorder of Deeds, 110 S. Main St. Courthouse, Huntsville, MO 65259. 816-277-4714, Fax: 660-277-3246. 8AM-4PM.

Felony, Misdemeanor, Civil Actions Over $45,000—Circuit Court, 223 N Williams, Moberly, MO 65270. 660-263-4474, Fax: 660-263-5966. 8AM-4:30PM. Access by: mail, fax, in person.

Misdemeanor, Civil Actions Under $45,000, Eviction, Small Claims, Probate—Associate Circuit Court, 223 N Williams, Moberly, MO 65270. 660-263-4450, Fax: 660-263-1007. 8AM-4:30PM. Access by: mail, in person.

Ray

Real Estate Recording—Ray County Recorder of Deeds, Courthouse, 2nd Floor, Richmond, MO 64085. 816-776-6140. 8AM-Noon, 1-4PM.

Felony, Misdemeanor, Civil Actions Over $45,000—Circuit Court, PO Box 594, Richmond, MO 64085. 660-776-3377, Fax: 660-776-6016. 8AM-4PM. Access by: mail, phone, fax, in person.

Misdemeanor, Civil Actions Under $25,000, Eviction, Small Claims, Probate—Associate Circuit Court, Courthouse, Richmond, MO 64085. 660-776-2335, Fax: 660-470-2064. 8AM-4PM. Access by: mail, fax, in person.

Reynolds

Real Estate Recording—Reynolds County Recorder of Deeds, Courthouse, Centerville, MO 63633., Fax: 573-648-2296. 8AM-4PM.

Felony, Misdemeanor, Civil Actions Over $45,000—Circuit Court, PO Box 76, Centerville, MO 63633. 573-648-2494, Fax: 573-648-2296. 8AM-4PM. Access by: mail, phone, in person.

Misdemeanor, Civil Actions Under $45,000, Eviction, Small Claims, Probate—Associate Circuit Court, PO Box 39, Centerville, MO 63633. 573-648-2494, Fax: 573-648-2296. 8AM-4PM. Access by: mail, phone, in person.

Ripley

Real Estate Recording—Ripley County Recorder of Deeds, 100 Courthouse Square, Suite 3, Doniphan, MO 63935., Fax: 573-966-5014. 8AM-4PM.

Felony, Misdemeanor, Civil Actions Over $25,000—Circuit Court, Courthouse, Doniphan, MO 63935. 573-996-2818, Fax: 573-996-5014. 8AM-4PM. Access by: mail, fax, in person.

Misdemeanor, Civil Actions Under $25,000, Eviction, Small Claims, Probate—Associate Circuit Court, 100 Court Sq., Courthouse, Doniphan, MO 63935. 573-996-2013, Fax: 573-996-5014. 8AM-4PM. Access by: mail, phone, fax, in person.

Saline

Real Estate Recording—Saline County Recorder of Deeds, Courthouse, Room 206, Marshall, MO 65340. 816-886-3636, Fax: 660-886-2603. 8:30AM-Noon, 1-5PM.

Felony, Misdemeanor, Civil Actions Over $45,000—Circuit Court, PO Box 597, Marshall, MO 65340. 660-886-2300. 8:00AM-5:00PM. Access by: mail, in person.

Misdemeanor, Civil Actions Under $25,000, Eviction, Small Claims—Associate Circuit Court, PO Box 751, Marshall, MO 65340. 660-886-6988, Fax: 660-886-2919. 8AM-5PM. Access by: mail, phone, in person.

Schuyler

Real Estate Recording—Schuyler County Recorder of Deeds, Courthouse, Highway 136 East, Lancaster, MO 63548. 816-457-3825, Fax: 660-457-3016. 8AM-4PM.

Felony, Misdemeanor, Civil Actions Over $45,000—Circuit Court, PO Box 186, Lancaster, MO 63548. 660-457-3784, Fax: 660-457-3016. 8AM-4PM. Access by: mail, in person.

Misdemeanor, Civil Actions Under $45,000, Eviction, Small Claims, Probate—Associate Circuit Court, Box 158, Lancaster, MO 63548. 660-457-3755, Fax: 660-457-3016. 8:15AM-4PM. Access by: mail, in person.

Scotland

Real Estate Recording—Scotland County Recorder of Deeds, 117 South Market St. Ste 106, Memphis, MO 63555. 816-465-2529, Fax: 660-465-8673. 9AM-Noon,1-4PM.

Felony, Misdemeanor, Civil Actions Over $45,000—Circuit Court, Courthouse, Rm 106, Memphis, MO 63555. 660-465-8605, Fax: 660-465-8673. 9AM-4PM. Access by: mail, in person.

Misdemeanor, Civil Actions Under $45,000, Eviction, Small Claims, Probate—Associate Circuit Court, Courthouse, Rm 102, 117 S Market, Memphis, MO 63555. 660-465-2404, Fax: 660-465-8673. 8AM-4:30PM. Access by: mail, phone, in person.

Scott

Real Estate Recording—Scott County Recorder of Deeds, Courthouse, Highway 61, Benton, MO 63736. 573-545-3543. 8:30AM-5PM.

Felony, Misdemeanor, Civil Actions Over $25,000—Circuit Court, PO Box 277, Benton, MO 63736. 573-545-3596, Fax: 573-545-3597. 8:30AM-12, 1-5PM. Access by: mail, fax, in person.

Misdemeanor, Civil Actions Under $45,000, Eviction, Small Claims, Probate—Associate Circuit Court, PO Box 249, Benton, MO 63736. 573-545-3576, Fax: 573-545-4231. 8:30AM-5PM. Access by: mail, phone, in person.

Shannon

Real Estate Recording—Shannon County Recorder of Deeds, Courthouse, Eminence, MO 65466. 573-226-3614, Fax: 573-226-5321. 8AM-Noon, 12:30-4:30PM.

Felony, Misdemeanor, Civil Actions Over $45,000—Circuit Court, PO Box 148, Eminence, MO 65466. 573-226-3315, Fax: 573-226-5321. 8AM-4:30PM. Access by: mail, in person.

Misdemeanor, Civil Actions Under $45,000, Eviction, Small Claims, Probate—Associate Circuit Court, PO Box 845, Eminence, MO 65466-0845. 573-226-5515, Fax: 573-226-5321. 8AM-4:30PM. Access by: mail, in person.

Shelby

Real Estate Recording—Shelby County Recorder of Deeds, Courthouse, Shelbyville, MO 63469. 573-633-2574, Fax: 573-633-1004. 8AM-4:30PM.

Felony, Misdemeanor, Civil Actions Over $45,000—Circuit Court, PO Box 176, Shelbyville, MO 63469. 573-633-2151, Fax: 573-633-1004. 8AM-4:30PM. Access by: mail, in person.

Misdemeanor, Civil Actions Under $45,000, Eviction, Small Claims, Probate—Associate Circuit Court, PO Box 206, Shelbyville, MO 63469. 573-633-2251, Fax: 573-633-2142. 8AM-4PM. Access by: mail, phone, fax, in person.

St. Charles

Real Estate Recording—St. Charles County Recorder of Deeds, 201 North 2nd, Room 338, St. Charles, MO 63301. 636-947-2676, Fax: 636-949-7512. 8AM-5PM.

Felony, Misdemeanor, Civil Actions Over $25,000—Circuit Court, 300 N 2nd St, St. Charles, MO 63301. 636-949-7900, Fax: 636-949-7390. 8:30AM-5PM. Access by: mail, in person.

Civil Actions Under $25,000, Eviction, Small Claims, Probate—Associate Circuit Court, 300 N 2nd, Suite 436, St. Charles, MO 63301. 636-949-3043. 8:30AM-5:00PM. Access by: mail, in person.

St. Clair

Real Estate Recording—St. Clair County Recorder of Deeds, Courthouse Square, Osceola, MO 64776. 417-646-8068, Fax: 417-646-2401. 8AM-4:30PM.

Felony, Misdemeanor, Civil, Eviction, Small Claims, Probate—Circuit & Associate Circuit Courts, PO Box 493, Osceola, MO 64776. 417-646-2226, Fax: 417-646-2401. 8AM-4:30PM. Access by: mail, in person.

St. Francois

Real Estate Recording—St. Francois County Recorder of Deeds, Courthouse, Farmington, MO 63640. 573-756-3349. 8AM-4PM.

Felony, Misdemeanor, Civil Actions Over $25,000—Circuit Court, Division I & II, 1 N Washington, 3rd Floor, Farmington, MO 63640. 573-756-4551, Fax: 573-756-3733. 8AM-5PM. Access by: mail, fax, in person.

Misdemeanor, Civil Actions Under $25,000, Eviction, Small Claims, Probate—Associate Circuit Court, County Courthouse, 2nd Fl, Farmington, MO 63640. 573-756-5755, Fax: 573-756-8173. 8AM-5PM. Access by: mail, in person.

St. Louis

Real Estate Recording—St. Louis City Recorder, Tucker & Market Streets, City Hall Room 127, St. Louis, MO 63103. 315-255-0065, Fax: 314-622-4175. 9AM-5PM.

St. Louis County Recorder of Deeds, 41 S. Central Ave. 4th Floor, Clayton, MO 63105. 8AM-5PM.

Felony, Misdemeanor, Civil—Circuit Court of St. Louis County, 7900 Carondolet, Clayton, MO 63105-1766. 315-287-0850, Fax: 314-854-8739. 8AM-5PM. Access by: mail, phone, fax, in person.

Civil Actions Under $25,000, Eviction, Small Claims, Probate—Associate Circuit-Civil Division, 7900 Carondolet, Clayton, MO 63105. 315-287-4623, Fax: 314-889-2689. 8AM-5PM. Access by: mail, phone, in person.

Misdemeanor—Associate Circuit Court-Criminal Division, 7900 Carondolet, Clayton, MO 63105. 315-287-0045, Fax: 314-889-2689. Access by: mail, in person.

St. Louis City

Civil, Eviction, Small Claims, Probate—Circuit & Associate Circuit Courts, 10 N Tucker, Civil Courts Bldg, St Louis, MO 63101. 315-255-4316, Fax: 314-622-4537. 8:00AM-5:00PM. Access by: mail, in person.

Felony, Misdemeanor—City of St Louis Circuit Court, 1320 Market, St Louis, MO 63103. 315-265-2131, Fax: 314-622-3202. 8AM-5PM. Access by: mail, in person.

Ste. Genevieve

Real Estate Recording—Ste. Genevieve County Recorder of Deeds, 3rd Street, Court House, Ste. Genevieve, MO 63670., Fax: 573-883-5312. 8AM-4:30PM.

Felony, Misdemeanor, Civil Actions Over $25,000—Circuit Court, 55 S 3rd, Rm 23, Ste Genevieve, MO 63670. 573-883-2705, Fax: 573-883-9351. 8AM-5PM. Access by: in person.

Misdemeanor, Civil Actions Under $45,000, Eviction, Small Claims, Probate—Associate Circuit Court, 3rd and Market, Ste Genevieve, MO 63670. 573-883-2265, Fax: 573-883-9351. 8AM-5PM. Access by: mail, in person.

Stoddard

Real Estate Recording—Stoddard County Recorder of Deeds, Courthouse Square, Prairie St. Bloomfield, MO 63825. 573-568-3327, Fax: 573-568-2545. 8:30AM-4:30PM.

Felony, Misdemeanor, Civil Actions Over $45,000—Circuit Court, PO Box 30, Bloomfield, MO 63825. 573-568-4640, Fax: 573-568-2271. 8:30AM-4:30PM. Access by: mail, fax, in person.

Civil Actions Under $25,000, Eviction, Small Claims, Probate—Division III & Probate, PO Box 518, Bloomfield, MO 63825. 573-568-2181, Fax: 573-568-3229. 7:30AM-4PM. Access by: mail, phone, fax, in person.

Misdemeanor—Associate Circuit Court-Criminal Division II, PO Box 218, Bloomfield, MO 63825. 573-568-4671, Fax: 573-568-2299. 8:30AM-4:30PM. Access by: in person.

Stone

Real Estate Recording—Stone County Recorder of Deeds, Courthouse Square, Galena, MO 65656., Fax: 417-357-8131. 8AM-4PM.

Felony, Misdemeanor, Civil Actions Over $25,000—Circuit Court, PO Box 18, Galena, MO 65656. 417-357-6114, Fax: 417-357-6163. 7:30AM-4PM. Access by: mail, phone, fax, in person.

Misdemeanor, Civil Actions Under $25,000, Eviction, Small Claims, Probate—Circuit Court-Division II & III, PO Box 186, Galena, MO 65656. 417-357-6511, Fax: 417-357-6163. 7:30AM-4PM. Access by: mail, phone, fax, in person.

Sullivan

Real Estate Recording—Sullivan County Recorder of Deeds, Courthouse, Milan, MO 63556. 816-265-4514, Fax: 660-265-5071. 9AM-Noon, 1-4:30PM.

Felony, Misdemeanor, Civil Actions Over $45,000—Circuit Court, Courthouse, Milan, MO 63556-1358. 660-265-4717, Fax: 660-265-5071. 9:00AM-4:30PM. Access by: in person.

Misdemeanor, Civil Actions Under $45,000, Eviction, Small Claims, Probate—Associate Circuit Court, Courthouse, Milan, MO 63556. 660-265-3303, Fax: 660-265-4711. 9AM-4:30PM. Access by: mail, in person.

Taney

Real Estate Recording—Taney County Recorder of Deeds, Main & David, Courthouse, Forsyth, MO 65653. 417-546-4584. 8AM-5PM.

Felony, Misdemeanor, Civil Actions Over $45,000—Circuit Court, PO Box 335, Forsyth, MO 65653. 417-546-7230, Fax: 417-546-6133. 8AM-5PM. Access by: mail, in person.

Misdemeanor, Civil Actions Under $25,000, Eviction, Small Claims, Probate—Associate Circuit Court, PO Box 129, Forsyth, MO 65653. 417-546-7212, Fax: 417-546-4513. 8AM-5PM. Access by: mail, in person.

Texas

Real Estate Recording—Texas County Recorder of Deeds, 210 North Grand, P.O. Box 237, Houston, MO 65483. 417-967-2589, Fax: 417-967-4220. 8AM-5PM.

Felony, Misdemeanor, Civil Actions Over $45,000—Circuit Court, 210 N Grand, Houston, MO 65483. 417-967-3742, Fax: 417-967-4220. 8AM-5PM. Access by: mail, fax, in person.

Misdemeanor, Civil Actions Under $45,000, Eviction, Small Claims, Probate—Associate Circuit Court, County Courthouse, Houston, MO 65483. 417-967-3663, Fax: 417-967-4128. 8AM-5PM. Access by: mail, phone, fax, in person.

Vernon

Real Estate Recording—Vernon County Recorder of Deeds, Courthouse, Nevada, MO 64772. 417-448-2516. 8:30AM-Noon, 1-4:30PM.

Felony, Misdemeanor, Civil Actions Over $45,000—Circuit Court, Courthouse, 3rd Fl, Nevada, MO 64772. 417-448-2525, Fax: 417-448-2512. 8AM-4:30PM. Access by: mail, fax, in person.

Misdemeanor, Civil Actions Under $45,000, Eviction, Small Claims, Probate—Associate Circuit Court, County Courthouse, Nevada, MO 64772. 417-448-2550, Fax: 417-448-2512. 8:30AM-4:30PM. Access by: mail, fax, in person.

Warren

Real Estate Recording—Warren County Recorder of Deeds, 104 West Boone's Lick Rd. Warrenton, MO 63383. 315-253-9021. 8AM-4:30PM.

Felony, Misdemeanor, Civil Actions Over $45,000—Circuit Court, 104 W Main, Warrenton, MO 63383. 636-456-3363, Fax: 636-456-2422. 8AM-4:30PM. Access by: in person.

Misdemeanor, Civil Actions Under $25,000, Eviction, Small Claims, Probate—Associate Circuit Court, Warren County Courthouse, 104 W Main, Warrenton, MO 63383. 636-456-3375, Fax: 636-456-2422. 8:30AM-4:30PM. Access by: mail, phone, fax, in person.

Washington

Real Estate Recording—Washington County Recorder of Deeds, 102 North Missouri Street, Potosi, MO 63664. 573-438-2031, Fax: 573-438-7900. 8AM-5PM.

Felony, Misdemeanor, Civil Actions Over $45,000—Circuit Court, PO Box 216, Potosi, MO 63664. 573-438-4171, Fax: 573-438-7900. 8AM-5PM. Access by: mail, in person.

Misdemeanor, Civil Actions Under $45,000, Eviction, Small Claims, Probate—Associate Circuit Court, 102 N Missouri St, Potosi, MO 63664. 573-438-3691, Fax: 573-438-7900. 8AM-5PM. Access by: mail, phone, fax, in person.

Wayne

Real Estate Recording—Wayne County Recorder of Deeds, 106 Walnut, Courthouse, Greenville, MO 63944. 573-224-3221, Fax: 573-224-3225. 8:30AM-Noon, 1-4:30PM.

Felony, Misdemeanor, Civil Actions Over $45,000—Circuit Court, PO Box 187A, Greenville, MO 63944. 573-224-3221, Fax: 573-224-3225. 8:30AM-4:30PM. Access by: mail, in person.

Misdemeanor, Civil Actions Under $45,000, Eviction, Small Claims, Probate—Associate Circuit Court, PO Box 188-A, Greenville, MO 63944. 573-224-3221, Fax: 573-224-3225. 8:30AM-4:30PM. Access by: mail, phone, fax, in person.

Webster

Real Estate Recording—Webster County Recorder of Deeds, Courthouse, Marshfield, MO 65706. 417-468-2108, Fax: 417-468-3786. 8AM-4PM.

Felony, Misdemeanor, Civil Actions Over $25,000—Circuit Court, PO Box 529, Marshfield, MO 65706. 417-859-2006, Fax: 417-468-3786. 8AM-5PM. Access by: mail, fax, in person.

Misdemeanor, Civil Actions Under $45,000, Eviction, Small Claims, Probate—Associate Circuit Court, Courthouse, Marshfield, MO 65706. 417-859-2041, Fax: 417-468-3786. 8AM-4:30PM. Access by: mail, phone, fax, in person.

Worth

Real Estate Recording—Worth County Recorder of Deeds, Courthouse on the Square, Grant City, MO 64456. 816-564-2154, Fax: 660-564-2432. 8:30AM-Noon, 1-4:30PM.

Felony, Misdemeanor, Civil Actions Over $45,000—Circuit Court, PO Box 340, Grant City, MO 64456. 660-564-2210, Fax: 660-564-2432. 8:30AM-4:30PM. Access by: mail, in person.

Misdemeanor, Civil Actions Under $45,000, Eviction, Small Claims, Probate—Associate Circuit Court, PO Box 428, Grant City, MO 64456. 660-564-2152, Fax: 660-564-2432. 9AM-4:30PM. Access by: mail, in person.

Wright

Real Estate Recording—Wright County Recorder of Deeds, Courthouse Square, Hartville, MO 65667., Fax: 417-741-7504. 8AM-4:30PM.

Felony, Misdemeanor, Civil Actions Over $45,000—Circuit Court, PO Box 39, Hartville, MO 65667. 417-741-7121, Fax: 417-741-7504. 8AM-4:30PM. Access by: mail, in person.

Misdemeanor, Civil Actions Under $25,000, Eviction, Small Claims, Probate—Associate Circuit Court, PO Box 58, Hartville, MO 65667. 417-741-6450, Fax: 417-741-7504. 8AM-4:30PM. Access by: mail, phone, fax, in person.

Federal Courts

US District Court

Eastern District of Missouri

Cape Girardeau Division 339 Broadway, Room 240, Cape Girardeau, MO 63701573-335-8538 Fax: 573-335-0379 Counties: Bollinger, Butler, Cape Girardeau, Carter, Dunklin, Madison, Mississippi, New Madrid, Pemiscot, Perry, Reynolds, Ripley, Scott, Shannon, Stoddard, Wayne. www.moed.uscourts.gov
Hannibal Division c/o St Louis Division, Room 260, 1114 Market St, St Louis, MO 63101314-539-2315 Fax: 314-539-2929 Counties: Adair, Audrain, Chariton, Clark, Knox, Lewis, Linn, Macon, Marion, Monroe, Montgomery, Pike, Ralls, Randolph, Schuyler, Scotland, Shelby. www.moed.uscourts.gov
St Louis Division Room 260, 1114 Market St, St Louis, MO 63101314-539-2315, Record Room: 314-539-7336 Fax: 314-539-

2929 Counties: Crawford, Dent, Franklin, Gasconade, Iron, Jefferson, Lincoln, Maries, Phelps, St. Charles, Ste. Genevieve, St. Francois, St. Louis, Warren, Washington, City of St. Louis. www.moed.uscourts.gov

Western District of Missouri

Jefferson City-Central Division 131 W High St, Jefferson City, MO 65101573-636-4015 Fax: 573-636-3456 Counties: Benton, Boone, Callaway, Camden, Cole, Cooper, Hickory, Howard, Miller, Moniteau, Morgan, Osage, Pettis.
Joplin-Southwestern Division c/o Kansas City Division, 201 US Courthouse, 811 Grand Ave, Kansas City, MO 64106816-426-2811 Fax: 816-426-2819 Counties: Barry, Barton, Jasper, Lawrence, McDonald, Newton, Stone, Vernon.
Kansas City-Western Division Clerk of Court, 201 US Courthouse, 811 Grand Ave, Kansas City, MO 64106816-426-2811

Fax: 816-426-2819 Counties: Bates, Carroll, Cass, Clay, Henry, Jackson, Johnson, Lafayette, Ray, St. Clair, Saline.

Springfield-Southern Division 222 N John Q Hammons Pkwy, Suite 1400, Springfield, MO 65806417-865-3869 Fax: 417-865-7719 Counties: Cedar, Christian, Dade, Dallas, Douglas, Greene, Howell, Laclede, Oregon, Ozark, Polk, Pulaski, Taney, Texas, Webster, Wright.

St Joseph Division PO Box 387, 201 S 8th St, St Joseph, MO 64501, Civil Docket Phone: 816-279-2428, Criminal Docket Phone: 816-426-2811 Fax: 816-279-0177 Counties: Andrew, Atchison, Buchanan, Caldwell, Clinton, Daviess, De Kalb, Gentry, Grundy, Harrison, Holt, Livingston, Mercer, Nodaway, Platte, Putnam, Sullivan, Worth.

US Bankruptcy Court

Eastern District of Missouri

St Louis Division 7th Floor, 211 N Broadway, St Louis, MO 63102-2734314-425-4222 Fax: 314-425-4063 Counties: Adair, Audrain, Bollinger, Butler, Cape Girardeau, Carter, Chariton, Clark, Crawford, Dent, Dunklin, Franklin, Gasconade, Iron, Jefferson, Knox, Lewis, Lincoln, Linn, Macon, Madison, Maries, Marion, Mississippi, Monroe, Montgomery, New Madrid, Pemiscot,Perry, Phelps, Pike, Ralls, Randolph, Reynolds, Ripley, Schuyler, Scotland, Scott, Shannon, Shelby, St. Charles, St. Francois, St. Louis, St.Louis City, Ste. Genevieve, Stoddard, Warren, Washington, Wayne. www.moeb.uscourts.gov

Western District of Missouri

Kansas City-Western Division Room 913, 811 Grand Ave, Kansas City, MO 64106816-426-3321 Fax: 816-426-3364 Counties: Andrew, Atchison, Barry, Barton, Bates, Benton, Boone, Buchanan, Caldwell, Callaway, Camden, Carroll, Cass, Cedar, Christian, Clay, Clinton, Cole, Cooper, Dade, Dallas, Daviess, De Kalb, Douglas, Gentry, Greene, Grundy, Harrison, Henry, Hickory, Holt,Howard, Howell, Jackson, Jasper, Johnson, Laclede, Lafayette, Lawrence, Livingston, McDonald, Mercer, Miller, Moniteau, Morgan, Newton, Nodaway, Oregon, Osage, Ozark, Pettis, Platte, Polk, Pulaski, Putnam, Ray, Saline, St. Clair, Sullivan, Taney, Texas,Vernon, Webster, Worth, Wright.

Attorney General's Office

PO Box 201401   406-444-2026
Helena, MT 59620   Fax: 406-444-3549

www.doj.state.mt.us

Governor's Office

1625 11th Ave   406-444-3111
Helena, MT 59620-0801   Fax: 406-444-5529

www.state.mt.us/governor/governor.htm

State Archives

225 N Roberts St   406-444-2694
Helena, MT 59620-1201   Fax: 406-444-2696

www.his.state.mt.us

Capital:	Helena
	Lewis and Clark County
Time Zone:	MST
Number of Counties:	56
Population:	878,810
Web Site:	www.mt.gov

Search Unclaimed Property Online

There is no Internet-based search for unclaimed property for this state.

State Agencies

Criminal Records

Department of Justice, Criminal History Records Program, 303 N Roberts, Room 374, Helena, MT 59620-1418; 406-444-3625; Fax: 406-444-0689; 8AM-5PM. Access by: mail.

Corporation Records
Limited Liability Company Records
Fictitious Name
Limited Partnerships
Assumed Name
Trademarks/Servicemarks

Business Services Bureau, Secretary of State, PO Box 202801, Helena, MT 59620; 406-444-3665; Fax: 406-444-3976; 8AM-5PM. Access by: mail, phone, in person. www.mt/gov/sos

Uniform Commercial Code
Federal Tax Liens

Business Services Bureau, Secretary of State, PO Box 202801, Helena, MT 59620-2801 (State Capitol, Rm 225, Helena, MT 59620); 406-444-3665; Fax: 406-444-3976; 8AM-5PM. Access by: mail, online. www.mt.gov/sos

State Tax Liens

Records not available from state agency.

Records are at the county level.

Workers' Compensation Records

State Compensation Fund, PO Box 4759, Helena, MT 59604-4759 (5 S. Last Chance Gulch, Helena, MT 59601); 406-444-6485; Fax: 406-444-7796; 8AM-5PM. Access by: mail. www.stfund.mt.us

Birth Certificates

Montana Department of Health, Vital Records, PO Box 4210, Helena, MT 59604 (111 N Sanders, Rm 209, Helena, MT 59601); 406-444-4228; Fax: 406-444-1803; 8AM-5PM. Access by: mail, fax.

Death Records

Montana Department of Health, Vital Records, PO Box 4210, Helena, MT 59604; 406-444-4228; Fax: 406-444-1803; 8AM-5PM. Access by: mail.

Marriage Certificates
Divorce Records

Records not available from state agency.

Marriage and divorce records are found at county of issue. The State is required by law to maintain an index of these records. The index is from 1943 to present. The State can direct you to the correct county for a fee of $10.00 per 5 years searched.

Accident Reports

Montana Highway Patrol, Accident Records, 2550 Prospect Ave, Helena, MT 59620-1419; 406-444-3278; Fax: 406-444-4169; 8AM-5PM. Access by: mail, phone, in person.

Driver Records

Motor Vehicle Division, Driver's Services, PO Box 201430, Helena, MT 59620-1430 (Records Unit, 303 N Roberts, Room 262, Helena, MT 59620); 406-444-4590; Fax: 406-444-1631; 8AM-5PM. Access by: mail. www.doj.state.mt.us

Vehicle Ownership
Vehicle Identification
Boat & Vessel Ownership
Boat & Vessel Registration

Department of Justice, Title and Registration Bureau, 1032 Buckskin Drive, Deer Lodge, MT 59722; 406-846-6000; Fax: 406-846-6039; 8AM-5PM. Access by: mail, phone, in person.

Legislation-Current/Pending
Legislation-Passed

State Legislature of Montana, State Capitol, PO Box 201706, Helena, MT 59620-1706; 406-444-3064; Fax: 406-444-3036; 8AM-5PM. Access by: mail, phone, in person, online. www.leg.state.mt.us

Voter Registration

Secretary of State, Election Records, PO Box 202801, Helena, MT 59620; 406-444-4732; Fax: 406-444-3976; 8AM-5PM. Access by:, phone, fax, in person. www.state.mt.us/sos

GED Certificates

Office of Public Instruction, GED Program, PO Box 202501, Helena, MT 59620-2501; 406-444-4438; Fax: 406-444-1373; 7AM-4PM M-F.

Hunting License Information
Fishing License Information

Fish, Wildlife & Parks Department, Department of Fish & Wildlife, PO Box 200701, Helena, MT 59620-0701 (1420 E 6th Ave, Helena, MT 59620); 406-444-2950; Fax: 406-444-4952; 8AM-5PM. Access by: mail. http://fwp.state.mt.us

County Courts & Recording Offices

About the Courts...

Administration

Court Administrator, Justice Building   406-444-2621
215 N Sanders, Room 315 (PO Box 203002) Fax: 406-444-0834
Helena, MT 59620

Court Structure

The District Courts have no minimum amount for civil judgment cases. Justice Courts may handle civil actions under $7000. The Small Claims limit is $3000. Many Montana Justices of the Peace maintain case record indexes on their personal PCs which does speed the retrieval process.

Online Access

There is no statewide internal or external online computer system available. Those courts with computer systems use them for internal purposes only.

About the Recording Offices...

Organization

57 counties, 56 recording offices. The recording officer is County Clerk and Recorder (Clerk of District Court for state tax liens). Yellowstone National Park is considered a county, but is not included as a filing location. The entire state is in the Mountain Time Zone (MST).

UCC Records

Financing statements are filed at the state level, except for consumer goods and real estate related collateral. All counties will perform UCC searches. Use search request form UCC-11. Search fees are usually $7.00 per debtor name. Copy fees vary.

Lien Records

Federal tax liens on personal property of businesses are filed with the Secretary of State. Other federal tax liens are filed with the county Clerk and Recorder. State tax liens are filed with the Clerk of District Court. Usually tax liens on personal property filed with the Clerk and Recorder are in the same index with UCC financing statements. Most counties will perform tax lien searches, some as part of a UCC search and others for a separate fee, usually $7.00 per name. Copy fees vary.

Real Estate Records

Many Montana counties will perform real estate searches. Search and copy fees vary. Certification usually costs $2.00 per document.

County Courts & Recording Offices

Beaverhead

Real Estate Recording—Beaverhead County Clerk and Recorder, 2 South Pacific, Dillon, MT 59725. 406-822-3550, Fax: 406-683-5776. 8AM-5PM.

Felony, Civil Actions Over $5,000, Eviction, Probate—District Court, Beaverhead County Courthouse, 2 S Pacific St, Dillon, MT 59725. 406-822-4542, Fax: 406-683-5776. 8AM-5PM. Access by: mail, fax, in person.

Misdemeanor, Civil Actions Under $5,000, Eviction, Small Claims—Dillon Justice Court, 2 S Pacific, Cluster #16, Dillon, MT 59725. 406-822-3538, Fax: 406-683-5776. 8AM-Noon. Access by: mail, in person.

Misdemeanor, Civil Actions Under $7,000, Eviction, Small Claims—Beaverhead County Justice Court, PO Box 107, Lima, MT 59739. 406-377-3967. 4-6PM. Access by: mail, in person.

Big Horn

Real Estate Recording—Big Horn County Clerk and Recorder, 121 West 3rd Street, Hardin, MT 59034. 406-796-2484, Fax: 406-665-1608. 8AM-5PM.

Felony, Civil Actions Over $7,000, Eviction, Probate—District Court, 121 West 3rd St #221, PO Box 908, Hardin, MT 59034. 406-795-2482, Fax: 406-665-1540. 8AM-5PM. Access by: mail, phone, fax, in person.

Misdemeanor, Civil Actions Under $5,000, Eviction, Small Claims—Justice Court, PO Box 908, Hardin, MT 59034. 406-796-2484, Fax: 406-665-1608. 8AM-5PM. Access by: mail, in person.

Blaine

Real Estate Recording—Blaine County Clerk and Recorder, 400 Ohio Street, Chinook, MT 59523. 406-466-2909, Fax: 406-357-2199. 8AM-5PM.

Felony, Civil Actions Over $5,000, Eviction, Probate—District Court, PO Box 969, Chinook, MT 59523. 406-454-6870, Fax: 406-357-2199. 8AM-5PM. Access by: mail, fax, in person.

Misdemeanor, Civil Actions Under $5,000, Eviction, Small Claims—Harlem Justice Court, PO Box 354, Harlem, MT 59526. 406-447-8216, Fax: 406-353-2361. 9AM-Noon. Access by: mail, in person. Special note: Most requests referred to Chinook.

Misdemeanor, Civil Actions Under $7,000, Eviction, Small Claims—Chinook Justice Court, PO Box 1266, Chinook, MT 59523. 406-454-6850. 8AM-5PM. Access by: mail, in person.

Broadwater

Real Estate Recording—Broadwater County Clerk and Recorder, 515 Broadway, Townsend, MT 59644. 406-375-6214, Fax: 406-266-3674. 8AM-Noon, 1-5PM.

Felony, Civil Actions Over $5,000, Eviction, Probate—District Court, 515 Broadway, Townsend, MT 59644. 406-375-6252, Fax: 406-266-5354. 8AM-Noon, 1-5PM. Access by: mail, phone, in person.

Misdemeanor, Civil Actions Under $7,000, Eviction, Small Claims—Justice Court, 515 Broadway, Townsend, MT 59644. 406-365-5425, Fax: 406-266-4720. 8AM-5PM. Access by: mail, in person.

Carbon

Real Estate Recording—Carbon County Clerk and Recorder, Courthouse, 17 W. 11th St, Red Lodge, MT 59068. 406-557-6254, Fax: 406-446-2640. 8AM-5PM.

Felony, Civil Actions Over $5,000 Probate—District Court, PO Box 948, Red Lodge, MT 59068. 406-563-4025, Fax: 406-446-2640. 8AM-5PM. Access by: mail, phone, fax, in person. Special note: Also, this court holds youth, adoption and sanity records.

Misdemeanor, Civil Actions Under $5,000, Eviction, Small Claims—Carbon County Justice Court, Box 2, Red Lodge, MT 59068. 406-563-4040, Fax: 406-446-1911. 8AM-5PM. Access by: mail, in person.

Misdemeanor, Civil Actions Under $7,000—Joliet City Court, PO Box 210, Joliet, MT 59041. 409-275-2231. 8AM-1PM on 1st, 2nd &3rd Wed of month. Access by: mail, in person.

Carter

Real Estate Recording—Carter County Clerk and Recorder, Courthouse, 101 Park Street, Ekalaka, MT 59324. 406-883-7224, Fax: 406-775-8750. 8AM-Noon, 1-5PM.

Felony, Civil Actions Over $5,000, Eviction, Probate—District Court, PO Box 322, Ekalaka, MT 59324. 406-873-5063, Fax: 406-775-8714. 8AM-5PM. Access by: mail, fax, in person.

Misdemeanor, Civil Actions Under $5,000, Eviction, Small Claims—Justice Court, PO Box 72, Ekalaka, MT 59324-0072. 406-883-7254, Fax: 406-775-8714. 8AM-5PM TH. Access by: mail, in person. Special note: 1st & 3rd Thurs of month here, 2nd & 4th Thurs of month in Alzada (406-775-8749).

Cascade

Real Estate Recording—Cascade County Clerk and Recorder, 415 2nd Ave North, Great Falls, MT 59401. 406-568-2231, Fax: 406-454-6802. 8AM-5PM.

Felony, Civil Actions Over $5,000, Eviction, Probate—District Court, County Courthouse, 415 2nd Ave North, Great Falls, MT 59401. 406-566-2341. 8AM-5PM. Access by: mail, phone, in person.

Misdemeanor, Civil Actions Under $7,000, Eviction, Small Claims—Cascade Justice Court, Cascade County Courthouse, 415 2nd Ave N, Great Falls, MT 59401. 406-568-2231, Fax: 406-454-6877. 8AM-5PM. Access by: mail, in person.

Chouteau

Real Estate Recording—Chouteau County Clerk and Recorder, 1308 Franklin, Fort Benton, MT 59442. 406-759-5172, Fax: 406-622-3012. 8AM-5PM.

Felony, Civil Actions Over $5,000, Eviction, Probate—District Court, PO Box 459, Ft Benton, MT 59442. 406-758-5680, Fax: 406-622-3028. 8AM-5PM. Access by: mail, phone, fax, in person.

Misdemeanor, Civil Actions Under $5,000, Eviction, Small Claims—Big Sandy Justice Court, PO Box 234, Big Sandy, MT 59520. 406-487-2651. 1-5PM Th. Access by: mail, in person.

Misdemeanor, Civil Actions Under $7,000, Eviction, Small Claims—Ft Benton Justice Court, PO Box 459, Ft Benton, MT 59442. 406-759-5455, Fax: 406-622-3815. 8AM-4PM M,W. Access by: mail, phone, in person.

Custer

Real Estate Recording—Custer County Clerk and Recorder, 1010 Main Street, Miles City, MT 59301., Fax: 406-233-3452. 8AM-5PM.

Felony, Civil Actions Over $5,000, Eviction, Probate—District Court, 1010 Main, Miles City, MT 59301-3418. 406-342-5547, Fax: 406-233-3450. 8AM-5PM. Access by: mail, in person.

Misdemeanor, Civil Actions Under $5,000, Eviction, Small Claims—Justice Court, 1010 Main St, Miles City, MT 59301-3418. 406-353-4971, Fax: 406-233-3452. 8AM-5PM. Access by: mail, in person.

Daniels

Real Estate Recording—Daniels County Clerk and Recorder, 213 Main Street, Scobey, MT 59263. 406-632-4821. 8AM-5PM.

Felony, Civil Actions Over $5,000, Eviction, Probate—District Court, PO Box 67, Scobey, MT 59263. 406-622-5502. 8AM-5PM. Access by: mail, phone, in person.

Misdemeanor, Civil Actions Under $5,000, Eviction, Small Claims—Justice Court, PO Box 838, Scobey, MT 59263. 406-632-4892. 8AM-5PM. Access by: mail, in person.

Dawson

Real Estate Recording—Dawson County Clerk and Recorder, 207 West Bell, Glendive, MT 59330., Fax: 406-377-2022. 8AM-5PM.

Felony, Civil Actions Over $5,000, Eviction, Probate—District Court, 207 W Bell, Glendive, MT 59330. 406-485-3548, Fax: 406-377-2022. 8AM-5PM. Access by: mail, in person.

Misdemeanor, Civil Actions Under $5,000, Eviction, Small Claims—Justice Court, 207 W Bell, Glendive, MT 59330. 406-482-6885, Fax: 406-365-2022. 8AM-5PM. Access by: in person.

Deer Lodge

Real Estate Recording—Deer Lodge County Clerk and Recorder, 800 South Main St. Courthouse, Anaconda, MT 59711. 406-683-2383, Fax: 406-563-4001. 8AM-5PM.

Felony, Civil Actions Over $5,000, Eviction, Probate—District Court, 800 S Main, Anaconda, MT 59711. 406-665-2275, Fax: 406-563-4001. 8AM-5PM. Access by: mail, in person.

Misdemeanor, Civil Actions Under $5,000, Eviction, Small Claims—Justice Court, 800 S Main, Anaconda, MT 59711. 406-665-1505, Fax: 406-563-4028. 8AM-5PM. Access by: mail, phone, fax, in person.

Fallon

Real Estate Recording—Fallon County Clerk and Recorder, 10 West Fallon Avenue, Baker, MT 59313. 406-932-5150, Fax: 406-778-3431. 8AM-5PM.

Felony, Civil Actions Over $5,000, Eviction, Probate—District Court, PO Box 1521, Baker, MT 59313. 406-932-5151, Fax: 406-778-2815. 8AM-5PM. Access by: mail, in person.

Misdemeanor, Civil Actions Under $5,000, Eviction, Small Claims—Justice Court, Box 846, Baker, MT 59313. 406-883-7258. 11:30AM-4:30PM M-W. Access by: mail, phone, in person.

Fergus

Real Estate Recording—Fergus County Clerk and Recorder, 712 West Main, Lewistown, MT 59457. 406-653-1590, Fax: 406-538-9023. 8AM-5PM.

Felony, Civil Actions Over $5,000, Eviction, Probate—District Court, PO Box 1074, Lewistown, MT 59457. 406-635-4466, Fax: 406-538-6076. 8AM-5PM. Access by: mail, phone, fax, in person.

Misdemeanor, Civil Actions Under $5,000, Eviction, Small Claims—Justice Court, 121 8th Ave South, Lewistown, MT 59457. 406-637-5575. 9AM-4PM. Access by: mail, in person.

Flathead

Real Estate Recording—Flathead County Clerk and Recorder, 800 South Main, Courthouse, Kalispell, MT 59901. 406-846-3680, Fax: 406-758-5865. 8AM-5PM.

Felony, Civil Actions Over $5,000, Eviction, Probate—District Court, 800 S Main, Kalispell, MT 59901. 406-843-5392. 8AM-5PM. Access by: mail, phone, in person.

Misdemeanor, Civil Actions Under $5,000, Eviction, Small Claims—Justice Court, 800 S Main St, Kalispell, MT 59901. 406-846-3680. 8AM-5PM. Access by: mail, in person.

Gallatin

Real Estate Recording—Gallatin County Clerk and Recorder, 311 West Main, Room 204, Bozeman, MT 59715. 406-758-5660. 8AM-5PM.

Felony, Civil Actions Over $5,000, Eviction, Probate—District Court, 615 S 16th, Rm 302, Bozeman, MT 59715. 406-723-8262, Fax: 406-582-2176. 8AM-5PM. Access by: mail, in person.

Misdemeanor, Civil Actions Under $5,000, Eviction, Small Claims—Belgrade Justice and City Court, 91 E Central, Belgrade, MT 59714. 406-487-2671, Fax: 406-388-4996. 8AM-5PM. Access by: mail, in person.

Misdemeanor, Civil Actions Under $7,000, Eviction, Small Claims—Bozeman Justice Court, 615 S 16th St, Bozeman, MT 59715. 406-748-2934, Fax: 406-582-2163. 8AM-5PM. Access by: mail, in person.

Garfield

Real Estate Recording—Garfield County Clerk and Recorder, Courthouse, 700 Kramer, Jordan, MT 59337. 406-654-1118, Fax: 406-557-2625. 8AM-5PM.

Felony, Civil Actions Over $5,000, Eviction, Probate—District Court, PO Box 8, Jordan, MT 59337. 406-665-1504, Fax: 406-557-2625. 8AM-5PM. Access by: mail, phone, in person.

Misdemeanor, Civil Actions Under $7,000, Eviction, Small Claims—Justice Court, PO Box 482, Jordan, MT 59337. 406-654-1742, Fax: 406-557-2735. 8AM-5PM Wed. Access by: mail, in person.

Glacier

Real Estate Recording—Glacier County Clerk and Recorder, 512 East Main, Cut Bank, MT 59427. 408-866-8331, Fax: 406-873-2125. 8AM-5PM.

Felony, Civil, Eviction, Probate—District Court, 512 E Main St, Cut Bank, MT 59427. 409-244-7621, Fax: 406-873-5627. 8AM-5PM. Access by: mail, phone, fax, in person.

Misdemeanor, Civil Actions Under $5,000, Eviction, Small Claims—Justice Court, 512 E Main St, Cut Bank, MT 59427. 409-244-7680, Fax: 406-873-4218. 8AM-Noon, 1-5PM. Access by: mail, in person.

Golden Valley

Real Estate Recording—Golden Valley County Clerk and Recorder, 107 Kemp, Ryegate, MT 59074. 406-758-5660, Fax: 406-568-2598. 8AM-5PM.

Felony, Civil Actions Over $5,000, Eviction, Probate—District Court, PO Box 10, Ryegate, MT 59074. 406-723-8262, Fax: 406-568-2598. 8AM-5PM. Access by: mail, fax, in person.

Misdemeanor, Civil Actions Under $5,000, Eviction, Small Claims—Justice Court, PO Box 10, Ryegate, MT 59074. 406-723-8262, Fax: 406-568-2598. 8AM-5PM Tues. Access by: mail, phone, fax, in person.

Granite

Real Estate Recording—Granite County Clerk and Recorder, 220 North Sansome, Philipsburg, MT 59858. 408-739-1503, Fax: 406-859-3817. 8AM-Noon,1-5PM.

Felony, Civil Actions Over $5,000, Eviction, Probate—District Court, PO Box 399, Philipsburg, MT 59858-0399. 408-454-2155, Fax: 406-859-3817. 8AM-Noon, 1-5PM. Access by: mail, phone, fax, in person.

Misdemeanor, Civil Actions Under $5,000, Eviction, Small Claims—Philipsburg Justice Court, PO Box 356, Philipsburg, MT 59858. 408-299-2974, Fax: 406-859-3817. 11AM-Noon, 1-5PM MWF. Access by: mail, in person.

Misdemeanor, Civil Actions Under $7,000, Eviction, Small Claims—Drummond Justice Court, PO Box 159, Drummond, MT 59832. 406-429-5311, Fax: 406-288-3050. 8AM-4PM M,W,F. Access by: mail, in person.

Hill

Real Estate Recording—Hill County Clerk and Recorder, 315 4th Street, Courthouse, Havre, MT 59501. 406-363-3111, Fax: 406-265-2445. 8AM-5PM.

Felony, Civil Actions Over $5,000, Eviction, Probate—District Court, Hill County Courthouse, Havre, MT 59501. 406-357-3230, Fax: 406-265-1273. 8AM-5PM. Access by: mail, phone, fax, in person.

Misdemeanor, Civil Actions Under $5,000, Eviction, Small Claims—Justice Court, County Courthouse, Havre, MT 59501. 406-357-3280, Fax: 406-265-5487. 8AM-5PM. Access by: mail, in person.

Jefferson

Real Estate Recording—Jefferson County Clerk and Recorder, Corner Centennial & Washington, Boulder, MT 59632. 406-323-1078, Fax: 406-225-4149. 8AM-5PM.

Felony, Civil Actions Over $5,000, Eviction, Probate—District Court, PO Box H, Boulder, MT 59632. 406-322-5320, Fax: 406-225-4149. 8AM-Noon, 1-5PM. Access by: mail, in person.

Misdemeanor, Civil Actions Under $7,000, Eviction, Small Claims—Justice Court, PO Box H, Boulder, MT 59632. 406-322-5332. 8AM-4PM. Access by: mail, in person.

Judith Basin

Real Estate Recording—Judith Basin County Clerk and Recorder, Courthouse, Stanford, MT 59479. 406-721-5700, Fax: 406-566-2211. 8AM-5PM.

Felony, Civil Actions Over $5,000, Eviction, Probate—District Court, PO Box 307, Stanford, MT 59479. 406-683-5821, Fax: 406-566-2211. 8AM-5PM. Access by: mail, phone, in person.

Misdemeanor, Civil Actions Under $5,000, Eviction, Small Claims—Hobson Justice Court, PO Box 276, Hobson, MT 59452. 406-487-5432. 4-9PM. Access by: mail, in person.

Misdemeanor, Civil Actions Under $7,000, Eviction, Small Claims—Stanford Justice Court, PO Box 339, Stanford, MT 59479. 406-683-5831. 9AM-Noon MWF. Access by: mail, in person.

Lake

Real Estate Recording—Lake County Clerk and Recorder, 106 4th Avenue East, Polson, MT 59860. 409-246-5121, Fax: 406-883-7283. 8AM-5PM.

Felony, Civil Actions Over $5,000, Probate—District Court, 106 4th Ave E, Polson, MT 59860. 409-246-5150, Fax: 406-883-7343. 8AM-5PM. Access by: mail, phone, fax, in person.

Misdemeanor, Civil Actions Under $5,000, Eviction, Small Claims—Justice Court, 106 4th Ave E, Polson, MT 59860. 409-246-5185, Fax: 406-883-7283. 8AM-5PM. Access by: mail, phone, fax, in person.

Lewis and Clark

Real Estate Recording—Lewis and Clark County Clerk and Recorder, 316 North Park Avenue, Helena, MT 59601. 406-566-2277. 8AM-5PM.

Felony, Civil Actions Over $5,000, Eviction, Probate, Small Claims—District Court, 228 Broadway, PO Box 158, Helena, MT 59624. 406-566-2277, Fax: 406-447-8275. 8AM-5PM. Access by: mail, fax, in person, online. www.co.lewis-clark.mt.us

Misdemeanor, Civil Actions Under $5,000, Eviction, Small Claims—Justice Court, 228 Broadway, Helena, MT 59601. 406-563-8421, Fax: 406-447-8275. 8AM-Noon, 1-5PM. Access by: mail, in person.

Liberty

Real Estate Recording—Liberty County Clerk and Recorder, 101 First Street East, Chester, MT 59522. 406-859-3006, Fax: 406-759-5395. 8AM-5PM.

Felony, Civil Actions Over $5,000, Eviction, Probate—District Court, PO Box 549, Chester, MT 59522. 406-859-3712, Fax: 406-759-5996. 8AM-5PM. Access by: mail, phone, in person.

Misdemeanor, Civil Actions Under $7,000, Eviction, Small Claims—Justice Court, PO Box 170, Chester, MT 59522. 406-846-3680, Fax: 406-759-5395. 9AM-5PM T. Access by: mail, in person.

Lincoln

Real Estate Recording—Lincoln County Clerk and Recorder, 512 California Avenue, Libby, MT 59923. 406-429-5551, Fax: 406-293-8577. 8AM-5PM.

Felony, Civil Actions Over $5,000, Eviction, Probate—District Court, 512 California Ave, Libby, MT 59923. 406-429-5311, Fax: 406-293-9816. 8AM-5PM. Access by: mail, in person.

Misdemeanor, Civil Actions Under $5,000, Eviction, Small Claims—Eureka Justice Court #2, PO Box 403, Eureka, MT 59917. 406-434-2651, Fax: 406-296-3829. 8AM-Noon, 1-5PM. Access by: mail, in person.

Libby Justice Court #1, 418 Mineral Ave, Libby, MT 59923. 406-434-2271, Fax: 406-293-5948. 8AM-5PM. Access by: mail, in person.

Madison

Real Estate Recording—Madison County Clerk and Recorder, 110 West Wallace, Virginia City, MT 59755. 407-847-1300. 8AM-Noon, 1-5PM.

Felony, Civil Actions Over $5,000, Eviction, Probate—District Court, PO Box 185, Virginia City, MT 59755. 407-836-5715, Fax: 406-843-5207. 8AM-5PM. Access by: mail, fax, in person.

Misdemeanor, Civil Actions Under $5,000, Eviction, Small Claims—Justice Court, PO Box 277, Virginia City, MT 59755. 407-847-1300, Fax: 406-843-5517. 8AM-5PM. Access by: mail, phone, in person.

McCone

Real Estate Recording—McCone County Clerk and Recorder, 206 Second Avenue, Circle, MT 59215., Fax: 406-485-2689. 8AM-5PM.

Felony, Civil Actions Over $5,000, Eviction, Probate—District Court, PO Box 199, Circle, MT 59215. 406-622-5024, Fax: 406-485-3410. 8AM-5PM. Access by: mail, in person.

Misdemeanor, Civil Actions Under $5,000, Eviction, Small Claims—Justice Court, PO Box 192, Circle, MT 59215. 406-622-5032. 2-5PM Wed. Access by: mail, in person.

Meagher

Real Estate Recording—Meagher County Clerk and Recorder, 15 West Main, White Sulphur Springs, MT 59645. 406-653-1590, Fax: 406-547-3388. 8AM-Noon, 1-5PM.

Felony, Civil Actions Over $5,000, Eviction, Probate—District Court, PO Box 443, White Sulphur Springs, MT 59645. 406-653-6266, Fax: 406-547-3388. 8AM-5PM. Access by: mail, phone, in person.

Misdemeanor, Civil Actions Under $7,000, Eviction, Small Claims—Justice Court, PO Box 698, White Sulphur Springs, MT 59645. 406-654-1023, Fax: 406-547-3388. 8AM-5PM M-Th. Access by: mail, in person.

Mineral

Real Estate Recording—Mineral County Clerk and Recorder, 300 River Street, Superior, MT 59872. 407-343-3543, Fax: 406-822-3579. 8AM-5PM.

Felony, Civil Actions Over $5,000, Probate—District Court, PO Box 129, Superior, MT 59872. 407-264-5350, Fax: 406-822-3579. 8AM-Noon, 1-5PM. Access by: mail, phone, fax, in person.

Misdemeanor, Civil Actions Under $5,000, Eviction, Small Claims—Justice Court, PO Box 658, Superior, MT 59872. 407-323-4330, Fax: 406-822-3579. 8AM-5PM. Access by: mail, fax, in person.

Missoula

Real Estate Recording—Missoula County Clerk and Recorder, 200 West Broadway, Missoula, MT 59802., Fax: 406-721-4043. 8AM-5PM.

Felony, Civil Actions Over $5,000, Probate—District Court, 200 W Broadway, Missoula, MT 59802. 406-632-4893, Fax: 406-523-4899. 8AM-5PM. Access by: mail, fax, in person.

Misdemeanor, Civil Actions Under $5,000, Eviction, Small Claims—Justice Court, Dept 1, 200 W Broadway, Missoula, MT 59802. 406-827-4316, Fax: 406-721-4043. 8AM-5PM. Access by: mail, in person.

Musselshell

Real Estate Recording—Musselshell County Clerk and Recorder, 506 Main Street, Courthouse, Roundup, MT 59072., Fax: 406-323-3303. 8AM-5PM.

Felony, Civil Actions Over $5,000, Eviction, Probate—District Court, PO Box 357, Roundup, MT 59072. 406-446-1221, Fax: 406-323-1710. 8AM-5PM. Access by: mail, in person.

Misdemeanor, Civil Actions Under $5,000, Eviction, Small Claims—Justice Court, PO Box 660, Roundup, MT 59072. 406-436-2503, Fax: 406-323-3452. 9AM-Noon, 1-3PM. Access by: mail, phone, fax, in person.

Park

Real Estate Recording—Park County Clerk and Recorder, 414 East Callendar, Livingston, MT 59047. 406-322-4577, Fax: 406-222-4199. 8AM-5PM.

Felony, Civil Actions Over $5,000, Eviction, Probate—District Court, PO Box 437, Livingston, MT 59047. 406-293-7781, Fax: 406-222-4128. 8AM-5PM. Access by: mail, phone, in person.

Misdemeanor, Civil Actions Under $5,000, Eviction, Small Claims—Justice Court, 414 E Callender, Livingston, MT 59047. 406-296-2622, Fax: 406-222-4103. 8AM-Noon, 1-5PM. Access by: mail, phone, fax, in person.

Petroleum

Real Estate Recording—Petroleum County Clerk and Recorder, 201 East Main, Winnett, MT 59087. 406-538-5418, Fax: 406-429-6328. 8AM-5PM.

Felony, Civil Actions Over $5,000, Eviction, Probate—District Court, PO Box 226, Winnett, MT 59087. 406-523-4780, Fax: 406-429-6328. 8AM-5PM. Access by: mail, phone, in person.

Misdemeanor, Civil Actions Under $7,000, Eviction, Small Claims—Justice Court, PO Box 223, Winnett, MT 59087. 406-538-5026, Fax: 406-429-6328. 9AM-Noon Th. Access by: mail, fax, in person.

Phillips

Real Estate Recording—Phillips County Clerk and Recorder, 314 S. 2nd Avenue West, Malta, MT 59538. 406-787-6607, Fax: 406-654-2429. 8AM-5PM.

Felony, Civil Actions Over $5,000, Eviction, Probate—District Court, PO Box 530, Malta, MT 59538. 406-778-2883, Fax: 406-654-1023. 8AM-5PM. Access by: mail, phone, fax, in person.

Misdemeanor, Civil Actions Under $7,000, Eviction, Small Claims—Justice Court, PO Box 1396, Malta, MT 59538. 406-778-7114, Fax: 406-654-1213. 10AM-4PM. Access by: mail, fax, in person.

Pondera

Real Estate Recording—Pondera County Clerk and Recorder, 20 4th Avenue S.W. Conrad, MT 59425. 406-423-5503, Fax: 406-278-4070. 8AM-5PM.

Felony, Civil Actions Over $5,000, Eviction, Probate—9th Judicial District Court, 20 Fourth Ave SW, Conrad, MT 59425. 406-378-2203, Fax: 406-278-4081. 8AM-5PM. Access by: mail, fax, in person.

Misdemeanor, Civil Actions Under $5,000, Eviction, Small Claims—Justice Court, 20 Fourth Ave SW, Conrad, MT 59425. 406-388-3760, Fax: 406-278-4070. 9AM-4PM. Access by: mail, in person.

Powder River

Real Estate Recording—Powder River County Clerk and Recorder, Courthouse Square, Broadus, MT 59317. 406-557-2233. 8AM-5PM.

Felony, Civil Actions Over $5,000, Eviction, Probate—District Court, PO Box 239, Broadus, MT 59317. 406-547-3954, Fax: 406-436-2325. 8AM-Noon, 1-5PM. Access by: mail, fax, in person.

Misdemeanor, Civil Actions Under $7,000, Eviction, Small Claims—Justice Court, PO Box 488, Broadus, MT 59317. 406-557-2733, Fax: 406-436-2866. 9AM-3:30PM M-Th. Access by: mail, in person.

Powell

Real Estate Recording—Powell County Clerk and Recorder, 409 Missouri Avenue, Deer Lodge, MT 59722. 408-249-2690. 8AM-5PM.

Felony, Civil Actions Over $5,000, Eviction, Probate—District Court, 409 Missouri Ave, Deer Lodge, MT 59722. 408-299-2281, Fax: 406-846-2742. 8AM-5PM. Access by: mail, in person.

Misdemeanor, Civil Actions Under $5,000, Eviction, Small Claims—Justice Court, 409 Missiouri, Deer Lodge, MT 59722. 407-889-4176. 8AM-5PM. Access by: mail, in person.

Prairie

Real Estate Recording—Prairie County Clerk and Recorder, Courthouse, 217 W. Park, Terry, MT 59349., Fax: 406-635-5576. 8AM-5PM.

Felony, Civil Actions Over $5,000, Eviction, Probate—District Court, PO Box 125, Terry, MT 59349. 406-775-8714. 8AM-5PM. Access by: mail, in person.

Misdemeanor, Civil Actions Under $5,000, Eviction, Small Claims—Justice Court, PO Box 40, Terry, MT 59349. 406-765-2310. 1-2PM. Access by: mail, in person.

Ravalli

Real Estate Recording—Ravalli County Clerk and Recorder, 205 Bedford, Courthouse, Hamilton, MT 59840. 406-466-5611, Fax: 406-363-1880. 8AM-5PM.

Felony, Civil Actions Over $7,000, Probate—District Court, Ravalli County Courthouse, Box 5014, Hamilton, MT 59840. 406-482-6945, Fax: 406-375-6327. 8AM-5PM. Access by: mail, fax, in person.

Misdemeanor, Civil Actions Under $7,000, Eviction, Small Claims—Justice Court, Courthouse Box 5023, Hamilton, MT 59840. 406-485-3410, Fax: 406-375-6383. 8-12, 1-5. Access by: mail, phone, in person.

Richland

Real Estate Recording—Richland County Clerk and Recorder, 201 West Main Street, Sidney, MT 59270., Fax: 406-482-3731. 8AM-5PM.

Felony, Civil Actions Over $5,000, Eviction, Probate—District Court, 201 W Main, Sidney, MT 59270. 406-586-2342, Fax: 406-482-3731. 8AM-5PM. Access by: mail, phone, fax, in person.

Misdemeanor, Civil Actions Under $7,000, Eviction, Small Claims—Justice Court, 123 W Main, Sidney, MT 59270. 406-585-1315, Fax: 406-482-4766. 8AM-5PM. Access by: mail, fax, in person.

Roosevelt

Real Estate Recording—Roosevelt County Clerk and Recorder, 400 Second Avenue South, Wolf Point, MT 59201. 406-775-8735, Fax: 406-653-6202. 8AM-5PM.

Felony, Civil Actions Over $5,000, Eviction, Probate—District Court, County Courthouse, Wolf Point, MT 59201. 406-778-2883, Fax: 406-653-6203. 8AM-5PM. Access by: mail, fax, in person.

Misdemeanor, Civil Actions Under $5,000, Eviction, Small Claims—Culbertson Justice Court Post #2, PO Box 421, Culbertson, MT 59218. 406-932-5154, Fax: 406-787-6193. 9AM-3PM M-Th. Access by: mail, in person.

Wolf Point Justice Court Post #1, County Courthouse, Wolf Point, MT 59201. 406-775-8754, Fax: 406-653-3100. 8-11:30AM, 12:30-5PM. Access by: in person.

Rosebud

Real Estate Recording—Rosebud County Clerk and Recorder, 1200 Main Street, Forsyth, MT 59327., Fax: 406-356-7551. 8AM-5PM.

Felony, Civil Actions Over $5,000, Eviction, Probate—District Court, PO Box 48, Forsyth, MT 59327. 406-454-6780, Fax: 406-356-7551. 8AM-5PM. Access by: mail, fax, in person.

Misdemeanor, Civil Actions Under $5,000, Eviction, Small Claims—Justice Court, PO Box 575, Department Two, Colstrip, MT 59323. 406-843-4230, Fax: 406-748-4832. 8AM-5PM. Access by: mail, in person.

Misdemeanor, Civil Actions Under $7,000, Eviction, Small Claims—Justice Court #1, PO Box 504, Forsyth, MT 59327. 406-447-8327. 8AM-5PM. Access by: mail, in person.

Sanders

Real Estate Recording—Sanders County Clerk and Recorder, Courthouse, 1111 Main St. Thompson Falls, MT 59873. 407-836-2060, Fax: 406-827-4388. 8AM-5PM.

Felony, Civil Actions Over $5,000, Eviction, Probate—District Court, PO Box 519, Thompson Falls, MT 59873. 407-665-4356, Fax: 406-827-0094. 8AM-5PM. Access by: mail, in person.

Misdemeanor, Civil Actions Under $7,000, Eviction, Small Claims—Justice Court, PO Box 519, Thompson Falls, MT 59873. 407-671-1116, Fax: 406-827-0094. 8AM-5PM. Access by: mail, fax, in person.

Sheridan

Real Estate Recording—Sheridan County Clerk and Recorder, 100 West Laurel Avenue, Plentywood, MT 59254. 406-873-5063, Fax: 406-765-2609. 8AM-5PM.

Felony, Civil Actions Over $5,000, Eviction, Probate—District Court, 100 W Laurel, Plentywood, MT 59254. 406-859-3831, Fax: 406-765-2602. 8AM-Noon, 1-5PM. Access by: mail, phone, in person.

Misdemeanor, Civil Actions Under $5,000, Eviction, Small Claims—Justice Court, 100 W Laurel, Plentywood, MT 59254. 406-873-5063, Fax: 406-765-2129. 8AM-5PM. Access by: mail, fax, in person.

Silver Bow

Real Estate Recording—Silver Bow County Clerk and Recorder, 155 West Granite, Butte, MT 59701. 406-827-4398, Fax: 406-782-6637. 8AM-5PM.

Felony, Civil Actions Over $5,000, Probate—District Court, 155 W Granite St, Butte, MT 59701. 406-843-4230, Fax: 406-723-1280. 8AM-5PM. Access by: mail, fax, in person.

Misdemeanor, Civil Actions Under $5,000, Eviction, Small Claims—Justice Court #1 & #2, 155 W Granite St, Butte, MT 59701. 406-827-4318. 8AM-5PM. Access by: mail, in person. Special note: There are two Justice Courts at this location. Both courts must be searched for records.

Stillwater

Real Estate Recording—Stillwater County Clerk and Recorder, 400 Third Avenue North, Columbus, MT 59019. 406-436-2320, Fax: 406-322-4698. 8AM-5PM.

Felony, Civil Actions Over $5,000, Eviction, Probate—District Court, PO Box 367, Columbus, MT 59019. 406-436-2444, Fax: 406-322-4698. 8AM-5PM. Access by: mail, phone, in person.

Misdemeanor, Civil Actions Under $5,000, Eviction, Small Claims—Justice Court, PO Box 77, Columbus, MT 59019. 406-434-5501, Fax: 406-322-5838. 8AM-5PM. Access by: mail, phone, fax, in person.

Sweet Grass

Real Estate Recording—Sweet Grass County Clerk and Recorder, Courthouse, 200 W. 1st Ave. Big Timber, MT 59011. 409-267-8286, Fax: 406-932-4777. 8AM-5PM.

Felony, Civil Actions Over $5,000, Eviction, Probate—District Court, PO Box 698, Big Timber, MT 59011. 409-267-8309, Fax: 406-932-5433. 8AM-Noon, 1-5PM. Access by: mail, phone, in person.

Misdemeanor, Civil Actions Under $5,000, Eviction, Small Claims—Justice Court, PO Box 1432, Big Timber, MT 59011. 409-267-8276, Fax: 406-932-5433. 8AM-5PM. Access by: mail, fax, in person.

Teton

Real Estate Recording—Teton County Clerk and Recorder, Courthouse, Choteau, MT 59422., Fax: 406-466-2138. 8AM-5PM.

Felony, Civil Actions Over $5,000, Eviction, Probate—District Court, PO Box 487, Choteau, MT 59422. 406-582-2165, Fax: 406-466-2138. 8AM-5PM. Access by: mail, phone, fax, in person.

Misdemeanor, Civil Actions Under $5,000, Eviction, Small Claims—Justice Court, PO Box 337, Choteau, MT 59422. 406-582-2191, Fax: 406-466-2138. 1-5PM. Access by: mail, fax, in person.

Toole

Real Estate Recording—Toole County Clerk and Recorder, 226 1st Street South, Shelby, MT 59474. 406-547-3941, Fax: 406-434-2467. 8AM-5PM.

Felony, Civil Actions Over $5,000, Eviction, Probate—District Court, PO Box 850, Shelby, MT 59474. 406-538-9220, Fax: 406-434-7225. 8AM-Noon, 1-5PM. Access by: mail, phone, fax, in person.

Misdemeanor, Civil Actions Under $5,000, Eviction, Small Claims—Justice Court, PO Box 738, Shelby, MT 59474. 406-547-3641. 10AM-4PM. Access by: mail, in person.

Treasure

Real Estate Recording—Treasure County Clerk and Recorder, 307 Rapelje Ave. Hysham, MT 59038. 406-446-1440, Fax: 406-342-5445. 8AM-Noon,1-5PM.

Felony, Civil Actions Over $5,000, Eviction, Probate—District Court, PO Box 392, Hysham, MT 59038. 406-447-8202, Fax: 406-342-5445. 8AM-5PM. Access by: mail, phone, fax, in person.

Misdemeanor, Civil Actions Under $5,000, Eviction, Small Claims—Justice Court, PO Box 267, Hysham, MT 59038. 406-446-1225. 9AM-Noon. Access by: mail, in person.

Valley

Real Estate Recording—Valley County Clerk and Recorder, 501 Court Square, Box 2, Glasgow, MT 59230. 406-323-1413, Fax: 406-228-9027. 8AM-5PM.

Felony, Civil Actions Over $5,000, Eviction, Probate—District Court, 501 Court Sq #4, Glasgow, MT 59230. 406-342-5532, Fax: 406-228-4601. 8AM-5PM. Access by: mail, phone, fax, in person.

Misdemeanor, Civil Actions Under $5,000, Eviction, Small Claims—Justice Court, 501 Court Sq #10, Glasgow, MT 59230. 406-342-5545, Fax: 406-228-4601. 8AM-5PM. Access by: mail, phone, in person.

Wheatland

Real Estate Recording—Wheatland County Clerk and Recorder, Courthouse, Harlowton, MT 59036. 406-765-2310, Fax: 406-632-5654. 8AM-5PM.

Felony, Civil Actions Over $5,000, Eviction, Probate—District Court, Box 227, Harlowton, MT 59036. 406-765-2310, Fax: 406-632-4873. 8AM-5PM. Access by: mail, phone, in person.

Misdemeanor, Civil Actions Under $7,000, Eviction, Small Claims—Justice Court, PO Box 524, Harlowton, MT 59036. 406-759-5615, Fax: 406-632-5654. 10AM-1PM T,Th. Access by: mail, phone, in person.

Wibaux

Real Estate Recording—Wibaux County Clerk and Recorder, 200 South Wibaux Street, Wibaux, MT 59353. 406-962-3133, Fax: 406-796-2625. 8AM-5PM.

Felony, Civil Actions Over $5,000, Eviction, Probate—District Court, PO Box 292, Wibaux, MT 59353. 407-264-5245, Fax: 406-796-2484. 8AM-5PM, Closed 12-1. Access by: mail, phone, fax, in person.

Misdemeanor, Civil Actions Under $7,000, Eviction, Small Claims—Justice Court, PO Box 445, Wibaux, MT 59353. 407-264-5350. 1-5PM M&W, 8AM-12 F. Access by: mail, in person.

Yellowstone

Real Estate Recording—Yellowstone County Clerk and Recorder, 217 North 27th, Room 401, Billings, MT 59101. 406-356-2638, Fax: 406-256-2736. 8AM-5PM.

Felony, Civil Actions Over $5,000, Probate—District Court, PO Box 35030, Billings, MT 59107. 406-356-7322, Fax: 406-256-2995. 8AM-5PM. Access by: mail, in person.

Misdemeanor, Civil Actions Under $7,000, Eviction, Small Claims—Justice Court, PO Box 35032, Billings, MT 59107. 406-357-2335, Fax: 406-256-2898. 8AM-5PM. Access by: mail, fax, in person.

Federal Courts

US District Court

Billings Division Clerk, Room 5405, Federal Bldg, 316 N 26th St, Billings, MT 59101406-247-7000 Fax: 406-247-7008 Counties: Big Horn, Carbon, Carter, Custer, Daniels, Dawson, Fallon, Garfield, Golden Valley, McCone, Musselshell, Park, Petroleum, Phillips, Powder River, Prairie, Richland, Roosevelt, Rosebud, Sheridan, Stillwater, Sweet Grass, Treasure, Valley, Wheatland,Wibaux, Yellowstone, Yellowstone National Park.

Butte Division Room 273, Federal Bldg, Butte, MT 59701406-782-0432 Fax: 406-782-0537 Counties: Beaverhead, Deer Lodge, Gallatin, Madison, Silver Bow.

Great Falls Division Clerk, PO Box 2186, Great Falls, MT 59403406-727-1922 Fax: 406-727-7648 Counties: Blaine, Cascade, Chouteau, Fergus, Glacier, Hill, Judith Basin, Liberty, Pondera, Teton, Toole.

Helena Division Federal Bldg, Drawer 10015, Helena, MT 59626406-441-1355 Fax: 406-441-1357 Counties: Broadwater, Jefferson, Lewis and Clark, Meagher, Powell.

Missoula Division Russell Smith Courthouse, PO Box 8537, Missoula, MT 59807406-542-7260 Fax: 406-542-7272 Counties: Flathead, Granite, Lake, Lincoln, Mineral, Missoula, Ravalli, Sanders.

US Bankruptcy Court

Butte Division PO Box 689, Butte, MT 59703406-782-3354 Fax: 406-782-0537 Counties: All counties in Montana.

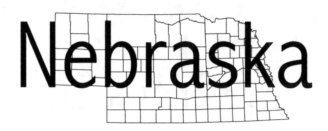

Attorney General's Office
2115 State Capitol
Lincoln, NE 68509
www.nol.org/home/ago

402-471-2682
Fax: 402-471-3297

Governor's Office
PO Box 94848
Lincoln, NE 68509-4848
www.gov.nol.org

402-471-2244
Fax: 402-471-6031

State Archives
PO Box 82554
Lincoln, NE 68501-2554
www.nebraskahistory.org

402-471-4771
Fax: 402-471-3100

Capital: Lincoln
Lancaster County

Time Zone: CST*

* Nebraska's 19 western-most counties are MST:
Arthur, Banner, Box Butte, Chase, Cherry, Cheyenne,
Dawes, Deuel, Dundy, Garden, Grant, Hooker, Keith,
Kimball, Morrill, Perkins, Scotts Bluff, Sheridan, Sioux.

Number of Counties: 93

Population: 1,656,870

Web Site: www.state.ne.us

Search Unclaimed Property Online
www.treasurer.org/search1.html

State Agencies

Criminal Records
Nebraska Highway Patrol, CID, PO Box 94907, Lincoln, NE 68509-4907 (1500 Nebraska Highway 2, Lincoln, NE 68502); 402-479-4924, 402-479-4978, 402-471-4545; 8AM-4PM. Access by: mail.

Corporation Records
Limited Liability Company Records
Limited Partnerships
Trade Names
Trademarks/Servicemarks
Secretary of State, Corporation Commission, 1301 State Capitol Bldg, Lincoln, NE 68509; 402-471-4079; Fax: 402-471-3666;

8AM-5PM. Access by: mail, phone, in person, online. www.nol.org.home/SOS

Sales Tax Registrations
Revenue Department, Revenue Operations Division, PO Box 94818, Lincoln, NE 68509-4818 (301 Centennial Mall South, Lincoln, NE 68509); 402-471-5695; Fax: 402-471-5608; 8AM-5PM. Access by: mail, phone, in person. www.nol.org/revenue

Uniform Commercial Code
Federal Tax Liens

UCC Division, Secretary of State, PO Box 95104, Lincoln, NE 68509 (1305 State Capitol Bldg, Lincoln, NE 68509); 402-471-4080; Fax: 402-471-4429; 7:30AM-5PM. Access by: mail, phone, in person, online.

State Tax Liens

Records not available from state agency.

Records are with the Register at the county level.

Workers' Compensation Records

Workers' Compensation Court, PO Box 98908, Lincoln, NE 68509-8908 (State Capitol, 13th Floor, Lincoln, NE 68509); 402-471-6468, 800-599-5155 In-state; Fax: 402-471-2700; 8AM-5PM. Access by: mail, online.

Birth Certificates

NE Health & Human Services System, Vital Statistics Section, PO Box 95065, Lincoln, NE 68509-5065 (301 Centennial Mall S, 3rd Floor, Lincoln, NE 68509); 402-471-2871; 8AM-5PM. Access by: mail, phone, in person. www.hhs.state.ne.us/cedindex.htm

Death Records

Health and Human Services System, Vital Statistics Section, PO Box 95065, Lincoln, NE 68509-5065; 402-471-2871; 8AM-5PM. Access by: mail, phone, in person. www.hhs.state.ne.us/cedindex.htm

Marriage Certificates

Health and Human Services System, Vital Statistics Section, PO Box 95065, Lincoln, NE 68509-5065; 402-471-2871; 8AM-5PM. Access by: mail, phone, in person. www.hhs.state.ne.us/cedindex.htm

Divorce Records

Health and Humna Services System, Vital Statistics Section, PO Box 95065, Lincoln, NE 68509-5065; 402-471-2871; 8AM-5PM. Access by: mail, phone, in person. www.hhs.state.ne.us/cedindex.htm

Accident Reports

Department of Roads, Accident Records Bureau, Box 94669, Lincoln, NE 68509 (1500 Nebraska Highway 2, Lincoln, NE 68502); 402-479-4645; Fax: 402-479-4325; 8AM-5PM. Access by: mail, phone, in person.

Driver Records

Department of Motor Vehicles, Driver Records Division, PO Box 94789, Lincoln, NE 68509-4789 (301 Centennial Mall, S, Lincoln, NE 68509); 402-471-4343; 8AM-5PM. Access by: mail, online. www.nol.org/home/dmv/driverec.htm

Vehicle Ownership
Vehicle Identification
Boat & Vessel Ownership

Department of Motor Vehicles, Titles and Registration Section, PO Box 94789, Lincoln, NE 68509 (301 Centennial Mall, S, Lincoln, NE 68509); 402-471-3918; 8AM-5PM. Access by: mail, online. www.nol.org/home/DMV

Boat & Vessel Registration

Records not available from state agency.

All boats must be registered. Records are found at the county recorder offices.

Legislation-Current/Pending
Legislation-Passed

Clerk of Legislature Office, PO Box 94604, Lincoln, NE 68509-4604 (State Capitol, 1445 K Street, Room 2018, Lincoln, NE 68509); 402-471-2271; Fax: 402-471-2126; 8AM-5PM. Access by: mail, phone, in person, online. www.unicam.state.ne.us

Voter Registration

Restricted access.

Individual look-ups must be done at the county level. The state has developed a new statewide system. Current law dictates that the database can only be sold for political purposes, and not for commercial purposes. A CD can be purchased for $500.

Secretary of State, Election Divisions, PO Box 94608, Lincoln, NE 68509; 402-471-2554; Fax: 402-471-3237; 8AM-5PM www.nol.org/home/SOS

GED Certificates

NE Dept of Education, Adult Education, PO Box 94987, Lincoln, NE 68509 (301 Centennial Mall S, Lincoln, NE 68509); 402-471-2475; Fax: 402-471-0117;.

Hunting License Information
Fishing License Information

Game & Parks Commission, PO Box 30370, Lincoln, NE 68503 (2200 N 33rd St, Lincoln, NE 68503); 402-471-0641; Fax: 402-471-5528; 8AM-5PM. Access by: mail, phone, in person.

County Courts & Recording Offices

About the Courts...

Administration

Court Administrator   402-471-2643
PO Box 98910   Fax: 402-471-2197
Lincoln, NE 68509-8910
http://court.nol.org

Court Structure

The District Court is the court of general jurisdiction. The County Court is limited to $15,000 in civil judgment matters. The number of judicial districts went from 21 to the current 12 in July 1992.

County Courts have juvenile jurisdiction in all but 3 counties. Douglas, Lancaster, and Sarpy counties have separate Juvenile Courts. Probate is handled by County Courts. Many have records on microfiche back to the mid/late 1800s.

Searching Hints

Most Nebraska courts require the public to do their own in-person searches and will not respond to written search requests. The State Attorney General has recommended that courts not perform searches because of the time involved and possible legal liability concerns.

Online Access

Implementation of a statewide, internal online access system is underway. The goal is statewide access by the year 2000. All internal online courts allow public access at their offices. Douglas county offers remote online. Remote access by the public for all the courts will be considered in the future.

About the Recording Offices...

Organization

93 counties, 109 recording offices. The recording officers are County Clerk (UCC and some state tax liens) and Register of Deeds (real estate and most tax liens). Most counties have a combined Clerk/Register office, which are designated "County Clerk" in this section. Sixteen counties have separate offices for County Clerk and for Register of Deeds - Adams, Cass, Dakota, Dawson, Dodge, Douglas, Gage, Hall, Lancaster, Lincoln, Madison, Otoe, Platte, Sarpy, Saunders, and Scotts. Bluff. In combined offices, the Register of Deeds is frequently a different person from the County Clerk. 74 counties are in the Central Time Zone (CST) and 19 are in the Mountain Time Zone (MST).

UCC Records

Financing statements are filed at the state level, and real estate related collateral are filed with the County Clerk. All non-real estate UCC filings are entered into a statewide database that is accessible from any county office. All but five counties will perform UCC searches. Use search request form UCC-11. The UCC statute allows for telephone searching. Search fees are usually $3.50 per debtor name. Copy fees vary.

Lien Records

All federal and some state tax liens are filed with the County Register of Deeds. Some state tax liens on personal property are filed with the County Clerk. Most counties will perform tax lien searches, some as part of a UCC search, and others for a separate fee, usually $3.50 per name in each index. Copy fees vary.

Real Estate Records

Some Nebraska counties will perform real estate searches, including owner of record from the legal description of the property. Address search requests and make checks payable to the Register of Deeds, not the County Clerk. Fees vary.

County Courts & Recording Offices

Adams

Real Estate Recording—Adams County Clerk, 500 W. 4th, #109, Hastings, NE 68901. Fax: 402-461-7185. 9AM-5PM.

Adams County Register of Deeds, 500 W. 4th, Room 100, Hastings, NE 68901. 402-746-2716, Fax: 402-461-7154. 9AM-5PM.

Felony, Civil Actions Over $15,000—District Court, PO Box 9, Hastings, NE 68902. 402-746-2877, Fax: 402-461-7269. 8:30AM-5PM. Access by: in person.

Misdemeanor, Civil Actions Under $15,000, Eviction, Small Claims, Probate—Adams County Court, PO Box 95, Hastings, NE 68902-0095. 402-746-2777, Fax: 402-461-7144. 8AM-5PM. Access by: in person.

Antelope

Real Estate Recording—Antelope County Clerk, Courthouse, 501 Main St. Neligh, NE 68756. 405-258-1309, Fax: 402-887-4719. 8:30AM-5PM.

Felony, Civil Actions Over $15,000—District Court, PO Box 45, Neligh, NE 68756. 405-262-1070, Fax: 402-887-4160. 8:30AM-5PM. Access by: in person.

Misdemeanor, Civil Actions Under $15,000, Eviction, Small Claims, Probate—Antelope County Court, 501 Main, Neligh, NE 68756. 405-258-1491, Fax: 402-887-4160. 8:30AM-5PM. Access by: in person.

Arthur

Real Estate Recording—Arthur County Clerk, Main Street, Courthouse, Arthur, NE 69121. Fax: 308-764-2216. 8AM-4PM.

Felony, Misdemeanor, Civil, Eviction, Small Claims, Probate—District and County Court, PO Box 126, Arthur, NE 69121. 308-928-2171, Fax: 308-764-2216. 8AM-4PM. Access by: mail, phone, fax, in person.

Banner

Real Estate Recording—Banner County Clerk, State Street, Courthouse, Harrisburg, NE 69345. 308-547-2223, Fax: 308-436-4180. 8AM-Noon, 1-5PM.

Felony, Civil Actions Over $15,000—District Court, PO Box 67, Harrisburg, NE 69345. 308-547-2225, Fax: 308-436-4180. 8AM-5PM. Access by: mail, fax, in person.

Misdemeanor, Civil Actions Under $15,000, Eviction, Small Claims, Probate—Banner County Court, PO Box 67, Harrisburg, NE 69345. 308-587-2363, Fax: 308-436-4180. 8AM-Noon, 1-5PM. Access by: mail, fax, in person.

Blaine

Real Estate Recording—Blaine County Clerk, Lincoln Avenue, Courthouse, Brewster, NE 68821. 308-728-5606, Fax: 308-547-2228. 8AM-Noon, 1-4PM.

Felony, Civil Actions Over $15,000—District Court, Lincoln Ave, Box 136, Brewster, NE 68821. 308-728-3831, Fax: 308-547-2228. 8AM-4PM. Access by: mail, fax, in person.

Misdemeanor, Civil Actions Under $15,000, Eviction, Small Claims, Probate—Blaine County Court, Lincoln Ave, Box 123, Brewster, NE 68821. 308-745-1513, Fax: 308-547-2228. 8AM-4PM. Access by: mail, phone, fax, in person.

Boone

Real Estate Recording—Boone County Clerk, 222 South 4th Street, Albion, NE 68620. 402-497-3791, Fax: 402-395-6592. 8:30AM-5PM.

Felony, Civil Actions Over $15,000—District Court, 222 Fourth St, Albion, NE 68620. 402-497-3021, Fax: 402-395-6592. 8:30AM-5PM. Access by: mail, phone, fax, in person.

Misdemeanor, Civil Actions Under $15,000, Eviction, Small Claims, Probate—Boone County Court, 222 S 4th St, Albion, NE 68620. 402-497-3891, Fax: 402-395-6592. 8AM-5PM. Access by: mail, fax, in person.

Box Butte

Real Estate Recording—Box Butte County Clerk, 5th Box Butte, Courthouse, Suite 203, Alliance, NE 69301. 308-882-5266, Fax: 308-762-2867. 8:30AM-4:30PM.

Felony, Civil Actions Over $15,000—District Court, 515 Box Butte Suite 300, Alliance, NE 69301. 308-882-4690, Fax: 308-762-7703. 9AM-5PM. Access by: in person.

Misdemeanor, Civil Actions Under $15,000, Eviction, Small Claims, Probate—Box Butte County Court, PO Box 613, Alliance, NE 69301. 308-882-4756, Fax: 308-762-6802. 8:30AM-5PM. Access by: mail, phone, fax, in person.

Boyd

Real Estate Recording—Boyd County Clerk, Thayer Street, Courthouse, Butte, NE 68722. 405-236-2727, Fax: 402-775-2146. 8:15AM-Noon, 1-5PM.

Felony, Civil Actions Over $15,000—District Court, PO Box 26, Butte, NE 68722. 405-228-2967, Fax: 402-775-2146. 8:45AM-5PM. Access by: mail, in person.

Misdemeanor, Civil Actions Under $15,000, Eviction, Small Claims, Probate—Boyd County Court, PO Box 396, Butte, NE 68722. 405-227-4782, Fax: 402-775-2146. 8AM-5PM W,Th. Access by: mail, phone, fax, in person.

Brown

Real Estate Recording—Brown County Clerk, Courthouse, 148 W. 4th St. Ainsworth, NE 69210. 402-461-7120, Fax: 402-387-0918. 8AM-5PM.

Felony, Civil Actions Over $15,000—District Court, 148 W Fourth St, Ainsworth, NE 69210. 402-461-7143, Fax: 402-387-0918. 8AM-5PM. Access by: mail, phone, fax, in person.

Misdemeanor, Civil Actions Under $15,000, Eviction, Small Claims, Probate—Brown County Court, 148 W Fourth St, Ainsworth, NE 69210. 402-461-7264, Fax: 402-387-0918. 8AM-5PM. Access by: mail, in person.

Buffalo

Real Estate Recording—Buffalo County Register of Deeds, 16th & Central Avenue, Kearney, NE 68847. 308-327-2123, Fax: 308-236-1291. 8AM-5PM.

Felony, Civil Actions Over $15,000—District Court, PO Box 520, Kearney, NE 68848. 308-324-5606, Fax: 308-233-3693. 8AM-5PM. Access by: mail, in person.

Misdemeanor, Civil Actions Under $15,000, Eviction, Small Claims, Probate—Buffalo County Court, PO Box 520, Kearney, NE 68848. 308-324-4261, Fax: 308-236-1243. 8AM-5PM. Access by: in person.

Burt

Real Estate Recording—Burt County Clerk, Courthouse, 111 N. 13th St. Tekamah, NE 68061. 402-441-7328, Fax: 402-374-1955. 8AM-4:30PM.

Felony, Civil Actions Over $15,000—District Court, 111 N 13th St, Tekamah, NE 68061. 402-441-7425, Fax: 402-374-2746. 8AM-4:30PM. Access by: mail, in person.

Misdemeanor, Civil Actions Under $15,000, Eviction, Small Claims, Probate—Burt County Court, 111 N 13th St, PO Box 87, Tekamah, NE 68061. 402-441-7295, Fax: 402-374-2746. 8AM-4:30PM. Access by: in person.

Butler

Real Estate Recording—Butler County Clerk, 451 5th Street, David City, NE 68632. 402-426-6888, Fax: 402-367-3329. 8:30AM-5PM.

Felony, Civil Actions Over $15,000—District Court, 451 5th St, David City, NE 68632-1666. 402-426-6899, Fax: 402-367-3249. 8:30AM-5PM. Access by: mail, phone, fax, in person.

Misdemeanor, Civil Actions Under $15,000, Eviction, Small Claims, Probate—Butler County Court, 451 5th St, David City, NE 68632-1666. 402-436-6621, Fax: 402-367-3249. 8AM-Noon, 1-5PM. Access by: mail, fax, in person.

Cass

Real Estate Recording—Cass County Clerk, Courthouse, Room 202, 346 Main St. Plattsmouth, NE 68048. Fax: 402-296-9327. 8AM-5PM.

Cass County Register of Deeds, County Courthouse, 346 Main St. Plattsmouth, NE 68048. 402-563-4905, Fax: 402-296-9327. 8AM-5PM.

Felony, Civil Actions Over $15,000—District Court, Cass County Courthouse, 346 Main Street, Plattsmouth, NE 68048. 402-375-3885, Fax: 402-296-9345. 8AM-5PM. Access by: in person.

Misdemeanor, Civil Actions Under $15,000, Eviction, Small Claims, Probate—Cass County Court, Cass County Courthouse, Plattsmouth, NE 68048. 402-375-2260. 8AM-5PM. Access by: in person.

Cedar

Real Estate Recording—Cedar County Clerk, Courthouse, Hartington, NE 68739. 402-367-7480, Fax: 402-254-7410. 8AM-5PM.

Felony, Civil Actions Over $15,000—District Court, PO Box 796, Hartington, NE 68739-0796. 402-367-7460, Fax: 402-254-6954. 8AM-5PM. Access by: fax, in person.

Misdemeanor, Civil Actions Under $15,000, Eviction, Small Claims, Probate—Cedar County Court, 101 S Broadway Ave, Hartington, NE 68739. 402-372-6003, Fax: 402-254-6954. 8AM-5PM. Access by: in person.

Chase

Real Estate Recording—Chase County Clerk, 921 Broadway, Courthouse, Imperial, NE 69033. 309-345-3863, Fax: 308-882-5390. 8AM-4PM.

Felony, Civil Actions Over $15,000—District Court, PO Box 1299, Imperial, NE 69033. 309-467-3312, Fax: 308-882-5390. 8AM-4PM. Access by: mail, phone, fax, in person.

Misdemeanor, Civil Actions Under $15,000, Eviction, Small Claims, Probate—Chase County Court, PO Box 1299, Imperial, NE 69033. 309-345-3817, Fax: 308-882-5679. 7:30AM-4:30PM. Access by: mail, phone, in person.

Cherry

Real Estate Recording—Cherry County Clerk, 365 North Main, Valentine, NE 69201. 402-444-5425, Fax: 402-376-3095. 8:30AM-4:30PM.

Felony, Civil Actions Over $15,000—District Court, 365 N Main St, Valentine, NE 69201. 402-444-7018, Fax: 402-376-3830. 8:30AM-4:30PM. Access by: in person.

Misdemeanor, Civil Actions Under $15,000, Eviction, Small Claims, Probate—Cherry County Court, 365 N Main St, Valentine, NE 69201. 402-444-7272, Fax: 402-376-3830. 8AM-5PM. Access by: in person.

Cheyenne

Real Estate Recording—Cheyenne County Clerk, 1000 10th Avenue, Sidney, NE 69162. 308-327-2362, Fax: 308-254-4293. 8AM-5PM.

Felony, Civil Actions Over $15,000—District Court, PO Box 217, Sidney, NE 69162. 308-327-2692, Fax: 308-254-4293. 8AM-Noon,1-5PM. Access by: in person.

Misdemeanor, Civil Actions Under $15,000, Eviction, Small Claims, Probate—Cheyenne County Court, 1000 10th Ave, Sidney, NE 69162. 308-334-5383, Fax: 308-254-4641. 8AM-5PM. Access by: mail, in person.

Clay

Real Estate Recording—Clay County Clerk, 111 West Fairfield Street, Clay Center, NE 68933. 404-730-4640, Fax: 402-762-3250. 8:30AM-5PM.

Felony, Civil Actions Over $15,000—District Court, 111 W Fairfield St, Clay Center, NE 68933. 404-730-5000, Fax: 402-762-3250. 8:30AM-5PM. Access by: in person.

Misdemeanor, Civil Actions Under $15,000, Eviction, Small Claims, Probate—Clay County Court, 111 W Fairfield St, Clay Center, NE 68933. 404-730-5078, Fax: 402-762-3250. 8:30AM-5PM. Access by: in person.

Colfax

Real Estate Recording—Colfax County Clerk, 411 East 11th Street, Schuyler, NE 68661. 402-387-2864, Fax: 402-352-8515. 8:30AM-5PM.

Felony, Civil Actions Over $15,000—District Court, 411 E 11th St, PO Box 429, Schuyler, NE 68661. 402-395-2513, Fax: 402-352-2847. 8:30AM-5PM. Access by: in person.

Misdemeanor, Civil Actions Under $15,000, Eviction, Small Claims, Probate—Colfax County Court, 411 E 11th St, Box 191, Schuyler, NE 68661. 402-395-2057, Fax: 402-352-2847. 8AM-5PM. Access by: in person.

Cuming

Real Estate Recording—Cuming County Clerk, Courthouse, 200 S. Lincoln, West Point, NE 68788. 402-439-2223, Fax: 402-372-6013. 8:30AM-4:30PM.

Felony, Civil Actions Over $15,000—District Court, 200 S Lincoln, Rm 200, West Point, NE 68788. 402-439-2222, Fax: 402-372-6017. 8:30AM-4:30PM. Access by: in person.

Misdemeanor, Civil Actions Under $15,000, Eviction, Small Claims, Probate—Cuming County Court, 200 S Lincoln, Rm 103, West Point, NE 68788. 402-439-2221, Fax: 402-372-6017. 8:30AM-4:30PM. Access by: in person.

Custer

Real Estate Recording—Custer County Clerk, 431 South 10th, Broken Bow, NE 68822. 308-995-6561. 9AM-5PM.

Felony, Civil Actions Over $15,000—District Court, 431 S 10th Ave, Broken Bow, NE 68822. 308-995-6115, Fax: 308-872-5826. 9AM-5PM. Access by: mail, phone, fax, in person.

Misdemeanor, Civil Actions Under $15,000, Eviction, Small Claims, Probate—Custer County Court, 431 South 10th Ave, Broken Bow, NE 68822. 309-246-6085, Fax: 308-872-6052. 8AM-12 1-5PM. Access by: in person.

Dakota

Real Estate Recording—Dakota County Clerk, 1601 Broadway, Courthouse Square, Dakota City, NE 68731. Fax: 402-494-9228. 8AM-4:30PM.

Dakota County Register of Deeds, 1601 Broadway, Courthouse Square, Dakota City, NE 68731. 405-273-0213. 8AM-4:30PM.

Felony, Civil Actions Over $15,000—District Court, PO Box 66, Dakota City, NE 68731. 405-262-1070, Fax: 402-987-2117. 8AM-4:30PM. Access by: in person.

Misdemeanor, Civil Actions Under $15,000, Eviction, Small Claims, Probate—Dakota County Court, PO Box 385, Dakota City, NE 68731. 405-273-3624, Fax: 402-987-2185. 8AM-4:30PM. Access by: in person.

Dawes

Real Estate Recording—Dawes County Clerk, 451 Main Street, Courthouse, Chadron, NE 69337. 308-546-2245, Fax: 308-432-0106. 8:30AM-4:30PM.

Felony, Civil Actions Over $15,000—District Court, PO Box 630, Chadron, NE 69337. 308-546-2249, Fax: 308-432-0110. 8:30AM-4:30PM. Access by: mail, phone, in person.

Misdemeanor, Civil Actions Under $15,000, Eviction, Small Claims, Probate—Dawes County Court, PO Box 806, Chadron, NE 69337. 308-547-2222, Fax: 308-432-0110. 7:30AM-4:30PM. Access by: in person.

Dawson

Real Estate Recording—Dawson County Clerk, 700 North Washington Street, Lexington, NE 68850. Fax: 308-324-6106. 8AM-4:30PM UCC; 8AM-5PM Real Property.

Dawson County Register of Deeds, County Courthouse, 700 N. Washington, Lexington, NE 68850. 308-367-8641. 8AM-Noon, 1-5PM.

Felony, Civil Actions Over $15,000—District Court, PO Box 429, Lexington, NE 68850. 308-385-5025, Fax: 308-324-3374. 8AM-5PM. Access by: in person.

Misdemeanor, Civil Actions Under $15,000, Eviction, Small Claims, Probate—Dawson County Court, 700 N Washington St, Lexington, NE 68850. 308-385-5135. 8AM-5PM. Access by: in person.

Deuel

Real Estate Recording—Deuel County Clerk, 3rd & Vincent, Chappell, NE 69129. 309-286-5901, Fax: 308-874-3472. 8AM-4PM.

Felony, Civil Actions Over $15,000—District Court, PO Box 327, Chappell, NE 69129. 309-286-5941, Fax: 308-874-3472. 8AM-4PM. Access by: mail, phone, fax, in person.

Misdemeanor, Civil Actions Under $15,000, Eviction, Small Claims, Probate—Deuel County Court, PO Box 514, Chappell, NE 69129. 309-246-6435, Fax: 308-874-2994. 8AM-4PM. Access by: mail, in person.

Dixon

Real Estate Recording—Dixon County Clerk, Courthouse, 302 Third St. Ponca, NE 68770. 402-987-2114, Fax: 402-755-4276. 8AM-4:30PM.

Felony, Civil Actions Over $15,000—District Court, PO Box 395, Ponca, NE 68770. 402-987-2131, Fax: 402-755-2632. 8AM-Noon, 1-5PM. Access by: in person.

Misdemeanor, Civil Actions Under $15,000, Eviction, Small Claims, Probate—Dixon County Court, PO Box 497, Ponca, NE 68770. 402-887-4870, Fax: 402-755-2632. 8AM-4:30PM. Access by: in person.

Dodge

Real Estate Recording—Dodge County Clerk, 435 North Park, Courthouse - Room 102, Fremont, NE 68025. Fax: 402-727-2764. 8:30AM-4:30PM.

Dodge County Register of Deeds, 435 North Park, Room 201, Fremont, NE 68025. 402-775-2581. 8:30AM-4:30PM.

Felony, Civil Actions Over $15,000—District Court, PO Box 1237, Fremont, NE 68026. 402-821-2375, Fax: 402-727-2773. 8:30AM-4:30PM. Access by: in person.

Misdemeanor, Civil Actions Under $15,000, Eviction, Small Claims, Probate—Dodge County Court, 428 N Broad St, Fremont, NE 68025. 402-821-2131, Fax: 402-727-2762. 8AM-5PM. Access by: in person.

Douglas

Real Estate Recording—Douglas County Clerk, 1819 Farnam St. Room H08, Omaha, NE 68183. Fax: 402-444-6456. 8AM-5PM-County Clerk; 8AM-4:30PM Reg. of Deeds.

Douglas County Register of Deeds, 1819 Farnam, Room H09, Omaha, NE 68183. 402-727-2780, Fax: 402-444-6693. 8:30AM-4:30PM.

Felony, Civil Actions Over $15,000—District Court, 1819 Farnam, Omaha, NE 68183. 402-727-2755. 8:30AM-4:30PM. Access by: mail, in person.

Misdemeanor, Civil Actions Under $15,000, Eviction, Small Claims, Probate—Douglas County Court, 1819 Farnam, 2nd Fl, Omaha, NE 68183. 402-727-2750. 8AM-4:30PM. Access by: mail, in person.

Dundy

Real Estate Recording—Dundy County Clerk, Courthouse, Benkelman, NE 69021. 308-458-2488. 8AM-5PM.

Felony, Civil Actions Over $15,000—District Court, PO Box 506, Benkelman, NE 69021. 308-458-2433. 8AM-5PM. Access by: mail, phone, in person.

Misdemeanor, Civil Actions Under $15,000, Eviction, Small Claims, Probate—Dundy County Court, PO Box 377, Benkelman, NE 69021. 308-534-4350. 8AM-4:30PM. Access by: mail, phone, in person.

Fillmore

Real Estate Recording—Fillmore County Clerk, Courthouse, 900 G st. Geneva, NE 68361. 404-371-2836, Fax: 402-759-4307. 8AM-5PM.

Felony, Civil Actions Over $15,000—Fillmore County District Court, PO Box 147, Geneva, NE 68361-0147. 404-371-2261, Fax: 402-759-4440. 8AM-Noon, 1-5PM. Access by: mail, phone, fax, in person.

Misdemeanor, Civil Actions Under $15,000, Eviction, Small Claims, Probate—Fillmore County Court, PO Box 66, Geneva, NE 68361. 402-987-2145, Fax: 402-759-4440. 8AM-5PM. Access by: mail, fax, in person.

Franklin

Real Estate Recording—Franklin County Clerk, 405 15th Avenue, Franklin, NE 68939. 308-534-4350, Fax: 308-425-6289. 8:30AM-4:30PM.

Felony, Civil Actions Over $15,000—District Court, PO Box 146, Franklin, NE 68939. 308-534-4350, Fax: 308-425-6289. 8:30AM-4:30PM. Access by: in person.

Misdemeanor, Civil Actions Under $15,000, Eviction, Small Claims, Probate—Franklin County Court, PO Box 174, Franklin, NE 68939. 308-536-2165, Fax: 308-425-6289. 8:30AM-4:30PM M-F. Access by: mail, in person.

Frontier

Real Estate Recording—Frontier County Register of Deeds, 1 Wellington Street, Stockville, NE 69042. Fax: 308-367-8730. 8:30AM-Noon, 1-5PM.

Felony, Civil Actions Over $15,000—District Court, PO Box 40, Stockville, NE 69042. 308-436-6621, Fax: 308-367-8730. 9AM-4:30PM. Access by: mail, in person.

Misdemeanor, Civil Actions Under $15,000, Eviction, Small Claims, Probate—Frontier County Court, PO Box 38, Stockville, NE 69042. 308-436-5268, Fax: 308-367-8730. 9AM-4:30PM. Access by: mail, in person.

Furnas

Real Estate Recording—Furnas County Clerk, Courthouse, 912 R Street, Beaver City, NE 68926. 308-345-4583. 8AM-4PM.

Felony, Civil Actions Over $15,000—District Court, PO Box 413, Beaver City, NE 68926. 308-345-6515, Fax: 308-268-2345. 10AM-Noon, 1-3PM. Access by: mail, in person.

Misdemeanor, Civil Actions Under $15,000, Eviction, Small Claims, Probate—Furnas County Court, 912 R St (PO Box 373), Beaver City, NE 68926. 308-346-4123, Fax: 308-268-2345. 8AM-4PM. Access by: in person.

Gage

Real Estate Recording—Gage County Clerk, 612 Grant St. Courthouse, Beatrice, NE 68310. Fax: 402-223-1371. 8AM-5PM.

Gage County Register of Deeds, 612 Grant St. Beatrice, NE 68310. 402-336-2840. 8AM-4:30PM.

Felony, Civil Actions Over $15,000—District Court, PO Box 845, Beatrice, NE 68310. 402-352-3322, Fax: 402-223-1313. 8AM-5PM. Access by: mail, in person.

Misdemeanor, Civil Actions Under $15,000, Eviction, Small Claims, Probate—Gage County Court, PO Box 219, Beatrice, NE 68310. 402-352-2105. 8AM-5PM. Access by: mail, in person.

Garden

Real Estate Recording—Garden County Clerk, 611 Main Street, Courthouse, Oshkosh, NE 69154. 308-928-2173, Fax: 308-772-4143. 8AM-4PM.

Felony, Civil Actions Over $15,000—District Court, PO Box 486, Oshkosh, NE 69154. 308-942-3115, Fax: 308-772-4143. 8AM-4PM. Access by: mail, fax, in person.

Misdemeanor, Civil Actions Under $15,000, Eviction, Small Claims, Probate—Garden County Court, PO Box 465, Oshkosh, NE 69154. 308-928-2179. 8AM-4PM. Access by: in person.

Garfield

Real Estate Recording—Garfield County Clerk, 250 South 8th Street, Burwell, NE 68823. 308-432-0105. 9AM-Noon, 1-5PM.

Felony, Civil Actions Over $15,000—District Court, PO Box 218, Burwell, NE 68823. 308-432-0109. 9AM-5PM. Access by: mail, in person.

Misdemeanor, Civil Actions Under $15,000, Eviction, Small Claims, Probate—Garfield County Court, PO Box 431, Burwell, NE 68823. 308-428-3625, Fax: 308-346-5064. 9AM-4PM. Access by: mail, fax, in person.

Gosper

Real Estate Recording—Gosper County Clerk, Courthouse, 507 Smith Ave. Elwood, NE 68937. 308-942-6035. 8:30AM-4:30PM.

Felony, Civil Actions Over $15,000—District Court, PO Box 136, Elwood, NE 68937. 308-946-2171. 8:30AM-4:30PM. Access by: in person.

Misdemeanor, Civil Actions Under $15,000, Eviction, Small Claims, Probate—Gosper County Court, PO Box 55, Elwood, NE 68937. 308-942-6035, Fax: 308-785-2036. 8:30AM-4:30PM. Access by: in person.

Grant

Real Estate Recording—Grant County Clerk, Harrison Avenue, Courthouse, Hyannis, NE 69350. 308-636-2441, Fax: 308-458-2485. 8AM-Noon,1-4PM.

Felony, Civil Actions Over $15,000—District Court, PO Box 139, Hyannis, NE 69350. 308-645-2261, Fax: 308-458-2485. 8AM-4PM. Access by: mail, fax, in person.

Misdemeanor, Civil Actions Under $15,000, Eviction, Small Claims, Probate—Grant County Court, PO Box 97, Hyannis, NE 69350. 308-636-2677, Fax: 308-458-2283. 8AM-4PM. Access by: mail, phone, in person.

Greeley

Real Estate Recording—Greeley County Clerk, Courthouse, Greeley, NE 68842. 308-536-2675, Fax: 308-428-6500. 8AM-5PM.

Felony, Civil Actions Over $15,000—District Court, PO Box 287, Greeley, NE 68842. 308-546-2244, Fax: 308-428-6500. 8AM-4PM. Access by: mail, in person.

Misdemeanor, Civil Actions Under $15,000, Eviction, Small Claims, Probate—Greeley County Court, PO Box 302, Greeley, NE 68842. 308-536-2365, Fax: 308-428-6500. 8AM-5PM. Access by: in person.

Hall

Real Estate Recording—Hall County Clerk, 121 South Pine, Grand Island, NE 68801. Fax: 308-385-5094. 8:30AM-5PM.

Hall County Register of Deeds, 121 South Pine, Grand Island, NE 68801. 308-436-6641. 8:30AM-5PM.

Felony, Civil Actions Over $15,000—District Court, PO Box 1926, Grand Island, NE 68802. 308-458-2422, Fax: 308-385-5110. 8AM-5PM. Access by: mail, in person.

Misdemeanor, Civil Actions Under $15,000, Eviction, Small Claims, Probate—Hall County Court, 111 W 1st Suite 1, Grand Island, NE 68801. 308-436-6648. 8:30AM-5PM. Access by: in person.

Hamilton

Real Estate Recording—Hamilton County Clerk, Courthouse, 1111 13th St. - Suite 1, Aurora, NE 68818. 402-768-6325, Fax: 402-694-2396. 8AM-5PM.

Felony, Civil Actions Over $15,000—District Court, PO Box 201, Aurora, NE 68818-0201. 402-775-2211, Fax: 402-694-2250. 8AM-5PM. Access by: in person.

Misdemeanor, Civil Actions Under $15,000, Eviction, Small Claims, Probate—Hamilton County Court, PO Box 323, Aurora, NE 68818. 402-775-2391, Fax: 402-694-2250. Access by: in person.

Harlan

Real Estate Recording—Harlan County Clerk, 706 West 2nd Street, Alma, NE 68920. 309-467-4621, Fax: 308-928-2592. 8:30AM-4:30PM.

Felony, Civil Actions Over $15,000—District Court, PO Box 698, Alma, NE 68920. 309-477-2214, Fax: 308-928-2170. 8:30AM-4:30PM. Access by: mail, phone, in person.

Misdemeanor, Civil Actions Under $15,000, Eviction, Small Claims, Probate—Harlan County Court, PO Box 379, Alma, NE 68920. 309-477-2284, Fax: 308-928-2170. 8:30AM-4:30PM. Access by: in person.

Hayes

Real Estate Recording—Hayes County Clerk, Troth Street, Courthouse, Hayes Center, NE 69032. 308-352-4542. 8AM-4PM.

Felony, Civil Actions Over $15,000—District Court, PO Box 370, Hayes Center, NE 69032. 308-367-8629, Fax: 308-286-3208. 8AM-4PM. Access by: mail, fax, in person.

Misdemeanor, Civil Actions Under $15,000, Eviction, Small Claims, Probate—Hayes County Court, PO Box 370, Hayes Center, NE 69032. 308-352-4643. 9AM-Noon, 1-4PM T (Clerk's hours). Access by: mail, in person.

Hitchcock

Real Estate Recording—Hitchcock County Clerk, 229 East D, Trenton, NE 69044. 308-425-6202, Fax: 308-334-5351. 8:30AM-4PM.

Felony, Civil Actions Over $15,000—District Court, PO Box 248, Trenton, NE 69044. 308-425-6265, Fax: 308-334-5351. 8:30AM-4PM. Access by: mail, phone, fax, in person.

Misdemeanor, Civil Actions Under $15,000, Eviction, Small Claims, Probate—Hitchcock County Court, PO Box 366, Trenton, NE 69044. 308-423-2374. 8:30AM-4PM. Access by: mail, phone, in person.

Holt

Real Estate Recording—Holt County Clerk, 204 North 4th, O'Neill, NE 68763. 402-385-3318, Fax: 402-336-2885. 8AM-4:30PM.

Felony, Civil Actions Over $15,000—District Court, PO Box 755, O'Neill, NE 68763. 402-387-2705, Fax: 402-336-3601. 8AM-4:30PM. Access by: mail, phone, fax, in person.

Misdemeanor, Civil Actions Under $15,000, Eviction, Small Claims, Probate—Holt County Court, 204 N 4th St, O'Neill, NE 68763. 402-387-2650, Fax: 402-336-1663. 8AM-4:30PM. Access by: mail, in person.

Hooker

Real Estate Recording—Hooker County Clerk, 303 NW 1st, Courthouse, Mullen, NE 69152. 308-668-2475. 8:30AM-Noon, 1-4:30PM.

Felony, Civil Actions Over $15,000—District Court, PO Box 184, Mullen, NE 69152. 308-668-2443, Fax: 308-546-2490. 8:30AM-Noon, 1-4:30PM. Access by: mail, phone, fax, in person.

Misdemeanor, Civil Actions Under $15,000, Eviction, Small Claims, Probate—Hooker County Court, PO Box 184, Mullen, NE 69152. 308-728-3700, Fax: 308-546-2490. 8:30AM-4:30PM. Access by: mail, fax, in person.

Howard

Real Estate Recording—Howard County Clerk, 612 Indian Street, St. Paul, NE 68873. 308-874-3308, Fax: 308-754-4727. 8AM-5PM.

Felony, Civil Actions Over $15,000—District Court, PO Box 25, St Paul, NE 68873. 308-874-3307, Fax: 308-754-4727. 8AM-5PM. Access by: mail, in person.

Misdemeanor, Civil Actions Under $15,000, Eviction, Small Claims, Probate—Howard County Court, 612 Indian St Suite #6, St Paul, NE 68873. 308-874-2909. 8AM-5PM. Access by: in person.

Jefferson

Real Estate Recording—Jefferson County Register of Deeds, 411 4th, Courthouse, Fairbury, NE 68352. 402-852-2388, Fax: 402-729-2016. 9AM-5PM UCC; 9AM-Noon, 1-5PM Real Property.

Felony, Civil Actions Over $15,000—District Court, Jefferson County Courthouse, 411 Fourth Street, Fairbury, NE 68352. 402-821-2823, Fax: 402-729-2016. 9AM-5PM. Access by: mail, fax, in person.

Misdemeanor, Civil Actions Under $15,000, Eviction, Small Claims, Probate—Jefferson County Court, 411 Fourth St, Fairbury, NE 68352. 402-852-2380, Fax: 402-729-2016. 8AM-Noon, 1-5PM. Access by: mail, in person.

Johnson

Real Estate Recording—Johnson County Clerk, Courthouse, Tecumseh, NE 68450. Fax: 402-335-3975. 8AM-12:30PM, 1-4:30PM.

Felony, Civil Actions Over $15,000—District Court, PO Box 416, Tecumseh, NE 68450. 402-385-3058, Fax: 402-335-3975. 8AM-Noon, 1-4:30PM. Access by: mail, phone, fax, in person.

Misdemeanor, Civil Actions Under $15,000, Eviction, Small Claims, Probate—Johnson County Court, PO Box 285, Tecumseh, NE 68450. 402-385-3136, Fax: 402-335-3070. 8AM-4:30PM. Access by: in person.

Kearney

Real Estate Recording—Kearney County Clerk, 424 North Colorado, Minden, NE 68959. 308-995-2281, Fax: 308-832-1748. 8:30AM-5PM.

Felony, Civil Actions Over $15,000—District Court, PO Box 208, Minden, NE 68959. 308-946-2461, Fax: 308-832-0636. 8:30AM-5PM. Access by: in person.

Misdemeanor, Civil Actions Under $15,000, Eviction, Small Claims, Probate—Kearney County Court, PO Box 377, Minden, NE 68959. 308-946-2812, Fax: 308-832-0636. 8:30AM-5PM. Access by: in person.

Keith

Real Estate Recording—Keith County Clerk, 511 North Spruce, Ogallala, NE 69153. 308-346-4125, Fax: 308-284-6277. 8AM-4PM.

Felony, Civil Actions Over $15,000—District Court, PO Box 686, Ogallala, NE 69153. 308-352-4415, Fax: 308-284-3978. 8AM-4PM. Access by: mail, fax, in person.

Misdemeanor, Civil Actions Under $15,000, Eviction, Small Claims, Probate—Keith County Court, PO Box 358, Ogallala, NE 69153. 308-346-4161, Fax: 308-284-6825. 8AM-5PM M-Th; 7AM-4PM F. Access by: in person.

Keya Paha

Real Estate Recording—Keya Paha County Clerk, Courthouse, Springview, NE 68778. 402-747-5441, Fax: 402-497-3799. 8AM-Noon,1-5PM.

Felony, Civil Actions Over $15,000—District Court, PO Box 349, Springview, NE 68778. 402-747-5371, Fax: 402-497-3799. 8AM-5PM. Access by: mail, fax, in person.

Misdemeanor, Civil Actions Under $15,000, Eviction, Small Claims, Probate—Keya Paha County Court, PO Box 275, Springview, NE 68778. 402-747-3487. 8AM-Noon M; 8AM-4:30PM Th,F. Access by: in person.

Kimball

Real Estate Recording—Kimball County Clerk, 114 East Third Street, Kimball, NE 69145. 308-286-3315, Fax: 308-235-3654. 8AM-5PM M-Th; 8AM-4PM F.

Felony, Civil Actions Over $15,000—District Court, 114 E 3rd St, Kimball, NE 69145. 308-324-3241, Fax: 308-235-3654. 8AM-5PM M-Th, 8AM-4PM F. Access by: in person.

Misdemeanor, Civil Actions Under $15,000, Small Claims, Probate—Kimball County Court, 114 E 3rd St, Kimball, NE 69145. 308-286-3413. 8AM-5PM. Access by: in person.

Knox

Real Estate Recording—Knox County Clerk (ex-officio Register of Deeds), 206 Main Street, Center, NE 68724. 402-375-1622, Fax: 402-288-3654. 8:30AM-4:30PM.

Felony, Civil Actions Over $15,000—District Court, PO Box 126, Center, NE 68724. 402-374-2605, Fax: 402-288-4275. 8:30AM-4:30PM. Access by: in person.

Misdemeanor, Civil Actions Under $15,000, Eviction, Small Claims, Probate—Knox County Court, PO Box 125, Center, NE 68724. 402-374-2191, Fax: 402-288-4275. 8:30AM-4:30PM. Access by: in person.

Lancaster

Real Estate Recording—Lancaster County Clerk, 555 South 10th Street, County-City Building, Lincoln, NE 68508. Fax: 402-441-8728. 7:30AM-4:30PM.

Lancaster County Register of Deeds, 555 South 10th Street, Lincoln, NE 68508. 402-684-3933, Fax: 402-441-7012. 8AM-4:30PM.

Felony, Civil Actions Over $15,000—District Court, 555 S Tenth St, Lincoln, NE 68508. 402-684-3601, Fax: 402-441-6190. 8AM-4:30PM. Access by: mail, phone, in person. www.ci.lincoln.ne.us/cnty/discrt/index.htm

Misdemeanor, Civil Actions Under $15,000, Eviction, Small Claims, Probate—Lancaster County Court, 129 N 10th, Lincoln, NE 68508. 402-684-3515. 8AM-4:30PM. Access by: in person. www.ci.lincoln.ne.us/cnty/discrt/index.htm

Lincoln

Real Estate Recording—Lincoln County Clerk, Courthouse, Room 101, 301 North Jeffers, North Platte, NE 69101. 9AM-5PM.

Lincoln County Reister of Deeds, 301 N. Jeffers, Room 103, North Platte, NE 69101. 308-645-2266, Fax: 308-534-5287. 9AM-5PM.

Felony, Civil Actions Over $15,000—District Court, 301 N Jeffers Third Floor, PO Box 1616, North Platte, NE 69101. 308-654-3235. 8AM-5PM. Access by: in person.

Misdemeanor, Civil Actions Under $15,000, Eviction, Small Claims, Probate—Lincoln County Court, PO Box 519, North Platte, NE 69103. 308-645-2262, Fax: 308-534-6468. 8AM-5PM. Access by: in person.

Logan

Real Estate Recording—Logan County Clerk, Courthouse, Stapleton, NE 69163. 308-754-4852. 8:30AM-4:30PM M,T,W,Th; 8:30AM-4PM F.

Felony, Civil Actions Over $15,000—District Court, PO Box 8, Stapleton, NE 69163. 308-754-4343. 8:30AM-4:30PM M-Th; 8:30AM-4PM F. Access by: mail, in person.

Misdemeanor, Civil Actions Under $15,000, Eviction, Small Claims, Probate—Logan County Court, PO Box 8, Stapleton, NE 69163. 308-762-6293. 8AM-Noon, 1-4:30PM M-Th; 8:30AM-Noon, 1-4PM F. Access by: mail, phone, fax, in person.

Loup

Real Estate Recording—Loup County Clerk, Courthouse, Taylor, NE 68879. 309-543-3359, Fax: 308-942-6015. 8:30AM-Noon, 1-5PM M,T,W,Th; 8:30AM-Noon F.

Felony, Civil Actions Over $15,000—District Court, PO Box 146, Taylor, NE 68879. 309-543-6619, Fax: 308-942-6015. 8:30AM-4:30PM M-Th, 8:30AM-Noon F. Access by: in person.

Misdemeanor, Civil Actions Under $15,000, Eviction, Small Claims, Probate—Loup County Court, PO Box 146, Taylor, NE 68879. 309-547-3041, Fax: 308-942-6015. 8:30AM-4:30PM M-Th, 8:30AM-Noon F. Access by: in person.

Madison

Real Estate Recording—Madison County Clerk, Clara Davis Drive, Courthouse, Madison, NE 68748. Fax: 402-454-6682. 8:30AM-5PM.

Madison County Register of Deeds, Clara Davis Drive, Courthouse, Madison, NE 68748. 402-729-2019. 8:30AM-5PM.

Felony, Civil Actions Over $15,000—District Court, PO Box 249, Madison, NE 68748. 402-729-2312, Fax: 402-454-6528. 8AM-5PM. Access by: in person.

Misdemeanor, Civil Actions Under $15,000, Eviction, Small Claims, Probate—Madison County Court, PO Box 230, Madison, NE 68748. 402-729-2411, Fax: 402-454-3438. 8:30AM-5PM. Access by: in person.

McPherson

Real Estate Recording—McPherson County Clerk, 5th & Anderson, Courthouse, Tryon, NE 69167. 308-754-4192, Fax: 308-587-2363. 8:30AM-Noon, 1-4:30PM.

Felony, Civil Actions Over $15,000—District Court, PO Box 122, Tryon, NE 69167. 308-745-1513, Fax: 308-587-2363. 8:30AM-4:30PM. Access by: mail, fax, in person.

Misdemeanor, Civil Actions Under $15,000, Eviction, Small Claims, Probate—McPherson County Court, PO Box 122, Tryon, NE 69167. 308-745-1513, Fax: 308-587-2363. 8:30AM-Noon, 1-4:30PM. Access by: mail, fax, in person.

Merrick

Real Estate Recording—Merrick County Clerk, Courthouse, Central City, NE 68826. 309-547-3041, Fax: 308-946-2332. 8AM-5PM.

Felony, Civil Actions Over $15,000—District Court, PO Box 27, Central City, NE 68826. 309-582-2524, Fax: 308-946-3692. 8AM-5PM. Access by: in person.

Misdemeanor, Civil Actions Under $15,000, Eviction, Small Claims, Probate—Merrick County Court, County Courthouse, PO Box 27, Central City, NE 68826. 309-582-7122. 8AM-5PM. Access by: in person, online.

Morrill

Real Estate Recording—Morrill County Clerk, 6th & Main Street, Courthouse, Bridgeport, NE 69336. 308-334-5646, Fax: 308-262-1469. 8AM-4:30PM.

Felony, Civil Actions Over $15,000—District Court, PO Box 824, Bridgeport, NE 69336. 308-345-1904. 8AM-Noon, 1-4:30PM. Access by: mail, phone, in person.

Misdemeanor, Civil Actions Under $15,000, Eviction, Small Claims, Probate—Morrill County Court, PO Box 418, Bridgeport, NE 69336. 308-334-5544. 8AM-4:30PM. Access by: in person.

Nance

Real Estate Recording—Nance County Clerk, 209 Esther Street, Fullerton, NE 68638. 308-654-3236, Fax: 308-536-2742. 8AM-5PM.

Felony, Civil Actions Over $15,000—District Court, PO Box 338, Fullerton, NE 68638. 308-654-3376, Fax: 308-536-2742. 8AM-5PM. Access by: mail, phone, fax, in person.

Misdemeanor, Civil Actions Under $15,000, Eviction, Small Claims, Probate—Nance County Court, PO Box 837, Fullerton, NE 68638. 308-668-2422, Fax: 308-536-2742. 8AM-5PM. Access by: mail, fax, in person.

Nemaha

Real Estate Recording—Nemaha County Clerk, 1824 N Street, Courthouse, Auburn, NE 68305. 402-372-6011, Fax: 402-274-4389. 8AM-5PM.

Felony, Civil Actions Over $15,000—District Court, 1824 N St, Auburn, NE 68305. 402-374-2000, Fax: 402-274-4478. 8AM-5PM. Access by: in person.

Misdemeanor, Civil Actions Under $15,000, Eviction, Small Claims, Probate—Nemaha County Court, 1824 N St, Auburn, NE 68305. 402-372-6004, Fax: 402-274-4605. 8AM-Noon, 1-5PM. Access by: in person. Special note: This court also handles adoption, juvenile, and preliminary felony hearings.

Nuckolls

Real Estate Recording—Nuckolls County Clerk, 150 South Main, Courthouse, Nelson, NE 68961. Fax: 402-225-4301. 8:30AM-4:30PM.

Felony, Civil Actions Over $15,000—District Court, PO Box 362, Nelson, NE 68961. 402-362-4038. 8:30AM-4:30PM. Access by: in person.

Misdemeanor, Civil Actions Under $15,000, Eviction, Small Claims, Probate—Nuckolls County Court, PO Box 372, Nelson, NE 68961. 402-352-8506, Fax: 402-225-2371. 8AM-4:30PM. Access by: in person.

Otoe

Real Estate Recording—Otoe County Clerk, 1021 Central Avenue, Nebraska City, NE 68410. Fax: 402-873-9506. 8AM-5PM.

Otoe County Register of Deeds, 1021 Central Ave. Room 203, Nebraska City, NE 68410. 405-255-0728, Fax: 402-873-6130. 8AM-Noon, 1-5PM.

Felony, Civil Actions Over $15,000—District Court, 1021 Central Ave, Rm 209, PO Box 726, Nebraska City, NE 68410. 405-257-6236. 8AM-Noon, 1-5PM. Access by: in person.

Misdemeanor, Civil Actions Under $15,000, Eviction, Small Claims, Probate—Otoe County Court, 1021 Central Ave, Rm 109, PO Box 487, Nebraska City, NE 68410-0487. 405-257-6262, Fax: 402-873-6130. 8AM-5PM. Access by: mail, phone, fax, in person.

Pawnee

Real Estate Recording—Pawnee County Clerk, 625 6th Street, Pawnee City, NE 68420. 405-247-3393, Fax: 402-852-2963. 8AM-4PM.

Felony, Civil Actions Over $15,000—District Court, PO Box 431, Pawnee City, NE 68420. 405-254-7404. 8AM-4PM. Access by: mail, phone, in person.

Misdemeanor, Civil Actions Under $15,000, Eviction, Small Claims, Probate—Pawnee County Court, PO Box 471, Pawnee City, NE 68420. 405-247-5151, Fax: 402-852-2388. 8AM-4:30PM. Access by: in person. Special note: Probate requests are accepted by mail.

Perkins

Real Estate Recording—Perkins County Clerk, 200 Lincoln Avenue, Grant, NE 69140. 308-436-5260, Fax: 308-352-2455. 8AM-4PM.

Felony, Civil Actions Over $15,000—District Court, PO Box 156, Grant, NE 69140. 308-436-5265, Fax: 308-352-2455. 8AM-4PM. Access by: mail, fax, in person.

Misdemeanor, Civil Actions Under $15,000, Eviction, Small Claims, Probate—Perkins County Court, PO Box 222, Grant, NE 69140. 308-432-0116, Fax: 308-352-2455. 8AM-4PM. Access by: mail, phone, fax, in person.

Phelps

Real Estate Recording—Phelps County Clerk, Courthouse, Holdrege, NE 68949. 309-672-6953, Fax: 308-995-4368. 9AM-5PM.

Felony, Civil Actions Over $15,000—District Court, PO Box 462, Holdrege, NE 68949. 309-672-6065. 9AM-5PM. Access by: in person.

Misdemeanor, Civil Actions Under $15,000, Eviction, Small Claims, Probate—Phelps County Court, PO Box 255, Holdrege, NE 68949. 309-734-5179, Fax: 308-995-6562. 8AM-5PM. Access by: mail, in person.

Pierce

Real Estate Recording—Pierce County Clerk, 111 West Court, Courthouse - Room 1, Pierce, NE 68767. 402-376-2590, Fax: 402-329-6439. 8:30AM-4:30PM.

Felony, Civil Actions Over $15,000—District Court, 111 W Court St, Rm 12, Pierce, NE 68767. 402-376-1580, Fax: 402-329-6412. 8:30 AM-4:30PM. Access by: in person.

Misdemeanor, Civil Actions Under $15,000, Eviction, Small Claims, Probate—Pierce County Court, 111 W Court St, Rm 11, Pierce, NE 68767. 402-376-1840, Fax: 402-329-6412. 8:30AM-5PM. Access by: in person.

Platte

Real Estate Recording—Platte County Clerk, 2610 14th Street, Columbus, NE 68601. Fax: 402-564-4614. 8AM-5PM.

Platte County Register of Deeds, 2610 14th Street, Columbus, NE 68601. 402-755-2881. 8AM-5PM.

Felony, Civil Actions Over $15,000—District Court, PO Box 1188, Columbus, NE 68602-1188. 402-755-2701, Fax: 402-562-6718. 8:30AM-5PM. Access by: in person.

Misdemeanor, Civil Actions Under $15,000, Eviction, Small Claims, Probate—Platte County Court, PO Box 538, Columbus, NE 68602-0538. 402-755-2355, Fax: 402-562-8158. 8AM-5PM. Access by: in person.

Polk

Real Estate Recording—Polk County Clerk, Courthouse Square, Osceola, NE 68651. 402-887-4650. 8AM-5PM.

Felony, Civil Actions Over $15,000—District Court, PO Box 447, Osceola, NE 68651. 402-873-9575, Fax: 402-747-8299. 8AM-Noon,1-5PM. Access by: in person.

Misdemeanor, Civil Actions Under $15,000, Eviction, Small Claims, Probate—Polk County Court, PO Box 506, Osceola, NE 68651. 402-887-4247, Fax: 402-747-2656. 8AM-5PM. Access by: in person.

Red Willow

Real Estate Recording—Red Willow County Clerk, 502 Norris Avenue, McCook, NE 69001. 308-428-3535, Fax: 308-345-7307. 8AM-4PM.

Felony, Civil Actions Over $15,000—District Court, 520 Norris Ave (PO Box 847), McCook, NE 69001. 308-428-2705, Fax: 308-345-7907. 8AM-4PM. Access by: mail, phone, fax, in person.

Misdemeanor, Civil Actions Under $15,000, Eviction, Small Claims, Probate—Red Willow County Court, 520 Norris Ave, McCook, NE 69001. 308-425-6288, Fax: 308-345-1503. 8AM-4PM. Access by: mail, in person.

Richardson

Real Estate Recording—Richardson County Clerk, Courthouse, 1700 Stone, Falls City, NE 68355. 402-367-7450, Fax: 402-245-3725. 8:30AM-5PM.

Felony, Civil Actions Over $15,000—District Court, 1700 Stone St, Falls City, NE 68355. 402-362-4925, Fax: 402-245-3725. 8:30AM-5PM. Access by: in person.

Misdemeanor, Civil Actions Under $15,000, Eviction, Small Claims, Probate—Richardson County Court, 1700 Stone St Room 205, Falls City, NE 68355. 402-362-4949, Fax: 402-245-3352. 8AM-5PM. Access by: in person.

Rock

Real Estate Recording—Rock County Clerk, 400 State Street, Bassett, NE 68714. 402-762-3651. 9AM-Noon, 1-5PM.

Felony, Civil Actions Over $15,000—District Court, PO Box 367, Bassett, NE 68714. 402-768-6227, Fax: 402-684-2741. 9AM-5PM. Access by: mail, phone, fax, in person.

Misdemeanor, Civil Actions Under $15,000, Eviction, Small Claims, Probate—Rock County Court, PO Box 249, Bassett, NE 68714. 402-768-6116, Fax: 402-684-2741. 8AM-5PM. Access by: in person.

Saline

Real Estate Recording—Saline County Clerk, 215 South Court, Wilber, NE 68465. 405-238-5596, Fax: 402-821-3381. 8AM-5PM.

Felony, Civil Actions Over $15,000—District Court, 215 S Court St, Wilber, NE 68465. 405-238-7301, Fax: 402-821-2132. 8AM-Noon, 1-5PM. Access by: in person.

Misdemeanor, Civil Actions Under $15,000, Eviction, Small Claims, Probate—Saline County Court, 215 S Court St, Wilber, NE 68465. 405-237-0246, Fax: 402-821-2132. 8AM-5PM. Access by: mail, fax, in person.

Sarpy

Real Estate Recording—Sarpy County Clerk, 1210 Golden Gate Drive, Suite 1118, Papillion, NE 68046. Fax: 402-593-4360. 8AM-4:45PM M,T,Th,F; 8AM-6PM W.

Sarpy County Register of Deeds, 1210 Golden Gate Drive #1109, Papillion, NE 68046. 402-593-2267, Fax: 402-593-2338. 8AM-4:45PM.

Felony, Civil Actions Over $15,000—District Court, 1210 Golden Gate Dr, Ste 3141, Papillion, NE 68046. 402-759-3811, Fax: 402-593-4403. 8AM-4:45PM. Access by: mail, phone, in person.

Misdemeanor, Civil Actions Under $15,000, Eviction, Small Claims, Probate—Sarpy County Court, 1210 Golden Gate Dr, Ste 3142, Papillion, NE 68046. 402-759-3514. 8AM-4:45PM. Access by: in person.

Saunders

Real Estate Recording—Saunders County Clerk, 5th & Chestnut, Courthouse, Wahoo, NE 68066. Fax: 402-443-5010. 8AM-5PM.

Saunders County Register of Deeds, 5th & Chestnut, Courthouse, Wahoo, NE 68066. 402-694-6188, Fax: 402-443-5010. 8AM-5PM.

Felony, Civil Actions Over $15,000—District Court, County Courthouse, Wahoo, NE 68066. 402-694-2291, Fax: 402-443-5010. 8AM-5PM. Access by: in person.

Misdemeanor, Civil Actions Under $15,000, Eviction, Small Claims, Probate—Saunders County Court, 433 N Chestnut, Wahoo, NE 68066. 402-694-3533, Fax: 402-443-5010. 8AM-5PM. Access by: in person.

Scotts Bluff

Real Estate Recording—Scotts Bluff County Clerk, 1825 10th Street, Administration Office Building, Gering, NE 69341. Fax: 308-436-3178. 8AM-4:30PM.

Scotts Bluff County Register of Deeds, 1825 10th Street, Administration Office Building, Gering, NE 69341. 308-587-2363. 8AM-4:30PM.

Felony, Civil Actions Over $15,000—District Court, 1725 10th St, PO Box 47, Gering, NE 69341-0047. 308-587-2363, Fax: 308-436-6759. 8AM-4:30PM. Access by: mail, in person.

Misdemeanor, Civil Actions Under $15,000, Eviction, Small Claims, Probate—Scotts Bluff County Court, 1725 10th St, Gering, NE 69341. 308-636-2311. 8AM-5PM. Access by: in person.

Seward

Real Estate Recording—Seward County Clerk, 529 Seward Street, Seward, NE 68434. 402-762-3505, Fax: 402-643-9243. 8AM-5PM.

Felony, Civil Actions Over $15,000—District Court, PO Box 36, Seward, NE 68434. 402-762-3595. 8AM-5PM. Access by: in person.

Misdemeanor, Civil Actions Under $15,000, Eviction, Small Claims, Probate—Seward County Court, PO Box 37, Seward, NE 68434. 402-759-3812, Fax: 402-643-2950. 8AM-5PM. Access by: in person.

Sheridan

Real Estate Recording—Sheridan County Clerk, 301 East 2nd Street, Rushville, NE 69360. 308-423-2058. 8:30AM-4:30PM.

Felony, Civil Actions Over $15,000—District Court, PO Box 581, Rushville, NE 69360. 308-385-5144, Fax: 308-327-2712. 8:30AM-4:30PM. Access by: mail, in person.

Misdemeanor, Civil Actions Under $15,000, Eviction, Small Claims, Probate—Sheridan County Court, PO Box 430, Rushville, NE 69360. 308-423-2346, Fax: 308-327-2936. 8AM-4:30PM. Access by: mail, fax, in person.

Sherman

Real Estate Recording—Sherman County Clerk, Courthouse, 630 "O" Street, Loup City, NE 68853. 308-872-5761, Fax: 308-745-1820. 8:30AM-4:30PM.

Felony, Civil Actions Over $15,000—District Court, 630 O St, PO Box 456, Loup City, NE 68853. 308-872-2921, Fax: 308-745-1820. 8:30AM-4:30PM. Access by: mail, in person.

Misdemeanor, Civil Actions Under $15,000, Eviction, Small Claims, Probate—Sherman County Court, 630 O St, PO Box 55, Loup City, NE 68853. 308-872-2121. 8:30AM-4:30PM. Access by: mail, fax, in person.

Sioux

Real Estate Recording—Sioux County Clerk, Courthouse, Harrison, NE 69346. 308-785-2450. Fax: 308-668-2443. 8AM-5PM.

Felony, Civil Actions Over $15,000—District Court, PO Box 158, Harrison, NE 69346. 308-785-2531, Fax: 308-668-2443. 8AM-5PM. Access by: mail, in person.

Misdemeanor, Civil Actions Under $15,000, Eviction, Small Claims, Probate—Sioux County Court, PO Box 477, Harrison, NE 69346. 308-785-2611. 8AM-Noon. Access by: mail, phone, in person.

Stanton

Real Estate Recording—Stanton County Clerk, 804 Ivy Street, Stanton, NE 68779. 402-643-4895, Fax: 402-439-2229. 8:30AM-4:30PM.

Felony, Civil Actions Over $15,000—District Court, PO Box 347, Stanton, NE 68779. 402-643-4574, Fax: 402-439-2229. 8:30AM-4:30PM. Access by: mail, fax, in person.

Misdemeanor, Civil Actions Under $15,000, Eviction, Small Claims, Probate—Stanton County Court, 804 Ivey St, PO Box 536, Stanton, NE 68779. 402-643-3341, Fax: 402-439-2229. 8:30AM-5PM. Access by: in person.

Thayer

Real Estate Recording—Thayer County Clerk, 225 N. 4th, Hebron, NE 68370. 405-223-9467. 8AM-4:30PM.

Felony, Civil Actions Over $15,000—District Court, PO Box 297, Hebron, NE 68370. 404-730-6100, Fax: 402-768-7232. 8AM-Noon, 1-5PM. Access by: mail, fax, in person.

Misdemeanor, Civil Actions Under $15,000, Eviction, Small Claims, Probate—Thayer County Court, PO Box 94, Hebron, NE 68370. 405-224-7446, Fax: 402-768-7232. 8AM-5PM. Access by: mail, in person.

Thomas

Real Estate Recording—Thomas County Clerk, 503 Main Street, Thedford, NE 69166. 308-762-6975, Fax: 308-645-2623. 8AM-Noon, 1-4PM M-Th; 8AM-Noon, 1-3PM F.

Felony, Civil Actions Over $15,000—District Court, PO Box 226, Thedford, NE 69166. 308-762-6800, Fax: 308-645-2623. 8AM-Noon,1-4PM. Access by: mail, fax, in person.

Misdemeanor, Civil Actions Under $15,000, Eviction, Small Claims, Probate—Thomas County Court, PO Box 233, Thedford, NE 69166. 308-764-2203, Fax: 308-645-2623. 8AM-Noon, 1-4PM. Access by: mail, fax, in person.

Thurston

Real Estate Recording—Thurston County Clerk, 106 South 5th Street, Pender, NE 68047. 402-454-3311, Fax: 402-385-3544. 8:30AM-5PM.

Felony, Civil Actions Over $15,000—District Court, PO Box 216, Pender, NE 68047. 402-454-3311, Fax: 402-385-2762. 8:30AM-5PM. Access by: in person.

Misdemeanor, Civil Actions Under $15,000, Eviction, Small Claims, Probate—Thurston County Court, County Courthouse, PO Box 129, Pender, NE 68047. 402-454-3311, Fax: 402-385-3143. 8:30AM-Noon,1-5PM. Access by: in person.

Valley

Real Estate Recording—Valley County Clerk, 125 South 15th, Ord, NE 68862. 308-832-2730. 8AM-5PM.

Felony, Civil Actions Over $15,000—District Court, 125 S 15th St, Ord, NE 68862. 308-832-1742, Fax: 308-728-7725. 8AM-5PM. Access by: mail, fax, in person.

Misdemeanor, Civil Actions Under $15,000, Eviction, Small Claims, Probate—Valley County Court, 125 S 15th St, Ord, NE 68862. 308-832-2719, Fax: 308-728-7725. 8AM-5PM. Access by: mail, phone, fax, in person.

Washington

Real Estate Recording—Washington County Clerk, 1555 Colfax Street, Blair, NE 68008. 402-563-4913, Fax: 402-426-6825. 8AM-4:30PM.

Felony, Civil Actions Over $15,000—District Court, PO Box 431, Blair, NE 68008. 402-593-2248, Fax: 402-426-6898. 8AM-4:30PM. Access by: in person.

Misdemeanor, Civil Actions Under $15,000, Eviction, Small Claims, Probate—Washington County Court, 1555 Colfax St, Blair, NE 68008. 402-563-4906, Fax: 402-426-6840. 8AM-4:30PM. Access by: in person.

Wayne

Real Estate Recording—Wayne County Clerk, 510 Pearl Street, Wayne, NE 68787. 402-443-8129, Fax: 402-375-3702. 8:30AM-5PM.

Felony, Civil Actions Over $15,000—District Court, 510 Pearl St, Wayne, NE 68787. 402-443-8119. 8:30AM-5PM. Access by: in person.

Misdemeanor, Civil Actions Under $15,000, Eviction, Small Claims, Probate—Wayne County Court, 510 Pearl St, Wayne, NE 68787. 402-443-8113, Fax: 402-375-1622. 8:30AM-5PM. Access by: in person.

Webster

Real Estate Recording—Webster County Clerk, 621 North Cedar, Court House, Red Cloud, NE 68970. 402-873-6440, Fax: 402-746-2710. 8AM-4:30PM.

Felony, Civil Actions Over $15,000—District Court, 621 N Cedar, Red Cloud, NE 68970. 402-852-2963, Fax: 402-746-2710. 8:30AM-4:30PM. Access by: mail, phone, fax, in person.

Misdemeanor, Civil Actions Under $15,000, Eviction, Small Claims, Probate—Webster County Court, 621 N Cedar, Red Cloud, NE 68970. 402-873-3589, Fax: 402-746-2771. 8:30AM-4:30PM. Access by: in person.

Wheeler

Real Estate Recording—Wheeler County Clerk, Courthouse, Bartlett, NE 68622. 308-772-3696, Fax: 308-654-3442. 9AM-Noon, 1-5PM.

Felony, Civil Actions Over $15,000—District Court, PO Box 127, Bartlett, NE 68622. 308-772-3622, Fax: 308-654-3442. 9AM-Noon, 1-5PM. Access by: in person.

Misdemeanor, Civil Actions Under $15,000, Eviction, Small Claims, Probate—Wheeler County Court, PO Box 127, Bartlett, NE 68622. 308-772-3924, Fax: 308-654-3442. 9AM-4PM. Access by: mail, in person.

York

Real Estate Recording—York County Clerk, Courthouse, 510 Lincoln Ave. York, NE 68467. 402-426-6833, Fax: 402-362-2651. 8:30AM-5PM.

Felony, Civil Actions Over $15,000—District Court, 510 Lincoln Ave, York, NE 68467. 402-395-6184, Fax: 402-362-2577. 8:30AM-5PM. Access by: in person. Special note: The SSN does not show up in the computer index, but will show in the case files.

Misdemeanor, Civil Actions Under $15,000, Eviction, Small Claims, Probate—York County Court, 510 Lincoln Ave, York, NE 68467. 402-396-4411, Fax: 402-362-2577. 8AM-5PM. Access by: in person.

Federal Courts

US District Court

Lincoln Division PO Box 83468, Lincoln, NE 68501402-437-5225 Counties: Nebraska cases may be filed in any of the three courts at the option of the attorney, except that filings in the North Platte Division must be during trial session.. www.ned.uscourts.gov

North Platte Division c/o Lincoln Division, PO Box 83468, Lincoln, NE 68501402-221-4761 Fax: 402-221-3160 Counties: Nebraska cases may be filed in any of the three courts at the option of the attorney, except that filings in the North Platte Division must be during trial session. Some case records may be in the Omaha Division as well as the Lincoln Division. www.ned.uscourts.gov

Omaha Division PO Box 129, DTS, Omaha, NE 68101402-221-4761 Fax: 402-221-3160 Counties: Nebraska cases may be filed in any of the three courts at the option of the attorney, except that filings in the North Platte Division must be during trial session.. www.ned.uscourts.gov

US Bankruptcy Court

Lincoln Division 460 Federal Bldg, 100 Centennial Mall N, Lincoln, NE 68508402-437-5100 Fax: 402-437-5454 Counties: Adams, Antelope, Boone, Boyd, Buffalo, Butler, Cass, Clay, Colfax, Fillmore, Franklin, Gage, Greeley, Hall, Hamilton, Harlan, Holt, Howard, Jefferson, Johnson, Kearney, Lancaster, Madison, Merrick, Nance, Nemaha, Nuckolls, Otoe, Pawnee, Phelps, Platte,Polk, Richardson, Saline, Saunders, Seward, Sherman, Thayer, Webster, Wheeler, York. Cases from the North Platte Division may also be assigned here.

North Platte Division c/o Omaha Division, PO Box 129, DTS, Omaha, NE 68101402-221-4687 Counties: Arthur, Banner, Blaine, Box Butte, Brown, Chase, Cherry, Cheyenne, Custer, Dawes, Dawson, Deuel, Dundy, Frontier, Furnas, Garden, Garfield, Gosper, Grant, Hayes, Hitchcock, Hooker, Keith, Keya Paha, Kimball, Lincoln, Logan, Loup, McPherson, Morrill,Perkins, Red Willow, Rock, Scotts Bluff, Sheridan, Sioux, Thomas, Valley. Cases may be randomly allocated to Omaha or Lincoln.

Omaha Division PO Box 428, DTS, Omaha, NE 68101-4281402-221-4687 Counties: Burt, Cedar, Cuming, Dakota, Dixon, Dodge, Douglas, Knox, Pierce, Sarpy, Stanton, Thurston, Washington, Wayne.

Nevada

Attorney General's Office
100 N Carson St   775-684-1100
Carson City, NV 89710   Fax: 775-684-1108
www.state.nv.us/ag

Governor's Office
Capitol Building   775-684-5670
Carson City, NV 89710
www.state.nv.us/gov/gov.htm

State Archives
100 N Stewart St   775-684-3360
Carson City, NV 89701-4285
www.clan.lib.nv.us/docs/NSLA/nsia.htm

Capital:	Carson City
	Carson City County
Time Zone:	PST
Number of Counties:	17
Number of Filing Locations:	17
Population:	1,676,809
Web Site:	www.state.nv.us

Search Unclaimed Property Online

http://treasurer.state.nv.us/
unclaimed/search.htm

State Agencies

Criminal Records
Nevada Highway Patrol, Record & ID Services, 555 Wright Way, Carson City, NV 89711-0585; 775-687-1600; Fax: 775-687-1843; 8AM-5PM. Access by: mail.

Corporation Records
Limited Partnerships
Limited Liability Company Records
Limited Partnership Records
Secretary of State, Status Division, 101 N Carson, #3, Carson City, NV 89701-4786; 775-684-5208, 900-535-3355 Status Line; Fax: 775-684-5725; 8AM-5PM. Access by: mail, phone, in person, online. http://sos.state.nv.us

Trademarks/Servicemarks
Secretary of State, Corporate Expedite Office, 555 E. Washington Ave, #2900, Las Vegas, NV 89101;, 702-486-2885; Fax: 702-486-2888; 8AM-5PM. Access by: mail, phone, in person. www.sos.state.nv.us

Uniform Commercial Code
Federal Tax Liens
State Tax Liens
UCC Department, Secretary of State, 220 N Carson St, Carson City, NV 89701-4201; 775-684-5708; Fax: 775-684-5630; 8AM-5PM. Access by: mail, online.

Assumed Name
Fictitious Name
Records not available from state agency.

Records are at the county level.

Workers' Compensation Records
State Industrial Insurance System, Workers Compensation Division, 515 E Musser St, Carson City, NV 89714; 775-886-1000; 8AM-5PM. Access by: mail.

Birth Certificates

Nevada Department of Health, Office of Vital Statistics, 505 E King St, Rm 102, Carson City, NV 89701-4749; 775-684-4242, 775-684-4280 Message Phone; Fax: 775-684-4156; 9AM-4PM. Access by: mail, phone, in person.

Death Records

Nevada Department of Health, Office of Vital Statistics, 505 E King St, Rm 102, Carson City, NV 89701-4749; 775-684-4242, 775-684-4280 Message Phone; Fax: 775-684-4156; 9AM-4PM. Access by: mail.

Marriage Certificates
Divorce Records

Restricted access.

Marriage and Divorce records are found at county of issue. However, the agency has an index and will relate the county and date of the event. The fee is $8.00. Call (775) 684-4242.

Nevada Department of Health, Office of Vital Statistics, 505 E King St, Rm 102, Carson City, NV 89701-4749; 702-687-4481;

Accident Reports

Department of Motor Vehicles, Highway Patrol Division, 555 Wright Way, Carson City, NV 89711; 775-684-4870; Fax: 775-684-4879; 8AM-5PM. Access by: mail.

Driver Records

Department of Motor Vehicles and Public Safety, Records Section, 555 Wright Way, Carson City, NV 89711-0250; 775-684-4590, 800-992-7945 In-state; 8AM-5PM. Access by: mail, phone, in person. www.state.nv.us/dmv_ps

Vehicle Ownership
Vehicle Identification

Department of Motor Vehicles and Public Safety, Motor Vehicle Record Section, 555 Wright Way, Carson City, NV 89711-0250;

775-684-4590; Fax: 775-684-4740; 8AM-5PM. Access by: mail, phone, in person. www.state.nv.us/dmv_ps

Boat & Vessel Ownership
Boat & Vessel Registration

Division of Wildlife, Boat Registration, PO Box 10678, Reno, NV 89520; 775-688-1511; 8AM-5PM M-F.

Legislation-Current/Pending
Legislation-Passed

Nevada Legislature, 401 S Carson St, Carson City, NV 89701-4747; 775-684-6827 Bill Status Only, 775-684-6800 Main Number, 775-684-6835 Publications, 775-684-6827 Research Library; Fax: 775-684-6600; 8AM-5PM. Access by: mail, phone, in person, online. www.leg.state.nv.us

Voter Registration

Records not available from state agency.

Records are open to the public at the county level. All data is released except for SSNs.

GED Certificates

Department of Education, State GED Administration, 700 E 5th Street, Carson City, NV 89701; 775-687-9104; Fax: 775-687-0114; 8AM-5PM. Access by: mail.

Hunting License Information
Fishing License Information

Division of Wildlife, PO Box 10678, Reno, NV 89520 (1100 Valley Rd, Reno, NV 89512); 775-688-1500; Fax: 775-688-1595; 8AM-12; 1PM-5PM. Access by: mail. www.state.nv.us/cnr/ndwildlife

County Courts & Recording Offices

About the Courts...

Administration

Supreme Court of Nevada,
Administrative Office of the Courts   775-687-5076
Capitol Complex, 201 S Carson St   Fax: 775-687-5079
Carson City, NV 89701

Court Structure

There are 17 District Courts within 9 judicial districts. The 56 Justice Courts are named for the township of jurisdiction. Probate is handled by the District Courts.

Searching Hints

Many Nevada Justice Courts are small and have very few records. Their hours of operation vary widely and contact is difficult. It is recommended that requesters call ahead for information prior to submitting a written request or attempting an in-person retrieval.

Online Access

Some Nevada Courts have internal online computer systems, but none have external access nor is such access planned in the near future. Planning began June 1998 for a statewide court automation system, with implementation planned within 2-3 years.

About the Recording Offices...

Organization

16 counties and one independent city, 17 recording offices. The recording officer is County Recorder. Carson City has a separate filing office. The entire state is in the Pacific Time Zone (PST).

UCC Records

Financing statements are filed at the state level, except for consumer goods, crops and real estate related collateral, which are filed only with the County Recorder. All recording offices will perform UCC searches. Search fees are $15.00 per debtor name using the approved UCC-3 request form and $20.00 using a non-Nevada. Copies cost $1.00 per page.

Lien Records

Federal tax liens on personal property of businesses are filed with the Secretary of State. Federal tax liens on personal property of individuals are filed with the County Recorder. Although not called state tax liens, employment withholding judgments have the same effect and are filed with the County Recorder. Most counties will provide tax lien searches for a fee of $15.00 per name - $20.00 if the standard UCC request form is not used.

Real Estate Records

Most counties will not provide real estate searches. Copies cost $1.00 per page and certification fees are usually $4.00 per document.

County Courts & Recording Offices

Carson

Real Estate Recording—Carson City Recorder, 885 E. Musser St. Ste 1628, Carson City, NV 89701. 702-887-2092. 8AM-5PM.

Carson City

Felony, Misdemeanor, Civil Actions Over $7,500, Probate—1st Judicial District Court, 885 E Musser St #3031, Carson City, NV 89701-4775. 775-887-2082, Fax: 775-887-2177. 9AM-5PM. Access by: mail, in person.

Civil Actions Under $7,500, Eviction, Small Claims—Justice Court Dept II, 111 W. Telegraph St, Suite 100, Carson City, NV 89701. 775-887-2275, Fax: 775-887-2297. 8:30AM-4:30PM. Access by: mail, phone, fax, in person.

Misdemeanor—Justice Court Dept I, 885 E Musser St #2007, Carson City, NV 89701-4775. 775-887-2121, Fax: 775-887-2297. 9AM-4PM M-W/9AM-5PM Th/9AM-3:30PM F. Access by: mail, phone, fax, in person.

Churchill

Real Estate Recording—Churchill County Recorder, 155 N. Taylor, Suite 131, Fallon, NV 89406. 702-423-6028, Fax: 775-423-8933. 8AM-5PM.

Felony, Misdemeanor, Civil Actions Over $7,500, Probate—3rd Judicial District Court, 73 N Maine St, Ste B, Fallon, NV 89406. 775-423-6080, Fax: 775-423-8578. 8AM-Noon, 1-5PM. Access by: mail, fax, in person.

Misdemeanor, Civil Actions Under $7,500, Eviction, Small Claims—Justice Court, 73 N Maine St, Fallon, NV 89406. 775-423-2845, Fax: 775-423-0472. 8AM-Noon, 1-5PM. Access by: mail, in person.

Clark

Real Estate Recording—Clark County Recorder, 500 S. Grand Central Parkway, 2nd Floor, Las Vegas, NV 89106. 702-455-4323, Fax: 702-455-5644. 8AM-5PM.

Felony, Misdemeanor, Civil Actions Over $7,500, Probate—8th Judicial District Court, 200 S 3rd (PO Box 551601), Las Vegas, NV 89155. 702-455-3156, Fax: 702-455-4929. 8AM-4PM. Access by: mail, in person. co.clark.nv.us

Misdemeanor, Civil Actions Under $7,000, Eviction, Small Claims—Laughlin Township Justice Court, PO Box 2305, 101 Civiv Way #2, Laughlin, NV 89029. 702-298-4622, Fax: 702-298-7508. 8AM-5PM. Access by: mail, fax, in person.

Misdemeanor, Civil Actions Under $7,500, Eviction, Small Claims—Boulder Township Justice Court, 505 Avenue G, Boulder City, NV 89005. 702-455-8000, Fax: 702-455-8003. 7:30AM-5PM. Access by: mail, fax, in person.

Bunkerville Justice Court, 190 W Virgin St, Bunkerville, NV 89007. 702-346-5711, Fax: 702-346-7212. 7AM-5PM M-Th. Access by: mail, phone, fax, in person.

Goodsprings Township Jean Justice Court, 1 Main St (PO Box 19155), Jean, NV 89019. 702-874-1405, Fax: 702-874-1612. 7AM-5PM M-Th. Access by: mail, phone, fax, in person.

Henderson Township Justice, 243 Water St, Henderson, NV 89015. 702-455-7951, Fax: 702-455-7935. 7AM-6PM M-Th. Access by: mail, in person.

Las Vegas Township Justice, 200 S 3rd, 2nd Fl, PO Box 552511, Las Vegas, NV 89155-2511. 702-455-4435, Fax: 702-455-4529. 8AM-5PM. Access by: mail, phone, fax, in person.

Mesquite Township Justice Court, PO Box 1209, Mesquite, NV 89024. 702-346-5298, Fax: 702-346-7319. 8AM-5PM M,T; 8AM-Noon F. Access by: mail, phone, in person.

Moapa Township Justice Court, 1340 E Com Hwy, PO Box 280, Moapa, NV 89025. 702-864-2333, Fax: 702-864-2585. 8AM-5PM M-Th. Access by: mail, fax, in person.

Moapa Valley Township Justice Court, 320 N Moapa Valley Blvd, PO Box 337, Overton, NV 89040. 702-397-2840, Fax: 702-397-2842. 7AM-4PM M-Th. Access by: mail, in person.

North Las Vegas Township Justice, 1916 N Bruce, N Las Vegas, NV 89030. 702-455-7802, Fax: 702-455-7831. 8:30AM-5PM. Access by: mail, phone, in person. Special note: Judge must approve all search requests.

Searchlight Township Justice, PO Box 815, Searchlight, NV 89046. 702-297-1252, Fax: 702-297-1263. 7AM-5:30PM M-Th. Access by: mail, fax, in person.

Douglas

Real Estate Recording—Douglas County Recorder, 1616 8th Street, Minden, NV 89423. 702-782-9022, Fax: 775-783-6413. 9AM-5PM.

Felony, Civil Actions Over $7,500, Probate—9th Judicial District Court, Box 218, Minden, NV 89423. 775-782-9820, Fax: 775-782-9954. 8AM-5PM. Access by: mail, in person. Special note: Misdemeanors are handled by the East Fork Justice Court.

Misdemeanor, Civil Actions Under $7,500, Eviction, Small Claims—E Fork Justice Court, PO Box 218, Minden, NV 89423. 775-782-9955, Fax: 775-782-9964. 8AM-5PM. Access by: mail, in person.

Tahoe Justice Court, PO Box 7169, Stateline, NV 89449. 775-588-8100, Fax: 775-588-6844. 9AM-5PM. Access by: mail, phone, fax, in person.

Elko

Real Estate Recording—Elko County Recorder, 571 Idaho St. Room 103, Elko, NV 89801. 702-738-5694, Fax: 775-738-3299. 9AM-5PM.

Felony, Gross Misdemeanor, Civil Actions Over $7,500, Probate—4th Judicial District Court, 571 Idaho St, 3rd Flr, Elko, NV 89801. 775-753-4600, Fax: 775-753-4610. 9AM-5PM. Access by: mail, phone, fax, in person.

Misdemeanor, Civil Actions Under $7,500, Eviction, Small Claims—Carlin Justice Court, PO Box 789, Carlin, NV 89822. 775-754-6321, Fax: 775-754-6893. 8AM-5PM. Access by: mail, in person.

Eastline Justice Court, PO Box 2300, Wendover, NV 89883. 775-664-2305, Fax: 775-664-2979. 9AM-4PM. Access by: mail, in person.

Elko Justice Court, PO Box 176, Elko, NV 89803. 775-738-8403, Fax: 775-738-8416. 9AM-Noon, 1-5PM. Access by: mail, fax, in person. Special note: There is a small Justice Court located in Tecoma Township at PO Box 8, Montello, NV 89830, 775-776-2544.

Jackpot Justice Court, PO Box 229, Jackpot, NV 89825. 775-755-2456, Fax: 775-755-2727. 9AM-Noon, 1-5PM. Access by: mail, fax, in person.

Jarbidge Justice Court, PO Box 26001, Jarbidge, NV 89826-2001. 775-488-2331. Access by: in person. Special note: This is "unincorporated ghost town." No criminal or civil cases in more than 20 years. Mostly marriages, fish and game violations. Only 40 year round residents here.

Mountain City Justice Court, Courthouse, Mountain City, NV 89831. 775-763-6621, Fax: 775-763-6621. Access by: mail, in person. Special note: New records held in Elko Justice Court; older ones may soon be transferred also. Limited cases heard here. Phone listed is sheriff's office. Only 49 people living here.

Wells Justice Municipal Court, PO Box 297, Wells, NV 89835. 775-752-3726, Fax: 775-752-3363. 9AM-Noon,1-5PM. Access by: mail, in person.

Esmeralda

Real Estate Recording—Esmeralda County Recorder, 458 Crook Street, Courthouse, Goldfield, NV 89013. 702-485-6367, Fax: 775-485-3524. 8AM-Noon,1-5PM.

Felony, Misdemeanor, Civil Actions Over $7,500, Probate—5th Judicial District Court, PO Box 547, Goldfield, NV 89013. 775-485-6367, Fax: 775-485-6376. 8AM-5PM. Access by: mail, fax, in person.

Misdemeanor, Civil Actions Under $7,500, Eviction, Small Claims—Esmeralda Justice Court, PO Box 370, Goldfield, NV 89013. 775-485-6359, Fax: 775-485-3524. 8AM-5PM. Access by: mail, phone, fax, in person.

Eureka

Real Estate Recording—Eureka County Recorder, 701 S. Main Street, Eureka, NV 89316. 702-237-5262, Fax: 775-237-5614. 8AM-Noon, 1-5PM.

Felony, Misdemeanor, Civil Actions Over $7,500, Probate—7th Judicial District Court, PO Box 677, Eureka, NV 89316. 775-237-5262, Fax: 775-237-6015. 8AM-Noon, 1-5PM. Access by: mail, phone, fax, in person.

Misdemeanor, Civil Actions Under $7,500, Eviction, Small Claims—Beowawe Justice Court, PO Box 211065A, Crescent Valley, NV 89821. 775-468-0244, Fax: 775-468-0323. 8AM-5PM. Access by: mail, in person.

Eureka Justice Court, PO Box 496, Eureka, NV 89316. 775-237-5540, Fax: 775-237-6016. 8AM-Noon,1-5PM. Access by: mail, phone, fax, in person.

Humboldt

Real Estate Recording—Humboldt County Recorder, 25 West 4th Street, Winnemucca, NV 89445. 702-623-6444. 8AM-5PM.

Felony, Misdemeanor, Civil Actions Over $7,500, Probate—6th Judicial District Court, 50 W Fifth St, Winnemucca, NV 89445. 775-623-6343, Fax: 775-623-6309. 8AM-5PM. Access by: mail, phone, fax, in person.

Misdemeanor, Civil Actions Under $7,500, Eviction, Small Claims—Union Justice Court, PO Box 1218, Winnemucca, NV 89446. 775-623-6377, Fax: 775-623-6439. 7AM-5PM. Access by: mail, fax, in person.

Lander

Real Estate Recording—Lander County Recorder, 315 South Humboldt, Battle Mountain, NV 89820. 702-635-5127, Fax: 775-635-8272. 8AM-5PM.

Felony, Misdemeanor, Civil Actions Over $7,500, Probate—6th Judicial District Court, 315 S Humboldt, Battle Mountain, NV 89820. 775-635-5738, Fax: 775-635-5761. 8AM-5PM. Access by: mail, phone, fax, in person.

Misdemeanor, Civil Actions Under $7,500, Eviction, Small Claims—Argenta Justice Court, 315 S Humboldt, Battle Mountain, NV 89820. 775-635-5151, Fax: 775-635-0604. 8AM-5PM. Access by: mail, phone, fax, in person.

Austin Justice Court, PO Box 100, Austin, NV 89310. 775-964-2380, Fax: 775-964-2327. 8AM-5PM M, 8AM-Noon T-Th. Access by: mail, in person.

Lincoln

Real Estate Recording—Lincoln County Recorder, 1 Main Street, Courthouse, Pioche, NV 89043. 702-962-5805, Fax: 775-962-5180. 9AM-5PM.

Felony, Misdemeanor, Civil Actions Over $7,500, Probate—7th Judicial District Court, PO Box 90, Pioche, NV 89043. 775-962-5390, Fax: 702-962-5180. 9AM-5PM. Access by: mail, fax, in person.

Misdemeanor, Civil Actions Under $7,500, Eviction, Small Claims—Meadow Valley Justice Court, PO Box 36, Pioche, NV 89043. 775-962-5140, Fax: 775-962-5877. 9AM-5PM. Access by: mail, phone, fax, in person.

Pahranagat Valley Justice Court, PO Box 449, Alamo, NV 89001. 775-725-3357, Fax: 775-725-3566. 9AM-5PM. Access by: mail, fax, in person.

Lyon

Real Estate Recording—Lyon County Recorder, 31 South Main Street, Yerington, NV 89447. 702-463-3341, Fax: 775-463-6585. 8AM-5PM.

Felony, Misdemeanor, Civil Actions Over $7,500, Probate—3rd Judicial District Court, PO Box 816, Yerington, NV 89447. 775-463-6503, Fax: 775-463-6575. 8AM-5PM. Access by: mail, phone, in person.

Misdemeanor, Civil Actions Under $10,000, Eviction, Small Claims—Smith Valley Justice Court, PO Box 141, Smith, NV 89430. 775-465-2313, Fax: 775-465-2153. 8AM-Noon Fri or by appointment. Access by: mail, phone, fax, in person.

Misdemeanor, Civil Actions Under $7,500, Eviction, Small Claims—Dayton Township Justice Court, PO Box 490, Dayton, NV 89403. 775-246-6233, Fax: 775-246-6203. 8AM-5PM. Access by: mail, phone, fax, in person.

Fernley Justice Court, PO Box 497, Fernley, NV 89408. 775-575-3355, Fax: 775-575-3359. 8AM-5PM. Access by: mail, phone, fax, in person.

Mason Valley Justice Court, 30 Nevin Way, Yerington, NV 89447. 775-463-6639, Fax: 775-463-6610. 8AM-5PM. Access by: mail, phone, in person.

Mineral

Real Estate Recording—Mineral County Recorder, 105 South A Street, P.O. Box 1447, Hawthorne, NV 89415. 702-945-2446, Fax: 775-945-1749. 8AM-5PM.

Felony, Misdemeanor, Civil Actions Over $7,500, Probate—5th Judicial District Court, PO Box 1450, Hawthorne, NV 89415. 775-945-2446, Fax: 775-945-0706. 8AM-5PM. Access by: mail, phone, fax, in person.

Misdemeanor, Civil Actions Under $7,500, Eviction, Small Claims—Hawthorne Justice Court, PO Box 1660, Hawthorne, NV 89415. 775-945-3859, Fax: 775-945-0700. 8AM-5PM. Access by: mail, phone, in person.

Mina Justice Court, PO Box 415, Mina, NV 89422. 775-573-2547, Fax: 775-573-2244. 9AM-Noon, 2-4PM. Access by: mail, phone, fax, in person.

Schurz Justice Court, PO Box 265, Schurz, NV 89427. 775-773-2241, Fax: 775-773-2030. 9AM-4PM Fri only. Access by: mail, fax, in person.

Nye

Real Estate Recording—Nye County Recorder, 101 Radar Rd. Tonopah, NV 89049. 702-482-8194, Fax: 775-482-8111. 8AM-Noon, 1-5PM.

Felony, Misdemeanor, Civil Actions Over $7,500, Probate—5th Judicial District Court, PO Box 1031, Tonopah, NV 89049. 775-482-8131, Fax: 775-482-8133. 8AM-5PM. Access by: mail, phone, fax, in person.

Misdemeanor, Civil Actions Under $7,500, Eviction, Small Claims—Beatty Justice Court, PO Box 805, Beatty, NV 89003. 775-553-2951, Fax: 752-553-2136. 8AM-5PM. Access by: mail, phone, in person.

Gabbs Justice Court, PO Box 533, Gabbs, NV 89409. 775-285-2379, Fax: 775-285-4263. 9AM-4PM M-Th. Access by: mail, phone, in person.

Tonopah Justice Court, PO Box 1151, Tonopah, NV 89049. 775-482-8153. 8AM-Noon, 1-5PM. Access by: mail, phone, in person.

Pershing

Real Estate Recording—Pershing County Recorder, Courthouse, 400 Main Street, Lovelock, NV 89419. 702-273-2208, Fax: 775-273-7058. 8AM-5PM.

Felony, Civil Actions Over $7,500, Probate—6th Judicial District Court, PO Box 820, Lovelock, NV 89419. 775-273-2208, Fax: 775-273-7058. 9AM-5PM. Access by: mail, phone, fax, in person. Special note: Misdemeanors are handled by the Lake Justice Court.

Misdemeanor, Civil Actions Under $7,500, Eviction, Small Claims—Lake Township Justice Court, PO Box 8, Lovelock, NV 89419. 775-273-2753, Fax: 775-273-0416. 8AM-5PM. Access by: mail, phone, fax, in person.

Storey

Real Estate Recording—Storey County Recorder, B Street, Courthouse, Virginia City, NV 89440. 702-847-0969, Fax: 775-847-1009. 9AM-5PM.

Felony, Misdemeanor, Civil Actions Over $7,500, Probate—1st Judicial District Court, PO Drawer D, Virginia City, NV 89440. 775-847-0969, Fax: 775-847-0949. 9AM-5PM. Access by: mail, phone, fax, in person.

Misdemeanor, Civil Actions Under $7,500, Eviction, Small Claims—Virginia City Justice Court, PO Box 674, Virginia City, NV 89440. 775-847-0962, Fax: 775-847-0915. 9AM-5PM. Access by: mail, phone, fax, in person.

Washoe

Real Estate Recording—Washoe County Recorder, 1001 East 9th Street, Reno, NV 89512. 702-328-2510. 8AM-5PM.

Felony, Misdemeanor, Civil Actions Over $7,500, Probate—2nd Judicial District Court, PO Box 11130, Reno, NV 89520. 775-328-3110, Fax: 775-328-3515. 8AM-5PM. Access by: mail, in person.

Misdemeanor, Civil Actions Under $7,500, Eviction, Small Claims—Reno Justice Court, PO Box 30083, Reno, NV 89520.

775-325-6501, Fax: 775-325-6510. 8AM-5PM. Access by: mail, phone, in person.

Sparks Justice Court, 630 Greenbrae Dr, Sparks, NV 89431. 775-352-3000. 8AM-5PM. Access by: mail, in person.

White Pine

Real Estate Recording—White Pine County Recorder, Courthouse Plaza, Ely, NV 89301. 702-289-4783, Fax: 775-289-1541. 9AM-5PM.

Felony, Misdemeanor, Civil Actions Over $7,500, Probate—7th Judicial District Court, PO Box 659, Ely, NV 89301. 775-289-2341, Fax: 775-289-2544. 9AM-5PM. Access by: mail, phone, fax, in person.

Misdemeanor, Civil Actions Under $7,500, Eviction, Small Claims—Ely Justice Court, PO Box 396, Ely, NV 89301. 775-289-2678, Fax: 775-289-3392. 9AM-5PM. Access by: mail, phone, fax, in person.

Lund Justice Court, PO Box 87, Lund, NV 89317. 775-238-5400, Fax: 775-238-5400. 10AM-2:30PM M,W,F. Access by: mail, fax, in person.

Federal Courts

US District Court

Las Vegas Division Room 4425, 300 Las Vegas Blvd S, Las Vegas, NV 89101702-388-6351 Counties: Clark, Esmeralda, Lincoln, Nye.
Reno Division Room 301, 400 S Virginia St, Reno, NV 89501775-686-5800, Record Room: 775-686-5909, Civil Docket Phone: 775-686-5845, Criminal Docket Phone: 775-686-5844 Fax: 702-686-5851 Counties: Carson City, Churchill, Douglas, Elko, Eureka, Humboldt, Lander, Lyon, Mineral, Pershing, Storey, Washoe, White Pine.

US Bankruptcy Court

Las Vegas Division Room 2130, 300 Las Vegas Blvd S, Las Vegas, NV 89101702-388-6257 Counties: Clark, Esmeralda, Lincoln, Nye. www.nvb.uscourts.gov
Reno-Northern Division Room 4005, 300 Booth St, Reno, NV 89509775-784-5559 Counties: Carson City, Churchill, Douglas, Elko, Eureka, Humboldt, Lander, Lyon, Mineral, Pershing, Storey, Washoe, White Pine. www.nvb.uscourts.gov

New Hampshire

Attorney General's Office

33 Capitol St 603-271-3658
Concord, NH 03301-6397 Fax: 603-271-2110
www.state.nh.us/doj/ag.html

Governor's Office

107 N Main St, Rm 208 603-271-2121
Concord, NH 03301 Fax: 603-271-6998
www.state.nh.us/governor/index.htm

State Archives

71 S Fruit St 603-271-2236
Concord, NH 03301 Fax: 603-271-2272
www.state.nh.us/state/archives.htm

Capital:	Concord
	Merrimack County
Time Zone:	EST
Number of Counties:	10
Population:	1,172,709
Web Site:	www.state.nh.us

Search Unclaimed Property Online

www.state.nh.us/treasury/
search.html

State Agencies

Criminal Records

State Police Headquarters, Criminal Records, James H. Hayes Bldg, 10 Hazen Dr, Concord, NH 03305; 603-271-2538; 8:15AM-4:15PM. Access by: mail.

Corporation Records
Limited Partnership Records
Limited Liability Company Records
Trademarks/Servicemarks
Trade Names
Limited Liability Partnerships

Secretary of State, Corporation Division, State House, Room 204, Concord, NH 03301; 603-271-3246, 603-271-3244; Fax: 603-271-3247; 8AM-4:30PM. Access by: mail, phone, in person. www.state.nh.us/sos

Uniform Commercial Code
Federal Tax Liens
State Tax Liens

UCC Division, Secretary of State, 25 Capitol St, State House Annex, 3rd Floor, Concord, NH 03301; 603-271-3276; 9AM-3:30PM (searches). Access by: mail.

Workers' Compensation Records

Labor Department, Workers Compensation Division, State Office Park S, 95 Pleasant St, Concord, NH 03301; 603-271-3174; Fax: 603-271-6149; 8AM-4:30PM. Access by: mail.

Birth Certificates

Office of Health Management, Bureau of Vital Records, 6 Hazen Dr, Concord, NH 03301-6527; 603-271-4650, 603-271-4654; Fax: 603-271-3447; 8:30AM-4PM. Access by: mail, phone, in person.

Death Records

Division of Public Health Services, Bureau of Vital Records, 6 Hazen Dr, Concord, NH 03301-6527; 603-271-4650, 603-271-4654; Fax: 603-271-3447; 8:30AM-4PM. Access by: mail, phone, in person.

Marriage Certificates

Office of Health Management, Bureau of Vital Records & Health Statistics, 6 Hazen Dr, Concord, NH 03301-6527; 603-271-4650, 603-271-4654; Fax: 603-271-3447; 8:30AM-4PM. Access by: mail, phone, in person.

Divorce Records

Division of Public Health Services, Bureau of Vital Records, 6 Hazen Dr, Concord, NH 03301-6527; 603-271-4650, 603-271-4654; Fax: 603-271-3447; 8:30AM-4PM. Access by: mail, phone, in person.

Accident Reports

Department of Safety, Accident Reproduction Section, 10 Hazen Dr, Concord, NH 03305; 603-271-2128; 8:15AM-4:15PM. Access by: mail.

Driver Records

Department of Motor Vehicles, Driving Records, 10 Hazen Dr, Concord, NH 03305; 603-271-2322; 8:15AM-4:15PM. Access by: mail, online.

Vehicle Identification

Department of Safety, Bureau of Title, 10 Hazen Dr, Concord, NH 03305; 603-271-3111 Bureau of Title, 603-271-2251 Registrations; 8:15AM-4:15PM. Access by: mail.

Vehicle Ownership
Boat & Vessel Registration

Department of Safety, Registration, Ten Hazen Court, Concord, NH 03305; 603-271-2251, 603-271-2333 Boat Desk; 8:15AM-4:15PM. Access by: mail.

Legislation-Current/Pending
Legislation-Passed

New Hampshire State Library, 20 Part St, Concord, NH 03301; 603-271-2239; Fax: 603-271-2205; 8AM-4:30PM. Access by: mail, phone, in person, online. www.state.nh.us/gencourt/gencourt.htm

Voter Registration

Records not available from state agency.

All records are kept by Town Clerks. Records are open.

GED Certificates

Department of Education, GED Testing, 101 Pleasant Street, Concord, NH 03301; 603-271-6699; Fax: 603-271-3454; 7:30AM-4PM.

Hunting License Information
Fishing License Information

Fish & Game Department, Licensing Department, Two Hazen Dr, Concord, NH 03301; 603-271-3421; Fax: 603-271-5829; 8AM-4:30PM. Access by: mail. www.wildlife.state.nh.us

County Courts & Recording Offices

About the Courts...

Administration

Administrative Office of the Courts   603-271-2521
Supreme Court Bldg, Noble Dr   Fax: 603-271-3977
Concord, NH 03301
www.state.nh.us/courts/home.htm

Court Structure

The Superior Court is the court of General Jurisdiction. Felony cases include Class A misdemeanors.

The District Court upper civil limit was increased to $25,000 from $10,000 on 1/1/93. Filing a civil case in the monetary "overlap" area between the Superior Court minimum and the District Court maximum is at the discretion of the filer.

There are only 2 Municipal Courts left in New Hampshire: Rye and Greenville. They may remain in operation for as long as 7 years. These courts are closed as the judge retires and the case load and records are absorbed by the nearest District Court.

Searching Hints

A statutory search fee has been implemented in the District Courts, as follows:

Computer search - $10.00 for up to 10 names in one request; $25.00 for 10 or more names in one request; $25.00 per hour for search time beyond one hour.

Manual search - $25.00 per hour.

If the search requires both types, the fee is the total for each.

Online Access

There is no remote online computer access available.

About the Recording Offices...

Organization

238 cities/towns and 10 counties, 10 recording offices and 242 UCC filing offices. The recording officers are Town/City Clerk (UCC) and Register of Deeds (real estate only). Each town/city profile indicates the county in which the town/city is located. Be careful to distinguish the following names that are identical for both a town/city and a county - Grafton, Hillsborough, Merrimack, Strafford, and Sullivan. Many towns are so small that their mailing addresses are within another town. The following unincorporated towns do not have a Town Clerk, so all liens are located at the corresponding county: Cambridge (Coos), Dicksville (Coos), Green's Grant (Coos), Hale's Location (Carroll), Millsfield (Coos), and Wentworth's Location (Coos). The entire state is in the Eastern Time Zone (EST).

UCC Records

This is a dual filing state. Financing statements are filed at the state level and with the Town/City Clerk, except for consumer goods and farm related collateral, which are filed only with the Town/City Clerk, and real estate related collateral, which are filed with the county Register of Deeds. Most recording offices will perform UCC searches. Use search request form UCC-11. Search fees are usually $5.00 per debtor name using the standard UCC-11 request form and $7.00 using a non-standard form. Copy fees are usually $.75 per page.

Lien Records

Federal and state tax liens on personal property of businesses are filed with the Secretary of State. Other federal and state tax liens on personal property are filed with the Town/City Clerk. Federal and state tax liens on real property are filed with the county Register of Deeds. There is wide variation in indexing and searching practices among the recording offices. Where a search fee of $7.00 is indicated, it refers to a non-standard request form such as a letter.

Real Estate Records

Real estate transactions are recorded at the county level, and property taxes are handled at the town/city level. Local town real estate ownership and assessment records are usually located at the Selectman's Office. Each town/city profile indicates the county in which the town/city is located. Most counties will not perform real estate searches. Copy fees vary. Certification fees generally are $2.00 per document.

County Courts & Recording Offices

Acworth

Real Estate Recording—Acworth Town Clerk, Town Hall, South Acworth, NH 3601. 6:30-8PM M-W; 9-11AM Sat.

Albany

Real Estate Recording—Albany Town Clerk, Town Hall, Conway, NH 3818. Fax: 603-447-2877. 4:30-7PM M; 5-7PM W; 9AM-Noon alternate Sat Summer; every Sat Winter.

Alexandria

Real Estate Recording—Alexandria Town Clerk, 44 Perkins Hill Road, Alexandria, NH 3222. Fax: 603-744-1079. 9AM-5PM M-T; 10AM-7PM Th; 10AM-5PM F.

Allenstown

Real Estate Recording—Allenstown Town Clerk, 68 School St. Allenstown, NH 3275. Fax: 603-485-5045. 8:30AM-5PM.

Alstead

Real Estate Recording—Alstead Town Clerk, Main St. Alstead, NH 3602. Fax: 603-835-2986. 11AM-4PM M-W; 2-7PM Th.

Alton

Real Estate Recording—Alton Town Clerk, Town Hall, 1 Monument Sq. Alton, NH 3809. 603-875-2161, Fax: 603-875-3894. 8:30AM-4:30PM.

Amherst

Real Estate Recording—Amherst Town Clerk, 2 Main Street, Town Hall, Amherst, NH 3031. 603-673-6041, Fax: 603-673-6794. 9AM-3PM M-F; 5:30-8PM Mon.

Andover

Real Estate Recording—Andover Town Clerk, Main St. Andover, NH 3216. 603-735-5516, Fax: 603-735-6975. 10AM-1PM T,Th; 6:30-8:30PM W; 9AM-Noon Sat.

Antrim

Real Estate Recording—Antrim Town Clerk, Main St. Antrim, NH 3440. Fax: 603-588-2969. 8AM-Noon, 1-4PM, 6-8PM M; 8AM-Noon W,Th.

Ashland

Real Estate Recording—Ashland Town Clerk, 20 Highland Street, Ashland, NH 3217. Fax: 603-968-3776. 8AM-4PM M-W & F; 8AM-5PM Th.

Atkinson

Real Estate Recording—Atkinson Town Clerk, 21 Academy Avenue, Town Hall, Atkinson, NH 3811. Fax: 603-362-5305. 8:30AM-4:30PM M; 8:30AM-4PM T-F.

Auburn

Real Estate Recording—Auburn Town Clerk, Town Hall, 47 Chester Road, Auburn, NH 3032. Fax: 603-483-0518. 9AM-2PM M,W,Th; 9AM-Noon F.

Barnstead

Real Estate Recording—Barnstead Town Clerk, Town Hall, 108 S. Barnstead Rd. Center Barnstead, NH 3225. Fax: 603-269-4072. 9AM-4:30PM M,W,Th,F; 9AM-7PM T.

Barrington

Real Estate Recording—Barrington Town Clerk, 41 Province Lane, Barrington, NH 3825. Fax: 603-664-5179. 8AM-2PM M,T,Th; 4-6PM W; 8AM-Noon F.

Bartlett

Real Estate Recording—Bartlett Town Clerk, Town Hall Road, Intervale, NH 3845. 8AM-4PM M-W & F; 8-11AM Sat.

Bath

Real Estate Recording—Bath Town Clerk, West Bath Road, Town Hall, Bath, NH 3740. 603-747-2454. 8AM-12, 1PM-4PM M,W,Th; 8AM-12, 5:30-8:30PM T.

Bedford

Real Estate Recording—Bedford Town Clerk, 24 North Amherst Road, Bedford, NH 3110. Fax: 603-472-4573. 8AM-4:30PM M,W,Th,F; 7AM-4:30PM T.

Belknap

Real Estate Recording—Belknap County Register of Deeds, 64 Court St. Laconia, NH 3246. Fax: 603-527-5429. 8:30AM-4PM.

Felony, Civil Actions Over $1,500—Superior Court, 64 Court St, Laconia, NH 03246. 603-524-3570. 8AM-4:30PM. Access by: mail, phone, in person.

Misdemeanor, Civil Actions Under $20,000, Eviction, Small Claims—Laconia District Court, 26 Academy St, PO Box 1010, Laconia, NH 03247. 603-524-4128. 8AM-4:30PM. Access by: mail, in person. Special note: Adoptions handled by probate court.

Probate—Probate Court, 64 Court St, PO Box 1343, Laconia, NH 03247-1343. 603-524-0903. 8AM-4PM. Access by: mail, in person.

Belmont

Real Estate Recording—Belmont Town Clerk, 45 Main Street, Town Hall, Belmont, NH 3220. Fax: 603-267-8305. 8:30AM-5PM.

Bennington

Real Estate Recording—Bennington Town Clerk, 7 School Street, #101, Bennington, NH 3442. Fax: 603-588-8005. 9AM-1PM T; 4:30-8:30PM Th; 9AM-Noon Sat.

Benton

Real Estate Recording—Benton Town Clerk, 547 Bradley Hill Rd. Benton, NH 3785. Fax: 603-787-6883. 6:30-8:30PM M Evening.

Berlin

Real Estate Recording—Berlin City Clerk, 168 Main Street, City Hall, Berlin, NH 3570. 603-752-1610, Fax: 603-752-8586. 8:30AM-4:30PM.

Bethlehem

Real Estate Recording—Bethlehem Town Clerk, Town Building, 2155 Main St. Bethlehem, NH 3574. Fax: 603-869-2280. 4:30-7PM M; 9AM-1PM T,Th; 12-3:30 W; 9-10:30AM F; 9-11AM 1st Sat of month.

Boscawen

Real Estate Recording—Boscawen Town Clerk, 17 High Street, Boscawen, NH 3303. 603-796-2343, Fax: 603-796-2316. 8:30AM-12:30PM, 1-5PM T,Th; 8:30AM-12:30PM,1-7PM W.

Bow

Real Estate Recording—Bow Town Clerk, 10 Grandview Road, Bow, NH 3304. 7:30AM-3:45PM.

Bradford

Real Estate Recording—Bradford Town Clerk, 75 Main Street, Town Hall, Bradford, NH 3221. Fax: 603-938-5900. 2-7PM M; 8AM-5PM T; 8AM-Noon F.

Brentwood

Real Estate Recording—Brentwood Town Clerk, 1 Dalton Road, Brentwood, NH 3833. Fax: 603-642-6310. 9AM-4:30PM T-F; 7-9PM T; 9AM-Noon Sat Sept-May.

Bridgewater

Real Estate Recording—Bridgewater Town Clerk, Kathy A. Vestal, 955 River Rd. Plymouth, NH 3264. 6PM-8:30PM W; 8:30-10AM Sat.

New Hampshire

Bristol

Real Estate Recording—Bristol Town Clerk, 230 Lake Street, Suite A, Bristol, NH 3222. Fax: 603-744-2521. 8:30AM-4PM; 6-8PM Th.

Brookfield

Real Estate Recording—Brookfield Town Clerk, 2 Piney Rd. Cedar Park, Sanbornville, NH 3872. 603-522-6551. 1-8PM M.

Brookline

Real Estate Recording—Brookline Town Clerk, Main Street, Town Hall, Brookline, NH 3033. Fax: 603-673-8136. 8AM-Noon (Closed M).

Campton

Real Estate Recording—Campton Town Clerk, Main Street, Campton, NH 3223. Fax: 603-726-9817. 9AM-3:30PM.

Canaan

Real Estate Recording—Canaan Town Clerk, Church Street, Canaan, NH 3741. Fax: 603-523-4526. 9-Noon, 1-4PM M,W,F; 9AM-Noon T,Th,Sat; 6-8PM W.

Candia

Real Estate Recording—Candia Town Clerk, 74 High Street, Candia, NH 3034. Fax: 603-483-0252. 8:30-11AM M; 5:30PM-8PM T,Th; 9AM-1PM W,F.

Canterbury

Real Estate Recording—Canterbury Town Clerk, 10 Hackleboro Road, Canterbury, NH 3224. 10AM-2PM M; 11AM-6PM T; 5-8:30PM Th.

Carroll

Real Estate Recording—Carroll County Register of Deeds, Route 171, 95 Water Village Rd. Ossipee, NH 3864. Fax: 603-539-5239. 9AM-5PM.

Carroll Town Clerk, School Road, Twin Mountain, NH 3595. Fax: 603-846-5754. 9AM-Noon, 6-8PM M; 9AM-3PM T,W,Th.

Felony, Civil Actions Over $1,500—Superior Court, PO Box 433, Ossipee, NH 03864. 603-539-2201. 8AM-4:30PM. Access by: mail, in person.

Misdemeanor, Civil Actions Under $25,000, Eviction, Small Claims—Northern Carroll County District Court, PO Box 940, Conway, NH 03818. 603-356-7710. 8:30AM-4:30PM. Access by: mail, phone, in person.

Southern Carroll County District Court, PO Box 421, Ossipee, NH 03864. 603-539-4561. 8AM-4PM. Access by: mail, in person. Special note: The former Wolfeboro District Court has been combined with this court.

Probate—Probate Court, PO Box 419, Ossipee, NH 03864. 603-539-4123, Fax: 603-539-4761. 8:30AM-4:30PM (phone is answered from 11:30 AM-4:30 PM. Access by: mail, in person.

Center Harbor

Real Estate Recording—Center Harbor Town Clerk, Main Street, Center Harbor, NH 3226. Fax: 603-253-8420. 9A-3P ex. W; 9A-12, 6:30-8:30P W; Winter: 9A-12, 6.

Charlestown

Real Estate Recording—Charlestown Town Clerk, 26 Railroad Street, Charlestown, NH 3603. 8AM-1PM, 1:30-6PM M; 8AM-1PM, 1:30-4PM T-F.

Chatham

Real Estate Recording—Chatham Town Clerk, Route 113 North Chatham, Center Conway, NH 3813. 4-7PM T.

Cheshire

Real Estate Recording—Cheshire County Register of Deeds, 33 West Street, Keene, NH 3431. Fax: 603-352-7678. 8:30-4:30PM.

Felony, Civil Actions Over $1,500—Superior Court, PO Box 444, Keene, NH 03431. 603-352-6902. 9AM-4:30PM. Access by: mail, in person.

Misdemeanor, Civil Actions Under $25,000, Eviction, Small Claims—Jaffrey-Peterborough District Court, 7 Knight St, PO Box 39, Jaffrey, NH 03452-0039. 603-532-8698. 8AM-4PM. Access by: mail, in person.

Keene District Court, PO Box 364, Keene, NH 03431. 603-352-2559. 8AM-4PM. Access by: mail, in person.

Probate—Probate Court, 12 Court St, Keene, NH 03431. 603-357-7786. 8AM-4:30PM. Access by: mail, in person.

Chester

Real Estate Recording—Chester Town Clerk, 1 Chester Street, Chester, NH 3036. 9AM-12:45PM.

Chesterfield

Real Estate Recording—Chesterfield Town Clerk, 504 Route 63, Chesterfield, NH 3443. 9AM-5:30PM M,W; 5-8PM Th.

Chichester

Real Estate Recording—Chichester Town Clerk, 54 Main St. Chichester, NH 3234. Fax: 603-798-3170. 1-6:30PM M,T; 9AM-1PM W.

Claremont

Real Estate Recording—Claremont UCC Filing Officer, City Hall - Finance Office, 58 Tremont Square, Claremont, NH 3743. Fax: 603-542-7014. 9AM-5PM.

Clarksville

Real Estate Recording—Clarksville Town Clerk, RFD 1, Box 460, Pittsburg, NH 3592. 7-8:30PM T; 7-8PM Th.

Colebrook

Real Estate Recording—Colebrook Town Clerk, 10 Bridge Street, Colebrook, NH 3576. Fax: 603-237-9852. 9AM-5PM M; 9AM-3PM T,Th,F; 1PM-3PM W.

Columbia

Real Estate Recording—Columbia Town Clerk, RR 1, Box 383-P, Colebrook, NH 3576. Fax: 603-237-8270. 3-5PM M,W; Noon-3PM F.

Concord

Real Estate Recording—Concord City Clerk, 41 Green Street, Room 2, Concord, NH 3301. Fax: 603-228-2724. 8AM-4:30PM.

Conway

Real Estate Recording—Conway Town Clerk, 1634 Main St. Center Conway, NH 3813. Fax: 603-447-1348. 9AM-5PM.

Coos

Real Estate Recording—Coos County Register of Deeds, Coos County Courthouse, 55 School St, Suite 103, Lancaster, NH 3584. Fax: 603-788-4291. 8AM-4PM.

Felony, Civil Actions Over $1,500—Superior Court, 55 School St #301, Lancaster, NH 03584. 603-788-4900. 8AM-4:15PM. Access by: mail, phone, in person.

Misdemeanor, Civil Actions Under $25,000, Eviction, Small Claims—Berlin District Court, 220 Main St, Berlin, NH 03570. 603-752-3160. 8AM-4PM. Access by: mail, in person.

Colebrook District Court, PO Box 5, Colebrook, NH 03576. 603-237-4229. 8AM-Noon,1-4PM. Access by: mail, in person.

Gorham District Court, PO Box 176, Gorham, NH 03581. 603-466-2454, Fax: 603-466-3631. 8AM-4PM. Access by: mail, in person.

Lancaster District Court, 55 School St, Suite 201, Lancaster, NH 03584. 603-788-4485. 8:30AM-4PM. Access by: mail, in person.

Probate—Probate Court, 55 School St #104, Lancaster, NH 03584. 603-788-2001. 8AM-4PM. Access by: mail, in person.

Cornish

Real Estate Recording—Cornish Town Clerk, Townhouse Rd. Cornish Flat, NH 3745. Fax: 603-675-5605. 9AM-Noon,4-7PM M,Th; 9AM-Noon F; 9AM-Noon last Sat of month.

Croydon

Real Estate Recording—Croydon Town Clerk, HC 63 Box 9, Newport, NH 3773. 9AM-1PM M-Th; 6PM-8PM W & Th.

Dalton

Real Estate Recording—Dalton Town Clerk, 741 Dalton Rd, Dalton, NH 3598. 603-837-9802, Fax: 603-837-9642. 1-6PM M; 8AM-4PM T-F.

Danbury

Real Estate Recording—Danbury Town Clerk, Box 4A High St. Danbury, NH 3230. Fax: 603-768-3313. 5-7PM T; 1-7PM W; 7:30AM-Noon 1st & last Sat.

Danville

Real Estate Recording—Danville Town Clerk, 127 Pine St. Danville, NH 3819. Fax: 603-382-3363. 9AM-Noon M; 4-8PM T; 9AM-1PM, 4-8PM W; 4-8PM Th.

Deerfield

Real Estate Recording—Deerfield Town Clerk, 8 Raymond Road, Deerfield, NH 3037. Fax: 603-463-2820. 8AM-7PM M; 8AM-2:30PM T-F.

Deering

Real Estate Recording—Deering Town Clerk, Route 149, RR #1 Box 166, Town Hall, Hillsborough, NH 3244. Fax: 603-464-3248. 9AM-3PM M & W; 3PM-7PM Th.

Derry

Real Estate Recording—Derry Town Clerk, 48 East Broadway, Derry, NH 3038. Fax: 603-432-6131. 7AM-4PM M,T,Th,F; 7AM-7PM W.

Dorchester

Real Estate Recording—Dorchester Town Clerk, Route 118, Rumney, NH 3266. 603-786-2764. 9AM-Noon, 3-6PM W; 9-11AM 2nd & 4th Sat.

Dover

Real Estate Recording—Dover City Clerk, 288 Central Avenue, City Hall, Dover, NH 3820. Fax: 603-790-6322. 8AM-4PM M,T,Th,F; 8AM-6PM W.

Dublin

Real Estate Recording—Dublin Town Clerk, Main Street, Town Hall, Dublin, NH 3444. Fax: 603-563-9221. 7-9PM M; 10AM-5PM W; 10Am-Noon Th.

Dummer

Real Estate Recording—Dummer Town Clerk, 1420 East Side River Rd. Dummer, NH 3588. By appointment.

Dunbarton

Real Estate Recording—Dunbarton Town Clerk, 1011 School St. Dunbarton, NH 3045. Fax: 603-774-5541. 9AM-Noon W; 5:30PM-9PM TH; 9AM-Noon F.

Durham

Real Estate Recording—Durham Town Clerk, 15 Newmarket Road, Town Hall, Durham, NH 3824. 603-868-5571, Fax: 603-868-5572. 8AM-5PM.

East Kingston

Real Estate Recording—East Kingston Town Clerk, 24 Depot Rd. East Kingston, NH 3827. Fax: 603-642-8406. 6-8PM M; 8:30AM-12:30PM T,Th,F; 4-6PM Th; Closed W.

Easton

Real Estate Recording—Easton Town Clerk, 381 Easton Valley Road, Easton, NH 3580. Fax: 603-823-7780. 10AM-Noon M; 4PM-6PM Th.

Eaton

Real Estate Recording—Eaton Town Clerk, Rt. 153, Eaton Center, NH 3832. Fax: 603-447-2840. 9-11AM M; 7-9PM T.

Effingham

Real Estate Recording—Effingham Town Clerk, Rt. 153 and Old Pound Road, South Effingham, NH 3882. Fax: 603-539-7799. 9AM-2PM M-W; 7-9PM Th.

Ellsworth

Real Estate Recording—Ellsworth Town Clerk, Ellsworth Pond Road, RR 1, Box 852, Plymouth, NH 3264. 603-726-8668. By Appointment.

Enfield

Real Estate Recording—Enfield Town Clerk, Main Street, Enfield, NH 3748. Fax: 603-632-5182. 9AM-3PM M-W & F; 11AM-7PM Th.

Epping

Real Estate Recording—Epping Town Clerk, 157 Main Street, Epping, NH 3042. Fax: 603-679-3302. Noon-8PM M; 9AM-6PM W; 9AM-3PM F.

Epsom

Real Estate Recording—Epsom Town Clerk, 946 Suncook Valley Hwy, Epsom, NH 3234. Fax: 603-736-8539. 8AM-1PM, 4:30-6:30PM M; 8AM-2:30PM Th,F; 8AM-Noon 2nd & last Sat.

Errol

Real Estate Recording—Errol Town Clerk, Town Hall, Errol, NH 3579. 603-482-3351, Fax: 603-482-3804. 9-11AM M; 5-7:30PM T; 8:30-11AM Th.

Exeter

Real Estate Recording—Exeter Town Clerk, 10 Front Street, Exeter, NH 3833. Fax: 603-772-4709. 8:30AM-3:30PM.

Farmington

Real Estate Recording—Farmington Town Clerk, Main Street, Town Hall, Farmington, NH 3835. 603-755-3657, Fax: 603-755-9128. 9AM-5PM.

Fitzwilliam

Real Estate Recording—Fitzwilliam Town Clerk, Town Hall, 13 NH Rte. 119 West, Fitzwilliam, NH 3447. Fax: 603-585-7744. 8:30AM-12:30 PM M,F; 1-5PM T,Th; 6-9PM W.

Francestown

Real Estate Recording—Francestown Town Clerk, 15 New Boston Rd. Francestown, NH 3043. Fax: 603-547-2818. 8AM-Noon M-Th; 6:30-7:30PM Mon & Th.

Franconia

Real Estate Recording—Franconia Town Clerk, Town Hall, 421 Main St. Franconia, NH 3580. Fax: 603-823-5581. 8AM-Noon T-Th.

Franklin

Real Estate Recording—Franklin City Clerk, 316 Central Street, Franklin, NH 3235. 8AM-5PM.

Freedom

Real Estate Recording—Freedom Town Clerk, Maple St. Freedom, NH 3836. Fax: 603-539-8270. 6:30PM-8PM M & W; 9AM-Noon Sat.

Fremont

Real Estate Recording—Fremont Town Clerk, 259 South Rd. Fremont, NH 3044. Fax: 603-895-3149. 9:30AM-1:30PM T,W,F; 3-8PM Th.

Gilford

Real Estate Recording—Gilford Town Clerk, 47 Cherry Valley Road, Town Hall, Gilford, NH 3246. Fax: 603-528-1183. 8AM-5PM.

Gilmanton

Real Estate Recording—Gilmanton Town Clerk, Route 107, Academy Building, Gilmanton, NH 3237. Fax: 603-267-6701. 9AM-Noon,7-8:30PM M; 9AM-Noon, 1-4PM W,F; 9AM-Noon Th.

Gilsum

Real Estate Recording—Gilsum Town Clerk, 109 Alstead Hill Rd. Gilsum, NH 3448. Fax: 603-352-0845. 6-8PM T; 10AM-Noon W.

Goffstown

Real Estate Recording—Goffstown Town Clerk, 16 Main Street, Goffstown, NH 3045. Fax: 603-497-8993. 8:30AM-4:30PM M,T,F; 8:30AM-12 W; 8:30AM-6PM Th.

Gorham

Real Estate Recording—Gorham Town Clerk, 20 Park Street, Gorham, NH 3581. Fax: 603-466-3100. 8:30AM-Noon, 1-5PM M, W, F; 8:30AM-1PM, 2-5PM T,Th.

Goshen

Real Estate Recording—Goshen Town Clerk, Town Hall, Goshen, NH 3752. 8:30AM-Noon, 1-5PM M,W,F.

Grafton

Real Estate Recording—Grafton County Register of Deeds, Route 10, North Haverhill, NH 3774. Fax: 603-787-2363. 7:30AM-4:30PM (Research); 8AM-3:45PM(Recording).

Grafton Town Clerk, Library Rd. Grafton, NH 3240. Fax: 603-523-4397. 7-9PM M; 9AM-Noon W; 9AM-Noon, 7-9PM Th; 9AM-Noon last Sat of month.

Felony, Civil Actions Over $1,500—Superior Court, RR1 Box 65, North Haverhill, NH 03774. 603-787-6961. 8AM-4:30PM. Access by: mail, in person.

Misdemeanor, Civil Actions Under $25,000, Eviction, Small Claims—Haverhill District Court, RR1 Box 65, North Haverhill, NH 03785. 603-787-6626. 8:30AM-4:30PM. Access by: mail, in person.

Lebanon District Court, 38 Centerra Parkway, Lebanon, NH 03766. 603-643-3555. 8AM-4PM. Access by: mail, in person.

Littleton District Court, 134 Main St, Littleton, NH 03561. 603-444-7750. 8AM-4PM. Access by: mail, in person.

Plymouth District Court, 26 Green St, Plymouth, NH 03264. 603-536-3326. 8AM-4PM. Access by: mail, in person.

Probate—Probate Court, RR1 Box 65C, North Haverhill, NH 03774-9700. 603-787-6931. 8AM-4PM. Access by: mail, phone, in person.

Grantham

Real Estate Recording—Grantham Town Clerk, 34 Dunbar Hill Road, Grantham, NH 3753. 603-863-5608, Fax: 603-863-4499. 7:30AM-4:30PM M-Th.

Greenfield

Real Estate Recording—Greenfield Town Clerk, Francestown Road, Greenfield, NH 3047. Fax: 603-547-2782. 6PM-7:30PM M,Th.

Greenland

Real Estate Recording—Greenland Town Clerk, 575 Portsmouth Avenue, Greenland, NH 3840. Fax: 603-430-3761. 9AM-4:30PM; Noon-8PM M.

Greenville

Real Estate Recording—Greenville Town Clerk, 46 Main Street, Greenville, NH 3048. Fax: 603-878-4645. 10AM-4PM T,Th; 10AM-4PM, 7-9PM W.

Groton

Real Estate Recording—Groton Town Clerk, North Groton Road, Groton, NH 3241. 10AM-6PM M,F; 10AM-2PM 1st & last Sat.

Hampstead

Real Estate Recording—Hampstead Town Clerk, 11 Main Street, Town Office Building, Hampstead, NH 3841. Fax: 603-329-6628. 8AM-4PM (F open until Noon).

Hampton

Real Estate Recording—Hampton Town Clerk, 136 Winnacunnet Road, Hampton, NH 3842. Fax: 603-929-5917. 9AM-6:30PM M; 9AM-5PM T-F.

Hampton Falls

Real Estate Recording—Hampton Falls Town Clerk, 1 Drinkwater Road, Town Hall, Hampton Falls, NH 3844. Fax: 603-926-1848. 9AM-Noon,1-4PM, 6:30-7:30PM M,T,Th.

Hancock

Real Estate Recording—Hancock Town Clerk, School Street, Hancock, NH 3449. 603-525-4441, Fax: 603-525-9327. 7PM-9PM M; 3-6PM Wed.

Hanover

Real Estate Recording—Hanover Town Clerk, 41 South Main Street, Hanover, NH 3755. 603-643-4123, Fax: 603-643-1720. 8:30AM-4:30PM.

Harrisville

Real Estate Recording—Harrisville Town Clerk, Selectman's Office, Chesham Rd. Harrisville, NH 3450. Fax: 603-827-2917. 9-11AM, 4:30-7PM T; 4:30-7PM W.

Hart's Location

Real Estate Recording—Hart's Location Town Clerk, Route 302, Hart's Location, NH 3812. By Appointment.

Haverhill

Real Estate Recording—Haverhill Town Clerk, RR 1 Box 23A, N. Haverhill, NH 3774. Fax: 603-787-2226. 9AM-4:30PM.

Hebron

Real Estate Recording—Hebron Town Clerk, Cooper Rd. East Hebron, NH 3232. 6-8PM W; 4-6PM 1st Sat of month.

Henniker

Real Estate Recording—Henniker Town Clerk, 2 Depot Hill Road, Henniker, NH 3242. Fax: 603-428-4366. 8AM-5:30PM M; 8AM-Noon T;8AM-4:30PM W,F;last Sat of month 10am-12.

Hill

Real Estate Recording—Hill Town Clerk, Town Hall, 32B Crescent Street, Hill, NH 3243. Fax: 603-934-1094. 6-9PM T; 1-3PM W; 9AM-3PM Th.

Hillsborough

Real Estate Recording—Hillsborough County Treasurer, 19 Temple Street, Nashua, NH 3060. Fax: 603-594-4137. 8AM-3:45PM.

Hillsborough Town Clerk, 29 School Street, Hillsborough, NH 3244. Fax: 603-464-4270. 9AM-5PM.

Felony, Civil Actions Over $1,500—Superior Court-North District, 300 Chestnut St Rm 127, Manchester, NH 03101. 603-424-9951. 8AM-4PM. Access by: mail, in person.

Superior Court-South District, 30 Spring St, Nashua, NH 03061. 603-883-6461. 8AM-4PM. Access by: mail, in person.

Misdemeanor, Civil Actions Under $25,000, Eviction, Small Claims—Goffstown District Court, PO Box 129, Goffstown, NH 03045. 603-497-2597. 8AM-4PM. Access by: mail, in person.

Hillsborough District Court, PO Box 763, Hillsborough, NH 03244. 603-464-5811. 8AM-3:30PM. Access by: mail, in person.

Manchester District Court, PO Box 456, Manchester, NH 03105. 603-624-6510. 8AM-4PM. Access by: mail, in person.

Merrimack District Court, PO Box 324, Merrimack, NH 03054-0324. 603-424-9916. 8:30AM-3PM. Access by: mail, in person.

Milford District Court, PO Box 148, Amherst, NH 03031. 603-673-2900. 8AM-4PM. Access by: mail, in person.

Nashua District Court, Walnut St Oval, Nashua, NH 03060. 603-880-3333. 8AM-4:15PM. Access by: mail, in person.

Probate—Probate Court, PO Box P, Nashua, NH 03061-6015. 603-882-1231, Fax: 603-882-1620. 8AM-4PM. Access by: mail, in person.

Hinsdale

Real Estate Recording—Hinsdale Town Clerk, 27 Spring Street, Hinsdale, NH 3451. 8:30AM-5PM T-Th; 1PM-7PM F.

Holderness

Real Estate Recording—Holderness Town Clerk, Route 3, Town Hall, Holderness, NH 3245. Fax: 603-968-9954. 9:30AM-2:30PM M-F; 9:30AM-4:30PM 1st & 3rd Th.

Hollis

Real Estate Recording—Hollis Town Clerk, 7 Monument Square, Hollis, NH 3049. Fax: 603-465-3701. 8AM-1PM M,W,F; 7-9PM Mon, 1st & 3rd T; 8-11AM 1st Sat of month.

Hooksett

Real Estate Recording—Hooksett Town Clerk, 16 North Main Street, Hooksett, NH 3106. Fax: 603-485-4423. 8AM-4:30PM.

Hopkinton

Real Estate Recording—Hopkinton Town Clerk, 44 Cedar St. Contoocook, NH 3229. 603-746-3180, Fax: 603-746-4011. 8AM-5PM.

Hudson

Real Estate Recording—Hudson Town Clerk, 12 School Street, Hudson, NH 3051. 603-886-6000. 8:30AM-4:30PM.

Jackson

Real Estate Recording—Jackson Town Clerk, Route 16B, Town Hall, Jackson, NH 3846. Fax: 603-383-6980. 3-7PM M; 8:30AM-12:30PM T-Th.

Jaffrey

Real Estate Recording—Jaffrey Town Clerk, 10 Goodnow St. Jaffrey, NH 3452. 603-532-7445, Fax: 603-532-7862. 9AM-4PM M-W; 9AM-4PM, 6-8PM Th; 9AM-Noon F.

Jefferson

Real Estate Recording—Jefferson Town Clerk, Town Hall, Main Street, Jefferson, NH 3583. Fax: 603-586-4553. 1:30PM-4:30PM M; 9AM-11:30AM T; 3-7PM Th.

Keene

Real Estate Recording—Keene City Clerk, 3 Washington Street, Keene, NH 3431. 603-357-9801, Fax: 603-357-9884. 8:30AM-5PM.

Kensington

Real Estate Recording—Kensington Town Clerk, Town Hall, 95 Amesbury Rd. Rte 150, Kensington, NH 3833. Fax: 603-778-4949. 8:30-11:30AM M & Th; 6-8PM T; 8:30-11:30AM, 6-8PM W.

Kingston

Real Estate Recording—Kingston Town Clerk, 163 Main Street, Kingston, NH 3848. 603-643-8195, Fax: 603-642-3204. 8:30AM-Noon,1-4PM, 7-9PM M,T; 8:30AM-Noon, 1-4PM W-F.

Laconia

Real Estate Recording—Laconia City Clerk, 45 Beacon Street East, City Hall, Laconia, NH 3246. 603-524-1520, Fax: 603-524-1520. 8:30AM-4:30PM.

Lancaster

Real Estate Recording—Lancaster Town Clerk, 25 Main Street, Lancaster, NH 3584. 603-788-3391, Fax: 603-788-2114. 8:30AM-5PM.

Landaff

Real Estate Recording—Landaff Town Clerk, 23 Jim Noyes Hill Rd. Landaff, NH 3585. 603-835-2907, Fax: 603-838-6220. 5PM-7PM T.

Langdon

Real Estate Recording—Langdon Town Clerk, Village Rd. Box 158A, Langdon Town Hall, Langdon, NH 3602. Fax: 603-835-2389. 10AM-Noon, 3-6PM T.

Lebanon

Real Estate Recording—Lebanon City Clerk, 51 North Park Street, Lebanon, NH 3766. Fax: 603-448-4891. 8AM-5PM.

Lee

Real Estate Recording—Lee Town Clerk, 7 Mast Road, Town Hall, Lee, NH 3824. 603-659-5414, Fax: 603-659-7202. 8:30AM-4:30PM M,W,F; 8:30AM-6PM 2nd & 4th M.

Lempster

Real Estate Recording—Lempster Town Clerk, 856 US Route 10, East Lempster, NH 3605. 603-863-3213, Fax: 603-863-8105. 9AM-Noon M,T,Th,F; 9AM-Noon, 5-7PM W.

Lincoln

Real Estate Recording—Lincoln Town Clerk, Main Street, Lincoln, NH 3251. 603-745-8971, Fax: 603-745-6743. 8AM-4PM.

Lisbon

Real Estate Recording—Lisbon Town Clerk, 21 School Street, Lisbon, NH 3585. Fax: 603-838-6790. 9AM-Noon, 1PM-4:30PM.

Litchfield

Real Estate Recording—Litchfield Town Clerk, 2 Liberty Way, Suite 3, Litchfield, NH 3052. 8AM-3PM M-F; 6:30PM-8PM Mon; 10AM-Noon last Sat of month.

Littleton

Real Estate Recording—Littleton Town Clerk, 26 Union Street, Littleton, NH 3561. Fax: 603-444-1715. 8AM-12:30PM, 1-4PM.

Londonderry

Real Estate Recording—Londonderry Town Clerk, 50 Nashua Rd. Suite 100, Londonderry, NH 3053. 603-432-1126, Fax: 603-432-1142. 8:30AM-5PM.

Loudon

Real Estate Recording—Loudon Town Clerk, South Village Road, Loudon, NH 3301. 603-798-4541, Fax: 603-798-4546. 3-9PM T; 9AM-4PM W,Th.

Lyman

Real Estate Recording—Lyman Town Clerk, 65 Parker Hill Farm, Lyman, NH 3585. 603-838-6009, Fax: 603-838-6818. 8AM-11:30AM, 1-5PM M; 8AM-2PM T; 8AM-Noon W & Th; Closed F.

Lyme

Real Estate Recording—Lyme Town Clerk, 38 Union St. Lyme, NH 3768. Fax: 603-795-4637. 9AM-12:30PM, 4:30-6:30pm M,W; 9am-12:30PM F.

Lyndeborough

Real Estate Recording—Lyndeborough Town Clerk, Clerk's Office, Citizens Hall Road, Lyndeborough, NH 3082. 8AM-Noon, 1-3PM, 5-8PM M;.

Madbury

Real Estate Recording—Madbury Town Clerk, 13 Town Hall Road, Madbury, NH 3820. Fax: 603-742-2505. 8AM-1PM M,W,F;.

Madison

Real Estate Recording—Madison Town Clerk, Route 113, Madison, NH 3849. Fax: 603-367-4547. 9AM-3:30PM M,T,W,F; 9AM-Noon Sat.

Manchester

Real Estate Recording—Manchester City Clerk, One City Hall Plaza, Manchester, NH 3101. Fax: 603-624-6481. 9AM-5PM.

Marlborough

Real Estate Recording—Marlborough Town Clerk, 236 E. Main St. Town Hall, Marlborough, NH 3455. 603-876-3842, Fax: 603-876-3313. 9AM-4:30PM M,T,Th; 9AM-Noon W; 9AM-2PM F.

Marlow

Real Estate Recording—Marlow Town Clerk, c/o David Stewart, Sand Pond Rd. Marlow, NH 3456. Fax: 603-446-6212. 4:30-7PM F; 10AM-12:30 Sat.

Mason

Real Estate Recording—Mason Town Clerk, 16 Darling Hill Rd. Mason, NH 3048. Fax: 603-878-6146. 1-4PM T; 9AM-Noon, 7-9PM Th.

Meredith

Real Estate Recording—Meredith Town Clerk, 41 Main Street, Meredith, NH 3253. Fax: 603-279-1042. 8AM-4PM.

Merrimack

Real Estate Recording—Merrimack County Register of Deeds, 163 North Main St. Concord, NH 3301. Fax: 603-226-0868. 8AM-4:15PM.

Merrimack Town Clerk, 6 Baboosic Lake Road, Merrimack, NH 3054. 603-424-3531. 8:30AM-4:30PM M-F; 2nd & 4th M 8:30AM-7PM.

Felony, Civil Actions Over $1,500—Superior Court, PO Box 2880, Concord, NH 03302-2880. 603-225-5501. 8:30AM-4PM. Access by: mail, phone, in person.

Misdemeanor, Civil Actions Under $25,000, Eviction, Small Claims—Concord District Court, 32 Clinton St, PO Box 3420, Concord, NH 03302-3420. 603-271-6400. 8AM-4PM; Drive-up hours: 8AM-4:30PM. Access by: mail, in person. Special note: The former Pittsfield District Court has been combined with this court.

Franklin District Court, PO Box 172, Franklin, NH 03235. 603-934-3290. 8AM-4PM. Access by: mail, in person.

Henniker District Court, 2 Depot St, Henniker, NH 03242. 603-428-3214. 8AM-4PM. Access by: mail, in person.

Hooksett District Court, 101 Merrimack, Hooksett, NH 03106. 603-485-9901. 8:30AM-4PM. Access by: mail, in person.

New London District Court, PO Box 1966, New London, NH 03257. 603-526-6519. 8:30AM-4PM. Access by: mail, in person.

Probate—Probate Court, 163 N Main St, Concord, NH 03301. 603-224-9589. 8AM-4:30PM. Access by: mail, in person.

Middleton

Real Estate Recording—Middleton Town Clerk, Middleton Town Offices, 182 Kings Highway, Middleton, NH 3887. 603-473-2134, Fax: 603-473-2577. 2-7PM M; 9AM-3PM T,Th; 9AM-Noon W.

Milan

Real Estate Recording—Milan Town Clerk, Bridge Street, Milan, NH 3588. Fax: 603-449-2142. 9AM-4PM, 6PM-8PM M; 9AM-4PM T; 1-4PM, 6-8PM Th.

Milford

Real Estate Recording—Milford Town Clerk, 1 Union Square, Milford, NH 3055. Fax: 603-673-2273. 8AM-4:30PM; 8AM-7PM 2nd & 4th M.

Milton

Real Estate Recording—Milton Town Clerk, Route 125, Town Office, Milton, NH 3851. 603-652-4501, Fax: 603-652-4120. 8AM-12;30PM, 1:30-5PM M,T,F; 8AM-Noon, 2-7PM Th.

Monroe

Real Estate Recording—Monroe Town Clerk, 50 Main St. Town Hall, Monroe, NH 3771. Fax: 603-638-2021. 8:30AM-Noon, 4-6PM M; 6-9PM T; 8:30AM-Noon F or by appointment.

Mont Vernon

Real Estate Recording—Mont Vernon Town Clerk, Clerk's Office, McCollom Bldg.-Main St. Mont Vernon, NH 3057. Fax: 603-672-9021. 9AM-Noon T,Th, & last Sat of the month; 5-8PM M & W.

Moultonborough

Real Estate Recording—Moultonborough Town Clerk, Town Hall, 36 Holland St. Moultonborough, NH 3254. 603-476-2347, Fax: 603-476-5835. 9AM-Noon, 1-4PM M,W,F.

Nashua

Real Estate Recording—Nashua City Clerk, 229 Main Street, Nashua, NH 3061. Fax: 603-594-3451. 8AM-5PM.

Nelson

Real Estate Recording—Nelson Town Clerk, Nelson Village, Old Brick Schoolhouse, Nelson, NH 3457. 603-847-9043, Fax: 603-847-9043. 9AM-Noon T; 6PM-9PM W; 9AM-1PM Th.

New Boston

Real Estate Recording—New Boston Town Clerk, 7 Meeting House Hill, New Boston, NH 3070. 603-487-5571, Fax: 603-487-2885. 8AM-4PM, 6-8PM M; 8AM-4PM W,F; 4-8PM Th.

New Castle

Real Estate Recording—New Castle Town Clerk, Town Hall, 49 Main St. New Castle, NH 3854. Fax: 603-431-7710. 9AM-1PM M,W,F.

New Durham

Real Estate Recording—New Durham Town Clerk, 4 Main Street, New Durham, NH 3855. Fax: 603-859-6644. 9AM-4PM M-F; 9AM-Noon Sat.

New Hampton

Real Estate Recording—New Hampton Town Clerk, Main Street, New Hampton, NH 3256. Fax: 603-744-5106. 8AM-4PM M-W,F; 1-8PM Th.

New Ipswich

Real Estate Recording—New Ipswich Town Clerk, 661 Turnpike Rd. New Ipswich, NH 3071. 603-878-2772, Fax: 603-878-3855. 9AM-4PM M,W,Th; 1-7PM T.

New London

Real Estate Recording—New London Town Clerk, 120 Main Street, New London, NH 3257. 603-526-4046, Fax: 603-526-9494. 8:30AM-12:30PM, 1:30-4PM.

Newbury

Real Estate Recording—Newbury Town Clerk, Route 103, Old Newbury School, Newbury, NH 3255. 603-763-4940. 6PM-9PM M; 8:30AM-3:30PM T-F.

Newfields

Real Estate Recording—Newfields Town Clerk, 65 Main St. Newfields, NH 3856. 603-772-7199, Fax: 603-772-9004. 9AM-1PM, 6-8PM T; 9AM-1PM W & Th.

Newington

Real Estate Recording—Newington Town Clerk, 205 Nimble Hill Road, Town Offices, Newington, NH 3801. Fax: 603-436-7188. 10AM-3PM T-Th.

Newmarket

Real Estate Recording—Newmarket Town Clerk, 186 Main Street, Town Hall, Newmarket, NH 3857. Fax: 603-659-8508. 8AM-4:30PM.

Newport

Real Estate Recording—Newport Town Clerk, 15 Sunapee Street, Newport, NH 3773. 603-863-3000, Fax: 603-863-8008. 8AM-4:30PM.

Newton

Real Estate Recording—Newton Town Clerk, South Main Street, Town Hall, Newton, NH 3858. 603-382-4405, Fax: 603-382-9140. 9AM-1PM; 5-9PM Th.

North Hampton

Real Estate Recording—North Hampton Town Clerk, 237 Atlantic Avenue, North Hampton, NH 3862. Fax: 603-964-1514. 8:30AM-2PM M-F; 6:30-8PM Mon.

Northfield

Real Estate Recording—Northfield Town Clerk, 21 Summer Street, Northfield, NH 3276. Fax: 603-286-3328. 8:30AM-5PM M,T,Th,F.

Northumberland

Real Estate Recording—Northumberland Town Clerk, 2 State Street, Groveton, NH 3582. Fax: 603-636-1450. 9AM-Noon, 1-4PM.

Northwood

Real Estate Recording—Northwood Town Clerk, 818 First NH Turnpike, Town Hall, Northwood, NH 3261. Fax: 603-942-9107. 9AM-1PM, 4-7PM T,F; 9AM-Noon 2nd & last Sat.

Nottingham

Real Estate Recording—Nottingham Town Clerk, Town Hall, Nottingham, NH 3290. Fax: 603-679-1013. 4-8PM M,W; 1-5PM T; 8AM-1PM Th,Sat.

Orford

Real Estate Recording—Orford Town Clerk, Clerk's Office, RR 1 Box 243, Orford, NH 3777. 2-7PM T; 6-8PM W; 8-11AM Th.

Ossipee

Real Estate Recording—Ossipee Town Clerk, 55 Main St. Center Ossipee, NH 3814. Fax: 603-539-4183. 8:30AM-4:30PM.

Pelham

Real Estate Recording—Pelham Town Clerk, 6 Main Street, Town Hall, Pelham, NH 3076. Fax: 603-635-6954. 8AM-4PM (open until 7PM T).

Pembroke

Real Estate Recording—Pembroke Town Clerk, 311 Pembroke Street, Pembroke, NH 3275. Fax: 603-485-3967. 8AM-4PM.

Peterborough

Real Estate Recording—Peterborough Town Clerk, 1 Grove Street, Peterborough, NH 3458. Fax: 603-924-8001. 8AM-4:30PM M-F; 5-7PM Th.

Piermont

Real Estate Recording—Piermont Town Clerk, 573 Route 25C, Piermont, NH 3779. Fax: 603-272-4947. 1-7PM T,W.

Pittsburg

Real Estate Recording—Pittsburg Town Clerk, Spruce Lane, Pittsburg, NH 3592. Fax: 603-538-6697. 3:30-7:30PM T-Th; 9AM-1PM Sat.

Pittsfield

Real Estate Recording—Pittsfield Town Clerk, 85 Main St. Pittsfield, NH 3263. Fax: 603-435-7922. 8AM-1PM, 2-6:30PM M; 8AM-2PM T; 8AM-1PM, 2-5PM W-F.

Plainfield

Real Estate Recording—Plainfield Town Clerk, Town Clerk's Office, Box 380, Meriden, NH 3770. Fax: 603-469-3642. 7-8:30PM T; 2-4PM, 7-8:30PM W; 2-4PM Th.

Plaistow

Real Estate Recording—Plaistow Town Clerk, 145 Main Street, Town Hall, Suite 2, Plaistow, NH 3865. 603-382-8469, Fax: 603-382-7183. 8:30AM-7PM M; 8:30AM-4:30PM T-F.

Plymouth

Real Estate Recording—Plymouth Town Clerk, 6 PO Square, Town Hall, Plymouth, NH 3264. Fax: 603-536-0036. 8:30AM-4PM.

Portsmouth

Real Estate Recording—Portsmouth City Clerk, 1 Junkins Avenue, Portsmouth, NH 3801. 603-431-2000, Fax: 603-427-1526. 8:30AM-5PM.

Randolph

Real Estate Recording—Randolph Town Clerk, RD 1, Town Hall, Randolph, NH 3570. Fax: 603-466-2777. 9-11AM M; 7-9PM W.

Raymond

Real Estate Recording—Raymond Town Clerk, Epping Street, Town Office Building, Raymond, NH 3077. Fax: 603-895-0903. 8AM-7PM M; 8AM-5PM T-F.

Richmond

Real Estate Recording—Richmond Town Clerk, 105 Old Homestead Hwy. Richmond, NH 3470. 9AM-Noon, 1-4PM, 6-8PM M; 9AM-Noon T; 9AM-Noon, 1-4PM W; 9AM-Noon Th.

Rindge

Real Estate Recording—Rindge Town Clerk, 49 Payson Hill Rd. Town Office, Rindge, NH 3461. Fax: 603-899-2101. 9AM-1PM, 2-4PM M-F; 6-8PM T,W.

Rochester

Real Estate Recording—Rochester City Clerk, 31 Wakefield Street, City Hall, Rochester, NH 3867. Fax: 603-335-7565. 8AM-5PM.

Rockingham

Real Estate Recording—Rockingham County Register of Deeds, #10 Route 125, Kingston, NH 3833. Fax: 603-642-8548. 8AM-4PM.

Felony, Civil Actions Over $1,500—Superior Court, PO Box 1258, Kingston, NH 03848. 603-642-5256. 8AM-4PM. Access by: in person.

Misdemeanor, Civil Actions Under $25,000, Eviction, Small Claims—Auburn District Court, 5 Priscilla Lane, Auburn, NH 03032. 603-624-2084. 8AM-4PM. Access by: mail, in person.

Derry District Court, 10 Manning St, Derry, NH 03038. 603-434-4676. 8AM-4PM. Access by: mail, phone, in person.

Exeter District Court, PO Box 394, Exeter, NH 03833. 603-772-2931. 8AM-4PM. Access by: mail, in person.

Hampton District Court, PO Box 10, Hampton, NH 03843-0010. 603-926-8117. 8AM-4PM. Access by: mail, in person.

Plaistow District Court, PO Box 129, Plaistow, NH 03865. 603-382-4651, Fax: 603-382-4952. 8AM-4PM. Access by: mail, in person.

Portsmouth District Court, 111 Parrott Ave, Portsmouth, NH 03801. 603-431-2192. 8AM-4PM. Access by: mail, in person.

Salem District Court, 35 Geremonty Dr, Salem, NH 03079. 603-893-4483. 8AM-4PM. Access by: mail, in person.

Probate—Probate Court, PO Box 789, Kingston, NH 03848. 603-642-7117. 8AM-4PM.

Rollinsford

Real Estate Recording—Rollinsford Town Clerk, 667 Main Street, Rollinsford, NH 3869. Fax: 603-740-0254. 9AM-1PM M-W,F; 3-7PM Th.

Roxbury

Real Estate Recording—Roxbury Town Clerk, 404 Branch Rd. Roxbury, NH 3431. 7PM-8PM M.

Rumney

Real Estate Recording—Rumney Town Clerk, 15 Quincy Bog Road, Rumney, NH 3266. Fax: 603-786-2237. 9AM-1PM M,W,Th,F; 5-8PM Wed.

Rye

Real Estate Recording—Rye Town Clerk, 10 Central Road, Rye, NH 3870. Fax: 603-964-4132. 8AM-4:30PM M; 8AM-4:30PM T-F.

Salem

Real Estate Recording—Salem Town Clerk, 33 Geremonty Drive, Municipal Building, Salem, NH 3079. Fax: 603-898-1223. 8:30AM-5PM.

Salisbury

Real Estate Recording—Salisbury Town Clerk, RFD Box 180, Franklin Rd. Salisbury, NH 3268. Fax: 603-648-6658. 6-8:30PM T; 2-4:30PM, 6-8:30PM W.

Sanbornton

Real Estate Recording—Sanbornton Town Clerk, Town Offices Bldg. 573 Sanborn Rd. Sanbornton, NH 3269. Fax: 603-286-9544. 8AM-6PM M; 8AM-4PM T,Th,F;.

Sandown

Real Estate Recording—Sandown Town Clerk, 320 Main Street, Town Hall, Sandown, NH 3873. Fax: 603-887-5163. 8AM-Noon,1-3PM.

Sandwich

Real Estate Recording—Sandwich Town Clerk, Town Hall, 8 Maple St. Center Sandwich, NH 3227. Fax: 603-284-6819. 7-9PM 1st M; 9AM-3PM T,Th; 9AM-Noon last Sat of month.

Seabrook

Real Estate Recording—Seabrook Town Clerk, 99 Lafayette Rd. Seabrook, NH 3874. Fax: 603-474-8007. 9AM-12:30PM, 1-4PM.

Sharon

Real Estate Recording—Sharon Town Clerk, 586 Jarmany Hill Road, Sharon, NH 3458. 6-8PM T.

Shelburne

Real Estate Recording—Shelburne Town Clerk, 881 North Road, Philbrook Farm Inn, Shelburne, NH 3581. By appointment.

Somersworth

Real Estate Recording—Somersworth City Clerk, 157 Main Street, Somersworth, NH 3878. Fax: 603-692-7338. 9AM-5PM M,W,F; 8AM-5PM T & Th.

South Hampton

Real Estate Recording—South Hampton Town Clerk, 304 Main Ave. South Hampton, NH 3827. 7-8:30PM M,T; 12:30-2PM W; 9:30-11:30AM F.

Springfield

Real Estate Recording—Springfield Town Clerk, 759 New London Road, Springfield, NH 3284. Fax: 603-763-3336. 10AM-Noon, 1-4PM M-F; 4-8PM Th; Summer hours: 9AM-Noon, 1-4PM, 4-8PM Th.

Stark

Real Estate Recording—Stark Town Clerk, 1189 Stark Hwy. Groveton, NH 3582. Fax: 603-636-6199. 10AM-4PM T,Th.

Stewartstown

Real Estate Recording—Stewartstown Town Clerk, High Street, West Stewartstown, NH 3597. 9:30AM-1PM, 4-6PM T,Th; 9:30AM-1PM W,F.

Stoddard

Real Estate Recording—Stoddard Town Clerk, 2175 Route 9, Stoddard, NH 3464. Fax: 603-446-7770. 9AM-2PM, 4-6PM T,Th.

Strafford

Real Estate Recording—Strafford County Register of Deeds, County Farm Road, Dover, NH 3820. 603-742-1458, Fax: 603-749-5130. 8:30AM-4:30PM.

Strafford Town Clerk, Town Hall, Strafford, NH 3884. Fax: 603-664-7276. 9AM-Noon, 4-8PM M & T; 9AM-Noon W.

Felony, Civil Actions Over $1,500—Superior Court, PO Box 799, Dover, NH 03821-0799. 603-742-3065. 8:30AM-4:30PM. Access by: mail, in person.

Misdemeanor, Civil Actions Under $25,000, Eviction, Small Claims—Dover District Court, 25 St Thomas St, Dover, NH 03820. 603-742-7202. 8AM-4PM. Access by: mail, in person.

Durham District Court, 1 New Market Rd, Durham, NH 03824. 603-868-2323. 8:30AM-4PM. Access by: mail, in person.

Rochester District Court, 76 N Main St, Rochester, NH 03866. 603-332-3516. 8AM-4:30PM. Access by: mail, in person.

Somersworth District Court, 2 Pleasant St, Somersworth, NH 03878-2543. 603-692-5967, Fax: 603-692-5752. 8AM-5:30PM. Access by: mail, phone, in person. Special note: The first 3 Tuesdays of the month the court is open until 8:30PM.

Probate—Probate Court, PO Box 799, Dover, NH 03821-0799. 603-742-2550. 8AM-4:30PM. Access by: mail, phone, in person.

Stratford

Real Estate Recording—Stratford Town Clerk, Fire Station, North Stratford, NH 3590. Fax: 603-922-5533. 9AM-Noon, 1-4PM M-W; 8-11AM Th.

Stratham

Real Estate Recording—Stratham Town Clerk, 10 Bunker Hill Avenue, Stratham, NH 3885. Fax: 603-772-5937. 8:30AM-4PM.

Sugar Hill

Real Estate Recording—Sugar Hill Town Clerk, 1448 Main St. Town Hall, Sugar Hill, NH 3585. Fax: 603-823-8446. 4-6PM M; 9-Noon T-Th; 10-Noon Sat.

Sullivan

Real Estate Recording—Sullivan County Register of Deeds, 20 Main Street, Newport, NH 3773. Fax: 603-863-0013. 8AM-4PM.

Sullivan Town Clerk, South Road, Box 228, Keene, NH 3431. 603-847-2340. 8AM-9AM.

Felony, Civil Actions Over $1,500—Superior Court, 22 Main St, Newport, NH 03773. 603-863-3450. 8AM-4:30PM. Access by: mail, in person.

Misdemeanor, Civil Actions Under $25,000, Eviction, Small Claims—Claremont District Court, PO Box 313, Claremont, NH 03743. 603-542-6064. 8AM-4PM. Access by: mail, phone, in person.

Newport District Court, PO Box 581, Newport, NH 03773. 603-863-1832. 8AM-4PM. Access by: mail, phone, in person.

Probate—Probate Court, PO Box 417, Newport, NH 03773. 603-863-3150. 8AM-4:30PM. Access by: mail, phone, in person.

Sunapee

Real Estate Recording—Sunapee Town Clerk, 23 Edgemont Road, Sunapee, NH 3782. Fax: 603-763-4925. 9AM-5PM M,T,Th,F; 9AM-1PM W.

Surry

Real Estate Recording—Surry Town Clerk, 1 Village Rd. Surry, NH 3431. Fax: 603-355-1380. 6PM-9PM T.

Sutton

Real Estate Recording—Sutton Town Clerk, Main St. South Sutton, NH 3221. Fax: 603-927-4631. 9AM-4PM M,T,Th,F; 4-8PM W.

Swanzey

Real Estate Recording—Swanzey Town Clerk, 620 Old Homestead, East Swanzey, NH 3446. Fax: 603-352-6250. 9AM-5PM.

Tamworth

Real Estate Recording—Tamworth Town Clerk, Town Hall, Tamworth, NH 3886. Fax: 603-323-2347. 9AM-Noon, 1PM-4PM.

Temple

Real Estate Recording—Temple Town Clerk, Rte. 45, Temple, NH 3084. 603-878-3873, Fax: 603-878-5067. 9AM-1PM, 7-9PM T; 9AM-1PM W,Th.

Thornton

Real Estate Recording—Thornton Town Clerk, RFD 1, Box 830-B, Campton, NH 3223. 603-764-9450, Fax: 603-726-2078. 8AM-4PM.

Tilton

Real Estate Recording—Tilton Town Clerk, 257 Main Street, Tilton, NH 3276. 603-286-4521, Fax: 603-286-3519. 8:30AM-4:15PM.

Troy

Real Estate Recording—Troy Town Clerk, Town Hall, 16 Central Square, Troy, NH 3465. Fax: 603-242-3430. 9AM-4:30PM M-W; 1-7PM Th; 9AM-1:30PM.F.

Tuftonboro

Real Estate Recording—Tuftonboro Town Clerk, Town Hall, Center Tuftonboro, NH 3816. Fax: 603-569-4328. 9AM-1PM, 2-4PM M,W,F.

Unity

Real Estate Recording—Unity Town Clerk, HCR 66, Box 176A, Newport, NH 3773. Fax: 603-542-9736. 9AM-5PM M,F; 9AM-6PM W; 11AM-3PM Th.

Wakefield

Real Estate Recording—Wakefield Town Clerk, 2 High St. Sanbornville, NH 3872. Fax: 603-522-6794. 8:30AM-4PM T-F; 8:30AM-1:30PM Sat.

Walpole

Real Estate Recording—Walpole Town Clerk, Town Hall-Town Clerk's Office, Elm St. Walpole, NH 3608. 7AM-Noon, 1-4PM T,W,F; 6-7PM W.

Warner

Real Estate Recording—Warner Town Clerk, Main St. Warner, NH 3278. Fax: 603-456-3647. 8AM-3PM M-Th; 6-8PM Tue.

Warren

Real Estate Recording—Warren Town Clerk, Rte. 25, RR 1 Box 2008, Warren, NH 3279. Fax: 603-764-9315. 6:30PM-8:30PM W,Th.

Washington

Real Estate Recording—Washington Town Clerk, Clerk's Office, Washington, NH 3280. 603-495-3667, Fax: 603-495-3299. 5-9PM Th; 9AM-3PM F; 9AM-1PM 2nd & last Sat.

Waterville Valley

Real Estate Recording—Waterville Valley Town Clerk, Clerk's Office, Waterville Valley, NH 3215. Fax: 603-236-2056. 8AM-4:30PM.

Weare

Real Estate Recording—Weare Town Clerk, Town Office Bldg. 15 Flanders Memorial Dr. Weare, NH 3281. Fax: 603-529-4554. 8AM-4PM; 8AM-7PM W.

Webster

Real Estate Recording—Webster Town Clerk, 945 Battle St. Rte 127, Webster, NH 3303. 9AM-Noon, 1-4PM M, W; 7-9PM Mon.

Wentworth

Real Estate Recording—Wentworth Town Clerk,

Westmoreland

Real Estate Recording—Westmoreland Town Clerk, 108 Pierce Lane, Westmoreland, NH 3467. 603-399-4471. 7-8:30PM M,W; 10AM-1PM F.

Whitefield

Real Estate Recording—Whitefield Town Clerk, 7 Jefferson Road, Whitefield, NH 3598. 603-837-2551, Fax: 603-837-3148. 9AM-4PM M-W,F; 9AM-6PM Th.

Wilmot

Real Estate Recording—Wilmot Town Clerk, Town Clerk's Office, Kearsarge Valley Rd. Wilmot, NH 3287. Fax: 603-526-2523. 9AM-1PM T; 4-7PM W; 9AM-1PM Th; 9AM-Noon 1st & last Sat of month.

Wilton

Real Estate Recording—Wilton Town Clerk, 42 Main Street, Wilton, NH 3086. Fax: 603-654-6663. 9AM-4PM M,T,F; 9AM-7PM Th.

Winchester

Real Estate Recording—Winchester Town Clerk, Main Street, Winchester, NH 3470. Fax: 603-239-4710. 8AM-5PM M-W & F; 8AM-Noon, 4PM-8PM Th.

Windham

Real Estate Recording—Windham Town Clerk, 3 North Lowell Road, P.O. Box 120, Windham, NH 3087. 603-432-7732, Fax: 603-425-6582. 9AM-8PM M; 9AM-5PM, T-F.

Windsor

Real Estate Recording—Windsor Town Clerk, HC68, Box 378, Rte. 31, Washington Rd. Hillsborough, NH 3244. 7PM-9PM W.

Wolfeboro

Real Estate Recording—Wolfeboro Town Clerk, 84 South Main Street, Wolfeboro, NH 3894. Fax: 603-569-8167. 8AM-4PM.

Woodstock

Real Estate Recording—Woodstock Town Clerk, Clerk's Office, 165 Lost River Rd. North Woodstock, NH 3262. 603-745-9085, Fax: 603-745-2393. 8AM-4PM.

Federal Courts

US District Court

Concord Division Warren B Rudman Courthouse, 55 Pleasant St, #110, Concord, NH 03301603-225-1423 Counties: Belknap, Carroll, Cheshire, Coos, Grafton, Hillsborough, Merrimack, Rockingham, Strafford, Sullivan.

US Bankruptcy Court

Manchester Division Room 404, 275 Chestnut St, Manchester, NH 03101603-666-7532, Record Room: 603-666-7626 Fax: 603-666-7408 Counties: Belknap, Carroll, Cheshire, Coos, Grafton, Hillsborough, Merrimack, Rockingham, Strafford, Sullivan. www.nhb.uscourts.gov

New Jersey

Attorney General's Office
25 Market St, CN-080   609-292-8740
Trenton, NJ 08625-0080   Fax: 609-292-3508
www.state.nj.us/lps

Governor's Office
125 W State St, CN001   609-292-6000
Trenton, NJ 08625-0001   Fax: 609-292-3454
www.state.nj.us/governor/office.htm

State Archives
185 W. State Street, PO Box 307   609-633-8334
Trenton, NJ 08625-0307   Fax: 609-396-2454
www.state.nj.us/state/darm/darm.html

Capital:	Trenton
	Mercer County
Time Zone:	EST
Number of Counties:	21
Population:	8,052,849
Web Site:	www.state.nj.us

Search Unclaimed Property Online
www.state.nj.us/treasury/taxation/unclaimsrch.htm

State Agencies

Criminal Records
Division of State Police, Records and Identification Section, PO Box 7068, West Trenton, NJ 08628-0068; 609-882-2000 x2878; Fax: 609-530-5780; 9AM-5PM. Access by: mail.

Corporation Records
Limited Liability Company Records
Fictitious Name
Limited Partnerships
Department of Treasury, Division of Commercial Recording, PO 308, Trenton, NJ 08625 (225 W State St, 3rd Fl, Trenton, NJ 08608); 609-292-9292; 8:30AM-5:00PM. Access by: mail, phone, in person, online. www.state.nj.us/njbgs

Trademarks/Servicemarks
Department of State, Trademark Division, PO Box 453, Trenton, NJ 08625 (820 Bear Tavern Rd, 2nd Floor, West Trenton, NJ 08628); 609-530-6422; 8AM-5PM. Access by: mail.

Uniform Commercial Code
UCC Section, Secretary of State, PO 303, Trenton, NJ 08625 (225 West State St, Trenton, NJ 08608); 609-292-9292; 8AM-5PM. Access by: mail. www.state.nj.us/njbgs

Federal Tax Liens
State Tax Liens
Records not available from state agency.

Federal tax liens are filed at the county, state tax liens filed at the Superior Court in Trenton.

Sales Tax Registrations
Records not available from state agency.

Sales tax information is considered confidential. The only way to verify if an entity has a license is to ask to look at the certificate at the place of business, per Joan Bench, Chief of Taxpayer Services Branch.

Workers' Compensation Records
Labor Department, Division of Workers Compensation, John Fitch Plaza, CN381, Trenton, NJ 08625 (Labor Building, 6th Floor, John Fitch Plaza, Trenton, NJ 08625); 609-292-6026; Fax: 609-984-3924; 8:30AM-4:30PM. Access by: mail.

Birth Certificates
Department of Health & Senior Services, Bureau of Vital Statistics, PO Box 370, Trenton, NJ 08625-0370 (S Warren St,

Room 504, Health & Agriculture Building, Trenton, NJ 08625); 609-292-4087, 609-633-2860 Credit Card Requests; Fax: 609-392-4292; 9AM-5PM. Access by: mail, phone, in person. www.state.nj.us/health

Divorce Records

Clerk of Superior Court, Records Center, PO Box 967, Trenton, NJ 08625-0967 (Corner of Jerser & Tremont Streets, Building #2, Trenton, NJ 08625); 609-777-0092; Fax: 609-777-0094; 8:30AM-4PM. Access by: mail.

Death Records

Department of Health, Bureau of Vital Statistics, PO Box 370, Trenton, NJ 08625-0370; 609-292-4087, 609-633-2860 Credit Card Requests; Fax: 609-392-4292; 9AM-4PM. Access by: mail, phone, fax, in person.

Death Records

Department of Health, Bureau of Vital Records, PO Box 370, Trenton, NJ 08625-0370; 505-827-2338; Fax: 505-984-1048; 8AM-5PM (Counter Service: 9AM-4PM). Access by: mail, phone, fax, in person.

Marriage Certificates

Department of Health & Senior Services, Bureau of Vital Statistics, PO Box 370, Trenton, NJ 08625-0370; 609-292-4087, 609-633-2860 Credit Card Requests; Fax: 609-392-4292; 8:45AM-5PM. Access by: mail, phone, in person.

Accident Reports

New Jersey State Police, Criminal Justice Records Bureau, PO Box 7068, West Trenton, NJ 08628-0068; 609-882-2000 x2234; 8AM-5PM. Access by: mail. www.state.nj.us/lps/njsp/index.html

Driver Records

Motor Vehicle Services, Driver History Abstract Unit, PO Box 142, Trenton, NJ 08666; 609-292-6500, 888-486-3339 In-state only, 609-292-6500 Suspensions; 8AM-5PM. Access by: mail, online. www.state.nj.us/mvs

Vehicle Ownership
Vehicle Identification
Boat & Vessel Ownership
Boat & Vessel Registration

Motor Vehicle Services, Certified Information Unit, PO Box 146, Trenton, NJ 08666; 609-292-6500, 888-486-3339 In-state; 8AM-5PM. Access by: mail. www.state.nj.us/mvs

Legislation-Current/Pending
Legislation-Passed

New Jersey State Legislature, State House Annex, PO Box 068, Room B01, Trenton, NJ 08625-0068; 609-292-4840 Bill Status Only, 609-292-6395 Copy Room, 800-792-8630 In State Only; Fax: 609-777-2440; 8:30AM-5PM. Access by: mail, phone, in person, online. www.njleg.state.nj.us

Voter Registration

Records not available from state agency.

The Commissioner of Registration maintains these records at the county level. Although these county agencies may permit individual look-ups, records may may only be purchased for political purposes.

GED Certificates

GED Office, CNN 500, Trenton, NJ 08675-0500; 609-777-1050;. Access by: mail. www.state.nj.us/njded/students/ged

Hunting License Information
Fishing License Information

Records not available from state agency.

They do not have a central database. You must contact the vendor where the license was purchased.

County Courts & Recording Offices

About the Courts...

Administration

Administrative Office of the Courts   609-984-0275
RJH Justice Complex, Courts Bldg 7th Floor, CN 037Fax: 609-984
Trenton, NJ 08625
www.state.nj.us/judiciary

Court Structure

Each Superior Court has 2 divisions; one for the Civil Division and another for the Criminal Division. Search requests should be addressed separately to each division.

The Special Civil Part of the Superior Court acts like a division of the court, and handles only the smaller civil claims. The small claims limit is now $2,000, up from $1,500 in 1994. The Superior Court designation refers to the court where criminal cases and civil claims over $10,000 are heard. Probate is handled by Surrogates.

Searching Hints

Effective 1/1/95, all court employees became state employees and each section is responsible for its own fees. Note that Cape May County offices are located in the city of Cape May Court House, and not in the city of Cape May.

Online Access

Online computer access is available through the ACMS, AMIS, and FACTS systems.

ACMS (Automated Case Management System) contains data on all active civil cases statewide from the Law Division-Civil Part, Chancery Division-Equity Part, the Special Civil Part for 21 counties, and the Appellate Division.

AMIS (Archival Management Information System) contains closed case information.

FACTS (Family Automated Case Tracking System) contains information on dissolutions from all counties.

The fee is $1.00 per minute of use. For further information and/or an Inquiry System Guidebook containing hardware and software requirements and an enrollment form, write to: Superior Court Clerk's Office, Electronic Access, Program, 25 Market St, CN971, Trenton NJ 08625, FAX 609-292-6564, or call 609-292-4987

About the Recording Offices...

Organization

21 counties, 21 recording offices. The recording officer title varies depending upon the county. It is either Register of Deeds or County Clerk.

UCC Records

Financing statements are filed at the state level, except for consumer goods, farm related and real estate related collateral, which are filed only with the County Clerk. Only 12 recording offices will perform UCC searches. Use search request form UCC-11. Search fees are usually $25.00 per debtor name and copy fees vary.

Lien Records

All federal tax liens are filed with the County Clerk/Register of Deeds and are indexed separately from all other liens. State tax liens comprise two categories - certificates of debt are filed with the Clerk of Superior Court (some, called docketed judgments are filed specifically with the Trenton court), and warrants of execution are filed with the County Clerk/Register of Deeds. Few counties will provide tax lien searches. Refer to The Sourcebook of County Court Records for information about New Jersey Superior Courts.

Real Estate Records

No counties will provide real estate searches. Copy and certification fees vary. Assessment and tax offices are at the municipal level.

County Courts & Recording Offices

Atlantic

Real Estate Recording—Atlantic County Clerk, 5901 Main Street, Courthouse-CN 2005, Mays Landing, NJ 8330. Fax: 609-625-4738. 8:30AM-7PM M,W; 8:30AM-4:30PM T,Th,F.

Felony—Superior Court-Criminal Division, Criminal Courthouse, 5909 Main St, Mays Landing, NJ 08330. 609-625-7000, Fax: 609-645-5875. 8:30AM-4:30PM. Access by: mail, in person.

Civil Actions Over $10,000, Probate—Superior Court-Civil Division, Civil Courthouse, Mays Landing, NJ 08330. 609-625-7000, Fax: 609-645-5875. 8:30AM-4:30PM. Access by: mail, in person.

Civil Actions Under $10,000, Eviction, Small Claims—Special Civil Part, 1201 Bacharach Blvd. Atlantic City, NJ 08401. 609-345-6700, Fax: 609-343-2214. 8:30AM-4:30PM. Access by: mail, in person.

Bergen

Real Estate Recording—Bergen County Clerk, Justice Center Room 214, 10 Main St. Hackensack, NJ 7601. 201-646-3000. 9AM-4PM.

Felony—Superior Court-Criminal Division, 10 Main St, Rm 134, Justice Center, Hackensack, NJ 07601. 201-646-2783, Fax: 201-342-9083. 8:30AM-4:30PM. Access by: mail, fax, in person.

Civil Actions Over $10,000, Probate—Superior Court-Civil Division, 10 Main St. Rm 119, Justice Center, Hackensack, NJ 07601. 201-646-2289, Fax: 201-752-4031. 8:30AM-4:30PM. Access by: mail, in person.

Civil Actions Under $10,000, Eviction, Small Claims—Special Civil Part, 10 Main St. Rm 430, Justice Center, Hackensack, NJ 07601. 201-621-4997. 8:30AM-5PM. Access by: mail, in person.

Burlington

Real Estate Recording—Burlington County Clerk, 49 Rancocas Road, Courts Facility-1st Floor, Mount Holly, NJ 8060. Fax: 609-265-0696. 8AM-4:30PM.

Felony—Superior Court-Criminal Division, 49 Rancocas Rd, Mount Holly, NJ 08060. 609-518-2568. 8AM-5PM. Access by: mail, in person.

Civil Actions Over $10,000, Probate—Superior Court-Civil Division, 49 Rancocas Rd, Mount Holly, NJ 08060. 609-265-5075. 8AM-5PM. Access by: mail, in person.

Civil Actions Under $10,000, Eviction, Small Claims—Special Civil Part, 49 Rancocas Rd. Mount Holly, NJ 08060. 609-265-5075, Fax: 609-265-3199. 8AM-5PM. Access by: mail, fax, in person.

Camden

Real Estate Recording—Camden County Clerk's Office, Courthouse Room 102, 520 Market Street, Camden, NJ 8102. Fax: 856-225-5316. 9AM-4PM.

Felony—Superior Court-Criminal Division, Hall of Justice, 101 S 5th St, Camden, NJ 08103. 856-225-7452. 8AM-4PM. Access by: mail, in person.

Civil Actions Over $10,000, Probate—Superior Court-Civil Division, Hall of Justice, 101 S 5th St, Camden, NJ 08103. 856-225-7494. 8AM-4PM. Access by: mail, in person.

Civil Actions Under $10,000, Eviction, Small Claims—Special Civil Part, Hall of Justice Complex, 101 S. 5th St. Camden, NJ 08103. 856-225-7433. 8:30AM-4:30PM. Access by: mail, in person.

Cape May

Real Estate Recording—Cape May County Clerk, 7 North Main Street, DN 109, Cape May Court House, NJ 8210. Fax: 609-465-8625. 8:30AM-4:30PM.

Felony—Superior Court-Criminal Division, DN-209-B 4 More Rd, Cape May Court House, NJ 08210. 609-463-6550, Fax: 609-463-6458. 8:30AM-4:30PM. Access by: fax, in person.

Civil Actions Over $10,000, Probate—Superior Court, Civil Division-Law, DN-203, 9 N Main St, Cape May Court House, NJ 08210. 609-463-6500, Fax: 609-463-6465. 8:30AM-4:30PM. Access by: mail, in person.

Civil Actions Under $10,000, Eviction, Small Claims—Superior Court, Civil Division-Special Civil Part, DN-203, 9 N. Main St, Cape May Court House, NJ 08210. 609-463-6502, Fax: 609-463-6465. 8:30AM-4:30PM. Access by: mail, in person.

Cumberland

Real Estate Recording—Cumberland County Clerk, 60 W. Broad St. Courthouse, Room A137, Bridgeton, NJ 8302. Fax: 856-455-1410. 8:30AM-4PM.

Felony—Superior Court-Criminal Division, PO Box 757, Bridgeton, NJ 08302. 856-453-4300, Fax: 856-451-7152. 8:30AM-4:30PM. Access by: mail, in person.

Civil Actions Over $10,000, Probate—Superior Court-Civil Division, PO Box 757, Bridgeton, NJ 08302. 856-453-4300, Fax: 856-451-7152. 8:30AM-4:30PM. Access by: mail, in person.

Civil Actions Under $10,000, Eviction, Small Claims—Special Civil Part, PO Box 10, Bridgeton, NJ 08302. 856-453-4350. 8:30AM-4:30PM. Access by: mail, phone, in person.

Essex

Real Estate Recording—Essex County Register of Deeds, 465 Martin Luther King Boulevard, Hall of Records, Room 130, Newark, NJ 7102. Fax: 973-621-6114. 9AM-4PM.

Felony—Superior Court-Criminal Division, Rm 610, Essex County Court Bldg, Newark, NJ 07102-1681. 973-623-5960, Fax: 973-623-5963. 8:30AM-4:30PM. Access by: mail, fax, in person.

Civil Actions Over $10,000, Probate—Superior Court-Civil Division, 465 Dr. Martin Luther King Blvd Room 237, Newark, NJ 07102-1681. 973-693-6460. 8:30AM-4:30PM. Access by: mail, fax, in person.

Civil Actions Under $10,000, Eviction, Small Claims—Special Civil Part, 470 Martin Luther King Blvd, Newark, NJ 07102. 973-693-6494, Fax: 973-621-5914. 8:30AM-4:30PM. Access by: mail, in person.

Gloucester

Real Estate Recording—Gloucester County Clerk, 1 North Broad Street, Corner of Broad & Delaware, Woodbury, NJ 8096. 856-853-3353, Fax: 856-853-3327. 8:30AM-4PM.

Felony—Superior Court-Criminal Division, PO Box 187, Woodbury, NJ 08096. 856-853-3531. 8:30AM-4:30 PM. Access by: mail, in person.

Civil Actions Over $10,000, Probate—Superior Court-Civil Division, 1 North Broad St, Woodbury, NJ 08096. 856-853-3250. 8:30AM-4:30 PM. Access by: mail, in person.

Civil Actions Under $10,000, Eviction, Small Claims—Special Civil Part, Old Courthouse, 1 N Broad St. Woodbury, NJ 08096. 856-853-3392, Fax: 856-853-3429. 8:30AM-4:30PM. Access by: mail, in person.

Hudson

Real Estate Recording—Hudson County Register of Deeds, 595 Newark Ave, Room 105, Jersey City, NJ 7306. Fax: 201-795-5179. 9AM-4PM.

Felony—Superior Court-Criminal Division, 595 Newark Ave, Jersey City, NJ 07306. 201-795-6680. 8:30AM-4:30PM. Access by: mail, in person.

Civil Actions Over $10,000, Probate—Superior Court-Civil Division, 583 Newark Ave, Jersey City, NJ 07306. 201-795-6723. 8:30AM-4:30PM. Access by: mail, in person.

Civil Actions Under $10,000, Eviction, Small Claims—Special Civil Part, 595 Newark Ave, Jersey City, NJ 07306. 201-646-3237. 8:30AM-4:30PM. Access by: in person.

Hunterdon

Real Estate Recording—Hunterdon County Clerk, 71 Main Street, Hall of Records, Flemington, NJ 8822. Fax: 908-782-4068. 8:30AM-4PM.

Felony—Superior Court-Criminal Division, 65 Park Ave, Flemington, NJ 08822. 908-806-4338, Fax: 908-806-4378. 8:30AM-4:30PM. Access by: mail, fax, in person.

Civil Actions Over $10,000, Probate—Superior Court-Civil Division, County Justice Center, 65 Park Ave, Flemington, NJ 08822. 908-806-5123. 8:30AM-4:30PM. Access by: mail, in person.

Civil Actions Under $10,000, Eviction, Small Claims—Special Civil Part, Hunterdon County Courthouse, 65 Park Ave, 2nd Floor, Flemington, NJ 08822. 908-788-1216. 8:30AM-4:30PM. Access by: mail, phone, in person.

Mercer

Real Estate Recording—Mercer County Clerk, 209 South Broad Street, Courthouse, Room 100, Trenton, NJ 8650. Fax: 609-989-1111. 8:30AM-4PM.

Felony—Superior Court-Criminal Division, 209 S. Broad, PO Box 8068, Trenton, NJ 08650-0068. 609-989-6453, Fax: 609-278-3530. 8:30AM-4:30PM; Search Hours: 9AM-3:30PM. Access by: mail, in person.

Civil Actions Over $10,000, Probate—Superior Court-Civil Division, 75 S Broad, PO Box 8068, Trenton, NJ 08650-0068. 609-989-6454, Fax: 609-278-8010. 8:30AM-4:30PM. Access by: mail, fax, in person.

Civil Actions Under $10,000, Eviction, Small Claims—Special Civil Part, Box 8068, Trenton, NJ 08650. 609-989-6206, Fax: 609-278-2721. 8:30AM-4:30PM. Access by: mail, in person.

Middlesex

Real Estate Recording—Middlesex County Clerk, 1 JFK Square between Patterson & Bayard, Main Lobby in East Wing of Courthouse, New Brunswick, NJ 8903. 908-754-3482. 8:30AM-4PM.

Felony—Superior Court-Criminal Division, PO Box 2673, New Brunswick, NJ 08903. 732-981-3135. 8:30AM-4:30PM. Access by: mail, in person.

Civil Actions Over $10,000, Probate—Superior Court-Civil Division, PO Box 2633, New Brunswick, NJ 08903. 732-981-3301. 8:30AM-4:30PM. Access by: mail, in person.

Civil Actions Under $10,000, Eviction, Small Claims—Special Civil Part, PO Box 1146, New Brunswick, NJ 08903. 732-981-3200. 8:30AM-4:30PM. Access by: mail, phone, in person.

Monmouth

Real Estate Recording—Monmouth County Clerk, Hall of Records, Main Street, Room 102, Freehold, NJ 7728. 8:30AM-4:30PM.

Felony—Superior Court-Criminal Division, PO Box 1271, Rm 143, Freehold, NJ 07728-1271. 732-431-7880, Fax: 732-409-7564. 8:30AM-4:30PM. Access by: in person.

Civil Actions Over $10,000, Probate—Superior Court-Civil Division, PO Box 1255, Freehold, NJ 07728-1255. 732-431-8783. 8:30AM-4:30PM. Access by: mail, in person.

Civil Actions Under $10,000, Eviction, Small Claims—Special Civil Part, Courthouse, Courthouse and Monument St. Freehold, NJ 07728. 732-577-6749. 8:30AM-4:30PM. Access by: mail, in person.

Morris

Real Estate Recording—Morris County Clerk, Administration & Records Bldg. Court Street, Morristown, NJ 7960. Fax: 973-285-5231. 8:30AM-4PM.

Felony—Superior Court-Criminal Division, PO Box 910, Morristown, NJ 07960-0910. 973-285-6119, Fax: 973-455-0615. 8:30AM-4:30PM. Access by: mail, fax, in person.

Civil Actions Over $10,000, Probate—Superior Court-Civil Division, PO Box 910, Morristown, NJ 07960-0910. 973-285-6165, Fax: 973-829-8413. 7:45AM-5PM. Access by: in person.

Civil Actions Under $10,000, Eviction, Small Claims—Special Civil Part, PO Box 910 and Court St, Morristown, NJ 07963-0910. 973-285-6150. 8:30AM-4:30PM. Access by: mail, in person.

Ocean

Real Estate Recording—Ocean County Clerk, 118 Washington Street, 1st Floor Room 108, Toms River, NJ 8753. Fax: 732-349-4336. 8:30AM-4PM.

Felony—Superior Court-Criminal Division, PO Box 2191, Justice Complex, Rm 220, Toms River, NJ 08754-2191. 732-929-2009. 8:30AM-4:30PM. Access by: mail, in person.

Civil Actions Over $10,000, Probate—Superior Court-Civil Division, 118 Washington, Toms River, NJ 08754. 732-929-2035. 8:30AM-4:30PM. Access by: mail, in person.

Civil Actions Under $10,000, Eviction, Small Claims—Special Civil Part, Box 2191, Toms River, NJ 08754. 732-929-2016, Fax: 732-506-5398. 8AM-4:30PM. Access by: mail, fax, in person.

Passaic

Real Estate Recording—Passaic County Register of Deeds, 77 Hamilton Street, Courthouse, Paterson, NJ 7505. 201-795-6723. 8:30AM-4:30PM; Vault Hours: 7:45AM-5:45PM.

Felony—Superior Court-Criminal Division, 77 Hamilton St. Paterson, NJ 07505-2108. 973-881-4126, Fax: 973-881-4563. 8:30AM-4:30PM. Access by: mail, in person.

Civil Actions Over $10,000, Probate—Superior Court-Civil Division, 77 Hamilton St. Paterson, NJ 07505-2108. 973-881-4125. 8:30AM-4:30PM. Access by: mail, phone, in person.

Civil Actions Under $10,000, Eviction, Small Claims—Special Civil Part, 71 Hamilton St. Paterson, NJ 07505. 973-247-8238. 8:30AM-4:30PM. Access by: mail, in person.

Salem

Real Estate Recording—Salem County Clerk, 92 Market Street, Salem, NJ 8079. Fax: 856-935-8882. 8:30AM-4:30PM.

Felony—Superior Court-Criminal Division, PO Box 78, Salem, NJ 08079-1913. 856-935-7510. 8:30AM-4:30PM. Access by: mail, in person.

Civil Actions Over $10,000, Probate—Superior Court-Civil Division, PO Box 78, Salem, NJ 08079-1913. 856-935-7510. 8:30AM-4:30PM. Access by: mail, phone, fax, in person.

Civil Actions Under $10,000, Eviction, Small Claims—Special Civil Part, PO Box 29, Salem, NJ 08079. 856-935-7510, Fax: 856-935-6551. 8:30AM-4:30PM. Access by: mail, phone, fax, in person.

Somerset

Real Estate Recording—Somerset County Clerk, 20 Grove St. Administration Building, Somerville, NJ 8876. 908-231-7000. 8:15AM-4:15PM.

Felony—Superior Court-Criminal Division, PO Box 3000, Somerville, NJ 08876-1262. 908-231-7662. 8:30AM-4:30PM. Access by: mail, in person.

Civil Actions Over $10,000, Probate—Superior Court-Civil Division, PO Box 3000, Somerville, NJ 08876-1262. 908-231-7055. 8:30AM-4:30PM. Access by: mail, phone, in person.

Civil Actions Under $10,000, Eviction, Small Claims—Special Civil Part, Courthouse, Bridge and Main St, PO Box 3000, Somerville, NJ 08876-1262. 908-231-7014. 8:30AM-4:30PM. Access by: mail, in person.

Sussex

Real Estate Recording—Sussex County Clerk, 4 Park Place, Hall of Records, Newton, NJ 7860. Fax: 973-383-7493. 8:30AM-4:30PM.

Felony—Superior Court-Criminal Division, 43-47 High St, Sussex Judicial Center, Newton, NJ 07860. 973-579-0933. 8:30AM-4:30PM. Access by: mail, phone, in person.

Civil Actions Over $10,000, Probate—Superior Court-Civil Division, 43-47 High St, Sussex Judicial Center, Newton, NJ 07860. 973-579-0914. 8:30AM-4:30PM. Access by: mail, phone, in person.

Civil Actions Under $10,000, Eviction, Small Claims—Special Civil Part, 43-47 High St. Newton, NJ 07860. 973-579-0918. 8:30AM-4:30PM. Access by: mail, phone, in person.

Union

Real Estate Recording—Union County Clerk, 2 Broad Street, Courthouse, Room 115, Elizabeth, NJ 7207. Fax: 908-558-2589. 8:30AM-4:30PM.

Felony—Superior Court-Criminal Division, County Courthouse-New Annex,Rm 201, Elizabeth, NJ 07207. 908-659-3376, Fax: 908-659-3391. 8:30AM-4:30PM. Access by: mail, phone, in person.

Civil Actions Over $10,000—Superior Court-Civil Division, 2 Broad St, Elizabeth, NJ 07207. 908-659-4176, Fax: 908-659-4185. 8:30AM-4:30PM. Access by: mail, phone, in person.

Civil Actions Under $10,000, Eviction, Small Claims—Special Civil Part, 2 Broad St, Elizabeth, NJ 07207. 908-527-4322. 8:30AM-4:30PM. Access by: mail, phone, in person.

Warren

Real Estate Recording—Warren County Clerk, 413 Second Street, Courthouse, Belvidere, NJ 7823. 8:30AM-4PM.

Felony—Warren County Superior Court, Criminal Case Management Division, PO Box 900, Belvidere, NJ 07823. 908-475-6990, Fax: 908-475-6982. 8:30AM-4:30PM. Access by: mail, in person.

Civil Actions Over $10,000, Probate—Superior Court-Civil Division, PO Box 900, Belvidere, NJ 07823. 908-475-6140. 8:30AM-4:30PM. Access by: mail, in person.

Civil Actions Under $10,000, Eviction, Small Claims—Special Civil Part, 314 2nd St, PO Box 900, Belvidere, NJ 07823. 908-475-6140. 8:30AM-4:30PM. Access by: mail, in person.

Federal Courts

US District Court

Camden Division Clerk, PO Box 2797, Camden, NJ 08101856-757-5021 Fax: 609-757-5370 Counties: Atlantic, Burlington, Camden, Cape May, Cumberland, Gloucester, Salem. www.njuscourts.org

Newark Division ML King, Jr Federal Bldg. & US Courthouse, 50 Walnut St, Room 4015, Newark, NJ 07101973-645-3730, Record Room: 973-645-6465 Counties: Bergen, Essex, Hudson, Middlesex, Monmouth, Morris, Passaic, Sussex, Union. Monmouth County was transferred from Trenton Division in late 1997; closed cases remain in Trenton. www.njuscourts.org

Trenton Division Clerk, US District Court, Room 2020, 402 E State St, Trenton, NJ 08608609-989-2065 Counties: Hunterdon, Mercer, Ocean, Somerset, Warren. Monmouth County was transferred to Newark Division in late 1997; closed Monmouth cases remain in Trenton. www.njuscourts.org

US Bankruptcy Court

Camden Division 15 N 7th St, 3rd Fl, Camden, NJ 08102856-757-5485 Counties: Atlantic, Burlington, Camden, Cape May, Cumberland, Gloucester, Salem. www.njuscourts.org

Newark Division ML King Jr Federal Bldg, 50 Walnut St, 3rd Fl, Newark, NJ 07102973-645-4764 Counties: Bergen, Essex, Hudson, Morris, Passaic, Sussex. Also Elizabeth, Springfield and Hillside townships in Union County. www.njuscourts.org

Trenton Division Clerk of Court, 402 E State St, 1st Fl, Trenton, NJ 08608609-989-2128 Counties: Hunterdon, Mercer, Middlesex, Monmouth, Ocean, Somerset, Warren, Union except the townships of Elizabeth, Hillside and Springfield. www.njuscourts.org

New Mexico

Attorney General's Office
PO Drawer 1508   505-827-6000
Santa Fe, NM 87504-1508 Fax: 505-827-5826
www.ago.state.nm.us

Governor's Office
State Capitol, Room 400 505-827-3000
Santa Fe, NM 87503   Fax: 505-827-3026
www.governor.state.nm.us

State Archives
1205 Camino Carols Rey   505-476-7908
Santa Fe, NM 87505   Fax: 505-476-7909
www.state.nm.us/cpr

Capital:	Santa Fe
	Santa Fe County
Time Zone:	MST
Number of Counties:	33
Population:	1,729,751
Web Site:	www.state.nm.us

Search Unclaimed Property Online
There is no Internet-based search for unclaimed property for this state.

State Agencies

Criminal Records
Department of Public Safety, Records Bureau, PO Box 1628, Santa Fe, NM 87504-1628 (4491 Serrillos Rd, Santa Fe, NM 87504); 505-827-9181; Fax: 505-827-3396; 8AM-5PM. Access by: mail.

Corporation Records
Limited Liability Company Records
State Corporation Commission, Corporate Department, PO Box 1269, Santa Fe, NM 87504-1269 (1120 Paseo de Peralta, Pera Bldg 4th Fl, Rm 418, Santa Fe, NM 87501); 505-827-4502 Main Number, 800-947-4722 In-state Only, 505-827-4510 Good Standing, 505-827-4513 Copy Request; Fax: 505-827-4387; 8AM-12:00: 1PM-5PM. Access by: mail, phone, in person, online. www.nmprc.state.nm.us

Trademarks/Servicemarks
Trade Names
Secretary of State, Trademarks Division, State Capitol, Santa Fe, NM 87503; 505-827-3600; Fax: 505-827-3611; 8AM-5PM. Access by: mail, phone, in person. www.sos.state.nm.us

Sales Tax Registrations
Taxation & Revenue Department, Tax Administrative Services Division, PO. Box 630, Santa Fe, NM 87504-0630 (Montoya Bldg, 1100 S St Francis Drive, Santa Fe, NM 87501); 505-827-0700; Fax: 505-827-0469; 8AM-5PM. Access by: mail, phone, in person. www.state.nm.us/tax

Uniform Commercial Code
UCC Division, Secretary of State, State Capitol Bldg, Rm 420, Santa Fe, NM 87503; 505-827-3610; Fax: 505-827-3611; 8AM-5PM. Access by:, online. www.sos.state.nm.us/ucc/ucchome.htm

Federal Tax Liens
State Tax Liens
Records not available from state agency.

Records are filed with the Clerk at the county level.

Workers' Compensation Records
Restricted access.

Workers Compensation Administration, PO Box 27198, Albuquerque, NM 87125-7198 (2410 Centre Ave, SE, Albuquerque, NM 87106) (2410 Centre Ave, SE, Albuquerque, NM 87106); 505-841-6000, 800-255-7965 In-State Toll Free; Fax: 505-841-6060; 8AM-5PM
www.state.nm.us/wca

Birth Certificates

Department of Health, Bureau of Vital Records, PO Box 26110, Santa Fe, NM 87502 (1105 South St Francis Dr, Santa Fe, NM 87502); 505-827-2338; Fax: 505-984-1048; 8AM-5:00PM (Counter Service: 9AM-4PM). Access by: mail, phone, in person.

Marriage Certificates
Divorce Records

Records not available from state agency.

Marriage and Divorce records are found at county of issue.

Accident Reports

Department of Public Safety, Records, PO Box 1628, Santa Fe, NM 87504-1628 (New Mexico State Police Complex, 4491 Cerrillos Rd, Santa Fe, NM 87504); 505-827-9300; Fax: 505-827-3396; 8AM-5PM. Access by: mail.

Driver Records

Motor Vehicle Division, Driver Services Bureau, PO Box 1028, Santa Fe, NM 87504-1028 (Joseph M. Montoya Bldg, 1100 S St. Francis Dr, 2nd Floor, Santa Fe, NM 87504); 505-827-2234; Fax: 505-827-2267; 8AM-5PM. Access by: mail, online.

Vehicle Ownership
Vehicle Identification
Boat & Vessel Ownership
Boat & Vessel Registration

Motor Vehicle Division, Vehicle Services Bureau, PO Box 1028, Santa Fe, NM 87504-1028 (Joseph M. Montoya Bldg, 1100 S St. Francis Dr, 2nd Floor, Santa Fe, NM 87504); 505-827-4636, 505-827-1004; Fax: 505-827-0395; 8AM-5PM. Access by: mail, online.

Legislation-Current/Pending
Legislation-Passed

Legislative Council Service, State Capitol Bldg, Room 411, Santa Fe, NM 87501; 505-986-4600, 505-986-4350 Bill Room (During Session Only); Fax: 505-986-4610; 8AM-5PM. Access by: mail, online. legis.state.nm.us

Voter Registration

Restricted access.
Individual look-ups must be done at the county level. This agency will sell its database, but for restricted purposes only (not for commercial purposes).
Secretary of State, Bureau of Elections, State Capitol Annex, Ste 300, Santa Fe, NM 87503; 505-827-3620; Fax: 505-827-4954; 8AM-5PM

GED Certificates

Department of Education, Licensing unit, 300 Don Gaspar, Rm 124, Santa Fe, NM 87501-2786; 505-827-6702; Fax: 505-827-6696; 8AM-5PM.

Hunting License Information
Fishing License Information

Game & Fish Department, PO Box 25112, Santa Fe, NM 87504 (Villagra Bldg, 408 Galisto St, Santa Fe, NM 87504); 505-827-7911 Switchboard; Fax: 505-827-7915; 8AM-12PM; 1PM-5PM.
www.gmfsh.state.nm.us

County Courts & Recording Offices

About the Courts...

Administration

Administrative Office of the Courts   505-827-4800
Supreme Court Building Room 25   Fax: 505-827-7549
Santa Fe, NM 87503
www.nmcourts.com

Court Structure

The 30 District Courts in 13 districts are the courts of general jurisdiction. Magistrate Courts and the Bernalillo Metropolitan Court have jurisdiction in cases up to $5000. Probate Courts handle "informal" (uncontested) probate cases, and the District Courts handle "formal" (contested) probate cases.

Searching Hints

There are some "shared" courts in New Mexico, with one county handling cases arising in another. Records are held at the location(s) indicated in the text.

Online Access

The web site ofers free acces to District and Magistrate Court case information. In general, records are availavel from June 1997.

Also, online computer access is available for the Bernalillo, Dona Ana, San Juan county court systems through New Mexico Technet. There is a $50.00 set up fee, a $.50 per minute connect time fee, and other fees based on type of search. The system is available 24 hours a day. Call 505-345-6555 for more information.

There is a free case look-up on the Internet at www.nmcourts.com/disclaim.htm. Be aware that that the site is subject to downtime.

All magistrate courts and the Bernalillo Metropolitan Court have public access terminals to access civil records only.

About the Recording Offices...

Organization

33 counties, 33 recording offices. The recording officer is County Clerk. Most counties maintain a grantor/grantee index and a miscellaneous index. The entire state is in the Mountain Time Zone (MST).

UCC Records

Financing statements are filed at the state level, except for consumer goods, farm related and real estate related collateral, which are filed only with the County Clerk. Only a few recording offices will perform UCC searches. Use search request form UCC-11. Search and copy fees vary.

Lien Records

All federal and state tax liens are filed with the County Clerk. Most counties will not provide tax lien searches.

Real Estate Records

Most counties will not perform real estate searches. Copy and certification fees vary.

County Courts & Recording Offices

Bernalillo

Real Estate Recording—Bernalillo County Clerk, 1 Civic Plaza NW, Level 6, Albuquerque, NM 87102. Fax: 505-768-4631. 8AM-4:30PM.

Felony, Civil, Probate—2nd Judicial District Court, PO Box 488, Albuquerque, NM 87103. 505-841-7425, Fax: 505-841-7446. 8AM-5PM. Access by: mail, in person, online.

Misdemeanor, Civil Actions Under $5,000, Eviction, Small Claims—Metropolitan Court, 401 Roma NW, Albuquerque, NM 87102. 505-841-8110, Fax: 505-841-8192. 8AM-5PM. Access by: mail, phone, fax, in person, online. www.metrocourt.nmcjnet.org

Probate—County Clerk, #1 Civic Plaza NW, Albuquerque, NM 87102. 505-768-4247. 8AM-4:30PM. Access by: mail, phone, in person.

Catron

Real Estate Recording—Catron County Clerk, Main Street, Reserve, NM 87830. Fax: 505-533-6400. 8AM-4:30PM.

Felony, Civil, Probate—7th Judicial District Court, PO Drawer 1129, Socorro, NM 87801. 505-835-0050, Fax: 505-838-5217. 8AM-4PM. Access by: mail, phone, in person. Special note: This court is also responsible for Socorro County.

Misdemeanor, Civil Actions Under $5,000, Eviction, Small Claims—Reserve Magistrate Court, PO Box 447, Reserve, NM 87830. 505-533-6474, Fax: 505-533-6623. 8AM-5PM. Access by: mail, phone, fax, in person.

Misdemeanor, Civil Actions Under $7,500, Eviction, Small Claims—Quemado Magistrate Court, PO Box 283, Quemado, NM 87829. 505-773-4604, Fax: 505-773-4688. 8AM-5PM. Access by: mail, phone, fax, in person.

Probate—County Clerk, PO Box I, Socorro, NM 87801. 505-835-0423, Fax: 505-835-1043. 8AM-5PM. Access by: mail, phone, in person.

Chaves

Real Estate Recording—Chaves County Clerk, 401 North Main, Courthouse, Roswell, NM 88201. Fax: 505-624-6523. 7AM-5PM.

Felony, Civil, Probate—5th Judicial District Court, Box 1776, Roswell, NM 88202. 505-622-2212, Fax: 505-624-9510. 8AM-Noon,1-5PM. Access by: mail, in person.

Misdemeanor, Civil Actions Under $5,000, Eviction, Small Claims—Magistrate Court, 200 E 4th St, Roswell, NM 88201. 505-624-6088, Fax: 505-624-6092. 8AM-4PM. Access by: mail, in person.

Probate—County Clerk, Box 580, Roswell, NM 88202. 505-624-6614, Fax: 505-624-6523. 7AM-5PM. Access by: mail, in person.

Cibola

Real Estate Recording—Cibola County Clerk, 515 West High Street, Grants, NM 87020. Fax: 505-285-5434. 8AM-5PM.

Felony, Civil, Probate—13th Judicial District Court, Box 758, Grants, NM 87020. 505-287-8831, Fax: 505-285-5755. 8AM-4PM. Access by: mail, fax, in person.

Misdemeanor, Civil Actions Under $7,500, Eviction, Small Claims—Magistrate Court, 515 W High, PO Box 130, Grants, NM 87020. 505-285-4605. 8AM-4PM. Access by: mail, in person.

Probate—County Clerk, 515 W. High, PO Box 19, Grants, NM 87020. 505-287-8107, Fax: 505-285-5434. 8AM-5PM. Access by: mail.

Colfax

Real Estate Recording—Colfax County Clerk, Third Street & Savage Avenue, Courthouse, Raton, NM 87740. Fax: 505-445-4031. 8AM-Noon, 1-5PM.

Felony, Civil, Probate—8th Judicial District Court, Box 160, Raton, NM 87740. 505-445-5585, Fax: 505-445-2626. 8AM-4PM. Access by: mail, phone, in person.

Misdemeanor, Civil Actions Under $5,000, Eviction, Small Claims—Cimarron Magistrate Court, PO Drawer 367, Highway 21, Cimarron, NM 87714. 505-376-2634. Access by: in person.

Raton Magistrate Court, PO Box 68, Raton, NM 87740. 505-445-2220, Fax: 505-445-8966. 8AM-5PM. Access by: mail, fax, in person.

Springer Magistrate Court, 300 Colbert Ave. PO Box 778, Springer, NM 87747. 505-483-2417, Fax: 505-483-0127. 8AM-Noon, 1-5PM. Access by: mail, fax, in person.

Probate—County Clerk, PO Box 159, Raton, NM 87740. 505-445-5551, Fax: 505-445-4031. 8AM-5PM. Access by: mail, in person.

Curry

Real Estate Recording—Curry County Clerk, 700 N. Main Street, Suite 7, Clovis, NM 88101. Fax: 505-763-4232. 8AM-5PM.

Felony, Civil, Probate—9th Judicial District Court, Curry County Courthouse, Clovis, NM 88101. 505-762-9148, Fax: 505-763-5160. 8AM-4PM. Access by: in person.

Misdemeanor, Civil Actions Under $5,000, Eviction, Small Claims—Magistrate Court, 900 Main St, Clovis, NM 88101. 505-762-3766, Fax: 505-769-1437. 8AM-4PM. Access by: mail, fax, in person.

Probate—District Court, Curry County Courthouse, 700 N Main, Clovis, NM 88101. 505-762-9148, Fax: 505-763-5160. 8AM-4PM. Access by: in person.

De Baca

Real Estate Recording—De Baca County Clerk, 514 Ave. C, Courthouse Square, Fort Sumner, NM 88119. Fax: 505-355-2441. 8AM-Noon, 1-4:30PM.

Felony, Civil, Probate—10th Judicial District Court, Box 910, Ft. Sumner, NM 88119. 505-355-2896, Fax: 505-355-2896. 8AM-4:30PM. Access by: mail, phone, in person.

Misdemeanor, Civil Actions Under $5,000, Eviction, Small Claims—Magistrate Court, Box 24, Ft Sumner, NM 88119. 505-355-7371, Fax: 505-355-7149. 8AM-5PM. Access by: mail, phone, in person.

Probate—County Clerk, 514 Ave C, Box 347, Ft. Sumner, NM 88119. 505-355-2601, Fax: 505-355-2441. 8AM-Noon, 1-4:30PM. Access by: mail, in person.

Dona Ana

Real Estate Recording—Dona Ana County Clerk, 251 West Amador, Room 103, Las Cruces, NM 88005. Fax: 505-647-7464. 8AM-5PM.

Felony, Civil, Probate—3rd Judicial District Court, 201 W Puecho, Suite A, Las Cruces, NM 88005. 505-523-8200, Fax: 505-523-8290. 8AM-Noon, 1-5PM. Access by: mail, in person, online.

Misdemeanor, Civil Actions Under $5,000, Eviction, Small Claims—Anthony Magistrate Court, PO Box 1259, Anthony, NM 88021. 505-233-3147. 8AM-Noon, 1-5PM. Access by: mail, phone, in person.

Las Cruces Magistrate Court, 151 N Church, Las Cruces, NM 88001. 505-524-2814, Fax: 505-525-2951. 8AM-Noon, 1-5PM. Access by: mail, phone, fax, in person.

Eddy

Real Estate Recording—Eddy County Clerk, 101 W. Greene St. Room 312, Carlsbad, NM 88220. Fax: 505-234-1793. 8AM-5PM.

Felony, Civil, Probate—5th Judicial District Court, Box 1838, Carlsbad, NM 88221. 505-885-4740, Fax: 505-887-7095. 8AM-Noon, 1-5PM. Access by: mail, phone, in person. www.fifthdistrictcourt.com

Misdemeanor, Civil Actions Under $5,000, Eviction, Small Claims—Artesia Magistrate Court, 611 Mahone Dr Ste A, Artesia,

NM 88210. 505-746-2481, Fax: 505-746-6763. 8AM-4PM. Access by: mail, phone, fax, in person.

Misdemeanor, Civil Actions Under $7,500, Eviction, Small Claims—Carlsbad Magistrate Court, 302 N Main St, Carlsbad, NM 88220. 505-883-3218. 8AM-4PM. Access by: mail, phone, fax, in person.

Probate—County Clerk, Eddy County Probate Judge, Rm 100, PO Box 850, Carlsbad, NM 88220. 505-885-4008, Fax: 505-887-1039. 8AM-5PM. Access by: mail, in person.

Grant

Real Estate Recording—Grant County Clerk, 201 North Cooper, Silver City, NM 88061. Fax: 505-538-8926. 8:30AM-5PM.

Felony, Civil, Probate—6th Judicial District Court, Box 2339, Silver City, NM 88062. 505-538-3250, Fax: 505-588-5439. 8AM-5PM. Access by: mail, in person.

Misdemeanor, Civil Actions Under $5,000, Eviction, Small Claims—Silver City Magistrate Court, 1620 E Pine St, Silver City, NM 88061. 505-538-3811, Fax: 505-538-8079. 8AM-5PM; Public hours 9AM-5PM. Access by: mail, in person.

Misdemeanor, Civil Actions Under $7,500, Eviction, Small Claims—Bayard Magistrate Court, PO Box 125, Bayard, NM 88023. 505-537-3402, Fax: 505-537-7365. 8AM-5PM. Access by: mail, in person.

Probate—County Clerk, Box 898, Silver City, NM 88062. 505-538-2979, Fax: 505-538-8926. 8AM-5PM. Access by: mail, phone.

Guadalupe

Real Estate Recording—Guadalupe County Clerk, 420 Parker Avenue, Courthouse-Suite 1, Santa Rosa, NM 88435. 505-472-3133, Fax: 505-472-3735. 8AM-5PM.

Felony, Civil, Probate—4th Judicial District Court, 420 Parker Ave Suite #5, Guadalupe County Courthouse, Santa Rosa, NM 88435. 505-472-3888, Fax: 505-472-3888. 8AM-5PM. Access by: in person.

Misdemeanor, Civil Actions Under $5,000, Eviction, Small Claims—Santa Rosa Magistrate Court, 603 Parker Ave, Santa Rosa, NM 88435. 505-472-3237. 8AM-Noon, 1-5PM. Access by: mail, in person.

Vaughn Magistrate Court, PO Box 246, Vaughn, NM 88353. 505-584-2345. 8AM-Noon, 1-5PM. Access by: mail, in person.

Probate—County Clerk, 4200 Parker Ave Courthouse, Santa Rosa, NM 88435. 505-472-3791, Fax: 505-472-3735. 8AM-5PM. Access by: mail, in person.

Harding

Real Estate Recording—Harding County Clerk, Third & Pine, Mosquero, NM 87733. 505-673-2928, Fax: 505-673-2922. 8AM-4PM.

Felony, Civil, Probate—10th Judicial District Court, Box 1002, Mosquero, NM 87733. 505-673-2252, Fax: 505-673-2252. 9AM-3PM M-W,F. Access by: mail, phone, fax, in person.

Misdemeanor, Civil Actions Under $5,000, Eviction, Small Claims—Magistrate Court, Box 9, Roy, NM 87743. 505-485-2549, Fax: 505-485-2407. 8AM-4:30PM. Access by: mail, phone, fax, in person.

Probate—County Clerk, County Clerk, Box 1002, Mosquero, NM 87733. 505-673-2301, Fax: 505-673-2922. 8AM-5PM. Access by: mail, in person.

Hidalgo

Real Estate Recording—Hidalgo County Clerk, 300 Shakespeare Street, Lordsburg, NM 88045. 505-542-9313. 9AM-5PM.

Felony, Civil, Probate—6th Judicial District Court, PO 608, Lordsburg, NM 88045. 505-542-3411, Fax: 505-542-3481. 8AM-Noon, 1-5PM. Access by: mail, phone, fax, in person.

Misdemeanor, Civil Actions Under $7,500, Eviction, Small Claims—Magistrate Court, 420 Wabash Ave, Lordsburg, NM 88045. 505-542-3582. 8AM-5PM. Access by: mail, in person.

Probate—Hildago County Probate Court, 300 S Shakespeare, Lordsburg, NM 88045. 505-542-9512, Fax: 505-542-3414. 9AM-Noon. Access by: mail, phone, in person.

Lea

Real Estate Recording—Lea County Clerk, 100 Main Street, Courthouse, Lovington, NM 88260. Fax: 505-396-3293. 8AM-5PM.

Felony, Civil, Probate—5th Judicial District Court, 100 N. Main, Box 6C, Lovington, NM 88260. 505-396-8571, Fax: 505-396-2428. 8AM-5PM. Access by: mail, fax, in person.

Misdemeanor, Civil Actions Under $5,000, Eviction, Small Claims—Eunice Magistrate Court, PO Box 240, Eunice, NM 88231. 505-394-3368, Fax: 505-394-3335. Access by: mail, in person.

Lovington Magistrate Court, 100 W Central, Suite D, Lovington, NM 88260. 505-396-6677, Fax: 505-396-6163. 8AM-4PM. Access by: mail, in person.

Tatum Magistrate Court, PO Box 918, Tatum, NM 88267. 505-398-5300, Fax: 505-398-5310. 8AM-4PM. Access by: mail, phone, fax, in person.

Misdemeanor, Civil Actions Under $7,500, Eviction, Small Claims—Hobbs Magistrate Court, 2110 N Alto Dr, Hobbs, NM 88240-3455. 505-397-3621, Fax: 505-393-9121. 8AM-4PM. Access by: mail, in person.

Probate—County Clerk, Box 1507, Lovington, NM 88260. 505-396-8531, Fax: 505-396-5684. 8AM-5PM. Access by: in person.

Lincoln

Real Estate Recording—Lincoln County Clerk, 300 Central Avenue, Carrizozo, NM 88301. 505-648-2397, Fax: 505-648-2576. 8AM-5PM.

Felony, Civil, Probate—12th Judicial District Court, Box 725, Carrizozo, NM 88301. 505-648-2432, Fax: 505-648-2581. 8AM-4PM. Access by: in person.

Misdemeanor, Civil Actions Under $5,000, Eviction, Small Claims—Ruidoso Magistrate court, 301 W Highway 70 #2, Ruidoso, NM 88345. 505-378-7022, Fax: 505-378-8508. 8AM-4PM. Access by: mail, in person.

Probate—County Clerk, Box 338, Carrizozo, NM 88301. 505-648-2394, Fax: 505-648-2576. 8AM-5PM. Access by: mail, in person. Special note: This court will not do searches.

Los Alamos

Real Estate Recording—Los Alamos County Clerk, 2300 Trinity Drive, Room 100, Los Alamos, NM 87544. 505-662-8070. 8AM-5PM.

Felony, Misdemeanor, Civil, Eviction, Small Claims, Probate—1st Judicial District Court, Access by: in person. Special note: All civil and criminal cases handled by Santa Fe District Court.

Misdemeanor, Civil Actions Under $5,000, Eviction, Small Claims—Magistrate Court, 1319 Trinity Dr, Los Alamos, NM 87544. 505-662-2727, Fax: 505-661-6258. 8AM-5PM. Access by: mail, in person.

Probate—County Clerk, Box 30, Los Alamos, NM 87544. 505-662-8010, Fax: 505-662-8008. 8AM-5PM. Access by: mail.

Luna

Real Estate Recording—Luna County Clerk, 700 South Silver, Courthouse, Deming, NM 88030. Fax: 505-546-4708. 8AM-5PM.

Felony, Civil, Probate—6th Judicial District Court, Luna County Courthouse Room 40, Deming, NM 88030. 505-546-9611, Fax: 505-546-2994. 8AM-4PM. Access by: mail, fax, in person.

Misdemeanor, Civil Actions Under $5,000, Eviction, Small Claims—Magistrate Court, 912 S Silver St, Deming, NM 88030. 505-546-9321, Fax: 505-546-4896. 8AM-Noon, 1-5PM. Access by: mail, fax, in person, online. www.nmcourts.com

Probate—County Clerk, PO Box 1838, Deming, NM 88031. 505-546-0491, Fax: 505-546-4708. 8AM-5PM. Access by: mail, in person.

McKinley

Real Estate Recording—McKinley County Clerk, 201 West Hill Avenue, Courthouse, Gallup, NM 87301. 505-722-4459. 8AM-5PM.

Felony, Civil, Probate—11th Judicial District Court, 201 W. Hill, Room 4, Gallup, NM 87301. 505-863-6816, Fax: 505-722-9172. 8AM-Noon, 1-5PM. Access by: mail, phone, in person.

Misdemeanor, Civil Actions Under $5,000, Eviction, Small Claims—Magistrate Court, 285 S Boardman Dr, Gallup, NM 87301. 505-722-6636. 8AM-4PM. Access by: mail, in person.

Probate—County Clerk, 201 W. Hill, Room 21, Gallup, NM 87301. 505-863-6866, Fax: 505-863-1419. 8AM-5PM. Access by: mail, in person.

Mora

Real Estate Recording—Mora County Clerk, Main Street, Mora, NM 87732. 505-387-2756, Fax: 505-387-9023. 8AM-5PM.

Felony, Civil, Probate—4th Judicial District Court, PO Box 1540, Las Vegas, NM 87701. 505-425-7281, Fax: 505-425-6307. 8AM-Noon, 1-5PM. Access by: in person.

Misdemeanor, Civil Actions Under $5,000, Eviction, Small Claims—Magistrate Court, 1927 7th Street, Las Vegas, NM 87701-4957. 505-425-5204. 8AM-4PM (closed for lunch). Access by: mail, in person.

Probate—County Clerk, Box 360, Mora, NM 87732. 505-387-2448, Fax: 505-387-9023. 8AM-5PM. Access by: mail, in person.

Otero

Real Estate Recording—Otero County Clerk, 1000 New York Avenue, Room 108, Alamogordo, NM 88310. 505-437-2030, Fax: 505-443-2922. 7:30AM-6PM.

Felony, Civil, Probate—12th Judicial District Court, 1000 New York Ave, Rm 209, Alamogordo, NM 88310-6940. 505-437-7310, Fax: 505-434-8886. 8AM-4PM. Access by: in person.

Misdemeanor, Civil Actions Under $5,000, Eviction, Small Claims—Magistrate Court, 263 Robert H Bradley Dr, Alamogordo, NM 88310-8288. 505-437-9000, Fax: 505-439-1365. 8AM-4PM. Access by: mail, in person.

Probate—County Clerk, 1000 New York Ave, Rm 108, Alamogordo, NM 88310. 505-437-4942, Fax: 505-443-2922. 7:30AM-6PM. Access by: mail, in person.

Quay

Real Estate Recording—Quay County Clerk, 301 South Third Street, Tucumcari, NM 88401. Fax: 505-461-0513. 8AM-Noon,1-5PM.

Felony, Civil, Probate—10th Judicial District Court, Box 1067, Tucumcari, NM 88401. 505-461-2764, Fax: 505-461-4498. 8AM-5PM. Access by: mail, phone, fax, in person.

Misdemeanor, Civil Actions Under $5,000, Eviction, Small Claims—San Jon Magistrate Court, PO Box 35, San Jon, NM 88434. 505-576-2591, Fax: 505-576-2773. 8AM-Noon,1-5PM. Access by: mail, in person. Special note: The work of this court is currently being handled by the Tucumcari court (505-461-1700).

Misdemeanor, Civil Actions Under $7,500, Eviction, Small Claims—Tucumcari Magistrate Court, PO Box 1301, Tucumcari, NM 88401. 505-461-1700, Fax: 505-461-4522. 8AM-Noon, 1-5PM. Access by: mail, phone, fax, in person. Special note: At press time, the court is closed. All inquires are referred to the Magistrate Court in Tucumcari - 505-461-1700.

Probate—County Clerk, Box 1225, Tucumcari, NM 88401. 505-461-0510, Fax: 505-461-0513. 8AM-5PM. Access by: mail, in person.

Rio Arriba

Real Estate Recording—Rio Arriba County Clerk, Courthouse, Tierra Amarilla, NM 87575. 505-588-7727. 8AM-4:30PM.

Felony, Civil, Probate—1st Judicial District Court, Access by: in person. Special note: All civil and criminal cases handled by Santa Fe District Court.

Misdemeanor, Civil Actions Under $5,000, Eviction, Small Claims—Rio Arriba Magistrate Court-Division 1, PO Box 538, Chama, NM 87520. 505-756-2278. 8AM-Noon, 1-5PM. Access by: mail, in person.

Rio Arriba Magistrate Court-Division 2, 410 Paseo de Onate, Espanola, NM 87532. 505-753-2532. 8AM-4PM. Access by: mail, in person.

Roosevelt

Real Estate Recording—Roosevelt County Clerk, 101 West First, Portales, NM 88130. 505-356-4081, Fax: 505-356-8562. 8AM-5PM.

Felony, Civil, Probate—9th Judicial District Court, 109 West 1st St, Suite 207, Portales, NM 88130. 505-356-4463, Fax: 505-356-5168. 8AM-4PM. Access by: in person.

Misdemeanor, Civil Actions Under $5,000, Eviction, Small Claims—Magistrate Court, 42427 US Hwy 70, Portales, NM 88130. 505-356-8569, Fax: 505-359-6883. 8AM-4PM. Access by: mail, in person.

Probate—County Clerk, Roosevelt County Courthouse, Portales, NM 88130. 505-356-8562, Fax: 505-356-3560. 8AM-5PM. Access by: mail, in person.

San Juan

Real Estate Recording—San Juan County Clerk, 100 S. Oliver Dr. Suite 200, Aztec, NM 87410. Fax: 505-334-3635. 7AM-5:30PM.

Felony, Civil, Probate—11th Judicial District Court, 103 S. Oliver, Aztec, NM 87410. 505-334-6151, Fax: 505-334-1940. 8AM-Noon, 1-5PM. Access by: in person, online.

Misdemeanor, Civil Actions Under $5,000, Eviction, Small Claims—Farmington Magistrate Court, 950 W Apache St, Farmington, NM 87401. 505-326-4338, Fax: 505-325-2618. 8AM-4PM. Access by: mail, fax, in person.

Misdemeanor, Civil Actions Under $7,500, Eviction, Small Claims—Aztec Magistrate Court, 101 S Oliver Dr Ste 1, Aztec, NM 87410. 505-334-9479. 8AM-Noon, 1-5PM. Access by: mail, in person.

Probate—County Clerk, Box 550, Aztec, NM 87410. 505-334-9471, Fax: 505-334-3635. 7AM-5:30PM. Access by: mail, in person.

San Miguel

Real Estate Recording—San Miguel County Clerk, Courthouse, Las Vegas, NM 87701. Fax: 505-425-7019. 8AM-Noon, 1-5PM.

Felony, Civil, Probate—4th Judicial District Court, PO Box 1540, Las Vegas, NM 87701. 505-425-7281, Fax: 505-425-6307. 8AM-Noon, 1-5PM. Access by: mail, phone, in person. Special note: Also handles cases for Mora County.

Misdemeanor, Civil Actions Under $5,000, Eviction, Small Claims—Magistrate Court, 1900 Hot Springs Blvd, Las Vegas, NM 87701. 505-425-5204, Fax: 505-425-0422. 8AM-4PM. Access by: mail, in person.

Probate—County Clerk, San Miguel County Clerk, Las Vegas, NM 87701. 505-425-9331, Fax: 505-454-7199. 8AM-Noon, 1-5PM. Access by: mail, in person.

Sandoval

Real Estate Recording—Sandoval County Clerk, 711 Camino Del Pueblo, Courthouse, 2nd Floor, Bernalillo, NM 87004. 505-867-2945, Fax: 505-771-8610. 8AM-5PM.

Felony, Civil, Probate—13th Judicial District Court, PO Box 130, Bernalillo, NM 87004. 505-867-2376. 8AM-Noon, 1-5PM. Access by: mail, in person.

Misdemeanor, Civil Actions Under $5,000, Eviction, Small Claims—Bernalillo Magistrate Court, PO Box 818, Bernalillo, NM 87004. 505-867-5202. 8AM-4PM. Access by: mail, in person.

Cuba Magistrate Court, 16B Cordova St, Cuba, NM 87013. 505-289-3519. 8AM-Noon, 1-5PM. Access by: in person.

Probate—County Clerk, Box 40, Bernalillo, NM 87004. 505-867-7572, Fax: 505-828-2862. 8AM-5PM. Access by: mail, phone, fax, in person.

Santa Fe

Real Estate Recording—Santa Fe County Clerk, 102 Grant Avenue, Santa Fe, NM 87504. 505-986-6253, Fax: 505-995-2767. 8AM-5PM.

Felony, Civil, Probate—1st Judicial District Court, Box 2268, Santa Fe, NM 87504. 505-476-0189, Fax: 505-827-7998. 8AM-4PM. Access by: mail, phone, in person. Special note: Because this court also handles the counties of Los Alamos and Rio Arriba, you must indicate which county you are searching.

Misdemeanor, Civil Actions Under $5,000, Eviction, Small Claims—Magistrate Court, Rte 11, Box 21M, Pojoaque, NM 87501. 505-455-7938, Fax: 505-455-3053. 8AM-Noon,1-5PM. Access by: mail, phone, in person.

Probate—County Clerk, Box 276, Santa Fe, NM 87501. 505-986-6279, Fax: 505-986-6362. 8AM-5PM. Access by: mail, in person.

Sierra

Real Estate Recording—Sierra County Clerk, 311 Date Street, Truth or Consequences, NM 87901. Fax: 505-894-2516. 8AM-5PM.

Felony, Civil, Probate—7th Judicial District Court, PO Box 3009, Truth or Consequences, NM 87901. 505-894-7167, Fax: 505-894-7168. 8AM-4PM. Access by: mail, phone, in person.

Misdemeanor, Civil Actions Under $5,000, Eviction, Small Claims—Magistrate Court, 100 Date St, Truth or Consequences, NM 87901. 505-894-3051, Fax: 505-894-0476. 8AM-Noon,1-5PM. Access by: mail, in person.

Probate—County Clerk, 311 Date St. Truth or Consequences, NM 87901. 505-894-2840, Fax: 505-894-2516. 8AM-5PM. Access by: mail, in person.

Socorro

Real Estate Recording—Socorro County Clerk, 200 Church Street, Socorro, NM 87801. Fax: 505-835-1043. 8AM-5PM.

Felony, Civil, Probate—7th Judicial District Court, Access by: in person. Special note: All civil and criminal cases are handled by Catron District Court.

Misdemeanor, Civil Actions Under $5,000, Eviction, Small Claims—Magistrate Court, 404 Park St, Socorro, NM 87801. 505-835-2500. 8AM-Noon, 1-5PM. Access by: mail, phone, in person.

Taos

Real Estate Recording—Taos County Clerk, 105 Albright Street, Suite D, Taos, NM 87571. Fax: 505-751-8637. 8AM-5PM.

Felony, Civil, Probate—8th Judicial District Court, 105 Albright St Ste H, Taos, NM 87571. 505-758-3173, Fax: 505-758-1281. 8AM-4PM. Access by: in person.

Misdemeanor, Civil Actions Under $5,000, Eviction, Small Claims—Questa Magistrate Court, PO Box 586, Questa, NM 87556. 505-586-0761, Fax: 505-586-0428. 8AM-Noon,1-5PM. Access by: mail, phone, fax, in person.

Taos Magistrate Court, Box 1121, Taos, NM 87571. 505-758-4030, Fax: 505-751-0983. 8AM-4PM. Access by: mail, in person.

Probate—County Clerk, 105 Albright, Suite D, Taos, NM 87571. 505-758-8266, Fax: 505-751-3391. 8AM-5PM. Access by: mail, in person.

Torrance

Real Estate Recording—Torrance County Clerk, 9th & Allen Streets, Estancia, NM 87016. Fax: 505-384-4080. 8AM-5PM.

Felony, Civil, Probate—7th Judicial District Court, County Courthouse, PO Box 78, Estancia, NM 87016. 505-384-2974, Fax: 505-384-2229. 8AM-5PM. Access by: mail, in person.

Misdemeanor, Civil Actions Under $5,000, Eviction, Small Claims—Moriarty Magistrate Court, PO Box 1968, Moriarty, NM 87035. 505-832-4476, Fax: 505-832-1563. 8AM-4PM. Access by: mail, phone, fax, in person.

Probate—County Clerk, Box 48, Estancia, NM 87016. 505-384-2221, Fax: 505-384-4080. 8AM-Noon, 1-5PM. Access by: mail, in person.

Union

Real Estate Recording—Union County Clerk, 200 Court Street, Courthouse, Clayton, NM 88415. Fax: 505-374-2763. 9AM-5PM.

Felony, Civil, Probate—8th Judicial District Court, Box 310, Clayton, NM 88415. 505-374-9577, Fax: 505-374-2089. 8AM-Noon, 1-5PM. Access by: mail, in person.

Misdemeanor, Civil Actions Under $5,000, Eviction, Small Claims—Magistrate Court, 118 Walnut St, Clayton, NM 88415. 505-374-9472, Fax: 505-374-9368. 8AM-Noon, 1-5PM. Access by: mail, phone, fax, in person.

Probate—County Clerk, PO Box 430, Clayton, NM 88415. 505-374-9491, Fax: 505-374-2763. 9AM-Noon, 1-5PM. Access by: in person.

Valencia

Real Estate Recording—Valencia County Clerk, 444 Luna Avenue, Los Lunas, NM 87031. 505-866-2090, Fax: 505-866-2023. 8AM-4:30PM.

Felony, Civil, Probate—13th Judicial District Court, Box 1089, Los Lunas, NM 87031. 505-865-4291, Fax: 505-865-8801. 8AM-5PM. Access by: mail, in person.

Misdemeanor, Civil Actions Under $5,000, Eviction, Small Claims—Belen Magistrate Court, 237 N Main St, Belen, NM 87002. 505-864-7509, Fax: 505-864-9532. 8AM-Noon,1-5PM. Access by: mail, fax, in person.

Los Lunas Magistrate Court, 121 SE Don Diego, Los Lunas, NM 87031. 505-865-4637. 8AM-4PM. Access by: mail, fax, in person.

Probate—County Clerk, Box 969, Los Lunas, NM 87031. 505-866-2073, Fax: 505-866-2023. 8AM-4:30PM. Access by: mail, phone, in person.

Federal Courts

US District Court

Albuquerque Division PO Box 689, Albuquerque, NM 87103505-248-8052, Record Room: 505-248-8045, Civil Docket Phone: 505-248-8128, Criminal Docket Phone: 505-248-8128 Fax: 505-248-8124 Counties: All counties in New Mexico. Cases may be assigned to any of its three divisions. www.nmcourt.fed.us
Las Cruces Division 200 E Griggs, Room C-242, Las Cruces, NM 88001505-527-6800 Fax: 505-527-6817 Counties: All counties in New Mexico. Cases may be assigned to any of its three divisions. www.nmcourt.fed.us

Santa Fe Division PO Box 2384, Santa Fe, NM 87504-2384505-988-6481 Fax: 505-988-6473 Counties: All counties in New Mexico. Cases may be assigned to any of the three divisions. www.nmcourt.fed.us

US Bankruptcy Court

Albuquerque Division PO Box 546, Albuquerque, NM 87103505-248-6500 Fax: 505-248-6540 Counties: All counties in New Mexico. www.nmcourt.fed.us

Attorney General's Office

State Capitol
Albany, NY 12224
www.oag.state.ny.us

518-474-7330
Fax: 518-473-9909

Governor's Office

Executive Chamber, State Capitol
Albany, NY 12224
www.state.ny.us/governor

518-474-8390
Fax: 518-474-8390

State Archives

Cultural Education
Center Room 11D40
Albany, NY 12230
www.sara.nysed.gov

518-474-8955
Fax: 518-473-9985

Capital:	Albany
	Albany County
Time Zone:	EST
Number of Counties:	62
Population:	18,137,226
Web Site:	www.state.ny.us

Search Unclaimed Property Online

www.osc.state.ny.us/cgi-bin/db2www/ouffrm.d2w/input

State Agencies

Criminal Records

Restricted access.
Thirteen counties in New York can be searched from the Unified Court System in New York City. Call Rene Elias at 212-428-2810 for more information.
Division of Criminal Justice Services, 4 Tower Place, Albany, NY 12203; 518-457-6043; Fax: 518-457-6550; 8AM-5PM

Corporation Records
Limited Partnership Records
Limited Liability Company Records
Limited Liability Partnerships

Division of Corporations, Department of State, 41 State St, Albany, NY 12231; 518-473-2492 General Information, 900-835-2677 Corporate Searches; 8AM-4:30PM. Access by: mail, phone, in person. www.dos.state.ny.us

Trademarks/Servicemarks

Department of State, Miscellaneous Records,, **NY** ; 518-474-4770; Fax: 518-473-0730; 8:30AM-4:30PM. Access by: mail, phone, in person.

Sales Tax Registrations

Sales Tax Registration Bureau, WA Harriman Campus, Building 8, Rm 408, Albany, NY 12227; 518-457-0259; Fax: 518-457-0453; 7AM-5PM. Access by: mail, phone, in person.

Uniform Commercial Code
Federal Tax Liens
State Tax Liens

UCC Division, Department of State, 41 State Street, Albany, NY 12231; 518-474-4763; 8AM-4:30PM. Access by: mail. www.dos.state.ny.us/corp/uccfaq.html

State Court Administrator

NY State Office of Court Administration, Empire State Plaza, Agency Bldg #4, Suite 2001, Albany, NY 12223; 518-473-1196; Fax: 518-473-6860; 9AM-5PM. www.courts.state.ny.us

Workers' Compensation Records

NY Workers' Compensation Board, Director of Claims Office, 180 Livingston St, Room 416, Brooklyn, NY 11248; 718-802-6621; Fax: 718-834-2116; 9AM-5PM. Access by: mail. www.wcb.state.ny.us

Birth Certificate-New York City
Death Records-New York City

Department of Health, Bureau of Vital Records, PO Box 3776, Church St Station, New York, NY 10013 (125 Worth St, Room 133, New York, NY 10013); 212-788-4520, 212-442-1999; Fax: 212-962-6105; 9AM-4PM. Access by: mail, phone, in person. www.ci.nyc.ny.us/health

Birth Certificates

Vital Records Section, Certification Unit, PO Box 2602, Albany, NY 12220-2602 (733 Broadway, #202, Albany, NY 12337); 518-474-3038, 518-474-3077; Fax: 518-474-9168; 8:30AM-4:30PM. Access by: mail, phone, in person.

Divorce Records-New York City

New York County Clerk's Office, Division of Old Records, 60 Centre Street, Rm 166, New York City, NY 10007; 212-374-4376; 9AM-3PM, M-F.

Marriage Certificate-New York City

City Clerk's Office, Department of Records & Information Services, 1 Centre Street, Rm 252, New York, NY 10007; 212-669-8898; 9AM-4:30PM M-TH; 9AM-1PM F. Access by: mail.

Death Records

Vital Records Section, certification Unit, PO Box 2602, Albany, NY 12220-2602; 518-474-3038, 518-474-3077; Fax: 518-474-9168; 8:30AM-4:30PM. Access by: mail.

Marriage Certificates

Vital Records Section, Certification Unit, PO Box 2602, Albany, NY 12220-2602; 518-474-3038, 518-474-3077; 8:30AM-4:30PM. Access by: mail.

Divorce Records

Vital Records Section, Certification Unit, PO Box 2602, Albany, NY 12220-2602; 518-474-3038, 518-474-3077; 8:30AM-4:30PM. Access by: mail.

Accident Reports

DMV Certified Document Center, Accident Report Section, Empire State Plaza, Swan St Bldg, Albany, NY 12228; 518-474-0710; 8AM-4:30PM. Access by: mail.

Driver Records

Department of Motor Vehicles, MV-15 Processing, 6 Empire State Plaza, Room 430, Albany, NY 12228; 518-474-0642, 518-473-5595; 8AM-5PM. Access by: mail, online. www.nydmv.state.ny.us

Vehicle Ownership
Vehicle Identification
Boat & Vessel Ownership
Boat & Vessel Registration

Department of Motor Vehicles, MV-15 Processing, 6 Empire State Plaza, Room 430, Albany, NY 12228; 518-474-0710, 518-474-8510; 8AM-5PM. Access by: mail, online. www.nydmv.state.ny.us/index.htm

Legislation-Current/Pending
Legislation-Passed

NY Senate Document Room, State Capitol, State Street Rm 317, Albany, NY 12247;, 518-455-2312 Senate Document Room, 518-455-3216 Calls Without Bill Numbers, 518-455-5164 Assembly Document Room; 9AM-5PM. Access by: mail, phone, in person, online. www.senate.state.ny.us

Voter Registration

Records not available from state agency.

Records may only be viewed or purchased at the county level. Purchases are restricted for political purposes only.

GED Certificates

NY State Education Dept, GED Testing, PO Box 7348, Albany, NY 12224-0348; 518-474-5906; Fax: 518-474-3041; 9AM-12PM, 1PM-4PM M-F.

Hunting License Information
Fishing License Information

Records not available from state agency.

They do not have a central database. Only vendors have the names and addresses.

County Courts & Recording Offices

About the Courts...

Administration

Office of Administration, Empire State Plaza   518-473-1196
Agency Plaza #4, Suite 2001   Fax: 518-473-6860
Albany, NY 12223
www.courts.state.ny.us

Court Structure

New York State has two sites for Administration; in addition to the Albany address above, there is a New York City office at this address: Office of Administration, 270 Broadway Room 1400, New York NY 10007, and telephone: 212-428-2100.

"Supreme Courts" are the highest trial courts in the state, equivalent to Circuit or District Courts in other states; they are not appeals courts. Many New York City courts are indexed by plaintiff only. After 1992 the small claims limit was raised from $2,000 to $3,000.

Records for Supreme and County Courts are maintained by County Clerks. In most counties, the address for the clerk is the same as for the court. Exceptions are noted in the court profiles.

Searching Hints

Supreme and County Court records are generally maintained in the County Clerk's Office, which outside of New York City may index civil cases by defendant, whereas the court itself maintains only a plaintiff index.

Fees for Supreme and County Courts are generally as follows: $5.00 per 2 year search per name for a manual search, and $16.00 per name for a computer or OCA search; $.50 per page (minimum $1.00) for copies; and $4.00 for certification. City Courts charge $5.00 for certification. Effective 4-1-95, no New York court will accept credit cards for any transaction.

Online Access

Civil case information from the 13 largest counties is available through DataCase, a database index of civil case information publicly available at terminals located at Supreme and County courts. In addition to the civil case index, DataCase also includes judgment docket and lien information, New York County Clerk system data, and the New York State attorney registration file. Remote access is also available at a fee of $1.00 per minute. Call 800-494-8981 for more remote access information.

About the Recording Offices...

Organization

62 counties, 62 recording offices. The recording officers are County Clerk (New York City Register in the counties of Bronx, Kings, New York, and Queens). The entire state is in the Eastern Time Zone (EST).

UCC Records

This is a dual filing state. Financing statements are filed both at the state level and with the County Clerk, except for consumer goods, cooperatives (as in cooperative apartments), farm related and real estate related collateral, which are filed only with the County Clerk. All counties will perform UCC searches. Use search request form UCC-11. Search fees are usually $7.00 per debtor name using the approved UCC-11 request form and sometimes $12.00 using a non-New York form. Copies usually cost $1.50 per page.

Lien Records

Federal tax liens on personal property of businesses are filed with the Secretary of State. Other federal tax liens are filed with the County Clerk. State tax liens are filed with the County Clerk, with a master list - called state tax warrants - available at the Secretary of State's office. Federal tax liens are usually indexed with UCC Records. State tax liens are usually indexed with other miscellaneous liens and judgments. Some counties include federal tax liens as part of a UCC search, and others will search tax liens for a separate fee. Search fees and copy fees vary.

Real Estate Records

Some counties will perform real estate searches. Certified copy fees are usually $1.00 per page with a $4.00 minimum. Tax records are located at the Treasurer's Office.

County Courts & Recording Offices

Albany

Real Estate Recording—Albany County Clerk, County Courthouse, Room 128, Albany, NY 12207. Fax: 518-487-5099. 9AM-5PM.

Felony, Civil—Supreme and County Court, Courthouse Rm 128, 16 Eagle St, Albany, NY 12207. 518-487-5118, Fax: 518-487-5099. 9AM-5PM. Access by: mail, in person. www.albanycounty.com/clerk

Civil Actions Under $15,000, Eviction, Small Claims—Albany City Court-Civil Part, City Hall Rm 209, Albany, NY 12207. 518-434-5115, Fax: 518-434-5034. 8:30AM-5PM. Access by: mail, in person.

Misdemeanor—Albany City Court-Misdemeanors, Morton & Broad St, Albany, NY 12202. 518-449-7109, Fax: 518-462-8074. 8AM-4PM. Access by: mail, phone, in person.

Probate—Surrogate's Court, Courthouse, Albany, NY 12207. 518-487-5393. 9AM-5PM. Special note: Search fee is $25.00 for up to 25 year search, $70 over.

Allegany

Real Estate Recording—Allegany County Clerk, Courthouse, 7 Court St. Belmont, NY 14813. 716-268-9282, Fax: 716-268-9659. 9AM-5PM (June-August 8:30AM-4PM).

Felony, Civil—Supreme and County Court, 7 Court Street, Belmont, NY 14813. 716-268-5813, Fax: 716-268-7090. 9AM-5PM. Access by: mail, phone, fax, in person.

Probate—Surrogate Court, Courthouse, Belmont, NY 14813. 716-268-5815, Fax: 716-268-7090. 9AM-5PM Sept-May; 8:30AM-4PM June-Aug. Access by: mail, phone, in person.

Bronx

Real Estate Recording—Bronx City Register, 1932 Arthur Avenue, Bronx, NY 10457. 9AM-4PM.

Civil Actions Over $25,000—Supreme Court-Civil Division, 851 Grand Concourse, Bronx, NY 10451. 718-590-3641, Fax: 718-590-8122. 9AM-5PM. Access by: mail, in person.

Felony—Supreme Court-Criminal Division, 215 E 161st St, Bronx, NY 10451. 718-417-3149. 9:30AM-4:30PM, Closed 12-2. Access by: mail, in person.

Civil Actions Under $25,000, Eviction, Small Claims—Civil Court of the City of New York-Bronx Branch, 851 Grand Concourse, Bronx, NY 10451. 718-590-3601. 9AM-5PM. Access by: in person.

Probate—Surrogate Court, 851 Grand Concourse, Bronx, NY 10451. 718-590-3611, Fax: 718-537-5158. 9AM-5PM.

Broome

Real Estate Recording—Broome County Clerk, 44 Hawley Street, Binghamton, NY 13901. 607-778-2161, Fax: 607-778-2243. 9AM-5PM.

Felony, Civil—Supreme and County Court, PO Box 2062, Binghamton, NY 13902. 607-778-2448, Fax: 607-778-6426. 9AM-5PM. Access by: mail, in person.

Probate—Surrogate Court, Courthouse Rm 109, Binghamton, NY 13901. 607-778-2111, Fax: 607-778-2308. 9AM-5PM. Special note: $25 search fee.

Cattaraugus

Real Estate Recording—Cattaraugus County Clerk, 303 Court Street, Little Valley, NY 14755. 716-938-9111, Fax: 716-938-6009. 9AM-5PM.

Felony, Civil—Supreme and County Court, 303 Court St, Little Valley, NY 14755. 716-938-9111, Fax: 716-938-6413. 9AM-5PM. Access by: mail, phone, in person.

Probate—Surrogate Court, 303 Court St, Little Valley, NY 14755. 716-938-9111, Fax: 716-938-6983. 9AM-5PM. Access by: mail, in person. Special note: Public can search, but if court has to search there is a fee.

Cayuga

Real Estate Recording—Cayuga County Clerk, 160 Genesee Street, Auburn, NY 13021. 315-328-4187, Fax: 315-253-1006. 9AM-5PM (July-Aug 8AM-4PM).

Felony, Civil—Supreme and County Court, 160 Genesee St, Auburn, NY 13021-3424. 315-331-2744, Fax: 315-253-1586. 9AM-5PM Sept-June; 8AM-4PM July-Aug. Access by: mail, in person.

Probate—Surrogate Court, Courthouse, Auburn, NY 13021-3471. 315-343-0415, Fax: 315-255-4322. 1-4PM T, 9AM-Noon Th; Summer hours 1-3:30PM T, 9AM-Noon Th. Access by: mail, in person.

Chautauqua

Real Estate Recording—Chautauqua County Clerk, Corner of North Erie and E. Chautauqua, Courthouse, Mayville, NY 14757. Fax: 716-753-4310. 9AM-5PM.

Civil—Supreme and County Court-Civil Records, PO Box 170, Mayville, NY 14757. 716-753-4331. 9AM-5PM/Summer 8:30AM-4:30PM. Access by: mail, in person.

Felony—Supreme and County Court-Criminal Records, Courthouse, PO Box 190, Mayville, NY 14757. 716-753-4331, Fax: 716-753-4993. 9AM-5PM/Summer 8:30AM-4:30PM. Access by: mail, in person.

Probate—Surrogate Court, Gerace Office Bldg, Rm 231 (PO Box C), Mayville, NY 14757-0299. 716-753-4339, Fax: 716-753-4600. 9AM-5PM.

Chemung

Real Estate Recording—Chemung County Clerk, 210 Lake Street, Elmira, NY 14902. Fax: 607-737-2897. 8:30AM-4:30PM.

Civil—Supreme and County Court-Civil Records, 210 Lake St, Elmira, NY 14901. 607-737-2920, Fax: 607-737-2897. 8:30AM-4:30PM. Access by: mail, in person.

Felony—Supreme and County Court-Criminal Records, PO Box 588, Elmira, NY 14902-0588. 607-737-2844. 8:30AM-4:30PM. Access by: mail, phone, fax, in person.

Probate—Surrogate Court, 224 Lake St, PO Box 588, Elmira, NY 14901. 607-737-2946, Fax: 607-737-2874. 9AM-5PM. Access by: mail, phone, in person.

Chenango

Real Estate Recording—Chenango County Clerk, 5 Court Street, Norwich, NY 13815. 607-337-1822. 8:30AM-5PM.

Felony, Civil—Supreme and County Court, County Office Bldg, Norwich, NY 13815-1676. 607-337-1450. 8:30AM-5PM. Access by: mail, in person.

Probate—Surrogate Court, County Office Bldg, 5 Court St, Norwich, NY 13815. 607-337-1822, Fax: 607-337-1834. 9AM-Noon, 1-5PM. Access by: mail, in person.

Clinton

Real Estate Recording—Clinton County Clerk, 137 Margaret Street, Government Center, Plattsburgh, NY 12901. 518-565-4730, Fax: 518-565-4780. 8AM-5PM.

Felony, Civil—Supreme and County Court, County Government Center, 137 Margaret St, Plattsburgh, NY 12901. 518-565-4715, Fax: 518-565-4708. 9AM-5PM. Access by: mail, in person.

Probate—Surrogate Court, 137 Margaret St, Plattsburgh, NY 12901-2933. 518-565-4630, Fax: 518-565-4769. 9AM-5PM. Access by: mail, in person.

Columbia

Real Estate Recording—Columbia County Clerk, 560 Warren St. Hudson, NY 12534. 518-828-0513, Fax: 518-828-5299. 9AM-5PM.

Felony, Civil—Supreme and County Court, 560 Warren Street, Hudson, NY 12534. 518-828-3339, Fax: 518-828-5299. 9AM-5PM. Access by: mail, in person.

Probate—Surrogate Court, Courthouse, 401 Union St, Hudson, NY 12534. 518-828-0414, Fax: 518-828-1603. 9AM-5PM. Access by: mail, in person.

Cortland

Real Estate Recording—Cortland County Clerk, Courthouse, Suite 101, 46 Greenbush St. Cortland, NY 13045. 607-753-5040, Fax: 607-758-5500. 9AM-5PM.

Felony, Civil—Supreme and County Court, 46 Greenbush St, Ste 301, Cortland, NY 13045. 607-753-5010, Fax: 607-756-3409. 9AM-5PM. Access by: mail, in person.

Probate—Surrogate Court, 46 Greenbush St, Ste 301, Cortland, NY 13045. 607-753-5355, Fax: 607-756-3409. 9AM-5PM.

Delaware

Real Estate Recording—Delaware County Clerk, Court House Square, Delhi, NY 13753. 607-746-2121, Fax: 607-746-6924. 8:30AM-5PM.

Felony, Civil—Supreme and County Court, 3 Court St, Delhi, NY 13753. 607-746-2131, Fax: 607-746-3253. 9AM-5PM. Access by: mail, in person.

Probate—Surrogate Court, 3 Court St, Delhi, NY 13753. 607-746-2126, Fax: 607-746-3253.

Dutchess

Real Estate Recording—Dutchess County Clerk, 22 Market Street, Poughkeepsie, NY 12601. 914-431-2025. 9AM-4:45PM.

Felony, Civil—Supreme and County Court, 22 Market St, Poughkeepsie, NY 12601-3203. 914-486-2125, Fax: 914-486-2138. 9AM-5PM. Access by: mail, in person. Special note: Criminal index computer search available at OCA. See state introduction.

Probate—Surrogate Court, 10 Market St, Poughkeepsie, NY 12601. 914-486-2235, Fax: 914-486-2234. 9AM-5PM. Access by: mail, in person.

Erie

Real Estate Recording—Erie County Clerk, 25 Delaware Avenue, County Hall, Buffalo, NY 14202. 716-858-3236, Fax: 716-858-6550. 9AM-5PM; Summer Hours July 1st-Sept 1st, 9AM-4:30PM.

Felony, Civil—Supreme and County Court, 25 Delaware Ave, Buffalo, NY 14202. Fax: 716-858-6550. 9AM-5PM. Access by: mail, in person. Special note: Criminal index available from OCA. See state introduction.

Probate—Surrogate Court, 92 Franklin St, Buffalo, NY 14202. 716-854-7867, Fax: 716-853-3741. 9AM-5PM. Access by: mail, in person.

Essex

Real Estate Recording—Essex County Clerk, 100 Court Street, Elizabethtown, NY 12932. 518-873-3310, Fax: 518-873-3548. 8AM-5PM.

Felony, Civil—Supreme and County Courts, Essex County Government Center, Court St, PO Box 217, Elizabethtown, NY 12932. 518-873-3370, Fax: 518-873-3376. 8:30AM-5PM. Access by: mail, in person.

Probate—Surrogate Court, 100 Court St, PO Box 505, Elizabethtown, NY 12932. 518-873-3384. 9AM-5PM.

Franklin

Real Estate Recording—Franklin County Clerk, 63 West Main Street, Malone, NY 12953. 518-483-6767, Fax: 518-483-9143. 9AM-5PM Jan-May; & Sept-Dec; 8AM-4PM June-Aug.

Felony, Civil—Supreme and County Court, 63 W Main St, Malone, NY 12953-1817. 518-481-1748. 9AM-5PM. Access by: mail, in person.

Probate—Surrogate Court, Courthouse, 63 W Main St, Malone, NY 12953-1817. 518-481-1736. 9AM-5PM Sept-May; 8AM-4PM June-Aug. Access by: mail, in person.

Fulton

Real Estate Recording—Fulton County Clerk, 223 West Main Street, Johnstown, NY 12095. Fax: 518-762-3839. 9AM-5PM (July-August 9AM-4PM).

Felony, Civil—Supreme and County Court, County Bldg, West Main St, Johnstown, NY 12095. 518-736-5539, Fax: 518-762-5078. 9AM-5PM. Access by: mail, in person.

Probate—Surrogate Court, County Bldg, West Main St, Johnstown, NY 12095. 518-736-5685, Fax: 518-762-6372. 8AM-5PM (8AM-4PM July-August). Access by: mail, in person.

Genesee

Real Estate Recording—Genesee County Clerk, County Bldg #1, Main & Court Sts. Batavia, NY 14020. Fax: 716-344-8521. 8:30AM-5PM.

Felony, Civil—Supreme and County Courts, PO Box 379, Batavia, NY 14021-0379. 716-344-2550, Fax: 716-344-8521. 8:30AM-5PM. Access by: mail, fax, in person. Special note: All records maintained at County Clerk's office, PO Box 379, Batavia, NY 14021.

Probate—Genessee County Surrogate's Court, 1 West Main St, Batavia, NY 14020. 716-344-2550, Fax: 716-344-8517. 9AM-5PM. Special note: $25.00 search fee.

Greene

Real Estate Recording—Greene County Clerk, 320 Main Street, Catskill, NY 12414. 518-943-4152, Fax: 518-943-2146. 9AM-5PM (June-August 8:30AM-4:30PM).

Felony, Misdemeanor, Civil—Supreme and County Court, Courthouse, Catskill, NY 12414. 518-943-2050, Fax: 518-943-2146. 9AM-5PM. Access by: mail, phone, fax, in person.

Probate—Surrogate Court, Courthouse, 320 Main St, Catskill, NY 12414. 518-943-2484, Fax: 518-943-4372. 9AM-5PM.

Hamilton

Real Estate Recording—Hamilton County Clerk, County Clerk's Office Bldg. Rte. 8, Lake Pleasant, NY 12108. 518-548-7911. 8:30AM-4:30PM.

Felony, Civil—Supreme and County Court, Courthouse, Route 8, Box 204, Lake Pleasant, NY 12108. 518-548-7111. 8:30AM-4:30PM. Access by: mail, in person.

Probate—Surrogate Court, PO Box 780, Indian Lake, NY 12842. 518-648-5411, Fax: 518-648-6286. 8:30AM-4:30PM. Access by: mail, in person.

Herkimer

Real Estate Recording—Herkimer County Clerk, 109 Mary Street, Suite 1111, Herkimer, NY 13350. 315-963-3785, Fax: 315-866-4396. 9AM-4:45PM (June-August 8:30AM-3:45PM).

Felony, Civil—Supreme and County Court, 301 N Washington Street, Herkimer County Office Bldg, Herkimer, NY 13350-1993. 315-964-1165, Fax: 315-866-1802. 9AM-5PM Sept-May; 8:30AM-4PM June-Aug. Access by: mail, phone, in person.

Probate—Surrogate Court, 301 N Washington St #5548, Herkimer, NY 13350. 315-963-3900, Fax: 315-866-1722. 9AM-5PM Sept-May; 8:30AM-4PM June-Aug. Access by: mail, in person.

Jefferson

Real Estate Recording—Jefferson County Clerk, 175 Arsenal Street, Watertown, NY 13601. 315-826-3772, Fax: 315-785-5048. 9AM-5PM (8:30AM-4PM July-Aug).

Felony, Civil—Supreme and County Court, Jefferson County Clerk's Office-Court Records, 175 Arsenal St, County Building, Watertown, NY 13601-3783. 315-826-7912, Fax: 315-785-5048. 9AM-5PM June-Sept; 8:30AM-4PM July-Aug. Access by: mail, in person. www.sunyjefferson.edu/jc

Probate—Jefferson County Surrogates Court, County Office Bldg, 7th Flr, 175 Arsenal St, Watertown, NY 13601-2562. 315-826-3432, Fax: 315-785-5194. 9AM-5PM Sept-May; 8:30AM-4PM June-Aug. Access by: mail, in person.

Kings

Real Estate Recording—Department of Finance, Municipal Building, 1st Floor, Room 2, 210 Joralemon Street, Brooklyn, NY 11201. 718-669-2746, Fax: 718-802-3745.

Civil Actions Over $25,000—Supreme Court-Civil Division, 360 Adams St, Brooklyn, NY 11201. 718-643-5894, Fax: 718-643-8187. 9AM-5PM. Access by: in person.

Felony, Misdemeanor—Supreme Court-Criminal, 120 Schermerhorn St, Brooklyn, NY 11210. 214-653-5740, Fax: 212-417-5856. 9:30AM-4:30PM. Access by: mail, in person.

Probate—Surrogate Court, 2 Johnson St, Brooklyn, NY 11201. 718-643-5262, Fax: 718-643-6237. 9AM-5PM.

Lewis

Real Estate Recording—Lewis County Clerk, 7660 State Street, Courthouse Building, Lowville, NY 13367. 315-429-8581, Fax: 315-376-3768. 8:30AM-4:30PM.

Felony, Civil—Supreme and County Court, Courthouse, PO Box 232, Lowville, NY 13367. 315-429-8612, Fax: 315-376-3768. 8:30AM-4:30PM. Access by: mail, in person.

Probate—Surrogate Court, Courthouse, 7660 State St, Lowville, NY 13367-1396. 315-429-9631, Fax: 315-376-4145. 8:30AM-4:30PM. Special note: Fee is $25 for under 25 years to $70 for over 70 years.

Livingston

Real Estate Recording—Livingston County Clerk, Government Center, 6 Court St. Room 201, Geneseo, NY 14454. 716-243-7050. 8:30AM-4:30PM Oct 1-May 30; 8AM-4PM June 1-Sept 30.

Felony, Civil—Supreme and County Court, 6 Court St, Rm 201, Geneseo, NY 14454. 716-243-7010. 8:30AM-4:30PM Oct-May; 8AM-4PM June-Sept. Access by: mail, in person.

Probate—Surrogate Court, 2 Court St, Geneseo, NY 14454. 716-243-7095. 9AM-5PM.

Madison

Real Estate Recording—Madison County Clerk, North Court Street, County Office Building, Wampsville, NY 13163. Fax: 315-366-2615. 9AM-5PM.

Felony, Civil—Supreme and County Court, County Office Bldg, Wampsville, NY 13163. 315-388-5629, Fax: 315-366-2615. 9AM-5PM. Access by: mail, in person.

Probate—Surrogate Court, Courthouse, PO Box 607, Wampsville, NY 13163. 315-389-4487, Fax: 315-366-2539. 9AM-5PM. Access by: mail, in person.

Monroe

Real Estate Recording—Monroe County Clerk, 39 West Main Street, Rochester, NY 14614. 716-428-5290, Fax: 716-428-5447. 9AM-5PM.

Felony, Civil—Supreme and County Court, County Office Bldg, 39 Main Street West, Rochester, NY 14614. 716-428-5151, Fax: 716-428-4698. 9AM-5PM. Access by: mail, fax, in person, online.

Probate—Surrogate's Court, Hall of Justice, Rm 541, Rochester, NY 14614-2186. 716-428-5200, Fax: 716-428-2650. 9AM-4PM. Access by: mail, in person.

Montgomery

Real Estate Recording—Montgomery County Clerk, County Office Building, Fonda, NY 12068. 518-853-8175. 8:30AM-4PM.

Felony, Civil—Supreme and County Court, Montgomery County Office Bldg, PO Box 1500, Fonda, NY 12068. Fax: 518-853-3596. 9AM-5PM; 8:30AM-4PM (civil). Access by: mail, in person.

Probate—Surrogate Court, PO Box 1500, Fonda, NY 12068-1500. 518-853-8108, Fax: 518-853-8148. 9AM-5PM. Access by: mail, in person. Special note: Court also handles administration of estates, guardianships and adoptions.

Nassau

Real Estate Recording—Nassau County Clerk, 240 Old Country Road, Mineola, NY 11501. 516-571-5021, Fax: 516-742-4099. 9AM-4:45PM.

Civil Actions Over $15,000—Supreme Court, Supreme Court Bldg, Supreme Court Dr, Mineola, NY 11501. 516-571-1660. 9AM-5PM. Access by: mail, in person. Special note: All records are maintained at the County Clerk's Office, 240 Old County Rd, Mineola, NY, 11501, 516-571-2664/2272.

Felony—County Court, 262 Old Country Rd, Mineola, NY 11501. 516-571-2720, Fax: 516-571-2160. 9AM-5PM. Access by: mail, in person. Special note: Criminal index search available at OCA. See state introduction.

Civil Actions Under $15,000, Eviction, Small Claims—District Court-1st and 2nd Districts, 99 Main St, Hempstead, NY 11550. 516-572-2266. 9AM-5PM. Access by: mail, in person. Special note: Records for 2nd District are separate prior to 1980.

District Court-4th District, 87 Bethpage Rd, Hicksville, NY 11801. 516-571-7090. 9AM-5PM. Access by: mail, in person.

Misdemeanor, Civil Actions Under $15,000, Eviction, Small Claims—Glen Cove City Court, 13 Glen St, Glen Cove, NY 11542-2704. 516-676-0109, Fax: 516-676-1570. 9AM-5PM. Access by: mail, in person.

Long Beach City Court, 1 West Chester St, Long Beach, NY 11561. 516-431-1000, Fax: 516-889-3511. 9AM-5PM. Access by: mail, in person.

Probate—Surrogate Court, 262 Old Country Rd, Mineola, NY 11501. 516-571-2082, Fax: 516-571-3864. 9AM-5PM.

New York

Real Estate Recording—New York City Register, 31 Chambers Street, Room 202, New York, NY 10007. 214-653-5950, Fax: 212-788-8521. 9AM-4PM.

Civil Actions Over $25,000—Supreme Court-Civil Division, County Clerk, 60 Centre St, Room 103, New York City, NY 10007. 213-974-5259. 9AM-3PM. Access by: mail, in person.

Felony, Misdemeanor—Supreme Court-Criminal Division, 100 Center St, New York, NY 10013. 214-548-4202. 9:30AM-12:30PM 2-4:30PM. Access by: mail, in person.

Civil Actions Under $25,000, Eviction, Small Claims—Civil Court of the City of New York, 111 Centre St, New York, NY 10013. 213-974-6135, Fax: 212-374-5709. 9AM-5PM. Access by: mail, in person.

Probate—Surrogate Court, 31 Chambers St, New York City, NY 10007. 213-974-6151. 9AM-5PM. Access by: mail, in person.

Niagara

Real Estate Recording—Niagara County Clerk, 175 Hawley Street, Lockport, NY 14094. 716-439-7031, Fax: 716-439-7066. 9AM-5PM (Summer 8:30AM-4:30PM).

Felony, Civil Actions Over $25,000—Supreme Court, 775 3rd St, Niagara Falls, NY 14302. 716-278-1800, Fax: 716-439-7066. 9AM-5PM. Access by: mail, in person. Special note: All records are maintained at County Clerk's Office, 75 Hawley St, Lockport, NY 14094 (716-439-7030).

Felony, Civil Actions Under $25,000—County Court, Courthouse, 175 Hawley St, Lockport, NY 14094. 716-439-7022, Fax: 716-439-4023. 9AM-5PM. Access by: mail, fax, in person.

Probate—Niagara County Surrogate's Court, Niagara County Courthouse, 175 Hawley St, Lockport, NY 14094. 716-439-7130, Fax: 716-439-7157. 9AM-5PM. Access by: in person.

Oneida

Real Estate Recording—Oneida County Clerk, 800 Park Avenue, Utica, NY 13501. 315-839-5400, Fax: 315-798-6440. 8:30AM-5PM.

Felony, Civil—Supreme and County Court, 800 Park Ave, Utica, NY 13501. 315-841-8007. 9AM-5PM. Access by: mail, phone, in person.

Probate—Oneida County Surrogate's Court, 800 Park Ave, 8th Fl, Utica, NY 13501. 315-837-4835, Fax: 315-797-9237. 9AM-5PM Sept-May; 8:30AM-4PM June-Aug.

Onondaga

Real Estate Recording—Onondaga County Clerk, 401 Montgomery St. Room 200, Syracuse, NY 13202. 315-497-0066, Fax: 315-435-3455. 8AM-5PM.

Felony, Civil—Supreme and County Court, 401 Montgomery St Room 200, Syracuse, NY 13202. 315-495-3333. 8AM-5PM. Access by: mail, in person.

Probate—Surrogate Court, Onondaga Courthouse, Rm 209, 401 Montgomery St, Syracuse, NY 13202. 315-493-6345, Fax: 315-435-2113. 8:30AM-5PM. Access by: mail, in person.

Ontario

Real Estate Recording—Ontario County Clerk, Ontario County Municipal Bldg. 20 Ontario St. Canandaigua, NY 14424. 716-396-4432, Fax: 716-393-2951. 8:30AM-5PM.

Felony, Civil—Supreme and County Court, 27 N Main St, Rm 130, Canandaigua, NY 14424-1447. 716-396-4239, Fax: 716-396-4576. 9AM-5PM. Access by: mail, phone, in person. Special note: Records are maintained at County Clerk's office, 25 Pleasant St. Canandaigua, NY 14424, 716-396-4205.

Probate—Surrogate's Court, 27 N Main St, Canandaigua, NY 14424-1447. 716-396-4055, Fax: 716-396-4576. 9AM-5PM. Access by: in person.

Orange

Real Estate Recording—Orange County Clerk, 255-275 Main Street, Goshen, NY 10924. Fax: 914-291-2691. 9AM-5PM.

Felony, Civil—Supreme and County Court, 255 Main St, Goshen, NY 10924. 914-291-3080, Fax: 914-291-2691. 9AM-5PM. Access by: mail, in person. Special note: Criminal index computer search available at OCA. See state introduction.

Probate—Surrogate Court, Park Place, PO Box 329, Goshen, NY 10924. 914-291-2193, Fax: 914-291-2196. 9AM-5PM; Vault closes at 4PM. Access by: mail, in person.

Orleans

Real Estate Recording—Orleans County Clerk, 3 South Main Street, Courthouse Square, Albion, NY 14411. 716-589-5353, Fax: 716-589-0181. 9AM-5PM (July-August 8:30AM-4PM).

Felony, Civil—Supreme and County Court, Courthouse, County Clerk's Office, Albion, NY 14411-9998. 716-589-5458, Fax: 716-589-1618. 9AM-5PM. Access by: mail, phone, in person.

Probate—Surrogate Court, Courthouse Sq, Albion, NY 14411-9998. 716-589-4457, Fax: 716-589-0632. 9AM-5PM. Access by: mail, in person.

Oswego

Real Estate Recording—Oswego County Clerk, 46 East Bridge Street, Oswego, NY 13126. 315-376-5344, Fax: 315-343-8383. 9AM-5PM.

Felony, Civil—Supreme and County Court, 46 E Bridge St, Oswego, NY 13126. 315-376-5333, Fax: 315-349-8383. 9AM-5PM. Access by: mail, in person.

Probate—Surrogate Court, Courthouse, East Oneida St, Oswego, NY 13126-2693. 315-376-5326, Fax: 315-349-8514. 9AM-5PM Sept-May; 8:30AM-3:30 PM June-Aug. Access by: mail, in person.

Otsego

Real Estate Recording—Otsego County Clerk, 197 Main Street, Cooperstown, NY 13326. Fax: 607-547-7544. 9AM-5PM (July-August 9AM-4PM).

Felony, Civil—Supreme and County Court, 197 Main St, Cooperstown, NY 13326. 607-547-4276, Fax: 607-547-7544. 9AM-5PM; 9AM-4PM July-Aug. Access by: mail, in person.

Probate—Surrogate Court, Otsego County Office Bldg, 197 Main St, Cooperstown, NY 13326. 607-547-4338, Fax: 607-547-7566. 9AM-5PM. Access by: mail, in person.

Putnam

Real Estate Recording—Putnam County Clerk, 40 Gleneida Ave. Carmel, NY 10512. 914-225-3641, Fax: 914-228-0231. 9AM-5PM (Summer 8AM-4PM).

Felony, Civil—Supreme and County Court, 40 Gleneida Ave, Carmel, NY 10512. 914-225-3641, Fax: 914-228-0231. 9AM-5PM. Access by: mail, in person. Special note: Criminal index search available at OCA. See state introduction.

Probate—Surrogate Court-Putnam County, 1 County Center, Carmel, NY 10512. 914-225-3641, Fax: 914-228-5761. 9AM-5PM. Access by: mail, in person.

Queens

Real Estate Recording—Queens City Register, 144-06 94th Ave. Jamaica, NY 11435. 9AM-4PM.

Civil Actions Over $25,000—Supreme Court-Civil Division, 88-11 Sutphin Blvd, Jamaica, NY 11435. 718-520-3136, Fax: 718-520-4731. 9AM-5PM, no cashier transactions after 4:45PM. Access by: mail, in person.

Felony, Misdemeanor—Supreme Court-Criminal Division, 125-01 Queens Blvd, Kew Gardens, NY 11415. 718-520-3494. 9:30AM-4:30PM. Access by: mail, in person.

Probate—Surrogate Court, 88-11 Sutphin Blvd, Jamaica, NY 11435. 718-520-3132. 9AM-5PM.

Rensselaer

Real Estate Recording—Rensselaer County Clerk, Courthouse, Congress & 2nd Street, Troy, NY 12180. 518-270-2751. 8:30AM-5PM.

Felony, Civil—Supreme and County Court, Congress & 2nd Sts, Troy, NY 12180. 518-270-4080, Fax: 518-271-7998. 9AM-5PM. Access by: mail, in person. www.rensco.com

Probate—Surrogate Court, Courthouse, Troy, NY 12180. 518-270-3724, Fax: 518-272-5452. 9AM-5PM.

Richmond

Real Estate Recording—Richmond County Clerk, 18 Richmond Terrace, County Courthouse, Staten Island, NY 10301. 9AM-5PM.

Civil Actions Over $25,000—Supreme Court-Civil Division, 18 Richmond Terrace, Staten Island, NY 10301. 718-390-5389. 9AM-5PM. Access by: in person.

Felony, Misdemeanor—Supreme Court-Criminal Division, 67 Targee St, Staten Island, NY 10304. 718-390-5354. 9:30AM-4:30PM, Closed 12-2. Access by: mail, in person.

Probate—Surrogate Court, 18 Richmond Terrace, Rm 201, Staten Island, NY 10301. 718-390-5400. 9AM-5PM.

Rockland

Real Estate Recording—Rockland County Clerk, 27 New Hempstead Road, New City, NY 10956. Fax: 914-638-5647. 7AM-7PM M-Th; 7AM-6PM F.

Felony, Civil—Supreme and County Court, 27 New Hempstead Rd, New City, NY 10956. 914-638-5070, Fax: 914-638-5647. 7AM-6PM. Access by: mail, in person, online. Special note: Criminal index computer search available at OCA. See state introduction.

Probate—Surrogate Court, 1 S Main St, New City, NY 10956. 914-638-5330, Fax: 914-638-5632. 9AM-5PM. Access by: mail, in person.

Saratoga

Real Estate Recording—Saratoga County Clerk, 40 McMaster Street, Ballston Spa, NY 12020. 518-885-5381, Fax: 518-884-4726. Search hours: 8AM-5PM; Recording & Filing hours: 8AM-4:15PM.

Felony, Civil—Supreme and County Court, 40 McMaster St, Ballston Spa, NY 12020. 518-885-2213, Fax: 518-884-4726. 9AM-5PM. Access by: mail, in person.

Probate—Surrogate Court, 30 McMaster St, Bldg 3, Ballston Spa, NY 12020. 518-884-4722. 9AM-5PM.

Schenectady

Real Estate Recording—Schenectady County Clerk, 620 State Street, Schenectady, NY 12305. 518-388-4262, Fax: 518-388-4224. 9AM-5PM.

Felony, Civil—Supreme and County Court, 612 State St, Schenectady, NY 12305. 518-388-4322, Fax: 518-388-4520. 9AM-5PM. Access by: mail, in person.

Probate—Surrogate Court, 612 State St, Schenectady, NY 12305. 518-388-4293, Fax: 518-377-6378. 9AM-5PM.

Schoharie

Real Estate Recording—Schoharie County Clerk, 300 Main Street, County Office Building, Schoharie, NY 12157. 518-295-8386, Fax: 518-295-8338. 8:30AM-5PM.

Felony, Civil—Supreme and County Court, PO Box 549, Schoharie, NY 12157. 518-295-8316, Fax: 518-295-8338. 8:30AM-5PM. Access by: mail, in person.

Probate—Surrogate Court, Courthouse, 300 Main St, PO Box 669, Schoharie, NY 12157-0669. 518-295-8383, Fax: 518-295-8451. 9AM-5PM. Access by: mail, in person.

Schuyler

Real Estate Recording—Schuyler County Clerk, 105 Ninth Street Unit 8, County Office Building, Watkins Glen, NY 14891. 607-535-8181. 9AM-5PM.

Felony, Civil—Supreme and County Court, Courthouse, Watkins Glen, NY 14891. 607-535-7760, Fax: 607-535-4918. 9AM-5PM. Access by: mail, fax, in person.

Probate—Surrogate Court, County Courthouse, 105 Ninth St, Watkins Glen, NY 14891. 607-535-7144, Fax: 607-535-4918. 9AM-5PM. Access by: mail, in person.

Seneca

Real Estate Recording—Seneca County Clerk, 1 DiPronio Drive, Waterloo, NY 13165. 315-598-2958, Fax: 315-539-3789. 8:30AM-5PM.

Felony, Civil—Supreme and County Court, 1 DiPronio Dr, Waterloo, NY 13165-1396. 315-598-7082, Fax: 315-539-9479. 8:30AM-5PM. Access by: mail, fax, in person.

Probate—Surrogate Court, 48 W Williams St, Waterloo, NY 13165-1393. 315-599-7786, Fax: 315-539-7929. 9AM-5PM.

St. Lawrence

Real Estate Recording—St. Lawrence County Clerk, 48 Court Street, Canton, NY 13617. 315-437-6456, Fax: 315-379-2302. 8:30AM-4:30PM.

Felony, Civil—Supreme and County Court, 48 Court St, Canton, NY 13617-1199. 315-435-2426, Fax: 315-379-2302. 8:30AM-4:30PM. Access by: mail, fax, in person.

Probate—Surrogate Court, 48 Court St, Canton, NY 13617. 315-435-2226, Fax: 315-379-2372. 9AM-5PM Sept-June; 8AM-4PM July-Aug. Access by: mail, in person.

Steuben

Real Estate Recording—Steuben County Clerk, 3 East Pulteney Square, County Office Building, Bath, NY 14810. 607-324-7421, Fax: 607-776-7158. 8:30AM-5PM (July-August 8:30AM-4:30PM).

Felony, Civil—Supreme and County Court, 3 E Pulteney Square, Bath, NY 14810-1575. 607-776-7879. 9AM-5PM. Access by: mail, phone, in person.

Probate—Surrogate Court, 13 E Pulteney Square, Bath, NY 14810-1598. 607-776-9631, Fax: 607-776-4987. 9AM-5PM. Access by: mail, in person.

Suffolk

Real Estate Recording—Suffolk County Clerk, 310 Center Drive, Riverhead, NY 11901. 516-852-1500, Fax: 516-852-2004. 9AM-5PM.

Felony, Civil—Suffolk County Court, 310 Centre Dr, Attn: Court Actions, Riverhead, NY 11901. 516-852-2016, Fax: 516-852-2004. 9AM-5PM. Access by: mail, in person. Special note: Criminal index computer search available at OCA. See state introduction. www.co.suffolk.ny.us/clerk/

Probate—Surrogate Court, 320 Centre Dr, Riverhead, NY 11901. 516-852-1745, Fax: 516-852-1777. 9AM-5PM.

Sullivan

Real Estate Recording—Sullivan County Clerk, 100 North Street, Government Center, Monticello, NY 12701. 914-794-3000. 9AM-5PM.

Probate—Surrogate Court, The Government Center, 100 N St, PO Box 5012, Monticello, NY 12701. 914-794-3000, Fax: 914-794-0310. 9AM-5PM. Access by: mail, in person.

Tioga

Real Estate Recording—Tioga County Clerk, 16 Court Street, Owego, NY 13827. Fax: 607-687-4612. 9AM-5PM.

Felony, Civil—Supreme and County Court, PO Box 307, Owego, NY 13827. 607-687-0544, Fax: 607-687-3240. 9AM-5PM. Access by: mail, in person.

Probate—Surrogate Court, PO Box 10, Owego, NY 13827. 607-687-1303, Fax: 607-687-3240. 9AM-5PM.

Tompkins

Real Estate Recording—Tompkins County Clerk, 320 North Tioga Street, Ithaca, NY 14850. 9AM-5PM.

Felony, Civil—Supreme and County Court, 320 N Tioga St, Ithaca, NY 14850. 607-274-5453, Fax: 607-274-5445. 9AM-5PM. Access by: mail, fax, in person.

Probate—Surrogate Court, PO Box 70, Ithaca, NY 14851. 607-277-0622, Fax: 607-277-2572. 9AM-5PM. Access by: mail, in person.

Ulster

Real Estate Recording—Ulster County Clerk, 240-244 Fair Street, County Office Building, Kingston, NY 12401. 914-331-9300, Fax: 914-340-3299. 9AM-5PM.

Felony, Civil—Supreme and County Court, PO Box 1800, Kingston, NY 12401. 914-340-3288, Fax: 914-340-3299. 9AM-5PM. Access by: mail, phone, in person, online.

Probate—Surrogate Court, PO Box 1800, Kingston, NY 12402-1800. 914-340-3000, Fax: 914-340-3352. 9AM-5PM. Access by: mail, in person.

Warren

Real Estate Recording—Warren County Clerk, Municipal Center, 1340 State Route 9, Lake George, NY 12845. Fax: 518-761-6551. 9AM-5PM.

Felony, Civil—Supreme and County Court, Rt US 9, Lake George, NY 12845. 518-761-6430, Fax: 518-761-6253. 9AM-5PM. Access by: mail, phone, fax, in person.

Probate—Surrogate Court, Municipal Center, 1340 Rt US 9, Lake George, NY 12845. 518-761-6514, Fax: 518-761-6465. 9AM-5PM. Access by: in person.

Washington

Real Estate Recording—Washington County Clerk, 383 Broadway, Bldg A, Fort Edward, NY 12828. 518-746-2130, Fax: 518-746-2166. 8:30AM-4:30PM.

Felony, Civil—Supreme and County Court, 383 Broadway, Fort Edward, NY 12828. 518-746-2520. 8:30AM-4:30PM. Access by: mail, in person.

Probate—Surrogate Court, 383 Broadway, Fort Edward, NY 12828. 518-746-2546, Fax: 518-746-2547. 8:30AM-4:30PM. Access by: mail, in person.

Wayne

Real Estate Recording—Wayne County Clerk, 9 Pearl Street, Lyons, NY 14489. 316-273-6319, Fax: 315-946-5978. 9AM-5PM.

Felony, Civil—Supreme and County Courts, 9 Pearl St, PO Box 608, Lyons, NY 14489-0608. 316-273-6493, Fax: 315-946-5978. 9AM-5PM. Access by: mail, phone, fax, in person.

Probate—Surrogate Court, 54 Broad St, Lyons, NY 14489-1134. 316-257-2852, Fax: 315-946-5433. 9AM-4PM.

Westchester

Real Estate Recording—Westchester County Clerk, 110 Dr. Martin Luther King Jr. Blvd. White Plains, NY 10601. Fax: 914-285-3172. 8AM-5:45PM.

Felony, Civil—Supreme and County Court, 110 Dr Martin L King Blvd, White Plains, NY 10601. 914-285-3070, Fax: 914-285-3172. 8AM-5:45PM. Access by: mail, in person. Special note: Criminal index computer search available at OCA. See state introduction. www.westchesterclerk.com

Probate—Surrogate Court, 140 Grand St, 8th Floor, White Plains, NY 10601. 914-285-3712, Fax: 914-285-3728. 9AM-5PM. Access by: mail, in person.

Wyoming

Real Estate Recording—Wyoming County Clerk, 143 North Main Street, Warsaw, NY 14569. 716-786-8800, Fax: 716-786-3703. 9AM-5PM.

Felony, Civil—Supreme and County Court, 147 N Main St, Warsaw, NY 14569. 716-786-2253, Fax: 716-786-3703. 9AM-5PM. Access by: mail, phone, fax, in person. Special note: All records maintained at County Clerk's office.

Probate—Surrogate Court, 143 N Main St, Warsaw, NY 14569. 716-786-3148, Fax: 716-786-3800. 9AM-5PM. Access by: mail, in person.

Yates

Real Estate Recording—Yates County Clerk, 110 Court Street, Penn Yan, NY 14527. 315-594-8074, Fax: 315-536-5545. 9AM-5PM.

Felony, Civil—Supreme and County Court, 110 Court St, Penn Yan, NY 14527-1191. 315-593-8400, Fax: 315-536-5545. 8:30AM-5PM. Access by: mail, in person.

Probate—Surrogate Court, 108 Court St, Penn Yan, NY 14527. 315-594-2719, Fax: 315-536-5190. 9AM-5PM.

Federal Courts

US District Court

Eastern District of New York

Brooklyn Division Brooklyn Courthouse, 225 Cadman Plaza E, Room 130, Brooklyn, NY 11201718-260-2600, Record Room: 718-260-2285, Civil Docket Phone: 718-260-2610, Criminal Docket Phone: 718-260-2610 Counties: Kings, Queens, Richmond. Cases from Nassau and Suffolk may also be heard here. www.nyed.uscourts.gov

Hauppauge Division 300 Rabro Dr, Hauppauge, NY 11788516-582-1100 Fax: 516-582-1417 Counties: Suffolk. www.nyed.uscourts.gov

Uniondale Division 2 Uniondale Ave, Room 303, Uniondale, NY 11553516-485-6500 Counties: Nassau. www.nyed.uscourts.gov

Northern District of New York

Albany Division 445 Broadway, Room 222, James T Foley Courthouse, Albany, NY 12207-2924518-431-0279 Counties: Albany, Clinton, Columbia, Essex, Greene, Rensselaer, Saratoga, Schenectady, Schoharie, Ulster, Warren, Washington. www.nynd.uscourts.gov

Binghamton Division 15 Henry St, Binghamton, NY 13901607-773-2893, Civil Docket Phone: 607-773-2638 Counties: Broome, Chenango, Delaware, Franklin, Jefferson, Lewis, Otsego, St. Lawrence, Tioga. www.nynd.uscourts.gov

Syracuse Division PO Box 7367, Syracuse, NY 13261-7367315-448-0507 Counties: Cayuga, Cortland, Fulton, Hamilton, Herkimer, Madison, Montgomery, Onondaga, Oswego, Tompkins. www.nynd.uscourts.gov

Utica Division Alexander Pirnie Bldg, 10 Broad St, Utica, NY 13501315-793-8151 Counties: Oneida. www.nynd.uscourts.gov

Southern District of New York

New York City Division 500 Pearl St, New York, NY 10007212-805-0136 Counties: Bronx, New York. Some cases from the counties in the White Plains Division are also assigned to the New York Division. www.nysd.uscourts.gov

White Plains Division 300 Quarropas St, White Plains, NY 10601914-390-4000 Counties: Dutchess, Orange, Putnam, Rockland, Sullivan, Westchester. Some cases may be assigned to New York Division. www.nysd.uscourts.gov

Western District of New York

Buffalo Division Room 304, 68 Court St, Buffalo, NY 14202716-551-4211 Fax: 716-551-4850 Counties: Allegany, Cattaraugus, Chautauqua, Erie, Genesee, Niagara, Orleans, Wyoming. Prior to 1982, this division included what is now the Rochester Division.

Rochester Division Room 2120, 100 State St, Rochester, NY 14614716-263-6263 Fax: 716-263-3178 Counties: Chemung, Livingston, Monroe, Ontario, Schuyler, Seneca, Steuben, Wayne, Yates.

US Bankruptcy Court

Eastern District of New York

Brooklyn Division 75 Clinton St, Brooklyn, NY 11201718-330-2188 Counties: Kings, Queens, Richmond. Kings and Queens County Chapter 11 cases may also be assigned to Westbury. Other Queens County cases may be assigned to Westbury Division. Nassau County Chapter 11 cases may be assigned here.

Hauppauge Division 601 Veterans Memorial Hwy, Hauppauge, NY 11788516-361-8038 Counties: Suffolk. Suffolk County Chapter 11 cases may also be assigned to Westbury Division. Nassau County Chapter 11 cases may be assigned here. Other cases for western Suffolk County may also be assigned to Westbury Division.

Westbury Division 1635 Privado Rd, Westbury, NY 11590516-832-8801 Counties: Nassau. Chapter 11 cases for Nassau County may also be assigned to the Brooklyn or Hauppauge Divisions. Kings and Suffolk County Chapter 11 cases may be assigned here. Any Queens County cases may be assigned here. Non-Chapter 11 cases from westernSuffolk County may also be assigned here.

Northern District of New York

Albany Division James T Foley Courthouse, 445 Broadway #327, Albany, NY 12207518-431-0188 Counties: Albany, Clinton, Essex, Franklin, Fulton, Jefferson, Montgomery, Rensselaer, Saratoga, Schenectady, Schoharie, St. Lawrence, Warren, Washington. www.nynb.uscourts.gov

Utica Division Room 230, 10 Broad St, Utica, NY 13501315-793-8101 Fax: 315-793-8128 Counties: Broome, Cayuga, Chenango, Cortland, Delaware, Hamilton, Herkimer, Lewis, Madison, Oneida, Onondaga, Otsego, Oswego, Tioga, Tompkins. www.nynb.uscourts.gov

Southern District of New York

New York Division Room 511, 1 Bowling Green, New York, NY 10004-1408212-668-2870 Counties: Bronx, New York. www.nysb.uscourts.gov

Poughkeepsie Division 176 Church St, Poughkeepsie, NY 12601914-551-4200 Fax: 914-452-8375 Counties: Columbia, Dutchess, Greene, Orange, Putnam, Sullivan, Ulster. www.nysb.uscourts.gov

White Plains Division 300 Quarropas St, White Plains, NY 10601914-390-4060 Counties: Rockland, Westchester. www.nysb.uscourts.gov

Western District of New York

Buffalo Division 310 US Courthouse, 68 Court St, Buffalo, NY 14202716-551-4130 Counties: Allegany, Cattaraugus, Chautauqua, Erie, Genesee, Niagara, Orleans, Wyoming.

Rochester Division Room 1220, 100 State St, Rochester, NY 14614716-263-3148 Counties: Chemung, Livingston, Monroe, Ontario, Schuyler, Seneca, Steuben, Wayne, Yates.

North Carolina

Attorney General's Office
PO Box 629
Raleigh, NC 27602-0629
919-716-6400
Fax: 919-716-6750
www.jus.state.nc.us

Governor's Office
20301 Mail Service Center
Raleigh, NC 27699-0301
919-733-4240
Fax: 919-715-3175
www.governor.state.nc.us

State Archives
109 E Jones St
Raleigh, NC 27601-2807
919-733-3952
Fax: 919-733-1354
www.ah.dcr.state.nc.us

Capital:	Raleigh
	Wake County
Time Zone:	EST
Number of Counties:	100
Population:	7,425,183
Web Site:	www.state.nc.us

Search Unclaimed Property Online
There is no Internet-based search for unclaimed property for this state.

State Agencies

Criminal Records
Restricted access.
State Bureau of Investigation, Identification Section, 407 N Blount St, Raleigh, NC 27601-1009; 919-662-4500 x300; Fax: 919-662-4380; 7:30AM-5PM

Corporation Records
Limited Partnerships
Limited Liability Company Records
Trademarks/Servicemarks
Secretary of State, Corporations Section, 300 N Salisbury St, Raleigh, NC 27603-5909; 919-733-4201 Corporations, 919-733-4129 Trademarks; Fax: 919-733-1837; 8AM-5PM. Access by: mail, phone, in person, online. www.secstate.state.nc.us/business

Uniform Commercial Code
Federal Tax Liens
UCC Division, Secretary of State, 300 North Salisbury St, #302, Raleigh, NC 27603-5909; 919-733-4205; Fax: 919-733-9700; 7:30AM-5PM. Access by: mail, online. www.secstate.state.nc.us/secstate/ucc.htm

Sales Tax Registrations
Restricted access.
This agency refuses to release any information about registrants, but will validate a number if presented with one.
Revenue Department, Sales & Use Tax Division, PO Box 25000, Raleigh, NC 27640 (501 N Wilmington Street, Raleigh, NC 27604) (501 N Wilmington Street, Raleigh, NC 27604); 919-733-3661; Fax: 919-715-6086; 8AM-5PM
www.dor.state.us/dor

State Tax Liens
Records not available from state agency.
Tax lien data is found at the county level.

Workers' Compensation Records
NC Industrial Commission, Dobbs Bldg, 430 N Salisbury-6th floor, Raleigh, NC 27611; 919-733-1989; 8AM-5PM. Access by: mail. www.comp.state.nc.us

Birth Certificates

Dept of Environment, Health & Natural Resources, Vital Records Section, PO Box 29537, Raleigh, NC 27626-0537 (225 N McDowell St, Raleigh, NC 27603); 919-733-3526; Fax: 919-829-1359; 8AM-4PM. Access by: mail, phone, in person.

Death Records

Dept of Environment, Health & Natural Resources, Vital Records Section, PO Box 29537, Raleigh, NC 27626-0537; 919-733-3526; Fax: 919-829-1359; 8AM-4PM. Access by: mail, phone, in person.

Marriage Certificates

Dept of Environment, Health & Natural Resources, Vital Records Section, PO Box 29537, Raleigh, NC 27626-0537; 919-733-3526; Fax: 919-829-1359; 8AM-4PM. Access by: mail, phone, in person.

Divorce Records

Dept of Environment, Health & Natural Resources, Vital Records Section, PO Box 29537, Raleigh, NC 27626-0537; 919-733-3526; Fax: 919-829-1359; 8AM-4PM. Access by: mail, phone, in person.

Accident Reports

Division of Motor Vehicles, Traffic Records Section, 1100 New Bern Ave, Room 101, Raleigh, NC 27697; 919-733-7250; Fax: 919-733-9605; 8AM-5PM. Access by: mail, fax.

Driver Records

Division of Motor Vehicles, Driver's License Section, 1100 New Bern Ave, Raleigh, NC 27697; 919-715-7000; 8AM-5PM. Access by: mail, online. www.dmv.dot.state.nc.us

Vehicle Ownership
Vehicle Identification

Division of Motor Vehicles, Registration/Correspondence Unit, 1100 New Bern Ave, Raleigh, NC 27697; 919-715-7000; 8AM-5PM. Access by: mail. www.dmv.dot.state.nc.us

Boat & Vessel Ownership
Boat & Vessel Registration

North Carolina Wildlife Resources Commission, 322 Chapanoke Rd, Raleigh, NC 27603; 919-662-4370; Fax: 919-662-4379; 8AM-5PM M-F. www.state.nc.us/Wildlife

Legislation-Current/Pending
Legislation-Passed

North Carolina General Assembly, State Legislative Bldg, 16 W. Jones Street, 1st Fl, Raleigh, NC 27603; 919-733-7779 Bill Numbers, 919-733-3270 Archives, 919-733-5648 Order Desk; 8:30AM-5:30PM. Access by: mail, phone, in person, online. www.ncga.state.nc.us

Voter Registration

Restricted access.
There is no statewide system, although one will be in place by early 2000. Records are open to the public and must be accessed at the county level through the County Director of Elections.
State Board of Elections, PO Box 2169, Raleigh, NC 27602-2169; 919-733-7173; Fax: 919-715-0125; 8AM-5PM www.sboe.state.nc.us/BOE

GED Certificates

Department of Community Colleges, GED Office, 5024 Mail Service Center, Raleigh, NC 27699-5024; 919-733-7051 x744; Fax: 919-715-5796; 8AM-4PM. Access by: mail, phone, in person.

Hunting License Information
Fishing License Information

Records not available from state agency.

They only maintain a database of lifetime license holders and consider the information to be confidential.

County Courts & Recording Offices

About the Courts...

Administration

Administrative Office of the Courts, Justice Bldg   919-733-7107
2 E Morgan St   Fax: 919-715-5779
Raleigh, NC 27602
www.aoc.state.nc.us

Court Structure

The Superior Court is the court of general jurisdiction, the District Court is limited. Most ounties combine the courts.

Searching Hints

Most courts recommend that civil searches be done in person or by a retriever and that only criminal searches be requested in writing (for a $5.00 search fee). Many courts have archived their records prior to 1968 in the Raleigh State Archives, 919-733-5722.

Online Access

An internal online computer system links all North Carolina civil and criminal courts. There is no external access.

About the Recording Offices...

Organization

100 counties, 100 recording offices. The recording officers are Register of Deeds and Clerk of Superior Court (tax liens). The entire state is in the Eastern Time Zone (EST).

UCC Records

This is a dual filing state. Financing statements are filed both at the state level and with the Register of Deeds, except for consumer goods, farm related and real estate related collateral. All counties will perform UCC searches. Use search request form UCC-11. Search fees are usually $15.00 per debtor name. Copies usually cost $1.00 per page.

Lien Records

Federal tax liens on personal property of businesses are filed with the Secretary of State. Other federal and all state tax liens are filed with the county Clerk of Superior Court, not with the Register of Deeds. (Oddly, even tax liens on real property are also filed with the Clerk of Superior Court, not with the Register of Deeds.) Refer to The Sourcebook of County Court Records for information about North Carolina Superior Courts.

Real Estate Records

Counties will not perform real estate searches. Copy fees are usually $1.00 per page. Certification usually costs $3.00 for the first page and $1.00 for each additional page of a document.

County Courts & Recording Offices

Alamance

Real Estate Recording—Alamance County Register of Deeds, 118 West Harden Street, Graham, NC 27253. 910-570-1318. 8AM-5PM.

Felony, Misdemeanor—Superior-District Court, 212 West Elm St, Suite 105, Graham, NC 27253. 360-336-9440. 8AM-5PM. Access by: mail, in person.

Civil, Eviction, Small Claims, Probate—Superior-District Court, Civil, 1 Court Square, Graham, NC 27253. 360-336-9350. 8AM-5PM. Access by: in person.

Alexander

Real Estate Recording—Alexander County Register of Deeds, 201 First Street SW, Suite 1, Taylorsville, NC 28681., Fax: 828-632-1119. 8AM-5PM.

Felony, Misdemeanor, Civil, Eviction, Small Claims, Probate—Superior-District Court, PO Box 100, Taylorsville, NC 28681. 828-632-2215, Fax: 828-632-3550. 8AM-5PM. Access by: mail, in person.

Alleghany

Real Estate Recording—Alleghany County Register of Deeds, 12 N. Main Street, Sparta, NC 28675. 910-372-4179, Fax: 336-372-2061. 8AM-5PM.

Felony, Misdemeanor, Civil, Eviction, Small Claims, Probate—Superior-District Court, PO Box 61, Sparta, NC 28675. 360-249-3842, Fax: 336-372-4899. 8AM-5PM. Access by: mail, fax, in person.

Anson

Real Estate Recording—Anson County Register of Deeds, Green Street Courthouse, Wadesboro, NC 28170. 704-694-6219, Fax: 704-694-6135. 8:30AM-5PM.

Felony, Misdemeanor, Civil, Eviction, Small Claims, Probate—Superior-District Court, PO Box 1064, Wadesboro, NC 28170. 704-694-2314, Fax: 704-695-1161. 8AM-5PM. Access by: mail, in person.

Ashe

Real Estate Recording—Ashe County Register of Deeds, East Main Street, Courthouse, Jefferson, NC 28640. 8AM-5PM.

Felony, Misdemeanor, Civil, Eviction, Small Claims, Probate—Superior-District Court, PO Box 95, Jefferson, NC 28640. 360-249-3441, Fax: 336-246-4276. 8AM-5PM. Access by: mail, in person.

Avery

Real Estate Recording—Avery County Register of Deeds, 200 Montezuma St. Newland, NC 28657. 704-732-8200. 8AM-4:30PM.

Felony, Misdemeanor, Civil, Eviction, Small Claims, Probate—Superior-District Court, PO Box 115, Newland, NC 28657. 828-733-2900, Fax: 828-733-8410. 8AM-4:30PM. Access by: mail, in person.

Beaufort

Real Estate Recording—Beaufort County Register of Deeds, 112 West Second Street, Courthouse, Washington, NC 27889. 8:30AM-5PM.

Felony, Misdemeanor, Civil, Eviction, Small Claims, Probate—Superior-District Court, PO Box 1403, Washington, NC 27889. 919-946-5184. 8:30AM-5:30PM. Access by: mail, in person.

Bertie

Real Estate Recording—Bertie County Register of Deeds, Corner of King & Dundee, Windsor, NC 27983., Fax: 919-794-5327. 8:30AM-5PM.

Felony, Misdemeanor, Civil, Eviction, Small Claims, Probate—Superior-District Court, PO Box 370, Windsor, NC 27983. 919-794-3039, Fax: 919-794-2482. 8AM-5PM. Access by: mail, fax, in person.

Bladen

Real Estate Recording—Bladen County Register of Deeds, Courthouse Drive, Elizabethtown, NC 28337., Fax: 910-862-6716. 8:30AM-5PM.

Felony, Misdemeanor, Civil, Eviction, Small Claims, Probate—Superior-District Court, PO Box 2619, Elizabethtown, NC 28337. 910-862-2143. 8:30AM-5PM. Access by: mail, in person.

Brunswick

Real Estate Recording—Brunswick County Register of Deeds, 75 Courthouse Dr. Bolivia, NC 28422. 910-253-4331, Fax: 910-253-2703. 8:30AM-5PM.

Felony, Misdemeanor, Civil, Eviction, Small Claims, Probate—Superior-District Court, PO Box 127, Bolivia, NC 28422. 910-253-8502, Fax: 910-253-7652. 8:30AM-5:00PM. Access by: mail, in person.

Buncombe

Real Estate Recording—Buncombe County Register of Deeds, 60 Court Plaza, Room 110, Asheville, NC 28801., Fax: 828-255-5829. 8:30AM-5PM.

Felony, Misdemeanor, Civil, Eviction, Small Claims, Probate—Superior-District Court, 60 Court Plaza, Asheville, NC 28801-3519. 828-255-4702, Fax: 828-251-6257. 8:30AM-5PM. Access by: mail, in person.

Burke

Real Estate Recording—Burke County Register of Deeds, 201 South Green Street, Courthouse, Morganton, NC 28655., Fax: 828-438-5463. 8AM-5PM.

Felony, Misdemeanor, Civil, Eviction, Small Claims, Probate—Superior-District Court, PO Box 796, Morganton, NC 28680. 828-432-2800, Fax: 828-438-5460. 8AM-5PM. Access by: mail, fax, in person.

Cabarrus

Real Estate Recording—Cabarrus County Register of Deeds, 65 Church Street S.E. Concord, NC 28025., Fax: 704-788-9898. 8AM-5PM.

Felony, Misdemeanor, Civil, Eviction, Small Claims, Probate—Superior-District Court, PO Box 70, Concord, NC 28026-0070. 704-786-4137. 8:30AM-5PM. Access by: mail, in person.

Caldwell

Real Estate Recording—Caldwell County Register of Deeds, 905 West Avenue N.W. County Office Building, Lenoir, NC 28645., Fax: 828-757-1294. 8AM-5PM.

Felony, Misdemeanor, Civil, Eviction, Small Claims, Probate—Superior-District Court, PO Box 1376, Lenoir, NC 28645. 828-757-1375, Fax: 828-757-1479. 8AM-5PM. Access by: mail, fax, in person.

Camden

Real Estate Recording—Camden County Register of Deeds, County Courthouse, 117 North 343, Camden, NC 27921. 8AM-5PM.

Felony, Misdemeanor, Civil, Eviction, Small Claims, Probate—Superior-District Court, PO Box 219, Camden, NC 27921. 919-331-4871, Fax: 919-331-4827. 8AM-5PM. Access by: mail, in person.

Carteret

Real Estate Recording—Carteret County Register of Deeds, Courthouse Square, Beaufort, NC 28516., Fax: 252-728-7693. 8AM-5PM.

Felony, Misdemeanor, Civil, Eviction, Small Claims, Probate—Superior-District Court, Carteret County, Courthouse

Square, Beaufort, NC 28516. 254-435-2334, Fax: 252-728-6502. 8AM-5PM. Access by: mail, phone, in person.

Caswell

Real Estate Recording—Caswell County Register of Deeds, 139 E. Church St. Courthouse, Yanceyville, NC 27379. 910-694-4193, Fax: 336-694-1405. 8AM-5PM.

Felony, Misdemeanor, Civil, Eviction, Small Claims, Probate—Superior-District Court, PO Drawer 790, Yanceyville, NC 27379. 360-374-6383, Fax: 336-694-7338. 8AM-5PM. Access by: mail, in person.

Catawba

Real Estate Recording—Catawba County Register of Deeds, Catawba County Justice Center, 100 S. West Blvd. Newton, NC 28658. 8AM-5PM.

Felony, Misdemeanor, Civil, Eviction, Small Claims, Probate—Superior-District Court, PO Box 790, Newton, NC 28658. 828-464-5216. 8AM-5PM. Access by: mail, in person.

Chatham

Real Estate Recording—Chatham County Register of Deeds, 12 East St. Pittsboro, NC 27312. 8AM-4:30PM.

Felony, Misdemeanor, Civil, Eviction, Small Claims, Probate—Superior-District Court, PO Box 369, Pittsboro, NC 27312. 919-542-3240. 8AM-5PM. Access by: mail, phone, in person.

Cherokee

Real Estate Recording—Cherokee County Register of Deeds, 75 Peachtree St. Suite 102, Murphy, NC 28906., Fax: 828-837-8414. 8AM-5PM.

Felony, Misdemeanor, Civil, Eviction, Small Claims, Probate—Superior-District Court, 75 Peachtree St, Rm 201, Murphy, NC 28906. 828-837-2522. 8AM-5PM. Access by: mail, in person.

Chowan

Real Estate Recording—Chowan County Register of Deeds, 101 South Broad Street, Courthouse, Edenton, NC 27932. 8AM-5PM.

Felony, Misdemeanor, Civil, Eviction, Small Claims, Probate—Superior-District Court, N.C. Courier Box 106319, PO Box 588, Edenton, NC 27932. 253-798-7474, Fax: 252-482-2190. 9AM-5PM. Access by: mail, in person.

Clay

Real Estate Recording—Clay County Register of Deeds, 54 Church St. Hayesville, NC 28904., Fax: 828-389-9749. 8AM-5PM.

Felony, Misdemeanor, Civil, Eviction, Small Claims, Probate—Superior-District Court, PO Box 506, Hayesville, NC 28904. 828-389-8334, Fax: 828-389-3329. 8AM-5PM. Access by: mail, fax, in person.

Cleveland

Real Estate Recording—Cleveland County Register of Deeds, 311 East Marion St. Room 151, Shelby, NC 28150. 704-484-4807, Fax: 704-484-4909. 8AM-5PM.

Felony, Misdemeanor, Civil, Eviction, Small Claims, Probate—Superior-District Court, 100 Justice Place, Shelby, NC 28150. 704-484-4851, Fax: 704-480-5487. 8AM-5PM. Access by: mail, fax, in person.

Columbus

Real Estate Recording—Columbus County Register of Deeds, Courthouse, Whiteville, NC 28472, Fax: 910-640-2547. 8:30AM-5PM.

Felony, Misdemeanor, Civil, Eviction, Small Claims, Probate—Superior-District Court, PO Box 1587, Whiteville, NC 28472. 910-641-3000, Fax: 910-641-3027. 8AM-5PM. Access by: mail, in person.

Craven

Real Estate Recording—Craven County Register of Deeds, 406 Craven Street, New Bern, NC 28560., Fax: 252-636-1937. 8AM-5PM.

Felony, Misdemeanor, Civil, Eviction, Small Claims, Probate—Superior-District Court, PO Box 1187, New Bern, NC 28563. 253-851-5131, Fax: 252-514-4891. 8AM-5PM. Access by: mail, in person.

Cumberland

Real Estate Recording—Cumberland County Register of Deeds, 117 Dick Street, Room 114, Fayetteville, NC 28302., Fax: 910-323-1456. 8AM-5PM.

Felony, Misdemeanor, Civil, Eviction, Small Claims, Probate—Superior-District Court, PO Box 363, Fayetteville, NC 28302. 8:30AM-5PM. Access by: mail, in person.

Currituck

Real Estate Recording—Currituck County Register of Deeds, 101 Courthouse Road, Currituck, NC 27929., Fax: 252-232-3906. 8AM-5PM.

Felony, Misdemeanor, Civil, Eviction, Small Claims, Probate—Superior-District Court, PO Box 175, Currituck, NC 27929. 252-527-6231, Fax: 252-232-3722. 8AM-5PM. Access by: mail, fax, in person.

Dare

Real Estate Recording—Dare County Register of Deeds, 300 Queen Elizabeth Avenue, Courthouse, PO Box 70, Manteo, NC 27954. 8:30AM-5PM.

Felony, Misdemeanor, Civil, Eviction, Small Claims, Probate—Superior-District Court, PO Box 1849, Manteo, NC 27954. 253-591-7455, Fax: 252-473-1620. 8:30AM-5PM. Access by: mail, in person.

Davidson

Real Estate Recording—Davidson County Register of Deeds, 110 West Center Street, Court House, Lexington, NC 27292., Fax: 336-238-2318. 8AM-5PM.

Felony, Misdemeanor, Civil, Eviction, Small Claims, Probate—Superior-District Court, PO Box 1064, Lexington, NC 27293-1064., Fax: 336-249-6951. 8AM-5PM. Access by: mail, in person.

Davie

Real Estate Recording—Davie County Register of Deeds, 123 South Main Street, Mocksville, NC 27028. 8:30AM-5PM.

Felony, Misdemeanor, Civil, Eviction, Small Claims, Probate—Superior-District Court, 140 S Main St, Mocksville, NC 27028., Fax: 336-751-4720. 8:30AM-5PM. Access by: mail, in person.

Duplin

Real Estate Recording—Duplin County Register of Deeds, Courthouse, Kenansville, NC 28349., Fax: 910-296-2344. 8AM-5PM.

Felony, Misdemeanor, Civil, Eviction, Small Claims, Probate—Superior-District Court, PO Box 189, Kenansville, NC 28349., Fax: 910-296-2310. 8AM-5PM. Access by: mail, phone, fax, in person.

Durham

Real Estate Recording—Durham County Register of Deeds, 200 East Main Street, Ground Floor, Durham, NC 27701., Fax: 919-560-0497. 8:30-5PM.

Felony, Misdemeanor, Civil, Eviction, Small Claims, Probate—Superior-District Court, PO Box 1772, Durham, NC 27702. 8:30AM-5PM. Access by: mail, in person.

Edgecombe

Real Estate Recording—Edgecombe County Register of Deeds, 301 St. Andrew Street, Courthouse, Tarboro, NC 27886. 919-641-7834, Fax: 919-641-1771. 7:30AM-5PM.

Felony, Misdemeanor, Civil, Eviction, Small Claims, Probate—Superior-District Court, PO Drawer 9, Tarboro, NC 27886., Fax: 919-823-1278. 8AM-5PM. Access by: mail, in person.

Forsyth

Real Estate Recording—Forsyth County Register of Deeds, 102 W. Third St, Upper Plaza, Winston-Salem, NC 27101. 910-727-2655, Fax: 336-727-2341. 8AM-5PM.

Felony, Misdemeanor, Civil, Eviction, Small Claims, Probate—Superior-District Court, PO Box 20099, Winston Salem, NC 27120-0099. 360-378-2163, Fax: 336-761-2018. 8AM-5PM. Access by: mail, in person.

Franklin

Real Estate Recording—Franklin County Register of Deeds, 113 South Main Street, Louisburg, NC 27549., Fax: 919-496-1457. 8AM-5PM.

Felony, Misdemeanor, Civil, Eviction, Small Claims, Probate—Superior-District Court, 102 S Main St, Louisburg, NC 27549. 919-496-5104, Fax: 919-496-0407. 8:30AM-5PM. Access by: mail, fax, in person.

Gaston

Real Estate Recording—Gaston County Register of Deeds, 325 N. Marietta St. Gastonia, NC 28052., Fax: 704-862-7519. 8:30AM-5PM.

Felony, Misdemeanor, Civil, Eviction, Small Claims, Probate—Superior-District Court, PO Box 340, Gastonia, NC 28053. 704-868-5801. 8AM-5PM. Access by: mail, in person.

Gates

Real Estate Recording—Gates County Register of Deeds, Court Street, Gatesville, NC 27938., Fax: 919-357-0850. 9AM-5PM.

Felony, Misdemeanor, Civil, Eviction, Small Claims, Probate—Superior-District Court, PO Box 31, Gatesville, NC 27938. 252-728-8500, Fax: 252-357-1047. 8AM-5PM. Access by: mail, in person.

Graham

Real Estate Recording—Graham County Register of Deeds, Main Street, Courthouse, Robbinsville, NC 28771. 704-479-7962, Fax: 828-479-7988. 8:30AM-4:30PM.

Felony, Misdemeanor, Civil, Eviction, Small Claims, Probate—Superior-District Court, PO Box 1179, Robbinsville, NC 28771. 828-479-7986, Fax: 828-479-6417. 8AM-5PM M-Th; 8AM-4:30PM Fri. Access by: mail, in person.

Granville

Real Estate Recording—Granville County Register of Deeds, 101 Main Street, Courthouse, Oxford, NC 27565., Fax: 919-603-1345. 8:30AM-5PM.

Felony, Misdemeanor, Civil, Eviction, Small Claims, Probate—Superior-District Court, Courthouse, 101 Main Street, Oxford, NC 27565. 919-693-2649, Fax: 919-693-8944. Access by: mail, phone, in person.

Greene

Real Estate Recording—Greene County Register of Deeds, Greene Street, Courthouse, Snow Hill, NC 28580. 8AM-5PM.

Felony, Misdemeanor, Civil, Eviction, Small Claims, Probate—Superior-District Court, PO Box 675, Snow Hill, NC 28580. 919-747-3505. 8AM-5PM. Access by: mail, in person.

Guilford

Real Estate Recording—Guilford County Register of Deeds, 505 E. Green St. Room 132, High Point, NC 27260. 8AM-5PM.

Felony, Misdemeanor, Civil, Eviction, Small Claims, Probate—Superior-District Court, 201 S Eugene, PO Box 3008, Greensboro, NC 27402. 8:30AM-5PM. Access by: mail, in person.

Halifax

Real Estate Recording—Halifax County Register of Deeds, Ferrell Lane, Halifax, NC 27839., Fax: 252-583-1273. 8:30AM-5PM.

Felony, Misdemeanor, Civil, Eviction, Small Claims, Probate—Superior-District Court, PO Box 66, Halifax, NC 27839.

254-435-2201, Fax: 252-583-1005. 8:30AM-5PM. Access by: mail, in person.

Harnett

Real Estate Recording—Harnett County Register of Deeds, Courthouse, 729 Main Street, Lillington, NC 27546., Fax: 910-814-3841. 8AM-5PM.

Felony, Misdemeanor, Civil, Eviction, Small Claims, Probate—Superior-District Court, PO Box 849, Lillington, NC 27546. 910-893-5164, Fax: 910-893-3683. 8:15AM-5:15PM. Access by: mail, in person.

Haywood

Real Estate Recording—Haywood County Register of Deeds, Courthouse, 215 N. Main St. Waynesville, NC 28786., Fax: 828-452-6762. 8AM-5PM.

Felony, Misdemeanor, Civil, Eviction, Small Claims, Probate—Superior-District Court, 420 N. Main, Waynesville, NC 28786. 828-456-3540, Fax: 828-456-4937. 8:30AM-5PM. Access by: mail, in person.

Henderson

Real Estate Recording—Henderson County Register of Deeds, Suite 129, 200 N. Grove St. Hendersonville, NC 28792. 8:30AM-5PM.

Felony, Misdemeanor, Civil, Eviction, Small Claims, Probate—Superior-District Court, PO Box 965, Hendersonville, NC 28793. 828-697-4860. 8AM-5PM. Access by: mail, in person.

Hertford

Real Estate Recording—Hertford County Register of Deeds, Courthouse, Winton, NC 27986. 919-358-7815, Fax: 252-358-7806. 8:30AM-5PM.

Felony, Misdemeanor, Civil, Eviction, Small Claims, Probate—Superior-District Court, PO Box 86, Winton, NC 27986. 252-792-2515, Fax: 252-358-0793. 8AM-5PM. Access by: mail, in person.

Hoke

Real Estate Recording—Hoke County Register of Deeds, 304 N. Main St. Raeford, NC 28376., Fax: 910-875-9515. 8AM-5PM.

Felony, Misdemeanor, Civil, Eviction, Small Claims, Probate—Superior-District Court, PO Drawer 1569, Raeford, NC 28376. 910-875-3728, Fax: 910-904-1708. 8:30AM-5PM. Access by: mail, in person.

Hyde

Real Estate Recording—Hyde County Register of Deeds, Courthouse Square, Swanquarter, NC 27885. 919-926-4101, Fax: 919-926-3082. 8AM-5PM.

Felony, Misdemeanor, Civil, Eviction, Small Claims, Probate—Superior-District Court, PO Box 337, Swanquarter, NC 27885. 919-926-4101, Fax: 919-926-1002. 8:30AM-5:30PM. Access by: mail, phone, in person. Special note: Phone requesting only for general inquires.

Iredell

Real Estate Recording—Iredell County Register of Deeds, 221 Water Street, Statesville, NC 28677., Fax: 704-878-3055. 8AM-5PM.

Felony, Misdemeanor, Civil, Eviction, Small Claims, Probate—Superior-District Court, PO Box 186, Statesville, NC 28687., Fax: 704-878-3261. 8AM-5PM. Access by: mail, phone, in person.

Jackson

Real Estate Recording—Jackson County Register of Deeds, 401 Grindstaff Cove Rd. Sylva, NC 28779., Fax: 828-586-6879. 8:30AM-5PM.

Felony, Misdemeanor, Civil, Eviction, Small Claims, Probate—Superior-District Court, 401 Grindstaff Cove Rd, Sylva, NC 28779. 828-586-7512, Fax: 828-586-9009. 8:30AM-5PM. Access by: mail, in person.

Johnston

Real Estate Recording—Johnston County Register of Deeds, Market Street, Courthouse Square, Smithfield, NC 27577. 8AM-5PM.

Felony, Misdemeanor, Civil, Eviction, Small Claims, Probate—Superior-District Court, PO Box 297, Smithfield, NC 27577. 919-934-3192, Fax: 919-934-5857. 8AM-5PM. Access by: mail, in person.

Jones

Real Estate Recording—Jones County Register of Deeds, 101 Market St. Trenton, NC 28585., Fax: 919-448-1357. 8AM-5PM.

Felony, Misdemeanor, Civil, Eviction, Small Claims, Probate—Superior-District Court, PO Box 280, Trenton, NC 28585. 919-448-7351, Fax: 919-448-1608. 8AM-5PM. Access by: mail, in person.

Lee

Real Estate Recording—Lee County Register of Deeds, 1408 South Horner Blvd. Sanford, NC 27331., Fax: 919-774-5063. 8AM-5PM.

Felony, Misdemeanor, Civil, Eviction, Small Claims, Probate—Superior-District Court, PO Box 4209, Sanford, NC 27331. 919-708-4400, Fax: 919-775-3483. 8AM-5PM. Access by: mail, in person.

Lenoir

Real Estate Recording—Lenoir County Register of Deeds, County Courthouse, 130 S. Queen St. Kinston, NC 28501. 919-527-7174, Fax: 252-523-6139. 8:30AM-5PM.

Felony, Misdemeanor, Civil, Eviction, Small Claims, Probate—Superior-District Court, PO Box 68, Kinston, NC 28502-0068. 254-386-3417, Fax: 252-527-9154. 8AM-5PM. Access by: mail, in person.

Lincoln

Real Estate Recording—Lincoln County Register of Deeds, Courthouse, Lincolnton, NC 28092., Fax: 704-732-9049. 8AM-5PM.

Felony, Misdemeanor, Civil, Eviction, Small Claims, Probate—Superior-District Court, PO Box 8, Lincolnton, NC 28093. 704-736-8566, Fax: 704-736-8718. 8AM-5PM. Access by: mail, in person.

Macon

Real Estate Recording—Macon County Register of Deeds, 5 West Main Street, Franklin, NC 28734., Fax: 828-369-6382. 8AM-5PM.

Felony, Misdemeanor, Civil, Eviction, Small Claims, Probate—Superior-District Court, PO Box 288, Franklin, NC 28744. 828-349-2000, Fax: 828-369-2515. 8:30AM-5PM. Access by: mail, in person.

Madison

Real Estate Recording—Madison County Register of Deeds, Courthouse, Marshall, NC 28753. 8:30AM-5PM.

Felony, Misdemeanor, Civil, Eviction, Small Claims, Probate—Superior-District Court, PO Box 217, Marshall, NC 28753. 828-649-2531. 8AM-5PM. Access by: mail, in person.

Martin

Real Estate Recording—Martin County Register of Deeds, 305 East Main Street, Williamston, NC 27892., Fax: 252-792-1684. 8AM-5PM.

Felony, Misdemeanor, Civil, Eviction, Small Claims, Probate—Superior-District Court, PO Box 807, Williamston, NC 27892. 254-559-3151, Fax: 252-792-6668. 8AM-5PM. Access by: mail, in person.

McDowell

Real Estate Recording—McDowell County Register of Deeds, 1 South Main Street, Courthouse, Marion, NC 28752. 704-652-7121, Fax: 828-652-4727. 8:30AM-5PM.

Felony, Misdemeanor, Civil, Eviction, Small Claims, Probate—Superior-District Court, PO Drawer 729, Marion, NC 28752. 828-652-7717. 8:30AM-5PM. Access by: mail, in person.

Mecklenburg

Real Estate Recording—Mecklenburg County Register of Deeds, 720 East 4th Street, Ste. 100, Charlotte, NC 28202., Fax: 704-336-7699.

Felony, Misdemeanor, Civil, Eviction, Small Claims, Probate—Superior-District Court, 800 E 4th St, Charlotte, NC 28202. 8AM-5PM. Access by: mail, in person. www.aoc.state.nc.us/www/public/courts/mecklenburg.htm

Mitchell

Real Estate Recording—Mitchell County Register of Deeds, Crimson Laurel Way, Administrative Building, Bakersville, NC 28705., Fax: 828-688-3666. 8AM-5PM.

Felony, Misdemeanor, Civil, Eviction, Small Claims, Probate—Superior-District Court, PO Box 402, Bakersville, NC 28705. 828-688-2161, Fax: 828-688-2168. 8:30AM-5PM. Access by: mail, in person.

Montgomery

Real Estate Recording—Montgomery County Register of Deeds, 102 East Spring St. Troy, NC 27371., Fax: 910-576-2209. 8AM-5PM.

Felony, Misdemeanor, Civil, Eviction, Small Claims, Probate—Superior-District Court, PO Box 527, Troy, NC 27371. 910-576-4211, Fax: 910-576-5020. 8AM-5PM. Access by: mail, phone, fax, in person.

Moore

Real Estate Recording—Moore County Register of Deeds, 100 Dowd Street, Carthage, NC 28327., Fax: 910-947-6396. 8AM-5PM.

Felony, Misdemeanor, Civil, Eviction, Small Claims, Probate—Superior-District Court, PO Box 936, Carthage, NC 28327. 910-947-2396, Fax: 910-947-1444. 8AM-5PM. Access by: mail, in person.

Nash

Real Estate Recording—Nash County Register of Deeds, 224 W. Washington Street, Nashville, NC 27856., Fax: 919-459-9889. 8AM-5PM.

Felony, Misdemeanor, Civil, Eviction, Small Claims, Probate—Superior-District Court, PO Box 759, Nashville, NC 27856., Fax: 919-459-6050. 8AM-5PM. Access by: mail, in person.

New Hanover

Real Estate Recording—New Hanover County Register of Deeds, 316 Princess Street, Room 216, Wilmington, NC 28401., Fax: 910-341-4323. 8:30AM-4:45PM.

Felony, Misdemeanor, Civil, Eviction, Small Claims, Probate—Superior-District Court, PO Box 2023, Wilmington, NC 28402. 910-341-4430, Fax: 910-251-2676. 8AM-5PM. Access by: mail, in person.

Northampton

Real Estate Recording—Northampton County Register of Deeds, Courthouse, Jackson, NC 27845. 8AM-5PM.

Felony, Misdemeanor, Civil, Eviction, Small Claims, Probate—Superior-District Court, PO Box 217, Jackson, NC 27845. 254-386-3518, Fax: 252-534-1308. 8:30AM-5PM. Access by: mail, in person.

Onslow

Real Estate Recording—Onslow County Register of Deeds, 109 Old Bridge Street, Jacksonville, NC 28540. 8AM-5PM.

Felony, Misdemeanor, Civil, Eviction, Small Claims, Probate—Superior-District Court, 625 Court St, Jacksonville, NC 28540. 910-455-4458. 8AM-5PM. Access by: mail, in person.

Orange

Real Estate Recording—Orange County Register of Deeds, 200 South Cameron Street, Hillsborough, NC 27278., Fax: 919-644-3015. 8AM-5PM.

Felony, Misdemeanor, Civil, Eviction, Small Claims, Probate—Superior-District Court, 106 E Margaret Lane, Hillsborough, NC 27278. 919-732-8181, Fax: 919-644-3043. 8AM-5PM. Access by: mail, in person.

Pamlico

Real Estate Recording—Pamlico County Register of Deeds, Courthouse, Bayboro, NC 28515. 8AM-5PM.

Felony, Misdemeanor, Civil, Eviction, Small Claims, Probate—Superior-District Court, PO Box 38, Bayboro, NC 28515. 919-745-3881, Fax: 919-745-3399. 8AM-5PM. Access by: mail, in person.

Pasquotank

Real Estate Recording—Pasquotank County Register of Deeds, 206 East Main Street, Room D102, Elizabeth City, NC 27909., Fax: 252-335-5106. 8AM-5PM.

Felony, Misdemeanor, Civil, Eviction, Small Claims, Probate—Superior-District Court, PO Box 449, Elizabeth City, NC 27907-0449. 252-583-5061. 8AM-5PM. Access by: mail, in person.

Pender

Real Estate Recording—Pender County Register of Deeds, 102 Wright Street, Courthouse, Burgaw, NC 28425., Fax: 910-259-1299. 8AM-5PM (Recording 8AM-4:30PM).

Felony, Misdemeanor, Civil, Eviction, Small Claims, Probate—Superior-District Court, PO Box 308, Burgaw, NC 28425. 910-259-1229, Fax: 910-259-1292. 8AM-5PM. Access by: mail, fax, in person.

Perquimans

Real Estate Recording—Perquimans County Register of Deeds, 128 North Church Street, Hertford, NC 27944., Fax: 252-426-7443. 8:30AM-5PM.

Felony, Misdemeanor, Civil, Eviction, Small Claims, Probate—Superior-District Court, PO Box 33, Hertford, NC 27944. 252-793-3013. 8AM-5PM. Access by: mail, in person.

Person

Real Estate Recording—Person County Register of Deeds, Courthouse Square, Roxboro, NC 27573. 8:30AM-5PM.

Felony, Misdemeanor, Civil, Eviction, Small Claims, Probate—Superior-District Court, 105 S Main St, Roxboro, NC 27573., Fax: 336-597-0568. 8:30AM-5PM. Access by: mail, in person.

Pitt

Real Estate Recording—Pitt County Register of Deeds, 3rd & Evans Streets, Courthouse, Greenville, NC 27834. 8AM-5PM.

Felony, Misdemeanor, Civil, Eviction, Small Claims, Probate—Superior-District Court, PO Box 6067, Greenville, NC 27834. 919-830-6400, Fax: 919-830-3144. 8AM-5PM. Access by: mail, in person.

Polk

Real Estate Recording—Polk County Register of Deeds, 102 Courthouse Street, Columbus, NC 28722. 704-894-8500, Fax: 828-894-5781. 8:30AM-5PM.

Felony, Misdemeanor, Civil, Eviction, Small Claims, Probate—Superior-District Court, PO Box 38, Columbus, NC 28722. 828-894-8231, Fax: 828-894-5752. 8AM-5PM. Access by: mail, in person.

Randolph

Real Estate Recording—Randolph County Register of Deeds, 158 Worth Street, Asheboro, NC 27203. 8AM-5PM.

Felony, Misdemeanor, Civil, Eviction, Small Claims, Probate—Superior-District Court, PO Box 1925, Asheboro, NC 27204-1925., Fax: 336-318-6709. 8AM-5PM. Access by: mail, in person.

Richmond

Real Estate Recording—Richmond County Register of Deeds, 114 E Franklin St. Suite 101, Rockingham, NC 28379., Fax: 910-997-8499. 8AM-5PM.

Felony, Misdemeanor, Civil, Eviction, Small Claims, Probate—Superior-District Court, PO Box 724, Rockingham, NC 28380., Fax: 910-997-9126. 8AM-5PM. Access by: mail, in person.

Robeson

Real Estate Recording—Robeson County Register of Deeds, 500 North Elm Street, Courthouse - Room 102, Lumberton, NC 28358., Fax: 910-671-3041. 8:15AM-5:15PM.

Felony, Misdemeanor, Civil, Eviction, Small Claims, Probate—Superior-District Court, PO Box 1084, Lumberton, NC 28358. 910-737-5035, Fax: 910-618-5598. 8:30AM-5PM. Access by: mail, in person.

Rockingham

Real Estate Recording—Rockingham County Register of Deeds, County Courthouse, Suite 99, 1086 NC 65, Wentworth, NC 27375. 8AM-5PM.

Felony, Misdemeanor, Civil, Eviction, Small Claims, Probate—Superior-District Court, PO Box 127, Wentworth, NC 27375. 360-249-3751. 8AM-5PM. Access by: mail, in person.

Rowan

Real Estate Recording—Rowan County Register of Deeds, 402 North Main Street, County Office Building, Salisbury, NC 28144. 704-633-3871. 8AM-5PM.

Felony, Misdemeanor, Civil, Eviction, Small Claims, Probate—Superior-District Court, PO Box 4599, 210 N Main St, Salisbury, NC 28144. 704-639-7505. 8AM-5PM. Access by: mail, in person.

Rutherford

Real Estate Recording—Rutherford County Register of Deeds, Courthouse, Room A-202, 229 N. Main St. Rutherfordton, NC 28139., Fax: 828-287-6470. 8:30AM-5PM.

Felony, Misdemeanor, Civil, Eviction, Small Claims, Probate—Superior-District Court, PO Box 630, Rutherfordton, NC 28139. 8:30AM-5PM. Access by: mail, in person.

Sampson

Real Estate Recording—Sampson County Register of Deeds, Main St. Courthouse, Room 109, Clinton, NC 28328., Fax: 910-592-1803. 8AM-5:15PM.

Felony, Misdemeanor, Civil, Eviction, Small Claims, Probate—Superior-District Court, Courthouse, Clinton, NC 28328. 910-592-5191, Fax: 910-592-5502. 8AM-5PM. Access by: mail, phone, in person.

Scotland

Real Estate Recording—Scotland County Register of Deeds, 212 Biggs Street, Courthouse, Room 250, Laurinburg, NC 28352., Fax: 910-277-3133. 8AM-5PM.

Felony, Misdemeanor, Civil, Eviction, Small Claims, Probate—Superior-District Court, PO Box 769, Laurinburg, NC 28353. 910-277-3240. 8:30AM-5PM. Access by: mail, in person.

Stanly

Real Estate Recording—Stanly County Register of Deeds, 201 South Second Street, Albemarle, NC 28001. 8:30AM-5PM.

Felony, Misdemeanor, Civil, Eviction, Small Claims, Probate—Superior-District Court, PO Box 668, Albemarle, NC 28002-0668. 704-982-2161, Fax: 704-982-8107. 8:30AM-5PM. Access by: mail, in person.

Stokes

Real Estate Recording—Stokes County Register of Deeds, Main Street, Government Center, Danbury, NC 27016., Fax: 336-593-9360. 8:30AM-5PM.

Felony, Misdemeanor, Civil, Eviction, Small Claims, Probate—Superior-District Court, PO Box 256, Danbury, NC 27016. 360-337-7109. 8AM-5PM. Access by: mail, in person.

Surry

Real Estate Recording—Surry County Register of Deeds, 114 W. Atkins St. Courthouse, Dobson, NC 27017. 910-386-9230, Fax: 336-401-8151. 8:15AM-5PM.

Felony, Misdemeanor, Civil, Eviction, Small Claims, Probate—Superior-District Court, PO Box 345, Dobson, NC 27017. 360-336-9319, Fax: 336-386-9879. 8AM-5PM. Access by: mail, in person.

Swain

Real Estate Recording—Swain County Register of Deeds, 101 Mitchell Street, Bryson City, NC 28713., Fax: 828-488-6947. 8:30AM-4:30PM.

Felony, Misdemeanor, Civil, Eviction, Small Claims, Probate—Superior-District Court, PO Box 1397, Bryson City, NC 28713. 828-488-2288, Fax: 828-488-9360. 8:30AM-5PM. Access by: mail, in person.

Transylvania

Real Estate Recording—Transylvania County Register of Deeds, 12 East Main Street, Courthouse, Brevard, NC 28712. 8:30AM-5PM.

Felony, Misdemeanor, Civil, Eviction, Small Claims, Probate—Superior-District Court, 12 E Main St, Brevard, NC 28712. 828-884-3120, Fax: 828-883-2161. 8AM-5PM. Access by: mail, in person.

Tyrrell

Real Estate Recording—Tyrrell County Register of Deeds, 403 Main Street, Columbia, NC 27925., Fax: 919-796-0148. 9AM-5PM.

Felony, Misdemeanor, Civil, Eviction, Small Claims, Probate—Superior-District Court, PO Box 406, Columbia, NC 27925. 919-796-6281, Fax: 919-796-0008. 8:30AM-5PM. Access by: mail, in person.

Union

Real Estate Recording—Union County Register of Deeds, 500 North Main Street, Room 205, Monroe, NC 28112. 9AM-5PM.

Felony, Misdemeanor, Civil, Eviction, Small Claims, Probate—Superior-District Court, PO Box 5038, Monroe, NC 28111. 704-283-4313. 8AM-5PM. Access by: mail, in person.

Vance

Real Estate Recording—Vance County Register of Deeds, 122 Young Street, Courthouse, Suite F, Henderson, NC 27536. 8:30AM-5PM.

Felony, Misdemeanor, Civil, Eviction, Small Claims, Probate—Superior-District Court, 122 Young St, Henderson, NC 27536. 919-492-0031. 8AM-5PM. Access by: mail, in person.

Wake

Real Estate Recording—Wake County Register of Deeds, 300 S. Salisbury St. Room 104, Raleigh, NC 27601. 919-856-6600. 8:30AM-5:15PM.

Felony, Misdemeanor, Civil, Eviction, Small Claims, Probate—Superior-District Court, PO Box 351, Raleigh, NC 27602. 919-755-4105. 8:30AM-5:00PM. Access by: mail, in person.

Warren

Real Estate Recording—Warren County Register of Deeds, Main Street, Courthouse, Warrenton, NC 27589. 919-257-3337, Fax: 919-257-1524. 8:30AM-5PM.

Felony, Misdemeanor, Civil, Eviction, Small Claims, Probate—Superior-District Court, PO Box 709, Warrenton, NC 27589. 252-534-1631, Fax: 252-257-5529. 8:30AM-5PM. Access by: mail, in person.

Washington

Real Estate Recording—Washington County Register of Deeds, 120 Adams Street, Courthouse, Plymouth, NC 27962. 8:30AM-5PM.

Felony, Misdemeanor, Civil, Eviction, Small Claims, Probate—Superior-District Court, PO Box 901, Plymouth, NC 27962. 254-582-2632, Fax: 252-793-1081. 8AM-5PM. Access by: mail, in person.

Watauga

Real Estate Recording—Watauga County Register of Deeds, 842 West King St. Suite 9, Boone, NC 28607., Fax: 828-265-7632. 8AM-5PM.

Felony, Misdemeanor, Civil, Eviction, Small Claims, Probate—Superior-District Court, Courthouse Suite 13, 842 West King St, Boone, NC 28607-3525. 828-265-5364, Fax: 828-262-5753. 8AM-5PM. Access by: mail, in person.

Wayne

Real Estate Recording—Wayne County Register of Deeds, William Street, Courthouse, Goldsboro, NC 27530. 8AM-5PM.

Felony, Misdemeanor, Civil, Eviction, Small Claims, Probate—Superior-District Court, PO Box 267, Goldsboro, NC 27530., Fax: 919-731-2037. 8AM-5PM. Access by: mail, in person.

Wilkes

Real Estate Recording—Wilkes County Register of Deeds, Courthouse, 500 Courthouse Dr. Wilkesboro, NC 28697. 8:30AM-5PM.

Felony, Misdemeanor, Civil, Eviction, Small Claims, Probate—Superior-District Court, 500 Courthouse Drive, PO Box 58, Wilkesboro, NC 28697., Fax: 336-667-1985. 8AM-5PM. Access by: mail, in person.

Wilson

Real Estate Recording—Wilson County Register of Deeds, 101 N. Goldsboro St. Wilson, NC 27893. 919-399-2902, Fax: 252-399-2942. 8AM-5PM.

Felony, Misdemeanor, Civil, Eviction, Small Claims, Probate—Superior-District Court, PO Box 1608, Wilson, NC 27893., Fax: 252-291-8049. 9AM-5PM. Access by: mail, in person.

Yadkin

Real Estate Recording—Yadkin County Register of Deeds, Courthouse, Yadkinville, NC 27055., Fax: 336-679-2703. 8AM-5PM.

Felony, Misdemeanor, Civil, Eviction, Small Claims, Probate—Superior-District Court, PO Box 95, Yadkinville, NC 27055. 360-337-7164, Fax: 336-679-4378. 8AM-5PM. Access by: mail, in person.

Yancey

Real Estate Recording—Yancey County Register of Deeds, Courthouse, Room #4, Burnsville, NC 28714., Fax: 828-682-4520. 9AM-5PM.

Felony, Misdemeanor, Civil, Eviction, Small Claims, Probate—Superior-District Court, 110 Town Square, Burnsville, NC 28714. 828-682-2122. 8:30AM-5PM. Access by: mail, phone, in person.

Federal Courts

US District Court

Eastern District of North Carolina

Elizabeth City Division c/o Raleigh Division, PO Box 25670, Raleigh, NC 27611919-856-4370 Counties: Bertie, Camden, Chowan, Currituck, Dare, Gates, Hertford, Northampton, Pasquotank, Perquimans, Tyrrell, Washington.

Greenville-Eastern Division Room 209, 201 S Evans St, Greenville, NC 27858-1137252-830-6009, Criminal Docket Phone: 919-856-4370 Fax: 919-830-2793 Counties: Beaufort, Carteret, Craven, Edgecombe, Greene, Halifax, Hyde, Jones, Lenoir, Martin, Pamlico, Pitt.

Raleigh Division Clerk's Office, PO Box 25670, Raleigh, NC 27611919-856-4370, Civil Docket Phone: 919-856-4422 Fax: 919-856-4160 Counties: Cumberland, Franklin, Granville, Harnett, Johnston, Nash, Vance, Wake, Warren, Wayne, Wilson.

Wilmington Division PO Box 338, Wilmington, NC 28402910-815-4663 Fax: 910-815-4518 Counties: Bladen, Brunswick, Columbus, Duplin, New Hanover, Onslow, Pender, Robeson, Sampson.

Middle District of North Carolina

Greensboro Division Clerk's Office, PO Box 2708, Greensboro, NC 27402336-332-6000, Civil Docket Phone: 336-332-6030, Criminal Docket Phone: 336-332-6020 Counties: Alamance, Cabarrus, Caswell, Chatham, Davidson, Davie, Durham, Forsyth, Guilford, Hoke, Lee, Montgomery, Moore, Orange, Person, Randolph, Richmond, Rockingham, Rowan, Scotland, Stanly, Stokes, Surry, Yadkin. www.ncmd.uscourts.gov

Western District of North Carolina

Asheville Division Clerk of the Court, Room 309, US Courthouse Bldg, 100 Otis St, Asheville, NC 28801-2611828-771-7200 Fax: 828-271-4343 Counties: Avery, Buncombe, Haywood, Henderson, Madison, Mitchell, Transylvania, Yancey. http://www.ncwd.net

Bryson City Division c/o Asheville Division, Clerk of the Court, Room 309, US Courthouse, 100 Otis St, Asheville, NC 28801-2611828-771-7200 Counties: Cherokee, Clay, Graham, Jackson, Macon, Swain. http://208.141.47.221/

Charlotte Division Clerk, Room 210, 401 W Trade St, Charlotte, NC 28202704-350-7400 Counties: Anson, Gaston, Mecklenburg, Union. http://208.141.47.221/

Shelby Division c/o Asheville Division, Clerk of the Court, Room 309, US Courthouse, 100 Otis St, Asheville, NC 28801-2611828-771-7200 Counties: Burke, Cleveland, McDowell, Polk, Rutherford. http://208.141.47.221/

Statesville Division PO Box 466, Statesville, NC 28687704-873-7112 Fax: 704-873-0903 Counties: Alexander, Alleghany, Ashe, Caldwell, Catawba, Iredell, Lincoln, Watauga, Wilkes. http://208.141.47.221/

US Bankruptcy Court

Eastern District of North Carolina

Raleigh Division PO Box 1441, Raleigh, NC 27602919-856-4752 Counties: Franklin, Granville, Harnett, Johnston, Vance, Wake, Warren. www.nceb.uscourts.gov

Raleigh Division PO Box 1441, Raleigh, NC 27602919-856-4752 Counties: Franklin, Granville, Harnett, Johnston, Vance, Wake, Warren. www.nceb.uscourts.gov

Wilson Division PO Drawer 2807, Wilson, NC 27894-2807252-237-0248 Counties: Beaufort, Bertie, Bladen, Brunswick, Camden, Carteret, Chowan, Columbus, Craven, Cumberland, Currituck, Dare, Duplin, Edgecombe, Gates, Greene, Halifax, Hertford, Hyde, Jones, Lenoir, Martin, Nash, New Hanover, Northampton, Onslow, Pamlico, Pasquotank,Pender, Perquimans, Pitt, Robeson, Sampson, Tyrrell, Washington, Wayne, Wilson. www.nceb.uscourts.gov

Wilson Division PO Drawer 2807, Wilson, NC 27894-2807252-237-0248 Counties: Beaufort, Bertie, Bladen, Brunswick, Camden, Carteret, Chowan, Columbus, Craven, Cumberland, Currituck, Dare, Duplin, Edgecombe, Gates, Greene, Halifax, Hertford, Hyde, Jones, Lenoir, Martin, Nash, New Hanover, Northampton, Onslow, Pamlico, Pasquotank,Pender, Perquimans, Pitt, Robeson, Sampson, Tyrrell, Washington, Wayne, Wilson. www.nceb.uscourts.gov

Middle District of North Carolina

Greensboro Division PO Box 26100, Greensboro, NC 27420-6100336-333-5647 Counties: Alamance, Cabarrus, Caswell, Chatham, Davidson, Davie, Durham, Guilford, Hoke, Lee, Montgomery, Moore, Orange, Person, Randolph, Richmond, Rockingham, Rowan, Scotland, Stanly. www.ncmb.uscourts.gov

Greensboro Division PO Box 26100, Greensboro, NC 27420-6100336-333-5647 Counties: Alamance, Cabarrus, Caswell, Chatham, Davidson, Davie, Durham, Guilford, Hoke, Lee, Montgomery, Moore, Orange, Person, Randolph, Richmond, Rockingham, Rowan, Scotland, Stanly. www.ncmb.uscourts.gov

Winston-Salem Division 226 S Liberty St, Winston-Salem, NC 27101336-631-5340 Counties: Forsyth, Stokes, Surry, Yadkin. www.ncmb.uscourts.gov

Winston-Salem Division 226 S Liberty St, Winston-Salem, NC 27101336-631-5340 Counties: Forsyth, Stokes, Surry, Yadkin. www.ncmb.uscourts.gov

Western District of North Carolina

Charlotte Division 401 W Trade St, Charlotte, NC 28202704-350-7500 Counties: Alexander, Alleghany, Anson, Ashe, Avery, Buncombe, Burke, Caldwell, Catawba, Cherokee, Clay, Cleveland, Gaston, Graham, Haywood, Henderson, Iredell, Jackson, Lincoln, Macon, Madison, McDowell, Mecklenburg, Mitchell, Polk, Rutherford, Swain,Transylvania, Union, Watauga, Wilkes, Yancey. www.ncbankruptcy.org

Attorney General's Office
600 E Boulevard Ave   701-328-2210
Bismarck, ND 58505-0040   Fax: 701-328-2226
www.expedition.bismarck.ag.state.nd.us/ndag

Governor's Office
600 E Boulevard Ave, 1st Floor   701-328-2200
Bismarck, ND 58505-0001   Fax: 701-328-2205
www.health.state.nd.us/gov

State Archives
N Dakota Heritage Center,
612 E Boulevard Ave   701-328-2666
Bismarck, ND 58505-0830   Fax: 701-328-3710
www.state.nd.us/hist

Capital: Bismark
                                  Burleigh County

Time Zone: CST

Number of Counties: 53

Population: 640,883

Web Site: www.state.nd.us

Search Unclaimed Property Online

http://data.land.state.nd.us/abp/
abpsearch.asp

State Agencies

Criminal Records
Bureau of Criminal Investigation, PO Box 1054, Bismarck, ND 58502-1054 (4205 N State St, Bismarck, ND 58501); 701-328-5500; Fax: 701-328-5510; 8AM-5PM. Access by: mail. www.state.nd.us/ndag

Corporation Records
Limited Liability Company Records
Limited Partnership Records
Trademarks/Servicemarks
Fictitious Name
Assumed Name
Secretary of State, Business Information/Registration, 600 E Boulevard Ave, Dept 108, Bismarck, ND 58505-0500; 701-328-4284; Fax: 701-328-2992; 8AM-5PM. Access by: mail, phone, in person. www.state.nd.us/sec

Sales Tax Registrations
State Tax Commission, Sales & Special Tax Division, State Capitol, 600 E Boulevard Ave, Bismarck, ND 58505-0599; 701-328-3470; Fax: 701-328-3700; 8AM-5PM. Access by: mail, phone, in person. www.state.nd.us/taxdpt

Uniform Commercial Code
Federal Tax Liens
State Tax Liens
UCC Division, Secretary of State, 600 E Boulevard Ave, 1st Fl, Bismarck, ND 58505-0500; 701-328-3662; Fax: 701-328-4214; 8AM-5PM. Access by: mail, phone, in person, online. www.state.nd.us/sec

Workers' Compensation Records
Workers Compensation Bureau, 500 E Front Ave, Bismarck, ND 58504-5685; 701-328-3800; Fax: 701-328-3820; 8AM-5PM. Access by: mail.

Birth Certificates
ND Department of Health, Vital Records, State Capitol, 600 E Blvd, 1st Floor, Bismarck, ND 58505-0200; 701-328-2360; Fax: 701-328-1850; 7:30AM-5PM. Access by: mail, phone, in person. www.ehs.health.state.nd

Death Records

ND Department of Health, Vital Records, State Capitol, 600 E Blvd, 1st Floor, Bismarck, ND 58505-0200; 701-328-2360; Fax: 701-328-1850; 7:30AM-5PM. Access by: mail, phone, in person. www.ehs.health.state.nd

Marriage Certificates

ND Department of Health, Vital Records, State Capitol, 600 E Blvd, 1st Floor, Bismarck, ND 58505-0200; 701-328-2360; Fax: 701-328-1850; 7:30AM-5PM. Access by:, phone, in person. www.ehs.health.state.nd

Divorce Records

Records not available from state agency.

The State has an index to direct people to which county has the records. The index contains records from July 1, 1949 to present.

Accident Reports

Driver License & Traffic Safety Division, CRASH Records Section, 608 E Boulevard Ave, Bismarck, ND 58505-0700; 701-328-4397; Fax: 701-328-2435; 8AM-5PM. Access by: mail. www.state.nd.us/dot

Driver Records

Department of Transportation, Driver License & Traffic Safety Division, /08 E Boulevard Ave, Bismarck, ND 58505-0700; 701-328-2603; Fax: 701-328-2435; 8AM-5PM. Access by: mail. www.state.nd.us/dot

Vehicle Ownership
Vehicle Identification

Department of Transportation, Records Section/Motor Vehicle Div., 608 E Boulevard Ave, Bismarck, ND 58505-0780; 701-328-2725; Fax: 701-328-3500; 8AM-4:50PM. Access by: mail.

Boat & Vessel Ownership
Boat & Vessel Registration

North Dakota Game & Fish Department, 100 N Bismarck Expressway, Bismarck, ND 58501; 701-328-6335; Fax: 701-328-6352; 8AM-5PM M-F. www.state.nd.us/gnf

Legislation-Current/Pending
Legislation-Passed

North Dakota Legislative Council, State Capitol, 600 E Boulevard Ave, Bismarck, ND 58505; 701-328-2916, 701-328-2900 Secretary of State, 701-328-2992 Sec of State fax; 8AM-5PM. Access by: mail, phone, in person, online. www.state.nd.us/lr

Voter Registration

Records not available from state agency.

Records are maintained at the county level by the County Auditors. Records are open to the public.

GED Certificates

Department of Public Instruction, GED Testing, 600 E Blvd Ave, Bismarck, ND 58505-0440; 701-328-2393; Fax: 701-328-4770; 8AM-4:30PM. www.dpi.state.nd.us

Hunting License Information
Fishing License Information

ND Game & Fish Department, 100 N Bismarck Expressway, Bismarck, ND 58501; 701-328-6300; Fax: 701-328-6352; 8AM-5PM. Access by: mail. www.state.nd.us/gnf

County Courts & Recording Offices

About the Courts...

Administration

Court Administrator, North Dakota Supreme Court 701-328-4216
600 E Blvd, 1st Floor Judicial Wing   Fax: 701-328-4480
Bismarck, ND 58505-0530
www.court.state.nd.us

Court Structure

In 1995, the County Courts were merged with the District Courts across the entire state. County court records are maintained by the 53 District Courts in the 7 judicial districts. We recommend stating "include all County Court cases" in search requests. There are 76 Municipal Courts that handle traffic cases.

Searching Hints

In Summer, 1997, the standard search fee in District Courts increased to $10.00 per name, and the certification fee increased to $10.00 per document. Copy fees remain at $.50 per page.

Online Access

A statewide computer system for internal purposes is in operation in most counties, with the main exception of Cass (Fargo), which has its own system. The Cass system will be converted to the statewide system by the end of 1999. No decision has been made whether to allow remote public access.

About the Recording Offices...

Organization

53 counties, 53 recording offices. The recording officer is. Register of Deeds. The entire state is in the Central Time Zone (CST).

UCC Records

Financing statements may be filed either at the state level or with any Register of Deeds, except for real estate related collateral, which are filed only with the Register of Deeds. All counties access a statewide computer database of filings and will perform UCC searches. Use search request form UCC-11. Various search options are available, including by federal tax identification number or Social Security number The search with copies costs $7.00 per debtor name, including three pages of copies and $1.00 per additional page. Copies may be faxed for an additional fee of $3.00.

Lien Records

Federal tax liens on personal property of businesses are filed with the Secretary of State. Other federal and all state tax liens are filed with the county Register of Deeds. All counties will perform tax lien searches. Some counties automatically include business federal tax liens as part of a UCC search because they appear on the statewide database. (Be careful - federal tax liens on individuals may only be in the county lien books, not on the statewide system.) Separate searches are usually available at $5.00-7.00 per name. Copy fees vary. Copies may be faxed.

Real Estate Records

Some counties will perform real estate searches by name or by legal description. Copy fees are usually $1.00 per page. Certified copies usually cost $5.00 for the first page and $2.00 for each additional page. Copies may be faxed.

County Courts & Recording Offices

Adams

Real Estate Recording—Adams County Register of Deeds, 602 Adams Avenue, Courthouse, Hettinger, ND 58639. 701-567-2537, Fax: 701-567-2910. 8:30AM-Noon, 1-5PM.

Felony, Misdemeanor, Civil, Eviction, Small Claims, Probate—Southwest Judicial District Court, 602 Adams Ave, PO Box 469, Hettinger, ND 58639. 701-567-2460, Fax: 701-567-2910. 8:30AM-5PM. Access by: mail, phone, fax, in person.

Barnes

Real Estate Recording—Barnes County Register of Deeds, 231 NE Third Street, Valley City, ND 58072. 701-845-8505, Fax: 701-845-8538. 8AM-5PM.

Felony, Misdemeanor, Civil, Eviction, Small Claims, Probate—Southeast Judicial District Court, PO Box 774, Valley City, ND 58072. 701-845-8512, Fax: 701-845-1341. 8AM-5PM. Access by: mail, phone, fax, in person.

Benson

Real Estate Recording—Benson County Register of Deeds, Courthouse, Minnewaukan, ND 58351. 701-473-5458, Fax: 701-473-5571. 8:30AM-Noon, 12:30-4:30PM.

Felony, Misdemeanor, Civil, Eviction, Small Claims, Probate—Northeast Judicial District Court, PO Box 213, Minnewaukan, ND 58351. 701-473-5345, Fax: 701-473-5571. 8:30AM-4:30PM. Access by: mail, phone, fax, in person.

Billings

Real Estate Recording—Billings County Register of Deeds, Courthouse, 4th & Pacific, Medora, ND 58645. 701-623-4484, Fax: 701-623-4896. 9AM-Noon, 1-5PM.

Felony, Misdemeanor, Civil, Eviction, Small Claims, Probate—Southwest Judicial District Court, PO Box 138, Medora, ND 58645. 701-623-4492, Fax: 701-623-4896. 9AM-Noon, 1-5PM. Access by: mail, fax, in person.

Bottineau

Real Estate Recording—Bottineau County Register of Deeds, 314 West 5th Street, Bottineau, ND 58318. 701-228-2035, Fax: 701-228-3658. 8:30AM-5PM.

Felony, Misdemeanor, Civil, Eviction, Small Claims, Probate—Northeast Judicial District Court, 314 W 5th St, Bottineau, ND 58318. 701-228-3983, Fax: 701-228-2336. Access by: mail, phone, fax, in person.

Bowman

Real Estate Recording—Bowman County Register of Deeds, 104 West 1st Street, Courthouse, Bowman, ND 58623. 701-523-3665, Fax: 701-523-5443. 8:30AM-5PM.

Felony, Misdemeanor, Civil, Eviction, Small Claims, Probate—Southwest Judicial District Court, PO Box 379, Bowman, ND 58623. 701-523-3450, Fax: 701-523-5443. 8:30AM-Noon, 1-5PM. Access by: mail, phone, in person.

Burke

Real Estate Recording—Burke County Register of Deeds, Main Street, Courthouse, Bowbells, ND 58721. 701-377-2917, Fax: 701-377-2020. 8:30AM-Noon, 1-5PM.

Felony, Misdemeanor, Civil, Eviction, Small Claims, Probate—Northwest Judicial District Court, PO Box 219, Bowbells, ND 58721. 701-377-2718, Fax: 701-377-2020. 8:30AM-Noon, 1-5 PM. Access by: mail, phone, fax, in person.

Burleigh

Real Estate Recording—Burleigh County Register of Deeds, 221 North 5th Street, Bismarck, ND 58501. 701-222-6696, Fax: 701-222-6717. 8AM-5PM.

Felony, Misdemeanor, Civil, Eviction, Small Claims, Probate—South Central Judicial District Court, PO Box 1055, Bismarck, ND 58502. 701-222-6690, Fax: 701-222-6689. 8AM-5PM. Access by: mail, in person.

Cass

Real Estate Recording—Cass County Register of Deeds, 211 Ninth Street South, Fargo, ND 58103. 701-241-5611, Fax: 701-241-5621. 8AM-5PM.

Felony, Misdemeanor, Civil, Eviction, Small Claims, Probate—East Central Judicial District Court, 211 South 9th St, Fargo, ND 58108. 701-241-5645, Fax: 701-241-5636. 8AM-5PM. Access by: mail, in person.

Cavalier

Real Estate Recording—Cavalier County Register of Deeds, 901 3rd Street, Langdon, ND 58249. 701-256-2549, Fax: 701-256-2566. 8:30AM-4:30PM.

Felony, Misdemeanor, Civil, Eviction, Small Claims, Probate—Northeast Judicial District Court, 901 Third St, Langdon, ND 58249. 701-256-2124, Fax: 701-256-2124. 8:30AM-4:30PM. Access by: mail, phone, fax, in person.

Dickey

Real Estate Recording—Dickey County Register of Deeds, 309 North 2nd, Courthouse, Ellendale, ND 58436., Fax: 701-349-4639. 8:30AM-5PM.

Felony, Misdemeanor, Civil, Eviction, Small Claims, Probate—Southeast Judicial District Court, PO Box 336, Ellendale, ND 58436. 701-349-3249, Fax: 701-349-3560. 9AM-Noon, 1-5PM. Access by: mail, in person.

Divide

Real Estate Recording—Divide County Register of Deeds, Courthouse, 300 2nd Ave. North, Crosby, ND 58730. 701-965-6312, Fax: 701-965-6943. 8:30AM-Noon, 1-5PM.

Felony, Misdemeanor, Civil, Eviction, Small Claims, Probate—Northwest Judicial District Court, PO Box 68, Crosby, ND 58730. 701-965-6831, Fax: 701-965-6943. 8:30AM-Noon, 1-5PM. Access by: mail, phone, fax, in person.

Dunn

Real Estate Recording—Dunn County Register of Deeds, Courthouse, 205 Owens St. Manning, ND 58642. 701-573-4446, Fax: 701-573-4444. 8AM-Noon, 12:30-4:30PM.

Felony, Misdemeanor, Civil, Eviction, Small Claims, Probate—District Court, PO Box 136, Manning, ND 58642-0136. 701-573-4447, Fax: 701-573-4444. 8AM-Noon,12:30-4:30PM. Access by: mail, fax, in person.

Eddy

Real Estate Recording—Eddy County Register of Deeds, 524 Central Avenue, New Rockford, ND 58356. 701-947-5315, Fax: 701-947-2067. 8AM-Noon, 12:30-4PM.

Felony, Misdemeanor, Civil, Eviction, Small Claims, Probate—Southeast Judicial District Court, 524 Central Ave, New Rockford, ND 58356. 701-947-2813, Fax: 701-947-2067. 8AM-4PM. Access by: mail, fax, in person.

Emmons

Real Estate Recording—Emmons County Register of Deeds, Courthouse, Linton, ND 58552. 701-254-4802, Fax: 701-254-4012. 8:30AM-Noon, 1-5PM.

Felony, Misdemeanor, Civil, Eviction, Small Claims, Probate—South Central Judicial District Court, PO Box 905, Linton, ND 58552. 701-254-4812, Fax: 701-254-4012. 8:30AM-Noon, 1-5PM. Access by: mail, fax, in person.

Foster

Real Estate Recording—Foster County Register of Deeds, 1000 Central Avenue, Carrington, ND 58421. 701-652-2323, Fax: 701-652-2173. 8:30AM-4:30PM.

Felony, Misdemeanor, Civil, Eviction, Small Claims, Probate—Southeast Judicial District Court, PO Box 257, Carrington, ND 58421. 701-652-1001, Fax: 701-652-2173. 8:30AM-4:30PM. Access by: mail, phone, fax, in person.

Golden Valley

Real Estate Recording—Golden Valley County Register of Deeds, 150 1st Avenue S.E. Courthouse, Beach, ND 58621. 701-872-4411, Fax: 701-872-4383. 8AM-Noon, 1-4PM.

Felony, Misdemeanor, Civil, Eviction, Small Claims, Probate—Southwest Judicial District Court, PO Box 9, Beach, ND 58621-0009. 701-872-4352, Fax: 701-872-4383. 8-Noon, 1-4PM. Access by: mail, fax, in person.

Grand Forks

Real Estate Recording—Grand Forks County Register of Deeds, County Office Bldg. 124 South 4th St. Grand Forks, ND 58201. 701-780-8295, Fax: 701-780-8212. 8AM-5PM.

Felony, Misdemeanor, Civil, Eviction, Small Claims, Probate—Northeast Central Judicial District Court, PO Box 5939, Grand Forks, ND 58206-5939. 701-780-8214. 8AM-5PM. Access by: mail, in person.

Grant

Real Estate Recording—Grant County Register of Deeds, Courthouse, Carson, ND 58529. 701-622-3422, Fax: 701-622-3717. 8AM-4PM.

Felony, Misdemeanor, Civil, Eviction, Small Claims, Probate—South Central Judicial District Court, PO Box 258, Carson, ND 58529. 701-622-3615, Fax: 701-622-3717. 8AM-Noon, 12:30-4PM. Access by: mail, phone, fax, in person.

Griggs

Real Estate Recording—Griggs County Register of Deeds, Courthouse, 45th & Rollins, Cooperstown, ND 58425. 701-797-2411, Fax: 701-797-3587. 8AM-12, 1-4:30PM.

Felony, Misdemeanor, Civil, Eviction, Small Claims, Probate—Southeast Judicial District Court, PO Box 326, Cooperstown, ND 58425. 701-797-2772, Fax: 701-797-3587. 8AM-Noon, 1-4:30PM. Access by: mail, phone, fax, in person.

Hettinger

Real Estate Recording—Hettinger County Register of Deeds, Courthouse, 336 Pacific Ave. Mott, ND 58646. 701-824-2655, Fax: 701-824-2717. 8AM-4:30PM.

Felony, Misdemeanor, Civil, Eviction, Small Claims, Probate—Southwest Judicial District Court, PO Box 668, Mott, ND 58646. 701-824-2645, Fax: 701-824-2717. 8AM-Noon, 1-4:30PM. Access by: mail, phone, fax, in person.

Kidder

Real Estate Recording—Kidder County Register of Deeds, Courthouse, 120 East Broadway, Steele, ND 58482. 701-475-2442, Fax: 701-475-2202. 9AM-5PM.

Felony, Misdemeanor, Civil, Eviction, Small Claims, Probate—District Court, PO Box 66, Steele, ND 58482. 701-475-2632, Fax: 701-475-2202. 9AM-5PM. Access by: mail, fax, in person.

La Moure

Real Estate Recording—La Moure County Register of Deeds, Courthouse, 202 4th Ave. N.E. La Moure, ND 58458. 701-883-5103, Fax: 701-883-5304. 9AM-5PM.

Felony, Misdemeanor, Civil, Eviction, Small Claims, Probate—Southeast Judicial District Court, PO Box 128, LaMoure, ND 58458. 701-883-5193, Fax: 701-883-5304. 9AM-Noon, 1-5PM. Access by: mail, phone, fax, in person.

Logan

Real Estate Recording—Logan County Register of Deeds, Highway 3, Courthouse, Napoleon, ND 58561. 701-754-2286, Fax: 701-754-2270. 8:30AM-Noon, 1-4:30PM.

Felony, Misdemeanor, Civil, Eviction, Small Claims, Probate—South Central Judicial District Court, PO Box 6, Napoleon, ND 58561. 701-754-2751, Fax: 701-754-2270. 8:30AM-4:30PM. Access by: mail, fax, in person.

McHenry

Real Estate Recording—McHenry County Register of Deeds, 407 S. Main, Room 206, Towner, ND 58788. 701-537-5731, Fax: 701-537-5969. 8AM-Noon, 1-4:30PM.

Felony, Misdemeanor, Civil, Eviction, Small Claims, Probate—Northeast Judicial District Court, PO Box 147, Towner, ND 58788. 701-537-5729, Fax: 701-537-5969. 8AM-4:30PM. Access by: mail, phone, fax, in person.

McIntosh

Real Estate Recording—McIntosh County Register of Deeds, 112 North East 1st, Ashley, ND 58413. 701-288-3342, Fax: 701-288-3671. 8AM-4:30PM.

Felony, Misdemeanor, Civil, Eviction, Small Claims, Probate—South Central Judicial District Court, PO Box 179, Ashley, ND 58413. 701-288-3450, Fax: 701-288-3671. 8AM-4:30PM. Access by: mail, phone, fax, in person.

McKenzie

Real Estate Recording—McKenzie County Register of Deeds, 201 West 5th Street, Watford City, ND 58854., Fax: 701-842-3902. 8:30AM-Noon, 1-5PM.

Felony, Misdemeanor, Civil, Eviction, Small Claims, Probate—Northwest District Court, PO Box 524, Watford City, ND 58854. 701-842-3452, Fax: 701-842-3916. 8:30AM-Noon, 1-5PM. Access by: mail, phone, fax, in person.

McLean

Real Estate Recording—McLean County Register of Deeds, 712 5th Avenue, Courthouse, Washburn, ND 58577. 701-462-8541, Fax: 701-462-3633. 8AM-Noon, 12:30-4:30PM.

Felony, Misdemeanor, Civil, Eviction, Small Claims, Probate—South Central Judicial District Court, PO Box 1108, Washburn, ND 58577. 701-462-8541, Fax: 701-462-8212. 8AM-Noon, 12:30-4:30PM. Access by: mail, in person.

Mercer

Real Estate Recording—Mercer County Register of Deeds, 1021 Arthur Street, Stanton, ND 58571., Fax: 701-745-3364. 8AM-4PM.

Felony, Misdemeanor, Civil, Eviction, Small Claims, Probate—District Court, PO Box 39, Stanton, ND 58571. 701-745-3262, Fax: 701-745-3364. 8AM-4PM. Access by: mail, fax, in person.

Morton

Real Estate Recording—Morton County Register of Deeds, 210 2nd Avenue, Mandan, ND 58554. 701-667-3310, Fax: 701-667-3453. 8AM-Noon, 1-5PM.

Felony, Misdemeanor, Civil, Eviction, Small Claims, Probate—South Central Judicial District Court, 210 2nd Ave NW, Mandan, ND 58554. 701-667-3358. 8AM-5PM. Access by: mail, in person.

Mountrail

Real Estate Recording—Mountrail County Register of Deeds, North Main, Courthouse, Stanley, ND 58784. 701-628-2935, Fax: 701-628-2276. 8:30AM-Noon, 1-4:30PM.

Felony, Misdemeanor, Civil, Eviction, Small Claims, Probate—Northwest Judicial District Court, PO Box 69, Stanley, ND 58784. 701-628-2915, Fax: 701-628-3975. 8:30AM-4:30PM. Access by: mail, phone, fax, in person.

Nelson

Real Estate Recording—Nelson County Register of Deeds, Courthouse, 210 W. B Ave. Lakota, ND 58344. 701-247-2840, Fax: 701-247-2412. 8:30AM-Noon, 1-5PM.

Felony, Misdemeanor, Civil, Eviction, Small Claims, Probate—Northeast Central Judicial District Court, PO Box 565, Lakota, ND 58344. 701-247-2462, Fax: 701-247-2412. 8:30AM-5PM. Access by: mail, phone, fax, in person.

Oliver

Real Estate Recording—Oliver County Register of Deeds, Courthouse, Center, ND 58530. 701-794-8737, Fax: 701-794-3476. 8AM-Noon, 1-4PM.

Felony, Misdemeanor, Civil, Eviction, Small Claims, Probate—South Central Judicial District Court, Box 125, Center, ND 58530. 701-794-8777, Fax: 701-794-3476. 8AM-4PM. Access by: mail, phone, fax, in person.

Pembina

Real Estate Recording—Pembina County Register of Deeds, 301 Dakota Street W. 10, Cavalier, ND 58220. 701-265-4465, Fax: 701-265-4876. 8:30AM-5PM.

Felony, Misdemeanor, Civil, Eviction, Small Claims, Probate—Pembina County District Court, 301 Dakota St West #6, Cavalier, ND 58220-4100. 701-265-4275, Fax: 701-265-4876. 8:30AM-5PM. Access by: mail, phone, fax, in person.

Pierce

Real Estate Recording—Pierce County Register of Deeds, 240 S.E. 2nd Street, Rugby, ND 58368. 701-776-6841, Fax: 701-776-5707. 9AM-Noon, 1PM-5PM.

Felony, Misdemeanor, Civil, Eviction, Small Claims, Probate—Northeast Judicial District Court, 240 SE 2nd St, Rugby, ND 58368. 701-776-6161, Fax: 701-776-5707. 9AM-5PM. Access by: mail, phone, fax, in person.

Ramsey

Real Estate Recording—Ramsey County Register of Deeds, 524 4th Avenue #30, Devils Lake, ND 58301. 701-662-7021, Fax: 701-662-7093. 8AM-Noon,1-5PM.

Felony, Misdemeanor, Civil, Eviction, Small Claims, Probate—Northeast Judicial District Court, 524 4th Ave #4, Devils Lake, ND 58301. 701-662-7066, Fax: 701-662-7049. 8AM-5PM. Access by: mail, fax, in person.

Ransom

Real Estate Recording—Ransom County Register of Deeds, Courthouse, Lisbon, ND 58054. 701-683-5823, Fax: 701-683-5827. 8:30AM-Noon, 1-4:30PM.

Felony, Misdemeanor, Civil, Eviction, Small Claims, Probate—Southeast Judicial District Court, PO Box 626, Lisbon, ND 58054. 701-683-5823, Fax: 701-683-5827. 8:30AM-4:30PM. Access by: mail, phone, fax, in person.

Renville

Real Estate Recording—Renville County Register of Deeds, 205 Main Street East, Mohall, ND 58761. 701-756-6304, Fax: 701-756-6398. 9AM-4:30PM.

Felony, Misdemeanor, Civil, Eviction, Small Claims, Probate—Northeast Judicial District Court, PO Box 68, Mohall, ND 58761. 701-756-6398, Fax: 701-756-6398. 9AM-4:30PM. Access by: mail, fax, in person.

Richland

Real Estate Recording—Richland County Register of Deeds, 418 2nd Avenue North, Courthouse, Wahpeton, ND 58075., Fax: 701-642-7820. 8AM-5PM.

Felony, Misdemeanor, Civil, Eviction, Small Claims, Probate—Southeast Judicial District Court, 418 2nd Ave North, Wahpeton, ND 58074. 701-642-7818, Fax: 701-671-1512. 8AM-5PM. Access by: mail, in person.

Rolette

Real Estate Recording—Rolette County Register of Deeds, 102 NE 2nd, Rolla, ND 58367. 701-477-3207, Fax: 701-477-5770. 8:30AM-12:30PM, 1-4:30PM.

Felony, Misdemeanor, Civil, Eviction, Small Claims, Probate—Northeast Judicial District Court, PO Box 460, Rolla, ND 58367. 701-477-3816, Fax: 701-477-5770. 8:30AM-4:30PM. Access by: mail, phone, in person.

Sargent

Real Estate Recording—Sargent County Register of Deeds, 645 Main Street, Forman, ND 58032. 701-724-6241, Fax: 701-724-6244. 9AM-Noon, 12:30-4:30PM.

Felony, Misdemeanor, Civil, Eviction, Small Claims, Probate—Southeast Judicial District Court, 355 Main St (PO Box 176), Forman, ND 58032. 701-724-6241, Fax: 701-724-6244. 9AM-Noon, 12:30-4:30PM. Access by: mail, phone, fax, in person.

Sheridan

Real Estate Recording—Sheridan County Register of Deeds, 215 2nd Street, Courthouse, McClusky, ND 58463. 701-363-2206, Fax: 701-363-2953. 9AM-Noon,1-5PM.

Felony, Misdemeanor, Civil, Eviction, Small Claims, Probate—South Central Judicial District Court, PO Box 636, McClusky, ND 58463. 701-363-2207, Fax: 701-363-2953. 9AM-Noon, 1-5PM. Access by: mail, in person.

Sioux

Real Estate Recording—Sioux County Register of Deeds, Courthouse, Fort Yates, ND 58538., Fax: 701-854-3854. 9AM-5PM.

Felony, Misdemeanor, Civil, Eviction, Small Claims, Probate—South Central Judicial District Court, Box L, Fort Yates, ND 58538. 701-854-3853, Fax: 701-854-3854. 9AM-5PM. Access by: mail, phone, fax, in person.

Slope

Real Estate Recording—Slope County Register of Deeds, Courthouse, Amidon, ND 58620. 701-879-6271, Fax: 701-879-6278. 9AM-Noon, 1-5PM.

Felony, Misdemeanor, Civil, Eviction, Small Claims, Probate—Southwest Judicial District Court, PO Box JJ, Amidon, ND 58620. 701-879-6275, Fax: 701-879-6278. 9AM-5PM. Access by: mail, fax, in person.

Stark

Real Estate Recording—Stark County Register of Deeds, Sims & 3rd Avenue, Courthouse, Dickinson, ND 58601., Fax: 701-264-7628. 8AM-5PM.

Felony, Misdemeanor, Civil, Eviction, Small Claims, Probate—District Court, PO Box 130, Dickinson, ND 58602., Fax: 701-264-7640. 7AM-5PM. Access by: mail, in person.

Steele

Real Estate Recording—Steele County Register of Deeds, Washington Street, Courthouse, Finley, ND 58230. 701-524-2890, Fax: 701-524-1325.

Felony, Misdemeanor, Civil, Eviction, Small Claims, Probate—East Central Judicial District Court, PO Box 296, Finley, ND 58230. 701-524-2152, Fax: 701-524-1325. 8AM-Noon; 1-4:30PM. Access by: mail, in person.

Stutsman

Real Estate Recording—Stutsman County Register of Deeds, 511 2nd Avenue S.E. Courthouse, Jamestown, ND 58401. 701-252-9036, Fax: 701-251-1603. 8AM-Noon; 1-5PM.

Felony, Misdemeanor, Civil, Eviction, Small Claims, Probate—Southeast Judicial District Court, 511 2nd Ave SE, Jamestown, ND 58401. 701-252-9042, Fax: 701-251-1006. 8AM-5PM. Access by: mail, in person.

Towner

Real Estate Recording—Towner County Register of Deeds, Courthouse, 315 2nd Street, Cando, ND 58324. 701-968-4347, Fax: 701-968-4344. 8:30AM-Noon, 1-5PM.

Felony, Misdemeanor, Civil, Eviction, Small Claims, Probate—Northeast Judicial District Court, Box 517, Cando, ND 58324. 701-968-4345, Fax: 701-968-4344. 8:30AM-5PM. Access by: mail, phone, fax, in person.

Traill

Real Estate Recording—Traill County Register of Deeds, 13 1st Street N.W. Courthouse, Hillsboro, ND 58045. 701-436-4457, Fax: 701-436-4457. 8AM-Noon, 12:30PM-4:30PM.

Felony, Misdemeanor, Civil, Eviction, Small Claims, Probate—East Central Judicial District Court, PO Box 805, Hillsboro, ND 58045. 701-436-4454, Fax: 701-436-5124. 8AM-4:30PM. Access by: mail, phone, fax, in person.

Walsh

Real Estate Recording—Walsh County Register of Deeds, 600 Cooper Avenue, Courthouse, Grafton, ND 58237. 701-352-2541, Fax: 701-352-3340. 8:30-Noon, 12:30-5PM.

Felony, Misdemeanor, Civil, Eviction, Small Claims, Probate—Northeast Judicial District Court, 600 Cooper Ave, Grafton, ND 58237. 701-352-0350, Fax: 701-352-1104. 8:30AM-5PM. Access by: mail, phone, fax, in person.

Ward

Real Estate Recording—Ward County Register of Deeds, 315 S.E. Third Street, Courthouse, Minot, ND 58705., Fax: 701-857-6414. 8AM-4:30PM.

Felony, Misdemeanor, Civil, Eviction, Small Claims, Probate—Northwest Judicial District Court, PO Box 5005, Minot, ND 58702-5005. 701-857-6460, Fax: 701-857-6469. 8AM-4:30PM. Access by: mail, in person.

Wells

Real Estate Recording—Wells County Register of Deeds, Court Street, Courthouse, P.O. Box 125, Fessenden, ND 58438. 701-547-3161, Fax: 701-547-3719. 8AM-Noon, 1-4:30PM.

Felony, Misdemeanor, Civil, Eviction, Small Claims, Probate—Southeast Judicial District Court, PO Box 596, Fessenden, ND 58438. 701-547-3122, Fax: 701-547-3719. 8AM-4:30PM. Access by: mail, in person.

Williams

Real Estate Recording—Williams County Treasurer/Recorder, 205 East Broadway, Williston, ND 58801. 701-572-1737, Fax: 701-572-1759. 8AM-5PM.

Felony, Misdemeanor, Civil, Eviction, Small Claims, Probate—Northwest Judicial District Court, PO Box 2047, Williston, ND 58802. 701-572-1720, Fax: 701-572-1760. 9AM-5PM. Access by: mail, in person.

Federal Courts

US District Court

Bismarck-Southwestern Division PO Box 1193, Bismarck, ND 58502701-250-4295 Fax: 701-250-4259 Counties: Adams, Billings, Bowman, Burleigh, Dunn, Emmons, Golden Valley, Grant, Hettinger, Kidder, Logan, McIntosh, McLean, Mercer, Morton, Oliver, Sioux, Slope, Stark.
Fargo-Southeastern Division PO Box 870, Fargo, ND 58107701-239-5377 Fax: 701-239-5270 Counties: Barnes, Cass, Dickey, Eddy, Foster, Griggs, La Moure, Ransom, Richland, Sargent, Steele, Stutsman. Rolette County cases prior to 1995 may be located here.
Grand Forks-Northeastern Division c/o Fargo-Southeastern Division, PO Box 870, Fargo, ND 58107701-239-5377 Fax: 701-239-5270 Counties: Benson, Cavalier, Grand Forks, Nelson, Pembina, Ramsey, Towner, Traill, Walsh.
Minot-Northwestern Division c/o Bismarck Division, PO Box 1193, Bismarck, ND 58502701-250-4295 Fax: 701-250-4259 Counties: Bottineau, Burke, Divide, McHenry, McKenzie, Mountrail, Pierce, Renville, Rolette, Sheridan, Ward, Wells, Williams. Case records from Rolette County prior to 1995 may be located in Fargo-Southeastern Division.

US Bankruptcy Court

Fargo Division PO Box 1110, Fargo, ND 58107701-239-5129 Counties: All counties in North Dakota. www.ndb.uscourts.gov

Attorney General's Office
30 E Broad St, 17th Floor   614-466-4320
Columbus, OH 43215-3428   Fax: 614-644-6135
www.ag.state.oh.gov

Governor's Office
77 S High St, 30th Floor   614-466-3555
Columbus, OH 43215   Fax: 614-466-9354
www.state.oh.us/gov

State Archives
1982 Velma Ave   614-297-2300
Columbus, OH 43211-2497   Fax: 614-297-2546
www.ohiohistory.org

Capital:	Columbus
	Franklin County
Time Zone:	EST
Number of Counties:	88
Population:	11,186,331
Web Site:	www.state.oh.us

Search Unclaimed Property Online

http://www2.state.oh.us/com/unfd/thqry1.htm

State Agencies

Criminal Records
Ohio Bureau of Investigation, Identification Division, PO Box 365, London, OH 43140 (1580 State Rte 56, London, OH 43140); 614-466-8204, 614-852-2556; Fax: 614-852-4453; 8AM-5:45PM. Access by: mail.

Corporation Records
Fictitious Name
Limited Partnership Records
Assumed Name
Trademarks/Servicemarks
Limited Liability Company Records
Secretary of State, Attn: Certification Desk, 30 E Broad St, 14th Floor, Columbus, OH 43266-0418; 614-466-3910, 614-466-1776 Forms and Copies, 614-466-0590 Name Availability; Fax: 614-466-2892; 8AM-5PM. Access by: mail, phone, in person. www.state.oh.us/sos/info.html

Uniform Commercial Code
UCC Division, 14th Floor, Secretary of State, 30 E Broad St, State Office Tower, Columbus, OH 43215; 614-466-3623, 614-466-3126; Fax: 614-466-2892; 8AM-5PM. Access by: mail, phone, in person. www.state.oh.us/sos/ucc.html

Sales Tax Registrations
Restricted access.
This agency refuses to release any information about registrants. Taxation Department, Sale & Use Tax Division, 30 E Broad St, 20th Floor, Columbus, OH 43215; 614-466-7351, 888-405-4039; Fax: 614-466-4977; 8AM-5PM M-F www.state.oh.us/tax

Federal Tax Liens
State Tax Liens
Records not available from state agency.

Records are not housed by a state agency. You must secure from the local county recorder offices.

Workers' Compensation Records
Bureau of Workers Compensation, Customer Assistance, 30 W Spring St, Fl 10, Columbus, OH 43215-2241; 800-644-6292; Fax: 614-752-4732; 7:30AM-5:30PM. Access by: mail, phone, in person. www.ohiobwc.com

Birth Certificates

Ohio Department of Health, Bureau of Vital Statistics, PO Box 15098, Columbus, OH 43215-0098 (35 E Chestnut, 6th Floor, Columbus, OH 43215); 614-466-2531; Fax: 614-466-6604; 7:45AM-4:30PM. Access by: mail. www.odh.state.oh.us/records/records-f.htm

Death Records

Ohio Department of Health, Bureau of Vital Statistics, PO Box 15098, Columbus, OH 43215-0098; 614-466-2531; Fax: 614-466-6604; 7:45AM-4:30PM. Access by: mail. www.odh.state.oh.us/records/records-f.htm

Marriage Certificates
Divorce Records

Records not available from state agency.

Marriage and Divorce records are found at county of issue.

Accident Reports

Department of Public Safety, Central Records Unit, PO Box 182074, Columbus, OH 43218-2074; 614-752-1593; Fax: 614-644-9749; 8AM-4:45PM. Access by: mail.

Driver Records

Department of Public Safety, Bureau of Motor Vehicles, 1970 W Broad St, Columbus, OH 43223-1102; 614-752-7600; 8AM-5:30PM M-T-W; 8AM-4:30PM TH-F. Access by: mail, phone, in person, online. www.ohio.gov/odps

Vehicle Ownership
Vehicle Identification

Bureau of Motor Vehicles, Motor Vehicle Title Records, 1970 W Broad St, Columbus, OH 43223-1102; 614-752-7671; Fax: 614-752-8929; 8AM-5:30PM M-T-W; 8AM-4:30PM TH-F. Access

by: mail, phone, in person, online. www.state.oh.us/odps/division/bmv/bmv/html

Boat & Vessel Ownership
Boat & Vessel Registration

Natural Resources Department, Division of Watercraft, 4435 Fountain Square Dr Bldg A, Columbus, OH 43224-1300; 614-265-6480; Fax: 614-267-8883; 8AM-5PM. Access by: mail. www.dnr.state.oh.us/odnr/watercraft

Legislation-Current/Pending
Legislation-Passed

Ohio House of Representatives, 77 S High Street, Columbus, OH 43266 (Ohio Senate, State House, Columbus, OH 43215); 614-466-8842 In-State Only, 614-466-9745 Out-of-State; 8:30AM-5PM. Access by:, phone, in person. www.legislature.state.oh.us

Voter Registration

Secretary of State, Elections Division, 30 E Broad St, 14th Floor, Columbus, OH 43266-0418; 614-466-2585; Fax: 614-752-4360; 8AM-5PM. Access by: mail. www.state.oh.us/sos

GED Certificates

Department of Education, State GED Office, 65 S Front Street, Room 210, Columbus, OH 43215-4183; 614-466-4868; Fax: 614-752-9445; 8-4:45. www.ode.ohio.gov/www/ae/ae_ged.html

Hunting License Information
Fishing License Information

Records not available from state agency.

They do not have a central database. Only vendors have the names and addresses, which are kept for one year.

County Courts & Recording Offices

About the Courts...

Administration

Administrative Director, Supreme Court of Ohio   614-466-2653
30 E Broad St, 3rd Fl   Fax: 614-752-8736
Columbus, OH 43266-0419
www.sconet.state.oh.us

Court Structure

The Court of Common Pleas is the general jurisdiction court and County Courts have limited jurisdiction. Effective July 1, 1997, the dollar limits for civil cases in County and Municipal Courts were raised as follows: County Court - from $3,000 to $15,000; Municipal Court - from $10,000 to $15,000. In addition the small claims limit was raised from $2,000 to $3,000. Probate courts are separate from the Court of Common Pleas, but Probate Court phone numbers are given with that court in each county.

Online Access

There is no statewide computer system, but a number of counties offer online access.

About the Recording Offices...

Organization

88 counties, 88 recording offices. The recording officer is County Recorder and Clerk of Common Pleas Court (state tax liens). The entire state is in the Eastern Time Zone (EST).

UCC Records

This is a dual filing state. Financing statements are filed both at the state level and with the County Recorder, except for consumer goods, farm related and real estate related collateral, which are filed only with the County Recorder. All counties will perform UCC searches. Use search request form UCC-11. Search fees are usually $9.00 per debtor name. Copies usually cost $1.00 per page.

Lien Records

All federal tax liens are filed with the County Recorder. All state tax liens are filed with the Clerk of Common Pleas Court. Refer to The Sourcebook of County Court Records for information about Ohio courts. Federal tax liens are filed in the "Official Records" of each county. Most counties will not perform a federal tax lien search.

Real Estate Records

Counties will not perform real estate searches. Copy fees are usually $1.00 per page. Certification usually costs $.50 per document. Tax records are located at the Auditor's Office.

County Courts & Recording Offices

Adams

Real Estate Recording—Adams County Recorder, 110 West Main, Courthouse, West Union, OH 45693. Fax: 937-544-5051. 8AM-4PM.

Felony, Civil Actions Over $3,000, Probate—Common Pleas Court, 110 W Main, West Union, OH 45693. 937-544-2344, Fax: 937-544-8911. 8:30AM-4PM. Access by: in person.

Misdemeanor, Civil Actions Under $15,000, Small Claims—County Court, 110 W Main, Rm 25, West Union, OH 45693. 937-544-2011, Fax: 937-544-8911. 8AM-4PM. Access by: mail, in person.

Allen

Real Estate Recording—Allen County Recorder, 301 North Main Street, Room 204, Lima, OH 45801. 8AM-4:30PM.

Felony, Civil Actions Over $15,000, Probate—Common Pleas Court, PO Box 1243, Lima, OH 45802. 419-228-3700, Fax: 419-222-8427. 8AM-4:30PM. Access by: mail, fax, in person. Special note: Probate is a separate court.

Misdemeanor, Civil Actions Under $15,000, Eviction, Small Claims—Lima Municipal Court, 109 N Union St (PO Box 1529), Lima, OH 45802. 419-221-5275, Fax: 419-228-2305. 8AM-5PM. Access by: mail, phone, fax, in person. www.bright.net/~limamuni

Ashland

Real Estate Recording—Ashland County Recorder, Courthouse, 142 W. 2nd St. Ashland, OH 44805. Fax: 419-281-5715. 8AM-4PM.

Felony, Civil Actions Over $10,000, Probate—Common Pleas Court, 142 W 2nd St, Ashland, OH 44805. 419-289-0000. 8AM-4PM. Access by: mail, in person.

Misdemeanor, Civil Actions Under $15,000, Eviction, Small Claims—Ashland Municipal Court, PO Box 385, Ashland, OH 44805. 419-289-8137, Fax: 419-289-8545. 8AM-5PM. Access by: mail, in person. www.ashland-ohio.com

Ashtabula

Real Estate Recording—Ashtabula County Recorder, 25 West Jefferson Street, Jefferson, OH 44047. Fax: 440-576-3231. 8AM-4:30PM.

Felony, Civil Actions Over $10,000, Probate—Common Pleas Court, 25 W Jefferson St, Jefferson, OH 44047. 440-576-3637, Fax: 440-576-2819. 8AM-4:30PM. Access by: in person.

Misdemeanor, Civil Actions Under $15,000, Small Claims—County Court Eastern Division, 25 W Jefferson St, Jefferson, OH 44047. 440-576-3617. 8AM-4:30PM. Access by: mail, in person.

County Court Western Division, 117 W Main St, Geneva, OH 44041. 440-466-1184, Fax: 440-466-7171. 8AM-4:30PM. Access by: in person.

Misdemeanor, Civil Actions Under $15,000, Eviction, Small Claims—Ashtabula Municipal Court, 110 W 44th St, Ashtabula, OH 44004. 440-992-7110, Fax: 440-998-5786. 8AM-4:30PM. Access by: in person. Special note: 440-992-7109 gives a directory.

Athens

Real Estate Recording—Athens County Recorder, Room 236, 15 South Court, Athens, OH 45701. 614-592-3731, Fax: 740-592-3229. 8AM-4PM.

Felony, Civil Actions Over $10,000, Probate—Common Pleas Court, PO Box 290, Athens, OH 45701-0290. 740-592-3242. 8AM-4PM. Access by: in person.

Misdemeanor, Civil Actions Under $15,000, Eviction, Small Claims—Athens Municipal Court, City Hall, 8 East Washington St, Athens, OH 45701. 740-592-3328, Fax: 740-592-3331. 8AM-4PM. Access by: in person.

Auglaize

Real Estate Recording—Auglaize County Recorder, Courthouse, Suite 101, 201 S. Willipie St. Wapakoneta, OH 45895. 419-738-2110, Fax: 419-738-4115. 8AM-4:30PM.

Felony, Civil Actions Over $10,000, Probate—Common Pleas Court, PO Box 409, Wapakoneta, OH 45895. 419-738-4219. 8AM-4:30PM. Access by: in person.

Misdemeanor, Civil Actions Under $15,000, Eviction, Small Claims—Auglaize County Municipal Court, PO Box 409, Wapakoneta, OH 45895. 419-738-2923. 8AM-4:30PM. Access by: in person.

Belmont

Real Estate Recording—Belmont County Recorder, Courthouse, Room 105, 101 Main St. St. Clairsville, OH 43950. 614-695-2120. 8:30AM-4:30PM.

Felony, Civil Actions Over $3,000, Probate—Common Pleas Court, Main St, Courthouse, St Clairsville, OH 43950. 740-695-2121. 8:30AM-4:30PM. Access by: mail, in person.

Misdemeanor, Civil Actions Under $15,000, Small Claims—County Court Eastern Division, 400 W 26th St, Bellaire, OH 43906. 740-676-4490. 8AM-4PM. Access by: mail, in person.

County Court Northern Division, PO Box 40, Martins Ferry, OH 43935. 740-633-3147, Fax: 740-633-6631. 8AM-4PM. Access by: mail, in person.

County Court Western Division, 147 W Main St, St Clairsville, OH 43950. 740-695-2875, Fax: 740-695-7285. 8AM-4PM. Access by: mail, fax, in person.

Brown

Real Estate Recording—Brown County Recorder, Administration Building, 800 Mt. Orab Pike, Georgetown, OH 45121. 937-378-6705, Fax: 937-378-2848. 8AM-4PM.

Felony, Civil Actions Over $3,000, Probate—Common Pleas Court, 101 S Main, Georgetown, OH 45121. 937-378-3100. 8AM-4PM. Access by: mail, in person.

Misdemeanor, Civil Actions Under $15,000, Eviction, Small Claims—County Court, 770 Mount Orab Pike, Georgetown, OH 45121. 937-378-6358, Fax: 937-378-2462. 8AM-4PM. Access by: mail, in person.

Butler

Real Estate Recording—Butler County Recorder, 130 High Street, Hamilton, OH 45011. Fax: 513-887-3198. 8AM-4:30PM.

Felony, Civil Actions Over $3,000, Probate—Common Pleas Court, 101 High St, Hamilton, OH 45011. 513-887-3996, Fax: 513-887-3089. 8:30AM-4:30PM. Access by: in person, online.

Misdemeanor, Civil Actions Under $15,000, Small Claims—County Court Area #1, 118 West High, Oxford, OH 45056. 513-523-4748, Fax: 513-523-4737. 8:30AM-4:30PM. Access by: mail, phone, in person.

County Court Area #2, Butler County Courthouse, 101 High St, 3rd Fl, Hamilton, OH 45011. 513-887-3459. 8AM-5PM. Access by: phone, in person.

County Court Area #3, 9113 Cincinnati, Dayton Rd, West Chester, OH 45069. 513-867-5070, Fax: 513-777-0558. 8:30AM-4:30PM. Access by: mail, in person.

Carroll

Real Estate Recording—Carroll County Recorder, Courthouse, 119 Public Square, Carrollton, OH 44615. Fax: 330-627-4295. 8AM-4PM.

Felony, Civil Actions Over $15,000, Probate—Common Pleas Court, PO Box 367, Carrollton, OH 44615. 334-275-3363, Fax: 330-627-6734. 8AM-4PM. Access by: mail, in person.

Misdemeanor, Civil Actions Under $15,000, Small Claims—County Court, Courthouse, 3rd Fl, Carrollton, OH 44615.

334-275-3507, Fax: 330-627-6656. 8AM-4PM. Access by: mail, in person.

Champaign

Real Estate Recording—Champaign County Recorder, 200 North Main Street, Urbana, OH 43078. Fax: 937-652-1515. 8AM-4PM.

Felony, Civil Actions Over $10,000, Probate—Common Pleas Court, 200 N Main St, Urbana, OH 43078. 937-653-2746. 8AM-4PM. Access by: mail, phone, in person. Special note: Probate is separate court at phone number given.

Misdemeanor, Civil Actions Under $15,000, Eviction, Small Claims—Champaign County Municipal Court, PO Box 85, Urbana, OH 43078. 937-653-7376. 8AM-4PM. Access by: mail, in person.

Clark

Real Estate Recording—Clark County Recorder, 31 North Limestone Street, Springfield, OH 45502. 937-328-2432, Fax: 937-328-4620. 8AM-4:30PM.

Felony, Civil Actions Over $10,000, Probate—Common Pleas Court, 101 N Limestone St, Springfield, OH 45502. 937-328-2458, Fax: 937-328-2436. 8AM-4:30PM. Access by: in person.

Misdemeanor, Civil Actions Under $15,000, Eviction, Small Claims—Clark County Municipal Court, 50 E Columbia St, Springfield, OH 45502. 937-328-3700. 8AM-5PM. Access by: mail, in person.

Clermont

Real Estate Recording—Clermont County Recorder, 101 E. Main Street, Batavia, OH 45103. 513-732-7254, Fax: 513-732-7891. 8AM-5PM.

Felony, Civil Actions Over $10,000, Probate—Common Pleas Court, 270 Main St, Batavia, OH 45103. 513-732-7130, Fax: 513-732-7050. 8:30AM-4:30PM. Access by: in person.

Misdemeanor, Civil Actions Under $15,000, Eviction, Small Claims—Clermont County Municipal Court, 289 Main St, Batavia, OH 45103. 8:30AM-4:30PM. Access by: mail, in person.

Clinton

Real Estate Recording—Clinton County Recorder, 46 S. South Street, Courthouse, Wilmington, OH 45177. 937-382-2224, Fax: 937-383-6653. 8AM-4PM.

Felony, Civil Actions Over $15,000, Probate—Common Pleas Court, 46 S South St, Wilmington, OH 45177. 937-382-2316, Fax: 937-383-3455. 7:30AM-4:30PM. Access by: mail, fax, in person. Special note: Probate fax is 937-383-1158.

Misdemeanor, Civil Actions Under $15,000, Eviction, Small Claims—Clinton County Municipal Court, 69 N South St, Wilmington, OH 45177. 937-382-8985, Fax: 937-383-0130. 8AM-3:30PM. Access by: mail, phone, in person.

Columbiana

Real Estate Recording—Columbiana County Recorder, County Courthouse, Room 104, 105 South Market St. Lisbon, OH 44432. Fax: 330-424-5067. 8AM-4PM.

Felony, Civil Actions Over $10,000, Probate—Common Pleas Court, 105 S Market St, Lisbon, OH 44432. 330-742-8863, Fax: 330-424-3960. 8AM-4:30PM. Access by: in person.

Misdemeanor, Civil Actions Under $15,000, Small Claims—County Court East Area, 31 North Market St, East Palestine, OH 44413. 330-742-8900, Fax: 330-426-6328. 8AM-4PM. Access by: mail, in person.

County Court Northwest Area, 130 Penn Ave, Salem, OH 44460. 330-675-2557. 8AM-4PM. Access by: mail, in person.

County Court Southwest Area, 41 N Park Ave, Lisbon, OH 44432. 330-740-2460, Fax: 330-424-6658. 8AM-4PM. Access by: mail, in person.

Misdemeanor, Civil Actions Under $15,000, Eviction, Small Claims—East Liverpool Municipal Court, 126 W 6th St, East Liverpool, OH 43920. 330-740-2104, Fax: 330-385-1566. 8AM-4PM. Access by: mail, phone, fax, in person.

Coshocton

Real Estate Recording—Coshocton County Recorder, 349 Main Street, Courthouse Annex, Coshocton, OH 43812. 614-622-2713, Fax: 740-622-0190. 8AM-4PM.

Felony, Civil Actions Over $10,000, Probate—Common Pleas Court, 318 Main St, Coshocton, OH 43812. 740-622-1456. 8AM-4PM. Access by: mail, in person.

Misdemeanor, Civil Actions Under $15,000, Eviction, Small Claims—Coshocton Municipal Court, 760 Chesnut St, Coshocton, OH 43812. 740-622-2871, Fax: 740-623-5928. 8AM-4:30PM M-W,F; 8AM-Noon Th. Access by: mail, phone, fax, in person.

Crawford

Real Estate Recording—Crawford County Recorder, 112 East Mansfield Street, Bucyrus, OH 44820. Fax: 419-562-6061. 8:30AM-4:30PM.

Felony, Civil Actions Over $3,000, Probate—Common Pleas Court, PO Box 470, Bucyrus, OH 44820. 419-562-2766, Fax: 419-562-8011. 8:30AM-4:30PM. Access by: mail, in person.

Misdemeanor, Civil Actions Under $15,000, Eviction, Small Claims—Crawford County Municipal Court, PO Box 550, Bucyrus, OH 44820. 419-562-2731. 8:30AM-4:30PM. Access by: mail, in person.

Crawford County Municipal Court Eastern Division, 301 Harding Way East, Galion, OH 44833. 419-468-6819, Fax: 419-468-6828. 8:30AM-4:30PM. Access by: mail, in person.

Cuyahoga

Real Estate Recording—Cuyahoga County Recorder, 1219 Ontario Street, Room 220, Cleveland, OH 44113. Fax: 216-443-8193. 8:30AM-4:30PM.

Felony, Civil Actions Over $10,000, Probate—Common Pleas Court-General Div, 1200 Ontario St, Cleveland, OH 44113. 217-243-5419, Fax: 216-443-5424. 8:30AM-4:30PM. Access by: mail, phone, in person. Special note: Probate is a separate division with separate records and personnel.

Civil Actions Under $15,000, Eviction, Small Claims—Cleveland Municipal Court-Civil Division, 1200 Ontario St, Cleveland, OH 44113. 217-285-6612, Fax: 216-664-4065. 8AM-3:50PM. Access by: mail, fax, in person.

Misdemeanor—Cleveland Municipal Court-Criminal Division, 1200 Ontario St, Cleveland, OH 44113. 217-285-4218. 8AM-3:50PM. Access by: mail, in person.

Misdemeanor, Civil Actions Under $15,000, Eviction, Small Claims—Bedford Municipal Court, 65 Columbus Rd, Bedford, OH 44146. 440-232-3420, Fax: 440-232-2510. 8:30AM-4:30PM. Access by: mail, fax, in person.

Berea Municipal Court, 11 Berea Commons, Berea, OH 44017. 440-826-5860, Fax: 440-891-3387. 8:30AM-5PM. Access by: mail, phone, fax, in person.

Cleveland Heights Municipal Court, 40 Severence Circle, Cleveland Heights, OH 44118. 216-664-4790, Fax: 216-291-2459. 8AM-5PM. Access by: in person, online.

East Cleveland Municipal Court, 14340 Euclid Ave, East Cleveland, OH 44112. 217-322-3830. 8:30AM-4:30PM. Access by: mail, in person.

Euclid Municipal Court, 555 E 222 St, Euclid, OH 44123-2099. 216-529-6700. 8:30AM-4:30PM. Access by: mail, in person.

Garfield Heights Municipal Court, 5555 Turney Rd, Garfield Heights, OH 44125. 217-253-2352. 8:30AM-4:30PM. Access by: mail, phone, in person.

Lakewood Municipal Court, 12650 Detroit Ave, Lakewood, OH 44107. 217-277-2100, Fax: 216-529-7687. 8AM-5PM. Access by: mail, fax, in person.

Lyndhurst Municipal Court, 5301 Mayfield Rd, Lyndhurst, OH 44124. 217-243-8581. 8:30AM-5PM. Access by: mail, in person.

Parma Municipal Court, 5750 W 54th St, Parma, OH 44129. 440-884-4000, Fax: 440-885-8937. 8:30AM-4:30PM. Access by: mail, phone, fax, in person. Special note: The court is making changes to block the SSN from appearing on record requests.

Rocky River Municipal Court, 21012 Hilliard Blvd, Rocky River, OH 44116. 440-333-0066, Fax: 440-356-5613. 8:30AM-4:30PM. Access by: mail, phone, fax, in person.

Shaker Heights Municipal Court, 3355 Lee Rd, Shaker Heights, OH 44120. 217-253-4011, Fax: 216-491-1314. 8:30AM-5PM. Access by: mail, phone, in person.

South Euclid Municipal Court, 1349 S Green Rd, South Euclid, OH 44121. 216-681-2021, Fax: 216-381-1195. 8:30AM-5PM. Access by: mail, in person.

Darke

Real Estate Recording—Darke County Recorder, 504 South Broadway, Courthouse, Greenville, OH 45331. 937-547-7365. 8:30AM-4:30PM.

Felony, Civil Actions Over $3,000, Probate—Common Pleas Court, Courthouse, Greenville, OH 45331. 937-547-7335, Fax: 937-547-7305. 8:30AM-4:30PM. Access by: mail, in person. Special note: Probate is a separate court at the number given.

Misdemeanor, Civil Actions Under $15,000, Small Claims—County Court, Courthouse, Greenville, OH 45331-1990. 937-547-7340, Fax: 937-547-7378. 8:30AM-4:30PM. Access by: mail, in person.

Defiance

Real Estate Recording—Defiance County Recorder, 221 Clinton Street, Courthouse, Defiance, OH 43512. Fax: 419-782-3421. 8:30AM-4:30PM.

Felony, Civil Actions Over $10,000, Probate—Common Pleas Court, PO Box 716, Defiance, OH 43512. 419-782-1936. 8:30AM-4:30PM. Access by: in person.

Misdemeanor, Civil Actions Under $15,000, Eviction, Small Claims—Defiance Municipal Court, 324 Perry St, Defiance, OH 43512. 419-782-5756, Fax: 419-782-2018. 8AM-5PM. Access by: mail, in person.

Delaware

Real Estate Recording—Delaware County Recorder, 91 North Sandusky Street, Courthouse, Delaware, OH 43015. 614-368-1790. 8:30AM-4:30PM.

Felony, Civil Actions Over $10,000, Probate—Common Pleas Court, 91 N Sandusky, Delaware, OH 43015. 740-368-1850, Fax: 740-368-1849. 8:30AM-4:30PM. Access by: mail, in person.

Misdemeanor, Civil Actions Under $15,000, Eviction, Small Claims—Delaware Municipal Court, 70 N Union St, Delaware, OH 43015. 740-363-1296, Fax: 740-368-1583. 8AM-5PM. Access by: mail, phone, in person.

Erie

Real Estate Recording—Erie County Recorder, Erie County Office Bldg, Room 225, 247 Columbus Ave. Sandusky, OH 44870. 419-627-7201, Fax: 419-627-6639. 8AM-4PM.

Felony, Civil Actions Over $10,000, Probate—Common Pleas Court, 323 Columbus Ave, Sandusky, OH 44870. 419-627-7705, Fax: 419-627-6873. 8AM-4PM M-Th/8AM-5PM F. Access by: in person.

Misdemeanor, Civil Actions Under $15,000, Small Claims—Erie County Court, 150 W Mason Rd, Milan, OH 44846. 419-499-4689, Fax: 419-499-3300. 8AM-4PM. Access by: mail, phone, in person.

Misdemeanor, Civil Actions Under $15,000, Eviction, Small Claims—Sandusky Municipal Court, 222 Meigs St, Sandusky, OH 44870. 419-627-5917, Fax: 419-627-5950. 7AM-4PM. Access by: mail, phone, fax, in person.

Vermilion Municipal Court, 687 Delatur St, Vermilion, OH 44089. 440-967-6543, Fax: 440-967-1467. 8AM-4PM. Access by: mail, fax, in person.

Fairfield

Real Estate Recording—Fairfield County Recorder, 210 East Main Street, Courthouse, Lancaster, OH 43130. 614-687-7094, Fax: 740-687-7104. 8AM-4PM.

Felony, Civil Actions Over $10,000, Probate—Common Pleas Court, 224 E Main (PO Box 370), 2nd Flr, Lancaster, OH 43130-0370. 740-687-7030. 8AM-4PM. Access by: mail, phone, in person.

Misdemeanor, Civil Actions Under $15,000, Eviction, Small Claims—Lancaster Municipal Court, PO Box 2390, Lancaster, OH 43130. 740-687-6621. 8AM-4PM. Access by: mail, in person.

Fayette

Real Estate Recording—Fayette County Recorder, 110 East Court Street, Courthouse Building, Washington Court House, OH 43160. Fax: 740-333-3530. 9AM-4PM.

Felony, Civil Actions Over $10,000, Probate—Common Pleas Court, 110 E Court St, Washington Court House, OH 43160. 740-335-6371. 9AM-4PM. Access by: mail, in person. Special note: Probate is a separate court at number given.

Misdemeanor, Civil Actions Under $15,000, Eviction, Small Claims—Municipal Court, Washington Courthouse, 119 N Main St, Washington Court House, OH 43160. 740-636-2350, Fax: 740-636-2359. 8AM-4PM. Access by: mail, in person.

Franklin

Real Estate Recording—Franklin County Recorder, 373 S. High Street, 18th Floor, Columbus, OH 43215. Fax: 614-462-4312. 8AM-5PM.

Felony, Civil Actions Over $10,000, Probate—Common Pleas Court, 369 S High St, Columbus, OH 43215-6311. 8AM-5PM. Access by: mail, in person.

Civil Actions Under $15,000, Eviction, Small Claims—Franklin County Municipal Court, Civil Division, 375 S High St, 3rd Flr, Columbus, OH 43215. 614-645-7220, Fax: 614-645-6919. 8AM-5PM. Access by: mail, phone, fax, in person, online. www.fcmcclerk.com

Misdemeanor—Franklin County Municipal Court, 375 S High St, 2nd Flr, Columbus, OH 43215. 614-645-7223. Open 24 hours a day. Access by: mail, in person, online. www.fcmcclerk.com

Fulton

Real Estate Recording—Fulton County Recorder, Courthouse, Room 103, 210 S. Fulton St. Wauseon, OH 43567. 419-337-9200, Fax: 419-337-9282. 8:30AM-4:30PM.

Felony, Civil Actions Over $3,000, Probate—Common Pleas Court, 210 S Fulton, Wauseon, OH 43567. 419-337-9230. 8:30AM-4:30PM. Access by: in person.

Misdemeanor, Civil Actions Under $15,000, Small Claims—County Court Eastern District, 128 N Main St, Swanton, OH 43558. 419-826-5636, Fax: 419-825-3324. 8:30AM-4:30PM. Access by: mail, in person.

County Court Western District, 224 S Fulton St, Wauseon, OH 43567. 419-337-9212, Fax: 419-337-9286. 8:30AM-4:30PM. Access by: mail, in person.

Gallia

Real Estate Recording—Gallia County Recorder, 18 Locust Street, Room 1265, Gallipolis, OH 45631. 614-446-6004, Fax: 740-446-4804. 8AM-4PM.

Felony, Civil Actions Over $10,000, Probate—Common Pleas Court-Gallia County Courthouse, 18 Locust St, Rm 1290, Gallipolis, OH 45631-1290. 740-446-4612, Fax: 740-441-2094. 8AM-4PM. Access by: in person.

Misdemeanor, Civil Actions Under $15,000, Eviction, Small Claims—Gallipolis Municipal Court, 518 2nd Ave, Gallipolis, OH 45631. 614-446-9400, Fax: 614-446-2070. 9AM-4:30PM. Access by: mail, phone, in person.

Geauga

Real Estate Recording—Geauga County Recorder, 231 Main Street, Courthouse Annex, Chardon, OH 44024. 8AM-4:30PM.

Felony, Civil Actions Over $10,000, Probate—Common Pleas Court, 100 Short Court, Chardon, OH 44024. 440-285-2222, Fax: 440-286-2127. 8AM-4:30PM. Access by: in person.

Misdemeanor, Civil Actions Under $15,000, Eviction, Small Claims—Chardon Municipal Court, 111 Water St, Chardon, OH

44024. 440-286-2670, Fax: 440-286-2679. 8AM-4:30PM. Access by: mail, in person.

Greene

Real Estate Recording—Greene County Recorder, 69 Greene Street, 3rd Floor, Xenia, OH 45385. 937-376-5065, Fax: 937-376-5386. 8AM-4:30PM.

Felony, Civil Actions Over $10,000, Probate—Common Pleas Court, 45 N Detroit St (PO Box 156), Xenia, OH 45385. 937-376-5292, Fax: 937-376-5309. 8AM-4PM. Access by: in person.

Misdemeanor, Civil Actions Under $15,000, Eviction, Small Claims—Xenia Municipal Court, 101 N Detroit, Xenia, OH 45385. 937-376-7294, Fax: 937-376-7288. 8AM-4:30PM. Access by: mail, fax, in person.

Misdemeanor, Civil Actions Under $20,000, Eviction, Small Claims—Fairborn Municipal Court, 44 W Hebble Ave, Fairborn, OH 45324. 937-754-3040, Fax: 937-879-4422. 7:30AM-4:30PM. Access by: mail, in person.

Guernsey

Real Estate Recording—Guernsey County Recorder, Courthouse D-202, Wheeling Avenue, Cambridge, OH 43725. 8AM-4PM.

Felony, Civil Actions Over $10,000, Probate—Common Pleas Court, 801 E Wheeling Ave D-300, Cambridge, OH 43725. 740-432-9230, Fax: 740-432-7807. 8:30AM-4PM. Access by: in person. Special note: Probate is a separte division with separate records and personnel.

Misdemeanor, Civil Actions Under $15,000, Eviction, Small Claims—Cambridge Municipal Court, 134 Southgate Parkway, Cambridge, OH 43725. 740-439-5585, Fax: 740-439-5666. 8:30AM-4:30PM. Access by: mail, phone, in person.

Hamilton

Real Estate Recording—Hamilton County Recorder, 138 East Court Street, Room 101-A, Cincinnati, OH 45202. 513-632-8380, Fax: 513-946-4577. 8AM-4PM.

Felony, Civil Actions Over $10,000, Probate—Common Pleas Court, 1000 Main St, Room 315, Cincinnati, OH 45202. 513-632-8283, Fax: 513-763-4860. 8AM-4PM. Access by: mail, phone, fax, in person, online. Special note: Probate is separate court at telephone number given. www.courtclerk.org

Civil Actions Under $15,000, Eviction, Small Claims—Hamilton County Municipal Court, 1000 Main St, Cincinnati, OH 45202. 513-632-8891, Fax: 513-632-7325. 8AM-4PM. Access by: mail, phone, fax, in person. www.courtclerk.org

Hancock

Real Estate Recording—Hancock County Recorder, 300 South Main Street, Courthouse, Findlay, OH 45840. Fax: 419-424-7828. 8:30AM-4:30PM.

Felony, Civil Actions Over $10,000, Probate—Common Pleas Court, 300 S Main St, Findlay, OH 45840. 419-424-7037. 8:30AM-4:30PM. Access by: mail, in person.

Misdemeanor, Civil Actions Under $15,000, Eviction, Small Claims—Findlay Municipal Court, PO Box 826, Findlay, OH 45839. 419-424-7141, Fax: 419-424-7803. 8AM-5PM. Access by: mail, in person.

Hardin

Real Estate Recording—Hardin County Recorder, One Courthouse Square, Suite 220, Kenton, OH 43326. 419-674-2246, Fax: 419-675-2802. 8:30AM-4PM; 8:30AM-6PM F.

Felony, Civil Actions Over $10,000, Probate—Common Pleas Court, Courthouse, Ste 310, Kenton, OH 43326. 419-674-2278, Fax: 419-674-2273. 8:30AM-4PM M-Th; 8:30AM-6PM F. Access by: mail, in person.

Misdemeanor, Civil Actions Under $15,000, Eviction, Small Claims—Hardin County Municipal Court, PO Box 250, Kenton, OH 43326. 419-674-4362, Fax: 419-674-4096. 8:30AM-4PM. Access by: mail, in person.

Harrison

Real Estate Recording—Harrison County Recorder, 100 West Market Street, Courthouse, Cadiz, OH 43907. 614-942-8864, Fax: 740-942-4693. 8:30AM-4:30PM.

Felony, Civil Actions Over $3,000, Probate—Common Pleas Court, 100 W Market, Cadiz, OH 43907. 740-942-8863, Fax: 740-942-4693. 8:30AM-4:30PM. Access by: mail, phone, fax, in person.

Misdemeanor, Civil Actions Under $15,000, Small Claims—Harrison County Court, Courthouse, 100 W Market St, Cadiz, OH 43907. 740-942-8865, Fax: 740-942-4693. 8:30AM-4:30PM. Access by: in person.

Henry

Real Estate Recording—Henry County Recorder, Courthouse, Room 202, 660 North Perry St. Napoleon, OH 43545. Fax: 419-592-1652. 8:30AM-4:30PM.

Felony, Civil Actions Over $10,000, Probate—Common Pleas Court, PO Box 71, Napoleon, OH 43545. 419-592-5886, Fax: 419-599-0803. 8:30AM-4:30PM. Access by: mail, in person. Special note: Probate Court's address is PO Box 70.

Misdemeanor, Civil Actions Under $15,000, Eviction, Small Claims—Napoleon Municipal Court, PO Box 502, Napoleon, OH 43545. 419-592-2851, Fax: 419-592-1805. 8:30AM-5PM. Access by: mail, phone, fax, in person.

Highland

Real Estate Recording—Highland County Recorder, 119 Governor Foraker, County Administration Building, Hillsboro, OH 45133. 937-393-9951, Fax: 937-393-5855. 8:30AM-4PM.

Felony, Civil Actions Over $10,000, Probate—Common Pleas Court, PO Box 821, Hillsboro, OH 45133. 937-393-9957, Fax: 937-393-6878. 8AM-4:30PM. Access by: mail, in person. Special note: Probate is a separate court.

Misdemeanor, Civil Actions Under $15,000, Eviction, Small Claims—Hillsboro County Municipal Court, 108 Governor Trimble Pl, Hillsboro, OH 45133. 937-393-3022, Fax: 937-393-3273. 7AM-3:30PM M,T,Th,F; 7AM-Noon W. Access by: mail, phone, fax, in person.

Hocking

Real Estate Recording—Hocking County Recorder, 1 East Main Street, Courthouse, Logan, OH 43138. Fax: 740-385-0377. 8:30AM-4PM.

Felony, Civil Actions Over $10,000, Probate—Common Pleas Court, PO Box 108, Logan, OH 43138. 740-385-2616, Fax: 740-385-1822. 8:30AM-4PM. Access by: mail, phone, fax, in person. Special note: Probate is a separate court at the number given.

Misdemeanor, Civil Actions Under $15,000, Eviction, Small Claims—Hocking County Municipal Court, 1 E Main St (PO Box 950), Logan, OH 43138-1278. 740-385-2250. 8:30AM-4PM. Access by: mail, in person.

Holmes

Real Estate Recording—Holmes County Recorder, 75 E. Clinton St. Suite 101, Millersburg, OH 44654. 334-361-3725. 8:30AM-4:30PM.

Felony, Civil Actions Over $10,000, Probate—Common Pleas Court, 1 E Jackson St #301, Millersburg, OH 44654. 334-347-2688, Fax: 330-674-0289. 8:30AM-4:30PM. Access by: mail, fax, in person. Special note: Juvenile and probate court at suite 201.

Misdemeanor, Civil Actions Under $15,000, Small Claims—County Court, 1 E Jackson St, Ste 101, Millersburg, OH 44654. 334-361-3737, Fax: 330-674-5514. 8:30AM-4:30PM. Access by: mail, phone, fax, in person.

Huron

Real Estate Recording—Huron County Recorder, 2 East Main Street, Norwalk, OH 44857. Fax: 419-663-4052. 8AM-4:30PM.

Felony, Civil Actions Over $10,000, Probate—Common Pleas Court, 2 E Main St, Norwalk, OH 44857. 419-668-5113, Fax: 419-663-4048. 8AM-4:30PM. Access by: mail, fax, in person. Special note: Probate is separate court at phone number given.

Misdemeanor, Civil Actions Under $15,000, Eviction, Small Claims—Bellevue Municipal Court, 117 N Sandusky, PO Box 305, Bellevue, OH 44811. 419-483-5880, Fax: 419-484-8060. 8:30AM-4:30PM. Access by: mail, phone, in person.

Norwalk Municipal Court, 45 N Linwood, Norwalk, OH 44857. 419-663-6750, Fax: 419-663-6749. 8:30AM-4:30PM. Access by: mail, fax, in person.

Jackson

Real Estate Recording—Jackson County Recorder, 226 E. Main St. Courthouse, Suite 1, Jackson, OH 45640. 614-286-2402. 8AM-4PM.

Felony, Civil Actions Over $10,000, Probate—Common Pleas Court, 226 Main St, Jackson, OH 45640. 740-286-2006, Fax: 740-286-4061. 8AM-4PM. Access by: mail, in person.

Misdemeanor, Civil Actions Under $15,000, Eviction, Small Claims—Jackson County Municipal Court, 226 Main St, Jackson, OH 45640-1764. 740-286-2718, Fax: 740-286-4061. 8AM-4PM. Access by: in person.

Jefferson

Real Estate Recording—Jefferson County Recorder, 3rd & Market Street, Courthouse, Steubenville, OH 43952. 614-283-8511. 8:30AM-4:30PM.

Felony, Civil Actions Over $500, Probate—Common Pleas Court, 301 Market St (PO Box 1326), Steubenville, OH 43952. 740-283-8583. 8:30AM-4:30PM. Access by: mail, in person. Special note: Probate is at PO Box 649 and can be reached at 740-283-8653. www.uov.net/jeffcodp/index.htm

Misdemeanor, Civil Actions Under $15,000, Small Claims—County Court #1, 1007 Franklin Ave, Toronto, OH 43964. 740-537-2020. 8:30AM-4:30PM. Access by: mail, in person.

County Court #2, PO Box 2207, Wintersville, OH 43953. 740-264-7644. 8:30AM-4PM. Access by: mail, in person.

County Court #3, PO Box 495, Dillonvale, OH 43917. 740-769-2903. 8:30AM-4PM. Access by: mail, in person.

Misdemeanor, Civil Actions Under $15,000, Eviction, Small Claims—Steubenville Municipal Court, 123 S 3rd St, Steubenville, OH 43952. 740-283-6020, Fax: 740-283-6167. 8:30AM-4PM. Access by: mail, in person.

Knox

Real Estate Recording—Knox County Recorder, 106 East High Street, Mount Vernon, OH 43050. 8AM-4PM.

Felony, Civil Actions Over $10,000, Probate—Common Pleas Court, 111 E High St, Mt Vernon, OH 43050. 740-393-6788. 8AM-4PM, til 6PM on Wed. Access by: in person.

Misdemeanor, Civil Actions Under $15,000, Eviction, Small Claims—Mount Vernon Municipal Court, 5 North Gay St, Mount Vernon, OH 43050. 740-393-9510, Fax: 740-393-5349. 8AM-4PM. Access by: mail, phone, in person.

Lake

Real Estate Recording—Lake County Recorder, 105 Main Street, Painesville, OH 44077. 216-664-4870, Fax: 440-350-5940. 8AM-4:30PM.

Felony, Civil Actions Over $10,000, Probate—Common Pleas Court, PO Box 490, Painesville, OH 44077. 440-350-2658. 8AM-4:30PM. Access by: in person.

Misdemeanor, Civil Actions Under $15,000, Eviction, Small Claims—Mentor Municipal Court, 8500 Civic Center Blvd, Mentor, OH 44060-2418. Fax: 440-974-5742. 8:30AM-4:30 PM. Access by: in person.

Painesville Municipal Court, 7 Richmond St (PO Box 601), Painesville, OH 44077. 440-639-4990, Fax: 440-352-0028. 8AM-4:30PM. Access by: mail, fax, in person. Special note: Civil & Probation Fax# 440-639-4932.

Willoughby Municipal Court, One Public Square, Willoughby, OH 44094-7888. Fax: 440-953-4149. 7:30AM-4:30 PM. Access by: mail, in person.

Lawrence

Real Estate Recording—Lawrence County Recorder, 111 South 4th Street, Courthouse, Ironton, OH 45638. Fax: 740-533-4411. 8AM-4PM.

Felony, Civil Actions Over $10,000, Probate—Common Pleas Court, PO Box 208, Ironton, OH 45638. 740-533-4355. 8:30AM-4PM. Access by: mail, in person.

Misdemeanor, Civil Actions Under $15,000, Eviction, Small Claims—Lawrence County Municipal Court, PO Box 126, Chesapeake, OH 45619. 740-867-3128, Fax: 740-867-3547. 8:30AM-4PM. Access by: mail, phone, fax, in person.

Ironton Municipal Court, PO Box 237, Ironton, OH 45638. 740-532-3062, Fax: 740-533-6088. 8:30AM-4PM. Access by: mail, in person.

Licking

Real Estate Recording—Licking County Recorder, 20 South Second Street, Third Floor, Newark, OH 43055. Fax: 740-349-1415. 8:30AM-4:30PM.

Felony, Civil Actions Over $10,000, Probate—Common Pleas Court, PO Box 4370, Newark, OH 43058-4370. 740-349-6171, Fax: 740-349-6945. 8AM-4:30PM. Access by: in person.

Misdemeanor, Civil Actions Under $15,000, Eviction, Small Claims—Licking County Municipal Court, 40 W Main St, Newark, OH 43055. 740-349-6627. 8AM-4:30PM. Access by: mail, phone, fax, in person.

Logan

Real Estate Recording—Logan County Recorder, 100 South Madriver, Suite A, Bellefontaine, OH 43311. Fax: 937-599-7287. 8:30AM-4:30PM.

Felony, Civil Actions Over $10,000, Probate—Common Pleas Court, 101 S Main St Rm 18, Bellefontaine, OH 43311-2097. 937-599-7275. 8:30AM-4:30PM. Access by: in person.

Misdemeanor, Civil Actions Under $15,000, Eviction, Small Claims—Bellefontaine Municipal Court, 226 W Columbus Ave, Bellefontaine, OH 43311. 937-599-6127. 8AM-4:30PM. Access by: in person.

Lorain

Real Estate Recording—Lorain County Recorder, 226 Middle Avenue, Elyria, OH 44035. Fax: 440-329-5199. 8AM-4:30PM.

Felony, Civil Actions Over $10,000, Probate—Common Pleas Court, 226 Middle Ave, Elyria, OH 44035. 440-329-5536, Fax: 440-329-5404. 8AM-4:30PM. Access by: mail, in person. www.lorain.county.com/clerk

Misdemeanor, Civil Actions Under $15,000, Eviction, Small Claims—Avon Lake Municipal Court, 150 Avon Beldon Rd, Avon Lake, OH 44012. 440-930-4103. 8:30AM-4:30PM. Access by: mail, phone, in person. Special note: The court is upgrading their computer system in late 1999 and will refrain from disclosing the SSN to the public.

Elyria Municipal Court, 328 Broad St (PO Box 1498), Elyria, OH 44036. 440-323-5743, Fax: 440-323-0785. 8AM-4:25PM. Access by: mail, fax, in person.

Lorain Municipal Court, 100 W Erie Ave, Lorain, OH 44052. 440-244-2286. 8:30AM-4:30PM. Access by: in person.

Oberlin Municipal Court, 85 S Main St, Oberlin, OH 44074. 440-775-7229, Fax: 440-775-0619. 8AM-4PM. Access by: in person.

Vermilion Municipal Court, 687 Decatour St, Vermilion, OH 44089-1152. 440-967-6543, Fax: 440-967-1467. 8AM-4PM. Access by: mail, fax, in person.

Lucas

Real Estate Recording—Lucas County Recorder, 1 Government Center #700, Jackson, Street, Toledo, OH 43604. 419-245-4303. 8AM-5PM.

Felony, Civil Actions Over $10,000, Probate—Common Pleas Court, 700 Adams, Courthouse, Toledo, OH 43624. 419-245-4483, Fax: 419-245-4487. 8AM-4:45PM. Access by: mail, fax, in person.

Misdemeanor, Civil Actions Under $15,000, Eviction, Small Claims—Maumee Municipal Court, 400 Conant St, Maumee, OH 43537-3397. Fax: 419-897-7129. 8AM-4:30PM. Access by: mail, phone, fax, in person. Special note: The court expects to provide Internet access to records sometime in 2000. www.maumee.org

Oregon Municipal Court, 5330 Seaman Rd, Oregon, OH 43616. Fax: 419-698-7013. 8:30AM-4:30PM. Access by: mail, phone, fax, in person.

Sylvania Municipal Court, 6700 Monroe St, Sylvania, OH 43560-1995. 419-885-8975, Fax: 419-885-8987. 7:30AM-4PM. Access by: mail, fax, in person.

Toledo Municipal Court, 555 N Erie St, Toledo, OH 43624-1391. 419-245-1926, Fax: 419-245-1801. 8AM-4:30PM civil; 8AM-5:45PM M-F, 8-11:30AM Sat crim & traffic. Access by: mail, in person.

Madison

Real Estate Recording—Madison County Recorder, Courthouse, Room 40, 1 N. Main St. London, OH 43140. 614-852-1936. 8AM-4PM.

Felony, Civil Actions Over $10,000, Probate—Common Pleas Court, PO Box 227, London, OH 43140. 740-852-9776. 8AM-4PM. Access by: in person.

Misdemeanor, Civil Actions Under $15,000, Eviction, Small Claims—Madison County Municipal Court, Main & High St, PO Box 646, London, OH 43140. 740-852-1669, Fax: 740-852-0812. 8AM-4PM. Access by: mail, phone, fax, in person.

Mahoning

Real Estate Recording—Mahoning County Recorder, 120 Market Street, Youngstown, OH 44503. 334-578-2066, Fax: 330-740-2006. 8AM-4:30PM.

Felony, Civil Actions Over $10,000, Probate—Common Pleas Court, 120 Market St, Youngstown, OH 44503. 334-567-1156, Fax: 330-740-2105. 8AM-4PM. Access by: mail, phone, fax, in person.

Misdemeanor, Civil Actions Under $15,000, Small Claims—County Court #2, 127 Boardman Canfield Rd, Boardman, OH 44512. 334-567-1123, Fax: 330-740-2035. 8:30AM-4PM. Access by: mail, in person.

County Court #3, 605 E Ohio Ave, Sebring, OH 44672. 334-684-5620, Fax: 330-938-6518. 8:30AM-4PM. Access by: mail, in person.

County Court #4, 6000 Mahoning Ave, Youngstown, OH 44515-2288. 334-567-1123, Fax: 330-740-2036. 8:30AM-4PM. Access by: mail, phone, fax, in person.

County Court #5, 72 N Broad St, Canfield, OH 44406. 330-938-9873, Fax: 330-740-2034. 8:30AM-4PM. Access by: mail, fax, in person.

Civil Actions Under $15,000, Eviction, Small Claims—Youngstown Municipal Court-Civil Records, PO Box 6047, Youngstown, OH 44501-6047. 334-585-2753, Fax: 330-742-8786. 8AM-4PM. Access by: mail, phone, fax, in person.

Misdemeanor—Youngstown Municipal Court-Criminal Records, 25 S Phelphs St, Youngstown, OH 44503. 334-624-4257, Fax: 330-742-8786. 8AM-4PM. Access by: mail, fax, in person.

Misdemeanor, Civil Actions Under $15,000, Eviction, Small Claims—Campbell Municipal Court, 351 Tenney Ave, Campbell, OH 44405. 334-682-9112, Fax: 330-755-3058. 8AM-4PM. Access by: mail, fax, in person.

Struthers Municipal Court, 6 Elm St, Struthers, OH 44471. 334-677-4800, Fax: 330-755-2790. 8AM-4PM; Public access only on Tuesday and Thursday. Access by: mail, in person.

Marion

Real Estate Recording—Marion County Recorder, 171 E. Center St. Marion, OH 43302. 614-387-5871, Fax: 740-383-1190. 8:30AM-4:30PM.

Felony, Civil Actions Over $10,000—Common Pleas Court, 100 N Main St, Marion, OH 43301. 740-387-8128, Fax: 740-383-1190. 8:30AM-4:30PM. Access by: mail, in person.

Misdemeanor, Civil Actions Under $15,000, Eviction, Small Claims—Marion Municipal Court, 233 W Center St, Marion, OH 43302-0326. 740-387-2020, Fax: 740-382-5274. 8:30AM-4:30PM. Access by: mail, in person.

Medina

Real Estate Recording—Medina County Recorder, County Administration Bldg, 144 N. Broadway, Medina, OH 44256. 8AM-4:30PM.

Felony, Civil Actions Over $10,000, Probate—Common Pleas Court, 93 Public Square, Medina, OH 44256. 334-566-4622. 8AM-4:30PM. Access by: mail, in person.

Misdemeanor, Civil Actions Under $15,000, Eviction, Small Claims—Medina Municipal Court, 135 N Elmwood, Medina, OH 44256. 334-548-2252, Fax: 330-225-1108. 8AM-4:30PM. Access by: mail, in person, online. www.medinamunicipalcourt.org

Wadsworth Municipal Court, 120 Maple St, Wadsworth, OH 44281-1825. 330-678-9170, Fax: 330-335-2723. 8AM-4PM. Access by: mail, fax, in person.

Meigs

Real Estate Recording—Meigs County Recorder, 100 East Second Street, Courthouse, Pomeroy, OH 45769. 614-992-2004, Fax: 740-992-2867. 8:30AM-4:30PM.

Felony, Civil Actions Over $3,000, Probate—Common Pleas Court, PO Box 151, Pomeroy, OH 45769. 740-992-5290, Fax: 740-992-4429. 8:30AM-4:30PM. Access by: in person. Special note: Probate fax is 740-992-6727.

Misdemeanor, Civil Actions Under $15,000, Small Claims—Meigs County Court, Courthouse, Pomeroy, OH 45769. 740-992-2279, Fax: 740-992-2270. 8:30AM-4:30PM. Access by: in person.

Mercer

Real Estate Recording—Mercer County Recorder, 101 North Main Street, Courthouse Square-Room 203, Celina, OH 45822. 419-586-2259, Fax: 419-586-3541. 8:30AM-5PM M; 8:30AM-4PM T-F.

Felony, Civil Actions Over $10,000, Probate—Common Pleas Court, 101 N Main St, Rm 205, PO Box 28, Celina, OH 45822. 419-586-6461, Fax: 419-586-5826. 8:30AM-4PM. Access by: in person.

Misdemeanor, Civil Actions Under $15,000, Eviction, Small Claims—Celina Municipal Court, PO Box 362, Celina, OH 45822. 419-586-6491, Fax: 419-586-4735. 8AM-5PM. Access by: mail, phone, fax, in person.

Miami

Real Estate Recording—Miami County Recorder, 201 West Main Street, Troy, OH 45373. 937-332-6929, Fax: 937-332-6806. 7:30AM-4:30PM.

Felony, Civil Actions Over $10,000, Probate—Common Pleas Court & Court of Appeals, Safety Bldg, 201 West Main St, 3rd Flr, Troy, OH 45373. 937-332-6855, Fax: 937-332-7069. 8AM-4PM. Access by: mail, in person. Special note: Probate is a separate division at the phone number given above.

Misdemeanor, Civil Actions Under $15,000, Eviction, Small Claims—Miami County Municipal Court, 201 West Main St, Troy, OH 45373. 937-332-6920, Fax: 937-332-6932. 8AM-4PM. Access by: mail, phone, fax, in person. Special note: If the SSN is not provided by the party doing the search, the court personnel will mask the SSN before providing copies.

Monroe

Real Estate Recording—Monroe County Recorder, 101 North Main Street, Courthouse, Room 20, Woodsfield, OH 43793. 614-472-1521. 8AM-4PM.

Felony, Civil Actions Over $3,000, Probate—Common Pleas Court, 101 N Main St Rm 26, Woodsfield, OH 43793. 740-472-0761, Fax: 740-472-2518. 8:30AM-4:30PM. Access by: mail, in person.

Misdemeanor, Civil Actions Under $15,000, Small Claims—County Court, 101 N Main St, Woodsfield, OH 43793. 740-472-5181. 9AM-4:30PM. Access by: mail, phone, in person.

Montgomery

Real Estate Recording—Montgomery County Recorder, 451 West Third Street, 5th Floor, County Administration Building, Dayton, OH 45402. Fax: 937-225-5980. 8AM-4PM.

Felony, Civil Actions Over $10,000, Probate—Common Pleas Court, 41 N Perry St, Dayton, OH 45422. 937-225-4512, Fax: 937-496-7389. 8:30AM-4:30PM. Access by: mail, fax, in person. www.erinet.com/mcoclerk

Misdemeanor, Civil Actions Under $15,000, Small Claims—County Court-District #2, 6111 Taylorsville Rd, Huber Heights, OH 45424. 937-496-7231, Fax: 937-496-7236. 8AM-4PM M & F; Noon-7PM T-Th. Access by: mail, phone, fax, in person.

First District Court- Area 1 (Trotwood), 3100 Shiloh Springs Rd, Trotwood, OH 45426. 937-837-3351, Fax: 937-837-0948. Noon-7PM M,W; 8AM-4PM T,Th,F. Access by: mail, in person.

Civil Actions Under $15,000, Eviction, Small Claims—Dayton Municipal Court-Civil Division, 301 W 3rd St, PO Box 968, Dayton, OH 45402-0968. 937-443-4480, Fax: 937-443-4468. 8AM-4:30PM. Access by: mail, phone, in person.

Misdemeanor—Dayton Municipal Court-Criminal Division, 301 W 3rd St, Rm 331, Dayton, OH 45402. 937-443-4314, Fax: 937-443-4490. 8AM-4:30PM. Access by: mail, in person.

Dayton Municipal Court-Traffic Division, 301 W 3rd St, PO Box 968, Dayton, OH 45402. 937-443-4313, Fax: 937-443-0497. 8AM-4:30PM. Access by: mail, phone, in person. Special note: Difficult to provide case information prior to 1995.

Misdemeanor, Civil Actions Under $15,000, Eviction, Small Claims—Kettering Municipal Court, 3600 Shroyer Rd, Kettering, OH 45429. 937-296-2461, Fax: 937-296-3284. 8:30AM-4:30PM. Access by: mail, in person.

Miamisburg Municipal Court, 10 N First St, Miamisburg, OH 45342. 937-866-2203, Fax: 937-866-0135. 8AM-4PM. Access by: mail, in person.

Oakwood Municipal Court, 30 Park Ave, Dayton, OH 45419. 937-293-3058. 8:30AM-4PM. Access by: mail, in person.

Vandalia Municipal Court, PO Box 429, Vandalia, OH 45377. 937-898-3996, Fax: 937-898-6648. 8AM-4PM. Access by: mail, phone, fax, in person.

Morgan

Real Estate Recording—Morgan County Recorder, 19 East Main Street, McConnelsville, OH 43756. 614-962-4475, Fax: 740-962-3364. 8AM-4PM.

Felony, Civil Actions Over $3,000, Probate—Common Pleas Court, 19 E Main St, McConnelsville, OH 43756. 740-962-4752, Fax: 740-962-4589. 8AM-4PM M-Th; 8AM-5PM F. Access by: mail, in person.

Misdemeanor, Civil Actions Under $15,000, Small Claims—Morgan County Court, 37 E Main St, McConnelsville, OH 43756. 740-962-4031, Fax: 740-962-4035. 8AM-4PM. Access by: mail, phone, fax, in person.

Morrow

Real Estate Recording—Morrow County Recorder, 48 East High Street, Mount Gilead, OH 43338. 419-947-6070, Fax: 419-947-3709. 8:30AM-4PM.

Felony, Civil Actions Over $3,000, Probate—Common Pleas Court, 48 E High St, Mount Gilead, OH 43338. 419-947-2085, Fax: 419-947-5421. 8AM-4PM. Access by: mail, phone, fax, in person.

Misdemeanor, Civil Actions Under $15,000, Small Claims—County Court, 48 E High St, Mount Gilead, OH 43338. 419-947-5045, Fax: 419-947-1860. 7:30AM-5PM. Access by: mail, in person.

Muskingum

Real Estate Recording—Muskingum County Recorder, Corner 4th & Main, Courthouse, Zanesville, OH 43701. 614-455-7118, Fax: 740-455-7943. 8:30AM-4:30PM.

Felony, Civil Actions Over $15,000, Probate—Common Pleas Court, 401 Main St, Zanesville, OH 43701. 740-455-7104. 8:30AM-4:30PM. Access by: mail, in person.

Misdemeanor, Civil Actions Under $15,000, Small Claims—County Court, 27 N 5th St, Zanesville, OH 43701. 740-455-7138, Fax: 740-455-7157. 8:30AM-4PM. Access by: mail, fax, in person.

Misdemeanor, Civil Actions Under $15,000, Eviction, Small Claims—Zanesville Municipal Court, PO Box 566, Zanesville, OH 43702. 740-454-3269, Fax: 740-455-0739. 9AM-4:30PM. Access by: mail, in person.

Noble

Real Estate Recording—Noble County Recorder, 260 Courthouse, Room 2E, Caldwell, OH 43724. 8AM-4PM M-W; 8-11:30AM Th; 8AM-4PM,5-7PM F.

Felony, Civil Actions Over $3,000, Probate—Common Pleas Court, 350 Courthouse, Caldwell, OH 43724. 740-732-4408, Fax: 740-732-5702. 8-11:30AM,12:30-4PM M-W; 8-11:30AM Th; 8-11:30AM, 12:30-7PM F. Access by: mail, phone, fax, in person. Special note: Probate office is separate from this court.

Misdemeanor, Civil Actions Under $15,000, Small Claims—Noble County Court, 100 Courthouse, Caldwell, OH 43724. 740-732-5795. 8:30AM-4PM M-W,F; 8:30-11:30AM Th. Access by: mail, in person.

Ottawa

Real Estate Recording—Ottawa County Recorder, 315 Madison Street, Room 204, Port Clinton, OH 43452. Fax: 419-734-6919. 8:30AM-4:30PM.

Felony, Civil Actions Over $10,000, Probate—Common Pleas Court, 315 Madison St, Port Clinton, OH 43452. 419-734-6755. 8:30AM-4:30PM. Access by: in person. Special note: Probate is a separate court at 315 Madison St.

Misdemeanor, Civil Actions Under $15,000, Eviction, Small Claims—Ottawa County Municipal Court, 1860 East Perry St, Port Clinton, OH 43452. 419-734-4143, Fax: 419-732-2862. 8:30AM-4:30PM. Access by: in person.

Paulding

Real Estate Recording—Paulding County Recorder, Courthouse, 115 N. Williams St. Paulding, OH 45879. Fax: 419-399-2862. 8AM-4PM.

Felony, Civil Actions Over $3,000, Probate—Common Pleas Court, 115 N Williams St Rm 104, Paulding, OH 45879. 419-399-8210, Fax: 419-399-8248. 8AM-4PM. Access by: mail, fax, in person.

Misdemeanor, Civil Actions Under $15,000, Small Claims—County Court, 201 E Carolina St, Suite 2, Paulding, OH 45879. 419-399-5370, Fax: 419-399-3421. 8AM-4PM. Access by: mail, fax, in person.

Perry

Real Estate Recording—Perry County Recorder, 105 Main Street, Courthouse, New Lexington, OH 43764. 614-342-2074. 8:30AM-4:30PM.

Felony, Civil Actions Over $3,000, Probate—Common Pleas Court, PO Box 67, New Lexington, OH 43764. 740-342-1022. 8AM-4PM. Access by: in person.

Misdemeanor, Civil Actions Under $15,000, Small Claims—Perry County Court, PO Box 207, New Lexington, OH 43764-0207. 740-342-3156, Fax: 740-342-2189. 8:30AM-4:30PM M,W,F. Access by: in person.

Pickaway

Real Estate Recording—Pickaway County Recorder, 207 South Court Street, Circleville, OH 43113. 614-474-2370, Fax: 740-477-6361. 8AM-4PM.

Felony, Civil Actions Over $10,000, Probate—Common Pleas Court, County Courthouse, 207 Court Street PO Box 270, Circleville, OH 43113. 740-474-5231. 8AM-4PM. Access by: mail, in person.

Misdemeanor, Civil Actions Under $15,000, Eviction, Small Claims—Circleville Municipal Court, PO Box 128, Circleville, OH 43113. 740-474-3171, Fax: 740-477-8291. 8AM-4PM. Access by: mail, phone, fax, in person.

Pike

Real Estate Recording—Pike County Recorder, Courthouse, 100 E. 2nd St. Waverly, OH 45690. 614-947-2713, Fax: 740-947-7997. 8AM-4PM.

Felony, Civil Actions Over $15,000, Probate—Common Pleas Court, 100 East 2nd St, Waverly, OH 45690. 740-947-2715, Fax:

740-947-1729. 8:30AM-4PM. Access by: in person. Special note: Probate is a separate court at the number given.

Misdemeanor, Civil Actions Under $15,000, Small Claims—Pike County Court, 106 N Market St, Waverly, OH 45690. 740-947-4003. 8:30AM-4PM. Access by: mail, phone, fax, in person.

Portage

Real Estate Recording—Portage County Recorder, 449 South Meridian Street, Ravenna, OH 44266. 330-674-1876, Fax: 330-297-7349. 8AM-4:30PM.

Felony, Civil Actions Over $10,000, Probate—Common Pleas Court, PO Box 1035, Ravenna, OH 44266. 330-674-4901, Fax: 330-297-4554. 8AM-4PM. Access by: in person.

Misdemeanor, Civil Actions Under $15,000, Eviction, Small Claims—Portage County Municipal Court, PO Box 958, Ravenna, OH 44266. 330-674-1896, Fax: 330-297-3526. 8AM-4PM. Access by: in person.

Portage Municipal Court, Kent Branch, 214 S Water, Kent, OH 44240. 334-428-2520, Fax: 330-677-9944. 8AM-4PM. Access by: mail, phone, in person.

Preble

Real Estate Recording—Preble County Recorder, Courthouse, 101 East Main St. Eaton, OH 45320. 8AM-4:30PM.

Felony, Civil, Probate—Common Pleas Court, 101 E Main, 3rd Fl, Eaton, OH 45320. 937-456-8160, Fax: 937-456-9548. 8AM-4:30PM. Access by: mail, in person. Special note: Probate office is separate from this court.

Misdemeanor, Civil Actions Under $15,000, Eviction, Small Claims—Eaton Municipal Court, PO Box 65, Eaton, OH 45320. 937-456-4941, Fax: 937-456-4685. 8AM-Noon, 1-4:30PM. Access by: mail, in person. www.eatonmc.com

Putnam

Real Estate Recording—Putnam County Recorder, 245 East Main Street, Courthouse - Suite 202, Ottawa, OH 45875. Fax: 419-523-4403. 8:30AM-4:30PM.

Felony, Civil Actions Over $3,000, Probate—Common Pleas Court, 245 E Main, Rm 301, Ottawa, OH 45875. 419-523-3110, Fax: 419-523-5284. 8:30AM-4:30PM. Access by: mail, fax, in person. Special note: Probate is a separate court at number given.

Misdemeanor, Civil Actions Under $15,000, Small Claims—Putnam County Court, 245 E Main, Rm 303, Ottawa, OH 45875. 419-523-3110, Fax: 419-523-5284. 8:30AM-4:30PM. Access by: mail, in person.

Richland

Real Estate Recording—Richland County Recorder, 50 Park Avenue East, Mansfield, OH 44902. Fax: 419-774-5603. 8AM-4PM.

Felony, Civil Actions Over $10,000, Probate—Common Pleas Court, 50 Park Ave E, 2nd Floor, PO Box 127, Mansfield, OH 44901. 419-774-5549. 8AM-4PM. Access by: in person.

Misdemeanor, Civil Actions Under $15,000, Eviction, Small Claims—Mansfield Municipal Court, PO Box 1228, Mansfield, OH 44901. 419-755-9617, Fax: 419-755-9647. 8AM-4PM. Access by: mail, phone, fax, in person.

Ross

Real Estate Recording—Ross County Recorder, 2 North Paint St. Suite E, Courthouse, Chillicothe, OH 45601. 614-774-7370, Fax: 740-702-3006. 8:30AM-4:30PM.

Felony, Civil Actions Over $10,000, Probate—Common Pleas Court, County Courthouse, 2 N Paint St, Ste A, Chillicothe, OH 45601. 740-702-3010, Fax: 740-702-3018. 8AM-4PM. Access by: mail, phone, fax, in person.

Misdemeanor, Civil Actions Under $15,000, Eviction, Small Claims—Chillicothe Municipal Court, 26 S Paint St, Chillicothe, OH 45601. 740-773-3515, Fax: 740-774-1101. 7:30AM-4:30PM. Access by: mail, in person.

Sandusky

Real Estate Recording—Sandusky County Recorder, 100 N. Park Ave. Courthouse, Fremont, OH 43420. 419-334-6233. 8AM-4:30PM.

Felony, Civil Actions Over $3,000, Probate—Common Pleas Court, 100 N Park Ave, Fremont, OH 43420. 419-334-6161, Fax: 419-334-6164. 8AM-4:30PM. Access by: in person.

Misdemeanor, Civil Actions Under $15,000, Small Claims—County Court #1, 123 W Buckeye St, Clyde, OH 43410. 419-547-0915, Fax: 419-547-9198. 8AM-4:30PM. Access by: mail, phone, fax, in person.

County Court #2, 128 E Main St, Woodville, OH 43469. 419-849-3961, Fax: 419-849-3932. 8AM-4:30PM. Access by: mail, phone, fax, in person.

Misdemeanor, Civil Actions Under $15,000, Eviction, Small Claims—Fremont Municipal Court, PO Box 886, Fremont, OH 43420-0071. 419-332-1579, Fax: 419-332-1570. 8AM-4:30PM. Access by: mail, fax, in person.

Scioto

Real Estate Recording—Scioto County Recorder, 602 7th Street, Room 110, Portsmouth, OH 45662. Fax: 740-353-7358. 8AM-4:30PM.

Felony, Civil Actions Over $10,000, Probate—Common Pleas Court, 602 7th St, Portsmouth, OH 45662. 740-355-8226. 8AM-4:30PM. Access by: in person.

Misdemeanor, Civil Actions Under $15,000, Eviction, Small Claims—Portsmouth Municipal Court, 728 2nd St, Portsmouth, OH 45662. 740-354-3283, Fax: 740-353-6645. 8AM-4PM. Access by: mail, phone, fax, in person.

Seneca

Real Estate Recording—Seneca County Recorder, 103 South Washington Street, Room 7, Tiffin, OH 44883. 8:30AM-4:30PM.

Felony, Civil Actions Over $10,000, Probate—Common Pleas Court, 103 S Washington St, Tiffin, OH 44883. 419-447-0671, Fax: 419-443-7919. 8:30AM-4:30PM. Access by: mail, phone, in person.

Misdemeanor, Civil Actions Under $15,000, Eviction, Small Claims—Fostoria Municipal Court, PO Box 985, Fostoria, OH 44830. 419-435-8139, Fax: 419-435-1150. 8:30AM-5PM. Access by: mail, phone, fax, in person.

Tiffin Municipal Court, PO Box 694, Tiffin, OH 44883. 419-448-5412, Fax: 419-448-5419. 8:30AM-4:30PM. Access by: mail, fax, in person.

Shelby

Real Estate Recording—Shelby County Recorder, 129 East Court Street, Shelby County Annex, Sidney, OH 45365. 513-498-7281, Fax: 937-498-7272. 7:30AM-4PM M-Th; 7:30AM-6PM F.

Felony, Civil Actions Over $10,000, Probate—Common Pleas Court, PO Box 809, Sidney, OH 45365. 937-498-7221, Fax: 937-498-7824. 8:30AM-4:30PM M-Th; 8:30AM-6PM F. Access by: in person.

Misdemeanor, Civil Actions Under $15,000, Eviction, Small Claims—Sidney Municipal Court, 201 W Poplar, Sidney, OH 45365. 513-498-8109, Fax: 513-498-8179. 8AM-4:30PM. Access by: mail, phone, fax, in person.

Stark

Real Estate Recording—Stark County Recorder, 110 Central Plaza South, Suite 170, Canton, OH 44702. Fax: 330-438-0394. 8:30AM-4:30PM (Recording: 8:30AM-4PM).

Civil Actions Over $10,000, Probate—Common Pleas Court-Civil Division, PO Box 21160, Canton, OH 44701. 330-753-2262, Fax: 330-438-0853. 8:30AM-4:30PM. Access by: mail, phone, in person.

Felony—Common Pleas Court-Criminal Division, PO Box 21160, Canton, OH 44701-1160. 330-755-1800, Fax: 330-438-0853. 8:30AM-4:30PM. Access by: mail, phone, fax, in person.

Misdemeanor, Civil Actions Under $15,000, Eviction, Small Claims—Canton Municipal Court, 218 Cleveland Ave SW, PO Box

24218, Canton, OH 44702-4218. 330-872-0302, Fax: 330-489-3075. 8AM-4:30PM. Access by: mail, phone, fax, in person.

Massillon Municipal Court, Two James Duncan Plaza, Massillion, OH 44646-6690. Fax: 330-830-3648. 8:30AM-4:30PM. Access by: mail, fax, in person.

Summit

Real Estate Recording—Summit County Recorder, 175 South Main Street, Akron, OH 44308. 334-335-6575. 7:30AM-4PM.

Felony, Civil Actions Over $10,000, Probate—Common Pleas Court, 209 S High St, Akron, OH 44308. 334-298-0516, Fax: 330-643-2213. 8AM-4PM. Access by: mail, in person. Special note: Probate is a separate court at the number given.

Misdemeanor, Civil Actions Under $15,000, Eviction, Small Claims—Akron Municipal Court, 217 S High St, Rm 837, Akron, OH 44308. Fax: 330-375-2427. 8AM-4:30PM. Access by: mail, in person.

Barberton Municipal Court, Municipal Bldg, 576 W Park Ave, Barberton, OH 44203-2584. 334-624-4334, Fax: 330-848-6779. 8AM-5PM. Access by: mail, phone, fax, in person.

Cuyahoga Falls Municipal Court, 2310 Second St, Cuyahoga Falls, OH 44222. 8AM-8PM. Access by: mail, phone, in person.

Trumbull

Real Estate Recording—Trumbull County Recorder, 160 High Street N.W. Warren, OH 44481. Fax: 330-675-2404. 8:30AM-4:30PM.

Felony, Civil Actions Over $10,000, Probate—Common Pleas Court, 160 High St, Warren, OH 44481. 334-382-3521. 8:30AM-4:30PM. Access by: mail, in person.

Misdemeanor, Civil Actions Under $15,000, Eviction, Small Claims—Trumbull County Court Central, 180 N Mecca St, Cortland, OH 44410. 334-295-2223, Fax: 330-637-5021. 8AM-4PM. Access by: mail, phone, fax, in person.

Misdemeanor, Civil Under $15,000, Eviction, Small Claims—Trumbull County Court East, 7130 Brookwood Dr, Brookfield, OH 44403. 330-755-2165, Fax: 330-448-6310. 8:30AM-4:30PM. Access by: mail, phone, fax, in person.

Misdemeanor, Civil Actions Under $15,000, Eviction, Small Claims—Girard Municipal Court, City Hall, 100 W Main St, Girard, OH 44420-2522. Fax: 330-545-7045. 8AM-4PM. Access by: mail, fax, in person. Special note: Traffic Records at 330-545-3049.

Newton Falls Municipal Court, 19 N Canal St, Newton Falls, OH 44444-1302. 334-683-6106, Fax: 330-872-3899. 8AM-4:30PM. Access by: mail, fax, in person.

Niles Municipal Court, 15 East St, Niles, OH 44446-5051. 334-347-2519, Fax: 330-544-9025. 8AM-4PM. Access by: mail, fax, in person.

Warren Municipal Court, 141 South St SE (PO Box 1550), Warren, OH 44482. Fax: 330-841-2760. 8AM-4:30PM. Access by: mail, fax, in person.

Tuscarawas

Real Estate Recording—Tuscarawas County Recorder, 125 East High Avenue, New Philadelphia, OH 44663. 330-740-2001. 8AM-4:30PM.

Felony, Civil Actions Over $15,000, Probate—Common Pleas Court, 125 E High (PO Box 628), New Philadelphia, OH 44663. 330-726-5546, Fax: 330-343-4682. 8AM-4:30PM. Access by: in person. Special note: Probate is a separate court.

Misdemeanor, Civil Actions Under $15,000, Small Claims—County Court, 220 E 3rd, Uhrichsville, OH 44683. 740-922-4795, Fax: 740-922-7020. 8AM-4:30PM. Access by: mail, fax, in person. Special note: Probation Office phone: 740-922-3653 & 922-4360. Probation Office hours: 8AM-4:30PM.

Misdemeanor, Civil Actions Under $15,000, Eviction, Small Claims—New Philadelphia Municipal Court, 166 E High Ave, New Philadelphia, OH 44663. 330-723-3641, Fax: 330-364-6885. 8AM-4PM. Access by: mail, in person.

Union

Real Estate Recording—Union County Recorder, 233 West Sixth St. Marysville, OH 43040. 513-645-3029, Fax: 937-642-3397. 8:30AM-4PM.

Felony, Civil Actions Over $10,000, Probate—Common Pleas Court, County Courthouse, 215 W 5th, PO Box 605, Marysville, OH 43040. 937-645-3006, Fax: 937-645-3162. 8:30AM-4PM. Access by: mail, in person.

Misdemeanor, Civil Actions Under $15,000, Eviction, Small Claims—Marysville Municipal Court, PO Box 322, Marysville, OH 43040. 937-644-9102, Fax: 937-644-1228. 8AM-4PM. Access by: mail, phone, fax, in person. www.munict.ci.marysville.oh.us

Van Wert

Real Estate Recording—Van Wert County Recorder, 121 East Main Street, Courthouse - Room 206, Van Wert, OH 45891. 419-238-5177, Fax: 419-238-5410. 8:30AM-5PM M; 8:30AM-4PM T-F.

Felony, Civil Actions Over $10,000, Probate—Common Pleas Court, PO Box 366, 121 E Main St, Van Wert, OH 45891. 419-238-1022, Fax: 419-238-4760. 8AM-4PM. Access by: in person.

Misdemeanor, Civil Actions Under $15,000, Eviction, Small Claims—Van Wert Municipal Court, 124 S Market, Van Wert, OH 45891. 419-238-5767. 8AM-4PM. Access by: mail, in person.

Vinton

Real Estate Recording—Vinton County Recorder, East Main Street, Courthouse, McArthur, OH 45651. 614-596-5690. 8:30AM-4PM.

Felony, Civil Actions Over $3,000, Probate—Common Pleas Court, County Courthouse, 100 E Main St, McArthur, OH 45651. 740-596-3001, Fax: 740-596-3001. 8:30AM-4PM M-F. Access by: mail, in person.

Misdemeanor, Civil Actions Under $15,000, Small Claims—Vinton County Court, County Courthouse, McArthur, OH 45651. 740-596-5000, Fax: 740-596-4702. 8:30AM-4PM. Access by: mail, phone, in person.

Warren

Real Estate Recording—Warren County Recorder, 320 East Silver Street, Lebanon, OH 45036. 513-933-1300, Fax: 513-695-2949. 8:30AM-4:30PM.

Felony, Civil Actions Over $3,000, Probate—Common Pleas Court, PO Box 238, Lebanon, OH 45036. 513-933-1120, Fax: 513-933-2965. 8:30AM-4:30PM. Access by: mail, phone, in person.

Misdemeanor, Civil Actions Under $15,000, Small Claims—County Court, 550 Justice Dr, Lebanon, OH 45036. 513-933-1370. 8AM-4:30PM. Access by: mail, phone, in person.

Misdemeanor, Civil Actions Under $15,000, Eviction, Small Claims—Franklin Municipal Court, 35 E 4th Street, Franklin, OH 45006-2484. 513-746-2858, Fax: 513-743-7751. 8:30AM-5PM. Access by: mail, phone, fax, in person.

Mason Municipal Court, 200 W Main St, Mason, OH 45040-1620. 513-398-7901, Fax: 513-459-8085. 7:30AM-4PM. Access by: mail, phone, fax, in person.

Misdemeanor, Civil Actions, Eviction, Small Claims—Lebanon Muncipal Court, City Building, Lebanon, OH 45036-1777. 513-932-7210, Fax: 513-933-7212. 8AM-4PM. Access by: mail, fax, in person.

Washington

Real Estate Recording—Washington County Recorder, 205 Putnam Street, Courthouse, Marietta, OH 45750. 614-373-6623, Fax: 740-373-9643. 8AM-5PM.

Felony, Civil Actions Over $10,000, Probate—Common Pleas Court, 205 Putnam St, Marietta, OH 45750. 740-373-6623. 8AM-4:15PM. Access by: in person.

Misdemeanor, Civil Actions Under $15,000, Eviction, Small Claims—Marietta Municipal Court, PO Box 615, Marietta, OH 45750. 740-373-4474, Fax: 740-373-2547. 8AM-5PM. Access by: mail, phone, in person. www.mariettacourt.com

Wayne

Real Estate Recording—Wayne County Recorder, 428 West Liberty Street, Wooster, OH 44691. 330-643-2201, Fax: 330-287-5685. 8AM-4:30PM.

Felony, Civil Actions Over $15,000, Probate—Common Pleas Court, PO Box 507, Wooster, OH 44691. 330-643-2587, Fax: 330-287-5416. 8AM-4:30PM. Access by: mail, phone, in person. Special note: Probate is a separate court at number given.

Misdemeanor, Civil Actions Under $15,000, Eviction, Small Claims—Wayne County Municipal Court, 538 N Market St, Wooster, OH 44691. 330-652-5863, Fax: 330-263-4043. 8AM-4:30PM. Access by: in person.

Williams

Real Estate Recording—Williams County Recorder, 1 Courthouse Square, Bryan, OH 43506. 8:30AM-4:30PM.

Felony, Civil Actions Over $10,000, Probate—Common Pleas Court, 1 Courthouse Square, Bryan, OH 43506. 419-636-1551, Fax: 419-636-7877. 8:30AM-4:30PM. Access by: in person.

Misdemeanor, Civil Actions Under $15,000, Eviction, Small Claims—Bryan Municipal Court, 516 E High, PO Box 546, Bryan, OH 43506. 419-636-6939, Fax: 419-636-3417. 8:30AM-4:30PM. Access by: mail, fax, in person.

Wood

Real Estate Recording—Wood County Recorder, 1 Courthouse Square, Bowling Green, OH 43402. 419-354-9130. 8:30AM-4:30PM.

Felony, Civil Actions Over $10,000, Probate—Common Pleas Court, Courthouse Square, Bowling Green, OH 43402. 419-354-9280, Fax: 419-354-9241. 8:30AM-4:30PM. Access by: mail, phone, fax, in person.

Misdemeanor, Civil Actions Under $15,000, Eviction, Small Claims—Bowling Green Municipal Court, PO Box 326, Bowling Green, OH 43402. 419-352-5263, Fax: 419-352-9407. 8:30AM-4:30PM. Access by: mail, phone, fax, in person.

Perrysburg Municipal Court, 300 Walnut, Perrysburg, OH 43551. 419-872-7900, Fax: 419-872-7905. 8AM-4:30PM. Access by: mail, phone, fax, in person, online.

Wyandot

Real Estate Recording—Wyandot County Recorder, Courthouse, 109 S. Sandusky Ave. Upper Sandusky, OH 43351. Fax: 419-294-6405. 8:30AM-4:30PM.

Felony, Civil Actions Over $10,000, Probate—Common Pleas Court, 109 S Sandusky Ave, Upper Sandusky, OH 43351. 419-294-1432. 8:30AM-4:30PM. Access by: mail, fax, in person.

Misdemeanor, Civil Actions Under $15,000, Eviction, Small Claims—Upper Sandusky Municipal Court, 119 N 7th St, Upper Sandusky, OH 43351. 419-294-3354, Fax: 419-090-4747. 8AM-4:30PM. Access by: mail, in person.

Federal Courts

US District Court

Northern District of Ohio

Akron Division 568 Federal Bldg, 2 S Main St, Akron, OH 44308330-375-5407 Counties: Carroll, Holmes, Portage, Stark, Summit, Tuscarawas, Wayne. Cases filed prior to 1995 for counties in the Youngstown Division may be located here. www.ohnd.uscourts.gov
Cleveland Division 201 Superior Ave, NE, Cleveland, OH 44114216-522-4355 Fax: 216-522-2140 Counties: Ashland, Ashtabula, Crawford, Cuyahoga, Geauga, Lake, Lorain, Medina, Richland. Cases prior to July 1995 for the counties of Ashland, Crawford, Medina and Richland are located in the Akron Division. Cases filed prior to 1995 from the counties in theYoungstown Division may be located here. www.ohnd.uscourts.gov
Toledo Division 114 US Courthouse, 1716 Spielbusch, Toledo, OH 43624419-259-6412 Counties: Allen, Auglaize, Defiance, Erie, Fulton, Hancock, Hardin, Henry, Huron, Lucas, Marion, Mercer, Ottawa, Paulding, Putnam, Sandusky, Seneca, Van Wert, Williams, Wood, Wyandot. www.ohnd.uscourts.gov
Youngstown Division 337 Federal Bldg, 125 Market St, Youngstown, OH 44503-1787330-746-1726 Fax: 330-746-2027 Counties: Columbiana, Mahoning, Trumbull. This division was reactivated in the middle of 1995. Older cases will be found in Akron or Cleveland. www.ohnd.uscourts.gov

Southern District of Ohio

Cincinnati Division Clerk, US District Court, 324 Courthouse Bldg, 100 E 5th St, Cincinnati, OH 45202513-564-7500 Fax: 513-564-7505 Counties: Adams, Brown, Butler, Clermont, Clinton, Hamilton, Highland, Lawrence, Scioto, Warren.
Columbus Division Office of the clerk, Room 260, 85 Marconi Blvd, Columbus, OH 43215614-719-3000 Fax: 614-469-5953 Counties: Athens, Belmont, Coshocton, Delaware, Fairfield, Fayette, Franklin, Gallia, Guernsey, Harrison, Hocking, Jackson, Jefferson, Knox, Licking, Logan, Madison, Meigs, Monroe, Morgan, Morrow, Muskingum, Noble, Perry, Pickaway, Pike, Ross, Union, Vinton,Washington.
Dayton Division Federal Bldg, 200 W 2nd, Room 712, Dayton, OH 45402513-512-1400 Counties: Champaign, Clark, Darke, Greene, Miami, Montgomery, Preble, Shelby.

US Bankruptcy Court

Northern District of Ohio

Akron Division 455 Federal Bldg, 2 S Main, Akron, OH 44308330-375-5840 Counties: Medina, Portage, Summit. www.ohnb.uscourts.gov
Canton Division Frank T Bow Federal Bldg, 201 Cleveland Ave SW, Canton, OH 44702330-489-4426 Fax: 330-489-4434 Counties: Ashland, Carroll, Crawford, Holmes, Richland, Stark, Tuscarawas, Wayne. www.ohnb.uscourts.gov
Cleveland Division Key Tower, 31st Floor, 127 Public Square, Cleveland, OH 44114216-522-4373 Counties: Cuyahoga, Geauga, Lake, Lorain. www.ohnb.uscourts.gov
Toledo Division Room 411, 1716 Spielbusch Ave, Toledo, OH 43624419-259-6440 Counties: Allen, Auglaize, Defiance, Erie, Fulton, Hancock, Hardin, Henry, Huron, Lucas, Marion, Mercer, Ottawa, Paulding, Putnam, Sandusky, Seneca, Van Wert, Williams, Wood, Wyandot. www.ohnb.uscourts.gov
Youngstown Division PO Box 147, Youngstown, OH 44501330-746-7027 Counties: Ashtabula, Columbiana, Mahoning, Trumbull. www.ohnb.uscourts.gov

Southern District of Ohio

Cincinnati Division Atrium Two, Suite 800, 221 E Fourth St, Cincinnati, OH 45202513-684-2572 Counties: Adams, Brown, Clermont, Hamilton, Highland, Lawrence, Scioto and a part of Butler.
Columbus Division 170 N High St, Columbus, OH 43215614-469-6638 Counties: Athens, Belmont, Coshocton, Delaware, Fairfield, Fayette, Franklin, Gallia, Guernsey, Harrison, Hocking, Jackson, Jefferson, Knox, Licking, Logan, Madison, Meigs, Monroe, Morgan, Morrow, Muskingum, Noble, Perry, Pickaway, Pike, Ross, Union, Vinton,Washington.
Dayton Division 120 W 3rd St, Dayton, OH 45402937-225-2516 Counties: Butler, Champaign, Clark, Clinton, Darke, Greene, Miami, Montgomery, Preble, Shelby, Warren; parts of Butler County are handled by Cincinnati Division.

Oklahoma

Attorney General's Office
2300 N Lincoln, #112   405-521-3921
Oklahoma City, OK 73105   Fax: 405-521-6246
www.oag.state.ok.us/oagweb.nsf

Governor's Office
State Capitol, Suite 212   405-521-2342
Oklahoma City, OK 73105   Fax: 405-521-3353
www.state.ok.us/~governor

State Archives
200 NE 18th   405-522-3577
Oklahoma City, OK 73105-3298 Fax: 405-525-7804
www.odl.state.ok.us

Capital:	Oklahoma City
	Oklahoma County
Time Zone:	CST
Number of Counties:	77
Population:	3,317,091
Web Site:	www.state.ok.us

Search Unclaimed Property Online

www.kocotv.com/5oys/fortune.html

State Agencies

Criminal Records
State Bureau of Investigation, Criminal History Reporting, 6600 N Harvey, Bldg 6, #300, Oklahoma City, OK 73116; 405-848-6724; 8AM-5PM. Access by: mail. www.osbi.state.ok.us

Corporation Records
Limited Liability Company Records
Limited Partnerships
Trademarks/Servicemarks
Limited Liability Partnerships
Secretary of State, 2300 N Lincoln Blvd, Rm 101, Oklahoma City, OK 73105-4897; 405-521-3911, 900-825-2424 Corporate Records; Fax: 405-521-3771; 8AM-5PM. Access by: mail, phone, in person. www.oklaosf.state.ok.us/~sos

Sales Tax Registrations
Taxpayer Assistance, 2501 N Lincoln Blvd, Oklahoma City, OK 73194; 405-521-3160; Fax: 405-521-3826; 7:30AM-4:30PM. Access by: mail, phone, in person. oktax.state.ok.us

Uniform Commercial Code
UCC Recorder, Oklahoma County Clerk, 320 R.S. Kerr Ave, County Office Bldg, Rm 105, Oklahoma City, OK 73102; 405-278-1521; Fax: 405-278-1810; 8AM-5PM. Access by: mail. www.oklahomacounty.org

Federal Tax Liens
State Tax Liens
Records not available from state agency.

All state tax liens and federal tax liens are filed at the local level. Federal tax liens are businesses are files with the Clerk of Oklahoma County.

Workers' Compensation Records
Workers Compensation Court, 1915 W Stiles, Oklahoma City, OK 73105-4918; 405-522-8600, 405-522-8640 Records Dept; Fax: 405-552-8647; 8AM-5PM. Access by: mail, phone, in person.

Birth Certificates
State Department of Health, Vital Records Service, PO Box 53551, Oklahoma City, OK 73152 (1000 NE 10th St, Oklahoma City, OK 73117); 405-271-4040; 8:30AM-4PM. Access by: mail. www.health.state.ok.us/program/vital/brec.html

Death Records

State Department of Health, Vital Records Service, PO Box 53551, Oklahoma City, OK 73152; 405-271-4040; 8:30AM-4PM. Access by: mail. www.health.state.ok.us/program/vital/brec.html

Marriage Certificates
Divorce Records

Records not available from state agency.

Marriage and Divorce records are found at county level. The record should be requested from the county courthouse in the county where the marriage or divorce was filed or granted.

Accident Reports

Department of Public Safety, Records Management Division, PO Box 11415, Oklahoma City, OK 73136 (3600 Martin Luther King Blvd, Room 206, Oklahoma City, OK 73111); 405-425-2192; Fax: 405-425-2046; 8AM-4:45PM. Access by: mail. www.dps.state.ok.us

Driver Records

MVR Desk, Records Management Division, PO Box 11415, Oklahoma City, OK 73136 (3600 Martin Luther King Blvd, Oklahoma City, OK 73111); 405-425-2262; 8AM-4:45PM. Access by: mail. www.dps.state.ok.us/dls

Vehicle Ownership
Vehicle Identification
Boat & Vessel Ownership
Boat & Vessel Registration

Oklahoma Tax Commission, Motor Vehicle Division, Attn: Research, 2501 N Lincoln Blvd, Oklahoma City, OK 73194; 405-521-3221; 7:30AM-4:30PM. Access by: mail. www.oktax.state.ok.us/oktax

Legislation-Current/Pending
Legislation-Passed

Oklahoma Legislature, State Capitol, Bill Status Info-Rm B-30, Copies-Rm 310, Oklahoma City, OK 73105; 405-521-5642 Bill Status Only, 405-521-5515 Bill Distribution, 405-528-2546 Biils in Progress; Fax: 405-521-5507; 8:30AM-4:30PM. Access by: mail, phone, in person. www.state.ok.us/osfdocs/leghp.html

Voter Registration

State Election Board, State Capitol-Rm B6, Box 53156, Oklahoma City, OK 73152; 405-521-2391; Fax: 405-521-6457; 8AM-5PM. Access by: mail, phone, in person. www.state.ok.us/~elections

GED Certificates

State Dept of Education, Lifelong Learning, 2500 N Lincoln Blvd, Oklahoma City, OK 73105; 405-521-3321; Fax: 405-521-6205;. http://sde.state.ok.us

Hunting License Information
Fishing License Information

Records not available from state agency.

They do not have a central database. Vendors do not have names and addresses either. However, a list of license vendors can be obtained for $150.00.

County Courts & Recording Offices

About the Courts...

Administration

Administrative Director of Courts   405-521-2450
1915 N Stiles #305   Fax: 405-521-6815
Oklahoma City, OK 73105
www.oscn.net

Court Structure

There are 80 District Courts in 26 judicial districts. Cities with populations in excess of 200,000 (Oklahoma City and Tulsa) have municipal criminal courts of record. Cities with less than 200,000 do not have such courts.

Small claims limit was raised from $3000 to $4500 in 1998.

Online Access

Online computer access, for internal use only, is available through the Case Processing System (CPS) for 9 counties, with a goal of including all Oklahoma counties at some future time. Access is available only through a "state terminal."

Case information is available in bulk form for downloading to computer. For information, call the Administrative Director of Courts, 405-521-2450.

About the Recording Offices...

Organization

77 counties, 77 recording offices. The recording officer is County Clerk. The entire state is in the Central Time Zone (CST).

UCC Records

Financing statements are filed centrally with the County Clerk of Oklahoma County, except for consumer goods, which are dual filed, and farm related and real estate related collateral, which are filed with the County Clerk. All counties will perform UCC searches. Use search request form UCC-4. Search fees are usually $5.00 per debtor name for a written request and $3.00 per name by telephone. Copies usually cost $1.00 per page.

Lien Records

Federal tax liens on personal property of businesses are filed with the County Clerk of Oklahoma County, which is the central filing office for the state. Other federal and all state tax liens are filed with the County Clerk. Usually state and federal tax liens on personal property are filed in separate indexes. Some counties will perform tax lien searches. Search fees vary.

Real Estate Records

Many counties will perform real estate searches by legal description. Copy fees are usually $1.00 per page. Certification usually costs $1.00 per document.

County Courts & Recording Offices

Adair

Real Estate Recording—Adair County Clerk, Division Street & Highway 59, Stilwell, OK 74960. Fax: 918-696-2603. 8AM-4:30PM.

Felony, Misdemeanor, Civil, Eviction, Small Claims, Probate—15th Judicial District Court, PO Box 426 (220 W Division), Stilwell, OK 74960. 918-696-7633. 8AM-4:30PM. Access by: mail, in person.

Alfalfa

Real Estate Recording—Alfalfa County Clerk, 300 South Grand, Cherokee, OK 73728. 406-233-3408. 8:30AM-4:30PM.

Felony, Misdemeanor, Civil, Eviction, Small Claims, Probate—4th Judicial District Court, County Courthouse, 300 S Grand, Cherokee, OK 73728. 580-596-3523. 8:30AM-4:30PM. Access by: mail, phone, in person.

Atoka

Real Estate Recording—Atoka County Clerk, 200 East Court Street, Atoka, OK 74525. 406-288-3446, Fax: 580-889-5063. 8:30AM-4:30PM.

Felony, Misdemeanor, Civil, Eviction, Small Claims, Probate—25th Judicial District Court, 200 E. Court St, Atoka, OK 74525. 580-889-3565. 8:30AM-4:30PM. Access by: mail, in person.

Beaver

Real Estate Recording—Beaver County Clerk, 111 West Second Street, Beaver, OK 73932. 406-256-2895, Fax: 580-625-3430. 9AM-5PM.

Felony, Misdemeanor, Civil, Eviction, Small Claims, Probate—1st Judicial District Court, PO Box 237, Beaver, OK 73932. 580-625-3191. 9AM-Noon, 1-5PM. Access by: mail, in person.

Beckham

Real Estate Recording—Beckham County Clerk, Courthouse, Room 102, 302 E. Main St. Sayre, OK 73662. 406-293-7781. 9AM-5PM.

Felony, Misdemeanor, Civil, Eviction, Small Claims, Probate—2nd Judicial District Court, PO Box 520, Sayre, OK 73662. 580-928-3330, Fax: 580-928-9278. 9AM-5PM. Access by: mail, fax, in person.

Blaine

Real Estate Recording—Blaine County Clerk, 212 North Weigel, Watonga, OK 73772. 406-256-2860, Fax: 580-623-5009. 8AM-4PM.

Felony, Misdemeanor, Civil, Eviction, Small Claims, Probate—4th Judicial District Court, 212 N. Weigle, Watonga, OK 73772. 580-623-5970. 8AM-4PM. Access by: mail, in person.

Bryan

Real Estate Recording—Bryan County Clerk, 402 West Evergreen, Durant, OK 74701. 406-293-7781, Fax: 580-924-3094. 8AM-Noon,1-5PM.

Felony, Misdemeanor, Civil, Eviction, Small Claims, Probate—19th Judicial District Court, Courthouse 3rd Fl, Durant, OK 74701. 580-924-1446. 8:00AM-12:00PM,1:00PM-5:00PM. Access by: mail, phone, in person.

Caddo

Real Estate Recording—Caddo County Clerk, Southwest Second & Oklahoma, Anadarko, OK 73005. 405-355-5763, Fax: 405-247-6510. 8:30AM-4:30PM.

Felony, Misdemeanor, Civil, Eviction, Small Claims, Probate—6th Judicial District Court, PO Box 10, Anadarko, OK 73005. 405-338-7050. 8:30AM-4:30PM. Access by: mail, in person.

Canadian

Real Estate Recording—Canadian County Clerk, 201 North Choctaw, El Reno, OK 73036. 405-382-3424, Fax: 405-422-2411. 8AM-4:30PM.

Felony, Misdemeanor, Civil, Eviction, Small Claims, Probate—26th Judicial District Court, PO Box 730, El Reno, OK 73036. 405-379-5371. 8AM-4:30PM. Access by: mail, in person.

Carter

Real Estate Recording—Carter County Clerk, 1st & B SW, Room 102, Ardmore, OK 73401. 405-321-6402. 8AM-5PM.

Felony, Misdemeanor, Civil, Eviction, Small Claims, Probate—20th Judicial District Court, PO Box 37, Ardmore, OK 73402. 580-223-5253. 8AM-Noon, 1-5PM. Access by: mail, in person.
www.brightok.net/chickasaw/ardmore/county/crtclerk.html

Cherokee

Real Estate Recording—Cherokee County Clerk, 213 West Delaware, Room 200, Tahlequah, OK 74464. 918-456-3321, Fax: 918-458-6508. 8AM-4:30PM (Recording hours 8AM-4PM).

Felony, Misdemeanor, Civil, Eviction, Small Claims, Probate—15th Judicial District Court, 213 W. Delaware, Tahlequah, OK 74464. 918-456-0691, Fax: 918-458-6587. 8AM-4:30PM. Access by: mail, phone, in person.

Choctaw

Real Estate Recording—Choctaw County Clerk, Courthouse, 300 E. Duke, Hugo, OK 74743. 405-682-7873, Fax: 580-326-6787. 8:30AM-4:30PM.

Felony, Misdemeanor, Civil, Eviction, Small Claims, Probate—17th Judicial District Court, 300 E. Duke, Hugo, OK 74743. 580-326-7554. 8AM-4PM. Access by: mail, phone, fax, in person.

Cimarron

Real Estate Recording—Cimarron County Clerk, Courthouse Square, Boise City, OK 73933. 406-233-3326, Fax: 580-544-3420. 8AM-Noon,1-5PM.

Felony, Misdemeanor, Civil, Eviction, Small Claims, Probate—1st Judicial District Court, PO Box 788, Boise City, OK 73933. 580-544-2221. 9AM-Noon,1-5PM. Access by: mail, phone, in person.

Cleveland

Real Estate Recording—Cleveland County Clerk, 201 South Jones, Room 204, Norman, OK 73069. 405-885-7620, Fax: 405-366-0229. 8:30AM-4:30PM.

Civil, Eviction, Small Claims, Probate—21st Judicial District Court-Civil Branch, 200 S. Peters, Norman, OK 73069. 405-622-3777. 8AM-5PM. Access by: mail, in person.

Felony, Misdemeanor—21st Judicial District Court-Criminal, 200 S. Peters, Norman, OK 73069. 405-623-5007. 8AM-5PM. Access by: mail, in person.

Coal

Real Estate Recording—Coal County Clerk, 4 North Main, Suite 1, Coalgate, OK 74538. Fax: 580-927-4003. 8AM-5PM.

Felony, Misdemeanor, Civil, Eviction, Small Claims, Probate—25th Judicial District Court, 4 N Main #9, Coalgate, OK 74538. 580-927-2281. 8AM-5PM. Access by: in person.

Comanche

Real Estate Recording—Comanche County Clerk, 315 SW 5th, Room 304, Lawton, OK 73501. 405-875-3264. 8:30AM-5PM.

Felony, Misdemeanor, Civil, Eviction, Small Claims, Probate—5th Judicial District Court, 315 SW 5th Street, Rm 504,

Lawton, OK 73501-4390. 580-355-4017. 8AM-5PM. Access by: mail, in person.

Cotton

Real Estate Recording—Cotton County Clerk, 301 North Broadway, Walters, OK 73572. 406-278-4026, Fax: 580-875-3756. 8AM-4:30PM.

Felony, Misdemeanor, Civil, Eviction, Small Claims, Probate—5th Judicial District Court, 301 N. Broadway, Walters, OK 73572. 580-875-3029. 8AM-4:30PM. Access by: mail, phone, in person.

Craig

Real Estate Recording—Craig County Clerk, Courthouse, Vinita, OK 74301. Fax: 918-256-3617. 8:30AM-4:30PM.

Felony, Misdemeanor, Civil, Eviction, Small Claims, Probate—12th Judicial District Court, 301 W. Canadian, Vinita, OK 74301. 918-256-6451. 8:30AM-4:30PM. Access by: mail, in person. Special note: SSNs are released to the public on criminal case matters, but not for civil cases.

Creek

Real Estate Recording—Creek County Clerk, 317 E. Lee, First Floor, Sapulpa, OK 74066. 8AM-5PM.

Felony, Misdemeanor, Civil, Eviction, Small Claims, Probate—24th Judicial District Court, PO Box 1410, Sapulpa, OK 74067. 918-227-2525, Fax: 918-227-5030. 8AM-5PM. Access by: in person.

Custer

Real Estate Recording—Custer County Clerk, 675 West "B" Street, Arapaho, OK 73620. 405-625-3161, Fax: 580-323-4421. 8AM-4PM.

Felony, Misdemeanor, Civil, Eviction, Small Claims, Probate—2nd Judicial District Court, Box D, Arapaho, OK 73620. 580-323-3233, Fax: 580-331-1121. 8AM-4PM. Access by: mail, in person.

Delaware

Real Estate Recording—Delaware County Clerk, 327 5th Street, Jay, OK 74346. Fax: 918-253-8352. 8AM-4:30PM.

Felony, Misdemeanor, Civil, Eviction, Small Claims, Probate—13th Judicial District Court, Box 407, Jay, OK 74346. 918-253-4420. 8:30AM-4:30PM. Access by: mail, in person.

Dewey

Real Estate Recording—Dewey County Clerk, Corner of Broadway & Ruble, Taloga, OK 73667. 405-735-2442. 8AM-4PM.

Felony, Misdemeanor, Civil, Eviction, Small Claims, Probate—4th Judicial District Court, Box 278, Taloga, OK 73667. 580-328-5521. 8AM-4PM. Access by: mail, in person.

Ellis

Real Estate Recording—Ellis County Clerk, 100 Courthouse Square, Arnett, OK 73832. 406-278-7681, Fax: 580-885-7258. 8:30AM-4:30PM.

Felony, Misdemeanor, Civil, Eviction, Small Claims, Probate—2nd Judicial District Court, Box 217, Arnett, OK 73832. 580-885-7255. 8:30AM-4:30PM. Access by: mail, phone, in person.

Garfield

Real Estate Recording—Garfield County Clerk, 114 West Broadway, Enid, OK 73701. 405-332-0183, Fax: 580-249-5951. 8AM-4PM.

Felony, Misdemeanor, Civil, Eviction, Small Claims, Probate—4th Judicial District Court, 114 W Broadway, Enid, OK 73701-4024. 580-237-0232. 8AM-4:30PM. Access by: mail, in person.

Garvin

Real Estate Recording—Garvin County Clerk, 201 West Grant, Pauls Valley, OK 73075. 405-336-2026, Fax: 405-238-6283. 8:30AM-4:30PM.

Felony, Misdemeanor, Civil, Eviction, Small Claims, Probate—21st Judicial District Court, PO Box 239, Pauls Valley, OK 73075. 405-335-3425. 8:30AM-4:30PM. Access by: mail, in person.

Grady

Real Estate Recording—Grady County Clerk, 4th & Choctaw, Chickasha, OK 73018. Fax: 405-222-4506. 8AM-4:30PM.

Felony, Misdemeanor, Civil, Eviction, Small Claims, Probate—6th Judicial District Court, PO Box 605, 328 Choctaw St, Chickasha, OK 73023. 405-323-2292. 8AM-4:30PM. Access by: in person.

Grant

Real Estate Recording—Grant County Clerk, 112 East Guthrie, Medford, OK 73759. 406-225-4055. 8AM-4:30PM.

Felony, Misdemeanor, Civil, Eviction, Small Claims, Probate—4th Judicial District Court, 112 E Guthrie, Medford, OK 73759. 580-395-2828. 8AM-4:30PM. Access by: mail, in person.

Greer

Real Estate Recording—Greer County Clerk, Courthouse Square, Mangum, OK 73554. 406-266-3445, Fax: 580-782-3803. 9AM-Noon,1-5PM.

Felony, Misdemeanor, Civil, Eviction, Small Claims, Probate—2nd Judicial District Court, PO Box 216, Mangum, OK 73554. 580-782-3665. 8:30AM-4:30PM. Access by: mail, in person.

Harmon

Real Estate Recording—Harmon County Clerk, Courthouse, 14 W. Hollis, Hollis, OK 73550. 406-278-4030.

Felony, Misdemeanor, Civil, Eviction, Small Claims, Probate—2nd Judicial District Court, 114 W. Hollis, Hollis, OK 73550. 580-688-3617. 8AM-5PM. Access by: mail, phone, in person.

Harper

Real Estate Recording—Harper County Clerk, 311 SE First Street, Buffalo, OK 73834. 406-265-5481. 8AM-4PM.

Felony, Misdemeanor, Civil, Eviction, Small Claims, Probate—1st Judicial District Court, Box 347, Buffalo, OK 73834. 580-735-2010. 8AM-4PM. Access by: mail, phone, in person.

Haskell

Real Estate Recording—Haskell County Clerk, 202 East Main, Courthouse, Stigler, OK 74462. 918-967-2441, Fax: 918-967-2885. 8AM-4:30PM.

Felony, Misdemeanor, Civil, Eviction, Small Claims, Probate—16th Judicial District Court, 202 E. Main, Stigler, OK 74462. 918-967-3323. 8AM-4:30PM. Access by: mail, phone, in person.

Hughes

Real Estate Recording—Hughes County Clerk, 200 North Broadway ST. #5, Holdenville, OK 74848. 406-222-4169. 8AM-4:30PM.

Felony, Misdemeanor, Civil, Eviction, Small Claims, Probate—22nd Judicial District Court, 200 N Broadway, Box 32, Holdenville, OK 74848. 406-222-4125. 8AM-4:30PM. Access by: mail, in person.

Jackson

Real Estate Recording—Jackson County Clerk, Main & Broadway, Courthouse-Room 203, Altus, OK 73522. 406-225-4251. 8AM-4PM.

Felony, Misdemeanor, Civil, Eviction, Small Claims, Probate—3rd Judicial District Court, 101 N. Main, Rm. 303, jackosn County Courthouse, Altus, OK 73521. 580-482-0448. 8AM-4PM. Access by: mail, in person.

Jefferson

Real Estate Recording—Jefferson County Clerk, 220 North Main, Courthouse - Room 103, Waurika, OK 73573. 405-327-0308, Fax: 580-228-3418. 8AM-4PM.

Felony, Misdemeanor, Civil, Eviction, Small Claims, Probate—5th Judicial District Court, 220 N. Main, Waurika, OK 73573. 580-228-2961. 8AM-4PM. Access by: mail, in person.

Johnston

Real Estate Recording—Johnston County Clerk, 414 West Main, Room 101, Tishomingo, OK 73460. 405-889-5283. 8:30AM-4:30PM.

Felony, Misdemeanor, Civil, Eviction, Small Claims, Probate—20th Judicial District Court, 414 W Main, Suite 201, Tishomingo, OK 73460. 580-371-3281. 8:30AM-4:30PM. Access by: mail, in person.

Kay

Real Estate Recording—Kay County Clerk, Courthouse, 201 S. Main, Newkirk, OK 74647. 405-882-3566, Fax: 580-362-3300. 8AM-4:30PM.

Felony, Misdemeanor, Civil, Eviction, Small Claims, Probate—8th Judicial District Court, Box 428, Newkirk, OK 74647. 580-362-3350. 8:00AM-4:30PM. Access by: mail, in person.

Kingfisher

Real Estate Recording—Kingfisher County Clerk, 101 South Main, Room #3, Kingfisher, OK 73750. Fax: 405-375-6033. 8AM-4:30PM.

Felony, Misdemeanor, Civil, Eviction, Small Claims, Probate—4th Judicial District Court, Box 328, Kingfisher, OK 73750. 405-928-2589. 8:30AM-4:30PM. Access by: mail, in person.

Kiowa

Real Estate Recording—Kiowa County Clerk, 316 South Main, Hobart, OK 73651. 406-265-5481, Fax: 580-726-6033. 9AM-5PM.

Felony, Misdemeanor, Civil, Eviction, Small Claims, Probate—3rd Judicial District Court, Box 854, Hobart, OK 73651. 580-726-5125. 9AM-5PM. Access by: mail, phone, in person.

Latimer

Real Estate Recording—Latimer County Clerk, 109 North Central, Room 103, Wilburton, OK 74578. 918-465-3450, Fax: 918-465-4001. 8AM-4:30PM.

Felony, Misdemeanor, Civil, Eviction, Small Claims, Probate—16th Judicial District Court, 109 N. Central, Rm 200, Wilburton, OK 74578. 918-465-2011. 8AM-4:30PM. Access by: mail, phone, in person.

Le Flore

Real Estate Recording—Le Flore County Clerk, 100 South Broadway, Poteau, OK 74953. 918-647-3525, Fax: 918-647-8930. 8AM-4:30PM.

Felony, Misdemeanor, Civil, Eviction, Small Claims, Probate—16th Judicial District Court, PO Box 688, Poteau, OK 74953. 918-647-3181. 8AM-4:30PM. Access by: mail, in person.

Lincoln

Real Estate Recording—Lincoln County Clerk, Courthouse, 800 Manvel Ave. Chandler, OK 74834. 405-379-3384. 8:30AM-4:30PM.

Felony, Misdemeanor, Civil, Eviction, Small Claims, Probate—23rd Judicial District Court, PO Box 307, Chandler, OK 74834. 405-375-3813. 8:30AM-4:30PM. Access by: mail, in person.

Logan

Real Estate Recording—Logan County Clerk, 301 East Harrison, Suite 102, Guthrie, OK 73044. 405-527-3261. 8:30AM-4:30PM.

Felony, Misdemeanor, Civil, Eviction, Small Claims, Probate—9th Judicial District Court, 301 E. Harrison, Rm 201, Guthrie, OK 73044. 405-527-3221. 8:30AM-4:30PM. Access by: mail, in person.

Love

Real Estate Recording—Love County Clerk, 405 West Main, Room 203, Marietta, OK 73448. 405-497-3349. 8AM-Noon, 12:30-4:30PM.

Felony, Misdemeanor, Civil, Eviction, Small Claims, Probate—20th Judicial District Court, 405 W. Main, Marietta, OK 73448. 580-276-2235. 8AM-4:30PM. Access by: mail, in person.

Major

Real Estate Recording—Major County Clerk, 9th & Broadway, Fairview, OK 73737. 405-326-6142, Fax: 580-227-2736. 8:30AM-4:30PM.

Felony, Misdemeanor, Civil, Eviction, Small Claims, Probate—4th Judicial District Court, 500 E Broadway, Fairview, OK 73737. 580-227-4690. 8:30AM-4:30PM. Access by: mail, phone, fax, in person.

Marshall

Real Estate Recording—Marshall County Clerk, Marshall County Courthouse, Room 101, Madill, OK 73446. 406-266-4720. 8:30AM-Noon, 12:30-5PM.

Felony, Misdemeanor, Civil, Eviction, Small Claims, Probate—20th Judicial District Court, Box 58, Madill, OK 73446. 580-795-3278. 8:30AM-5PM. Access by: mail, phone, in person.

Mayes

Real Estate Recording—Mayes County Clerk, Northeast 1st Street, Pryor, OK 74361. 918-825-0160, Fax: 918-825-2913. 9AM-5PM.

Felony, Misdemeanor, Civil, Eviction, Small Claims, Probate—12th Judicial District Court, Box 867, Pryor, OK 74362. 918-825-2185, Fax: 918-825-6446. 9AM-5PM. Access by: mail, phone, in person.

McClain

Real Estate Recording—McClain County Clerk, 2nd & Washington, Purcell, OK 73080. 406-228-8221. 8AM-4:30PM.

Felony, Misdemeanor, Civil, Eviction, Small Claims, Probate—21st Judicial District Court, 121 N. 2nd Rm 231, Purcell, OK 73080. 406-228-8221. 8AM-4:30PM. Access by: mail, in person.

McCurtain

Real Estate Recording—McCurtain County Clerk, 108 North Central, Idabel, OK 74745. 405-544-2261. 8AM-4PM.

Felony, Misdemeanor, Civil, Eviction, Small Claims, Probate—17th Judicial District Court, Box 1378, Idabel, OK 74745. 580-286-3693, Fax: 580-286-7095. 8AM-4PM. Access by: mail, in person.

McIntosh

Real Estate Recording—McIntosh County Clerk, 110 North 1st Street, Eufaula, OK 74432. 918-689-2491, Fax: 918-689-3385. 8AM-4PM.

Felony, Misdemeanor, Civil, Eviction, Small Claims, Probate—18th Judicial District Court, Box 426, Eufaula, OK 74432. 918-689-2282. 8AM-4PM. Access by: mail, in person.

Murray

Real Estate Recording—Murray County Clerk, 10th & Wyandotte, Sulphur, OK 73086. 406-256-2802, Fax: 580-622-6209. 7:30AM-Noon, 1-4:30PM.

Felony, Misdemeanor, Civil, Eviction, Small Claims, Probate—20th Judicial District Court, Box 578, Sulphur, OK 73086. 580-622-3223. 8AM-4:30PM, closed for lunch. Access by: mail, in person.

Muskogee

Real Estate Recording—Muskogee County Clerk, Corner of State & Court Streets, Muskogee, OK 74401. 918-682-0811. 8AM-4:30PM.

Felony, Misdemeanor, Civil, Eviction, Small Claims, Probate—15th Judicial District Court, Box 1350, Muskogee, OK 74402. 406-265-5481. 8AM-4:30PM. Access by: mail, in person.

Noble

Real Estate Recording—Noble County Clerk, 300 Courthouse Dr. Courthouse, Box 11, Room 201, Perry, OK 73077. 405-792-2463, Fax: 580-336-2481. 8AM-4PM.

Felony, Misdemeanor, Civil, Eviction, Small Claims, Probate—8th Judicial District Court, 300 Courthouse Dr, Box 14, Perry, OK 73077. 580-336-5187. 8AM-4:30PM. Access by: mail, in person.

Nowata

Real Estate Recording—Nowata County Clerk, 229 North Maple, Nowata, OK 74048. 918-273-3562, Fax: 918-273-2481. 8AM-4:30PM.

Felony, Misdemeanor, Civil, Eviction, Small Claims, Probate—11th Judicial District Court, 229 N. Maple, Nowata, OK 74048. 918-273-0127. 8AM-4:30PM. Access by: mail, in person.

Okfuskee

Real Estate Recording—Okfuskee County Clerk, 3rd & Atlanta, Okfuskee County Courthouse, Okemah, OK 74859. 918-623-1494, Fax: 918-623-0739. 8AM-4PM.

Felony, Misdemeanor, Civil, Eviction, Small Claims, Probate—24th Judicial District Court, Box 30, Okemah, OK 74859. 918-623-0525. 8:30AM-4:30PM. Access by: mail, phone, in person.

Oklahoma

Real Estate Recording—Oklahoma County Clerk, 320 Robert S. Kerr Avenue, Courthouse - Room 107, Oklahoma City, OK 73102. Fax: 405-278-2241. 8AM-5PM.

Felony, Misdemeanor, Civil, Eviction, Small Claims, Probate—7th Judicial District Court, 320 Robert S. Kerr St, Rm 409, Oklahoma City, OK 73102. 405-328-5501. 8AM-5PM. Access by: mail, in person.

Okmulgee

Real Estate Recording—Okmulgee County Clerk, 7th & Seminole, Courthouse, Okmulgee, OK 74447. 918-756-3848, Fax: 918-758-1261. 8AM-4:30PM.

Felony, Misdemeanor, Civil, Eviction, Small Claims, Probate—24th Judicial District Court-Henryetta Branch, 114 S 4th, Henryetta, OK 74437. 918-652-7142. 8:30AM-4:30PM. Access by: mail, phone, in person. Special note: You must search both courts in this county, records are not co-mingled.

24th Judicial District Court-Okmulgee Branch, 314 W 7th, Okmulgee, OK 74447. 918-756-3042. 8AM-4:30PM. Access by: mail, phone, in person.

Osage

Real Estate Recording—Osage County Clerk, 6th & Grandview, Courthouse, Pawhuska, OK 74056. 8:30AM-5PM.

Felony, Misdemeanor, Civil, Eviction, Small Claims, Probate—10th Judicial District Court, County Courthouse, 600 Grandview, Pawhuska, OK 74056. 918-287-4104. 9AM-5PM. Access by: mail, in person.

Ottawa

Real Estate Recording—Ottawa County Clerk, 102 E. Central, Suite 203, Miami, OK 74354. 9AM-Noon,1-5PM; Recording until 4:30PM.

Felony, Misdemeanor, Civil, Eviction, Small Claims, Probate—13th Judicial District Court, 102 E Central Ave, Suite 300, Miami, OK 74354. 918-542-2801. 9:00AM-5:00PM. Access by: mail, phone, in person.

Pawnee

Real Estate Recording—Pawnee County Clerk, Courthouse, Room 202, 500 Harrison St. Pawnee, OK 74058. 918-762-2418. 8AM-4:30PM.

Felony, Misdemeanor, Civil, Eviction, Small Claims, Probate—14th Judicial District Court, Courthouse, 500 Harrison St, Pawnee, OK 74058. 918-762-2547. 8AM-4:30PM. Access by: mail, in person.

Payne

Real Estate Recording—Payne County Clerk, 606 South Husband Street, Room 209, Stillwater, OK 74074. 406-266-3145. 8AM-5PM.

Felony, Misdemeanor, Civil, Eviction, Small Claims, Probate—9th Judicial District Court, 606 S. Husband Rm 308, Stillwater, OK 74074. 405-924-0748. 8AM-5PM. Access by: mail, in person.

Pittsburg

Real Estate Recording—Pittsburg County Clerk, 115 East Carl Albert Parkway, McAlester, OK 74501. 918-423-6895, Fax: 918-423-7304. 8AM-5PM.

Felony, Misdemeanor, Civil, Eviction, Small Claims, Probate—18th Judicial District Court, Box 460, McAlester, OK 74502. 918-423-4859. 8:30AM-5PM. Access by: mail, in person.

Pontotoc

Real Estate Recording—Pontotoc County Clerk, 100 W. 13th, Room 205, Ada, OK 74820. 405-747-9411, Fax: 580-332-9509. 8AM-5PM.

Felony, Misdemeanor, Civil, Eviction, Small Claims, Probate—22nd Judicial District Court, Box 427, Ada, OK 74820. 580-332-5763, Fax: 580-436-5613. 8AM-5PM. Access by: mail, phone, in person.

Pottawatomie

Real Estate Recording—Pottawatomie County Clerk, 325 North Broadway, Shawnee, OK 74801. 405-395-2274, Fax: 405-275-6898. 8:30AM-5PM.

Felony, Misdemeanor, Civil, Eviction, Small Claims, Probate—23rd Judicial District Court, 325 N. Broadway, Shawnee, OK 74801. 405-482-4371. 8:30AM-Noon, 1-5 PM. Access by: mail, in person.

Pushmataha

Real Estate Recording—Pushmataha County Clerk, 302 SW 'B', Antlers, OK 74523. 405-596-3148, Fax: 580-298-3626. 8AM-4:30PM.

Felony, Misdemeanor, Civil, Eviction, Small Claims, Probate—17th Judicial District Court, Push County Courthouse, Antlers, OK 74523. 580-298-2274. 8AM-4:30PM. Access by: mail, in person.

Roger Mills

Real Estate Recording—Roger Mills County Clerk, Broadway & L.L. Males Avenue, Cheyenne, OK 73628. 406-228-8221, Fax: 580-497-3488. 9AM-4:30PM.

Felony, Misdemeanor, Civil, Eviction, Small Claims, Probate—2nd Judicial District Court, Box 409, Cheyenne, OK 73628. 580-497-3361. 8AM-Noon, 1-4:30PM. Access by: mail, phone, in person.

Rogers

Real Estate Recording—Rogers County Clerk, 219 South Missouri, Claremore, OK 74017. 8AM-5PM.

Felony, Misdemeanor, Civil, Eviction, Small Claims, Probate—12th Judicial District Court, Box 839, Claremore, OK 74018. 918-341-5711. 8AM-4:30PM. Access by: mail, in person.

Seminole

Real Estate Recording—Seminole County Clerk, 100 South Wewoka, Courthouse, Wewoka, OK 74884. 405-372-4774, Fax: 405-257-6422. 8AM-4PM.

Felony, Misdemeanor, Civil, Eviction, Small Claims, Probate—22nd Judicial District Court-Seminole Branch, Box 1320, 401 Main St, Seminole, OK 74868. 406-225-4041. 8AM-Noon, 1-4PM. Access by: mail, phone, in person.

22nd Judicial District Court-Wewoka Branch, Box 130, Wewoka, OK 74884. 405-371-3082. 8AM-4PM. Access by: mail, in person.

Sequoyah

Real Estate Recording—Sequoyah County Clerk, 120 East Chickasaw, Sallisaw, OK 74955. Fax: 918-775-1218. 8AM-4PM.

Felony, Misdemeanor, Civil, Eviction, Small Claims, Probate—15th Judicial District Court, 120 E Chickasaw, Sallisaw, OK 74955. 918-775-4411. 8AM-4PM. Access by: mail, phone, in person.

Stephens

Real Estate Recording—Stephens County Clerk, 101 S. 11th St. Room 203, Duncan, OK 73533. 405-366-0217, Fax: 580-255-0991. 8:30AM-4:30PM.

Felony, Misdemeanor, Civil, Eviction, Small Claims, Probate—5th Judicial District Court, 101 S 11th Rm 301, Duncan, OK 73533. 580-255-8460. 8:30AM-4:30PM. Access by: mail, phone, in person.

Texas

Real Estate Recording—Texas County Clerk, 319 North Main, Guymon, OK 73942. 405-832-2667. 9AM-5PM.

Felony, Misdemeanor, Civil, Eviction, Small Claims, Probate—1st Judicial District Court, Box 1081, Guymon, OK 73942. 580-338-3003. 9AM-5PM. Access by: mail, in person.

Tillman

Real Estate Recording—Tillman County Clerk, 10th & Gladstone, Courthouse, Frederick, OK 73542. 405-782-5515, Fax: 580-335-3795. 8AM-4PM.

Felony, Misdemeanor, Civil, Eviction, Small Claims, Probate—3rd Judicial District Court, Box 116, Frederick, OK 73542. 580-335-3023. 8AM-4PM. Access by: mail, in person.

Tulsa

Real Estate Recording—Tulsa County Clerk, 500 South Denver Avenue, County Admin. Bldg.-Room 112, Tulsa, OK 74103. 918-596-5030, Fax: 918-596-5867. 8:30AM-5PM.

Felony, Misdemeanor, Civil, Eviction, Small Claims, Probate—14th Judicial District Court, 500 S. Denver, Tulsa, OK 74103-3832. 918-596-5000, Fax: 918-596-5216. 8:30AM-5PM. Access by: mail, in person.

Wagoner

Real Estate Recording—Wagoner County Clerk, 307 East Cherokee, Wagoner, OK 74467. 918-485-2149, Fax: 918-485-8677. 8AM-4:30PM.

Felony, Misdemeanor, Civil, Eviction, Small Claims, Probate—15th Judicial District Court, Box 249, Wagoner, OK 74477. 918-485-4508. 8:00AM-4:30PM. Access by: mail, phone, in person.

Washington

Real Estate Recording—Washington County Clerk, 420 South Johnstone, Room 102, Bartlesville, OK 74003. Fax: 918-337-2894. 8AM-5PM.

Felony, Misdemeanor, Civil, Eviction, Small Claims, Probate—11th Judicial District Court, 420 S Johnstone, Rm 212, Bartlesville, OK 74003. 918-337-2870, Fax: 918-337-2897. 8AM-5PM. Access by: mail, phone, fax, in person.

Washita

Real Estate Recording—Washita County Clerk, 100 East Main, Cordell, OK 73632. 406-276-3741. 8AM-4PM.

Felony, Misdemeanor, Civil, Eviction, Small Claims, Probate—3rd Judicial District Court, Box 397, Cordell, OK 73632,. 580-832-3836. 8AM-4PM. Access by: mail, in person.

Woods

Real Estate Recording—Woods County Clerk, Courthouse, 407 Government Street, Alva, OK 73717. 405-726-2362, Fax: 580-327-6230. 9AM-5PM.

Felony, Misdemeanor, Civil, Eviction, Small Claims, Probate—4th Judicial District Court, Box 924, Alva, OK 73717. 580-327-3119. 9AM-5PM. Access by: mail, in person.

Woodward

Real Estate Recording—Woodward County Clerk, 1600 Main Street, Woodward, OK 73801. 405-362-2523. 9AM-5PM.

Felony, Misdemeanor, Civil, Eviction, Small Claims, Probate—4th Judicial District Court, 1600 Main, Woodward, OK 73801. 580-256-3413. 9AM-5PM. Access by: mail, in person.

Federal Courts

US District Court

Eastern District of Oklahoma

Muskogee Division Clerk, PO Box 607, Muskogee, OK 74401918-687-2471 Fax: 918-687-2400 Counties: Adair, Atoka, Bryan, Carter, Cherokee, Choctaw, Coal, Haskell, Hughes, Johnston, Latimer, Le Flore, Love, McCurtain, McIntosh, Marshall, Murray, Muskogee, Okfuskee, Pittsburg, Pontotoc, Pushmataha, Seminole, Sequoyah, Wagoner.

Northern District of Oklahoma

Tulsa Division 411 US Courthouse, 333 W 4th St, Tulsa, OK 74103918-699-4700 Fax: 918-699-4756 Counties: Craig, Creek, Delaware, Mayes, Nowata, Okmulgee, Osage, Ottawa, Pawnee, Rogers, Tulsa, Washington.

Western District of Oklahoma

Oklahoma City Division Clerk, Room 1210, 200 NW 4th St, Oklahoma City, OK 73102405-231-4792, Criminal Docket Phone: 405-231-4955 Counties: Alfalfa, Beaver, Beckham, Blaine, Caddo, Canadian, Cimarron, Cleveland, Comanche, Cotton, Custer, Dewey, Ellis, Garfield, Garvin, Grady, Grant, Greer, Harmon, Harper, Jackson, Jefferson, Kay, Kingfisher, Kiowa, Lincoln, Logan, McClain, Major, Noble,Oklahoma, Payne, Pottawatomie, Roger Mills, Stephens, Texas, Tillman, Washita, Woods, Woodward.

US Bankruptcy Court

Eastern District of Oklahoma

Okmulgee Division PO Box 1347, Okmulgee, OK 74447918-758-0126 Fax: 918-756-9248 Counties: Adair, Atoka, Bryan, Carter, Cherokee, Choctaw, Coal, Haskell, Hughes, Johnston, Latimer, Le Flore, Love, Marshall, McCurtain, McIntosh, Murray, Muskogee, Okfuskee, Okmulgee, Pittsburg, Pontotoc, Pushmataha, Seminole, Sequoyah, Wagoner.

Northern District of Oklahoma

Tulsa Division 224 S. Boulder, Tulsa, OK 74103918-581-7181 Fax: 918-581-7645 Counties: Craig, Creek, Delaware, Mayes, Nowata, Osage, Ottawa, Pawnee, Rogers, Tulsa, Washington.

Western District of Oklahoma

Oklahoma City Division 1st Floor, Old Post Office Bldg, 215 Dean A McGee Ave, Oklahoma City, OK 73102405-231-5141 Fax: 405-231-5866 Counties: Alfalfa, Beaver, Beckham, Blaine, Caddo, Canadian, Cimarron, Cleveland, Comanche, Cotton, Custer, Dewey, Ellis, Garfield, Garvin, Grady, Grant, Greer, Harmon, Harper, Jackson, Jefferson, Kay, Kingfisher, Kiowa, Lincoln, Logan, Major, McClain, Noble,Oklahoma, Payne, Pottawatomie, Roger Mills, Stephens, Texas, Tillman, Washita, Woods, Woodward.

Attorney General's Office
1162 Court St NE   503-378-4400
Salem, OR 97310   Fax: 503-378-4017
www.doj.state.or.us

Governor's Office
160 State Capitol   503-378-3111
Salem, OR 97310   Fax: 503-378-6827
www.governor.state.or.us

State Archives
800 Summer St NE   503-373-0701
Salem, OR 97301   Fax: 503-373-0953
http://arcweb.sos.state.or.us

Capital:	Salem
	Marion County
Time Zone:	PST
Number of Counties:	36
Population:	3,243,487
Web Site:	www.state.or.us

Search Unclaimed Property Online

http://rogue.sscgis.state.or.us/dsl/search.cfm

State Agencies

Criminal Records
Oregon State Police, Identification Services Section, PO Box 4395, Salem, OR 97208-4396 (3772 Portland Rd NE, Salem, OR 97303); 503-378-3070; Fax: 503-378-2121; 8AM-5PM. Access by: mail, online. www.osp.state.or.us

Corporation Records
Limited Partnership Records
Trademarks/Servicemarks
Fictitious Name
Assumed Name
Limited Liability Company Records
Corporation Division, Public Service Building, 255 Capital St NE, #151, Salem, OR 97310-1327; 503-986-2200; Fax: 503-378-4381; 8AM-5PM. Access by: mail, phone, in person, online. www.sos.state.or.us/corporation/corphp.htm

Uniform Commercial Code
Federal Tax Liens
UCC Division, Secretary of State, 255 Capitol St NE, Suite 151, Salem, OR 97310-1327; 503-986-2200; Fax: 503-373-1166; 8AM-5PM. Access by: mail, online. www.sos.state.or.us/corporation/ucc/ucc.htm

State Tax Liens
Records not available from state agency.
Records are located at the county level.

Workers' Compensation Records
Department of Consumer & Business Srvs, Workers Compensation Division, 350 Winter Street NE, Salem, OR 97310; 503-945-7810; Fax: 503-945-7630; 8AM-5PM. Access by: mail. www.cbs.state.or.us/wed

Birth Certificates
Oregon State Health Division, Vital Records, PO Box 14050, Portland, OR 97293-0050 (800 NE Oregon St, #205, Portland, OR 97232); 503-731-4095 Recorded Message, 503-731-4108; Fax: 503-234-8417; 8AM-4:30PM. Access by: mail, phone, in

person. www.ohd.hr.state.or.us/
cdpe/chs/welcome.htm

Death Records

Oregon State Health Division, Vital Records, PO Box 14050,
Portland, OR 97293-0050; 503-731-4095 Recorded Message,
503-731-4108; Fax: 503-234-8417; 8AM-4:30PM. Access by:
mail, phone, in person. www.ohd.hr.state.or.us/
cdpe/chs/welcome.htm

Marriage Certificates

Oregon State Health Division, Vital Records, PO Box 14050,
Portland, OR 97293-0050; 503-731-4095 Recorded Message,
503-731-4108; Fax: 503-234-8417; 8AM-4:30PM. Access by:
mail, phone, in person. www.ohd.hr.state.or.us/
cdpe/chs/welcome.htm

Divorce Records

Oregon State Health Division, Vital Records, Suite 205, PO Box
14050, Portland, OR 97293-0050; 503-731-4095 Recorded
Message, 502-731-4108; Fax: 503-234-8417; 8AM-4:30PM.
Access by: mail, phone, in person.
www.ohd.hr.state.or.us/cdpe/chs/welcome.htm

Accident Reports

Motor Vehicle Division, Accident Reports & Information, 1905
Lana Ave, NE, Salem, OR 97314; 503-945-5098; Fax: 503-945-
5267; 8AM-5PM (until 8:30PM W). Access by: mail.

Driver Records

Driver and Motor Vehicle Services, Record Services, 1905 Lana
Ave, NE, Salem, OR 97314; 503-945-5000; 8AM-5PM. Access
by: mail, phone, in person. www.odot.state.or.us/
dmv/index.htm

Vehicle Ownership
Vehicle Identification

Driver and Motor Vehicle Services, Record Services Unit, 1905
Lana Ave, NE, Salem, OR 97314; 503-945-5000; Fax: 503-945-

5425; 8AM-5PM. Access by: mail, phone, in person.
www.odot.state.or.us/dmv/index.htm

Boat & Vessel Ownership
Boat & Vessel Registration

Oregon State Marine Board, PO Box 14145, Salem, OR 97309
(435 Commercial St NE, #400, Salem, OR 97301); 503-378-
8587; Fax: 503-378-4597; 8AM-5PM M-F.
www.osmb.state.or.us

Legislation-Current/Pending
Legislation-Passed

Oregon Legislative Assembly, State Capitol-Information
Services, State Capitol, Rm 49, Salem, OR 97310; 503-986-1180
Current Bill Information, 503-373-0701 Archives; Fax: 503-373-
1527; 8AM-5PM. Access by: mail, phone, in person, online.
www.leg.state.or.us

Voter Registration

Records not available from state agency.

Records are maintained at the county level and cannot be
purchased for commercial reasons.

GED Certificates

Community College & Workforce Development, GED Program,
255 Capitol St NE, Salem, OR 97310-1341; 503-378-8648 x373;
Fax: 503-378-8434; 8AM-5PM M-F.
www.odccwd.state.or.us

Hunting License Information
Fishing License Information

Fish & Wildlife Department, Licensing Division, PO Box 59,
Portland, OR 97207 (2501 SW 1st Ave, Portland, OR 97201);
503-872-5275; Fax: 503-872-5261; 8AM-5PM. Access by: mail,
phone, in person.

County Courts & Recording Offices

About the Courts...

About the Recording Offices...

Administration

Court Administrator, Supreme Court Building   503-986-5500
1163 State St   Fax: 503-986-5503
Salem, OR 97310

Court Structure

Effective January 15, 1998, the District and Circuit Courts were combined into "Circuit Courts." At the same time, three new judicial districts were created by splitting existing ones.

Searching Hints

Many Oregon courts indicated that in person searches would markedly improve request turnaround time as court offices are understaffed or spread very thin. Most Circuit Courts that have records on computer do have a public access terminal which will speed up in-person or retriever searches. Most records offices close from Noon to 1PM Oregon time for lunch. No staff is available during that period.

Online Access

Online computer access is available through the Oregon Judicial Information Network (OJIN). OJIN Online includes almost all cases filed in the Oregon state courts. Generally, the OJIN database contains criminal, civil, small claims, probate, and some, but not all, juvenile records. However, it does not contain any records from municipal nor county courts. There is a one time setup fee of $295.00, plus a monthly usage charge (minimum $10.00) based on transaction type, type of job, shift, and number of units/pages (which averages $10-13 per hour). For further information and/or a registration packet, write to: Oregon Judicial System, Information Systems Division, ATTN: Technical Support, 1163 State Street, Salem OR 97310, or call 800-858-9658.

Organization

36 counties, 36 recording offices. The recording officer is County Clerk. 35 counties are in the Pacific Time Zone (PST) and one is in the Mountain Time Zone (MST).

UCC Records

Financing statements are filed at the state level, except for real estate related collateral. All counties will perform UCC searches. Use search request form UCC-11. Search fees are vary from $3.75 to $12.50, and copy fees vary.

Lien Records

All federal tax liens on personal property are filed with the Secretary of State. Other federal tax liens and all state tax liens are filed with the County Clerk. Most counties will perform tax lien searches and include both with a UCC search for an extra $7.50 per name. Search fees vary widely.

Real Estate Records

Some counties will not perform real estate searches. Search fees vary. Many counties will search all liens together for $12.50 per name. Copy fees are usually $.25 per page. Certification usually costs $3.75 per document. The Assessor keeps tax and ownership records.

County Courts & Recording Offices

Baker

Real Estate Recording—Baker County Clerk, 1995 Third Street, Suite 150, Baker, OR 97814. 541-523-8233, Fax: 541-523-8240. 8AM-Noon,1-5PM.

Felony, Misdemeanor, Civil, Probate—Circuit Court, 1995 3rd St, #220, Baker City, OR 97814. 541-523-6305, Fax: 541-523-9738. 8AM-Noon, 1-3PM. Access by: mail, phone, fax, in person, online.

Benton

Real Estate Recording—Benton County Recorder, 120 NW 4th Street, Room 4, Corvallis, OR 97330. Fax: 541-754-2870. 8AM-5PM (Recording Hours: 9AM-4PM).

Felony, Misdemeanor, Civil, Eviction, Small Claims, Probate—Circuit Court, Box 1870, Corvallis, OR 97339. 541-757-6828, Fax: 541-766-6028. 8AM-Noon,1-5PM. Access by: mail, phone, in person, online.

Clackamas

Real Estate Recording—Clackamas County Clerk, 807 Main Street, Room 104, Oregon City, OR 97045. 8:30AM-5PM M,T,Th,F; 9:30AM-5PM W.

Felony, Misdemeanor, Civil, Eviction, Small Claims, Probate—Circuit Court, 807 Main St, Oregon City, OR 97045. 503-655-8447. 8:30AM-5PM. Access by: mail, in person, online.

Clatsop

Real Estate Recording—Clatsop County Clerk, 749 Commercial, Astoria, OR 97103. Fax: 503-325-9307. 8:30AM-5PM.

Felony, Civil Actions Over $10,000, Probate—Circuit Court, Box 835, Astoria, OR 97103. 503-325-8583, Fax: 503-325-9300. 8AM-Noon, 1-5PM. Access by: mail, phone, in person, online.

Misdemeanor, Civil Actions Under $10,000, Eviction, Small Claims—Circuit Court, Box 659, Astoria, OR 97103. 503-325-8536, Fax: 503-325-9300. 8AM-5PM. Access by: mail, in person, online.

Columbia

Real Estate Recording—Columbia County Clerk, Courthouse, St. Helens, OR 97051. Fax: 503-397-7266. 8:30AM-5PM (Recording 9AM-4PM).

Felony, Misdemeanor, Civil, Eviction, Small Claims, Probate—Circuit Court, Columbia County Courthouse, St. Helens, OR 97051. 503-397-2327, Fax: 503-397-3226. 8AM-Noon, 1-5PM. Access by: mail, in person, online.

Coos

Real Estate Recording—Coos County Clerk, Courthouse, 250 N. Baxter, Coquille, OR 97423. 541-396-3121, Fax: 541-396-4861. 8AM-5PM (Closed to public: Noon-1PM).

Felony, Misdemeanor, Civil, Eviction, Small Claims, Probate—Circuit Court, Courthouse, Coquille, OR 97423. 541-396-3121, Fax: 541-396-3456. 8AM-Noon,1-5PM. Access by: mail, phone, in person, online.

Crook

Real Estate Recording—Crook County Clerk, 300 East Third, Prineville, OR 97754. 541-447-6554, Fax: 541-447-1051. 8:30AM-5PM.

Felony, Misdemeanor, Civil, Eviction, Small Claims, Probate—Circuit Court, Crook County Courthouse, 300 NE Third St, Prineville, OR 97754. 541-447-6541. 8AM-5PM. Access by: mail, phone, in person.

Curry

Real Estate Recording—Curry County Clerk, 28821 Ellensburg Ave. Gold Beach, OR 97444. 503-247-7011, Fax: 541-247-6440. 8:30AM-5PM.

Felony, Misdemeanor, Civil, Eviction, Small Claims, Probate—Circuit Court, Box 810, Gold Beach, OR 97444. 541-247-4511. 8AM-5PM. Access by: mail, phone, in person, online.

Deschutes

Real Estate Recording—Deschutes County Clerk, 1340 NW Wall St. Bend, OR 97701. 541-388-6535, Fax: 541-389-6830. 8AM-5PM.

Felony, Misdemeanor, Civil, Eviction, Small Claims, Probate—Deschutes County Courts, 1100 NW Bond, Bend, OR 97701. 541-388-5300. 8AM-5PM. Access by: mail, phone, in person, online. www.empnet.com/deschutes-court/

Douglas

Real Estate Recording—Douglas County Clerk, 1036 SE Douglas, Room 221, Roseburg, OR 97470. 541-440-3311, Fax: 541-440-4408. 8AM-4PM.

Felony, Misdemeanor, Civil, Eviction, Small Claims, Probate—Circuit Court, 1036 S E Douglas Rm 202, Roseburg, OR 97470. 541-957-2470, Fax: 541-957-2462. 8AM-5PM. Access by: mail, phone, in person, online.

Gilliam

Real Estate Recording—Gilliam County Clerk, 221 South Oregon Street, Condon, OR 97823. 541-384-6321, Fax: 541-384-2166. 8:30AM-Noon, 1-5PM.

Felony, Misdemeanor, Civil—Circuit Court, Box 622, Condon, OR 97823. 541-384-3572, Fax: 541-384-2166. 1-5PM. Access by: mail, phone, in person, online.

Probate—County Court, 221 S Oregon, PO Box 427, Condon, OR 97823. 541-384-2311, Fax: 541-384-2166. 8:30AM-Noon, 1-5PM.

Grant

Real Estate Recording—Grant County Clerk, 201 South Humbolt, Suite 290, Canyon City, OR 97820. 541-575-1798, Fax: 541-575-2248. 8AM-5PM.

Felony, Misdemeanor, Civil—Circuit Court, Box 159, Canyon City, OR 97820. 541-575-1438, Fax: 541-575-2165. 8AM-Noon, 1-5PM. Access by: mail, in person, online.

Probate—County Court, 201 Humbolt St #290, Canyon City, OR 97820-6186. 541-575-1675, Fax: 541-575-2248. 8AM-5PM.

Harney

Real Estate Recording—Harney County Clerk, 450 North Buena Vista, Burns, OR 97720. Fax: 541-573-8370. 8:30AM-Noon, 1-5PM.

Felony, Misdemeanor, Civil—Circuit Court, 450 N. Buena Vista, Burns, OR 97720. 541-573-5207, Fax: 541-573-5715. 8AM-5PM. Access by: mail, phone, fax, in person, online.

Probate—County Court, PO Box 699, Burns, OR 97720. 541-573-6641, Fax: 541-573-8370. 8:30AM-Noon, 1-5PM.

Hood River

Real Estate Recording—Hood River County Recorder, 309 State Street, Hood River, OR 97031. Fax: 541-386-9392. 8AM-5PM (Recording 9AM-4PM).

Felony, Misdemeanor, Civil, Eviction, Small Claims, Probate—Circuit Court, 309 State St. Hood River, OR 97031. 541-386-1862, Fax: 541-386-3465. 8AM-Noon, 1-5PM. Access by: mail, phone, fax, in person, online.

Jackson

Real Estate Recording—Jackson County Clerk, 10 South Oakdale, Room 216A, Medford, OR 97501. 8AM-5PM.

Felony, Misdemeanor, Civil Actions, Eviction, Small Claims, Probat—Circuit Court, 100 S. Oakdale, Medford, OR 97501. 541-776-7171, Fax: 541-776-7057. 8AM-5PM. Access by: mail, in person, online.

Jefferson

Real Estate Recording—Jefferson County Clerk, 75 S.E. C Street, Madras, OR 97741. 541-475-4458, Fax: 541-475-4454. 8:30AM-5PM.

Felony, Misdemeanor, Civil, Eviction, Small Claims, Probate—Circuit Court, 75 SE C St. Madras, OR 97741-1750. 541-475-3317, Fax: 541-475-3421. 8AM-5PM. Access by: mail, in person, online.

Josephine

Real Estate Recording—Josephine County Clerk, Courthouse, 6 & C Streets, Grants Pass, OR 97526. 541-474-5235, Fax: 541-476-5246. 9AM-4PM.

Felony, Misdemeanor, Civil, Eviction, Small Claims, Probate—Circuit Court, Josephine County Courthouse, Rm 254, 500 NW 6th St, Grants Pass, OR 97526. 541-476-2309, Fax: 541-471-2079. 8AM-5PM. Access by: mail, fax, in person, online.

Klamath

Real Estate Recording—Klamath County Clerk, 305 Main St. Klamath Falls, OR 97601. Fax: 541-885-6757. 8AM-5PM; Recording Hours: 9AM-Noon, 1-4PM.

Felony, Misdemeanor, Civil, Eviction, Small Claims, Probate—Circuit Court, 316 Main Street, Klamath Falls, OR 97601. 541-883-5503, Fax: 541-882-6109. 8AM-5PM. Access by: mail, in person, online.

Lake

Real Estate Recording—Lake County Clerk, 513 Center Street, Lakeview, OR 97630. Fax: 541-947-6015. 8AM-5PM.

Felony, Misdemeanor, Civil, Eviction, Small Claims, Probate—Circuit Court, 513 Center St. Lakeview, OR 97630. 541-947-6051, Fax: 541-947-3724. 8AM-5PM. Access by: mail, in person, online.

Lane

Real Estate Recording—Deeds & Records, 125 East 8th Avenue, Eugene, OR 97401. 8AM-5PM; Recording 9AM-Noon, 1-4PM.

Felony, Misdemeanor, Civil, Eviction, Small Claims, Probate—Circuit Court, 125 E. 8th Ave. Eugene, OR 97401. 541-682-4020. 8AM-5PM. Access by: in person, online.

Lincoln

Real Estate Recording—Lincoln County Clerk, 225 West Olive Street, Room 201, Newport, OR 97365. Fax: 541-265-4950. 8:30AM-5PM.

Felony, Misdemeanor, Civil, Eviction, Small Claims, Probate—Lincoln County Courts, PO Box 100, Newport, OR 97365. 541-265-4236, Fax: 541-265-7561. 8AM-5PM. Access by: in person, online.

Linn

Real Estate Recording—Linn County Recorder, 300 SW 4th St. Courthouse Room 207, Albany, OR 97321. Fax: 541-926-5109. 8:30AM-5PM (Recording ends at 4PM).

Felony, Misdemeanor, Civil, Eviction, Small Claims, Probate—Circuit Court, PO Box 1749, Albany, OR 97321. 541-967-3845. 8AM-5PM. Access by: mail, in person, online.

Malheur

Real Estate Recording—Malheur County Clerk, 251 B Street West, Ste 4, Vale, OR 97918. Fax: 541-473-5523. 8:30AM-5PM.

Felony, Misdemeanor, Civil, Eviction, Small Claims—Circuit Court, 251 B St West, Vale, OR 97918. 541-473-5171, Fax: 541-473-2213. 8AM-5PM; 9AM-Noon, 1-4PM (Record Inquiry). Access by: mail, in person, online.

Probate—County Court, 251 B St W #5, Vale, OR 97918. 541-473-5123, Fax: 541-473-5168. 8AM-Noon, 1-4:30PM.

Marion

Real Estate Recording—Marion County Clerk, 100 High Street NE, Room 1331, Salem, OR 97301. Fax: 503-588-5237. 8:30AM-5PM.

Felony, Misdemeanor, Civil, Eviction, Small Claims, Probate—Lynn County Courts, 100 High St NE, 1st Floor, Salem, OR 97301. 503-588-5101, Fax: 503-373-4360. 8AM-5PM. Access by: mail, in person, online. http://marion-court.ojd.state.or.us

Morrow

Real Estate Recording—Morrow County Clerk, 100 Court Street, Heppner, OR 97836. 541-676-9061, Fax: 541-676-9876. 8AM-5PM.

Felony, Misdemeanor, Civil, Eviction, Small Claims, Probate—Circuit Court, PO Box 609, Heppner, OR 97836. 541-676-5264, Fax: 541-676-9902. 8AM-Noon, 1-4:45PM. Access by: mail, phone, fax, in person, online.

Multnomah

Real Estate Recording—Multnomah County Recorder, Room 308, 421 SW 6th Ave. Portland, OR 97204. 8AM-5PM; Phone hours: 9AM-4:30PM.

Felony, Misdemeanor, Civil Actions Over $10,000, Probate—Circuit Court, 1021 SW 4th Ave, Rm 131, Portland, OR 97204. 503-248-3003. 8AM-5PM. Access by: mail, in person, online.

Civil Actions Under $10,000, Eviction, Small Claims—Circuit Court-Civil Division, 1021 SW 4th Ave, Rm 210, Portland, OR 97204. 503-248-3022. 8AM-5PM. Access by: mail, phone, in person, online.

Polk

Real Estate Recording—Polk County Clerk, Courthouse, 850 Main St. Dallas, OR 97338. Fax: 503-623-0717. 8AM-5PM.

Felony, Misdemeanor, Civil, Eviction, Small Claims, Probate—Circuit Court, Polk County Courthouse, Rm 301, Dallas, OR 97338. Fax: 503-623-6614. 8AM-Noon, 1-5PM. Access by: mail, phone, fax, in person, online. Special note: Fax for criminal is 503-831-1779.

Sherman

Real Estate Recording—Sherman County Clerk, 500 Court Street, Moro, OR 97039. Fax: 541-565-3312. 8AM-5PM.

Felony, Misdemeanor, Civil—Circuit Court, PO Box 402, Moro, OR 97039. 541-565-3650. 1-5PM. Access by: mail, in person, online.

Probate—County Court, PO Box 365, Moro, OR 97039. 541-565-3606, Fax: 541-565-3312. 8AM-5PM. Access by: mail, in person.

Tillamook

Real Estate Recording—Tillamook County Clerk, 201 Laurel Avenue, Tillamook, OR 97141. 503-842-3425, Fax: 503-842-2721. 9AM-4PM.

Felony, Misdemeanor, Civil, Eviction, Small Claims, Probate—Circuit Court, 201 Laurel Ave, Tillamook, OR 97141. 503-842-8014, Fax: 503-842-2597. 8AM-5PM. Access by: mail, in person, online.

Umatilla

Real Estate Recording—Umatilla County, 216 SE 4th Street, Room 108, Pendleton, OR 97801. Fax: 541-278-5463. 8AM-5PM; Recording Hours 9AM-4PM.

Felony, Misdemeanor, Civil, Eviction, Small Claims, Probate—Circuit Court, PO Box 1307, Pendleton, OR 97801. 541-278-0341, Fax: 541-278-2071. 8AM-5PM. Access by: mail, in person, online.

Union

Real Estate Recording—Union County Clerk, 1001 4th St. Suite "D", La Grande, OR 97850. Fax: 541-963-1013. 8:30AM-5PM M-Th (Recording ends at 4:30PM); 9AM-4PM F.

Felony, Misdemeanor, Civil, Eviction, Small Claims, Probate—Circuit Court, 1008 K Ave, La Grande, OR 97850. 541-962-9500, Fax: 541-963-0444. 8AM-Noon, 1-5PM. Access by: mail, in person, online.

Wallowa

Real Estate Recording—Wallowa County Clerk, 101 South River, Room 100, Enterprise, OR 97828. Fax: 541-426-5901. 8:30AM-5PM.

Felony, Misdemeanor, Civil, Eviction, Small Claims, Probate—Circuit Court, 101 S River St, Rm 204, Enterprise, OR 97828. 541-426-4991, Fax: 541-426-4992. 8AM-5PM. Access by: mail, phone, in person, online.

Wasco

Real Estate Recording—Wasco County Clerk, 511 Washington St. Courthouse, The Dalles, OR 97058. Fax: 541-298-3607. 10AM-4PM.

Felony, Misdemeanor, Civil, Eviction, Small Claims, Probate—Circuit Court, PO Box 821, The Dalles, OR 97058. 541-296-3196, Fax: 541-298-5611. 8AM-Noon,1-5PM. Access by: mail, in person, online.

Washington

Real Estate Recording—Washington County Clerk, Public Services Building, 155 North First Avenue Suite 130, Hillsboro, OR 97124. 8:30AM-4:30PM.

Felony, Misdemeanor, Civil, Eviction, Small Claims, Probate—Circuit Court, 150 N 1st, Hillsboro, OR 97124. 503-648-

8888, Fax: 503-693-4971. 8-11:30AM, 12:30-3PM. Access by: mail, in person, online.

Wheeler

Real Estate Recording—Wheeler County Clerk, 701 Adams Street, Room 204, Fossil, OR 97830. 541-763-2078, Fax: 541-763-2026. 8:30AM-Noon, 1-5PM.

Felony, Misdemeanor, Civil—Circuit Court, PO Box 308, Fossil, OR 97830. 541-763-2541, Fax: 541-763-2026. 8:30AM-11:30AM. Access by: mail, phone, in person, online.

Probate—County Court, PO Box 327, Fossil, OR 97830. 541-763-2400, Fax: 541-763-4771. 9-5PM. Access by: mail, in person.

Yamhill

Real Estate Recording—Yamhill County Clerk, 535 NE 5th Street, McMinnville, OR 97128. Fax: 503-434-7520. 9AM-5PM.

Felony, Misdemeanor, Civil, Eviction, Small Claims, Probate—Circuit Court, 535 NE Fifth, McMinnville, OR 97128. 503-434-7530, Fax: 503-472-5805. 8AM-Noon, 1-5PM. Access by: mail, in person, online.

Federal Courts

US District Court

Eugene Division 100 Federal Bldg, 211 E 7th Ave, Eugene, OR 97401541-465-6423 Fax: 541-465-6344 Counties: Benton, Coos, Deschutes, Douglas, Lane, Lincoln, Linn, Marion. www.ord.uscourts.gov
Medford Division 201 James A Redden US Courthouse, 310 W 6th St, Medford, OR 97501541-776-3926 Fax: 541-776-3925 Counties: Curry, Jackson, Josephine, Klamath, Lake. Court set up in April 1994; Cases prior to that time were tried in Eugene. www.ord.uscourts.gov
Portland Division Clerk, 740 US Courthouse, 1000 SW 3rd Ave, Portland, OR 97204-2902503-326-8000, Record Room: 503-326-8020, Civil Docket Phone: 503-326-8008, Criminal Docket Phone: 503-326-8003 Fax: 503-326-8010 Counties: Baker, Clackamas, Clatsop, Columbia, Crook, Gilliam, Grant, Harney, Hood River,

Jefferson, Malheur, Morrow, Multnomah, Polk, Sherman, Tillamook, Umatilla, Union, Wallowa, Wasco, Washinton, Wheeler, Yamhill. www.ord.uscourts.gov

US Bankruptcy Court

Eugene Division PO Box 1335, Eugene, OR 97440541-465-6448 Counties: Benton, Coos, Curry, Deschutes, Douglas, Jackson, Josephine, Klamath, Lake, Lane, Lincoln, Linn, Marion.
Portland Division , 1001 SW 5th Ave, #700, Portland, OR 97204503-326-2231 Counties: Baker, Clackamas, Clatsop, Columbia, Crook, Gilliam, Grant, Harney, Hood River, Jefferson, Malheur, Morrow, Multnomah, Polk, Sherman, Tillamook, Umatilla, Union, Wallowa, Wasco, Washington, Wheeler, Yamhill.

Pennsylvania

Attorney General's Office
Strawberry Square, 16th Floor
Harrisburg, PA 17120
717-787-3391
Fax: 717-787-1190
www.attorneygeneral.gov

Governor's Office
225 Main Capitol Bldg
Harrisburg, PA 17120
717-787-2500
Fax: 717-772-8284
www.state.pa.us/PA_Exec/Governor/overview.html

State Archives
PO Box 1026
Harrisburg, PA 17108-1026
717-783-3281
Fax: 717-787-4822
state.pa.us/PA_Exec/Historical_Museum/DARMS/overview.htm

Capital:	Harrisburg
	Dauphin County
Time Zone:	EST
Number of Counties:	67
Population:	12,019,661
Web Site:	www.state.pa.us

Search Unclaimed Property Online

www.treasury.state.pa.us/
UPAdvertisIntro99.html

State Agencies

Criminal Records
State Police Central Repository, 1800 Elmerton Ave, Harrisburg, PA 17110-9758; 717-783-9973; Fax: 717-772-3681; 8:15AM-4:15PM. Access by: mail.

Corporation Records
Limited Partnership Records
Trademarks/Servicemarks
Fictitious Name
Assumed Name
Limited Liability Company Records
Corporation Bureau, Department of State, PO Box 8722, Harrisburg, PA 17105-8722 (308 North Office Bldg, Harrisburg, PA 17120); 717-787-1057; Fax: 717-783-2244; 8AM-5PM. Access by: mail, phone, in person. www.dos.state.pa.us/corp.htm

Sales Tax Registrations
Revenue Department, Sales Tax Division, Dept 280905, Harrisburg, PA 17128-0905; 717-783-9360; Fax: 717-783-5274; 7:30AM-5PM. Access by: mail, phone, in person. www.revenue.state.pa.us

Uniform Commercial Code
UCC Division, Department of State, PO Box 8721, Harrisburg, PA 17105-8721 (North Office Bldg, Rm 308, Harrisburg, PA 17120); 717-787-1057; Fax: 717-783-2244; 8AM-5PM. Access by: mail. www.dos.state.pa.us/corp.htm

Federal Tax Liens
State Tax Liens
Records not available from state agency.

All federal and state tax liens are filed at the Prothonotary of each county.

Workers' Compensation Records
Bureau of Workers' Compensation, 1171 S Cameron St, Rm 103, Harrisburg, PA 17104-2501; 717-772-4447; 8AM-5PM. Access by: mail.

Birth Certificates
PA Department of Health, Division of Vital Records, PO Box 1528, New Castle, PA 16103-1528 (101 S Mercer St, Room 401, New Castle, PA 16101); 724-656-3100 Message Phone; Fax: 724-652-8951; 8AM-4PM. Access by: mail, phone, in person.

Death Records

Department of Health, Division of Vital Records, PO Box 1528, New Castle, PA 16103-1528; 724-656-3100 Message Phone; Fax: 724-652-8951; 8AM-4PM. Access by: mail, phone, in person.

Marriage Certificates
Divorce Records

Records not available from state agency.

Marriage and divorce records are found at county or Prothonotary of issue.

Accident Reports

State Police Headquarters, Accident Records Unit, 1800 Elmerton Ave, Harrisburg, PA 17110; 717-783-5516; 8AM-5PM. Access by: mail.

Driver Records

Department of Transportation, Driver Record Services, PO Box 68695, Harrisburg, PA 17106-8695 (1101 S Front Street, Harrisburg, PA 17104); 717-391-6190, 800-932-4600 In-state only; 7:30AM-4:30PM. Access by: mail. www.dmv.state.pa.us

Vehicle Ownership
Vehicle Identification

Department of Transportation, Vehicle Record Services, PO Box 68691, Harrisburg, PA 17106-8691 (1101 South Front St, Harrisburg, PA 17104); 717-391-6190, 800-932-6000 In-state; 7:30AM-4:30PM. Access by: mail. www.dmv.state.pa.us

Boat & Vessel Ownership
Boat & Vessel Registration

Records not available from state agency.

Boat registration and ownership information is not open to the public. Liens are filed at UCC filing locations.

Legislation-Current/Pending
Legislation-Passed

Pennsylvania General Assembly, Main Capitol Bldg, Room 641, Harrisburg, PA 17120; 717-787-2342 History Room, 717-787-5320 House Bills, 717-787-6732 Senate Bills; House-8:30AM-4:30PM/Senate-8:30AM-5PM. Access by: mail, phone, in person.

Voter Registration

Records not available from state agency.

Records are kept at the county level and cannot be sold for commerical purposes.

GED Certificates

Commonwealth Diploma Program, GED Testing, 333 Market St 12th Fl, Harrisburg, PA 17126-0333; 717-787-6747; 8:30AM-4:30PM.

Fishing License Information

Fish & Boat Commission, Fishing License Division, PO Box 67000, Harrisburg, PA 17106 (3532 Walnut St, Harrisburg, PA 17106); 717-657-4518 Fishing License Division, 717-787-4250 Hunting License Division; Fax: 717-657-4549; 8AM-4PM. Access by: mail.

Hunting License Information

Records not available from state agency.

Hunting license information is not released to the public.

County Courts & Recording Offices

About the Courts...

About the Recording Offices...

Administration

Administrative Office of Pennsylvania Courts   717-795-2000
PO Box 719   Fax: 717-795-2050
Mechanicsburg, PA 17055
www.courts.aopc.org

Court Structure

The civil records clerk of the Court of Common Pleas is called the Prothonotary. Small claims cases are, usually, handled by the District Justice Courts/Magistrates. However, all small claims actions are recorded through the Prothonotary Section (civil) of the Court of Common Pleas, which then holds the records. It is not necessary to check with each District Justice Court, but rather to check with the Prothonotary for the county.

Probate is handled by the Register of Wills.

Searching Hints

Fees vary widely among jurisdictions. Many courts will not conduct searches due to a lack of personnel or, if they do search, turnaround time may be excessively lengthy. Many courts have public access terminals for in-person searches.

Online Access

Pennsylvania has an online computer system for internal access only to criminal cases, though some courts provide remote online access systems.

Organization

67 counties, 67 recording offices and 134 UCC filing offices. Each county has two different recording offices: the Prothonotary - their term for "Clerk" - accepts UCC and tax lien filings, and the Recorder of Deeds maintains real estate records. The entire state is in the Eastern Time Zone (EST).

UCC Records

This is a dual filing state. Financing statements are filed both at the state level and with the Prothonotary, except for real estate related collateral, which are filed with the Recorder of Deeds. Some county offices will not perform UCC searches. Use search request form UCC-11. Search fees are usually $57.50 per debtor name. Copies usually cost $.50-$2.00 per page. Counties also charge $5.00 per financing statement found on a search.

Lien Records

All federal and state tax liens on personal property and on real property are filed with the Prothonotary. Usually, tax liens on personal property are filed in the judgment index of the Prothonotary. Some Prothonotaries will perform tax lien searches. Search fees are usually $5.00 per name.

Real Estate Records

County Recorders of Deeds will not perform real estate searches. Copy fees and certification fees vary.

County Courts & Recording Offices

Adams

Real Estate Recording—Adams County Prothonotary, 111-117 Baltimore Street, Gettysburg, PA 17325. Fax: 717-334-0532. 8AM-4:30PM.

Adams County Recorder of Deeds, 111-117 Baltimore Street, County Courthouse Room 102, Gettysburg, PA 17325. 717-334-6781. 8AM-4:30PM.

Civil, Eviction—Court of Common Pleas-Civil, 111-117 Baltimore St Rm 104, Gettysburg, PA 17325. 717-334-6781. 8AM-4:30PM. Access by: mail, in person.

Felony, Misdemeanor—Court of Common Pleas-Criminal, 111-117 Baltimore St, Gettysburg, PA 17325. 717-334-6781. 8AM-4:30PM. Access by: mail, in person.

Probate—Register of Wills, 111-117 Baltimore St Rm 102, Gettysburg, PA 17325. 717-334-9826, Fax: 717-334-1758. 8AM-4:30PM.

Allegheny

Real Estate Recording—Allegheny County Prothonotary, 414 Grant Street, City County Building, Pittsburgh, PA 15219. 8:30AM-4:30PM.

Allegheny County Recorder of Deeds, 101 County Office Building, 542 Forbes Avenue, Pittsburgh, PA 15219. 412-355-4100, Fax: 412-350-6877. 8:30AM-4:30PM.

Civil, Eviction—Court of Common Pleas-Civil, City County Bldg, 414 Grant St, Pittsburgh, PA 15219. 412-350-4213, Fax: 412-350-5260. 8:30AM-4:30PM. Access by: mail, in person.

Felony, Misdemeanor—Court of Common Pleas-Criminal, 220 Courthouse, 436 Grant Street, Pittsburgh, PA 15219. 412-355-5378. 8:30AM-4:30PM. Access by: mail, in person.

Probate—Register of Wills, 414 Grant St, City County Bldg, PIttsburgh, PA 15219. 412-350-4180. 8:30AM-4:30PM. Access by: mail, in person. www.info.co.alleghany.pa.us.\

Armstrong

Real Estate Recording—Armstrong County Prothonotary, County Courthouse, 500 East Market Street, Kittanning, PA 16201. 8:30AM-4PM.

Armstrong County Recorder of Deeds, County Courthouse, 500 Market St. Kittanning, PA 16201. Fax: 724-548-3236. 8:30AM-4PM.

Civil, Eviction, Probate—Court of Common Pleas-Civil, 500 Market St, Kittanning, PA 16201. 724-548-3251, Fax: 724-548-3236. 8:30AM-4PM. Access by: in person.

Felony, Misdemeanor—Court of Common Pleas-Criminal, 500 Market St, Kittanning, PA 16201. 724-548-3252. 8:30AM-4PM. Access by: mail, in person.

Beaver

Real Estate Recording—Beaver County Prothonotary, Third Street, County Courthouse, Beaver, PA 15009. 8:30AM-4:30PM.

Beaver County Recorder of Deeds, 3rd Street, County Courthouse, Beaver, PA 15009. 412-728-5700, Fax: 724-728-3630. 8:30AM-4:30PM.

Civil, Eviction—Court of Common Pleas-Civil, Beaver County Courthouse, 3rd St, Beaver, PA 15009. 724-728-5700. 8:30AM-4:30PM. Access by: mail, in person.

Felony, Misdemeanor—Court of Common Pleas-Criminal, Beaver County Courthouse, 810 3rd St, Beaver, PA 15009. 724-728-5700, Fax: 724-728-8853. 8:30AM-4:30PM. Access by: mail, fax, in person.

Probate—Register of Wills, Beaver County Courthouse, 3rd St, Beaver, PA 15009. 724-728-5700, Fax: 724-728-9810. 8:30AM-4:30PM. Access by: mail, in person. Special note: Records are computerized since 1995, on books since 1800.

Bedford

Real Estate Recording—Bedford County Prothonotary, County Courthouse, Corner of Penn & Julliana, Bedford, PA 15522. 8:30AM-4:30PM.

Bedford County Recorder of Deeds, 200 South Juliana Street, County Courthouse, Bedford, PA 15522. 814-623-4846, Fax: 814-624-0488. 8:30AM-4:30PM.

Felony, Misdemeanor, Civil, Eviction—Court of Common Pleas-Criminal/Civil, Bedford County Courthouse, Bedford, PA 15522. 814-623-4833, Fax: 814-622-0991. 8:30AM-4:30PM. Access by: mail, in person.

Probate—Register of Wills, 200 S Juliana St, Bedford, PA 15522. 814-623-4836, Fax: 814-624-0488. 8:30AM-4:30PM.

Berks

Real Estate Recording—Berks County Prothonotary, 633 Court St. Reading, PA 19601. Fax: 610-478-6969. 8AM-4PM.

Berks County Recorder of Deeds, 633 Court St. 3rd Floor, Reading, PA 19601. 610-478-6645, Fax: 610-478-3359. 8AM-5PM.

Civil, Eviction—Court of Common Pleas-Civil, 2nd Floor, 633 Court St, Reading, PA 19601. 610-478-6970, Fax: 610-478-6969. 8AM-4PM. Access by: mail, fax, in person.

Felony, Misdemeanor—Court of Common Pleas-Criminal, 4th Floor, 633 Court St, Reading, PA 19601. 610-478-6550, Fax: 610-478-6570. 8AM-5PM. Access by: in person.

Probate—Register of Wills, 633 Court St 2nd Floor, Reading, PA 19601. 610-478-6600, Fax: 610-478-6251. 8AM-5PM. Access by: mail, in person. www.berksreqofwills.com

Blair

Real Estate Recording—Blair County Prothonotary, 423 Allegheny Street, Hollidaysburg, PA 16648. 8AM-4:30PM.

Blair County Recorder of Deeds, 423 Allegheny St. Suite 145, Hollidaysburg, PA 16648. 8AM-4PM.

Felony, Misdemeanor, Civil, Eviction—Court of Common Pleas-Criminal/Civil, 412 Allegheny Street, Hollidaysburg, PA 16648. 814-693-3080. 8AM-4:30PM. Access by: mail, in person.

Probate—Register of Wills, 423 Allegheny #145, Hollidaysburg, pa 16648-2022. 814-693-3095. 8AM-4PM.

Bradford

Real Estate Recording—Bradford County Prothonotary, Courthouse, 301 Main St. Towanda, PA 18848. 9AM-5PM.

Bradford County Recorder of Deeds, 301 Main Street, Courthouse, Towanda, PA 18848. 717-265-1700, Fax: 570-265-1721. 9AM-5PM.

Felony, Misdemeanor, Civil, Eviction—Court of Common Pleas-Criminal/Civil, Courthouse, 301 Main St, Towanda, PA 18848. 717-265-1705. 9AM-5PM. Access by: mail, in person.

Probate—Register of Wills, 301 Main St. Towanda, PA 18848. 717-265-1702. 9AM-5PM. Access by: mail, in person.

Bucks

Real Estate Recording—Bucks County Prothonotary, 55 East Court St. Courthouse, Doylestown, PA 18901. 8:15AM-4:15PM.

Bucks County Recorder of Deeds, Courthouse, 55 E. Court St. Doylestown, PA 18901. 216-291-4901. 8:15AM-4:15PM (Recording Hours 8:15AM-4PM).

Civil, Eviction—Court of Common Pleas-Civil, 55 E Court St, Doylestown, PA 18901. 570-348-6191. 8:15AM-4:15PM. Access by: in person.

Felony, Misdemeanor—Court of Common Pleas-Criminal, Bucks County Courthouse, Doylestown, PA 18901. 570-348-6389, Fax: 570-348-6379. 8AM-4:30PM. Access by: mail, in person, online.

Probate—Register of Wills, Bucks County Courthouse, Doylestown, PA 18901. 216-350-2631, Fax: 215-348-6156.

8:15AM-4:15PM M-F; 8:15AM-7:30PM 1st & 3rd Wed of month. Access by: mail, in person.

Butler

Real Estate Recording—Butler County Prothonotary, 300 S. Main Street, Courthouse, Butler, PA 16001. 8:30AM-4:30PM.

Butler County Recorder of Deeds, 124 West Diamond St. County Government Bldg. Butler, PA 16001. 412-284-5149, Fax: 724-285-9099. 8:30AM-4:30PM.

Civil, Eviction—Court of Common Pleas-Civil, Butler County Courthouse, PO Box 1208, Butler, PA 16001-1208. 724-284-5214. 8:30AM-4:30PM. Access by: in person.

Felony, Misdemeanor—Court of Common Pleas-Criminal, Butler County Courthouse, PO Box 1208, Butler, PA 16003-1208. 724-284-5233, Fax: 724-284-5244. 8:30AM-4:30PM. Access by: mail, in person, online.

Probate—Register of Wills, Butler County Courthouse, PO Box 1208, Butler, PA 16003-1208. 724-284-5348, Fax: 724-284-5278. 8:30AM-4:30PM. Access by: mail, in person.

Cambria

Real Estate Recording—Cambria County Prothonotary, 200 S. Center St. Ebensburg, PA 15931. Fax: 814-472-5632. 9AM-4PM.

Cambria County Recorder of Deeds, Cambria County Courthouse, 200 S. Center St. Ebensburg, PA 15931. 814-472-5440, Fax: 814-472-1412. 9AM-4PM.

Civil, Eviction—Court of Common Pleas-Civil, 200 S Center St, Ebensburg, PA 15931. 814-472-1636, Fax: 814-472-2353. 9AM-4PM. Access by: mail, in person.

Felony, Misdemeanor—Court of Common Pleas-Criminal, Cambria County Courthouse S Center St, Ebensburg, PA 15931. 814-472-1543. 9AM-4PM. Access by: mail, in person.

Probate—Register of Wills, 200 S Center St, Ebensburg, PA 15931. 814-472-5440. 9AM-4PM.

Cameron

Real Estate Recording—Cameron County Prothonotary, 20 E. 5th Street, Emporium, PA 15834. Fax: 814-486-0464. 8:30AM-4PM.

Cameron County Recorder of Deeds, 20 E. 5th Street, Emporium, PA 15834. 814-486-3348, Fax: 814-486-0464. 8:30AM-4PM.

Civil, Eviction—Court of Common Pleas-Civil, Cameron County Courthouse, East 5th St, Emporium, PA 15834. 814-486-3355, Fax: 814-468-0464. 8:30AM-4:30PM. Access by: mail, phone, fax, in person.

Felony, Misdemeanor—Court of Common Pleas-Criminal, 20 East 5th St, Emporium, PA 15834. 814-486-3349, Fax: 814-486-0464. 8:30AM-4PM. Access by: mail, phone, fax, in person.

Probate—Register of Wills, Cameron County Courthouse, East 5th St. Emporium, PA 15834. 814-486-3355, Fax: 814-486-0464. 8:30AM-4PM. Access by: in person.

Carbon

Real Estate Recording—Carbon County Prothonotary, 2 Broadway, County Courthouse, Jim Thorpe, PA 18229. Fax: 570-325-8047. 8:30AM-4:30PM.

Carbon County Recorder of Deeds, Courthouse Annexe, Rte. 209 & Hazard Square, Jim Thorpe, PA 18229. 717-325-2251. 8:30AM-4:30PM.

Civil, Eviction—Court of Common Pleas-Civil, PO Box 127, Courthouse, Jim Thorpe, PA 18229. 570-325-2481, Fax: 570-325-8047. 8:30AM-4:30PM. Access by: in person. www.aopc.org/counties/carbon

Felony, Misdemeanor—Court of Common Pleas-Criminal, County Courthouse, Jim Thorpe, PA 18229. 570-325-3637, Fax: 570-325-3525. 8:30AM-4PM. Access by: mail, phone, in person.

Probate—Register of Wills, PO Box 286, Jim Thorpe, PA 18229. 570-325-2261, Fax: 570-325-5098. 8:30AM-4:30PM.

Centre

Real Estate Recording—Centre County Prothonotary, Allegheny & High, County Courthouse, Bellefonte, PA 16823. 8:30AM-5PM.

Centre County Recorder of Deeds, 414 Holmes Ave. #1, Bellefonte, PA 16823. 814-355-6810, Fax: 814-355-8680. 8:30AM-5PM.

Felony, Misdemeanor, Civil, Eviction—Court of Common Pleas-Criminal/Civil, Centre County Courthouse, Bellefonte, PA 16823. 814-355-6796. 8:30AM-5PM. Access by: mail, phone, in person. http://countrystore.org/webpages/county/223.htm

Probate—Register of Wills, Willowbank Office Bldg, 414 Holmes Ave #2, Bellefonte, PA 16823. 814-355-6724. 8:30AM-5PM. www.countrystore.org/county/224.htm

Chester

Real Estate Recording—Chester County Prothonotary, 2 North High Street, Suite 130, County Courthouse, West Chester, PA 19380. Fax: 610-344-5903. 8:30AM-4:30PM.

Chester County Recorder of Deeds, Suite 100, 235 West Market St. West Chester, PA 19382. 610-344-6370, Fax: 610-344-6408. 8:30AM-4:30PM.

Civil, Eviction—Court of Common Pleas-Civil, 2 North High St, Ste 130, West Chester, PA 19380. 610-344-6300. 8:30AM-4:30PM. Access by: in person.

Felony, Misdemeanor—Court of Common Pleas-Criminal, 2 North High St #160, West Chester, PA 19380. 610-344-6135. 8:30AM-4:30PM. Access by: mail, in person, online.

Probate—Register of Wills, 2 North High St, Suite 109, West Chester, PA 19380-3073. 610-344-6335, Fax: 610-344-6218. 8:30AM-4:30PM. Access by: mail, in person.

Clarion

Real Estate Recording—Clarion County Prothonotary, Main Street, Courthouse, Clarion, PA 16214. Fax: 814-226-8069. 8:30AM-4:30PM.

Clarion County Recorder of Deeds, Courthouse, Corner of 5th Ave. & Main St. Clarion, PA 16214. 814-226-4000, Fax: 814-226-8069. 8:30AM-4:30PM.

Civil, Eviction—Court of Common Pleas-Civil, Clarion County Courthouse, Main St, Clarion, PA 16214. 814-226-1119, Fax: 814-226-8069. 8:30AM-4:30PM. Access by: mail, phone, fax, in person.

Felony, Misdemeanor—Court of Common Pleas-Criminal, Clarion County Courthouse, Main St, Clarion, PA 16214. 814-226-4000, Fax: 814-226-8069. 8AM-4:30PM. Access by: mail, phone, fax, in person.

Probate—Register of Wills, Clarion County Courthouse, Corner of 5th & Main, Clarion, PA 16214. 814-226-4000, Fax: 814-226-8069. 8:30AM-4:30PM. Access by: mail, in person.

Clearfield

Real Estate Recording—Clearfield County Prothonotary, Corner of 2nd & Market Streets, Clearfield, PA 16830. Fax: 814-765-6089. 8:30AM-4PM.

Clearfield County Recorder of Deeds, Corner of 2nd & Market Streets, Clearfield, PA 16830. 814-765-2641, Fax: 814-765-6089. 8:30AM-4PM.

Felony, Misdemeanor, Civil, Eviction—Court of Common Pleas-Criminal/Civil, 1 N 2nd St, Clearfield, PA 16830. 814-765-2641, Fax: 814-765-6089. 8:30AM-4PM. Access by: mail, in person.

Probate—Register of Wills & Clerk of Orphans Court, PO Box 361, Clearfield, PA 16830. 814-765-2641, Fax: 814-765-6089. 8:30AM-4PM. Access by: mail, in person.

Clinton

Real Estate Recording—Clinton County Prothonotary, 230 E. Water St. Courthouse, Lock Haven, PA 17745. 8AM-5PM M,T,Th,F; 8AM-12:30PM W.

Clinton County Recorder of Deeds, Corner of Water & Jay Streets, Courthouse, Lock Haven, PA 17745. 717-893-4004. 8:30AM-5PM.

Felony, Misdemeanor, Civil, Eviction—Court of Common Pleas-Criminal/Civil, 230 E Water St, Lock Haven, PA 17745. 570-893-4007. 8:30AM-5PM. Access by: in person.

Probate—Register of Wills, PO Box 943, Lock Haven, PA 17745. 570-893-4010. 8:30AM-5PM. Access by: in person.

Columbia

Real Estate Recording—Columbia County Prothonotary, 35 W. Main St. Courthouse, Bloomsburg, PA 17815. 8AM-4:30PM.

Columbia County Recorder of Deeds, 35 West Main Street, Court House, Bloomsburg, PA 17815. Fax: 570-389-5636. 8AM-4:30PM.

Felony, Misdemeanor, Civil, Eviction—Court of Common Pleas-Criminal/Civil, PO Box 380, Bloomsburg, PA 17815. 570-389-5600. 8AM-4:30PM. Access by: mail, phone, in person.

Probate—Court of Common Pleas, Columbia County Courthouse, PO Box 380, Bloomsburg, PA 17815. 570-389-5632, Fax: 570-784-0257. 8AM-4:30PM. Access by: mail, in person.

Crawford

Real Estate Recording—Crawford County Prothonotary, 903 Diamond Park, County Courthouse, Meadville, PA 16335. Fax: 814-337-5416. 8:30AM-4:30PM.

Crawford County Recorder of Deeds, Courthouse, 903 Diamond Park, Meadville, PA 16335. 814-333-1151, Fax: 814-337-5296. 8:30AM-4:30PM.

Civil, Eviction—Court of Common Pleas-Civil, Crawford County Courthouse, Meadville, PA 16335. 814-333-7324. 8:30AM-4:30PM. Access by: mail, in person.

Felony, Misdemeanor—Court of Common Pleas-Criminal, Crawford County Courthouse, Meadville, PA 16335. 814-336-1151, Fax: 814-337-7349. 8:30AM-4:30PM. Access by: mail, in person.

Probate—Register of Wills, 903 Diamond Park, Meadville, PA 16335. 814-336-1151. 8:30AM-4:30PM.

Cumberland

Real Estate Recording—Cumberland County Prothonotary, 1 Courthouse Square, County Courthouse, Carlisle, PA 17013. 8AM-4:30PM.

Cumberland County Recorder of Deeds, County Courthouse, 1 Courthouse Square, Carlisle, PA 17013. 717-240-6380, Fax: 717-240-6490. 8AM-4:30PM.

Civil, Eviction—Court of Common Pleas-Civil, Cumberland County Courthouse, Rm 100, One Courthouse Square, Carlisle, PA 17013-3387. 717-240-6195, Fax: 717-240-6573. 8AM-4:30PM. Access by: in person.

Felony, Misdemeanor—Court of Common Pleas-Criminal, Cumberland County Courthouse, East Wing, 1 Courthouse Sq, Carlisle, PA 17013-3387. 717-240-6250, Fax: 717-240-6571. 8AM-4:30PM. Access by: mail, in person.

Probate—Register of Wills, Cumberland County Courthouse, Rm 102, 1 Courthouse Sq, Carlisle, PA 17013. 717-240-6345, Fax: 717-240-6490. 8AM-4:30PM. Access by: mail, in person.

Dauphin

Real Estate Recording—Dauphin County Prothonotary, Front & Market Streets, Courthouse - Room 101, Harrisburg, PA 17101. 8:30AM-5.

Dauphin County Recorder of Deeds, Front & Market Streets, Courthouse, Harrisburg, PA 17101. 717-255-2676, Fax: 717-257-1521. 8:30AM-5PM.

Civil, Eviction—Court of Common Pleas-Civil, PO Box 945, Harrisburg, PA 17108. 717-255-2698. 8:30AM-5PM. Access by: mail, in person.

Felony, Misdemeanor—Court of Common Pleas-Criminal, Front & Market St, Harrisburg, PA 17101. 717-255-2692, Fax: 717-255-2694. 8:30AM-5PM. Access by: mail, in person.

Probate—Register of Wills, PO Box 1295, Harrisburg, PA 17101. 717-255-2656, Fax: 717-255-2749. 8:30AM-5PM. Access by: in person. www.dauphinc.org

Delaware

Real Estate Recording—Delaware County Office of Judicial Support, Delaware County Government Center Bldg. 201 West Front St. Room 127, Media, PA 19063. 8:30AM-4:30PM.

Delaware County Recorder of Deeds, 201 W. Front Street, Room 107, Government Center Building, Media, PA 19063. 610-891-4272. 8:30AM-4:30PM.

Felony, Misdemeanor, Civil, Eviction—Court of Common Pleas-Criminal/Civil, 201 W Front St, Media, PA 19063. 610-891-5399. 8:30AM-4:30PM. Access by: mail, in person.

Probate—Register of Wills, Delaware County Courthouse, 201 W Front St, Media, PA 19063. 610-891-4400, Fax: 610-891-4812. 8:30AM-4:30PM. Access by: in person. www.co.delaware.pa.us

Elk

Real Estate Recording—Elk County Prothonotary, Main Street, Courthouse, Ridgway, PA 15853. Fax: 814-776-5379. 8:30AM-4PM.

Elk County Recorder of Deeds, Main Street & Court Street, Courthouse, Ridgway, PA 15853. Fax: 814-776-5379. 8:30AM-4PM.

Felony, Misdemeanor, Civil, Eviction—Court of Common Pleas-Criminal/Civil, PO Box 237, Ridgway, PA 15853. 814-776-5344, Fax: 814-776-5379. 8:30AM-4PM. Access by: mail, phone, in person.

Probate—Register of Wills, PO Box 314, Ridgway, PA 15853. 814-776-5349, Fax: 814-776-5379. 8:30AM-4PM. Access by: mail, in person.

Erie

Real Estate Recording—Erie County Prothonotary, 140 West 6th Street, Room 120, Erie, PA 16501. 8:30AM-4:30PM.

Erie County Recorder of Deeds, 140 West 6th Street, Erie, PA 16501. 814-451-6080, Fax: 814-451-6213. 8:30AM-4:30PM.

Civil, Eviction—Court of Common Pleas-Civil, Erie County Courthouse, 140 West 6th St. Erie, PA 16501. 814-451-6076. 8:30AM-4:30PM. Access by: mail, in person. www.eriecountygov.org/cor

Felony, Misdemeanor—Court of Common Pleas-Criminal, Erie County Courthouse, 140 West 6th St, Erie, PA 16501. 814-451-6229, Fax: 814-451-6420. 8:30AM-4:30PM. Access by: mail, phone, in person.

Probate—Register of Wills, Erie County Courthouse 140 W 6th St. Erie, PA 16501. 814-451-6260. 8:30AM-4:30PM. Access by: mail.

Fayette

Real Estate Recording—Fayette County Prothonotary, 61 East Main Street, Courthouse, Uniontown, PA 15401. 8AM-4:30PM.

Fayette County Recorder of Deeds, 61 East Main Street, Courthouse, Uniontown, PA 15401. 412-430-1256, Fax: 724-430-1238. 8AM-4:30PM.

Civil, Eviction—Court of Common Pleas-Civil, 61 East Main St, Uniontown, PA 15401. 724-430-1272, Fax: 724-430-1265. 8AM-4:30PM. Access by: mail, in person.

Felony, Misdemeanor—Court of Common Pleas-Criminal, 61 East Main St, Uniontown, PA 15401. 724-430-1253, Fax: 724-438-8410. 8AM-4:30PM. Access by: mail, fax, in person.

Probate—Register of Wills, 61 East Main St, Uniontown, PA 15401. 724-430-1206. 8AM-4:30PM.

Forest

Real Estate Recording—Forest County Prothonotary, 526 Elm Street, Courthouse P.O. Box 423, Tionesta, PA 16353. Fax: 814-755-8837. 9AM-4PM.

Forest County Recorder of Deeds, 526 Elm Street, Courthouse P.O. Box 423, Tionesta, PA 16353. 814-755-3536, Fax: 814-755-8837. 9AM-4PM.

Felony, Misdemeanor, Civil, Eviction, Probate—Court of Common Pleas-Criminal/Civil, Forest County Courthouse, PO Box 423, Tionesta, PA 16353. 814-755-3526, Fax: 814-755-8837. 9AM-4PM. Access by: mail, in person.

Franklin

Real Estate Recording—Franklin County Prothonotary, 157 Lincoln Way East, County Court House, Chambersburg, PA 17201. Fax: 717-264-6772. 8:30AM-4:30PM.

Franklin County Recorder of Deeds, 157 Lincoln Way East, Chambersburg, PA 17201. 717-261-3120, Fax: 717-267-3438. 8:30AM-4:30PM.

Civil, Eviction—Court of Common Pleas-Civil, 157 Lincoln Way East, Chambersburg, PA 17201. 717-261-3858, Fax: 717-267-3438. 8:30AM-4:30PM. Access by: in person.

Felony, Misdemeanor—Court of Common Pleas-Criminal, 157 Lincoln Way East, Chambersburg, PA 17201. 717-261-3805, Fax: 717-261-3896. 8:30AM-4:30PM. Access by: mail, in person.

Probate—Register of Wills, 157 Lincoln Way East, Chambersburg, PA 17201. 717-261-3872, Fax: 717-267-3438. 8:30AM-4:30PM.

Fulton

Real Estate Recording—Fulton County Prothonotary, 201 North Second Street, Fulton County Courthouse, McConnellsburg, PA 17233. 8:30AM-4:30PM.

Fulton County Recorder of Deeds, 201 North Second Street, Fulton County Courthouse, McConnellsburg, PA 17233. 717-485-4454. 8:30AM-4:30PM.

Felony, Misdemeanor, Civil, Eviction—Court of Common Pleas-Criminal/Civil, Fulton County Courthouse, 201 N 2nd St, McConnellsburg, PA 17233. 717-485-4212, Fax: 717-485-5568. 8:30AM-4:30PM. Access by: mail, fax, in person.

Greene

Real Estate Recording—Greene County Prothonotary, 10 East High St. Room 105, Waynesburg, PA 15370. 8:30AM-4:30PM.

Greene County Recorder of Deeds, Courthouse, Waynesburg, PA 15370. 412-852-5225. 8:30AM-4:30PM.

Civil, Eviction—Court of Common Pleas, Fort Jackson County Bldg, Waynesburg, PA 15370. 724-852-5289. 8:30AM-4:30PM. Access by: mail, in person.

Felony, Misdemeanor—Court of Common Pleas-Criminal, Greene County Courthouse, Waynesburg, PA 15370. 724-852-5281, Fax: 724-627-4716. 8:30AM-4:30PM. Access by: mail, fax, in person.

Probate—Register of Wills, Greene County Courthouse, 10 E High St, Waynesburg, PA 15370. 724-852-5283. 8:30AM-4PM.

Huntingdon

Real Estate Recording—Huntingdon County Prothonotary, 223 Penn Street, Courthouse, Huntingdon, PA 16652. Fax: 814-643-4271. 8:30AM-4:30PM.

Huntingdon County Recorder of Deeds, 223 Penn Street, Courthouse, Huntingdon, PA 16652. 814-643-3523. 8:30AM-4:30PM.

Felony, Misdemeanor, Civil, Eviction—Court of Common Pleas-Criminal/Civil, PO Box 39, Courthouse, Huntingdon, PA 16652. 814-643-1610, Fax: 814-643-4172. 8:30AM-4:30PM. Access by: mail, phone, in person.

Probate—Register of Wills, Courthouse, 223 Penn St, Huntingdon, PA 16652. 814-643-2740. 8:30AM-4:30PM. Access by: in person.

Indiana

Real Estate Recording—Indiana County Prothonotary, 825 Philadelphia Street, Courthouse, 1st Floor, Indiana, PA 15701. Fax: 724-465-3868. 8AM-4:30PM.

Indiana County Recorder of Deeds, 825 Philadelphia Street, Courthouse, Indiana, PA 15701. 412-465-3845, Fax: 724-465-3863. 8AM-4:30PM.

Felony, Misdemeanor, Civil, Eviction—Court of Common Pleas-Criminal/Civil, County Courthouse, 825 Philadelphia St, Indiana, PA 15701. 724-465-3855, Fax: 724-465-3968. 8AM-4:30PM. Access by: mail, fax, in person.

Probate—Register of Wills, County Courthouse, 825 Philadelphia St, Indiana, PA 15701. 724-465-3860, Fax: 724-465-3863. 8AM-4:30PM. Access by: mail, in person.

Jefferson

Real Estate Recording—Jefferson County Prothonotary, 200 Main Street, Court House, Room 102, Brookville, PA 15825. 8:30AM-4:30PM.

Jefferson County Recorder of Deeds, 200 Main Street, Courthouse, Brookville, PA 15825. 814-849-1609, Fax: 814-849-1612. 8:30AM-4:30PM.

Felony, Misdemeanor, Civil, Eviction—Court of Common Pleas-Criminal/Civil, Courthouse, 200 Main St, Brookville, PA 15825. 814-849-1606, Fax: 814-849-1607. 8:30AM-4:30PM. Access by: mail, in person.

Probate—Register of Wills, Jefferson County Courthouse, 200 Main St, Brookville, PA 15825. 814-849-1610, Fax: 814-849-1612. 8:30AM-4:30PM.

Juniata

Real Estate Recording—Juniata County Prothonotary, Courthouse, Mifflintown, PA 17059. Fax: 717-436-7734. 8AM-4:30PM.

Juniata County Recorder of Deeds, Courthouse, Mifflintown, PA 17059. 717-436-8991, Fax: 717-436-7756. 8AM-4:30PM.

Felony, Misdemeanor, Civil, Eviction—Court of Common Pleas-Criminal/Civil, Juniata County Courthouse, Mifflintown, PA 17059. 717-436-7715, Fax: 717-436-7734. 8AM-4:30PM. Access by: mail, phone, in person.

Probate—Register of Wills, Juniata County Courthouse, PO Box 68, Mifflintown, PA 17059. 717-436-7709, Fax: 717-436-7756. 8AM-4:30PM M-F, 8AM-12PM Wed (June-Sept).

Lackawanna

Real Estate Recording—Lackawanna County Clerk of Judicial Records, 200 North Washington, Courthouse, Scranton, PA 18503. 9AM-4:00PM.

Lackawanna County Recorder of Deeds, 200 North Washington, Courthouse, Scranton, PA 18503. 570-963-6731. 9AM-4PM.

Civil, Eviction—Court of Common Pleas-Civil, Clerk of Judicial Records, PO Box 133, Scranton, PA 18503. 570-963-6724. 9AM-4PM. Access by: in person.

Felony, Misdemeanor—Court of Common Pleas-Criminal, Lackawanna County Courthouse, Scranton, PA 18503. 570-963-6759, Fax: 570-963-6459. 9AM-4PM. Access by: mail, in person.

Probate—Register of Wills, Registrar of Wills, County Courthouse, 200 N Washington Ave, Scranton, PA 18503. 570-963-6708, Fax: 570-963-6377. 9AM-4PM.

Lancaster

Real Estate Recording—Lancaster County Prothonotary, 50 North Duke Street, Lancaster, PA 17602. Fax: 717-293-7210. 8:30AM-5PM.

Lancaster County Recorder of Deeds, 50 North Duke Street, Lancaster, PA 17602. 717-299-8222. 8:30AM-4:30PM (for recording); 8:30AM-5PM (for the public).

Civil, Eviction—Court of Common Pleas-Civil, 50 N Duke St, PO Box 83480, Lancaster, PA 17608-3480. 717-299-8282, Fax: 717-293-7210. 8:30AM-5PM. Access by: mail, phone, fax, in person. www.co.lancaster.pa.us

Felony, Misdemeanor—Court of Common Pleas-Criminal, 50 North Duke St, Lancaster, PA 17602. 717-299-8275. 8:30AM-5PM. Access by: mail, in person.

Probate—Register of Wills, 50 N. Duke St. Lancaster, PA 17602. 717-299-8243, Fax: 717-295-3522. 8:30AM-5PM. www.co.lancaster.pa.us/wills.htm

Lawrence

Real Estate Recording—Lawrence County Prothonotary, 430 Court Street, Government Center, New Castle, PA 16101. Fax: 724-656-1988. 8AM-4PM.

Lawrence County Recorder of Deeds, 430 Court Street, Government Center, New Castle, PA 16101. 412-656-2183, Fax: 412-656-1966. 8AM-4PM.

Felony, Misdemeanor, Civil, Eviction—Court of Common Pleas-Criminal/Civil, 430 Court St, New Castle, PA 16101-3593. 724-656-2143, Fax: 724-656-1988. 8AM-4PM. Access by: mail, fax, in person.

Probate—, 430 Court St, New Castle, PA 16101-3593. 724-656-2128, Fax: 724-656-1966. 8AM-4PM.

Lebanon

Real Estate Recording—Lebanon County Prothonotary, 400 South 8th Street, Lebanon, PA 17042. 8:30AM-4:30PM.

Lebanon County Recorder of Deeds, 400 South 8th Street, Room 107, Lebanon, PA 17042. 717-274-2801. Recording Hours 8:30AM-4PM.

Civil, Eviction—Court of Common Pleas-Civil, Municipal Bldg, Rm 104, 400 S 8th St, Lebanon, PA 17042. 717-274-2801. 8:30AM-4:30PM. Access by: in person.

Felony, Misdemeanor—Court of Common Pleas-Criminal, Municipal Bldg, Rm 106, 400 S 8th St, Lebanon, PA 17042. 717-274-2801. 8:30AM-4:30PM. Access by: mail, phone, in person.

Probate—Register of Wills, Municipal Bldg, Rm 105, 400 S 8th St, Lebanon, PA 17042. 717-274-2801, Fax: 717-274-8094. 8:30AM-4:30PM. Access by: mail, in person.

Lehigh

Real Estate Recording—Lehigh County Clerk of Courts-Civil Division, 455 W. Hamilton St. Allentown, PA 18101. 8:30AM-4:30PM.

Lehigh County Recorder of Deeds, 455 W. Hamilton Street, Allentown, PA 18101. 610-820-3113, Fax: 610-820-2039. 8AM-4PM.

Civil, Eviction—Court of Common Pleas-Civil Division, 455 W Hamilton St, Allentown, PA 18101-1614. 610-782-3148, Fax: 610-770-3840. 8:30AM-4:30PM. Access by: mail, in person.

Felony, Misdemeanor—Court of Common Pleas-Criminal, 455 W Hamilton St, Allentown, PA 18101. 610-782-3077, Fax: 610-770-6797. 8:30AM-4:30PM. Access by: mail, fax, in person, online.

Probate—Register of Wills, 455 W Hamilton, Allentown, PA 18101-1614. 610-820-3170, Fax: 610-820-3439. 8AM-4PM. Access by: mail, in person.

Luzerne

Real Estate Recording—Luzerne County Prothonotary, 200 North River Street, County Court House, Wilkes-Barre, PA 18711. Fax: 570-825-1757. 9AM-4:30PM.

Luzerne County Recorder of Deeds, 200 North River Street, Courthouse, Wilkes-Barre, PA 18711. 570-825-1786. 9AM-4:30PM.

Civil, Eviction—Court of Common Pleas-Civil, 200 N River St, Wilkes Barre, PA 18711-1001. 570-825-1745, Fax: 570-825-1757. 9AM-4:30PM. Access by: mail, phone, in person.

Felony, Misdemeanor—Court of Common Pleas-Criminal, 200 N River St, Wilkes Barre, PA 18711. 570-825-1585, Fax: 570-825-1843. 8AM-4:30PM. Access by: mail, phone, fax, in person.

Probate—Register of Wills, 200 N River St, Wilkes Barre, PA 18711. 570-825-1672. 9AM-4:30PM. Access by: mail, in person.

Lycoming

Real Estate Recording—Lycoming County Prothonotary, 48 West Third Street, Williamsport, PA 17701. 8:30AM-5PM.

Lycoming County Recorder of Deeds, 48 West Third Street, Williamsport, PA 17701. 570-327-2249, Fax: 570-327-2511. 8:30AM-5PM.

Felony, Misdemeanor, Civil, Eviction—Court of Common Pleas-Criminal/Civil, 48 W 3rd St, Williamsport, PA 17701. 570-327-2251. 8:30AM-5PM. Access by: mail, in person.

Probate—Register of Wills, Lycoming Co Courthouse, 48 W 3rd St, Williamsport, PA 17701. 717-327-2258. 8:30AM-5PM.

McKean

Real Estate Recording—McKean County Prothonotary, Courthouse, 500 Main Street, Smethport, PA 16749. Fax: 814-887-3219. 8:30AM-4:30PM.

McKean County Recorder of Deeds, 500 W. Main St. Smethport, PA 16749. 814-887-5571, Fax: 814-887-7766. 8:30AM-4:30PM.

Felony, Misdemeanor, Civil, Eviction—Court of Common Pleas-Criminal and Civil, PO Box 273, Smethport, PA 16749. 814-887-3270, Fax: 814-887-3219. 8:30AM-4:30PM. Access by: mail, phone, fax, in person.

Probate—Register of Wills, PO Box 202, Smethport, PA 16749-0202. 814-887-3260, Fax: 814-887-2712. 8:30AM-4:30PM. Access by: mail, in person.

Mercer

Real Estate Recording—Mercer County Prothonotary, 105 North Diamond Street, County Courthouse, Mercer, PA 16137.

Mercer County Recorder of Deeds, North Diamond Street, Courthouse Room 109, Mercer, PA 16137. 412-662-3800, Fax: 412-662-2096. 8:30AM-4:30PM.

Civil, Eviction—Court of Common Pleas-Civil, 105 Mercer County Courthouse, Mercer, PA 16137. 724-662-3800. 8:30AM-4:30PM. Access by: mail, in person.

Felony, Misdemeanor—Court of Common Pleas-Criminal, 112 Mercer County Courthouse, Mercer, PA 16137. 724-662-3800. 8:30AM-4:30PM. Access by: mail, in person.

Probate—Register of Wills, 112 Mercer County Courthouse, Mercer, PA 16137. 724-662-3800, Fax: 724-662-1530. 8:30AM-4:30PM. Access by: in person.

Mifflin

Real Estate Recording—Mifflin County Prothonotary, 20 North Wayne Street, Lewistown, PA 17044. Fax: 717-248-5275. 8AM-4:30PM.

Mifflin County Recorder of Deeds, 20 North Wayne Street, Lewistown, PA 17044. 717-248-8439, Fax: 717-248-3695. 8AM-4:30PM.

Felony, Misdemeanor, Civil, Eviction—Court of Common Pleas-Criminal and Civil, 20 N Wayne St, Lewistown, PA 17044. 717-248-8146, Fax: 717-248-5275. 8AM-4:30PM. Access by: in person.

Probate—Register of Wills, 20 N. Wayne St. Lewistown, PA 17044. 717-242-1449. 8AM-4:30PM M-F.

Monroe

Real Estate Recording—Monroe County Prothonotary, N. 7th & Monroe Street, Courthouse, Room 303, Stroudsburg, PA 18360. 8:30AM-4:30PM.

Monroe County Recorder of Deeds, 7th & Monroe Street, Courthouse, Stroudsburg, PA 18360. 570-420-3510, Fax: 570-420-3537. 8:30AM-4:30PM.

Civil, Eviction—Court of Common Pleas-Civil, Monroe County Courthouse, Stroudsburg, PA 18360. 570-420-3570. 8:30AM-4:30PM. Access by: mail, in person.

Felony, Misdemeanor—Court of Common Pleas-Criminal, Monroe County Courthouse Rm 312, Stroudsburg, PA 18360-2190. 570-420-3710. 8:30AM-4:30PM. Access by: mail, in person.

Probate—Register of Wills, Monroe County Courthouse, Stroudsburg, PA 18360. 570-420-3540, Fax: 570-420-3537. 8:30AM-4:30PM.

Montgomery

Real Estate Recording—Montgomery County Prothonotary, Swede & Airy Streets, Courthouse, Room 100, Norristown, PA 19404. Fax: 610-278-5994. 8:30AM-4:15PM.

Montgomery County Recorder of Deeds, One Montgomery Plaza, Suite 303, Swede & Airy Sts. Norristown, PA 19404. 610-278-3066, Fax: 610-278-3869. 8:30AM-4:15PM.

Civil, Eviction—Court of Common Pleas-Civil, PO Box 311, Airy & Swede St, Norristown, PA 19404-0311. 610-278-3360. 8:30AM-4:15PM. Access by: mail, in person.

Felony, Misdemeanor—Court of Common Pleas-Criminal, PO Box 311, Airy & Swede St, Norristown, PA 19404-0311. 610-278-3346, Fax: 610-278-5188. 8:30AM-4:15PM. Access by: mail, in person, online. www.montcopa.org

Probate—Montgomery County Register in Wills, Clerk of Orphan's Court, Airy & Swede St, PO Box 311, Norristown, PA 19404. 610-278-3400, Fax: 610-278-3240. 8:30AM-4:15PM. Access by: mail, in person. www.montcopa.org/

Montour

Real Estate Recording—Montour County Prothonotary, 29 Mill Street, Courthouse, Danville, PA 17821. Fax: 570-271-3088. 9AM-4PM.

Montour County Recorder of Deeds, 29 Mill Street, Courthouse, Danville, PA 17821. 570-271-3016, Fax: 570-271-3071. 9AM-4PM.

Felony, Misdemeanor, Civil, Eviction—Court of Common Pleas-Criminal and Civil, Montour County Courthouse, 29 Mill St, Danville, PA 17821. 570-271-3010, Fax: 570-271-3088. 9AM-4PM. Access by: mail, phone, fax, in person.

Probate—Register of Wills, 29 Mill St, Danville, PA 17821. 570-271-3012, Fax: 570-271-3071. 9AM-4PM. Access by: mail, in person.

Northampton

Real Estate Recording—Northampton County Prothonotary, 669 Washington St. 2nd Floor, Room 207, Easton, PA 18042. 8:30AM-4:30PM.

Northampton County Recorder of Deeds, 669 Washington Streets, Government Center, Easton, PA 18042. Fax: 610-559-3103. 8:30AM-4:30PM.

Civil, Eviction—Court of Common Pleas-Civil, Gov't Center, 669 Washington St Rm 207, Easton, PA 18042-7498. 610-559-3060. 8:30AM-4:30PM. Access by: in person.

Felony, Misdemeanor—Court of Common Pleas-Criminal, 669 Washington St, Easton, PA 18042-7494. 610-559-3000, Fax: 610-262-4391. 8:30AM-4:30PM. Access by: mail, phone, fax, in person.

Probate—Register of Wills, Governnment Center, 669 Washington St, Easton, PA 18042. 610-559-3092, Fax: 610-559-3735. 8:30AM-4:30PM. Access by: mail, in person.

Northumberland

Real Estate Recording—Northumberland County Prothonotary, 201 Market Streets, Courthouse, Room 7, Sunbury, PA 17801. 9AM-4:30PM (M-open until 5PM).

Northumberland County Recorder of Deeds, 2nd & Market Streets, Court House, Sunbury, PA 17801. 570-988-4160. 9AM-4:30PM.

Civil, Eviction—Court of Common Pleas-Civil, County Courthouse, 2nd & Market St, 201 Market St, #7, Sunbury, PA 17801-3468. 570-988-4151. 9AM-5PM M; 9AM-4:30PM T-F. Access by: mail, in person.

Felony, Misdemeanor—Court of Common Pleas-Criminal, County Courthouse, 201 Market St, Rm 7, Sunbury, PA 17801-3468. 570-988-4148. 9AM-5PM M; 9AM-4:30PM T-F. Access by: mail, in person.

Probate—Register of Wills, County Courthouse, 201 Market St, Sunbury, PA 17801. 570-988-4143. 9AM-4:30PM. Access by: mail, in person.

Perry

Real Estate Recording—Perry County Prothonotary, Courthouse, New Bloomfield, PA 17068. 8AM-4PM.

Perry County Recorder of Deeds, Courthouse, New Bloomfield, PA 17068. 717-582-8984. 8AM-4PM.

Felony, Misdemeanor, Civil, Eviction—Court of Common Pleas-Criminal and Civil, PO Box 325, New Bloomfield, PA 17068. 717-582-2131. 8AM-4PM. Access by: mail, phone, fax, in person.

Probate—Register of Wills, PO Box 223, New Bloomfield, PA 17068. 717-582-2131, Fax: 717-582-8570. 8AM-4PM.

Philadelphia

Real Estate Recording—Philadelphia County Prothonotary, Broad & Market Streets, City Hall Room 262, Philadelphia, PA 19107.

Philadelphia County Recorder of Deeds, Broad & Market Streets, City Hall Room 153, Philadelphia, PA 19107. 216-443-8560.

Civil, Eviction—Court of Common Pleas-Civil, First Judicial District of PA, Room 284, City Hall, Philadelphia, PA 19107. 216-491-1300, Fax: 215-567-7380. 9AM-5PM. Access by: mail, in person.

Felony, Misdemeanor—Clerk of Quarter Session, 1301 Filbert St Ste 10, Philadelphia, PA 19107. 216-381-0400. 8AM-5PM. Access by: mail, in person.

Felony, Misdemeanor, Civil Actions Under $10,000, Eviction—Municipal Court, 34 S 11th St, 5th floor, Philadelphia, PA 19107. 216-475-1900, Fax: 215-569-9254. 9AM-5PM. Access by: mail, in person. Special note: Court has jurisdiction over certain criminal offenses with jail terms up to five years.

Probate—Register of Wills, City Hall Rm 180, Philadelphia, PA 19107. 216-461-6500, Fax: 215-686-6293. 8:30AM-4:30PM.

Pike

Real Estate Recording—Pike County Prothonotary, 412 Broad Street, Milford, PA 18337. 8:30AM-4:30PM.

Pike County Recorder of Deeds, 506 Broad Street, Milford, PA 18337. 570-296-3441. 8:30AM-4:30PM.

Felony, Misdemeanor, Civil, Eviction—Court of Common Pleas-Criminal and Civil, 412 Broad St, Milford, PA 18337. 570-296-7231. 8:30AM-4:30PM. Access by: mail, phone, in person.

Potter

Real Estate Recording—Potter County Prothonotary, Courthouse, Room 23, 1 E. 2nd St. Coudersport, PA 16915. Fax: 814-274-8284. 8:30AM-4:30PM.

Potter County Recorder of Deeds, Courthouse, Room 20, Coudersport, PA 16915. 814-274-9775. 8:30AM-4:30PM.

Felony, Misdemeanor, Civil, Eviction—Court of Common Pleas-Criminal and Civil, 1 E 2nd St Rm 23, Coudersport, PA 16915. 814-274-9740, Fax: 814-274-8284. 8:30AM-4:30PM. Access by: mail, phone, fax, in person.

Probate—Register of Wills, 1 E 2nd St, Coudersport, PA 16915. 814-274-8370. 8:30AM-4:30PM.

Schuylkill

Real Estate Recording—Schuylkill County Prothonotary, 401 N. Second St. Pottsville, PA 17901. 9AM-4PM.

Schuylkill County Recorder of Deeds, 401 N. Second St. Pottsville, PA 17901. 570-628-1433. 9AM-4PM.

Civil, Eviction—Court of Common Pleas-Civil, 401 N 2nd St, Pottsville, PA 17901-2528. 570-628-1270, Fax: 570-628-1108. 9AM-4PM. Access by: mail, in person.

Felony, Misdemeanor—Court of Common Pleas-Criminal, 410 N 2nd St, Pottsville, PA 17901. 570-622-5570, Fax: 570-628-1143. 9AM-4PM. Access by: mail, fax, in person.

Probate—Register of Wills, Courthouse 401 N 2nd St, Pottsville, PA 17901-2520. 570-628-1377, Fax: 570-628-1384. 9AM-4PM. Access by: mail, in person.

Snyder

Real Estate Recording—Snyder County Prothonotary, 9 West Market Street, Courthouse, Middleburg, PA 17842. Fax: 570-837-4275. 8:30AM-4PM.

Snyder County Recorder of Deeds, 9-11 West Market Street, Courthouse, Middleburg, PA 17842. 570-837-4221, Fax: 570-837-4299. 8:30AM-4PM.

Felony, Misdemeanor, Civil, Eviction—Court of Common Pleas-Criminal and Civil, Snyder County Courthouse, PO Box 217, Middleburg, PA 17842. 570-837-4202. 8:30AM-4PM. Access by: mail, in person.

Probate—Register of Wills, County Courthouse, PO Box 217, Middleburg, PA 17842. 570-837-4224. 8:30AM-4PM.

Somerset

Real Estate Recording—Somerset County Prothonotary, 111 East Union St. Suite 190, Somerset, PA 15501. Fax: 814-445-7991. 8:30AM-4PM.

Somerset County Recorder of Deeds, 111 E. Main St. Suite 140, Somerset, PA 15501. 814-445-2071. 8:30AM-4PM.

Civil, Eviction—Court of Common Pleas-Civil, 111 E Union St Suite 190, Somerset, PA 15501-0586. 814-445-2186, Fax: 814-445-7991. 8:30AM-4PM. Access by: mail, phone, fax, in person.

Felony, Misdemeanor—Court of Common Pleas-Criminal, 111 E Union St Suite 180, Somerset, PA 15501. 814-445-5154. 8:30AM-4PM. Access by: mail, phone, in person.

Probate—Register of Wills, 111 E Union St Suite 170, Somerset, PA 15501-0586. 814-445-1548, Fax: 814-445-7991. 8:30AM-4PM. Access by: mail, in person.

Sullivan

Real Estate Recording—Sullivan County Prothonotary, Main Street, Courthouse, Laporte, PA 18626. 8:30AM-4PM.

Sullivan County Recorder of Deeds, Main Street, Courthouse, Laporte, PA 18626. 570-946-7331. 8:30AM-4PM.

Felony, Misdemeanor, Civil, Eviction—Court of Common Pleas-Criminal and Civil, Main Street, Laporte, PA 18626. 570-946-7351, Fax: 570-946-4213. 8:30AM-4PM. Access by: mail, in person.

Susquehanna

Real Estate Recording—Susquehanna County Prothonotary, County Courthouse, Public Ave. Montrose, PA 18801. Fax: 570-278-9268. 8:30AM-4:30PM.

Susquehanna County Recorder of Deeds, Courthouse, Montrose, PA 18801. 570-278-4600, Fax: 570-278-9268. 8:30AM-4:30PM.

Civil, Eviction—Court of Common Pleas-Civil, Susquehanna Courthouse, PO Box 218, Montrose, PA 18801. 570-278-4600. 8:30AM-4:30PM. Access by: mail, in person.

Felony, Misdemeanor—Court of Common Pleas-Criminal, Susquehanna Courthouse, PO Box 218, Montrose, PA 18801. 570-278-4600. 8:30AM-4:30PM. Access by: mail, in person.

Probate—Register of Wills, Susquehanna County Courthouse, PO Box 218, Montrose, PA 18801. 570-278-4600, Fax: 570-278-9268. 8:30AM-4:30PM. Access by: in person.

Tioga

Real Estate Recording—Tioga County Prothonotary, 116 Main Street, Courthouse, Wellsboro, PA 16901. 9AM-4:30PM.

Tioga County Recorder of Deeds, 116 Main Street, Courthouse, Wellsboro, PA 16901. 570-723-9117. 9AM-4:30PM.

Felony, Misdemeanor, Civil, Eviction—Court of Common Pleas-Criminal and Civil, 116 Main St, Wellsboro, PA 16901. 570-724-9281. 9AM-4:30PM. Access by: mail, in person.

Probate—Register of Wills, 116 Main St, Wellsboro, PA 16901. 570-724-9260. 9AM-4:30PM.

Union

Real Estate Recording—Union County Prothonotary, 103 South 2nd Street, Courthouse, Lewisburg, PA 17837. 8:30AM-4:30PM.

Union County Recorder of Deeds, 103 South 2nd Street, Courthouse, Lewisburg, PA 17837. 570-524-8781. 8:30AM-4:30PM.

Felony, Misdemeanor, Civil, Eviction—Court of Common Pleas-Criminal and Civil, 103 S 2nd St, Lewisburg, PA 17837. 570-524-8751. 8:30AM-4:30PM. Access by: mail, phone, in person.

Probate—Union County Court, 103 S 2nd St, Lewisburg, PA 17837-1996. 570-524-8761. 8:30AM-4:30PM. Access by: in person.

Venango

Real Estate Recording—Venango County Prothonotary, Courthouse, Franklin, PA 16323. Fax: 814-432-9569. 8:30AM-4:30PM.

Venango County Recorder of Deeds, 1168 Liberty St. Franklin, PA 16323. 814-432-9525, Fax: 814-432-9569. 8:30AM-4:30PM.

Felony, Misdemeanor, Civil, Eviction—Court of Common Pleas-Criminal and Civil, Venango County Courthouse, Franklin, PA 16323. 814-432-9577, Fax: 814-432-9569. 8:30AM-4:30PM. Access by: mail, in person.

Probate—Register of Wills/Recorder of Deeds, 1168 Liberty St, Franklin, PA 16323. 814-432-9539, Fax: 814-432-9569. 8:30AM-4:30PM.

Warren

Real Estate Recording—Warren County Prothonotary, 4th & Market Streets, Courthouse, Warren, PA 16365. Fax: 814-723-8115.

Warren County Recorder of Deeds, 4th & Market Streets, Courthouse, Warren, PA 16365. 814-723-7550. 8:30AM-3:30PM.

Felony, Misdemeanor, Civil, Eviction—Court of Common Pleas-Criminal and Civil, 4th & Market St, Warren, PA 16365. 814-728-3530, Fax: 814-728-3452. 8:30AM-4:30PM. Access by: mail, fax, in person. http://users.penn.com/~wrncourt/

Probate—Register of Wills, Courthouse, 204 4th Ave, Warren, PA 16365. 814-723-7550, Fax: 814-723-8115. 8:30AM-4:30PM.

Washington

Real Estate Recording—Washington County Prothonotary, 1 S. Main St. Suite 1001, Courthouse, Washington, PA 15301. 9AM-4:30PM.

Washington County Recorder of Deeds, Washington County Courthouse, 1 South Main St. Room 1006, Washington, PA 15301. 412-228-6780, Fax: 412-228-6737. 9AM-4:30PM.

Civil, Eviction—Court of Common Pleas-Civil, 1 S Main St Suite 1001, Washington, PA 15301. 724-228-6770. 9AM-4:30PM. Access by: in person.

Felony, Misdemeanor—Court of Common Pleas-Criminal, Courthouse Ste 1005, 1 S Main St, Washington, PA 15301. 724-228-6787, Fax: 724-228-6890. 9AM-4:30PM. Access by: mail, in person, online.

Probate—Register of Wills, Courthouse, 1 S Main St Suite 1002, Washington, PA 15301. 724-228-6775. 9AM-4:30PM.

Wayne

Real Estate Recording—Wayne County Prothonotary, 925 Court Street, Courthouse, Honesdale, PA 18431. Fax: 570-253-0687. 8:30AM-4:30PM.

Wayne County Recorder of Deeds, 925 Court Street, Honesdale, PA 18431. 717-253-5970. 8:30AM-4:30PM.

Felony, Misdemeanor, Civil, Eviction—Court of Common Pleas-Criminal and Civil, 925 Court St, Honesdale, PA 18431. 570-253-5970, Fax: 570-253-0687. 8:30AM-4:30PM. Access by: in person.

Probate—Register of Wills, 925 Court St, Honesdale, PA 18431. 570-253-5970. 8:30AM-4:30PM.

Westmoreland

Real Estate Recording—Westmoreland County Prothonotary, Main Street, Courthouse Square Room 501, Greensburg, PA 15601. 8:30AM-4PM.

Westmoreland County Recorder of Deeds, Main Street, Courthouse Square Room 503, Greensburg, PA 15601. 412-830-3173, Fax: 724-832-8757. 8:30AM-4PM.

Civil, Eviction—Court of Common Pleas-Civil, Courthouse Sq, Rm 501, PO Box 1630, Greensburg, PA 15601-1168. 724-830-3500, Fax: 724-830-3517. 8:30AM-4PM. Access by: in person.

Felony, Misdemeanor—Court of Common Pleas-Criminal, Criminal Division, 203 Courthouse Square, Greensburg, PA 15601-1168. 724-830-3734, Fax: 724-830-3472. 8:30AM-4PM. Access by: mail, fax, in person, online.

Probate—Register of Wills, Registrar of Wills, 301 Courthouse Sq, Greensburg, PA 15601. 724-830-3177, Fax: 724-850-3976. 8:30AM-4PM.

Wyoming

Real Estate Recording—Wyoming County Prothonotary, 1 Courthouse Square, Wyoming County Courthouse, Tunkhannock, PA 18657. 8:30AM-4PM.

Wyoming County Recorder of Deeds, 1 Courthouse Square, Tunkhannock, PA 18657. 717-836-3200. 8:30AM-4PM.

Felony, Misdemeanor, Civil, Eviction—Court of Common Pleas-Criminal and Civil, Wyoming County Courthouse, Tunkhannock, PA 18657. 570-836-3200. 8:30AM-4PM. Access by: in person.

Probate—Register of Wills, County Courthouse, 1 Courthouse Sq, Tunkhannock, PA 18657. 570-836-3200. 8:30AM-4PM.

York

Real Estate Recording—York County Prothonotary, 28 East Market Street, York, PA 17401. Fax: 717-771-4629. 8:30AM-4:30PM.

York County Recorder of Deeds, 28 East Market Street, York, PA 17401. 717-771-9603, Fax: 717-771-9582. 8AM-4:30PM.

Civil, Eviction—Court of Common Pleas-Civil, York County Courthouse, 28E Market St, York, PA 17401. 717-771-9611. 8:30AM-4:30PM. Access by: mail, phone, in person.

Felony, Misdemeanor—Court of Common Pleas-Criminal, York County Courthouse 28 E Market St, York, PA 17401. 570-771-9612, Fax: 570-771-9096. 8:30AM-4:30PM. Access by: mail, fax, in person, online.

Probate—Register of Wills, York County Courthouse 28 E Market St, York, PA 17401. 570-771-9263, Fax: 570-771-4678. 8:30AM-4:15PM. Access by: mail, in person.

Federal Courts

US District Court

Eastern District of Pennsylvania

Allentown/Reading Division c/o Philadelphia Division, Room 2609, US Courthouse, 601 Market St, Philadelphia, PA 19106-1797215-597-7704, Record Room: 215-597-7721 Fax: 215-597-6390 Counties: Berks, Lancaster, Lehigh, Northampton, Schuylkill. www.paed.uscourts.gov
Philadelphia Division Room 2609, US Courthouse, 601 Market St, Philadelphia, PA 19106-1797215-597-7704, Record Room: 215-597-7721 Fax: 215-597-0303 Counties: Bucks, Chester, Delaware, Montgomery, Philadelphia. www.paed.uscourts.gov

Middle District of Pennsylvania

Harrisburg Division PO Box 983, Harrisburg, PA 17108-0983717-221-3920, Record Room: 717-221-3924 Fax: 717-221-3959 Counties: Adams, Cumberland, Dauphin, Franklin, Fulton, Huntingdon, Juniata, Lebanon, Mifflin, York.
Scranton Division Clerk's Office, PO Box 1148, Scranton, PA 18501570-207-5600, Criminal Docket Phone: 570-207-5606 Fax: 717-207-5650 Counties: Bradford, Carbon, Lackawanna, Luzerne, Monroe, Pike, Susquehanna, Wayne, Wyoming.
Williamsport Division PO Box 608, Williamsport, PA 17703570-323-6380 Fax: 717-323-0636 Counties: Cameron, Centre, Clinton, Columbia, Lycoming, Montour, Northumberland, Perry, Potter, Snyder, Sullivan, Tioga, Union.

Western District of Pennsylvania

Erie Division PO Box 1820, Erie, PA 16507814-453-4829 Counties: Crawford, Elk, Erie, Forest, McKean, Venango, Warren. www.pawd.uscourts.gov
Johnstown Division Penn Traffic Bldg, Room 208, 319 Washington St, Johnstown, PA 15901814-533-4504 Fax: 814-533-4519 Counties: Bedford, Blair, Cambria, Clearfield, Somerset. www.pawd.uscourts.gov

Pittsburgh Division US Post Office & Courthouse, Room 829, 7th Ave & Grant St, Pittsburgh, PA 15219412-644-3527, Record Room: 412-644-3533 Counties: Allegheny, Armstrong, Beaver, Butler, Clarion, Fayette, Greene, Indiana, Jefferson, Lawrence, Mercer, Washington, Westmoreland. www.pawd.uscourts.gov

US Bankruptcy Court

Eastern District of Pennsylvania

Philadelphia Division 4th Floor, 900 Market St, Philadelphia, PA 19107215-408-2800 Counties: Bucks, Chester, Delaware, Montgomery, Philadelphia. www.paeb.uscourts.gov
Reading Division Suite 300, The Madison, 400 Washington St, Reading, PA 19601610-320-5255 Counties: Berks, Lancaster, Lehigh, Northampton, Schuylkill. www.paeb.uscourts.gov

Middle District of Pennsylvania

Harrisburg Division PO Box 908, Harrisburg, PA 17101717-901-2800 Counties: Adams, Centre, Cumberland, Dauphin, Franklin, Fulton, Huntingdon, Juniata, Lebanon, Mifflin, Montour, Northumberland, Perry, Snyder, Union, York. www.paeb.uscourts.gov
Wilkes-Barre Division Room 217, 197 S Main St, Wilkes-Barre, PA 18701570-826-6450 Counties: Bradford, Cameron, Carbon, Clinton, Columbia, Lackawanna, Luzerne, Lycoming, Monroe, Pike, Potter, Sullivan, Susquehanna, Tioga, Wayne, Wyoming. www.paeb.uscourts.gov

Western District of Pennsylvania

Erie Division 717 State St, #501, Erie, PA 16501814-453-7580 Counties: Clarion, Crawford, Elk, Erie, Forest, Jefferson, McKean, Mercer, Venango, Warren.
Pittsburgh Division 600 Grant St #5414, Pittsburgh, PA 15219-2801412-644-2700 Counties: Allegheny, Armstrong, Beaver, Bedford, Blair, Butler, Cambria, Clearfield, Fayette, Greene, Indiana, Lawrence, Somerset, Washington, Westmoreland.

Rhode Island

Attorney General's Office
150 S Main St   401-274-4400
Providence, RI 02903   Fax: 401-222-1302
www.riaq.state.ri.us

Governor's Office
State House, Room 115   401-222-2080
Providence, RI 02903   Fax: 401-861-5894
www.rigovernor.com

State Archives
337 Westminster St   401-222-2353
Providence, RI 02903   Fax: 401-222-3199
www.state.ri.us/archives

Capital:	Providence
	Providence County
Time Zone:	EST
Number of Counties:	5
Population:	987,429
Web Site:	www.state.ri.us

Search Unclaimed Property Online
www.state.ri.us/treas/money1st.htm

State Agencies

Criminal Records
Department of Attorney General, Bureau of Criminal Identification, 150 S Main Street, Providence, RI 02903; 401-421-5268; 8AM-5PM. Access by: mail.
www.riaq.state.ri.us

Corporation Records
Fictitious Name
Limited Partnerships
Limited Liability Company Records
Limited Liability Partnerships
Secretary of State, Corporations Division, 100 N Main St, Providence, RI 02903; 401-222-3040; Fax: 401-222-1309; 8:30AM-4:30PM. Access by: mail, phone, in person, online.
www.sec.state.ri.us

Sales Tax Registrations
Taxation Division, Sales & Use Tax Office, One Capitol Hill, Providence, RI 02908-5890; 401-222-2937; Fax: 401-222-6006; 8:30AM-4PM. Access by: mail, phone, in person.
www.tax.state.ri.us

Trademarks/Servicemarks
Secretary of State, Trademark Division, 100 N Main St, Providence, RI 02903; 401-222-1487; Fax: 401-222-3879; 8:30AM-4:30PM. Access by: mail, phone, in person.

Uniform Commercial Code
UCC Division, Secretary of State, 100 North Main St, Providence, RI 02903; 401-222-2249; 8:30AM-4:30PM. Access by: mail, phone, in person.

Federal Tax Liens
State Tax Liens
Records not available from state agency.

All records are located at the county level.

Workers' Compensation Records
Department of Labor & Training, Division of Workers' Compensation, PO Box 3500, Providence, RI 02909-0500 (610 Manton Ave, Providence, RI 02909); 401-457-1800; Fax: 401-222-2127; 8:30AM-4PM. Access by: mail.
www.dlt.state.ri.us

Birth Certificates

State Department of Health, Division of Vital Records, 3 Capitol Hill, Room 101, Providence, RI 02908-5097; 401-222-2812, 401-222-2811; 8:30AM-4:30PM. Access by: mail.

Death Records

State Department of Health, Division of Vital Records, 3 Capitol Hill, Room 101, Providence, RI 02908-5097; 401-222-2812, 401-222-2811; 8:30AM-4:30PM;. Access by: mail, phone, in person.

Marriage Certificates

State Department of Health, Division of Vital Records, 3 Capitol Hill, Room 101, Providence, RI 02908-5097; 401-222-2812, 401-222-2811; 8:30AM-4:30PM M-F;. Access by: mail, phone, in person.

Divorce Records

Records not available from state agency.

Divorce records are found at one of the 4 county Family Courts.

Accident Reports

Rhode Island State Police, Accident Record Division, 311 Danielson Pike, North Scituate, RI 02857; 401-444-1143; Fax: 401-444-1133; 10AM-3:30PM M,T,TH,F. Access by: mail, phone, in person.

Driver Records

Division of Motor Vehicles, Driving Record Clerk, Operator Control, 345 Harris Ave, Providence, RI 02909; 401-222-2994; Fax: 401-222-6120; 8:30AM-4:30PM. Access by: mail.

Vehicle Ownership
Vehicle Identification

Registry of Motor Vehicles, c/o Registration Files, 286 Main Street, Pawtucket, RI 02860; 401-588-3020 x2552; 8:30AM-3:30PM. Access by: mail.

Boat & Vessel Ownership
Boat & Vessel Registration

Dept of Environmental Managment, Office of Boat Registration, 235 Promenade, Providence, RI 02908; 401-222-6647; Fax: 401-222-1181; 8:30AM-3:30PM M-F. www.state.ri.us/dem

Legislation-Current/Pending
Legislation-Passed

Secretary of State, State House, Room 38, Public Information Center, Providence, RI 02903; 401-222-3983 Bill Status Only, 401-222-2473 State Library, 401-222-1308 Fax Back Request Line; Fax: 401-222-1356; 8:30AM-4:30PM. Access by: mail, phone, in person. www.sec.state.ri.us

Voter Registration

Records not available from state agency.

The Local Board of Canvassers keeps records at the town and city level. Although records are open, they may not be purchased for commercial purposes.

GED Certificates

Department of Education, GED Testing, 255 Westminster, Providence, RI 02908; 401-222-4600 x2181; 7:30AM-4PM. Access by:, phone, in person.

Hunting License Information
Fishing License Information

RI DEM, 235 Promenade, Providence, RI 02908; 401-222-3576 License Issue Only; Fax: 401-222-1181; 8:30AM-3:30PM. Access by: mail, phone, in person. www.state.ri.us/dem

County Courts & Recording Offices

About the Courts...

Administration

Court Administrator, Supreme Court   401-222-3272
250 Benefit St   Fax: 401-222-3599
Providence, RI 02903
www.courts.state.ri.us

Court Structure

Rhode Island has five counties, but only four Superior/District Court Locations (2nd, 3rd, 4th, and 6th Districts). Bristol and Providence counties are completely merged at the Providence location. Civil claims between $5000 and $10,000 may be filed in either Superior or District Court at the discretion of the filer. Probate is handled by the Town Clerk at the 39 cities and towns across. Rhode Island.

Online Access

An online computer system for internal use is under development which will eventually include all state courts.

About the Recording Offices...

Organization

5 counties and 39 towns, 39 recording offices. The recording officer is Town/City Clerk (Recorder of Deeds). The Town/City Clerk usually also serves as. Recorder of Deeds. There is no county administration in Rhode Island. The entire state is in the Eastern Time Zone (EST).

Towns will not perform real estate searches. Copy fees are usually $1.50 per page. Certification usually costs $3.00 per document.

UCC Records

Financing statements are filed at the state level, except for farm related and real estate related collateral, which are filed with the Town/City Clerk. Most recording offices will not perform UCC searches. Use search request form UCC-11. Copy fees are usually $1.50 per page. Certification usually costs $3.00 per document.

Lien Records

All federal and state tax liens on personal property and on real property are filed with the Recorder of Deeds. Towns will not perform tax lien searches.

Real Estate Records

Towns will not perform real estate searches. Copy fees are usually $1.50 per page. Certification usually costs $3.00 per document.

County Courts & Recording Offices

Barrington

Real Estate Recording—Barrington Town Clerk, 283 County Road, Town Hall, Barrington, RI 2806. 8:30AM-4:30PM.

Bristol

Real Estate Recording—Bristol Town Clerk, 10 Court Street, Town Hall, Bristol, RI 2809. 8:30AM-4PM.

Felony, Civil Actions Over $10,000—Superior and District Courts, Access by: in person. Special note: All civil and criminal cases handled by the Providence County courts.

Probate—Barrington Town Hall, 283 County Road, Barrington, RI 02806. 401-728-2400. 8:30AM-4:30PM.

Bristol Town Hall, 10 Court Street, Bristol, RI 02809. 401-738-2000, Fax: 401-253-3080. 8:30AM-4PM. Access by: mail, in person.

Warren Town Hall, 514 Main Street, Warren, RI 02885. 401-728-0500, Fax: 401-245-7421. 9AM-4PM.

Burrillville

Real Estate Recording—Burrillville Town Clerk, 105 Harrisville Main Street, Town Hall, Harrisville, RI 2830. Fax: 401-568-0490. 8:30AM-4:30PM (Recording until 4PM).

Central Falls

Real Estate Recording—Central Falls City Clerk, 580 Broad Street, City Hall, Central Falls, RI 2863. Fax: 401-727-7476. 8:30AM-4:30PM.

Charlestown

Real Estate Recording—Charlestown Town Clerk, 4540 South County Trail, Charlestown, RI 2813. Fax: 401-364-1238. 8:30AM-4:30PM (Recording until 4PM).

Coventry

Real Estate Recording—Coventry Town Clerk, 1670 Flat River Road, Town Hall, Coventry, RI 2816. Fax: 401-822-9132. 8:30AM-4:30PM.

Cranston

Real Estate Recording—Cranston City Clerk, 869 Park Avenue, City Hall, Cranston, RI 2910. 8:30AM-4:30PM.

Cumberland

Real Estate Recording—Cumberland Town Clerk, 45 Broad Street, Town Hall, Cumberland, RI 2864. Fax: 401-724-1103. 8:30AM-4:30PM.

East Greenwich

Real Estate Recording—East Greenwich Town Clerk, Town Hall, 125 Main St. East Greenwich, RI 2818. Fax: 401-886-8625. 8:30AM-4:30PM.

East Providence

Real Estate Recording—East Providence City Clerk, 145 Taunton Avenue, City Hall, East Providence, RI 2914. Fax: 401-435-7501. 8AM-4PM; Recording Hours: 8AM-3:30PM.

Exeter

Real Estate Recording—Exeter Town Clerk, 675 Ten Rod Road, Town Hall, Exeter, RI 2822. Fax: 401-295-1248. 9AM-4PM.

Foster

Real Estate Recording—Foster Town Clerk, 181 Howard Hill Road, Town Hall, Foster, RI 2825. Fax: 401-392-9201. 9AM-3:30PM.

Glocester

Real Estate Recording—Glocester Town Clerk, 1145 Putnam Pike, Town Hall, Glocester/ Chepachet, RI 2814. Fax: 401-568-5850. 8AM-4:30PM.

Hopkinton

Real Estate Recording—Hopkinton Town Clerk, 1 Town House Road, Town Hall, Hopkinton, RI 2833. Fax: 401-377-7788. 8:30AM-4:30PM.

Jamestown

Real Estate Recording—Jamestown Town Clerk, 93 Narragansett Avenue, Town Hall, Jamestown, RI 2835. Fax: 401-423-7230. 8AM-4:30PM.

Johnston

Real Estate Recording—Johnston Town Clerk, 1385 Hartford Avenue, Town Hall, Johnston, RI 2919. Fax: 401-331-4271. 9AM-4:30PM.

Kent

Felony, Civil Actions Over $10,000—Superior Court, 222 Quaker Lane, Warwick, RI 02886-0107. 402-288-4491. 8:30AM-4:30PM. Access by: in person.

Misdemeanor, Civil Actions Under $10,000, Eviction, Small Claims—3rd Division District Court, 222 Quaker Lane, Warwick, RI 02886-0107. 402-296-9334. 8:30AM-4:30PM. Access by: in person.

Probate—Coventry Town Hall, 1670 Flat River Road, Coventry, RI 02816. 402-296-9339, Fax: 401-822-9132. 8:30AM-4:30PM. Access by: mail, in person.

East Greenwich Town Hall, 125 Main St, East Greenwich, RI 02818. 402-336-1662, Fax: 401-886-8625. 8:30AM-4:30PM.

Warwick City Hall, 3275 Post Road, Warwick, RI 02886. 402-245-3511, Fax: 401-738-6639. 8:30AM-4:30PM. Access by: mail, in person.

West Greenwich Town Hall, 280 Victory Highway, West Greenwich, RI 02817. 401-822-1311, Fax: 401-392-3805. 9AM-4PM M,T,Th,F; 9AM-4PM, 7-9PM W. Access by: mail, in person.

West Warwick Town Hall, 1170 Main Street, West Warwick, RI 02893-4829. 402-329-4335, Fax: 401-822-9266. 8:30AM-4:30PM; 8:30AM-4PM June 1st-Labor Day.

Lincoln

Real Estate Recording—Lincoln Town Clerk, 100 Old River Road, Town Hall, Lincoln, RI 2865. Fax: 401-333-3648. 9AM-4:30PM.

Little Compton

Real Estate Recording—Little Compton Town Clerk, 40 Commons, Town Hall, Little Compton, RI 2837. Fax: 401-635-2470. 8AM-4PM.

Middletown

Real Estate Recording—Middletown Town Clerk, 350 East Main Road, Town Hall, Middletown, RI 2842. Fax: 401-848-0500. 9AM-5PM.

Narragansett

Real Estate Recording—Narragansett Town Clerk, 25 Fifth Avenue, Town Hall, Narragansett, RI 2882. Fax: 401-783-9637. 8:30AM-4:30PM.

New Shoreham

Real Estate Recording—New Shoreham Town Clerk, Old Town Road, Town Hall, Block Island, RI 2807. Fax: 401-466-3219. 9AM-3PM.

Newport

Real Estate Recording—Newport City Clerk, 43 Broadway, Town Hall, Newport, RI 2840. 9AM-5PM (Recording Hours 9AM-4PM).

Felony, Civil Actions Over $10,000—Superior Court, Florence K Murray Judicial Complex, 45 Washington Sq, Newport, RI 02840.

402-329-6335. 8:30AM-4:30PM (July and August till 4PM). Access by: mail, in person.

Misdemeanor, Civil Actions Under $10,000, Eviction, Small Claims—2nd Division District Court, Eisenhower Square, Newport, RI 02840. 402-335-2871. 8:30AM-4:30PM (4PM-summer months). Access by: in person.

Probate—Jamestown Town Hall, 93 Narragansett Avenue, Jamestown, RI 02835. 401-822-9174, Fax: 401-423-7230. 8AM-4:30PM. Access by: mail, in person.

Little Compton Town Hall, 40 Commons, PO Box 226, Little Compton, RI 02837. 402-223-1315, Fax: 401-635-2470. 8AM-4PM.

Middletown Town Hall, 350 East Main Road, Middletown, RI 02842. 402-336-1291, Fax: 401-845-0400. 9AM-5PM.

Newport City Hall, 43 Broadway, Newport, RI 02840. 402-335-3050, Fax: 401-849-8757. 8:30AM-4:30PM.

Portsmouth Town Hall, 2200 East Main Road, PO Box 115, Portsmouth, RI 02871. 402-225-2371. 9AM-4PM.

Tiverton Town Hall, 343 Highland Road, Tiverton, RI 02878. 401-886-8603, Fax: 401-624-8640. 8:30AM-4PM.

North Kingstown

Real Estate Recording—North Kingstown Town Clerk, 80 Boston Neck Road, Town Hall, North Kingstown, RI 2852. Fax: 401-885-7373. 8:30AM-4:30PM.

North Providence

Real Estate Recording—North Providence Town Clerk, 2000 Smith Street, Town Hall, North Providence, RI 2911. 401-683-2101, Fax: 401-233-1409. 8:30AM-4:30PM (Summer hours 8:30 AM-4PM).

North Smithfield

Real Estate Recording—North Smithfield Town Clerk, 1 Main Street, Town Hall, Slatersville, RI 2876. Fax: 401-766-0016. 8AM-4PM (Recording until 3:30PM).

Pawtucket

Real Estate Recording—Pawtucket City Clerk, 137 Roosevelt Avenue, City Hall, Pawtucket, RI 2860. Fax: 401-728-8932. 8:30AM-4:30PM; Recording until 3:30PM.

Portsmouth

Real Estate Recording—Portsmouth Town Clerk, 2200 East Main Road, Town Hall, Portsmouth, RI 2871. Recording Hours 9AM-3:45PM.

Providence

Real Estate Recording—Providence City Recorder of Deeds, 25 Dorrance Street, City Hall, Providence, RI 2903. 8:30AM-4:30PM (Recording Hours 8:30AM-4PM).

Felony, Civil Actions Over $10,000—Providence/Bristol Superior Court, 250 Benefit St, Providence, RI 02903. 401-635-4400. 8:30AM-4:30PM. Access by: in person.

Misdemeanor, Civil Actions Under $10,000, Eviction, Small Claims—6th Division District Court, 1 Dorrance Plaza 2nd Floor, Providence, RI 02903. 401-647-2547. 8:30AM-4:30PM. Access by: mail, in person.

Probate—Burrillville Town Hall, 105 Harrisville Main Street, Harrisville, RI 02830. 401-846-9600, Fax: 401-568-0490. 8:30AM-4:30PM.

Central Falls City Hall, 580 Broad Street, Central Falls, RI 02863. 402-225-4341, Fax: 401-727-7476. 8:30AM-4:30PM. Access by: in person.

Cranston City Hall, 869 Park Avenue, Cranston, RI 02910. 401-822-9216, Fax: 401-461-9650. 8:30AM-4:30PM.

Cumberland Town Hall, 45 Broad Street, PO Box 7, Cumberland, RI 02864. 402-245-2812, Fax: 401-724-1103. 8:30AM-4:30PM.

East Providence City Hall, 145 Taunton Avenue, East Providence, RI 02914. 401-822-9201, Fax: 401-438-7501. 8AM-4PM.

Foster Town Hall, 181 Howard Hill Road, Foster, RI 02825. 401-789-9331, Fax: 401-397-9736. 9AM-4PM.

Glocester Town Hall, 1145 Putnam Pike, Glocester/ Chepachet, RI 02814. 401-847-0009, Fax: 401-568-5850. 8AM-4:30PM. Access by: mail, in person.

Johnston Town Hall, 1385 Hartford Avenue, Johnston, RI 02919. 401-782-4131, Fax: 401-553-8835. 9AM-4:30PM. Access by: in person.

Lincoln Town Hall, 100 Old River Road, Lincoln, RI 02865. 401-767-2200, Fax: 401-333-3648. 9AM-4:30PM.

North Providence Town Hall, 2000 Smith Street, North Providence, RI 02911. 401-647-7466, Fax: 401-233-1409. 8:30AM-4:30PM.

North Smithfield Town Hall, 1 Main Street, Slatersville, RI 02876. 402-254-7441, Fax: 401-766-0016. 8AM-4PM.

Pawtucket City Hall, 137 Roosevelt Avenue, Pawtucket, RI 02860. 402-245-2023, Fax: 401-728-8932. 8:30AM-4:30PM.

Providence City Hall, 25 Dorrance Street, Providence, RI 02903. 401-822-1771, Fax: 401-861-6208. 8:45AM-4:15PM. Access by: mail, in person.

Scituate Town Hall, 195 Danielson Pike, PO Box 328, North Scituate, RI 02857. 402-223-1332. 9AM-4PM.

Smithfield Town Hall, 64 Farnum Pike, Smithfield, RI 02917. 401-727-7400, Fax: 401-232-7244. 9AM-4PM. Access by: mail, in person.

Woonsocket City Hall, 169 Main Street, Woonsocket, RI 02895. 402-254-7421, Fax: 401-765-0022. 8:30AM-4PM.

Richmond

Real Estate Recording—Richmond Town Clerk, 5 Richmond Townhouse Rd. Town Hall, Wyoming, RI 2898. Fax: 401-539-1089. 9AM-4PM (6-7:30PM M).

Scituate

Real Estate Recording—Scituate Town Clerk, 195 Danielson Pike, Town Hall, North Scituate, RI 2857. 402-223-1323. 8:30AM-4PM.

Smithfield

Real Estate Recording—Smithfield Town Clerk, 64 Farnum Pike, Town Hall, Esmond, RI 2917. Fax: 401-232-7244. 9AM-4PM.

South Kingstown

Real Estate Recording—South Kingstown Town Clerk, 180 High Street, Town Hall, Wakefield, RI 2879. 402-288-4484. 8:30AM-4:30PM.

Tiverton

Real Estate Recording—Tiverton Town Clerk, 343 Highland Road, Town Hall, Tiverton, RI 2878. Fax: 401-624-8640. 8:30AM-4PM.

Warren

Real Estate Recording—Warren Town Clerk, 514 Main Street, Town Hall, Warren, RI 2885. Fax: 401-245-7421. 9AM-4PM.

Warwick

Real Estate Recording—Warwick City Clerk, 3275 Post Road, Warwick, RI 2886. 402-254-6957, Fax: 401-738-6639. 8:30AM-4:30PM (Recording 8:30AM-4PM).

Washington

Felony, Civil Actions Over $10,000—Superior Court, 4800 Towerhill Rd, Wakefield, RI 02879. 402-274-3008. 8:30AM-4:30PM (Sept-June) 8:30AM-4PM (July & Aug). Access by: mail, phone, in person.

Misdemeanor, Civil Actions Under $10,000, Eviction, Small Claims—4th District Court, 4800 Towerhill Rd, Wakefield, RI 02879. 402-274-3319. 8:30AM-4:30PM. Access by: in person.

Probate—Charlestown Town Hall, 4540 South County Trail, Charlestown, RI 02813. 401-789-1044, Fax: 401-364-1238. 8:30AM-4:30PM.

Exeter Town Hall, 675 Ten Rod Road, Exeter, RI 02822. 401-762-6400, Fax: 401-295-1248. 9AM-4PM.

Hopkinton Town Hall, 1 Town House Road, Hopkinton, RI 02833. 401-789-9331, Fax: 401-377-7788. 8:30AM-4:30PM or by appointment. Access by: mail, in person.

Narragansett Town Hall, 25 Fifth Avenue, Narragansett, RI 02882. 402-274-3616, Fax: 401-783-9637. 8:30AM-4:30PM.

New Shoreham Town Hall, Old Town Road, PO Drawer 220, Block Island, RI 02807. 401-841-8330, Fax: 401-466-3219. 9AM-3PM.

North Kingstown Town Hall, 80 Boston Neck Road, North Kingstown, RI 02852-5762. 401-738-2000, Fax: 401-885-7373. 8:30AM-4:30PM. www.northkingstown.org

Richmond Town Hall, 5 Richmond Townhouse Rd. Wyoming, RI 02898. 401-841-8350, Fax: 401-539-1089. 9AM-4PM, 6-7:30PM M; 9AM-4PM T-F.

South Kingstown Town Hall, 180 High Street, Wakefield, RI 02879. 402-288-4277, Fax: 401-789-5280. 8:30AM-4:30PM. Access by: mail, in person.

Westerly Town Hall, 45 Broad Street, Westerly, RI 02891. 401-782-4121, Fax: 401-348-2571. 8:30AM-4:30PM. Access by: in person.

West Greenwich

Real Estate Recording—West Greenwich Town Clerk, 280 Victory Highway, Town Hall, West Greenwich, RI 2817. Fax: 401-392-3805.

West Warwick

Real Estate Recording—West Warwick Town Clerk, 1170 Main Street, Town Hall, West Warwick, RI 2893. 402-329-6245, Fax: 401-822-9266. 8:30AM-4:30PM (June-August 8:30AM-4PM).

Westerly

Real Estate Recording—Westerly Town Clerk, 45 Broad Street, Town Hall, Westerly, RI 2891. Fax: 401-348-2571. 8:30AM-4:30PM.

Woonsocket

Real Estate Recording—Woonsocket City Clerk, 169 Main Street, City Hall, Woonsocket, RI 2895. Fax: 401-765-4569. 8:30-4PM.

Federal Courts

US District Court

Providence Division Clerk's Office, One Exchange Terrace, Federal Bldg, Providence, RI 02903401-528-5100 Fax: 401-528-5112 Counties: All counties in Rhode Island.

US Bankruptcy Court

Providence Division 6th Floor, 380 Westminster Mall, Providence, RI 02903401-528-4477 Fax: 401-528-4470 Counties: All counties in Rhode Island. www.rib.uscourts.gov

South Carolina

Attorney General's Office
PO Box 11549   803-734-3970
Columbia, SC 29211   Fax: 803-734-4323
www.scattorneygeneral.org

Governor's Office
PO Box 11829   803-734-9818
Columbia, SC 29211   Fax: 803-734-9413
www.state.sc.us/governor

State Archives
8301 Parklane Rd   803-896-6100
Columbia, SC 29223   Fax: 803-896-6198
www.state.sc.us/scdah

Capital:	Columbia
	Richland County
Time Zone:	EST
Number of Counties:	46
Population:	3,760,181
Web Site:	www.state.sc.us

Search Unclaimed Property Online

www.state.sc.us/treas/uprop/
search.html

State Agencies

Criminal Records
South Carolina Law Enforcement Division (SLED), Criminal Records Section, PO Box 21398, Columbia, SC 29221 (440 Broad River Rd, Columbia, SC 29210); 803-737-9000, 803-737-4205; Fax: 803-896-7022; 8:30AM-5PM. Access by: mail.

Corporation Records
Trademarks/Servicemarks
Limited Partnerships
Limited Liability Company Records
Corporation Division, Capitol Complex, PO Box 11350, Columbia, SC 29211 (Edgar A. Brown Bldg, Room 525, Columbia, SC 29201); 803-734-2158; Fax: 803-734-2164; 8:30PM-5PM. Access by: mail, phone, in person, online.

Sales Tax Registrations
Revenue Department, Sales Tax Registration Section, PO Box 125, Columbia, SC 29214 (301 Gervais St, Columbia, SC 29214); 803-898-5872; Fax: 803-898-5888; 8:30AM-4:45PM. Access by: mail, phone, in person. www.dor.state.sc.us

Uniform Commercial Code
UCC Division, Secretary of State, PO Box 11350, Columbia, SC 29211 (Edgar Brown Bldg, 1205 Pendelton St #525, Columbia, SC 29201); 803-734-2175; Fax: 803-734-2164; 8:30AM-5PM. Access by: mail, phone, in person, online.

Federal Tax Liens
State Tax Liens
Records not available from state agency.

Tax lien data is found at the county level.

Fictitious Name
Assumed Name
Trade Names
Records not available from state agency.

Records are found at the county level.

Workers' Compensation Records
Workers Compensation Commission, PO Box 1715, Columbia, SC 29202 (1612 Marion St, Columbia, SC 29201); 803-737-5700; Fax: 803-737-5768; 8:30AM-5PM. Access by: mail. www.state.sc.us/wcc

Birth Certificates

South Carolina DHEC, Vital Records, 2600 Bull St, Columbia, SC 29201; 803-898-3630, 803-898-3631 Order Line; Fax: 803-799-0301; 8:30AM-4:30PM. Access by: mail, phone, in person.

Death Records

South Carolina DHEC, Vital Records, 2600 Bull St, Columbia, SC 29201; 803-898-3630, 803-898-3631 Order Line; Fax: 803-799-0301; 8:30AM-4:30PM. Access by: mail, phone, in person.

Marriage Certificates

South Carolina DHEC, Vital Records, 2600 Bull St, Columbia, SC 29201; 803-898-3630, 803-898-3631 Order Line; Fax: 803-799-0301; 8:30AM-4:30PM. Access by: mail, phone, fax, in person.

Divorce Records

South Carolina DHEC, Vital Records, 2600 Bull St, Columbia, SC 29201; 803-898-3630, 803-898-3631 Order Line; Fax: 803-799-0301; 8:30AM-4:30PM. Access by: mail, phone, in person.

Accident Reports

Accident Reports, PO Box 1498, Columbia, SC 29216-0040 (955 Park St, Columbia, SC 29201); 803-737-4000; Fax: 803-737-4483; 8:30AM-5PM. Access by: mail, phone, in person.

Driver License Information
Driver Records

Division of Motor Vehicles, Driver Records Section, PO Box 100178, Columbia, SC 29202-3178 (955 Park St, Columbia, SC 29201); 803-737-4000; Fax: 803-737-1077; 8:30AM-5PM. Access by: mail, online.

Vehicle Ownership
Vehicle Identification

Division of Motor Vehicles, Title and Registration Records Section, PO Box 1498, Columbia, SC 29216 (955 Park St, Columbia, SC 29201); 803-737-4000; 8:30AM-5PM. Access by: mail, phone, in person. www.state.sc.us/dps/dmv

Boat & Vessel Ownership
Boat & Vessel Registration

Dept of Natural Resources, Registration & Titles, PO Box 167, Columbia, SC 29202; 803-734-3857; Fax: 803-734-4138; 8:30AM-5PM. www.dnr.state.sc.us

Legislation-Current/Pending
Legislation-Passed

South Carolina Legislature, 937 Assembly Street, Rm 220, Columbia, SC 29201; 803-734-2060, 803-734-2145 Older Bills; 9AM-5PM. Access by: mail, phone, in person, online. www.leginfo.state.sc.us

Voter Registration

, State Election Commission, PO Box 5987, Columbia, SC 29205; 803-734-9060; Fax: 803-734-9366; 8:30AM-5PM. Access by: mail, phone, fax, in person. www.state.sc.us/scsec

Annual Reports, Directors and Officers

Department of Revenue, Annual Reports Division, 301 Gervias St, Columbia, SC 29201; 803-898-5866; Fax: 803-898-5885; 8:30AM-5PM. Access by: mail, phone, in person.

GED Certificates

GED Testing Office, 402 Rutledge Bldg, 1429 Senate St, Columbia, SC 29201; 803-734-8347; Fax: 803-734-8336; 8:30AM-5PM M-F. www.state.sc.us/sde

Hunting License Information
Fishing License Information

Records not available from state agency.

They do not have a central database. Licenses are kept on file within the License Division by the county and agent where the license was sold.

County Courts & Recording Offices

About the Courts...

Administration

Court Administration   803-734-1800
1015 Sumter St, 2nd Floor   Fax: 803-734-1821
Columbia, SC 29201
www.judicial.state.sc.us

Court Structure

There are 46 Circuit Courts in 16 circuits. The Clerk of the Circuit Court maintains the records of both civil and criminal divisions of the Circuit Court, Court of General Sessions, and Court of Common Pleas as well as for the Family Court. General Sessions and Common Pleas are co-located in every county. The over 370 Magistrate and Municipal Courts only handle misdemeanor cases involving 30 days or less jail time.

The maximum civil claim monetary amount for the Magistrate Courts increased from $2500 to $5000 as of January 1, 1996.

Searching Hints

If requesting a record in writing, it is recommended that the words "request that General Session, Common Pleas, and Family Court records be searched" be included in the request.
Most South Carolina courts will not conduct searches. However, if a name and case number are provided, many will pull and copy the record. Search fees vary widely as they are set by each county individually.

Online Access

There is no statewide online public access available. Charlestown County has Internet access.

About the Recording Offices...

Organization

46 counties, 46 recording offices. The recording officer is. Register of Mesne Conveyances or Clerk of Court (varies by county). The entire state is in the Eastern Time Zone (EST).

UCC Records

Financing statements are filed at the state level, except for consumer goods, farm related and real estate related collateral, which are filed with the Register. All recording offices will perform UCC searches. Use search request form UCC-4. Searches fees are usually $5.00 per debtor name. Copy fees are usually $1.00 per page.

Lien Records

All federal and state tax liens on personal property and on real property are filed with the Register of Mesne Conveyances (Clerk of Court). Some counties will perform tax lien searches. Search fees and copy fees vary.

Real Estate Records

Most counties will not perform real estate searches. Copy and certification fees vary. The Assessor keeps tax records.

County Courts & Recording Offices

Abbeville

Real Estate Recording—Abbeville Clerk of Court, Court Square, Abbeville, SC 29620. 864-459-2539. 9AM-5PM.

Felony, Misdemeanor, Civil Actions Over $5,000—Circuit Court, PO Box 99, Abbeville, SC 29620. 864-459-5074, Fax: 864-459-9188. 9AM-5PM. Access by: in person.

Probate—Probate Court, PO Box 70, Abbeville, SC 29620. 864-459-4626, Fax: 864-459-4982. 9AM-5PM. Access by: mail, phone, fax, in person.

Aiken

Real Estate Recording—Aiken County Register of Mesne Conveyances, 828 Richland Avenue West, Aiken, SC 29801. 803-642-2055. 8:30AM-5PM.

Felony, Misdemeanor, Civil Actions Over $5,000—Circuit Court, PO Box 583, Aiken, SC 29802. 803-642-1715, Fax: 803-642-1718. 8:30AM-5PM. Access by: in person.

Probate—Probate Court, 109 Park Ave, PO Box 1576, Aiken, SC 29802. 803-642-2001, Fax: 803-642-2007. 8:30AM-5PM.

Allendale

Real Estate Recording—Allendale Clerk of Court, Pine Street, Courthouse, Allendale, SC 29810. 803-584-3876, Fax: 803-584-7058.

Felony, Misdemeanor, Civil Actions Over $5,000—Circuit Court, PO Box 126, Allendale, SC 29810. 803-584-2737, Fax: 803-584-7058. 9AM-5PM. Access by: mail, phone, fax, in person.

Probate—Probate Court, PO Box 603, Allendale, SC 29810. 803-584-3157. 9AM-5PM. Access by: mail, in person.

Anderson

Real Estate Recording—Anderson County Register of Deeds, 100 South Main Street, Courthouse, Anderson, SC 29624. 864-260-4033, Fax: 864-260-4443. 8:30AM-5PM.

Felony, Misdemeanor, Civil Actions Over $5,000—Circuit Court, PO Box 8002, Anderson, SC 29622. 864-260-4053, Fax: 864-260-4715. 8:30AM-5PM. Access by: in person.

Probate—Probate Court, PO Box 8002, Anderson, SC 29622. 864-260-4049, Fax: 864-260-4811. 8AM-5PM. Access by: in person.

Bamberg

Real Estate Recording—Bamberg Clerk of Court, 110 North Main Street, Bamberg, SC 29003. 803-245-3003, Fax: 803-245-3088. 9AM-5PM.

Felony, Misdemeanor, Civil Actions Over $5,000—Circuit Court, PO Box 150, Bamberg, SC 29003. 803-245-3025, Fax: 803-245-3088. 9AM-5PM. Access by: mail, in person.

Probate—Probate Court, PO Box 180, Bamberg, SC 29003. 803-245-3008, Fax: 803-245-3027. 9AM-5PM.

Barnwell

Real Estate Recording—Barnwell Clerk of Court, Courthouse Building, Room 114, Barnwell, SC 29812. 803-541-1050, Fax: 803-541-1025. 9AM-5PM.

Felony, Misdemeanor, Civil Actions Over $5,000—Circuit Court, PO Box 723, Barnwell, SC 29812. 803-541-1020, Fax: 803-541-1025. 9AM-5PM. Access by: in person.

Probate—Probate Court, Room 108, County Courthouse, Barnwell, SC 29812. 803-541-1031, Fax: 803-541-1012. 9AM-5PM.

Beaufort

Real Estate Recording—Beaufort County Register of Deeds, 100 Ribaut Rd. Administration Bldg. Rm 205, Beaufort, SC 29902. Fax: 843-470-2709. 8AM-5PM.

Felony, Misdemeanor, Civil Actions Over $5,000—Circuit Court, PO Drawer 1128, Beaufort, SC 29901. 843-525-7306. 8AM-5PM. Access by: mail, in person.

Probate—Probate Court, PO Box 1083, Beaufort, SC 29901-1083. 843-470-5319, Fax: 843-470-5324. 8AM-5PM. Access by: mail, in person.

Berkeley

Real Estate Recording—Berkeley County Register of Deeds, 223 North Live Oak Drive, Moncks Corner, SC 29461. 803-761-3800, Fax: 843-719-4139. 9AM-5PM.

Felony, Misdemeanor, Civil Actions Over $5,000—Circuit Court, PO Box 219, Moncks Corner, SC 29461. 843-719-4406. 9AM-5PM. Access by: in person.

Probate—Probate Court, 300 B California Ave, Moncks Corner, SC 29461. 843-719-4519, Fax: 843-719-4527. 9AM-5PM. Access by: in person.

Calhoun

Real Estate Recording—Calhoun Clerk of Court, 302 S. F.R. Huff Drive, St. Matthews, SC 29135. 803-874-3519, Fax: 803-874-1942. 9AM-5PM.

Felony, Misdemeanor, Civil Actions Over $5,000—Circuit Court, 302 S Huff Dr, St Matthews, SC 29135. 803-874-3524, Fax: 803-874-1942. 9AM-5PM. Access by: mail, in person.

Probate—Probate Court, 302 S Huff Dr, St Matthews, SC 29135. 803-874-1942, Fax: 803-874-4575. Access by: mail, in person.

Charleston

Real Estate Recording—Charleston County Register of Mesne Conveyances, 2 Courthouse Square, Room 201, Meeting Street, Charleston, SC 29401. 803-723-6759, Fax: 843-720-2210. 8:30AM-5PM.

Felony, Misdemeanor, Civil Actions Over $5,000—Circuit Court, PO Box 70219, Charleston, SC 29415. 843-740-5700, Fax: 843-740-5887. 8:30AM-5PM. Access by: mail, in person, online. www3.charlestoncounty.org

Probate—Probate Court, 2144 Melbourne Ave, North Charleston, SC 294o5. 843-740-5890, Fax: 843-740-5897. 8:30AM-5PM. Access by: in person.

Cherokee

Real Estate Recording—Cherokee Clerk of Court, Courthouse, E. Floyd Baker Blvd. Gaffney, SC 29340. Fax: 864-487-2754. 8:30AM-5PM.

Felony, Misdemeanor, Civil Actions Over $5,000—Circuit Court, PO Drawer 2289, Gaffney, SC 29342. 864-487-2571, Fax: 864-487-2751. 8:30AM-5PM. Access by: in person.

Probate—Probate Court, PO Box 22, Gaffney, SC 29342. 864-487-2583, Fax: 864-902-8426. 9AM-5PM.

Chester

Real Estate Recording—Chester Clerk of Court, 140 Main Street, Chester, SC 29706. 803-385-2608, Fax: 803-581-7975. 8:30AM-5PM.

Felony, Misdemeanor, Civil Actions Over $5,000—Circuit Court, PO Drawer 580, Chester, SC 29706. 803-385-2605, Fax: 803-581-7975. 8:30AM-5PM. Access by: mail, in person.

Probate—Probate Court, PO Drawer 580, Chester, SC 29706. 803-385-2604, Fax: 803-581-5180. 8:30AM-5PM. Access by: mail, in person.

Chesterfield

Real Estate Recording—Chesterfield Clerk of Court, 200 West Main Street, Chesterfield, SC 29709. Fax: 843-623-3945. 8:30AM-5PM.

Felony, Misdemeanor, Civil Actions Over $5,000—Circuit Court, PO Box 529, Chesterfield, SC 29709. 843-623-2574, Fax: 843-623-6944. 8:30AM-5PM. Access by: mail, in person.

Probate—Probate Court, County Courthouse, 200 W Main St, Chesterfield, SC 29709. 843-623-2376, Fax: 843-623-3945. 8:30AM-5PM.

Clarendon

Real Estate Recording—Clarendon Clerk of Court, Boyce Street, Courthouse, Manning, SC 29102. Fax: 803-435-8258. 8:30AM-5PM.

Felony, Misdemeanor, Civil Actions Over $5,000—Circuit Court, PO Drawer E, Manning, SC 29102. 803-435-4444. 8:30AM-5PM. Access by: mail, in person.

Probate—Probate Court, PO Box 307, Manning, SC 29102. 803-435-8774, Fax: 803-435-8774. 8:30AM-5PM. Access by: mail, in person.

Colleton

Real Estate Recording—Colleton Clerk of Court, 101 Washington Street, Courthouse, Walterboro, SC 29488. Fax: 843-549-2875. 8:30AM-5PM.

Felony, Misdemeanor, Civil Actions Over $5,000—Circuit Court, PO Box 620, Walterboro, SC 29488. 843-549-5791, Fax: 843-549-2875. 8:30AM-5PM. Access by: mail, in person.

Probate—Probate Court, PO Box 1036, Walterboro, SC 29488-0031. 843-549-7216, Fax: 843-549-5571. 8:30AM-5PM. Access by: mail, in person.

Darlington

Real Estate Recording—Darlington Clerk of Court, Courthouse, Darlington, SC 29532. Fax: 843-398-4172. 8:30AM-5PM.

Felony, Misdemeanor, Civil Actions Over $5,000—Circuit Court, PO Box 1177, Darlington, SC 29540. 843-398-4339. 8:30AM-5PM. Access by: mail, in person.

Probate—Probate Court, Courthouse #1 Public Sq Rm 208, Darlington, SC 29532. 843-398-4310, Fax: 843-398-4172. 8:30AM-5PM. Access by: mail, in person.

Dillon

Real Estate Recording—Dillon Clerk of Court, 401 West Main Street, City-County Complex, Suite 201, Dillon, SC 29536. Fax: 843-774-1443. 8:30AM-5PM.

Felony, Misdemeanor, Civil Actions Over $5,000—Circuit Court, PO Drawer 1220, Dillon, SC 29536. 843-774-1425. 8:30AM-5PM. Access by: mail, in person.

Probate—Probate Court, PO Box 189, Dillon, SC 29536. 843-774-1423. 8:30AM-5PM.

Dorchester

Real Estate Recording—Dorchester County Register of Mesne Conveyances, 101 Ridge Street, St. George, SC 29477. 803-563-0165, Fax: 843-563-0277. 8:30AM-5PM (Recording 8:30AM-4:30PM).

Felony, Misdemeanor, Civil Actions Over $5,000—Circuit Court, 101 Ridge St, St George, SC 29477. 843-563-0160. 8:30AM-5PM. Access by: in person.

Probate—Probate Court, 101 Ridge St, St George, SC 29477. 843-563-0105, Fax: 843-832-0187. 8:30AM-5PM.

Edgefield

Real Estate Recording—Edgefield Clerk of Court, 129 Courthouse Square, Edgefield, SC 29824. Fax: 803-637-4117. 8:30AM-5PM.

Felony, Misdemeanor, Civil Actions Over $5,000—Circuit Court, PO Box 34, Edgefield, SC 29824. 803-637-4082, Fax: 803-637-4117. 8:30AM-5PM. Access by: mail, in person.

Probate—Probate Court, 124 Courthouse Square, Edgefield, SC 29824. 803-637-4076, Fax: 803-637-7157. 8:30AM-5PM. Access by: mail, in person.

Fairfield

Real Estate Recording—Fairfield Clerk of Court, Congress Street, Courthouse, Winnsboro, SC 29180. 803-635-1411. 9AM-5PM.

Felony, Misdemeanor, Civil Actions Over $5,000—Circuit Court, PO Drawer 299, Winnsboro, SC 29180. 803-635-1411. 9AM-5PM. Access by: in person.

Probate—Probate Court, PO Box 385, Winnsboro, SC 29180. 803-635-1411, Fax: 803-635-2767. 9AM-5PM. Access by: mail, in person.

Florence

Real Estate Recording—Florence Clerk of Court, 180 North Irby, Courthouse, Florence, SC 29501. 803-665-3041, Fax: 843-665-3097. 8:30AM-5PM.

Felony, Misdemeanor, Civil Actions Over $5,000—Circuit Court, Drawer E, City County Complex, Florence, SC 29501. 843-665-3031. 8:30AM-5PM. Access by: mail, in person.

Probate—Probate Court, 180 N Irby, MSC-L, Florence, SC 29501. 843-665-3085, Fax: 843-665-3068. 8:30AM-5PM. Access by: mail, phone, in person.

Georgetown

Real Estate Recording—Georgetown County Register of Deeds, 715 Prince Street, Georgetown, SC 29440. 803-527-5179. 8:30AM-5PM.

Felony, Misdemeanor, Civil Actions Over $5,000—Circuit Court, PO Box 1270, Georgetown, SC 29442. 843-546-5011, Fax: 843-546-2144. 8:30AM-5PM. Access by: mail, in person.

Probate—Probate Court, PO Box 1270, Georgetown, SC 29442. 843-527-6325, Fax: 843-546-4730. 8:30AM-5PM. Access by: mail, in person.

Greenville

Real Estate Recording—Greenville County Register of Deeds, 301 University Ridge, County Square Suite 1300, Greenville, SC 29601. 864-467-7210, Fax: 864-467-7107. 8:30AM-5PM.

Felony, Misdemeanor, Civil Actions Over $5,000—Circuit Court, 305 E. North St, Greenville, SC 29601. 864-467-8551, Fax: 864-467-8540. 8:30AM-5PM. Access by: in person.

Probate—Probate Court, 301 University Ridge, Ste 1200, Greenville, SC 29601. 864-467-7170, Fax: 864-467-7082. 8:30AM-5PM. Access by: mail, phone, fax, in person. www.greenvillecounty.org

Greenwood

Real Estate Recording—Greenwood Clerk of Court, Courthouse, 528 Monument St. Greenwood, SC 29646. 864-942-8528. 8:30AM-5PM.

Felony, Misdemeanor, Civil Actions Over $5,000—Circuit Court, Courthouse, Rm 114, 528 Monument St, Greenwood, SC 29646. 864-942-8612, Fax: 864-943-8620. 8:30AM-5PM. Access by: mail, in person.

Probate—Probate Court, PO Box 1210, Greenwood, SC 29648. 864-942-8625, Fax: 864-942-8620. 8:30AM-5PM. Access by: fax, in person.

Hampton

Real Estate Recording—Hampton Clerk of Court, Courthouse Square, Elm Street, Hampton, SC 29924. Fax: 803-943-7596. 8AM-5PM.

Felony, Misdemeanor, Civil Actions Over $5,000—Circuit Court, PO Box 7, Hampton, SC 29924. 803-943-7500. 8AM-5PM. Access by: mail, in person.

Probate—Probate Court, PO Box 601, Hampton, SC 29924. 803-943-7512, Fax: 803-943-7596. 8AM-5PM. Access by: mail, in person.

Horry

Real Estate Recording—Horry County Register of Deeds, 1316 1st St. Conway, SC 29526. Fax: 843-248-1566. 8AM-5PM.

Felony, Misdemeanor, Civil Actions Over $5,000—Circuit Court, PO Box 677, Conway, SC 29526. 843-248-1270, Fax: 843-248-1341. 8AM-5PM. Access by: mail, phone, in person.

Probate—Probate Court, PO Box 288, Conway, SC 29528. 843-248-1294, Fax: 843-248-1298. 8AM-5PM. Access by: in person.

Jasper

Real Estate Recording—Jasper Clerk of Court, 305 Russell Street, Ridgeland, SC 29936. Fax: 843-726-7782. 9AM-5PM.

Felony, Misdemeanor, Civil Actions Over $5,000—Circuit Court, PO Box 248, Ridgeland, SC 29936. 843-726-7710. 8:30AM-5PM. Access by: mail, in person.

Probate—Probate Court, PO Box 1028, Ridgeland, SC 29936. 843-726-7719, Fax: 843-726-7782. 9AM-5PM. Access by: mail, in person.

Kershaw

Real Estate Recording—Kershaw Clerk of Court, Courthouse - Room 313, 1121 Broad St. Camden, SC 29020. Fax: 803-425-1505. 8:30AM-5PM.

Felony, Misdemeanor, Civil Actions Over $5,000—Circuit Court, County Courthouse, Rm 313, PO Box 1557, Camden, SC 29020. 803-425-1500, Fax: 803-425-1505. 9AM-5PM. Access by: in person.

Probate—Probate Court, 1121 Broad St, Rm 302, Camden, SC 29020. 803-425-1500, Fax: 803-425-1526. 9AM-5PM. Access by: mail, in person.

Lancaster

Real Estate Recording—Lancaster Clerk of Court, 116 W. Dunlap Street, Lancaster, SC 29720. 803-285-7939, Fax: 803-416-9388. 8:30AM-5PM.

Felony, Misdemeanor, Civil Actions Over $5,000—Circuit Court, PO Box 1809, Lancaster, SC 29721. 803-285-1581, Fax: 803-285-6497. 8:30AM-5PM. Access by: mail, in person.

Probate—Probate Court, PO Box 1809, Lancaster, SC 29721. 803-283-3379, Fax: 803-283-3370. 8:30AM-5PM. Access by: mail, phone, in person.

Laurens

Real Estate Recording—Laurens Clerk of Court, Public Square, Laurens, SC 29360. 9AM-5PM.

Felony, Misdemeanor, Civil Actions Over $5,000—Circuit Court, PO Box 287, Laurens, SC 29360. 864-984-3538. 9AM-5PM. Access by: mail, in person.

Probate—Probate Court, PO Box 194, Laurens, SC 29360. 864-984-7315. 9AM-5PM. Access by: mail, phone, in person.

Lee

Real Estate Recording—Lee Clerk of Court, 123 South Main Street, Courthouse, Bishopville, SC 29010. Fax: 803-484-5043. 9AM-5PM.

Felony, Misdemeanor, Civil Actions Over $5,000—Circuit Court, PO Box 387, Bishopville, SC 29010. 803-484-5341, Fax: 803-484-6512. 9AM-5PM. Access by: mail, in person.

Probate—Lee County Probate Court, PO Box 24, Bishopville, SC 29010. 803-484-5341, Fax: 803-484-6512. 9AM-5PM. Access by: in person.

Lexington

Real Estate Recording—Lexington County Register of Deeds, 212 South Lake Drive, Lexington, SC 29072. 803-359-8217, Fax: 803-359-8189. 8AM-5PM.

Felony, Misdemeanor, Civil Actions Over $5,000—Circuit Court, Lexington County Courthouse, Rm 107, 139 East Main St, Lexington, SC 29072-33494. 803-359-8212, Fax: 803-359-8314. 8AM-5PM. Access by: mail, fax, in person.

Probate—Probate Court, County Courthouse, Rm 110, 139 E Main St, Lexington, SC 29072-3448. 803-359-8324. 8AM-5PM. Access by: mail, in person.

Marion

Real Estate Recording—Marion Clerk of Court, 100 West Court Street, Marion, SC 29571. Fax: 843-423-8306. 8:30AM-5PM.

Felony, Misdemeanor, Civil Actions Over $5,000—Circuit Court, PO Box 295, Marion, SC 29571. 843-423-8240. 8:30AM-5PM. Access by: in person.

Probate—Probate Court, PO Box 583, Marion, SC 29571. 843-423-8244, Fax: 843-423-0526. 8:30AM-5PM. Access by: mail, in person.

Marlboro

Real Estate Recording—Marlboro Clerk of Court, Main Street, Courthouse, Bennettsville, SC 29512. Fax: 843-479-5640. 8:30AM-5PM.

Felony, Misdemeanor, Civil Actions Over $5,000—Circuit Court, PO Drawer 996, Bennettsville, SC 29512. 843-479-5613, Fax: 843-479-5640. 8:30AM-5PM. Access by: mail, in person.

Probate—Probate Court, PO Box 455, Bennettsville, SC 29512. 843-479-5610. 8:30AM-5PM. Access by: mail, in person.

McCormick

Real Estate Recording—McCormick Clerk of Court, 133 South Mine Street, Courthouse, Room 102, McCormick, SC 29835. 864-465-2332, Fax: 864-465-0071. 9AM-5PM.

Felony, Misdemeanor, Civil Actions Over $5,000—Circuit Court, 133 S Mine St, McCormick, SC 29835. 864-465-2195, Fax: 864-465-0071. 9AM-5PM. Access by: mail, in person.

Probate—Probate Court, 133 S Mine St, McCormick, SC 29835. 864-465-2630, Fax: 864-465-0071. 9AM-5PM. Access by: mail, phone, in person.

Newberry

Real Estate Recording—Newberry Clerk of Court, Courthouse Room 5, 1226 College St. Newberry, SC 29108. 803-321-2130, Fax: 803-321-2111. 8:30AM-5PM.

Felony, Misdemeanor, Civil Actions Over $5,000—Circuit Court, PO Box 278, Newberry, SC 29108. 803-321-2110, Fax: 803-321-2102. 8:30AM-5PM. Access by: mail, in person.

Probate—Probate Court, PO Box 442, Newberry, SC 29108. 803-321-2118, Fax: 803-321-2119. 8:30AM-5PM. Access by: mail, in person.

Oconee

Real Estate Recording—Oconee Clerk of Court, 211 W. Main St. Walhalla, SC 29691. 803-638-4162. 8:30AM-5PM.

Felony, Misdemeanor, Civil Actions Over $5,000—Circuit Court, PO Box 678, Walhalla, SC 29691. 864-638-4280. 8:30AM-5PM. Access by: mail, in person.

Probate—Probate Court, PO Box 471, Walhalla, SC 29691. 864-638-4275, Fax: 864-638-4278. 8:30AM-5PM. Access by: in person.

Orangeburg

Real Estate Recording—Orangeburg County Register of Deeds, 190 Gibson St. Room 108, Orangeburg, SC 29115. 803-533-6130, Fax: 803-534-3848. 8:30AM-5PM.

Felony, Misdemeanor, Civil Actions Over $5,000—Circuit Court, PO Box 9000, Orangeburg, SC 29116. 803-533-6243, Fax: 803-534-3848. 8:30AM-5PM. Access by: in person.

Probate—Probate Court, PO Drawer 9000, Orangeburg, SC 29116-9000. 803-533-6280, Fax: 803-533-6279. 8:30AM-5PM. Access by: mail, in person.

Pickens

Real Estate Recording—Pickens Register of Deeds, 222 McDaniel Ave. B-5, Pickens, SC 29671. 864-898-5883, Fax: 864-898-5924. 8:30AM-5PM.

Felony, Misdemeanor, Civil Actions Over $5,000—Circuit Court, PO Box 215, Pickens, SC 29671. 864-898-5866, Fax: 864-898-5863. 8:30AM-5PM. Access by: mail, in person.

Probate—Probate Court, 222 McDaniel Ave B-16, Pickens, SC 29671. 864-898-5903, Fax: 864-898-5924. 8:30AM-5PM. Access by: mail, in person.

Richland

Real Estate Recording—Richland County Register of Deeds, 1701 Main Street, Columbia, SC 29201. Fax: 803-748-4807. 8:45AM-5PM.

Felony, Misdemeanor, Civil Actions Over $5,000—Circuit Court, PO Box 2766, Columbia, SC 29202. 803-748-4684, Fax: 803-748-5039. 8:30AM-5PM. Access by: mail, in person.

Probate—Probate Court, PO Box 192, Columbia, SC 29202. 803-748-4705, Fax: 803-748-5079. 8:30AM-5PM. Access by: mail, in person.

Saluda

Real Estate Recording—Saluda Clerk of Court, Courthouse, Saluda, SC 29138. 864-445-2875, Fax: 864-445-3772. 8:30AM-5PM.

Felony, Misdemeanor, Civil Actions Over $5,000—Circuit Court, County Courthouse, Saluda, SC 29138. 864-445-3303, Fax: 864-445-3772. 8:30AM-5PM. Access by: mail, fax, in person.

Probate—Probate Court, County Courthouse, Saluda, SC 29138. 864-445-7110, Fax: 864-445-9726. 8:30AM-5PM. Access by: mail, in person.

Spartanburg

Real Estate Recording—Spartanburg County Register of Mesne Conveyances, 366 North Church Street, County Administrative Offices, Spartanburg, SC 29303. 803-596-2603. 8:30AM-5PM.

Felony, Misdemeanor, Civil—Circuit Court, County Courthouse, 180 Magnolia St, Spartanburg, SC 29306. 864-596-2591, Fax: 864-596-2239. 8:30AM-5PM. Access by: in person.

Probate—Probate Court, 180 Magnolia St, Spartanburg, SC 29306-2392. 864-596-2556, Fax: 864-596-2011. 8:30AM-5PM. Access by: mail, in person.

Sumter

Real Estate Recording—Sumter County Register of Deeds, Courthouse, Room 202, 141 N. Main St. Sumter, SC 29150. 803-436-2213. 8:30AM-5PM.

Felony, Misdemeanor, Civil Actions Over $5,000—Circuit Court, 141 N Main, Sumter, SC 29150. 803-436-2227, Fax: 803-436-2223. 8:30AM-5PM. Access by: mail, in person.

Probate—Probate Court, 141 N Main, Rm 111, Sumter, SC 29150. 803-436-2166, Fax: 803-436-2407. 8:30AM-5PM. Access by: mail, in person.

Union

Real Estate Recording—Union Clerk of Court, 210 West Main Street, Union, SC 29379. Fax: 864-429-1715. 9AM-5PM.

Felony, Misdemeanor, Civil Actions Over $5,000—Circuit Court, PO Box 200, Union, SC 29379. 864-429-1630, Fax: 864-429-4454. 9AM-5PM. Access by: in person.

Probate—Probate Court, PO Box 447, Union, SC 29379. 864-429-1625, Fax: 864-429-1603. 9AM-5PM. Access by: mail, in person.

Williamsburg

Real Estate Recording—Williamsburg Clerk of Court, 125 West Main Street, Courthouse Square, Kingstree, SC 29556. Fax: 843-354-5813. 9AM-5PM.

Felony, Misdemeanor, Civil Actions Over $5,000—Circuit Court, 125 W Main St, Kingstree, SC 29556. 843-354-9321, Fax: 843-354-7821. 8:30AM-5PM. Access by: mail, in person.

Probate—Probate Court, PO Box 1005, Kingstree, SC 29556. 843-354-9321, Fax: 843-354-2106. 8:30AM-5PM. Access by: mail, in person.

York

Real Estate Recording—York Clerk of Court, 2 South Congress, York, SC 29745. 803-684-8528. 8AM-5PM.

Felony, Misdemeanor, Civil Actions Over $5,000—Circuit Court, PO Box 649, York, SC 29745. 803-688-8506. 8AM-5PM. Access by: mail, fax, in person.

Probate—Probate Court, PO Box 219, York, SC 29745. 803-684-8513. 8AM-5PM. Access by: mail, in person.

Federal Courts

US District Court

Anderson Division c/o Greenville Division, PO Box 10768, Greenville, SC 29603864-241-2700 Counties: Anderson, Oconee, Pickens. www.scd.uscourts.gov

Beaufort Division c/o Charleston Division, PO Box 835, Charleston, SC 29402843-579-1401 Fax: 803-579-1402 Counties: Beaufort, Hampton, Jasper. www.scd.uscourts.gov

Charleston Division PO Box 835, Charleston, SC 29402843-579-1401 Fax: 803-579-1402 Counties: Berkeley, Charleston, Clarendon, Colleton, Dorchester, Georgetown. www.scd.uscourts.gov

Columbia Division 1845 Assembly St, Columbia, SC 29201803-765-5816 Counties: Kershaw, Lee, Lexington, Richland, Sumter. www.scd.uscourts.gov

Florence Division PO Box 2317, Florence, SC 29503843-676-3820 Fax: 803-676-3831 Counties: Chesterfield, Darlington, Dillon, Florence, Horry, Marion, Marlboro, Williamsburg. www.scd.uscourts.gov

Greenville Division PO Box 10768, Greenville, SC 29603864-241-2700 Counties: Greenville, Laurens. www.scd.uscourts.gov

Greenwood Division c/o Greenville Division, PO Box 10768, Greenville, SC 29603864-241-2700 Counties: Abbeville, Aiken, Allendale, Bamberg, Barnwell, Calhoun, Edgefield, Fairfield, Greenwood, Lancaster, McCormick, Newberry, Orangeburg, Saluda. www.scd.uscourts.gov

Spartanburg Division c/o Greenville Division, PO Box 10768, Greenville, SC 29603864-241-2700 Counties: Cherokee, Chester, Spartanburg, Union, York. www.scd.uscourts.gov

US Bankruptcy Court

Columbia Division PO Box 1448, Columbia, SC 29202803-765-5436 Counties: All counties in South Carolina. www.scb.uscourts.gov

South Dakota

Attorney General's Office
State Capitol, 500 E Capitol Ave   605-773-3215
Pierre, SD 57501-5070   · Fax: 605-773-4106
www.state.sd.us/attorney/attorney.html

Governor's Office
State Capitol, 500 E Capitol Ave   605-773-3212
Pierre, SD 57501-5070   Fax: 605-773-4711
www.state.sd.us/governor/index.htm

State Archives
900 Governors Dr   605-773-3804
Pierre, SD 57501-2217   Fax: 605-773-6041
www.state.sd.us/deca/cultural

Capital: Pierre
Hughes County

Time Zone: CST*

* South Dakota's 18 western-most counties are MST: They are: Bennett, Butte, Corson, Custer, Dewey, Fall River, Haakon, Harding, Jackson, Lawrence, Meade, Mellette, Pennington, Perkins, Shannon, Stanley, Todd, Ziebach,

Number of Counties: 66

Population: 737,973

Web Site: www.state.sd.us

Search Unclaimed Property Online

There is no Internet-based search for this state; however, the URL for the agency responsible for unclaimed property is www.state.sd.us/state/executive/treasurer/prop.htm

State Agencies

Criminal Records
Division of Criminal Investigation, Office of Attorney General, 500 E Capitol, Pierre, SD 57501-5070; 605-773-3331; Fax: 605-773-4629; 8AM-5PM. Access by: mail.

Corporation Records
Limited Partnerships
Limited Liability Company Records
Trademarks/Servicemarks
Corporation Division, Secretary of State, 500 E Capitol Ave, Suite B-05, Pierre, SD 57501-5070; 605-773-4845; Fax: 605-773-4550; 8AM-5PM. Access by: mail, phone, in person. www.state.sd.us/sos/sos.htm

Sales Tax Registrations
Revenue Department, Business Tax Division, 445 E Capitol, Pierre, SD 57501-3100; 605-773-3311; Fax: 605-773-5129; 8AM-5PM. Access by: mail, phone, in person. www.state.sd.us/revenue

Uniform Commercial Code
Federal Tax Liens
UCC Division, Secretary of State, 500 East Capitol, Pierre, SD 57501-5077; 605-773-4422; Fax: 605-773-4550; 8AM-5PM. Access by: mail, phone, in person, online. www.state.sd.us/sos/sos.htm

Fictitious Name
Assumed Name
Records not available from state agency.

Records are located at the county level.

State Tax Liens
Records not available from state agency.

Records are filed at the county level.

Workers' Compensation Records
Labor Department, Workers Compensation Division, 700 Governors Dr, Pierre, SD 57501; 605-773-3681; Fax: 605-773-4211; 8AM-5PM. Access by: mail. www.state.sd.us/state

Birth Certificates
South Dakota Department of Health, Vital Records, 600 E Capitol, Pierre, SD 57501-2536; 605-773-4961, 605-773-3355 Message Phone; 8AM-5PM. Access by: mail, phone, in person.

Death Records
South Dakota Department of Health, Vital Records, 600 E Capitol, Pierre, SD 57501-2536; 605-773-4961, 605-773-3355 Message Phone; 8AM-5PM. Access by: mail, phone, in person.

Marriage Certificates
South Dakota Department of Health, Vital Records, 600 E Capitol, Pierre, SD 57501-2536; 605-773-4961, 605-773-3355 Message Phone; 8AM-5PM. Access by: mail, phone, in person.

Divorce Records
South Dakota Department of Health, Vital Records, 600 E Capitol, Pierre, SD 57501-2536; 605-773-4961, 605-773-3355 Message Phone; 8AM-5PM. Access by: mail, phone, in person.

Accident Reports
Department of Transportation, Accident Records, 700 E. Broadway, Pierre, SD 57501-2586; 605-773-3868; Fax: 605-773-4870; 8AM-5PM. Access by: mail.

Driver Records
Dept of Commerce & Regulation, Office of Driver Licensing, 118 W Capitol, Pierre, SD 57501; 605-773-6883; Fax: 605-773-3018; 8AM-5PM. Access by: mail. www.state.sd.us/dcr/dl/sddriver.htm

Vehicle Ownership
Vehicle Identification
Boat & Vessel Ownership
Boat & Vessel Registration
Division of Motor Vehicles, Information Section, 445 E Capitol Ave, Pierre, SD 57501-3100; 605-773-3541; Fax: 605-773-5129; 8AM-5PM. Access by: mail. www.sd.us/state/revenue

Legislation-Current/Pending
Legislation-Passed
South Dakota Legislature, Capitol Bldg - Legislative Documents, 500 E Capitol Ave, Pierre, SD 57501; 605-773-3835; Fax: 605-773-4576; 8AM-5PM. Access by: mail, phone, in person, online. www.state.sd.us/state/legis/lrc.htm.

Voter Registration
Records not available from state agency.

The county auditors hold records. There are no restrictions on usage.

GED Certificates
Department of Education, GED Testing, 700 Governors Drive, Pierre, SD 57501-2291; 605-773-4463; Fax: 605-773-4236; 8AM-5PM.

Hunting License Information
Fishing License Information
Game, Fish & Parks Department, License Division, 412 W Missouri, Pierre, SD 57501; 605-773-3926; Fax: 605-773-5842; 8AM-5PM. Access by: mail. www.state.sd.us/gfp

County Courts & Recording Offices

About the Courts...

Administration

State Court Administrator, State Capitol Building   605-773-3474
500 E Capitol Av   Fax: 605-773-5627
Pierre, SD 57501
www.state.sd.us/state/judicial

Court Structure

South Dakota has a statewide criminal record search database, administrated by the State Court Administrator's Office in Pierre. All criminal record information from July 1, 1989 forward, statewide, is contained in the database. To facilitate quicker access for the public, the state has designated 10 county record centers to process all mail or ongoing commercial accounts' criminal record requests. All mail requests are forwarded to, and commercial account requests are assigned to one of 10 specific county court clerks for processing a statewide search. Note that walk-in requesters seeking a single or minimum of requests may still obtain a record from their local county court. 6 counties (Buffalo, Campbell, Corson, Dewey, McPherson, and Ziebach) do not have computer terminals in-house. The criminal records from these 6 counties are entered into the database by court personnel from another location.

The fee is $15.00 per record. State authorized commercial accounts may order and receive records by fax, there is an additional $5.00 fee unless a non-toll free line is used.

Requesters who wish to set up a commercial account are directed to contact Jill Smith at the Court Administrator's Office in Pierre at the address mentioned above. Ms. Smith can also be reached at jill@ujs.state.sd.us.

Searching Hints

Most South Dakota courts do not allow the public to perform searches, but rather require the court clerk to do them for a fee of $15.00 per name (increased from $5.00 as of July 1, 1997). A special Record Search Request Form must be used. Searches will be returned with a disclaimer stating that the clerk is not responsible for the completeness of the search. Clerks are not required to respond to telephone or Fax requests. Many courts are not open all day so they prefer written requests.

Online Access

There is no statewide online access computer system currently available. Larger courts are being placed on computer systems at a rate of 4 to 5 courts per year. Access is intended for internal use only. Smaller courts place their information on computer cards that are later sent to Pierre for input by the state office.

About the Recording Offices...

Organization

66 counties, 66 recording offices. The recording officer is. Register of Deeds. 48 counties are in the Central Time Zone (CST) and 18 are in the Mountain Time Zone (MST).

UCC Records

Financing statements are filed at the state level, except for real estate related collateral, which are filed with the Register of Deeds. All recording offices will perform UCC searches. All counties have access to a statewide database of UCC filings. Use search request form UCC-11. Searches fees are usually $10.00 per debtor name. Copy fees are usually $1.00 per page.

Lien Records

Federal and state tax liens on personal property of businesses are filed with the Secretary of State. Other federal and state tax liens are filed with the county Register of Deeds. Most counties will perform tax lien searches. Search fees and copy fees vary.

Real Estate Records

Many counties will perform real estate searches. Search fees and copy fees vary. Certification usually costs $1.00 per document.

County Courts & Recording Offices

Aurora

Real Estate Recording—Aurora County Register of Deeds, Courthouse, 401 N. Main St. Plankinton, SD 57368. 605-942-7162, Fax: 605-942-7751. 8AM-Noon,1-5PM.

Felony, Misdemeanor, Civil, Eviction, Small Claims, Probate—Circuit Court, PO Box 366, Plankinton, SD 57368. 605-942-7165, Fax: 605-942-7751. 8AM-Noon, 1-5PM. Access by: mail, in person.

Beadle

Real Estate Recording—Beadle County Register of Deeds, 450-3rd St. SW, Huron, SD 57350. 605-352-6719, Fax: 605-352-1328. 8AM-5PM.

Felony, Misdemeanor, Civil, Eviction, Small Claims, Probate—Circuit Court, PO Box 1358, Huron, SD 57350. 605-353-7165. 8AM-5PM. Access by: mail, in person.

Bennett

Real Estate Recording—Bennett County Register of Deeds, 202 Main Street, Courthouse, Martin, SD 57551. 605-685-6092, Fax: 605-685-6311. 8AM-Noon, 12:30-4:30PM.

Felony, Misdemeanor, Civil, Eviction, Small Claims, Probate—Circuit Court, PO Box 281, Martin, SD 57551. 605-685-6969. 8AM-4:30PM. Access by: mail, in person.

Bon Homme

Real Estate Recording—Bon Homme County Register of Deeds, Cherry Street, Courthouse, Tyndall, SD 57066. 8AM-4:30PM.

Felony, Misdemeanor, Civil, Eviction, Small Claims, Probate—Circuit Court, PO Box 6, Tyndall, SD 57066. 605-589-4215, Fax: 605-589-4209. 8AM-4:30PM. Access by: mail, fax, in person.

Brookings

Real Estate Recording—Brookings County Register of Deeds, 314 6th Avenue, Courthouse, Brookings, SD 57006. 605-692-4731. 8AM-5PM.

Felony, Misdemeanor, Civil, Eviction, Small Claims, Probate—Circuit Court, 314 6th Ave, Brookings, SD 57006. 605-688-4200, Fax: 605-688-4952. 8AM-5PM. Access by: mail, in person.

Brown

Real Estate Recording—Brown County Register of Deeds, 25 Market Street, Aberdeen, SD 57402. Fax: 605-626-4010. 8AM-5PM.

Felony, Misdemeanor, Civil, Eviction, Small Claims, Probate—Circuit Court, 101 1st Ave SE, Aberdeen, SD 57401. 605-626-2451, Fax: 605-626-2491. 8AM-5PM. Access by: mail, in person.

Brule

Real Estate Recording—Brule County Register of Deeds, 300 South Courtland, Suite 110, Chamberlain, SD 57325. 8AM-Noon,1-5PM.

Felony, Misdemeanor, Civil, Eviction, Small Claims, Probate—Circuit Court, 300 S Courtland #111, Chamberlain, SD 57325-1599. 605-734-5443, Fax: 605-734-4151. 8AM-Noon, 1-5PM. Access by: mail, fax, in person.

Buffalo

Real Estate Recording—Buffalo County Register of Deeds, Main Street, Courthouse, Gannvalley, SD 57341. 605-293-3236, Fax: 605-293-3240. 9AM-5PM.

Felony, Misdemeanor, Civil, Eviction, Small Claims, Probate—Circuit Court, PO Box 148, Gann Valley, SD 57341. 605-293-3234, Fax: 605-293-3240. 9AM-Noon. Access by: mail, in person.

Butte

Real Estate Recording—Butte County Register of Deeds, 839 Fifth Avenue, Belle Fourche, SD 57717. 605-892-4456. 8AM-5PM.

Felony, Misdemeanor, Civil, Eviction, Small Claims, Probate—Circuit Court, PO Box 237, Belle Fourche, SD 57717. 605-892-2516, Fax: 605-892-2836. 8AM-Noon, 1-5PM. Access by: mail, in person.

Campbell

Real Estate Recording—Campbell County Register of Deeds, Courthouse, 111 2nd St. East, Mound City, SD 57646. 605-955-3388, Fax: 605-955-3308. 8AM-Noon,1-5PM.

Felony, Misdemeanor, Civil, Eviction, Small Claims, Probate—Circuit Court, PO Box 146, Mound City, SD 57646. 605-955-3536, Fax: 605-955-3308. 8AM-Noon T-W-TH. Access by: mail, in person.

Charles Mix

Real Estate Recording—Charles Mix County Register of Deeds, Courthouse, 400 E. Main, Lake Andes, SD 57356. Fax: 605-487-7221. 8AM-4:30PM.

Felony, Misdemeanor, Civil, Eviction, Small Claims, Probate—Circuit Court, PO Box 640, Lake Andes, SD 57356. 605-487-7511, Fax: 605-487-7221. 8AM-4:30PM. Access by: mail, fax, in person.

Clark

Real Estate Recording—Clark County Register of Deeds, 202 N. Commercial St. Clark, SD 57225. 605-532-5911, Fax: 605-532-5931. 8AM-5PM.

Felony, Misdemeanor, Civil, Eviction, Small Claims, Probate—Circuit Court, PO Box 294, Clark, SD 57225. 605-532-5851. 8AM-Noon, 1-5PM. Access by: mail, in person.

Clay

Real Estate Recording—Clay County Register of Deeds, 211 West Main Street, Suite 202, Vermillion, SD 57069. 605-624-3562. 8AM-5PM.

Felony, Misdemeanor, Civil, Eviction, Small Claims, Probate—Circuit Court, PO Box 377, Vermillion, SD 57069. 605-677-6755, Fax: 605-677-7105. 8AM-5PM. Access by: mail, in person.

Codington

Real Estate Recording—Codington County Register of Deeds, 14 1st Avenue S.E. Watertown, SD 57201. 605-886-3611, Fax: 602-882-6288. 8AM-5PM.

Felony, Misdemeanor, Civil, Eviction, Small Claims, Probate—Circuit Court, PO Box 1054, Watertown, SD 57201. 605-882-5095, Fax: 605-882-5106. 8AM-5PM. Access by: mail, in person.

Corson

Real Estate Recording—Corson County Register of Deeds, Courthouse, McIntosh, SD 57641. 605-273-4552, Fax: 605-273-4304. 8AM-Noon,1-5PM.

Felony, Misdemeanor, Civil, Eviction, Small Claims, Probate—Circuit Court, PO Box 175, McIntosh, SD 57641. 605-273-4201, Fax: 605-273-4233. 9:30AM-2:30PM. Access by: mail, in person.

Custer

Real Estate Recording—Custer County Register of Deeds, 420 Mount Rushmore Road, Custer, SD 57730. 605-673-2282, Fax: 605-673-3439. 8AM-5PM.

Felony, Misdemeanor, Civil, Eviction, Small Claims, Probate—Circuit Court, 420 Mt Rushmore Rd, Custer, SD 57730. 605-673-4816, Fax: 605-673-3416. 8AM-5PM. Access by: mail, in person.

Davison

Real Estate Recording—Davison County Register of Deeds, 200 East 4th, Courthouse, Mitchell, SD 57301. Fax: 605-995-8648. 8AM-5PM.

Felony, Misdemeanor, Civil, Eviction, Small Claims, Probate—Circuit Court, PO Box 927, Mitchell, SD 57301. 605-995-4705, Fax: 605-995-3134. 8AM-5PM. Access by: mail, in person.

Day

Real Estate Recording—Day County Register of Deeds, 710 West First Street, Webster, SD 57274. 605-345-3081, Fax: 605-345-4162. 8AM-5PM.

Felony, Misdemeanor, Civil, Eviction, Small Claims, Probate—Circuit Court, 710 W 1st St, Webster, SD 57274. 605-345-3771, Fax: 605-345-3818. 8AM-5PM. Access by: mail, in person.

Deuel

Real Estate Recording—Deuel County Register of Deeds, Courthouse, Clear Lake, SD 57226. 605-874-2483, Fax: 605-874-2916. 8AM-5PM.

Felony, Misdemeanor, Civil, Eviction, Small Claims, Probate—Circuit Court, PO Box 308, Clear Lake, SD 57226. 605-874-2120. 8AM-5PM. Access by: mail, in person.

Dewey

Real Estate Recording—Dewey County Register of Deeds, Courthouse, 710 C Street, Timber Lake, SD 57656. Fax: 605-865-3691. 8AM-Noon,1-5PM.

Felony, Misdemeanor, Civil, Eviction, Small Claims, Probate—Circuit Court, PO Box 96, Timber Lake, SD 57656. 605-865-3566. 9:30AM-Noon, 1-2:30PM. Access by: mail, in person.

Douglas

Real Estate Recording—Douglas County Register of Deeds, Courthouse, 1st & Braddock (Hwy 281), Armour, SD 57313. Fax: 605-724-2204. 8AM-Noon,1-5PM.

Felony, Misdemeanor, Civil, Eviction, Small Claims, Probate—Circuit Court, PO Box 36, Armour, SD 57313. 605-724-2585, Fax: 605-724-2204. 8AM-Noon, 1-5PM. Access by: mail, fax, in person.

Edmunds

Real Estate Recording—Edmunds County Register of Deeds, Courthouse, Ipswich, SD 57451. 605-426-6801, Fax: 605-426-6257. 8AM-Noon,1-5PM.

Felony, Misdemeanor, Civil, Eviction, Small Claims, Probate—Circuit Court, PO Box 384, Ipswich, SD 57451. 605-426-6671, Fax: 605-426-6671. 8AM-Noon, 1-5PM. Access by: mail, fax, in person.

Fall River

Real Estate Recording—Fall River County Register of Deeds, 906 North River Street, Hot Springs, SD 57747. 605-745-5145, Fax: 605-745-6835. 8AM-5PM.

Felony, Misdemeanor, Civil, Eviction, Small Claims, Probate—Circuit Court, 906 N River St, Hot Springs, SD 57747. 605-745-5131. 8AM-5PM. Access by: mail, in person. Special note: Also handles cases for Shannon County. Specify which county in any search request.

Faulk

Real Estate Recording—Faulk County Register of Deeds, Courthouse, Faulkton, SD 57438. 605-598-6232, Fax: 605-598-6680. 8AM-Noon,1-5PM.

Felony, Misdemeanor, Civil, Eviction, Small Claims, Probate—Circuit Court, PO Box 357, Faulkton, SD 57438. 605-598-6223, Fax: 605-598-6680. 9AM-3PM. Access by: mail, in person.

Grant

Real Estate Recording—Grant County Register of Deeds, 210 East Fifth Avenue, Milbank, SD 57252. 605-432-5651. 8AM-5PM.

Felony, Misdemeanor, Civil, Eviction, Small Claims, Probate—Circuit Court, PO Box 509, Milbank, SD 57252. 605-432-5482. 8AM-Noon, 1-5PM. Access by: mail, in person.

Gregory

Real Estate Recording—Gregory County Register of Deeds, Courthouse, Burke, SD 57523. 605-775-2605, Fax: 605-775-2596. 8AM-Noon,1-5PM.

Felony, Misdemeanor, Civil, Eviction, Small Claims, Probate—Circuit Court, PO Box 430, Burke, SD 57523. 605-775-2665. 8AM-Noon, 1-5PM. Access by: mail, in person.

Haakon

Real Estate Recording—Haakon County Register of Deeds, 130 South Howard, Courthouse, Philip, SD 57567. 605-859-2612. 8AM-Noon,1-5PM.

Felony, Misdemeanor, Civil, Eviction, Small Claims, Probate—Circuit Court, PO Box 70, Philip, SD 57567. 605-859-2627. 1-5PM. Access by: mail, in person.

Hamlin

Real Estate Recording—Hamlin County Register of Deeds, 300 4th St. Hayti, SD 57241. 605-783-3441. 8AM-Noon, 1-5PM.

Felony, Misdemeanor, Civil, Eviction, Small Claims, Probate—Circuit Court, PO Box 256, Hayti, SD 57241. 605-783-3751, Fax: 605-783-3201. 8AM-Noon, 1-5PM. Access by: mail, in person.

Hand

Real Estate Recording—Hand County Register of Deeds, 415 West 1st Avenue, Miller, SD 57362. 605-853-2136, Fax: 605-853-2769. 8AM-5PM.

Felony, Misdemeanor, Civil, Eviction, Small Claims, Probate—Circuit Court, PO Box 122, Miller, SD 57362. 605-853-3337, Fax: 605-853-2769. 8AM-5PM. Access by: mail, fax, in person.

Hanson

Real Estate Recording—Hanson County Register of Deeds, Courthouse, 720 5th Street, Alexandria, SD 57311. 605-239-4723, Fax: 605-239-4296. 8AM-Noon,1-5PM.

Felony, Misdemeanor, Civil, Small Claims, Probate—Circuit Court, PO Box 127, Alexandria, SD 57311. 605-239-4446, Fax: 605-239-4296. 8AM-5PM. Access by: mail, fax, in person.

Harding

Real Estate Recording—Harding County Register of Deeds, Courthouse, Buffalo, SD 57720. 605-375-3542, Fax: 605-375-3318. 8AM-Noon, 1-5PM.

Felony, Misdemeanor, Civil, Eviction, Small Claims, Probate—Circuit Court, PO Box 534, Buffalo, SD 57720. 605-375-3351. 9:30AM-Noon, 1-2:30PM. Access by: mail, fax, in person.

Hughes

Real Estate Recording—Hughes County Register of Deeds, 104 East Capital, Pierre, SD 57501. 605-224-9231, Fax: 605-773-7479. 8AM-5PM.

Felony, Misdemeanor, Civil, Eviction, Small Claims, Probate—Circuit Court, 104 E Capital, Pierre, SD 57501. 605-773-3713. 8AM-5PM. Access by: mail, in person.

Hutchinson

Real Estate Recording—Hutchinson County Register of Deeds, 140 Euclid Street, Room 37, Olivet, SD 57052. 605-387-2330, Fax: 605-387-4209. 8AM-Noon, 1-5PM.

Felony, Misdemeanor, Civil, Eviction, Small Claims, Probate—Circuit Court, 140 Euclid Rm 36, Olivet, SD 57052-2103. 605-387-4215, Fax: 605-387-4209. 8AM-Noon, 1-5PM. Access by: mail, fax, in person.

Hyde

Real Estate Recording—Hyde County Register of Deeds, 412 Commercial S.E. Courthouse, Highmore, SD 57345. 605-852-2510.

Felony, Misdemeanor, Civil, Eviction, Small Claims, Probate—Circuit Court, PO Box 306, Highmore, SD 57345. 605-852-2512, Fax: 605-852-3178. 8AM-12PM. Access by: mail, fax, in person.

Jackson

Real Estate Recording—Jackson County Register of Deeds, Main Street, Courthouse, Kadoka, SD 57453. 605-837-2423. 8AM-5PM.

Felony, Misdemeanor, Civil, Eviction, Small Claims, Probate—Circuit Court, PO Box 128, Kadoka, SD 57543. 605-837-2121. 8AM-Noon, 1-5PM. Access by: mail, in person.

Jerauld

Real Estate Recording—Jerauld County Register of Deeds, Courthouse, 205 So. Wallace, Wessington Springs, SD 57382. 605-539-1241. 8AM-12, 1PM-5PM.

Felony, Misdemeanor, Civil, Eviction, Small Claims, Probate—Circuit Court, PO Box 435, Wessington Springs, SD 57382. 605-539-1202. 8AM-5PM. Access by: mail, fax, in person.

Jones

Real Estate Recording—Jones County Register of Deeds, 310 Main Street, Courthouse, Murdo, SD 57559. 605-669-2122. 8AM-5PM.

Felony, Misdemeanor, Civil, Eviction, Small Claims, Probate—Circuit Court, PO Box 448, Murdo, SD 57559. 605-669-2361. 8AM-5PM. Access by: mail, in person.

Kingsbury

Real Estate Recording—Kingsbury County Register of Deeds, Courthouse, 201 2nd St. SE, De Smet, SD 57231. 605-854-3411, Fax: 605-854-3833. 8AM-Noon, 1-5PM.

Felony, Misdemeanor, Civil, Eviction, Small Claims, Probate—Circuit Court, PO Box 176, De Smet, SD 57231-0176. 605-854-3811, Fax: 605-854-3833. 8AM-Noon, 1-5PM. Access by: mail, in person.

Lake

Real Estate Recording—Lake County Register of Deeds, 200 East Center, Courthouse, Madison, SD 57042. 605-256-7618, Fax: 605-256-7622. 8AM-Noon, 1-5PM.

Felony, Misdemeanor, Civil, Eviction, Small Claims, Probate—Circuit Court, 200 E Center St, Madison, SD 57042. 605-256-5644. 8AM-Noon, 1-5PM. Access by: mail, in person.

Lawrence

Real Estate Recording—Lawrence County Register of Deeds, 90 Sherman Street, Deadwood, SD 57732. 8AM-5PM.

Felony, Misdemeanor, Civil, Eviction, Small Claims, Probate—Circuit Court, PO Box 626, Deadwood, SD 57732. 605-578-2040. 8AM-5PM. Access by: mail, fax, in person.

Lincoln

Real Estate Recording—Lincoln County Register of Deeds, 100 East 5th, Canton, SD 57013. Fax: 605-987-5932. 8AM-5PM.

Felony, Misdemeanor, Civil, Eviction, Small Claims, Probate—Circuit Court, 100 E 5th St, Canton, SD 57013. 605-987-5891. 8AM-5PM. Access by: mail, in person.

Lyman

Real Estate Recording—Lyman County Register of Deeds, 100 Main Street, Courthouse, Kennebec, SD 57544. 605-869-2295, Fax: 605-869-2203. 8AM-Noon, 1-5PM.

Felony, Misdemeanor, Civil, Eviction, Small Claims, Probate—Circuit Court, PO Box 235, Kennebec, SD 57544. 605-869-2277. 8AM-5PM. Access by: mail, in person.

Marshall

Real Estate Recording—Marshall County Register of Deeds, Vander Horck Avenue, Courthouse, Britton, SD 57430. 605-448-2451, Fax: 605-448-2116. 8AM-Noon, 1-5PM.

Felony, Misdemeanor, Civil, Eviction, Small Claims, Probate—Circuit Court, PO Box 130, Britton, SD 57430. 605-448-5213. 8AM-Noon, 1-5PM. Access by: mail, phone, in person.

McCook

Real Estate Recording—McCook County Register of Deeds, 130 West Essex Street, Salem, SD 57058. 605-425-2721, Fax: 605-425-2534. 8:30AM-4:30PM.

Felony, Misdemeanor, Civil, Eviction, Small Claims, Probate—Circuit Court, PO Box 504, Salem, SD 57058. 605-425-2781, Fax: 605-425-3144. 8AM-5PM. Access by: mail, fax, in person.

McPherson

Real Estate Recording—McPherson County Register of Deeds, Main Street, Courthouse, Leola, SD 57456. 605-439-3544, Fax: 605-439-3394. 8AM-12, 1PM-5PM.

Felony, Misdemeanor, Civil, Eviction, Small Claims, Probate—Circuit Court, PO Box 248, Leola, SD 57456. 605-439-3361, Fax: 605-439-3394. 8AM-Noon. Access by: mail, in person.

Meade

Real Estate Recording—Meade County Register of Deeds, 1425 Sherman Street, Sturgis, SD 57785. 605-347-5871, Fax: 605-347-5925. 8AM-5PM.

Felony, Misdemeanor, Civil, Eviction, Small Claims, Probate—Circuit Court, PO Box 939, Sturgis, SD 57785. 605-347-4411, Fax: 605-347-3526. 8AM-Noon, 1-5PM. Access by: mail, in person.

Mellette

Real Estate Recording—Mellette County Register of Deeds, Courthouse, White River, SD 57579. 605-259-3151. 8AM-Noon, 1-5PM.

Felony, Misdemeanor, Civil, Eviction, Small Claims, Probate—Circuit Court, PO Box 257, White River, SD 57579. 605-259-3230, Fax: 605-259-3194. 8AM-Noon. Access by: mail, phone, in person.

Miner

Real Estate Recording—Miner County Register of Deeds, Main Street, Courthouse, Howard, SD 57349. 605-772-4652, Fax: 605-772-4148. 8AM-Noon, 1-5PM.

Felony, Misdemeanor, Civil, Eviction, Small Claims, Probate—Circuit Court, PO Box 265, Howard, SD 57349. 605-772-4612, Fax: 605-772-1148. 8AM-5PM. Access by: mail, fax, in person.

Minnehaha

Real Estate Recording—Minnehaha County Register of Deeds, 415 North Dakota Avenue, Sioux Falls, SD 57104. 605-335-4212, Fax: 605-367-8314. 8AM-5PM.

Felony, Misdemeanor, Civil, Eviction, Small Claims, Probate—Circuit Court, 425 N Dakota Ave, Sioux Falls, SD 57104. 605-367-5900, Fax: 605-367-5916. 8AM-5PM. Access by: mail, in person.

Moody

Real Estate Recording—Moody County Register of Deeds, Pipestone Avenue, Courthouse, Flandreau, SD 57028. 605-997-3171. 8AM-5PM.

Felony, Misdemeanor, Civil, Eviction, Small Claims, Probate—Circuit Court, 101 E Pipestone, Flandreau, SD 57028. 605-997-3181, Fax: 605-997-3861. 8AM-5PM. Access by: mail, in person.

Pennington

Real Estate Recording—Pennington County Register of Deeds, 315 St. Joe Street, Rapid City, SD 57701. 605-394-2161. 8AM-5PM.

Felony, Misdemeanor, Civil, Eviction, Small Claims, Probate—Circuit Court, PO Box 230, Rapid City, SD 57709. 605-394-2575. 8AM-5PM. Access by: mail, in person.

Perkins

Real Estate Recording—Perkins County Register of Deeds, 100 E. Main St. Bison, SD 57620. 605-244-5613, Fax: 605-244-7289. 8AM-Noon,1-5PM.

Felony, Misdemeanor, Civil, Eviction, Small Claims, Probate—Circuit Court, PO Box 426, Bison, SD 57620-0426. 605-244-5626, Fax: 605-244-7110. 8AM-Noon, 1-5PM. Access by: mail, fax, in person.

Potter

Real Estate Recording—Potter County Register of Deeds, 201 South Exene, Gettysburg, SD 57442. 605-765-9403, Fax: 605-765-2412. 8AM-Noon, 1-5PM.

Felony, Misdemeanor, Civil, Eviction, Small Claims, Probate—Circuit Court, 201 S Exene, Gettysburg, SD 57442. 605-765-9472. 8AM-Noon, 1-5PM. Access by: mail, fax, in person.

Roberts

Real Estate Recording—Roberts County Register of Deeds, 411 East 2nd Avenue, Sisseton, SD 57262. 605-698-7245. 8AM-5PM.

Felony, Misdemeanor, Civil, Eviction, Small Claims, Probate—Circuit Court, 411 2nd Ave E, Sisseton, SD 57262. 605-698-3395, Fax: 605-698-7894. 8AM-5PM. Access by: mail, in person.

Sanborn

Real Estate Recording—Sanborn County Register of Deeds, Courthouse, Woonsocket, SD 57385. 605-796-4512, Fax: 605-796-4509.

Felony, Misdemeanor, Civil, Eviction, Small Claims, Probate—Circuit Court, PO Box 56, Woonsocket, SD 57385. 605-796-4515, Fax: 605-796-4509. 8AM-5PM. Access by: mail, fax, in person.

Shannon

Real Estate Recording—Shannon County Register of Deeds, 906 North River Street, Hot Springs, SD 57747. 605-745-5145. 8AM-5PM.

Felony, Misdemeanor, Civil, Eviction, Small Claims, Probate—Circuit Court, 906 N River St, Hot Springs, SD 57747. 605-745-5131. 8AM-5PM. Access by: mail, in person. Special note: Also handles cases for Fall River County. Specify which county in your search request.

Spink

Real Estate Recording—Spink County Register of Deeds, 210 East 7th Avenue, Redfield, SD 57469. 605-472-0880, Fax: 605-472-2301. 8AM-5PM.

Felony, Misdemeanor, Civil, Eviction, Small Claims, Probate—Circuit Court, 210 E 7th Ave, Redfield, SD 57469. 605-472-4535, Fax: 605-472-2877. 8AM-5PM. Access by: mail, phone, fax, in person.

Stanley

Real Estate Recording—Stanley County Register of Deeds, 8 East 2nd Avenue, Courthouse, Fort Pierre, SD 57532. 605-223-2648, Fax: 605-223-9948. 8AM-Noon,1-5PM.

Felony, Misdemeanor, Civil, Eviction, Small Claims, Probate—Circuit Court, PO Box 758, Fort Pierre, SD 57532. 605-773-3992, Fax: 605-773-6330. 8AM-5PM. Access by: mail, in person.

Sully

Real Estate Recording—Sully County Register of Deeds, 700 Ash Avenue, Courthouse, Onida, SD 57564. 605-258-2444, Fax: 605-258-2884. 8AM-Noon,1-5PM.

Felony, Misdemeanor, Civil, Eviction, Small Claims, Probate—Circuit Court, PO Box 188, Onida, SD 57564. 605-258-2535, Fax: 605-258-2382. 8AM-Noon. Access by: mail, in person.

Todd

Real Estate Recording—Todd County Register of Deeds, Courthouse, 200 E. 3rd St. Winner, SD 57580. Fax: 605-842-3621. 8AM-5PM.

Felony, Misdemeanor, Civil, Eviction, Small Claims, Probate—Circuit Court, 200 E 3rd St, PO Box 311, Winner, SD 57580. 605-842-2266, Fax: 605-842-2267. 8AM-5PM. Access by: mail, in person.

Tripp

Real Estate Recording—Tripp County Register of Deeds, Courthouse, 200 E. 3rd St. Winner, SD 57580. 605-842-1700, Fax: 605-842-3621. 8AM-5PM.

Felony, Misdemeanor, Civil, Eviction, Small Claims, Probate—Circuit Court, 200 E 3rd St, PO Box 377, Winner, SD 57580. 605-842-2266, Fax: 605-842-2267. 8AM-5PM. Access by: mail, in person.

Turner

Real Estate Recording—Turner County Register of Deeds, 400 South Main Street, Courthouse, Parker, SD 57053. 605-297-4425, Fax: 605-297-5556. 8:30AM-5PM.

Felony, Misdemeanor, Civil, Eviction, Small Claims, Probate—Circuit Court, PO Box 446, Parker, SD 57053. 605-297-3115, Fax: 605-297-3871. 8AM-5PM. Access by: mail, in person.

Union

Real Estate Recording—Union County Register of Deeds, Courthouse, 200 E. Main, Elk Point, SD 57025. Fax: 605-356-3047. 8:30AM-5PM.

Felony, Misdemeanor, Civil, Eviction, Small Claims, Probate—Circuit Court, PO Box 757, Elk Point, SD 57025. 605-356-2132. 8:30AM-5PM. Access by: mail, in person.

Walworth

Real Estate Recording—Walworth County Register of Deeds, Courthouse, Selby, SD 57472. 605-649-7737, Fax: 605-649-7867. 8AM-Noon,1-5PM.

Felony, Misdemeanor, Civil, Eviction, Small Claims, Probate—Circuit Court, PO Box 328, Selby, SD 57472. 605-649-7311, Fax: 605-649-7624. 8AM-5PM. Access by: mail, in person.

Yankton

Real Estate Recording—Yankton County Register of Deeds, 327 W. 3rd, Yankton, SD 57078. 605-665-2143. 9AM-5PM.

Felony, Misdemeanor, Civil, Eviction, Small Claims, Probate—Circuit Court, PO Box 155, Yankton, SD 57078. 605-668-3080. 8AM-5PM. Access by: mail, in person.

Ziebach

Real Estate Recording—Ziebach County Register of Deeds, Courthouse, Dupree, SD 57623. 605-365-5173. 8AM-5PM.

Felony, Misdemeanor, Civil, Eviction, Small Claims, Probate—Circuit Court, PO Box 306, Dupree, SD 57623. 605-365-5159. 9:30AM-Noon, 1-2:30PM. Access by: mail, in person.

Federal Courts

US District Court

Aberdeen Division c/o Pierre Division, Federal Bldg & Courthouse, 225 S Pierre St, Room 405, Pierre, SD 57501605-342-3066 Counties: Brown, Butte, Campbell, Clark, Codington, Corson, Day, Deuel, Edmunds, Grant, Hamlin, McPherson, Marshall, Roberts, Spink, Walworth. Judge Battey's closed case records are located at the Rapid City Division. www.sdd.uscourts.gov

Pierre Division Federal Bldg & Courthouse, Room 405, 225 S Pierre St, Pierre, SD 57501605-224-5849 Fax: 605-224-0806 Counties: Buffalo, Dewey, Faulk, Gregory, Haakon, Hand, Hughes, Hyde, Jackson, Jerauld, Jones, Lyman, Mellette, Potter, Stanley, Sully, Todd, Tripp, Ziebach. www.sdd.uscourts.gov

Rapid City Division Clerk's Office, Room 302, 515 9th St, Rapid City, SD 57701605-342-3066 Counties: Bennett, Custer, Fall River, Harding, Lawrence, Meade, Pennington, Perkins, Shannon. Judge Battey's closed cases are located here.. www.sdd.uscourts.gov

Sioux Falls Division Room 220, US Courthouse, 400 S Phillips Ave, Sioux Falls, SD 57102605-330-4447 Fax: 605-330-4312 Counties: Aurora, Beadle, Bon Homme, Brookings, Brule, Charles Mix, Clay, Davison, Douglas, Hanson, Hutchinson, Kingsbury, Lake, Lincoln, McCook, Miner, Minnehaha, Moody, Sanborn, Turner, Union, Yankton. www.sdd.uscourts.gov

US Bankruptcy Court

Pierre Division Clerk, Room 203, Federal Bldg, 225 S Pierre St, Pierre, SD 57501605-224-6013 Fax: 605-224-9808 Counties: Bennett, Brown, Buffalo, Butte, Campbell, Clark, Codington, Corson, Custer, Day, Deuel, Dewey, Edmunds, Fall River, Faulk, Grant, Gregory, Haakon, Hamlin, Hand, Harding, Hughes, Hyde, Jackson, Jerauld, Jones, Lawrence, Lyman, Marshall, McPherson, Meade,Mellette, Pennington, Perkins, Potter, Roberts, Shannon, Spink, Stanley, Sully, Todd, Tripp, Walworth, Ziebach. www.sdb.uscourts.gov

Sioux Falls Division PO Box 5060, Sioux Falls, SD 57117-5060605-330-4541 Fax: 605-330-4548 Counties: Aurora, Beadle, Bon Homme, Brookings, Brule, Charles Mix, Clay, Davison, Douglas, Hanson, Hutchinson, Kingsbury, Lake, Lincoln, McCook, Miner, Minnehaha, Moody, Sanborn, Turner, Union, Yankton. www.sdb.uscourts.gov

Tennessee

Attorney General's Office
425 5th Ave North   615-741-3491
Nashville, TN 37243-0497   Fax: 615-741-2009

Governor's Office
State Capitol, 1st Floor   615-741-2001
Nashville, TN 37243-0001   Fax: 615-532-9711
www.state.tn.us/governor

State Archives
403 7th Ave N   615-741-7996
Nashville, TN 37243-0312   Fax: 615-741-6471
www.state.tn.us/sos/statelib/tslahome.htm

Capital: Nashville
Davidson County

Time Zone: CST*

* Tennessee's 29 eastern-most counties are EST:
They are: Anderson, Blount, Bradley, Campbell, Carter,
Claiborne, Cocke, Grainger, Greene, Hamilton, Hancock,
Hawkins, Jefferson, Johnson, Knox, Loudon, McMinn,
Meigs, Monroe, Morgan, Polk, Rhea, Roane, Scott,
Sevier, Sullivan, Unicoi, Union, Washington.

Number of Counties: 95

Population: 5,368,198

Web Site: www.state.tn.us

Search Unclaimed Property Online

www.treasury.state.tn.us/unclaim/
unclaim-s.htm

State Agencies

Criminal Records
Restricted access.
Tennessee Bureau of Investigation, Records and Identification
Unit, 1148 Foster Ave, Menzler-Nix Bldg, Nashville, TN 37210;
615-741-0430; 24 hours daily

Corporation Records
Limited Partnership Records
Fictitious Name
Assumed Name
Limited Liability Company Records
Corporation Section, Secretary of State, Polk Bldg, 500
Deaderick St, #1800, Nashville, TN 37243-0306; 615-741-2286;
Fax: 615-741-7310; 8AM-4:30PM. Access by: mail, phone, in
person. www.state.tn.us/sos

Trademarks/Servicemarks
Trade Names
Secretary of State, Trademarks/Tradenames Division, James K.
Polk Bldg, Nashville, TN 37243-0306; 615-741-0531; Fax: 615-
741-7310; 8AM-4:30PM. Access by: mail, phone, in person.

Uniform Commercial Code
State Tax Liens
UCC Division, Secretary of State, James K Polk Bldg, Suite
1800, Nashville, TN 37243-0306; 615-741-3276; Fax: 615-741-
7310; 8AM-4:30PM. Access by: mail.
www.state.tn.us/sos

Sales Tax Registrations
Restricted access.
This agency refuses to make any information about registrants
available.

Revenue Department, Tax Enforcement Division, Andrew Jackson Bldg, 500 Deaderick St, Nashville, TN 37242-0100; 615-741-7071; Fax: 615-532-6339; 8AM-4:30PM

Workers' Compensation Records

Tennessee Department of Labor, Workers Compensation Division, 710 James Robertson Pwy, 2nd Floor, Nashville, TN 37243-0661; 615-741-2395; Fax: 615-532-1468; 8AM-4:30PM. Access by: mail.

Birth Certificates

Tennessee Department of Health, Office of Vital Records, 421 5th Ave North, 1st floor, Nashville, TN 37247-0460; 615-741-1763, 615-741-0778 Credit card order; Fax: 615-726-2559; 8AM-4PM. Access by: mail, phone, in person. www.state.tn.us/health

Death Records

Tennessee Department of Health, Office of Vital Records, 421 5th Ave North, 1st floor, Nashville, TN 37247-0460; 615-741-1763, 615-741-0778 Credit card order; Fax: 615-726-2559; 8AM-4PM. Access by: mail, phone, in person.

Marriage Certificates

Tennessee Department of Health, Office of Vital Records, 421 5th Ave North, 1st floor, Nashville, TN 37247-0460; 615-741-1763, 615-741-0778 Credit card order; Fax: 615-726-2559; 8AM-4PM. Access by: mail, phone, in person.

Divorce Records

Tennessee Department of Health, Office of Vital Records, 421 5th Ave North, 1st floor, Nashville, TN 37247-0460; 615-741-1763, 615-741-0778 Credit card order; Fax: 615-726-2559; 8AM-4PM. Access by: mail, phone, in person.

Accident Reports

Financial Responsibility Section, Records Unit, 1150 Foster Avenue, Nashville, TN 37210; 615-741-3954; 8AM-4:30PM. Access by: mail. www.state.tn.us/safety

Driver Records

Dept. of Safety, Financial Responsibility Section, Attn: Driving Records, 1150 Foster Ave, Nashville, TN 37249-4000; 615-741-3954; 8AM-4:30PM. Access by: mail.

Vehicle Ownership
Vehicle Identification

Titling and Registration Division, Information Unit, 44 Vantage Way #160, Nashville, TN 37243-8050; 615-741-3101 Titles; Fax: 615-401-6782; 8AM-4:30PM. Access by: mail.

Boat & Vessel Ownership
Boat & Vessel Registration

Wildlife Resources Agency, Boating Division, PO Box 40747, Nashville, TN 37204; 615-781-6500; Fax: 615-741-4606; 8AM-4:30PM. www.state.tn.us/twra

Legislation-Current/Pending
Legislation-Passed

Tennessee General Assembly, Office of Legislative Information Services, Rachel Jackson Bldg, 1st Floor, Nashville, TN 37243; 615-741-3511 Status, 615-741-0927 Bill Room; 8AM-4:30PM. Access by: mail, phone, in person. www.legislature.state.tn.us

Voter Registration

Records not available from state agency.

Records are held by the Administrator of Elections at the county level. Records can only be purchased for political related purposes.

GED Certificates

Department of Education, GED Records - Johnson Tower, 710 James Robertson Parkway, 7th Fl, Nashville, TN 37243-0387; 615-741-7054; Fax: 615-532-4899; 8AM-4:30PM.

Hunting License Information
Fishing License Information

Records not available from state agency.

There is not a central database of hunting or fishing licenses. You must contact the vendor where the license was sold. The Sportman License Division (615-781-6585) does hold information on 45,000 sportsman licenses (boating, etc).

County Courts & Recording Offices

About the Courts...

About the Recording Offices...

Administration

Administrative Office of the Courts	615-741-2687
511 Union St (Nashville City Center) #600	Fax: 615-741-6285
Nashville, TN 37243-0607	
www.tsc.state.tn.us	

Court Structure

Criminal cases are handled by the Circuit Courts and General Sessions Courts. All General Sessions Courts have raised the maximum civil case limit to $15,000 from $10,000. The Chancery Courts, in addition to handling probate, also hear certain types of equitable civil cases. Combined courts vary by county, and the counties of Davidson, Hamilton, Knox, and Shelby have separate Criminal Courts.

Probate is handled in the Chancery or County Courts, except in Shelby and Davidson Counties where it is handled by the Probate Court.

Online Access

There is currently no statewide, online computer system available, internal or external. The Tennessee Administrative Office of Courts (AOC) has provided computers and CD-ROM readers to state judges, and a computerization project (named TnCIS) to implement statewide court automation started in January 1997.

Organization

95 counties, 96 recording offices. The recording officer is. Register of Deeds. Sullivan County has two offices. 66 counties are in the Central Time Zone (CST) and 29 are in the Eastern Time Zone (EST).

UCC Records

Financing statements are filed at the state level, except for consumer goods, farm and real estate related collateral, which are filed with the Register of Deeds. Most recording offices will not perform UCC searches. Use search request form UCC-11. Search fees and copy fees vary.

Lien Records

All federal tax liens are filed with the county Register of Deeds. State tax liens are filed with the Secretary of State or the Register of Deeds. Counties will not perform tax lien searches.

Real Estate Records

Counties will not perform real estate searches. Certified copies usually cost $1.00 per page. Tax records are kept at the Assessor's Office.

County Courts & Recording Offices

Anderson

Real Estate Recording—Anderson County Register of Deeds, 100 North Main Street, Courthouse, Room 205, Clinton, TN 37716. Fax: 423-457-1638. 8:30AM-4:30PM.

Felony, Misdemeanor, Civil, Eviction, Small Claims—7th District Circuit Court and General Sessions, 100 Main St, Clinton, TN 37716. 423-457-5400. 8AM-4:30PM. Access by: in person.

Civil, Probate—Chancery Court, Anderson County Courthouse, PO Box 501, Clinton, TN 37717. 423-457-5400, Fax: 423-457-4828. 8:30AM-4:30PM. Access by: mail, phone, in person.

Bedford

Real Estate Recording—Bedford County Register of Deeds, 108 Northside Square, Shelbyville, TN 37160. 615-684-4363, Fax: 931-685-2086. 8AM-4PM M,T,Th,F; 8AM-4PM W; 8AM-Noon Sat.

Felony, Misdemeanor, Civil, Eviction, Small Claims—17th District Circuit Court and General Sessions, 1 Public Sq, Suite 200, Shelbyville, TN 37160. 931-684-3223. 8AM-4PM M-Th, 8AM-5PM Fri. Access by: in person.

Civil, Probate—Chancery Court, Chancery Court, 1 Public Sq, Suite 302, Shelbyville, TN 37160. 931-684-1672. 8AM-4PM M-Th, 8AM-5PM Fri. Access by: mail, in person.

Benton

Real Estate Recording—Benton County Register of Deeds, 1 E. Court Sq, Suite 105, Camden, TN 38320. 8AM-4PM; 8AM-5PM F.

Felony, Misdemeanor, Civil, Eviction, Small Claims—24th District Circuit Court, General Sessions and Juvenile, 1 East Court Sq Rm 207, Camden, TN 38320. 901-584-6711, Fax: 901-584-0475. 8AM-4PM M-Th; 8AM-5PM F. Access by: in person.

Civil, Probate—Chancery Court, 1 E Court Sq, Courthouse Rm 206, Camden, TN 38320. 901-584-4435, Fax: 901-584-5956. 8AM-4PM M-Th; 8AM-5PM F. Access by: in person.

Bledsoe

Real Estate Recording—Bledsoe County Register of Deeds, Main Street, Courthouse, Pikeville, TN 37367. Fax: 423-447-6856. 8AM-4PM M-W,F; 8AM-Noon Sat.

Felony, Misdemeanor, Civil, Eviction, Small Claims—12th District Circuit Court and General Sessions, PO Box 455, Pikeville, TN 37367. 423-447-6488, Fax: 423-447-6856. 8AM-4PM Access by: in person.

Civil, Probate—Chancery Court, PO Box 413, Pikeville, TN 37367. 423-447-2484, Fax: 423-447-6856. 8AM-4PM. Access by: mail, phone, fax, in person.

Blount

Real Estate Recording—Blount County Register of Deeds, 349 Court Street, Maryville, TN 37804. Fax: 423-273-5890. 8AM-4:30PM.

Felony, Misdemeanor, Civil, Eviction, Small Claims—5th District Circuit Court and General Sessions, 926 E Lamar Alexander Pkwy, Maryville, TN 37804-6201. 423-273-5400, Fax: 423-273-5411. 8AM-4:30PM. Access by: mail, in person.

Misdemeanor, Civil, Probate—County Court, 301 Court St, Maryville, TN 37804. 423-273-5400, Fax: 423-273-5411. 8AM-4:30PM. Access by: mail, in person.

Probate—Probate Court, 345 Court St, Maryville, TN 37804-5906. 423-982-4391. 9AM-5PM M-F, 9AM-12PM Sat. Access by: mail, in person.

Bradley

Real Estate Recording—Bradley County Register of Deeds, 155 North Ocoee, Courthouse, Room 102, Cleveland, TN 37311. Fax: 423-478-8888. 8:30AM-4:30PM M-Th; 8:30AM-5PM F.

Felony, Misdemeanor, Civil, Eviction, Small Claims—10th District Criminal, Circuit, and General Sessions Court, 155 N Ocoee St, PO Box 1167, Cleveland, TN 37311. 423-476-0544, Fax: 423-476-0488. 8:30AM-4:30PM M-Th, 8:30AM-5PM Fri. Access by: mail, in person.

Civil, Probate—Chancery Court, Chancery Court, 155 N. Ocoee St, Cleveland, TN 37311. 423-476-0526. 8:30AM-4:30PM M-Th, 8:30AM-5PM Fri. Access by: mail, in person.

Campbell

Real Estate Recording—Campbell County Register of Deeds, Courthouse, Suite 302, 570 Main Street, Jacksboro, TN 37757. Fax: 423-562-9833. 8AM-4:30PM.

Felony, Misdemeanor, Civil, Eviction, Small Claims—8th District Criminal, Circuit, and General Sessions Court, PO Box 26, Jacksboro, TN 37757. 423-562-2624. 8AM-4:30PM. Access by: mail, in person.

Civil, Probate—Chancery Court, PO Box 182, Jacksboro, TN 37757. 423-562-3496. 8AM-4:30PM. Access by: mail, in person.

Cannon

Real Estate Recording—Cannon County Register of Deeds, Courthouse, Woodbury, TN 37190. Fax: 615-563-5696. 8AM-4PM M,T,Th,F; 8AM-Noon Sat.

Felony, Misdemeanor, Civil, Eviction, Small Claims—16th District Circuit Court and General Sessions, County Courthouse Public Sq, Woodbury, TN 37190. 615-563-4461, Fax: 615-563-6391. 8AM-4:30PM M,T,Th,F; 8AM-Noon Wed. Access by: mail, in person.

Probate—County Court, Public Square, Woodbury, TN 37190. 615-563-4278, Fax: 615-563-5696. 8AM-4PM M,T,Th,F; 8AM-Noon Sat. Access by: mail.

Carroll

Real Estate Recording—Carroll County Register of Deeds, Carroll County Office Complex, 625 High St. Suite 104, Huntingdon, TN 38344. Fax: 901-986-1955. 8AM-4PM.

Felony, Misdemeanor, Civil, Eviction, Small Claims—24th District Circuit Court and General Sessions, PO Box 587, Huntingdon, TN 38344. 901-986-1931. 8AM-4PM. Access by: in person.

Civil, Probate—Chancery Court, PO Box 886, Huntingdon, TN 38344. 901-986-1920. 8AM-4PM. Access by: mail, in person.

Carter

Real Estate Recording—Carter County Register of Deeds, 801 East Elk Avenue, Elizabethton, TN 37643. 8:30AM-5PM.

Felony, Misdemeanor, Civil, Eviction, Small Claims—1st District Criminal, Circuit, and General Sessions Court, Carter County Justice Center, 900 E Elk Ave, Elizabethton, TN 37643. 423-542-1835, Fax: 423-542-3742. 8AM-5PM. Access by: in person.

Probate—County Court, Old Courthouse, Main St, Elizabethton, TN 37643. 423-542-1812. 8AM-5PM. Access by: mail, in person.

Cheatham

Real Estate Recording—Cheatham County Register of Deeds, 100 Public Square, Suite 117, Ashland City, TN 37015. 615-792-4298, Fax: 615-792-2039. 8AM-4PM.

Felony, Misdemeanor, Civil, Eviction, Small Claims—23rd District Circuit Court and General Sessions, 100 Public Sq, Ashland City, TN 37015. 615-792-3272, Fax: 615-792-3203. 8AM-4PM. Access by: mail, phone, in person. Special note: Circuit Court is room 225, General sessions is in room 223.

Civil, Probate—Chancery Court, Clerk & Master, Suite 106, Ashland City, TN 37015. 615-792-4620. 8AM-4PM. Access by: mail, phone, in person.

Chester

Real Estate Recording—Chester County Register of Deeds, Main Street, Courthouse, Henderson, TN 38340. 901-989-3993. 8AM-4PM.

Felony, Misdemeanor, Civil, Eviction, Small Claims—26th District Circuit Court and General Sessions, PO Box 133, Henderson, TN 38340. 901-989-2454. 8AM-4PM. Access by: mail, phone, fax, in person.

Civil, Probate—Chancery Court, Clerk & Master, PO Box 262, Henderson, TN 38340. 901-989-7171, Fax: 901-989-7176. 8AM-4PM. Access by: mail, in person.

Claiborne

Real Estate Recording—Claiborne County Register of Deeds, Main Street, Courthouse, Tazewell, TN 37879. 423-626-3275. 8:30AM-4PM.

Felony, Misdemeanor, Civil, Eviction, Small Claims—8th District Criminal, Circuit, and General Sessions Court, Box 34, Tazewell, TN 37879. 423-626-3334. 8:30AM-4PM M-F, 8:30AM-Noon Sat. Access by: mail, in person.

Civil, Probate—Chancery Court, PO Drawer G, Tazewell, TN 37879. 423-626-3284. 8:30AM-Noon, 1-4PM. Access by: mail, in person.

Clay

Real Estate Recording—Clay County Register of Deeds, East Lake Avenue, Celina, TN 38551. 615-243-2310. 8AM-4PM M,T,Th,F; 8AM-Noon Sat.

Felony, Misdemeanor, Civil, Eviction, Small Claims—13th District Criminal, Circuit, and General Sessions Court, PO Box 749, Celina, TN 38551. 931-243-2557. 8AM-4PM. Access by: in person.

Civil, Probate—Chancery Court, PO Box 332, Celina, TN 38551. 931-243-3145. 8AM-4PM M,T,Th,F; 8AM-Noon W & Sat. Access by: mail, in person.

Cocke

Real Estate Recording—Cocke County Register of Deeds, 111 Court Ave. Room 102, Courthouse, Newport, TN 37821. 423-623-3037. 8AM-4PM M,T,Th,F; 8AM-Noon W,Sat.

Felony, Misdemeanor, Civil Actions Over $15,000—4th District Circuit Court, 111 Court Ave Rm 201, Newport, TN 37821. 423-623-6124, Fax: 423-625-3889. 8:30AM-5PM. Access by: mail, in person.

Misdemeanor, Civil Actions Under $15,000, Eviction, Small Claims—General Sessions, 111 Court Ave, Newport, TN 37821. 423-623-8619, Fax: 423-623-9808. 8AM-4PM. Access by: mail, phone, in person.

Civil, Probate—Chancery Court, Courthouse Annex, 360 E Main St, Suite 103, Newport, TN 37821. 423-623-3321, Fax: 423-625-3642. 8AM-4:30PM. Access by: mail, phone, in person.

Coffee

Real Estate Recording—Coffee County Register of Deeds, 1341 McArthur St. Ste 2, Manchester, TN 37355. Fax: 931-723-8232. 8AM-4:30PM.

Felony, Misdemeanor, Civil, Eviction, Small Claims—14th District Circuit Court and General Sessions, PO Box 629, Manchester, TN 37349. 931-723-5110. 8AM-4:30PM. Access by: mail, in person.

Civil, Probate—Chancery Court, 101 W. Fort St, Box 5, Manchester, TN 37355. 931-723-5132. 8AM-4:30PM. Access by: mail, in person.

Crockett

Real Estate Recording—Crockett County Register of Deeds, Crockett County Courthouse, 1 S. Bells St. Suite 2, Alamo, TN 38001. 901-696-5454. 8AM-4PM.

Felony, Misdemeanor, Civil, Eviction, Small Claims—Circuit Court and General Sessions, 1 South Bell St, Ste 6 Courthouse, Alamo, TN 38001. 901-696-5462, Fax: 901-696-4101. 8AM-4PM. Access by: mail, in person.

Civil, Probate—Chancery Court, 1 South Bells St, Suite 5, Alamo, TN 38001. 901-696-5458, Fax: 901-696-4101. 8AM-4PM. Access by: mail, in person.

Cumberland

Real Estate Recording—Cumberland County Register of Deeds, 2 North Main St. Suite 204, Crossville, TN 38555. 615-484-5730. 8AM-4PM.

Felony, Misdemeanor, Civil, Eviction, Small Claims—13th District Criminal, Circuit, and General Sessions Court, 2 N Main St, Suite 302, Crossville, TN 38555. 931-484-6647, Fax: 931-484-1615. 8AM-4PM. Access by: in person.

Civil, Probate—Chancery Court, 2 N Main St, Suite 101, Crossville, TN 38555-4583. 931-484-4731. 8AM-4PM. Access by: mail, in person.

Davidson

Real Estate Recording—Davidson County Register of Deeds, 103 Metro Courthouse, Nashville, TN 37201. Fax: 615-880-2039. 8AM-4:30PM.

Misdemeanor, Civil Actions Under $10,000, Eviction, Small Claims—General Sessions Court, 100 James Robinson Parkway, Ben West Bldg Room 2, Nashville, TN 37201. 615-862-5195, Fax: 615-862-5924. 8AM-4:30PM. Access by: in person.

Civil Actions Over $15,000—Circuit Court, 506 Metro Courthouse, Nashville, TN 37201. 615-862-5181. 8AM-4:30PM. Access by: mail, in person. www.nashville.org/cir/

Felony, Misdemeanor—20th District Criminal Court, Metro Courthouse, Rm 305, Nashville, TN 37201. 615-862-5600, Fax: 615-862-5676. 8AM-4PM. Access by: mail, in person.

De Kalb

Real Estate Recording—De Kalb County Register of Deeds, 201 Courthouse, Smithville, TN 37166. 615-597-5176, Fax: 615-597-7420. 8AM-4:30PM M-Th; 8AM-5PM F.

Felony, Misdemeanor, Civil, Eviction, Small Claims—13th District Criminal, Circuit, and General Sessions Court, Public Sq, Smithville, TN 37166. 615-597-5711. 8AM-4:30PM M,T,W,Th; 8AM-5PM Fri. Access by: mail, in person.

Civil, Probate—Chancery Court, 1 Public Square, Rm 302, Smithville, TN 37166. 615-597-4360. 8AM-4PM. Access by: in person.

Decatur

Real Estate Recording—Decatur County Register of Deeds, Main Street, Courthouse, Decaturville, TN 38329. 901-852-3723. 8AM-4PM M,T,Th,F; 8AM-Noon W,Sat.

Felony, Misdemeanor, Civil, Eviction, Small Claims—24th District Circuit Court and General Sessions, PO Box 488, Decaturville, TN 38329. 901-852-3125, Fax: 901-852-2130. 8AM-4PM M,T,Th,F; 8AM-Noon W & Sat. Access by: in person.

Civil, Probate—Chancery Court, Clerk & Master, Decaturville, TN 38329. 901-852-3422, Fax: 901-852-2130. 9M-4PM M,T,Th,F; 9AM-Noon Sat. Access by: mail, phone, in person.

Dickson

Real Estate Recording—Dickson County Register of Deeds, Court Square, Courthouse, Charlotte, TN 37036. Fax: 615-789-3893. 8AM-4PM.

Felony, Misdemeanor, Civil Actions Over $15,000—23rd District Circuit Court, Court Square, PO Box 220, Charlotte, TN 37036. 615-789-7010, Fax: 615-789-7018. 8AM-4PM. Access by: mail, phone, fax, in person.

Civil Actions Under $10,000, Eviction, Small Claims—General Sessions, PO Box 217, Charlotte, TN 37036. 615-789-5414, Fax: 615-789-3456. 8AM-4PM. Access by: mail, phone, fax, in person.

Probate—County Court, Court Square, PO Box 220, Charlotte, TN 37036. 615-789-4171. 8AM-4PM. Access by: mail, in person.

Dyer

Real Estate Recording—Dyer County Register of Deeds, 1 Veteran's Square, Dyersburg, TN 38024. 901-286-7802, Fax: 901-288-7724. 8:30AM-4:30PM.

Felony, Misdemeanor, Civil, Eviction, Small Claims—29th District Circuit Court and General Sessions, PO Box 1360,

Dyersburg, TN 38025. 901-286-7809, Fax: 901-286-3580. 8:30AM-4:30PM. Access by: mail, in person.

Civil, Probate—Chancery Court, PO Box 1360, Dyersburg, TN 38024. 901-286-7818, Fax: 901-286-7812. 8:30AM-4:30PM M-Th, 8:30AM-5PM Fri. Access by: mail, in person.

Fayette

Real Estate Recording—Fayette County Register of Deeds, 1 Court Square, Courthouse, Somerville, TN 38068. 9AM-5PM.

Felony, Misdemeanor, Civil, Eviction, Small Claims—25th District Circuit Court and General Sessions, PO Box 670, Somerville, TN 38068. 901-465-5205, Fax: 901-465-5215. 9AM-5PM. Access by: mail, in person.

Civil, Probate—Chancery Court, PO Drawer 220, Somerville, TN 38068. 901-465-5220, Fax: 901-465-5215. 9AM-5PM. Access by: in person.

Fentress

Real Estate Recording—Fentress County Register of Deeds, Courthouse, Jamestown, TN 38556. 615-879-7717, Fax: 931-879-1579. 8AM-4PM.

Felony, Misdemeanor, Civil, Eviction, Small Claims—8th District Criminal, Circuit and General Sessions Court, PO Box 699, Jamestown, TN 38556. 931-879-7919. 8AM-4PM M-F; 8AM-Noon Sat. Access by: mail, in person.

Civil, Probate—Chancery Court, PO Box 151, Jamestown, TN 38556. 931-879-8615, Fax: 931-879-1575. 9AM-5PM M,T,Th,F; 9AM-Noon Wed. Access by: mail, in person.

Franklin

Real Estate Recording—Franklin County Register of Deeds, Public Square, Winchester, TN 37398. 615-967-2962. 8AM-4:30PM; 8AM-Noon Sat.

Felony, Misdemeanor, Civil, Eviction, Small Claims—12th District Circuit Court and General Sessions, 1 South Jefferson St, Winchester, TN 37398. 931-967-2923, Fax: 931-962-1479. 8AM-4:30PM. Access by: mail, in person.

Probate—Probate Court, 1 South Jefferson St, Winchester, TN 37398. 931-962-1485, Fax: 931-962-3394. 8AM-4:30PM. Access by: mail, in person.

Gibson

Real Estate Recording—Gibson County Register of Deeds, Courthouse, 1 Court Square, Trenton, TN 38382. Fax: 901-855-7650. 8AM-4:30PM; 8AM-Noon Sat.

Felony, Misdemeanor, Civil, Eviction, Small Claims—28th District Circuit Court and General Sessions, 295 N College, PO Box 147, Trenton, TN 38382. 901-855-7615, Fax: 901-855-7676. 8AM-4:30PM. Access by: mail, fax, in person.

Civil, Probate—Chancery Court, Clerk & Master, PO Box 290, Trenton, TN 38382. 901-855-7639, Fax: 901-855-7655. 8AM-4:30PM. Access by: mail, in person.

Giles

Real Estate Recording—Giles County Register of Deeds, Courthouse, Pulaski, TN 38478. 615-363-1676, Fax: 931-424-6101. 8AM-4PM.

Felony, Misdemeanor, Civil, Eviction, Small Claims—22nd District Circuit Court and General Sessions, PO Box 678, Pulaski, TN 38478. 931-363-5311, Fax: 931-424-4790. 8AM-4PM. Access by: mail, in person.

Probate—County Court, PO Box 678, Pulaski, TN 38478. 931-363-1509, Fax: 931-424-6101. 8AM-4PM M-F. Access by: mail, in person.

Grainger

Real Estate Recording—Grainger County Register of Deeds, Main Street, Highway 11W, Rutledge, TN 37861. 423-828-3514, Fax: 423-828-4284. 8:30AM-4:30PM M,T,Th,F; 8:30AM-Noon W,Sat.

Felony, Misdemeanor, Civil, Eviction, Small Claims—4th District Circuit Court and General Sessions, PO Box 157, Rutledge, TN 37861. 423-828-3605, Fax: 423-828-3339. 8:30AM-4:30PM. Access by: mail, in person.

Civil, Probate—Chancery Court, Clerk & Master, Rutledge, TN 37861. 423-828-4436, Fax: 423-828-4284. 8:30AM-4:30PM M,T,Th,F, 8:30AM-Noon Wed. Access by: mail, in person.

Greene

Real Estate Recording—Greene County Register of Deeds, Courthouse, 101 S. Main St. Suite 201, Greeneville, TN 37743. 423-638-4432. 8AM-4:30PM.

Felony, Misdemeanor, Civil, Eviction, Small Claims—3rd District Criminal, Circuit and General Sessions Court, 101 S Main, Geene County Courthouse, Suite 302, Greeneville, TN 37743. 423-638-4332, Fax: 423-638-7160. 8AM-4:30PM. Access by: mail, in person.

Probate—County Court Annex, 204 N Cutler St, #200, Greeneville, TN 37745. 423-798-1708, Fax: 423-798-1822. 8AM-4:30PM. Access by: mail, in person.

Grundy

Real Estate Recording—Grundy County Register of Deeds, Highway 56 & 108, City Hall, Altamont, TN 37301. Fax: 931-692-3627. 8AM-4PM M,T,Th,F; 8AM-Noon W,Sat.

Felony, Misdemeanor, Civil, Eviction, Small Claims—12th District Circuit Court and General Sessions, PO Box 161, Altamont, TN 37301. 931-692-3368, Fax: 931-692-2414. 8AM-4PM M,T,Th,F; 8AM-Noon W. Access by: mail, in person.

Civil, Probate—Chancery Court, PO Box 174, Altamont, TN 37301. 931-692-3455, Fax: 931-692-4125. 8AM-4PM M,T,Th,F; 8AM-Noon Wed & Sat. Access by: mail, phone, in person.

Hamblen

Real Estate Recording—Hamblen County Register of Deeds, 511 West 2nd North Street, Morristown, TN 37814. Fax: 423-587-9798. 8AM-4:30PM M-F; 9AM-Noon Sat.

Felony, Misdemeanor, Civil, Eviction, Small Claims—3rd District, Criminal, Circuit and General Sessions Court, 510 Allison St, Morristown, TN 37814. 423-586-5640, Fax: 423-585-2764. 8AM-4PM M-Th, 8AM-5PM Fri, 9-11:30AM Sat. Access by: mail, in person.

Civil—Chancery Court, 511 West 2nd North St, Morristown, TN 37814. 423-586-9112, Fax: 423-587-9798. 8AM-4PM M-Th; 8AM-4:30PM F. Access by: mail, phone, fax, in person.

Hamilton

Real Estate Recording—Hamilton County Register of Deeds, 625 Georgia Ave. Court House, Room 400, Chattanooga, TN 37402. 423-209-7270, Fax: 423-209-6561. 7:30AM-5PM.

Civil Actions Over $15,000—11th Judicial District Circuit Court, Room 500 Courthouse, 625 Georgia Ave, Chattanooga, TN 37402. 423-209-6700. 8AM-4PM. Access by: mail, in person. www.hamiltontn.gov

Civil Actions Under $15,000, Eviction, Small Claims—11th District General Sessions, Civil Division, 600 Market St, Room 111, Chattanooga, TN 37402. 423-209-7631, Fax: 423-209-7631. 7AM-4PM. Access by: mail, phone, in person. www.hamiltontn.gov/courts/sessions/default.htm

Felony, Misdemeanor—11th District Criminal Court, 600 Market St, Room 102, Chattanooga, TN 37402. 423-209-7500, Fax: 423-209-7501. 8AM-4PM. Access by: mail, in person.

Civil, Probate—Chancery Court, Chancery Court, Clerk & Master, Room 300, Chattanooga, TN 37402. 423-209-6615, Fax: 423-209-6601. 8AM-4PM. Access by: mail, phone, fax, in person. www.hamilton.gov/courts/clerkmaster

Hancock

Real Estate Recording—Hancock County Register of Deeds, Courthouse, Sneedville, TN 37869. 9AM-4PM; 9AM-Noon W,Sat.

Felony, Misdemeanor, Civil, Eviction, Small Claims—3rd District, Criminal, Circuit and General Sessions Court, PO Box 347, Sneedville, TN 37869. 423-733-2954, Fax: 423-733-2119. 8AM-4PM. Access by: mail, fax, in person.

Civil, Probate—Chancery Court, PO Box 277, Sneedville, TN 37869. 423-733-4524, Fax: 423-733-2762. 9AM-4PM. Access by: mail, in person.

Hardeman

Real Estate Recording—Hardeman County Register of Deeds, Courthouse, Bolivar, TN 38008. 8:30AM-4:30PM; 8:30AM-5PM F.

Felony, Misdemeanor, Civil, Eviction, Small Claims—25th District Circuit Court and General Sessions, Courthouse, 100 N Main, Bolivar, TN 38008. 901-658-6524, Fax: 901-658-4584. 8:30AM-4:30PM M-Th, 8AM-5PM Fri. Access by: in person.

Civil, Probate—Chancery Court, PO Box 45, Bolivar, TN 38008. 901-658-3142, Fax: 901-658-4580. 8:30AM-4:30PM M-Th, 8:30AM-5PM Fri. Access by: mail, in person.

Hardin

Real Estate Recording—Hardin County Register of Deeds, Courthouse, Savannah, TN 38372. 901-925-8180. 8AM-4:30PM M,T,Th,F; 8AM-Noon W.

Felony, Misdemeanor, Civil, Eviction, Small Claims—24th District Circuit Court and General Sessions, 601 Main St, Savannah, TN 38372. 901-925-3583, Fax: 901-926-2955. 8AM-4:30PM M,T,Th,F, 8AM-Noon Wed. Access by: in person.

Probate—County Court, 601 Main St, Savannah, TN 38372. 901-925-3921. 8AM-4:30PM M,T,TH,F, 8AM-12PM Wed & Sat. Access by: mail, in person.

Hawkins

Real Estate Recording—Hawkins County Register of Deeds, 100 E. Main Street, Courthouse - Room 101, Rogersville, TN 37857. Fax: 423-921-3170. 8AM-4PM; 8AM-Noon W,Sat.

Felony, Misdemeanor, Civil, Eviction, Small Claims—3rd District Criminal, Circuit and General Sessions Court, PO Box 9, Rogersville, TN 37857. 423-272-3397, Fax: 423-272-9646. 8AM-4PM. Access by: in person.

Civil, Probate—Chancery Court, PO Box 908, Rogersville, TN 37857. 423-272-8150. 8AM-4PM. Access by: in person.

Haywood

Real Estate Recording—Haywood County Register of Deeds, 1 North Washington, Courthouse, Brownsville, TN 38012. 901-772-1722. 8:30AM-5PM.

Felony, Misdemeanor, Civil, Eviction, Small Claims—28th District Circuit Court and General Sessions, 1 N Washington Ave, Brownsville, TN 38012. 901-772-1112, Fax: 901-772-3864. 8:30AM-5PM. Access by: mail, phone, in person.

Civil, Probate—Chancery Court, 1 N Washington, PO Box 356, Brownsville, TN 38012. 901-772-0122, Fax: 901-772-3864. 8:30AM-5PM. Access by: mail, in person.

Henderson

Real Estate Recording—Henderson County Register of Deeds, Courthouse, Lexington, TN 38351. 8AM-4:30PM M,T,Th,F; 8AM-Noon Sat.

Felony, Misdemeanor, Civil, Eviction, Small Claims—26th District Circuit Court and General Sessions, Henderson County Courthouse, Lexington, TN 38351. 901-968-2031, Fax: 901-967-9441. 8AM-4:30PM M,T,Th,F. Access by: mail, phone, in person.

Civil, Probate—Chancery Court, PO Box 67, Lexington, TN 38351. 901-968-2801, Fax: 901-967-5380. 8AM-4:30PM M,T,Th,F; 8AM-Noon Sat. Access by: mail, phone, in person.

Henry

Real Estate Recording—Henry County Register of Deeds, 101 West Washington St. Ste 104, Paris, TN 38242. 901-642-6633, Fax: 901-642-2123. 8:30AM-4:30PM.

Felony, Misdemeanor, Civil, Eviction, Small Claims—24th District Circuit Court and General Sessions, PO Box 429, Paris, TN 38242. 901-642-0461. 8AM-4:30PM. Access by: mail, phone, in person.

Probate—County Court, PO Box 24, Paris, TN 38242. 901-642-2412, Fax: 901-644-0947. 8AM-4:30PM. Access by: mail, in person.

Hickman

Real Estate Recording—Hickman County Register of Deeds, #1 Courthouse, Centerville, TN 37033. 7:30AM-4PM; 8AM-Noon Sat.

Felony, Misdemeanor, Civil, Eviction, Small Claims—21st District Circuit Court and General Sessions, 104 College Ave #204, Centerville, TN 37033. 931-729-2211, Fax: 931-729-6141. 8AM-4PM. Access by: in person.

Civil, Probate—Chancery Court, 104 College Ave #202, Centerville, TN 37033. 931-729-2522, Fax: 931-729-6141. 8AM-4PM. Access by: mail, in person.

Houston

Real Estate Recording—Houston County Register of Deeds, Main Street, Court Square, Erin, TN 37061. Fax: 931-289-4240. 8AM-4:30PM; 8AM-Noon Sat.

Felony, Misdemeanor, Civil, Eviction, Small Claims—23rd District Circuit Court and General Sessions, PO Box 403, Erin, TN 37061. 931-289-4673, Fax: 931-289-5182. 8AM-4:30PM. Access by: mail, phone, fax, in person.

Civil, Probate—Chancery Court, PO Box 332, Erin, TN 37061. 931-289-3870, Fax: 931-289-5679. 8AM-4PM. Access by: mail, in person.

Humphreys

Real Estate Recording—Humphreys County Register of Deeds, 102 Thompson Street, Courthouse Annex, Room 3, Waverly, TN 37185. 8AM-4:30PM.

Felony, Misdemeanor, Civil, Eviction, Small Claims—23rd District Circuit Court and General Sessions, Room 106, Waverly, TN 37185. 931-296-2461, Fax: 931-296-1651. 8AM-4:30PM. Access by: mail, phone, in person.

Probate—County Court, Clerk, Room 2 Courthouse Annex, Waverly, TN 37185. 931-296-7671, Fax: 931-296-5011. 8AM-4:30PM. Access by: mail, in person.

Jackson

Real Estate Recording—Jackson County Register of Deeds, 6 E. Madison Ave. Gainesboro, TN 38562. 8AM-4PM M,T,Th,F; 8AM-3PM W; 8AM-Noon Sat.

Felony, Misdemeanor, Civil, Eviction, Small Claims—15th District Criminal, Circuit and General Sessions Court, PO Box 205, Gainesboro, TN 38562. 931-268-9314, Fax: 931-268-4555. 8AM-4PM M,T,Th,F; 8AM-3PM W; 8AM-Noon Sat. Access by: mail, phone, fax, in person.

Probate—Jackson County Chancery Court, PO Box 733, Gainesboro, TN 38562-0733. 931-268-9216, Fax: 931-268-9060. 8AM-4PM M,T,Th,F; 8AM-3PM W. Access by: mail, in person. www.jacksonco.com

Jefferson

Real Estate Recording—Jefferson County Register of Deeds, 202 Main Street, Courthouse, Dandridge, TN 37725. 423-397-2101. 8AM-4PM; 8-11AM Sat.

Felony, Misdemeanor, Civil, Eviction, Small Claims—4th District Circuit Court and General Sessions, PO Box 671, Dandridge, TN 37725. 423-397-2786, Fax: 423-397-4894. 8AM-4PM M-F; 8-11AM Sat. Access by: mail, in person.

Probate—County Court, PO Box 710, Dandridge, TN 37725. 423-397-2935, Fax: 423-397-3839. 8AM-4PM M-F, 8AM-11PM Sat. Access by: mail, phone, fax, in person.

Johnson

Real Estate Recording—Johnson County Register of Deeds, 222 Main Street, Mountain City, TN 37683. Fax: 423-727-7047. 8:30AM-5PM M,T,Th,F; 8:30AM-Noon W,Sat.

Felony, Misdemeanor, Civil, Eviction, Small Claims—1st District Criminal, Circuit and General Sessions Court, PO Box 73, Mountain City, TN 37683. 423-727-9012, Fax: 423-727-7047. 8:30AM-5PM. Access by: mail, phone, in person.

Civil, Probate—Chancery Court, PO Box 196, Mountain City, TN 37683. 423-727-7853, Fax: 423-727-7047. 8:30AM-5PM. Access by: mail, in person.

Knox

Real Estate Recording—Knox County Register of Deeds, 400 W. Main Avenue, Room 224, Knoxville, TN 37902. 423-521-2305. 8AM-4:30PM.

Civil Actions Over $10,000—Circuit Court, 400 Main Ave, Room M-30, PO Box 379, Knoxville, TN 37901. 423-215-2400, Fax: 423-521-4251. 8AM-6PM. Access by: mail, phone, fax, in person.

Civil Actions Under $15,000, Eviction, Small Claims—General Sessions, 400 Main Ave, Knoxville, TN 37902. 423-215-2518. 8AM-4:30PM. Access by: mail, in person.

Felony, Misdemeanor—6th District Criminal Court, 400 Main Ave, Room 149, Knoxville, TN 37902. 423-215-2492, Fax: 423-215-4291. 8AM-5PM M-Th; 8AM-4:30PM F. Access by: mail, phone, fax, in person.

Civil, Probate—Chancery Court, 400 Main Ave, Knoxville, TN 37902. 423-215-2555, Fax: 423-215-2920. 8AM-4:30PM. Access by: mail, phone, fax, in person.

Lake

Real Estate Recording—Lake County Register of Deeds, 229 Church St. Box 5, Courthouse, Tiptonville, TN 38079. Fax: 901-253-6815. 9AM-4PM M,T,W,F; 8AM-Noon Th.

Felony, Misdemeanor, Civil, Eviction, Small Claims—29th District Circuit Court and General Sessions, 227 Church St, PO Box 11, Tiptonville, TN 38079. 901-253-7137, Fax: 901-253-9815. 8AM-4PM M-W & F; 8AM-Noon Th. Access by: mail, phone, in person.

Civil, Probate—Chancery Court, PO Box 12, Tiptonville, TN 38079. 901-253-8926. 9AM-4PM M-W & F, 8AM-Noon Th. Access by: mail, in person.

Lauderdale

Real Estate Recording—Lauderdale County Register of Deeds, Courthouse, Ripley, TN 38063. 901-635-0712, Fax: 901-635-9682. 8AM-4:30PM M,T,Th,F; 8AM-Noon W,Sat.

Felony, Misdemeanor, Civil Actions Over $15,000—25th District Circuit Court, Lauderdale County Justice Center, 675 Hwy 51 S, PO Box 509, Ripley, TN 38063. 901-635-0101, Fax: 901-635-0583. 8AM-4:30PM. Access by: mail, in person.

Civil Actions Under $15,000, Eviction, Small Claims—General Sessions Court, PO Box 509, Ripley, TN 38063. 901-635-2572, Fax: 901-635-9682. 8AM-4:30PM. Access by: mail, in person.

Probate—County Court, Courthouse, 100 Court Sq, Ripley, TN 38063. 901-635-2561. 8AM-4:30PM M,T,Th,F; 8AM-Noon W & Sat. Access by: mail.

Lawrence

Real Estate Recording—Lawrence County Register of Deeds, 240 West Gaines Street, N.B.U. #18, Lawrenceburg, TN 38464. Fax: 931-766-5602. 8AM-4:30PM.

Felony, Misdemeanor, Civil, Eviction, Small Claims—22nd District Circuit Court and General Sessions, NBU #12 240 W Gaines, Lawrenceburg, TN 38464. 931-762-4398, Fax: 931-766-2219. 8AM-4:30PM. Access by: in person.

Civil, Probate—County Court, 240 Gaines St, NBU #12, Lawrenceburg, TN 38464. 931-762-7700. 8AM-4:30PM. Access by: in person.

Lewis

Real Estate Recording—Lewis County Register of Deeds, Courthouse, Room 104, 110 N. Park Ave. Hohenwald, TN 38462. 8AM-4:30PM.

Felony, Misdemeanor, Civil, Eviction, Small Claims—21st Judicial District Circuit Court and General Sessions, Courthouse 110 Park Avenue N, Rm 201, Hohenwald, TN 38462. 931-796-3724, Fax: 931-796-6010. 8AM-4:30PM. Access by: in person.

Civil, Probate—Chancery Court, Chancery Court, Clerk & Master, Hohenwald, TN 38462. 931-796-3734, Fax: 931-796-6010. 8AM-4:30PM. Access by: mail, phone, fax, in person.

Lincoln

Real Estate Recording—Lincoln County Register of Deeds, Courthouse, Room 104, 112 Main St. Fayetteville, TN 37334. 615-433-1371. 8AM-4PM.

Felony, Misdemeanor, Civil, Eviction, Small Claims—17th Judicial District Circuit Court and General Sessions, 112 Main Ave

S, Rm 203, Fayetteville, TN 37334. 931-433-2334, Fax: 931-438-1577. 8AM-4PM. Access by: mail, phone, fax, in person.

Civil, Probate—Chancery Court, 112 Main Ave, Rm B109, Fayetteville, TN 37334. 931-433-1482, Fax: 931-433-9979. 8AM-4PM. Access by: mail, in person.

Loudon

Real Estate Recording—Loudon County Register of Deeds, 101 Mulberry St. Loudon, TN 37774. Fax: 423-458-9028. 8AM-4:30PM (M-open until 5:30PM).

Felony, Misdemeanor, Civil, Eviction, Small Claims—9th District Criminal & Circuit Court, PO Box 160, Loudon, TN 37774. 423-458-2042, Fax: 423-458-2043. 8AM-5:30PM Mon, 8AM-4:30PM T-F; 8AM-6:30PM(General Session Juv). Access by: mail, in person. Special note: General Sessions & Juvenile Court located at 12680 Hwy 11 W Suite 3, Lenoir City, TN 37771, 423-986-3505.

Probate—County Court, 101 Mulberry St #200, Loudon, TN 37774. 423-458-2726, Fax: 423-458-9891. 8AM-5:30PM Mon, 8AM-4:30PM T-F. Access by: mail, in person.

Macon

Real Estate Recording—Macon County Register of Deeds, Courthouse, Room 102, Lafayette, TN 37083. 615-666-3624, Fax: 615-666-5323. 8AM-4:30PM.

Felony, Misdemeanor, Civil, Eviction, Small Claims—15th District Criminal, Circuit, and General Sessions Court, Room 202, Lafayette, TN 37083. 615-666-2354, Fax: 615-666-3001. 8AM-4:30PM M-Th; 8AM-5PM F. Access by: in person.

Probate—County Court, County Court Clerk, Rm 104, Lafayette, TN 37083. 615-666-2333, Fax: 615-666-5323. 8AM-4:30PM M-W, Closed Thu, 8AM-5PM Fri, 8AM-1:30PM Sat. Access by: mail, in person.

Madison

Real Estate Recording—Madison County Register of Deeds, Courthouse, Room 109, 100 Main St. Jackson, TN 38301. 901-423-6027, Fax: 901-422-1171. 9AM-5PM.

Felony, Misdemeanor, Civil Actions Over $15,000—26th District Circuit Court, 515 S Liberty St, Jackson, TN 38301. 901-423-6035. 8AM-4PM. Access by: in person.

Civil Actions Under $15,000, Eviction, Small Claims—General Sessions, 515 S Liberty St, Jackson, TN 38301. 901-423-6041. 8AM-4PM. Access by: mail, in person.

Probate—General Sessions Division II, Probate Division, 110 Irby St, PO Box 1504, Jackson, TN 38302-1504. 901-988-3025, Fax: 901-422-6044. 8:30-12, 1-4PM. Access by: mail, phone, in person.

Marion

Real Estate Recording—Marion County Register of Deeds, Highway 41, Courthouse, Jasper, TN 37347. 8AM-4PM M-F; 8AM-Noon Sat.

Felony, Misdemeanor, Civil, Eviction, Small Claims—12th District Circuit Court and General Sessions, PO Box 789, Courthouse Sq, Jasper, TN 37347. 423-942-2134, Fax: 423-942-4160. 8AM-4PM. Access by: mail, phone, in person.

Civil, Probate—Chancery Court, PO Box 789, Jasper, TN 37347. 423-942-2601, Fax: 423-942-0291. 8AM-4PM. Access by: mail, in person.

Marshall

Real Estate Recording—Marshall County Register of Deeds, 1103 Courthouse Annex, Lewisburg, TN 37091. 8AM-4PM.

Felony, Misdemeanor, Civil, Eviction, Small Claims—17th District Circuit Court and General Sessions, Courthouse, Lewisburg, TN 37091. 931-359-0526, Fax: 931-359-0543. 8AM-4PM. Access by: in person.

Probate—County Court, 1107 Courthouse Annex, Lewisburg, TN 37091. 931-359-2181, Fax: 931-359-0543. 8AM-4PM. Access by: mail, in person.

Maury

Real Estate Recording—Maury County Register of Deeds, #1 Public Square, Columbia, TN 38401. 8AM-4PM.

Felony, Misdemeanor, Civil, Eviction, Small Claims, Probate—Circuit Court and General Sessions, Maury County Courthouse, 41 Public Square, Columbia, TN 38401. 931-381-3690, Fax: 931-381-5614. 8:30AM-4PM M,T,Th,F; 8:30AM-Noon W & Sat. Access by: mail, phone, fax, in person.

McMinn

Real Estate Recording—McMinn County Register of Deeds, 6 East Madison, Athens, TN 37303. 423-745-1291, Fax: 423-745-0095. 8:30AM-4PM.

Felony, Misdemeanor, Civil, Eviction, Small Claims, Probate—10th District Criminal, Circuit and General Sessions Court, PO Box 506, Athens, TN 37303. 423-745-1923, Fax: 423-745-1642. 8:30AM-4PM. Access by: mail, phone, fax, in person.

McNairy

Real Estate Recording—McNairy County Register of Deeds, Court Avenue, Courthouse, Selmer, TN 38375. Fax: 901-645-3656. 8AM-4:30PM M,T,Th,F; 8AM-Noon Sat.

Felony, Misdemeanor, Civil, Eviction, Small Claims—25th District Circuit Court and General Sessions, 300 Industrial Drive, Selmer, TN 38375. 901-645-1015, Fax: 901-645-1003. 8AM-4:30PM M-F; 8AM-Noon Sat. Access by: mail, in person.

Civil, Probate—Chancery Court, Chancery Court, Clerk & Master, Courthouse, Rm 205, Selmer, TN 38375. 901-645-5446, Fax: 901-645-3656. 8AM-4PM M,T,Th,F; Closed W. Access by: mail, in person.

Meigs

Real Estate Recording—Meigs County Register of Deeds, Courthouse, Decatur, TN 37322. 423-334-5119. 8AM-5PM M,T,Th,F; 8AM-Noon W & Sat.

Felony, Misdemeanor, Civil, Eviction, Small Claims—9th District Criminal, Circuit and General Sessions Court, PO Box 205, Decatur, TN 37322. 423-334-5821, Fax: 423-334-4819. 8AM-5PM M,T,Th,F; 8AM-12PM Sat. Access by: mail, in person.

Civil, Probate—Chancery Court, PO Box 5, Decatur, TN 37322. 423-334-5243. 8AM-5PM M,T,Th,F; 8:30AM-Noon Wed. Access by: mail, in person.

Monroe

Real Estate Recording—Monroe County Register of Deeds, 103 College Street - Suite 4, Madisonville, TN 37354. 423-442-2920. 8:30AM-4:30PM M,T,Th,F; 8:30AM-Noon W & Sat.

Felony, Misdemeanor, Civil, Eviction, Small Claims—10th District, Circuit and General Sessions Court, 105 College St, Madisonville, TN 37354. 423-442-2396, Fax: 423-442-9538. 8AM-4:30PM. Access by: mail, in person.

Civil, Probate—Chancery Court, PO Box 56, Madisonville, TN 37354. 423-442-2644, Fax: 423-420-0048. 8:30AM-4:30PM. Access by: mail, in person.

Montgomery

Real Estate Recording—Montgomery County Register of Deeds, 350 Pageant Ln, Suite 404, Clarksville, TN 37040. 615-648-5710, Fax: 931-553-5157. 8AM-4:30PM.

Felony, Civil Actions Over $10,000—19th District Circuit Court, PO Box 384, Clarksville, TN 37041-0384. 931-648-5700, Fax: 931-648-5731. 8:30AM-4:30PM. Access by: in person.

Misdemeanor, Civil Actions Under $10,000, Eviction, Small Claims—General Sessions, 120 Commerce St, Clarksville, TN 37040. 8:30AM-4:30PM. Access by: mail, in person.

Civil, Probate—Chancery Court, Chancery Court, Clerk & Master, Montgomery County Courthouse, Clarksville, TN 37040. 931-648-5703. 8AM-4:30PM. Access by: mail, in person.

Moore

Real Estate Recording—Moore County Register of Deeds, Courthouse, Lynchburg, TN 37352. 8AM-4:30PM; Closed Th; 8AM-Noon Sat.

Felony, Misdemeanor, Civil, Eviction, Small Claims—17th District Circuit Court and General Sessions, Courthouse, PO Box 206, Lynchburg, TN 37352. 931-759-7208, Fax: 931-759-7028. 8AM-4:30PM MTWF; 8AM-Noon Sat. Access by: mail, in person.

Civil, Probate—Chancery Court, PO Box 206, Lynchburg, TN 37352. 931-759-7028, Fax: 931-759-7028. 8AM-4:30PM M-W,F; 8AM-Noon Sat. Access by: mail, in person.

Morgan

Real Estate Recording—Morgan County Register of Deeds, Courthouse Square, Room 102, Wartburg, TN 37887. 8AM-4PM.

Felony, Misdemeanor, Civil, Eviction, Small Claims—9th District Criminal, Circuit and General Sessions Court, PO Box 163, Wartburg, TN 37887. 423-346-3503. 8AM-4PM. Access by: mail, in person.

Civil, Probate—Chancery Court, PO Box 789, Wartburg, TN 37887. 423-346-3881. 8AM-4PM. Access by: mail, phone, in person.

Obion

Real Estate Recording—Obion County Register of Deeds, 5 Bill Burnett Circle, Union City, TN 38261. Fax: 901-885-7515. 8AM-4:30PM.

Felony, Misdemeanor, Civil Actions Over $10,000—27th District Circuit Court, 7 Bill Burnett Circle, Union City, TN 38261. 901-885-1372, Fax: 901-885-7515. 8:30AM-4:30PM. Access by: mail, phone, in person.

Civil Actions Under $15,000, Eviction, Small Claims—General Sessions, 9 Bill Burnett Circle, Union City, TN 38281-0236. 901-885-1811, Fax: 901-885-7515. 9AM-4PM. Access by: mail, in person.

Civil, Probate—Chancery Court, PO Box 187, Union City, TN 38281. 901-885-2562, Fax: 901-885-7515. 8:30AM-4:30PM. Access by: mail, phone, in person.

Overton

Real Estate Recording—Overton County Register of Deeds, 317 East University St. Room 150, Livingston, TN 38570. 8AM-4:30PM.

Felony, Misdemeanor, Civil, Eviction, Small Claims—13th District Criminal, Circuit and General Sessions Court, Overton County Courthouse, 100 Court Sq, Livingston, TN 38570. 931-823-2312, Fax: 931-823-9728. 8AM-4:30PM M,T,Th,F, 8AM-Noon Wed & Sat. Access by: mail, in person.

Probate—County Court, Courthouse Annex, University St, Livingston, TN 38570. 931-823-2631, Fax: 931-823-7036. 8AM-4:30PM M,T,Th,F; 8AM-Noon W & Sat. Access by: mail, in person.

Perry

Real Estate Recording—Perry County Register of Deeds, Main Street, Courthouse, Linden, TN 37096. 615-589-2313. 8AM-4PM M,T,Th,F; Closed Wed; 8-11AM Sat.

Felony, Misdemeanor, Civil, Eviction, Small Claims—21st District Circuit Court and General Sessions, PO Box 91, Linden, TN 37096. 931-589-2218. 8AM-4PM. Access by: mail, in person.

Civil, Probate—Chancery Court, PO Box 251, Linden, TN 37096. 931-589-2217, Fax: 931-589-2350. 8AM-4PM. Access by: mail, in person.

Pickett

Real Estate Recording—Pickett County Register of Deeds, Main Street, Courthouse, Byrdstown, TN 38549. Fax: 931-864-6615. 8AM-4PM.

Felony, Misdemeanor, Civil, Eviction, Small Claims—13th District, Criminal, Circuit and General Sessions Court, PO Box 5, Byrdstown, TN 38549. 931-864-3958, Fax: 931-864-6885. 8AM-4PM. Access by: mail, in person.

Probate—County Court, PO Box 5 Courthoue Square, Byrdstown, TN 38549. 931-864-3879. 8AM-4PM M,T,Th,F, 8AM-Noon W & Sat. Access by: mail, in person.

Polk

Real Estate Recording—Polk County Register of Deeds, 411 Highway, Courthouse, Benton, TN 37307. 423-338-4545. 9AM-4:30PM; Closed Th; 9AM-Noon Sat.

Felony, Misdemeanor, Civil, Eviction, Small Claims—10th District Criminal, Circuit and General Sessions Court, PO Box 256, Benton, TN 37307. 423-338-4524, Fax: 423-338-4558. 8:30AM-4:30PM M-F; 9AM-Noon Sat. Access by: mail, in person.

Civil, Probate—Chancery Court, PO Drawer L, Benton, TN 37307. 423-338-4522, Fax: 423-338-4553. 8:30AM-4:30PM M-F, 8:30AM-Noon Sat. Access by: mail, in person.

Putnam

Real Estate Recording—Putnam County Register of Deeds, 300 East Spring Street, Courthouse - Room 3, Cookeville, TN 38501. 615-528-8845. 8AM-4PM.

Felony, Misdemeanor, Civil, Eviction, Small Claims—13th District Criminal, Circuit and General Sessions Court, 421 E Spring St, 1C-49A, Cookeville, TN 38501. 931-528-1508. 8AM-4PM. Access by: mail, in person.

Probate—County Court, PO Box 220, Cookeville, TN 38503-0220. 931-526-7106, Fax: 931-372-8201. 8AM-4:30PM. Access by: mail, in person.

Rhea

Real Estate Recording—Rhea County Register of Deeds, 1475 Market Street, Dayton, TN 37321. 423-775-7810. 8AM-4PM.

Felony, Misdemeanor, Civil, Eviction, Small Claims—12th District Circuit Court and General Sessions, 1475 Market St Rm 200, Dayton, TN 37321. 423-775-7805, Fax: 423-775-5553. 8AM-4PM M-Th; 8AM-5:30PM F. Access by: in person.

Probate—Probate Division, 1475 Market St, Rm 105, Dayton, TN 37321. 423-775-7806, Fax: 423-775-4064. 8AM-4:30PM. Access by: mail, in person.

Roane

Real Estate Recording—Roane County Register of Deeds, 200 Race Street, Courthouse, Kingston, TN 37763. 423-386-4938. 8:30AM-6PM M; 8:30AM-4:30PM T-F.

Felony, Misdemeanor, Civil, Eviction, Small Claims—9th District Criminal, Circuit, and General Sessions Court, PO Box 73, Kingston, TN 37763. 423-376-2390, Fax: 423-376-4458. 8:30AM-6PM Mon; 8:30AM-4:30PM T-F. Access by: mail, in person. Special note: General Sessions phone is 423-376-5584, their records are separate.

Civil, Probate—Chancery Court, PO Box 402, Kingston, TN 37763. 423-376-2487, Fax: 423-376-4318. 8:30AM-6PM Mon, 8:30AM-4:30PM T-F. Access by: mail, phone, in person.

Robertson

Real Estate Recording—Robertson County Register of Deeds, 525 S. Brown St. Springfield, TN 37172. 8AM-4:30PM.

Felony, Misdemeanor, Civil, Eviction, Small Claims—19th District Circuit Court and General Sessions, Room 200, Springfield, TN 37172. 615-382-2324, Fax: 615-384-8246. 8AM-4:30PM. Access by: mail, phone, fax, in person.

Civil, Probate—Chancery Court, 101 Robertson, County Courthouse, Springfield, TN 37172. 615-384-5650. 8:30AM-4:30PM. Access by: mail, in person.

Rutherford

Real Estate Recording—Rutherford County Register of Deeds, 319 North Maple St. Room 133, Murfreesboro, TN 37130. Fax: 615-898-7987. 8AM-4PM.

Felony, Misdemeanor, Civil Actions Over $15,000—16th District Circuit Court, Room 201, Murfreesboro, TN 37130. Fax: 615-849-9553. 8AM-4:15PM. Access by: in person.

Civil Actions Under $10,000, Eviction, Small Claims—General Sessions, Judicial Bldg, Room 101, Murfreesboro, TN 37130. 615-898-7831, Fax: 615-898-7835. 8AM-4:15PM. Access by: in person.

Probate—County Court, 319 N Maple St, Murfreesboro, TN 37130. 615-898-7798, Fax: 615-898-7830. 8AM-4PM M-Th; 8AM-5PM F. Access by: mail, in person.

Scott

Real Estate Recording—Scott County Register of Deeds, 283 Court St. Room 217, Huntsville, TN 37756. 423-663-2598. 8AM-4:30PM.

Felony, Misdemeanor, Civil, Eviction, Small Claims—8th District Criminal, Circuit, and General Sessions Court, PO Box 73,

Huntsville, TN 37756. 423-663-2440, Fax: 423-663-3803. 8AM-4:30PM. Access by: mail, phone, fax, in person.

Sequatchie

Real Estate Recording—Sequatchie County Register of Deeds, Cherry Street, Courthouse - 307E, Dunlap, TN 37327. Fax: 423-949-6554. 8AM-4PM; Closed Th; 8AM-Noon Sat.

Felony, Misdemeanor, Civil, Eviction, Small Claims—12th District Circuit Court and General Sessions, PO Box 551, Dunlap, TN 37327. 423-949-2618, Fax: 423-949-2902. 8AM-4PM. Access by: mail, phone, fax, in person.

Civil, Probate—Chancery Court, PO Box 1651, Dunlap, TN 37327. 423-949-3670, Fax: 423-949-2579. 8AM-4PM. Access by: mail, fax, in person.

Sevier

Real Estate Recording—Sevier County Register of Deeds, 125 Court Avenue, Courthouse Suite 209W, Sevierville, TN 37862. 423-453-2767. 8AM-4:30PM M-Th; 8AM-6PM F.

Felony, Misdemeanor, Civil, Eviction, Small Claims—4th District Circuit Court and General Sessions, 125 Court Ave 204 E, Sevierville, TN 37862. 423-453-5536, Fax: 423-453-6830. 8AM-4:30PM M-Th, 8AM-6PM Fri. Access by: mail, phone, in person.

Probate—County Court, 125 Court Ave, Suite 202, Sevierville, TN 37862. 423-453-5502, Fax: 423-453-6830. 8AM-4:30PM. Access by: mail, in person.

Shelby

Real Estate Recording—Shelby County Register of Deeds, 160 North Main St. Room 519, Memphis, TN 38103. Fax: 901-545-3837. 8AM-4:30PM.

Civil Actions Over $15,000—Circuit Court, 140 Adams Ave, Rm 224, Memphis, TN 38103. 901-576-4006, Fax: 901-576-4372. 8AM-4:30PM. Access by: mail, fax, in person.

Felony—30th District Criminal Court, 201 Poplar, Room 401, 4th Flr, Memphis, TN 38103. 901-576-5001, Fax: 901-576-3679. 8AM-4:30PM. Access by: mail, fax, in person.

Civil Actions Under $25,000, Eviction, Small Claims—General Sessions-Civil, 140 Adams, Room 106, Memphis, TN 38103. 901-576-4031, Fax: 901-576-2515. 8AM-4:30PM. Access by: mail, fax, in person.

Misdemeanor—General Sessions-Criminal, 201 Poplar, Room 81, Memphis, TN 38103. 901-576-5098, Fax: 901-576-3655. 8AM-4:30PM. Access by: mail, in person.

Probate—Probate Court, 140 Adams, Room 124, Memphis, TN 38103. 901-576-4040, Fax: 901-576-4746. 8AM-4:30PM. Access by: mail, phone, fax.

Smith

Real Estate Recording—Smith County Register of Deeds, 122 Turner High Circle, Suite 113, Carthage, TN 37030. Fax: 615-735-8263. 8AM-4PM.

Felony, Misdemeanor, Civil, Eviction, Small Claims—15th District Criminal, Circuit, and General Sessions Court, 211 Main St, Carthage, TN 37030. 615-735-0500, Fax: 615-735-8261. 8AM-4PM M-F; 8AM-Noon Sat. Access by: mail, phone, in person.

Civil, Probate—Chancery Court, 211 N Main St, Carthage, TN 37030. 615-735-2092, Fax: 615-735-8261. 8AM-4:30PM. Access by: mail, fax, in person.

Stewart

Real Estate Recording—Stewart County Register of Deeds, Courthouse, 225 Donelson Parkway, Dover, TN 37058. 615-232-7026. 8AM-4:30PM.

Felony, Misdemeanor, Civil, Eviction, Small Claims—23rd District Circuit Court and General Sessions, PO Box 193, Dover, TN 37058. 931-232-7042, Fax: 931-232-3111. 8AM-4:30PM. Access by: mail, in person.

Civil, Probate—Chancery Court, PO Box 102, Dover, TN 37058. 931-232-5665, Fax: 931-232-3111. 8AM-4:30PM. Access by: mail, in person.

Sullivan

Real Estate Recording—Sullivan County Register of Deeds, 801 Anderson St. Bristol, TN 37620. 423-323-6464. 8:30AM-5PM.

Sullivan County Register of Deeds, 3411 Highway 126, Courthouse, Blountville, TN 37617. 423-323-6464, Fax: 423-279-2771. 8AM-5PM.

Civil—Bristol Circuit Court-Civil Division, Courthouse, Rm 211, 801 Anderson St, Bristol, TN 37620. 423-989-4354. 8AM-5PM. Access by: mail, in person.

Civil Actions Over $10,000—Kingsport Circuit Court-Civil Division, 225 W Center St, Kingsport, TN 37660. 423-224-1724. 8AM-5PM. Access by: mail, phone, in person.

Felony, Misdemeanor—2nd District Circuit Court, 140 Blockville ByPass, PO Box 585, Blountville, TN 37617. 423-323-5158. 8AM-5PM. Access by: mail, in person.

Misdemeanor, Civil Actions Under $10,000, Eviction, Small Claims—Bristol General Sessions, Courthouse, 801 Broad St, Rm 211, Bristol, TN 37620. 423-989-4352. 8AM-4:30PM. Access by: mail, phone, in person.

Misdemeanor, Civil Actions Under $15,000, Eviction, Small Claims—Kingsport General Sessions, 200 Shelby St, Kingsport, TN 37660. 423-279-2752. 8AM-5PM. Access by: mail, phone, in person.

Civil, Probate—Chancery Court, PO Box 327, Blountville, TN 37617. 423-323-6483, Fax: 423-279-3280. 8AM-5PM. Access by: mail, in person.

Sumner

Real Estate Recording—Sumner County Register of Deeds, 355 N. Belvedere Dr. S.C. Admin. Bldg, Rm 201, Gallatin, TN 37066. 615-452-1260. 8AM-4:30PM.

Felony, Misdemeanor, Civil, Eviction, Small Claims—18th District Criminal, Circuit, and General Sessions Court, Public Sq, PO Box 549, Gallatin, TN 37066. 615-452-4367, Fax: 615-451-6027. 8AM-4:30PM. Access by: in person.

Civil, Probate—Chancery Court, Room 300, Sumner County Courthouse, Gallatin, TN 37066. 615-452-4282, Fax: 615-451-6031. 8AM-4:30PM. Access by: mail, phone, fax, in person.

Tipton

Real Estate Recording—Tipton County Register of Deeds, Court Square, Courthouse, Room 105, Covington, TN 38019. 901-476-0211, Fax: 901-476-0227. 8AM-5PM.

Felony, Misdemeanor, Civil, Eviction, Small Claims—25th District Circuit Court and General Sessions, 1801 S College, Rm 102, Covington, TN 38019. 901-475-3310. 8AM-5PM. Access by: mail, in person.

Civil, Probate—Chancery Court, Tipton County Courthouse, Court Sq, PO Box 87, Covington, TN 38019. 901-476-0209, Fax: 901-476-0246. 8AM-5PM. Access by: mail, phone, in person.

Trousdale

Real Estate Recording—Trousdale County Register of Deeds, 200 E. Main St. #8, Hartsville, TN 37074. Fax: 615-374-1100. 8AM-4:30PM.

Felony, Misdemeanor, Civil, Eviction, Small Claims—15th District Criminal, Circuit, and General Sessions Court, 200 East Main St, Rm 5, Hartsville, TN 37074. 615-374-3411, Fax: 615-374-1100. 8AM-4:30PM. Access by: in person.

Civil, Probate—Chancery Court, Courthouse Room 1, 200 E Main St, Hartsville, TN 37074. 615-374-2996, Fax: 615-374-1100. 8AM-4:30PM. Access by: mail, in person.

Unicoi

Real Estate Recording—Unicoi County Register of Deeds, 100 Main, 1st Floor, Courthouse, Erwin, TN 37650. 9AM-5PM; 9AM-Noon Sat.

Felony, Misdemeanor, Civil, Eviction, Small Claims—1st District Criminal, Circuit, and General Sessions Court, PO Box 2000, Erwin, TN 37650. 423-743-3541. 8AM-5PM. Access by: mail, in person.

Probate—Probate Court, PO Box 340, Erwin, TN 37650. 423-743-3381, Fax: 423-743-3219. 9AM-5PM M-F, 9AM-Noon Sat. Access by: mail, in person.

Union

Real Estate Recording—Union County Register of Deeds, Main Street, Maynardville, TN 37807. 423-992-5943. 8AM-4PMM,T,Th.F; 8AM-Noon W,Sat.

Felony, Misdemeanor, Civil, Eviction, Small Claims—8th District Criminal, Circuit, and General Sessions Court, 901 E Main Street, #220, Maynardville, TN 37807. 423-992-5493. 8AM-4PM M,T,Th,F; 8AM-Noon W & Sat. Access by: mail, in person.

Civil, Probate—Chancery Court, 901 Main St #215, Maynardville, TN 37807-3510. 423-992-5942. 8AM-4PM (6PM F). Access by: mail, phone, in person.

Van Buren

Real Estate Recording—Van Buren County Register of Deeds, Courthouse Square, Spencer, TN 38585. Fax: 931-946-7572. 8AM-5PM.

Felony, Misdemeanor, Civil, Eviction, Small Claims—31st District Circuit Court and General Sessions, PO Box 126, Spencer, TN 38585. 931-946-2153, Fax: 931-946-2388. 8AM-5PM. Access by: mail, phone, in person.

Probate—County Court, PO Box 126, Spencer, TN 38585. 931-946-2121, Fax: 931-946-2388. 8AM-4PM M,T,Th,F, 8AM-Noon Wed & Sat. Access by: mail, in person.

Warren

Real Estate Recording—Warren County Register of Deeds, 111 S. Court Square, McMinnville, TN 37110. 8AM-4:30PM M-Th; 8AM-5PM F.

Felony, Misdemeanor, Civil, Eviction, Small Claims—31st District Circuit Court and General Sessions, 111 Court Sq, PO Box 639, McMinnville, TN 37111. 931-473-2373, Fax: 931-473-3726. 8AM-4:30PM M-Th; 8AM-5PM F. Access by: mail, in person.

Civil, Probate—Chancery Court, PO Box 639, McMinnville, TN 37110. 931-473-2364, Fax: 931-473-3726. 8AM-4:30PM M-Th, 8AM-5PM F. Access by: mail, in person.

Washington

Real Estate Recording—Washington County Register of Deeds, Main Street, Courthouse, Jonesboro, TN 37659. Fax: 423-753-1743. 8AM-4:30PM.

Felony, Misdemeanor, Civil, Eviction, Small Claims—1st District Circuit Court and General Sessions, PO Box 356, Jonesborough, TN 37659. 423-753-1611, Fax: 423-753-1809. 8AM-5PM. Access by: mail, in person.

Civil Actions Over $10,000—Johnson City Law Court-Civil, 101 E Market St, Johnson City, TN 37604. 423-461-1475, Fax: 423-926-4862. 8AM-5PM. Access by: mail, in person.

Civil Actions Under $15,000, Eviction, Small Claims—General Sessions, 101 E Market St, Johnson City, TN 37604. 423-461-1412, Fax: 423-926-4862. 8AM-5PM. Access by: mail, in person.

Probate—Probate Court, PO Box 218, Jonesborough, TN 37659. 423-753-1623, Fax: 423-753-4716. 8AM-5PM. Access by: mail, in person.

Wayne

Real Estate Recording—Wayne County Register of Deeds, Court Square, Waynesboro, TN 38485. 615-722-3269, Fax: 931-722-5994. 8AM-4PM M,T,Th,F; 8AM-Noon W,Sat.

Felony, Misdemeanor, Civil, Eviction, Small Claims—22nd District Circuit Court and General Sessions, PO Box 869, Waynesboro, TN 38485. 931-722-5519, Fax: 931-722-5994. 8AM-4PM M,T,Th,F, 8AM-Noon W & Sat. Access by: mail, phone, fax, in person.

Civil, Probate—Chancery Court, PO Box 101, Waynesboro, TN 38485. 931-722-5517, Fax: 931-722-5994. 8AM-4PM. Access by: mail, in person.

Weakley

Real Estate Recording—Weakley County Register of Deeds, Courthouse, Room 102, Dresden, TN 38225. 901-364-3643, Fax: 901-364-5389. 8AM-4:30PM.

Felony, Misdemeanor, Civil, Eviction, Small Claims—27th District Circuit Court and General Sessions, PO Box 28, Dresden, TN 38225. 901-364-3455, Fax: 901-364-6765. 8AM-4:30PM. Access by: mail, fax, in person.

Civil, Probate—Chancery Court, PO Box 197, Dresden, TN 38225. 901-364-3454, Fax: 901-364-5247. 8AM-4:30PM. Access by: mail, in person.

White

Real Estate Recording—White County Register of Deeds, Courthouse Rm 118, 1 East Bockman Way, Sparta, TN 38583. Fax: 931-836-8418. 8AM-5PM.

Felony, Misdemeanor, Civil, Eviction, Small Claims—13th District Criminal, Circuit, and General Sessions Court, Courthouse, Room 304, Sparta, TN 38583. 931-836-3205, Fax: 931-836-3526. 8AM-5PM. Access by: in person.

Civil, Probate—Chancery Court, White County Courthouse, Sparta, TN 38583. 931-836-3787. 8AM-Noon. Access by: mail, phone, in person.

Williamson

Real Estate Recording—Williamson County Register of Deeds, 1320 West Main Street, Room 201, Franklin, TN 37064. 8AM-4:30PM.

Felony, Misdemeanor, Civil, Eviction, Small Claims—21st District Circuit Court and General Sessions, Room 107, Franklin, TN 37064. 615-790-5454, Fax: 615-790-5432. 8AM-4:30PM. Access by: mail, in person.

Civil, Probate—Chancery Court, Clerk & Master, Franklin, TN 37064. 615-790-5428, Fax: 615-790-5626. 8AM-4:30PM. Access by: mail, phone, in person.

Wilson

Real Estate Recording—Wilson County Register of Deeds, Wilson County Register, 228 East Main St. Lebanon, TN 37087. 615-444-0894, Fax: 615-443-3288. 8AM-4PM; 8AM-5PM F.

Felony, Misdemeanor, Civil, Eviction, Small Claims—15th District Criminal, Circuit, and General Sessions Court, PO Box 518, Lebanon, TN 37088-0518. 615-444-2042, Fax: 615-449-3420. 8AM-4PM M-Th, 8AM-5PM F. Access by: in person.

Probate—County Court, PO Box 918, Lebanon, TN 37088-0918. 615-443-2627, Fax: 615-443-2628. 8AM-4:30PM M-Th, 8AM-5PM Fri. Access by: mail, phone, in person.

Federal Courts

US District Court

Eastern District of Tennessee

Chattanooga Division Clerk's Office, PO Box 591, Chattanooga, TN 37401423-752-5200 Counties: Bledsoe, Bradley, Hamilton, McMinn, Marion, Meigs, Polk, Rhea, Sequatchie.

Greeneville Division 101 Summer St W, Greenville, TN 37743423-639-3105 Counties: Carter, Cocke, Greene, Hamblen, Hancock, Hawkins, Johnson, Sullivan, Unicoi, Washington.

Knoxville Division Clerk's Office, 800 Market St, Knoxville, TN 37902423-545-4228 Counties: Anderson, Blount, Campbell, Claiborne, Grainger, Jefferson, Knox, Loudon, Monroe, Morgan, Roane, Scott, Sevier, Union.

Winchester Division PO Box 459, Winchester, TN 37398931-967-1444 Counties: Bedford, Coffee, Franklin, Grundy, Lincoln, Moore, Van Buren, Warren.

Middle District of Tennessee

Columbia Division c/o Nashville Division, US Courthouse Room 800, 801 Broadway, Nashville, TN 37203615-736-5498 Counties: Giles, Hickman, Lawrence, Lewis, Marshall, Maury, Wayne. http://edge.edge.net/~uscourts

Cookeville Division c/o Nashville Division, US Courthouse Room 800, 801 Broadway, Nashville, TN 37203615-736-5498 Fax: 615-736-7488 Counties: Clay, Cumberland, De Kalb, Fentress, Jackson, Macon, Overton, Pickett, Putnam, Smith, White. http://edge.edge.net/~uscourts

Nashville Division US Courthouse, Room 800, 801 Broadway, Nashville, TN 37203615-736-5498, Record Room: 615-736-5498, Civil Docket Phone: 615-736-7178, Criminal Docket Phone: 615-736-7396 Fax: 615-736-7488 Counties: Cannon, Cheatham, Davidson, Dickson, Houston, Humphreys, Montgomery, Robertson, Rutherford, Stewart, Sumner, Trousdale, Williamson, Wilson. http://edge.edge.net/~uscourts

Western District of Tennessee

Jackson Division Federal Bldg, Room 101, 109 S Highland Ave, Jackson, TN 38301901-427-6586 Fax: 901-422-3367 Counties: Benton, Carroll, Chester, Crockett, Decatur, Gibson, Hardeman, Hardin, Haywood, Henderson, Henry, Lake, McNairy, Madison, Obion, Perry, Weakley.

Memphis Division Federal Bldg, Room 242, 167 N Main, Memphis, TN 38103901-495-1200, Record Room: 901-495-1206 Fax: 901-495-1250 Counties: Dyer, Fayette, Lauderdale, Shelby, Tipton.

US Bankruptcy Court

Eastern District of Tennessee

Chattanooga Division Historic US Courthouse, 31 E 11th St, Chattanooga, TN 37402423-752-5163 Counties: Bedford, Bledsoe, Bradley, Coffee, Franklin, Grundy, Hamilton, Lincoln, Marion, McMinn, Meigs, Moore, Polk, Rhea, Sequatchie, Van Buren, Warren.

Knoxville Division Suite 1501, 1st Tennessee Plaza, Knoxville, TN 37929423-545-4279 Counties: Anderson, Blount, Campbell, Carter, Claiborne, Cocke, Grainger, Greene, Hamblen, Hancock, Hawkins, Jefferson, Johnson, Knox, Loudon, Monroe, Morgan, Roane, Scott, Sevier, Sullivan, Unicoi, Union, Washington.

Middle District of Tennessee

Nashville Division Customs House, Room 200, 701 Broadway, Nashville, TN 37203615-736-5584 Counties: Cannon, Cheatham, Clay, Cumberland, Davidson, De Kalb, Dickson, Fentress, Giles, Hickman, Houston, Humphreys, Jackson, Lawrence, Lewis, Macon, Marshall, Maury, Montgomery, Overton, Pickett, Putnam, Robertson, Rutherford, Smith, Stewart, Sumner, Trousdale, Wayne, White, Williamson, Wilson. http://edge.edge.net/~uscourts

Western District of Tennessee

Jackson Division Room 312, 109 S Highland Ave, Jackson, TN 38301901-424-9751 Counties: Benton, Carroll, Chester, Crockett, Decatur, Gibson, Hardeman, Hardin, Haywood, Henderson, Henry, Lake, Madison, McNairy, Obion, Perry, Weakley. www.tnwb.uscourts.gov

Memphis Division Suite 413, 200 Jefferson Ave, Memphis, TN 38103901-544-3202, Record Room: 901-544-4429 Counties: Dyer, Fayette, Lauderdale, Shelby, Tipton. www.tnwb.uscourts.gov

Attorney General's Office

PO Box 12548   512-463-2100
Austin, TX 78711-2548   Fax: 512-463-2063
www.oag.state.tx.us

Governor's Office

PO Box 12428   512-463-2000
Austin, TX 78711   Fax: 512-463-1849
www.governor.state.tx.us

State Archives

PO Box 12927   512-463-5455
Austin, TX 78711-2927   Fax: 512-463-5436
www.tsl.state.tx.us

Capital:	Austin
	Travis County
Time Zone:	CST*

* Texas' two western-most counties are MST:
They are: El Paso and Hudspeth,

Number of Counties:	254
Population:	19,439,337
Web Site:	www.state.tx.us

Search Unclaimed Property Online

www.window.state.tx.us/comptrol/
unclpropr/upsearch.html

State Agencies

Criminal Records

Crime Records Service, Correspondence Section, PO Box 15999, Austin, TX 78761-5999 (5805 N Lamar, Austin, TX 78752); 512-424-5079; 8AM-5PM. Access by: mail. http://records.txdps.state.tx.us/dps/default.cfm

Corporation Records
Fictitious Name
Limited Partnership Records
Limited Liability Company Records
Assumed Name
Trademarks/Servicemarks

Secretary of State, Corporation Section, PO Box 13697, Austin, TX 78711-3697 (J Earl Rudder Bldg, 1019 Brazos, B-13, Austin, TX 78701); 512-463-5555 Information, 512-463-5578 Copies, 512-463-5576 Trademarks; Fax: 512-463-5709; 8AM-5PM. Access by: mail, phone, in person, online. www.sos.state.tx.us

Sales Tax Registrations

Controller of Public Accounts, LBJ Office Bldg, 111 E 17th St, Austin, TX 78774; 512-463-4600, 800-252-1386 Searches; Fax: 512-475-1610; 8AM-5PM. Access by: mail, phone, in person. www.window.state.tx.us

Uniform Commercial Code
Federal Tax Liens

UCC Section, Secretary of State, PO Box 13193, Austin, TX 78711-3193 (1019 Brazos St, Rm B-13, Austin, TX 78701); 512-475-2705; Fax: 512-475-2812; 8AM-5PM. Access by: mail, phone, in person, online. www.sos.state.tx.us

State Tax Liens

Records not available from state agency.

Records are located at the county level.

Workers' Compensation Records

Texas Workers' Compensation Commission, Southfield Building, 4000 South, IH-35, MS-92B, Austin, TX 78704-7491; 512-448-7900, 512-385-5161 Reprographics Department; Fax: 512-385-5232; 8AM-5PM. Access by: mail.

Birth Certificates

Texas Department of Health, Bureau of Vital Statistics, PO Box 12040, Austin, TX 78711-2040 (1100 W 49th St, Austin, TX 78756); 512-458-7111; Fax: 512-458-7506; 8AM-5PM. Access by: mail. www.tdh.state.tx.us/bvs

Death Records

Texas Department of Health, Bureau of Vital Statistics, PO Box 12040, Austin, TX 78711-2040; 512-458-7111; Fax: 512-458-7506; 8AM-5PM. Access by: mail. www.tdh.state.tx.us/bvs

Marriage Certificates

Texas Department of Health, Bureau of Vital Statistics, PO Box 12040, Austin, TX 78711-2040; 512-458-7111; Fax: 512-458-7506; 8AM-5PM. Access by: mail. www.tdh.state.tx.us/bvs

Divorce Records

Texas Department of Health, Bureau of Vital Statistics, PO Box 12040, Austin, TX 78711-2040; 512-458-7111; Fax: 512-458-7506; 8AM-5PM. Access by: mail. www.tdh.state.tx.us/bvs

Accident Reports

Texas Department of Public Safety, Accident Records Bureau, PO Box 15999, Austin, TX 78761-5999 (5805 N Lamar Blvd, Austin, TX 78752); 512-424-2600; 8AM-5PM. Access by: mail. www.txdps.state.ts.us

Driver Records

Department of Public Safety, Driver Records Section, PO Box 15999, Austin, TX 78761-5999 (5805 N Lamar Blvd, Austin, TX 78752); 512-424-2032; 8AM-5PM. Access by: mail. www.txdps.state.tx.us

Vehicle Ownership
Vehicle Identification

Department of Transportation, Vehicle Titles and Registration, 40th St and Jackson, Austin, TX 78779-0001; 512-465-7611; Fax: 512-465-7736; 8AM-5PM. Access by: mail, online.

Boat & Vessel Ownership
Boat & Vessel Registration

Parks & Wildlife Dept, 4200 Smith School Rd, Austin, TX 78744; 512-389-4828; 800-262-8755; 8AM-5PM. www.tpwd.state.tx.us/boat/boat.htm

Legislation-Current/Pending
Legislation-Passed

Legislative Reference Library, PO Box 12488, Austin, TX 78711-2488 (State Capitol Building, 2N.3, 1100 Congress, Austin, TX 78701); 512-463-1252 Bill Status, 512-463-0252 Senate Bill Copies, 512-463-1144 House Bill Copies; Fax: 512-475-4626; 8AM-5PM. Access by: mail, phone, in person, online. www.capitol.state.tx.us

Voter Registration

Restricted access.
To do individual look-ups, one must go to the Tax Assessor-Collector at the county level Records are open. The state will sell the entire database, for non-commercial purposes, in a variety of media and sort formats.
Secretary of State, Elections Division, PO Box 12060, Austin, TX 78711-2060; 800-252-8683; Fax: 512-475-2811; 8AM-5PM www.sos.state.tx.us

GED Certificates

Texas Education Association, GED Records, 1701 N Congress Ave, Austin, TX 78701-1494; 512-463-9292; Fax: 512-305-9493; 7:30AM-5PM M-F.

Hunting License Information
Fishing License Information

Parks & Wildlife Department, License Section, 4200 Smith School Rd, Austin, TX 78744; 512-389-4820; Fax: 512-389-4330; 8AM-5PM. Access by: mail. www/tpwd.state.tx.us

County Courts & Recording Offices

About the Courts...

About the Recording Offices...

Administration

Office of Court Administration   512-463-1625
PO Box 12066   Fax: 512-463-1648
Austin, TX 78711
www.courts.state.tx.us

Court Structure

The legal court structure for Texas takes up 30 pages in the "Texas Judicial Annual Report." Generally, Texas District Courts have general civil jurisdiction and exclusive felony jurisdiction, along with typical variations such as contested probate and divorce.

The County Court structure includes two forms of courts - "Constitutional" and "at Law" - which come in various configurations depending upon the county. County Courts' upper claim limits vary from $5,000 to $100,000. For civil matters up to $5000, we recommend searchers start at the Constitutional County Court as they, generally, offer a shorter waiting time for cases in urban areas. In addition, keep in mind that the Municipal Courts have, per the Texas manual, "limited civil penalties in cases involving dangerous dogs." In some counties the District Court or County Court handles evictions.

District Courts handle felonies. County Courts handle misdemeanors and general civil cases. Probate is handled in Probate Court in the 18 largest counties and in District Courts or County Courts at Law elsewhere. However, the County Clerk is responsible for the records in every county.

Online Access

There is no statewide, court-related online computer access available, internal or external. However, a number of counties do offer online access.

Organization

254 counties, 254 recording offices. The recording officer is County Clerk. 252 counties are in the Central Time Zone (CST) and 2 are in the Mountain Time Zone (MST).

Certain Assessor and property information is available through two companies:

www.taxnetusa.com - TaxNetUSA, 817-795-8378, Fax 817-795-8359. 42 Texas counties on the TaxNetUSA site are available on the Internet for no fee.

www.txcountydata.com - 36 Texas counties on the TXCOUNTYDATA site are available on the Internet for no fee.

UCC Records

Financing statements are filed at the state level, except for real estate related collateral, which are filed with the County Clerk. All recording offices will perform UCC searches. Searches fees are usually $10.00 per debtor name using the approved UCC-11 request form, plus $15.00 for using a non-Texas form. Copy fees are usually $1.00-1.50 per page with a minimum copy fee of $5.00.

Lien Records

Federal tax liens on personal property of businesses are filed with the Secretary of State. Other federal and all state tax liens are filed with the County Clerk. All counties will perform tax lien searches. Search fees and copy fees vary.

Real Estate Records

Some counties will perform real estate searches. Copy fees are usually $1.00 per page. Certification usually costs $5.00 per document. Each county has an "Appraisal District" which is responsible for collecting taxes.

County Courts & Recording Offices

Anderson

Real Estate Recording—Anderson County Clerk, 500 North Church Street, Palestine, TX 75801. 903-723-7408. 8AM-5PM.

Felony, Civil—District Court, PO Box 1159, Palestine, TX 75802-1159. 903-723-7412. 8AM-Noon, 1-5PM. Access by: mail, in person.

Misdemeanor, Civil, Probate—County Court, 500 N Church, Palestine, TX 75801. 903-723-7432. 8AM-5PM. Access by: mail, in person.

Andrews

Real Estate Recording—Andrews County Clerk, 215 N.W. 1st Street, Annex Building Room 121A, Andrews, TX 79714. Fax: 915-524-1473. 8AM-5PM.

Felony, Civil—District Court, PO Box 328, Andrews, TX 79714. 915-524-1417. 8AM-5PM. Access by: mail, in person.

Misdemeanor, Civil, Probate—County Court, PO Box 727, Andrews, TX 79714. 915-524-1426. 8AM-5PM. Access by: mail, phone, in person.

Angelina

Real Estate Recording—Angelina County Clerk, 215 East Lufkin Avenue, Lufkin, TX 75901. Fax: 409-634-8460. 8AM-4:30PM.

Felony, Civil—District Court, PO Box 908, Lufkin, TX 75902. 409-849-5711, Fax: 409-634-5915. 8AM-5PM. Access by: mail, in person.

Misdemeanor, Civil, Probate—County Court, PO Box 908, Lufkin, TX 75902. 409-864-1316, Fax: 409-634-8460. 8AM-5PM. Access by: mail, in person.

Aransas

Real Estate Recording—Aransas County Clerk, 301 North Live Oak, Rockport, TX 78382. 512-790-0132. 8AM-4:30PM.

Felony, Civil—District Court, 301 North Live Oak, Rockport, TX 78382. 401-466-3200. 8AM-5PM. Access by: mail, in person.

Misdemeanor, Civil, Probate—County Court, 301 N Live Oak, Rockport, TX 78382. 401-461-1000, Fax: 361-790-0125. 8AM-4:30PM. Access by: mail, in person.

Archer

Real Estate Recording—Archer County Clerk, Center & Main, Archer City, TX 76351. 817-574-4822. 8:30AM-5PM.

Felony, Misdemeanor, Civil, Eviction, Probate—District and County Court, PO Box 815, Archer City, TX 76351. 940-574-4615. 8:30AM-5PM. Access by: mail, phone, in person.

Armstrong

Real Estate Recording—Armstrong County Clerk, Trice Street, Courthouse, Claude, TX 79019. 806-226-3651, Fax: 806-226-2030. 8AM-Noon, 1-5PM.

Felony, Misdemeanor, Civil, Eviction, Probate—District and County Court, PO Box 309, Claude, TX 79019. 806-226-2081, Fax: 806-226-2030. 8AM-Noon, 1-5PM. Access by: mail, in person.

Atascosa

Real Estate Recording—Atascosa County Clerk, Circle Drive, Room 6-1, Jourdanton, TX 78026. 212-374-7915. 8AM-5PM.

Felony, Civil—District Court, #52 Courthouse Circle, Jourdanton, TX 78026. 830-769-3011. 8AM-Noon, 1-5PM. Access by: mail, in person.

Misdemeanor, Civil, Probate—County Court, Circle Dr Rm 6-1, Jourdanton, TX 78026. 830-769-2511. 8AM-5PM. Access by: mail, in person.

Austin

Real Estate Recording—Austin County Clerk, 1 East Main, Bellville, TX 77418. 410-479-1811, Fax: 409-865-0336. 8AM-5PM.

Felony, Civil—District Court, 1 East Main, Bellville, TX 77418-1598. 410-479-5800. 8AM-Noon, 1-5PM. Access by: mail, fax, in person.
www.austincounty.com/Courthouse/courthouse.html

Misdemeanor, Civil, Probate—County Court at Law, 1 E Main, Bellville, TX 77418. 410-479-0717, Fax: 409-865-0336. 8AM-5PM. Access by: mail, in person.

Bailey

Real Estate Recording—Bailey County Clerk, 300 South First, Suite 200, Muleshoe, TX 79347. 806-272-3239, Fax: 806-272-3879. 8AM-Noon, 1-5PM.

Felony, Civil—District Court, 300 S 1st St, Muleshoe, TX 79347. 806-272-3165, Fax: 806-272-3879. 8AM-5PM. Access by: mail, phone, in person.

Misdemeanor, Civil, Probate—County Court, 300 S 1st St, Muleshoe, TX 79347. 806-272-3044, Fax: 806-272-3879. 8AM-4PM. Access by: mail, in person.

Bandera

Real Estate Recording—Bandera County Clerk, 500 Main Street, Bandera, TX 78003. Fax: 830-796-8323. 8:30AM-4:30PM.

Felony, Misdemeanor, Civil, Eviction, Probate—District and County Court, PO Box 823, Bandera, TX 78003. 830-796-3332, Fax: 830-796-8323. 8AM-5PM. Access by: mail, fax, in person. Special note: The District Clerk can be reached at PO Box 2688 and 830-796-4606. PO and phone above is for County Clerk.

Bastrop

Real Estate Recording—Bastrop County Clerk, 803 Pine Street, Courthouse, Bastrop, TX 78602. 512-321-2460. 8AM-Noon, 1-5PM.

Felony, Civil—District Court, PO Box 770, Bastrop, TX 78602. 361-782-3563. 8AM-5PM. Access by: mail, in person.

Misdemeanor, Probate—County Court, PO Box 577, Bastrop, TX 78602. 361-782-3402. 8AM-Noon, 1-5PM. Access by: mail, phone, in person.

Baylor

Real Estate Recording—Baylor County Clerk, 101 South Washington, Seymour, TX 76380. 817-888-3553. 8:30AM-5PM.

Felony, Misdemeanor, Civil, Eviction, Probate—District and County Court, PO Box 689, Seymour, TX 76380. 940-888-3322. 8:30AM-5PM. Access by: mail, phone, in person.

Bee

Real Estate Recording—Bee County Clerk, 105 West Corpus Christi Street, Room 103, Beeville, TX 78102. Fax: 361-362-3247. 8AM-Noon, 1-5PM.

Felony, Civil—District Court, PO Box 666, Beeville, TX 78102-0666. 361-782-3812, Fax: 361-362-3282. 8AM-5PM. Access by: mail, in person.

Misdemeanor, Civil, Probate—County Court, 105 W Corpus Christi St Rm 103, Beeville, TX 78102. 361-790-0122, Fax: 361-362-3247. 8AM-Noon, 1-5PM. Access by: mail, phone, fax, in person.

Bell

Real Estate Recording—Bell County Clerk, 550 East 2nd Ave. Bldg D, Belton, TX 76513. 817-933-5255, Fax: 254-933-5176. 8AM-5PM.

Felony, Civil—District Court, 104 S Main St, PO Box 909, Belton, TX 76513. 256-463-2651, Fax: 254-933-5199. 8AM-5PM. Access by: mail, in person.

Misdemeanor, Civil, Probate—County Court, PO Box 480, Belton, TX 76513. 256-351-4790, Fax: 254-933-5176. 8AM-5PM. Access by: mail, in person.

Bexar

Real Estate Recording—Bexar County Clerk, Bexar County Courthouse, 100 Dolorosa, Room 108, San Antonio, TX 78205. Fax: 210-335-2813. 8AM-5PM.

Felony, Civil—District Court, 100 Dolorosa, County Courthouse, San Antonio, TX 78205. 210-374-2442, Fax: 210-335-2942. 8AM-5PM. Access by: mail, in person, online. www.co.bexar.tx.us

Civil—County Court-Civil Central Filing Department, 100 Dolorosa, San Antonio, TX 78205-3083. 210-393-7310. 8AM-5PM. Access by: mail, phone, in person. Special note: There are nine (9) hearing locations in this county where open cases are held. All closed cases are forwarded here.

Misdemeanor—County Court-Criminal, 300 Dolorosa, Suite 4101, San Antonio, TX 78205. 210-683-5116. 8AM-5PM. Access by: mail, in person, online.

Probate—Probate Court #2, 100 Dolorosa St, San Antonio, TX 78205. 210-544-0819. 8AM-5PM. Access by: mail, in person.

Blanco

Real Estate Recording—Blanco County Clerk, Courthouse, Pecan Street, Johnson City, TX 78636. 212-669-3913. 8AM-5PM.

Felony, Misdemeanor, Civil, Eviction, Probate—District and County Court, PO Box 65, Johnson City, TX 78636. 830-868-7357. 8AM-5PM. Access by: mail, in person.

Borden

Real Estate Recording—Borden County Clerk, 101 Main, Gail, TX 79738. 806-756-4386. 8AM-Noon, 1-5PM.

Felony, Misdemeanor, Civil, Eviction, Probate—District and County Court, PO Box 124, Gail, TX 79738. 806-756-4312. 8AM-5PM. Access by: mail, in person.

Bosque

Real Estate Recording—Bosque County Clerk, 103 River Street, Meridian, TX 76665. 817-435-2201. 8AM-5PM.

Felony, Civil—District Court, Main & Morgan St, Po Box 674, Meridian, TX 76665. 254-729-3206. 8AM-5PM. Access by: mail, in person.

Misdemeanor, Civil, Probate—County Court, PO Box 617, Meridian, TX 76665. 254-697-6596, Fax: 254-435-2152. 8AM-5PM. Access by: mail, in person.

Bowie

Real Estate Recording—Bowie County Clerk, 710 James Bowie Drive, New Boston, TX 75570. 903-628-2571, Fax: 903-628-6729. 8AM-5PM.

Felony, Misdemeanor, Civil—District Court, 710 James Bowie Dr, PO Box 248, New Boston, TX 75570. 903-628-6750. 8AM-5PM. Access by: mail, in person.

Misdemeanor, Civil, Eviction, Small Claims, Probate—County Court, PO Box 248, New Boston, TX 75570. 903-628-6740. 8AM-5PM. Access by: mail, in person.

Brazoria

Real Estate Recording—Brazoria County Clerk, 111 East Locust, Suite 200, Angleton, TX 77515. 410-398-2737, Fax: 409-864-1358. 8AM-5PM.

Felony, Civil—District Court, 111 E Locus #500, Angleton, TX 77515-4678. 410-479-0410. 8AM-5PM. Access by: mail, phone, in person.

Misdemeanor, Civil—County Court, 111 E Locust #200, Angleton, TX 77515. 410-386-2642, Fax: 409-848-1951. 8AM-5PM. Access by: mail, fax, in person.

Probate—Probate Court, County Courthouse, 111 E Locust, Angleton, TX 77515. 410-461-0200, Fax: 409-864-1031. 8AM-5PM.

Brazos

Real Estate Recording—Brazos County Clerk, 300 East 26th Street, Suite 120, Bryan, TX 77803. 8AM-5PM.

Felony, Civil—District Court, 300 E 26th St #216 (PO Box 2208), Bryan, TX 77806. 409-642-1208, Fax: 409-361-0197. 8AM-5PM. Access by: mail, in person.

Misdemeanor, Civil, Probate—County Court, 300 E 26th St #120, Bryan, TX 77803. 409-642-1118. 8AM-5PM. Access by: mail, in person. Special note: Court holds misdemeanor records prior to 1986 only. Newer cases are at the District Court.

Brewster

Real Estate Recording—Brewster County Clerk, 201 West Avenue E, Alpine, TX 79830. 915-837-3667, Fax: 915-837-1536. 9AM-Noon, 1-5PM.

Felony, Civil—District Court, PO Box 1024, Alpine, TX 79831. 915-837-0102, Fax: 915-837-1536. 9AM-12, 1-5PM. Access by: mail, phone, fax, in person.

Misdemeanor, Civil Probate—County Court, PO Box 119, Alpine, TX 79831. 915-837-3366, Fax: 915-837-1536. 9AM-5PM. Access by: mail, in person.

Briscoe

Real Estate Recording—Briscoe County Clerk, 415 Main Street, Silverton, TX 79257. Fax: 806-823-2359. 8AM-5PM.

Felony, Misdemeanor, Civil, Eviction, Probate—District and County Court, PO Box 375, Silverton, TX 79257. 806-823-2134, Fax: 806-823-2359. 8AM-5PM. Access by: mail, fax, in person.

Brooks

Real Estate Recording—Brooks County Clerk, 110 East Miller, Falfurrias, TX 78355. 512-325-5604, Fax: 361-325-4944. 8AM-5PM.

Felony, Civil—District Court, PO Box 534, Falfurrias, TX 78355. 361-668-5713, Fax: 361-325-5679. 8AM-5PM. Access by: mail, phone, fax, in person.

Misdemeanor, Civil, Probate—County Court, PO Box 427, Falfurrias, TX 78355. 361-668-5717. 8AM-5PM. Access by: mail, phone, fax, in person.

Brown

Real Estate Recording—Brown County Clerk, 200 South Broadway, Courthouse, Brownwood, TX 76801. 915-646-6033. 8:30AM-5PM.

Felony, Civil—District Court, 200 S Broadway, Brownwood, TX 76801. 915-646-5514. 8:30AM-5PM. Access by: mail, in person.

Misdemeanor, Civil, Probate—County Court, 200 S Broadway, Brownwood, TX 76801. 915-643-2594. 8:30AM-5PM. Access by: mail, in person.

Burleson

Real Estate Recording—Burleson County Clerk, 100 West Buck St. Sutie 203, Caldwell, TX 77836. 9AM-5PM.

Felony, Civil—District Court, 100 West Buck #303, Caldwell, TX 77836. 409-835-8509. 8AM-12, 1-5PM. Access by: mail, in person.

Misdemeanor, Civil, Probate—County Court, 100 West Buck #203, Caldwell, TX 77836. 409-835-8479. 9AM-5PM. Access by: mail, in person.

Burnet

Real Estate Recording—Burnet County Clerk, 220 South Pierce Street, Burnet, TX 78611. Fax: 512-756-5410. 8AM-5PM.

Felony, Civil—District Court, 220 S Pierce, Burnet, TX 78611. 512-756-5450. 8AM-5PM. Access by: mail, in person.

Misdemeanor, Civil, Probate—County Court, 220 S Pierce, Burnet, TX 78611. 512-756-5403, Fax: 512-756-5410. 8AM-5PM. Access by: mail, fax, in person.

Caldwell

Real Estate Recording—Caldwell County Clerk, 401 East Market, Lockhart, TX 78644. 512-398-1800. 8:30AM-Noon, 1-5PM.

Felony, Civil—District Court, 201 E San Antonio St, Lockhart, TX 78644. 512-398-1806. 8:30AM-Noon, 1-5PM. Access by: mail, in person.

Misdemeanor, Civil, Probate—County Court, PO Box 906, Lockhart, TX 78644. 512-398-1804. 8:30AM-Noon, 1-4:45PM. Access by: mail, in person.

Calhoun

Real Estate Recording—Calhoun County Clerk, 211 South Ann, Port Lavaca, TX 77979. 401-247-1900, Fax: 361-553-4420. 8AM-5PM.

Felony, Civil—District Court, 211 S Ann, Port Lavaca, TX 77979. 401-253-7000. 8AM-5PM. Access by: mail, in person.

Misdemeanor, Civil, Probate—County Court, 211 S Ann, Port Lavaca, TX 77979. 401-245-7340, Fax: 361-553-4420. 8AM-5PM. Access by: mail, phone, in person.

Callahan

Real Estate Recording—Callahan County Clerk, 100 W. 4th, Ste. 104, Courthouse, Baird, TX 79504. 915-854-1399, Fax: 915-854-1227. 8AM-5PM.

Felony, Civil—District Court, 100 W 4th St Suite 300, Baird, TX 79504-5396. 915-854-1800. 8AM-5PM. Access by: mail, in person.

Misdemeanor, Civil, Probate—County Court, 100 W 4th St, Suite 104, Baird, TX 79504-5300. 915-854-1217, Fax: 915-854-1227. 8AM-5PM. Access by: mail, in person.

Cameron

Real Estate Recording—Cameron County Clerk, 964 East Harrison, Brownsville, TX 78520. 210-765-9925, Fax: 956-554-0813. 8AM-5PM.

Felony, Civil—District Court, 974 E Harrison St, Brownsville, TX 78520. 956-544-0839. 8AM-Noon, 1-5PM. Access by: mail, in person.

Misdemeanor, Civil, Probate—County Court No. 1, 2 & 3, PO Box 2178, Brownsville, TX 78522-2178. 956-544-0848, Fax: 956-544-0894. 8AM-5PM. Access by: mail, fax, in person.

Camp

Real Estate Recording—Camp County Clerk, 126 Church Street, Room 102, Pittsburg, TX 75686. Fax: 903-856-0811. 8AM-Noon, 1-5PM.

Felony, Civil—District Court, 126 Church St Rm 203, Pittsburg, TX 75686. 903-856-3221. 8AM-5PM. Access by: mail, in person.

Misdemeanor, Civil, Probate—County Court, 126 Church St Rm 102, Pittsburg, TX 75686. 903-856-2731, Fax: 903-856-2309. 8AM-Noon, 1-5PM. Access by: mail, fax, in person.

Carson

Real Estate Recording—Carson County Clerk, 5th & Main Street, Courthouse, Panhandle, TX 79068. 806-537-3753. 8AM-Noon, 1-5PM.

Felony, Misdemeanor, Civil, Eviction, Probate—District and County Court, PO Box 487, Panhandle, TX 79068. 806-537-3873, Fax: 806-537-3724. 8AM-Noon, 1-5PM. Access by: mail, in person.

Cass

Real Estate Recording—Cass County Clerk, Main & Houston, Courthouse, Linden, TX 75563. 903-756-7626, Fax: 903-756-5732. 8AM-5PM.

Felony, Civil—District Court, PO Box 510, Linden, TX 75563. 903-756-7514. 8AM-5PM. Access by: mail, in person.

Misdemeanor, Probate—County Court, PO Box 449, Linden, TX 75563. 903-756-5071. 8AM-5PM. Access by: mail, in person.

Castro

Real Estate Recording—Castro County Clerk, 100 East Bedford, Room 101, Dimmitt, TX 79027. 806-647-5534. 8AM-5PM.

Felony, Misdemeanor, Civil, Eviction, Probate—District and County Court, 100 E Bedford, Rm 101, Dimmitt, TX 79027. 806-647-3338. 8AM-5PM. Access by: mail, in person.

Chambers

Real Estate Recording—Chambers County Clerk, 404 Washington Street, Anahuac, TX 77514. 409-436-4972, Fax: 409-267-4453. 8AM-5PM.

Felony, Civil—District Clerk, Drawer NN, Anahuac, TX 77514. 409-436-4922. 8AM-Noon, 1-5PM. Access by: mail, in person.

Misdemeanor, Civil, Probate—County Court, PO Box 728, Anahuac, TX 77514. 409-532-2381, Fax: 409-267-4453. 8AM-5PM. Access by: mail, in person.

Cherokee

Real Estate Recording—Cherokee County Clerk, 402 N. Main, Courthouse, Rusk, TX 75785. 903-683-4935, Fax: 903-683-2393. 8AM-5PM.

Felony, Civil—District Court, Drawer C, Rusk, TX 75785. 903-683-4533. 8AM-Noon, 1-5PM. Access by: mail, in person.

Misdemeanor, Civil, Probate—County Court, Cherokee County Clerk, PO Box 420, Rusk, TX 75785. 903-683-2350, Fax: 903-683-2393. 8AM-5PM. Access by: mail, in person.

Childress

Real Estate Recording—Childress County Clerk, 100 Avenue E NW, Childress, TX 79201. 817-937-6271, Fax: 940-937-3479. 8:30AM-Noon, 1-5PM.

Felony, Misdemeanor, Civil, Eviction, Probate—District and County Court, Courthouse Box 4, Childress, TX 79201. 940-937-6143, Fax: 940-937-3479. 8:30AM-Noon, 1-5PM. Access by: mail, in person.

Clay

Real Estate Recording—Clay County Clerk, 100 North Bridge, Henrietta, TX 76365. 8AM-5PM.

Felony, Civil—District Clerk, PO Box 568, Henrietta, TX 76365. 940-538-4561, Fax: 940-538-4431. 8AM-Noon, 1-5PM. Access by: mail, in person.

Misdemeanor, Civil, Probate—County Court, PO Box 548, Henrietta, TX 76365. 940-538-4631. 8AM-5PM. Access by: mail, in person.

Cochran

Real Estate Recording—Cochran County Clerk, 100 North Main, Courthouse, Morton, TX 79346. 806-266-5161, Fax: 806-266-9027. 8AM-5PM.

Felony, Misdemeanor, Civil, Eviction, Probate—District and County Court, County Courthouse Rm 102, Morton, TX 79346. 806-266-5450, Fax: 806-266-9027. 8AM-5PM. Access by: mail, fax, in person.

Coke

Real Estate Recording—Coke County Clerk, 13 East 7th Street, Courthouse, Robert Lee, TX 76945. 915-453-2713, Fax: 915-453-2297. 8AM-5PM.

Felony, Misdemeanor, Civil, Eviction, Probate—District and County Court, PO Box 150, Robert Lee, TX 76945. 915-453-2631, Fax: 915-453-2297. 8AM-5PM. Access by: mail, in person.

Coleman

Real Estate Recording—Coleman County Clerk, Courthouse, Coleman, TX 76834. 915-625-4221. 8AM-5PM.

Felony, Civil—District Court, PO Box 512, Coleman, TX 76834. 915-625-2568. 8AM-4:30PM. Access by: mail, in person.

Misdemeanor, Civil, Probate—County Court, PO Box 591, Coleman, TX 76834. 915-625-2889. 8AM-5PM. Access by: mail, in person.

Collin

Real Estate Recording—Collin County Clerk, 200 South McDonald, Annex "A", Suite 120, McKinney, TX 75069. 214-771-5251. 8AM-5PM (8AM-4PM Land Recording).

Felony, Civil—District Clerk, PO Box 578, McKinney, TX 75069. 972-548-4365. 8AM-5PM. Access by: mail, in person, online.

Misdemeanor, Civil, Probate—County Court, 210 S McDonald St Rm 542, McKinney, TX 75069. 972-548-4529, Fax: 972-548-4698. 8AM-5PM. Access by: mail, phone, fax, in person, online.

Collingsworth

Real Estate Recording—Collingsworth County Clerk, Courthouse, Room 3, 800 West Ave. Wellington, TX 79095. Fax: 806-447-5418. 9AM-5PM.

Felony, Misdemeanor, Civil, Eviction, Probate—District and County Court, County Courthouse, Rm 3, 800 West Ave, Box 10, Wellington, TX 79095. 806-447-2408, Fax: 806-447-5418. 9AM-5PM. Access by: mail, in person.

Colorado

Real Estate Recording—Colorado County Clerk, 400 Spring Street, Courthouse, Columbus, TX 78934. 409-883-7740, Fax: 409-732-8852. 8AM-5PM.

Felony, Civil—District Court, County Courthouse, 400 Spring St, Columbus, TX 78934. 409-882-7055. 8AM-Noon, 1-5PM. Access by: mail, in person.

Misdemeanor, Civil, Probate—County Court, PO Box 68, County Courthouse, Columbus, TX 78934. 409-873-2662, Fax: 409-732-8852. 8AM-5PM. Access by: mail, in person.

Comal

Real Estate Recording—Comal County Clerk, 100 Main Plaza, Suite 104, New Braunfels, TX 78130. 210-773-2413, Fax: 830-620-3410. 8AM-4:30PM.

Felony, Civil—District Court, 150 N Seguin Ste 304, New Braunfels, TX 78130-5161. 830-620-5574, Fax: 830-608-2006. 8AM-5PM. Access by: mail, fax, in person.

Misdemeanor, Civil, Probate—County Court at Law, 100 Main Plaza, Ste 303, New Braunfels, TX 78130. 830-620-5582, Fax: 830-608-2021. 8AM-4:30PM. Access by: mail, phone, fax, in person.

Comanche

Real Estate Recording—Comanche County Clerk, Courthouse, Comanche, TX 76442. 915-356-2838, Fax: 915-356-3710. 8:30-5PM.

Felony, Civil—District Court, County Courthouse, Comanche, TX 76442. 915-356-2342, Fax: 915-356-2150. 8:30AM-Noon, 1-5PM. Access by: mail, in person.

Misdemeanor, Civil, Probate—County Court, County Courthouse, Comanche, TX 76442. 915-356-2655. 8:30AM-5PM. Access by: mail, in person.

Concho

Real Estate Recording—Concho County Clerk, Courthouse, 152 North Roberts, Paint Rock, TX 76866. Fax: 915-732-2040. 8:30AM-5PM.

Felony, Misdemeanor, Civil, Eviction, Probate—District and County Court, PO Box 98, Paint Rock, TX 76866. 915-732-4322, Fax: 915-732-2040. 8:30AM-5PM. Access by: mail, in person.

Cooke

Real Estate Recording—Cooke County Clerk, Courthouse, Gainesville, TX 76240. 817-668-5423, Fax: 940-668-5440. 8AM-5PM.

Felony, Civil—District Court, County Courthouse, Gainesville, TX 76240. 940-668-5450. 8AM-5PM. Access by: mail, in person.

Misdemeanor, Civil, Probate—County Court, County Courthouse, Gainesville, TX 76240. 940-668-5422. 8AM-5PM. Access by: mail, in person.

Coryell

Real Estate Recording—Coryell County Clerk, Courthouse, Gatesville, TX 76528. Fax: 254-865-8631. 8AM-Noon, 1-5PM.

Felony, Civil—District Court, PO Box 4, Gatesville, TX 76528. 256-231-1750, Fax: 254-865-5064. 8AM-5PM. Access by: mail, fax, in person.

Misdemeanor, Civil, Probate—County Court, PO Box 237, Gatesville, TX 76528. 254-965-1486, Fax: 254-865-8631. 8AM-Noon, 1-5PM. Access by: mail, fax, in person.

Cottle

Real Estate Recording—Cottle County Clerk, Courthouse, 9th & Richards, Paducah, TX 79248. 806-492-3738.

Felony, Misdemeanor, Civil, Eviction, Probate—District and County Court, PO Box 717, Paducah, TX 79248. 806-492-3823. 9AM-Noon, 1-5PM. Access by: mail, in person.

Crane

Real Estate Recording—Crane County Clerk, 6th East Alford Street, Courthouse, Crane, TX 79731. 915-558-3372. 9AM-Noon, 1-5PM.

Felony, Misdemeanor, Civil, Eviction, Probate—District and County Court, PO Box 578, Crane, TX 79731. 915-558-3581. 9AM-12 1-5PM. Access by: mail, in person.

Crockett

Real Estate Recording—Crockett County Clerk, 907 Avenue D, Ozona, TX 76943. Fax: 915-392-2675. 8AM-5PM M-Th; 8AM-4PM F.

Felony, Misdemeanor, Civil, Eviction, Probate—District and County Court, PO Drawer C, Ozona, TX 76943. 915-392-2022. 8AM-5PM. Access by: mail, in person.

Crosby

Real Estate Recording—Crosby County Clerk, Aspen & Berkshire Streets, Courthouse, Crosbyton, TX 79322. 8AM-Noon, 1-5PM.

Felony, Civil—District Court, PO Box 495, Crosbyton, TX 79322. 806-675-2071, Fax: 806-675-2433. 8AM-Noon, 1-5PM. Access by: mail, phone, fax, in person.

Misdemeanor, Civil, Probate—County Court, PO Box 218, Crosbyton, TX 79322. 806-675-2334. 8AM-5PM. Access by: mail, in person.

Culberson

Real Estate Recording—Culberson County Clerk, 301 La Caverna, Courthouse, Van Horn, TX 79855. 915-283-2115, Fax: 915-283-9234. 8AM-Noon,1-5PM.

Felony, Misdemeanor, Civil, Eviction, Probate—District and County Court, PO Box 158, Van Horn, TX 79855. 915-283-2058. 8AM-5PM. Access by: mail, phone, in person.

Dallam

Real Estate Recording—Dallam County Clerk, 101 East 5th, Dalhart, TX 79022. Fax: 806-249-2252. 9AM-5PM.

Felony, Misdemeanor, Civil, Eviction, Probate—District and County Court, PO Box 1352, Dalhart, TX 79022. 806-249-4751, Fax: 806-249-2252. 9AM-5PM. Access by: mail, fax, in person.

Dallas

Real Estate Recording—Dallas County Clerk's Office, Records Bldg, 2nd Floor, 509 Main St. Dallas, TX 75202. 8AM-4:30PM.

Civil—District Court-Civil, 600 Commerce, Dallas, TX 75202-4606. 215-686-8859. 8AM-4:30PM. Access by: mail, in person.

Felony—Criminal District Courts 1-5, 133 N Industrial Blvd, Dallas, TX 75207. 215-686-6250, Fax: 214-653-5986. 8:00AM-4:30PM M-F. Access by: mail, phone, in person, online.

District Court-Criminal, 133 N Industrial Blvd, Dallas, TX 75207-4313. 215-348-6265, Fax: 214-653-5986. 8AM-4:30PM. Access by: mail, in person, online.

Misdemeanor—District Court-Misdemeanor, 133 N Industrial Blvd, Dallas, TX 75207-4313. 215-348-6244. 8AM-4:30PM. Access by: mail, in person, online.

Civil—County Court-Civil, 509 W Main 3rd Floor, Dallas, TX 75202. 215-686-2312. 8AM-4:30PM. Access by: mail, in person. Special note: No civil claims limit as of 05/23/97 in Dallas County.

Probate—Probate Court #3, Records Bldg, 2nd Floor, Dallas, TX 75202. 215-683-7700. 8AM-4:30PM.

Dawson

Real Estate Recording—Dawson County Clerk, North 1st & Main Street, Courthouse, Lamesa, TX 79331. 806-872-7474, Fax: 806-872-2473. 8:30AM-5PM.

Felony, Civil—District Court, Drawer 1268, Lamesa, TX 79331. 806-872-7373, Fax: 806-872-9513. 8:30AM-5PM. Access by: mail, fax, in person.

Misdemeanor, Civil, Probate—County Court, Drawer 1268, Lamesa, TX 79331. 806-872-3778, Fax: 806-872-2473. 8:30AM-5PM. Access by: mail, fax, in person.

De Witt

Real Estate Recording—De Witt County Clerk, 307 North Gonzales, Courthouse, Cuero, TX 77954. Fax: 361-275-8994. 8AM-Noon, 1-5PM.

Felony, Civil—District Court, PO Box 845, Cuero, TX 77954. 301-475-5621. 8AM-5PM. Access by: mail, phone, in person.

Misdemeanor, Probate—County Court, 307 N Gonzales, Cuero, TX 77954. 301-608-0660, Fax: 275-275-8994. 8AM-5PM. Access by: mail, phone, fax, in person.

Deaf Smith

Real Estate Recording—Deaf Smith County Clerk, 235 East 3rd, Room 203, Hereford, TX 79045. 806-364-0399, Fax: 806-363-7007. 8AM-5PM.

Felony, Civil—District Court, 235 E Third St Rm 304, Hereford, TX 79045. 806-364-3901, Fax: 806-363-7007. 8AM-5PM. Access by: mail, phone, fax, in person.

Misdemeanor, Civil, Probate—County Court, Deaf Smith Courthouse, 235 E Third, Room 203, Hereford, TX 79045. 806-363-7077. 8AM-5PM. Access by: mail, in person.

Delta

Real Estate Recording—Delta County Clerk, 200 West Dallas Avenue, Cooper, TX 75432. Fax: 903-395-2178. 8AM-5PM.

Felony, Misdemeanor, Civil, Eviction, Probate—District and County Court, PO Box 455, Cooper, TX 75432. 903-395-4110, Fax: 903-395-2211. 8AM-5PM. Access by: mail, phone, in person.

Denton

Real Estate Recording—Denton County Clerk, 401 West Hickory, Denton, TX 76201. 8AM-4:30PM.

Felony, Civil—District Court, PO Box 2146, Denton, TX 76202. 940-565-8530, Fax: 940-565-8607. 8AM-4:30PM. Access by: mail, in person, online. www.co.denton.tx.us

Misdemeanor, Civil, Probate—County Court, PO Box 2187, Denton, TX 76202. 8AM-4:30PM. Access by: mail, in person. http://justice.co.denton.texas.us

Dickens

Real Estate Recording—Dickens County Clerk, Montgomery St. & Hwy 82, Dickens, TX 79229. Fax: 806-623-5319. 8AM-Noon, 1-5PM.

Felony, Misdemeanor, Civil, Eviction, Probate—District and County Court, PO Box 120, Dickens, TX 79229. 806-623-5531, Fax: 806-623-5319. 8AM-5PM. Access by: mail, in person.

Dimmit

Real Estate Recording—Dimmit County Clerk, 103 North 5th Street, Carrizo Springs, TX 78834. Fax: 830-876-5036. 8AM-Noon, 1-5PM.

Felony, Civil—District Court, 103 N 5th, Carrizo Springs, TX 78834. 830-876-2321, Fax: 830-876-5036. 8AM-5PM. Access by: mail, in person.

Misdemeanor, Civil, Probate—County Court, 103 N 5th, Carrizo Springs, TX 78834. 830-876-3569, Fax: 210-876-5036. 8AM-5PM. Access by: mail, in person.

Donley

Real Estate Recording—Donley County Clerk, 300 South Sully, Clarendon, TX 79226. 806-874-2328, Fax: 806-874-5146. 8AM-Noon,1-5PM.

Felony, Misdemeanor, Civil, Eviction, Probate—District and County Court, PO Drawer U, Clarendon, TX 79226. 806-874-3436, Fax: 806-874-5146. 8AM-Noon, 1-5PM. Access by: mail, in person.

Duval

Real Estate Recording—Duval County Clerk, 400 East Gravis on Highway 44, San Diego, TX 78384. 8AM-Noon, 1-5PM.

Felony, Civil—District Court, PO Drawer 428, San Diego, TX 78384. 361-595-8548. 8AM-5PM. Access by: mail, phone, in person.

Misdemeanor, Civil, Probate—County Court, PO Box 248, San Diego, TX 78384. 361-595-8535. 8AM-Noon, 1-5PM. Access by: mail, in person.

Eastland

Real Estate Recording—Eastland County Clerk, 100 West Main, Courthouse, Eastland, TX 76448. 817-629-2672, Fax: 254-629-8125. 8AM-5PM.

Felony, Civil—District Court, PO Box 670, Eastland, TX 76448. 254-883-1408, Fax: 254-629-1558. 8AM-5PM. Access by: mail, phone, fax, in person.

Misdemeanor, Probate—County Court, PO Box 110, Eastland, TX 76448. 254-865-5911. 8AM-5PM. Access by: mail, in person.

Ector

Real Estate Recording—Ector County Clerk, 300 Grant Avenue, Courthouse, Room 111, Odessa, TX 79761. 915-335-3105, Fax: 915-498-4177. 8AM-4:30PM.

Felony, Civil—District Court, County Courthouse, 300 N Grant, Rm 301, Odessa, TX 79761. 915-335-3144, Fax: 915-335-3112. 8AM-5PM. Access by: mail, phone, fax, in person.

Misdemeanor, Civil, Probate—County Court, PO Box 707, Odessa, TX 79760. 915-498-4130. 8AM-4:30PM. Access by: mail, in person.

Edwards

Real Estate Recording—Edwards County Clerk, 400 Main, Rocksprings, TX 78880. 210-780-2312, Fax: 830-683-5376. 8AM-5PM.

Felony, Misdemeanor, Civil, Eviction, Probate—District and County Court, PO Box 184, Rocksprings, TX 78880. 830-683-2235, Fax: 830-683-5376. 8AM-Noon, 1-5PM. Access by: mail, fax, in person.

El Paso

Real Estate Recording—El Paso County Clerk, 500 E. San Antonio, Room 105, El Paso, TX 79901. 8AM-4:45PM.

Felony, Civil—District Court, 500 East San Antonio Rm 103, El Paso, TX 79901. 915-546-2021. 8AM-4:45PM. Access by: mail, in person.

Misdemeanor, Civil—County Court, 500 E San Antonio St Rm 105, El Paso, TX 79901. 915-546-2071. 8AM-4:45PM. Access by: mail, in person.

Probate—Probate Court, 500 E San Antonio, Rm 1201 A, El Paso, TX 79901. 915-546-2161, Fax: 915-533-4448. 8AM-5PM. Access by: mail, in person.

Ellis

Real Estate Recording—Ellis County Clerk, Records Building, 117 W. Franklin, Waxahachie, TX 75165. 972-923-5125. 8AM-5PM.

Felony, Civil—District Court, 101 W Main St County Courthouse, Waxahachie, TX 75165-3774. 972-923-5000. 8AM-5PM. Access by: mail, in person.

Misdemeanor, Civil, Probate—County Court, PO Box 250, Waxahachie, TX 75165. 972-923-5070. 8AM-4:45PM. Access by: mail, in person.

Erath

Real Estate Recording—Erath County Clerk, Courthouse, 100 W. Washington St. Stephenville, TX 76401. Fax: 254-965-5732. 8AM-Noon, 1-5PM.

Felony, Civil—District Court, 112 W College, Courthouse Annex, Stephenville, TX 76401. 256-574-9320, Fax: 254-965-7156. 8AM-Noon, 1-5PM. Access by: mail, in person.

Misdemeanor, Civil, Probate—County Court, Erath County Courthouse, Stephenville, TX 76401. 256-571-7758. 8AM-Noon, 1-5PM. Access by: mail, in person.

Falls

Real Estate Recording—Falls County Clerk, Corner of Business Hwy 6 and Hwy 7, Courthouse, Marlin, TX 76661. 256-332-8861, Fax: 254-883-1406. 8AM-Noon, 1-5PM.

Felony, Civil—District Court, 3rd Floor, PO Box 229, Marlin, TX 76661. 256-332-8850. 8AM-Noon, 1-5PM. Access by: mail, in person.

Misdemeanor, Civil, Probate—County Court, PO Box 458, Marlin, TX 76661. 256-245-4352. 8AM-5PM. Access by: mail, phone, in person.

Fannin

Real Estate Recording—Fannin County Clerk, Courthouse, Suite 102, 101 E. Sam Rayburn Dr. Bonham, TX 75418. Fax: 903-583-7811. 8AM-5PM.

Felony, Civil—District Court, Fannin County Courthouse Ste 201, Bonham, TX 75418. 903-583-7459, Fax: 903-640-1826. 8AM-Noon, 1-5PM. Access by: mail, fax, in person.

Misdemeanor, Civil, Probate—County Court, County Courthouse, 101 E Sam Rayburn Ste 102, Bonham, TX 75418. 903-583-7486, Fax: 903-583-7811. 8AM-5PM. Access by: mail, phone, in person.

Fayette

Real Estate Recording—Fayette County Clerk, 151 North Washington, Courthouse, La Grange, TX 78945. 410-543-6635. 8AM-Noon, 1-5PM.

Felony, Civil—District Court, Fayette County Courthouse, 151 N Washington, La Grange, TX 78945. 410-632-1221, Fax: 409-968-8621. 8AM-5PM. Access by: mail, in person.

Misdemeanor, Civil, Probate—County Court, PO Box 59, La Grange, TX 78945. 410-554-4227. 8AM-5PM. Access by: mail, phone, in person.

Fisher

Real Estate Recording—Fisher County Clerk, Corner of US Highway 180 & 70, Courthouse, Roby, TX 79543. 915-776-2351, Fax: 915-776-2815. 8AM-Noon, 1-5PM.

Felony, Civil—32nd District Court, PO Box 88, Roby, TX 79543. 915-776-2279, Fax: 915-776-2815. 8AM-5PM. Access by: mail, in person.

Misdemeanor, Civil, Probate—County Court, Box 368, Roby, TX 79543-0368. 915-776-2401. 8AM-Noon, 1-5PM. Access by: mail, in person.

Floyd

Real Estate Recording—Floyd County Clerk, Courthouse, Room 101, 100 Main St. Floydada, TX 79235. 806-983-2376. 8:30AM-12, 1-5PM.

Felony, Civil—District Court, PO Box 67, Floydada, TX 79235. 806-983-4923. 8:30AM-Noon, 1-4:45PM. Access by: mail, phone, in person.

Misdemeanor, Civil, Probate—County Court, Courthouse, Rm 101, Main Street, Floydada, TX 79235. 806-983-4900. 8:30AM-Noon, 1-5PM. Access by: mail, phone, in person.

Foard

Real Estate Recording—Foard County Clerk, 100 Main and Commerce, Crowell, TX 79227. Fax: 940-684-1947. 9AM-11:45AM, 1-4:30PM.

Felony, Misdemeanor, Civil, Eviction, Probate—District and County Court, PO Box 539, Crowell, TX 79227. 940-684-1365. 9AM-4:30PM. Access by: mail, in person.

Fort Bend

Real Estate Recording—Fort Bend County Clerk, 301 Jackson, Hwy 90A, Richmond, TX 77469. Fax: 281-341-8669. 8AM-4PM.

Felony, Civil—District Court, 301 Jackson, Richmond, TX 77469. 301-645-0685, Fax: 281-341-4519. 8AM-5PM. Access by: mail, phone, in person, online. Special note: Physical court location is 401 Jackson.

Misdemeanor, Civil, Probate—County Court, 301 Jackson St, Richmond, TX 77469. 301-663-3722, Fax: 281-341-4520. 8AM-4PM. Access by: mail, in person, online. Special note: Plans are to have the record index on the Internet by 03/00. www.co.fort-bend.tx.us

Franklin

Real Estate Recording—Franklin County Clerk, Corner of Dallas & Kaufman Streets, Courthouse, Mount Vernon, TX 75457. 903-537-2206, Fax: 903-537-2418. 8AM-5PM.

Felony, Civil—District Court, PO Box 68, Mount Vernon, TX 75457. 903-537-4786. 8AM-5PM. Access by: mail, in person.

Misdemeanor, Civil, Probate—County Court, PO Box 68, Mount Vernon, TX 75457. 903-537-4252, Fax: 903-537-2418. 8AM-5PM. Access by: mail, in person.

Freestone

Real Estate Recording—Freestone County Clerk, Courthouse Annex, 103 E. Main St. Suite 1, Fairfield, TX 75840. 903-389-2180. 8AM-5PM.

Felony, Civil—District Court, PO Box 722, Fairfield, TX 75840. 903-389-2534. 8AM-5PM. Access by: mail, in person.

Misdemeanor, Civil, Probate—County Court, PO Box 1017, Fairfield, TX 75840. 903-389-2635. 8AM-5PM. Access by: mail, in person.

Frio

Real Estate Recording—Frio County Clerk, 500 E San Antonio Street, # 6, Pearsall, TX 78061. 210-627-2621, Fax: 830-334-4881. 8AM-Noon, 1-5PM.

Felony, Civil—District Court, 500 E San Antonio Box 8, Pearsall, TX 78061. 830-334-8073, Fax: 830-334-0047. 8AM-5PM. Access by: mail, in person.

Misdemeanor, Civil, Probate—County Court, 500 E San Antonio St #6, Pearsall, TX 78061. 830-334-3200, Fax: 830-334-4881. 8AM-Noon, 1-5PM. Access by: mail, fax, in person.

Gaines

Real Estate Recording—Gaines County Clerk, 101 S. Main, Room 107, Seminole, TX 79360. 8AM-5PM.

Felony, Civil—District Court, 101 S Main Rm 213, Seminole, TX 79360. 915-758-4013, Fax: 915-758-4036. 8AM-Noon, 1-5PM. Access by: mail, phone, in person.

Misdemeanor, Civil, Probate—County Court, 101 S Main Rm 107, Seminole, TX 79360. 915-758-4003. 8AM-5PM. Access by: mail, phone, in person.

Galveston

Real Estate Recording—Galveston County Clerk, 722 Moody Avenue, Galveston, TX 77550. 409-883-7993. 8AM-5PM.

Felony, Civil—District Court, 722 Moody St Rm 404, Galveston, TX 77550. 409-968-3251, Fax: 409-766-2292. 8AM-5PM. Access by: mail, fax, in person.

Misdemeanor, Civil, Probate—County Court, PO Box 2450, Galveston, TX 77553-2450. 409-968-3548. 8AM-5PM. Access by: mail, in person, online.

Probate—Probate Court, PO Box 2450, Galveston, TX 77553-2450. 409-968-3055. 8AM-5PM. Access by: mail, in person.

Garza

Real Estate Recording—Garza County Clerk, 300 W. Main, Post, TX 79356. Fax: 806-495-4431. 8AM-Noon, 1-5PM.

Felony, Misdemeanor, Civil, Eviction, Probate—District and County Court, PO Box 366, Post, TX 79356. 806-495-4430, Fax: 806-495-4431. 8AM-Noon,1-5PM. Access by: mail, in person.

Gillespie

Real Estate Recording—Gillespie County Clerk, 101 West Main, Room 109, Unit #13, Fredericksburg, TX 78624. 213-744-4036, Fax: 830-997-9958. 8AM-4PM.

Felony, Civil—District Court, 101 W Main Rm 204, Fredericksburg, TX 78624. 830-997-6517. Public hours 8AM-Noon, 1-4PM. Access by: mail, in person.

Misdemeanor, Civil, Probate—County Court, 101 W Main Unit #13, Fredericksburg, TX 78624. 830-997-6515, Fax: 830-997-9958. 8AM-4PM. Access by: mail, in person.

Glasscock

Real Estate Recording—Glasscock County Clerk, Courthouse, 117 E. Currie, Garden City, TX 79739. 915-354-2415. 8AM-4PM.

Felony, Misdemeanor, Civil, Eviction, Probate—District and County Court, PO Box 190, 117 E Currie, Garden City, TX 79739. 915-354-2371. 8AM-4PM. Access by: mail, in person.

Goliad

Real Estate Recording—Goliad County Clerk, 127 N. Courthouse Square, Goliad, TX 77963. Fax: 361-645-3858. 8AM-5PM.

Felony, Misdemeanor, Civil, Eviction, Probate—District and County Court, PO Box 50, Goliad, TX 77963. 401-364-1200, Fax: 361-645-3858. 8AM-5PM. Access by: mail, in person.

Gonzales

Real Estate Recording—Gonzales County Clerk, 1709 Sarah DeWitt Dr. Courthouse, Gonzales, TX 78629. 210-774-4602, Fax: 830-672-2636. 8AM-5PM.

Felony, Civil—District Court, PO Box 34, Gonzales, TX 78629-0034. 830-672-2326, Fax: 830-672-9313. 8AM-Noon 1-5PM. Access by: mail, phone, fax, in person.

Misdemeanor, Civil, Probate—County Court, PO Box 77, Gonzales, TX 78629. 830-672-2801, Fax: 830-672-2636. 8AM-5PM. Access by: mail, fax, in person.

Gray

Real Estate Recording—Gray County Clerk, 205 North Russell, Courthouse, Pampa, TX 79065. 806-669-8009, Fax: 806-669-8054. 8:30AM-Noon, 1-5PM.

Felony, Civil—District Court, PO Box 1139, Pampa, TX 79066-1139. 806-669-8010, Fax: 806-669-8053. 8:30AM-5PM. Access by: mail, fax, in person.

Misdemeanor, Civil, Probate—County & Probate COurt, PO Box 1902, Pampa, TX 79066-1902. 806-669-8004, Fax: 806-669-8054. 8:30AM-5PM. Access by: mail, phone, fax, in person.

Grayson

Real Estate Recording—Grayson County Clerk, 100 West Houston #17, Sherman, TX 75090. 903-813-4251, Fax: 903-813-4382. 8AM-5PM.

Felony, Civil—District Court, 200 S Crockett Rm 120-A, Sherman, TX 75090-7167. 903-813-4352. 8AM-5PM. Access by: mail, in person.

Misdemeanor, Civil, Probate—County Court, 200 S Crockett, Sherman, TX 75090. 903-813-4336, Fax: 903-892-8300. 8AM-5PM. Access by: mail, in person.

Gregg

Real Estate Recording—Gregg County Clerk, 100 East Methvin, Suite 200, Longview, TX 75601. Fax: 903-237-2574. 8AM-5PM.

Felony, Civil—District Court, PO Box 711, Longview, TX 75606. 903-237-2663. 8AM-5PM. Access by: mail, phone, fax, in person.

Misdemeanor, Civil, Probate—County Court, PO Box 3049, Longview, TX 75606. 903-236-8430. 8AM-5PM. Access by: mail, in person.

Grimes

Real Estate Recording—Grimes County Clerk, Courthouse, 100 Main St. Anderson, TX 77830. 410-535-1600. 8AM-Noon, 1-4:45PM.

Felony, Civil—District Court, PO Box 234, Anderson, TX 77830. 410-535-1600, Fax: 409-873-2415. 8AM-4:45PM. Access by: mail, phone, fax, in person.

Misdemeanor, Civil, Probate—County Court, PO Box 209, Anderson, TX 77830. 410-535-1600. 8AM-4:45PM. Access by: mail, in person.

Guadalupe

Real Estate Recording—Guadalupe County Clerk, 101 East Court Street, Rm 209, Seguin, TX 78155. 8AM-4:30PM.

Felony, Civil—District Court, 101 E Court St, Seguin, TX 78155. 830-303-4188, Fax: 830-379-1943. 8AM-5PM. Access by: in person.

Misdemeanor, Civil, Probate—County Court, 101 E Court St, Seguin, TX 78155. 830-303-4188, Fax: 830-372-1206. 8AM-4:30PM. Access by: mail, in person.

Hale

Real Estate Recording—Hale County Clerk, 500 Broadway #140, Plainview, TX 79072. Fax: 806-296-7786. 8AM-Noon,1-5PM.

Felony, Civil—District Court, 500 Broadway #200, Plainview, TX 79072-8050. 806-291-5226, Fax: 806-291-5206. 8AM-5PM. Access by: mail, phone, in person.

Misdemeanor, Civil, Probate—County Court, 500 Broadway #140, Plainview, TX 79072-8030. 806-291-5261, Fax: 806-291-9810. 8AM-Noon, 1-5PM. Access by: mail, in person.

Hall

Real Estate Recording—Hall County Clerk, Courthouse, Box 8, Memphis, TX 79245. 806-259-2421, Fax: 806-259-5078. 8:30AM-5PM.

Felony, Misdemeanor, Civil, Eviction, Probate—District and County Court, County Courthouse, Memphis, TX 79245. 806-259-2627, Fax: 806-259-5078. 8:30AM-5PM. Access by: mail, phone, in person.

Hamilton

Real Estate Recording—Hamilton County Clerk, Main Street, Courthouse, Hamilton, TX 76531. Fax: 254-386-8727. 8AM-5PM.

Felony, Civil—District Court, County Courthouse, Hamilton, TX 76531. 254-629-2664, Fax: 254-386-8610. 8AM-5PM M-Th; 8AM-4:30PM F. Access by: mail, fax, in person.

Misdemeanor, Civil, Probate—County Court, County Courthouse, Hamilton, TX 76531. 254-697-3952, Fax: 254-386-8727. 8AM-5PM. Access by: mail, in person.

Hansford

Real Estate Recording—Hansford County Clerk, Hansford Co. Clerk, 1 N.W. Court, Spearman, TX 79081. Fax: 806-659-4168. 8:30AM-5PM.

Felony, Misdemeanor, Civil, Eviction, Probate—District and County Court, PO Box 397, Spearman, TX 79081. 806-659-4110, Fax: 806-659-4168. 8:30AM-5PM. Access by: mail, phone, fax, in person.

Hardeman

Real Estate Recording—Hardeman County Clerk, 300 Main Street, Quanah, TX 79252. 8:30AM-5PM.

Felony, Misdemeanor, Civil, Eviction, Probate—District and County Court, PO Box 30, Quanah, TX 79252. 940-663-2901. 8:30AM-5PM. Access by: mail, in person.

Hardin

Real Estate Recording—Hardin County Clerk, Courthouse Square, Highway 326, Kountze, TX 77625. 409-384-2461. 8AM-5PM.

Felony, Civil—District Court, PO Box 2997, Kountze, TX 77625. 409-384-2721. 8AM-4PM. Access by: mail, phone, in person.

Misdemeanor, Civil, Probate—County Court, PO Box 38, Kountze, TX 77625. 409-384-9481. 8AM-5PM. Access by: mail, in person.

Harris

Real Estate Recording—Harris County Clerk, 1001 Preston, 4th Floor, Houston, TX 77002. Fax: 713-755-8839. 8AM-4:30PM.

Felony, Civil Over $100,000—District Court, PO Box 4651, Houston, TX 77210. Fax: 713-755-5480. 8AM-5PM. Access by: mail, phone, fax, in person, online. www.hcdistrictclerk.com

Civil Under $100,000—County Court, Access by: mail, in person. www.co.harris.tx.us/ccl

Probate—Probate Court, 1115 Congress, 6th Floor, Houston, TX 77002. 713-755-6084, Fax: 713-755-4349. 6AM-5PM. Special note: Probate dockets available through the Harris County online system.

Harrison

Real Estate Recording—Harrison County Clerk, Corner of W. Houston & S. Wellington, Courthouse, Marshall, TX 75670. 903-935-4820. 8AM-5PM.

Felony, Civil—71st District Court, PO Box 1119, Marshall, TX 75671-1119. 903-935-4845. 8AM-5PM. Access by: mail, in person.

Misdemeanor, Civil, Probate—County Court, PO Box 1365, Marshall, TX 75671. 903-935-4858. 8AM-5PM. Access by: mail, in person.

Hartley

Real Estate Recording—Hartley County Clerk, 9th & Railroad, Channing, TX 79018. Fax: 806-235-2316. 8:30AM-Noon, 1-5PM.

Felony, Misdemeanor, Civil, Eviction, Probate—District and County Court, PO Box Q, Channing, TX 79018. 806-235-3582, Fax: 806-235-2316. 8:30AM-Noon, 1-5PM. Access by: mail, in person.

Haskell

Real Estate Recording—Haskell County Clerk, Courthouse, 1 Ave. D, Haskell, TX 79521. 817-864-3448, Fax: 940-864-6164. 8AM-5PM.

Felony, Civil—District Court, PO Box 27, Haskell, TX 79521. 940-864-2030. 8AM-Noon, 1-5PM M-Th; 8AM-4:30PM F. Access by: mail, in person.

Misdemeanor, Civil, Probate—County Court, PO Box 725, Haskell, TX 79521. 940-864-2451. 8AM-Noon, 1-5PM. Access by: mail, phone, fax, in person.

Hays

Real Estate Recording—Hays County Clerk, 137 N. Guadalupe, Hays County Records Building, San Marcos, TX 78666. 512-392-3669, Fax: 512-393-7337. 8AM-5PM.

Felony, Civil—District Court, 110 E Martin Luther King, Suite 123, San Marcos, TX 78666. 512-393-7660, Fax: 512-393-7674. 8AM-5PM. Access by: mail, phone, in person. www.co.hays.tx.us

Misdemeanor, Civil, Probate—County Court, Justice Center, 110 E Martin L King Dr, San Marcos, TX 78666. 512-393-7738, Fax: 512-393-7735. 8AM-5PM. Access by: mail, in person. www.co.hays.tx.us

Hemphill

Real Estate Recording—Hemphill County Clerk, 400 Main Street, Courthouse, Canadian, TX 79014. 806-323-6671. 8AM-5PM.

Felony, Misdemeanor, Civil, Eviction, Probate—District and County Court, PO Box 867, Canadian, TX 79014. 806-323-6212. 8AM-5PM. Access by: mail, in person.

Henderson

Real Estate Recording—Henderson County Clerk, Courthouse Square, South Side, First Floor, Athens, TX 75751. 903-675-6119. 8AM-5PM.

Felony, Civil—District Court, Henderson County Courthouse, Athens, TX 75751. 903-675-6115. 8AM-5PM. Access by: mail, in person.

Misdemeanor, Civil, Probate—County Court, PO Box 632, Athens, TX 75751. 903-675-6140. 8AM-5PM. Access by: mail, in person.

Hidalgo

Real Estate Recording—Hidalgo County Clerk, 100 North Closner, Courthouse, Edinburg, TX 78539. Fax: 956-318-2105. 7:30AM-5:30PM.

Felony, Civil—District Court, 100 N Closner, Box 87, Edinburg, TX 78540. 956-318-2200. 8AM-5PM. Access by: mail, in person.

Misdemeanor, Civil, Probate—County Court, PO Box 58, Edinburg, TX 78540. 956-318-2100. 7:30AM-5:30PM. Access by: mail, in person.

Hill

Real Estate Recording—Hill County Clerk, Courthouse, 126 S. Covington, Hillsboro, TX 76645. 254-757-5054. 8AM-5PM.

Felony, Misdemeanor, Civil—District Court, PO Box 634, Hillsboro, TX 76645. 254-865-5016. 8AM-5PM. Access by: mail, in person.

Probate—County Court, PO Box 398, Hillsboro, TX 76645. 254-757-5185. 8AM-5PM. Access by: mail, in person.

Hockley

Real Estate Recording—Hockley County Clerk, 800 Houston St. Ste 213, Levelland, TX 79336. 806-894-3718. 9AM-5PM.

Felony, Civil—District Court, 802 Houston St, Ste 316, Levelland, TX 79336. 806-894-8527, Fax: 806-894-3891. 9AM-5PM. Access by: mail, phone, in person.

Misdemeanor, Civil, Probate—County Court, County Courthouse, 802 Houston St Ste 213, Levelland, TX 79336. 806-894-3185. 9AM-5PM. Access by: mail, in person.

Hood

Real Estate Recording—Hood County Clerk, Courthouse, Room 5, 100 E Pearl, Granbury, TX 76048. 817-579-3208, Fax: 817-579-3227. 8AM-5PM.

Felony, Civil—District Court, County Courthouse, Granbury, TX 76048. 817-579-3236, Fax: 817-579-3239. 8AM-5PM. Access by: mail, in person.

Misdemeanor, Civil, Probate—County Court, PO Box 339, Granbury, TX 76048. 817-579-3222, Fax: 817-579-3227. 8AM-5PM. Access by: mail, in person.

Hopkins

Real Estate Recording—Hopkins County Clerk, 118 Church Street, Courthouse, Sulphur Springs, TX 75482. 903-885-2426, Fax: 903-885-2487. 8AM-5PM.

Felony, Civil—District Court, PO Box 391, Sulphur Springs, TX 75482. 903-438-4081. 8AM-5PM. Access by: mail, in person.

Misdemeanor, Civil, Probate—County Court, PO Box 288, Sulphur Springs, TX 75483. 903-885-3929, Fax: 903-885-2487. 8AM-5PM. Access by: mail, in person.

Houston

Real Estate Recording—Houston County Clerk, Courthouse Square, 401 E. Houston, Crockett, TX 75835. 409-828-3201. 8AM-4:30PM.

Felony, Civil—District Court, County Courthouse, 410 E Houston, PO Box 1186, Crockett, TX 75835. 409-826-3357, Fax: 409-544-8053. 8AM-5PM. Access by: mail, fax, in person.

Misdemeanor, Civil, Probate—County Court, PO Box 370, Crockett, TX 75835. 409-826-3357, Fax: 409-544-8053. 8AM-4:30. Access by: mail, in person.

Howard

Real Estate Recording—Howard County Clerk, 300 Main, Courthouse, Big Spring, TX 79720. Fax: 915-264-2215. 8AM-5PM.

Felony, Civil—District Court, PO Box 2138, Big Spring, TX 79721. 915-264-2223, Fax: 915-264-2256. 8AM-5PM. Access by: mail, in person.

Misdemeanor, Civil, Probate—County Court, PO Box 1468, Big Spring, TX 79721. 915-264-2213, Fax: 915-264-2215. 8AM-5PM. Access by: mail, phone, in person.

Hudspeth

Real Estate Recording—Hudspeth County Clerk, FM 1111, Courthouse Square, Sierra Blanca, TX 79851. Fax: 915-369-2361. 8AM-5PM.

Felony, Misdemeanor, Civil, Eviction, Probate—District and County Court, PO Drawer 58, Sierra Blanca, TX 79851. 915-369-2301, Fax: 915-369-3005. 8AM-5PM. Access by: mail, phone, fax, in person.

Hunt

Real Estate Recording—Hunt County Clerk, 2500 Lee Street, Courthouse, 2nd Fl. East End, Greenville, TX 75401. 903-408-4171. 8AM-5PM.

Felony, Civil—District Court, PO Box 1437, Greenville, TX 75403. 903-408-4172. 8AM-5PM. Access by: mail, in person.

Misdemeanor, Civil, Probate—County Court, PO Box 1316, Greenville, TX 75403-1316. 903-408-4130. 8AM-5PM. Access by: mail, in person.

Hutchinson

Real Estate Recording—Hutchinson County Clerk, 6th & Main, Courthouse, Stinnett, TX 79083. 806-878-4010. 9AM-5PM.

Felony, Civil—District Court, PO Box 580, Stinnett, TX 79083. 806-878-4017, Fax: 806-878-4023. 9AM-5PM. Access by: mail, in person.

Misdemeanor, Civil, Probate—County Court, PO Box 1186, Stinnett, TX 79083. 806-878-4002. 9AM-5PM. Access by: mail, in person.

Irion

Real Estate Recording—Irion County Clerk, 209 N. Parkview, Mertzon, TX 76941. 915-835-4111, Fax: 915-835-2008. 8AM-5PM.

Felony, Misdemeanor, Civil, Eviction, Probate—District and County Court, PO Box 736, Mertzon, TX 76941-0736. 915-835-2421, Fax: 915-835-2008. 8AM-5PM. Access by: mail, in person.

Jack

Real Estate Recording—Jack County Clerk, 100 Main Street, Jacksboro, TX 76458. 817-567-2251. 8AM-5PM.

Felony, Civil—District Court, 100 Main, County Courthouse, Jacksboro, TX 76458. 940-567-2141, Fax: 940-567-2696. 8AM-5PM. Access by: mail, in person.

Misdemeanor, Civil, Probate—County Court, 100 Main, Jacksboro, TX 76458. 940-567-2111. 8AM-Noon, 1-5PM. Access by: mail, phone, in person.

Jackson

Real Estate Recording—Jackson County Clerk, 115 West Main, Room 101, Edna, TX 77957. 401-421-7740. 8AM-5PM.

Felony, Civil—District Court, 115 W Main Rm 203, Edna, TX 77957. 401-435-7500. 8AM-5PM. Access by: mail, phone, in person.

Misdemeanor, Civil, Probate—County Court, 115 W Main Rm101, Edna, TX 77957. 401-423-7200. 8AM-5PM. Access by: mail, in person.

Jasper

Real Estate Recording—Jasper County Clerk, Courthouse, Room 103, Main at Lamar St. Jasper, TX 75951. 409-732-2155, Fax: 409-384-7198. 8AM-5PM.

Felony, Civil—District Court, County Courthouse #202, PO Box 2088, Jasper, TX 75951. 409-732-2536. 8AM-Noon, 1-5PM. Access by: mail, in person.

Misdemeanor, Civil, Probate—County Court, Rm 103, Courthouse, Main at Lamar, PO Box 2070, Jasper, TX 75951. 409-732-2865, Fax: 409-384-9745. 8AM-5PM. Access by: mail, in person.

Jeff Davis

Real Estate Recording—Jeff Davis County Clerk, Main Street, Fort Davis, TX 79734. 915-426-3242, Fax: 915-426-3760. 9AM-Noon, 1-5PM.

Felony, Misdemeanor, Civil, Eviction, Probate—District and County Court, PO Box 398, Fort Davis, TX 79734. 915-426-3251, Fax: 915-426-3760. 9AM-Noon, 1-5PM. Access by: mail, in person.

Jefferson

Real Estate Recording—Jefferson County Clerk, 1149 Pearl Street, Beaumont, TX 77701. 410-333-3750, Fax: 409-839-2394. 8AM-5PM.

Felony, Civil—District Court, PO Box 3707, Beaumont, TX 77704. 410-386-2365, Fax: 409-835-8527. 8AM-5PM. Access by: mail, in person.

Misdemeanor, Civil, Probate—County Court, PO Box 1151, Beaumont, TX 77704. 410-333-3716, Fax: 409-839-2394. 8AM-5PM. Access by: mail, fax, in person.

Jim Hogg

Real Estate Recording—Jim Hogg County Clerk, 102 East Tilley, Hebbronville, TX 78361. 401-232-0900, Fax: 361-527-5843. 9AM-5PM.

Felony, Misdemeanor, Civil, Eviction, Probate—District and County Court, PO Box 878, Hebbronville, TX 78361. 401-233-1000, Fax: 361-527-5843. 9AM-5PM. Access by: mail, in person.

Jim Wells

Real Estate Recording—Jim Wells County Clerk, 200 North Almond Street, Alice, TX 78332. 401-392-9200. 8AM-Noon, 1-5PM.

Felony, Civil—79th District Court, PO Drawer 2219, Alice, TX 78333. 401-397-5016. 8AM-Noon, 1-5PM. Access by: mail, in person.

Misdemeanor, Civil, Probate—County Court, PO Box 1459, 200 N Almond, Alice, TX 78333. 401-377-7777. 8:30AM-Noon, 1-5PM. Access by: mail, phone, in person.

Johnson

Real Estate Recording—Johnson County Clerk, 2 North Main, Room 101, Cleburne, TX 76031. 817-566-6341, Fax: 817-556-6326. 8AM-4:30PM.

Felony, Civil—District Court, PO Box 495, Cleburne, TX 76033-0495. 817-556-6300, Fax: 817-556-6210. 8AM-5PM. Access by: mail, fax, in person.

Misdemeanor, Civil, Probate—County Court, Room 104, PO Box 662, Cleburne, TX 76033-0662. 817-556-6300. 8AM-Noon, 1-4:30PM. Access by: mail, in person.

Jones

Real Estate Recording—Jones County Clerk, 12th & Commercial, Courthouse, Anson, TX 79501. 915-823-3742, Fax: 915-823-4223. 8AM-5PM.

Felony, Misdemeanor, Civil—District Court, PO Box 308, Anson, TX 79501. 915-823-3731, Fax: 915-823-3513. 8AM-5PM. Access by: mail, in person.

Karnes

Real Estate Recording—Karnes County Clerk, 101 North Panna Maria Ave. Courthouse - Suite 9, Karnes City, TX 78118. 212-428-2810, Fax: 830-780-4576. 8AM-5PM.

Felony, Civil—District Court, County Courthouse, 101 N Panna Maria, Karnes City, TX 78118. 830-780-2562, Fax: 830-780-3227. 8AM-Noon, 1-5PM. Access by: mail, in person.

Misdemeanor, Civil, Probate—County Court, 101 N Panna Maria Ave #9 Courthouse, Karnes City, TX 78118-2929. 830-780-3938, Fax: 830-780-4576. 8AM-5PM. Access by: mail, in person.

Kaufman

Real Estate Recording—Kaufman County Clerk, Courthouse, Kaufman, TX 75142. 972-932-4331, Fax: 972-932-7628. 8AM-5PM.

Felony, Civil—District Court, County Courthouse, Kaufman, TX 75142. 972-932-4331. 8AM-5PM. Access by: mail, in person.

Misdemeanor, Civil, Probate—County Court, County Courthouse, Kaufman, TX 75142. 972-932-4331. 8AM-5PM. Access by: mail, in person.

Kendall

Real Estate Recording—Kendall County Clerk, 201 East San Antonio, Suite 127, Boerne, TX 78006. Fax: 830-249-3472. 8AM-Noon, 1-5PM.

Felony, Civil—District Court, 210 E. San Antonia, #201, Boerne, TX 78006. 830-249-9343. 8:30AM-Noon, 1-5PM. Access by: mail, in person.

Misdemeanor, Civil, Probate—County Court, 204 E San Antonio #127, Boerne, TX 78006. 830-249-9343, Fax: 830-249-3472. 8AM-5PM. Access by: mail, in person.

Kenedy

Real Estate Recording—Kenedy County Clerk, 101 Mallory Street, Sarita, TX 78385. 361-645-2443, Fax: 361-294-5218. 8:30AM-Noon, 1-4:30PM.

Felony, Misdemeanor, Civil, Eviction, Probate—District and County Court, PO Box 227, Sarita, TX 78385. 361-595-8561, Fax: 361-294-5218. 8:30AM-Noon, 1PM-4:30PM. Access by: mail, in person.

Kent

Real Estate Recording—Kent County Clerk, Courthouse, Jayton, TX 79528. 806-237-3075, Fax: 806-237-2632. 8:30AM-Noon, 1-5PM.

Felony, Misdemeanor, Civil, Eviction, Probate—District and County Court, PO Box 9, Jayton, TX 79528. 806-237-3881, Fax: 806-237-2632. 8:30AM-Noon, 1-5PM. Access by: mail, in person.

Kerr

Real Estate Recording—Kerr County Clerk, Courthouse, Room 122, 700 Main, Kerrville, TX 78028. 210-563-2777, Fax: 830-792-2274. 8AM-5PM.

Felony, Civil—District Court, 700 Main, County Courthouse, Kerrville, TX 78028. 830-792-2281. 8AM-5PM. Access by: mail, in person.

Misdemeanor, Civil, Probate—County Court & County Court at Law, 700 Main St, #122, Kerrville, TX 78028-5389. 830-792-2255, Fax: 830-792-2274. 8AM-5PM. Access by: mail, in person.

Kimble

Real Estate Recording—Kimble County Clerk, 501 Main Street, Junction, TX 76849. 915-446-2847, Fax: 915-446-2986. 8AM-Noon, 1-5PM.

Felony, Misdemeanor, Civil, Probate—District and County Court, 501 Main St, Junction, TX 76849. 915-446-3353, Fax: 915-446-2986. 8AM-Noon, 1-5PM. Access by: mail, in person.

King

Real Estate Recording—King County Clerk, Courthouse, Highway 82, Guthrie, TX 79236. Fax: 806-596-4664. 9AM-Noon, 1-5PM.

Felony, Misdemeanor, Civil, Eviction, Probate—District and County Court, PO Box 135, Guthrie, TX 79236. 806-596-4412. 9AM-Noon, 1-5PM. Access by: mail, in person.

Kinney

Real Estate Recording—Kinney County Clerk, 501 Ann Street, Brackettville, TX 78832. 210-769-3024, Fax: 830-563-2644. 8AM-Noon, 1-5PM.

Felony, Misdemeanor, Civil, Probate—District and County Court, PO Drawer 9, Brackettville, TX 78832. 830-563-2521, Fax: 830-563-2644. 8AM-5PM. Access by: mail, phone, in person.

Kleberg

Real Estate Recording—Kleberg County Clerk, 700 East Kleberg Street, First Floor, East Wing, Kingsville, TX 78363. 401-333-1100. 8AM-Noon, 1-5PM.

Felony, Civil—District and County Court at Law, PO Box 312, Kingsville, TX 78364-0312. 401-351-6618, Fax: 361-595-8525. 8AM-Noon, 1-5 PM. Access by: mail, phone, fax, in person.

Misdemeanor, Probate—County Court-Criminal, PO Box 1327, Kingsville, TX 78364. 401-348-2500. 8AM-5PM. Access by: mail, in person. Special note: Court also handles civil cases dealing with occupational licenses and bond forfeitures.

Knox

Real Estate Recording—Knox County Clerk, Corner of Highway 6 & 82, Benjamin, TX 79505. 817-454-2251, Fax: 940-454-2022. 8AM-12, 1-5PM.

Felony, Misdemeanor, Civil, Eviction, Probate—District and County Court, PO Box 196, Benjamin, TX 79505. 940-454-2441. 8AM-Noon, 1-5PM. Access by: mail, in person.

La Salle

Real Estate Recording—La Salle County Clerk, Courthouse Square, Suite 107, Cotulla, TX 78014. Fax: 830-879-2933. 8AM-Noon, 1-5PM.

Felony, Civil—District Court, PO Box 340, Cotulla, TX 78014. 830-879-2421. 8AM-5PM. Access by: mail, in person.

Misdemeanor, Civil, Eviction, Probate—District and County Courts, PO Box 340, Cotulla, TX 78014. 830-879-2117, Fax: 830-879-2933. 8AM-5PM. Access by: mail, in person.

Lamar

Real Estate Recording—Lamar County Clerk, Courthouse, 119 N. Main #109, Paris, TX 75460. 8AM-5PM.

Felony, Civil—District Court, 119 N Main Rm 306, Paris, TX 75460. 903-737-2427. 8AM-5PM. Access by: mail, in person.

Misdemeanor, Civil, Probate—County Court, 119 N Main, Paris, TX 75460. 903-737-2420. 8AM-5PM. Access by: mail, phone, fax, in person.

Lamb

Real Estate Recording—Lamb County Clerk, 100 6th Street, Room 103 Box 3, Littlefield, TX 79339. 806-385-3770, Fax: 806-385-6485. 8:30AM-5PM.

Felony, Civil—District Court, 100 6th Rm 212, Courthouse, Littlefield, TX 79339. 806-385-4222. 8:30AM-Noon, 1-5PM. Access by: mail, in person.

Misdemeanor, Civil, Probate—County Court, County Courthouse, Rm 103, Box 3, Littlefield, TX 79339-3366. 806-385-4222, Fax: 806-385-6485. 8AM-5PM. Access by: mail, in person.

Lampasas

Real Estate Recording—Lampasas County Clerk, 400 Live Oak Street, Lampasas, TX 76550. 512-556-8058. 8AM-5PM.

Felony, Civil—District Court, PO Box 327, Lampasas, TX 76550. 512-556-8271, Fax: 512-556-8270. 8AM-5PM. Access by: mail, in person.

Misdemeanor, Civil, Probate—County Court, PO Box 347, Lampasas, TX 76550. 512-556-8271. 8AM-5PM. Access by: mail, in person.

Lavaca

Real Estate Recording—Lavaca County Clerk, 201 North LaGrange Street, Courthouse, Hallettsville, TX 77964. 512-798-2181. 8AM-5PM.

Felony, Civil—District Court, PO Box 306, Hallettsville, TX 77964. 401-539-2497. 8AM-Noon, 1-5PM. Access by: mail, phone, in person.

Misdemeanor, Civil, Probate—County Court, PO Box 326, Hallettsville, TX 77964. 401-568-4300. 8AM-5PM. Access by: mail, phone, in person.

Lee

Real Estate Recording—Lee County Clerk, 200 S. Main, Courthouse, Giddings, TX 78942. Fax: 409-542-2623. 8AM-5PM.

Felony, Civil—District Court, PO Box 176, Giddings, TX 78942. 409-787-3786, Fax: 409-542-2444. 8AM-Noon, 1-5PM. Access by: mail, in person.

Misdemeanor, Civil, Probate—County Court, PO Box 419, Giddings, TX 78942. 409-826-3357, Fax: 409-542-2623. 8AM-5PM. Access by: mail, in person.

Leon

Real Estate Recording—Leon County Clerk, Corner Cass and St. Mary Street, Courthouse Square, Centerville, TX 75833. 903-536-2915, Fax: 903-536-2431. 8AM-5PM.

Felony, Civil—District Court, PO Box 39, Centerville, TX 75833. 903-536-2227. 8AM-5PM. Access by: mail, in person.

Misdemeanor, Civil, Probate—County Court, PO Box 98, Centerville, TX 75833. 903-536-2352. 8AM-5PM. Access by: mail, in person.

Liberty

Real Estate Recording—Liberty County Clerk, 1923 Sam Houston, Room 209, Liberty, TX 77575. 8AM-5PM.

Felony, Civil—District Court, 1923 Sam Houston Rm 303, Liberty, TX 77575. 409-598-3581. 8AM-Noon, 1-5PM. Access by: mail, in person.

Misdemeanor, Civil, Probate—County Court, PO Box 369, Liberty, TX 77575. 409-598-4164. 8AM-5PM. Access by: mail, in person.

Limestone

Real Estate Recording—Limestone County Clerk, 200 West State Street, Groesbeck, TX 76642. 817-729-3314, Fax: 254-729-2951. 8AM-5PM.

Felony, Civil—District Court, PO Box 230, Groesbeck, TX 76642. 254-897-4427, Fax: 254-729-2960. 8AM-5PM. Access by: mail, phone, fax, in person.

Misdemeanor, Civil, Probate—County Court, PO Box 350, Groesbeck, TX 76642. 254-933-5165, Fax: 254-729-2951. 8AM-5PM. Access by: mail, in person.

Lipscomb

Real Estate Recording—Lipscomb County Clerk, Main Street, Courthouse, Lipscomb, TX 79056. 806-862-3821, Fax: 806-862-3004. 8:30AM-5PM.

Felony, Misdemeanor, Civil, Eviction, Probate—District and County Court, PO Box 70, Lipscomb, TX 79056. 806-862-3091, Fax: 806-862-3004. 8:30AM-Noon, 1-5PM. Access by: mail, fax, in person.

Live Oak

Real Estate Recording—Live Oak County Clerk, 301 Houston, George West, TX 78022. 361-798-3612. 8AM-Noon, 1-5PM.

Felony, Civil—District Court, PO Drawer O, George West, TX 78022. 361-888-0515. 8AM-5PM. Access by: mail, in person.

Misdemeanor, Civil, Probate—County Court, PO Box 280, George West, TX 78022. 361-888-0681. 8AM-5PM. Access by: mail, in person.

Llano

Real Estate Recording—Llano County Clerk, 107 W. Sandstone, Llano, TX 78643. 915-247-5056, Fax: 915-247-2406. 8AM-5PM.

Felony, Civil—District Clerk, PO Box 877, Llano, TX 78643-0877. 915-247-5036, Fax: 915-247-2446. 8AM-5PM. Access by: mail, in person.

Misdemeanor, Civil, Probate—County Court, PO Box 40, Llano, TX 78643-0040. 915-247-4455. 8AM-4:30PM. Access by: mail, in person.

Loving

Real Estate Recording—Loving County Clerk, Courthouse, 100 Bell St. Mentone, TX 79754. 915-377-2311, Fax: 915-377-2701. 9AM-Noon, 1-5PM.

Felony, Misdemeanor, Civil, Eviction, Probate—District and County Court, PO Box 194, Mentone, TX 79754. 915-377-2441, Fax: 915-377-2701. 9AM-Noon, 1-5PM. Access by: mail, fax, in person.

Lubbock

Real Estate Recording—Lubbock County Clerk, 904 Broadway, 2nd Floor Rm.207, Lubbock, TX 79401. Fax: 806-775-1660. 8:30-5PM.

Felony, Civil—District Court, PO Box 10536, Lubbock, TX 79408-3536. 806-775-1623, Fax: 806-775-1382. 8AM-5PM. Access by: mail, fax, in person.

Misdemeanor, Civil, Probate—County Courts, Courthouse, Room 207, PO Box 10536, Lubbock, TX 79408. 806-775-1051. 8:30AM-5PM. Access by: mail, in person.

Lynn

Real Estate Recording—Lynn County Clerk, Courthouse, Tahoka, TX 79373. 806-998-4055, Fax: 806-998-4151. 8:30AM-5PM.

Felony, Civil—District Court, PO Box 939, Tahoka, TX 79373. 806-998-4274, Fax: 806-998-4151. 8:30AM-5PM. Access by: mail, fax, in person.

Misdemeanor, Civil, Probate—County Court, PO Box 937, Tahoka, TX 79373. 806-998-4750, Fax: 806-998-4277. 8:30AM-5PM. Access by: mail, in person.

Madison

Real Estate Recording—Madison County Clerk, 101 West Main, Room 102, Madisonville, TX 77864. 409-634-4312, Fax: 409-348-5858. 8AM-5PM.

Felony, Civil—District Court, 101 W Main Rm 226, Madisonville, TX 77864. 409-634-8339. 8AM-Noon, 1-5PM. Access by: mail, in person.

Misdemeanor, Civil, Probate—County Court, 101 W Main Rm 102, Madisonville, TX 77864. 409-598-6361, Fax: 409-348-5858. 8AM-5PM. Access by: mail, in person.

Marion

Real Estate Recording—Marion County Clerk, 102 West Austin, Room 206, Jefferson, TX 75657. 903-665-2472. 8AM-Noon, 1-5PM.

Felony, Civil—District Court, PO Box 628, Jefferson, TX 75657. 903-665-2441. 8AM-5PM. Access by: mail, in person.

Misdemeanor, Probate—County Court, PO Box 763, Jefferson, TX 75657. 903-665-3971. 8AM-Noon, 1-5PM. Access by: mail, in person.

Martin

Real Estate Recording—Martin County Clerk, 301 North St. Peter Street, Stanton, TX 79782. Fax: 915-756-2992. 8AM-5PM.

Felony, Misdemeanor, Civil, Eviction, Probate—District and County Court, PO Box 906, Stanton, TX 79782. 915-756-3412. 8AM-Noon, 1-5PM. Access by: mail, in person.

Mason

Real Estate Recording—Mason County Clerk, 201 Ft. McKavitt, Mason, TX 76856. 915-347-5251. 8AM-Noon, 1-4PM.

Felony, Misdemeanor, Civil, Probate—District and County Court, PO Box 702, Mason, TX 76856. 915-347-5253, Fax: 915-347-6868. 8AM-Noon, 1-5PM. Access by: mail, in person.

Matagorda

Real Estate Recording—Matagorda County Clerk, 1700 7th Street, Room 202, Bay City, TX 77414. Fax: 409-244-7688. 8AM-5PM.

Felony, Civil—District Court, 1700 7th St Rm 307, Bay City, TX 77414-5092. 409-379-5341. 8AM-Noon, 1-5PM. Access by: mail, in person.

Misdemeanor, Civil, Probate—County Court, 1700 7th St Rm 202, Bay City, TX 77414-5094. 409-379-8127, Fax: 409-244-7688. 8AM-5PM. Access by: mail, in person.

Maverick

Real Estate Recording—Maverick County Clerk, 500 Quarry Street, Eagle Pass, TX 78852. 212-374-8233. 8AM-12, 1-5PM.

Felony, Civil—District Court, PO Box 3659, Eagle Pass, TX 78853. 830-773-2629. 8AM-5PM. Access by: mail, in person.

Misdemeanor, Civil, Probate—County Court, PO Box 4050, Eagle Pass, TX 78853. 830-773-2829. 8AM-5PM. Access by: mail, in person.

McCulloch

Real Estate Recording—McCulloch County Clerk, Courthouse, Brady, TX 76825. Fax: 915-597-1731. 8AM-5PM.

Felony, Civil—District Court, County Courthouse Rm 205, Brady, TX 76825. 915-597-0733, Fax: 915-597-0606. 8:30AM-5PM. Access by: mail, in person.

Misdemeanor, Civil, Probate—County Court, County Courthouse, Brady, TX 76825. 915-597-0733. 8AM-5PM. Access by: mail, in person.

McLennan

Real Estate Recording—McLennan County Clerk, 215 North 5th, Waco, TX 76701. Fax: 254-757-5146. 8AM-5PM.

Felony, Civil—District Court, PO Box 2451, Waco, TX 76703. 254-933-5197, Fax: 254-757-5060. 8AM-Noon, 1-5PM. Access by: mail, fax, in person.

Misdemeanor, Civil, Probate—County Court, PO Box 1727, Waco, TX 76703. 254-965-1482, Fax: 254-757-5146. 8AM-5PM. Access by: mail, in person.

McMullen

Real Estate Recording—McMullen County Clerk, River Street & Elm, Courthouse, Tilden, TX 78072. Fax: 361-274-3618. 8AM-4PM.

Felony, Misdemeanor, Civil, Eviction, Probate—District and County Court, PO Box 235, Tilden, TX 78072. 361-575-1478, Fax: 361-274-3618. 8AM-4PM. Access by: mail, in person.

Medina

Real Estate Recording—Medina County Clerk, Courthouse, Room 109, 16th St. Hondo, TX 78861. Fax: 830-741-6015. 8AM-Noon, 1-5PM.

Felony, Civil—District Court, County Courthouse Rm 209, Hondo, TX 78861. 830-741-6000. 8AM-Noon, 1-5PM. Access by: mail, in person.

Misdemeanor, Civil, Probate—County Court at Law, 1100 16th St, Rm 109, Hondo, TX 78861. 830-741-6041. 8AM-Noon, 1-5PM. Access by: mail, phone, in person.

Menard

Real Estate Recording—Menard County Clerk, 210 East San Saba, Menard, TX 76859. Fax: 915-396-2047. 8AM-Noon, 1-5PM.

Felony, Misdemeanor, Civil, Eviction, Probate—District and County Court, PO Box 1028, Menard, TX 76859. 915-396-4682, Fax: 915-396-2047. 8AM-Noon, 1-5PM. Access by: mail, fax, in person.

Midland

Real Estate Recording—Midland County Clerk, 200 West Wall Street, Suite 105, Midland, TX 79701. 915-688-1235, Fax: 915-688-8973. 8AM-5PM.

Felony, Civil—District Court, 200 W Wall #301, Midland, TX 79701. 915-688-1107. 8AM-5PM. Access by: mail, in person.

Misdemeanor, Civil, Probate—County Court, PO Box 211, Midland, TX 79702. 915-688-1070, Fax: 915-688-8973. 8AM-5PM. Access by: mail, in person.

Milam

Real Estate Recording—Milam County Clerk, 100 South Fannin, Cameron, TX 76520. 817-697-2331, Fax: 254-697-4433. 8AM-5PM.

Felony, Civil—District Court, PO Box 999, Cameron, TX 76520. 254-883-1419. 8AM-5PM. Access by: mail, in person.

Misdemeanor, Civil, Probate—County Court, PO Box 191, Cameron, TX 76520. 254-883-5591, Fax: 254-697-4433. 8AM-5PM. Access by: mail, in person.

Mills

Real Estate Recording—Mills County Clerk, 1011 4th Street, Goldthwaite, TX 76844. 915-648-2636, Fax: 915-648-2806. 8AM-Noon, 1-5PM.

Felony, Misdemeanor, Civil, Eviction, Probate—District and County Court, PO Box 646, Goldthwaite, TX 76844. 915-648-2711, Fax: 915-648-2806. 8AM-Noon, 1-5PM. Access by: mail, in person.

Mitchell

Real Estate Recording—Mitchell County Clerk, 349 Oak St. #103, Colorado City, TX 79512. 8AM-Noon, 1-5PM M,T,Th,F; 8AM-5PM W.

Felony, Civil—District Court, County Courthouse, Colorado City, TX 79512. 915-728-5918. 8AM-5PM. Access by: mail, in person.

Misdemeanor, Civil, Probate—County Court, 349 Oak St Rm 103, Colorado City, TX 79512. 915-728-3481, Fax: 915-728-8697. 8AM-Noon, 1-5PM. Access by: mail, fax, in person.

Montague

Real Estate Recording—Montague County Clerk, Rush & Washington, Courthouse, Montague, TX 76251. Fax: 940-894-3110. 8AM-5PM.

Felony, Civil—District Court, PO Box 155, Montague, TX 76251. 940-894-2571. 8AM-5PM. Access by: mail, in person.

Misdemeanor, Civil, Probate—County Court, PO Box 77, Montague, TX 76251. 940-894-2461. 8AM-5PM. Access by: mail, in person.

Montgomery

Real Estate Recording—Montgomery County Clerk, 210 West Davis, Suite 103, Conroe, TX 77301. Fax: 409-760-6990. 8:30AM-4:30PM.

Felony, Civil—District Court, PO Box 2985, Conroe, TX 77305. 409-787-2210. 8AM-5PM. Access by: mail, in person.

Misdemeanor, Civil, Probate—County Court, PO Box 959, Conroe, TX 77305. 409-787-2912, Fax: 409-760-6990. 8AM-5PM. Access by: mail, in person.

Moore

Real Estate Recording—Moore County Clerk, 715 Dumas Ave. Rm. 105, Dumas, TX 79029. 806-935-2019, Fax: 806-935-9004. 8:30AM-5PM.

Felony, Civil—District Court, 715 Dumas Ave #109, Dumas, TX 79029. 806-935-4218, Fax: 806-935-6325. 8:30AM-5PM. Access by: mail, in person.

Misdemeanor, Civil, Probate—County Court, 715 Dumas Ave Rm 105, Dumas, TX 79029. 806-935-6164, Fax: 806-935-9004. 8:30AM-5PM. Access by: mail, in person.

Morris

Real Estate Recording—Morris County Clerk, 500 Broadnax Street, Daingerfield, TX 75638. 903-645-2916. 8AM-5PM.

Felony, Civil—District Court, 500 Brodnax, Daingerfield, TX 75638. 903-645-2321. 8AM-5PM. Access by: mail, in person.

Misdemeanor, Probate—County Court, 500 Broadnax, Daingerfield, TX 75638. 903-645-3911. 8AM-5PM. Access by: mail, in person.

Motley

Real Estate Recording—Motley County Clerk, Main & Dundee, Courthouse, Matador, TX 79244. Fax: 806-347-2220. 9AM-5PM.

Felony, Misdemeanor, Civil, Eviction, Probate—District and County Court, PO Box 660, Matador, TX 79244. 806-347-2621, Fax: 806-347-2220. 9AM-Noon, 1-5PM. Access by: mail, in person.

Nacogdoches

Real Estate Recording—Nacogdoches County Clerk, 101 West Main, Room 205, Nacogdoches, TX 75961. 8AM-5PM.

Felony, Civil—District Court, 101 W Main #215, Nacogdoches, TX 75961. 409-828-3636, Fax: 409-560-7839. 8AM-5PM. Access by: mail, in person.

Misdemeanor, Civil, Probate—County Court, 101 W Main, Rm 205, Nacogdoches, TX 75961. 409-828-4130. 8AM-5PM. Access by: mail, in person.

Navarro

Real Estate Recording—Navarro County Clerk, 300 West Third Avenue, Courthouse - Suite 101, Corsicana, TX 75110. 903-654-3090. 8AM-5PM.

Felony, Civil—District Court, PO Box 1439, Corsicana, TX 75151. 903-654-3040, Fax: 903-654-3088. 8AM-5PM. Access by: mail, phone, fax, in person.

Misdemeanor, Civil, Probate—County Court, PO Box 423, Corsicana, TX 75151. 903-654-3035. 8AM-5PM. Access by: mail, in person.

Newton

Real Estate Recording—Newton County Clerk, Courthouse Square, Newton, TX 75966. 409-653-2909, Fax: 409-379-9049. 8AM-4:30PM.

Felony, Civil—District Court, PO Box 535, Newton, TX 75966. 409-653-2324. 8AM-4:30PM. Access by: mail, in person.

Misdemeanor, Civil, Probate—County Court, PO Box 484, Newton, TX 75966. 409-653-2353, Fax: 409-379-9049. 8AM-4:30PM. Access by: mail, in person.

Nolan

Real Estate Recording—Nolan County Clerk, 100 East 3rd, East Wing - Room 100-A, Sweetwater, TX 79556. 915-236-6932. 8:30AM-Noon, 1-5PM.

Felony, Civil—District Court, PO Box 1236, Sweetwater, TX 79556. 915-235-2111. 8:30AM-Noon, 1-5PM. Access by: mail, in person.

Misdemeanor, Civil, Probate—County Court, PO Drawer 98, Sweetwater, TX 79556-0098. 915-235-2462. 8:30AM-Noon, 1-5PM. Access by: mail, in person.

Nueces

Real Estate Recording—Recording Section, 901 Leopard St. Rm.201, Courthouse, Corpus Christi, TX 78401. 401-568-6206, Fax: 361-888-0329. 8AM-5PM.

Felony, Civil—District Court, PO Box 2987, Corpus Christi, TX 78403-2987. 401-625-6700, Fax: 361-888-0571. 8AM-5PM. Access by: mail, in person.

Misdemeanor, Civil, Probate—District Court, PO Box 2987, Corpus Christi, TX 78403-2987. Fax: 361-888-0571. 8AM-5PM. Access by: mail, in person.

Ochiltree

Real Estate Recording—Ochiltree County Clerk, 511 South Main, Perryton, TX 79070. 806-435-8120, Fax: 806-435-2081. 8:30AM-Noon, 1-5PM.

Felony, Civil—District Court, 511 S Main, Perryton, TX 79070. 806-435-8160, Fax: 806-435-4341. 8:30AM-5PM. Access by: mail, fax, in person.

Misdemeanor, Civil, Probate—County Court, 511 S Main St, Perryton, TX 79070. 806-435-8039, Fax: 806-435-2081. 8:30AM-Noon, 1-5PM. Access by: mail, fax, in person.

Oldham

Real Estate Recording—Oldham County Clerk, Highway 385 & Main Street, Courthouse, Vega, TX 79092. 8:30AM-5PM.

Felony, Misdemeanor, Civil, Eviction, Probate—District and County Court, PO Box 360, Vega, TX 79092. 806-267-2667. 8:30AM-Noon, 1-5PM. Access by: mail, in person.

Orange

Real Estate Recording—Orange County Clerk, 801 Division, Courthouse, Orange, TX 77630. 410-543-6600, Fax: 409-882-0379. 8:30AM-5PM.

Felony, Civil—District Court, PO Box 427, Orange, TX 77630. 410-543-6551. 8AM-5PM. Access by: mail, in person.

Misdemeanor, Civil, Probate—County Court, PO Box 1536, Orange, TX 77631-1536. 410-535-8801, Fax: 409-882-0379. 8:30AM-5PM. Access by: mail, phone, in person.

Palo Pinto

Real Estate Recording—Palo Pinto County Clerk, 520 Oak St. Courthouse, Palo Pinto, TX 76484. 817-659-1260. 8:30AM-4:30PM.

Felony, Civil—District Court, PO Box 189, Palo Pinto, TX 76484-0189. 940-659-1279. 8AM-4:30PM. Access by: mail, in person.

Misdemeanor, Civil, Probate—County Court, PO Box 219, Palo Pinto, TX 76484. 940-659-1277, Fax: 940-659-2590. 8:30AM-4:30PM. Access by: mail, in person.

Panola

Real Estate Recording—Panola County Clerk, Sabine & Sycamore, Courthouse Bldg. Room 201, Carthage, TX 75633. 903-693-0325, Fax: 903-693-2726. 8AM-5PM.

Felony, Civil—District Court, County Courthouse Rm 227, Carthage, TX 75633. 903-693-0306, Fax: 903-693-6914. 8AM-5PM. Access by: mail, in person.

Misdemeanor, Civil, Probate—County Court, County Courthouse Rm 201, Carthage, TX 75633. 903-693-0302. 8AM-5PM. Access by: mail, in person.

Parker

Real Estate Recording—Parker County Clerk, 1112 Santa Fe Drive, Weatherford, TX 76086. 817-596-0078. 8AM-5PM.

Felony, Civil—District Court, PO Box 340, Weatherford, TX 76086-0340. 817-599-6591. 8AM-5PM. Access by: mail, in person.

Misdemeanor, Civil—County Court, PO Box 819, Weatherford, TX 76086-0819. 817-599-6591. 8AM-Noon, 1-5PM. Access by: mail, in person.

Probate—Probate Court, 1112 Santa Fe Dr, PO Box 819, Weatherford, TX 76086. 817-594-7461. 8AM-5PM.

Parmer

Real Estate Recording—Parmer County Clerk, 400 Third Street, Farwell, TX 79325. 806-481-9152. 8:30AM-5PM.

Felony, Civil—District Court, PO Box 195, Farwell, TX 79325-0195. 806-481-3419, Fax: 806-481-9416. 8:30AM-Noon, 1-5PM. Access by: mail, fax, in person.

Misdemeanor, Civil, Probate—County Court, PO Box 356, Farwell, TX 79325. 806-481-3691. 8:30AM-5PM. Access by: mail, in person.

Pecos

Real Estate Recording—Pecos County Clerk, 103 West Callaghan Street, Fort Stockton, TX 79735. 915-336-3461, Fax: 915-336-7557. 8AM-5PM.

Felony, Civil—District Court, 400 S Nelson, Fort Stockton, TX 79735. 915-336-3503, Fax: 915-336-6437. 8AM-5PM. Access by: mail, fax, in person.

Misdemeanor, Civil, Probate—County Court, 103 W Callaghan, Fort Stockton, TX 79735. 915-336-7555, Fax: 915-336-7575. 8AM-5PM. Access by: mail, in person.

Polk

Real Estate Recording—Polk County Clerk, 101 West Church Street, Livingston, TX 77351. 409-567-2336, Fax: 409-327-6874. 8AM-5PM.

Felony, Civil—District Court, 101 W Church, Livingston, TX 77351. 409-567-2329. 8AM-5PM. Access by: mail, in person.

Misdemeanor, Civil, Probate—County Court at Law, PO Drawer 2119, Livingston, TX 77351. 409-560-7733, Fax: 409-327-6805. 8AM-5PM. Access by: mail, in person.

Potter

Real Estate Recording—Potter County Clerk, 500 S. Fillmore, Room 205, Amarillo, TX 79101. 806-379-2236, Fax: 806-379-2296. 8AM-5PM.

Felony, Civil—District Court, PO Box 9570, Amarillo, TX 79105-9570. 806-379-2300. 7:30AM-5:30PM. Access by: mail, phone, fax, in person, online.

Misdemeanor, Civil, Probate—County Court & County Courts at Law 1 & 2, PO Box 9638, Amarillo, TX 79105. 806-379-2285, Fax: 806-379-2296. 8AM-5PM. Access by: mail, in person. Special note: Limited civil records filed here, most are with the District Clerk.

www.co.potter.tx.us/countyclerk/index.html

Presidio

Real Estate Recording—Presidio County Clerk, Courthouse, 320 N. Highland, Marfa, TX 79843. 915-729-4076, Fax: 915-729-4313. 8AM-12, 1-5PM.

Felony, Misdemeanor, Civil, Eviction, Probate—District and County Court, PO Box 789, Marfa, TX 79843. 915-729-4812, Fax: 915-729-4313. 8AM-Noon, 1-4PM. Access by: mail, in person.

Rains

Real Estate Recording—Rains County Clerk, 100 Quitman Street, Emory, TX 75440. 903-473-2412. 8AM-5PM.

Felony, Misdemeanor, Civil, Eviction, Probate—District and County Court, PO Box 187, Emory, TX 75440. 903-473-2461. 8AM-5PM. Access by: mail, in person.

Randall

Real Estate Recording—Randall County Clerk, 401 15th Street, Canyon, TX 79015. 806-655-6256. 8AM-5PM (On Weekends by Appointment).

Felony, Civil—District Courts, PO Box 1096, Canyon, TX 79015. 806-655-6200, Fax: 806-655-6205. 8AM-5PM. Access by: mail, fax, in person.

Misdemeanor, Civil, Probate—County Court, PO Box 660, Canyon, TX 79015. 806-655-6330. 8AM-5PM. Access by: mail, in person.

Reagan

Real Estate Recording—Reagan County Clerk, 3rd at Plaza, Courthouse, Big Lake, TX 76932. 915-884-2090. 8:30AM-5PM.

Felony, Misdemeanor, Civil, Eviction, Probate—District and County Court, PO Box 100, Big Lake, TX 76932. 915-884-2442. 8:30AM-5PM. Access by: mail, in person.

Real

Real Estate Recording—Real County Clerk, Courthouse Square, Leakey, TX 78873. Fax: 830-232-6040. 8AM-5PM.

Felony, Misdemeanor, Civil, Eviction, Probate—District and County Court, PO Box 750, Leakey, TX 78873. 830-232-5202, Fax: 830-232-6040. 8AM-5PM. Access by: in person.

Red River

Real Estate Recording—Red River County Clerk, 200 North Walnut, Courthouse Annex, Clarksville, TX 75426. 903-427-3748. 8:30AM-5PM.

Felony, Civil—District Court, 400 N Walnut, Clarksville, TX 75426. 903-427-3761, Fax: 903-427-9004. 8:30AM-Noon, 1-5PM. Access by: mail, in person.

Misdemeanor, Probate—County Court, 200 N Walnut, Clarksville, TX 75426. 903-427-2401. 8:30AM-5PM. Access by: mail, phone, in person.

Reeves

Real Estate Recording—Reeves County Clerk, 100 East 4th Street, Room 101, Pecos, TX 79772. 915-445-2631, Fax: 915-445-5096. 8AM-5PM.

Felony, Civil—District Court, PO Box 848, Pecos, TX 79772. 915-445-2714, Fax: 915-445-7455. 8AM-Noon, 1-5PM. Access by: mail, in person.

Misdemeanor, Civil, Probate—County Court, PO Box 867, Pecos, TX 79772. 915-445-5467. 8AM-5PM. Access by: mail, in person.

Refugio

Real Estate Recording—Refugio County Clerk, 808 Commerce, Rm.112, Courthouse, Refugio, TX 78377. 401-232-0900. 8AM-5PM.

Felony, Civil—District Court, PO Box 736, Refugio, TX 78377. 401-222-6710. 8AM-Noon, 1-5PM. Access by: mail, in person.

Misdemeanor, Civil, Probate—County Court, PO Box 704, Refugio, TX 78377. 401-222-3250. 8AM-5PM. Access by: mail, in person.

Roberts

Real Estate Recording—Roberts County Clerk, Highway 60 & Kiowa Street, Courthouse, Miami, TX 79059. 806-868-3201, Fax: 806-868-3381. 8AM-Noon, 1-5PM.

Felony, Misdemeanor, Civil, Eviction, Probate—District and County Court, PO Box 477, Miami, TX 79059. 806-868-2341. 8AM-Noon, 1-5PM. Access by: mail, phone, in person.

Robertson

Real Estate Recording—Robertson County Clerk, Courthouse Square on Center Street, Room 104, Franklin, TX 77856. 410-313-2111. 8AM-5PM.

Felony, Civil—District Court, PO Box 250, Franklin, TX 77856. 410-313-2133. 8AM-5PM. Access by: mail, in person.

Misdemeanor, Civil, Probate—County Court, PO Box 1029, Franklin, TX 77856. 410-321-3300. 8AM-5PM. Access by: mail, in person.

Rockwall

Real Estate Recording—Rockwall County Clerk, 1101 Ridge Rd. S-101, Rockwall, TX 75087. 216-289-2888, Fax: 972-882-0229. 8AM-5PM.

Felony, Civil—District Court, 1101 Ridge Rd #209, Rockwall, TX 75087. 972-882-0260, Fax: 972-882-0268. 8AM-5PM. Access by: mail, in person.

Misdemeanor, Civil, Probate—County Court, 1101 Ridge Rd, Rockwall, TX 75087. 972-882-0220, Fax: 972-882-0229. 8AM-5PM. Access by: mail, in person.

Runnels

Real Estate Recording—County Clerk, Runnels County, Broadway & Hutchings, 600 Courthouse Square, Ballinger, TX 76821. 915-365-2428, Fax: 915-365-3408. 8:30AM-Noon, 1-5PM.

Felony, Civil—District Court, PO Box 166, Ballinger, TX 76821. 915-365-2638, Fax: 915-365-3408. 8:30AM-5PM. Access by: mail, phone, fax, in person.

Misdemeanor, Civil, Probate—County Court, PO Box 189, Ballinger, TX 76821. 915-365-2720. 8:30AM-Noon, 1-5PM. Access by: mail, phone, in person.

Rusk

Real Estate Recording—Rusk County Clerk, 115 North Main, Courthouse, Henderson, TX 75652. 8AM-5PM.

Felony, Civil—District Court, PO Box 1687, Henderson, TX 75653. 903-657-0353. 8AM-5PM. Access by: mail, in person.

Misdemeanor, Civil, Probate—County Court at Law, PO Box 1687, Henderson, TX 75653-1687. 903-657-0353. 8AM-5PM. Access by: mail, in person.

Sabine

Real Estate Recording—Sabine County Clerk, Corner of Oak & Main, Courthouse, Hemphill, TX 75948. 410-221-2580, Fax: 409-787-2044. 8AM-4PM.

Felony, Civil—District Court, PO Box 850, Hemphill, TX 75948. 410-222-1397. 8AM-4PM. Access by: mail, in person.

Misdemeanor, Probate—County Court, PO Drawer 580, Hemphill, TX 75948-0580. 410-222-1430. 8AM-4PM. Access by: mail, in person.

San Augustine

Real Estate Recording—San Augustine County Clerk, 106 Courthouse, 100 W. Columbia, San Augustine, TX 75972. 409-539-7885, Fax: 409-275-9579. 8AM-4:30PM.

Felony, Civil—District Court, County Courthouse Rm 202, San Augustine, TX 75972. 409-532-5542, Fax: 409-275-9579. 8AM-4:15PM. Access by: mail, in person.

Misdemeanor, Civil, Probate—County Court, County Courthouse Rm 106, San Augustine, TX 75972. 409-539-7855, Fax: 409-275-9579. 8AM-4:30PM. Access by: mail, phone, in person.

San Jacinto

Real Estate Recording—San Jacinto County Clerk, Corner of Church & Byrd, Courthouse, Coldspring, TX 77331. 409-873-2111. 8AM-4:30PM.

Felony, Civil—District Court, PO Box 369, Coldspring, TX 77331. 409-873-2111. 8AM-Noon, 1-5PM. Access by: mail, in person.

Misdemeanor, Civil, Probate—County Court, PO Box 669, Coldspring, TX 77331. 409-865-5911. 8AM-4:30PM. Access by: mail, in person.

San Patricio

Real Estate Recording—San Patricio County Clerk, 400 West Sinton Street, Sinton, TX 78387. Fax: 361-364-3825. 8AM-5PM.

Felony, Civil—District Court, PO Box 1084, Sinton, TX 78387. 361-790-0128. 8AM-5PM. Access by: mail, in person.

Misdemeanor, Civil, Probate—County Court, PO Box 578, Sinton, TX 78387. 361-798-2351, Fax: 361-364-3825. 8AM-5PM. Access by: mail, phone, fax, in person.

San Saba

Real Estate Recording—San Saba County Clerk, 500 East Wallace, San Saba, TX 76877. Fax: 915-372-5746. 8AM-Noon, 1-4:30PM.

Felony, Misdemeanor, Civil, Eviction, Probate—District and County Court, County Courthouse, 500 E Wallace #202, San Saba, TX 76877. 915-372-3375. 8AM-Noon, 1-5PM. Access by: mail, phone, in person.

Schleicher

Real Estate Recording—Schleicher County Clerk, Highway 277, Courthouse, Eldorado, TX 76936. Fax: 915-853-2603. 9AM-Noon, 1-5PM.

Felony, Misdemeanor, Civil, Eviction, Probate—District and County Court, PO Drawer 580, Eldorado, TX 76936. 915-853-2833, Fax: 915-853-2603. 9AM-Noon, 1-5PM. Access by: mail, in person.

Scurry

Real Estate Recording—Scurry County Clerk, 1806 25th Street, Suite 300, Snyder, TX 79549. 915-573-5382, Fax: 915-573-7396. 8:30AM-5PM.

Felony, Civil—132nd District Court, 1806 25th St #402, Snyder, TX 79549. 915-573-5641. 8AM-5PM. Access by: mail, in person.

Misdemeanor, Civil, Probate—County Court, County Courthouse, 1806 25th St Ste 300, Snyder, TX 79549. 915-573-5332. 8:30AM-5PM. Access by: mail, in person.

Shackelford

Real Estate Recording—Shackelford County Clerk, 225 S. Main, Albany, TX 76430. 915-762-2232. 8:30AM-Noon, 1-5PM.

Felony, Misdemeanor, Civil, Probate—District and County Court, PO Box 247, Albany, TX 76430. 915-762-2232. 8:30AM-5PM. Access by: mail, in person.

Shelby

Real Estate Recording—Shelby County Clerk, 200 San Augustine St. Suite A, Center, TX 75935. 409-835-8580. 8AM-4:30PM.

Felony, Civil—District Court, PO Drawer 1953, Center, TX 75935. 409-849-5711. 8AM-4:30PM. Access by: mail, in person.

Misdemeanor, Civil, Probate—County Court, PO Box 1987, Center, TX 75935. 409-849-5711, Fax: 409-598-3701. 8AM-4:30PM. Access by: mail, in person.

Sherman

Real Estate Recording—Sherman County Clerk, 701 North 3rd Street, Stratford, TX 79084. 806-396-5842, Fax: 806-366-5670. 8AM-Noon,1-5PM.

Felony, Misdemeanor, Civil, Eviction, Probate—District and County Court, PO Box 270, Stratford, TX 79084. 806-366-2371, Fax: 806-366-5670. 8AM-Noon, 1-5PM. Access by: mail, in person.

Smith

Real Estate Recording—Smith County Clerk, Courthouse, 100 Broadway, Rm.104, Tyler, TX 75702. 903-535-0555, Fax: 903-535-0684. 8AM-5PM.

Felony, Civil—District Courts, PO Box 1077, Tyler, TX 75710. 903-535-0666, Fax: 903-535-0683. 8AM-5PM. Access by: mail, in person.

Misdemeanor, Civil, Probate—County Court, PO Box 1018, Tyler, TX 75710. 903-535-0634, Fax: 903-535-0684. 8AM-5PM. Access by: mail, phone, in person.

Somervell

Real Estate Recording—Somervell County Clerk, 107 N.E. Vernon St. Glen Rose, TX 76043. 817-897-4814. 8AM-5PM.

Felony, Misdemeanor, Civil, Eviction, Probate—District and County Court, PO Box 1098, Glen Rose, TX 76043. 256-351-4640, Fax: 254-897-3233. 8AM-5PM. Access by: mail, in person.

Starr

Real Estate Recording—Starr County Clerk, Courthouse, Rio Grande City, TX 78582. Fax: 956-487-6227. 8AM-5PM.

Felony, Misdemeanor, Civil, Eviction, Probate—County Court at Law, Starr County Courthouse, Room 201, Rio Grande City, TX 78582. 956-487-2101, Fax: 956-487-6227. 8AM-5PM. Access by: mail, phone, fax, in person.

District and County Court, Starr County Courthouse, Room 304, Rio Grande City, TX 78582. 956-487-2610, Fax: 956-487-4885. 8AM-5PM. Access by: mail, in person.

Stephens

Real Estate Recording—Stephens County Clerk, Courthouse, Breckenridge, TX 76424. 817-559-3181. 8AM-5PM.

Felony, Civil—District Court, 200 W Walker, Breckenridge, TX 76424. 254-729-5504, Fax: 254-559-8127. 8:30AM-5PM. Access by: mail, fax, in person.

Sterling

Real Estate Recording—Sterling County Clerk, 609 4th Street, Courthouse, Sterling City, TX 76951. 915-378-8511. 8:30AM-Noon, 1-5PM.

Felony, Misdemeanor, Civil, Eviction, Probate—District and County Court, PO Box 55, Sterling City, TX 76951. 915-378-5191. 8:30AM-Noon, 1-5PM. Access by: mail, in person.

Stonewall

Real Estate Recording—Stonewall County Clerk, 510 South Broadway, Aspermont, TX 79502. 817-989-3520. 8AM-4:30PM.

Felony, Misdemeanor, Civil, Eviction, Probate—District and County Court, PO Drawer P, Aspermont, TX 79502. 940-989-2272. 8AM-Noon, 1-4:30PM. Access by: mail, phone, in person.

Sutton

Real Estate Recording—Sutton County Clerk, Sutton County Annex, 300 E. Oak, Suite 3, Sonora, TX 76950. 915-387-2886. 8:30AM-4:30PM.

Felony, Misdemeanor, Civil, Eviction, Probate—District and County Court, 300 E Oak, Ste 3, Sonora, TX 76950. 915-387-3815. 8:30AM-4:30PM. Access by: mail, in person.

Swisher

Real Estate Recording—Swisher County Clerk, Courthouse, 119 S. Maxwell, Tulia, TX 79088. Fax: 806-995-4121. 8AM-5PM.

Felony, Misdemeanor, Civil, Eviction, Probate—District and County Court, County Courthouse, Tulia, TX 79088. 806-995-4396, Fax: 806-995-4121. 8AM-5PM. Access by: mail, phone, fax, in person.

Tarrant

Real Estate Recording—Tarrant County Clerk, 100 West Weatherford, Courthouse, Room 180, Ft. Worth, TX 76196. 8AM-4:30PM.

Felony, Civil—District Court, 401 W Belknap, Fort Worth, TX 76196-0402. 817-884-1574, Fax: 817-884-1484. 8AM-5PM. Access by: mail, in person, online.

Misdemeanor, Civil—County Court, 100 W Weatherford Rm 250, Fort Worth, TX 76196. 817-884-1076. 7:30AM-4:30PM. Access by: mail, in person.

Probate—Probate Court, County Courthouse, 100 W Weatherford St, Probate Court #1 Rm 260A, Fort Worth, TX 76196. 817-884-1200, Fax: 817-884-3178. 8AM-4:30PM. Access by: mail, in person.

Taylor

Real Estate Recording—Taylor County Clerk, 300 Oak, Courthouse, Abilene, TX 79602. 915-674-1231, Fax: 915-674-1279. 8AM-5PM.

Felony, Civil—District Court, 300 Oak St, Abilene, TX 79602. 915-674-1316, Fax: 915-674-1307. 8AM-Noon, 1-5PM. Access by: mail, fax, in person.

Misdemeanor, Civil, Probate—County Court, PO Box 5497, Abilene, TX 79608. 915-674-1202, Fax: 915-674-1279. 8AM-5PM. Access by: mail, in person.

Terrell

Real Estate Recording—Terrell County Clerk, Courthouse Square, 108 Hackberry, Sanderson, TX 79848. Fax: 915-345-2653. 9AM-5PM.

Felony, Misdemeanor, Civil, Eviction, Probate—District and County Court, PO Drawer 410, Sanderson, TX 79848. 915-345-2391, Fax: 915-345-2653. 9AM-Noon, 1-5PM. Access by: mail, phone, fax, in person.

Terry

Real Estate Recording—Terry County Clerk, 500 West Main, Room 105, Brownfield, TX 79316. 806-637-3616, Fax: 806-637-4874. 8:30AM-5PM.

Felony, Civil—District Court, 500 W Main Rm 209E, Brownfield, TX 79316. 806-637-4202. 8:30AM-5PM. Access by: mail, in person.

Misdemeanor, Civil, Probate—County Court, 500 W Main Rm 105, Brownfield, TX 79316-4398. 806-637-8551, Fax: 806-637-4874. 8:30AM-5PM. Access by: mail, in person.

Throckmorton

Real Estate Recording—Throckmorton County Clerk, 105 Minter Street, Courthouse, Throckmorton, TX 76483. Fax: 940-849-3220. 8AM-5PM.

Felony, Misdemeanor, Civil, Eviction, Probate—District and County Court, PO Box 309, Throckmorton, TX 76483. 940-849-2501. 8AM-Noon, 1-5PM. Access by: mail, phone, in person.

Titus

Real Estate Recording—Titus County Clerk, 100 W. 1 St. 2nd Floor, Suite 204, Mount Pleasant, TX 75455. 903-572-8723, Fax: 903-577-6793. 8AM-5PM.

Felony, Civil—District Court, 105 W 1st St, PO Box 492, Mount Pleasant, TX 75455. 903-577-6721. 8AM-5PM. Access by: mail, in person.

Misdemeanor, Civil, Probate—County Court, 100 W 1st St #204, Mount Pleasant, TX 75455. 903-577-6796, Fax: 903-577-6793. 8AM-5PM. Access by: mail, in person.

Tom Green

Real Estate Recording—Tom Green County Clerk, 124 West Beauregard, San Angelo, TX 76903. 8AM-Noon, 1-4:30PM.

Felony, Civil—District Court, County Courthouse, 112 W Beauregard, San Angelo, TX 76903. 915-659-6579, Fax: 915-659-3241. 8AM-5PM. Access by: mail, in person.

Misdemeanor, Civil, Probate—County Court, 124 W Beauregard, San Angelo, TX 76903. 915-659-6555. 8AM-4:30PM. Access by: mail, in person.

Travis

Real Estate Recording—Travis County Clerk, 1000 Guadalupe, Room 222, Austin, TX 78701. 512-473-9000, Fax: 512-473-9075. 8AM-5PM.

Felony, Civil—District Court, PO Box 1748, Austin, TX 78767. Fax: 512-473-9549. 8AM-5PM. Access by: mail, phone, in person.

Misdemeanor, Civil, Probate—County Court, PO Box 1748, Austin, TX 78767-1748. Fax: 512-473-4220. 8AM-5PM. Access by: mail, phone, in person. www.co.travis.tx.us

Trinity

Real Estate Recording—Trinity County Clerk, First Street, Courthouse, Groveton, TX 75845. Fax: 409-642-3004. 8AM-5PM.

Felony, Civil—District Court, PO Box 548, Groveton, TX 75845. 409-865-5911. 8AM-5PM. Access by: mail, in person.

Misdemeanor, Civil, Probate—County Court, PO Box 456, Groveton, TX 75845. 409-865-5911, Fax: 409-642-3004. 8AM-5PM. Access by: mail, in person.

Tyler

Real Estate Recording—Tyler County Clerk, 110 W. Bluff, Room 110, Woodville, TX 75979. 409-560-7730. 8AM-4:30PM.

Felony, Civil—District Court, 203 Courthouse, 100 W Bluff, Woodville, TX 75979. 409-544-3255. 8AM-Noon, 1-4:30PM. Access by: mail, in person.

Misdemeanor, Civil, Probate—County Court, County Courthouse, Rm 110, 100 W Bluff, Woodville, TX 75979. 409-544-3255, Fax: 409-283-7296. 8AM-4:30PM. Access by: mail, in person.

Upshur

Real Estate Recording—Upshur County Clerk, Highway 154, Courthouse, Gilmer, TX 75644. 903-843-3083. 8AM-5PM.

Felony, Misdemeanor, Civil, Probate—County Court, PO Box 730, Gilmer, TX 75644. 903-843-4015. 8AM-5PM. Access by: mail, in person.

Upton

Real Estate Recording—Upton County Clerk, 205 East 10th Street, Rankin, TX 79778. 915-693-2401, Fax: 915-693-2129. 8AM-5PM.

Felony, Misdemeanor, Civil, Eviction, Probate—District and County Court, PO Box 465, Rankin, TX 79778. 915-693-2861, Fax: 915-693-2243. 8AM-5PM. Access by: mail, fax, in person.

Uvalde

Real Estate Recording—Uvalde County Clerk, Main & Getty, Courthouse, Uvalde, TX 78801. 210-620-5506. 8AM-5PM.

Felony, Civil—District Court, County Courthouse Suite #15, Uvalde, TX 78801. 830-278-3918. 8AM-5PM. Access by: mail, phone, in person.

Misdemeanor, Civil, Probate—County Court, PO Box 284, Uvalde, TX 78802. 830-278-6614. 8AM-5PM. Access by: mail, in person.

Val Verde

Real Estate Recording—Val Verde County Clerk, 100 Broadway St. Del Rio, TX 78840. 212-417-3149. 8AM-4:30PM.

Felony, Civil—District Court, PO Box 1544, Del Rio, TX 78841. 830-774-7538. 8AM-4:30PM. Access by: mail, in person.

Misdemeanor, Probate—County Court, PO Box 1267, Del Rio, TX 78841-1267. 830-774-7564. 8AM-4:30PM. Access by: mail, in person.

Van Zandt

Real Estate Recording—Van Zandt County Clerk, 121 East Dallas St, Courthouse - Room 202, Canton, TX 75103. Fax: 903-567-6722. 8AM-5PM.

Felony, Civil—District Court, 121 E Dallas St Rm 302, Canton, TX 75103. 903-567-6576, Fax: 903-567-4700. 8AM-5PM. Access by: mail, phone, in person.

Misdemeanor, Civil, Probate—County Court, 121 E Dallas St #202, Canton, TX 75103. 903-567-6503, Fax: 903-567-6722. 8AM-5PM. Access by: mail, in person.

Victoria

Real Estate Recording—Victoria County Clerk, 115 North Bridge Street #103, Victoria, TX 77901. 512-576-8588, Fax: 361-575-6276. 8AM-5PM.

Felony, Civil—District Court, PO Box 2238, Victoria, TX 77902. 401-294-3331, Fax: 361-572-5682. 8AM-5PM. Access by: mail, fax, in person.

Misdemeanor, Civil, Probate—County Court, 115 N Bridge, Rm 103, Victoria, TX 77901. 401-294-3891, Fax: 361-575-6276. 8AM-5PM. Access by: mail, fax, in person.

Walker

Real Estate Recording—Walker County Clerk, 1100 University Avenue, Huntsville, TX 77340. Fax: 409-436-4930. 8AM-5PM.

Felony, Civil—District Court, 1100 University Ave Rm 301, Huntsville, TX 77340. 409-766-2202. 8AM-Noon, 1-4:30PM. Access by: mail, in person.

Misdemeanor, Civil, Probate—County Court, PO Box 210, Huntsville, TX 77342-0210. 409-762-8621, Fax: 409-436-4922. 8AM-4:45PM. Access by: mail, in person.

Waller

Real Estate Recording—Waller County Clerk, 836 Austin Street, Room 217, Hempstead, TX 77445. 410-260-1370. 8AM-Noon, 1-5PM.

Felony, Civil—District Court, 836 Austin St Rm 318, Hempstead, TX 77445. 410-228-4181. 8AM-Noon, 1-5PM. Access by: mail, in person.

Misdemeanor, Civil, Probate—County Court, 836 Austin St, Rm 217, Hempstead, TX 77445. 410-228-0481. 8AM-Noon, 1-5PM. Access by: mail, in person.

Ward

Real Estate Recording—Ward County Clerk, Courthouse, 400 S. Allen St. Monahans, TX 79756. 915-943-2841, Fax: 915-942-6054. 8AM-5PM.

Felony, Civil—District Court, PO Box 440, Monahans, TX 79756. 915-943-2751, Fax: 915-943-3810. 8AM-5PM. Access by: mail, fax, in person.

Misdemeanor, Civil, Probate—County Court, County Courthouse, Monahans, TX 79756. 915-943-3294, Fax: 915-943-6054. 8AM-5PM. Access by: mail, in person.

Washington

Real Estate Recording—Washington County Clerk, 100 East Main, Suite 102, Brenham, TX 77833. 409-544-3255, Fax: 409-277-6278. 8AM-5PM.

Felony, Civil—District Court, 100 E Main #304, Brenham, TX 77833-3753. 409-542-3684. 8AM-5PM. Access by: mail, in person.

Misdemeanor, Civil, Probate—County Court, 100 E Main #102, Brenham, TX 77833. 409-542-2947, Fax: 409-277-6278. 8AM-5PM. Access by: mail, in person.

Webb

Real Estate Recording—Webb County Clerk, 1110 Victoria Street, Suite 201, Laredo, TX 78040. 210-997-6521, Fax: 956-721-2288.

Felony, Civil—District Court, PO Box 667, Laredo, TX 78042-0667. 956-721-2460, Fax: 956-721-2458. 8AM-5PM. Access by: mail, in person.

Misdemeanor, Civil Under $5,000, Probate—County Court, PO Box 29, Laredo, TX 78042. 956-721-2640, Fax: 956-721-2288. 8AM-5PM. Access by: mail, in person.

Wharton

Real Estate Recording—Wharton County Clerk, 100 East Milam, Wharton, TX 77488. 8AM-5PM.

Felony, Civil—District Court, PO Drawer 391, Wharton, TX 77488. 409-766-5112, Fax: 409-532-1299. 8AM-Noon, 1-5PM. Access by: mail, in person.

Misdemeanor, Civil, Probate—County Court, PO Box 69, Wharton, TX 77488. 409-766-2424. 8AM-5PM. Access by: mail, in person.

Wheeler

Real Estate Recording—Wheeler County Clerk, 400 Main Street, Courthouse, Wheeler, TX 79096. 806-826-3122, Fax: 806-826-3282. 8AM-5PM.

Felony, Civil—District Court, PO Box 528, Wheeler, TX 79096. 806-826-5931, Fax: 806-826-3282. 8AM-5PM. Access by: mail, phone, in person.

Misdemeanor, Civil, Probate—County Court, PO Box 465, Wheeler, TX 79096. 806-826-5544, Fax: 806-826-3282. 8AM-5PM. Access by: mail, in person.

Wichita

Real Estate Recording—Wichita County Clerk, 900 7th Street, Room 250, Wichita Falls, TX 76301. 817-766-8245. 8AM-5PM.

Felony, Civil—District Court, PO Box 718, Wichita Falls, TX 76307. 940-766-8190. 8AM-5PM. Access by: mail, phone, in person.

Misdemeanor, Probate—County Court, PO Box 1679, Wichita Falls, TX 76307. 940-766-8173. 8AM-5PM. Access by: mail, phone, in person.

Wilbarger

Real Estate Recording—Wilbarger County Clerk, Courthouse, 1700 Main St. #15, Vernon, TX 76384. 8AM-5PM.

Felony, Civil—District Court, 1700 Wilbarger Rm 33, Vernon, TX 76384. 940-553-3411, Fax: 940-553-2316. 8AM-5PM. Access by: mail, in person.

Misdemeanor, Civil, Probate—County Court, 1700 Wilbarger Rm 15, Vernon, TX 76384. 940-552-5486. 8AM-5PM. Access by: mail, in person.

Willacy

Real Estate Recording—Willacy County Clerk, 540 West Hidalgo Avenue, Courthouse Building, First Floor, Raymondville, TX 78580. 210-868-4566, Fax: 956-689-0937. 8AM-Noon, 1-5PM.

Felony, Civil—District Court, County Courthouse, Raymondville, TX 78580. 956-689-2532, Fax: 956-689-5713. 8AM-5PM. Access by: mail, in person.

Misdemeanor, Civil, Probate—County Court, 540 W Hidalgo, Raymondville, TX 78580. 956-689-2710. 8AM-Noon, 1-5PM. Access by: mail, in person.

Williamson

Real Estate Recording—Williamson County Clerk, Courthouse, 1st Floor, 710 S. Main St. Georgetown, TX 78626. 512-930-4424, Fax: 512-943-1616. 8AM-5PM.

Felony, Civil—District Court, PO Box 24, Georgetown, TX 78627. 512-943-1212, Fax: 512-943-1222. 8AM-5PM. Access by: mail, in person.

Misdemeanor, Civil, Probate—County Court, PO Box 18, (405 MLK St, 78626), Georgetown, TX 78627. Fax: 512-943-1154. 8AM-5PM M,T,Th,F. Access by: mail, in person.

Wilson

Real Estate Recording—Wilson County Clerk, 1420 3rd Street, Floresville, TX 78114. 210-721-2215. 8AM-5PM.

Felony, Civil—District Court, PO Box 812, Floresville, TX 78114. 830-393-7322, Fax: 830-393-7319. 8AM-Noon, 1-5PM. Access by: mail, fax, in person.

Misdemeanor, Civil, Probate—County Court, PO Box 27, Floresville, TX 78114. 830-393-7308. 8AM-5PM. Access by: mail, in person.

Winkler

Real Estate Recording—Winkler County Clerk, 100 East Winkler Street, Courthouse, Kermit, TX 79745. 915-586-6604. 8AM-5PM.

Felony, Civil—District Court, PO Box 1065, Kermit, TX 79745. 915-586-3359. 8:30AM-5PM. Access by: mail, in person.

Misdemeanor, Civil, Probate—County Court, PO Box 1007, Kermit, TX 79745. 915-586-3401. 8AM-5PM. Access by: mail, in person.

Wise

Real Estate Recording—Wise County Clerk, 200 North Trinity, Records Bldg. Decatur, TX 76234. 940-627-3540, Fax: 940-627-2138. 8AM-5PM.

Felony, Civil—District Court, PO Box 308, Decatur, TX 76234. 940-627-5535, Fax: 940-627-6926. 8AM-5PM. Access by: mail, in person.

Misdemeanor, Civil, Probate—County Court at Law, PO Box 359, Decatur, TX 76234. 940-627-3351, Fax: 940-627-2138. 8AM-5PM. Access by: mail, in person.

Wood

Real Estate Recording—Wood County Clerk, 1 Main Street, Courthouse, Quitman, TX 75783. 903-763-4186, Fax: 903-763-2902. 8AM-5PM.

Felony, Civil—District Court, PO Box 1707, Quitman, TX 75783. 903-763-2361, Fax: 903-763-1511. 8AM-Noon, 1-5PM. Access by: mail, in person.

Misdemeanor, Civil, Probate—County Court, PO Box 1796, Quitman, TX 75783. 903-763-2711, Fax: 903-763-2902. 8AM-5PM. Access by: mail, in person.

Yoakum

Real Estate Recording—Yoakum County Clerk, Courthouse, Cowboy Way & Avenue G, Plains, TX 79335. 806-456-8794, Fax: 806-456-2258. 8AM-5PM.

Felony, Civil—District Court, PO Box 899, Plains, TX 79355. 806-456-7453, Fax: 806-456-8767. 8AM-5PM. Access by: mail, phone, fax, in person.

Misdemeanor, Civil, Probate—County Court, PO Box 309, Plains, TX 79355. 806-456-2721, Fax: 806-456-6175. 8AM-5PM. Access by: mail, phone, fax, in person.

Young

Real Estate Recording—Young County Clerk, Young County Courthouse, 516 Fourth St. Room 104, Graham, TX 76450. 940-549-2633. 8:30AM-5PM.

Felony, Civil—District Court, 516 4th St Rm 201, Courthouse, Graham, TX 76450. 940-549-0029, Fax: 940-549-4874. 8:30AM-Noon, 1-5PM. Access by: mail, phone, fax, in person.

Misdemeanor, Civil, Probate—County Court, 516 4th St Rm 104, Graham, TX 76450. 940-549-8432. 8:30AM-Noon, 1-5PM. Access by: mail, in person.

Zapata

Real Estate Recording—Zapata County Clerk, 7th Avenue & Hidalgo Street, Zapata, TX 78076. 212-374-4704, Fax: 956-765-9933. 8AM-5PM.

Felony, Civil—District Court, PO Box 788, Zapata, TX 78076. 956-765-9930, Fax: 956-765-9931. 8AM-Noon, 1-5PM. Access by: mail, fax, in person.

Misdemeanor, Civil, Probate—County Court, PO Box 789, Zapata, TX 78076. 956-765-9915, Fax: 956-765-9933. 8AM-Noon, 1-5PM. Access by: mail, fax, in person.

Zavala

Real Estate Recording—Zavala County Clerk, Zavala Courthouse, Crystal City, TX 78839. 210-689-2772, Fax: 830-374-5955. 8AM-5PM.

Felony, Civil—District Court, PO Box 704, Crystal City, TX 78839. 830-374-3456. 8AM-Noon, 1-5PM. Access by: mail, phone, in person.

Misdemeanor, Civil, Probate—County Court, Zavala County Courthouse, Crystal City, TX 78839. 830-374-2331, Fax: 830-374-5955. 8AM-5PM. Access by: mail, in person.

Federal Courts

US District Court

Eastern District of Texas

Beaumont Division PO Box 3507, Beaumont, TX 77704409-654-7000 Counties: Hardin, Jasper, Jefferson, Liberty, Newton, Orange. www.txed.uscourts.gov
Marshall Division PO Box 1499, Marshall, TX 75671-1499903-935-2912, Criminal Docket Phone: 903-590-1000 Counties: Camp, Cass, Harrison, Marion, Morris, Upshur. www.txed.uscourts.gov
Sherman Division 101 E Pecan St, Sherman, TX 75090903-892-2921 Counties: Collin, Cooke, Delta*, Denton, Fannin*, Grayson, Hopkins*, Lamar*, Red River*. Counties marked with asterisk are called the Paris Division, whose case records are maintained here.. www.txed.uscourts.gov
Texarkana Division Clerk's Office, 500 State Line Ave, Room 302, Texarkana, TX 75501903-794-8561 Fax: 903-794-0600 Counties: Angelina, Bowie, Franklin, Houston, Nacogdoches, Polk, Sabine, San Augustine, Shelby, Titus, Trinity, Tyler. www.txed.uscourts.gov
Tyler Division Clerk, Room 106, 211 W Ferguson, Tyler, TX 75702903-590-1000 Counties: Anderson, Cherokee, Gregg, Henderson, Panola, Rains, Rusk, Smith, Van Zandt, Wood. www.txed.uscourts.gov

Northern District of Texas

Abilene Division PO Box 1218, Abilene, TX 79604915-677-6311 Counties: Callahan, Eastland, Fisher, Haskell, Howard, Jones, Mitchell, Nolan, Shackelford, Stephens, Stonewall, Taylor, Throckmorton. www.txnd.uscourts.gov
Amarillo Division 205 E 5th St, Amarillo, TX 79101806-324-2352 Counties: Armstrong, Briscoe, Carson, Castro, Childress, Collingsworth, Dallam, Deaf Smith, Donley, Gray, Hall, Hansford, Hartley, Hemphill, Hutchinson, Lipscomb, Moore, Ochiltree, Oldham, Parmer, Potter, Randall, Roberts, Sherman, Swisher, Wheeler. www.txnd.uscourts.gov
Dallas Division Room 14A20, 1100 Commerce St, Dallas, TX 75242214-767-0787, Record Room: 214-767-0789 Counties: Dallas,

Ellis, Hunt, Johnson, Kaufman, Navarro, Rockwall. www.txnd.uscourts.gov
Fort Worth Division Clerk's Office, 501 W Tenth St, Room 310, Fort Worth, TX 76102817-978-3132 Counties: Comanche, Erath, Hood, Jack, Palo Pinto, Parker, Tarrant, Wise. www.txnd.uscourts.gov
Lubbock Division Clerk, Room 105, 904 Broadway, Lubbock, TX 79401806-775-1300 Counties: Bailey, Borden, Cochran, Crosby, Dawson, Dickens, Floyd, Gaines, Garza, Hale, Hockley, Kent, Lamb, Lubbock, Lynn, Motley, Scurry, Terry, Yoakum. www.txnd.uscourts.gov
San Angelo Division Clerk's Office, Room 202, 33 E Twohig, San Angelo, TX 76903915-655-4506 Fax: 915-658-6826 Counties: Brown, Coke, Coleman, Concho, Crockett, Glasscock, Irion, Menard, Mills, Reagan, Runnels, Schleicher, Sterling, Sutton, Tom Green. www.txnd.uscourts.gov
Wichita Falls Division PO Box 1234, Wichita Falls, TX 76307940-767-1902 Fax: 940-767-2526 Counties: Archer, Baylor, Clay, Cottle, Foard, Hardeman, King, Knox, Montague, Wichita, Wilbarger, Young. www.txnd.uscourts.gov

Southern District of Texas

Brownsville Division PO Box 2299, Brownsville, TX 78522956-548-2500 Counties: Cameron, Willacy. www.txs.uscourts.gov
Corpus Christi Division Clerk's Office, 521 Starr St, Corpus Christi, TX 78401361-888-3142 Counties: Aransas, Bee, Brooks, Duval, Jim Wells, Kenedy, Kleberg, Live Oak, Nueces, San Patricio. www.txs.uscourts.gov
Galveston Division Clerk's Office, PO Drawer 2300, Galveston, TX 77553409-766-3530 Counties: Brazoria, Chambers, Galveston, Matagorda. www.txs.uscourts.gov
Houston Division PO Box 61010, Houston, TX 77208713-250-5500, Record Room: 713-250-5543, Civil Docket Phone: 713-250-5786, Criminal Docket Phone: 713-250-5598 Counties: Austin, Brazos, Colorado, Fayette, Fort Bend, Grimes, Harris, Madison, Montgomery, San Jacinto, Walker, Waller, Wharton. www.txs.uscourts.gov
Laredo Division PO Box 597, Laredo, TX 78042-0597956-723-3542, Civil Docket Phone: 956-726-2236, Criminal Docket Phone:

956-726-2236 Fax: 956-726-2289 Counties: Jim Hogg. La Salle. McMullen, Webb. Zapata. www.txs.uscourts.gov

McAllen Division Suite 1011, 10th Fl, 1701 W Business Hwy 83, McAllen, TX 78501956-618-8065 Counties: Hidalgo, Starr. www.txs.uscourts.gov

Victoria Division Clerk US District Court, PO Box 1541, Victoria, TX 77902361-788-5000 Counties: Calhoun, De Witt, Goliad, Jackson, Lavaca, Refugio, Victoria. www.txs.uscourts.gov

Western District of Texas

Austin Division Room 130, 200 W 8th St, Austin, TX 78701512-916-5896 Counties: Bastrop, Blanco, Burleson, Burnet, Caldwell, Gillespie, Hays, Kimble, Lampasas, Lee, Llano, McCulloch, Mason, San Saba, Travis, Washington, Williamson. www.txwd.uscourts.gov

Del Rio Division Room L100, 111 E Broadway, Del Rio, TX 78840830-703-2054 Counties: Edwards, Kinney, Maverick, Terrell, Uvalde, Val Verde, Zavala. www.txwd.ucourts.gov

El Paso Division US District Clerk's Office, Room 350, 511 E San Antonio, El Paso, TX 79901915-534-6725 Counties: El Paso. www.txwd.uscourts.gov

Midland Division Clerk, US District Court, 200 E Wall St, Midland, TX 79701915-686-4001 Counties: Andrews, Crane, Ector, Martin, Midland, Upton. www.tswd.uscourts.gov

Pecos Division US Courthouse, 410 S Cedar St, Pecos, TX 79772915-445-4228 Counties: Brewster, Culberson, Hudspeth, Jeff Davis, Loving, Pecos, Presidio, Reeves, Ward, Winkler. www.txwd.uscourts.gov

San Antonio Division US Clerk's Office, 655 E Durango, Suite G-65, San Antonio, TX 78206210-472-6550 Counties: Atascosa, Bandera, Bexar, Comal, Dimmit, Frio, Gonzales, Guadalupe, Karnes, Kendall, Kerr, Medina, Real, Wilson. www.txwd.uscourts.gov

Waco Division Clerk, PO Box 608, Waco, TX 76703254-750-1501 Counties: Bell, Bosque, Coryell, Falls, Freestone, Hamilton, Hill, Leon, Limestone, McLennan, Milam, Robertson, Somervell. www.txwd.uscourts.gov

US Bankruptcy Court

Eastern District of Texas

Beaumont Division Suite 100, 300 Willow, Beaumont, TX 77701409-839-2617 Counties: Angelina, Hardin, Houston, Jasper, Jefferson, Liberty, Nacogdoches, Newton, Orange, Polk, Sabine, San Augustine, Shelby, Trinity, Tyler. www.txeb.uscourts.gov

Marshall Division c/o Tyler Division, 200 E Ferguson, Tyler, TX 75702903-590-1212 x210 Fax: 903-590-1226 Counties: Camp, Cass, Harrison, Marion, Morris, Upshur. www.txeb.uscourts.gov

Plano Division Suite 300B, 660 N Central Expressway, Plano, TX 75074972-509-1240 Fax: 972-509-1245 Counties: Collin, Cooke, Delta, Denton, Fannin, Grayson, Hopkins, Lamar, Red River. www.txeb.uscourts.gov

Texarkana Division c/o Plano Division, Suite 300B, 660 N Central Expressway, Plano, TX 75074972-509-1240 Fax: 972-509-1245 Counties: Bowie, Franklin, Titus. www.txeb.uscourts.gov

Tyler Division 200 E Ferguson, 2nd Floor, Tyler, TX 75702903-590-1212 x210 Fax: 903-590-1226 Counties: Anderson, Cherokee, Gregg, Henderson, Panola, Rains, Rusk, Smith, Van Zandt, Wood. www.txeb.uscourts.gov

Northern District of Texas

Amarillo Division PO Box 15960, Amarillo, TX 79105806-324-2302 Counties: Armstrong, Briscoe, Carson, Castro, Childress, Collingsworth, Dallam, Deaf Smith, Donley, Gray, Hall, Hansford, Hartley, Hemphill, Hutchinson, Lipscomb, Moore, Ochiltree,

Oldham, Parmer, Potter, Randall, Roberts, Sherman, Swisher, Wheeler. www.txnb.uscourts.gov

Dallas Division 1100 Commerce St, Suite 12A24, Dallas, TX 75242-1496214-767-0814, Record Room: 214-767-3616 Counties: Dallas, Ellis, Hunt, Johnson, Kaufman, Navarro, Rockwall. www.txnb.uscourts.gov

Fort Worth Division 501 W 10th, Suite 147, Fort Worth, TX 76102817-978-3802 Counties: Comanche, Erath, Hood, Jack, Palo Pinto, Parker, Tarrant, Wise. www.txnb.uscourts.gov

Lubbock Division 306 Federal Bldg, 1205 Texas Ave, Lubbock, TX 79401806-472-7336 Counties: Bailey, Borden, Brown, Callahan, Cochran, Cooke, Coleman, Concho, Crockett, Crosby, Dawson, Dickens, Eastland, Fisher, Floyd, Gaines, Garza, Glasscock, Hale, Haskell, Hockley, Howard, Irion, Jones, Kent, Lamb, Lubbock, Lynn, Menard, Mills, Mitchell,Motley, Nolan, Reagan, Runnels, Schleicher, Scurry, Shackelford, Stephens, Sterling, Stonewall, Sutton, Taylor, Terry, Throckmorton, Tom Green, Yoakum. www.txnb.uscourts.gov

Wichita Falls Division c/o Dallas Division, Suite 12A24, 1100 Commerce St, Dallas, TX 75242-1496214-767-0814, Record Room: 214-767-0814 Counties: Archer, Baylor, Clay, Cottle, Foard, Hardeman, King, Knox, Montague, Wichita, Wilbarger, Young. www.txnb.uscourts.gov

Southern District of Texas

Corpus Christi Division Room 113, 615 Leopard St, Corpus Christi, TX 78476361-888-3484 Counties: Aransas, Bee, Brooks, Calhoun, Cameron, Duval, Goliad, Hidalgo, Jackson, Jim Wells, Kenedy, Kleberg, Lavaca, Live Oak, Nueces, Refugio, San Patricio, Starr, Victoria, Willacy.Files from Brownsville, Corpus Christi, McAllen and Victoria are maintained here. www.txs.uscourts.gov

Houston Division Room 1217, 515 Rusk Ave, Houston, TX 77002713-250-5500 Counties: Austin, Brazoria, Brazos, Chambers, Colorado, De Witt, Fayette, Fort Bend, Galveston, Grimes, Harris, Jim Hogg*, La Salle*, Madison, Matagorda, McMullen*, Montgomery, San Jacinto, Walker,Waller, Wharton, Webb* Zapata*. Open case records for the counties marked with an asterisk are being moved to the Laredo Division.. www.txs.uscourts.gov

Western District of Texas

Austin Division Homer Thornberry Judicial Bldg, 903 San Antonio, Room 322, Austin, TX 78701512-916-5237 Counties: Bastrop, Blanco, Burleson, Burnet, Caldwell, Gillespie, Hays, Kimble, Lampasas, Lee, Llano, Mason, McCulloch, San Saba, Travis, Washington, Williamson. www.txwb.uscourts.gov

El Paso Division PO Box 971040, El Paso, TX 79997-1040915-779-7362 Counties: El Paso. www.txwb.uscourts.gov

Midland/Odessa Division US Post Office Annex, Room P-163, 100 E Wall St, Midland, TX 79701915-683-1650 Counties: Andrews, Brewster, Crane, Culberson, Ector, Hudspeth, Jeff Davis, Loving, Martin, Midland, Pecos, Presidio, Reeves, Upton, Ward, Winkler. www.txwb.uscourts.gov

Pecos Division 410 S. Cedar, Pecos, TX 79772915-445-4228 Counties: Brewster, Culberson, Hudspeth, Jeff Davis, Loving, Pecos, Presidio, Reeves, Ward, Winkler. www.txwb.uscourts.gov

San Antonio Division PO Box 1439, San Antonio, TX 78295210-472-6720 Fax: 210-472-5916 Counties: Atascosa, Bandera, Bexar, Comal, Dimmit, Edwards, Frio, Gonzales, Guadalupe, Karnes, Kendall, Kerr, Kinney, Maverick, Medina, Real, Terrell, Uvalde, Val Verde, Wilson, Zavala. www.txwb.uscourts.gov

Waco Division PO Box 687, Waco, TX 76703254-754-1481 Counties: Bell, Bosque, Coryell, Falls, Freestone, Hamilton, Hill, Leon, Limestone, McLennan, Milam, Robertson, Somervell. www.txwb.uscourts.gov

Attorney General's Office

236 State Capitol
Salt Lake City, UT 84114
www.attygen.state.ut.us

801-538-9600
Fax: 801-366-0221

Governor's Office

210 State Capitol
Salt Lake City, UT 84114
www.governor.state.ut.us

801-538-1000
Fax: 801-538-1528

State Archives

PO Box 141021
Salt Lake City, UT 84114-1021
www.archives.state.ut.us

801-538-3013
Fax: 801-538-3354

Capital:	Salt Lake City
	Salt Lake County
Time Zone:	MST
Number of Counties:	29
Population:	2,059,148
Web Site:	www.state.ut.us

Search Unclaimed Property Online
www.up.state.ut.us/html_pages/ Search.htm

State Agencies

Criminal Records

Restricted access.
  Bureau of Criminal Identification, Box 148280, Salt Lake City, UT 84114-8280 (3888 West 5400 South, Salt Lake City, UT 84119) (3888 West 5400 South, Salt Lake City, UT 84119); 801-965-4445; Fax: 801-965-4749; 8AM-5PM

Corporation Records
Limited Liability Company Records
Fictitious Name
Limited Partnership Records
Assumed Name
Trademarks/Servicemarks

  Commerce Department, Corporate Division, PO Box 146705, Salt Lake City, UT 84114-6705 (160 E 300 S, 2nd fl, Salt Lake City, UT 84111); 801-530-4849 Call Center, 801-530-6205 Certified Records, 801-530-6034 Non-Certified, 801-530-6363 Good Standing; Fax: 801-530-6111; 8AM-5PM. Access by: mail, phone, in person, online. www.commerce.state.ut.us

Sales Tax Registrations

  Tax Commission, Taxpayer Services, 210 N 1950 W, Salt Lake City, UT 84134; 801-297-2200; Fax: 801-297-7697; 8AM-5PM. Access by: mail. www.tax.ex.state.ut.us

Uniform Commercial Code

  Department of Commerce, UCC Division, Box 146705, Salt Lake City, UT 84114-6705 (160 E 300 South, Heber M Wells Bldg, 2nd Floor, Salt Lake City, UT 84111); 801-530-4849; Fax: 801-530-6438; 8AM-5PM. Access by: mail, phone, in person, online. www.commerce.state.ut.us

Federal Tax Liens
State Tax Liens

Records not available from state agency.

  Records are found at the local level.

Workers' Compensation Records

  Labor Commission, Division of Industrial Accidents, PO Box 146610, Salt Lake City, UT 84114-6610 (160 E 300 S, 3rd Floor, Salt Lake City, UT 84114); 801-530-6800; Fax: 801-530-6804; 8AM-5PM. Access by: mail.

Birth Certificates

Department of Health, Bureau of Vital Records, Box 141012, Salt Lake City, UT 84114-1012 (288 N 1460 W, Salt Lake City, UT 84114); 801-538-6105; Fax: 801-538-9467; 9AM-5PM. Access by: mail. http://hlunix.state.ut.us/bvr/home.html

Death Records

Department of Health, Bureau of Vital Records, Box 141012, Salt Lake City, UT 84114-1012; 801-538-6105; Fax: 801-538-9467; 9AM-5PM. Access by: mail, phone, in person.

Divorce Records

Records not available from state agency.

Divorce records are not held by the state. You must go to the Clerk of the Court issuing the decree.

Marriage Certificates

Records not available from state agency.

Marriage records not held by the state. Query the County Recorder in county where marriage took place.

Driver Records

Department of Public Safety, Driver's License & Driving Records Section, PO Box 30560, Salt Lake City, UT 84130-0560 (4501 South 2700 West, 3rd Floor South, Salt Lake City, UT 84119); 801-965-4437; Fax: 801-965-4496; 8AM-5PM. Access by: mail. www.dl.state.ut.us

Vehicle Ownership
Vehicle Identification
Boat & Vessel Ownership
Boat & Vessel Registration

State Tax Commission, Motor Vehicle Records Section, 210 North 1950 West, Salt Lake City, UT 84134; 801-297-3507; Fax: 801-297-3578; 8AM-5PM. Access by: mail, phone, in person.

Accident Reports

Driver's License Division, Accident Reports Section, PO Box 30560, Salt Lake City, UT 84130-0560 (4501 South 2700 West, 3rd Floor, Salt Lake City, UT 84119); 801-965-4428; 8AM-5PM. Access by: mail.

Legislation-Current/Pending
Legislation-Passed

Utah Legislature, Research and General Counsel, 436 State Capitol, Salt Lake City, UT 84114; 801-538-1032, 801-538-1588 Bill Room, 801-538-1032 Older Passed Bills; Fax: 801-538-1712; 8AM-5PM. Access by: mail, phone, in person, online. www.le.state.ut.us

Voter Registration

Restricted access.
Records are at the county clerk offices. Records that have not been secured by the registrant are open to the public; however, the counties will not release the SSN or DL.
Office of Lt Governor, Elections Office, 115 State Capitol, Salt Lake City, UT 84114; 801-538-1041; Fax: 801-538-1133; 8AM-5PM www.governor.state.ut.us/elections

GED Certificates

State Office of Education, GED, 250 East 500 South, Salt Lake City, UT 84111; 801-538-7870; Fax: 801-538-7868; 8AM-5PM. www.usoe.k12.ut.us/adulted/ged/index.html

Hunting License Information
Fishing License Information

Utah Division of Wildlife Resources, PO Box 146301, Salt Lake City, UT 84114-6301 (1594 West North Temple, #2110, Salt Lake City, UT 84116); 801-538-4700; Fax: 801-538-4709; 8AM-5PM. Access by: mail. www.nr.state.us/dwr

County Courts & Recording Offices

About the Courts...

Administration

Court Administrator   801-578-3942
450 S State Street   Fax: 801-578-3843
Salt Lake City, UT 84114
http://courtlink.utcourts.gov

Court Structure

There are 41 District Courts in 8 judicial districts. Effective July 1, 1996, all Circuit Courts (the lower court) were combined with the District Courts (the higher court) in each county. It is reported that branch courts in larger counties such as Salt Lake which were formerly Circuit Courts have been elevated to District Courts, with full jurisdiction over felony as well as misdemeanor cases. Therefore, it may be necessary to search for felony records at more courts than prior to July 1, 1996. In written requests to District Courts, we recommend including a statement asking to "include Circuit Court cases in the search" to assure that index records from the former court are checked.

Searching Hints

A toll-free general information line is available daily from 8AM to 5PM at 888-640-COURT. Personal checks are generally accepted across the state. SASE are, generally, required across the state. Fees are set by statute as follows: Search Fee - $13.00 per hour; Certification Fee - $2.00 per document plus $.50 per page; Copy Fee - $.25 per page.

Online Access

Case index information from approximately 98% of all Utah court locations is available through XChange. Those counties not yet included as of July 1999 are Randolph, Junction, Kanob, Loa, Manilla, and Panguitch.

Fees include $25.00 registration and $30.00 per month plus $.10 per minute for usage. Information about XChange and the subscription agreement can be found on the Utah Internet site or call the Administrative Office of the Courts (AOC) at 801-578-3850.

About the Recording Offices...

Organization

29 counties 29 recording offices. The recording officers are County Recorder and Clerk of District Court (state tax liens). The entire state is in the Mountain Time Zone (MST).

UCC Records

Financing statements are filed at the state level, except for real estate related collateral, which are filed with the Register of Deeds (and at the state level in certain cases). Filing offices will not perform UCC searches. Copy fees vary. Certification usually costs $2.00 per document.

Lien Records

All federal tax liens are filed with the County Recorder. They do not perform searches. All state tax liens are filed with Clerk of District Court, many of which have on-line access. Refer to The Sourcebook of County Court Records for information about Utah District Courts.

Real Estate Records

County Recorders will not perform real estate searches. Copy fees vary, and certification fees are usually $2.00 per document.

County Courts & Recording Offices

Beaver

Real Estate Recording—Beaver County Recorder, 105 East Center, Beaver, UT 84713. Fax: 435-438-6481. 9AM-5PM.

Felony, Misdemeanor, Civil, Eviction, Small Claims, Probate—5th Judicial District Court, PO Box 1683, Beaver, UT 84713. 435-438-5309, Fax: 435-438-5395. 8AM-5PM. Access by: mail, fax, in person.

Box Elder

Real Estate Recording—Box Elder County Recorder, 1 South Main, Courthouse, Brigham City, UT 84302. Fax: 435-734-2038. 8AM-5PM.

Felony, Misdemeanor, Civil, Eviction, Small Claims, Probate—1st District Court, 43 N Main, PO Box 873, Brigham City, UT 84302. 435-734-4600, Fax: 435-734-4610. 8AM-5PM. Access by: mail, in person, online.

Cache

Real Estate Recording—Cache County Recorder, 179 North Main Street, Logan, UT 84321. Fax: 435-753-7120. 8AM-5PM.

Felony, Misdemeanor, Civil, Eviction, Small Claims, Probate—1st District Court, 140 N. 100 W. Logan, UT 84321. 435-750-1300, Fax: 435-750-1355. 8AM-5PM. Access by: mail, phone, in person, online.

Carbon

Real Estate Recording—Carbon County Recorder, Courthouse Building, 120 East Main, Price, UT 84501. Fax: 435-637-6757. 9AM-5PM.

Felony, Misdemeanor, Civil, Eviction, Small Claims, Probate—7th District Court, 149 E. 100 South, Price, UT 84501. 435-637-2150, Fax: 435-637-7349. 8AM-5PM. Access by: mail, phone, in person, online.

Daggett

Real Estate Recording—Daggett County Recorder, 95 North 1st West, Manila, UT 84046. 801-784-3154, Fax: 435-784-3335. 9AM-Noon,1-5PM.

Felony, Misdemeanor, Civil, Eviction, Probate—8th District Court, PO Box 219, Manila, UT 84046. 435-784-3154, Fax: 435-784-3335. 9AM-Noon, 1-5PM. Access by: mail, fax, in person.

Davis

Real Estate Recording—Davis County Recorder, 28 East State, Room 119, Farmington, UT 84025. 801-451-3243, Fax: 801-451-3111. 8:30AM-5PM.

Felony, Misdemeanor, Civil, Eviction, Small Claims, Probate—2nd District Court, PO Box 769, Farmington, UT 84025. 801-451-4400, Fax: 801-451-4470. 8AM-5PM. Access by: mail, phone, in person, online.

2nd District Court-Bountiful Department, 805 South Main, Bountiful, UT 84010. 801-298-6152, Fax: 801-397-7010. 8AM-5PM. Access by: mail, phone, fax, in person, online.

2nd District Court-Layton Department, 425 Wasatch Dr, Layton, UT 84041. 801-546-2484, Fax: 801-546-8224. 8AM-5PM. Access by: mail, in person, online.

Duchesne

Real Estate Recording—Duchesne County Recorder, 734 N. Center, Duchesne, UT 84021. 801-738-2435, Fax: 435-738-5522. 8:30AM-5PM.

Felony, Misdemeanor, Civil, Eviction, Small Claims, Probate—8th District Court, PO Box 990, Duchesne, UT 84021. 435-738-2753, Fax: 435-738-2754. 8AM-5PM. Access by: mail, in person, online.

Felony, Misdemeanor, Civil, Eviction, Probate—8th District Court-Roosevelt Department, PO Box 1286, Roosevelt, UT 84066.

435-722-0235, Fax: 435-722-0236. 8AM-5PM. Access by: mail, in person, online.

Emery

Real Estate Recording—Emery County Recorder, 95 East Main, Castle Dale, UT 84513. 801-381-2510, Fax: 435-381-5529. 8:30AM-5PM.

Felony, Misdemeanor, Civil, Eviction, Probate—7th District Court, PO Box 635, Castle Dale, UT 84513. 800-992-0172, Fax: 435-637-7349. 8AM-5PM. Access by: mail, phone, fax, in person, online.

Garfield

Real Estate Recording—Garfield County Recorder, 55 South Main, Panguitch, UT 84759. Fax: 435-676-8239. 9AM-Noon, 1-5PM.

Felony, Misdemeanor, Civil, Eviction, Small Claims, Probate—6th District Court, PO Box 77, Panguitch, UT 84759. 435-676-8826, Fax: 435-676-8239. 9AM-5PM. Access by: mail, fax, in person.

Grand

Real Estate Recording—Grand County Recorder, 125 East Center St. Moab, UT 84532. 801-295-1337, Fax: 435-259-2959. 8AM-5PM.

Felony, Misdemeanor, Civil, Eviction, Small Claims, Probate—7th District Court, 125 E. Center, Moab, UT 84532. 435-259-1349, Fax: 435-259-4081. 8AM-5PM. Access by: mail, phone, in person, online.

Iron

Real Estate Recording—Iron County Recorder, 68 South 100 East, Parowan, UT 84761. 8:30AM-5PM.

Felony, Misdemeanor, Civil, Eviction, Small Claims, Probate—5th District Court, 40 North 100 East, Cedar City, UT 84720. 435-586-7440, Fax: 435-586-4801. 8AM-5PM. Access by: mail, in person, online. Special note: Hearing location also in Parawon, but records held here.

Juab

Real Estate Recording—Juab County Recorder, 160 North Main, Nephi, UT 84648. 801-623-0096. 8:30AM-5PM.

Felony, Misdemeanor, Civil, Eviction, Probate—4th District Court, 160 N. Main, PO Box 249, Nephi, UT 84648. 435-623-0901, Fax: 435-623-0922. 8AM-5PM. Access by: mail, phone, in person, online.

Kane

Real Estate Recording—Kane County Recorder, 76 North Main #14, Kanab, UT 84741. 801-644-5659. 8AM-Noon, 1-5PM.

Felony, Misdemeanor, Civil, Eviction, Small Claims, Probate—6th District Court, 76 North Main, Kanab, UT 84741. 435-644-2458, Fax: 435-644-2052. 8AM-5PM. Access by: mail, phone, fax, in person.

Millard

Real Estate Recording—Millard County Recorder, 50 South Main, Fillmore, UT 84631. Fax: 435-743-4221. 8AM-5PM.

Felony, Misdemeanor, Civil, Eviction, Small Claims, Probate—4th District Court, 765 S Highway 99, #6, Fillmore, UT 84631. 435-743-6223, Fax: 435-743-6923. 8AM-5PM. Access by: mail, phone, in person, online.

Morgan

Real Estate Recording—Morgan County Recorder, 48 West Young Street, Morgan, UT 84050. 801-829-6811, Fax: 801-829-6176. 8AM-5PM.

Felony, Misdemeanor, Civil, Eviction, Small Claims, Probate—2nd District Court, PO Box 886, Morgan, UT 84050.

801-845-4020, Fax: 801-829-6176. 8AM-5PM. Access by: mail, phone, fax, in person, online.

Piute

Real Estate Recording—Piute County Recorder, Courthouse, Junction, UT 84740. Fax: 435-577-2433. 9AM-5PM.

Felony, Misdemeanor, Civil, Eviction, Small Claims, Probate—6th District Court, PO Box 99, Junction, UT 84740. 435-577-2840, Fax: 435-577-2433. 9AM-Noon, 1-5PM. Access by: mail, in person.

Rich

Real Estate Recording—Rich County Recorder, 20 South Main, Randolph, UT 84064. 801-793-5155. 9AM-Noon,1-5PM.

Felony, Misdemeanor, Civil, Eviction, Small Claims, Probate—1st District Court, PO Box 218, Randolph, UT 84064. 435-793-2415, Fax: 435-793-2410. 9AM-5PM. Access by: mail, phone, fax, in person.

Salt Lake

Real Estate Recording—Salt Lake County Recorder, 2001 South State Street, Room N-1600, Salt Lake City, UT 84190. 801-468-3404. 8AM-5PM.

Felony, Misdemeanor, Civil, Eviction, Small Claims, Probate—3rd District Court, 450 South State, Salt Lake City, UT 84111. 801-238-7300, Fax: 801-238-7404. 8AM-5PM. Access by: mail, phone, in person, online.

Felony, Misdemeanor, Civil, Eviction, Small Claims—3rd District Court-Murray Department, 5022 S. State St, Murray, UT 84107. 801-281-7700, Fax: 801-281-7736. 8AM-5PM. Access by: mail, fax, in person, online.

Felony, Misdemeanor, Civil, Eviction, Small Claims, Probate—3rd District Court-Salt Lake City, 451 South 2nd East, Salt Lake City, UT 84111. 801-238-7480, Fax: 801-238-7396. 8AM-5PM. Access by: mail, in person, online.

3rd District Court-Sandy Department, 210 West 10,000 South, Sandy, UT 84070-3282. 801-565-5714, Fax: 801-565-5703. 8AM-5PM. Access by: mail, phone, in person, online.

3rd District Court-West Valley Department, 3636 S. Constitution Blvd, West Valley, UT 84119. 801-963-8181, Fax: 801-967-9857. 8AM-5PM. Access by: mail, in person, online.

San Juan

Real Estate Recording—San Juan County Recorder, 117 South Main, Room 103, Monticello, UT 84535. 801-547-3237, Fax: 435-587-2425. 8AM-5PM.

Felony, Misdemeanor, Civil, Eviction, Probate—7th District Court, PO Box 68, Monticello, UT 84535. 435-587-2122, Fax: 435-587-2372. 8AM-5PM. Access by: mail, in person, online.

Sanpete

Real Estate Recording—Sanpete County Recorder, 160 North Main, Manti, UT 84642. 801-835-2101, Fax: 435-835-2143. 8:30AM-5PM.

Felony, Misdemeanor, Civil, Eviction, Small Claims, Probate—6th District Court, 160 N. Main, Manti, UT 84642. 435-835-2131, Fax: 435-835-2135. 8:30AM-5PM. Access by: mail, phone, fax, in person.

Sevier

Real Estate Recording—Sevier County Recorder, 250 North Main, Richfield, UT 84701. 801-896-9262, Fax: 435-896-8888. 8AM-5PM.

Felony, Misdemeanor, Civil, Eviction, Probate—6th District Court, 895 E 300 N, Richfield, UT 84701-2345. 435-896-2700, Fax: 435-896-8047. 8AM-5PM. Access by: mail, phone, fax, in person, online.

Summit

Real Estate Recording—Summit County Recorder, 54 North Main, Coalville, UT 84017. 801-336-4451, Fax: 435-336-3030. 8AM-5PM.

Felony, Misdemeanor, Civil, Eviction, Small Claims, Probate—3rd District Court, PO Box 128, Coalville, UT 84017.

435-336-4451, Fax: 435-336-3030. 8AM-5PM. Access by: mail, in person, online.

Felony, Misdemeanor, Civil Under $20,000, Eviction, Small Claims—3rd District Court-Park City Department, PO Box 1480, 455 Marsac Ave, Park City, UT 84060. 435-645-5070. 8AM-5PM. Access by: mail, in person, online.

Tooele

Real Estate Recording—Tooele County Recorder, 47 South Main Street, Courthouse, Tooele, UT 84074. 801-882-9190, Fax: 435-882-7317. 8:30AM-5PM.

Felony, Misdemeanor, Civil, Eviction, Small Claims, Probate—3rd District Court, 47 S. Main, Tooele, UT 84074. 435-842-3210, Fax: 435-882-8524. 8AM-5PM. Access by: mail, fax, in person, online.

Uintah

Real Estate Recording—Uintah County Recorder, 147 East Main St. County Building, Vernal, UT 84078. 801-781-5365, Fax: 435-781-5319. 8AM-5PM.

Felony, Misdemeanor, Civil, Eviction, Probate—8th District Court, PO Box 1015, Vernal, UT 84078. 435-789-7534, Fax: 435-789-0564. 8AM-5PM. Access by: mail, in person, online.

Utah

Real Estate Recording—Utah County Recorder, County Administration Bldg.-Room 1300, 100 East Center, Provo, UT 84606. Fax: 801-370-8181. 8:30AM-5PM.

Felony, Misdemeanor, Civil, Eviction, Small Claims, Probate—4th District Court, 125 North, 100 West, Provo, UT 84601. 801-429-1060, Fax: 801-429-1033. 8AM-5PM. Access by: mail, in person, online.

Felony, Misdemeanor, Civil, Eviction, Small Claims—4th District Court-Spanish Forks Department, 40 S Main St, Spanish Forks, UT 84660. 801-798-8674, Fax: 801-798-1377. 8AM-5PM. Access by: mail, in person, online.

Misdemeanor, Civil, Eviction, Small Claims—4th District Court-Orem Department, 97 E Center, Orem, UT 84057. 801-764-5870, Fax: 801-226-5244. 8AM-5PM. Access by: mail, in person, online.

4th District Court-American Fork Department, 98 N Center St, American Fork, UT 84003-1626. 801-756-9654, Fax: 801-763-0153. 8AM-5PM. Access by: mail, in person, online.

Wasatch

Real Estate Recording—Wasatch County Recorder, 25 North Main, Heber, UT 84032. 8AM-5PM.

Felony, Misdemeanor, Civil, Eviction, Small Claims, Probate—4th District Court, PO Box 730, Heber City, UT 84032. 435-654-4676, Fax: 435-654-5281. 8AM-5PM. Access by: mail, phone, fax, in person, online.

Washington

Real Estate Recording—Washington County Recorder, 197 East Tabernacle, St. George, UT 84770. 801-634-5711, Fax: 435-634-5718. 8AM-5PM.

Felony, Misdemeanor, Civil, Eviction, Small Claims, Probate—5th District Court, 220 North 200 East, St. George, UT 84770. 435-673-7225, Fax: 435-628-7870. 8AM-5PM. Access by: mail, in person, online.

Wayne

Real Estate Recording—Wayne County Recorder, 88 South Main, Loa, UT 84747. Fax: 435-836-2479. 8:30AM-5PM.

Felony, Misdemeanor, Civil, Eviction, Small Claims, Probate—6th District Court, PO Box 189, Loa, UT 84747. 435-836-2731, Fax: 435-836-2479. 9AM-5PM. Access by: mail, in person.

Weber

Real Estate Recording—Weber County Recorder, 2380 Washington Blvd, Suite 370, Ogden, UT 84401. 8AM-5PM.

Felony, Misdemeanor, Civil, Eviction, Small Claims, Probate—2nd District Court, 2525 Grant Ave, Ogden, UT 84401. 801-395-1081. 8AM-5PM. Access by: mail, phone, in person, online.

Felony, Misdemeanor—2nd District Court-Roy Department, 5051 South 1900 West, Roy, UT 84067. 801-774-1051, Fax: 801-774-1060. 8AM-5PM. Access by: mail, in person, online. Special note: Civil and small claims records here only prior to 01/01/90. Newer records maintained in Ogden.

Federal Courts

US District Court

Division Clerk's Office, Room 150, 350 S Main St, Salt Lake City, UT 84101801-524-6100 Fax: 801-526-1175 Counties: All counties in Utah. Although all cases are heard here, the district is divided into Northern and Central Divisions. The Northern Division includes the counties of Box Elder, Cache, Rich, Davis, Morgan and Weber, and the Central Division includes allother counties. www.utd.uscourts.gov

US Bankruptcy Court

Division Clerk of Court, Frank E Moss Courthouse, 350 S Main St, Room 301, Salt Lake City, UT 84101801-524-5157 Fax: 801-524-4409 Counties: All counties in Utah. Although all cases are handled here, the court divides itself into two divisions. The Northern Division includes the counties of Box Elder, Cache, Rich, Davis, Morgan and Weber, and the Central Division includes the remainingcounties. Court is held once per week in Ogden for Northern cases.. www.utb.uscourts.gov

Vermont

Attorney General's Office
109 State St   802-828-3171
Montpelier, VT 05609-1001   Fax: 802-828-2154
www.state.vt.us/atg

Governor's Office
109 State St   802-828-3333
Montpelier, VT 05609   Fax: 802-828-3339
www.state.vt.us/governor/index.htm

State Archives
26 Terrace-Redstone Bldg   802-828-2308
Montpelier, VT 05609-1103   Fax: 802-828-2496
www.sec.state.vt.us/archives/archdex.htm

Capital:	Montpelier
	Washington County
Time Zone:	EST
Number of Counties:	14
Population:	588,978
Web Site:	www.state.vt.us

Search Unclaimed Property Online
www.state.vt.us/treasurer/ abanprop.htm#_HOW_TO_LOOK

State Agencies

Criminal Records
Restricted access.
State Repository, Vermont Criminal Information Center, 103 S. Main St., Waterbury, VT 05671-2101; 802-244-8727; Fax: 802-244-1106; 8AM-4:30PM

Corporation Records
Limited Liability Company Records
Limited Liability Partnerships
Limited Partnerships
Trademarks/Servicemarks
Secretary of State, Corporation Division, 109 State St, Montpelier, VT 05609-1101 (81 River St, Heritage Bldg, Montpelier, VT 05602); 802-828-2386; Fax: 802-828-2853; 7:45AM-4:30PM. Access by: mail, phone, in person, online. sec.state.vt.us/soshome.htm

Sales Tax Registrations
Administrative Agency/Tax Department, Business Tax Division, 109 State St, Montpelier, VT 05609-1401; 802-828-2551; Fax: 802-828-5787; 7:45AM-4:30PM. Access by: mail, phone, in person.

Uniform Commercial Code
UCC Division, Secretary of State, 109 State St, Montpelier, VT 05609-1101 (81 River St, Heritage One, Montpelier, VT 05602); 802-828-2386; Fax: 802-828-2853; 7:45AM-4:30PM. Access by: mail, online. sec.state.vt.us/seek/ucc_seek.htm

Federal Tax Liens
State Tax Liens
Records not available from state agency.

Records are found at the local town level.

Workers' Compensation Records
Labor and Industry, Workers Compensation Division, Drawer 20, Montpelier, VT 05620-3401 (National Life Bldg, Montpelier, VT 05620); 802-828-2286; Fax: 802-828-2195; 7:45AM-4:30PM.

Access by: mail, phone, in person. state.vt.us/labind/workers.htm

Birth Certificates

Reference & Research, Vital Records Section, US Rte 2, Drawer 33, Montpelier, VT 05633-7601; 802-828-3286; 8AM-4:15PM. Access by: mail, phone, in person.

Death Records

Reference & Research, Vital Records, US Rte 2, Drawer 33, Montpelier, VT 05633-7601; 802-828-3286; 8AM-4:15PM. Access by: mail, phone, in person.

Marriage Certificates

Reference & Research, Vital Records Section, US Rte 2, Drawer 33, Montpelier, VT 05633-7601; 802-828-3286; 8AM-4:15PM. Access by: mail.

Divorce Records

Research & Reference, Vital Records Section, US Rte 2, Drawer 33, Montpelier, VT 05633-7601; 802-828-3286; 8AM-4:15PM. Access by: mail.

Driver Records
Driver License Information

Department of Motor Vehicles, DI - Records Unit, 120 State St, Montpelier, VT 05603; 802-828-2050; Fax: 802-828-2098; 7:45AM-4:30PM. Access by: mail, online. www.aot.state.vt.us/dmv/dmvhp.htm

Vehicle Ownership
Vehicle Identification
Boat & Vessel Ownership
Boat & Vessel Registration

Department of Motor Vehicles, Registration & License Information/Records, 120 State St, Montpelier, VT 05603; 802-

828-2000; 7:45AM-4:30PM. Access by: mail. www.aot.state.vt.us/dmv/dmvhp.htm

Accident Reports

Department of Motor Vehicles, Accident Report Section, 120 State St, Montpelier, VT 05603; 802-828-2050; 7:45AM-4PM. Access by: mail.

Legislation-Current/Pending
Legislation-Passed

Vermont General Assembly, State House-Legislative Council, 115 State Street, Drawer 33, Montpelier, VT 05633; 802-828-2231; Fax: 802-828-2424; 8AM-4:30PM. Access by: mail, phone, in person, online. www.leg.state.vt.us

Voter Registration

Records not available from state agency.

There is no statewide database. All records are kept at the municipal level.

GED Certificates

Department of Education, GED Testing, 120 State Street, Montpelier, VT 05620; 802-828-5161; Fax: 802-828-3146; 8AM-4:30PM.

Hunting License Information
Fishing License Information

Records not available from state agency.

They do maintain a central database on computer. Vendors forward records on a yearly basis (July).

County Courts & Recording Offices

About the Courts...

Administration

Administrative Office of Courts,
Court Administrator   802-828-3278
109 State St   Fax: 802-828-3457
Montpelier, VT 05609-0701
www.state.vt.us/courts

Court Structure

As of September, 1996, all small claims came under the jurisdiction of Superior Court, the court of general jurisdiction.. All counties have a diversion program in which 1st offenders go through a process that includes a letter of apology, community service, etc. and, after 2 years, the record is expunged. These records are never released.

There is one Probate Court per county except in the four southern counties (Bennington, Rutland, Windsor, and Windham) which have two each.

Searching Hints

There are statewide certification and copy fees, as follows: Certification Fee - $5.00 per document plus copy fee; Copy Fee - $.25 per page with a $1.00 minimum.

Online Access

There is no online computer access to the public; however, some courts offer calendar data over the Internet.

About the Recording Offices...

Organization

14 counties and 246 towns/cities, 246 recording offices. The recording officer is Town/City Clerk. There is no county administration in Vermont. Many towns are so small that their mailing addresses are in different towns. Four towns/cities have the same name as counties - Barre, Newport, Rutland, and St. Albans. The entire state is in the Eastern Time Zone (EST).

UCC Records

This has been a dual filing state until December 31, 1994. As of January 1, 1995, only consumer goods and real estate related collateral are filed with Town/City Clerks. Most recording offices will perform UCC searches. Use search request form UCC-11. Search fees are usually $10.00 per name, and copy fees vary.

Lien Records

All federal and state tax liens on personal property and on real property are filed with the Town/City Clerk in the lien/attachment book and indexed in real estate records. Most towns/cities will not perform tax lien searches.

Real Estate Records

Most towns/cities will not perform real estate searches. Copy fees and certification fees vary. Certified copies are generally very expensive at $6.00 per page total. Deed copies usually cost $2.00 flat.

County Courts & Recording Offices

Addison

Real Estate Recording—Addison Town Clerk, 65 Route 17 West, Addison, VT 5491. Fax: 802-759-2233. 8:30AM-Noon, 1-4:30PM.

Civil, Eviction, Small Claims—Superior Court, 7 Mahady Ct, Middlebury, VT 05753. 802-388-7741. 8:30AM-4:30PM. Access by: mail, in person.

Felony, Misdemeanor—District Court, 7 Mahady Ct, Middlebury, VT 05753. 802-388-4237. 8AM-4:30PM. Access by: mail, phone, in person.

Probate—Probate Court, 7 Mahady Court, Middlebury, VT 05753. 802-388-2612. 8AM-4:30PM.

Albany

Real Estate Recording—Albany Town Clerk, Main St. Albany, VT 5820. 9AM-4PM T,Th; 9AM-7PM W.

Alburg

Real Estate Recording—Alburg Town Clerk, Main Street, Alburg, VT 5440. Fax: 802-796-3939. 9AM-Noon,1-5PM.

Andover

Real Estate Recording—Andover Town Clerk, 953 Weston-Andover Rd. Andover, VT 5143. Fax: 802-875-6647. 9AM-1PM.

Arlington

Real Estate Recording—Arlington Town Clerk, Main Street, Town Hall, Arlington, VT 5250. 802-375-1260, Fax: 802-375-6474. 9AM-2PM.

Athens

Real Estate Recording—Athens Town Clerk, 56 Brookline Rd. Athens, VT 5143. 9AM-1PM or By Appointment.

Bakersfield

Real Estate Recording—Bakersfield Town Clerk, Town Road 3, Bakersfield, VT 5441. Fax: 802-527-4495. 9AM-Noon.

Baltimore

Real Estate Recording—Baltimore Town Clerk, 49 Harris Rd. Baltimore, VT 5143. Fax: 802-263-9423. By Appointmment Evenings M-F; 10AM-Noon Sat.

Barnard

Real Estate Recording—Barnard Town Clerk, North Rd. Barnard, VT 5031. 8AM-3:30PM M-W.

Barnet

Real Estate Recording—Barnet Town Clerk, US Route 5, Main Street, Barnet, VT 5821. Fax: 802-633-4315. 9AM-Noon, 1-4:30PM.

Barre

Real Estate Recording—Barre City Clerk, 12 North Main Street, Barre, VT 5641. Fax: 802-476-0264. 8:30AM-5PM.

Barre Town Clerk, Municipal Building, 149 Websterville Road, Websterville, VT 5678. Fax: 802-479-9332. 8AM-Noon, 1-4:30PM.

Barton

Real Estate Recording—Barton Town Clerk, 34 Main St. Barton, VT 5822. Fax: 802-525-8856. 8:30AM-5PM.

Belvidere

Real Estate Recording—Belvidere Town Clerk, RR 1, Box 1062, Belvidere Center, VT 5492.

Bennington

Real Estate Recording—Bennington Town Clerk, 205 South Street, Bennington, VT 5201. Fax: 802-442-1068. 8AM-5PM.

Civil, Eviction, Small Claims—Superior Court, 207 South St, PO Box 4157, Bennington, VT 05201. 802-447-2700, Fax: 802-447-2703. 8AM-4:30PM. Access by: mail, phone, in person.

Felony, Misdemeanor—District Court, 1 Veterans Memorial Dr, Bennington, VT 05201. 802-447-2727, Fax: 802-447-2750. 7:45AM-4:30PM. Access by: mail, phone, in person.

Probate—Probate Court-Bennington District, 207 South St, PO Box 65, Bennington, VT 05201. 802-447-2705, Fax: 802-447-2703. 9AM-Noon, 1:30-4PM. Access by: mail, in person.

Probate Court-Manchester District, PO Box 446, Manchester, VT 05254. 802-362-1410. 8AM-Noon, 1-4:20PM.

Benson

Real Estate Recording—Benson Town Clerk, Stage Street, Benson, VT 5731. Fax: 802-537-2611. 9AM-4:30PM M-Th; Closed F.

Berkshire

Real Estate Recording—Berkshire Town Clerk, RFD 1, Box 2560, Enosburg Falls, VT 5450. 9AM-Noon, 1-4PM M,T,Th,F; 9AM-Noon W.

Berlin

Real Estate Recording—Berlin Town Clerk, 108 Shed Rd. Berlin, VT 5602. 8:30AM-Noon,1-4:30PM (July-August 8:30AM-Noon, 1-3:30PM).

Bethel

Real Estate Recording—Bethel Town Clerk, South Main Street, Town Office, Bethel, VT 5032. Fax: 802-234-6840. 8AM-Noon T,F; 8AM-12:30, 1-4PM M,Th.

Bloomfield

Real Estate Recording—Bloomfield Town Clerk, 3399 VT Route 102, No. Stratford, NH, VT 5905. Fax: 802-962-5548. 9AM-3PM T or by appointment.

Bolton

Real Estate Recording—Bolton Town Clerk, 3045 Theodore Roosevelt Hwy, Waterbury, VT 5676. 802-434-5075, Fax: 802-434-6404. 7AM-3PM M-Th; 7AM-Noon F.

Bradford

Real Estate Recording—Bradford Town Clerk, Main Street, Bradford, VT 5033. Fax: 802-222-4728. 8:30AM-4:30PM.

Braintree

Real Estate Recording—Braintree Town Clerk, 932 VT Route 12A, Randolph, VT 5060. M 9AM-4:30PM; W 1:30-4:30PM; F 9AM-Noon.

Brandon

Real Estate Recording—Brandon Town Clerk, 49 Center Street, Brandon, VT 5733. Fax: 802-247-5481. 8:30AM-4PM.

Brattleboro

Real Estate Recording—Brattleboro Town Clerk, 230 Main Street, Brattleboro, VT 5301. Fax: 802-257-2312. 8:30AM-5PM.

Bridgewater

Real Estate Recording—Bridgewater Town Clerk, Route 4, Clerk's Office, Bridgewater, VT 5034. Fax: 802-672-5395. 8:30AM-2PM.

Bridport

Real Estate Recording—Bridport Town Clerk, Town Hall, Bridport, VT 5734. 8AM-4PM M-W,F; 8AM-Noon Th; Treasurer 9AM-4PM F.

Brighton

Real Estate Recording—Brighton Town Clerk, Main Street, Town Hall, Island Pond, VT 5846. Fax: 802-723-4405. 8AM-3:30PM M,T,W,F; 8AM-6PM Th.

Bristol

Real Estate Recording—Bristol Town Clerk, 1 South Street, Bristol, VT 5443. Fax: 802-843-3127. 8:30AM-4PM.

Brookfield

Real Estate Recording—Brookfield Town Clerk, Ralph Rd. Brookfield, VT 5036. 802-728-3391, Fax: 802-276-3926. 8:30AM-4:30PM M,T,F.

Brookline

Real Estate Recording—Brookline Town Clerk, PO Box 403, Brookline, VT 5345. 9AM-3PM M.

Brownington

Real Estate Recording—Brownington Town Clerk, 509 Dutton Brook Ln, Orleans, VT 5860. 802-754-6326, Fax: 802-754-8401. 1PM-3:30PM W; 9AM-Noon Th.

Brunswick

Real Estate Recording—Brunswick Town Clerk, Route 102, RFD 1, Box 470, Guildhall, VT 5905. M-Sat by appointment.

Burke

Real Estate Recording—Burke Town Clerk, Town Office, 212 School St. West Burke, VT 5871. Fax: 802-467-8623. 8AM-5PM M; 8AM-4PM T-F.

Burlington

Real Estate Recording—Burlington Clerk/Treasurer's Office, City Hall, Room 20, 149 Church St. Burlington, VT 5401. Fax: 802-865-7014. 8AM-7:30PM M; 8AM-4:30PM T-F.

Cabot

Real Estate Recording—Cabot Town Clerk, Main Street, Town Hall, Cabot, VT 5647. Fax: 802-563-2423. M 9-6; Tu 9-5; W 12-5; Th 9-5; F 9-1.

Calais

Real Estate Recording—Calais Town Clerk, 668 West County Rd. Calais, VT 5648. 8AM-5PM M,T,Th; 8AM-Noon Sat.

Caledonia

Civil, Eviction, Small Claims—Superior Court, Box 4129, St Johnsbury, VT 05819. 802-748-6600, Fax: 802-748-6603. 8AM-4:30PM. Access by: mail, phone, fax, in person.

Felony, Misdemeanor—District Court, 2176 Portland St, St Johnsbury, VT 05819. 802-748-6610, Fax: 802-748-6603. 8AM-4:30PM. Access by: mail, fax, in person. Special note: This is a temporary address, prior was 27 Main St.

Probate—Probate Court, 27 Main St, PO Box 406, St Johnsbury, VT 05819. 802-748-6605, Fax: 802-748-6603. 8AM-4:30PM. Access by: mail, in person.

Cambridge

Real Estate Recording—Cambridge Town Clerk, Clerk's Office, Jeffersonville, VT 5464. Fax: 802-644-8348. 8AM-Noon,1-4PM.

Canaan

Real Estate Recording—Canaan Town Clerk, 318 Christian Hill, Town Hall, Canaan, VT 5903. Fax: 802-266-7085. 9AM-3PM.

Castleton

Real Estate Recording—Castleton Town Clerk, Main Street, Town Hall, Castleton, VT 5735. 802-468-5319, Fax: 802-468-5482. 8:30AM-Noon, 1-4PM.

Cavendish

Real Estate Recording—Cavendish Town Clerk, High Street, Town Hall, Cavendish, VT 5142. Fax: 802-226-7790. 9AM-Noon, 1-4:30PM.

Charleston

Real Estate Recording—Charleston Town Clerk, Route 105, Town Hall, West Charleston, VT 5872. Fax: 802-895-2814. 8AM-3PM M,T,Th,F.

Charlotte

Real Estate Recording—Charlotte Town Clerk, 159 Ferry Road, Charlotte, VT 5445. Fax: 802-425-4241. 8AM-4PM.

Chelsea

Real Estate Recording—Chelsea Town Clerk, Main Street, Town Hall, Chelsea, VT 5038. 8AM-Noon, 1-4PM.

Chester

Real Estate Recording—Chester Town Clerk, Town Hall, 556 Elm St. Chester, VT 5143. Fax: 802-875-2237. 8AM-5PM.

Chittenden

Real Estate Recording—Chittenden Town Clerk, Holden Road, Town Hall, Chittenden, VT 5737. 10AM-2PM.

Civil, Eviction, Small Claims—Superior Court, 175 Main St.(PO Box 187), Burlington, VT 05402. 802-863-3467. 8AM-4:30PM. Access by: mail, phone, in person.

Felony, Misdemeanor—District Court, 32 Cherry St #300, Burlington, VT 05401. 802-651-1800. 8AM-4:30PM. Access by: mail, in person.

Probate—Probate Court, PO Box 511, Burlington, VT 05402. 802-651-1518. 8AM-4:30PM.

Clarendon

Real Estate Recording—Clarendon Town Clerk, Middle Road, North Clarendon, VT 5759. Fax: 802-775-4274. 10AM-4PM M,T; 10AM-3PM W,F.

Colchester

Real Estate Recording—Colchester Town Clerk, 172 Blakely Road, Colchester, VT 5446. Fax: 802-654-0757. 8AM-4PM.

Concord

Real Estate Recording—Concord Town Clerk, 374 Main St. Concord, VT 5824. Fax: 802-695-2220. 9AM-Noon,1-4PM (Closed Th); 9AM-7PM 1st & 3rd M.

Corinth

Real Estate Recording—Corinth Town Clerk, Cookeville Road, Town Hall, Corinth, VT 5039. Fax: 802-439-5850. 8:30AM-3PM M,T,Th,F.

Cornwall

Real Estate Recording—Cornwall Town Clerk, 2629 Route 30, Cornwall, VT 5753. Fax: 802-462-2606. 12:30PM-4:30PM T,W,Th,F.

Coventry

Real Estate Recording—Coventry Town Clerk, Coventry Community Center, Coventry, VT 5825. Fax: 802-754-2288. 9:30AM-4PM M,Th.

Craftsbury

Real Estate Recording—Craftsbury Town Clerk, Main Street, Town Hall, Craftsbury, VT 5826. Fax: 802-586-2823. 8:30AM-4PM T-F.

Danby

Real Estate Recording—Danby Town Clerk, Brook Road, Danby, VT 5739. Fax: 802-293-5311. 9AM-Noon, 1-4PM M-Th.

Danville

Real Estate Recording—Danville Town Clerk, Town Hall, 36 Rte 2 West, Danville, VT 5828. Fax: 802-684-9606. 8:30AM-4:30PM.

Derby

Real Estate Recording—Derby Town Clerk, 124 Main Street, Town Hall, Derby, VT 5829. Fax: 802-766-2027. 8AM-4PM.

Dorset

Real Estate Recording—Dorset Town Clerk, Mad Tom Road, Town Hall, East Dorset, VT 5253. Fax: 802-362-5156. 9AM-2PM (& by appointment).

Dover

Real Estate Recording—Dover Town Clerk, Route 100 North, Town Clerk's Office, Dover, VT 5356. Fax: 802-464-8721. 9AM-5PM.

Dummerston

Real Estate Recording—Dummerston Town Clerk, 1523 Middle Rd. Dummerston, VT 5346. Fax: 802-257-4671. 9AM-3PM M,T,Th,F; 11AM-5PM W.

Duxbury

Real Estate Recording—Duxbury Town Clerk, 3316 Crossett Hill, Waterbury, VT 5676. 8AM-5PM M-Th.

East Haven

Real Estate Recording—East Haven Town Clerk, 17 Maple St. East Haven, VT 5837. 3-7PM T; 8AM-Noon Th.

East Montpelier

Real Estate Recording—East Montpelier Town Clerk, Kelton Road, Town Municipal Building, East Montpelier, VT 5651. 9AM-5PM M-Th; 9AM-Noon F.

Eden

Real Estate Recording—Eden Town Clerk, 71 Old Schoolhouse Rd. Eden Mills, VT 5653. Fax: 802-635-1724. 8AM-Noon, 1-4PM M-Th.

Elmore

Real Estate Recording—Elmore Town Clerk, Town Hall, Towm Clerk's Office, Lake Elmore, VT 5657. 9AM-3PM T,W,Th.

Enosburg

Real Estate Recording—Enosburg Town Clerk, 239 Main Street, Enosburg Falls, VT 5450. Fax: 802-933-4832. 9AM-Noon,1-4PM.

Essex

Real Estate Recording—Essex Town Clerk, 81 Main Street, Essex Junction, VT 5452. Fax: 802-878-1353. 8AM-4:30PM.

Felony, Misdemeanor, Civil, Eviction, Small Claims—District and Superior Court, Box 75, Guildhall, VT 05905. 802-676-3910, Fax: 802-676-3463. 8AM-4:30PM. Access by: mail, phone, fax, in person.

Probate—Probate Court, PO Box 426, Island Pond, VT 05846. 802-723-4770. 8:30AM-Noon, 1-3:30PM.

Fair Haven

Real Estate Recording—Fair Haven Town Clerk, 3 North Park Place, Fair Haven, VT 5743. 802-265-3010, Fax: 802-265-2158. 8AM-Noon, 1PM-4PM.

Fairfax

Real Estate Recording—Fairfax Town Clerk, 67 Hunt Street, Town Office, Fairfax, VT 5454. 9AM-4PM.

Fairfield

Real Estate Recording—Fairfield Town Clerk, Town Hall, Fairfield, VT 5455. 10AM-2PM.

Fairlee

Real Estate Recording—Fairlee Town Clerk, Main Street, Fairlee, VT 5045. Fax: 802-333-9214. 9AM-2PM M,T,Th,F; 1-6PM W.

Fayston

Real Estate Recording—Fayston Town Clerk, 866 N. Fayston Rd. No. Fayston, VT 5660. 9AM-Noon, 12:30-3:30PM.

Ferrisburgh

Real Estate Recording—Ferrisburgh Town Clerk, Route 7, Town Hall, Ferrisburgh, VT 5456. Fax: 802-877-6757. 8AM-4PM; Summer Hours: 7:30AM-3:30PM.

Fletcher

Real Estate Recording—Fletcher Town Clerk, Town Office, Cambridge, VT 5444. Fax: 802-849-2500. 9AM-3:30PM M,T,Th,F; 9AM-Noon W.

Franklin

Real Estate Recording—Franklin Town Clerk, Haston Library, Franklin, VT 5457. 9AM-4PM M,T,F; 9AM-7PM Th; 9AM-Noon W.

Civil, Eviction, Small Claims—Superior Court, Box 808 Church St, St Albans, VT 05478. 802-524-3863, Fax: 802-524-7996. 8AM-4:30PM. Access by: mail, phone, fax, in person.

Felony, Misdemeanor—District Court, 36 Lake St, St Albans, VT 05478. 802-524-7997, Fax: 802-524-7946. 8AM-4:30PM. Access by: mail, phone, fax, in person.

Probate—Franklin Probate Court, 17 Church St, St Albans, VT 05478. 802-524-4112. 8AM-Noon, 1-4:30PM. Access by: in person.

Georgia

Real Estate Recording—Georgia Town Clerk, Route 7, Town Hall, St. Albans, VT 5478. Fax: 802-524-9794. 11AM-5PM, 7-9PM M; 8AM-4PMT,Th,F; Closed to public Wed.

Glover

Real Estate Recording—Glover Town Clerk, 51 Bean Hill, Glover, VT 5839. Fax: 802-525-6227. 8AM-4PM.

Goshen

Real Estate Recording—Goshen Town Clerk, 50 Carlisle Hill Rd. Goshen, VT 5733. 9-11AM T & Th.

Grafton

Real Estate Recording—Grafton Town Clerk, Main Street, Grafton, VT 5146. 9AM-Noon, 1-5PM M,T,Th,F.

Granby

Real Estate Recording—Granby Town Clerk, 9005 Granby Road, Granby, VT 5840. Fax: 802-328-3611. By appointment.

Grand Isle

Real Estate Recording—Grand Isle Town Clerk, 9 Hyde Road, Grand Isle, VT 5458. Fax: 802-372-8815. 8:30AM-Noon, 1-4:30PM.

Felony, Misdemeanor, Civil, Eviction, Small Claims—District and Superior Court, PO Box 7, North Hero, VT 05474. 802-372-8350, Fax: 802-372-3221. 8AM-4:30PM. Access by: mail, phone, fax, in person.

Probate—Probate Court, PO Box 7, North Hero, VT 05474. 802-372-8350, Fax: 802-372-3221. 8AM-4:30PM.

Granville

Real Estate Recording—Granville Town Clerk, Route 100, Granville, VT 5747. 9AM-3PM M-Th (Closed F).

Greensboro

Real Estate Recording—Greensboro Town Clerk, Town Hall, Greensboro, VT 5841. 8:30AM-Noon, 1-4PM T-F.

Groton

Real Estate Recording—Groton Town Clerk, 314 Scott Highway, Groton, VT 5046. Fax: 802-584-3276. 7:30AM-Noon, 1-3:30PM M-Th; 7:30-11:30AM F.

Guildhall

Real Estate Recording—Guildhall Town Clerk, Route 102, Guildhall, VT 5905. Fax: 802-676-3518. 1-3PM T,Th.

Guilford

Real Estate Recording—Guilford Town Clerk, 236 School Rd. Guilford, VT 5301. Fax: 802-257-5764. 9AM-4PM M,T,Th,F; 9AM-Noon, 6:30PM-8:30PM W.

Halifax

Real Estate Recording—Halifax Town Clerk, 246 Branch Rd. West Halifax, VT 5358. 9AM-4PM M,T,F; 9AM-Noon Sat.

Hancock

Real Estate Recording—Hancock Town Clerk, 48 Rt 125, Hancock, VT 5748. 8:30AM-3:30PM W,Th; 8:30AM-5PM T; Closed Fri.

Hardwick

Real Estate Recording—Hardwick Town Clerk, 2 Church Street, Hardwick, VT 5843. Fax: 802-472-6865. 9AM-4PM T-F.

Hartford

Real Estate Recording—Hartford Town Clerk, 15 Bridge Street, White River Junction, VT 5001. 8AM-Noon, 1-5PM.

Hartland

Real Estate Recording—Hartland Town Clerk, 5 Queechee Rd. Hartland, VT 5048. Fax: 802-436-2444. 8AM-4PM.

Highgate

Real Estate Recording—Highgate Town Clerk, Municipal Building, Route 78, Highgate Center, VT 5459. 8:30AM-12, 1PM-4:30PM.

Hinesburg

Real Estate Recording—Hinesburg Town Clerk, Main Street, Town Hall, Hinesburg, VT 5461. Fax: 802-482-5404. Noon-8PM M; 8AM-4PM T-F.

Holland

Real Estate Recording—Holland Town Clerk, 120 School Rd. Derby Line, VT 5830. Fax: 802-895-4440. 8AM-3PM M,T,Th,F.

Hubbardton

Real Estate Recording—Hubbardton Town Clerk, RR 1, Box 2828, Fair Haven, VT 5743. 9AM-2PM M,W,F.

Huntington

Real Estate Recording—Huntington Town Clerk, 4930 Main Rd. Huntington, VT 5462. 9AM-4PM M,T,W,Th; 8:30AM-2PM F.

Hyde Park

Real Estate Recording—Hyde Park Town Clerk, 344 VT 15 West, Hyde Park Town Clerk's Office, Hyde Park, VT 5655. Fax: 802-888-6878. 8AM-4PM.

Ira

Real Estate Recording—Ira Town Clerk, 808 Route 133, West Rutland, VT 5777. 9AM-2:30PM M; 2-7PM T.

Irasburg

Real Estate Recording—Irasburg Town Clerk, Route 58, Irasburg, VT 5845. 9AM-Noon, 1-4PM M,T,Th,F.

Isle La Motte

Real Estate Recording—Isle La Motte Town Clerk, Rt 129, Town Hall, Isle La Motte, VT 5463. Fax: 802-928-3002. 9AM-3PM T,Th; 9AM-Noon Sat.

Jamaica

Real Estate Recording—Jamaica Town Clerk, White Building behind J.A.Muzzy, in center of Jamaica Village, Jamaica, VT 5343. 9AM-Noon, 1-4PM T,W,Th,F.

Jay

Real Estate Recording—Jay Town Clerk, RFD 2, Box 136, Jay, VT 5859. 7AM-4PM (Closed M).

Jericho

Real Estate Recording—Jericho Town Clerk, 67 VT Route 15, Jericho, VT 5465. Fax: 802-899-5549. 8AM-5PM M-Th; 8AM-3PM F.

Johnson

Real Estate Recording—Johnson Town Clerk, 93 Pearl Street, Johnson, VT 5656. Fax: 802-635-9523. 7:30AM-4PM.

Kirby

Real Estate Recording—Kirby Town Clerk, Town of Kirby, 346 Town Hall Rd. Lyndonville, VT 5851. Fax: 802-626-9386. 8AM-3PM T,Th.

Lamoille

Civil, Eviction, Small Claims—Superior Court, Box 490, Hyde Park, VT 05655. 802-888-2207. 8AM-4:30PM. Access by: mail, in person.

Felony, Misdemeanor—District Court, PO Box 489, Hyde Park, VT 05655-0489. 802-888-3887, Fax: 802-888-2531. 8AM-4:30PM. Access by: mail, fax, in person.

Probate—Probate Court, PO Box 102, Hyde Park, VT 05655-0102. 802-888-3306, Fax: 802-888-1347. 8AM-12:30, 1-4:30PM.

Landgrove

Real Estate Recording—Landgrove Town Clerk, Casey Henson, Red Pine Dr.-End of Landgrove Hollow Rd, Londonderry, VT 5148. Fax: 802-824-3716. 9AM-Noon Th.

Leicester

Real Estate Recording—Leicester Town Clerk, 44 Schoolhouse Rd. Leicester, VT 5733. 1-4PM M-W; 9AM-1PM Th,F.

Lemington

Real Estate Recording—Lemington Town Clerk, 2549 RIver Rd. VT 102, Lemington, VT 5903. Noon-3PM W.

Lincoln

Real Estate Recording—Lincoln Town Clerk, 62 Quaker St. Lincoln, VT 5443. Fax: 802-453-2975. 9AM-4PM M,T,Th,F; 9AM-Noon Sat.

Londonderry

Real Estate Recording—Londonderry Town Clerk, Old School St. South Londonderry, VT 5155. 9AM-3PM T-F; 9AM-12 Sat.

Lowell

Real Estate Recording—Lowell Town Clerk, 2170 Rt. 100, Lowell, VT 5847. Fax: 802-744-2357. 9AM-2:30PM M & Th.

Ludlow

Real Estate Recording—Ludlow Town Clerk, 37 Depot Street, Ludlow, VT 5149. Fax: 802-228-2813. 8:30AM-4:30PM.

Lunenburg

Real Estate Recording—Lunenburg Town Clerk, Box 54 Main St. Lunenburg, VT 5906. 8:30AM-Noon, 1-4PM.

Lyndon

Real Estate Recording—Lyndon Town Clerk, 20 Park Avenue, Lyndonville, VT 5851. Fax: 802-626-1265. 7:30AM-4:30PM.

Maidstone

Real Estate Recording—Maidstone Town Clerk, 1174 State Rt. 102, Maidstone, VT 5905. 802-676-3950, Fax: 802-676-3210. 9-11AM M & Th.

Manchester

Real Estate Recording—Manchester Town Clerk, 6039 Main St. Manchester Center, VT 5255. Fax: 802-362-1315. 9AM-4 W-F; By Appointment M & T.

Marlboro

Real Estate Recording—Marlboro Town Clerk, Town Office, Marlboro, VT 5344. 9AM-2PM M,W,Th.

Marshfield

Real Estate Recording—Marshfield Town Clerk, 122 School St. Room 1, Marshfield, VT 5658. Fax: 802-426-3045. 8:30AM-Noon, 12:30-4:30PM T-F.

Mendon

Real Estate Recording—Mendon Town Clerk, 34 US Route 4, Rutland, VT 5701. Fax: 802-747-4592. 9AM-3PM.

Middlebury

Real Estate Recording—Middlebury Town Clerk, Municipal Building, 94 Main St. Middlebury, VT 5753. 8:30AM-5PM.

Middlesex

Real Estate Recording—Middlesex Town Clerk, 5 Church St. Middlesex, VT 5602. Fax: 802-223-0569. 8:30AM-Noon, 1-4:30PM M-Th.

Middletown Springs

Real Estate Recording—Middletown Springs Town Clerk, 10 Park Street, Middletown Springs, VT 5757. 1-4PM M,T,F; 9AM-Noon Sat.

Milton

Real Estate Recording—Milton Town Clerk, 43 Bombardier Rd. Milton, VT 5468. Fax: 802-893-1005. 8AM-5PM.

Monkton

Real Estate Recording—Monkton Town Clerk, RR 1, Box 2015, North Ferrisburg, VT 5473. 8AM-2PM M,T,Th,F; 8:30AM-Noon Sat.

Montgomery

Real Estate Recording—Montgomery Town Clerk, 3 Main Street, Montgomery Center, VT 5471. Fax: 802-326-4939. 9AM-Noon, 1-4PM M,T,Th,F; 9AM-Noon W.

Montpelier

Real Estate Recording—Montpelier City Clerk, 39 Main Street, City Hall, Montpelier, VT 5602. Fax: 802-223-9518. 8AM-4:30PM.

Moretown

Real Estate Recording—Moretown Town Clerk, Route 100B, Moretown, VT 5660. 9AM-4:30PM.

Morgan

Real Estate Recording—Morgan Town Clerk, Town Clerk Rd. Morgan, VT 5853. 9AM-Noon, 1-4PM M,T,Th,F.

Morristown

Real Estate Recording—Morristown Town Clerk, 18 Lower Main St. Morrisville, VT 5661. Fax: 802-888-6375. 8:30AM-4:30PM M,T,Th,F; 8:30AM-12:30PM W.

Mount Holly

Real Estate Recording—Mount Holly Town Clerk, 50 School Street, Mount Holly, VT 5758. Fax: 802-259-2391. 8:15AM-4PM M-Th; Closed Fri.

Mount Tabor

Real Estate Recording—Mount Tabor Town Clerk, Brooklyn Rd. Town Office, Mt. Tabor, VT 5739. 802-293-5589, Fax: 802-293-5287. 8AM-Noon, 1-4:30PM T; 8AM-Noon, 1-5PM W.

New Haven

Real Estate Recording—New Haven Town Clerk, 78 North St. New Haven, VT 5472. 9AM-3PM M,T,Th,F; 9AM-Noon W.

Newark

Real Estate Recording—Newark Town Clerk, RFD 1, Box 50C, West Burke, VT 5871. 9AM-4PM M,W,Th.

Newbury

Real Estate Recording—Newbury Town Clerk, Main St. Newbury, VT 5051. 7AM-1PM.

Newfane

Real Estate Recording—Newfane Town Clerk, 555 VT Rte. 30, Newfane, VT 5345. Fax: 802-365-7692. 9AM-1PM M; 9AM-3PM T-F; 9AM-Noon Sat.

Newport

Real Estate Recording—Newport City Clerk, 222 Main Street, Newport, VT 5855. Fax: 802-334-5632. 8AM-4:30PM.

Newport Town Clerk, Vance Hill, Newport Center, VT 5857. Fax: 802-334-6442. 9AM-5PM M,T,Th,F; 9AM-Noon W.

North Hero

Real Estate Recording—North Hero Town Clerk, 3549 US Rte. 2, North Hero, VT 5474. Fax: 802-372-3806. 9AM-3PM M-F; Sat 9AM-Noon.

Northfield

Real Estate Recording—Northfield Town Clerk, 51 South Main Street, Northfield, VT 5663. 802-485-5431, Fax: 802-485-8426. 8AM-4:30PM.

Norton

Real Estate Recording—Norton Town Clerk, 347 Nelson Rd. Norton, VT 5907. 9AM-5PM M,T,Th; 9AM-Noon F,Sat.

Norwich

Real Estate Recording—Norwich Town Clerk, 300 Main St. Norwich, VT 5055. Fax: 802-649-0123. 8:30AM-4:30PM M-F; 10AM-Noon Sat.

Orange

Real Estate Recording—Orange Town Clerk, US Rte 302, (3 miles east of East Barre), East Barre, VT 5649. Fax: 802-479-2673. 8AM-Noon, 1-4PM.

Felony, Misdemeanor, Civil, Eviction, Small Claims—District and Superior Court, 5 Court St, Chelsea, VT 05038-9746. 802-685-4870, Fax: 802-685-3246. 8AM-4:30PM. Access by: mail, phone, fax, in person.

Probate—Probate Court-Orange District, 5 Court Street, Chelsea, VT 05038-9746. 802-685-4610, Fax: 802-685-3246. 8AM-Noon, 1-4:30PM. Access by: mail, in person. Special note: The Bradford and Randolph Districts were consolidated into this one probate court as of June 1, 1994.

Orleans

Civil, Eviction, Small Claims—Superior Court, 247 Main St, Newport, VT 05855. 802-334-3344, Fax: 802-334-3385. 8AM-4:30PM. Access by: mail, phone, fax, in person.

Felony, Misdemeanor—District Court, 217 Main St, Newport, VT 05855. 802-334-3325. 8AM-4:30PM. Access by: mail, phone, in person.

Probate—Probate Court, 247 Main St, Newport, VT 05855. 802-334-3366. 8AM-Noon, 1-4:30PM. Access by: mail, in person.

Orwell

Real Estate Recording—Orwell Town Clerk, Main St. Orwell, VT 5760. 9:30AM-Noon, 1-3:30PM.

Panton

Real Estate Recording—Panton Town Clerk, RFD 3, Panton Corners, Vergennes, VT 5491. 9AM-4:30PM M,T.

Pawlet

Real Estate Recording—Pawlet Town Clerk, Town Hall, 122 School Street, Pawlet, VT 5761. Fax: 802-325-6109. 9AM-3PM T,W,Th; 9AM-Noon F.

Peacham

Real Estate Recording—Peacham Town Clerk, 79 Church St. Peacham, VT 5862. 8AM-Noon M,T,Th,F; 1-4PM Th; 4PM-7PM W.

Peru

Real Estate Recording—Peru Town Clerk, Main St. Peru, VT 5152. Fax: 802-824-3065. 8AM-4PM T & Th.

Pittsfield

Real Estate Recording—Pittsfield Town Clerk, Park Drive, Pittsfield, VT 5762. 802-746-8050. Noon-6PM T; 9AM-3PM W,Th.

Pittsford

Real Estate Recording—Pittsford Town Clerk, P.O. Box 10, Pittsford, VT 5763. Fax: 802-483-6612. 8AM-4:30PM.

Plainfield

Real Estate Recording—Plainfield Town Clerk, P.O. Box 217, Plainfield, VT 5667. Fax: 802-454-8461. 7:30AM-4PM.

Plymouth

Real Estate Recording—Plymouth Town Clerk, 68 Town Office Rd. Plymouth, VT 5056. Fax: 802-672-5466. 8:30-11:30AM, 12:30-3:30PM.

Pomfret

Real Estate Recording—Pomfret Town Clerk, Main St. Town Clerk, North Pomfret, VT 5053. 8AM-2:30PM M,W,F.

Poultney

Real Estate Recording—Poultney Town Clerk, 9 Main St. Suite 2, Poultney, VT 5764. 8:30AM-12:30, 1:30-4PM.

Pownal

Real Estate Recording—Pownal Town Clerk, Center St. Pownal, VT 5261. Fax: 802-823-0116. 9AM-2PM M,W,Th,F; 9AM-4PM T.

Proctor

Real Estate Recording—Proctor Town Clerk, 45 Main Street, Proctor, VT 5765. Fax: 802-459-2356. 8AM-4PM.

Putney

Real Estate Recording—Putney Town Clerk, Town Hall, Main Street, Putney, VT 5346. 9AM-2PM M, Th, F; 9AM-2PM, 7-9PM W; 9AM-Noon Sat.

Randolph

Real Estate Recording—Randolph Town Clerk, 7 Summer Street, Randolph, VT 5060. Fax: 802-728-5818. 8AM-Noon, 1-4:30PM.

Reading

Real Estate Recording—Reading Town Clerk, 799 Route 106, Reading, VT 5062. Fax: 802-454-7250. 9AM-Noon, 1-4PM, M,W,F.

Readsboro

Real Estate Recording—Readsboro Town Clerk, 301 Phelps Lane, Readsboro, VT 5350. Fax: 802-423-5423. 9AM-3PM.

Richford

Real Estate Recording—Richford Town Clerk, Main St. Town Hall, Richford, VT 5476. Fax: 802-848-7752. 8:30AM-4PM (F open until 5PM).

Richmond

Real Estate Recording—Richmond Town Clerk, 203 Bridge St. Richmond, VT 5477. Fax: 802-434-5570. 8AM-7PM M; 8AM-4PM T-Th; 8AM-1PM F.

Ripton

Real Estate Recording—Ripton Town Clerk, Rte 125, Ripton, VT 5766. 2-6PM M; 9AM-1PM T,W,Th,F.

Rochester

Real Estate Recording—Rochester Town Clerk, School St. Rochester, VT 5767. Fax: 802-767-6028. 8AM-4PM T-F.

Rockingham

Real Estate Recording—Rockingham Town Clerk, Municipal Bldg. 7 Village Square, Bellows Falls, VT 5101. Fax: 802-463-1228. 8:30AM-4:30PM.

Roxbury

Real Estate Recording—Roxbury Town Clerk, 1664 Roxbury Rd. Roxbury, VT 5669. 802-485-7595, Fax: 802-485-7860. 9AM-Noon, 1-4PM T-F.

Royalton

Real Estate Recording—Royalton Town Clerk, Basement - Royalton Memorial Library, Safford Street, South Royalton, VT 5068. Fax: 802-763-7967. 9AM-1PM, 2-5PM T-Th.

Rupert

Real Estate Recording—Rupert Town Clerk, Route 153, Sherman's Store Complex, West Rupert, VT 5776. 12:30-5:30PM M; 2-7PM W; 10AM-3PM Th.

Rutland

Real Estate Recording—Rutland City Clerk, 1 Strongs Avenue, City Hall, Rutland, VT 5701. 9AM-Noon, 1-4:45PM.

Rutland Town Clerk, Route 4 West, Center Rutland, VT 5736. Fax: 802-773-7295. 8AM-4:30PM.

Civil, Eviction, Small Claims—Superior Court, 83 Center St, Rutland, VT 05702. 802-775-4394, Fax: 802-775-2291. 8AM-4:30PM. Access by: mail, in person.

Felony, Misdemeanor—District Court, 92 State St, Rutland, VT 05701-2886. 802-786-5880. 8AM-4:30PM. Access by: mail, phone, in person.

Probate—Probate Court-Fair Haven District, 3 North Park Place, Fair Haven, VT 05743. 802-265-3380. 8AM-4PM.

Probate Court-Rutland District, 83 Center St, Rutland, VT 05701. 802-775-0114. 8AM-4:30PM.

Ryegate

Real Estate Recording—Ryegate Town Clerk, Town Highway #1, 18 South Bayley-Hazen Road, Ryegate, VT 5042. Fax: 802-584-3880. 1-5PM M-W; 9AM-1PM F.

Salisbury

Real Estate Recording—Salisbury Town Clerk, 25 Schoolhouse Rd. Salisbury, VT 5769. Fax: 802-352-9832. 2-6PM M; 9AM-Noon T & F; 9AM-Noon, 7:30AM-2PM W,Th.

Sandgate

Real Estate Recording—Sandgate Town Clerk, 3266 Sandgate Rd. Sandgate, VT 5250. 9AM-3PM T,W.

Searsburg

Real Estate Recording—Searsburg Town Clerk, Route 9, Wilmington, VT 5363. 8AM-Noon M,T,F.

Shaftsbury

Real Estate Recording—Shaftsbury Town Clerk, East St. Shaftsbury, VT 5262. 802-442-6242, Fax: 802-442-4043. 8AM-4PM M; 9AM-2PM T-F.

Sharon

Real Estate Recording—Sharon Town Clerk, Rt 132, Sharon, VT 5065. 7:30AM-12:30PM, 1:30-6PM T & Th; 7:30AM-12:30PM W.

Sheffield

Real Estate Recording—Sheffield Town Clerk, Town Highway #32, Sheffield, VT 5866. 9AM-2PM.

Shelburne

Real Estate Recording—Shelburne Town Clerk, Town Hall, 5376 Shelburne Rd. Shelburne, VT 5482. Fax: 802-985-9550. 8:30AM-4:30PM.

Sheldon

Real Estate Recording—Sheldon Town Clerk, Main St. Sheldon, VT 5483. 8AM-3PM.

Sherburne

Real Estate Recording—Sherburne Town Clerk, River Road, Killington, VT 5751. Fax: 802-422-3030. 9AM-3PM.

Shoreham

Real Estate Recording—Shoreham Town Clerk, 297 Main St. Shoreham, VT 5770. Fax: 802-897-2545. 9AM-4PM M-W & F.

Shrewsbury

Real Estate Recording—Shrewsbury Town Clerk, 9823 Cold River Rd. Shrewsbury, VT 5738. Fax: 802-492-3511. 1-6PM M,F; 10AM-2PM T,Th.

South Burlington

Real Estate Recording—South Burlington City Clerk, 575 Dorset Street, South Burlington, VT 5403. Fax: 802-658-4748. 8AM-4:30PM.

South Hero

Real Estate Recording—South Hero Town Clerk, 333 Rt.2, South Hero, VT 5486. 8:30AM-Noon, 1-4:30PM M-W; 8:30AM-Noon,1:30-6PM Th.

Springfield

Real Estate Recording—Springfield Town Clerk, 96 Main Street, Springfield, VT 5156. Fax: 802-885-1617. 8AM-4:30PM.

St. Albans

Real Estate Recording—St. Albans City Clerk, 100 N. Main, St. Albans, VT 5478. 7:30AM-4PM.

St. Albans Town Clerk, 579 Lake Road, St. Albans Bay, VT 5481. Fax: 802-524-9609. 8AM-4PM.

St. George

Real Estate Recording—St. George Town Clerk, 1 Barber Rd. St. George, VT 5495. Fax: 802-482-5548. 8AM-Noon.

St. Johnsbury

Real Estate Recording—St. Johnsbury Town Clerk, 1189 Main St. Suite 2, St. Johnsbury, VT 5819. Fax: 802-748-1268. 8AM-5PM (May-September 7AM-4PM).

Stamford

Real Estate Recording—Stamford Town Clerk, 986 Main Rd. Stamford, VT 5352. 11AM-4PM T & W; Noon-4PM, 7-9PM Th; Noon-4PM F.

Stannard

Real Estate Recording—Stannard Town Clerk,

Starksboro

Real Estate Recording—Starksboro Town Clerk, 3056 VT Route 116, Starksboro, VT 5487. Fax: 802-453-7293. 9AM-5PM M,T,Th,F.

Stockbridge

Real Estate Recording—Stockbridge Town Clerk, Blackmer Blvd. Stockbridge, VT 5772. Fax: 802-234-9371. 9AM-3PM T,Th; 9AM-Noon W,F.

Stowe

Real Estate Recording—Stowe Town Clerk, 67 Main St. Stowe, VT 5672. Fax: 802-253-6137. 7:30AM-4:30PM.

Strafford

Real Estate Recording—Strafford Town Clerk, Justin Morrill Highway, Strafford, VT 5072. 8AM-5PM T,W; 8AM-7PM Th; 8AM-Noon F.

Stratton

Real Estate Recording—Stratton Town Clerk, West Jamaica Rd. West Wardsboro, VT 5360. Fax: 802-896-6630. 9AM-3PM M-Th.

Sudbury

Real Estate Recording—Sudbury Town Clerk, 4694 Route 30, Sudbury, VT 5733. 9AM-4PM M; 9AM-1PM W,F.

Sunderland

Real Estate Recording—Sunderland Town Clerk, South Rd. East Arlington, VT 5252. 8AM-2PM M,T,Th,F; 8AM-Noon, 6-8PM W.

Sutton

Real Estate Recording—Sutton Town Clerk, State Aid #1, Sutton, VT 5867. Fax: 802-467-1052. 9AM-5PM M,T,Th,F; 9AM-Noon W.

Swanton

Real Estate Recording—Swanton Town Clerk, Academy Street, Swanton, VT 5488. 8AM-4PM.

Thetford

Real Estate Recording—Thetford Town Clerk, Rt. 113, Thetford Center, VT 5075. Fax: 802-785-2031. 6-8PM M; 8AM-3PM T-F.

Tinmouth

Real Estate Recording—Tinmouth Town Clerk, 515 North End Rd. Tinmouth, VT 5773. Fax: 802-446-2498. 8AM-Noon, 1-4PM M & Th.

Topsham

Real Estate Recording—Topsham Town Clerk, 69 VT Route 25, Topsham, VT 5086. 10AM-2PM M,T.

Townshend

Real Estate Recording—Townshend Town Clerk, Rte 30, Town Hall, Townshend, VT 5353. 9AM-4PM M-W & F.

Troy

Real Estate Recording—Troy Town Clerk, Main Street, North Troy, VT 5859. 8AM-Noon, 1-4PM.

Tunbridge

Real Estate Recording—Tunbridge Town Clerk, Main St. Tunbridge, VT 5077. Fax: 802-889-3744. 9:30AM-Noon, 1-4PM.

Underhill

Real Estate Recording—Underhill Town Clerk, 12 Pleasant Valley Rd. Underhill, VT 5489. Fax: 802-899-2137. 8AM-4PM M,T,Th,F; 8AM-7PM W.

Vergennes

Real Estate Recording—Vergennes City Clerk, 120 Main St. Vergennes, VT 5491. Fax: 802-877-1157. 8AM-4:30PM.

Vernon

Real Estate Recording—Vernon Town Clerk, 567 Governor Hunt Rd. Vernon, VT 5354. Fax: 802-254-3561. 8:30AM-4PM M-W; 8:30AM-6:30PM Th; 8:30AM-4PM F.

Vershire

Real Estate Recording—Vershire Town Clerk, RR 1, Box 66C, Vershire, VT 5079. 8:30AM-3PM T-Th.

Victory

Real Estate Recording—Victory Town Clerk, E. Finkle - River Rd. North Concord, VT 5858. By Appointment.

Waitsfield

Real Estate Recording—Waitsfield Town Clerk, RD2, Box 390, Bridge Street, Waitsfield, VT 5673. 9AM-Noon,1-4PM.

Walden

Real Estate Recording—Walden Town Clerk, 12 Vt. Rte. 215, West Danville, VT 5873. 9:30AM-4PM M,T,Th,F.

Vermont

Wallingford

Real Estate Recording—Wallingford Town Clerk, School St. Wallingford, VT 5773. 8AM-Noon, 1-4:30PM M-Th; 8AM-Noon F.

Waltham

Real Estate Recording—Waltham Town Clerk, Maple Street Ext. Vergennes, VT 5491. 9AM-Noon T; 9AM-Noon, 3-6PM Th.

Wardsboro

Real Estate Recording—Wardsboro Town Clerk, Main St. Wardsboro, VT 5355. Fax: 802-896-1000. 9AM-Noon, 1-4:30PM (Closed F).

Warren

Real Estate Recording—Warren Town Clerk, Main St. Town Clerk, Warren, VT 5674. 9AM-4:30PM.

Washington

Real Estate Recording—Washington Town Clerk, Clerk's Office, Rte. 100, Washington, VT 5675. 8:30AM-2PM M,T.

Civil, Eviction, Small Claims—Superior Court, 65 State St, Montpelier, VT 05602-3594. 802-828-2091. 8AM-4:30PM. Access by: mail, phone, in person.

Felony, Misdemeanor—District Court, 255 N Main, Barre, VT 05641. 802-479-4252. 8AM-4:30PM. Access by: mail, phone, in person.

Probate—Probate Court, 10 Elm Street, Montpelier, VT 05601. 802-828-3405. 8AM-Noon, 1-4:30PM M-Th; 8AM-Noon, 1-4PM F. Access by: mail, in person.

Waterbury

Real Estate Recording—Waterbury Town Clerk, 51 South Main Street, Waterbury, VT 5676. Fax: 802-244-1014. 8AM-4:30PM.

Waterford

Real Estate Recording—Waterford Town Clerk, 532 Maple St. Lower Waterford, VT 5848. Fax: 802-748-8196. 8:30AM-3:30PM M,Th,F; Noon-6PM T.

Waterville

Real Estate Recording—Waterville Town Clerk, 850 Vt. Rte. 109, Waterville, VT 5492. Fax: 802-644-8865. 9AM-1:30PM M,T,Th.

Weathersfield

Real Estate Recording—Weathersfield Town Clerk, Rt. 5, Ascutney Village at Martin Memorial Hall, Weathersfield, VT 5030. 9AM-4PM M-W; 9AM-5PM Th.

Wells

Real Estate Recording—Wells Town Clerk, Rt.30, Wells, VT 5774. 9AM-1PM.

West Fairlee

Real Estate Recording—West Fairlee Town Clerk, Rt 113, Town Clerk, West Fairlee, VT 5083. Fax: 802-333-9696. 10AM-4PM M,W,F.

West Haven

Real Estate Recording—West Haven Town Clerk, 2919 Main Rd. Fair Haven, VT 5743. 802-265-3675, Fax: 802-265-4880. 1-3:30PM M & W.

West Rutland

Real Estate Recording—West Rutland Town Clerk, 35 Marble St. West Rutland, VT 5777. Fax: 802-438-5133. 9AM-Noon, 1-3PM M-Th; Fri by appointment.

West Windsor

Real Estate Recording—West Windsor Town Clerk, Rt. 44 & Hartland-Brownsville Rd. Brownsville, VT 5037. Fax: 802-484-7212. 9AM-Noon, 1:30-4:30PM.

Westfield

Real Estate Recording—Westfield Town Clerk, RR 1 Box 171, Westfield, VT 5874. 8AM-Noon, 1PM-5PM M-Th.

Westford

Real Estate Recording—Westford Town Clerk, 1713 Vermont Route 128, Westford, VT 5494. Fax: 802-879-6503. 8:30AM-4:30PM.

Westminster

Real Estate Recording—Westminster Town Clerk, Town Hall, 3651 US Route 5, Westminster, VT 5158. Fax: 802-722-4255. 9AM-4PM.

Westmore

Real Estate Recording—Westmore Town Clerk, 54 Hinton Hill Rd. Orleans, VT 5860. Fax: 802-525-3007. 9AM-Noon, 1-4PM M-Th.

Weston

Real Estate Recording—Weston Town Clerk, 12 Lawrence Hill Rd. Weston, VT 5161. Fax: 802-824-4121. 9AM-1PM.

Weybridge

Real Estate Recording—Weybridge Town Clerk, 1727 Quaker Village Rd. Weybridge, VT 5753. Fax: 802-545-2450. 9AM-2PM M,T,Th,F.

Wheelock

Real Estate Recording—Wheelock Town Clerk, Rt.122, Lyndonville, VT 5851. Fax: 802-626-9094. 9AM-2PM T,Th,F.

Whiting

Real Estate Recording—Whiting Town Clerk, 29 S. Main St. Whiting, VT 5778. 9AM-Noon M,W,F.

Whitingham

Real Estate Recording—Whitingham Town Clerk, Municipal Center, Jacksonville, VT 5342. 802-368-2801, Fax: 802-368-7519. 9AM-2PM (5:30-7:30PM W); 1st Sat of month 9AM-2PM.

Williamstown

Real Estate Recording—Williamstown Town Clerk, 2470 VT Rt. 14, Williamstown, VT 5679. 8AM-Noon,12:30-4:30PM.

Williston

Real Estate Recording—Williston Town Clerk, 6400 Williston Rd. Williston, VT 5495. 8AM-4:30PM.

Wilmington

Real Estate Recording—Wilmington Town Clerk, Main Street, Wilmington, VT 5363. Fax: 802-464-1238. 8AM-Noon, 1PM-4PM.

Windham

Real Estate Recording—Windham Town Clerk, RR 1, Box 109, West Townshend, VT 5359. 10AM-3PM T,Th,F.

Civil, Eviction, Small Claims—Superior Court, Box 207, Newfane, VT 05345. 802-365-7979, Fax: 802-365-4360. 9AM-4PM. Access by: mail, phone, fax, in person.

Felony, Misdemeanor—District Court, 6 Putney Rd, Brattleboro, VT 05301. 802-257-2800, Fax: 802-257-2853. 8AM-4:30PM. Access by: mail, phone, fax, in person.

Probate—Probate Court-Marlboro District, PO Box 523, Brattleboro, VT 05302. 802-257-2898. 8AM-Noon, 1-4:30PM. Access by: mail, in person.

Probate Court-Westminster District, PO Box 47, Bellows Falls, VT 05101. 802-463-3019. 8AM-Noon,1-4:30PM. Access by: mail, in person.

Windsor

Real Estate Recording—Windsor Town Clerk, 147 Main Street, Windsor, VT 5089. 802-674-6788, Fax: 802-674-5610. 8AM-4PM (F open until 3:30PM).

Civil, Eviction, Small Claims—Superior Court, Box 458, Woodstock, VT 05091. 802-457-2121, Fax: 802-457-3446. 8AM-4:30PM. Access by: mail, phone, in person.

Felony, Misdemeanor—District Court, Windsor Circuit Unit 1, 10 Railroad Row, White River Junction, VT 05001-1962. 802-295-8865. 8AM-4:30PM. Access by: mail, phone, in person.

Probate—Probate Court-Hartford District, PO Box 275, Woodstock, VT 05091. 802-457-1503, Fax: 802-457-3446. 8AM-Noon, 1-4:30PM.

Probate Court-Windsor District, PO Box 402, North Springfield, VT 05150. 802-886-2284, Fax: 802-886-2285. 8AM-Noon, 1-4:30PM. Access by: mail, in person.

Winhall

Real Estate Recording—Winhall Town Clerk, River Rd. Bondville, VT 5340. 9AM-Noon (Closed Th).

Winooski

Real Estate Recording—Winooski City Clerk, 27 West Allen Street, Winooski, VT 5404. Fax: 802-655-6414. 8AM-5PM.

Wolcott

Real Estate Recording—Wolcott Town Clerk, 4186 VT Route 15, Wolcott, VT 5680. Fax: 802-888-2746. 8AM-4PM T-F; 6-8PM Tue.

Woodbury

Real Estate Recording—Woodbury Town Clerk, Rt 14, Town Clerk, Woodbury, VT 5681. 8:30AM-1PM T-Th; 6-8PM Th evening.

Woodford

Real Estate Recording—Woodford Town Clerk, HRC 65 Box 600, Bennington, VT 5201. Fax: 802-442-4895. 8:30AM-Noon M-Th.

Woodstock

Real Estate Recording—Woodstock Town Clerk, 31 The Green, Woodstock, VT 5091. Fax: 802-457-2329. 8:30AM-Noon, 1-3:30PM.

Worcester

Real Estate Recording—Worcester Town Clerk, 20 Worcester Village Rd. Worcester, VT 5682. Fax: 802-229-5216. 8AM-Noon, 1-3PM M,T,Th; 8AM-1PM F; 8-10AM Sat.

Federal Courts

US District Court

Burlington Division Clerk's Office, PO Box 945, Burlington, VT 05402-0945802-951-6301 Counties: Caledonia, Chittenden, Essex, Franklin, Grand Isle, Lamoille, Orleans, Washington. However, cases from all counties in the state are assigned randomly to either Burlington or Brattleboro. Brattleboro is a hearing location only, not listed here.

Rutland Division PO Box 607, Rutland, VT 05702-0607802-773-0245 Counties: Addison, Bennington, Orange, Rutland, Windsor, Windham. However, cases from all counties in the state are randomly assigned to either Burlington or Brattleboro. Brattleboro is a hearing location only, not listed here.

US Bankruptcy Court

Rutland Division PO Box 6648, Rutland, VT 05702-6648802-747-7625, Record Room: 802-747-7625 Fax: 802-747-7629 Counties: All counties in Vermont. www.vtb.uscourts.gov

Attorney General's Office
900 E Main St
Richmond, VA 23219
www.oag.state.va.us

804-786-2071
Fax: 804-786-1991

Governor's Office
Capitol Bldg, 3rd Floor
Richmond, VA 23219
www.state.va.us/governor

804-786-2211
Fax: 804-371-6351

State Archives
800 E. Broad St
Richmond, VA 23219-8000
http://leo.vsla.edu

804-692-3500
Fax: 804-692-3556

Capital:	Richmond
	Richmond City County
Time Zone:	EST
Number of Counties:	95
Population:	6,733,996
Web Site:	www.state.va.us

Search Unclaimed Property Online

There is no Internet-based search for this state; however, the URL for the agency responsible for unclaimed property is www.trs.state.va.us/ textfiles/UCP/Press.htm.

State Agencies

Criminal Records
Virginia State Police, CCRE, PO Box C-85076, Richmond, VA 23261-5076 (7700 Midlothian Turnpike, Richmond, VA 23235); 804-674-2084; Fax: 804-674-2277; 8AM-5PM. Access by: mail, online.

Corporation Records
Limited Liability Company Records
Fictitious Name
Limited Partnership Records
Assumed Name
State Corporation Commission, Clerks Office, PO Box 1197, Richmond, VA 23218-1197 (Tyler Bldg, 1st Floor, 1300 E Main St, Richmond, VA 23219); 804-371-9733, 804-371-9133 Other fax; Fax: 804-371-9744; 8:15AM-5PM. Access by: mail, phone, in person, online. dit1.state.va.us/scc/ division/clm/index.htm

Sales Tax Registrations
Taxation Department, Sales - Taxpayer Assistance, PO Box 1880, Richmond, VA 23218-1880 (2220 W Broad St, Richmond, VA 23220); 804-367-8037; Fax: 804-367-0971; 8:30AM-4:30PM. Access by: mail. www.state.va.us/tax/tax.html

Trademarks/Servicemarks
State Corporation Commission, Division of Security & Retail Franchises, PO Box 1197, Richmond, VA 23218-1197 (1300 E. Main, 9th Floor, Richmond, VA 23219); 804-371-9051; Fax: 804-371-9911; 8:15AM-5PM. Access by: mail, phone, in person. www.state.va.us/sec

Uniform Commercial Code
Federal Tax Liens
UCC Division, State Corporation Commission, PO Box 1197, Richmond, VA 23218-1197 (1300 E Main St, 1st Floor, Richmond, VA 23219); 804-371-9189; Fax: 804-371-9744; 8:15AM-5PM. Access by: mail, phone, in person, online. dit1.state.va.us/ecc/division/clk/index.htm

State Tax Liens

Records not available from state agency.

All information is found at the local city or county level.

Workers' Compensation Records

Workers' Compensation Commission, 1000 DMV Dr, Richmond, VA 23220; 804-367-8633; Fax: 804-367-9740; 8:15AM-5PM. Access by: mail.

Birth Certificates

State Health Department, Division of Vital Records, PO Box 1000, Richmond, VA 23218-1000 (109 Governor St, 2nd Floor, Richmond, VA 23219); 804-225-5000, 804-644-2723 VitalChek; Fax: 804-644-2550; 8AM-5PM. Access by: mail, phone, in person.

Death Records

State Health Department, Division of Vital Records, PO Box 1000, Richmond, VA 23218-1000; 804-225-5000, 804-644-2723 VitalChek; Fax: 804-644-2550; 8AM-5PM. Access by: mail, phone, in person.

Marriage Certificates

State Health Department, Division of Vital Records, PO Box 1000, Richmond, VA 23218-1000; 804-225-5000, 804-644-2723 VitalChek; Fax: 804-644-2550; 8AM-5PM. Access by: mail, phone, in person.

Divorce Records

State Health Department, Division of Vital Records, PO Box 1000, Richmond, VA 23218-1000; 804-225-5000, 804-644-2723 VitalChek; Fax: 804-644-2550; 8AM-5PM. Access by: mail, phone, in person.

Driver Records

Department of Motor Vehicles, Motorist Records Services, PO Box 27412, Richmond, VA 23269; 804-367-0538; 8:30AM-5:30PM M-F; 8:30AM-12:30PM S. Access by: mail, online. www.dmv.state.va.us

Vehicle Ownership
Vehicle Identification

Motorist Records Services, Customer Records Request Section, PO Box 27412, Richmond, VA 23269; 804-367-0538; 8:30AM-5:30PM M-F; 8:30AM-12:30PM S. Access by: mail, phone, in person, online. www.dmv.state.va.us

Accident Reports

Department of Motor Vehicles, Customer Record Requests, Rm 517, PO Box 27412, Richmond, VA 23269; 804-367-0538; Fax: 804-367-0390; 8:30AM-5:30PM M-F; 8:30AM-12:30PM S. Access by: mail. www.dmv.state.va.us

Boat & Vessel Ownership
Boat & Vessel Registration

Game & Inland Fisheries Dept, 4010 W Broad St, Richmond, VA 23230-1528; 804-367-0939; Fax: 804-367-1064; 8:15AM-5PM. Access by: online. www.dgif.state.va.us/boating

Legislation-Current/Pending
Legislation-Passed

House of Delegates, Legislative Information, PO Box 406, Richmond, VA 23218 (1st Floor, State Capitol Bldg, 9th and Grace Streets, Richmond, VA 23219); 804-698-1500; Fax: 804-786-3215; 8AM-5PM. Access by: mail, phone, in person, online. http://legis.state.va.us/vaonline/v.htm

Voter Registration

Restricted access.

Individual searches must be done at the county or city level with the General Registrars. The state will sell all or portions of its statewide database (95 counties, 40 cities) to organizations promoting voter registration and participation.

Secretary of the Commonwealth, State Board of Elections, 200 N 9th Street, #101, Richmond, VA 23219; 804-786-6551; Fax: 804-371-0194; 8:30AM-5PM

www.state.va.us

GED Certificates

Virginia Dept of Education, GED Services, PO Box 2120, Richmond, VA 23218-2120; 804-225-2020; Fax: 804-786-7243; 8:15AM-5PM.

Hunting License Information
Fishing License Information

Records not available from state agency.

They do not have a central database.

County Courts & Recording Offices

About the Courts...

Administration

Executive Secretary, Administrative Office of Courts804-786-6455
100 N 9th St 3rd Fl, Supreme Court Bldg   Fax: 804-786-4541
Richmond, VA 23219
www.courts.state.va.us

Court Structure

117 Circuit Courts in 31 districts are the courts of general jurisdiction. There are 123 District Courts of limited juridiction. Please note that a district can comprise a county or a city. Records of civil action from $1000 to $15,000 can be at either the Circuit or District Court as either can have jurisdiction. It is necessary to check both record locations as there is no concurrent database nor index.

The upper limit for civil actions in District Court was raised from $10,000 to $15,000 as of July 1, 1997.

Searching Hints

In most jurisdictions, the Certification Fee is $2.00 per document plus copy fee. The Copy Fee is $.50 per page.

Online Access

An online, statewide public access computer system is available, called Law Office Public Access System (LOPAS). The system allows remote access to the court case indexes and abstracts from most of the state's courts. In order to determine which courts are on LOPAS, you must obtain an ID and password (instructions below), and search on the system. A summary list of included courts is not available. Searching is by specific court; there is no combined index.

The system contains opinions from the Supreme Court and the Court of Appeals, as well as criminal and civil case information from Circuit and District Courts. The number of years of information provided varies widely from court to court, depending on when the particular court joined the Courts Automated Information System (CAIS).

The preferred communication software for LOPAS access is PROCOMM+. There are no sign-up or other fees to use LOPAS. Access is granted on a request-by-request basis. Anyone wishing to establish an account or receive information on LOPAS must contact Ken Mittendorf, Director of MIS, Supreme Court of Virginia, 100 N 9th St, Richmond VA 23219 or by phone at 804-786-6455 or Fax at 804-786-4542.

About the Recording Offices...

Organization

95 counties and 41 independent cities, 123 recording offices. The recording officer is Clerk of Circuit Court. Fourteen independent cities share the Clerk of Circuit Court with the county - Bedford, Emporia (Greenville County), Fairfax, Falls Church (Arlington or Fairfax County), Franklin (Southhampton County), Galax (Carroll County), Harrisonburg (Rockingham County), Lexington (Rockbridge County), Manassas and Manassas Park (Prince William County), Norton (Wise County), Poquoson (York County), South Boston (Halifax County), and Williamsburg (James City County. Charles City and James City are counties, not cities. The City of Franklin is not in Franklin County, the City of Richmond is not in Richmond County, and the City of Roanoke is not in Roanoke County. The entire state is in the Eastern Time Zone (EST).

UCC Records

This is a dual filing state. Financing statements are filed at the state level and with the Clerk of Circuit Court, except for consumer goods, farm and real estate related collateral, which are filed only with the Clerk of Circuit Court. Some recording offices will perform UCC searches. Use search request form UCC-11. Searches fees and copy fees vary.

Lien Records

Federal tax liens on personal property of businesses are filed with the State Corporation Commission. Other federal and all state tax liens are filed with the county Clerk of Circuit Court. They are usually filed in a "Judgment Lien Book." Most counties will not perform tax lien searches.

Real Estate Records

Only a few Clerks of Circuit Court will perform real estate searches. Copy fees and certification fees vary. The independent cities may have separate Assessor Offices.

County Courts & Recording Offices

Accomack

Real Estate Recording—Accomack County Clerk of the Circuit Court, 23316 Courthouse Avenue, Accomac, VA 23301. Fax: 757-787-1849. 9AM-5PM.

Felony, Civil Actions Over $15,000, Probate—2nd Circuit Court, PO Box 126, Accomac, VA 23301. 757-787-5776, Fax: 757-787-1849. 9AM-5PM. Access by: mail, fax, in person, online.

Misdemeanor, Civil Actions Under $15,000, Eviction, Small Claims—2A General District Court, PO Box 276, Accomac, VA 23301. 757-787-0920. 9AM-5PM. Access by: mail, phone, in person, online.

Albemarle

Real Estate Recording—Albemarle County Clerk of the Circuit Court, 501 E. Jefferson St. Room 225, Charlottesville, VA 22902. Fax: 804-293-0298. 8:30AM-4:30PM.

Felony, Misdemeanor, Civil, Eviction, Probate—16th Circuit and District Court, 501 E Jefferson St, Charlottesville, VA 22902. 804-972-4085, Fax: 804-972-4071. 8:30AM-4:30PM. Access by: mail, in person, online.

Alexandria City

Real Estate Recording—Alexandria City Clerk of the Circuit Court, 520 King Street, Room 307, Alexandria, VA 22314. 703-838-6420. 9AM-5PM.

Felony, Civil Actions Over $15,000, Probate—18th Circuit Court, 520 King St. #307, Alexandria, VA 22314. 703-838-4044. 9AM-5PM. Access by: in person.

Misdemeanor, Civil Actions Under $15,000, Eviction, Small Claims—18th Judicial District Court, 520 King St #201, PO Box 20206, Alexandria, VA 22314. 703-838-4041. 8AM-4PM. Access by: in person, online.

Alleghany

Real Estate Recording—Alleghany County Clerk of the Circuit Court, 266 West Main Street, Covington, VA 24426. 540-965-1630, Fax: 540-965-1732. 9AM-5PM; 9AM-Noon Sat.

Felony, Civil Actions Over $15,000, Probate—25th Circuit Court, PO Box 670, Covington, VA 24426. 540-965-1730, Fax: 540-965-1732. 8:45AM-5PM M-F; 9AM-Noon Sat. Access by: in person, online. www.alleghanycountyclerk.com

Misdemeanor, Civil Actions Under $15,000, Small Claims—25th General District Court, PO Box 139, Covington, VA 24426. 540-965-1720, Fax: 540-965-1722. 9AM-5PM. Access by: mail, fax, in person, online.

Amelia

Real Estate Recording—Amelia County Clerk of the Circuit Court, 16441 Court St. Courthouse, Amelia Court House, VA 23002. 804-561-2145. 8:30AM-4:30PM.

Felony, Civil Actions Over $15,000, Probate—11th Circuit Court, 16441 Court St, PO Box 237, Amelia, VA 23002. 804-561-2128. 8:30AM-4:30PM. Access by: mail, in person, online.

Misdemeanor, Civil Actions Under $15,000, Eviction, Small Claims—11th General District Court, PO Box 24, Amelia, VA 23002. 804-561-2456, Fax: 804-561-6956. 8:15AM-4:15PM. Access by: mail, in person, online.

Amherst

Real Estate Recording—Amherst County Clerk of the Circuit Court, 113 Taylor St. Amherst, VA 24521. 804-946-9318. 8AM-5PM.

Felony, Civil Actions Over $15,000, Probate—24th Circuit Court, PO Box 462, Amherst, VA 24521. 804-946-9321, Fax: 804-946-9323. 8AM-5PM. Access by: in person, online.

Misdemeanor, Civil Actions Under $15,000, Eviction, Small Claims—24th General District Court, PO Box 513, Amherst, VA 24521. 804-946-9351, Fax: 804-946-9359. 8AM-4:30PM. Access

by: in person, online. Special note: Has handled misdemeanor cases since 1985.

Appomattox

Real Estate Recording—Appomattox County Clerk of the Circuit Court, Courthouse Square, Court Street, Appomattox, VA 24522. 804-352-5200, Fax: 804-352-2781. 8:30AM-4:30PM.

Felony, Civil Actions Over $15,000, Probate—10th Circuit Court, PO Box 672, Appomattox, VA 24522. 804-352-5275, Fax: 804-352-2781. 8:30AM-4:30PM. Access by: in person, online.

Misdemeanor, Civil Actions Under $15,000, Eviction, Small Claims—10th General District Court, PO Box 187, Appomattox, VA 24522. 804-352-5540, Fax: 804-352-0717. 8:30AM-4:30PM. Access by: mail, fax, in person, online.

Arlington

Real Estate Recording—Arlington County Clerk of the Circuit Court, 1425 N. Courthouse Road #6700, Arlington, VA 22201. 8AM-5PM.

Felony, Civil Actions Over $15,000, Probate—17th Circuit Court, 1425 N Courthouse Rd, Arlington, VA 22201. 703-358-7010. 8AM-5PM. Access by: mail, in person, online.

Misdemeanor, Civil Actions Under $15,000, Eviction, Small Claims—17th General District Court, 1425 N Courthouse Rd, Rm 2500, Arlington, VA 22201. 703-228-4590, Fax: 703-228-4593. 8AM-4PM. Access by: mail, phone, in person, online.

Augusta

Real Estate Recording—Augusta County Clerk of the Circuit Court, 1 East Johnson Street, Courthouse, Staunton, VA 24401. 540-245-5660, Fax: 540-245-5318. 8AM-5PM.

Felony, Civil Actions Over $15,000, Probate—25th Circuit Court, PO Box 689, Staunton, VA 24402-0689. 540-245-5321, Fax: 540-245-5318. 8AM-5PM. Access by: mail, phone, in person, online.

Misdemeanor, Civil Actions Under $15,000, Eviction, Small Claims—25th General District Court, 6 E Johnson St, 2nd Floor, Staunton, VA 24401. 540-245-5300, Fax: 540-245-5302. 8:30AM-4:30PM. Access by: mail, in person, online.

Bath

Real Estate Recording—Bath County Clerk of the Circuit Court, Courthouse, Room 101, Warm Springs, VA 24484. 540-839-7256. 8:30AM-4:30PM.

Felony, Civil Actions Over $15,000, Probate—25th Circuit Court, PO Box 180, Warm Springs, VA 24484. 540-839-7226, Fax: 540-839-7222. 8:30AM-4:30PM. Access by: mail, in person, online.

Misdemeanor, Civil Actions Under $15,000, Eviction, Small Claims—25th General District Court, PO Box 96, Warm Springs, VA 24484. 540-839-7241, Fax: 540-839-7222. 8:30AM-4:30PM. Access by: mail, phone, in person, online.

Bedford

Real Estate Recording—Bedford County Clerk of the Circuit Court, Courthouse, Corner Court & Main Streets, Bedford, VA 24523. 540-586-7670. 8:30AM-5PM.

Felony, Civil Actions Over $15,000, Probate—24th Circuit Court, PO Box 235, Bedford, VA 24523. 540-586-7632, Fax: 540-586-6197. 8:30AM-5PM. Access by: in person, online.

Misdemeanor, Civil Actions Under $15,000, Eviction—24th General District Court, 123 E Main St, Rm 204, Bedford, VA 24523. 540-586-7637, Fax: 540-586-7684. 8AM-4PM. Access by: mail, in person, online.

Bland

Real Estate Recording—Bland County Clerk of the Circuit Court, #1 Courthouse Square, Bland, VA 24315. 540-688-3741, Fax: 540-688-4562. 8AM-6PM.

Felony, Civil Actions Over $15,000, Probate—27th Circuit Court, PO Box 295, Bland, VA 24315. 540-688-4562, Fax: 540-688-4562. 8AM-6PM. Access by: mail, phone, fax, in person, online.

Misdemeanor, Civil Actions Under $15,000, Eviction, Small Claims—27th General District Court, PO Box 157, Bland, VA 24315. 540-688-4433, Fax: 540-688-4789. 8AM-5PM. Access by: mail, phone, fax, in person, online.

Botetourt

Real Estate Recording—Botetourt County Clerk of the Circuit Court, Main St. and Roanoke St. Courthouse, Fincastle, VA 24090. 540-473-8254. 8:30AM-4:30PM.

Felony, Civil Actions Over $15,000, Probate—25th Circuit Court, PO Box 219, Fincastle, VA 24090. 540-473-8274, Fax: 540-473-8209. 8:30AM-4:30PM. Access by: mail, in person, online.

Misdemeanor, Civil Actions Under $15,000, Eviction, Small Claims—25th General District Court, PO Box 205, Fincastle, VA 24090-0205. 540-473-8244, Fax: 540-473-8344. 8AM-4PM. Access by: mail, in person, online.

Bristol City

Real Estate Recording—Bristol City Clerk of the Circuit Court, 497 Cumberland Street, Room 210, Bristol, VA 24201. 540-645-7311, Fax: 540-645-7345. 9AM-5PM.

Felony, Civil Actions Over $15,000, Probate—28th Circuit Court, 497 Cumberland St, Bristol, VA 24201. 540-645-7321, Fax: 540-645-7345. 9AM-5PM. Access by: mail, in person, online.

Misdemeanor, Civil Actions Under $15,000, Eviction, Small Claims—28th General District Court, 497 Cumberland St, Bristol, VA 24201. 540-645-7341, Fax: 540-645-7345. 8AM-5PM. Access by: mail, in person, online.

Brunswick

Real Estate Recording—Brunswick County Circuit Court, 216 N. Main St. Lawrenceville, VA 23868. 804-848-2512, Fax: 804-848-4307. 8:30AM-5PM.

Felony, Civil, Probate—6th Circuit Court, 216 N Main St, Lawrenceville, VA 23868. 804-848-2215, Fax: 804-848-4307. 8:30AM-5PM. Access by: in person, online.

Misdemeanor, Civil Actions Under $15,000, Eviction, Small Claims—6th General District Court, PO Box 66, 228 Main St, Lawrenceville, VA 23868-0066. 804-848-2315, Fax: 804-848-2550. 8:30AM-4:30PM. Access by: mail, in person, online.

Buchanan

Real Estate Recording—Buchanan County Clerk of the Circuit Court, Courthouse, Main & Walnut Sts. 2nd Floor, Grundy, VA 24614. 540-935-6551, Fax: 540-935-6574. 8:30AM-5PM.

Felony, Misdemeanor, Civil Actions Over $15,000, Probate—29th Circuit, PO Box 929, Grundy, VA 24614. 540-935-6575. 8:30AM-5PM. Access by: mail, phone, in person, online.

Civil Actions Under $15,000, Eviction, Small Claims—29th Judicial District Court, PO Box 654, Grundy, VA 24614. 540-935-6526, Fax: 540-935-5479. 8AM-4PM. Access by: mail, phone, fax, in person.

Buckingham

Real Estate Recording—Buckingham County Clerk of the Circuit Court, Highway 60, Courthouse, Buckingham, VA 23921. Fax: 804-959-2043. 8:30AM-4:30PM.

Felony, Civil Actions Over $15,000, Probate—10th Circuit Court, Route 60, PO Box 107, Buckingham, VA 23921. 804-969-4734, Fax: 804-969-2043. 8:30AM-4:30PM. Access by: mail, in person, online.

Misdemeanor, Civil Actions Under $15,000, Eviction, Small Claims—Buckingham General District Court, PO Box 127, Buckingham, VA 23921. 804-969-4755, Fax: 804-969-1762. 8:30AM-4:30PM. Access by: mail, fax, in person, online.

Buena Vista City

Real Estate Recording—Clerk of Circuit Court, 2039 Sycamore Ave. Buena Vista, VA 24416. Fax: 540-261-8623. 8:30AM-5PM.

Felony, Misdemeanor, Civil, Eviction, Probate—25th Circuit and District Court, 2039 Sycamore Ave, Buena Vista, VA 24416.

540-261-8627, Fax: 540-261-8625. 8:30AM-5PM. Access by: mail, in person, online.

Campbell

Real Estate Recording—Campbell County Clerk of the Circuit Court, Main Street, New Courthouse, Rustburg, VA 24588. 8:30AM-4:30PM.

Felony, Civil Actions Over $15,000, Probate—24th Circuit Court, State RD 501 Village Hwy, PO Box 7, Rustburg, VA 24588. 804-592-9517. 8:30AM-4:30PM. Access by: mail, in person, online.

Misdemeanor, Civil Actions Under $15,000, Eviction, Small Claims—24th General District Court, 1st Floor, New Courthouse Bldg, PO Box 97, Rustburg, VA 24588. 804-332-9546, Fax: 804-332-9694. 8AM-4PM. Access by: in person, online.

Caroline

Real Estate Recording—Caroline County Clerk of the Circuit Court, Main St. & Courthouse Lane, Bowling Green, VA 22427. 8:30AM-5PM (Recording Hours 8:30AM-4:30PM).

Felony, Civil Actions Over $15,000, Probate—15th Circuit Court, Main St & Courthouse Ln, PO Box 309, Bowling Green, VA 22427-0309. 804-633-5800. 9AM-5PM. Access by: in person, online.

Misdemeanor, Civil Actions Under $15,000, Eviction, Small Claims—15th General District Court, PO Box 511, Bowling Green, VA 22427. 804-633-5720, Fax: 804-633-3033. 8AM-4PM. Access by: mail, in person, online.

Carroll

Real Estate Recording—Carroll County Clerk of the Circuit Court, 515 North Main Street, Courthouse, Hillsville, VA 24343. Fax: 540-728-0255. 8AM-5PM.

Felony, Civil Actions Over $15,000, Probate—27th Circuit Court, PO Box 218, Hillsville, VA 24343. 540-728-3117. 8AM-5PM. Access by: mail, in person, online.

Misdemeanor, Civil Actions Under $15,000, Eviction, Small Claims—Carroll Combined District Court, PO Box 698, Hillsville, VA 24343. 540-728-7751, Fax: 540-728-2582. 8AM-4:30PM. Access by: in person, online.

Charles City

Real Estate Recording—Charles City County Clerk of the Circuit Court, 10700 Courthouse Road, Intersection of Rts 5 and 155, Charles City, VA 23030. Fax: 804-829-5647. 8:30AM-4:30PM.

Felony, Civil Actions Over $15,000, Probate—9th Circuit Court, 10700 Courthouse Rd, PO Box 86, Charles City, VA 23030-0086. 804-829-9212, Fax: 804-829-5647. 8:30AM-4:30PM. Access by: mail, in person, online.

Misdemeanor, Civil Actions Under $15,000, Eviction, Small Claims—9th General District Court, Charles City Courthouse, 10700 Courthouse Rd, Charles City, VA 23030. 804-829-9224, Fax: 504-829-5109. 8:30AM-4:30PM. Access by: mail, in person, online.

Charlotte

Real Estate Recording—Charlotte County Clerk of the Circuit Court, Courthouse, Charlotte Court House, VA 23923. 804-542-5725, Fax: 804-542-4336. 8:30AM-4:30PM.

Felony, Civil Actions Over $15,000, Probate—10th Circuit Court, #8 LeGrande Ave PO Box 38, Charlotte Courthouse, VA 23923. 804-542-5147. 8:30AM-4:30PM. Access by: mail, in person.

Misdemeanor, Civil Actions Under $15,000, Eviction, Small Claims—Charlotte General District Court, PO Box 127, Charlotte Courthouse, VA 23923. 804-542-5600, Fax: 804-542-5902. 8:30AM-4:30PM. Access by: in person, online.

Charlottesville City

Real Estate Recording—Charlottesville City Clerk of the Circuit Court, 315 East High Street, Charlottesville, VA 22902. 804-296-5851. 8:30AM-4:30PM.

Felony, Civil Actions Over $15,000, Probate—16th Circuit Court, 315 E High St, Charlottesville, VA 22902. 804-295-3182. 8:30AM-4:30PM. Access by: in person, online.

Misdemeanor, Civil Actions Under $15,000, Eviction, Small Claims—Charlottesville General District Court, 606 E Market St,

PO Box 2677, Charlottesville, VA 22902. 804-970-3385, Fax: 804-970-3387. 8:30AM-4:30PM. Access by: mail, in person, online.

Chesapeake City

Real Estate Recording—Chesapeake Clerk of the Circuit Court, 300 Cedar Road, Chesapeake, VA 23322. Fax: 757-436-8750. 8:30AM-5PM.

Felony, Civil Actions Over $15,000, Probate—1st Circuit Court, PO Box 15205, Chesapeake, VA 23328-5205. 757-382-6111. 8:30AM-5PM. Access by: mail, in person, online.

Misdemeanor, Civil Actions Under $15,000, Eviction, Small Claims—1st General District Court, 308 Shea Dr, Chesapeake, VA 23322-5571. Fax: 757-382-8529. 8AM-4PM. Access by: mail, in person, online. Special note: Indicate division (civil, criminal or traffic) in address.

Chesterfield

Real Estate Recording—Chesterfield County Clerk of the Circuit Court, 9500 Courthouse Road, Chesterfield, VA 23832. Fax: 804-796-5625. 8:30AM-5PM (Recording hours: 8:30AM-4PM M-Th; 8:30AM-3PM F).

Felony, Civil Actions Over $15,000, Probate—12th Circuit Court, 9500 Courthouse Rd, PO Box 125, Chesterfield, VA 23832. 804-748-1241, Fax: 804-796-5625. 8:30AM-5PM. Access by: mail, in person, online. www.co.chesterfield.va.us/cc-main.htm

Misdemeanor, Civil Actions Under $15,000, Eviction, Small Claims—12th General District Court, PO Box 144, Chesterfield, VA 23832. 804-748-1231. 8AM-4PM. Access by: mail, in person, online.

Clarke

Real Estate Recording—Clarke County Clerk of the Circuit Court, 102 North Church Street, Courthouse, Berryville, VA 22611. 540-955-5160, Fax: 540-955-0284. 9AM-5PM.

Felony, Civil Actions Over $15,000, Probate—26th Circuit Court, PO Box 189, Berryville, VA 22611. 540-955-5116, Fax: 540-955-0284. 9AM-5PM. Access by: mail, in person, online.

Misdemeanor, Civil Actions Under $15,000, Eviction, Small Claims—26th General District Court, 104 N Church St (PO Box 612), Berryville, VA 22611. 540-955-5128, Fax: 540-955-1195. 8:30AM-4:30PM. Access by: in person, online.

Clifton Forge City

Real Estate Recording—Clifton Forge City Clerk of the Circuit Court, 547 Main St. Clifton Forge, VA 24422. 9AM-5PM.

Felony, Civil Actions Over $15,000, Probate—25th Circuit Court, 547 Main St, PO Box 27, Clifton Forge, VA 24422. 540-863-8536. 9AM-5PM. Access by: mail, in person, online.

Misdemeanor, Civil Actions Under $15,000, Eviction, Small Claims—25th General District Court, 547 Main St, Clifton Forge, VA 24422. 540-863-2510, Fax: 540-863-2543. 9AM-5PM. Access by: mail, in person, online.

Colonial Heights City

Real Estate Recording—Clerk, Colonial Heights Circuit Court, 401 Temple Avenue, Courthouse, Colonial Heights, VA 23834. 8:30AM-5PM.

Felony, Civil Actions Over $15,000, Probate—12th Circuit Court, 401 Temple Ave, PO Box 3401, Colonial Heights, VA 23834. 804-520-9364. 8:30AM-5PM. Access by: mail, in person, online.

Misdemeanor, Civil Actions Under $15,000, Eviction, Small Claims—12th General District Court, 401 Temple Ave, PO Box 279, Colonial Heights, VA 23834. 804-520-9346. 8AM-4PM. Access by: mail, in person, online.

Craig

Real Estate Recording—Craig County Clerk of the Circuit Court, 303 Main Street, Courthouse, New Castle, VA 24127. 540-864-5641. 9AM-5PM.

Felony, Civil Actions Over $15,000, Probate—25th Circuit Court, PO Box 185, New Castle, VA 24127-0185. 540-864-6141. 9AM-5PM. Access by: in person, online.

Misdemeanor, Civil Actions Under $15,000, Eviction, Small Claims—25th General District Court, Craig County General District Court, PO Box 232, New Castle, VA 24127. 540-864-5989. 8:15AM-4:45PM. Access by: in person, online.

Culpeper

Real Estate Recording—Culpeper County Clerk of the Circuit Court, 135 West Cameron St. Room 103, Culpeper, VA 22701. 540-825-2035. 8:30AM-4:30PM.

Felony, Civil Actions Over $15,000, Probate—16th Circuit Court, 135 W Cameron St, Culpeper, VA 22701-3097. 540-727-3438. 8:30AM-4:30PM. Access by: in person, online.

Misdemeanor, Civil Actions Under $15,000, Eviction, Small Claims—16th General District Court, 135 W Cameron St, Culpeper, VA 22701. 540-727-3417, Fax: 540-727-3474. 8:30AM-4:30PM. Access by: mail, fax, in person, online.

Cumberland

Real Estate Recording—Cumberland County Clerk of the Circuit Court, County Office Building, Cumberland, VA 23040. 804-492-4297, Fax: 804-492-4876. 8:30AM-4:30PM.

Felony, Civil Actions Over $15,000, Probate—10th Circuit Court, PO Box 8, Cumberland, VA 23040. 804-492-4442. 8:30AM-4:30PM. Access by: in person, online.

Misdemeanor, Civil Actions Under $15,000, Eviction, Small Claims—10th General District Court, PO Box 24, Cumberland, VA 23040. 804-492-4848, Fax: 804-492-9455. 8:30AM-4:30PM. Access by: mail, phone, fax, in person, online.

Danville

Real Estate Recording—Danville City Clerk of the Circuit Court, 212 Lynn Street, Danville, VA 24541. 804-799-5140, Fax: 804-799-6502. 8:30AM-5PM.

Danville City

Felony, Civil Actions Over $15,000, Probate—22nd Circuit Court, PO Box 3300, Danville, VA 24543. 804-799-5168, Fax: 804-799-6502. 8:30AM-5PM. Access by: in person, online.

Misdemeanor, Civil Actions Under $15,000, Eviction, Small Claims—22nd General District Court, PO Box 3300, Danville, VA 24543. 804-799-5179, Fax: 804-797-8814. 8:30AM-4:30PM. Access by: mail, phone, fax, in person, online.

Dickenson

Real Estate Recording—Dickenson County Clerk of the Circuit Court, Main Street, Courthouse, Clintwood, VA 24228. 540-926-1610, Fax: 540-926-6465. 8:30AM-4:30PM.

Felony, Civil Actions Over $15,000, Probate—29th Circuit Court, PO Box 190, Clintwood, VA 24228. 540-926-1616, Fax: 540-926-6454. 8:30AM-4:30PM. Access by: mail, phone, in person, online.

Misdemeanor, Civil Actions Under $15,000, Eviction, Small Claims—29th General District Court, PO Box 128, Clintwood, VA 24228. 540-926-1630, Fax: 540-926-4815. 8:30AM-4:30PM. Access by: mail, phone, in person, online.

Dinwiddie

Real Estate Recording—Dinwiddie County Clerk of the Circuit Court, Courthouse, 14008 Boydton Plank Rd. Dinwiddie, VA 23841. 804-469-4510. 9AM-5PM.

Felony, Civil Actions Over $15,000, Probate—11th Circuit Court, PO Box 63, Dinwiddie, VA 23841. 804-469-4540. 8:30AM-4:30PM. Access by: mail, in person, online.

Misdemeanor, Civil Actions Under $15,000, Eviction, Small Claims—11th General District Court, PO Box 280, Dinwiddie, VA 23841. 804-469-4533, Fax: 804-469-4412. 8:30AM-4:30PM. Access by: mail, in person, online.

Emporia City

Misdemeanor, Civil Actions Under $15,000, Eviction, Small Claims—6th General District Court, 315 S Main, Emporia, VA 23847. 804-634-5400. 8:30AM-4:30PM. Access by: mail, in person, online.

Essex

Real Estate Recording—Essex County Clerk of the Circuit Court, 305 Prince Street, Tappahannock, VA 22560. 804-443-4371. 9AM-5PM.

Felony, Civil Actions Over $15,000, Probate—15th Circuit Court, PO Box 445, 305 prince St, Tappahannock, VA 22560. 804-443-3541. 9AM-5PM. Access by: in person.

Misdemeanor, Civil Actions Under $15,000, Eviction, Small Claims—15th General District Court, PO Box 66, Tappahannock, VA 22560. 804-443-3744, Fax: 804-443-4122. 8AM-12:30PM, 1-4:30PM. Access by: mail, in person, online.

Fairfax

Real Estate Recording—Fairfax County Clerk of the Circuit Court, 4110 Chain Bridge Road, 3rd Floor, Fairfax, VA 22030. 8AM-4PM.

Felony, Civil Actions Over $15,000, Probate—19th Circuit Court, 4110 Chain Bridge Rd, Fairfax, VA 22030. 8AM-4PM. Access by: in person. www.co.fairfax.va.us/courts

Misdemeanor, Civil Actions Under $15,000, Eviction, Small Claims—19th General District Court, 4110 Chain Bridge Rd, Fairfax, VA 22030. 703-246-2153, Fax: 703-591-2349. 8AM-4PM. Access by: phone, in person. Special note: Traffic division at 703-352-1912. www.co.fairfax.va.us/courts

Misdemeanor—19th General District Court, 10455 Armstrong St #304, Fairfax, VA 22030. 703-385-7866, Fax: 703-352-3195. 8:30AM-4:30PM. Access by: mail, in person. Special note: Find Circuit Court cases and General District civil cases for this city in the Fairfax County listing.

Falls Church City

Misdemeanor, Civil Actions Under $15,000, Eviction, Small Claims—17th District Courts Combined, Falls Church District, 300 Park Ave, Falls Church, VA 22046-3305. 703-241-5096, Fax: 703-241-1407. 8AM-4PM. Access by: mail, fax, in person, online. Special note: Small claims phone is 703-248-5157; juvenile and domestic relations is 703-248-5099.

Fauquier

Real Estate Recording—Fauquier County Clerk of the Circuit Court, First Floor, 40 CulpeperSt. Warrenton, VA 20186. 540-347-8691. 8AM-4:30PM.

Felony, Civil Actions Over $15,000, Probate—20th Circuit Court, 40 Culpepper St, Warrenton, VA 20186-3298. 540-347-8610. 8AM-4:30PM. Access by: in person, online.

Misdemeanor, Civil Actions Under $15,000, Eviction, Small Claims—20th General District Court, 6 Court St, Warrenton, VA 20186. Fax: 540-347-5756. 8:30AM-4:30PM. Access by: in person, online.

Floyd

Real Estate Recording—Floyd County Clerk of the Circuit Court, 100 East Main Street, Room 200, Floyd, VA 24091. 540-745-9357. 8:30AM-4:30PM; 8:30AM-Noon Sat (Closed Sat if holiday weekend).

Felony, Civil Actions Over $15,000, Probate—27th Circuit Court, 100 East Main St, #200, Floyd, VA 24091. 540-745-9330. 8:30AM-4:30PM M-F, 8:30AM-Noon Sat. Access by: in person, online.

Misdemeanor, Civil Actions Under $15,000, Eviction, Small Claims—27th General District Court, 100 East Main St, Floyd, VA 24091-2101. 540-745-9327, Fax: 540-745-9329. 8AM-4:30PM. Access by: mail, in person, online.

Fluvanna

Real Estate Recording—Fluvanna County Clerk of the Circuit Court, Clerk's Office Bldg. Court Green & Rt. 15, Palmyra, VA 22963. 804-589-8012, Fax: 804-589-6004. 8AM-4:30PM.

Felony, Civil Actions Over $15,000, Probate—16th Circuit Court, PO Box 299, Palmyra, VA 22963. 804-589-8011, Fax: 804-589-6004. 8:30AM-4:30PM. Access by: mail, fax, in person, online.

Misdemeanor, Civil Actions Under $15,000, Eviction, Small Claims—16th General District Court, Fluvanna County Courthouse, PO Box 417, Palmyra, VA 22963. 804-589-8022, Fax: 804-589-6934. 8:30AM-4:30PM. Access by: mail, in person, online.

Franklin

Real Estate Recording—Franklin County Clerk of the Circuit Court, Courthouse Building, Rocky Mount, VA 24151. Fax: 540-483-3042. 8:30AM-5PM.

Felony, Civil Actions Over $15,000, Probate—22nd Circuit Court, PO Box 190, Courtland, VA 23837. 757-653-2200. 8:30AM-5PM. Access by: mail, in person, online.

Franklin City

Misdemeanor, Civil Actions Under $15,000, Eviction, Small Claims—22nd General District Court, PO Box 569, Rocky Mount, VA 24151. 540-483-3060, Fax: 540-483-3036. 8:30AM-4:30PM. Access by: in person, online.

Frederick

Real Estate Recording—Frederick County Clerk of the Circuit Court, 5 North Kent Street, Winchester, VA 22601. 540-662-6611, Fax: 540-545-8711. 9AM-5PM.

Felony, Misdemeanor, Civil, Eviction, Probate—26th Circuit and District Court, 5 North Kent St, Winchester, VA 22601. 540-667-5770. 9AM-5PM. Access by: mail, in person, online.

Fredericksburg City

Real Estate Recording—Fredericksburg City Clerk of the Circuit Court, 815 Princess Anne Street, Fredericksburg, VA 22401. 8AM-4PM.

Felony, Civil Actions Over $15,000, Probate—15th Circuit Circuit Court, 815 Princess Anne St, PO Box 359, Fredericksburg, VA 22404-0359. 540-372-1066. 8AM-4PM. Access by: in person, online.

Misdemeanor, Civil Actions Under $15,000, Eviction, Small Claims—15th General District Court, PO Box 180, Fredericksburg, VA 22404. 540-372-1044. 8AM-4PM. Access by: mail, in person, online.

Galax City

Circuit Court, Special note: See Carroll County for Hillsville area and Grayson County for Independence area.

Misdemeanor, Civil Actions Under $15,000, Eviction, Small Claims—27th General District Court, 353 N Main St, PO Box 214, Galax, VA 24333-0214. 540-236-8731, Fax: 540-236-2754. 8:30AM-4:30PM. Access by: mail, in person, online. Special note: Circuit Court jurisdiction for this city can be in Carroll County or Grayson County depending on side of the side the offense occured.

Giles

Real Estate Recording—Giles County Clerk of the Circuit Court, 501 Wenonah Avenue, Pearisburg, VA 24134. 540-921-1240, Fax: 540-921-3825. 9AM-5PM.

Felony, Civil Actions Over $15,000, Probate—27th Circuit Court, 501 Wenonah Ave, Pearisburg, VA 24134. 540-921-1722, Fax: 540-921-3825. 9AM-5PM. Access by: mail, in person, online.

Misdemeanor, Civil Actions Under $15,000, Eviction, Small Claims—27th General District Court, 120 N Main St, #1, Pearisburg, VA 24134. 540-921-3533, Fax: 540-921-2752. 8:30AM-4:30PM. Access by: mail, fax, in person, online.

Gloucester

Real Estate Recording—Gloucester County Clerk of the Circuit Court, Courts & Office Bldg. Room 207, 6489 Main Street, Gloucester, VA 23061. 804-693-2141, Fax: 804-693-2186. 8AM-4:30PM.

Felony, Civil Actions Over $15,000, Probate—9th Circuit Court, Box N, Gloucester, VA 23061-0570. 804-693-2502, Fax: 804-693-2186. 8AM-4:30PM. Access by: mail, phone, fax, in person, online. www.co.gloucester.va.us

Misdemeanor, Civil Actions Under $15,000, Eviction, Small Claims—9th General District Court, PO Box 873, Gloucester, VA 23061. 804-693-4860, Fax: 804-693-6669. 8:30AM-4:30PM. Access by: mail, fax, in person, online.

Goochland

Real Estate Recording—Goochland County Clerk of the Circuit Court, 2938 River Road West, Goochland, VA 23063. 8:30AM-5PM.

Felony, Civil Actions Over $15,000, Probate—16th Circuit Court, PO Box 196, Goochland, VA 23063. 804-556-5353. 8:30AM-5PM. Access by: in person, online.

Misdemeanor, Civil Actions Under $15,000, Eviction, Small Claims—General District Court, PO Box 47, Goochland, VA 23063. 804-556-5309. 8:30AM-4:30PM. Access by: in person, online.

Grayson

Real Estate Recording—Grayson County Clerk of the Circuit Court, 129 Davis Street, Independence, VA 24348. 540-773-2571, Fax: 540-773-3338. 8AM-5PM.

Felony, Civil Actions Over $15,000, Probate—27th Circuit Court, PO Box 130, Independence, VA 24348. 540-773-2231, Fax: 540-773-3338. 8AM-5PM. Access by: mail, in person, online.

Misdemeanor, Civil Actions Under $15,000, Eviction, Small Claims—27th General District Court, PO Box 280, Independence, VA 24348. 540-773-2011. 8AM-4:30PM. Access by: mail, in person, online.

Greene

Real Estate Recording—Greene County Clerk of the Circuit Court, Courthouse, Court Square, Stanardsville, VA 22973. 804-985-5214, Fax: 804-985-6723. 8:15AM-4:30PM; Recording Hours: 8:15AM-4:15PM.

Felony, Civil Actions Over $15,000, Probate—16th Circuit Court, PO Box 386, Stanardsville, VA 22973. 804-985-5208, Fax: 804-985-6723. 8:30AM-4:30PM; Recording until 4:15 PM. Access by: mail, in person, online.

Misdemeanor, Civil Actions Under $15,000, Eviction, Small Claims—16th General District Court, Greene County Courthouse (PO Box 245), Stanardsville, VA 22973. 804-985-5224. 8AM-4:30PM. Access by: mail, in person, online.

Greensville

Real Estate Recording—Greensville County Clerk of the Circuit Court, 308 South Main Street, Emporia, VA 23847. 804-348-4208, Fax: 804-348-4020. 9AM-5PM.

Felony, Civil Actions Over $15,000, Probate—6th Circuit Court, PO Box 631, Emporia, VA 23847. 804-348-4215. 9AM-5PM. Access by: in person, online.

Misdemeanor, Civil Actions Under $15,000, Eviction, Small Claims—Greenville/Emporia Combined Court, 315 S Main, Emporia, VA 23847. 804-348-4266. 8:30AM-4:30PM. Access by: in person, online.

Halifax

Real Estate Recording—Halifax County Clerk of the Circuit Court, Courthouse Square, Halifax, VA 24558. 804-476-2025, Fax: 804-476-2890. 8:30AM-4:30PM.

Felony, Civil Actions Over $15,000, Probate—10th Circuit Court, PO Box 729, Halifax, VA 24558. 804-476-6211. 8:30AM-5PM. Access by: mail, in person, online.

Misdemeanor, Civil Actions Under $15,000, Eviction, Small Claims—10th General District Court, Halifax County Courthouse, PO Box 458, Halifax, VA 24558. 804-476-3385, Fax: 804-476-3387. 8:30AM-4:30PM. Access by: mail, fax, in person, online.

Hampton City

Real Estate Recording—Hampton Clerk of the Circuit Court, 101 Kingsway Mall, Hampton, VA 23669. 757-727-6374. 8:30AM-5PM.

Felony, Civil Actions Over $15,000, Probate—8th Circuit Court, 101 King's Way, PO Box 40, Hampton, VA 23669-0040. 757-727-6105. 8:30AM-5PM. Access by: mail, in person, online.

Misdemeanor, Civil Actions Under $15,000, Eviction, Small Claims—8th General District Court, Courthouse, Po Box 70, Hampton, VA 23669-0070. 8AM-4PM. Access by: mail, in person, online.

Hanover

Real Estate Recording—Hanover County Clerk of the Circuit Court, 7507 Library Dr. 2nd Floor, Hanover, VA 23069. 8:30AM-4:30PM.

Felony, Civil Actions Over $15,000, Probate—15th Circuit Court, 7507 Library Dr, PO Box 39, Hanover, VA 23069. 804-537-6143, Fax: 804-534-6278. 8:30AM-4:30PM. Access by: in person, online.

Misdemeanor, Civil Actions Under $15,000, Eviction, Small Claims—15th General District Court, Hanover County Courthouse, PO Box 176, Hanover, VA 23069. 804-537-6000, Fax: 804-365-6290. 8AM-4PM. Access by: mail, in person, online.

Harrisonburg City

Circuit and District Courts, Special note: See Rockingham County.

Henrico

Real Estate Recording—Henrico Circuit Court Clerk, 4301 East Parham Road, Richmond, VA 23228. 8AM-4PM; (Recording Hours 8AM-3:30PM).

Felony, Civil Actions Over $15,000, Probate—14th Circuit Court, PO Box 27032, Richmond, VA 23273-7032. 8AM-4:30PM. Access by: mail, in person, online.

Misdemeanor, Civil Actions Under $15,000, Eviction, Small Claims—14th General District Court, PO Box 27032, Richmond, VA 23273. 804-501-4723, Fax: 804-501-4141. 8AM-4PM. Access by: in person, online.

Henry

Real Estate Recording—Henry County Clerk of the Circuit Court, 3160 Kings Mountain Rd. #B, Martinsville, VA 24112. 9AM-5PM.

Felony, Civil Actions Over $15,000, Probate—21st Circuit Court, 3160 Kings Mountain Rd Suite B, Martinsville, VA 24112. 540-634-4880. 9AM-5PM. Access by: mail, in person, online.

Misdemeanor, Civil Actions Under $15,000, Eviction, Small Claims—21st General District Court, 3160 King's Mountain Rd Ste A, Martinsville, VA 24112. 540-634-4815, Fax: 540-634-4825. 9AM-5PM. Access by: in person, online.

Highland

Real Estate Recording—Highland County Clerk of the Circuit Court, Spruce Street, Courthouse, Monterey, VA 24465. 540-465-2265, Fax: 540-468-3447. 8:45AM-4:30PM.

Felony, Civil Actions Over $15,000, Probate—25th Circuit Court, PO Box 190, Monterey, VA 24465. 540-468-2447, Fax: 540-468-3447. 8:45AM-4:30PM. Access by: mail, in person, online.

Misdemeanor, Civil Actions Under $15,000, Eviction, Small Claims—25th General District Court, Highland County Courthouse, PO Box 88, Monterey, VA 24465. 540-468-2445, Fax: 540-468-3447. 8:30AM-4:30PM. Access by: mail, fax, in person, online.

Hopewell City

Real Estate Recording—Hopewell City Clerk of the Circuit Court, 100 E. Broadway, Room 251, Hopewell, VA 23860. 8:30AM-4:30PM.

Felony, Civil Actions Over $15,000, Probate—6th Circuit Court, 100 E Broadway, PO Box 354, 2nd Fl, Hopewell, VA 23860. 804-541-2239, Fax: 804-541-2438. 8:30AM-4:30PM. Access by: mail, in person, online.

Misdemeanor, Civil Actions Under $15,000, Eviction, Small Claims—Hopewell District Court, 100 E Broadway, Hopewell, VA 23860. 804-541-2257, Fax: 804-541-2364. 8:30AM-4:30PM. Access by: mail, in person, online.

Isle of Wight

Real Estate Recording—Isle of Wight County Clerk of the Circuit Court, 17122 Monument Circle, Hwy 258, Courthouse, Isle of Wight, VA 23397. 757-357-3191. 9AM-5PM.

Felony, Civil Actions Over $15,000, Probate—5th Circuit Court, 17122 Monument Circle, PO Box 110, Isle of Wight, VA 23397. 757-357-3191. 9AM-5PM. Access by: in person, online. Special note: The Clerk can be reached at 757-365-6233.

Misdemeanor, Civil Actions Under $15,000, Eviction, Small Claims—5th General District Court, Isle of Wight Courthouse, PO Box 122, Isle of Wight, VA 23397. 757-357-3191, Fax: 757-365-6246. 8AM-4PM. Access by: in person, online. Special note: The Clerk can be reached at 757-365-6244.

James City

Real Estate Recording—Williamsburg-James City County Clerk of the Circuit Court, 321-45 Court Street West, Room 28, Williamsburg, VA 23185. 757-229-6705. 8:30AM-4:30PM.

5elony, Civil Actions Over $15,000, Probate—Williamsburg-James City County Circuit Court, 5201 Monticello Ave #6, Williamsburg, VA 23188-8218. 757-564-2242, Fax: 757-564-2250. 8:30AM-4:30PM. Access by: mail, in person, online.

9th General District Court, James City County Courthouse, PO Box 3005, Williamsburg, VA 23187. 757-564-2400, Fax: 757-564-2410. 7:30AM-4PM. Access by: mail, fax, in person, online.

King and Queen

Real Estate Recording—King and Queen County Clerk of the Circuit Court, Route 681, Allen's Circle, Courthouse, King and Queen Court House, VA 23085. 804-785-6321, Fax: 804-785-5698. 9AM-5PM.

Felony, Civil Actions Over $15,000, Probate—9th Circuit Court, PO Box 67, King & Queen Court House, VA 23085. 804-785-5984, Fax: 804-785-5698. 9AM-5PM. Access by: in person, online.

Misdemeanor, Civil Actions Under $15,000, Eviction—King & Queen Courthouse, PO Box 86, King William Courthouse, VA 23085-0086. 804-785-5982, Fax: 804-785-5694. 8:30AM-1PM. Access by: mail, fax, in person, online.

King George

Real Estate Recording—King George County Clerk of the Circuit Court, 9483 Kings Highway, Courthouse, King George, VA 22485. 540-775-2571. 8:30AM-4:30PM.

Felony, Civil Actions Over $15,000, Probate—15th Circuit Court, PO Box 105, King George, VA 22485. 540-775-3322. 8:30AM-4:30PM. Access by: mail, in person, online.

Misdemeanor, Civil Actions Under $15,000, Eviction, Small Claims—15th Judicial District King George Combined Court, County Courthouse PO Box 279, King George, VA 22485. 540-775-3573. 8AM-4:30PM. Access by: mail, in person, online.

King William

Real Estate Recording—King William County Clerk of the Circuit Court, Route 619, 227 Courthouse Lane, King William, VA 23086. 804-769-4950. 8:30AM-4:30PM.

Felony, Civil Actions Over $15,000, Probate—9th Circuit Court, 227 Courthouse Lane, PO Box 216, King William, VA 23086. 804-769-4938. 8:30AM-4:30PM. Access by: mail, in person.

Misdemeanor, Civil Actions Under $15,000, Eviction, Small Claims—King William General District Court, PO Box 5, King William, VA 23086. 804-769-4948, Fax: 804-769-4971. 8:30AM-4:30PM. Access by: mail, fax, in person, online.

Lancaster

Real Estate Recording—Lancaster County Clerk of the Circuit Court, Courthouse, 8311 Maryball Rd. Lancaster, VA 22503. 9AM-5PM.

Felony, Civil Actions Over $15,000, Probate—15th Circuit Court, Courthouse Building, PO Box 99, Lancaster, VA 22503. 804-462-5611. 9AM-5PM. Access by: mail, in person, online.

Misdemeanor, Civil Actions Under $15,000, Eviction, Small Claims—15th General District Court, PO 129, Lancaster, VA 22503. 804-462-0012. 8:30AM-4:30PM. Access by: mail, in person, online.

Lee

Real Estate Recording—Lee County Clerk of the Circuit Court, Main Street, Courthouse, Jonesville, VA 24263. 540-346-7716, Fax: 540-346-3440. 8:30AM-5PM; 9AM-Noon Sat.

Felony, Civil Actions Over $15,000, Probate—30th Circuit Court, PO Box 326, Jonesville, VA 24263. 540-346-7763, Fax: 540-

346-3440. 8:30AM-5PM M-F, 9AM-Noon Sat. Access by: mail, phone, fax, in person, online.

Misdemeanor, Civil Actions Under $15,000, Eviction, Small Claims—30th General District Court, Lee County Courthouse, PO Box 306, Jonesville, VA 24263. 540-346-7729, Fax: 540-346-7701. 8AM-4:30PM. Access by: mail, fax, in person, online.

Lexington City

Circuit and District Courts, Special note: See Rockbridge County.

Loudoun

Real Estate Recording—Loudoun County Clerk of the Circuit Court, 18 E. Market St. Leesburg, VA 20176. 703-777-0280. 9AM-4PM.

Felony, Civil Actions Over $15,000, Probate—20th Circuit Court, 18 N King St, PO Box 550, Leesburg, VA 20178. 703-777-0270, Fax: 703-777-0676. 9AM-5PM. Access by: mail, phone, in person, online.

Misdemeanor, Civil Actions Under $15,000, Eviction—20th General District Court, 18 E Market St, 2nd Flr, Leesburg, VA 20176. 703-777-0312, Fax: 703-777-0311. 8:30AM-4:30PM. Access by: mail, in person, online.

Louisa

Real Estate Recording—Louisa County Clerk of the Circuit Court, 314 W. Main Street, Courthouse, Louisa, VA 23093. 8:30AM-5PM (Stop Recording 4:15PM).

Felony, Civil Actions Over $15,000, Probate—16th Circuit Court, Box 37, Louisa, VA 23093. 540-967-5312, Fax: 540-967-2705. 8:30AM-5PM. Access by: mail, in person, online.

Misdemeanor, Civil Actions Under $15,000, Eviction, Small Claims—16th General District Court, PO Box 452, Louisa, VA 23093. 540-967-5330, Fax: 540-967-2369. 8:30AM-4:30PM. Access by: in person, online.

Lunenburg

Real Estate Recording—Lunenburg County Clerk of the Circuit Court, Courthouse, Lunenburg, VA 23952. 8:30AM-4:30PM.

Felony, Civil Actions Over $15,000, Probate—10th Circuit Court, Courthouse, Lunenburg, VA 23952. 804-696-2230, Fax: 804-696-3931. 8:30AM-4:30PM. Access by: mail, fax, in person, online.

Misdemeanor, Civil Actions Under $15,000, Eviction, Small Claims—10th General District Court, 1143 Courthouse Road, Lunenburg, VA 23952. 804-696-5508, Fax: 804-696-3665. 8:30AM-5PM. Access by: mail, in person, online.

Lynchburg City

Real Estate Recording—Lynchburg City Clerk of the Circuit Court, 900 Court Street, Lynchburg, VA 24504. 804-847-1520, Fax: 804-847-1864. 8:30AM-4:45PM.

Felony, Civil Actions Over $15,000, Probate—24th Circuit Court, 900 Court St, PO Box 4, Lynchburg, VA 24505-0004. 804-847-1590, Fax: 804-847-1864. 8:30AM-4:45PM. Access by: mail, in person, online.

Civil Actions Under $15,000, Eviction, Small Claims—24th General District Court-Civil Division, 905 Court St, PO Box 60, Lynchburg, VA 24505. 804-847-1639, Fax: 804-847-1779. 8:30AM-4:30PM. Access by: mail, in person.

Misdemeanor—24th General District Court-Criminal Division, 905 Court St, Lynchburg, VA 24504. 804-847-1560, Fax: 804-847-1779. 8:30AM-4:30PM. Access by: in person, online.

Madison

Real Estate Recording—Madison County Clerk of the Circuit Court, 100 Court Square, Madison, VA 22727. 540-948-4409, Fax: 540-948-3759. 8:30AM-4:30PM.

Felony, Civil Actions Over $15,000, Probate—16th Circuit Court, PO Box 220, Madison, VA 22727. 540-948-6888, Fax: 540-948-3759. 8:30AM-4:30PM. Access by: mail, in person, online.

Misdemeanor, Civil Actions Under $15,000, Eviction, Small Claims—16th General District Court, Madison County Courthouse, PO Box 470, Madison, VA 22727. 540-948-4657. 8:30AM-4:30PM. Access by: mail, phone, fax, in person, online.

Manassas City

Circuit and District Courts, Special note: See Prince William County.

Manassas Park City

Circuit and District Courts, Special note: See Prince William County.

Martinsville City

Real Estate Recording—Martinsville City Clerk of the Circuit Court, 55 West Church Street, Martinsville, VA 24112. Fax: 540-656-5232. 9AM-5PM.

Felony, Civil Actions Over $15,000, Probate—21st Circuit Court, PO Box 1206, Martinsville, VA 24114-1206. 540-656-5106, Fax: 540-656-5232. 9AM-5PM. Access by: mail, in person, online.

Misdemeanor, Civil Actions Under $15,000, Eviction, Small Claims—21st General District Court, PO Box 1402, Martinsville, VA 24112. 540-656-5125, Fax: 540-638-8584. 9AM-5PM. Access by: in person, online.

Mathews

Real Estate Recording—Mathews County Clerk of the Circuit Court, Courthouse Square, Mathews, VA 23109. 8AM-4PM.

Felony, Civil Actions Over $15,000, Probate—9th Circuit Court, PO Box 463, Mathews, VA 23109. 804-725-2550. 8AM-4PM. Access by: mail, in person, online.

Misdemeanor, Civil Actions Under $15,000, Eviction, Small Claims—9th General District Court, PO Box 169, Saluda, VA 23149. 804-758-4312. 8:30AM-4:30PM. Access by: mail, in person, online.

Mecklenburg

Real Estate Recording—Mecklenburg County Clerk of the Circuit Court, 393 Washington Street, Boydton, VA 23917. 8:30AM-5PM.

Felony, Civil Actions Over $15,000, Probate—10th Circuit Court, PO Box 530, Boydton, VA 23917. 804-738-6191, Fax: 804-738-6861. 8:30AM-4:30PM. Access by: in person, online.

Misdemeanor, Civil Actions Under $15,000, Eviction, Small Claims—10th General District Court, 1294 Jefferson Street (PO Box 306), Boydton, VA 23917. 804-738-6191. 8:30AM-4:30PM. Access by: mail, fax, in person, online.

Middlesex

Real Estate Recording—Middlesex County Clerk of the Circuit Court, Route 17 Courthouse, Saluda, VA 23149. 8:30AM-4:30PM.

Felony, Civil Actions Over $15,000, Probate—9th Circuit Court, PO Box 158, Saluda, VA 23149. 804-758-5317, Fax: 804-758-0792. 8:30AM-4:30PM. Access by: in person, online.

Misdemeanor, Civil Actions Under $15,000, Eviction, Small Claims—9th General District Court, PO Box 169, Saluda, VA 23149. 804-758-4312. 8:30AM-4:30PM. Access by: mail, in person, online.

Montgomery

Real Estate Recording—Montgomery County, Courthouse, 1 East Main #B5, Christiansburg, VA 24073. Fax: 540-382-6937. 8:30AM-4:30PM.

Felony, Civil Actions Over $15,000, Probate—27th Circuit Court, 1 E Main St, Suite B-5, Christiansburg, VA 24073. 540-382-5760, Fax: 540-382-6937. 8:30AM-4:30PM. Access by: in person, online.

Misdemeanor, Civil Actions Under $15,000, Eviction, Small Claims—27th General District Court, Montgomery County Courthouse, 1 E Main St, Suite 201, Christiansburg, VA 24073. 540-382-5735, Fax: 540-382-6988. 8:30AM-4:30PM. Access by: mail, fax, in person, online.

Nelson

Real Estate Recording—Nelson County Clerk of the Circuit Court, 84 Courthouse Square, Lovingston, VA 22949. 804-263-4079, Fax: 804-263-8313. 9AM-5PM.

Felony, Civil Actions Over $15,000, Probate—24th Circuit Court, PO Box 10, Lovingston, VA 22949. 804-263-4069, Fax: 804-263-8313. 9AM-5PM. Access by: in person, online.

Misdemeanor, Civil Actions Under $15,000, Eviction, Small Claims—24th General District Court, Nelson County Courthouse, 84 Courthouse St, PO Box 55, Lovingston, VA 22949. 804-263-4245, Fax: 804-263-4264. 8AM-4:30PM. Access by: mail, fax, in person, online.

New Kent

Real Estate Recording—New Kent County Clerk of the Circuit Court, 12001 Courthouse Circle, Courthouse, New Kent, VA 23124. 804-966-9615, Fax: 804-966-9528. 8:30AM-4:30PM.

Felony, Civil Actions Over $15,000, Probate—9th Circuit Court, PO Box 98, 2001 Court House Circle, New Kent, VA 23124. 804-966-9520, Fax: 804-966-9528. 8:30AM-4:30PM. Access by: in person, online.

Misdemeanor, Civil Actions Under $15,000, Eviction, Small Claims—9th General District Court, PO Box 127, New Kent, VA 23124. 804-966-9530, Fax: 804-966-9535. 8:30AM-4:30PM. Access by: mail, in person, online.

Newport News City

Real Estate Recording—Newport News Clerk of the Circuit Court, 2500 Washington Avenue, Courthouse, Newport News, VA 23607. 757-247-8731, Fax: 757-926-8531. 8AM-4:45PM.

Felony, Civil Actions Over $15,000, Probate—7th Circuit Court, 2500 Washington Ave, Newport News, VA 23607. 757-926-8561, Fax: 757-926-8531. 8AM-4:45PM. Access by: mail, in person, online.

Misdemeanor, Civil Actions Under $15,000, Eviction, Small Claims—7th General District Court, 2500 Washington Ave, Newport News, VA 23607. Fax: 757-926-8496. 7:30AM-4PM. Access by: mail, in person, online.

Norfolk City

Real Estate Recording—Norfolk City Clerk of the Circuit Court, 100 St. Paul's Blvd. Norfolk, VA 23510. 757-441-2931. 9AM-5PM.

Felony, Civil Actions Over $15,000, Probate—4th Circuit Court, 100 St Paul's Blvd, Norfolk, VA 23510. 757-664-4380, Fax: 757-664-4581. 9AM-5PM. Access by: mail, in person, online.

Misdemeanor, Civil Actions Under $15,000, Eviction, Small Claims—4th General District Court, 811 E City Hall Ave, Norfolk, VA 23510. 757-664-4910. 8AM-4PM. Access by: mail, in person, online.

Northampton

Real Estate Recording—Northampton County Clerk of the Circuit Court, 16404 Courthouse Rd. Courthouse, Eastville, VA 23347. 757-678-0450, Fax: 757-678-5410. 9AM-5PM.

Felony, Civil Actions Over $15,000, Probate—2nd Circuit Court, PO Box 36, Eastville, VA 23347. 757-678-0465, Fax: 757-678-5410. 9AM-5PM. Access by: mail, phone, fax, in person, online.

Misdemeanor, Civil Actions Under $15,000, Eviction, Small Claims—Northampton General District Court, PO Box 125, Eastville, VA 23347. 757-678-0466. 8AM-5PM. Access by: mail, in person, online.

Northumberland

Real Estate Recording—Northumberland County Clerk of the Circuit Court, Highway 360, Courthouse, 39 Judicial Place, Heathsville, VA 22473. 804-580-4600. 8:30AM-4:45PM.

Felony, Civil Actions Over $15,000, Probate—15th Circuit Court, PO Box 217, Heathsville, VA 22473. 804-580-3700, Fax: 804-580-2261. 8:30AM-4:45PM. Access by: mail, in person, online.

Misdemeanor, Civil Actions Under $15,000, Eviction, Small Claims—15th General District Court, Northumberland Courthouse, PO Box 114, Heathsville, VA 22473. 804-580-4323, Fax: 804-580-6702. 8AM-4:30PM. Access by: in person, online.

Norton City

Circuit and District Courts, Special note: See Wise County.

Nottoway

Real Estate Recording—Nottoway County Clerk of the Circuit Court, State Route 625, Courthouse, Nottoway, VA 23955. Fax: 804-645-2201. 8:30AM-4:30PM.

Felony, Civil Actions Over $15,000, Probate—11th Circuit Court, Courthouse, PO Box 25, Nottoway, VA 23955. 804-645-9043, Fax: 804-645-2201. 8:30AM-4:30PM. Access by: mail, in person, online.

Misdemeanor, Civil Actions Under $15,000, Eviction, Small Claims—11th General District Court, Courthouse, Nottoway, VA 23955. 804-645-9312. 8AM-4:15PM. Access by: mail, in person, online.

Orange

Real Estate Recording—Orange County Clerk of the Circuit Court, 109 West Main Street, Orange, VA 22960. 540-672-2656, Fax: 540-672-2939. 8:30AM-4:30PM.

Felony, Civil Actions Over $15,000, Probate—16th Circuit Court, PO Box 230, Orange, VA 22960. 540-672-4030, Fax: 540-672-2939. 8:30AM-4:30PM. Access by: mail, phone, fax, in person, online.

Misdemeanor, Civil Actions Under $15,000, Eviction, Small Claims—16th General District Court, Orange County Courthouse, PO Box 821, Orange, VA 22960. 540-672-3150, Fax: 540-672-9438. 8:30AM-4:30PM. Access by: mail, in person, online.

Page

Real Estate Recording—Page County Clerk of the Circuit Court, 116 South Court Street, Suite A, Luray, VA 22835. 540-743-3975, Fax: 540-743-2338. 9AM-5PM.

Felony, Civil Actions Over $15,000, Probate—26th Circuit Court, 116 S Court St, Suite A, Luray, VA 22835. 540-743-4064, Fax: 540-743-2338. 9AM-5PM. Access by: in person, online.

Misdemeanor, Civil Actions Under $15,000, Eviction, Small Claims—26th General District Court, 116 S Court St, Luray, VA 22835. 540-743-5705. 8AM-4:30PM. Access by: mail, in person, online.

Patrick

Real Estate Recording—Patrick County Clerk of the Circuit Court, Courthouse, 101 West Blue Ridge St. Stuart, VA 24171. 540-694-7257, Fax: 540-694-6943. 9AM-5PM.

Felony, Civil Actions Over $15,000, Probate—21st Circuit Court, PO Box 148, Stuart, VA 24171. 540-694-7213. 9AM-5PM. Access by: in person, online.

Misdemeanor, Civil Actions Under $15,000, Eviction, Small Claims—21st General District Court, PO Box 149, Stuart, VA 24171. 540-694-7258, Fax: 540-694-5614. 8:30AM-5PM. Access by: mail, in person, online.

Petersburg City

Real Estate Recording—Petersburg City Clerk of the Circuit Court, 7 Courthouse Ave. Petersburg, VA 23803. 804-733-2321, Fax: 804-732-5548. 8AM-4PM (Recording until 4PM).

Felony, Civil Actions Over $15,000, Probate—11th Circuit Court, 7 Courthouse Ave, Petersburg, VA 23803. 804-733-2367, Fax: 804-732-5548. 8AM-4:30PM. Access by: in person, online.

Misdemeanor, Civil Actions Under $15,000, Eviction, Small Claims—11th Judicial District Court, 35 E Tabb St, Petersburg, VA 23803. 804-733-2374, Fax: 804-733-2375. 8AM-4PM. Access by: mail, fax, in person, online.

Pittsylvania

Real Estate Recording—Pittsylvania County Clerk of the Circuit Court, 1 North Main Street, Courthouse, Chatham, VA 24531. 8:30AM-5PM.

Felony, Civil Actions Over $15,000, Probate—22nd Circuit Court, PO Drawer 31, Chatham, VA 24531. 804-432-2041. 8:30AM-5PM. Access by: in person, online.

Misdemeanor, Civil Actions Under $15,000, Eviction, Small Claims—22nd General District Court, Pittsylvania Courthouse Annex 2nd Flr, PO Box 695, Chatham, VA 24531. 804-432-7879, Fax: 804-432-7915. 8:30AM-4:30PM. Access by: in person, online.

Poquoson City

Circuit and District Courts, Special note: See York County.

Portsmouth City

Real Estate Recording—Portsmouth City Clerk of the Circuit Court, 601 Crawford Street, Portsmouth, VA 23704. 804-393-8651. 9AM-5PM.

Felony, Civil Actions Over $15,000, Probate—3rd Circuit Court, PO Drawer 1217, Portsmouth, VA 23705. 757-393-8671, Fax: 757-399-4826. 8:30AM-5PM. Access by: mail, in person, online.

Misdemeanor, Civil Actions Under $15,000, Eviction, Small Claims—General District Court, PO Box 129, Portsmouth, VA 23705. Fax: 757-393-8634. 8:30AM-4:30PM. Access by: mail, in person, online. Special note: Traffic Division: 757-393-8506.

Powhatan

Real Estate Recording—Powhatan County Clerk of the Circuit Court, 3880 Old Buckingham Road, Powhatan, VA 23139. 804-598-5626. 8:30AM-5PM.

Felony, Civil Actions Over $15,000, Probate—11th Circuit Court, PO Box 37, Powhatan, VA 23139-0037. 804-598-5660, Fax: 804-598-5608. 8:30AM-5PM. Access by: mail, in person.

Misdemeanor, Civil Actions Under $15,000, Eviction, Small Claims—11th General District Court, Courthouse, PO Box 113, Powhatan, VA 23139-0113. 804-598-5665, Fax: 804-598-5648. 8:30AM-5PM. Access by: mail, phone, fax, in person, online.

Prince Edward

Real Estate Recording—Prince Edward County Clerk of the Circuit Court, 124 North Main Street, Courthouse, Farmville, VA 23901. 804-392-3404. 9AM-4:30PM.

Felony, Civil Actions Over $15,000, Probate—Circuit Court, 111 South Street, Court House, Farmville, VA 23901. 804-392-5145. 8:30AM-4:30PM. Access by: in person, online.

Misdemeanor, Civil Actions Under $15,000, Eviction, Small Claims—General District Court, PO Box 41, Farmville, VA 23901-0041. 804-392-4024, Fax: 804-392-3800. 8:30AM-4:30PM. Access by: mail, in person, online.

Prince George

Real Estate Recording—Prince George County Clerk of the Circuit Court, 6601 Courts Dr. Prince George, VA 23875. 804-733-2620. Recording Hours 8:30AM-4:30PM.

Felony, Civil Actions Over $15,000, Probate—6th Circuit Court, PO Box 98, Prince George, VA 23875. 804-733-2640, Fax: 804-733-2602. 8:30AM-5PM. Access by: mail, in person, online.

Misdemeanor, Civil Actions Under $15,000, Eviction, Small Claims—6th General District Court, P.C. Courthouse, PO Box 187, Prince George, VA 23875. 804-733-2783. 8:30AM-4:30PM. Access by: mail, in person, online.

Prince William

Real Estate Recording—Prince William County Clerk of the Circuit Court, 9311 Lee Avenue, Room 300, Manassas, VA 20110. Fax: 703-792-4721. 8:30AM-3:45PM (Actual Recording); 8:30AM-5PM (General Information).

Felony, Civil Actions Over $15,000, Probate—31st Circuit Court, 9311 Lee Ave, Manassas, VA 20110. 703-792-6015, Fax: 703-792-4721. 8:30AM-5PM. Access by: mail, in person. www.pwcgov.org/ccourt

Misdemeanor, Civil Actions Under $15,000, Eviction, Small Claims—31st General District Court, 9311 Lee Ave, Manassas, VA 20110. Fax: 703-792-6121. 8AM-4PM. Access by: mail, in person, online.

Pulaski

Real Estate Recording—Pulaski County Clerk of the Circuit Court, Suite 101, 45 3rd St. NW, Pulaski, VA 24301. 540-980-7785, Fax: 540-980-7835. 8:30AM-4:30PM.

Felony, Civil Actions Over $15,000, Probate—27th Circuit Court, 45 3rd St NW Suite 101, Pulaski, VA 24301. 540-980-7825, Fax: 540-980-7835. 8:30AM-4:30PM. Access by: in person, online.

Misdemeanor, Civil Actions Under $15,000, Eviction, Small Claims—27th General District Court, 45 3rd St NW Ste 102, Pulaski, VA 24301. 540-980-7470, Fax: 540-980-7792. 8:30AM-4:30PM. Access by: in person, online.

Radford

Real Estate Recording—Radford City Clerk of the Circuit Court, 619 Second Street, Courthouse, Radford, VA 24141. 540-731-3661, Fax: 540-731-3612. 8:30AM-5PM (No machine receipts after 4:30PM).

Radford City

Felony, Civil Actions Over $15,000, Probate—27th Circuit Court, 619 2nd St, Radford, VA 24141. 540-731-3610, Fax: 540-731-3612. 8:30AM-5PM (no machine receipts after 4:30PM). Access by: mail, fax, in person, online.

Misdemeanor, Civil Actions Under $15,000, Eviction, Small Claims—27th General District Court, 619 2nd St, Radford, VA 24141. 540-731-3609, Fax: 540-731-3692. 8:30AM-4:30PM. Access by: mail, fax, in person, online.

Rappahannock

Real Estate Recording—Clerk of the Circuit Court, 238 Gay Street, Clerk's Office, Washington, VA 22747. 540-675-3334. 8:30AM-4:30PM.

Felony, Civil Actions Over $15,000, Probate—20th Circuit Court, 238 Gay Street (PO Box 517), Washington, VA 22747. 540-675-3621. 8:30AM-4:30PM. Access by: mail, in person, online.

Misdemeanor, Civil Actions Under $15,000, Eviction, Small Claims—20th Combined District Court, PO Box 206, Washington, VA 22747. 540-675-3518. 8:30AM-4:30PM. Access by: mail, in person, online.

Richmond

Real Estate Recording—Richmond City Clerk of the Circuit Court, 400 N. 9th St. Richmond, VA 23219. 9AM-3:30PM.

Richmond County Clerk of the Circuit Court, 101 Court Circle, Warsaw, VA 22572. 9AM-5PM.

Felony, Civil Actions Over $15,000, Probate—15th Circuit Court, 101 Court Circle, PO Box 1000, Warsaw, VA 22572. 804-333-3781. 9AM-5PM. Access by: mail, phone, in person, online.

Misdemeanor, Civil Actions Under $15,000, Eviction, Small Claims—15th General District Court, Richmond County Courthouse, PO Box 1000, Warsaw, VA 22572. 804-333-4616. 8AM-4:30PM. Access by: mail, in person, online.

Richmond City

Felony, Civil Actions Over $15,000, Probate—13th Circuit Court, John Marshall Courts Building, 400 N 9th St, Richmond, VA 23219. 804-646-6505, Fax: 804-646-6562. 9AM-4:45PM. Access by: in person, online. www.ncsc.dni.us\court\richmond\richmond.htm

13th Circuit Court-Division II, Manchester Courthouse, 10th and Hull St, Richmond, VA 23224-0129. 804-780-5370, Fax: 804-319-3122. 8:45AM-4:45PM. Access by: mail, in person, online.

Civil Actions Under $15,000, Eviction, Small Claims—13th General District Court, Civil Division, 400 N 9th St Rm 203, Richmond, VA 23219. 804-646-6461. 8AM-4PM. Access by: mail, phone, in person.

Misdemeanor—13th General District Court, Division II, 905 Decatur St, Richmond, VA 23224. 804-646-5387, Fax: 804-232-7862. 8AM-4:30PM. Access by: mail, in person, online.

Roanoke

Real Estate Recording—Roanoke City Clerk of the Circuit Court, 315 Church Ave S.W. Room 357, Roanoke, VA 24016. 540-333-3555. 8:30AM-4:30PM.

Roanoke County Clerk of the Circuit Court, 305 East Main Street, Salem, VA 24153. Fax: 540-387-6145. 8:30AM-4:30PM.

Felony, Civil Actions Over $15,000, Probate—23rd Judicial Circuit Court, PO Box 1126, Salem, VA 24153-1126. 540-387-6261. 8:30AM-4:30PM. Access by: in person, online. www.co.roanoke.va.us

Misdemeanor, Civil Actions Under $15,000, Eviction, Small Claims—23rd General District Court, PO Box 997, Salem, VA 24153. 540-387-6168, Fax: 540-387-6066. 8:30AM-4:30PM. Access by: mail, in person, online. www.co.roanoke.va.us

Roanoke City

Felony, Civil Actions Over $15,000, Probate—23rd Circuit Court, PO Box 2610, Roanoke, VA 24010-2610. 8:30AM-4:30PM. Access by: in person, online. www.co.roanoke.va.us

Misdemeanor, Civil Actions Under $15,000, Eviction, Small Claims—General District Court, 315 W Church Ave, 2nd Flr, Roanoke, VA 24016-5007. 8AM-4PM. Access by: mail, in person, online.

Rockbridge

Real Estate Recording—Rockbridge County Clerk of the Circuit Court, 2 South Main Street, Court House, Lexington, VA 24450. 540-772-2056, Fax: 540-463-3850. 8:30AM-4:30PM.

Felony, Civil Actions Over $15,000, Probate—25th Circuit Court, Courthouse Square, 2 S Main St, Lexington, VA 24450. 540-463-2232, Fax: 540-463-3850. 8:30AM-4:30PM. Access by: mail, phone, in person, online.

Misdemeanor, Civil Actions Under $15,000, Eviction, Small Claims—District Court, 150 S Main St, Lexington, VA 24450. 540-463-3631. 8:30AM-4:30PM. Access by: mail, in person, online.

Rockingham

Real Estate Recording—Rockingham County Clerk of the Circuit Court, Courthouse, Harrisonburg, VA 22801. Fax: 540-564-3127. 9AM-5PM; Th-until 6PM.

Felony, Civil Actions Over $15,000, Probate—26th Circuit Court, Courthouse, Harrisonburg, VA 22801. Fax: 540-564-3127. 9AM-5PM. Access by: in person, online.

Misdemeanor, Civil Actions Under $15,000, Eviction, Small Claims—26th General District Court, 53 Court Square, Harrisonburg, VA 22801. 540-564-3130, Fax: 540-564-3096. 8AM-4PM. Access by: mail, phone, fax, in person, online.

Russell

Real Estate Recording—Russell County Clerk of the Circuit Court, Main Street, Courthouse, Lebanon, VA 24266. 540-889-8028, Fax: 540-889-8003. 8:30AM-4:30PM.

Felony, Civil Actions Over $15,000, Probate—29th Circuit Court, PO Box 435, Lebanon, VA 24266. 540-889-8023, Fax: 540-889-8003. 8:30AM-4:30PM. Access by: mail, fax, in person, online.

Misdemeanor, Civil Actions Under $15,000, Eviction, Small Claims—29th General District Court, Russell County Courthouse, PO Box 65, Lebanon, VA 24266. 540-889-8051, Fax: 540-889-8091. 8:30AM-4:30PM. Access by: mail, phone, fax, in person, online.

Salem

Real Estate Recording—Salem City Clerk of the Circuit Court, 2 East Calhoun Street, Salem, VA 24153. Fax: 540-375-4039. 8:30AM-5PM.

Salem City

Felony, Civil Actions Over $15,000, Probate—23rd Circuit Court, 2 E Calhoun St, PO Box 891, Salem, VA 24153. 540-375-3067, Fax: 540-375-4039. 8:30AM-5PM. Access by: mail, in person, online.

Misdemeanor, Civil Actions Under $15,000, Eviction, Small Claims—23rd General District Court, 2 E Calhoun St, Salem, VA 24153. 540-375-3044, Fax: 540-375-4024. 8AM-4PM. Access by: in person, online.

Scott

Real Estate Recording—Scott County Clerk of the Circuit Court, 104 East Jackson Street, Courthouse, Suite 2, Gate City, VA 24251. 540-386-7742. 8AM-Noon,1-5PM.

Felony, Civil Actions Over $15,000, Probate—30th Circuit Court, 104 E Jackson St, Suite 2, Gate City, VA 24251. 540-386-3801. 8AM-Noon, 1-5PM. Access by: mail, phone, in person, online.

Misdemeanor, Civil Actions Under $15,000, Eviction, Small Claims—30th General District Court, 104 E Jackson St, Suite 9, Gate City, VA 24251. 540-386-7341. 8AM-4PM. Access by: mail, in person, online.

Shenandoah

Real Estate Recording—Shenandoah County Clerk of the Circuit Court, 112 South Main Street, Woodstock, VA 22664. 540-459-6180, Fax: 540-459-6155. 9AM-5PM.

Felony, Civil Actions Over $15,000, Probate—26th Circuit Court, 112 S Main St, PO Box 406, Woodstock, VA 22664. 540-459-6150, Fax: 540-459-6155. 9AM-5PM. Access by: mail, in person, online.

Misdemeanor, Civil Actions Under $15,000, Eviction, Small Claims—26th General District Court, W Court St, PO Box 189, Woodstock, VA 22664. 540-459-6130, Fax: 540-459-6139. 8:30AM-4:30PM. Access by: in person, online.

Smyth

Real Estate Recording—Smyth County Clerk of the Circuit Court, Courthouse, Room 144, 109 West Main, Marion, VA 24354. 540-783-5711, Fax: 540-783-4430. 9AM-5PM.

Felony, Civil Actions Over $15,000, Probate—28th Circuit Court, PO Box 1025, Marion, VA 24354. 540-783-7186, Fax: 540-783-4430. 9AM-5PM. Access by: mail, in person, online.

Misdemeanor, Civil Actions Under $15,000, Eviction, Small Claims—28th General District Court, Smythe County Courthouse, Rm 231, 109 W Main St, Marion, VA 24354. 540-782-4047, Fax: 540-782-4048. 8:30AM-4:30PM. Access by: mail, phone, in person, online.

South Boston City

Circuit and District Courts, Special note: See Halifax County.

Southampton

Real Estate Recording—Southampton County Clerk of the Circuit Court, 22350 Main Street, Courthouse - Room 106, Courtland, VA 23837. 8:30AM-5PM.

Felony, Civil Actions Over $15,000, Probate—5th Circuit Court, PO Box 190, Courtland, VA 23837. 757-653-2200. 8:30AM-5PM. Access by: mail, in person, online.

Misdemeanor, Civil Actions Under $15,000, Eviction, Small Claims—5th General District Court, PO Box 347, Courtland, VA 23837. 757-653-2673. 8:30AM-5PM. Access by: mail, in person, online.

Spotsylvania

Real Estate Recording—Spotsylvania County Clerk of the Circuit Court, 9113 Courthouse Rd, Spotsylvania, VA 22553. Fax: 540-582-2169. 8AM-4:30PM (Recording Real Property 3:30PM).

Felony, Civil Actions Over $15,000, Probate—15th Circuit Court, 9113 Courthouse Rd, PO Box 96, Spotsylvania, VA 22553. 540-582-7090, Fax: 540-582-2169. 8AM-4:30PM. Access by: in person, online.

Misdemeanor, Civil Actions Under $15,000, Eviction, Small Claims—15th General District Court, Judicial Center, PO Box 339, Spotsylvania, VA 22553. 540-582-7110. 8AM-4PM. Access by: mail, in person, online.

Stafford

Real Estate Recording—Stafford County Clerk of the Circuit Court, 1300 Courthouse Rd. Stafford, VA 22554. 540-659-8700. 8AM-4PM.

Felony, Civil Actions Over $15,000, Probate—15th Circuit Court, PO Box 69, Stafford, VA 22554. 540-659-8750. 8:30AM-4PM. Access by: mail, in person, online.

Misdemeanor, Civil Actions Under $15,000, Eviction, Small Claims—15th General District Court, 1300 Courthouse Rd, PO Box 940, Stafford, VA 22555. 540-658-8763, Fax: 540-720-4834. 8:AM-4PM. Access by: mail, fax, in person, online.

Staunton City

Real Estate Recording—Staunton City Clerk of the Circuit Court, 113 East Beverly Street, Staunton, VA 24401. Fax: 540-332-3970. 8:30AM-5PM.

Felony, Civil Actions Over $15,000, Probate—25th Circuit Court, PO Box 1286, Staunton, VA 24402-1286. 540-332-3874, Fax: 540-332-3970. 8:30AM-5PM. Access by: in person, online.

Misdemeanor, Civil Actions Under $15,000, Eviction, Small Claims—25th General District Court, 113 E Beverly St, Staunton, VA 24401-4390. 540-332-3878, Fax: 540-332-3985. 8:30AM-4:30PM. Access by: mail, in person, online.

Suffolk City

Real Estate Recording—Suffolk City Clerk of the Circuit Court, Godwin Courts Bldg. 150 N. Main St. Suffolk, VA 23434. 8:30AM-5PM.

Felony, Civil Actions Over $15,000, Probate—Suffolk Circuit Court, PO Box 1604, Suffolk, VA 23439-1604. 757-923-2251, Fax: 757-934-3490. 8:30AM-5PM. Access by: in person, online.

Misdemeanor, Civil Actions up to $15,000, Eviction, Small Claims—5th General District Court, 524 N Main St, PO Box 1648, Suffolk, VA 23434. 757-923-2281, Fax: 757-925-1790. 8AM-4PM. Access by: mail, in person, online.

Surry

Real Estate Recording—Surry County Clerk of the Circuit Court, 28 Colonial Trail East, Courthouse, Surry, VA 23883. 804-294-5206. 9AM-5PM.

Felony, Civil Actions Over $15,000, Probate—6th Circuit Court, 28 Colonial Trail East, PO Box 203, Surry, VA 23883. 757-294-3161, Fax: 757-294-3162. 9AM-5PM. Access by: in person.

Misdemeanor, Civil Actions Under $15,000, Eviction, Small Claims—6th General District Court, Hwy 10 and School St, PO Box 332, Surry, VA 23883. 757-294-5201, Fax: 757-294-0312. 8:30AM-4:30PM. Access by: in person, online.

Sussex

Real Estate Recording—Sussex County Clerk of the Circuit Court, Route 735, 15088 Courthouse Road, Sussex, VA 23884. 757-246-5511. 9AM-5PM.

Felony, Civil Actions Over $15,000, Probate—6th Circuit Court, PO Box 1337, Sussex, VA 23884. 804-246-5511, Fax: 804-246-2203. 9AM-5PM. Access by: mail, in person, online.

Misdemeanor, Civil Actions Under $15,000, Eviction, Small Claims—6th Judicial District Sussex Court, Sussex Cnty Courthouse 15098 Courthouse Rd Rt 735, PO Box 1315, Sussex, VA 23884. 804-246-5511, Fax: 804-246-6604. 8:30AM-4:30PM. Access by: mail, in person, online.

Tazewell

Real Estate Recording—Tazewell County Clerk of the Circuit Court, 101 Main Street, Tazewell, VA 24651. 540-988-7541, Fax: 540-988-7501. 8AM-4:30PM.

Felony, Civil Actions Over $15,000, Probate—29th Circuit Court, PO Box 968, Tazewell, VA 24651-0968. 540-988-7541, Fax: 540-988-7501. 8AM-4:30PM. Access by: mail, in person, online.

Misdemeanor, Civil Actions Under $15,000, Eviction, Small Claims—29th General District Court, PO Box 566, Tazewell, VA 24651. 540-988-9057, Fax: 540-988-6202. 8AM-4:30PM. Access by: mail, in person, online.

Virginia Beach City

Real Estate Recording—Virginia Beach Clerk of the Circuit Court, Judicial Center, 2305 Judicial Blvd. Virginia Beach, VA 23456. Fax: 757-426-5686. 8:30AM-5PM.

Felony, Civil Actions Over $15,000, Probate—2nd Circuit Court, 2305 Judicial Blvd, Virginia Beach, VA 23456-9002. 757-427-4181, Fax: 757-426-5686. 8:30AM-5PM. Access by: in person, online.

Misdemeanor, Civil Actions Under $15,000, Eviction, Small Claims—2nd General District Court, 2305 Judicial Blvd, Judicial Center, Virginia Beach, VA 23456-9057. 757-427-8531, Fax: 757-427-1065. 8:30AM-4PM. Access by: mail, phone, fax, in person, online.

Warren

Real Estate Recording—Warren County Clerk of the Circuit Court, 1 East Main Street, Front Royal, VA 22630. 540-635-2215, Fax: 540-636-3274. 9AM-5PM.

Felony, Civil Actions Over $15,000, Probate—Circuit Court, 1 East Main St, Front Royal, VA 22630. 540-635-2435, Fax: 540-636-3274. 9AM-5PM. Access by: mail, phone, fax, in person, online.

Misdemeanor, Civil Actions Under $15,000, Eviction, Small Claims—26th General District Court, 1 East Main St, Front Royal, VA 22630. 540-635-2335, Fax: 540-636-8233. 8AM-4:30PM. Access by: mail, in person, online.

Washington

Real Estate Recording—Washington County Clerk of the Circuit Court, 189 E. Main St. Abingdon, VA 24210. 540-676-6272, Fax: 540-676-6218. 7:30AM-5PM.

Felony, Civil Actions Over $15,000, Probate—Circuit Court of Washington County, PO Box 289, Abingdon, VA 24212-0289. 540-676-6224, Fax: 540-676-6218. 7:30AM-5PM; Recording Hours: 7:30AM-4PM. Access by: mail, in person, online.

Misdemeanor, Civil Actions Under $15,000, Eviction, Small Claims—28th General District Court, 191 E Main St, Abingdon, VA 24210. 540-676-6279, Fax: 540-676-6293. 8:30AM-5PM. Access by: mail, fax, in person, online.

Waynesboro City

Real Estate Recording—Waynesboro City Clerk of the Circuit Court, 250 South Wayne Avenue, Waynesboro, VA 22980. 540-942-6606. 8:30AM-5PM.

Felony, Civil Actions Over $15,000, Probate—25th Circuit Court, 250 S Wayne Ave, PO Box 910, Waynesboro, VA 22980. 540-942-6616, Fax: 540-542-6774. 8:30AM-5PM. Access by: in person, online.

Misdemeanor, Civil Actions Under $15,000, Eviction, Small Claims—25th General District Court-Waynesboro, 250 S Wayne, PO Box 1028, Waynesboro, VA 22980. 540-942-6636, Fax: 540-942-6793. 8:30AM-4:30PM. Access by: mail, in person, online.

Westmoreland

Real Estate Recording—Westmoreland County Clerk of the Circuit Court, Courthouse, Rte. 3 and Polk St. Montross, VA 22520. 804-493-0124. 9AM-5PM.

Felony, Civil Actions Over $15,000, Probate—15th Circuit Court, PO Box 307, Montross, VA 22520. 804-493-0108, Fax: 804-493-0393. 9AM-5PM. Access by: in person, online.

Misdemeanor, Civil Actions Under $15,000, Eviction, Small Claims—15th General District Court, PO Box 688, Montross, VA 22520. 804-493-0105. 8AM-4:30PM. Access by: mail, in person, online.

Williamsburg City

Circuit and District Courts, Special note: See James City County.

Winchester City

Real Estate Recording—Winchester City Clerk of the Circuit Court, 5 N. Kent Street, Winchester, VA 22601. 9AM-5PM.

Felony, Civil Actions Over $15,000, Probate—26th Circuit Court, 5 N Kent St, Winchester, VA 22601. 540-667-5770, Fax: 540-667-6638. 9AM-5PM. Access by: mail, in person, online.

Misdemeanor, Civil Actions Under $15,000, Eviction, Small Claims—26th General District Court, 5 N Kent St, PO Box 526, Winchester, VA 22604. 540-722-7208, Fax: 540-722-1063. 8AM-4PM. Access by: mail, phone, in person, online.

Wise

Real Estate Recording—Wise County/City of Norton Clerk of the Circuit Court, 206 E. Main St. Courthouse, Wise, VA 24293. 540-328-3666, Fax: 540-328-0039. 8:30PM-5PM.

Felony, Civil Actions Over $15,000, Probate—30th Circuit Court, PO Box 1248, Wise, VA 24293-1248. 540-328-6111, Fax: 540-328-6111. 8:30AM-5PM. Access by: mail, phone, fax, in person, online. www.courtbar.org

Misdemeanor, Civil Actions Under $15,000, Eviction, Small Claims—30th General District Court, Wise County Courthouse, PO Box 829, Wise, VA 24293. 540-328-3426, Fax: 540-328-4576. 8AM-4PM. Access by: mail, phone, in person, online.

Wythe

Real Estate Recording—Wythe County Clerk of the Circuit Court, 225 South Fourth Street, Room 105, Wytheville, VA 24382. 540-223-6070, Fax: 540-223-6057. 8:30AM-5PM.

Felony, Civil Actions Over $15,000, Probate—27th Circuit Court, 225 S Fourth St, Rm 105, Wytheville, VA 24382. 540-223-6050, Fax: 540-223-6057. 8:30AM-5PM. Access by: mail, in person, online.

Misdemeanor, Civil Actions Under $15,000, Eviction, Small Claims—27th General District Court, 225 S. Fourth St. Rm 203, Wytheville, VA 24382-2595. 540-223-6075, Fax: 540-223-6087. 8AM-4:30PM. Access by: in person, online.

York

Real Estate Recording—York County Clerk of the Circuit Court, 300 Ballard St. Yorktown, VA 23690. 757-890-3420, Fax: 757-890-3364. 8:15AM-5PM.

Felony, Civil Actions Over $15,000, Probate—9th Circuit Court, PO Box 371, Yorktown, VA 23690. 757-890-3350, Fax: 757-890-3364. 8:30AM-5PM. Access by: mail, in person, online.

Misdemeanor, Civil Actions Under $15,000, Eviction, Small Claims—9th Judicial District Court, York County GDC, PO Box 316, Yorktown, VA 23690-0316. 757-890-3450, Fax: 757-890-3459. 8:30AM-4:30PM. Access by: mail, fax, in person, online.

St. Croix

Real Estate Recording—St. Croix Recorder of Deeds, 1131 King Street, Suite 101, Christiansted, VI 820. Fax: 809-773-0330. 8AM-5PM.

St. Thomas

Real Estate Recording—St. Thomas Recorder, Division of Corporations & Trademarks, Kongens Gabe #18, St. Thomas, VI 802. Fax: 809-774-6953. 8AM-5PM.

Federal Courts

US District Court

Eastern District of Virginia

Alexandria Division 401 Courthouse Square, Alexandria, VA 22314703-299-2100, Record Room: 703-299-2128, Civil Docket Phone: 703-299-2101, Criminal Docket Phone: 703-299-2102 Counties: Arlington, Fairfax, Fauquier, Loudoun, Prince William, Stafford, City of Alexandria, City of Fairfax, City of Falls Church, City of Manassas, City of Manassas Park.

Newport News Division Clerk's Office, PO Box 494, Newport News, VA 23607757-244-0539 Counties: Gloucester, James City, Mathews, York, City of Hampton, City of Newport News, City of Poquoson, City of Williamsburg.

Norfolk Division US Courthouse, Room 193, 600 Granby St, Norfolk, VA 23510, Civil Docket Phone: 757-441-3250, Criminal Docket Phone: 757-441-3253 Counties: Accomack, City of Chesapeake, City of Franklin, Isle of Wight, City of Norfolk,Northampton, City of Portsmouth, City of Suffolk, Southampton, City of Virginia Beach.

Richmond Division Lewis F Powell, Jr Courthouse Bldg, 1000 E Main St, Room 307, Richmond, VA 23219-3525, Civil Docket Phone: 804-771-2611, Criminal Docket Phone: 804-771-2612 Counties: Amelia, Brunswick, Caroline, Charles City, Chesterfield, Dinwiddie, Essex, Goochland, Greensville, Hanover, Henrico, King and Queen, King George, King William, Lancaster, Lunenburg, Mecklenburg, Middlesex, New Kent, Northumberland, Nottoway, City ofPetersburg, Powhatan, Prince Edward, Prince George, Richmond, City of Richmond, Spotsylvania, Surry, Sussex,

Westmoreland, City of Colonial Heights, City of Emporia, City of Fredericksburg, City of Hopewell.

Western District of Virginia

Abingdon Division Clerk's Office, PO Box 398, Abingdon, VA 24212540-628-5116 Fax: 540-628-1028 Counties: Buchanan, City of Bristol, Russell, Smyth, Tazewell, Washington.

Big Stone Gap Division PO Box 490, Big Stone Gap, VA 24219540-523-3557 Fax: 540-523-6214 Counties: Dickenson, Lee, Scott, Wise, City of Norton.

Charlottesville Division Clerk, Room 304, 255 W Main St, Charlottesville, VA 22902804-296-9284 Counties: Albemarle, Culpeper, Fluvanna, Greene, Louisa, Madison, Nelson, Orange, Rappahannock, City of Charlottesville.

Danville Division PO Box 52, Danville, VA 24543-0053804-793-7147 Fax: 804-793-0284 Counties: Charlotte, Halifax, Henry, Patrick, Pittsylvania, City of Danville, City of Martinsville, City of South Boston.

Harrisonburg Division Clerk, PO Box 1207, Harrisonburg, VA 22801540-434-3181 Counties: Augusta, Bath, Clarke, Frederick, Highland, Page, Rockingham, Shenandoah, Warren, City of Harrisonburg, City of Staunton, City of Waynesboro, City of Winchester.

Lynchburg Division Clerk, PO Box 744, Lynchburg, VA 24505804-847-5722 Counties: Amherst, Appomattox, Bedford, Buckingham, Campbell, Cumberland, Rockbridge, City of Bedford, City of Buena Vista, City of Lexington, City of Lynchburg.

Roanoke Division Clerk, PO Box 1234, Roanoke, VA 24006540-857-2224, Civil Docket Phone: 540-857-2224, Criminal Docket Phone: 540-857-2661 Counties: Alleghany, Bland, Botetourt, Carroll, Craig, Floyd, Franklin, Giles, Grayson, Montgomery, Pulaski, Roanoke, Wythe, City of Covington, City of Clifton Forge, City of Galax, City of Radford, City of Roanoke, City of Salem.

US Bankruptcy Court

Eastern District of Virginia

Alexandria Division PO Box 19247, Alexandria, VA 22320-0247703-557-1716 Counties: City of Alexandria, Arlington, Fairfax, City of Fairfax, City of Falls Church, Fauquier, Loudoun, City of Manassas, City of Manassas Park, Prince William, Stafford. www.vaeb.uscourts.gov

Newport News Division 825 Diligence Dr, Suite 201, Newport News, VA 23606757-595-9805 Counties: Gloucester, City of Hampton, James City, Mathews, City of Newport News, City of Poquoson, City of Williamsburg, York. www.vaeb.uscourts.gov

Norfolk Division PO Box 1938, Norfolk, VA 23501-1938757-441-6651 Counties: Accomack, City of Cape Charles, City of Chesapeake, City of Franklin, Isle of Wight, City of Norfolk, Northampton, City of Portsmouth, Southampton, City of Suffolk, City of Virginia Beach. www.vaeb.uscourts.gov

Richmond Division Office of the clerk, 1100 E Main St, Room 310, Richmond, VA 23219-3515804-771-2878 Counties: Amelia, Brunswick, Caroline, Charles City, Chesterfield, City of Colonial Heights, Dinwiddie, City of Emporia, Essex, City of Fredericksburg, Goochland, Greensville, Hanover, Henrico, City of Hopewell, King and Queen, King George, King William,Lancaster, Lunenburg, Mecklenburg, Middlesex, New Kent, Northumberland, Nottoway, City of Petersburg, Powhatan, Prince Edward, Prince George, Richmond, City of Richmond, Spotsylvania, Surry, Sussex, Westmoreland. www.vaeb.uscourts.gov

Western District of Virginia

Harrisonburg Division PO Box 1407, Harrisonburg, VA 22801540-434-8327 Fax: 540-434-9715 Counties: Alleghany, Augusta, Bath, City of Buena Vista, Clarke, City of Clifton Forge, City of Covington, Frederick, City of Harrisonburg, Highland, City of Lexington, Page, Rappahannock, Rockbridge, Rockingham, Shenandoah, City of Staunton, Warren, City ofWaynesboro, City of Winchester. www.vawb.uscourts.gov

Lynchburg Division PO Box 6400, Lynchburg, VA 24505804-845-0317 Counties: Albemarle, Amherst, Appomattox, Bedford, City of Bedford, Buckingham, Campbell, Charlotte, City of Charlottesville, Culpeper, Cumberland, City of Danville, Fluvanna, Greene, Halifax, Henry, Louisa, City of Lynchburg, Madison, City of Martinsville,Nelson, Orange, Patrick, Pittsylvania, City of South Boston. www.vawb.uscourts.gov

Roanoke Division PO Box 2390, Roanoke, VA 24010540-857-2391 Counties: Bland, Botetourt, City of Bristol, Buchanan, Carroll, Craig, Dickenson, Floyd, Franklin, City of Galax, Giles, Grayson, Lee, Montgomery, City of Norton, Pulaski, City of Radford, Roanoke, City of Roanoke, Russell, City of Salem, Scott, Smyth, Tazewell,Washington, Wise, Wythe. www.vawb.uscourts.gov

Attorney General's Office
PO Box 40100   360-753-6200
Olympia, WA 98504-0100   Fax: 360-586-8474
www.wa.gov/ago/COG.htm

Governor's Office
PO Box 40002   360-902-4111
Olympia, WA 98504-0002   Fax: 360-753-4110
www.wa.gov/governor

State Archives
PO Box 40238   360-753-5485
Olympia, WA 98504-0238   Fax: 360-664-8814

Capital:	Olympia
	Thurston County
Time Zone:	PST
Number of Counties:	39
Population:	5,610,362
Web Site:	access.wa.gov

Search Unclaimed Property Online
http://dor.wa.gov/index.asp?/ unclaim/search.htm

State Agencies

Criminal Records
Washington State Patrol, Identification Section, PO Box 42633, Olympia, WA 98504-2633 (403 Cleveland Ave, #A, Tumwater, WA 98501); 360-705-5100; 8AM-5PM. Access by: mail, online. www.wa.gov/wsp/wsphome.htm

Corporation Records
Trademarks/Servicemarks
Limited Partnerships
Limited Liability Company Records
Secretary of State, Corporations Division, PO Box 40234, Olympia, WA 98504-0234 (505 E Union, 2nd Floor, Olympia, WA 98504); 360-753-7115, 900-463-6000 Records; Fax: 360-664-8781; 8AM-4PM. Access by: mail, phone, in person, online. www.wa.gov/sec/corps.htm

Sales Tax Registrations
Revenue Department, Taxpayer Account Administration, PO Box 47476, Olympia, WA 98504-7476 (415 Gen Admin Bldg, Olympia, WA 98504); 360-902-7180, 800-647-7706; Fax: 360-586-5543; 8AM-5PM. Access by: mail, phone, in person. www.wa.gov/dor/wador.htm

Trade Names
Master License Service, Business & Professions Div, PO Box 9034, Olympia, WA 98507-9034 (405 Black Lake Blvd, Olympia, WA 98507); 360-664-1400, 900-463-6000 Trade Name Search; Fax: 360-753-9668; 8AM-5PM. Access by: mail, phone, in person, online. www.wa.gov/dol

Uniform Commercial Code
Federal Tax Liens
Department of Licensing, UCC Records, PO Box 9660, Olympia, WA 98507-9660 (1125 Washington St SE, Olympia, WA 98501); 360-753-2523; Fax: 360-586-1404; 8AM-5PM. Access by: mail, online. www.wa.gov/dol/bpd/uccfront.htm

State Tax Liens
Records not available from state agency.

State tax liens are filed at the county level.

Workers' Compensation Records
Labor and Industries, Workers Compensation Division, PO Box 44285, Olympia, WA 98504-4285 (7273 Linderson Way SW, Tumwater, WA 98501); 360-902-4937; Fax: 360-902-5529; 8AM-5PM. Access by: mail.

Birth Certificates

Department of Health, Center for Health Statistics, PO Box 9709, Olympia, WA 98507-9709 (1112 S Quince St, 1st Fl, Olympia, WA 98501); 360-236-4300 Main Number, 360-236-4313 Credit Card Ordering; Fax: 360-352-2586; 8 AM - 4:30 PM. Access by: mail, phone, fax, in person. www.doh.wa.gov

Death Records

Department of Health, Vital Records, PO Box 9709, Olympia, WA 98507-9709; 360-236-4300 Main Number, 360-236-4313 Credit Card Ordering; Fax: 360-352-2586; 8 AM - 4:30 PM. Access by: mail, phone, in person.

Marriage Certificates

Department of Health, Vital Records, PO Box 9709, Olympia, WA 98507-9709; 360-236-4300 Main Number, 360-236-4313 Credit Card Ordering; Fax: 360-352-2586; 8 AM - 4:30 PM. Access by: mail, phone, in person.

Divorce Records

Department of Health, Vital Records, PO Box 9709, Olympia, WA 98507-9709; 360-753-5936 Main Number, 360-753-4379 Credit Card Ordering; Fax: 360-352-2586; 8 AM - 4:30 PM. Access by: mail, phone, in person.

Accident Reports

State Patrol, Collision Reports, PO Box 42628, Olympia, WA 98504-2628; 360-412-9417; Fax: 360-493-9417; 8AM-5PM. Access by: mail. www.wa.gov/wsp/wsphome.htm

Driver Records

Department of Licensing, Driver Services Division, PO Box 9030, Olympia, WA 98507-9030 (1125 Washington Street SE, Olympia, WA 98504); 360-902-3921, 360-902-3900 General Information; Fax: 360-586-9044; 8AM-4:30PM. Access by: mail. www.wa.gov/dol

Vehicle Ownership
Vehicle Identification
Boat & Vessel Ownership
Boat & Vessel Registration

Department of Licensing, Licensing Records, 1125 S Washington MS-48001, Olympia, WA 98504; 360-902-4000; Fax: 360-902-3827; 8AM-5PM. Access by: mail, phone, in person. www.wa.gov/dol

Legislation-Current/Pending
Legislation-Passed

Washington Legislature, State Capitol, Room 120, 1st Floor, Olympia, WA 98504-0600; 360-753-5000 Information, 800-562-6000 Local Only, 360-786-7573 Bill Room; Fax: 360-786-1293; 9AM-5PM. Access by: mail, phone, in person, online. http://leginfo.leg.wa.gov

Voter Registration

Records not available from state agency.

All voter information is kept at the local level by the County Auditor (except King County where records are kept by the Dept of Records and Elections). Individual look-ups will not receive SSNs, DOBs, and telephone numbers.

GED Certificates

State Board for Community & Technical Colleges, GED Records, PO Box 42495, Olympia, WA 98504-2495 (319 7th Ave, Olympia, WA 98504); 360-753-6748; Fax: 360-664-8808; 8AM-5PM. www.sbctc.ctc.edu

Hunting License Information
Fishing License Information

Department of Fish & Wildlife, Attn: Public Disclosure Officer, 600 Capitol Way, N, Olympia, WA 98501-1091; 360-902-2250; Fax: 360-902-2171; 8AM-5PM. www.wa.gov/wdfw

County Courts & Recording Offices

About the Courts...

Administration

Court Administrator, Temple of Justice 360-357-2121
PO Box 41174 Fax: 360-357-2127
Olympia, WA 98504
http://198.187.0.226/courts/home.htm

Court Structure

District Courts retain civil records for 10 years from date of final disposition, then the records are destroyed. District Courts retain criminal records forever.

Washington has a mandatory arbitration requirement for civil disputes for $35,000 or less. However, either party may request a trial in Superior Court if dissatisfied with the arbitrator's decision.

The limit for civil actions in District Court has been increased from $25,000 to $35,000.

Searching Hints

SASE is required in every jurisdiction that responds to written search requests.

Online Access

Appellate, Superior, and District Court records are available online. The Superior Court Management Information System (SCOMIS), the Appellate Records System (ACORDS) and the District/Municipal Court Information System (DISCIS) are on the Judicial Information System's JIS-Link. Case records available through JIS-Link from 1977 include criminal, civil, domestic, probate, and judgments. JIS-Link is generally available Monday through Friday from 6:30AM to Midnight Washington time (PST or PDT). Equipment requirements are a PC running Windows or MS-DOS, and a Hayes-compatible modem. There is a one-time installation fee of $100.00 per site, and a connect time charge of $25.00 per hour (approximately $.42 per minute). For additional information and/or a registration packet, contact: JISLink Coordinator, Office of the Administrator for the Courts, 1206 S Quince St., PO Box 41170, Olympia WA 98504-1170, 360-357-2407.

About the Recording Offices...

Organization

39 counties, 39 recording offices. The recording officer is County Auditor. County records are usually combined in a Grantor/Grantee index. The area code for some counties has been changed from 206 to 360, effective January 1, 1995. The entire state is in the Pacific Time Zone (PST).

UCC Records

Financing statements are filed at the state level, except for real estate related collateral, which are filed with the County Auditor. Most recording offices will perform UCC searches. Use search request form UCC-11R. Searches fees and copy fees vary.

Lien Records

All federal tax liens on personal property are filed with the Department of Licensing. Other federal and all state tax liens are filed with the County Auditor. Most counties will perform tax lien searches. Search fees are usually $8.00 per hour.

Real Estate Records

Many County Auditors will perform real estate searches, including record owner. Search fees and copy fees vary. Copies usually cost $1.00 per page and $2.00 for certification per document. If the Auditor does not provide searches, contact the Assessor for record owner information. Contact the Treasurer (Finance Department in King County) for information about unpaid real estate taxes.

County Courts & Recording Offices

Adams

Real Estate Recording—Adams County Auditor, 210 West Broadway, Ritzville, WA 99169. 509-659-0090, Fax: 509-659-3254. 8:30AM-4:30PM.

Felony, Civil, Eviction, Probate—Superior Court, 210 W Broadway (PO Box 187), Ritzville, WA 99169-0187. 509-659-3257, Fax: 509-659-0118. 8:30AM-Noon, 1-4:30PM. Access by: mail, phone, fax, in person, online.

Misdemeanor, Civil Actions Under $35,000, Small Claims—Othello District Court, 165 N 1st, Othello, WA 99344. 509-488-3935, Fax: 509-488-3480. 8:30AM-4:30PM. Access by: mail, phone, fax, in person, online.

Ritzville District Court, 210 W Broadway, Ritzville, WA 99169. 509-659-1002, Fax: 509-659-0118. 8:30AM-4:30PM. Access by: mail, fax, in person, online.

Asotin

Real Estate Recording—Asotin County Auditor, 135 2nd Street, Asotin, WA 99402. 509-243-2014, Fax: 509-243-2087. 9AM-5PM.

Felony, Civil, Eviction, Probate—Superior Court, PO Box 159, Asotin, WA 99402-0159. 509-243-2081, Fax: 509-243-4978. 9AM-5PM. Access by: mail, phone, fax, in person, online.

Misdemeanor, Civil Actions Under $35,000, Small Claims—District Court, PO Box 429, Asotin, WA 99402-0429. 509-243-2027, Fax: 509-243-4978. 8AM-5PM. Access by: mail, fax, in person, online.

Benton

Real Estate Recording—Benton County Auditor, 620 Market Street, Courthouse, Prosser, WA 99350. 509-786-2255, Fax: 509-786-5528. 8AM-5PM.

Felony, Civil, Eviction, Probate—Superior Court, 7320 W Quinault, Kennewick, WA 99336-7690. 509-735-8388. 8AM-4PM. Access by: mail, fax, in person.

Misdemeanor, Civil Actions Under $35,000, Small Claims—District Court, 7320 W Quinault, Kennewick, WA 99336. 509-735-8476, Fax: 509-736-3069. 7:30AM-Noon, 1-4:30PM. Access by: mail, in person, online.

Chelan

Real Estate Recording—Chelan County Auditor, 350 Orondo, Courthouse, Wenatchee, WA 98801. 509-664-5405, Fax: 509-664-5246. 8:30AM-5PM.

Felony, Civil, Eviction, Probate—Superior Court, 401 Washington (PO Box 3025), Wenatchee, WA 98807-3025. 509-664-5380, Fax: 509-664-2611. 8:30AM-5PM. Access by: mail, phone, fax, in person, online.

Misdemeanor, Civil Actions Under $35,000, Small Claims—Chelan County District Court, PO Box 2182, Courthouse 4th Fl, Wenatchee, WA 98807. 509-664-5393, Fax: 509-664-5456. 8:30AM-5PM. Access by: mail, fax, in person, online.

Clallam

Real Estate Recording—Clallam County Auditor, 223 East Fourth Street, Port Angeles, WA 98362. 360-786-5550, Fax: 360-417-2517. 8AM-4:30PM.

Felony, Civil, Eviction, Probate—Superior Court, 223 E Fourth St, PO Box 863, Port Angeles, WA 98362-3098. 360-786-5450, Fax: 360-417-2495. 8AM-5PM. Access by: mail, phone, in person, online. www.wa.gov/clallam

Misdemeanor, Civil Actions Under $35,000, Small Claims—District Court One, 223 E 4th St, Port Angeles, WA 98362. 360-786-5430, Fax: 360-417-2470. 8AM-5PM. Access by: mail, phone, fax, in person, online.

District Court Two, PO Box 1937, Forks, WA 98331. 360-679-7359, Fax: 360-374-2100. 8AM-5PM. Access by: mail, in person, online.

Clark

Real Estate Recording—Clark County Auditor, 12th & Franklin, Vancouver, WA 98660. 361-332-7234, Fax: 360-737-6007. 8AM-5PM.

Felony, Civil, Eviction, Probate—Superior Court, 1200 Franklin St, PO Box 5000, Vancouver, WA 98668. 361-332-7244. 8:30AM-4:30PM. Access by: mail, phone, in person, online.

Misdemeanor, Civil Actions Under $35,000, Small Claims—District Court, PO Box 5000, Vancouver, WA 98666-5000. Fax: 360-737-6044. 8:30AM-4:30PM. Access by: mail, phone, fax, in person, online.

Columbia

Real Estate Recording—Columbia County Auditor, 341 East Main St. Dayton, WA 99328. 509-382-2641, Fax: 509-382-4830. 8:30AM-4:30PM.

Felony, Civil, Eviction, Probate—Superior Court, 341 E Main St, Dayton, WA 99328. 509-382-4321, Fax: 509-382-4830. 8:30AM-Noon, 1-4:30PM. Access by: mail, phone, fax, in person, online.

Misdemeanor, Civil Actions Under $35,000, Small Claims—District Court, 341 E Main St, Dayton, WA 99328-1361. 509-382-4812, Fax: 509-382-4830. 8:30AM-4:30PM. Access by: mail, in person, online.

Cowlitz

Real Estate Recording—Cowlitz County Auditor, 207 Fourth Avenue North, Kelso, WA 98626. 360-875-9354, Fax: 360-414-5552. 8AM-5PM.

Felony, Civil, Eviction, Probate—Superior Court, 312 SW First Ave, Kelso, WA 98626-1724. 360-875-9320, Fax: 360-577-2323. 8:30-11:30AM, 12:30-4:30PM. Access by: mail, phone, fax, in person, online.

Misdemeanor, Civil Actions Under $35,000, Small Claims—District Court, 312 SW First Ave, Kelso, WA 98626-1724. 360-875-9421. 8:30AM-5PM. Access by: mail, in person, online.

Douglas

Real Estate Recording—Douglas County Auditor, 213 South Rainier, Waterville, WA 98858. 509-884-9428, Fax: 509-884-9468. 8AM-5PM; (Recording hours: 8AM-4PM).

Felony, Civil, Eviction, Probate—Superior Court, PO Box 488, Waterville, WA 98858-0516. 509-745-9063, Fax: 509-745-8027. 8AM-5PM. Access by: mail, phone, fax, in person, online. Special note: Clerk is reached at 509-745-8529.

Misdemeanor, Civil Actions Under $35,000, Small Claims—District Court-Bridgeport, 1206 Columbia Ave (PO Box 730), Bridgeport, WA 98813-0730. 509-686-2034, Fax: 509-686-4671. 8:30AM-4:30PM. Access by: mail, fax, in person, online. Special note: If record not found in this court, request forwarded to East Wenatchee (South) court.

District Court-East Wenatchee, 110 3rd St NE, East Wenatchee, WA 98802. 509-884-3536, Fax: 509-884-5973. 8:30AM-4:30PM. Access by: mail, fax, in person, online. Special note: If record not found in this court, request forwarded to Bridgeport (North) Court.

Ferry

Real Estate Recording—Ferry County Auditor, 350 East Delaware #2, Republic, WA 99166. 509-775-5238, Fax: 509-775-5208. 8AM-4PM.

Felony, Civil, Probate—Superior Court, 350 E Delaware #4, Republic, WA 99166. 509-775-5245. 8AM-4PM. Access by: mail, phone, in person, online.

Misdemeanor, Civil Actions Under $35,000, Small Claims—District Court, 350 E Delaware Ave #6, Republic, WA 99166-9747. 509-775-5244, Fax: 509-775-5221. 8AM-4PM. Access by: mail, fax, in person, online.

Franklin

Real Estate Recording—Franklin County Auditor, 1016 North Fourth Street, Pasco, WA 99301. 509-545-3518, Fax: 509-545-2142. 8:30AM-5PM.

Felony, Civil, Eviction, Probate—Superior Court, 1016 N 4th St, Pasco, WA 99301. 509-545-3525. 8:30AM-5PM. Access by: mail, in person, online.

Misdemeanor, Civil Actions Under $35,000, Small Claims—District Court, 1016 N 4th St, Pasco, WA 99301. 509-545-3593, Fax: 509-545-3588. 8:30AM-Noon, 1-5PM. Access by: mail, in person, online.

Garfield

Real Estate Recording—Garfield County Auditor, Corner of 8th & Main, Pomeroy, WA 99347. 509-843-1531, Fax: 509-843-3941. 8:30AM-5PM.

Felony, Civil, Eviction, Probate—Superior Court, PO Box 915, Pomeroy, WA 99347-0915. 509-843-3731, Fax: 509-843-1224. 8:30AM-Noon, 1-5PM. Access by: mail, phone, fax, in person, online.

Misdemeanor, Civil Actions Under $35,000, Small Claims—District Court, PO Box 817, Pomeroy, WA 99347-0817. 509-843-1002. 8:30AM-5PM. Access by: mail, in person, online.

Grant

Real Estate Recording—Grant County Auditor, 1st & C Street NW, Ephrata, WA 98823. 509-754-2011. 8AM-5PM.

Felony, Civil, Eviction, Probate—Superior Court, PO Box 37, Ephrata, WA 98823-0037. 509-754-2011, Fax: 509-754-5638. 8AM-5PM. Access by: mail, phone, fax, in person, online.

Misdemeanor, Civil Actions Under $35,000, Small Claims—District Court, PO Box 37, Ephrata, WA 98823-0037. 509-754-2011, Fax: 509-754-6099. 8AM-5PM. Access by: mail, in person, online.

Grays Harbor

Real Estate Recording—Grays Harbor County Auditor, 101 W. Broadway, Ste. 2, Montesano, WA 98563. 360-642-9417, Fax: 360-249-3330. 8AM-5PM.

Felony, Civil, Eviction, Probate—Superior Court, 102 W Broadway, Rm 203, Montesano, WA 98563-3606. 360-652-9552, Fax: 360-249-6381. 8AM-5PM. Access by: mail, phone, fax, in person, online.

Misdemeanor, Civil Actions Under $35,000, Small Claims—District Court No 1, 102 W Broadway, Rm 202, PO Box 647, Montesano, WA 98563-0647. 360-577-3073, Fax: 360-249-6382. 8AM-Noon, 1-5PM. Access by: mail, phone, fax, in person, online.

District Court No 2, PO Box 142, Aberdeen, WA 98520-0035. 360-829-0411, Fax: 360-532-7704. 8AM-Noon, 1-5PM. Access by: mail, phone, fax, in person, online.

Island

Real Estate Recording—Island County Auditor, 6th & Main, Coupeville, WA 98239. 361-325-5604, Fax: 360-240-5553. 8AM-4:30PM.

Felony, Civil, Eviction, Probate—Superior Court, PO Box 5000, Coupeville, WA 98239-5000. 361-325-5604. 8AM-4:30PM. Access by: mail, phone, fax, in person, online.

Misdemeanor, Civil Actions Under $35,000, Small Claims—District Court, 800 S 8th Ave, Oak Harbor, WA 98277. 361-279-3322, Fax: 360-675-8231. 8AM-4:30PM. Access by: mail, fax, in person, online. Special note: Records requests are done as time permits. Bottom of priority list.

Jefferson

Real Estate Recording—Jefferson County Auditor, 1820 Jefferson Street, Port Townsend, WA 98368. 360-779-5600, Fax: 360-385-9228. 9AM-5PM.

Felony, Civil, Eviction, Probate—Superior Court, PO Box 1220, Port Townsend, WA 98368-0920. 360-740-1203. 9AM-5PM. Access by: mail, phone, in person, online.

Misdemeanor, Civil Actions Under $35,000, Small Claims—District Court, PO Box 1220, Port Townsend, WA 98368-0920. 360-740-2704, Fax: 360-385-9367. 9AM-5PM. Access by: mail, phone, fax, in person, online. www.co.jefferson.wa.us

King

Real Estate Recording—King County Records, 500 4th Avenue, Administration Building, Room 311, Seattle, WA 98104. 206-296-7688, Fax: 206-205-8396. 8:30AM-4:30PM; Recording Hours 8:30AM-3:30PM.

Felony, Misdemeanor, Civil, Eviction, Probate—Superior Court, 516 Third Ave, E-609 Courthouse, Seattle, WA 98104-2386. 206-388-3366. 8:30AM-4:30AM. Access by: mail, in person, online.

Misdemeanor, Civil Actions Under $35,000, Small Claims—District Court (Aukeen Division), 1210 S Central, Kent, WA 98032-7426. 206-296-7784. 8:30AM-4:30PM. Access by: mail, in person, online.

District Court (Bellevue Div), 585 112th Ave SE, Bellevue, WA 98004. 206-296-3664, Fax: 206-296-0589. 8:30AM-4:30PM. Access by: mail, in person, online.

District Court (Federal Way Division), 33506 10th Pl South, Federal Way, WA 98003-6396. 206-296-9300, Fax: 206-296-0590. 8:30AM-4:30PM. Access by: mail, phone, in person, online.

District Court (Issaquah Division), 5415 220th Ave SW, Issaquah, WA 98029-6839. 206-296-7740, Fax: 206-296-0591. 8:30AM-4:30PM. Access by: mail, in person, online.

District Court (Renton Division), 3407 NE 2nd St, Renton, WA 98056-4193. 206-296-3565, Fax: 206-296-0593. 8:30AM-4:30PM. Access by: mail, phone, fax, in person, online. www.metrokc.gov

District Court (Seattle Division), 516 Third Ave E-327 Courthouse, Seattle, WA 98104-3273. 206-296-3650. 8:30AM-4:30PM. Access by: mail, in person, online. www.metrokc.gov.kcdc

District Court (Shoreline Division), 18050 Meridian Ave N, Shoreline, WA 98133-4642. 206-296-3850, Fax: 206-296-0594. 8:30AM-4:30PM. Access by: mail, phone, fax, in person, online. www.metrokc.gov/kcdc

District Court (Southwest Division), 601 SW 149th St, Seattle, WA 98166. 206-296-3532, Fax: 206-296-0585. 8:30AM-4:30PM. Access by: mail, in person, online.

District Court (Southwest Division-Vashon), 19021 99th SW (PO Box 111), Vashon, WA 98070-0111. 206-296-3667, Fax: 206-296-0578. 8:30AM-Noon, 1:15-4:30PM 2nd & 4th F of the month. Access by: mail, fax, in person, online.

District Court NE Division, 8601 160th Ave NE, Redmond, WA 98052-3548. 206-296-3679. 8:30AM-4:30PM. Access by: mail, in person, online.

Kitsap

Real Estate Recording—Kitsap County Auditor, 614 Division Street, Room 106 /MS 31, Port Orchard, WA 98366. 361-575-0581, Fax: 360-337-4645. 8AM-4:30PM.

Felony, Civil, Eviction, Probate—Superior Court, 614 Division St, Port Orchard, WA 98366-4699. 360-678-5111, Fax: 360-337-4927. 8AM-4:30PM. Access by: mail, in person, online. www.wa.gov/kitsap/departments/clerk/index.html

Misdemeanor, Civil Actions Under $35,000, Small Claims—District Court, 614 Division St, MS 25, Port Orchard, WA 98366-4614. 360-676-6777, Fax: 360-337-4865. 8:30AM-4:30PM. Access by: mail, phone, fax, in person, online.

District Court North, 19050 Jensen Way NE, Poulsbo, WA 98370-0910. 361-364-6290, Fax: 360-895-4865. 8:30AM-12:15PM; 1:15-4:30PM. Access by: in person, online.

Kittitas

Real Estate Recording—Kittitas County Auditor, 205 West 5th, Room 105, Ellensburg, WA 98926. 509-962-7535, Fax: 509-962-7687. 9AM-5PM.

Felony, Misdemeanor, Civil, Eviction, Probate—Superior Court, 205 W 5th Rm 210, Ellensburg, WA 98926. 509-962-7531, Fax: 509-962-7667. 9AM-Noon, 1-5PM. Access by: mail, phone, fax, in person, online.

Misdemeanor, Civil Actions Under $35,000, Small Claims—District Court Lower Kittitas, 5th and Main, Rm 180,

Ellensburg, WA 98926. 509-962-7511. 9AM-5PM. Access by: mail, in person, online.

District Court Upper Kittitas, 618 E First, Cle Elum, WA 98922. 509-674-5533, Fax: 509-674-4209. 8AM-5PM. Access by: mail, fax, in person, online.

Klickitat

Real Estate Recording—Klickitat County Auditor, 205 S. Columbus Avenue, MS-CH-2, Goldendale, WA 98620. 509-773-4664, Fax: 509-773-4244. 9AM-5PM.

Felony, Civil, Eviction, Probate—Superior Court, 205 S Columbus, Rm 204, Goldendale, WA 98620. 509-773-5744. 9AM-5PM. Access by: mail, phone, in person, online.

Misdemeanor, Civil Actions Under $35,000, Small Claims—East District Court, 205 S Columbus, MS-CH11, Goldendale, WA 98620-9290. 509-773-4670. 8AM-12, 1-5pm. Access by: mail, phone, in person, online.

West District Court, PO Box 435, White Salmon, WA 98672-0435. 509-493-1190, Fax: 509-493-4469. 8AM-5PM. Access by: mail, in person.

Lewis

Real Estate Recording—Lewis County Auditor, 351 NW North Street, Chehalis, WA 98532. 361-362-3242, Fax: 360-740-1421. 8AM-5PM.

Felony, Misdemeanor, Civil, Eviction, Probate—Superior Court, 360 NW North St, MS:CLK 01, Chehalis, WA 98532-1900. 361-364-6225, Fax: 360-748-1639. 8AM-5PM. Access by: mail, phone, in person, online.

Misdemeanor, Civil Actions Under $35,000, Small Claims—District Court, PO Box 336, Chehalis, WA 98532-0336. 361-362-3245, Fax: 360-740-2779. 8AM-5PM. Access by: mail, fax, in person, online.

Lincoln

Real Estate Recording—Lincoln County Auditor, 450 Logan, Davenport, WA 99122. 509-725-5061, Fax: 509-725-0820. 8:30AM-4:30PM.

Felony, Misdemeanor, Civil, Eviction, Probate—Superior Court, Box 68, Davenport, WA 99122-0396. 509-725-1401, Fax: 509-725-1150. 8AM-5PM. Access by: mail, phone, in person, online.

Misdemeanor, Civil Actions Under $35,000, Small Claims—District Court, PO Box 329, Davenport, WA 99122-0329. 509-725-2281. 8:30AM-5PM. Access by: mail, in person, online. Special note: Small office with limited time allowable for searches.

Mason

Real Estate Recording—Mason County Auditor, 411 North 5th Street, Shelton, WA 98584. 360-795-3461, Fax: 360-427-8425. 8:30AM-5PM.

Felony, Civil, Eviction, Probate—Superior Court, PO Box 340, Shelton, WA 98584. 360-795-3558. 8:30AM-5PM. Access by: mail, phone, in person, online.

Misdemeanor, Civil Actions Under $35,000, Small Claims—District Court, PO Box "O", Shelton, WA 98584-0090. 360-795-8005, Fax: 360-427-7776. 8:30AM-5PM. Access by: mail, in person.

Okanogan

Real Estate Recording—Okanogan County Auditor, Courthouse, 149 North 3rd, Okanogan, WA 98840. 509-422-7180. 8:30AM-5PM.

Felony, Misdemeanor, Civil, Eviction, Probate—Superior Court, PO Box 72, Okanogan, WA 98840. 509-422-7275, Fax: 509-422-7277. 8AM-5PM. Access by: mail, phone, fax, in person, online.

Misdemeanor, Civil Actions Under $35,000, Small Claims—District Court, PO Box 980, Okanogan, WA 98840-0980. 509-422-7170, Fax: 509-422-7174. 8AM-5PM. Access by: mail, phone, fax, in person, online.

Pacific

Real Estate Recording—Pacific County Auditor, 300 Memorial Drive, South Bend, WA 98586. 361-553-4630, Fax: 360-875-9333. 8AM-5PM.

Felony, Civil, Eviction, Probate—Superior Court, PO Box 67, South Bend, WA 98586. 361-553-4411, Fax: 360-875-9321. 8AM-5PM. Access by: mail, phone, in person, online.

Misdemeanor, Civil Actions Under $35,000, Small Claims—District Court North, Box 134, South Bend, WA 98586-0134. 361-553-4620, Fax: 360-875-9362. 8:30AM-5PM. Access by: mail, phone, fax, in person, online.

District Court South, PO Box 794, Ilwaco, WA 98624. 360-876-7135, Fax: 360-642-9417. 8AM-Noon, 1-5PM. Access by: mail, phone, fax, in person, online.

Pend Oreille

Real Estate Recording—Pend Oreille County Auditor, West 625 4th Street, Newport, WA 99156. 509-447-3612, Fax: 509-447-2475. 8AM-4:30PM.

Felony, Civil, Eviction, Probate—Superior Court, 229 S Garden Ave (PO Box 5020), Newport, WA 99156-5020. 509-447-2435, Fax: 509-447-2734. 8AM-4:30PM. Access by: mail, phone, in person.

Misdemeanor, Civil Actions Under $35,000, Small Claims—District Court, PO Box 5030, Newport, WA 99156-5030. 509-447-4110, Fax: 509-447-5724. 8AM-4:30PM. Access by: mail, phone, fax, in person, online.

Pierce

Real Estate Recording—Pierce County Auditor, 2401 South 35th Street, Room 200, Tacoma, WA 98409. 207-255-3044, Fax: 253-798-2761. 8:30AM-4:30PM.

Felony, Civil, Eviction, Probate—Superior Court, 930 Tacoma Ave South, Rm 110, Tacoma, WA 98402. 254-582-4030, Fax: 253-597-3428. 8:30AM-4:30PM. Access by: mail, in person, online. www.co.pierce.wa.us/linx

Misdemeanor, Civil Actions Under $35,000, Small Claims—District Court #1, 930 Tacoma Ave S, Rm 601, Tacoma, WA 98402-2175. 254-582-4042, Fax: 253-798-6166. 8:30AM-4:30PM. Access by: mail, in person, online.

District Court #2, 6659 Kimball Dr, Suite E-503, Gig Harbor, WA 98335-1229. 254-629-1583, Fax: 253-858-2184. 8:30AM-4:30PM. Access by: mail, phone, fax, in person.

District Court #3, PO Box 105, Eatonville, WA 98328-0105. 361-527-4031, Fax: 360-832-8911. 8:30AM-4:30PM. Access by: mail, in person, online.

District Court #4, PO Box 110, Buckley, WA 98321-0110. 361-527-3164, Fax: 360-829-3098. 8:30AM-4PM. Access by: mail, phone, in person, online.

San Juan

Real Estate Recording—San Juan County Auditor, 350 Court Street, Friday Harbor, WA 98250. 360-699-2295, Fax: 360-378-6256. 8AM-4:30PM.

Felony, Misdemeanor, Civil, Eviction, Probate—Superior Court, 350 Court St, #7, Friday Harbor, WA 98250. 360-699-2252, Fax: 360-378-3967. 8AM-4:30PM. Access by: mail, phone, fax, in person, online.

Misdemeanor, Civil Actions Under $35,000, Small Claims—District Court, PO Box 127, Friday Harbor, WA 98250-0127. 360-740-1115, Fax: 360-378-4099. 8AM-5PM. Access by: mail, in person.

Skagit

Real Estate Recording—Skagit County Auditor, 700 So. 2nd St. 2nd Floor, Admin. Bldg. Mount Vernon, WA 98273. 360-676-6770, Fax: 360-336-9429. 8:30AM-4:30PM.

Felony, Civil, Eviction, Probate—Superior Court, PO Box 837, Mount Vernon, WA 98273-0837. 360-676-6774. 8:30AM-4:30PM. Access by: mail, in person, online.

Misdemeanor, Civil Actions Under $35,000, Small Claims—District Court, 600 S 3rd, Mount Vernon, WA 98273. 360-675-5988, Fax: 360-336-9318. 8:30AM-4:30PM. Access by: mail, phone, fax, in person, online.

Skamania

Real Estate Recording—Skamania County Auditor, 240 Vancouver Avenue, Stevenson, WA 98648. 509-427-9410, Fax: 509-427-4165. 8:30AM-5PM.

Felony, Misdemeanor, Civil, Eviction, Probate—Superior Court, PO Box 790, Stevenson, WA 98648. 509-427-9431, Fax: 509-427-7386. 8:30AM-5PM. Access by: mail, phone, in person, online.

Misdemeanor, Civil Actions Under $35,000, Small Claims—District Court, PO Box 790, Stevenson, WA 98648. 509-427-9430, Fax: 509-427-7386. 8:30AM-5PM. Access by: mail, phone, fax, in person, online.

Snohomish

Real Estate Recording—Snohomish County Auditor, Dept. R. M/S # 204, 3000 Rockefeller Avenue, Everett, WA 98201. 206-475-9555, Fax: 425-259-2777. 9AM-5PM.

Felony, Civil Actions, Eviction, Probate—Superior Court, 3000 Rockefeller, MS 605, Everett, WA 98201. 425-388-3466. 8:30AM-5PM. Access by: mail, phone, in person, online. www.co.snohomish.wa.us

Misdemeanor, Civil Actions Under $35,000, Small Claims—Cascade District Court, 415 E Burke, Arlington, WA 98223. 361-274-3215, Fax: 360-435-0873. 9AM-5PM. Access by: mail, in person, online.

Everett District Court, 3000 Rockefeller Ave MS 508, Everett, WA 98201. 425-388-3331, Fax: 425-388-3565. 8AM-5PM. Access by: mail, phone, fax, in person, online.

Evergreen Division, 14414 179th Ave SE, PO Box 625, Monroe, WA 98272-0625. 360-832-6000, Fax: 360-794-6644. 8:30AM-5PM. Access by: mail, phone, in person.

South District Court, 20520 68th Ave W, Lynnwood, WA 98036-7406. 425-774-8803, Fax: 425-744-6820. 8:30AM-5PM. Access by: mail, in person, online.

Spokane

Real Estate Recording—Spokane County Auditor, West 1116 Broadway, Spokane, WA 99260. 509-456-4713, Fax: 509-477-6451. 8:30AM-5PM.

Felony, Civil, Eviction, Probate—Superior Court, W 1116 Broadway, Spokane, WA 99260. 509-456-2211. 8:30AM-5PM. Access by: mail, phone, in person, online.

Misdemeanor, Civil Actions Under $35,000, Small Claims—District Court, Public Safety Bldg, W 1100 Mallon, Spokane, WA 99260. 509-456-4770. 8:30AM-5PM. Access by: mail, in person, online.

Stevens

Real Estate Recording—Stevens County Auditor, 215 South Oak St. Colville, WA 99114. 509-684-2593, Fax: 509-684-8310. 8AM-4:30PM.

Felony, Civil, Eviction, Probate—Superior Court, 215 S Oak Rm 206, Colville, WA 99114. 509-684-7520. 8AM-Noon, 1-4:30PM. Access by: mail, phone, in person, online.

Misdemeanor, Civil Actions Under $35,000, Small Claims—District Court, 215 S Oak Rm 213, Colville, WA 99114. 509-684-5249, Fax: 509-684-7571. 8AM-Noon, 1-4:30PM. Access by: mail, phone, in person, online.

Thurston

Real Estate Recording—Thurston County Auditor, 2000 Lakeridge Drive SW, Olympia, WA 98502. 361-449-2733, Fax: 360-786-5223. 8AM-5PM.

Felony, Misdemeanor, Civil, Eviction, Probate—Superior Court, 2000 Lakeridge Dr SW, Bldg 2, Olympia, WA 98502. 361-449-2641. 8AM-5PM. Access by: mail, phone, in person. www.co.thurston.wa.us

Misdemeanor, Civil Actions Under $35,000, Small Claims—District Court, 2000 Lakeridge Dr SW, Bldg 3, Olympia, WA 98502. 361-449-2733, Fax: 360-754-3359. 9AM-5PM. Access by: mail, phone, fax, in person, online.

Wahkiakum

Real Estate Recording—Wahkiakum County Auditor, 64 Main Street, Cathlamet, WA 98612. 361-526-4223, Fax: 360-795-0824. 8AM-4PM.

Felony, Misdemeanor, Civil, Eviction, Probate—Superior Court, PO Box 116, Cathlamet, WA 98612. 361-526-2721, Fax: 360-795-8813. 8AM-4PM. Access by: mail, in person, online.

Misdemeanor, Civil Actions Under $35,000, Small Claims—District Court, PO Box 144, Cathlamet, WA 98612. 361-526-2233, Fax: 360-795-6506. 8AM-4PM. Access by: mail, phone, fax, in person, online.

Walla Walla

Real Estate Recording—Walla Walla County Auditor, 315 West Main Street, Walla Walla, WA 99362. 509-527-3212, Fax: 509-526-4806. 9AM-5PM.

Felony, Civil, Eviction, Probate—Superior Court, PO Box 836, Walla Walla, WA 99362. 509-527-3221, Fax: 509-527-3214. 9AM-4PM. Access by: mail, phone, in person, online.

Misdemeanor, Civil Actions Under $35,000, Small Claims—District Court, 1646 Plaza Way, Walla Walla, WA 99362-4325. 509-527-3236. 9AM-4PM. Access by: mail, in person, online.

Whatcom

Real Estate Recording—Whatcom County Auditor, 311 Grand Avenue, Bellingham, WA 98225. 361-294-5220, Fax: 360-738-4556. 8:30AM-4:30PM.

Felony, Civil, Eviction, Probate—Superior Court, PO Box 1144, Bellingham, WA 98227. 361-294-5304, Fax: 360-676-7727. 8:30AM-Noon, 1-4:30PM. Access by: mail, phone, in person, online.

Misdemeanor, Civil Actions Under $35,000, Small Claims—District Court, 311 Grand Ave, Bellingham, WA 98225. 361-279-3322, Fax: 360-738-2452. 8AM-4:30PM. Access by: mail, in person, online.

Whitman

Real Estate Recording—Whitman County Auditor, North 404 Main, 2nd Floor, Colfax, WA 99111. 509-397-6230, Fax: 509-397-6351. 8AM-5PM (Recording Until 2:30PM).

Felony, Civil, Eviction, Probate—Superior Court, Box 390, Colfax, WA 99111. 509-397-6244, Fax: 509-397-3546. 8AM-5PM. Access by: mail, phone, fax, in person, online.

Misdemeanor, Civil Actions Under $35,000, Small Claims—District Court, PO Box 249, Pullman, WA 99163. 509-332-2065, Fax: 509-332-5740. 8AM-5PM. Access by: mail, fax, in person, online.

District Court, N 404 Main St, Colfax, WA 99111. 509-397-6260, Fax: 509-397-5584. 8AM-5PM; Public Hours: 8:30AM-4:30PM. Access by: mail, phone, fax, in person, online.

Yakima

Real Estate Recording—Yakima County Auditor, 128 N. 2nd St. #117, Yakima, WA 98901. 509-575-4091, Fax: 509-574-1341. 9AM-4:30PM.

Felony, Civil, Eviction, Probate—Superior Court, 128 N 2nd St, Rm 323, Yakima, WA 98901. 509-574-1430. 8:30AM-4:30PM. Access by: mail, phone, in person, online.

Misdemeanor, Civil Actions Under $35,000, Small Claims—District Court, 128 N 2nd St, Rm 225, Yakima, WA 98901-2631. 509-574-1800, Fax: 509-574-1831. 8:30AM-4:30PM. Access by: mail, phone, fax, in person, online.

Federal Courts

US District Court

Eastern District of Washington

Spokane Division PO Box 1493, Spokane, WA 99210-1493509-353-2150 Counties: Adams, Asotin, Benton, Chelan, Columbia, Douglas, Ferry, Franklin, Garfield, Grant, Lincoln, Okanogan, Pend Oreille, Spokane, Stevens, Walla Walla, Whitman. Also, some cases from Kittitas, Klickitat and Yakima are heard here. www.waed.uscourts.gov
Yakima Division PO Box 2706, Yakima, WA 98907509-575-5838 Counties: Kittitas, Klickitat, Yakima. Cases assigned primarily to Judge McDonald are here. Some cases from Kittitas, Klickitat and Yakima are heard in Spokane.. www.waed.uscourts.gov

Western District of Washington

Seattle Division Clerk of Court, 215 US Courthouse, 1010 5th Ave, Seattle, WA 98104206-553-5598, Record Room: 206-553-5598, Civil Docket Phone: 206-553-4080, Criminal Docket Phone: 206-553-4080 Counties: Island, King, San Juan, Skagit, Snohomish, Whatcom. www.wawd.uscourts.gov
Tacoma Division Clerk's Office, Room 3100, 1717 Pacific Ave, Tacoma, WA 98402-3200253-593-6313 Counties: Clallam, Clark, Cowlitz, Grays Harbor, Jefferson, Kitsap, Lewis, Mason, Pacific,

Pierce, Skamania, Thurston, Wahkiakum. www.wawd.uscourts.gov

US Bankruptcy Court

Eastern District of Washington

Spokane Division PO Box 2164, Spokane, WA 99210-2164509-353-2404 Counties: Adams, Asotin, Benton, Chelan, Columbia, Douglas, Ferry, Franklin, Garfield, Grant, Kittitas, Klickitat, Lincoln, Okanogan, Pend Oreille, Spokane, Stevens, Walla Walla, Whitman, Yakima. www.waeb.uscourts.gov

Western District of Washington

Seattle Division Clerk of Court, 315 Park Place Bldg, 1200 6th Ave, Seattle, WA 98101206-553-7545 Fax: 206-553-0131 Counties: Clallam, Island, Jefferson, King, Kitsap, San Juan, Skagit, Snohomish, Whatcom. www.wawb.uscourts.gov
Tacoma Division Suite 2100, 1717 Pacific Ave, Tacoma, WA 98402-3233253-593-6310 Counties: Clark, Cowlitz, Grays Harbor, Lewis, Mason, Pacific, Pierce, Skamania, Thurston, Wahkiakum. www.wawb.uscourts.gov

West Virginia

Attorney General's Office
State Capitol, Bldg 1, Rm E-26   304-558-2021
Charleston, WV 25305-0220   Fax: 304-558-0140
www.state.wv.us/wvag

Governor's Office
1900 Kanawha Blvd, East   304-558-2000
Charleston, WV 25305-0370   Fax: 304-342-7025
www.state.wv.us/governor

State Archives
1900 Kanawha Blvd E   304-558-0220
Charleston, WV 25305-0300   Fax: 304-558-2779
www.wvlc.wvnet.edu/history/historyw.html

Capital:	Charleston
	Kanawha County
Time Zone:	EST
Number of Counties:	55
Population:	1,815,787
Web Site:	www.state.wv.us

Search Unclaimed Property Online

http://wvtreasury.com/search_
unclaimed_property_databa.htm

State Agencies

Criminal Records
State Police, Criminal Identification Bureau, Records Section, 725 Jefferson Rd, South Charleston, WV 25309; 304-746-2277; Fax: 304-746-2402; 8AM-5PM. Access by: mail. www.wvstatepolice.com

Corporation Records
Limited Liability Company Records
Limited Partnerships
Trademarks/Servicemarks
Secretary of State, Corporation Division, State Capitol Bldg, Room W139, Charleston, WV 25305-0776; 304-558-8000; Fax: 304-558-0900; 8:30AM-4:30PM. Access by: mail, phone, in person.

Sales Tax Registrations
Tax Administration Department, Revenue Division, PO Box 2389, Charleston, WV 25330 (1001 E Lee St E, Charleston, WV 25330); 304-558-8500; Fax: 304-558-8733; 8:30AM-4:30PM. Access by: mail, phone, in person. www.wvweb.net/taxdiv

Uniform Commercial Code
UCC Division, Secretary of State, State Capitol Bldg, Rm W131, Charleston, WV 25305; 304-558-6000; Fax: 304-558-5758; 8:30AM-4:30PM. Access by: mail, phone, in person. www.state.wv.us/sos

Federal Tax Liens
State Tax Liens
Records not available from state agency.

All tax liens are filed at the county level.

Workers' Compensation Records
Workers Compensation Division, Records Management, 4510 Pennsylvania, Charleston, WV 25302; 304-558-5587; Fax: 304-558-1908; 8AM-4:30PM. Access by: mail. www.state.wv.us/bep

Birth Certificates
Bureau of Public Health, Vital Records, State Capitol Complex Bldg 3-Rm 516, Charleston, WV 25305; 304-558-2931; 8AM-4PM. Access by: mail, phone, in person. www.wvdhhr.org/bph/oehp/hsc/vr/birtcert.htm

Death Records

Bureau of Public Health, Vital Records, State Capitol Complex Bldg 3-Rm 516, Charleston, WV 25305; 304-558-2931; 8AM-4PM. Access by: mail, phone, in person.

Marriage Certificates

Bureau of Public Health, Vital Records, State Capitol Complex Bldg 3-Rm 516, Charleston, WV 25305; 304-558-2931; 8AM-4PM. Access by: mail, phone, in person.

Divorce Records

Records not available from state agency.

Records are maintained by the Clerk of Court in the county of divorce.

Accident Reports

Department of Public Safety, Traffic Records Section, 725 Jefferson Rd, South Charleston, WV 25309-1698; 304-746-2128; Fax: 304-746-2206; 8:30AM-4:30PM. Access by: mail, phone, fax, in person.

Driver License Information
Driver Records

Division of Motor Vehicles, Driver Improvement Unit, Building 3, Rm 124, State Capitol Complex, Charleston, WV 25317; 304-558-0238; Fax: 304-558-0037; 8:30AM-4:30PM. Access by: mail, online. www.state.wv.us/dmv

Vehicle Ownership
Vehicle Identification
Boat & Vessel Ownership
Boat & Vessel Registration

Division of Motor Vehicles, Information Services, 1606 Washington St East, Charleston, WV 25311; 304-558-0282; Fax: 304-558-1012; 8:30AM-4:30PM. Access by: mail. www.state.wv.us/dmv

Legislation-Current/Pending
Legislation-Passed

West Virginia State Legislature, State Capitol, Documents, Charleston, WV 25305; 304-347-4830, 800-642-8650 Local; 8:30AM-4:30PM. Access by: mail, phone, in person, online. wvlc.wvnet.edu/legisinfo/legisht.html

Voter Registration

Records not available from state agency.

Voter information is held by the county clerks. There is no statewide system. All information is public record.

GED Certificates

Dept of Education, GED Office, 1900 Kanawha Blvd E, Bldg 6, Rm 230, Charleston, WV 25305-0330; 304-558-6315;.

Hunting License Information
Fishing License Information

Natural Resources Department, Licensing Division, 1900 Kanawha Blvd E, Bldg 3, Room 658, Charleston, WV 25305; 304-558-2758; Fax: 304-558-6208; 8:30AM-4:30PM. Access by: mail. wvweb.com/www/hunting

County Courts & Recording Offices

About the Courts...

Administration

Administrative Office, State Court of Appeals   304-558-0145
1900 Kanawha Blvd, 1 E 100 State Capitol   Fax: 304-558-1212
Charleston, WV 25305
www.state.wv.us/wvsca

Court Structure

The 55 Circuit Courts and the courts of general jurisdiction. The upper limit for civil claims in the Magistrate Courts was changed to $5000 from $3000 effective July 1994. Probate is handled by the Circuit Court. Records are held at the County Commissioner's Office.

Searching Hints

There is a statewide requirement that search turnaround times not exceed 10 days. However, most courts do far better than that limit. There is a discrepancy in what courts will and will not release with the decisions resting with the judges and clerks in the various jurisdictions.

Online Access

There is no statewide online computer system, internal or external. Most courts with a computer system use FORTUNE software; however, no external access is permitted.

About the Recording Offices...

Organization

55 counties, 55 recording offices. The recording officer is County Clerk. The entire state is in the Eastern Time Zone (EST).

UCC Records

Financing statements are filed at the state level, except for real estate related collateral, which are filed only with the Register of Deeds, and consumer goods, which are filed in both places. Many recording offices will perform UCC searches. Use search request form UCC-11. Searches fees and copy fees vary.

Lien Records

All federal and state tax liens are filed with the County Clerk. Most counties will not perform tax lien searches.

Real Estate Records

Most County Clerks will not perform real estate searches. Copy fees are usually $1.50 up to two pages and $1.00 for each additional page. Certification usually costs $1.00 per document.

County Courts & Recording Offices

Barbour

Real Estate Recording—Barbour County Clerk, 8 North Main Street, Courthouse, Philippi, WV 26416. 304-526-8642. 8:30AM-4:30PM.

Felony, Civil Actions Over $5,000, Probate—Circuit Court, 8 N Main St, Philippi, WV 26416. 304-526-8672. 8:30AM-4:30PM. Access by: mail, phone, in person. Special note: Probate is handled by the County Clerk at this address.

Misdemeanor, Civil Actions Under $5,000, Eviction, Small Claims—Magistrate Court, PO Box 541, Philippi, WV 26416. 304-538-2593. 8AM-4PM. Access by: mail, phone, in person.

Berkeley

Real Estate Recording—Berkeley County Clerk, 100 West King Street, Room 1, Martinsburg, WV 25401. 304-329-0047, Fax: 304-267-1794. 9AM-5PM.

Felony, Civil Actions Over $5,000, Probate—Circuit Court, 110 W King St, Martinsburg, WV 25401-3210. 304-291-7244. 9AM-5PM. Access by: mail, phone, fax, in person. Special note: Probate is handled by Fiduciary Records Clerk, 100 W King St, Room 2, Martinsburg, WV 25401.

Misdemeanor, Civil Actions Under $5,000, Eviction, Small Claims—Berkeley County Magistrate Court, 120 W John St, Martinsburg, WV 25401. 304-291-7296, Fax: 304-263-9154. 9AM-4PM. Access by: mail, in person.

Boone

Real Estate Recording—Boone County Clerk, 200 State Street, Madison, WV 25130. 304-457-3454, Fax: 304-369-7329. 8AM-4PM.

Felony, Civil Actions Over $5,000, Probate—Circuit Court, 200 State St, Madison, WV 25130. 304-455-8219, Fax: 304-369-7326. 8AM-4PM. Access by: mail, phone, fax, in person. Special note: Probate is handled by County Clerk, 200 State St, Madison, WV 25130.

Misdemeanor, Civil Actions Under $5,000, Eviction, Small Claims—Magistrate Court, 200 State St. Madison, WV 25130. 304-457-2881, Fax: 304-369-1932. 8AM-4PM. Access by: mail, in person.

Braxton

Real Estate Recording—Braxton County Clerk, 300 Main Street, Sutton, WV 26601. 304-824-7887, Fax: 304-765-2093. 8AM-4PM.

Felony, Civil Actions Over $5,000, Probate—Circuit Court, 300 Main St, Sutton, WV 26601. 304-845-1400, Fax: 304-765-2093. 8AM-4PM. Access by: mail, phone, fax, in person.

Misdemeanor, Civil Actions Under $5,000, Eviction, Small Claims—Magistrate Court, 307 Main St, Sutton, WV 26601. 304-845-2130, Fax: 304-765-3756. 8:30AM-4:30PM. Access by: mail, in person.

Brooke

Real Estate Recording—Brooke County Clerk, 632 Main Street, Courthouse, Wellsburg, WV 26070. Fax: 304-737-4023. 9AM-5PM; Sat 9AM-Noon.

Felony, Civil Actions Over $5,000, Probate—Circuit Court, Brooke County Courthouse, Wellsburg, WV 26070. 304-822-4720. 9AM-5PM. Access by: mail, in person. Special note: Probate is handled by County Clerk, 632 Main St, Courthouse, Wellsburg, WV 26070.

Misdemeanor, Civil Actions Under $5,000, Eviction, Small Claims—Magistrate Court, 632 Main St, Wellsburg, WV 26070. 304-799-6603, Fax: 304-737-1509. 9AM-4PM. Access by: in person.

Cabell

Real Estate Recording—Cabell County Clerk, Cabell County Courthouse, 750 Fifth Ave. Room 108, Huntington, WV 25701. 304-624-8640, Fax: 304-526-8632. 8:30AM-4:30PM.

Felony, Civil Actions Over $5,000, Probate—Circuit Court, PO Box 0545, Huntington, WV 25710-0545. 304-587-4260, Fax: 304-526-8699. 8:30AM-4:30PM. Access by: mail, in person.

Misdemeanor, Civil Actions Under $5,000, Eviction, Small Claims—Magistrate Court, 750 5th Ave, Basement, Rm B 113 Courthouse, Huntington, WV 25701. 304-624-8550, Fax: 304-526-8646. 8:30AM-4:30PM. Access by: in person.

Calhoun

Real Estate Recording—Calhoun County Clerk, Main Street, Courthouse, Grantsville, WV 26147. 304-372-2011, Fax: 304-354-6725. 8:30AM-4PM.

Felony, Civil Actions Over $5,000, Probate—Circuit Court, PO Box 266, Grantsville, WV 26147. 304-422-3444, Fax: 304-354-6910. 8:30AM-4PM, 8:30AM-Noon 1st Sat ea month. Access by: mail, phone, fax, in person.

Misdemeanor, Civil Actions Under $5,000, Eviction, Small Claims—Magistrate Court, PO Box 186, Grantsville, WV 26147. 304-372-2011, Fax: 304-354-6698. 8:30AM-4PM. Access by: mail, in person.

Clay

Real Estate Recording—Clay County Clerk, Courthouse, 207 Main St. Clay, WV 25043. 304-684-2285, Fax: 304-587-7329. 8AM-4PM.

Felony, Civil Actions Over $5,000, Probate—Circuit Court, PO Box 129, Clay, WV 25043. 304-675-6840, Fax: 304-587-4346. 8AM-4PM. Access by: mail, phone, fax, in person.

Misdemeanor, Civil Actions Under $5,000, Eviction, Small Claims—Magistrate Court, PO Box 393, Clay, WV 25043. 304-675-4400, Fax: 304-587-2727. 8:30AM-4:30PM. Access by: mail, phone, in person.

Doddridge

Real Estate Recording—Doddridge County Clerk, 118 East Court Street, Room 102, West Union, WV 26456. 307-322-3441. 8:30AM-4PM.

Felony, Civil Actions Over $5,000, Probate—Circuit Court, 118 E. Court St, West Union, WV 26456. 307-322-3857. 8:30AM-4PM. Access by: mail, phone, in person.

Misdemeanor, Civil Actions Under $5,000, Eviction, Small Claims—Magistrate Court, PO Box 207, West Union, WV 26456. 307-324-6655, Fax: 304-873-2643. 8AM-4PM. Access by: mail, fax, in person.

Fayette

Real Estate Recording—Fayette County Clerk, Courthouse, Fayetteville, WV 25840. 304-643-4409. 8AM-4PM.

Felony, Civil Actions Over $5,000, Probate—Circuit Court, 100 Court St, Fayetteville, WV 25840. 8AM-4PM. Access by: mail, phone, in person. Special note: Probate is handled by County Clerk, PO Box 569, Fayetteville, WV 25840.

Misdemeanor, Civil Actions Under $5,000, Eviction, Small Claims—Magistrate Court, 100 Court St, Fayetteville, WV 25840. 304-647-6609, Fax: 304-574-2458. 9AM-9PM M-F, 9AM-Noon Sat. Access by: in person.

Gilmer

Real Estate Recording—Gilmer County Clerk, 10 Howard Street, Courthouse, Glenville, WV 26351. 304-538-7869, Fax: 304-462-5134. 8AM-4PM.

Felony, Civil Actions Over $5,000, Probate—Circuit Court, Gilmer County Courthouse, Glenville, WV 26351. 304-538-6836, Fax: 304-462-5134. 8AM-4PM. Access by: mail, phone, in person.

Misdemeanor, Civil Actions Under $5,000, Eviction, Small Claims—Magistrate Court, Courthouse Annex, Glenville, WV 26351. 304-564-3311, Fax: 304-462-8582. 8:30AM-4PM. Access by: mail, phone, fax, in person.

Grant

Real Estate Recording—Grant County Clerk, 5 Highland Avenue, Petersburg, WV 26847. 304-272-5648, Fax: 304-257-2593. 8:30AM-4:30PM.

Felony, Civil Actions Over $5,000, Probate—Circuit Court, 5 Highland Ave, Petersburg, WV 26847. 304-272-6721, Fax: 304-257-2593. 8:30AM-4:30PM. Access by: mail, phone, fax, in person.

Misdemeanor, Civil Actions Under $5,000, Eviction, Small Claims—Magistrate Court, 5 Highland Ave (PO Box 216), Petersburg, WV 26847. 304-275-3641, Fax: 304-257-2593. 9AM-4PM. Access by: mail, phone, fax, in person.

Greenbrier

Real Estate Recording—Greenbrier County Clerk, 200 North Court Street, Lewisburg, WV 24901. 304-737-3662, Fax: 304-647-6666. 8:30AM-4:30PM.

Felony, Civil Actions Over $5,000, Probate—Circuit Court, PO Drawer 751, Lewisburg, WV 24901. 304-758-2137, Fax: 304-647-6666. 8:30AM-4:30PM. Access by: mail, in person.

Misdemeanor, Civil Actions Under $5,000, Eviction, Small Claims—Magistrate Court, 200 North Court St, Lewisburg, WV 24901. 304-758-4551, Fax: 304-647-3612. 8:30AM-4:30PM. Access by: mail, phone, fax, in person.

Hampshire

Real Estate Recording—Hampshire County Clerk, Main Street, Courthouse, Romney, WV 26757. 304-927-4750, Fax: 304-822-4039. 9AM-4PM (F open until 8PM).

Felony, Civil Actions Over $5,000, Probate—Circuit Court, PO Box 343, Romney, WV 26757. 305-275-1155. 9AM-4PM M-F 5PM-8PM Friday evening. Access by: mail, in person. Special note: Probate handled by County Clerk, PO Box 806, Romney, WV 26757.

Misdemeanor, Civil Actions Under $5,000, Eviction, Small Claims—Magistrate Court, 239 W Birch Ln, PO Box 881, Romney, WV 26757. 304-927-2750, Fax: 304-822-3981. 8:30AM-4PM. Access by: mail, phone, in person.

Hancock

Real Estate Recording—Hancock County Clerk, 102 Court Street, New Cumberland, WV 26047. 304-643-2163, Fax: 304-564-5941. 8:30AM-4:30PM; Recording Hours: 8:30AM-4PM.

Felony, Civil Actions Over $5,000, Probate—Circuit Court, PO Box 428, New Cumberland, WV 26047. 304-637-3700, Fax: 304-564-5014. 8:30AM-4:30PM. Access by: mail, fax, in person. Special note: Probate can be reached at PO Box 367.

Misdemeanor, Civil Actions Under $5,000, Eviction, Small Claims—Magistrate Court, 106 Court St, New Cumberland, WV 26047. 304-643-2263, Fax: 304-564-3852. 8AM-4PM M-W, F; 8AM-9PM Th. Access by: mail, phone, fax, in person.

Hardy

Real Estate Recording—Hardy County Clerk, 204 Washington Street, Courthouse - Room 111, Moorefield, WV 26836. 304-624-8645, Fax: 304-538-6832. 9AM-4PM; Sat 9AM-Noon.

Felony, Civil Actions Over $5,000, Probate—Circuit Court, 204 Washington St, RM 237, Moorefield, WV 26836. 304-636-5885, Fax: 304-538-6197. 9AM-4PM. Access by: mail, phone, fax, in person.

Misdemeanor, Civil Actions Under $5,000, Eviction, Small Claims—Magistrate Court, 204 Washington St, Moorefield, WV 26836. 304-636-2100, Fax: 304-538-2072. 9AM-4PM. Access by: mail, phone, fax, in person.

Harrison

Real Estate Recording—Harrison County Clerk, 301 West Main Street, Courthouse, Clarksburg, WV 26301. 304-684-3513, Fax: 304-624-8673. 8:30AM-4PM.

Felony, Civil Actions Over $5,000, Probate—Circuit Court, 301 W. Main, Suite 301, Clarksburg, WV 26301-2967. 304-684-7197, Fax: 304-624-8710. 8:30AM-4PM. Access by: in person. Special note: Probate is handled by County Clerk, 301 W Main St, Courthouse, Clarksburg, WV 26301.

Misdemeanor, Civil Actions Under $5,000, Eviction, Small Claims—Magistrate Court, 306 Washington Ave Rm 222, Clarksburg, WV 26301. 304-725-3233, Fax: 304-624-8640. 8AM-4PM. Access by: mail, phone, fax, in person.

Jackson

Real Estate Recording—Jackson County Clerk, Court & Main Streets, P.O. Box 800, Ripley, WV 25271. 304-462-7241, Fax: 304-372-5259. 9AM-4PM; 9AM-Noon Sat.

Felony, Civil Actions Over $5,000, Probate—Circuit Court, PO Box 427, Ripley, WV 25271. 304-462-7441, Fax: 304-372-5259. 9AM-4PM M-F, 9AM-Noon Sat. Access by: mail, phone, in person.

Misdemeanor, Civil Actions Under $5,000, Eviction, Small Claims—Magistrate Court, PO Box 368, Ripley, WV 25271. 304-457-3676, Fax: 304-372-7132. 9AM-4PM. Access by: mail, in person.

Jefferson

Real Estate Recording—Jefferson County Clerk, 100 East Washington Street, Courthouse, Charles Town, WV 25414. 304-788-2625, Fax: 304-728-1957. 9AM-5PM (F open until 7PM).

Felony, Civil Actions Over $5,000, Probate—Circuit Court, PO Box 584, Charles Town, WV 25414. 304-792-8550, Fax: 304-725-7916. 9AM-5PM. Access by: in person.

Misdemeanor, Civil Actions Under $5,000, Eviction, Small Claims—Magistrate Court, PO Box 607, Charles Town, WV 25414. 304-772-3321, Fax: 304-728-3235. 7:30AM-4:30PM. Access by: mail, phone, fax, in person.

Kanawha

Real Estate Recording—Kanawha County Clerk, 409 Virginia Street East, Charleston, WV 25301. 304-424-1700, Fax: 304-357-0585. 8AM-4PM M-W,F; 8AM-7PM Th.

Felony, Civil Actions Over $5,000, Probate—Circuit Court, PO Box 2351, Charleston, WV 25328. 304-425-7952, Fax: 304-357-0473. 8AM-5PM. Access by: in person. Special note: Probate is handled by County Clerk, 409 Virginia St East, Charleston, WV 25301.

Misdemeanor, Civil Actions Under $5,000, Eviction, Small Claims—Magistrate Court, 111 Court St, Charleston, WV 25333. 304-424-1910, Fax: 304-357-0205. 8:30AM-4:30PM. Access by: mail, in person.

Lewis

Real Estate Recording—Lewis County Clerk, 110 Center Avenue, Courthouse, Weston, WV 26452. 304-354-6910, Fax: 304-269-8202. 8:30AM-4:30PM.

Felony, Civil Actions Over $5,000, Probate—Circuit Court, PO Box 69, Weston, WV 26452. 304-354-6698, Fax: 304-269-8249. 8:30AM-4:30PM. Access by: mail, phone, fax, in person.

Misdemeanor, Civil Actions Under $5,000, Eviction, Small Claims—Magistrate Court, 111 Court St, PO Box 260, Weston, WV 26452. 304-357-0210, Fax: 304-269-8253. 8:30AM-Noon, 1-4:30PM. Access by: mail, phone, fax, in person.

Lincoln

Real Estate Recording—Lincoln County Clerk, 8000 Court Avenue, Hamlin, WV 25523. 305-275-1155, Fax: 304-824-7972. 9AM-4:30PM.

Felony, Civil Actions Over $5,000, Probate—Circuit Court, PO Box 338, Hamlin, WV 25523. 305-294-4641, Fax: 304-824-7909. 9AM-4:30PM. Access by: mail, phone, fax, in person.

Misdemeanor, Civil Actions Under $5,000, Eviction, Small Claims—Magistrate Court, PO Box 573, Hamlin, WV 25523. 305-292-3550, Fax: 304-824-5280. 9AM-4:30PM. Access by: mail, phone, fax, in person. Special note: Searches performed by court only on second and fourth Thursday of each month.

Logan

Real Estate Recording—Logan County Clerk, Stratton & Main Street, Courthouse, Room 101, Logan, WV 25601. Fax: 304-792-8621. 8:30AM-4:30PM.

Felony, Civil Actions Over $5,000, Probate—Circuit Court, Logan County Courthouse, Rm 311, Logan, WV 25601. 304-872-

7829, Fax: 304-792-8555. 8:30AM-4:30PM. Access by: mail, in person.

Misdemeanor, Civil Actions Under $5,000, Eviction, Small Claims—Magistrate Court, Logan County Courthouse, Logan, WV 25601. 304-873-1000, Fax: 304-752-0790. 8:30AM-4:30PM. Access by: mail, in person.

Marion

Real Estate Recording—Marion County Clerk, 217 Adams Street, Courthouse, Fairmont, WV 26554. 304-436-8587, Fax: 304-367-5448. 8:30AM-4:30PM.

Felony, Civil Actions Over $3,000—Circuit Court, PO Box 1269, Fairmont, WV 26554. 304-455-8218, Fax: 304-367-5374. 8:30AM-4:30PM. Access by: mail, phone, fax, in person.

Misdemeanor, Civil Actions Under $5,000, Eviction, Small Claims—Magistrate Court, 200 Jackson St, Fairmont, WV 26554. 304-455-5040, Fax: 304-367-5337. 8:30AM-4:30PM M-W, F; 8:30AM-9PM Th. Access by: mail, phone, in person.

Marshall

Real Estate Recording—Marshall County Clerk, 7th Street & Tomlinson Avenue, Moundsville, WV 26041. 307-235-9243, Fax: 304-845-5891. 8:30AM-4:30PM (F open until 5:30PM).

Felony, Civil Actions Over $5,000, Probate—Circuit Court, Marshall County Courthouse, 7th St, Moundsville, WV 26041. 307-235-9266, Fax: 304-845-3948. 8:30AM-4:30PM M-Th; 8:30AM-5:30PM F. Access by: mail, fax, in person.

Mason

Real Estate Recording—Mason County Clerk, 200 6th Street, Point Pleasant, WV 25550. 304-758-4811, Fax: 304-675-2521. 8:30AM-4:30PM.

Felony, Civil Actions Over $5,000, Probate—Circuit Court, PO Box 402, Point Pleasant, WV 25550. 304-765-2830, Fax: 304-675-7419. 8:30AM-4:30PM. Access by: mail, phone, fax, in person.

Misdemeanor, Civil Actions Under $5,000, Eviction, Small Claims—Magistrate Court, Corner of 6th St and Viand, Point Pleasant, WV 25550. 304-765-2837, Fax: 304-675-5949. 8:30AM-4:30PM. Access by: mail, phone, in person.

McDowell

Real Estate Recording—McDowell County Clerk, 90 Wyoming Street, Suite 109, Welch, WV 24801. 304-472-2053, Fax: 304-436-8576. 9AM-5PM.

Felony, Civil Actions Over $5,000, Probate—Circuit Court, PO Box 400, Welch, WV 24801. 304-472-2370. 9AM-5PM. Access by: mail, in person. Special note: Probate is handled by Coutny Clerk, 90 Wyoming St, Ste 109, Welch, WV 24801.

Misdemeanor, Civil Actions Under $5,000, Eviction, Small Claims—Magistrate Court, PO Box 447, Welch, WV 24801. 304-478-2606, Fax: 304-436-8575. 9AM-5PM. Access by: mail, phone, fax, in person.

Mercer

Real Estate Recording—Mercer County Clerk, 1501 Main St. Princeton, WV 24740. 304-472-1180, Fax: 304-487-8351. 8:30AM-4PM.

Felony, Civil Actions Over $5,000, Probate—Circuit Court, 1501 W. Main St, Princeton, WV 24740. 304-587-4256, Fax: 304-487-8351. 8:30AM-4:30PM. Access by: mail, phone, in person.

Misdemeanor, Civil Actions Under $5,000, Eviction, Small Claims—Magistrate Court, 120 Scott Street, Princeton, WV 24740. 304-466-7129. 8:30AM-4:30PM. Access by: in person.

Mineral

Real Estate Recording—Mineral County Clerk, 150 Armstrong Street, Keyser, WV 26726. Fax: 304-788-4109. 8:30AM-5PM.

Felony, Civil Actions Over $5,000, Probate—Circuit Court, 150 Armstrong St, Keyser, WV 26726. 304-872-3630, Fax: 304-788-4109. 8:30AM-5PM. Access by: mail, fax, in person.

Misdemeanor, Civil Actions Under $5,000, Eviction, Small Claims—Magistrate Court, 105 West St, Keyser, WV 26726. 304-872-7810, Fax: 304-788-9835. 8:30AM-4:30PM. Access by: mail, phone, in person.

Mingo

Real Estate Recording—Mingo County Clerk, 75 E. 2nd Ave. Williamson, WV 25661. Fax: 304-235-0565. 8:30AM-4:30PM.

Felony, Civil Actions Over $5,000, Probate—Circuit Court, PO Box 435, Williamson, WV 25661. 304-265-2480. 8:30AM-4:30PM M-W,F; 8:30AM-6:30PM Th. Access by: mail, in person. Special note: Probate is handled by County Clerk, 75 E 2nd Ave, Williamson, WV 25661.

Misdemeanor, Civil Actions Under $5,000, Eviction, Small Claims—Magistrate Court, PO Box 986, Williamson, WV 25661. 304-265-5766, Fax: 304-235-3179. 8:30AM-4:30PM. Access by: mail, phone, in person.

Monongalia

Real Estate Recording—Monongalia County Clerk, 243 High Street, Courthouse - Room 123, Morgantown, WV 26505. 304-367-5360, Fax: 304-291-7233. 9AM-7PM M; 9AM-5PM T-F.

Felony, Civil Actions Over $5,000, Probate—Circuit Court, County Courthouse, 243 High St Rm 110, Morgantown, WV 26505. 304-367-5330, Fax: 304-291-7273. 9AM-7PM M; 9AM-5PM T-F. Access by: mail, in person. Special note: A disclaimer for the Clerk must be included by mail requesters. Probate is handled by County Clerk, 243 High St, Room 123, Morgantown, WV 26505.

Misdemeanor, Civil Actions Under $5,000, Eviction, Small Claims—Magistrate Court, 265 Spruce St, Morgantown, WV 26505. 304-369-3925, Fax: 304-284-7313. 8AM-7PM. Access by: mail, fax, in person.

Monroe

Real Estate Recording—Monroe County Clerk, Main Street, Union, WV 24983. 304-847-2421. 8:30AM-4:30PM.

Felony, Civil Actions Over $5,000, Probate—Circuit Court, PO Box 350, Union, WV 24983. 304-847-2006, Fax: 304-772-5051. 8AM-4PM. Access by: mail, phone, in person.

Misdemeanor, Civil Actions Under $5,000, Eviction, Small Claims—Magistrate Court, PO Box 4, Union, WV 24983. 304-847-2613, Fax: 304-772-4357. 8:30AM-4:30PM. Access by: mail, fax, in person.

Morgan

Real Estate Recording—Morgan County Clerk of County Commission, 202 Fairfax Street, Suite 100, Berkeley Springs, WV 25411. 304-275-6597. 9AM-5PM M,T,Th; 9AM-1PM W; 9AM-7PM F.

Felony, Civil Actions Over $5,000, Probate—Circuit Court, 202 Fairfax St, Ste 101, Berkeley Springs, WV 25411-1501. 304-275-4222, Fax: 304-258-8557. 9AM-5PM MTTh, 9AM-1PM Wed, 9AM-7PM Fri. Access by: in person.

Misdemeanor, Civil Actions Under $5,000, Eviction, Small Claims—Magistrate Court, 202 Fairfax St, Ste 202, Berkeley Springs, WV 25411. 304-291-7240, Fax: 304-258-8639. 9AM-4:30PM. Access by: in person.

Nicholas

Real Estate Recording—Nicholas County Clerk, 700 Main Street, Suite 2, Summersville, WV 26651. 307-283-2929, Fax: 304-872-9600. 8:30AM-4:30PM.

Felony, Civil Actions Over $5,000, Probate—Circuit Court, 700 Main St, Summersville, WV 26651. 307-322-1105. 8:30AM-4:30PM. Access by: mail, in person. Special note: Probate is handled by County Clerk, 700 Main St, Ste 2, Summersville, WV 26651.

Misdemeanor, Civil Actions Under $5,000, Eviction, Small Claims—Magistrate Court, 511 Church St, Suite 206 2nd Flr, Summersville, WV 26651. 307-322-2092, Fax: 304-872-7888. 8:30AM-4:30PM. Access by: in person.

Ohio

Real Estate Recording—Ohio County Clerk, 205 City County Building, Wheeling, WV 26003. 304-264-1980, Fax: 304-234-3829. 8:30AM-5PM.

Felony, Civil Actions Over $5,000, Probate—Circuit Court, 1500 Chapline St, City & County Bldg Rm 403, Wheeling, WV

26003. 304-264-1956, Fax: 304-232-0550. 8:30AM-5PM. Access by: mail, fax, in person.

Misdemeanor, Civil Actions Under $5,000, Eviction, Small Claims—Magistrate Court, Courthouse Annex, 46 15th St, Wheeling, WV 26003. 304-265-1322, Fax: 304-234-3898. 8:30AM-4:30PM. Access by: mail, phone, fax, in person.

Pendleton

Real Estate Recording—Pendleton County Clerk, Main Street, Courthouse, Franklin, WV 26807. 304-425-8366, Fax: 304-358-2473. 8:30AM-4PM; Sat 8:30AM-Noon.

Felony, Civil Actions Over $5,000, Probate—Circuit Court, PO Box 846, Franklin, WV 26807. 304-436-8535, Fax: 304-358-2152. 8:30AM-4PM. Access by: mail, phone, fax, in person.

Misdemeanor, Civil Actions Under $5,000, Eviction, Small Claims—Magistrate Court, PO Box 637, Franklin, WV 26807. 304-436-8528, Fax: 304-358-3870. 8:30AM-4PM. Access by: mail, phone, fax, in person.

Pleasants

Real Estate Recording—Pleasants County Clerk, Courthouse, 301 Court Lane, Room 101, St. Marys, WV 26170. 304-765-5678, Fax: 304-684-9315. 8:30AM-4:30PM.

Felony, Civil Actions Over $5,000, Probate—Circuit Court, 301 Court Lane, Rm 101, St. Mary's, WV 26170. 304-772-3017, Fax: 304-684-3514. 8:30AM-4:30PM. Access by: in person. Special note: Probate is handled by County Clerk, 301 Court Lane, Room 101, St Mary's, WV 26170.

Misdemeanor, Civil Actions Under $5,000, Eviction, Small Claims—Magistrate Court, 301 Court Lane, Rm B-6, St Mary's, WV 26170. 304-772-3018, Fax: 304-684-9315. 8:30AM-4:30PM. Access by: mail, phone, in person.

Pocahontas

Real Estate Recording—Pocahontas County Clerk, 900C 10th Avenue, Marlinton, WV 24954. 304-873-2694. 9AM-4:30PM.

Felony, Civil Actions Over $5,000, Probate—Circuit Court, 900-D 10th Ave, Marlinton, WV 24954. 304-873-2331. 9AM-4:30PM. Access by: mail, phone, in person.

Misdemeanor, Civil Actions Under $5,000, Eviction, Small Claims—Magistrate Court, 900 10th Ave, Marlinton, WV 24954. 304-927-2540, Fax: 304-799-6331. 9AM-4:30PM. Access by: mail, in person.

Preston

Real Estate Recording—Preston County Clerk, 101 West Main Street, Room 201, Kingwood, WV 26537. 304-369-7391, Fax: 304-329-0198. 9AM-5PM (F open until 7PM).

Felony, Civil Actions Over $5,000, Probate—Circuit Court, 101 W. Main St, Rm 301, Kingwood, WV 26537. 304-369-7364, Fax: 304-329-0372. 9AM-5PM M-Th, 9AM-7PM Fri. Access by: mail, phone, fax, in person. Special note: Probate is handled by County Clerk, 101 W Main St, Room 201, Kingwood, WV 26537.

Misdemeanor, Civil Actions Under $5,000, Eviction, Small Claims—Magistrate Court, 328 Tunnelton, Kingwood, WV 26537. 304-372-2011, Fax: 304-329-0855. 8:30AM-4:30PM. Access by: mail, in person.

Putnam

Real Estate Recording—Putnam County Clerk, 3389 Winfield Rd. Winfield, WV 25213. 304-647-6632, Fax: 304-586-0200. 8AM-4PM.

Felony, Civil Actions Over $5,000, Probate—Circuit Court, Putnam County Judicial Bldg, 3389 Winfield Rd, Winfield, WV 25213. 304-647-6626, Fax: 304-586-0221. 8AM-4PM M-W & F, 8AM-7PM Th. Access by: mail, phone, fax, in person.

Misdemeanor, Civil Actions Under $5,000, Eviction, Small Claims—Magistrate Court, 3389 Winfield Rd, Winfield, WV 25213. 304-675-3810, Fax: 304-586-0234. 8:30AM-4:30PM. Access by: mail, in person.

Raleigh

Real Estate Recording—Raleigh County Clerk, 215 Main Street, Courthouse, Beckley, WV 25801. 304-269-8230, Fax: 304-255-9352. 8:30AM-4PM.

Felony, Civil Actions Over $5,000, Probate—Circuit Court, 215 Main St, Beckley, WV 25801. 304-269-8210, Fax: 304-255-9353. 8:30AM-4:30PM. Access by: mail, phone, fax, in person. Special note: Probate is handled by County Clerk, 215 Main St, Courthouse, Beckley, WV 25801.

Misdemeanor, Civil Actions Under $5,000, Eviction, Small Claims—Magistrate Court, 115 W Prince St, Suite A, Beckley, WV 25801. 304-269-8222, Fax: 304-255-9354. 8AM-4PM. Access by: in person.

Randolph

Real Estate Recording—Randolph County Clerk, 2 Randolph Avenue, Elkins, WV 26241. 304-725-9761.

Felony, Civil Actions Over $5,000, Probate—Circuit Court, Courthouse, Elkins, WV 26241. 304-732-8000, Fax: 304-636-5989. 8AM-4:30PM. Access by: in person.

Misdemeanor, Civil Actions Under $5,000, Eviction, Small Claims—Magistrate Court, #2 Randolph Ave, Elkins, WV 26241. 304-725-9761, Fax: 304-636-2510. 8AM-4:30PM. Access by: mail, phone, fax, in person.

Ritchie

Real Estate Recording—Ritchie County Clerk, 115 East Main Street, Courthouse - Room 201, Harrisville, WV 26362. 304-732-8000. 8AM-4PM.

Felony, Civil Actions Over $5,000, Probate—Circuit Court, 115 E. Main St, Harrisville, WV 26362. 304-732-8000. 8AM-4PM. Access by: mail, phone, in person.

Misdemeanor, Civil Actions Under $5,000, Eviction, Small Claims—Magistrate Court, 319 E. Main St, Harrisville, WV 26362. 304-737-1321, Fax: 304-643-2098. 8AM-4PM. Access by: mail, phone, fax, in person.

Roane

Real Estate Recording—Roane County Clerk, 200 Main Street, Spencer, WV 25276. 307-328-2628, Fax: 304-927-0079. 9AM-4PM; 9AM-Noon Sat.

Felony, Civil Actions Over $5,000, Probate—Circuit Court, PO Box 122, Spencer, WV 25276. 307-328-2662, Fax: 304-927-4165. 9AM-Noon, 1-4PM M-F; 9AM-Noon Sat. Access by: mail, phone, fax, in person.

Misdemeanor, Civil Actions Under $5,000, Eviction, Small Claims—Magistrate Court, PO Box 663, Spencer, WV 25276. 307-332-1134, Fax: 304-927-2754. 9AM-4PM. Access by: in person.

Summers

Real Estate Recording—Summers County Clerk, 120 Ballengee Street, Courthouse, Hinton, WV 25951. 304-564-3355, Fax: 304-466-7128. 8:30AM-4:30PM.

Felony, Civil Actions Over $5,000, Probate—Circuit Court, PO Box 1058, Hinton, WV 25951. 304-564-3311, Fax: 304-466-7124. 8:30AM-4:30PM. Access by: mail, phone, fax, in person.

Misdemeanor, Civil Actions Under $5,000, Eviction, Small Claims—Magistrate Court, PO Box 1059, Hinton, WV 25951. 304-574-1200, Fax: 304-466-4912. 8:30AM-4:30PM. Access by: mail, phone, fax, in person.

Taylor

Real Estate Recording—Taylor County Clerk, 214 West Main Street, Room 101, Courthouse, Grafton, WV 26354. 304-354-6333, Fax: 304-265-3016.

Felony, Civil Actions Over $5,000, Probate—Circuit Court, 214 W. Main St, Rm 104, Grafton, WV 26354. 304-329-2764. 8:30AM-Noon, 1-4:30PM. Access by: mail, phone, in person.

Misdemeanor, Civil Actions Under $5,000, Eviction, Small Claims—Magistrate Court, 214 W. Main St, Grafton, WV 26354. 304-329-0105, Fax: 304-265-5708. 8:30AM-4:30PM. Access by: mail, phone, fax, in person.

Tucker

Real Estate Recording—Tucker County Clerk, Courthouse, 215 First St. Parsons, WV 26287. Fax: 304-478-4464. 8AM-4PM.

Felony, Civil Actions Over $5,000, Probate—Circuit Court, 215 1st St #2, Parsons, WV 26287. 304-586-0234, Fax: 304-478-4464. 8AM-4PM. Access by: in person.

Misdemeanor, Civil Actions Under $5,000, Eviction, Small Claims—Magistrate Court, 201 Walnut St, Parsons, WV 26287. 304-587-2131, Fax: 304-478-4836. 8:30AM-4:30PM. Access by: mail, phone, in person.

Tyler

Real Estate Recording—Tyler County Clerk, Corner of Main & Court Street, Middlebourne, WV 26149. 304-824-3336, Fax: 304-758-2126. 8AM-4PM.

Felony, Civil Actions Over $5,000, Probate—Circuit Court, PO Box 8, Middlebourne, WV 26149. 304-824-5001, Fax: 304-758-4008. 8AM-4PM. Access by: mail, phone, in person.

Misdemeanor, Civil Actions Under $5,000, Eviction, Small Claims—Magistrate Court, PO Box 127, Middlebourne, WV 26149. 304-822-5022. 9AM-4PM. Access by: mail, in person.

Upshur

Real Estate Recording—Upshur County Clerk, 40 W. Main Street, Courthouse - Room 101, Buckhannon, WV 26201. 304-574-1200, Fax: 304-472-1029. 8AM-4:30PM.

Felony, Civil Actions Over $5,000, Probate—Circuit Court, 38 W. Main St, Rm 304, Buckhannon, WV 26201. 304-586-0204, Fax: 304-472-2168. 8AM-4:30PM. Access by: mail, fax, in person. Special note: Probate is handled by County Clerk, 40 W Main, Courthouse, Room 101, Buckhannon, WV 26201.

Misdemeanor, Civil Actions Under $5,000, Eviction, Small Claims—Magistrate Court, 38 W Main, Rm 204 Courthouse Annex, Buckhannon, WV 26201. 304-586-0203. 8AM-4PM. Access by: mail, in person.

Wayne

Real Estate Recording—Wayne County Clerk, Courthouse, Room 108, 700 Hendricks Street, Wayne, WV 25570. 304-358-2214, Fax: 304-272-5318. 8AM-4PM M-W, F; 8AM-8PM Th.

Felony, Civil Actions Over $5,000, Probate—Circuit Court, PO Box 38, Wayne, WV 25570. 304-357-0440. 8AM-4PM M,T,W,F; 8AM-8PM Th. Access by: mail, phone, in person. Special note: Probate is handled by County Clerk, PO Box 248, Wayne, WV 25570.

Misdemeanor, Civil Actions Under $5,000, Eviction, Small Claims—Magistrate Court, PO Box 667, Wayne, WV 25570. 304-357-0400. 8AM-4PM M-W, F; 8AM-8PM Th. Access by: mail, phone, in person.

Webster

Real Estate Recording—Webster County Clerk, Courthouse - Room G-1, 2 Court Square, Webster Springs, WV 26288. 307-235-9370, Fax: 304-847-7671. 8:30AM-4PM.

Felony, Civil Actions Over $5,000, Probate—Circuit Court, 2 Court Square, Rm G-4, Webster Springs, WV 26288. 307-283-1244, Fax: 304-847-7671. 8:30AM-4PM. Access by: mail, phone, fax, in person.

Misdemeanor, Civil Actions Under $5,000, Eviction, Small Claims—Magistrate Court, 2 Court Square, Rm B-1, Webster Springs, WV 26288. 307-283-2523, Fax: 304-847-7747. 8:30AM-4PM. Access by: mail, in person.

Wetzel

Real Estate Recording—Wetzel County Clerk, Main Street, Courthouse, New Martinsville, WV 26155. 304-487-8369, Fax: 304-455-3256. 9AM-4:30PM M,T,W,F; 9AM-4PM Th; 9AM-Noon Sat.

Felony, Civil Actions Over $5,000—Circuit Court, PO Box 263, New Martinsville, WV 26155. 304-526-8622, Fax: 304-455-5256. 9AM-4:30PM. Access by: mail, phone, in person.

Misdemeanor, Civil Actions Under $5,000, Eviction, Small Claims—Magistrate Court, PO Box 147, New Martinsville, WV 26155. 304-478-2665, Fax: 304-455-2859. 8:30AM-4:30PM. Access by: mail, fax, in person.

Wirt

Real Estate Recording—Wirt County Clerk, Courthouse Square, Elizabeth, WV 26143. 304-358-7067, Fax: 304-275-3418. 8:30AM-4PM.

Felony, Civil Actions Over $5,000, Probate—Circuit Court, PO Box 465, Elizabeth, WV 26143. 304-367-5303, Fax: 304-275-3642. 8:30AM-4PM. Access by: mail, phone, fax, in person.

Misdemeanor, Civil Actions Under $5,000, Eviction, Small Claims—Magistrate Court, PO Box 249, Elizabeth, WV 26143. 304-358-2343, Fax: 304-275-3642. 8:30AM-4PM. Access by: mail, in person.

Wood

Real Estate Recording—Wood County Clerk, 3rd & Market Sts. Room 201, Parkersburg, WV 26101. 304-466-7112. 8:30AM-4:30PM.

Felony, Civil Actions Over $5,000, Probate—Circuit Court, Wood County Judicial, #2 Government Sq, Parkersburg, WV 26101-5353. 304-466-7103. 8:30AM-4:30PM. Access by: mail, phone, in person. Special note: Probate is handled by County Clerk, PO Box 1474, Parkersburg, WV 26102.

Misdemeanor, Civil Actions Under $5,000, Eviction, Small Claims—Magistrate Court, 208 Avery St, Parkersburg, WV 26101. 304-462-7812, Fax: 304-422-2451. 8:30AM-4:30PM. Access by: mail, fax, in person.

Wyoming

Real Estate Recording—Wyoming County Clerk, Main Street, Courthouse, Pineville, WV 24874. 304-792-8651, Fax: 304-732-9659. 8AM-4PM.

Felony, Civil Actions Over $5,000, Probate—Circuit Court, PO Box 190, Pineville, WV 24874. 304-799-4710. 9AM-4PM. Access by: mail, phone, in person.

Misdemeanor, Civil Actions Under $5,000, Eviction, Small Claims—Magistrate Court, PO Box 598, Pineville, WV 24874. 304-799-4604, Fax: 304-732-7247. 9AM-4PM M-Th, 9AM-6PM Fri. Access by: mail, phone, in person.

Federal Courts

US District Court

Northern District of West Virginia

Clarksburg Division PO Box 2857, Clarksburg, WV 26302-2857304-622-8513 Counties: Braxton, Calhoun, Doddridge, Gilmer, Harrison, Lewis, Marion, Monongalia, Pleasants, Ritchie, Taylor, Tyler. www.wvnd.uscourts.gov
Elkins Division PO Box 1518, Elkins, WV 26241304-636-1445 Fax: 304-636-5746 Counties: Barbour, Grant, Hardy, Mineral,

Pendleton, Pocahontas, Preston, Randolph, Tucker, Upshur, Webster. www.wvnd.uscourts.gov
Martinsburg Division Room 207, 217 W King St, Martinsburg, WV 25401304-267-8225 Fax: 304-264-0434 Counties: Berkeley, Hampshire, Jefferson, Morgan. www.wvnd.uscourts.gov
Wheeling Division Clerk, PO Box 471, Wheeling, WV 26003304-232-0011 Fax: 304-233-2185 Counties: Brooke, Hancock, Marshall, Ohio, Wetzel. www.wvnd.uscourts.gov

Southern District of West Virginia

Beckley Division PO Drawer 5009, Beckley, WV 25801304-253-7481 Fax: 304-253-3252 Counties: Fayette, Greenbrier, Nicholas, Raleigh, Wyoming.

Bluefield Division Clerk's Office, PO Box 4128, Bluefield, WV 24701304-327-9798 Counties: McDowell, Mercer, Monroe, Summers.

Charleston Division PO Box 2546, Charleston, WV 25329304-347-5114, Record Room: 304-347-5527 Counties: Boone, Clay, Kanawha, Logan, Putnam, Roane.

Huntington Division Clerk of Court, PO Box 1570, Huntington, WV 25716304-529-5588 Fax: 304-529-5131 Counties: Cabell, Lincoln, Mason, Mingo, Wayne.

Parkersburg Division Clerk of Court, PO Box 1526, Parkersburg, WV 26102304-420-6490 Fax: 304-420-6363 Counties: Jackson, Wirt, Wood.

US Bankruptcy Court

Northern District of West Virginia

Wheeling Division PO Box 70, Wheeling, WV 26003304-233-1655 Counties: Barbour, Berkeley, Braxton, Brooke, Calhoun, Doddridge, Gilmer, Grant, Hampshire, Hancock, Hardy, Harrison, Jefferson, Lewis, Marion, Marshall, Mineral, Monongalia, Morgan, Ohio, Pendleton, Pleasants, Pocahontas, Preston, Randolph, Ritchie, Taylor,Tucker, Tyler, Upshur, Webster, Wetzel.

Southern District of West Virginia

Charleston Division PO Box 3924, Charleston, WV 25339304-347-5114 Counties: Boone, Cabell, Clay, Fayette, Greenbrier, Jackson, Kanawha, Lincoln, Logan, Mason, McDowell, Mercer, Mingo, Monroe, Nicholas, Putnam, Raleigh, Roane, Summers, Wayne, Wirt, Wood, Wyoming.

Wisconsin

Attorney General's Office
PO Box 7857
Madison, WI 53707-7857
608-266-1221
Fax: 608-267-2779
www.doj.state.wi.us

Governor's Office
PO Box 7863
Madison, WI 53707-7863
608-266-1212
Fax: 608-267-8983
www.wisgov.state.wi.us

State Archives
816 State St
Madison, WI 53706
608-264-6450
Fax: 608-264-6486
www.shsw.wisc.edu

Capital:	Madison
	Dane County
Time Zone:	CST
Number of Counties:	72
Population:	5,169,677
Web Site:	www.state.wi.us

Search Unclaimed Property Online

http://prd1.state.wi.us/servlet/
trdUnclaimProperty

State Agencies

Criminal Records
Wisconsin Department of Justice, Crime Information Bureau, Record Check Unit, PO Box 2688, Madison, WI 53701-2688 (123 W Washington Ave, Madison, WI 53703); 608-266-5764; 8AM-4:30PM. Access by: mail, online. www.doj.state.wi.us

Corporation Records
Limited Partnership Records
Limited Liability Company Records
Department of Financial Institutions, Division of Corporate & Consumer Services, PO Box 7846, Madison, WI 53707-7846 (345 W Washington Ave, 3rd Floor, Madison, WI 53703); 608-261-7577; Fax: 608-267-6813; 7:45AM-4:30PM. Access by: mail, phone, in person. www.wdfi.org

Trademarks/Servicemarks
Trade Names
Secretary of State, Tradenames/Trademarks Division, PO Box 7848, Madison, WI 53707-7848 (30 W Mifflin St, 10th Floor, Madison, WI 53702); 608-266-5653; Fax: 608-266-3159; 7:45AM-4:30PM. Access by: mail, phone, in person. ttp://badger.state.wi.us/agencies/sos

Sales Tax Registrations
Revenue Department, Income, Sales, & Excise Tax Division, PO Box 8933, Madison, WI 53708-8933 (125 S Webster, Madison, WI 53702); 608-266-1911; Fax: 608-261-6240; 7:45AM-4:30PM. Access by: mail, phone, fax, in person. www.dor.state.wi.us

Uniform Commercial Code
Federal Tax Liens
State Tax Liens
Department of Financial Institutions, CCS/UCC, PO Box 7847, Madison, WI 53707-7847 (345 W Washington Ave 3rd Fl, Madison, WI 53703); 608-261-9548; Fax: 608-264-7965; 7:45AM-4:30PM. Access by: mail, phone, in person, online. www.wdfi.org

Workers' Compensation Records
Dept of Workforce Development, Worker's Compensation Division, PO Box 7901, Madison, WI 53707-7901 (201 E Washington Ave, Madison, WI 53707); 608-266-1340; 7:45AM-4:30PM. Access by: mail. dwd.state.wi.us/wc

Birth Certificates

The Center of Health Statistics, Vital Records, PO Box 309, Madison, WI 53701 (One W Wilson St, Room 158, Madison, WI 53702); 608-266-1372, 608-266-1371 Message Phone; Fax: 608-255-2035; 8AM-4:15PM. Access by: mail.

Death Records

The Center of Health Statistics, Vital Records, PO Box 309, Madison, WI 53701; 608-266-1372, 608-266-1371; Fax: 608-255-2035; 8AM-4:15PM. Access by: mail.

Marriage Certificates

The Center of Health Statistics, Vital Records, PO Box 309, Madison, WI 53701; 608-266-1372, 608-266-1371; Fax: 608-255-2035; 8AM-4:15PM. Access by: mail.

Divorce Records

The Center of Health Statistics, Vital Records, PO Box 309, Madison, WI 53701; 608-266-1372, 608-266-1371; Fax: 608-255-2035; 8AM-4:15PM. Access by: mail.

Accident Reports

Division of Motor Vehicles, Traffic Accident Section, PO Box 7919, Madison, WI 53707-7919 (4802 Sheboygan Ave, Room 804, Madison, WI 53707); 608-266-8753; Fax: 608-267-0606; 7:30AM-4:30PM. Access by: mail, phone, in person. www.dot.state.wi.us

Driver Records

Division of Motor Vehicles, Records & Licensing Section, PO Box 7995, Madison, WI 53707-7995 (4802 Sheboygan Ave, Room 301, Madison, WI 53707); 608-266-2353; Fax: 608-267-3636; 7:30AM-4:30PM. Access by: mail, phone, in person, online.

Vehicle Ownership
Vehicle Identification

Department of Transportation, Vehicle Records Section, PO Box 7911, Madison, WI 53707-7911 (4802 Sheboygan Ave, Room 205, Madison, WI 53707); 608-266-3666, 608-266-1466 Registration Laws; Fax: 608-267-6966; 7:30AM-4:30PM. Access by: mail.

Boat & Vessel Ownership
Boat & Vessel Registration

Department of Natural Resources, Boat Registration, PO Box 7236, Madison, WI 53707-7924 (101 S Webster, Madison, WI 53703); 608-266-2107; Fax: 608-264-6130; 7:45AM-4:30PM. Access by: mail. www.dnr/state.wi.us

Legislation-Current/Pending
Legislation-Passed

Wisconsin Legislative, Legislative Reference Bureau, PO Box 2037, Madison, WI 53701-2037 (100 N. Hamilton Street, Madison, WI 53703); 608-266-0341, 800-362-9472 Bill Status; Fax: 608-266-5648; 7:45AM-4:30PM. Access by: mail, phone, in person, online. www.legis.state.wi.us

Voter Registration

Records not available from state agency.

All records are maintained at the municipal level. Although records are open to the public, be advised that not all municipalities maintain voter lists. Not all voters are registered.

GED Certificates

Department of Public Instruction, GED Program, PO Box 7841, Madison, WI 53707-7841 (125 S Webster, Madison, WI 53707); 608-267-9245, 800-441-4563; Fax: 608-264-9552;. Access by: mail, phone, in person. www.dpi.state.wi.us

Hunting License Information
Fishing License Information

Records not available from state agency.

They do not have a central database. Only vendors have the names and addresses and they supply to local county clerks. On 03/99 a new automated issuance system will be implemented which will change availability.

County Courts & Recording Offices

About the Courts...

Administration

Director of State Courts, Supreme Court   608-266-6828
PO Box 1688   Fax: 608-267-0980
Madison, WI 53701
www.courts.state.wi.us

Court Structure

The Circuit Court is the court of general jurisdiction. Probate filing is a function of the Circuit Court; however, each county has a Register in Probate who maintains and manages the probate records. The Register in Probate, also, maintains guardianship and mental health records, most of which are sealed but may be opened for cause with a court order. In some counties, the Register also maintains termination and adoption records, but practices vary widely across the state.

Most Registers in Probate are putting pre-1950 records on microfilm and destroying the hard copies. This is done as "time and workloads permit," so microfilm archiving is not uniform across the state. The small claims limit was raised to $5000 in mid-1995.

Searching Hints

The statutory fee schedule for the Circuit Courts is as follows: Search Fee - $5.00 per name; Copy Fee - $1.25 per page; Certification Fee - $5.00. In about half the Circuit Courts, no search fee is charged if the case number is provided. There is normally no search fee charged for in-person searches.

The fee schedule for probate is as follows: Search Fee - $4.00 per name; Certification Fee - $3.00 per document plus copy fee; Copy Fee - $1.00 per page.

Online Access

Wisconsin Circuit Court Access (WCCA) allows users to view circuit court case information through the Wisconsin court system   web   site   -- http://ccap.court.state.wi.us/internetcourt access. No data is available for Outagamie, Portage and Walworth counties or for Ozaukee, Waukesha (criminal court), and Wood counties. Searches can be conducted statewide or county by county. WCCA provides detailed information about circuit cases and for civil cases, the program displays judgment and judment party information. WCCA also offers the ability to generate reports. Although, due to statutory requirements, WCCA users will not be able to view restricted cases.. In addition, public access terminals are available at each court.

About the Recording Offices...

Organization

72 counties, 72 recording offices. The recording officers are Register of Deeds and Clerk of Court (state tax liens). The entire state is in the Central Time Zone (CST).

UCC Records

Financing statements are filed at the state level, except for consumer goods, farm and real estate related collateral, which are filed only with the Register of Deeds. All recording offices will perform UCC searches, and many will accept a search by phone. Use search request form UCC-11 for mail-in searches. Searches fees are usually $10.00 per debtor name. Copy fees are usually $1.00 per page.

Lien Records

Federal tax liens on personal property of businesses are filed with the Secretary of State. Other federal tax liens are filed with the county Register of Deeds. State tax liens are filed with the Clerk of Court. Refer to The Sourcebook of County Court Records for information about Wisconsin courts. Many Registers will perform federal tax lien searches. Search fees and copy fees vary.

Real Estate Records

Registers will not perform real estate searches. Copy fees and certification fees vary. Assessor telephone numbers are for local municipalities or for property listing agencies. Counties do not have assessors. Copies usually cost $2.00 for the first page and $1.00 for each additional page. Certification usually costs $.25 per document. The Treasurer maintains property tax records.

County Courts & Recording Offices

Adams

Real Estate Recording—Adams County Register of Deeds, 402 Main Street, Friendship, WI 53934. 8AM-4:30PM.

Felony, Misdemeanor, Civil, Eviction, Small Claims—Circuit Court, PO Box 220, Friendship, WI 53934. 608-339-4208, Fax: 608-339-6414. 8AM-4:30PM. Access by: mail, phone, in person.

Probate—Register in Probate, PO Box 200, Friendship, WI 53934. 608-339-4213, Fax: 608-339-6414. 8AM-4:30PM. Access by: mail, in person.

Ashland

Real Estate Recording—Ashland County Register of Deeds, 201 West Main Street, Room 206, Ashland, WI 54806. Fax: 715-682-7032. 8AM-4PM.

Felony, Misdemeanor, Civil, Eviction, Small Claims—Circuit Court, Courthouse 210 W Main St Rm 307, Ashland, WI 54806. 715-682-7016, Fax: 715-682-7919. 8AM-Noon, 1-4PM. Access by: mail, phone, fax, in person.

Probate—Register in Probate, Courthouse Rm 203, 201 W Main, Ashland, WI 54806. 715-682-7009. 8AM-Noon, 1-4PM. Access by: mail, in person.

Barron

Real Estate Recording—Barron County Register of Deeds, 330 East LaSalle, Room 201, Barron, WI 54812. 715-537-6270, Fax: 715-537-6277. 8AM-4PM.

Felony, Misdemeanor, Civil, Eviction, Small Claims—Circuit Court, Barron County Courthouse, 330 E LaSalle Ave, Barron, WI 54812. 715-537-6265, Fax: 715-537-6269. 8AM-4PM. Access by: in person.

Probate—Register in Probate, Courthouse Rm 218, Barron, WI 54812. 715-537-6261, Fax: 715-537-6277. 8AM-4PM. Access by: mail, in person.

Bayfield

Real Estate Recording—Bayfield County Register of Deeds, 117 East 5th, Washburn, WI 54891. 8AM-4PM.

Felony, Misdemeanor, Civil, Eviction, Small Claims—Circuit Court, 117 E 5th, Washburn, WI 54891. 715-373-6108, Fax: 715-373-6153. 8AM-4PM. Access by: mail, in person.

Probate—Register in Probate, 117 E 5th, PO Box 86, Washburn, WI 54891. 715-373-6108, Fax: 715-373-6155. 8AM-4PM. Access by: mail, in person.

Brown

Real Estate Recording—Brown County Register of Deeds, 305 E. Walnut, Room 260, Green Bay, WI 54301. Fax: 920-448-4449. 8AM-4:30PM.

Felony, Misdemeanor, Civil, Eviction, Small Claims—Circuit Court, PO Box 23600, Green Bay, WI 54305-3600. 920-448-4161, Fax: 920-448-4156. 8AM-4:30PM. Access by: mail, in person.

Probate—Register in Probate, PO Box 23600, Green Bay, WI 54305-3600. 920-448-4275, Fax: 920-448-6208. 8AM-Noon, 1-4:30PM. Access by: mail, in person.

Buffalo

Real Estate Recording—Buffalo County Register of Deeds, 407 Second Street, Alma, WI 54610. 608-685-6215, Fax: 608-685-6213. 8AM-4:30PM.

Felony, Misdemeanor, Civil, Eviction, Small Claims—Circuit Court, 407 S 2nd, PO Box 68, Alma, WI 54610. 608-685-6212, Fax: 608-685-6211. 8AM-4:30PM. Access by: mail, phone, in person.

Probate—Register in Probate, 407 S 2nd, PO Box 68, Alma, WI 54610. 608-685-6202, Fax: 608-685-6213. 8AM-4:30PM. Access by: mail, phone, in person.

Burnett

Real Estate Recording—Burnett County Register of Deeds, 7410 County Road K #103, Siren, WI 54872. 715-349-2187. 8:30AM-4:30PM.

Felony, Misdemeanor, Civil, Eviction, Small Claims—Circuit Court, 7410 County Road K #115, Siren, WI 54872. 715-349-2147. 8:30AM-4:30PM. Access by: mail, in person.

Probate—Register in Probate, 7410 County Road K #110, Siren, WI 54872. 715-349-2177, Fax: 715-349-7659. 8:30AM-4:30PM. Access by: mail, in person.

Calumet

Real Estate Recording—Calumet County Register of Deeds, 206 Court Street, Chilton, WI 53014. Fax: 920-849-1469. 8AM-4:30PM.

Felony, Misdemeanor, Civil, Eviction, Small Claims—Circuit Court, 206 Court St, Chilton, WI 53014. 920-849-1414, Fax: 920-849-1483. 8AM-4:30PM. Access by: mail, in person.

Probate—Register in Probate, 206 Court St, Chilton, WI 53014-1198. 920-849-1455, Fax: 920-849-1483. 8AM-Noon, 1-4:30PM. Access by: mail, in person.

Chippewa

Real Estate Recording—Chippewa County Register of Deeds, 711 North Bridge Street, Chippewa Falls, WI 54729. 715-726-7965, Fax: 715-726-4582. 8AM-4:30PM.

Felony, Misdemeanor, Civil, Eviction, Small Claims—Circuit Court, 711 N Bridge St, Chippewa Falls, WI 54729-1879. 715-726-7758, Fax: 715-726-7786. 8AM-4:30PM. Access by: mail, in person.

Probate—Register in Probate, 711 N Bridge St, Chippewa Falls, WI 54729. 715-726-7737, Fax: 715-726-7786. 8AM-4:30PM. Access by: mail, in person.

Clark

Real Estate Recording—Clark County Register of Deeds, 517 Court Street, Room 303, Neillsville, WI 54456. Fax: 715-743-5154. 8AM-Noon, 12:30-5PM.

Felony, Misdemeanor, Civil, Eviction, Small Claims—Circuit Court, 517 Court St, Neillsville, WI 54456-1971. 715-743-5181, Fax: 715-743-5154. 8AM-5PM. Access by: mail, in person.

Probate—Register in Probate, 517 Court St, Rm 403, Neillsville, WI 54456. 715-743-5172, Fax: 715-743-4350. 8AM-5PM. Access by: mail, in person. Special note: There is a $4.00 search fee.

Columbia

Real Estate Recording—Columbia County Register of Deeds, 400 DeWitt Street, Portage, WI 53901. 608-742-9613, Fax: 608-742-9602. 8AM-4:30PM.

Felony, Misdemeanor, Civil, Eviction, Small Claims—Circuit Court, PO Box 587, Portage, WI 53901. 608-742-2191, Fax: 608-742-9601. 8AM-4:30PM. Access by: mail, in person.

Probate—Register in Probate, 400 DeWitt, PO Box 221, Portage, WI 53901. 608-742-9636, Fax: 608-742-9601. 8AM-4:30PM. Access by: mail, in person.

Crawford

Real Estate Recording—Crawford County Register of Deeds, 220 North Beaumont Road, Prairie du Chien, WI 53821. 608-326-0219, Fax: 608-326-0220. 8AM-4:30PM.

Felony, Misdemeanor, Civil, Eviction, Small Claims—Circuit Court, 220 N Beaumont Rd, Prairie Du Chien, WI 53821. 608-326-0211. 8AM-4:30PM. Access by: mail, in person.

Probate—Register in Probate, 220 N Beaumont Rd, Prairie Du Chien, WI 53821. 608-326-0206, Fax: 608-326-0288. 8AM-4:30PM. Access by: mail, phone, in person.

Dane

Real Estate Recording—Dane County Register of Deeds, 210 Martin Luther King Jr. Blvd. Room 110, Madison, WI 53709. Fax: 608-267-3110. 7:45AM-4PM.

Felony, Misdemeanor, Civil, Eviction, Small Claims—Circuit Court, 210 Martin Luther King Jr Blvd, Rm GR10, Madison, WI 53709. 608-266-4311, Fax: 608-267-8859. 7:45AM-4:30PM. Access by: mail, fax, in person.

Probate—Register in Probate, 210 Martin Luther King Jr Blvd, Rm 305, Madison, WI 53709. 608-266-4331. 7:45AM-4:30PM. Access by: mail, in person.

Dodge

Real Estate Recording—Dodge County Register of Deeds, 127 East Oak Street, Administration Building, Juneau, WI 53039. 414-386-3781, Fax: 920-386-3902. 8AM-4:30PM.

Felony, Misdemeanor, Civil, Eviction, Small Claims—Circuit Court, 105 N Main, Juneau, WI 53039. 920-386-3820, Fax: 920-386-3587. 8AM-4:30PM. Access by: mail, in person.

Probate—Register in Probate, 105 N Main St, Juneau, WI 53039-1056. 920-386-3550, Fax: 920-386-3587. 8AM-4:30PM. Access by: mail, in person. Special note: $4.00 search fee, records computerized since 1992.

Door

Real Estate Recording—Door County Register of Deeds, 421 Nebraska Street, Sturgeon Bay, WI 54235. 414-746-2286, Fax: 920-746-2525. 8AM-4:30PM.

Felony, Misdemeanor, Civil, Eviction, Small Claims—Circuit Court, PO Box 670, Sturgeon Bay, WI 54235. 920-746-2205, Fax: 920-746-2381. 8AM-4:30PM. Access by: mail, in person.

Probate—Register in Probate, PO Box 670, 421 Nebraska St, Rm C375, Sturgeon Bay, WI 54235-2470. 920-746-2482, Fax: 920-746-2470. 8AM-4:30PM. Access by: mail, fax, in person.

Douglas

Real Estate Recording—Douglas County Register of Deeds, 1313 Belknap Street, Courthouse - Room 108, Superior, WI 54880. Fax: 715-395-1553. 8AM-4:30PM.

Felony, Misdemeanor, Civil, Eviction, Small Claims—Circuit Court, 1313 Belknap, Superior, WI 54880. Fax: 715-395-1421. 8AM-4:30PM. Access by: mail, in person.

Probate—Register in Probate, 1313 Belknap, Superior, WI 54880. 715-395-1229, Fax: 715-395-1421. 8AM-4:30PM. Access by: mail, in person.

Dunn

Real Estate Recording—Dunn County Register of Deeds, 800 Wilson Avenue, Menomonie, WI 54751. Fax: 715-232-1324. 8AM-4:30PM.

Felony, Misdemeanor, Civil, Eviction, Small Claims—Circuit Court, Stokke Parkway #1500, Menomonie, WI 54751. 715-232-2611. 8AM-4:30PM. Access by: mail, in person.

Probate—Register in Probate, 615 Parkway Dr #1300, Menomonie, WI 54751. 715-232-1449, Fax: 715-232-6971. 8AM-4:30PM. Access by: mail, in person.

Eau Claire

Real Estate Recording—Eau Claire County Register of Deeds, 721 Oxford Avenue, Courthouse, Room 1310, Eau Claire, WI 54703. 715-839-4745. 8AM-5PM.

Felony, Misdemeanor, Civil, Eviction, Small Claims—Record Search, 721 Oxford Ave, Eau Claire, WI 54703. 715-839-4816, Fax: 715-839-4817. 8AM-5PM. Access by: mail, in person.

Probate—Register in Probate, 721 Oxford Ave, Eau Claire, WI 54703. 715-839-4823. 8AM-5PM. Access by: mail, in person.

Florence

Real Estate Recording—Florence County Register of Deeds, 501 Lake Avenue, Florence, WI 54121. Fax: 715-528-5470. 8:30AM-Noon, 12:30-4PM.

Felony, Misdemeanor, Civil, Eviction, Small Claims—Circuit Court, PO Box 410, Florence, WI 54121. 715-528-3205, Fax: 715-528-5470. 8:30AM-4PM. Access by: mail, in person.

Probate—Register in Probate, PO Box 410, Florence, WI 54121. 715-528-3205, Fax: 715-528-5470. 8:30AM-Noon, 1-4PM. Access by: mail.

Fond du Lac

Real Estate Recording—Fond du Lac County Register of Deeds, 160 South Macy Street, Fond du Lac, WI 54935. 920-929-3010.

Felony, Misdemeanor, Civil, Eviction, Small Claims—Circuit Court, PO Box 1355, Fond du Lac, WI 54936-1355. 920-929-3041, Fax: 920-929-3933. 8AM-4:30PM. Access by: mail, in person.

Probate—Register in Probate, PO Box 1355, Fond du Lac, WI 54936-1355. 920-929-3084, Fax: 920-929-7058. 8AM-Noon, 1-4:30PM. Access by: mail, in person.

Forest

Real Estate Recording—Forest County Register of Deeds, 200 E. Madison Street, Crandon, WI 54520. 715-478-3829. 8:30AM-Noon, 1-4:30PM.

Felony, Misdemeanor, Civil, Eviction, Small Claims—Circuit Court, 200 E Madison St, Crandon, WI 54520. 715-478-3323, Fax: 715-478-2430. 8:30AM-4:30PM. Access by: mail, in person.

Probate—Register in Probate, 200 E Madison St, Crandon, WI 54520. 715-478-2418, Fax: 715-478-2430. 8:30AM-4:30PM. Access by: mail, in person.

Grant

Real Estate Recording—Grant County Register of Deeds, 130 West Maple, Lancaster, WI 53813. Fax: 608-723-7370. 8AM-4:30PM.

Felony, Misdemeanor, Civil, Eviction, Small Claims—Circuit Court, PO Box 110, Lancaster, WI 53813. 608-723-2752, Fax: 608-723-7370. 8AM-4:30PM. Access by: mail, in person.

Probate—Register in Probate, 130 W Maple St, Lancaster, WI 53813. 608-723-2697, Fax: 608-723-7370. 8AM-4:30PM. Access by: mail, in person. Special note: $4.00 search fee, records computerized since 1993.

Green

Real Estate Recording—Green County Register of Deeds, 1016 16th Avenue, Courthouse, Monroe, WI 53566. Fax: 608-328-2835. 8AM-5PM.

Felony, Misdemeanor, Civil, Eviction, Small Claims—Circuit Court, 1016 16th Ave, Monroe, WI 53566. 608-328-9433, Fax: 608-328-2835. 8AM-5PM. Access by: mail, in person.

Probate—Register in Probate, 1016 16th Ave, Monroe, WI 53566. 608-328-9567, Fax: 608-328-2835. 8AM-12, 1PM-5PM. Access by: mail, in person.

Green Lake

Real Estate Recording—Green Lake County Register of Deeds, 492 Hill Street, Green Lake, WI 54941. Fax: 920-294-4009. 8AM-4:30PM.

Felony, Misdemeanor, Civil, Eviction, Small Claims—Circuit Court, 492 Hill St, PO Box 3188, Green Lake, WI 54941. 920-294-4142, Fax: 920-294-4150. 8AM-4:30PM. Access by: mail, in person.

Probate—Register in Probate, 492 Hill St, Green Lake, WI 54941. 920-294-4044, Fax: 920-294-4150. 8AM-4:30PM. Access by: mail, in person.

Iowa

Real Estate Recording—Iowa County Register of Deeds, 222 North Iowa Street, Dodgeville, WI 53533. Fax: 608-935-3024. 8:30AM-4:30PM.

Felony, Misdemeanor, Civil, Eviction, Small Claims—Circuit Court, 222 N Iowa St, Dodgeville, WI 53533. 608-

935-0395, Fax: 608-935-0386. 8:30AM-4:30PM. Access by: mail, in person.

Probate—Register in Probate, 222 N Iowa St, Dodgeville, WI 53533. 608-935-5812, Fax: 608-935-0368. 8:30AM-Noon, 12;30-4:30PM. Access by: mail, fax, in person.

Iron

Real Estate Recording—Iron County Register of Deeds, 300 Taconite Street, Hurley, WI 54534. Fax: 715-561-2928. 8AM-4PM.

Felony, Misdemeanor, Civil, Eviction, Small Claims—Circuit Court, 300 Taconite St, Hurley, WI 54534. 715-561-4084, Fax: 715-561-4054. 8AM-4PM. Access by: mail, phone, in person.

Probate—Register in Probate, 300 Taconite St, Hurley, WI 54534. 715-561-3434, Fax: 715-561-4054. 8AM-4PM. Access by: mail, in person.

Jackson

Real Estate Recording—Jackson County Register of Deeds, 307 Main, Black River Falls, WI 54615. Fax: 715-284-0261. 8AM-4:30PM.

Felony, Misdemeanor, Civil, Eviction, Small Claims—Circuit Court, 307 Main St, Black River Falls, WI 54615. 715-284-0208, Fax: 715-284-0270. 8AM-4:30PM. Access by: mail, in person. www.co.jackson.wi.us

Probate—Register in Probate, 307 Main St, Black River Falls, WI 54615. 715-284-0213, Fax: 715-284-0277. 8AM-4:30PM. Access by: mail, in person.

Jefferson

Real Estate Recording—Jefferson County Register of Deeds, 320 South Main Street, Courthouse, Room 102, Jefferson, WI 53549. 414-674-7250. 8AM-4:30PM.

Felony, Misdemeanor, Civil, Eviction, Small Claims—Circuit Court, 320 S Main St, Jefferson, WI 53549. 920-674-7150, Fax: 920-674-7425. 8AM-4:30PM. Access by: mail, in person.

Probate—Register in Probate, 320 S Main St, Jefferson, WI 53549. 920-674-7245, Fax: 920-675-0134. 8AM-4:30PM. Access by: mail, in person.

Juneau

Real Estate Recording—Juneau County Register of Deeds, Courthouse, 220 E. State St. Mauston, WI 53948. Fax: 608-849-9369. 8AM-Noon, 12:30-4:30PM.

Felony, Misdemeanor, Civil, Eviction, Small Claims—Circuit Court, 220 E State St, Mauston, WI 53948. 608-847-9356, Fax: 608-847-9360. 8AM-Noon, 12:30-4:30PM. Access by: mail, in person.

Probate—Register in Probate, 220 E State St Rm 205, Mauston, WI 53948. 608-847-9346, Fax: 608-847-9349. 8AM-4:30PM. Access by: mail, in person.

Kenosha

Real Estate Recording—Kenosha County Register of Deeds, 1010 56 St. Kenosha, WI 53140. Fax: 262-653-2564. 8AM-5PM.

Felony, Misdemeanor, Civil, Eviction, Small Claims—Circuit Court, 912 56th St, Kenosha, WI 53140. 270-247-3626, Fax: 262-653-2435. 8AM-5PM. Access by: mail, in person.

Probate—Register in Probate, Courthouse Rm 302, 912 56th St, Kenosha, WI 53140. 270-259-3040, Fax: 262-653-2435. 8AM-5PM. Access by: mail, in person. Special note: $4.00 per search, records indexed on computer (1992) and cards.

Kewaunee

Real Estate Recording—Kewaunee County Register of Deeds, 613 Dodge Street, Kewaunee, WI 54216. Fax: 920-388-7195. 8AM-4:30PM.

Felony, Misdemeanor, Civil, Eviction, Small Claims—Circuit Court, 613 Dodge St, Kewaunee, WI 54216. 920-388-7144, Fax: 920-388-3139. 8:30AM-4:30PM. Access by: mail, phone, in person.

Probate—Register in Probate, 613 Dodge St, Kewaunee, WI 54216. 920-388-4410, Fax: 920-388-3139. 8AM-4:30PM. Access by: mail, in person.

La Crosse

Real Estate Recording—La Crosse County Register of Deeds, 400 North 4th Street, Room 106, Administrative Center, La Crosse, WI 54601. 608-785-9711, Fax: 608-785-9704. 8:30AM-5PM.

Felony, Misdemeanor, Civil, Eviction, Small Claims—Circuit Court, 201 W Main St Rm 307, La Crosse, WI 54601. 608-785-9590, Fax: 608-789-7821. 8:30AM-5PM. Access by: mail, phone, in person.

Probate—Register in Probate, 333 Vine St, Rm 1201, La Crosse, WI 54601. 608-785-9882. 8:30AM-5PM. Access by: mail, in person.

Lafayette

Real Estate Recording—Lafayette County Register of Deeds, 626 Main Street, Darlington, WI 53530. Fax: 608-776-4991. 8AM-4:30PM.

Felony, Misdemeanor, Civil, Eviction, Small Claims—Circuit Court, 626 Main St, Darlington, WI 53530. 608-776-4832. 8AM-4:30PM. Access by: mail, in person.

Probate—Register in Probate, 626 Main St, Darlington, WI 53530. 608-776-4811. 8AM-4:30PM. Access by: mail, in person.

Langlade

Real Estate Recording—Langlade County Register of Deeds, 800 Clermont Street, Antigo, WI 54409. 715-627-6204, Fax: 715-627-6303. 8:30AM-4:30PM.

Felony, Misdemeanor, Civil, Eviction, Small Claims—Circuit Court, 800 Clermont St, Antigo, WI 54409. 715-627-6215. 8:30AM-4:30PM. Access by: mail, in person.

Probate—Register in Probate, 800 Clermont St, Antigo, WI 54409. 715-627-6303, Fax: 715-627-6213. 8:30AM-4:30PM. Access by: mail, in person. Special note: There is a $4.00 search fee.

Lincoln

Real Estate Recording—Lincoln County Register of Deeds, 1110 East Main, Courthouse, Merrill, WI 54452. Fax: 715-536-0360. 8:15AM-4:30PM.

Felony, Misdemeanor, Civil, Eviction, Small Claims—Circuit Court, 1110 E Main St, Merrill, WI 54452. 715-536-0319, Fax: 715-536-6528. 8:15AM-4:30PM. Access by: mail, in person.

Probate—Register in Probate, 1110 E Main St, Merrill, WI 54452. 715-536-0342, Fax: 715-536-5230. 8:15AM-Noon, 1-4:30PM. Access by: mail, in person.

Manitowoc

Real Estate Recording—Manitowoc County Register of Deeds, 1010 South 8th Street, Courthouse, Manitowoc, WI 54220. 414-683-4020, Fax: 920-683-2702. 8:30AM-5PM M; 8:30AM-4:30PM T-F.

Felony, Misdemeanor, Civil, Eviction, Small Claims—Circuit Court, PO Box 2000, Manitowoc, WI 54221-2000. 920-683-4030. 8:30AM-5PM M; 8:30AM-4:30PM T-F. Access by: mail, phone, in person.

Probate—Register in Probate, 1010 S 8th St Rm 116, Manitowoc, WI 54220. 920-683-4016, Fax: 920-683-5182. 8:30AM-4:30PM. Access by: mail, in person.

Marathon

Real Estate Recording—Marathon County Register of Deeds, 500 Forest Street, Courthouse, Wausau, WI 54403. 715-847-5241, Fax: 715-261-1488. 8AM-5PM.

Felony, Misdemeanor, Civil, Eviction, Small Claims—Circuit Court, 500 Forest St, Wausau, WI 54403. 715-261-1300, Fax: 715-261-1319. 8AM-5PM (Summer hours 8AM-4:30PM Memorial-Labor Day). Access by: mail, in person.

Probate—Register in Probate, 500 Forest St, Wausau, WI 54403. 715-847-5218, Fax: 715-847-5200. 8AM-5PM. Access by: mail, in person.

Marinette

Real Estate Recording—Marinette County Register of Deeds, 1926 Hall Avenue, Courthouse, Marinette, WI 54143. 715-732-7430, Fax: 715-732-7532. 8:30AM-4:30PM.

Felony, Misdemeanor, Civil, Eviction, Small Claims—Circuit Court, 1926 Hall Ave, Marinette, WI 54143-1717. 715-732-7450. 8:30AM-4:30PM. Access by: mail, in person.

Probate—Register in Probate, 1926 Hall Ave, Marinette, WI 54143-1717. 715-732-7475, Fax: 715-732-7496. 8:30AM-Noon, 1-4:30PM. Access by: mail, in person.

Marquette

Real Estate Recording—Marquette County Register of Deeds, 77 West Park, Montello, WI 53949. 608-297-9148, Fax: 608-297-7606. 8AM-Noon, 12:30-4:30PM.

Felony, Misdemeanor, Civil, Eviction, Small Claims—Circuit Court, PO Box 187, Montello, WI 53949. 608-297-9102, Fax: 608-297-9188. 8AM-Noon, 12:30-4:30PM. Access by: mail, in person.

Probate—Register in Probate, 77 W Park St, PO Box 749, Montello, WI 53949. 608-297-9105, Fax: 608-297-9188. 8AM-4:30PM.

Menominee

Real Estate Recording—Menominee County Register of Deeds, Courthouse Lane, Keshena, WI 54135. 715-799-3001, Fax: 715-799-1322. 8AM-Noon, 1-4:30PM.

Felony, Misdemeanor, Civil, Eviction, Small Claims—Circuit Court, PO Box 279, Keshena, WI 54135. 715-799-3313, Fax: 715-799-1322. 8AM-4:30PM. Access by: mail, in person.

Probate—Register in Probate, 311 N Main St, Shawano, WI 54166. 715-526-8631, Fax: 715-526-4915. 8AM-4:30PM. Access by: mail, in person. Special note: Tribal probate records only in Keshena (Menominee County); Non-tribal records are in Shawano County.

Milwaukee

Real Estate Recording—Milwaukee County Register of Deeds, 901 North 9th Street, Milwaukee, WI 53233. 414-278-4033, Fax: 414-223-1257. 8AM-4:30PM.

Civil, Eviction, Small Claims—Circuit Court-Civil, 901 9th St Rm G-9, Milwaukee, WI 53233. 414-278-4128, Fax: 414-223-1256. 8AM-4PM. Access by: mail, in person.

Felony, Misdemeanor—Circuit Court-Criminal Division, 821 W State St, Milwaukee, WI 53233. 414-278-4588, Fax: 414-223-1262. 8AM-5PM. Access by: mail, fax, in person. Special note: Address Room 136 for felonies and Room 124 for misdemeanors.

Probate—Register in Probate, 901 N 9th St Rm 207, Milwaukee, WI 53233. 414-278-4444, Fax: 414-223-1814. 8AM-4:30PM. Access by: mail, in person.

Monroe

Real Estate Recording—Monroe County Register of Deeds, Administrative Center, 202 S. "K" St. Sparta, WI 54656. 608-269-8710. 8AM-4:30PM.

Felony, Misdemeanor, Civil, Eviction, Small Claims—Circuit Court, PO Box 186, Sparta, WI 54656. 608-269-8745. 8AM-4:30PM. Access by: mail, in person.

Probate—Register in Probate, 112 S Court, Rm 301, Sparta, WI 54656-1765. 608-269-8701, Fax: 608-269-8950. 8AM-4:30PM. Access by: mail, phone, in person.

Oconto

Real Estate Recording—Oconto County Register of Deeds, 301 Washington Street, Room 2035, Oconto, WI 54153. 414-834-6813. 8AM-4PM.

Felony, Misdemeanor, Civil, Eviction, Small Claims—Circuit Court, 301 Washington St, Oconto, WI 54153. 920-834-6855, Fax: 920-834-6867. 8AM-4PM. Access by: mail, in person.

Probate—Register in Probate, 301 Washington St, Oconto, WI 54153. 920-834-6839, Fax: 920-834-6867. 8AM-4PM. Access by: mail, in person.

Oneida

Real Estate Recording—Oneida County Register of Deeds, Oneida Avenue, 1 Courthouse Square, Rhinelander, WI 54501. 715-369-6137, Fax: 715-369-6222. 8AM-4:30PM.

Felony, Misdemeanor, Civil, Eviction, Small Claims—Circuit Court, PO Box 400, Rhinelander, WI 54501. 715-369-6120. 8AM-4:30PM. Access by: mail, in person.

Probate—Register in Probate, PO Box 400, Rhinelander, WI 54501. 715-369-6159. 8AM-12, 1-4:30PM. Access by: mail, in person.

Outagamie

Real Estate Recording—Outagamie County Register of Deeds, 410 South Walnut St. CAB 205, Appleton, WI 54911. 414-832-5065, Fax: 920-832-2177. 8:30AM-5PM.

Felony, Misdemeanor, Civil, Eviction, Small Claims—Circuit Court, 320 S Walnut St, Appleton, WI 54911. 920-832-5130, Fax: 920-832-5115. 8:30AM-5PM. Access by: mail, in person. Special note: Small claims and eviction records at 920-832-5135.

Probate—Register in Probate, 320 S Walnut St, Appleton, WI 54911. 920-832-5601, Fax: 920-832-5115. 8:30AM-Noon, 1-5PM. Access by: mail, in person.

Ozaukee

Real Estate Recording—Ozaukee County Register of Deeds, 121 West Main Street, Port Washington, WI 53074. 262-636-3238, Fax: 262-284-8100. 8:30AM-5PM.

Felony, Misdemeanor, Civil, Eviction, Small Claims—Circuit Court, 1201 S Spring St, Port Washington, WI 53074. 262-653-2664, Fax: 262-284-8491. 8:30AM-5PM. Access by: mail, in person. www.co.ozaukee.wi.us/departments/clerkofcourts.htm

Probate—Register in Probate, PO Box 994, Port Washington, WI 53074. 262-636-3333, Fax: 262-284-8491. 8:30AM-5PM. Access by: mail, in person.

Pepin

Real Estate Recording—Pepin County Register of Deeds, 740 7th Avenue West, County Government Center, Durand, WI 54736. 715-672-8850, Fax: 715-672-8677. 8:30AM-Noon, 12:30PM-4:30PM.

Felony, Misdemeanor, Civil, Eviction, Small Claims—Circuit Court, PO Box 39, Durand, WI 54736. 715-672-8861, Fax: 715-672-8521. 8:30AM-Noon, 12:30-4:30PM. Access by: mail, in person.

Probate—Register in Probate, PO Box 39, Durand, WI 54736. 715-672-8859, Fax: 715-672-8753. 8:30AM-Noon, 1-4:30PM. Access by: mail, in person.

Pierce

Real Estate Recording—Pierce County Register of Deeds, 414 West Main Street, Ellsworth, WI 54011. 715-273-3531, Fax: 715-273-6861. 8AM-5PM.

Felony, Misdemeanor, Civil, Eviction, Small Claims—Circuit Court, PO Box 129, Ellsworth, WI 54011. 715-273-3531. 8:30AM-4:30PM. Access by: mail, in person.

Probate—Register in Probate, PO Box 97, Ellsworth, WI 54011. 715-273-3531, Fax: 715-273-6855. 8AM-5PM. Access by: mail, in person.

Polk

Real Estate Recording—Polk County Register of Deeds, 100 Polk County Plaza, Suite 160, Balsam Lake, WI 54810. 715-485-3161, Fax: 715-485-9202. 8:30AM-4:30PM.

Felony, Misdemeanor, Civil, Eviction, Small Claims—Circuit Court, 100 Polk Plaza, PO Box 549, Balsam Lake, WI 54810. 715-485-9299, Fax: 715-485-9262. 8:30AM-4:30PM. Access by: mail, in person.

Probate—Register in Probate, 100 Polk Plaza, Suite 230, Balsam Lake, WI 54810. 715-485-9238, Fax: 715-485-9275. 8:30AM-4:30PM. Access by: mail, in person.

Portage

Real Estate Recording—Portage County Register of Deeds, 1516 Church Street, County-City Building, Stevens Point, WI 54481. 715-346-1428, Fax: 715-345-5361. 7:30AM-4:30PM.

Felony, Misdemeanor, Civil, Eviction, Small Claims—Circuit Court (Branches 1, 2 & 3), 1516 Church St, Stevens Point, WI 54481. 715-346-1351, Fax: 715-346-1236. 7:30AM-4:30PM. Access by: mail, in person, online.

Probate—Register in Probate, 1516 Church St, Stevens Point, WI 54481. 715-346-1362, Fax: 715-346-1486. 7:30AM-4:30PM. Access by: mail, phone, in person.

Price

Real Estate Recording—Price County Register of Deeds, 126 Cherry, Phillips, WI 54555. 715-339-2615. 8AM-Noon, 1-4:30PM.

Felony, Misdemeanor, Civil, Eviction, Small Claims—Circuit Court, Courthouse, 126 Cherry St, Phillips, WI 54555. 715-339-2353, Fax: 715-339-3089. 8AM-Noon, 1-4:30PM. Access by: mail, phone, in person.

Probate—Register in Probate, Courthouse, 126 Cherry St, Phillips, WI 54555. 715-339-3078, Fax: 715-339-3089. 8AM-4:30PM. Access by: mail, in person.

Racine

Real Estate Recording—Racine County Register of Deeds, 730 Wisconsin Avenue, Racine, WI 53403. 270-237-3561, Fax: 262-636-3851. 8AM-5PM.

Felony, Misdemeanor, Civil, Eviction, Small Claims, Probate—Circuit Court, 730 Wisconsin Ave, Racine, WI 53403. 270-247-1733, Fax: 262-636-3341. 8AM-5PM. Access by: mail, in person.

Probate—Register in Probate, 730 Wisconsin Ave, Racine, WI 53403. 270-236-3944, Fax: 262-636-3341. 8AM-5PM. Access by: mail, in person.

Richland

Real Estate Recording—Richland County Register of Deeds, Seminary Street, Courthouse, Richland Center, WI 53581. 608-647-3658. 8:30AM-4:30PM.

Felony, Misdemeanor, Civil, Eviction, Small Claims—Circuit Court, PO Box 655, Richland Center, WI 53581. 608-647-3956, Fax: 608-647-6134. 8:30AM-4:30PM. Access by: mail, in person.

Probate—Register in Probate, PO Box 427, Richland Center, WI 53581. 608-647-2626, Fax: 608-647-6134. 8:30AM-Noon, 1-4:30PM. Access by: mail, in person.

Rock

Real Estate Recording—Rock County Register of Deeds, 51 South Main Street, Janesville, WI 53545. 8AM-5PM.

Felony, Misdemeanor, Civil, Eviction, Small Claims—Circuit Court, 51 S Main, Janesville, WI 53545. 608-743-2200, Fax: 608-743-2223. 8AM-5PM. Access by: mail, in person.

Circuit Court-South, Jaynesville Courthouse, 51 S Main St, Janesville, WI 53545. 608-364-2010. 8AM-5PM. Access by: mail, in person.

Probate—Register in Probate, 51 S Main, Janesville, WI 53545. 608-757-5635. 8AM-5PM. Access by: mail, in person.

Rusk

Real Estate Recording—Rusk County Register of Deeds, 311 Miner Avenue, Ladysmith, WI 54848. 715-532-2105, Fax: 715-532-2194. 8AM-4:30PM.

Felony, Misdemeanor, Civil, Eviction, Small Claims—Circuit Court, 311 Miner Ave East, Ladysmith, WI 54848. 715-532-2108. 8AM-4:30PM. Access by: mail, in person.

Probate—Register in Probate, 311 E Miner Ave, Ladysmith, WI 54848. 715-532-2147, Fax: 715-532-2266. 8AM-4:30PM. Access by: mail, in person.

Sauk

Real Estate Recording—Sauk County Register of Deeds, 505 Broadway St. Baraboo, WI 53913. 608-355-3276, Fax: 608-355-3292. 8AM-4:30PM.

Felony, Misdemeanor, Civil, Eviction, Small Claims—Circuit Court, 515 Oak Street, Baraboo, WI 53913. 608-355-3287. 8AM-4:30PM. Access by: mail, fax, in person.

Probate—Register in Probate, 515 Oak St, Baraboo, WI 53913. 608-355-3226. 8AM-4:30PM. Access by: mail, in person.

Sawyer

Real Estate Recording—Sawyer County Register of Deeds, 406 Main, Hayward, WI 54843. 715-634-4868, Fax: 715-634-6839. 8AM-4PM.

Felony, Misdemeanor, Civil, Eviction, Small Claims—Circuit Court, PO Box 508, Hayward, WI 54843. 715-634-4887. 8AM-4PM. Access by: mail, in person.

Probate—Register in Probate, PO Box 447, Hayward, WI 54843. 715-634-7519. 8AM-4PM. Access by: mail, in person.

Shawano

Real Estate Recording—Shawano County Register of Deeds, 311 North Main, Shawano, WI 54166. 715-524-9130, Fax: 715-524-5157. 8AM-4:30PM.

Felony, Misdemeanor, Civil, Eviction, Small Claims—Circuit Court, 311 N Main Rm 206, Shawano, WI 54166. 715-526-9347, Fax: 715-526-4915. 8AM-4:30PM. Access by: mail, in person.

Probate—Register in Probate, 311 N Main, Shawano, WI 54166. 715-526-8631, Fax: 715-526-4915. 8AM-4:30PM. Access by: mail, in person.

Sheboygan

Real Estate Recording—Sheboygan County Register of Deeds, 500 New York Ave. 2nd Floor, Sheboygan, WI 53081. 414-459-3015. 8AM-5PM.

Felony, Misdemeanor, Civil, Eviction, Small Claims—Circuit Court, 615 N 6th St, Sheboygan, WI 53081. 920-459-3068, Fax: 920-459-3921. 8AM-5PM. Access by: mail, in person.

Probate—Register in Probate, 615 N 6th St, Sheboygan, WI 53081. 920-459-3050, Fax: 920-459-3921. 8AM-5PM. Access by: mail, in person. Special note: There is a $4.00 search fee.

St. Croix

Real Estate Recording—St. Croix County Register of Deeds, 1101 Carmichael Rd. Hudson, WI 54016. 715-386-4645, Fax: 715-386-4687. 8AM-5PM.

Felony, Misdemeanor, Civil, Eviction, Small Claims—Circuit Court, 1101 Carmichael Rd, Hudson, WI 54016. 715-386-4630. 8AM-5PM. Access by: mail, in person.

Probate—Register in Probate, 1101 Carmichael Rd, Rm 2242, Hudson, WI 54016. 715-386-4618, Fax: 715-381-4401. 8AM-5PM. Access by: mail, phone, in person.

Taylor

Real Estate Recording—Taylor County Register of Deeds, 224 South 2nd Street, Medford, WI 54451. 715-748-1466. 8:30AM-4:30PM.

Felony, Misdemeanor, Civil, Eviction, Small Claims—Circuit Court, 224 S 2nd St, Medford, WI 54451-1811. 715-748-1425, Fax: 715-748-2465. 8:30AM-4:30PM. Access by: mail, in person.

Probate—Register in Probate, 224 S 2nd, Medford, WI 54451. 715-748-1435, Fax: 715-748-2465. 8:30AM-4:30PM. Access by: mail, in person.

Trempealeau

Real Estate Recording—Trempealeau County Register of Deeds, Courthouse, 36245 Main St. Whitehall, WI 54773. 8AM-4:30PM.

Felony, Misdemeanor, Civil, Eviction, Small Claims—Circuit Court, 36245 Main St, Whitehall, WI 54773. 715-538-2311. 8AM-4:30PM. Access by: mail, fax, in person.

Probate—Register in Probate, 36245 Main St, PO Box 67, Whitehall, WI 54773. 715-538-2311, Fax: 715-538-4400. 8AM-4:30PM. Access by: mail, in person.

Vernon

Real Estate Recording—Vernon County Register of Deeds, 400 Court House Square St. Court House Annex, Viroqua, WI 54665. 608-637-3222. 8:30AM-4:30PM.

Felony, Misdemeanor, Civil, Eviction, Small Claims—Circuit Court, PO Box 426, Viroqua, WI 54665. 608-637-5340, Fax: 608-637-5554. 8:30AM-4:30PM. Access by: mail, phone, in person.

Probate—Register in Probate, PO Box 448, Viroqua, WI 54665. 608-637-5347, Fax: 608-637-5554. 8:30AM-4:30PM. Access by: mail, in person.

Vilas

Real Estate Recording—Vilas County Register of Deeds, 330 Court St. Eagle River, WI 54521. 715-479-3610, Fax: 715-479-3605. 8AM-4PM.

Felony, Misdemeanor, Civil, Eviction, Small Claims—Circuit Court, 330 Court St, Eagle River, WI 54521. 715-479-3632, Fax: 715-479-3740. 8AM-4PM. Access by: mail, in person.

Probate—Register in Probate, 330 Court St, Eagle River, WI 54521. 715-479-3642, Fax: 715-479-3740. 8AM-4PM. Access by: mail, in person.

Walworth

Real Estate Recording—Walworth County Register of Deeds, Courthouse - Room 102, 100 W. Walworth St. Elkhorn, WI 53121. 270-265-2451, Fax: 262-741-4221. 8AM-5PM (UCC 8AM-4:30PM).

Felony, Misdemeanor, Civil, Eviction, Small Claims—Circuit Court, PO Box 1001, Elkhorn, WI 53121. 270-259-5000, Fax: 262-741-4379. 8AM-5PM. Access by: mail, in person.

Probate—Register in Probate, PO Box 1001, Elkhorn, WI 53121. 270-265-5631, Fax: 262-741-4182. 8AM-5PM. Access by: mail, phone, fax, in person.

Washburn

Real Estate Recording—Washburn County Register of Deeds, 10 4th Avenue, Shell Lake, WI 54871. Fax: 715-468-4699. 8AM-4:30PM.

Felony, Misdemeanor, Civil, Eviction, Small Claims—Circuit Court, PO Box 339, Shell Lake, WI 54871. 715-468-7468, Fax: 715-468-7836. 8AM-4:30PM. Access by: mail, in person.

Probate—Register in Probate, PO Box 316, Shell Lake, WI 54871. 715-468-4688, Fax: 715-468-4678. 8AM-4:30PM. Access by: mail, in person.

Washington

Real Estate Recording—Washington County Register of Deeds, 432 East Washington Street, Room 2084, West Bend, WI 53095. 262-653-6678, Fax: 262-335-6866. 8AM-4:30PM.

Felony, Misdemeanor, Civil, Eviction, Small Claims—Circuit Court, PO Box 1986, West Bend, WI 53095-7986. 262-741-4251, Fax: 262-335-4776. 8AM-4:30PM. Access by: mail, in person.

Probate—Register in Probate, PO Box 82, West Bend, WI 53095-0082. 262-741-4224, Fax: 262-306-2224. 8AM-4:30PM. Access by: mail, in person.

Waukesha

Real Estate Recording—Waukesha County Register of Deeds, 1320 Pewaukee Rd. Room 110, Waukesha, WI 53188. 270-236-2594. 8AM-4:30PM.

Felony, Misdemeanor, Civil, Eviction, Small Claims—Circuit Court, 515 W Moreland Blvd, Waukesha, WI 53188. Fax: 262-896-8228. 8AM-4:30PM M,T,Th,F; 7:30AM-5:30PM F. Access by: mail, in person.

Probate—Register in Probate, 515 W Moreland, Rm 375, Waukesha, WI 53188. 262-741-4256. 8AM-4:30PM M,T,Th,F; 7:30AM-5:30PM W. Access by: mail, in person.

Waupaca

Real Estate Recording—Waupaca County Register of Deeds, 811 Harding Street, Waupaca, WI 54981. 715-258-6220, Fax: 715-258-6212. 8AM-4PM.

Felony, Misdemeanor, Civil, Eviction, Small Claims—Circuit Court, 811 Harding St, Waupaca, WI 54981. 715-258-6460. 8AM-4PM. Access by: mail, in person.

Probate—Register in Probate, 811 Harding St, Waupaca, WI 54981. 715-258-6429, Fax: 715-258-6440. 8AM-4PM. Access by: mail, in person.

Waushara

Real Estate Recording—Waushara County Register of Deeds, 209 South St. Marie, Wautoma, WI 54982. 414-787-4631, Fax: 920-787-0425. 8AM-4:30PM.

Felony, Misdemeanor, Civil, Eviction, Small Claims—Circuit Court, PO Box 507, Wautoma, WI 54982. 920-787-0441, Fax: 920-787-0481. 8AM-4:30PM. Access by: mail, in person.

Probate—Register in Probate, PO Box 508, Wautoma, WI 54982. 920-787-0448. 8AM-4:30PM. Access by: mail, in person.

Winnebago

Real Estate Recording—Winnebago County Register of Deeds, Courthouse, Room 30, 415 Jackson Street, Oshkosh, WI 54901. 414-236-4777. 8AM-4:30PM.

Felony, Misdemeanor, Civil, Eviction, Small Claims—Circuit Court, PO Box 2808, Oshkosh, WI 54903-2808. 920-236-4848, Fax: 920-424-7780. 8AM-4:30PM. Access by: mail, in person.

Probate—Register in Probate, PO Box 2808, Oshkosh, WI 54903-2808. 920-236-4833, Fax: 920-424-7536. 8AM-Noon, 1-4:30PM. Access by: mail, in person. Special note: Records are open to the pubic, there is a $4.00 search fee.

Wood

Real Estate Recording—Wood County Register of Deeds, 400 Market Street, Wisconsin Rapids, WI 54494. 715-421-8484. 8AM-4:30PM.

Felony, Misdemeanor, Civil, Eviction, Small Claims—Circuit Court, 400 Market St, Po Box 8095, Wisconsin Rapids, WI 54494-958095. 715-421-8490. 8AM-Noon, 1-4:45PM. Access by: mail, in person.

Probate—Register in Probate, Wood County Courthouse, PO Box 8095, Wisconsin Rapids, WI 54495-8095. 715-421-8520, Fax: 715-421-8808. 8AM-4:30PM. Access by: mail, in person. Special note: This court also holds guardianships, juveniles, mentals and adoption records.

Federal Courts

US District Court

Eastern District of Wisconsin

Milwaukee Division Clerk's Office, Room 362, 517 E Wisconsin Ave, Milwaukee, WI 53202414-297-3372 Counties: Brown, Calumet, Dodge, Door, Florence, Fond du Lac, Forest, Green Lake, Kenosha, Kewaunee, Langlade, Manitowoc, Marinette, Marquette, Menominee, Milwaukee, Oconto, Outagamie, Ozaukee, Racine, Shawano, Sheboygan, Walworth, Washington, Waukesha, Waupaca,Waushara, Winnebago. www.wied.uscourts.gov

Western District of Wisconsin

Madison Division PO Box 432, Madison, WI 53701608-264-5156 Counties: Adams, Ashland, Barron, Bayfield, Buffalo, Burnett, Chippewa, Clark, Columbia, Crawford, Dane, Douglas, Dunn, Eau Claire, Grant, Green, Iowa, Iron, Jackson, Jefferson, Juneau, La Crosse, Lafayette, Lincoln, Marathon, Monroe, Oneida, Pepin, Pierce, Polk,Portage, Price, Richland, Rock, Rusk, Sauk, Sawyer, St. Croix, Taylor, Trempealeau, Vernon, Vilas, Washburn, Wood. www.wiw.uscourts.gov

Wyoming

Attorney General's Office
123 State Capitol   307-777-7841
Cheyenne, WY 82002   Fax: 307-777-6869
www.state.wy.us/~ag/index.html

Governor's Office
State Capitol Building, Rm 124   307-777-7434
Cheyenne, WY 82002-0010   Fax: 307-632-3909
www.state.wy.us/governor/governor_home.html

State Archives
Barrett Bldg   307-777-7826
Cheyenne, WY 82002   Fax: 307-777-7044
http://commerce.state.wy.us/cr/archives

Capital:	Cheyenne
	Laramie County
Time Zone:	MST
Number of Counties:	23
Population:	479,743
Web Site:	www.state.wy.us

Search Unclaimed Property Online

www.state.wy.us/~sot/
text_find.html

State Agencies

Criminal Records
Division of Criminal Investigation, Criminal Record Section, 316 W 22nd St, Cheyenne, WY 82002; 307-777-7523; Fax: 307-777-7252; 8:30-10:30AM; 1:30-3:30PM. Access by: mail.

Corporation Records
Limited Liability Company Records
Limited Partnership Records
Fictitious Name
Trademarks/Servicemarks
Corporations Division, Secretary of State, State Capitol, Cheyenne, WY 82002; 307-777-7311; Fax: 307-777-5339; 8AM-5PM. Access by: mail, phone, in person, online. soswy.state.wy.us

Sales Tax Registrations
Revenue Department, Excise Tax Division, Herscher Bldg, 122 W 25th St, Cheyenne, WY 82002; 307-777-5203; Fax: 307-777-7722; 8AM-5PM. Access by: mail, phone, in person. revenue.state.wy.us

Uniform Commercial Code
Federal Tax Liens
UCC Division, Secretary of State, The Capitol, Cheyenne, WY 82002-0020 (Capitol Bldg, RM 110, Cheyenne, WY 82002); 307-777-5372, 307-777-5338; Fax: 307-777-5988; 8AM-5PM. Access by: mail, online.

State Tax Liens
Records not available from state agency.

All state tax liens are filed at the county level.

Workers' Compensation Records
Employment Department, Workers Compensation Division, 122 W 25th St, Cheyenne, WY 82002 (Herschler Bldg, 2nd Floor E, 122 W 25th St, Cheyenne, WY 82002); 307-777-7159; Fax: 307-777-5946; 8AM-4:30PM. Access by: mail. www.wydoe.state.wy.us/wscd

Birth Certificates
Wyoming Department of Health, Vital Records Services, Hathaway Bldg, Cheyenne, WY 82002; 307-777-7591; Fax: 307-635-4103; 8AM-5PM. Access by: mail.

Death Records

Wyoming Department of Health, Vital Records Services, Hathaway Bldg, Cheyenne, WY 82002; 307-777-7591; Fax: 307-635-4103; 8AM-5PM. Access by: mail, fax.

Marriage Certificates

Wyoming Department of Health, Vital Records Services, Hathaway Bldg, Cheyenne, WY 82002; 307-777-7591; Fax: 307-635-4103; 8AM-5PM. Access by: mail.

Divorce Records

Wyoming Department of Health, Vital Records Services, Hathaway Bldg, Cheyenne, WY 82002; 307-777-7591; Fax: 307-635-4103; 8AM-5PM. Access by: mail, phone, fax, in person.

Driver License Information
Driver Records

Wyoming Department of Transportation, Driver Services, 5300 Bishop Blvd, Cheyenne, WY 82009-3340; 307-777-4800; Fax: 307-777-4773; 8AM-5PM. Access by: mail. http://wydotweb.state.wy.us

Vehicle Ownership
Vehicle Identification

Motor Vehicle Services, Licensing and Titling Section, PO Box 1708, Cheyenne, WY 82003-1708 (5300 Bishop Blvd, Cheyenne, WY 82002); 307-777-4709; Fax: 307-777-4772; 8AM-5PM. Access by: mail.

Accident Reports

Department of Transportation, Accident Records Section, 5300 Bishop Blvd, Cheyenne, WY 82009-3340; 307-777-4450; Fax: 307-777-4250; 8AM-5PM. Access by: mail.

Boat & Vessel Ownership
Boat & Vessel Registration

Wyoming Game & Fish Dept, Watercraft Section, 5400 Bishop Blvd, Cheyenne, WY 82006; 307-777-4575; Fax: 307-777-4610; 8AM-5PM M-F. Access by: mail, phone, in person. gf.state.wy.us

Legislation-Current/Pending
Legislation-Passed

Wyoming Legislature, State Capitol, Room 213, Cheyenne, WY 82002; 307-777-7881; 8AM-5PM. Access by: mail, phone, in person. legisweb.state.wy.us

Voter Registration

Restricted access.
Individual look-ups must be done at the county level. The SSN and DOB are not released. The state will sell all or part of its database, but only for political reasons. Commercial use is not permitted.
Secretary of State, Election Division, Wyoming State Capitol, Cheyenne, WY 82002-0020; 307-777-7186; Fax: 307-777-7640; 8AM-5PM
http://soswy.state.wy.us

GED Certificates

Dept of Education, GED Program, Hathaway Bldg, 2nd Fl, 2300 Capitol Ave, Cheyenne, WY 82002-0050; 307-777-6911, 307-777-7039 Info Line; Fax: 307-777-6234; 8AM-5PM M-F. www.k12.wy.us/alt ed.html#GED

Hunting License Information
Fishing License Information

Game & Fish Department, License Section, 5400 Bishop Blvd, Cheyenne, WY 82006; 307-777-4600 Licensing Section; Fax: 307-777-4610; 8AM-5PM. Access by: mail, phone, in person. gf.state.wy.us

County Courts & Recording Offices

About the Courts...

Administration

Court Administrator   307-777-7590
2301 Capitol Av, Supreme Court Bldg   Fax: 307-777-3447
Cheyenne, WY 82002
www.courts.state.wy.us

Court Structure

Some counties have County Courts and others have Justice Courts, thus each county has a District Court and either a County or Justice Court. County Courts handle civil claims up to $7,000 while Justice Courts handle civil claims up to $3,000. The District Courts take cases over the applicable limit in each county, not just over $7,000. Three counties have two county courts each: Fremont, Park, and Sweetwater. Cases may be filed in either of the two courts in those counties, and records requests are referred between the two courts.

The Park and Sublette County Justice Courts were eliminated on January 2, 1995 and were replaced by County Courts, where the prior records are now located.

Probate is handled by the District Court.

Online Access

Wyoming's statewide case management system is for internal use only. Planning is underway for a new case management system that will ultimately allow public access.

About the Recording Offices...

Organization

23 counties, 23 recording offices. The recording officer is County Clerk. The entire state is in the Mountain Time Zone (MST).

UCC Records

Financing statements are usually filed with the County Clerk. Accounts receivable and farm products require filing at the state level as well. All recording offices will perform UCC searches. Use search request form UCC-11. Searches fees are usually $10.00 per debtor name. Copy fees vary.

Lien Records

Federal tax liens on personal property of businesses are filed with the Secretary of State. Other federal and all state tax liens are filed with the County Clerk. Most counties will perform tax lien searches. Search fees are usually $10.00 per name.

Real Estate Records

County Clerks will not perform real estate searches. Copy fees are usually $1.00 per page, and certification fees are usually $2.00 per document. The Assessor maintains property tax records.

County Courts & Recording Offices

Albany

Real Estate Recording—Albany County Clerk, 525 Grand Ave. Room 202, Laramie, WY 82070. Fax: 307-721-2544. 9AM-5PM.

Felony, Civil Actions Over $3,000, Probate—2nd Judicial District Court, County Courthouse, 525 Grand, Rm 305, Laramie, WY 82070. 308-235-2831. 9AM-5PM. Access by: mail, phone, in person.

Misdemeanor, Civil Actions Under $7,000, Eviction, Small Claims—Albany County Court, County Courthouse, 525 Grand, Rm 105, Laramie, WY 82070. 308-236-1246, Fax: 307-742-5610. 8AM-5PM. Access by: mail, in person.

Big Horn

Real Estate Recording—Big Horn County Clerk, 420 West C Street, Basin, WY 82410. 307-754-5163, Fax: 307-568-9375. 8AM-5PM.

Felony, Civil Actions Over $3,000, Probate—5th Judicial District Court, PO Box 670, Basin, WY 82410. 307-746-4778, Fax: 307-568-2791. 8AM-Noon, 1-5PM. Access by: mail, fax, in person.

Misdemeanor, Civil Actions Under $7,000, Small Claims—County Court, PO Box 749, Basin, WY 82410. 307-746-3547, Fax: 307-568-2554. 8AM-5PM. Access by: mail, fax, in person.

Campbell

Real Estate Recording—Campbell County Clerk, 500 South Gillette Avenue, Suite 220, Gillette, WY 82716. Fax: 307-687-6455. 8AM-5PM.

Felony, Civil Actions Over $7,000, Probate—6th Judicial District Court, PO Box 817, Gillette, WY 82717. 307-872-6460, Fax: 307-687-6209. 8AM-5PM. Access by: mail, phone, fax, in person.

Misdemeanor, Civil Actions Under $7,000, Eviction, Small Claims—Campbell County Court, 500 S Gillette Ave #301, Gillette, WY 82716. 307-872-6440, Fax: 307-687-6214. 8AM-5PM. Access by: mail, in person.

Carbon

Real Estate Recording—Carbon County Clerk, 415 West Pine, P.O. Box 6, Courthouse, Rawlins, WY 82301. 307-527-8690, Fax: 307-328-2690. 8AM-5PM.

Felony, Civil Actions Over $3,000, Probate—2nd Judicial District Court, PO Box 67, Rawlins, WY 82301. 307-527-8590, Fax: 307-328-2629. 8AM-5PM. Access by: mail, phone, fax, in person.

Misdemeanor, Civil Actions Under $3,000, Eviction, Small Claims—County Court, Attn: Chief Clerk, Courthouse, Rawlins, WY 82301. 307-527-7163, Fax: 307-324-9465. 8AM-5PM. Access by: mail, in person.

Converse

Real Estate Recording—Converse County Clerk, 107 North 5th Street, Suite 114, Douglas, WY 82633. 307-674-2940, Fax: 307-358-4065. 9AM-5PM.

Felony, Civil Actions Over $7,000, Probate—8th Judicial District Court, Box 189, Douglas, WY 82633. 307-674-2960, Fax: 307-358-6703. 9AM-5PM. Access by: mail, phone, fax, in person.

Misdemeanor, Civil Actions Under $7,000, Eviction, Small Claims—Converse County Court, PO Box 45, Douglas, WY 82633. 307-638-4225, Fax: 307-358-2501. 8AM-5PM. Access by: mail, fax, in person.

Crook

Real Estate Recording—Crook County Clerk, 309 Cleveland Street, P.O. Box 37, Sundance, WY 82729. 307-358-2196, Fax: 307-283-1091. 8AM-5PM.

Felony, Civil Actions Over $7,000, Probate—6th Judicial District Court, Box 904, Sundance, WY 82729. 307-358-3120, Fax: 307-283-2996. 8AM-5PM. Access by: mail, in person.

Misdemeanor, Civil Actions Under $3,000, Small Claims—Justice Court, PO Box 117, Sundance, WY 82729. 307-358-3165, Fax: 307-283-1091. 8AM-5PM. Access by: mail, in person.

Fremont

Real Estate Recording—Fremont County Clerk, 450 N. 2nd Street, Courthouse - Room 220, Lander, WY 82520. 307-367-2556, Fax: 307-332-1132. 8AM-5PM.

Felony, Civil Actions Over $7,000, Probate—9th Judicial District Court, PO Box 370, Lander, WY 82520. 307-532-2155, Fax: 307-332-1143. 8AM-Noon, 1-5PM. Access by: mail, phone, fax, in person.

Misdemeanor, Civil Actions Under $7,000, Eviction, Small Claims—Dubois County Court, Box 952, Dubois, WY 82513. 307-684-5720, Fax: 307-455-2567. 8AM-Noon. Access by: mail, in person. Special note: This is a satellite of the Lander Court.

Fremont County Court, 450 N. 2nd, Rm 230, Lander, WY 82520. 307-532-2938, Fax: 307-332-1152. 8AM-5PM. Access by: mail, phone, fax, in person.

Riverton County Court, 818 S Federal Blvd, Riverton, WY 82501. 308-262-1177, Fax: 307-857-3635. 8AM-5PM. Access by: mail, fax, in person.

Goshen

Real Estate Recording—Goshen County Clerk, 2125 East A Street, Torrington, WY 82240. 307-742-5747, Fax: 307-532-7375. 8AM-4PM.

Felony, Civil Actions Over $7,000, Probate—8th Judicial District Court, Clerk of District Court, PO Box 818, Torrington, WY 82240. 307-733-2533, Fax: 307-532-8608. 7:30AM-4PM. Access by: mail, in person.

Misdemeanor, Civil Actions Under $7,000, Eviction, Small Claims—Goshen County Court, Drawer BB, Torrington, WY 82240. 307-733-7713, Fax: 307-532-5101. 7AM-4PM. Access by: mail, in person.

Hot Springs

Real Estate Recording—Hot Springs County Clerk, 415 Arapahoe Street, Courthouse, Thermopolis, WY 82443. 308-268-2195, Fax: 307-864-5116. 8AM-5PM.

Felony, Civil Actions Over $3,000, Probate—5th Judicial District Court, 415 Arapahoe St, Thermopolis, WY 82443. 308-262-1261, Fax: 307-864-3210. 8AM-5PM. Access by: mail, in person.

Misdemeanor, Civil Actions Under $3,000, Small Claims—Justice Court, 417 Arapahoe St, Thermopolis, WY 82443. 308-268-4015, Fax: 307-864-5116. 8AM-5PM. Access by: mail, in person.

Johnson

Real Estate Recording—Johnson County Clerk, 76 North Main Street, Buffalo, WY 82834. 308-235-2242, Fax: 307-684-2708. 8AM-5PM.

Felony, Civil Actions Over $7,000, Probate—4th Judicial District Court, 76 N Main, Buffalo, WY 82834. 307-877-9056, Fax: 307-684-5146. 8AM-5PM. Access by: mail, phone, in person.

Misdemeanor, Civil Actions Under $3,000, Small Claims—Justice Court, 639 Fort St. Buffalo, WY 82834. 307-877-4431, Fax: 307-684-5585. 8AM-5PM. Access by: mail, in person.

Laramie

Real Estate Recording—Laramie County Clerk, Room 1600, 309 West 20th St. Cheyenne, WY 82001. 307-864-3323, Fax: 307-633-4240. 8:30AM-5PM.

Felony, Civil Actions Over $7,000, Probate—1st Judicial District Court, 309 W 20th St, Suite 3205, PO Box 787, Cheyenne, WY 82001. 307-783-0320, Fax: 307-633-4277. 8AM-5PM. Access by: mail, phone, fax, in person.
http://webgate.co.laramie.wy.us/dc/dc.html

Misdemeanor, Civil Actions Under $7,000, Eviction, Small Claims—Laramie County Court, 309 W 20th St Rm 2300, Cheyenne, WY 82001. 307-856-7259, Fax: 307-633-4392. 8AM-5PM. Access by: mail, fax, in person.

Lincoln

Real Estate Recording—Lincoln County Clerk, 925 Sage, Courthouse, Kemmerer, WY 83101. Fax: 307-877-3101. 8AM-5PM.

Felony, Civil Actions Over $7,000, Probate—3rd Judicial District Court, PO Drawer 510, Kemmerer, WY 83101. 308-286-3214, Fax: 307-877-6263. 8AM-5PM. Access by: mail, phone, fax, in person.

Misdemeanor, Civil Actions Under $7,000, Eviction, Small Claims—County Court, PO Box 949, Kemmerer, WY 83101. 308-284-3849, Fax: 307-877-4936. 8AM-5PM. Access by: mail, fax, in person.

Natrona

Real Estate Recording—Natrona County Clerk, 200 North Center, Casper, WY 82601. 307-352-6817, Fax: 307-235-9367. 8AM-5PM.

Felony, Civil Actions Over $7,000, Probate—7th Judicial District Court, Clerk of District Court, PO Box 2510, Casper, WY 82602. 307-347-2702, Fax: 307-235-9493. 8AM-5PM. Access by: mail, phone, fax, in person.

Misdemeanor, Civil Actions Under $7,000, Eviction, Small Claims—Natrana County Court, PO Box 1339, Casper, WY 82602. 307-347-4821, Fax: 307-235-9331. 8AM-5PM. Access by: mail, phone, fax, in person. Special note: All search requests must be in writing.

Niobrara

Real Estate Recording—Niobrara County Clerk, 424 South Elm, Lusk, WY 82225. 307-532-5151, Fax: 307-334-3013. 8AM-4PM.

Felony, Civil Actions Over $3,000, Probate—8th Judicial District Court, Clerk of District Court, PO Box 1318, Lusk, WY 82225. 307-568-2367, Fax: 307-334-2703. 8AM-Noon, 1-4PM. Access by: mail, phone, fax, in person.

Misdemeanor, Civil Actions Under $3,000, Small Claims—Justice Court, PO Box 209, Lusk, WY 82225. 307-568-2381, Fax: 307-334-3846. 9AM-Noon, 1-5PM. Access by: mail, fax, in person.

Park

Real Estate Recording—Park County Clerk, Courthouse, 1002 Sheridan Ave. Cody, WY 82414. 307-684-7271, Fax: 307-527-8626. 8AM-5PM.

Felony, Civil Actions Over $7,000, Probate—5th Judicial District Court, Clerk of District Court, PO Box 1960, Cody, WY 82414. 307-721-2508, Fax: 307-527-8676. 8AM-5PM. Access by: mail, phone, fax, in person.

Misdemeanor, Civil Actions Under $7,000, Eviction, Small Claims—County Court-Cody, 1002 Sheridan Ave. Cody, WY 82414. 307-684-7302. 8AM-5PM. Access by: mail, in person. Special note: On January 2, 1995 this court changed status from a Justice Court to a County Court.

County Court-Powell, 109 W. 14th, Powell, WY 82435. 308-254-2814. 8AM-5PM. Access by: mail, in person.

Platte

Real Estate Recording—Platte County Clerk, 800 9th Street, Wheatland, WY 82201. 307-367-4373, Fax: 307-322-5402. 8AM-5PM.

Felony, Civil Actions Over $3,000, Probate—8th Judicial District Court, PO Box 158, Wheatland, WY 82201. 307-455-2920, Fax: 307-322-5402. 8AM-5PM. Access by: mail, in person.

Misdemeanor, Civil Actions Under $3,000, Small Claims—Justice Court, PO Box 306, Wheatland, WY 82201. 307-367-4376, Fax: 307-322-5402. 8AM-5PM. Access by: mail, in person.

Sheridan

Real Estate Recording—Sheridan County Clerk, 224 South Main Street, Suite B-2, Sheridan, WY 82801. 307-872-6389, Fax: 307-674-2529. 8AM-5PM.

Felony, Civil Actions Over $7,000, Probate—4th Judicial District Court, 224 S. Main, Suite B-11, Sheridan, WY 82801. 307-864-5161, Fax: 307-674-2909. 8AM-5PM. Access by: mail, in person.

Misdemeanor, Civil Actions Under $7,000, Eviction, Small Claims—County Court, 224 S. Main, Suite B-7, Sheridan, WY 82801. 307-864-3616, Fax: 307-674-2944. 8AM-5PM. Access by: mail, in person.

Sublette

Real Estate Recording—Sublette County Clerk, 21 South Tyler Avenue, Pinedale, WY 82941. 307-682-2190, Fax: 307-367-6396. 8AM-5PM.

Felony, Civil Actions Over $7,000, Probate—9th Judicial District Court, PO Box 292, Pinedale, WY 82941. 307-682-3424, Fax: 307-367-6474. 8AM-5PM. Access by: mail, phone, fax, in person.

Misdemeanor, Civil Actions Under $7,000, Eviction, Small Claims—Sublette County Court, PO Box 1796, Pinedale, WY 82941. 307-674-6522, Fax: 307-367-2658. 8AM-5PM. Access by: mail, in person.

Sweetwater

Real Estate Recording—Sweetwater County Clerk, 80 West Flaming Gorge Way, Green River, WY 82935. 308-268-4025, Fax: 307-872-6337. 9AM-5PM.

Felony, Civil Actions Over $7,000, Probate—3rd Judicial District Court, PO Box 430, Green River, WY 82935. 308-284-3231, Fax: 307-872-6439. 9AM-5PM. Access by: mail, phone, fax, in person.

Misdemeanor, Civil Actions Under $7,000, Eviction, Small Claims—Green River County Court, PO Drawer 1720, Green River, WY 82935. 308-284-3693, Fax: 307-872-6375. 8AM-5PM. Access by: mail, in person.

Sweetwater County Court, PO Box 2028, Rock Springs, WY 82902. 307-633-4298, Fax: 307-352-6758. 8AM-5PM. Access by: mail, fax, in person.

Teton

Real Estate Recording—Teton County Clerk, 200 S. Willow, Jackson, WY 83001. Fax: 307-739-8681. 8AM-5PM.

Felony, Civil Actions Over $7,000, Probate—9th Judicial District Court, PO Box 4460, Jackson, WY 83001. 308-235-3591, Fax: 307-734-1562. 8AM-5PM. Access by: mail, phone, fax, in person.

Misdemeanor, Civil Actions Under $3,000, Small Claims—Justice Court, PO Box 2906, Jackson, WY 83001. 308-236-1228, Fax: 307-733-8694. 8AM-5PM. Access by: mail, in person.

Uinta

Real Estate Recording—Uinta County Clerk, 225 9th Street, Evanston, WY 82930. Fax: 307-783-0511. 8AM-5PM.

Felony, Civil Actions Over $7,000, Probate—3rd Judicial District Court, PO Drawer 1906, Evanston, WY 82931. 308-254-2929, Fax: 307-783-0400. 8AM-5PM. Access by: mail, phone, fax, in person.

Misdemeanor, Civil Actions Under $7,000, Eviction, Small Claims—Uinta County Court, 225 9th St, 2nd Fl, Evanston, WY 82931. 308-262-0812, Fax: 307-789-5062. 8AM-5PM. Access by: mail, in person.

Washakie

Real Estate Recording—Washakie County Clerk, 10th & Big Horn, Courthouse, Worland, WY 82401. Fax: 307-347-9366. 8AM-5PM.

Felony, Civil Actions Over $3,000, Probate—5th Judicial District Court, PO Box 862, Worland, WY 82401. 307-633-4270,

Fax: 307-347-4325. 8AM-5PM. Access by: mail, phone, fax, in person.

Misdemeanor, Civil Actions Under $3,000, Small Claims—Justice Court, PO Box 927, Worland, WY 82401. 307-568-2578, Fax: 307-347-4325. 8AM-5PM. Access by: mail, in person.

Weston

Real Estate Recording—Weston County Clerk, One West Main, Newcastle, WY 82701. Fax: 307-746-9505. 8AM-5PM.

Felony, Civil Actions Over $7,000, Probate—6th Judicial District Court, 1 W Main, Newcastle, WY 82701. 308-254-2733,

Fax: 307-746-4778. 8AM-5PM. Access by: mail, phone, fax, in person.

Misdemeanor, Civil Actions Under $3,000, Small Claims—Justice Court, 6 W Warwick, Newcastle, WY 82701. 308-236-1250, Fax: 307-746-3558. 8:30AM-4:30PM. Access by: mail, fax, in person.

Federal Courts

US District Court

Casper Division 111 South Wolcott, Room 121, Casper, WY 82601307-261-5440 Counties: Cases from any county in the state may be assigned here. www.ck10.uscourts.gov/wyoming/district
Cheyenne Division PO Box 727, Cheyenne, WY 82003307-772-2145 Counties: All counties in Wyoming. Some criminal records are held in Casper. www.ck10.uscourts.gov/wyoming/district

US Bankruptcy Court

Cheyenne Division PO Box 1107, Cheyenne, WY 82003307-772-2191 Counties: All counties in Wyoming. www.wyb.uscourts.gov

Free Internet Access to Public Records

Listed in this section are over 300 state, county, city and federal (court) URLs where you can access public record information for free.

Please note that recently a number of US District and Bankruptcy Courts began making indexes and case information available to the public over the Internet. At present there is no fee for these courts. However, a user fee, approved by the Judicial Conference of the United States, may be applied in the future.

Also, please note that this list does not contain URLs for state occupational licensing boards or registrations. However, BRB Publications has researched over 1,200 free access sites to these records and these sites are profiled within several of our products. Call 800-929-3811 for further details on these products.

This list is also maintained online. For a hyperlinked version, visit www.brbpub.com.

A word of caution to those of you who professionally search or use public records—-some of these sites will not offer the same thorough and conclusive results as a hands-on search.

State Sites

Alabama - Corporation
www.sos.state.al.us

Alabama - UCC
www.sos.state.al.us

Alaska - Corporation
www.dced.state.ak.us/bsc/bsc.htm

Alaska - Dept of Commerce - Business names/owners
www.dced.state.ak.us/occ/buslic.htm

Arizona - UCC
www.sosaz.com

Arkansas - Corp
www.sosweb.state.ar.us/corps/incorp

Arkansas - Trademark
www.sosweb.state.ar.us/corps/trademk

California - Corporations
http://204.147.113.12/list.html

Colorado - Marriage and Divorce
www.state.co.us/gov_dir/cdphe_dir/hs/search.html

Colorado - UCC
www.dos1.state.co.us/ucc/uccsearch.stm

Connecticut - Civil Court Records Statewide
www.jud2.state.ct.us

Connecticut - UCC and Corporation
www.concord.state.ct.us

Florida - UCC, Corporation, Trademark
www.sunbiz.org

Georgia - Corporation
www.sos.state.ga.us/corporations

Iowa - Corporation
www.sos.state.ia.us/corpweb

Iowa - UCC
www.sos.state.ia.us/uccweb

Kentucky - UCC & Corporation (UCC is limited)
www.sos.state.ky.us

Kentucky - Vital Records (marriage, divorce, death)
http://ukcc.uky.edu:80/~vitalrec

Louisiana - Corporations
www.sec.state.la.us/crping.htm

Maine - Corporation
www.state.me.us/sos/corpinfo.htm

Maine - Vital Records (death from 1960 through 1996)
http://thor.ddp.state.me.us/archives/plsql/archdev.death_archiv
e.search_form

Maine - Vital Records (marriage from 1892 through 1996)
http://thor.ddp.state.me.us/archives/plsql/archdev.Marriage_archi
ve.search_form

Maryland - Real Estate
http://192.94.47.83/sdat/CICS

Maryland - Trademarks & Service Marks
www.sos.state.md.us/sos/admin2/html/trade.html

Maryland - UCC
www.dat.state.md.us/bsfd

Michigan - Vital Records (death from 1971 to 1996)
www.ancestry.com/ancestry/search/3171.htm

Missouri - Corporations
http://168.166.2.55/corporations

Nevada - Corporation
http://sos.state.nv.us

New Jersey - Property (also MD)
www.taxrecords.com

New Mexico - Corporation
www.nmprc.state.nm.us/ftq.htm

New Mexico - Court Records Statewide
www.nmcourts.com/disclaim.htm

New Mexico - UCC
www.sos.state.nm.us/UCC/UCCHOME.HTM

North Carolina - Corporation
www.state.nc.us/secstate

Oregon - UCC
www.sos.state.or.us/cgi-bin/uccsrch.htm

Texas - Corporation
http://records.txdps.state.us/dps/default.cfm

Texas - Sex Offenders
www.window.texas.gov/taxinfo/coasintr.html

Vermont - UCC & Corporation
www.sec.state.vt.us

Washington - Business Records
http://dor.wa.gov/prd

Wisconsin - Statewide Circuit Court Records
http://ccap.courts.state.wi.us/internetcourtaccess
Note—Outagamie and Walworth counties are not online. Portage has only probate data. 5 other counties are restrictive in their case data, but will eventually have all case types online.

Wyoming - Corporation
http://soswy.state.wy.us/corporat/webtips.htm

County/City Sites

AK - City of Fairbanks - Property Records
www.co.fairbanks.ak.us/database/aurora/default.asp

AK - City of Juneau - Property Records
http://record.org/juneau_tax/search_tax_form.html

AK - Kenai Peninsula Borough - Assessor
www.borough.kenai.ak.us/assesingdept/Parcel/SEARCH.HTM

AR - Benton County - Assessor, Circuit Court
http://208.154.254.51:5061

AZ - Maricopa County - Assessor
www.maricopa.gov/assessor/default.asp

AZ - Maricopa County - Recorder
http://recorder.maricopa.gov/recdocdata/GetRecDataSelect.asp

AZ - Maricopa County - Superior Court
www.superiorcourt.maricopa.gov

AZ - Pima County - Consolidated Justice Courts
http://iissvr.jp.co.pima.az.us/webinfo/findcase.asp

CA - Alameda County - Property Tax & Assessor
www.co.alameda.ca.us/aswping/index.htm

CA - City of Ontario - Assessor
http://158.61.82.251/gis/par.htm

CA - City of Redding - Assessor (no name searching)
www.ci.redding.ca.us

CA - Los Angeles Municipal Courts - Civil
www.latrialcourts.org/civilon.htm

CA - San Bernardino - Recorder & Fict Names
www.co.san-bernardino.ca.us/ACR

CA - San Diego County - Assessor/Recorder
www.co.san-diego.ca.us/cnty/cntydepts/general/assessor/online.html

CA - San Mateo County - Assessor
http://204.114.51.6/index.htm

CO - Arapahoe County - Assessor (no name searching)
www.co.arapahoe.co.us/as/ResForm.htm

CO - Denver County - Assessor
www.denvergov.org/realproperty.asp

CO - El Paso - Assessor
www.co.el-paso.co.us/assessor

CO - Jefferson County/Golden - Assessor
http://buffy.co.jefferson.co.us/cgi-bin/mis/ats/assr

CO - La Plata County - Assessor
www.laplatainfo.com/search2.html

CO - Larimer County - Property
www.valuate.net/comps/newsearch.asp

CO - Mesa County - Assessor
www.co.mesa.co.us/Assessor/assessor1.htm

CO - Park County - Assessor
www.parkco.org

CO - Pitkin County - Assessor
http://aimwebdomain.aspen.com/db/pca/pcareg1.asp

CT - Civil Court Records Statewide
www.jud2.state.ct.us

DE - New Castle City - Assessor
www.2isystems.com/newcastle/index.htm

FL - Brevard County - Property Appraiser
www.appraiser.co.brevard.fl.us/asp/disclaimer.asp

FL - Broward County - Property Appraiser
www.bcpa.net/search_1.htm

FL - Charlotte County - Property Appraiser
www.ccappraiser.com/record.asp?

FL - Citrus County - Assessor
www.pa.citrus.fl.us

FL - Escambia County - Property Tax
www.co.escambia.fl.us/ectc/taxiq.html

FL - Highlands County - Property Appraiser
www.appraiser.co.highlands.fl.us/search.html

FL - Hillsborough County - Property Appraiser
www.propappr.co.hillsborough.fl.us/padb/address.htm

FL - Jacksonville City - Property Records
www.ci.jax.fl.us/pub/depot.htm#prop

FL - Lake County - Property Appraiser
www.lakecopropappr.com

FL - Lee County - Property Appraiser
www.property-appraiser.lee.fl.us/Queries/Query.htm

FL - Leon County - Court and County Clerk's Office
www.clerk.leon.fl.us

FL - Leon County - Property Appraiser
www.co.leon.fl.us/propappr/prop.htm

FL - Manatee County - Property Appraiser
www.manateepao.com

FL - Marion County - Property Appraiser
www.propappr.marion.fl.us

FL - Martin County - Property Appraiser
www.martin.fl.us/GOVT/co/pa/pa.html

FL - Orange County - Property Appraiser
www.property-appraiser.co.orange.fl.us/ocpa/owa/disclaimer

FL - Orange County - Recorder's Office
www.comptroller.co.orange.fl.us

FL - Palm Beach County - Property Appraiser
www.co.palm-beach.fl.us/papa

FL - Pinellas County - Property Appraiser
www.pao.co.pinellas.fl.us

FL - Santa Rosa County - Property Appraiser
www.srcpa.org/agree.html

FL - Sarasota County - Property Appraiser
www.sarasotaproperty.net/scpa_recs.htm

FL - Seminole County - Property Appraiser
http://ntweb.scpafl.org

FL - St. Johns County - Property Appraiser
www.co.st-johns.fl.us/Const-Officers/Prop-App/index.html

FL - St. Lucie County - Property Appraiser
www.paslc.org/Agree.htm

FL - Volusia County - Property Appraiser
http://critpath.ent.db.erau.edu/vc_search.html

GA - Cobb County - Superior Court Records
www.clerksuperiorcourt.w1.com

GA - Dougherty County - Civil, Criminal, and Probate
www.dougherty.ga.us/docotax.htm

GA - Dougherty County - Real Estate, Tax Records, UCC
www.dougherty.ga.us/docotax.htm

GA - Fayette County - Tax Digest (real estate)
www.admin.co.fayette.ga.us/intro.htm

IA - Polk County - Assessor
www.assess.co.polk.ia.us

IA - Pottawattamie County - Assessor/Recorder
www.pottco.org

IL - Cook County - Assessor's Office (no name searching)
www.assessor.co.cook.il.us/startsearch.html

IL - Macon County - Circuit Court
www.court.co.macon.il.us

IL - Vanderburgh County - Assessor
www.assessor.evansville.net

KS - Douglas County - Real Estate
http://hometown.lawrence.com/valuation

KS - Johnson County - Real Estate (no name searching)
www.jocoks.com/appraiser/disclaim.html

KS - Sedgwick County - Property Tax
www.sedgwick.ks.us/property/index.html

KS - Wyandotte County - Property Tax
www.courthouseusa.com/wyanadd.htm

MA - City of Boston - Assessor
www.ci.boston.ma.us/assessing/search.asp

MA - City of Cambridge - Assessor
http://www2.ci.cambridge.ma.us/assessor/index.html

MA - City of Newton - Appraiser
www.appgeo.com/clients/newton

MA - Concord Town - Assessor
www.concordnet.org/finance/Assessor.html

MA - Essex County - Registry of Deeds
http://207.244.88.10/deedsonline.asp

MA - Falmouth Town - Assessor
www.town.falmouth.ma.us/proping.html

MA - Plymouth - Registry of Deeds
http://regdeeds.co.plymouth.ma.us/tview.html

MA - Provincetown - Assessor
www.provincetowngov.org/assessor.html

MA - Town of Brookline - Assessor
www.town.brookline.ma.us/Assessors/property.asp

MA - Town of Mashpee - Assessor
www.capecod.net/mashpee/assess

MA - Town of Reading - Assessor
www.ziplink.net/~reading1/assessor.htm

MA - Town of Walpole - Assessor (no name searching)
www.walpole.ma.us/thdassesorproperty.htm

MD - All Counties - Tax Records
http://209.3.171.137/cgi-bin/DOTAXMAPFORM?account=c6000059

ME - Bath City - Assessor
www.cityofbath.com/assessing/INDEX.HTM

ME - Cape Elizabeth Town - Assessor
www.capeelizabeth.com/taxdata.html

ME - Kennebunk Town - Assessor - Real Estate
www.kennebunk.maine.org/assessor/database/home.html

ME - Town of York - Property Assessor
www.raynorshyn.com/com/yorknet/accsel.cfm

MI - City of Walker - Assessor
http://walker.data-web.net/query.php3

MI - Eaton County - Real Estate
www.co.eaton.mi.us/CNTSRV/ONLINE.HTM

MN - Carver County - Assessor
www.co.carver.mn.us/Prop_Tax/default.asp

MN - Hennepin County - Property Information
http://www2.co.hennepin.mn.us/pins/main.htm

MO - Jackson County - Civil and Probate
http://168.166.59.61/casenet/welcome.asp

MO - Montgomery County - Civil and Probate
http://168.166.59.61/casenet/welcome.asp

MO - St Charles County - Assessor
www.win.org/library/library_office/assessment

MO - St Charles County - Property
www.dailywatch.com/stlouis/realper2.asp

MO - St Louis County - Property
www.dailywatch.com/stlouis/realper2.asp

MT - Yellowstone County - Assessor
www.ystone.mt.gov?GIS/index.asp

NC - Cabarrus County - Assessor
www.co.cabarrus.nc.us/Pages/GIS.html

NC - Catawba County - Assessor, Real Estate
www.gis.catawba.nc.us/maps/public.htm

NC - Dare County - Assessor, Real Estate
www.co.dare.nc.us/interactive/setup.htm

NC - Davidson County - Assessor, Real Estate
www.co.davidson.nc.us/asp/taxsearch.asp

NC - Forsyth County - Recorders
http://maps.co.forsyth.nc.us/index.html

NC - Haywood County - Real Estate
www.undersys.com/haywood/haywoodframe.html

NC - Mecklenburg County - Tax Records
http://209.3.171.149/cgi-bin/DOTAXMAPFORM?account=c6000059

NC - Wilson County - Real Estate
www.wilson-co.com/wctax.html

NE - Douglas County - Assessor
http://zulu.co.douglas.ne.us/pages/assessor/framevalinfo.htm

NE - Lancaster County - Assessor
www.ci.lincoln.ne.us/database.htm

NE - Sarpy County - Property
www.sarpy.com/publicaccess/capslookup.htm

NH - City of Portsmouth - Assessor
www.portsmouthnh.com/realestate/index.htm

NH - Merrimack County - Registry of Deeds
www.nhdeeds.com

NJ - All Counties - Tax Records
http://209.3.171.146/cgi-bin/DOTAXMAPFORM?account=c6000059

NJ - Atlantic County - Tax Records
http://taxrecords.com/cgi-bin/DOTAXMAPFORM?account=c6000059

NJ - Cape County - Tax Records
http://taxrecords.com/cgi-bin/DOTAXMAPFORM?account=c6000059

NJ - Counties along Jersey Shore - Real Estate
www.philly.com/packages/njshore/lookup.htm

NJ - Ocean County - Tax Records
http://209.3.171.250/cgi-bin/DOTAXMAPFORM?account=c6000059

NM - County Court Records Statewide
www.nmcourts.com/disclaim.htm

NM - Dona Ana County - Assessor's Office
www.co.dona-ana.nm.us/newpages/assr/txparcel.html

NM - Dona Ana County - Real Property
www.co.dona-ana.nm.us/assr/txparcel.html

NV - Clark County - Assessor
www.co.clark.nv.us/assessor/Disclaimer.htm

NV - Clark County - Real Estate, UCC, and Vital Records
www.co.clark.nv.us/recorder/recindex.htm

NV - Douglas County - Property
www.co.douglas.nv.us/assessor/menu.html

NY - 57 NY Cities & Counties - Property
http://land.netacc.net

NY - Schenectady - Assessor
www.scpl.org/assessments

NY - Tompkins County - Assessor
http://md2020.hypermart.net/tentative.html

NY - Town of Erwin - Assessor
www.pennynet.org/erwin/er95tax.htm

OH - Franklin County - Real Estate (Auditor)
http://198.234.34.195/auditor

OH - Greene County - Real Estate
www.co.greene.oh.us/gismapserver.htm

OH - Hamilton County - Common Pleas and Municipal Courts
www.courtclerk.org/case.htm

OH - Logan County - Real Estate (Auditor)
http://www2.co.logan.oh.us/logan208/LandRover.asp

OH - Trumball County - Real Estate (Auditor)
http://co.auditor,trumball.oh.us/trumv208/LandRover.asp

OK - Oklahoma County - Assessor/Property Records
www.oklahomacounty.org/assessor/default.htm

OK - Oklahoma County - Real Estate and UCC
www.oklahomacounty.org/coclerk

OR - Deschutes County - Assessor
www.deschutes.org

OR - Linn County - Assessor
www.co.linn.or.us/assessor/PropSearch.asp

OR - Tillamook County - Assessor
www.co.tillamook.or.us/Service/Tax_Assessment/frmain.asp

PA - Berks County - Marriage and Birth
www.berksregofwills.com

PA - Delaware County - Tax Records
http://209.3.171.148/cgi-bin/DOTAXMAPFORM?account=c6000059

PA - Montgomery County - Assessor
www.montcopa.org/reassessment/boahome0.htm

PA - Montgomery County - Tax Records
http://209.3.171.148/cgi-bin/DOTAXMAPFORM?account=c6000059

SC - Greenwood County - Real Estate
www.akanda.com/grnwood/Search/search.htm

TX - Bell County Assessor
www.texastax.com/bell/index.asp

TX - Bexar County - Assessor
www.bcad.org/property.htm

TX - Denton County - District Court
http://justice.co.denton.tx.us

TX - Harris County - Assessor and Voter Registration
www.tax.co.harris.tx.us

TX - Newton County - Death Records
www.jas.net/~newton/txnewton/deaths/death.htm

TX - Potter County - Court Records
www.idocket.com

TX - Potter-Randall Counties - Assessor
www.prad.org

TX - 42 Counties
www.taxnetusa.com

> Links to the Assessor and RE name searches for these counties: Archer, Bandera, Brazoria, Brazos, Caldwell, Cameron, Chambers, Collin, Dallas, Denton, Ellis, El Paso, Erath, Fannin, Franklin, Galveston, Grayson, Gregg, Guadalupe, Hardin, Harrison, Hays, Henderson, Hidalgo, Hill, Jack, Jefferson, Kaufman, Kendall, Lubbuck, McLennan, Rockwell, Rusk, Smith, Tarrent, Tayler, Travis, VanZandt, Webb, Wichita, Williamson (go straight to basic search, login not needed)

TX - 33 Counties
www.txcountydata.com

> Links to the Assessor and RE name searches for these counties: Angelina, Aransas, Austin, Bastrop, Brazoria, Brazos, Brown, Burleson, Burnet, Caldwell, Calhoun, Collin, Denton, Fort Bend, Gillespie, Gregg, Hays, Kendall, Kerr, Lamb, Liberty, Limestone, Llano, Maverick, Parmer, Rockwell, San Jacinto, Somervell, Upshur, Valverde, Waller, Washington, Wharton (use the "other counties" search)

VA - City of Bedford
www.ci.bedford.va.us/proptax/lookup.html

VA - Fairfax County - Real estate (no name searching)
www.co.fairfax.va.us/dta/re/notice.asp

VA - Montgomery County - Real Estate
www.andassoc.com/gismaps/Montgomery/MCPlus.htm

VA - Wise County & City of Norton - Land Records
www.courtbar.org

WA - Pierce County - Assessor (cannot search by name)
www.co.pierce.wa.us/abtus/ourorg/at/at.htm

WA - Pierce County - Civil Court Records
www.co.pierce.wa.us/cfapps/linx/index.htm

WI - Almost All Counties* - Circuit Court Records
http://ccap.courts.state.wi.us/internetcourtaccess

WI - Milwaukee City - Assessor's Office
www.ci.mil.wi.us/citygov/assessor/assessments.htm

> *Note—Outagamie and Walworth counties are not online. Portage has only probate data. 5 other counties are restrictive in their case data, but will eventually have all case types online.

Federal Courts Sites

RACER - Free, For Now

Most of the online access systems (such as PACER and RACER) charge $.06 a minute to access. However, there are a handful of courts that offer their own online access at no fee and a few RACER courts that have not converted to the $.06 fee. Please be aware that some the courts listed below use RACER and may convert at anytime to a pay system.

Arkansas – District - Eastern
www.are.uscourts.gov/case_information.htm
Requires free registration.

Arkansas – District - Western
www.arwd.uscourts.gov/mailform.html
Offers case information sent directly to your e-mailbox. Simply visit the site above and input the information you are looking for, and the system will automatically send the results to you by e-mail.

Idaho - Bankruptcy
www.id.uscourts.gov/wconnect/wc.dll?usbc_racer~main

Idaho - District
www.id.uscourts.gov/wconnect/wc.dll?usdc_racer~main

Illinois - Bankruptcy - Northern
http://207.41.17.23/wc.dll?usbcn_racer~main

Indiana – Bankruptcy - Southern
www.insb.uscourts.gov/public/casesearch.asp
You may search using case number, party name, social security number and/or tax ID number.

Indiana – District – Southern
www.insd.uscourts.gov/casesearch.htm

Kentucky - District - Western
http://38.244.24.106/default.html

Minnesota - Bankruptcy
www.mnb.uscourts.gov/cgi-bin/mnb-450-main.pl

Nevada - Bankruptcy
www.nvb.uscourts.gov

New Jersey - Bankruptcy
http://38.149.170.80/wconnect/wc.dll?usbc_racer~main

North Carolina – Bankruptcy - Western
www.ncbankruptcy.org/view.html

North Carolina – District - Western
http://208.141.47.221/dc/search.html
You can search using case number, name and/or filing date. This service is only available for documents filed AFTER 03/01/99. The service is currently free to use.

Rhode Island - Bankruptcy
www.rib.uscourts.gov
Requires free registration.

South Dakota - District
www.sdd.uscourts.gov

Virginia – District - Eastern
To search by name visit: www.vaeb.uscourts.gov/home/SearchNM.html
To search by case number:
www.vaeb.uscourts.gov/home/SearchCSNUM.html

Washington – Bankruptcy - Eastern
http://204.227.177.194/wconnect/wc.dll?usbcn_racer~main

Wyoming - Bankruptcy
http://209.64.46.86/wconnect/wc.dll?usbc_racer~main

Searching Electronic Filed Federal Cases

Electronic Filing of documents is becoming more widespread. The following federal courts offer electronic filing for law firms and practitioners. Keep in mind that searching is available ONLY for cases that were filed electronically NOT all cases.

California – Bankruptcy - Southern
http://ecf.casb.uscourts.gov/cgi-bin/PublicCaseFiled-Rpt.pl

Georgia – Bankruptcy - Northern
http://ecf.ganb.uscourts.gov/cgi-bin/PublicCaseFiled-Rpt.pl

Missouri – District - Western
http://ecf.mowd.uscourts.gov/cgi-bin/PublicCaseFiled-Rpt.pl

New York – District - Eastern
http://ecf.nyed.uscourts.gov/cgi-bin/PublicCaseFiled-Rpt.pl

New York – Bankruptcy - Southern
http://ecf.nysb.uscourts.gov/cgi-bin/PublicCaseFiled-Rpt.pl

Ohio – District - Northern
http://ecf.ohnd.uscourts.gov/cgi-bin/PublicCaseFiled-Rpt.pl

Oregon - District
http://ecf.ord.uscourts.gov/cgi-bin/PublicCaseFiled-Rpt.pl

Using a Public Record Vendor

Hiring Someone to Obtain the Record

There are five main categories of public record professionals: distributors and gateways; search firms; local document retrievers; investigative firms; and information brokers.

Distributors and Gateways (Proprietary Database Vendors)

Distributors are automated public record firms who combine public sources of bulk data and/or online access to develop their own database product(s). Primary Distributors include companies that collect or buy public record information from its source and reformat the information in some useful way. They tend to focus on one or a limited number of types of information, although a few firms have branched into multiple information categories.

Gateways are companies that either compile data from or provide an automated gateway to Primary Distributors. Gateways thus provide "one-stop shopping" for multiple geographic areas and/or categories of information.

Companies can be both Primary Distributors and Gateways. For example, a number of online database companies are both primary distributors of corporate information and also gateways to real estate information from other Primary Distributors

Search Firms

Search firms are companies that furnish public record search and document retrieval services through outside online services and/or through a network of specialists, including their own employees or correspondents (see Retrievers below). There are three types of Search Firms.

Search Generalists offer a full range of search capabilities in many public record categories over a wide geographic region. They may rely on gateways, primary distributors and/or networks of retrievers. They combine online proficiency with document retrieval expertise.

Search Specialists focus either on one geographic region—like Ohio—or on one specific type of public record information—like driver/vehicle records.

Application Specialists focus on one or two types of services geared to specific needs. In this category are pre-employment screening firms and tenant screening firms. Like investigators, they search many of the public record categories in order to prepare an overall report about a person or business.

Local Document Retrievers

Local document retrievers use their own personnel to search specific requested categories of public records usually in order to obtain documentation for legal compliance (e.g., incorporations), for lending, and for litigation. They do not usually review or interpret the results or issue reports in the sense that investigators do, but rather return documents with the results of searches. They tend to be localized, but there are companies that offer a national network of retrievers and/or correspondents. The retriever or his/her personnel goes directly to the agency to look up the information. A retriever may be relied upon for strong knowledge in a local area, whereas a search generalist has a breadth of knowledge and experience in a wider geographic range.

The 725+ members of the **Public Record Retriever Network (PRRN)** can be found, by state and counties served, at www.brbpub.com. This organization has set industry standards for the retrieval of public record documents and operates under a Code of Professional Conduct. Using one of these record retrievers is an excellent way to access records in those jurisdictions that do not offer online access.

Private Investigation Firms

Investigators use public records as tools rather than as ends in themselves, in order to create an overall, comprehensive "picture" of an individual or company for a particular purpose. They interpret the information they have gathered in order to identify further investigation tracks. They summarize their results in a report compiled from all the sources used.

Many investigators also act as Search Firms, especially as tenant or pre-employment screeners, but this is a different role from the role of Investigator per se, and screening firms act very much like investigators in their approach to a project. In addition, an investigator may be licensed, and may perform the types of services traditionally thought of as detective work, such as surveillance.

Information Brokers

There is one additional type of firm that occasionally utilizes public records. **Information Brokers** (IB) gather information that will help their clients make informed business decisions. Their work is usually done on a custom basis with each project being unique. IB's are extremely knowledgeable in online research of full text databases and most specialize in a particular subject area, such as patent searching or competitive intelligence. The Association of Independent Information Professionals (AIIP), at www.aiip.org, has over 750 experienced professional information specialist members from 21 countries. *The Burwell World Directory of Information Brokers,* found in print and CD-ROM (972-732-0160) is an excellent source of IB's in over 48 countries.

Which Type of Vendor is Right for You?

With all the variations of vendors and the categories of information, the obvious question is; "How do I find the right vendor to go to for the public record information I need?" Before you start calling every interesting online vendor that catches your eye, you need to narrow your search to the **type** of vendor for your needs. To do this, ask yourself the following questions—

What is the Frequency of Usage?

If you have on-going, recurring requests for a particular type of information, it is probably best to choose a different vendor then if you have infrequent requests. Setting up an account with a primary distributor, such as Metromail, will give you an inexpensive per search fee, but the monthly minimum requirements will be prohibitive to the casual requester, who would be better off finding a vendor who accesses or is a gateway to Metromail. **EDITOR'S NOTE**: Check out Metromail and similar vendors at www.publicrecordsources.com.

What is the Complexity of the Search?

The importance of hiring a vendor who understands and can interpret the information in the final format increase with the complexity of the search. Pulling a driving record in Maryland is not difficult, but doing an online criminal record search in Maryland, when only a portion of the felony records are online, is not so easy.

Thus, part of the answer to determining which vendor or type of vendor to use is to become conversant with what is (and is not) available from government agencies. Without knowing what is available (and what restrictions apply), you cannot guide the search process effectively. Once you are comfortable knowing the kinds of information available in the public record, you are in a position to find the best method to access needed information.

What are the Geographic Boundaries of the Search?

A search of local records close to you may require little assistance, but a search of records nationally or in a state 2,000 miles away will require seeking a vendor who covers the area you need to search. Many national primary distributors and gateways combine various local and state databases into one large comprehensive system available for searching. However, if your record searching is narrowed by a region or locality, an online source that specializes in a specific geographic region, like Superior Information Services in NJ, may be an alternative to a national vendor. Keep in mind that many national firms allow you to order a search online, even though results cannot be delivered immediately and some hands-on local searching is required.

Of course, you may want to use the government agency online system if available for the kind of information you need.

Eleven Questions to Ask a Public Records Vendor

(Or a Vendor Who Uses Online Sources)

The following discussion focuses specifically on automated sources of information because many valuable types of public records have been entered into a computer and, therefore, require a computer search to obtain reliable results. The original version of this article was authored by **Mr. Leroy Cook**, Director of ION and The Investigators Anywhere Resource Line (800-338-3463). Mr. Cook has graciously allowed us to edit the article and reprint it for our readers.

1. Where does he or she get the information?

You may feel awkward asking a vendor where he or she obtained the information you are purchasing. The fake Rolex watch is a reminder that even buying physical things based on looks alone—without knowing where they come from—is dangerous.

Reliable information vendors *will* provide verification material such as the name of the database or service accessed, when it was last updated, and how complete it is.

It is important that you know the gathering process in order to better judge the reliability of the information being purchased. There *are* certain investigative sources that a vendor will not be willing to disclose to a you. However, that type of source should not be confused with the information that is being sold item by item. Information technology has changed so rapidly that some information brokers may still confuse "items of information" with "investigative reports." Items of information sold as units are *not* investigative reports. The professional reputation of an information vendor is a guaranty of sorts. Still, because information as a commodity is so new, there is little in the way of an implied warranty of fitness.

2. How often is the information database source updated?

Any answer *except* a clear, concise date and time or the vendor's personal knowledge of an ongoing system's methods of maintaining information currency is a reason to keep probing. Ideally, the mechanism by which you purchase items of information *should* include an update or statement of accuracy—as a part of the reply—*without* having to ask.

3. How long does it take for the new information or changes to get into the system?

In view of the preceding question, this one might seem repetitive, but it *really* is a different issue. Microfiche or a database of records may have been updated last week at a courthouse or a DMV, but the department's computer section may also be working with a three-month backlog. In this case, a critical incident occurring one month ago would *not* show up in the information updated last week. The importance of timeliness is a variable to be determined by you, but to be truly informed you need to know how "fresh" the information is.

4. What are the searchable fields? Which fields are mandatory?

If your knowledge of "fields" and "records" is limited to the places where cattle graze and those flat, round things that play music, you *could* have a problem telling a good database from a bad one. An MVR vendor, for example, should be able to tell you that a subject's middle initial is critical when pulling an Arizona driving record. You don't have to become a programmer to use a computer and you needn't know a database management language to benefit from databases, *but* it is very helpful to understand how databases are constructed and (*at the least*) what fields, records, and indexing procedures are used.

As a general rule, the computerized, public-record information world is not standardized from county to county or from state to state; in the same way, there is little standardization within or between information vendors. Look at the system documentation from the vendor. The manual should include this sort of information.

5. How much latitude is there for error (misspellings or inappropriate punctuation) in a data request?

If the vendor's requirements for search data appear to be concise and meticulous, then you're probably on the right track. Some computer systems will tell (or "flag") an operator when they make a mistake such as omitting important punctuation or using an unnecessary comma. Other systems allow you to make inquiries by whatever means or in whatever format you like—and then tell you the requested information has *not* been found. In this instance, the desired information may *actually* be there, but the computer didn't understand the question because of the way in which it was asked. It is easy to misinterpret "no record found" as "there is no record." Please take note that the meanings of these two phrases are quite different.

6. What method is used to place the information in the repository and what error control or edit process is used?

In some databases, information may be scanned in or may be entered by a single operator as it is received and, in others, information may be entered *twice* to allow the computer to catch input errors by searching for non-duplicate entries. You don't have to know *everything* about all the options, but the vendor selling information in quantity *should*.

7. How many different databases or sources does the vendor access *and* how often?

The chance of obtaining an accurate search of a database increases with the frequency of access and the vendor's/searcher's level of knowledge. If he or she only makes inquiries once a month—and the results are important—you may need to find someone who sells data at higher volume. The point here is that it is better to find someone who specializes in the type of information you are seeking than it is to utilize a vendor who *can* get the information, but actually specializes in another type of data.

8. Does the price include assistance in interpreting the data received?

A report that includes coding and ambiguous abbreviations may look impressive in your file, but may not be too meaningful. For all reports, except those you deal with regularly, interpretation assistance can be *very* important. Some information vendors offer searches for information they really don't know much about through sources that they only use occasionally. Professional pride sometimes prohibits them from disclosing their limitations—until *you* ask the right questions.

9. Do vendors "keep track" of requesters and the information they seek (usage records)?

This may not seem like a serious concern when you are requesting information you're legally entitled to; however, there *is* a possibility that your usage records could be made available to a competitor. Most probably, the information itself is *already* being (or will be) sold to someone else, but you may not necessarily want *everyone* to know what you are requesting and how often. If the vendor keeps records of who-asks-what, the confidentiality of that information should be addressed in your agreement with the vendor.

10. Will the subject of the inquiry be notified of the request?

If your inquiry is sub rosa or if the subject's discovery of the search could lead to embarrassment, double check! There are laws that mandate the notification of subjects when certain types of inquires are made into their files. If notification is required, the way it is accomplished could be critical.

11. Is the turnaround time and cost of the search made clear at the outset?

You should be crystal clear about what you expect and/or need; the vendor should be succinct when conveying exactly what will be provided and how much it will cost. Failure to address these issues can lead to disputes and hard feelings.

These are excellent questions and concepts to keep in mind when searching for the right public record vendor to meet your needs.

Private Online Sources of Public Records

If you go to a search engine and surf for "public records," you will find a myriad of sites offering access to public records. Many tout access to 10,000 databases and offer "national" searches. Most of these sites are legitimate, reputable vendors. Some sites even collect, purchase and store the data themselves, such as KnowX, a subsidiary of Information America and one of the largest private companies in the information industry. However, the majority of sites you will find are usually intermediaries — companies that access records upon demand from either government agencies or from private enterprise and then resell the data to the end user.

So, who are these private enterprise companies that have developed their own databases and how have they done this? Actually, there are not that many (if you don't count all the direct marketing companies). These private enterprise companies create their databases in one of two ways: they buy records in bulk from government agencies; or they send people to the government agencies and compile information using laptop computers or copy machines. This information can be sliced, diced and merged to create a powerful proprietary database for internal use or for resale purposes.

The pages that follow are profiles of these commercial database vendors, preceded by an index of typical application or use by their clientele. The profiles include product descriptions, methods of distribution, and general statements regarding their capabilities. This list is not limited to only companies proving online access. You will find many media outlets, including CD-ROM, disk, tapes and microfiche, and even good old-fashioned telephone service. Every vendor may not be here, but what you will find is quite extensive.

Keep in mind many of these companies are sources and do not necessarily sell their products to casual or infrequent users. However, people who use public records extensively will find these pages invaluable.

The first part of this section is a series of indices based on the "applications" or practical uses of the each company's services. Following these eighteen indexes, there are full profiles of each company. The indexes are:

Asset/Lien Searching/Verification
Background Info – Business
Background Info – Individuals
Collections
Competitive Intelligence
Direct Marketing
Employment Screening
Filing/Recording Documents
Fraud Prevention/Detection
Genealogical Research
General Business Information
Government Document Retrieval
Insurance Underwriting
Legal Compliance
Lending/Leasing
Locating People/Businesses
Litigation
Real Estate Transactions
Tenant Screening

If you find a company that may possibly fit you public record searching needs, call them or visit their web site.

For a more inclusive and updated list of online searchable of source, gateways and distributors of public records, visit www.publicrecordsources.com.

Application Indexes

Searching/Verification Asset/Lien

Access Louisiana
AccuSearch Inc
Amerestate Inc
Attorneys Title Insurance Fund
Banko Inc
Cal Info
Capitol Lien Records & Research Inc
ChoicePoint Inc
ChoicePoint, formally CDB Infotek
Commercial Information Systems Inc
Confi-Chek
Court PC of Connecticut
CourtH.com
Datalink
DataQuick
DCS Information Systems
Diversified Information Services Corp
Dun & Bradstreet
Electronic Property Information Corp (EPIC)
Experian Business Information Solutions
Finder Group, The
First American Real Estate Solutions
IDM Corporation
Information America Inc
Intranet Inc
IRSC
KnowX
Law Bulletin Information Network
LIDA Credit Agency Inc
Lloyds Maritime Information Services Inc
Logan Information Services
Logan Registration Service Inc
Merlin Information Services
Motznik Computer Services Inc
National Service Information
Northwest Location Services
OPEN (Online Professional Electronic
    Network)
Pallorium Inc
Paragon Document Research
Professional Services Bureau
Property Data Center Inc
PROTEC
Public Data Corporation
Publook Information Service
Richland County Abstract Co

Search Company of North Dakota LLC
Search Network Ltd
Search Systems
Security Search & Abstract Co
SKLD Information Services LLC
Southeastern Public Records Inc
Southwest InfoNet
Specialty Services
Superior Information Services LLC
The Search Company Inc
Todd Wiegele Research Co Inc
Tyler-McLennon Inc
UCC Retrievals Inc
Unisearch Inc
US Corporate Services
US Document Services Inc
Western Regional Data Inc

Background Info - Business

AcuSearch Investigations & Services LLC
American Business Information Inc
ARISTOTLE
Avantex Inc
Burrelles Information Services
Cal Info
CCH Washington Service Bureau
ChoicePoint Inc
ChoicePoint, formally CDB Infotek
CompuServe
Corporate Screening Services Inc
Court PC of Connecticut
CourtLink
Daily Report, The
Datalink
Derwent Information
Dialog Corporation, The
Disclosure Incorporated
Dun & Bradstreet
EdVerifY Inc
Electronic Property Information Corp (EPIC)
Experian Business Information Solutions
Fidelifacts
Finder Group, The
First American Real Estate Solutions
Gale Group Inc, The
Hollingsworth Court Reporting Inc
Hoovers Inc
Inform Alaska Inc

Information America Inc
Information Network of Arkansas
IRSC
KnowX
LIDA Credit Agency Inc
Lloyds Maritime Information Services Inc
Logan Registration Service Inc
Martindale-Hubbell
Merlin Information Services
Motznik Computer Services Inc
National Service Information
Offshore Business News & Research
OPEN (Online Professional Electronic
    Network)
OSHA DATA
Owens Online Inc
Paragon Document Research
PROTEC
Publook Information Service
RC Information brokers
San Diego Daily Transcript/San Diego Source
SEAFAX Inc
Search Company of North Dakota LLC
Search Systems
Specialty Services
Tax Analysts
The Search Company Inc
Thomson & Thomson
UMI Company
US Document Services Inc
USADATA.com
WinStar Telebase Inc

Background Info – Individuals

AcuSearch Investigations & Services LLC
Agency Records
Ameridex Information Systems
Avert Inc
BiblioData
Cal Info
CCH Washington Service Bureau
ChoicePoint Inc
CompuServe
Confi-Chek
Corporate Screening Services Inc
Court PC of Connecticut
CourtLink
CQ Staff Directories Ltd
Credentials LLC

CrimeLine Information Systems
Daily Report, The
Electronic Property Information Corp (EPIC)
Equifax Credit Services Division
Fidelifacts
Finder Group, The
First American Real Estate Solutions
Hogan Information Services
Infocon Corporation
Inform Alaska Inc
Information Inc
Informus Corporation
Logan Registration Service Inc
MDR/Minnesota Driving Records
Military Information Enterprises Inc
National Credit Information Network NCI
National Information Bureau Ltd
Offshore Business News & Research
OPEN (Online Professional Electronic
    Network)
Owens Online Inc
PROTEC
RC Information brokers
Software Computer Group Inc
Specialty Services
The Search Company Inc
Thomson & Thomson
Todd Wiegele Research Co Inc
VitalChek Network

Collections

Banko Inc
Case Record Info Services
Commercial Information Systems Inc
Equifax Credit Services Division
Haines & Company Inc
Household Drivers Reports Inc (HDR Inc)
Information Inc
Informus Corporation
Merlin Information Services
Northwest Location Services
RC Information brokers
Record Information Services Inc
Search Systems
Trans Union
WinStar Telebase Inc

Competitive Intelligence

American Business Information Inc
Aurigin Systems Inc
BiblioData
Burrelles Information Services
CCH Washington Service Bureau
CompuServe
Confi-Chek
Daily Report, The
DataTech Research
Derwent Information
Dialog Corporation, The
Disclosure Incorporated
FOIA Group Inc
Hoovers Inc
IRSC
KnowX
LEXIS-NEXIS
MicroPatent USA
Paragon Document Research
Public Record Research Library
Search Systems
Thomson & Thomson
UMI Company
US Corporate Services
USADATA.com
West Group
WinStar Telebase Inc

Direct Marketing

Accutrend Corporation
Amerestate Inc
American Business Information Inc
ARISTOTLE
Avantex Inc
Banko Inc
Case Record Info Services
CQ Staff Directories Ltd
Daily Report, The
DataQuick
Dialog Corporation, The
Experian Target Marketing Services
Haines & Company Inc
IDM Corporation
Intranet Inc
Lloyds Maritime Information Services Inc
Logan Information Services
MDR/Minnesota Driving Records
Metromail Corporation

Nebrask@ Online
OSHA DATA
Property Data Center Inc
Record Information Services Inc
SKLD Information Services LLC
Southeastern Public Records Inc
Thomson & Thomson
USADATA.com
Western Regional Data Inc
WinStar Telebase Inc

Employment Screening

Access Indiana Information Network
AcuSearch Investigations & Services LLC
American Driving Records
Avantex Inc
Avert Inc
Business Information Service
ChoicePoint Inc
Commercial Information Systems Inc
Corporate Screening Services Inc
CourtLink
Credentials LLC
DAC Services
Database Technologies Inc
Datalink
DCS Information Systems
EdVerifY Inc
Equifax Credit Services Division
Experian Consumer Credit
Felonies R Us
Fidelifacts
Hogan Information Services
Hollingsworth Court Reporting Inc
Information Inc
Information Network of Arkansas
Information Network of Kansas
Informus Corporation
IQ Data Systems
Law Bulletin Information Network
LIDA Credit Agency Inc
Logan Information Services
National Credit Information Network NCI
OPEN (Online Professional Electronic
    Network)
Pallorium Inc
Paragon Document Research
PROTEC
Search Company of North Dakota LLC

Software Computer Group Inc
Specialty Services
TML Information Services Inc
Todd Wiegele Research Co Inc
Tyler-McLennon Inc
Virginia Information Providers Network

IRSC
Merlin Information Services
Metromail Corporation
National Fraud Center
Offshore Business News & Research
PROTEC

Filing/Recording Documents

Access Indiana Information Network
AccuSearch Inc
AcuSearch Investigations & Services LLC
Amerestate Inc
Banko Inc
Capitol Lien Records & Research Inc
CCH Washington Service Bureau
Chattel Mortgage Reporter Inc
CourtH.com
Daily Report, The
Diversified Information Services Corp
Hollingsworth Court Reporting Inc
National Service Information
Professional Services Bureau
Richland County Abstract Co
San Diego Daily Transcript/San Diego Source
Search Company of North Dakota LLC
Search Network Ltd
Security Search & Abstract Co
SKLD Information Services LLC
Southwest InfoNet
Tyler-McLennon Inc
UCC Retrievals Inc
US Corporate Services
US Document Services Inc

Fraud Prevention/Detection

Cambridge Statistical Research Associates
Carfax
ChoicePoint, formally CDB Infotek
Commercial Information Systems Inc
DAC Services
Database Technologies Inc
Datalink
DCS Information Systems
Felonies R Us
Household Drivers Reports Inc (HDR Inc)
IDM Corporation
Investigators Anywhere Resource Line
IQ Data Systems

Genealogical Research

Ameridex Information Systems
CQ Staff Directories Ltd
Everton Publishers
Gale Group Inc, The
Infocon Corporation
Military Information Enterprises Inc
RC Information brokers
VitalChek Network

General Business Information

Accutrend Corporation
Agency Records
American Business Information Inc
Banko Inc
BRC Inc
Business Information Service
CompuServe
CrimeLine Information Systems
Database Technologies Inc
DataTech Research
DCS Information Systems
Dialog Corporation, The
Disclosure Incorporated
Dun & Bradstreet
Federal Filings Inc
Felonies R Us
Finder Group, The
Hollingsworth Court Reporting Inc
Hoovers Inc
Inform Alaska Inc
Information Network of Arkansas
Information Network of Kansas
Intranet Inc
LEXIS-NEXIS
Lloyds Maritime Information Services Inc
MicroPatent USA
National Information Bureau Ltd
Offshore Business News & Research
Owens Online Inc
Public Data Corporation

Public Record Research Library
Publook Information Service
SEAFAX Inc
Search Systems
Tax Analysts
Trans Union
UMI Company
West Group
WinStar Telebase Inc

Government Document Retrieval

Access Indiana Information Network
AccuSearch Inc
ARISTOTLE
CCH Washington Service Bureau
Congressional Information Service Inc
Conrad Grundlehner Inc
CQ Staff Directories Ltd
Database Technologies Inc
DataTech Research
Dialog Corporation, The
FOIA Group Inc
Hollingsworth Court Reporting Inc
Inform Alaska Inc
KnowX
LEXIS-NEXIS
Loren Data Corp
OSHA DATA
Public Record Research Library
Publook Information Service
Software Computer Group Inc
Southwest InfoNet
The Search Company Inc
US Document Services Inc
West Group

Insurance Underwriting

A.M. Best Company
Access Indiana Information Network
Agency Records
American Driving Records
DAC Services
Datalink
Diversified Information Services Corp
Electronic Property Information Corp (EPIC)
Explore Information Services
Haines & Company Inc
Household Drivers Reports Inc (HDR Inc)
Information Network of Arkansas

Information Network of Kansas
Insurance Information Exchange (iiX)
MDR/Minnesota Driving Records
Nebrask@ Online
Property Data Center Inc
Silver Plume
TML Information Services Inc
Trans Union
Tyler-McLennon Inc
Virginia Information Providers Network
VISTA Information Solutions

Legal Compliance

Access Indiana Information Network
Access Louisiana
AccuSearch Inc
Agency Records
ARISTOTLE
Aurigin Systems Inc
Avantex Inc
Congressional Information Service Inc
Conrad Grundlehner Inc
Corporate Screening Services Inc
CrimeLine Information Systems
Derwent Information
Disclosure Incorporated
Federal Filings Inc
Information Network of Kansas
Investigators Anywhere Resource Line
Legi-Slate Inc
LEXIS-NEXIS
MicroPatent USA
National Service Information
Nebrask@ Online
OSHA DATA
Public Data Corporation
Security Search & Abstract Co
Superior Information Services LLC
Tax Analysts
Thomson & Thomson
UCC Guide Inc, The
UCC Retrievals Inc
Unisearch Inc
VISTA Information Solutions
West Group
Western Regional Data Inc

Lending/Leasing

AccuSearch Inc
Amerestate Inc
Business Information Service
Capitol Lien Records & Research Inc
Chattel Mortgage Reporter Inc
ChoicePoint, formally CDB Infotek
CourtH.com
DataQuick
Derwent Information
Equifax Credit Services Division
Experian Business Information Solutions
Experian Consumer Credit
First American Real Estate Solutions
Haines & Company Inc
Hogan Information Services
IDM Corporation
Information America Inc
Information Network of Kansas
IQ Data Systems
National Information Bureau Ltd
National Service Information
Nebrask@ Online
Professional Services Bureau
Property Data Center Inc
Publook Information Service
Real Estate Guide Inc, The
SEAFAX Inc
Search Network Ltd
Southwest InfoNet
Superior Information Services LLC
Trans Union
Tyler-McLennon Inc
UCC Guide Inc, The
Unisearch Inc
US Corporate Services
VISTA Information Solutions

Litigation

Access Louisiana
Agency Records
Business Information Service
Capitol Lien Records & Research Inc
Chattel Mortgage Reporter Inc
ChoicePoint Inc
Confi-Chek
Conrad Grundlehner Inc
Court PC of Connecticut
CourtLink

CrimeLine Information Systems
Database Technologies Inc
Disclosure Incorporated
Federal Filings Inc
Felonies R Us
Fidelifacts
FOIA Group Inc
Household Drivers Reports Inc (HDR Inc)
Infocon Corporation
Inform Alaska Inc
Information America Inc
Information Inc
Intranet Inc
Investigators Anywhere Resource Line
LIDA Credit Agency Inc
MicroPatent USA
Motznik Computer Services Inc
Northwest Location Services
Offshore Business News & Research
OPEN (Online Professional Electronic
    Network)
OSHA DATA
Pallorium Inc
Paragon Document Research
RC Information brokers
Southeastern Public Records Inc
Southwest InfoNet
Specialty Services
Superior Information Services LLC
Tax Analysts
The Search Company Inc
Todd Wiegele Research Co Inc
UCC Retrievals Inc
Virginia Information Providers Network

Locating People/Businesses

AcuSearch Investigations & Services LLC
American Business Information Inc
Ameridex Information Systems
ARISTOTLE
Cambridge Statistical Research Associates
ChoicePoint, formally CDB Infotek
Commercial Information Systems Inc
Confi-Chek
Court PC of Connecticut
CourtH.com
CQ Staff Directories Ltd
CrimeLine Information Systems
DataQuick

DCS Information Systems
Finder Group, The
Folks Finders Ltd
Haines & Company Inc
Hoovers Inc
Household Drivers Reports Inc (HDR Inc)
Information America Inc
Informus Corporation
IQ Data Systems
IRSC
KnowX
Law Bulletin Information Network
Merlin Information Services
Metromail Corporation
Military Information Enterprises Inc
Motznik Computer Services Inc
National Credit Information Network NCI
Northwest Location Services
Owens Online Inc
Pallorium Inc
Public Data Corporation
Public Record Research Library
Western Regional Data Inc

Diversified Information Services Corp
Electronic Property Information Corp (EPIC)
Environmental Data Resources Inc
First American Real Estate Solutions
IDM Corporation
Infocon Corporation
LIDA Credit Agency Inc
Logan Information Services
Motznik Computer Services Inc
Professional Services Bureau
Property Data Center Inc
Real Estate Guide Inc, The
Record Information Services Inc
Richland County Abstract Co
San Diego Daily Transcript/San Diego Source
Security Search & Abstract Co
SKLD Information Services LLC
Southeastern Public Records Inc
Todd Wiegele Research Co Inc
Trans Union
Unisearch Inc
US Corporate Services
Western Regional Data Inc

Real Estate Transactions

Amerestate Inc
Attorneys Title Insurance Fund
BRC Inc
Business Information Service
Capitol Lien Records & Research Inc
Chattel Mortgage Reporter Inc
CourtH.com
DataQuick

Tenant Screening

American Driving Records
AmRent
Experian Consumer Credit
Felonies R Us
Hogan Information Services
Information Inc
Logan Information Services
National Credit Information Network NCI

Vendor Profiles

A.M. Best Company

Ambest Rd
Oldwick, NJ 08858-9988
Telephone: **Fax:**
908-439-2200 908-439-3296
www.ambest.com

Applications: Insurance Underwriting, Insurance Ratings

Proprietary Products:

Name/Desc: Best Database Services
Info Provided: SEC/Other Financial
Media: Online Database, CD-ROM, Disk, Magnetic Tape, Call-back
Coverage: US

Statement of Capabilities:
A.M. Best Company, known worldwide as The Insurance Information Source, was the first company to report on the financial condition of of insurance companies. A.M. Best strives to perform a constructive and objective role in the insurance industry toward the prevention and detection of insurer solvency. The company's exclusive Best's Ratings are the original and most recognized insurer financial strength ratings. A.M. Best provides quantitative and qualitative evaluations, and offers information through more than 50 reference publications and services. Since its inception a century ago, A.M. Best has provided financial services to professionals with timely, accurate and comprehensive insurance information. A.M. Best's London office can be reached at 011-44-171-264-2260. A.M. Best International, also based in London, can be reached at 011-44-181-579-1091.

Access Indiana Information Network

150 W Market #530
Indianapolis, IN 46204-2806
Telephone: **Fax:**
317-233-2106 317-233-2011
www.ai.org

Applications: Employment Screening, Filing/Recording Documents, Government Document Retrieval, Insurance Underwriting, Legal Compliance

Proprietary Products:

Name/Desc: Premium Services
Info Provided: Driver and/or Vehicle, Licenses/Registrations/Permits, Uniform Commercial Code, Litigation/Judgments/Tax Liens
Media: Internet, E-mail
Coverage: IN

Name/Desc: Free Services
Info Provided: Legislation/Regulation
Media: Internet, E-mail
Coverage: IN

Statement of Capabilities:
AIIN is a comprehensive, one-stop source for electronic access to State of Indiana government information. This network is owned by the state of Indiana. Access to the public records listed here requires a subscription fee and per-use fee. Specialties include drivers records, vehicle title and lien information, vehicle registration records, physician and nurse license verification, Secretary of State records (including UCC and Corporation information) and information on the Indiana General Assembly. See the Internet site for more information.

Access Louisiana

400 Travis St #1308
Shreveport, LA 71101
Telephone: **Fax:**
800-489-5620 800-705-8953
318-227-9730

Applications: Asset/Lien Searching/Verification, Legal Compliance, Litigation

Proprietary Products:

Name/Desc: LA UCC
Info Provided: Uniform Commercial Code, Addresses/Telephone Numbers and Social Security (Numbers)
Media: Printed Report
Coverage: LA

Name/Desc: LA Corporate Data
Info Provided: Corporate/Trade Name Data, Trademarks/Patents and Addresses/Telephone Numbers
Media: Printed Report

Coverage: LA

Statement of Capabilities:

Access Louisiana is a statewide legal research company with a physical presence in every Louisiana parish. Services include: public records (UCC, accounts, receivable, state/federal tax liens, suits, chattel mortgages, bankruptcy records), corporate filing/retrieval, court records and registered agent services. They have extensive knowledge of where information is recorded and how to effectively retrieve Louisiana public records.

AccuSearch Inc

PO Box 3248
Houston, TX 77253-3248
Telephone: **Fax:**
800-833-5778 713-831-9891
713-864-7639

www.accusearchinc.com
accualr@accusearchinc.com

Applications: Asset/Lien Searching/Verification, Filing/Recording Documents, Legal Compliance, Government Document Retrieval, Lending/Leasing

Proprietary Products:

Name/Desc: AccuSearch
Info Provided: Corporate/Trade Name, Uniform Commercial Code
Media: Direct Online
Coverage: TX,CA,PA,IL,WA,OH,OR,MO

Name/Desc: AccuSearch
Info Provided: Bankruptcy
Media: Direct Online
Coverage: CA,IL,TX

Statement of Capabilities:

AccuSearch provides immediate access to UCC, corporate, charter, real property and bankruptcy search services via IBM-compatible PCs or over the telephone. Instantaneous access is available for each online database listed. Each online or over-the-phone search is followed by same-day mailing or faxing of the search report and any copies requested. AccuSearch also performs any of the above searches for any county or state nationwide. AccuSearch's Direct Access system allows multi-page, formatted reports which eliminates print screens, and selective ordering of UCC copies.

Accutrend Corporation

6021 S Syracuse Wy #111
Denver, CO 80111
Telephone: **Fax:**
800-488-0011 303-488-0133
303-488-0011

www.accutrend.com

Applications: Direct Marketing, General Business Information

Proprietary Products:

Name/Desc: New Business Database
Info Provided:
Licenses/Registrations/Permits and Corporate/Trade Name Data
Media: CD-ROM, Internet, Magnetic Tape and Lists or labels
Coverage: US

Statement of Capabilities:

Accutrend Corporation compiles a new business database monthly that contains 175 to 200 million new business registrations, licenses and incorporations. Data is collected from all levels of government and is enhanced with demographic overlays.

ACS Inc

PO Box 4889
Syracuse, NY 13221
Telephone: **Fax:**
315-437-1283 315-437-3223
Applications: General Business Information, UCCs, Real Estate Transactions

Proprietary Products:

Name/Desc: ACS
Info Provided: Real Estate/Assessor
Media: Direct Online
Coverage: ME-county registries, also Illinois and Ohio.

Statement of Capabilities:

ACS, formerly BRC, specializes in online access to recorders, county clerks and registrars across the country. Fees are involved. Online access capabilities are expanding in MI & PA; other states will follow.

AcuSearch Investigations & Services LLC

PO Box 100613
Denver, CO 80250

Telephone:　　**Fax:**
303-756-9687　　303-756-9687
AcuSearch9@aol.com

Applications:　　　　Background Info -
Business, Background Info - Individuals,
Employment Screening, Filing/Recording
Documents, Locating People/Businesses

Proprietary Products:

Name/Desc: CO Criminal Information
Info Provided: Criminal Information
Media: Call-back Only
Coverage: CO

Statement of Capabilities:
AcuSearch specializes in locating and
obtaining pertinent information for financial
institutions, businesses and individuals. Instant
access to nationwide people, credit, and vehicle
info. 24 hour turnaround time on all Colorado
and Washington criminal/civil, driving/plate
records, and process service. They provide in
depth investigation in trademark matters.
Owner Layla Flora is a Univ. of Colorado
graduate and has extensive case investigation
experience in civil and criminal matters.
Guarantees quality and professional service.

Agency Records

PO Box 310175
Newington, CT 06131
Telephone:　　**Fax:**
800-777-6655　　860-666-4247
860-667-1490

www.agencyrecords.com

Applications:　　　　Background Info -
Individuals, Litigation, General Business
Information, Insurance Underwriting, Legal
Compliance

Proprietary Products:

Name/Desc: ARI
Info Provided: Criminal Information
Media: Direct Online to Your Computer,
Gateway via Another Online Svc, Automated
Telephone Look-Up, and Auto-Activated Fax-
on-Demand
Coverage: CT

Name/Desc: MN Court Convictions (15 years)
Info Provided: Criminal Information
Media: Direct Online to Your Computer,
Gateway via Another Online Svc, Automated
Telephone Look-Up, and Auto-Activated Fax-
on-Demand

Coverage: MN
Name/Desc: FL Workers' Compensation
Claims (20 years)
Info Provided: Workers' Compensation
Media: Direct Online to Your Computer,
Gateway via Another Online Svc, Automated
Telephone Look-Up, and Auto-Activated Fax-
on-Demand
Coverage: FL

Statement of Capabilities:
Agency Records provides instant access to
MVRs for FL, AL, SC, NC, WV, NJ, NY, CT,
VT, NH, and ME. They also provide instant
access to court convictions for Connecticut and
Minnesota. They offer computer, fax and
phone ordering as well as volume discounts.
Public companies may be invoiced.

Amerestate Inc

8160 Corporate Park Dr #200
Cincinnati, OH 45242
Telephone:　　**Fax:**
800-582-7300　　513-489-4409
513-489-7300

www.amerestate.com

sales@amerestate.com

Applications:　　　　Asset/Lien
Searching/Verification, Direct Marketing,
Filing/Recording Documents,
Lending/Leasing, Real Estate Transactions

Proprietary Products:

Name/Desc: PaceNet for Windows
Info Provided: Real Estate/Assessor,
Mortgage Data and Addresses/Telephone
Numbers
Media: CD-ROM and Direct Online to Your
Computer
Coverage: KY, MI, OH

Name/Desc: PaceNet Online
Info Provided: Real Estate/Assessor
Media: Direct Online to Your Computer
Coverage: KY, MI, OH

Name/Desc: Pace Books
Info Provided: Real Estate/Assessor
(Mortgage Data) and Addresses/Telephone
Numbers
Media: Printed Report
Coverage: KY, MI, OH

Name/Desc: PaceNet Mortgage Heads

Info Provided: Real Estate/Assessor (Mortgage Data) and Addresses/Telephone Numbers
Media: Direct Online to Your Computer
Coverage: KY, MI, OH

Name/Desc: Prospect Services
Info Provided: Real Estate/Assessor (Mortgage Data) and Addresses/Telephone Numbers
Media: Disk, Lists or labels, Magnetic Tape and Printed Report
Coverage: KY, MI , OH

Statement of Capabilities:
Amerestate maintains databases of existing real estate ownership and gathers and verifies data from courthouse public records and other sources on all real estate sales. They collect most information manually, assuring accuracy, completeness and timely information. Property addresses are standardized and updated quarterly to current CASS standards required by the USPS. Amerestate has recently introduced PaceNet Mortgage Leads, a product specifically designed for those in the lending industry who want to target prospects for refinance, lines of credit or seconds.

American Business Information Inc
PO Box 27347
Omaha, NE 68127
Telephone: **Fax:**
800-808-4636   402-331-5990
402-593-4500

www.infousa.com

Applications: Background Info - Business, Competitive Intelligence, Direct Marketing, General Business Information, Locating People/Businesses
Proprietary Products:

Name/Desc: Business Sales Leads
Info Provided: Addresses/Telephone Numbers, Credit Information, Foreign Country Information, News/Current Events and SEC/Other Financial
Media: CD-ROM, Direct Online to Your Computer, Disk, Gateway Via Another Online Service, Internet, Lists or labels, Magnetic Tape, Printed Report, Publication/Directory and Software
Coverage: US

Name/Desc: Consumer Sales Leads

Info Provided: Addresses/Telephone Numbers, Credit Information, Driver and/or Vehicle, Genealogical Information and Real Estate/Assessor
Media: CD-ROM, Direct Online to Your Computer, Disk, Gateway Via Another Online Service, Internet, Lists or labels, Magnetic Tape, Printed Report, Publication/Directory and Software
Coverage: US

Statement of Capabilities:
American Business Information compiles business information from telephone directories and other public sources. Over the past 20+ years, they have provided services to over 2 million customers. They telephone verify every name in their database before they offer it for sale. They phone-verify address changes from the USPS NCOA program. Their info is available in a variety of ways including online (SalesLeadsUSA.com), CD-ROM, and by telephone (Directory Assistance Plus). A division produces the Pro-CD Disk and another operates Digital Directory Assistance. For business leads call 800-555-5335. For SalesLeads USA call 402-593-4593.

American Driving Records
PO Box 160147
Sacramento, CA 95816-9998
Telephone: **Fax:**
800-766-6877   800-800-0817
916-456-3200   916-456-3332

www.mvrs.com

sales@mvrs.com

Applications: Insurance Underwriting, Employment Screening, Tenant Screening
Proprietary Products:

Name/Desc: ADR
Info Provided: Driver and/or Vehicle
Media: Online, Fax, Printed Report
Coverage: US

Statement of Capabilities:
Amercian Driving Record (ADR) services include driving records, registration information, and special processing for the insurance industry such as automatic checking (ACH), calculating underwriting points, and ZapApp (tm) - an automated insurance application from the agency to the carrier.

Driving records can be instant, same day or overnight, depending on the state.

Ameridex Information Systems

PO Box 51314
Irvine, CA 92619-1314
Fax:
714-731-2116
http://kadima.com

Applications: Background Info - Individuals, Locating People/Businesses, Genealogical Research

Proprietary Products:

Name/Desc: SSDI
Info Provided: Addresses/Telephone Numbers
Media: CD-ROM, Online, Lists
Coverage: US

Name/Desc: Military
Info Provided: Military Service
Media: CD-ROM, Direct Online, List
Coverage: US

Name/Desc: Live Index
Info Provided: Addresses/Telephone Numbers
Media: CD-ROM, Direct Online, Lists
Coverage: US

Statement of Capabilities:
Ameridex presents several unique databases for people tracing on the Internet. Over 220 million names and 180 million with a date of birth are compiled from multiple public record sources. Speciality databases include a nationwide death index with supplements and an active military personnel database.

AmRent

9990 Richmond #100
Houston, TX 77042
Telephone: **Fax:**
800-324-3681 800-324-4595
713-266-1870 713-266-9146

Applications: Tenant Screening

Proprietary Products:

Name/Desc: AmRent
Info Provided: Tenant History
Media: Available on Trans Registry and Call-in
Coverage: IL, TX

Statement of Capabilities:
AmRent furnishes background checks in relation to their tenant screening services, utilizing proprietary in-house database information and public records. AmRent is an affiliate of Trans Registry, a database of tenant history and eviction information accumulated from affiliates nationwide.

ARISTOTLE

205 Pennsylvania Ave SW
Washington, DC 20003
Telephone: **Fax:**
800-296-2747 202-543-6407
202-543-8345

www.products.aristotle.org

Applications: Background Info - Business, Legal Compliance, Direct Marketing, Government Document Retrieval, Locating People/Businesses

Proprietary Products:

Name/Desc: ARISTOTLE
Info Provided: Voter Registration and Addresses/Telephone Numbers
Media: CD-ROM, Magnetic Tape and Online Database
Coverage: US

Statement of Capabilities:
ARISTOTLE maintains a nationwide file of registered voters. Information obtained from 3,400 counties and municipalities is standardized and enhanced with listed phone number, postal correction and national change of address, census geography, and age and vote history. Twenty-six states have no significant restrictions on the commercial use of their voter registration information.

Attorneys Title Insurance Fund

PO Box 628600
Orlando, FL 32862
Telephone: **Fax:**
800-336-3863 407-240-1106
407-240-3863

www.thefund.com

Applications: Real Estate Transactions, Asset/Lien Searching/Verification

Proprietary Products:

Name/Desc: The Fund
Info Provided: Real Estate/Assessor,
Litigation/Judgments/Tax Liens
Media: Online, Disk, Printed Report, Magnetic
Tape
Coverage: FL-31 counties

Statement of Capabilities:
Although the primary business of The Fund (as
they are called) is to issue title insurance, they
offer access to over 100 million real estate
records from 31 major counties in FL. The
Fund has 14 branch offices and is expanding to
SC and IL. Online users can access public
records including mortgages, deeds, liens,
assessments, right-of-way data, and even
judgment and divorce proceedings.

Aurigin Systems Inc

1975 Landings Drive
Mountain View, CA 94043
Telephone: **Fax:**
650-237-0900   650-237-0910
http://aurigin.com
info@aurigin.com
Applications: Legal Compliance,
Competitive Intelligence
Proprietary Products:

Name/Desc: SmartPatent
Info Provided: Trademarks/Patents
Media: Online, Software
Coverage: US, Itl

Statement of Capabilities:
Aurigin, formally known as SmartPatents Inc,
offers the Aurigin IPAM System to manage a
company's intellectual asset management
needs. Other important products are
SmartPatent Electronic Patents, indexed
patents from the US Patent and Trademark
Office, and the SmartPatent Workbench, a
desktop software application.

Avantex Inc

Green Hills Corporate Center
2675 Morgantown Rd #3300Reading, PA
19607
Telephone: **Fax:**
800-998-8857   800-544-9252
610-796-2385   610-796-2392
www.avantext.com

dara@avantex.com
Applications: Background Info -
Business, Direct Marketing, Employment
Screening, Legal Compliance
Proprietary Products:

Name/Desc: FAA Data
Info Provided: Aviation/Vessels,
Addresses/Telephone Numbers,
Legislation/Regulations
Media: CD-ROM
Coverage: US

Statement of Capabilities:
Avantext product line includes 6 powerful CDs
for the aviation industry. The FAA Data CD
includes a full listing of pilots and aircraft
owners, schools, technicians, dealers and much
more.

Avert Inc

301 Remington St
Fort Collins, CO 80524
Telephone: **Fax:**
800-367-5933   800-237-4011
970-484-7722   970-221-1526

www.avert.com
info@avert.com
Applications: Background Info -
Individuals, Employment Screening
Proprietary Products:

Name/Desc: Workers' Compensation History
Info Provided: Workers Compensation
Media: Direct Online, Printed Report, E-mail,
Call Back
Coverage: FL, IA, ME, MD, MI, MS, NE, OR

Name/Desc: First Check
Info Provided: Social Security (Numbers)
Media: Direct Online, Printed Report, E-mail,
Call Back
Coverage: US

Name/Desc: Credit & Name Link
Info Provided: Credit Information
Media: Direct Online, Printed Report, E-mail,
Call Back
Coverage: US

Statement of Capabilities:
Avert helps employers minimize risk and hire
safe, honest and competent employees. Use
Avert's on-line ordering system, OrderXpert,
and retrieve reports to your desktop. Avert
offers services such as KnowledgeLink Help

Desk for building a compliant pre-employment screening program to fit the need. Legal and fair to all parties, Avert is a good outsource for pre-employment screening as well as providing a proactive approach to reducing fraud, theft, turnover, and violence in the workplace.

Banko Inc

607 Marquette Ave #500
Minneapolis, MN 55402
Telephone: **Fax:**
800-533-8897   612-321-0325
612-332-2427
www.BANKO.com
SALES@BANKO.com

Applications: Asset/Lien
Searching/Verification, Collections, Direct Marketing, Filing/Recording Documents, General Business Information

Proprietary Products:

Statement of Capabilities:
Banko Inc. provides up to the minute information about bankruptcy suppression and notification in a variety of electronic formats.

BiblioData

PO Box 61
Needham Heights, MA 02494
Telephone: **Fax:**
781-444-1154   781-449-4584
www.bibliodata.com
ina@bibliodata.com

Applications: Current Events,
Competitive Intelligence, Background Info - Individuals, Risk Management

Proprietary Products:

Name/Desc: BiblioData
Info Provided: News/Current Events, Addresses/Telephone Numbers
Media: Internet
Coverage: US

Statement of Capabilities:
BiblioData publishes informative newsletters directly related to the online industry. Their products are targeted for researchers and librarians.

Burrelles Information Services

75 East Northfield Rd
Livingston, NJ 07039
Telephone:
800-631-1160
973-992-6600
http://burrelles.com
info@burrelles.com

Applications: Current Events,
Background Info - Business, Competitive Intelligence

Proprietary Products:

Name/Desc: BIO
Info Provided: News/Current Events
Media: Direct Online, CD-ROM, Publication
Coverage: US, Itl

Statement of Capabilities:
For over 100 years Burrelle's has been monitoring, organizing, and delivering media data to clients. Products include Press Clipping, NewsExpress, NewsAlert, Media Direcories, Broadcast Transcripts, and Web Clips. The BIO - Burrelle's Information Office, is software to receive and use information from Burrelle's.

Business Information Service

531 S Holland
Bellville, TX 77418
Telephone: **Fax:**
409-865-2547   409-865-8918
Applications: General Business
Information, Lending/Leasing, Real Estate Transactions, Litigation, Employment Screening

Proprietary Products:

Name/Desc: Local Public Record
Info Provided: Real Estate/Assessor, Litigation/Judgments/Tax Liens, Uniform Commercial Code and Criminal Information
Media: Publication
Coverage: TX -Austin, Colorado, Waller, Washington Counties

Name/Desc: Bankruptcies
Info Provided: Bankruptcy
Media: Publication
Coverage: TX-Austin, Colorado, Waller, Washington

Statement of Capabilities:
Business Information Service (BIS) provides its information in the form of monthly subscription publications

Cal Info

316 W 2nd St #102
Los Angeles, CA 90012
Telephone: **Fax:**
213-687-8710 213-687-8778
http://members.aol.com/calinfola
calinfola@aol.com

Applications: Background Info - Business, Background Info - Individuals, Asset/Lien Searching/Verification

Proprietary Products:

Name/Desc: Guide to State Statutes
Info Provided: Legislation/Regulation (State Statutes)
Media: Directory
Coverage: US

Name/Desc: Administrative Guide to State Regulations
Info Provided: Legislation/Regulation
Media: Publication

Statement of Capabilities:
Cal Info offers an information research and retrieval service that finds answers to questions that affect law firms and businesses every day. Their personnel are trained to search computerized databases as well as the more traditional information sources, including libraries, publishers, government agencies, courts, trade unions and associations.. They provide company reports, financial data, product information, people information, journals and news stories, real estate information, legal research, public records research, government information and document retrieval.

Cambridge Statistical Research Associates

53 Wellesley
Irvine, CA 92612
Telephone: **Fax:**
800-327-2772 800-327-2720
949-250-8579 949-250-8591

Applications: Locating People/Businesses, Fraud Prevention/Detection

Proprietary Products:

Name/Desc: Death Master File
Info Provided: Social Security (Numbers)
Media: CD-ROM, Direct Online and Printed Report
Coverage: US

Statement of Capabilities:
CSRA traces its origin to an actuarial and programming service established in 1979. In recent years, its efforts moved toward bringing large mainframe databases to the desktop computing platform, including CD-ROM. CSRA specializes in nationwide death index by name and Social Security Number, death auditing service, database consulting, genealogical and probate research, and address trace service.

Capitol Lien Records & Research Inc

1010 N Dale
St Paul, MN 55117
Telephone: **Fax:**
800-845-4077 800-845-4080
651-488-0100 651-488-0300

Applications: Asset/Lien Searching/Verification, Filing/Recording Documents, Lending/Leasing, Litigation, Real Estate Transactions

Proprietary Products:

Name/Desc: UCC
Info Provided: Uniform Commercial Code
Media: Disk
Coverage: MN

Statement of Capabilities:
Capitol Lien Records & Research provides UCC, federal and state tax lien searches, real estate searches, document retrievals, bankruptcy searches, judgment searches, corporate documents, a weekly tax lien report, environmental lien searches, Phase 1, 2 and 3 environmental searches, watercraft, and aircraft and vessel searches. An online ordering system accepting credit cards is provided to clients.

Carfax

3975 Fair Ridge Dr #200N
Fairfax, VA 22033
Telephone: **Fax:**
703-934-2664 703-218-2465
www.carfax.com

Applications: Fraud Prevention/Detection, Risk Management
Proprietary Products:

Name/Desc: Vehicle History Service
Info Provided: Driver and/or Vehicle
Media: Internet and Direct Online to Your Computer
Coverage: US

Name/Desc: Motor Vehicle Title Information
Info Provided: Driver and/or Vehicle
Media: Direct Online Database, Available on CompuServe and Call-in
Coverage: US

Name/Desc: VINde (VIN Validity Check Program)
Info Provided: Software/Training
Media: Disk
Coverage: US

Statement of Capabilities:
With the largest online vehicle history database (728 million vehicle records), Carfax can generate a Vehicle History Report based on a VIN in less than one second. They collect data from a variety of sources including state DMVs and salvage pools. Reports include details from previous titles, city and state, odometer rollbacks, junk and flood damage, etc, reducing the risk of handling used vehicles with hidden problems that affect their value.

Case Record Info Services

2648 E Workman Ave #512
West Covina, CA 91791
Telephone: **Fax:**
626-967-6682 626-967-3782
caserecord@yahooo.com
Applications: Collections, Direct Marketing
Proprietary Products:

Name/Desc: Judgment Lists
Info Provided: Litigation/Judgments/Tax Liens
Media: Disk, Lists or labels and Printed Report
Coverage: CA

Statement of Capabilities:
Case Record Info Services provides judgment lists in California. Their data is used by bulk data providers, collection and mediation companies. They are also members of the American Arbitration Association.

CCH Washington Service Bureau

655 15th Street NW
Washington, DC 20005
Telephone: **Fax:**
800-955-5219 202-508-0694
202-508-0600
www.wsb.com
custserve@wsb.com
Applications: Background Info - Business, Background Info - Individuals, Competitive Intelligence, Filing/Recording Documents, Government Document Retrieval
Proprietary Products:

Name/Desc: SECnet
Info Provided: SEC/Other Financial
Media: Direct Online to Your Computer and Internet
Coverage: US

Statement of Capabilities:
With an average of over seven years of SEC document experience, their research specialists can tackle tough assignments and meet the most pressing deadlines. Whether clients require examples of precedent language or detailed intelligence on a specific firm or industry, CCH Washington Service Bureau will quickly provide the precise information. Using state-of-the-art proprietary databases, their research specialists quickly deliver a wide range of corporate and transactional information.

Chattel Mortgage Reporter Inc

300 W Washington #808
Chicago, IL 60606
Telephone: **Fax:**
312-214-1048 312-214-1054
www.chattelmtg.com
searches@chattelmtg.com
Applications: Lending/Leasing, Filing/Recording Documents, Real Estate Transactions, Litigation
Proprietary Products:

Name/Desc: Chattel Mortgage Reporter
Info Provided: Uniform Commercial Code
Media: Call-in, Fax, Online and E-mail
Coverage: IL-Cook County

Statement of Capabilities:
CMR is a national public record service organization specializing in Illinois. They have more than 95 years of experience, with emphasis on public record research in Cook County, IL and the counties surrounding the Chicago area. For fast copy retrieval, their UCC database for Cook County is backed up by microfilm dating back to 1973.

ChoicePoint Inc

1000 Alderman Dr
Alphretta, GA 30005

Telephone: **Fax:**
770-752-6000 770-752-6005
www.choicepointinc.com

Applications: Background Info - Business, Employment Screening, Asset/Lien Searching/Verification, Background Info - Individuals, Litigation

Proprietary Products:

Name/Desc: Corp Data
Info Provided: Corporation/Trade Name Data
Media: Direct Online
Coverage: US

Name/Desc: Bankruptcy
Info Provided: Bankruptcy
Media: Direct Online
Coverage: US

Name/Desc: UCC
Info Provided: UCC Fillings and Tax Liens
Media: Direct Online Database
Coverage: US

Name/Desc: Real Property
Info Provided: Real Estate/Assessor
Media: Direct Online
Coverage: US

Name/Desc: Litigation
Info Provided: Litigation/Judgments/Tax Liens
Media: Direct Online
Coverage: US

Name/Desc: Licenses
Info Provided: Licenses/Registrations/Permits (Physicians)
Media: Direct Online
Coverage: US

Name/Desc: Fict. Bus Names
Info Provided: Corporate/Trade Name Data (Fictitious Business Names)
Media: Direct Online

Coverage: US
Name/Desc: MVRs
Info Provided:
Media: Direct Online
Coverage: US

Statement of Capabilities:
ChoicePoint is a leading provider of intelligence information to help businesses, governments, and individuals to better understand with whom they do business. ChoicePoint services the risk management information needs of the property and casualty insurance market, the life and health insurance market, and business and government, including asset-based lenders and professional service providers. The company, with many branch offices nationwide, was spun off/out from Equifax in 1997. They offer a variety of useful online products.

ChoicePoint, formally CDB Infotek

6 Hutton Centre Dr #600
Santa Ana, CA 92707

Telephone: **Fax:**
800-427-3747 714-708-1000
714-708-2000

www.cdb.com

Applications: Locating People/Businesses, Asset/Lien Searching/Verification, Background Info - Business, Fraud Prevention/Detection, Lending/Leasing

Proprietary Products:

Name/Desc: Real Property Ownership & Transfers
Info Provided: Real Estate/Assessor
Media: Direct Online
Coverage: US

Name/Desc: Corporate & Limited Partnerships
Info Provided: Corporate/Trade Name Data
Media: Direct Online Database
Coverage: US

Name/Desc: Uniform Commercial Code
Info Provided: Uniform Commerical Code
Media: Direct Online Database
Coverage: US

Name/Desc: Bankruptcies, Tax Liens, Judgments, Notices of Default
Info Provided: Bankruptcy and Litigation/Judgments/Tax Liens
Media: Direct Online Databases

Coverage: US

Name/Desc: Address Inspector
Info Provided: Addresses/Telephone Numbers
Media: Direct Online Database
Coverage: US

Statement of Capabilities:
ChoicePoint (CDB Infotek) offers nationwide public records information, including instant access to more than 4 billion records and 1,600 targeted databases to efficiently locate people or businesses, conduct background research, identify assets, control fraud, conduct due diligence, etc. Subscribers learn search strategies at free, year-round seminars and have toll-free access to customer service representatives for help. ChoicePoint also offers direct marketing lists, monitoring services, hard copy document retrieval and high-volume processing services.

Commercial Information Systems Inc

4747 SW Kelly #110
Portland, OR 97201-4221
Telephone: **Fax:**
800-454-6575 503-222-7405
503-222-7422

www.cis-usa.com
cis@cis-usa.com

Applications: Asset/Lien Searching/Verification, Collections, Employment Screening, Fraud Prevention/Detection, Locating People/Businesses

Proprietary Products:

Name/Desc: Aircraft Registrations
Info Provided: Aviation/Vessels
Media: Direct Online to Your Computer, Fax, Printed Report
Coverage: US

Name/Desc: UCCs
Info Provided: Uniform Commercial Code
Media: Direct Online to Your Computer, Fax, Printed Report
Coverage: CA, ID, OR, WA

Name/Desc: Corporations & Limited Partnerships
Info Provided: Corporate/Trade Name Data
Media: Direct Online to Your Computer, Fax, Printed Report
Coverage: CA, ID, OR, WA

Name/Desc: Professional Licenses
Info Provided: Licenses/Registrations/Permits
Media: Direct Online to Your Computer, Fax, Printed Report
Coverage: ID, OR, WA

Name/Desc: Real Estate Records
Info Provided: Real Estate/Assessor
Media: Direct Online to Your Computer, Fax, Printed Report
Coverage: ID, NV, OR, WA

Name/Desc: Criminal Records, Litigation/Judgments/Tax Liens
Info Provided: Criminal Information
Media: Direct Online to Your Computer, Fax, Printed Report
Coverage: ID, OR, WA, CA

Name/Desc: Fish & Wildlife Records
Info Provided: Licenses/Registrations/Permits
Media: Direct Online to Your Computer, Fax, Printed Report
Coverage: ID, OR, NV

Name/Desc: Driver's License & Registration
Info Provided: Hazardous Materials
Media: Direct Online to Your Computer, Fax, Printed Report
Coverage: ID, OR

Name/Desc: Hazardous Materials
Info Provided: Environmental
Media: Direct Online to Your Computer, Fax, Printed Report

Statement of Capabilities:
Commercial Information Systems (CIS) is an online/on-site database of public records serving business and government entities. They provide direct access to selected public and private database records on a national level through special gateway relationships. The CIS integrated regional database aggregates, commingles and cross-matches records at the state level by name, address, city, state, ZIP Code, birth date, driver's license, vehicle plates and other identifiers with a search engine that allows a subscriber to return all related records on a common identifier. The CIS system is always available through a PC and modem. CIS provides the communication software. Internet access is expected. CIS also provides information on a manual retrieval basis, including credit bureau products and services as well as special data mining capabilities

tailored to a clients' specific research or volume searching needs.

CompuServe

PO Box 20212
Columbus, OH 43220
Telephone: **Fax:**
800-848-8199 614-457-0348
614-457-8600

www.compuserve.com

Applications: General Business Information, Background Info - Business, Background Info - Individuals, Competitive Intelligence

Proprietary Products:

Name/Desc: Quest Research Center
Info Provided: Trademarks/Patents, News/Current Events,
Media: Internet
Coverage: US

Name/Desc: Phonefile
Info Provided: Addresses/Telephone Numbers
Coverage: US

Statement of Capabilities:
Now a subsidiary of AOL, CompuServe is available in 185 countries and provides comprehensive services for serious Internet online users at home, in the workplace, and globally. Business and professional resources, latest news and information, are but a few of CompuServe's powerful communications capabilities.

Confi-Chek

1816 19th ST
Sacramento, CA 95814
Telephone: **Fax:**
800-821-7404 800-758-5859
916-443-4822 916-443-7420

www.Confi-check.com

Applications: Asset/Lien Searching/Verification, Background Info - Individuals, Competitive Intelligence, Litigation, Locating People/Businesses

Proprietary Products:

Name/Desc: Confi-Chek Online
Info Provided: Criminal History
Media: Direct Online
Coverage: CA

Statement of Capabilities:
Confi-Check provides instant access to national and local records throughout the US. They also offer asset services. Their web site has almost all state records. Dial-up and fax call-in services are also available.

Congressional Information Service Inc

4520 East-West Highway
Bethesda, MD 20814-3389
Telephone: **Fax:**
800-638-8380 301-654-4033
301-654-1550

www.cispubs.com

Applications: Legal Compliance, Government Document Retrieval, Current Events

Proprietary Products:

Name/Desc: Current Issues Sourcefile
Info Provided: Legislation/Regulations
Media: CD-ROM, Disk, Publication
Coverage: US

Statement of Capabilities:
Congressional Information Service is an international publisher of reference, research, and current awareness information products and services. Many of their products deal with economic and demographic issues. Their multiple databases are offered in electronic format and through partners such as LEXIS-NEXIS.

Conrad Grundlehner Inc

8605 Brook Rd
McLean, VA 22102-1504
Telephone: **Fax:**
703-506-9648 703-506-9580
Applications: Legal Compliance, Government Document Retrieval, Litigation

Proprietary Products:

Name/Desc: Conrad Grundlehner
Info Provided: Bankruptcy, Litigation/Judgments/Tax Liens
Media: Disk, Magnetic Tape
Coverage: DC, MD, NC, VA, WV

Statement of Capabilities:
Conrad Grundlehner Inc (CGI) was among the first companies to use portable computers to collect legal data at courts and recording

offices. The use of notebook computers combined with electronic transmission of data to the customer reduces the time between data collection and its availability to the customer. CGI's information processing expertise also allows it to provide a high degree of customized service to its customers. Data can be delivered in a wide variety of ways on a broad spectrum of media.

Corporate Screening Services Inc

PO Box 36129
Cleveland, OH 44136
Telephone: **Fax:**
800-229-8606   888-815-4567
440-816-0500   440-243-4204

www.corporate-screening.com

Applications: Background Info - Individuals, Background Info - Business, Employment Screening, Legal Compliance

Proprietary Products:

Name/Desc: CSS EASE
Info Provided: Credit Information, Driver and/or Vehicle, Education/Employment, Licenses/Registrations/Permits, Litigation/Judgments/Tax Liens, Social Security (Numbers) and Workers' Compensation
Media: Internet
Coverage: US

Statement of Capabilities:
Corporate Screening utilizes a national network of resources for public record search and retrieval services. They offer complete pre-employment and business background investigative packages; can customize to fit needs. Complies with FCRA. Their applicant Screening Engine (CSS EASE) allows registered users to access complete investigative results and updates over the Internet. This has recently expanded to include online public record search ordering, free and easy to use.

Court PC of Connecticut

PO Box 11081
Greenwich, CT 06831-1081
Telephone: **Fax:**
203-531-7866   203-531-6899
Applications: Litigation, Background Info - Business, Asset/Lien

Searching/Verification, Locating People/Businesses, Background Info - Individuals

Proprietary Products:

Name/Desc: Superior Index
Info Provided: Litigation/Judgments/Tax Liens, Criminal Information
Media: Fax-on-Demand and Printed Report
Coverage: CT

Statement of Capabilities:
Court PC is Connecticut's comprehensive source of docket search information from Superior Court and US District Court cases. Their database contains records of civil filings from 1984, family/divorce from 1988, and criminal conviction data from 1991. Indexes are used to supplement PACER data from 1970 to present. They also provide current corporation, UCC and tax lien data from the Connecticut Secretary of State database, and statewide real estate information from computerized assessor lists.

CourtH.com

PO Box 70558
Houston, TX 77270-0558
Telephone: **Fax:**
800-925-4225   713-683-0493
713-683-0491

www.courth.com

orders@courth.com

Applications: Asset/Lien Searching/Verification, Filing/Recording Documents, Lending/Leasing, Locating People/Businesses, Real Estate Transactions

Proprietary Products:

Name/Desc: Courthouse Research
Info Provided: Corporate/Trade Name Data, Real Estate/Assessor, Litigation/judgments/Tax Liens
Media: Direct Online, Internet
Coverage: TX

Statement of Capabilities:
Our Internet service provides access to 30 databases of public information from marriage records to property records to bankruptcies. Our proprietary database consists of public records from Harris, Montgomery, and Fort Bend counties. These records are easily searched on our web site.

CourtLink

400 112th Ave NE #250
Bellevue, WA 98004
Telephone: **Fax:**
800-774-7317   425-974-1419
425-974-5000

www.courtlink.com
goconnor@courtlink.com

Applications: Background Info -
Business, Background Info - Individuals,
Litigation, Risk Management, Employment
Screening

Proprietary Products:

Name/Desc: CourtLink
Info Provided: Bankruptcy,
Litigation/Judgments/Tax Liens
Media: Online Database, Printed Reports and
Lists or Labels
Coverage: US

Statement of Capabilities:
Based in Bellevue, WA, CourtLink partners
with courts throughout the country to help
them creat grant electronic public access to
docket information.   CourtLink currently
provides real-time electronic public access to
over 450 federal, state and local courts
nationwide. Users gain access to the complete
federal system as well as a select number of
local courts through a simple Windows
interface. State and local content includes
access to courts in WA, OR, NY, TX, VA, and
MD. At the end of February, new software will
be released which will include access to
Riverside County CA and to North Carolina.
There are many benefits that CourtLink can
provide, including one central source of
accessing multiple courts. Possible uses of the
system include litigation history, employee
screening, discovery, case management and
background checks. Search results include case
summaries, names of parties and attorneys,
dockets, judgments, claims, creditors and
charges. Currently, over 1,500 organizations
use CourtLink including over 80% of the 250
largest law firms in the country. During the
third quarter of 1999, CourtLink will be
providing complete web based access. With the
migration, the number of courts accessible
through CourtLink will expand at a rapid rate.
More   information   is   available   at
www.courtlink.com.

CQ Staff Directories Ltd

815 Slaters Ln
Alexandria, VA 22314
Telephone: **Fax:**
800-252-1722   703-739-0234
703-739-0900

www.staffdirectories.com

Applications: Locating
People/Businesses, Background Info -
Individuals, Direct Marketing, Genealogical
Research, Government Document Retrieval

Proprietary Products:

Name/Desc: Congressional Staff Directory
Info Provided: Addresses/Telephone
Numbers
Media: Publication, CD-ROM, Disk, and
available on Lexis, LegiSlate and America
Online
Coverage: US

Name/Desc: Federal Staff Directory
Info Provided: Addresses/Telephone
Numbers
Media: Publication, CD-ROM and available
on Lexis.
Coverage: US

Name/Desc: Judicial Staff Directory (Federal)
Info Provided: Addresses/Telephone
Numbers
Media: Publication, CD-ROM and avaiable on
Lexis
Coverage: US

Name/Desc: Military Personnel (Active-US)
Info Provided: Addresses/Telephone
Numbers
Media: CD-ROM
Coverage: US

Statement of Capabilities:
Staff Directories is a leading publisher of
directory information about federal employees,
including Congress, the federal judiciary, and
the US military.

Credentials LLC

550 Frontage Road #3500
Northfield, IL 60093
Telephone: **Fax:**
847-446-7422   847-446-7424
www.degreechk.com
tmckechney@degreechk.com

Applications: Background Info - Individuals, Employment Screening

Proprietary Products:

Name/Desc: Degreechk
Info Provided: Education/Employment
Media: Internet, E-mail, Fax
Coverage: US

Statement of Capabilities:
Credentials LLC offers 24 hour, 365 day Internet access to degree verification from participating colleges and universities. All verification transactions are uniquely audit-trailed and confirmed to the user via fax or e-mail. In addition to online databases provided by participating schools, the system includes an off-line, archival search capability for degrees that are not included in the online database. This feature is important since most school databases only date back to the early or mid-1980s. Frequently, these archival searches can be completed in less than an hour with final results automatically e-mailed or faxed to the inquirer. A Preferred Client Package, which includes wholesale pricing and billing options, is available to the employment screening firms. All interactions with degreechk.com are fully encrypted for security. Other important security features are detailed on the web site. While the menu of schools is currently limited, significant growth is expected over the next 18 months. Degreechk.com will broadcast (e-mail) notification of new school additions to the menu.

CrimeLine Information Systems

113 Latigo Lane
Canon City, CO 81212
Telephone: **Fax:**
800-332-7999   800-462-5823
www.cdrominvestigations.com
caligast@rmi.net

Applications: Background Info - Individuals, General Business Information, Legal Compliance, Litigation, Locating People/Businesses

Proprietary Products:

Name/Desc: CA Criminal
Info Provided: Criminal Information
Media: CD-ROM, Direct Online to Your Computer and Call back
Coverage: AZ, CA, CO

Name/Desc: CA Professional Licenses
Info Provided: Licenses/Registration/Permits
Media: CD-ROM, Direct Online to Your Computer and Call back
Coverage: CA

Name/Desc: CA Corporate Records
Info Provided: Corporate/Trade Name Data
Media: CD-ROM, Direct Online to Your Computer and Call back
Coverage: CA

Statement of Capabilities:
Crimeline provides a criminal background checking database as well as research on corporate requirements, professional licenses, Board of Equalization, fictitious business names, and others. Features online and CD-ROM technology at competitive prices.

DAC Services

4500 S 129th E Ave
Tulsa, OK 74134
Telephone: **Fax:**
800-331-9175   918-664-4366
918-664-9991

www.dacservices.com

Applications: Insurance Underwriting, Employment Screening, Risk Management, Fraud Prevention/Detection

Proprietary Products:

Name/Desc: Transportation Employment History; Drug/Alcohol Test Results, Security Guard Employment History
Info Provided: Education/Employment
Media: Direct Online
Coverage: US

Name/Desc: Driving Records
Info Provided: Driver and/orVehicle
Media: Direct Online Database
Coverage: US

Name/Desc: 20/20 Insight
Info Provided: Criminal Information
Media: Direct Online Database
Name/Desc: Claims and Injury Reports
Info Provided: Workers' Compensation
Media: Direct Online Database
Coverage: AR, FL, IA, IL, KS, MA, MD, ME, MI, MS, ND, NE, OH, OK, OR, TX

Statement of Capabilities:
DAC has serviced employers and insurance businesses for more than 15 years, providing employment screening and underwriting/risk

assessment tools. CDLIST contains summary information on more than 6,000,000 drivers. Customers request information by PC and modem via toll-free lines. Computer access is available through networks and mainframe-to-mainframe connections. Customers may opt to call or fax requests to their service representative toll-free.

Daily Report, The

310 H Street
Bakersfield, CA 93304-2914
Telephone: **Fax:**
800-803-6127   805-322-9084
805-322-3226

www.thedailyreport.com
inquires@thedailyreport.com

Applications: Background Info - Business, Background Info - Individuals, Direct Marketing, Filing/Recording Documents, Competitive Intelligence

Proprietary Products:

Name/Desc: The Daily Report
Info Provided: Addresses/Telephone Numbers, Licenses/Registrations/Permits, Criminal Information, Litigation/Judgments/Tax Liens
Media: Internet
Coverage: CA

Database Technologies Inc

4530 Blue Lake Dr
Boca Raton, FL 33431
Telephone: **Fax:**
800-279-7710   561-982-5872
561-982-5000

www.dbtonline.com

Applications: Employment Screening, Fraud Prevention/Detection, General Business Information, Government Document Retrieval, Litigation

Proprietary Products:

Name/Desc: AutoTrackXP
Info Provided: Driver and/or Vehicle, Addresses/Telephone Numbers, Real Estate/Assessor, Corporate/Trade Name Data
Media: Direct Online to Your Computer, Internet
Coverage: US

Name/Desc: AutoTrackXP
Info Provided: Driver and/or Vehicle
Media: Direct Online
Coverage: US

Statement of Capabilities:
DBT Online, Inc. is a leading nationwide provider of organized online public record data and other information.DBT Online's database is one of the country's largest depositories of public records combined with other information, containing more than 4.5 billion records and more than 25 terabytes of data storage capacity. DBT Online's customers use its online information services to detect fraudulent activity, assist law enforcement efforts, locate people and assets, and verify information and identities, as well as many other purposes. AutoTrackXP, DBT Online's product offers powerful search capabilities current and historical records on individuals and businesses. Whether you are investigating fraud, conducting criminal and civil investigations, locating witnesses, finding missing children or locating and verifying assets, AutoTrackXP can deliver comprehensive information right to your desktop. DBT Online employs a state-of-the-art security systems that firewalls, encryption and acitve intrusion detection. Furthermore, we continually test and review our security systems to ensure that they remain the best in the industry. We offer these records in a uniquely integrated and cross-referenced system that is instantly accessible 7 days a week, 24 hours a day.

Datalink

PO Box 188416
Sacramento, CA 95818
Telephone: **Fax:**
800-742-2375   916-452-5096
916-456-7454

www.datalinkservices.com
sales@datalinkservices.com

Applications: Asset/Lien Searching/Verification, Background Info - Business, Employment Screening, Fraud Prevention/Detection, Insurance Underwriting

Proprietary Products:

Name/Desc: Driving, Vehicle & Dealer Records
Info Provided: Driver and/or Vehicle and Dealer Records
Media: Direct Online to Your Computer, Fax-on-Demand, Printed Report and Software
Coverage: US

Statement of Capabilities:
Datalink is a public record research firm that accesses records nationwide. Located just 2 blocks from the California DMV, they provide fast, accurate information to clients. They provide electronic record retrieval for California driving and vehicle records and dealer searches through a proprietary software program. They use a nationwide database to access most state DMV records. A commitment to customer service is their top priority. Their staff has over 15 years in the record research industry, providing reliable technical support on searches.

DataQuick
9171 Towne Centre Dr #600
San Diego, CA 92122
Telephone:
619-455-6900
www.dataquick.com

Applications: Real Estate Transactions, Lending/Leasing, Asset/Lien Searching/Verification, Direct Marketing, Locating People/Businesses

Proprietary Products:

Name/Desc: DataQuick
Info Provided: Real Estate/Assessor
Media: Direct Online, Tape, Disk, Print
Coverage: US

Statement of Capabilities:
A leading name in real property information products, Axiom/DataCheck services the title, mortgage, real estate and insurance industries. They provide property details such as: ownership and address information; sale and loan details; characteristics such as sq footage etc.; and historical sales and data such as previous transactions for marketing and research purposes. They cover household development demographics and market trend data.

DataTech Research
726 Wilson Ave.
Green Bay, WI 54303
Telephone: **Fax:**
920-592-9617 920-592-9645
REILAND@NETNET.NET

Applications: Competitive Intelligence, General Business Information, Government Document Retrieval

Statement of Capabilities:
DataTech Research specializes in Federal and State procurement consulting and research, and provides daily observance of State and Federal acquisitions requests, and timely research of government agency forecasts and acquisitions in any market. Navy veteran Mark Reiland has worked with large and small companies in purchasing and defense contract administration. DataTech helps companies do business with the government, providing timely, accurate information on various government agencies.

DCS Information Systems
500 N Central Expressway #280
Plano, TX 75074
Telephone: **Fax:**
800-394-3274 972-422-3621
972-422-3600

www.dnis.com

Applications: Fraud Prevention/Detection, Locating People/Businesses, Asset/Lien Searching/Verification, Employment Screening, General Business Information

Proprietary Products:

Name/Desc: AmeriFind (DNIS)
Info Provided: Addresses/Telephone Numbers, Credit Information (Header), Real Estate/Assessor and Driver and/or Vehicle
Media: Direct Online, Internet
Coverage: US

Name/Desc: Texas Systems
Info Provided: Driver and/or Vehicle, Criminal Convictions, Credit Information (Header), Real Estate/Assessor, Vital Records (marriage & divorce)
Media: Online, Internet
Coverage: TX

Statement of Capabilities:
DCS' national products, DNIS and AmeriFind are very comprehensive national skip tracing, locating, fraud prevention and investigation tools. The TEXAS product provides comprehensive, up to date, information on Texas drivers and vehicle owners, with up to 12 years' history. These systems provide the users with search capabilities not available from other suppliers. DCS offers customized information solutions for large volume users. The new AmeriFind product is available via the internet.

Derwent Information

1725 Duke Street #250
Alexandria, VA 22314
Telephone: **Fax:**
800-337-9368 703-838-0450
703-706-4220

www.derwent.com
info@derwent.com

Applications: Background Info - Business, Competitive Intelligence, Legal Compliance, Lending/Leasing, Current Events
Proprietary Products:

Name/Desc: Derwent World Patents Index Derwent World Patent Index
Info Provided: Trademarks/Patents, Corporate/Trade Name Data
Media: Direct Online to Your Computer, Internet, Publication/Directory, Printed Report,
Coverage: US,itl

Name/Desc: Patent Explorer
Info Provided: Trademarks/Patents, Corporate/Trade Name Data
Media: US, Itl
Coverage: US, Itl

Statement of Capabilities:
With offices in London, Tokyo, and Alexandria, Derwent provides international patent information and recruitment data oriented to chemicals, engineering, and pharm. They are parent company to The Thomson Corporation. Online hosts include Dialog Corp, Questel.Orbit, DIMDI, and STN as well as their own various media and networks, some customized to client's needs. Additional offices in Japan and London.

Dialog Corporation, The

2440 W El Camino Real
Mountain View, CA 94040
Telephone: **Fax:**
800-334-2564 650-254-7070
650-254-7000

www.dialog.com

Applications: General Business Information, Competitive Intelligence, Direct Marketing, Government Document Retrieval, Background Info - Business
Proprietary Products:

Name/Desc: Profound; DIALOG Web
Info Provided: Foreign Country Information, Corporate/Trade Name Data, Trademarks/Patents, Legislation/Regulation, SEC/Other Financial
Media: Direct Online to Your Computer, Internet, CD-ROM, Software
Coverage: US,Itl

Name/Desc: Profound LiveWire
Info Provided: News/Current Events
Media: Direct Online
Coverage: US

Statement of Capabilities:
The Dialog Corporation provides comprehensive, authoritative sources of information to professionals worldwide. The company was created by the merger of MAID plc and Knight-Rider Information Inc. The Dialog Corporation's complete line of Internet, intranet, CD-ROM and Windows-based products and services have been designed to specifically address individual as well as enterprise-wide information solutions. They include DIALOGWeb, DataStar Web, DIALOG Select, Profound, DIALOG@Site, and Profound LiveWire.

Disclosure Incorporated

5161 River Rd
Bethesda, MD 20816
Telephone: **Fax:**
800-945-3647 301-657-1962
301-951-1300

www.disclosure.com

Applications: Background Info - Business, Competitive Intelligence, General Business Information, Legal Compliance, Litigation

Proprietary Products:

Name/Desc: Compact D/SEC
Info Provided: SEC/Other Financial
Media: CD-ROM, Magnetic Tape, Online Database, Microfiche and Publication
Coverage: US

Name/Desc: Compact D/Canada
Info Provided: SEC/Other Financial
Media: CD-ROM and Publication
Coverage: CD

Name/Desc: Compact D/'33
Info Provided: SEC/Other Financial
Media: CD-ROM
Coverage: US

Name/Desc: Laser D SEC
Info Provided: SEC/Other Financial
Media: CD-ROM
Coverage: US

Name/Desc: Laser D International
Info Provided: SEC/Other Financial
Media: CD-ROM
Coverage: US, Itl

Name/Desc: Worldscope Global
Info Provided: SEC/Other Financial
Media: CD-ROM, Magnetic Tape, Online Database and Publication
Coverage: US, Itl

Statement of Capabilities:
Disclosure has specialized in public company information over the past 20 years. Their newest product, Global Access, provides online access to all EDGAR files. Disclosure's information products have grown from SEC documents filed by US public companies to include virtually every document available to the public. A subsidiary, FDR Information Centers, provides search and retrieval services. Disclosure was the first company to offer SEC documents via CD-ROM. Disclosure later teamed with Wright Investors' Service to provide Worldscope, an extensive database of international companies.

Diversified Information Services Corp

67 East Weldon #220
Phoenix, AZ 85012
Telephone: **Fax:**
602-532-0111   602-532-0393
www.discplats.qpg.com
discplats@aol.com

Applications: Asset/Lien Searching/Verification, Filing/Recording Documents, Insurance Underwriting, Real Estate Transactions

Proprietary Products:

Name/Desc: Real Property Records
Info Provided: Real Estate/Assessor
Media: Direct Online, Disk, CD-ROM, Printed Report, Fax
Coverage: AZ-Maricopa

Statement of Capabilities:
Diversified Information Services is owned by North American Title Agency, Old Republic Title Insurance Agency, Transnation Title, Lawyers Title of Arizona, Fidelity National Title Agency, Stewart Title & Trust of Phoenix, and Nations Title Agency.

Dun & Bradstreet

1 Diamond Hill Rd
Murray Hill, NJ 07974
Telephone:
800-234-3867
908-665-5000

www.dnb.com

Applications: Risk Management, General Business Information, Asset/Lien Searching/Verification, Background Info - Business

Proprietary Products:

Name/Desc: D & B Public Record Search
Info Provided: Addresses/Telephone Numbers, Bankruptcy, Corporate/Trade Name Data, Credit Information, Litigation/Judgments/Tax Liens and Uniform Commercial Code
Media: Call-in Only, Direct Online to Your Computer, Internet, Printed Report, Software and Disk
Coverage: US

Name/Desc: Business Credit Information
Info Provided: Credit Information
Media: Direct Online Database and Call-Back
Coverage: US

Statement of Capabilities:
Dun & Bradstreet's Public Records Search database is one of the most extensive commercial public record information sites available. It is probably the only online database of corporate, UCC, litigation and tax lien information about businesses that covers

all 50 states, the Virgin Islands, Puerto Rico and the District of Columbia. The 800 number listed above is for business credit information.

EdVerifY Inc

880 Jupiter Park Drive
Jupiter, FL 33458
Telephone:
877-338-3743
http://edverify.com

Applications: Background Info - Business, Employment Screening

Proprietary Products:

Name/Desc: EdVerifY.com
Info Provided: Education/Employment
Media: Internet, E-mail, Fax
Coverage: US

Statement of Capabilities:
With the creation of the National Student Records Clearinghouse, EdVerifY is redefining educational verification by providing a one-stop service for educational verification of new hires. It allows employers an efficient due diligence strategy for protection against material misrepresentation on job applications. By consolidating the Directory Information as defined by FERPA, EdVerify acts as the institution's agent and satisfies requests from eligible requesters. All records are matched to the information provided by the student on the application for employement. EdVerifY will provide all records matching the Social Security Number, as provided by the requester. The proprietary database of participating schools is expanding rapidly. Schools not in the database are processed within hours in most cases.

Electronic Property Information Corp (EPIC)

227 Alexander St #206
Rochester, NY 14607
Telephone: **Fax:**
716-454-7390   716-454-7409
Applications: Real Estate
Transactions, Insurance Underwriting, Asset/Lien Searching/Verification, Background Info - Business, Background Info - Individuals

Proprietary Products:

Name/Desc: OPRA
Info Provided: Real Estate/Assessor, Uniform Commerical Code, Litigation/Judgments/Tax Liens and Wills/Probate
Media: Direct Online
Coverage: NY-Erie, Monroe Counties

Name/Desc: OPRA
Info Provided: Bankruptcy
Media: Direct Online Database
Coverage: NY-Northern & Western Districts

Statement of Capabilities:
EPIC provides online access to their proprietary database of all public records affecting real property in Erie and Monroe Counties, NY and bankruptcy records for New York's Western and Northern Districts. In addition to helping create abstracts and write title insurance, the database has been used for collections, asset search, and individual and business screening applications.

Environmental Data Resources Inc

3530 Post Rd
Southport, CT 06490
Telephone: **Fax:**
800-352-0050   800-231-6802
203-255-6606   203-255-1976
www.edrnet.com

Applications: Real Estate
Transactions, Risk Management

Proprietary Products:

Name/Desc: NEDIS, WasteMonitor, Sanborn Maps
Info Provided: Environmental, Licenses/Registratoins/Permits, and Real Estate/Assessor
Media: Online Database, Call-in
Coverage: US

Statement of Capabilities:
Environmental Data Resources (EDR) is an information company specializing in providing data on environmental liabilities associated with companies and properties. EDR provides this data to environmental consulting firms, banks, insurance companies, law firms, corporations and accounting firms. EDR has compiled and organized more than 600 separate government databases, obtained at the federal, state and local levels, into an environmental database referred to as NEDIS,

the National Environmental Data Information System. The WasteMonitor database contains detailed information about more than 5000 non-hazardous waste disposal facilities and more than 500 hazardous treatment, storage and disposal facilities. EDR Sanborn owns the largest and most complete collection of fire insurance maps, with more than 12,000 communities surveyed, dating back to the 1800s.

Equifax Credit Services Division

1600 Peachtree St NW
Atlanta, GA 30309
Telephone:
888-202-4025
404-885-8000
www.equifax.com

Applications: Background Info - Individuals, Employment Screening, Lending/Leasing, Collections

Proprietary Products:

Name/Desc: Acrofile
Info Provided: Credit Information
Media: Direct Online to Your Computer, Internet
Coverage: US

Name/Desc: Persona
Persona
Info Provided: Addresses/Telephone Numbers, Education/Employment, Social Security (Numbers), Credit Information
Media: Direct Online to Your Computer, Internet
Coverage: US

Statement of Capabilities:
Equifax, like its 2 major competitors Experian and Trans Union, provides a full range of consumer credit and related information. Equifax credit services include consumer credit, locate services, fraud detection, and accounts receivable management. They operate globally - in 18 countries with sales in 40. North American Information Services is an Equifax company. Media Relations telephone is 404-888-5452. Consumers may order a credit report at 800-685-1111 or discuss its content at 888-909-7304. Government entities can fax Equifax at 404-885-8215, or e-mail at govetrelequifax.com.

Everton Publishers

PO Box 368
Logan, UT 84323
Telephone:
800-443-6325
801-752-6022
www.everton.com
leverton@everton.com

Applications: Genealogical Research

Proprietary Products:

Name/Desc: Everton's Online Search
Info Provided: Addresses/Telephone Numbers, Social Security (Numbers)
Media: Direct Online
Coverage: US

Statement of Capabilities:
Everton Publishers publish "The Genealogical Helper."

Experian Business Information Solutions

600 City Parkway West
8th FlOrange, CA 92868
Telephone:
800-831-5614
www.experian.com

Applications: Lending/Leasing, Asset/Lien Searching/Verification, Background Info - Business

Proprietary Products:

Name/Desc: Business Credit Information
Info Provided: Uniform Commercial Code, Bankruptcy, Litigation/Judgments/Tax Liens, Corporate/Trade Name Data
Media: Direct Online to Your Computer, Printed Report
Coverage: US

Statement of Capabilities:
Experian Business Information Solutions is the business credit arm of Experian. Although this division is located in Orange, CA, they prefer inquiries to go through the main Experian switchboard (800-831-5614 in Allen, TX) first, then allow access to the California site at 714-385-7000.

Experian Consumer Credit

425 Martingale Rd #600
Schaumburg, IL 60173
Telephone:
800-831-5614
www.experian.com

Applications: Lending/Leasing,
Employment Screening, Tenant Screening
Proprietary Products:

Name/Desc: Consumer File
Consumer File
Info Provided: Credit Information,
Addresses/Telephone Numbers
Media: Direct Online to Your Computer,
Printed Report
Coverage: US

Statement of Capabilities:
As the consumer credit arm of Experian,
formerly TRW, data from here may be used for
a variety of purposes related to individuals,
subject to permissible purposes. Individuals
who need assistance with reports should call
888-397-3742.

Experian Target Marketing Services

701 Experian Parkway
Allen, TX 70013
Telephone: **Fax:**
800-527-3933 972-390-5001
972-390-5000

www.experian.com

Applications: Direct Marketing
Proprietary Products:

Name/Desc: Various Experian Databases
Various Experian Databases
Info Provided: Addresses/Telephone
Numbers, Driver and/or Vehicle
Media: Disk, Magnetic Tape, Printed Report
Coverage: US

Statement of Capabilities:
Experian Target Marketing Services is a list
compiler that utilizes Experian's overall
information - collected from such sources as
the NCOA file - to provide support to direct
marketers to businesses and individuals. Their
MV database includes 42+ million vehicle
owners and vehicle characteristics in 32 states
and is available when and where legally
permissible. Combining vehicle selections
with their demographic, lifestyle, and other

selections allows for higher focused targeting.
Other Experian divisions are profiled
separately.

Explore Information Services

4920 Moundview Dr
Red Wing, MN 55066
Telephone: **Fax:**
800-531-9125 651-385-2281
651-385-2284

www.exploredata.com

Applications: Insurance Underwriting
Proprietary Products:

Name/Desc: EARS
Info Provided: Driver and/or Vehicle
Media: Direct Online, Magnetic Tape and
Disk
Coverage: CO, FL, IA, KY, ME, MN, MO,
NE, NH, OH, TN, UT, WI

Statement of Capabilities:
Their Electronically Accessed Reunderwriting
Service (EARS), is a database of driver
information, including violation history, that
can be customized for use by insurance
industry clients. RiskAlert is a service that
identifies all licensed drivers in a household.

Federal Filings Inc

601 Pennsylvania Ave NW
South Bldg #700 Washington, DC 20004-2601
Telephone: **Fax:**
800-487-6162 202-393-0974
202-393-7400

www.fedfil.com

Applications: General Business
Information, Litigation, Legal Compliance
Proprietary Products:

Name/Desc: EDGAR
Info Provided: SEC/Other Financial
Media: Direct Online
Coverage: US

Name/Desc: Federal Filings Business News
Info Provided: News/Current Events
Media: Direct Online Database, Newsletters
Coverage: US

Statement of Capabilities:
Federal Filings provides a number of different
services based on access to federal records,
including SEC filings, bankruptcy and civil

court cases, and research at other federal agencies in Washington, DC such as the FCC. SEC services include monitoring specific public company filings. Court services include monitoring companies for new cases and new pleadings in existing cases. Copies of 10Ks and 10Qs may be ordered through their online system. Federal Filings also has a library of bankruptcy documents dating back to 1988.

Felonies R Us

1423 W 3rd #21
Little Rock, AR 72201

Telephone: **Fax:**
501-376-4719   501-376-4619

Applications: Employment Screening, Fraud Prevention/Detection, General Business Information, Litigation, Tenant Screening

Proprietary Products:

Name/Desc: AR Felonies
Info Provided: Criminal Information
Media: Fax-on-Demand and Printed Report
Coverage: AR

Statement of Capabilities:
Felonies 'R' Us maintains an updated criminal database obtained from the Arkansas Administrative Office of the Courts. Able to run statewide searches, they retrieve documents desired by the client.

Fidelifacts

50 Broadway
New York, NY 10004

Telephone: **Fax:**
800-678-0007   212-248-5619
212-425-1520

www.fidelifacts.com
norton@fidelifacts.com

Applications: Background Info - Business, Background Info - Individuals, Employment Screening, Litigation

Proprietary Products:

Name/Desc: Fidelifacts Data Bank
Info Provided: Criminal Information
Media: Call-in
Coverage: NY

Statement of Capabilities:
Among the oldest companies engaged in the business of providing background reports on individuals for employment purposes and on

companies, Fidelifacts has a network of investigators in offices around the country, and local personnel who examine public records in less populated areas. Fidelifacts specialty is conducting background investigations, reference checks, screening checks of job applicants and due diligence investigations. They also provide asset location services, skip tracing and other services on legal matters. Their in-house database lists 1,500,000 names of persons arrested, indicted, convicted, and otherwise had problems with the law. Data is primarily for metro New York area, but also includes SEC/NASD filings where unlawful activity may be a question. Note: their office is located 1/2 block from the NY State Office of Court Administration and they have personnel there on a daily basis.

Finder Group, The

PO Box 11740
Kansas City, KS 64138

Telephone: **Fax:**
800-501-8455   816-737-5225
816-737-5005

finder@solve.net

Applications: Asset/Lien Searching/Verification, Background Info - Business, Background Info - Individuals, General Business Information, Locating People/Businesses

Statement of Capabilities:
The Finder Group is a professional search firm designed to bridge the gap between end users and repositories. Economical access to public records includes criminal, civil, MVR, asset, background and address information. A web site is planned with links to sites for public record searching.

First American Real Estate Solutions

5601 E. La Palma Ave
Anaheim, CA 92807

Telephone: **Fax:**
800-345-7334   800-406-2907
714-701-2150   714-701-9231

www.firstAm.com

Applications: Real Estate Transactions, Lending/Leasing, Asset/Lien Searching/Verification, Background Info - Business, Background Info - Individuals

Proprietary Products:

Name/Desc: Real Property Database
Info Provided: Real Estate/Assessor
Media: Online Database, CD-ROM and Microfiche
Coverage: AL, AZ, CA, CO, DC, DE, FL, GA, HI, IL, IN, LA, MA, MD, MI, MN, MS, NC, NJ, NM, NY, NV, OH, OK, OR, PA, SC, TN, TX, UT, VA, VI, WA, WI

Statement of Capabilities:
Now independent of Experian Inc, First American Real Estate Solutions is now part of the First American Financial Corporation. They are a leading provider of real estate information from major counties in most US states. Call for specific coverage and access via online database, CD-ROM and microfiche information.

FOIA Group Inc

1090 Vermont Ave NW # 800
Washington, DC 20005
Telephone: **Fax:**
202-408-7028   202-347-8419
www.FOIA.com
FOIA@FOIA.com

Applications: Competitive Intelligence, Government Document Retrieval, Litigation

Proprietary Products:

Name/Desc: FOIA-Ware
Info Provided: Software/Training
Media: Internet, Software and Disk
Coverage: US

Statement of Capabilities:
FOIA specializes in the Freedom of Information Act and State Open Records Act protocols. They help prepare and file FOIA requests, monitor and review documents, and service the legal profession and others seeking information through the Act. They also offer agency and customer competitive research and surveys. FOIA Group attorneys provide whistleblower assistance.

Folks Finders Ltd

PO Box 880
Neoga, IL 62447
Telephone: **Fax:**
800-277-3318   800-476-0782

www.pimall.com/folkfinders/folkfind.htm
Applications: Locating People/Businesses

Proprietary Products:

Name/Desc: Birth Index
Info Provided: Vital Records
Media: Printed Report
Coverage: NYC, IL, CA, OH, KY, MI, NJ, CT, NC, ND. Oky

Name/Desc: Birth Records Index
Name/Desc: Cemetery Internment
Info Provided: Vital Records
Media: US

Statement of Capabilities:
Folks Finders specializes in finding folks, missing persons, that may not object to being located. Most service charges are based on a "NO FIND-NO FEE" philosophy. Categories of searches include no-name pension beneficiaries, health-science related searches, and adoption searches. As part of their expertise, they obtain and provide vital records worldwide. They have begun "alternate identity" locating. They also market actual original certified "Celebrity" death certificates for the serious collector. Branch offices are located in: Delvan, WI; Paducah, KY; Bradenton, FL; San Jose, CA; Marshall, TX; and Wallingford, CT.

Gale Group Inc, The

27500 Drake Rd
Framington Hills, MI 48331-3535
Telephone: **Fax:**
800-877-4253
248-699-4253

www.gale.com
galeord@gale.com

Applications: Background Info - Business, Current Events, Genealogical Research

Proprietary Products:

Name/Desc: GaleNet
Info Provided: Associations/Trade Groups, Addresses/Telephone Numbers and Corporate/Trade Name Data
Media: Direct Online
Coverage: US, Itl

Statement of Capabilities:
As a major publisher of academic, educational, and business research companies serving libraries, educational institutions, and businesses in all major international markets, The Gale Group provides much of its material online through products such as Associations Unlimited, Biography and Genealogy Master Index, Brands and Their Companies, Gale Business Resources, and Peterson's Publications. It was formed Sept. '98 with the merger of Gale Research, Information Access Co., and Primary Source Material.

Haines & Company Inc

8050 Freedom Ave
North canton, OH 44720

Telephone: **Fax:**
800-843-8452   330-494-0226
330-494-9111

www.haines.com
criscros@haines.com

Applications: Collections, Direct Marketing, Insurance Underwriting, Lending/Leasing, Locating People/Businesses

Proprietary Products:

Name/Desc: Criss+Cross Directory
Info Provided: Addresses/Telephone Numbers
Media: Publication/Directory
Coverage: US

Name/Desc: Criss+Cross Plus CD-ROM
Info Provided: Address/Telephone Numbers
Media: CD-ROM
Coverage: US

Name/Desc: Criss+Cross Plus Real Estate
Info Provided: Real Estate/Assessor
Media: CD-ROM
Coverage: US

Name/Desc: Criss+Cross Plus Online
Info Provided: Address/Telephone Numbers, Real Esate/Assessor
Media: Direct Online to Your Computer
Coverage: US

Name/Desc: Criss+Cross Natl Look-Up Library
Info Provided: Addresses/Telephone Numbers
Media: Call-in Only
Coverage: US

Name/Desc: Americalist

Media: Disk, Lists or labels and Magnetic Tape
Coverage: US

Statement of Capabilities:
Varied products and full-service capabilities allow Haines & Company to satisfy the marketing and research needs of most industries. County Real Estate on CD-ROM has been noted for its ease of use, speed and marketing power. They also offer cross-reference directories in book form or on CD-ROM in 71 major markets, also business and residential lists on labels, manuscripts, CD-ROM, off the Internet or bulletin boards (24-hour turnaround time available). Using their target list or a customer-provided list, they can provide complete direct marketing services, graphic design, printing and database maintenance -- all in-house.

Hogan Information Services

14000 Quail Springs Parkway #4000
Oklahoma, OK 73134

Telephone:
405-278-6954

www.hoganinfo.com
hogan.data@firstdatacorp.com

Applications: Lending/Leasing, Risk Management, Employment Screening, Tenant Screening, Background Info - Individuals

Proprietary Products:

Name/Desc: Hogan Online
Info Provided: Bankruptcy
Media: Direct Online, Disk, Lists, Labels, Magnetic Tape
Coverage: US

Statement of Capabilities:
Hogan Information Services provides high-quality national public record information to credit bureaus, bankcard issuers, collection agencies, retail institutions, and other businesses through various First Data business units. Founded in 1990, in 1996 Hogan Information Services became a business unit of First Data Corp. Hogan gathers public record information on laptop computers in over 8,000 courthouses nationwide for business to business applications. They specialize in helping businesses make smarter decisions and manage risk by using public record information.

Hollingsworth Court Reporting Inc

10761 Perkins Rd #A
Baton Rouge, LA 70810
Telephone: **Fax:**
225-769-3386 225-769-1814
www.hcrinc.com
Nora@hcrinc.com

Applications: General Business
Information, Background Info - Business,
Employment Screening, Government
Document Retrieval, Filing/Recording
Documents
Proprietary Products:

Name/Desc: Public Record Report
Info Provided: Litigation/Judgments/Tax
Liens
Media: Direct Online, E-mail, FTP, Internet
Coverage: AL, AR, FL, GA, LA, MS, TN

Name/Desc: Tenant Eviction Report
Info Provided:
Judgments/Possessions/Complaints
Media: Direct Online, E-mail, FTP, Internet
Coverage: AL, AR, FL, GA, IL, LA, MS, TN

Statement of Capabilities:
HCR offers regional public record information
including access to 25 million records. We
have judgment, lien & eviction information.
We also process criminal record searches with
a 48 hour turnaround time.

Hoovers Inc

1033 La Posada Drive #250
Austin, TX 78752
Telephone: **Fax:**
800-486-8666 512-374-4505
512-374-4500
www.hoovers.com
info@hoovers.com

Applications: General Business
Information, Background Info - Business,
Competitive Intelligence, Locating
People/Businesses
Proprietary Products:

Name/Desc: Hoover's Company Profiles
Info Provided: Addresses/Telephone
Numbers, Corporate/Trade Name Data,
News/Current Events
Media: Direct Online to Your Computer,
Printed Report, Internet

Coverage: US, Itl
Name/Desc: Real-Time SEC Documents
Info Provided: SEC/Other Financial
Media: Direct Online to Your Computer,
Printed Report, Internet
Coverage: US

Statement of Capabilities:
Hoovers offers a wide range of company
information, much for investing purposes.
Their published materials are distributed
electronically and in print, and they claim their
databases are among the least expensive
sources of information on operations,
strategies, etc. of major US and global and
private companies.

Household Drivers Reports Inc (HDR Inc)

902 S Friendswood Dr Suite F
Friendswood, TX 77546
Telephone: **Fax:**
800-899-4437 281-996-1947
281-996-5509
www.hdr.com
sthomas@hdr.com

Applications: Fraud
Prevention/Detection, Litigation, Collections,
Insurance Underwriting, Locating
People/Businesses
Proprietary Products:

Name/Desc: Corp Data
Info Provided: Corporation/Trade Name Data
Media: Direct Online to Your Computer
Coverage: TX

Name/Desc: Criminal Information
Info Provided: Criminal Information
Media: Direct Online to Your Computer
Coverage: TX

Name/Desc: Driver & Vehicle
Info Provided: Driver and/or Vehicle
Media: Direct Online to Your Computer
Coverage: TX

Name/Desc: Vital Records
Info Provided: Vital Records
Media: Direct Online to Your Computer
Coverage: TX

Statement of Capabilities:
Household Drivers Report Inc has been in the
information business since 1989, at which time

it pioneered its first online database. From your PC, HDR subscribers can access the information available through HDR's online system with the slightest amount of information. The HDR system offers the unique capability of wildcard searches. With only a partial last name, plate, VIN or address, HDR can locate that person or business and identify a wealth of information. Their driver and vehicle information is updated weekly. HDR is an online, real time database system, providing results to you within minutes. They offer a "no-hit, no-charge" feautre on their online searches as well as a competitive pricing structure. The system is available to qualified professionals in law enforcement, private investigatioon, insurance fraud investigation, business professionals and security investigations. HDR offers customize information solutions for large volume users. They operate strictly in compliance with the myriad of state and federal laws. The HDR system allows you access to the following: Texas: driver license records, vehicle registration records, business records, vehicle by manufacturer, automatic driver update report, criminal conviction records, sex offender records, marriage, death, divorce records; Nationwide: moving violation reports. New databases are added periodically.

IDM Corporation

3550 W Temple St
Los Angeles, CA 90004
Telephone: **Fax:**
877-436-3282 213-389-9569
213-389-2793

Applications: Asset/Lien
Searching/Verification, Direct Marketing,
Fraud Prevention/Detection, Lending/Leasing,
Real Estate Transactions

Proprietary Products:

Name/Desc: Tax, Assessor and Recorders
Info Provided: Real Estate/Assessor
Media: Disk and Direct Online to Your
Computer
Coverage: US

Statement of Capabilities:
IDM Corporation is one of the largest source providers of real estate public records. They convert 900 tax/assessor counties and 500 recorder's counties to a uniform format. Their

assessment files are updated once per year, and recorder's are updated weekly.

Infocon Corporation

PO Box 568
Ebensburg, PA 15931-0568
Telephone: **Fax:**
814-472-6066 814-472-5019
Applications: Background Info -
Individuals, Real Estate Transactions,
Litigation, Risk Management, Genealogical
Research

Proprietary Products:

Name/Desc: INFOCON County Access
System
Info Provided: Criminal Information, Vital
Records, Voter Registration,
Litigation/Judgments/Tax Liens, Real
Estate/Assessor
Media: Direct Online to Your Computer
Coverage: PA-12 Western Counties

Statement of Capabilities:
The Infocon County Access System offers online access to civil, criminal, real estate, and vital record information in Pennsylvania counties of Armstrong, Bedford, Blair, Butler, Clarion, Clinton, Erie, Huntingdon, Lawrence, Mifflin, Potter, and Pike. Fees are involved, access is through a remote 800 number.

Inform Alaska Inc

PO Box 190908
Anchorage, AK 99519-0908
Telephone: **Fax:**
907-258-4636 907-277-8294
InformAlaska@att.net

Applications: Background Info -
Business, Background Info - Individuals,
General Business Information, Litigation,
Government Document Retrieval

Proprietary Products:

Statement of Capabilities:
Inform Alaska is unique for performing "retrospective" searches in prior-dated issues of Alaskan newspapers and Journals. Inform Alaska is the publisher of Alaska Court Review, a monthly summary and index of all the Alaska Supreme Court and Court of Appeals opinions. Sample copies are sent upon request. Owner is attorney with 20 years

experience in state government, legal affairs, legislation, and agency administration.

Information America Inc

Marquis One Tower #1400
245 Peachtree Center AveAtlanta, GA 30303

Telephone: **Fax:**
800-235-4008 800-845-6319
404-479-6500

www.infoam.com

Applications: Lending/Leasing, Background Info - Business, Asset/Lien Searching/Verification, Litigation, Locating People/Businesses

Proprietary Products:

Name/Desc: Bankruptcy Records
Info Provided: Bankruptcy
Media: Online Database and Call back
Coverage: US

Name/Desc: Corporations and Partnerships
Info Provided: Corporate/Trade Name Data
Media: Online Database and Call back
Coverage: US

Name/Desc: Lawsuits, Judgments, Liens
Info Provided: Litigation/Judgments/Tax Liens
Media: Direct Online Database and Call back
Coverage: US

Name/Desc: Professional Licenses
Info Provided: Licenses/Registrations/Permits
Media: Direct Online Database and Call back
Coverage: AZ, CA, CO, CT, FL, GA, IL, IN, LA, MA, MD, MI, NJ, OH, PA, SC, TN, TX, VA, WI

Name/Desc: Real Estate, Liens and Judgments
Info Provided: Real Estate/Assessor, Litigation/Judgments/Tax Liens
Media: Direct Online Database and Call back
Coverage: US

Name/Desc: UCCs
Info Provided: Uniform Commerical Code
Media: Direct Online Database and Call back
Coverage: US

Name/Desc: Watercraft Locator/Aircraft Locator
Info Provided: Aviation/Vessels
Media: Direct Online Database and Call back
Coverage: US

Name/Desc: Business Finder/People Finder
Info Provided: Motor Vehicle Records

Media: Direct Online Database, Internet and Call back
Coverage: US

Name/Desc: Motor Vehicle Records
Info Provided: Driver and/or Vehicle
Media: Direct Online to Your Computer

Statement of Capabilities:
Information America combines and links public records and courthouse documents with information from private sources to address the relationships between corporations, people and their assets. Banks, financial service companies, corporations, law firms and government agencies across the nation use their online and document retrieval services to obtain background data on businesses, locate assets and people, retrieve official public records and solve business problems. Information America was founded by a practicing attorney and a computer systems expert acquainted with the needs of government, legal and corporate customers. A related company, Document Resources, is a national search firm.

Information Inc

PO Box 382
Hermitage, TN 37076

Telephone: **Fax:**
615-884-8000 615-889-6492
www.members.aol.com/infomant n/info.html
infomantn@aol.com

Applications: Background Info - Individuals, Collections, Employment Screening, Litigation, Tenant Screening

Proprietary Products:

Name/Desc: Arrest Database
Info Provided: Criminal Information
Media: Direct Online to Your Computer
Coverage: TN-Nashville

Statement of Capabilities:
Information Inc provides a real time criminal arrest database for Davidson County, TN. This includes all agencies in the 20th Judicial District of Tennessee.

Information Network of Arkansas

425 West Capitol Ave #3565
Little Rock, AR 72201

Telephone:
800-392-6069
501-324-8900

www.state.ar.us/ina/about_in
a.html

info@ark.org

Applications: Background Info - Business, General Business Information, Employment Screening, Insurance Underwriting

Proprietary Products:

Name/Desc: INA
Info Provided: Driver and/or Vehicle
Media: Internet
Coverage: AR

Statement of Capabilities:
The Information Network of Arkansas was created by the Arkansas Legislature with the responsibility of assisting the state in permitting citizens to access public records. More categories of records will soon be available. There is a fee for driving record access; there may not be fees for other record categories.

Information Network of Kansas

534 S Kansas Ave #1210
Topeka, KS 66603
Telephone: **Fax:**
800-452-6727   785-296-5563
785-296-5059

www.ink.org

Applications: General Business Information, Employment Screening, Insurance Underwriting, Lending/Leasing, Legal Compliance

Proprietary Products:

Name/Desc: Premium Services
Info Provided: Driver and/or Vehicle, Uniform Commercial Code, Corporate/Trade Name Data, Legislation/Regulations, Real Estate/Assessor
Media: Internet, Direct Online
Coverage: KS

Name/Desc: Premium Services
Info Provided: Litigation/Judgements/Tax Liens
Media: Internet, Direct Online
Coverage: KS-Johnson, Sedgwick, Shawnee, Wyandotte

Name/Desc: Premium Services
Info Provided: Criminal Information
Media: Direct Online, Internet
Coverage: KS- Sedgwick, Shawnee, Wyandotte

Statement of Capabilities:
INK is the official source for electronic access to the State of Kansas government information. Access to public record information listed here requires a subscription.

Informus Corporation

2001 Airport Rd #201
Jackson, MS 39208
Telephone: **Fax:**
800-364-8380   800-660-8340
601-664-1900

www.informus.com

info@informus.com

Applications: Employment Screening, Locating People/Businesses, Background Info - Individuals, Collections

Proprietary Products:

Name/Desc: Informus
Info Provided: Workers' Compensation
Media: Direct Online, Printed Report
Coverage: MS, US

Name/Desc: IntroScan
Info Provided: Addresses/Telephone Numbers, Social Security (Numbers)
Media: Direct Online, Printed Report
Coverage: US

Statement of Capabilities:
Informus provides an online pre-employment screening and public record retrieval service. Online access is available through the Internet. Some searches provide instant information, depending on state and category.

Insurance Information Exchange (iiX)

PO Box 30001
College Station, TX 77842-3001
Telephone: **Fax:**
800-683-8553   409-696-5584
www.iix.com
Applications: Insurance Underwriting
Proprietary Products:

Name/Desc: Motor Vehicle Reports
Info Provided: Driver and/or Vehicle

Media: Direct Online to Your Computer, Fax-on-Demand, Internet and Printed Report
Coverage: US

Name/Desc: UDI
Info Provided: Driver and/or Vehicle
Media: Direct Online to Your Computer, Fax-on-Demand, Internet and Printed Report
Coverage: US

Name/Desc: CLUE
Info Provided: Driver and/or Vehicle
Media: Direct Online to Your Computer
Coverage: US

Name/Desc: UNCLE
Info Provided: Driver and/or Vehicle
Media: Direct Online to Your Computer
Coverage: US

Name/Desc: A+
Info Provided: Driver and/or Vehicle
Media: Direct Online to Your Computer
Coverage: US

Name/Desc: MVP
Info Provided: Driver and/or Vehicle
Media: Direct Online to Your Computer
Coverage: US

Statement of Capabilities:
iiX is an established provider of information systems to the insurance industry. Their services and products include MVR, claims, undisclosed driver, and other underwriting services. Users still call this system AMS or AMSI. They are one of the leading providers of driving records to search firms and investigators.

Intranet Inc

107 E Erwin
Tyler, TX 75702
Telephone: **Fax:**
903-593-9817   903-593-8183
Applications: Asset/Lien
Searching/Verification, Litigation, General Business Information, Direct Marketing
Proprietary Products:

Name/Desc: Bankscan
Info Provided: Bankruptcy
Media: Disk
Coverage: TX

Statement of Capabilities:
Intranet specializes in bankruptcy research and retrieval services for the state of Texas.

Investigators Anywhere Resource Line

PO Box 40970
Mesa, AZ 85274-0970
Telephone: **Fax:**
800-338-3463   480-730-8103
480-730-8088

www.IONINC.com
IONPRRN@IONINC.com

Applications: Risk Management, Litigation, Legal Compliance, Litigation, Fraud Prevention/Detection
Proprietary Products:

Name/Desc: Resource Line
Info Provided: Addresses/Telephone Numbers
Media: Call-in
Coverage: US, Itl

Statement of Capabilities:
Investigators Anywhere Resources' Resource Line service provides access to over 30,000 investigators, prescreened for excellence of service levels. Callers are matched to appropriate investigators. No fee to the callers except for international and non-commercial projects.

IQ Data Systems

1401 El Camino Ave, 5th Fl
Sacramento, CA 95815
Telephone: **Fax:**
800-264-6517   800-528-2813
916-418-9000   916-418-1000

www.jim@iqdata.com
jim@iqdata.com

Applications: Locating People/Businesses, Employment Screening, Fraud Prevention/Detection, Lending/Leasing, Document Retrieval
Proprietary Products:

Name/Desc: IQ Data
Info Provided: Uniform Commercial Code, Bankruptcy, Real Estate/Assessor, Litigation/Judgments/Tax Liens, Addresses/Telephone Numbers, Corporate/Trade Name Data
Media: Internet

Coverage: US

Info Provided: Driver and/or Vehicle, Credit Information
Media: Internet
Coverage: US

Statement of Capabilities:
IQ Data Systems is a leading nationwide online public record information provider. Accurate, up-to-date cost effective and instant easy-to-access national data to verify information and identities, conduct background checks, locate people/business/assets, detect fraud, find criminal/civil/financial records, assist law enforcement and more. Empowering corporations, government agencies and individuals to maximize the use and value of public record information. IQ Data's cutting edge technology and proprietary databases direct its customers to make better, timely and more informed decisions.

IRSC

3777 N Harbor Blvd
Fullerton, CA 92835
Telephone: **Fax:**
800-640-4772   714-526-5836
714-526-8485

www.irsc.com

Applications: Asset/Lien Searching/Verification, Background Info - Business, Competitive Intelligence, Fraud Prevention/Detection, Locating People/Businesses

Proprietary Products:

Name/Desc: IRSC
Info Provided: Social Security (Numbers), Education/Employment, Aviation/Vessels, Credit Information, Addresses/Telephone Numbers, Environmental, Uniform Commercial Code and Litigation/Judgments/Tax Liens
Media: Direct Online
Coverage: US

Name/Desc: IRSC
Info Provided: Corporate/Trade Name Data
Media: Direct Online Database
Coverage: US

Name/Desc: IRSC
Info Provided: Bankruptcy
Media: Direct Online Database
Coverage: US

Name/Desc: IRSC (Criminal Court Index)
Info Provided: Criminal Information
Media: Direct Online Database
Coverage: US

Name/Desc: IRSC
Info Provided: Workers' Compensation
Media: Direct Online Database
Coverage: Ak, AL, AR, AZ, CA, CO, DC, DE, FL, IA, ID, IL, IN, KS, KY, MA, MD, ME, MI, MO, MT, NE, NH, NM, NV, OH, OK, OR, RI, SC, SD, TX, UT, VA, VT, WY

Name/Desc: IRSC
Info Provided: Real Estate/Assessor
Media: Direct Online Database
Coverage: AK, AL, AR, AZ, CA, CO, CT, DC, DE, FL, GA, HI, IL, KY, LA, MA, MD, MI, MN, MO, MS, NC, NJ, NV, NY, OH, OK, PA, SC, TN, TX, UT, VA, WI

Name/Desc: IRSC
Info Provided: Driver and/or Vehicle
Coverage: US

Statement of Capabilities:
Information Resource Service Company (IRSC) has an investigative database that accesses more than one billion records about individuals and businesses. Their database is available online 24 hours a day. They do not charge for connect time. A Windows-based front end program is available.

KnowX

245 Peachtree Center Ave #1400
Atlanta, GA 30303
www.search3.knowx.com
support@knowx.com

Applications: Asset/Lien Searching/Verification, Background Info - Business, Competitive Intelligence, Locating People/Businesses, Government Document Retrieval

Proprietary Products:

Name/Desc: KnowX
Info Provided: Addresses/Telephone Numbers, Bankruptcy, Licenses/Registrations/Permits, Corporate/Trade Name Data, Aviation/Vessels, Litigation/Judgments/Tax Liens, Uniform Commercial Code
Media: Direct Online to Your Computer, Internet
Coverage: US

Statement of Capabilities:
KnowX, a division of Information America (owned by West Group and Thomson Corp.) is one of the most comprehensive sources of public records available on the Internet. Included is aircraft ownership, bankruptcies, business directories, partnerships, DBAs, DEAs, death records, Duns, judgments, liens, lawsuits, licensing, residencies, real property foreclosures & refinancings, tax records, property transfers, sales permits, stock ownership, UCC and watercraft records.

Law Bulletin Information Network

415 N State
Chicago, IL 60610-4674
Telephone: **Fax:**
312-644-7800   312-527-2890
www.lawbulletin.com
Applications: Asset/Lien Searching/Verification, Locating People/Businesses, Employment Screening
Proprietary Products:

Name/Desc: Access Plus
Info Provided: Real Estate/Assessor
Media: Direct Online
Coverage: IL-Cook County

Name/Desc: Access Plus
Info Provided: Litigation/Judgments/Tax Liens
Media: Direct Online Database
Coverage: IL-Central, North Counties

Name/Desc: Access Plus
Info Provided: Addresses/Telephone Numbers
Media: Direct Online Database
Coverage: IL

Statement of Capabilities:
The Law Bulletin Publishing Company's Information Network, called access Plus, provides both online and access to Illinois Courts, vital public record information, corporate documents, realty sales, etc. They offer other useful DocuCheck services online, and also licensed investigative services.

Legi-Slate Inc

10 G Street NE #500
Washington, DC 20002
Telephone: **Fax:**
800-733-1131   202-898-3030

202-898-2300
www.legislate.com
legislate@legislate.com
Applications: Current Events, Legal Compliance
Proprietary Products:

Name/Desc: Legi-Slate
Info Provided: Legislation/Regulations
Media: Direct Online
Coverage: US

Statement of Capabilities:
Legi-Slate provides expert guidance on federal and state government issues. Includes federal regulations, analysis, news, and current events, with timely delivery and responsive customized support.

LEXIS-NEXIS

PO Box 933
Dayton, OH 45401-0933
Telephone:
800-227-9597
937-865-6800
www.lexis-nexis.com
Applications: Legal Compliance, Current Events, General Business Information, Competitive Intelligence, Government Document Retrieval
Proprietary Products:

Name/Desc: LEXIS Law Publishing
Info Provided: Litigation/Judgments/Tax Liens
Media: Direct Online to Your Computer, Internet
Coverage: US

Name/Desc: Shepard's
Info Provided: Litigation/Judgments/Tax Liens
Media: Direct Online to Your Computer, Internet
Coverage: US

Name/Desc: Congressional Information Service
Info Provided: Legislation/Regulation
Media: Direct Online to Your Computer, CD-ROM
Coverage: US

Statement of Capabilities:
For more than 10 years, LEXIS-NEXIS has been building one of the largest collection of

public records in the US, and today is an industry leader in providing information to a variety of professionals in law, law enforcement, business, research, and academia. Four main business units are LEXIS, NEXIS, Reed Technologies & Information Systems, and Martindale-Hubbell. Their Quick-Check provides clients with company news and credit rating changes, brokerage reports, SEC filings, trends and views/analysis of companies, their debts, equities, and earnings estimates, etc.

LIDA Credit Agency Inc

450 Sunrise Hwy
Rockville Centre, NY 11570
Telephone: **Fax:**
516-678-4600 516-678-4611
Applications: Litigation, Real Estate
Transactions, Background Info - Business,
Asset/Lien Searching/Verification,
Employment Screening
Proprietary Products:

Name/Desc: LIDA
Info Provided: Litigation/Judgments/Tax
Liens
Media: Printed Report and Call-back
Coverage: DE, NJ, NY, PA

Statement of Capabilities:
LIDA's management averages more than 35 years in public record research, investigations and credit/financial reporting. Among their 17 member staff are five licensed and bonded private investigators. They specialize in Metro New York City, including the five boroughs and surrounding counties.

Lloyds Maritime Information Services Inc

1200 Summer St
Stamford, CT 06905
Telephone: **Fax:**
800-423-8672 203-358-0437
203-359-8383
www.lmis.com
lmisusa@llplimited.com
Applications: General Business
Information, Direct Marketing, Background
Info - Business, Asset/Lien
Searching/Verification

Proprietary Products:

Name/Desc: SEADATA
Info Provided: Aviation/Vessels
Media: Direct Online to Your Computer,
Internet
Coverage: US, Itl

Name/Desc: APEX (Analysis of Petroleum
Exports)
Info Provided: Economic/Demographic
Media: Disk
Coverage: US, Itl

Name/Desc: SeaSearcher
Info Provided: Aviation/Vessels
Media: Direct Online to Your Computer,
Internet
Coverage: US, Itl

Name/Desc: AS+ (Analysis Software +)
Info Provided: Economic/Demographic
Media: Disk
Coverage: US, Itl

Statement of Capabilities:
Lloyd's Maritime Information Services (LMIS) provides the maritime business community with access to the world's most authoritative, up-to-date and comprehensive source of computerized international maritime information, derived from the databases of it's two principles LLP Ltd. (now part of the Informa Group) and Lloyd's Register. This gives access to an unparaled range of information on the world commercial shipping fleet of vessels of 100gt and above (some 85,000+ vessels) and a vast resource for colecting, maintaining and verifying the data. The LMIS mission is to provide decision ready data. Data can be provided as a custom built service on CD Rom, diskette or via e-mail and can also be accessed through a wide range of standard products such as the online systems SeaSearcher and SeaData and the PC databases AS+ and Fleet Information Database. The Market Intelligence Division of LMIS provides industry specific products for the oil and liner markets as well as producing the prestigious Lloyd's Shipping Economist magazine and offering ad-hoc consultancy services, forecasting and market research..

Logan Information Services
636-B Piney Forest Rd #172
Danville, VA 24540

Telephone: **Fax:**
888-640-8613   804-836-6709
804-791-0808

LISINC@gamewood.net

Applications: Direct Marketing,
Employment Screening, Real Estate
Transactions, Tenant Screening, Asset/Lien
Searching/Verification

Proprietary Products:

Name/Desc: Driving Records
Info Provided: Driver and/or Vehicle
Media: Direct Online to Your Computer and
Printed Report
Coverage: CA

Name/Desc: LIS 5
Info Provided: Litigation/Judgments/Tax
Liens, Tenant History, Uniform Commercial
Code, Voter Registration and
Education/Employment
Media: Printed Report and Internet
Coverage: NC, VA

Statement of Capabilities:
Logan Information Services is an information
retrieval and verification company providing
public records research services to some of the
country's largest and best known corporations.
Their services include criminal, civil and real
estate record searches. One of the principals of
the organization was a key employee for a
major consumer information provider; he has
trained his staff to ensure that each report will
be accurately prepared and timely received.
Turnaround time on searches is 24-48 hours,
depending on the type of search requested.
"Rush" service is available on all searches.

Logan Registration Service Inc

PO Box 161644
Sacramento, CA 95816
Telephone: **Fax:**
800-524-4111   916-457-5789
916-457-5787

Applications: Asset/Lien
Searching/Verification, Background Info -
Business, Background Info - Individuals

Statement of Capabilities:
Logan has more than 20 year experience
working with California driver and vehicle
records. They are an online vendor that allows
their DMV authorized clients to retrieve driver
and vehicle registration records in seconds with

a computer software program that is available
free of charge. Clients are also able to access
needed records via phone or fax.

Loren Data Corp

4640 Admiralty Way #430
Marina Del Rey, CA 90292
Telephone:
800-745-6736
310-827-7400

www.LD.com

Applications: Government Document
Retrieval

Proprietary Products:

Name/Desc: Commerce Business Daily
Info Provided: Environmental, Military
Service, News/Current Events,
Legislation/Regulation
Media: E-mail
Coverage: US

Name/Desc: World-Wide EDI
Info Provided: Contracts
Media: E-mail
Coverage: US

Statement of Capabilities:
Loren Data Corp provides customers with
access to government business, helping make
bids and gain government contracts. They offer
free access and e-mail based subscription
services for their publication Commerce
Business Daily, CBD.

Martindale-Hubbell

121 Chanlon Road
New Providence, NJ 07974
Telephone: **Fax:**
800-526-4902   908-464-3553
908-464-6800

www.martindale.com

info@martindale.com

Applications: Background Info -
Business

Proprietary Products:

Name/Desc: Martindale-Hubbell Law
Directory (Attorneys and Law Firms)
Info Provided: Addresses/Telephone
Numbers, Education/Employment
Media: Available on LEXIS, Publication,
Printed Reports, CD-ROM and Lists or Laels
Coverage: US, Itl

Statement of Capabilities:

Martindale-Hubbell's database is now regarded as the primary source for attorney and law firm information around the world. Their flagship product, Martindale-Hubbell Law Directory consists of more the 900,000 listings, organized by city, state, county, and province with extensive cross-references and indexes. Products are available in four media: hardbound print, CR-ROM, via LEXIS/NEXIS (a sister company) and Internet via the Martindale-Hubbell Lawyer Locator. Their data includes corporate law departments, legal-related services such as P.I.s, title search companies, law digests.

MDR/Minnesota Driving Records

1710 Douglas Dr. N #103
Golden Valley, MN 55422-4313

Telephone: **Fax:**
800-644-6877 612-595-8079
612-755-1164

Applications: Insurance Underwriting, Risk Management, Background Info - Individuals, Direct Marketing

Proprietary Products:

Name/Desc: MDR
Info Provided: Driver and/or Vehicle
Media: Automated Telephone Lookup, Printed Report and Lists or Labels
Coverage: US

Statement of Capabilities:

MDR provides an automated touch-tone call-in service for driver information in Minnesota, letting clients retrieve a record with a verbal response in less than one minute, followed by a fax hard copy within minutes. Service available 24 hours a day every day. The service is endorsed by the Minnesota Insurance Agents Assoc.

Merlin Information Services

215 S Complex Dr
Kalispell, MT 59901

Telephone: **Fax:**
800-367-6646 406-755-8568
406-755-8550

www.merlindata.com/redirect.
asp

Applications: Locating People/Businesses, Asset/Lien Searching/Verification, Background Info - Business, Collections, Fraud Prevention/Detection

Proprietary Products:

Name/Desc: California Criminal
Info Provided: Criminal Information
Media: CD-ROM and Internet
Coverage: CA

Name/Desc: CA Brides and Grooms
Info Provided: Vital Records
Media: CD-ROM and Internet
Coverage: CA

Name/Desc: CA Statewide Property
Info Provided: Real Estate/Assessor
Media: CD-ROM and Internet
Coverage: CA

Name/Desc: CA Civil Superior Indexes
Info Provided: Litigation/Judgments/Tax Liens
Media: CD-ROM and Internet
Coverage: CA

Name/Desc: CA Sales, Use Tax, Prof. Licenses, Alcohol Bev Control Lic
Info Provided: Licenses/Registrations/Permits (Professional Licenses)
Media: CD-ROM and Internet
Coverage: CA

Name/Desc: UCC Index
Info Provided: Uniform Commercial Code (Filing Index)
Media: CD-ROM and Internet
Coverage: CA

Name/Desc: Investigator's National New Business Filings
Info Provided: Corporation/Trade Name Data, Occupational Licenses/Business Registrations/Permits, News/Current Events
Media: CD-ROM, Direct Online, Magnetic Tape
Coverage: CA, US

Name/Desc: National People Finder, national Credt Headers
Info Provided: Trace Wizard National Residential Locator
Media: CD-ROM and Internet
Coverage: US

Name/Desc: Trace Wizard National Residential Locator

Info Provided: Addresses/Telephone Numbers, Vital Records, Driver and/or vehicle, Voter Registration, Credit Header Info
Media: CD-ROM, Direct Online, Magnetic Tape

Statement of Capabilities:
Merlin Information Services produces unique search and retrieval systems to search public record and proprietary information databases. Merlin specializes in new technology for combined media search and retrieval using both CD-ROM and the Internet. Merlin's proprietary databases and several national databases are available on the Internet at their web site. They also sell public record related CD-ROM products produced by a number of other publishers, including voter registration records, DMV records, and Social Security death records. Their list of available gateways and databases is so exhaustive that this profile could not list the CA Fictitious Business Names index, CA Corporations, Limited Partnerships, and Limited Liability Corporations, and National Bankrupties index.

Metromail Corporation
360 East 22nd St
Lombard, IL 60148
Telephone: **Fax:**
800-927-2238 708-916-1336
www.metromail.com

Applications: Locating People/Businesses, Fraud Prevention/Detection, Direct Marketing

Proprietary Products:

Name/Desc: MetroSearch
Info Provided: Addresses/Telephone Numbers
Media: CD-ROM
Coverage: US

Name/Desc: Cole Directory
Info Provided: Addresses/Telephone Numbers
Media: CD-ROM, Publication
Coverage: US

Statement of Capabilities:
MetroNet includes direct access to the electronic directory assistance databases of the Regional Bells (RBOC's). Regional editions of the MetroSearch CD-ROM products and call-in services are featured.

MicroPatent USA
250 Dodge Ave
East Haven, CT 06512
Telephone: **Fax:**
800-648-6787 203-466-5054
203-466-5055
http://micropat.com
info@micropat.com

Applications: Legal Compliance, Competitive Intelligence, General Business Information, Litigation, Research & Development

Proprietary Products:

Name/Desc: WPS
Info Provided: Trademarks/Patents
Media: Direct Online, CD-ROM, E-mail
Coverage: US, Itl

Name/Desc: TradeMark Checker
Info Provided: Trademarks/Patents
Media: CD-ROM
Coverage: US, Itl

Name/Desc: Mark Search Plus
Info Provided: Trademark
Media: Direct Online, CD-ROM
Coverage: US, Itl

Statement of Capabilities:
Micropatent is a global leader in the production and distribution of patent and trademark information. MicroPatent is committed to developing intellectual property systems with its sophisticated and talented programming staff. MicroPatent Europe is located in London, England.

Military Information Enterprises Inc
PO Box 17118
Spartanburg, SC 29301
Telephone: **Fax:**
800-937-2133 864-595-0813
864-595-0981
www.militaryusa.com
thelocator@aol.com

Applications: Background Info - Individuals, Genealogical Research, Locating People/Businesses

Proprietary Products:

Name/Desc: Nationwide Locator Online
Info Provided: Military Svc (Files and Military Service)
Media: Internet
Coverage: US

Statement of Capabilities:
Military Information Enterprises specializes in current and former military locates and background checks. They also publish books on locating people. The principal served 28 years in the US Army and is a licensed private investigator in South Carolina and Texas.

Motznik Computer Services Inc

8301 Briarwood St #100
Anchorage, AK 99518-3332
Telephone:
907-344-6254
Applications: Asset/Lien Searching/Verification, Locating People/Businesses, Real Estate Transactions, Litigation, Background Info - Business
Proprietary Products:

Name/Desc: Alaska Public Information Access System
Info Provided: Aviation/Vessels, Bankruptcy, Licenses/Registrations/Permits, Litigation/Judgments/Tax Liens, Criminal Information, Corporate/Trade Name Data, Uniform Commercial Code, Real Estate/Assessor, Voter Registration and Driver and/or Vehicle
Media: Direct Online Database, Call back
Coverage: AK

Statement of Capabilities:
Motznik Computer Services' product is a comprehensive information research system that provides access to a wide selection of Alaska public files online. Information that can be researched includes: tax liens, UCC, address, real property, Anchorage civil suits, commercial fishing vessels, judgments, motor vehicles, partnerships, bankruptcies, aircraft, permanent fund filing, businesses, Anchorage criminal cases and commercial fishing permits. MV data does not include driver information.

National Credit Information Network NCI

PO Box 31221
Cincinnati, OH 45231-0221
Telephone: **Fax:**
800-374-1400 513-522-1702
513-522-3832

www.wdia.com

Applications: Background Info - Individuals, Locating People/Businesses, Employment Screening, Tenant Screening
Proprietary Products:

Name/Desc: Evictalert
Info Provided: Tenant History
Media: Printed Report, Fax and Call back
Coverage: IN, KY, OH

Name/Desc: NCI Network
Info Provided: Credit Information, Addresses/Telephone Numbers, Social Security (Numbers), Voter Registration, Driver and/or Vehicle
Media: Direct Online to Your Computer and Internet
Coverage: US

Statement of Capabilities:
National Credit Information Network (NCI) specializes in interfacing with credit and public record databases for online searches with immediate response time. Online ordering is available for setup and for searches using a credit card. Access is available through their Internet site. A variety of packages include applicant identity, SSNs, DMVs, education, reference and credential verification, criminal history, bankruptcy and civil history, workers comp claims, and more.

National Fraud Center

Four Horsham Business Center
300 Welsh Rd #200Horsham, PA 19044
Telephone: **Fax:**
800-999-5658 215-657-7071
215-657-0800

www.nationalfraud.com

Applications: Fraud Prevention/Detection, Risk Management
Proprietary Products:

Name/Desc: NFC Online
Info Provided: Software/Training
Media: CD-ROM, Disk and Call-in

Coverage: US, Itl

Name/Desc: Bank Fraud Database
Info Provided: Criminal Information
Media: Online Database and Call-in
Coverage: US, Itl

Name/Desc: Insurance Fraud Database
Info Provided: Criminal Information
Media: Direct Online Database and Call-in
Coverage: US, Itl

Name/Desc: Organized Crime Database
Info Provided: Criminal Information
Media: Direct Online Database and Call-in
Coverage: US, Itl

Name/Desc: Government Fraud Database
Info Provided: Criminal Information
Media: Direct Online Database and Call-in
Coverage: US, Itl

Name/Desc: The Fraud Bulletin
Info Provided: Criminal History
Media: Publication
Coverage: US

Name/Desc: Fraud Alert
Info Provided: Criminal Information
Media: Publication
Coverage: US

Name/Desc: Cellular Fraud Database
Info Provided: Check Fraud Database
Media: Direct Online Database
Coverage: US

Name/Desc: Check Fraud Database
Info Provided: Criminal Information
Media: Direct Online Database

Statement of Capabilities:
National Fraud Center combines its diverse databases into a system: NFConline. They utilize a fraud prevention, an interdiction program, and risk management tools to discover and prevent fraud and risk. They also specialize in pro-active measures such as security policies, training, and installation of security devices to protect corporations from future losses.

National Information Bureau Ltd
14 Washington Rd Bldg 2
Princeton Junction, NJ 08550
Telephone: **Fax:**
609-936-2900   609-936-2859
http://nib.com

Applications: Background Info - Individuals, General Business Information, Lending/Leasing
Proprietary Products:

Name/Desc: BACAS
Info Provided: Credit Information
Media: Direct Online, Software
Coverage: US

Statement of Capabilities:
National Information Bureau (NIB) offers Courier, a combination of accessible to multiple databases for public record retrieval. Other state-of-the-art products include Ca$he, RTK, and BACAS.

National Service Information
145 Baker St
Marion, OH 43301
Telephone: **Fax:**
740-387-6806   740-382-1256
www.nsii.net

Applications: Asset/Lien Searching/Verification, Filing/Recording Documents, Background Info - Business, Lending/Leasing, Legal Compliance
Proprietary Products:

Name/Desc: NSI - Online
Info Provided: Corporate/Trade Name Data, Uniform Commercial Code
Media: Internet
Coverage: IN, OH, WI

Statement of Capabilities:
Founded in 1989, National Service Information is engaged in the search, filing and document retrieval of public record information. Having offices in Marion, OH and Indianapolis, IN, they consider Ohio, Indiana and Kentucky their local market in addition to 4300 different jurisdictions they search nationwide. They recently unveiled a comprehensive database to allow clients to perform public record searches via the Web. Their web site allows you to perform state level UCC lien and corporate detail searches for Ohio, and state level UCCs for Indiana. NSI also provides the option of requesting copies of microfilmed UCC lien images.

Nebrask@ Online

301 South 13th #301
Lincoln, NE 68508

Telephone: **Fax:**
800-747-8177   402-471-7817
402-471-7810

www.nol.org
INFO@NOL.org

Applications: Asset/Lien
Searching/Verification and Filing, Legal
Compliance, Insurance Underwriting,
Lending/Leasing, Direct Marketing

Proprietary Products:

Name/Desc: Nebrask@ Online
Info Provided: Driver and/or Vehicle,
Corporate/Trade Name Data and Uniform
Commercial Code
Media: Magnetic Tape and Online Database
Coverage: NE

Name/Desc: Nebrask@ Online
Info Provided: Litigation/Judgments/Tax
Liens and Addresses/Telephone Numbers
Media: Direct Online Database
Coverage: NE

Statement of Capabilities:
Nebrask@ Online is a State of Nebraska
information system that provides electronic
access to state, county, local, association and
other public information. Some agency and
association data is updated daily, weekly or
monthly, Subscribers connect via 800 #, local
#s, or the Internet 24-hours per day. There are
sign-up and connect fees if not accessing via
the Internet. Interactive access to premium
services (those with a statutory fee) requires an
annual subscription.

New Mexico Technet

5921 Jefferson NE
Albuquerque, NM 87109

Telephone: **Fax:**
505-345-6555   505-345-6559
www.technet.nm.org

Proprietary Products:

Name/Desc: New Mexico Technet
Info Provided: Driver and/or Vehicle,
Litigation/Judgments/Tax Liens and
Corporate/Trade Name Data
Media: Online
Coverage: NM

Statement of Capabilities:
New Mexico Technet is a self-supporting, non-
profit corporation operating to provide
management of a statewide fiber optic
computer network serving the needs of New
Mexico, its state universities and statewide
research, educational and economic-
development interests. Technet serves as the
primary connection point to the Internet for
other Internet Service Providers, business,
government and private users in New Mexico.
Technet offers a full range of Internet services
from dial-up to direct connections and web
page services, to co-located services and New
Mexico MVR requests.

Northwest Location Services

1416 E Main Ave #E
Puyallup, WA 98372

Telephone: **Fax:**
253-848-7767   253-848-4414
http://search.nwlocation.com
/nwmain.htm

Applications: Locating
People/Businesses, Asset/Lien
Searching/Verification, Collections, Litigation

Proprietary Products:

Name/Desc: Superior Courts
Northwest Online
Info Provided: Staewide Court Filings
Media: Internet
Coverage: WA

Name/Desc: Business Licenses
Info Provided: Licenses/Registration/Permits
Media: Internet
Coverage: WA

Name/Desc: People Finder
Info Provided: Name/Address/SSN/DOB
Media: Internet
Coverage: WA

Statement of Capabilities:
Serving investigative, legal and business
professionals, Northwest Location Services
specializes in witness location, skip tracing,
asset research and other information services,
with an eye on protecting privacy and the
public safety. Licensed and bonded in
Washington, they are allied with Northwest
Online and Digital Research Company who
produces CD-ROM database products for
investigators, attorneys and collection
agencies.

Offshore Business News & Research

123 SE 3rd Ave #173
Miami, FL 33131
Telephone: **Fax:**
305-372-6267   305-372-8724
www.offshorebusiness.com
INFOOFFSHOREBUSINESS.com

Applications: Background Info -
Business, Background Info - Individuals, Fraud
Prevention/Detection, General Business
Information, Litigation
Proprietary Products:

Name/Desc: BE Supreme Court
Info Provided: Litigation/Judgments/Tax
Liens and Bankruptcy
Media: Internet
Coverage: BE/Fix

Name/Desc: Grand Court of the CI
Info Provided: Litigation/Judgments/Tax
Liens and Bankruptcy
Media: Internet
Coverage: CI/Fix

Name/Desc: BE Business
Info Provided: Corporate/Trade Name Data,
Legislation/Regulation and Real
Estate/Assessor
Media: Internet
Coverage: BE/Fix

Name/Desc: Cayman Business
Info Provided: Corporate/Trade Name Data
and Bankruptcy
Media: Internet
Coverage: CI/Fix

Name/Desc: BA Business
Info Provided: Corporate/Trade Name Data
Media: Internet
Coverage: BA/Fix

Statement of Capabilities:
Offshore owns litigation databases covering
Bermuda and the Cayman Islands. They offer
24 hour daily access, year around via the
Internet. They publish investigative newsletters
covering Bermuda and the Caribbean.

OPEN (Online Professional Electronic Network)

PO Box 549
Columbus, OH 43216-0549

Telephone: **Fax:**
888-381-5656   614-481-6980
614-481-6999

www.openonline.com

Applications: Background Info -
Business, Background Info - Individuals,
Employment Screening, Asset/Lien
Searching/Verification, Litigation
Proprietary Products:

Name/Desc: OPEN
OPEN
Info Provided: Real Estate/Assessor,
Bankruptcy, Uniform Commercial Code,
Corporate/Trade Name Data,
Addresses/Telephone Numbers, Social
Security (Numbers), Workers' Compensation,
Education/Employment, Credit Information,
Criminal Information, Driver and/or Vehicle
Media: Direct Online to Your Computer
Coverage: US

Name/Desc: Arrest Records
Info Provided: Criminal Information
Media: Direct Online to Your Computer
Coverage: OH,IN,MN,AL,MI

Statement of Capabilities:
OPEN provides real-time,direct access to a
large range of nationwide public records and
proprietary information, such as driver records,
commercial and consumer credit reports,
bankruptcies, liens and judgments. The service
is subscription-based and is available to
professionals and businesses for a variety of
applications including background checks,
skip-traces, verification of information such as
addresses, phone numbers, SSNs, previous
employment and educational background.
OPEN provides free software, account start-
up,and toll-free technical support with no
monthly minimum.

OSHA DATA

12 Hoffman St
Maplewood, NJ 07040-1114
Telephone:
973-378-8011
www.oshadata.com
mcarmel@oshadata.com

Applications: Litigation, Legal
Compliance, Direct Marketing, Background
Info - Business, Government Document
Retrieval

Proprietary Products:

Name/Desc: OSHA Data Gateway
Info Provided: Legislation/Regulation
Media: Printed Report, Fax
Coverage: US

Statement of Capabilities:
OSHA DATA's database contains corporate regulator violation records for every business inspected since July 1972. Information includes not only OSHA data, but also wage and hour, EEOC, insurance, NLRB asbestos and other regulatory types. The database is updated quarterly. Consultation and software for the utilization of the data are available.

Owens Online Inc

251 Lyndhurst St
Dunedin, FL 34698-7577
Telephone: **Fax:**
800-745-4656   727-738-8275
727-738-1245

www.owens.com

email@owens.com

Applications: Background Info - Business, Background Info - Individuals, General Business Information, Locating People/Businesses

Statement of Capabilities:
Owens Online specializes in international credit reports on businesses and individuals. They provide worldwide coverage, with 9 million foreign credit reports online. Single orders are welcomed and there are no complex unit contracts.

Pallorium Inc

PO Box 155-Midwood Station
Brooklyn, NY 11230
Telephone: **Fax:**
212-969-0286   800-275-4329
www.pallorium.com

Applications: Asset/Lien Searching/Verification, Locating People/Businesses, Employment Screening, Risk Management, Litigation

Proprietary Products:

Name/Desc: Skiptrace America
Info Provided: Aviation/Vessels, Driver and/or Vehicle, Vital Records and Voter Registration
Media: Direct Online to Your Computer
Coverage: US

Name/Desc: People Finder California
Info Provided: Aviation/Vessels, Driver and/or Vehicle, Vital Records and Voter Registration
Media: Direct Online to Your Computer
Coverage: CA

Name/Desc: People Finder Texas
Info Provided: Aviation/Vessels, Driver and/or Vehicle, Vital Records and Voter Registration
Media: Direct Online to Your Computer
Coverage: TX

Name/Desc: People Finder Tri-State
Info Provided: Aviation/Vessels, Driver and/or Vehicle, Vital Records and Voter Registration
Media: Direct Online to Your Computer
Coverage: CT, NJ, NY

Name/Desc: People Finder Florida
Info Provided: Aviation/Vessels, Driver and/or Vehicle, Vital Records and Voter Registration
Media: Direct Online to Your Computer
Coverage: FL

Name/Desc: People Finder Gulf Coast
Info Provided: Aviation/Vessels, Driver and/or Vehicle, Vital Records and Voter Registration
Media: Direct Online to Your Computer
Coverage: AL, GA, LA, MS

Name/Desc: People Finder West I & II
Info Provided: Aviation/Vessels, Driver and/or Vehicle, Vital Records and Voter Registration
Media: Direct Online to Your Computer
Coverage: AZ, CO, NM, OR, UT, WA

Name/Desc: People Finder Great Lakes
Info Provided: People Finder New England
Media: Direct Online to Your Computer
Coverage: ID, IL, MI, OH

Name/Desc: People Finder New England
Info Provided: Aviation/Vessels, Driver and/or Vehicle, Vital Records and Voter Registration
Media: Direct Online to Your Computer

Statement of Capabilities:

Pallorium (PallTech Online) services are divided into three areas: the electronic mail system, which links all users (800 investigative/security professionals); the bulletin board system, which provides a forum for the free exchange of information among all approved subscribers (public or private law enforcement only); and the investigative support system, which provides investigative support to approved users. PallTech's searches include aircraft record locator, national financial asset tracker, bankruptcy filings locator, business credit reports, consumer credit reports, NCOA trace, criminal records, national vehicle records, current employment locator, NYC registered voters by address, court and governmental jurisdiction identifier, ZIP Code locator and more searches in the US, Canada, Israel and Hong Kong. New products are CD-ROMs of addresses and personal information for a number of states, totaling more than one billion records.

Paragon Document Research

PO Box 65216
St Paul, MN 55165
Telephone: **Fax:**
800-892-4235 800-847-7369
651-222-6844 651-222-2281
www.banc.com

Applications: Asset/Lien Searching/Verification, Background Info - Business, Competitive Intelligence, Employment Screening, Litigation

Proprietary Products:

Name/Desc: Pdrlog
Info Provided: Uniform Commercial Code
Media: Lists or Labels
Coverage: US

Statement of Capabilities:

Paragon Document Research's services include searches throughout state and county levels of Minnesota, Montana, North Dakota and South Dakota covering UCC, Tax Liens, Bankruptcy filings, past and present litigation, searches for ownership of, and liens on DMV reports, assumed name searches, name reservations and corporate agents. There are no correspondent fees applied.

Plat System Services Inc

12450 Wayzata Blvd #108
Minnetonka, MN 55305-1926
Telephone: **Fax:**
612-544-0012 612-544-0617
www.platsystems.com

Proprietary Products:

Name/Desc: System90
Info Provided: Real Estate/Assessor
Media: Disk, Lists or labels, Direct Online to Your Computer and Printed Report, Internet
Coverage: MN- Minneapolis, St. Paul

Name/Desc: CompUmap
Info Provided: Addresses/Telephone Numbers and Real Estate/Assessor
Media: Direct Online to Your Computer, Internet
Coverage: MN-Minneapolis and St Paul

Name/Desc: PID Directory
Info Provided: Real Estate/Assessor
Media: Reports, Lists or Labels, Publication and Disk
Coverage: MN-Minneapolis, St. Paul

Statement of Capabilities:

Plat System Services has a variety of services available including online services updated weekly, PID directories published annually, commercial sold reports monthly, residential sold reports monthly, custom reports updated weekly, and other monthly reports such as contract for deeds, and commercial buyers and sellers reports. They also offer mailing lists and labels, diskettes updated weekly, and PLAT books updated semi-annually. They provide computerized county plat maps.

Professional Services Bureau

315 S College #245
Lafayette, LA 70503
Telephone: **Fax:**
800-960-2214 318-235-5318
318-234-9933
casey@casepi.com

Applications: Asset/Lien Searching/Verification, Real Estate Transactions, Filing/Recording Documents, Lending/Leasing, Document Retrieval

Proprietary Products:

Name/Desc: PSB Database
Info Provided: Addresses/Telephone
Numbers, Credit Information, Social Security
(Numbers), Criminal Information
Media: Direct Online, Print, Disk, Magnetic
Tape
Coverage: LA

Statement of Capabilities:
Professional Services Bureau is a full service
public record agency covering Louisiana and
Mississippi. They offer background, criminal,
employment, insurance, financial, activity
checks, fraud, and missing person
investigations, also surveillance and process
service. They perform courthouse research,
document filing and retrieval at all municipal,
state and federal courts. Other services are title
abstracting, notary services and claims
adjusting. Their firm has proprietary sources of
background information in South Louisiana.
All 64 Louisiana parishes can be researched in
about 48 hours; about 72 hours for Mississippi.

Property Data Center Inc

7100 E Bellevue #110
Greenwood Village, CO 80111
Telephone: **Fax:**
303-850-9586   303-850-9637
www.pdclane.net

Applications: Real Estate
Transactions, Asset/Lien
Searching/Verification, Direct Marketing,
Lending/Leasing, Insurance Underwriting
Proprietary Products:

Name/Desc: Real Property Assessments
Info Provided: Real Estate/Assessor
Media: Direct Online to Your Computer, Disk,
Lists or labels, Magnetic Tape and Printed
Report
Coverage: CO

Name/Desc: Real Property Taxes
Info Provided: Real Estate/Assessor
Media: Direct Online to Your Computer, Disk,
Lists or labels, Magnetic Tape and Printed
Report
Coverage: CO

Name/Desc: Sales, Warranty/Quit Claim
Deeds
Name/Desc: Owner Phone Numbers

Info Provided: Addresses/Telephone
Numbers
Media: Direct Online Database, Disk,
Magnetic Tape, Printed Reports and Lists or
Labels
Coverage: CO

Name/Desc: PDC
Info Provided: Real Estate/Assessor
Media: Direct Online Database, Disk,
Magnetic Tape, Printed Reports and Lists or
Labels
Coverage: CO

Statement of Capabilities:
Property Data Center's PDC database includes
three million real property ownership and deed
transfer records for the metro Denver area, plus
counties of Adams, Arapahoe, Boulder,
Denver, Douglas, El Paso, Eagle, Elbert,
Jefferson, Larimer, Mesa, Pitkin, Pueblo,
Summit, Weld. Data is accessible by owner,
location, and indicators such as property value.
They specialize in lender marketing data, new
owners, sold comparables, mapping data and
direct mail lists.

PROTEC

PO Box 54866
Cincinnati, OH 45254
Telephone: **Fax:**
800-543-7651   513-528-4402
513-528-4400

procaq007@fuse.net

Applications: Asset/Lien
Searching/Verification, Background Info -
Business, Background Info - Individuals,
Employment Screening, Fraud
Prevention/Detection
Proprietary Products:

Name/Desc: Consta-Trac
Info Provided: Identifiers-DOB, Social
Security (Numbers), Addresses/Telephone
Numbers
Media: Printed Report
Coverage: US

Statement of Capabilities:
PROTEC has 35 years of concurrent exposure
to the information highway, beginning its
database system in 1979 using its own
information. Since that beginning, they have
remained unique in responsible information
gathering, being useful in fraud detection and

factual data gathering. Their newest and most successful database is "CONSTRA-TRAC" - a master compilation of over 700 record systems and special use cross-check histories from individuals, businesses, societies, and public record data.

Public Data Corporation

38 East 29th St
New York, NY 10016
Telephone: **Fax:**
212-519-3063   212-519-3067
www.pdcny.com

Applications: General Business Information, Legal Compliance, Locating People/Businesses, Asset/Lien Searching/Verification, Background Info - Business/Individuals

Proprietary Products:

Name/Desc: Public Data
Info Provided: Real Estate/Assessor, Environmental, Litigation/Judgments/Tax Liens and Uniform Commercial Code
Media: Call-in, Disk, Magnetic Tape and Online Database
Coverage: NY

Statement of Capabilities:
Public Data Corporation's 24 million records database includes real estate, lien, bankruptcy, environmental and other records for the boroughs of Manhattan, Bronx, Brooklyn, Queens. Information is updated daily.

Public Record Research Library

4653 S Lakeshore #3
Tempe, AZ 85282
Telephone: **Fax:**
800-939-2811   800-929-3810
602-838-8909   602-838-8324
http://brbpub.com
brb@brbpub.com

Applications: General Business Information, Government Document Retrieval, Risk Management, Locating People/Businesses, Competitive Intelligence

Proprietary Products:

Name/Desc: PRRS
Info Provided: Addresses/Telephone Numbers, Legislation/Regulations
Media: CD-ROM, Disk, Publication

Coverage: US

Statement of Capabilities:
The Public Record Research Library is a series of in-depth databases formatted into books, CDs and soon to be online. BRB is recognized as the nation's leading research and reference publisher of public record related information. The principals of the parent company are directors of the Public Record Retriever Network, the nation's largest organization of public record professionals. Over 26,000 government and private enterprises are analyzed in-depth regarding regulations and access of public records and public information. The Public Record Research System (PRRS) is available on CD, loose-leaf print, and as a customized database.

Publook Information Service

PO Box 450
Worthington, OH 43085-0450
Telephone: **Fax:**
877-478-2566   740-928-2036
740-928-2035
http://publook.com
mail@publook.com

Applications: Asset/Lien Searching/Verification, Background Info - Business, General Business Information, Lending/Leasing, Government Document Retrieval

Proprietary Products:

Name/Desc: Corp Data
Info Provided: Corporate/Trade Name Data, Addresses/Telephone Numbers, Trademarks/Patents, Licenses/Registrations/Permits
Media: Direct Online, Call Back, Fax, E-mail (Internet), Printed Report
Coverage: OH

Name/Desc: UCC Data
Info Provided: Uniform Commercial Code
Media: Direct Online, Call Back, Fax, E-mail (Internet), Printed Report
Coverage: OH

Statement of Capabilities:
Publook.com features immediate Internet web access to its proprietary databases of Ohio Secretary of State corporations, trade names, trademarks and UCC filings information. Search corporation, debtor names by keywords,

search by debtor address, secured party name, secured party address, filing number. Search corporations by agent/business address, agent/business associate name, charter number. Information is updated weekly. No subscription fees, no charge if no hits, pay a flat fee per search that hits results.

RC Information brokers

PO Box 1114
Framingham, MA 01701-0206
Telephone: **Fax:**
508-651-1126   508-657-2414
psconnor@gis.net

Applications: Background Info - Business, Background Info - Individuals, Collections, Genealogical Research, Litigation

Proprietary Products:

Name/Desc: MassData
Info Provided: Addresses/Telephone Numbers and Vital Records
Media: Disk, Call-in Only and Internet
Coverage: MA

Statement of Capabilities:
RC Information Brokers provide "critical information support" to attorneys, licensed private investigators and other professionals. RCIB specializes in supporting attorneys seeking information on individuals for litigation, credit checks, internal financial investigations and background checks. Information support is also available for major financial centers outside the US, especially London. Specific proprietary databases include "MassData" compiled from various databases archived over the past 22 years on current and previous residents of Massachusetts. Turnaround time depends on specific needs and caseload. Locating Massachusetts individuals past and present including adoption cases is their specialty.

Real Estate Guide Inc, The

PO Box 338
Ravena, NY 12143
Telephone: **Fax:**
800-345-3822   800-252-0906
www.eguides.com

Applications: Real Estate Transactions, Lending/Leasing

Proprietary Products:

Name/Desc: Real Estate Filing Guide
Info Provided: Real Estate/Assessor
Media: Print and CD-ROM
Coverage: US

Statement of Capabilities:
The Real Estate Filing Guide is a 4,400 page, 6 volume quarterly-updated service used by real estate documentation specialists for the purpose of accurately recording those documents in any of the 3,600 county recording offices nationwide. It is available in print and CD-ROM. Firms wishing to integrate this information with internal documentation systems may license the underlying databases.

Record Information Services Inc

Box 1183
St Charles, IL 60174
Telephone: **Fax:**
630-365-6490   630-365-6524
www.public-record.com
metcalf@elnet.com

Applications: Collections, Direct Marketing, Real Estate Transactions

Proprietary Products:

Name/Desc: Foreclosures
Info Provided: Litigation/Judgments/Tax Liens
Media: Disk, Fax-on-Demand, Internet, Lists or labels and Printed Report
Coverage: IL

Name/Desc: Bankruptcies
Info Provided: Bankruptcy
Media: Disk, Fax-on-Demand, Internet, Lists or labels and Printed Report
Coverage: IL

Name/Desc: Judgments
Info Provided: Litigation/Judgments/Tax Liens
Media: Disk, Direct Online to Your Computer, Fax-on-Demand, Printed Report and Software
Coverage: IL

Name/Desc: State & Federal Tax Liens
Info Provided: Litigation/Judgments/Tax Liens
Media: Disk, Direct Online to Your Computer, Fax-on-Demand, Printed Report and Software
Coverage: IL

Name/Desc: Business Licenses

Info Provided:
Licenses/Registrations/Permits
Media: Disk, Direct Online to Your Computer,
Fax-on-Demand, Printed Report and Software
Coverage: IL

Name/Desc: News Incorporations
Info Provided:
Licenses/Registrations/Permits
Media: Disk, Direct Online to Your Computer,
Fax-on-Demand, Printed Report and Software
Coverage: IL

Name/Desc: New Homeowners
Info Provided: Real Estate/Assessor
Media: Disk, Direct Online to Your Computer,
Fax-on-Demand, Printed Report and Software
Coverage: IL

Statement of Capabilities:
Record Information Services provides complete and timely public record data that is delivered through state-of-the-art technology. Custom reports are available upon request.

Richland County Abstract Co
POB 910
Wahpeton, ND 58074-0910
Telephone: **Fax:**
701-642-3781 701-642-3852
Applications: Real Estate
Transactions, Filing/Recording Documents,
Asset/Lien Searching/Verification
Proprietary Products:

Name/Desc: Judgment & Tax Liens
Info Provided: Litigation/Judgments/Tax
Liens
Media: Disk and Printed Report
Coverage: MN, ND

Statement of Capabilities:
Richland County Abstract specializes in providing real estate information for the states of Minnesota and North Dakota.

San Diego Daily Transcript/San Diego Source
2131 Third Ave
San Diego, CA 92101
Telephone:
800-697-6397
619-232-4381
www.sddt.com

editor@sddt.com
Applications: Filing/Recording
Documents, Real Estate Transactions,
Background Info - Business
Proprietary Products:

Name/Desc: San Diego Source
Info Provided: Litigation/Judgments/Tax
Liens and Uniform Commercial Code
Media: Internet
Coverage: CA

Name/Desc: US Bankruptcy Court Filings
Info Provided: Bankruptcy
Media: Internet
Coverage: US

Statement of Capabilities:
The San Diego Source is a leading California web site for public record information and business data. Site visitors can perform customized searches on one or more than fifteen databases. Links with Transcripts Online are provided.

SEAFAX Inc
PO Box 15340
Portland, ME 04112-5340
Telephone: **Fax:**
800-777-3533 800-876-3533
207-773-3533 207-773-9564
www.seafax.com

Applications: Background Info -
Business, General Business Information,
Lending/Leasing
Proprietary Products:

Name/Desc: Business Reports
Info Provided: Credit Information
Media: Fax-on-Demand and Internet
Coverage: US

Statement of Capabilities:
Seafax is an information provider for the seafood industry, offering complete credit monitoring services, accounts receivable discounting, customized marketing data, contingent collections services, outsourcing, receivables management, and consulting services. Seafax provides one central location for the information for conducting business in the seafood industry.

Search Company of North Dakota LLC

1008 E Capitol Ave
Bismarck, ND 58501-1930

Telephone: **Fax:**
701-258-5375   701-258-5375
mkautzma@btigate.com

Applications: Current Events,
Filing/Recording Documents, Asset/Lien
Searching/Verification, Background Info -
Business, Employment Screening

Proprietary Products:

Name/Desc: North Dakota Records
Info Provided: Addresses/Telephone
Numbers, Social Security Numbers,
Litigation/Judgments/Tax Liens,
Licenses/Registrations/Permits, Driver and/or
Vehicle, Criminal Information and Bankruptcy
Media: Printed Report, Fax-on-Demand and
Lists or labels
Coverage: ND

Name/Desc: ND UCC
Info Provided: Uniform Commercial Code,
Litigation/Judgments/Tax Liens
Media: Printed Report, Fax-on-Demand and
Lists or labels
Coverage: ND

Statement of Capabilities:
We will provide any and all city, county, state,
or federal record searching or filing in North
Dakota. Over 15 years of experience in all
aspects of public record searching, retrieval, or
filing.

Search Network Ltd

Two Corporate Place #210
1501 42nd StWest Des Moines, IA 50266-
1005

Telephone: **Fax:**
800-383-5050   800-383-5060
515-223-1153   515-223-2814
http://searchnetworkltd.com

Applications: Lending/Leasing,
Filing/Recording Documents, Asset/Lien
Searching/Verification

Proprietary Products:

Name/Desc: Search Network
Info Provided: Uniform Commercial Code
Media: Direct Online Database, Printed
Reports, Lists or Labels, Publication and
Microfilm

Coverage: IA, KS

Statement of Capabilities:
In business for over 30 years, Search Network
provides full service public record search
information. The company maintains an on-site
UCC database for Iowa and Kansas. Same day
searches and copies are available as well as
personal filing service for UCC and corporate
documents. Since 1980, they have offered
direct online access to their databases of UCC
filing/records information in Iowa and Kansas

Search Systems

PO Box 544
Newbury Park, CA 91319-0544

Telephone: **Fax:**
800-350-2232   805-375-4042
805-375-4041

www.pac-info.com
tjkoster@pac-info.com

Applications: Asset/Lien
Searching/Verification, Background Info -
Business, Collections, Competitive
Intelligence, General Business Information

Statement of Capabilities:
Search Systems specializes in four primary
services; skip tracing, asset evaluations, asset
recovery, and information services. They locate
the right person (verify the identity and
guarantee that the address is correct); analyze
public record information; determine business
ownership; perform bank, employment and
property searches for asset recovery; and do
research and problem-solving.

Security Search & Abstract Co

926 Pine St
Philadelphia, PA 19107

Telephone: **Fax:**
800-345-9494   800-343-4294
215-592-0660   215-592-0998

Applications: Real Estate
Transactions, Legal Compliance, Asset/Lien
Searching/Verification, Filing/Recording
Documents

Proprietary Products:

Name/Desc: Security Search
Info Provided: Real Estate/Assessor
Media: Call-in
Coverage: PA

Silver Plume

4775 Walnut St #2B
Boulder, CO 80301
Telephone: **Fax:**
800-677-4442 303-449-1199
303-444-0695

www.silverplume.iix.com

Applications: Insurance Underwriting
Proprietary Products:

Name/Desc: Insurance Industry Rates, Forms and Manuals
Info Provided: Legislation/Regulations
Media: CD-ROM, Magnetic Tape
Coverage: US

Statement of Capabilities:
Silver Plume supplies most of the widely-used manuals in the property and casualty insurance industry in electronic format. All manuals are updated monthly and distributed to subscribing agencies and companies to provide convenient access to vital information without the hassles.

SKLD Information Services LLC

720 S Colorado Blvd #1000N
Denver, CO 80246
Telephone: **Fax:**
800-727-6358 303-260-6391
303-820-0883
www.skld.com
sales@skld.com

Applications: Real Estate
Transactions, Asset/Lien Searching/Verification, Direct Marketing, Filing/Recording Documents
Proprietary Products:

Name/Desc: New Homeowners List
Info Provided: Real Estate/Assessor
Media: Disk, Magnetic Tape, Call-back, and Labels
Coverage: CO

Statement of Capabilities:
SKLD Information Services maintains a complete database of public record information keyed from documents recorded in County Recorder offices since 1990. Information is available to enhance existing databases, create new homeowner mailing lists, report on real estate loan transaction information, and as mortgage marketing data. With archived county recorded documents in their in-house microfilm library, SKLD can provide quick turnaround times. Reports available include: real estate loan activity reports, warranty deed/trust deed match, trust deed report, owner carry 1 and 2 reports, notice of election and demand, and new homeowners list.

Software Computer Group Inc

PO Box 3042
Charleston, WV 25331-3042
Telephone:
800-795-8543
304-343-6480

www.swcg-inc.com
info@swcg-inc.com

Applications: Background Info -
Individuals, Employment Screening, Government Document Retrieval, Risk Management
Proprietary Products:

Name/Desc: Circuit Express
Info Provided: Criminal Information, Litigation/judgments/Tax Liens
Media: Direct Online
Coverage: WV

Statement of Capabilities:
The Circuit Express product brings civil and criminal public information records from the Circuit Courts in West Virginia to you onlinet. You can locate cases by name or case filing type. Not all counties are available. Fees include a sign-up fee, and monthly fee with connect charges. There is an additional system for magistrate courts; however, this service is only available to government agencies.

Southeastern Public Records Inc

208 W Chicago Rd #4
Sturgis, MI 49091
Telephone: **Fax:**
616-659-8131 616-659-1169
www.instantimpact.com/spr
jimbarfield@msn.com

Applications: Asset/Lien
Searching/Verification, Litigation, Direct Marketing, Real Estate Transactions

Proprietary Products:

Name/Desc: Michigan Public Records
Info Provided: Addresses/Telephone
Numbers, Bankruptcy,
Litigation/Judgments/Tax Liens
Media: CD-ROM, Magnetic Tape, Call back,
Gateway, Fax, Printed Report, E-mail,
Software (results in the form of software)
Coverage: MI

Name/Desc: Georgia Public Records
Info Provided: Addresses/Telephone
Numbers, Bankruptcy,
Litigation/Judgments/Tax Liens
Media: CD-ROM, Magnetic Tape, Call back,
Gateway, Fax, Printed Report, E-mail,
Software (results in the form of software)
Coverage: GA

Statement of Capabilities:
Southeastern Public Records can deliver bulk
data up to 3,000,000 records within 48 hours of
verifying customer specifications. Smaller
batches of data available in 1 to 48 hours if
needed. Verification of any judgment, tax lien,
or bankruptcy at its original place of filing in
all covered areas. All data is recorded from its
original source by one of our certified
collectors on software developed by us for that
particular purpose. Our databases contain 15
years of historical data in Michigan and 10
years in Georgia. Our key personnel include: a
full time onsite Internet/web specialist; full
time onsite database development specialists;
several full time personnel with extensive
knowledge of legal recording, mortgages,
major credit bureaus, and all civil public
records at all levels.

Southwest InfoNet

2252 N 44th St #1007
Phoenix, AZ 85008-7201
Telephone: **Fax:**
800-579-1892   800-549-1925
602-286-6804   602-286-6712
www.unisearch.com
paulstr24@aol.com

Applications: Asset/Lien
Searching/Verification, Filing/Recording
Documents, Government Document Retrieval,
Lending/Leasing, Litigation

Proprietary Products:

Name/Desc: WALDO
Info Provided: Uniform Commercial Code
Media: Internet and Direct Online to Your
Computer
Coverage: CA, IL, WA

Statement of Capabilities:
Southwest InfoNet's normal turnaround time is
24-48 hours. Projects are generally billed by
the number of names searched or records
located. Copy costs and disbursements are
added to the search charge. Their large
microfilm library allows immediate copy
retrieval for many states. Their web site
includes news, jurisdiction updates and online
ordering.

Specialty Services

8491 Hospital Dr #151
Douglasville, GA 30134
Telephone: **Fax:**
770-942-8264   770-942-5355
Applications: Asset/Lien
Searching/Verification, Background Info -
Business, Background Info - Individuals,
Employment Screening, Litigation

Proprietary Products:

Name/Desc: Fulco
Info Provided: Criminal Information and
Litigation/Judgments/Tax Liens
Media: Fax-on-Demand
Coverage: US

Statement of Capabilities:
Speciality Services specializes in record
retrieval from county, state and federal courts
as well as criminal/civil backgrounds for pre-
employment screening, litigation support,
insurance fraud investigation assistance, asset
reports, UCC searches, title work, etc.

Superior Information Services LLC

PO Box 8787
Trenton, NJ 08650-0787
Telephone: **Fax:**
800-848-0489   800-883-0677
609-883-7000   609-883-0677
www.superiorinfo.com

Applications: Litigation,
Lending/Leasing, Legal Compliance,
Asset/Lien Searching/Verification

Proprietary Products:

Name/Desc: Superior Online
Info Provided: Litigation/Judgments/Tax Liens and Bankruptcy
Media: Direct Online
Coverage: DC, DE, MD, NC, NJ, NY, PA, VA

Name/Desc: Superior Online
Info Provided: Corporate/Trade Name Data
Media: Direct Online Database
Coverage: NY, PA

Name/Desc: Superior Online
Info Provided: Uniform Commercial Code
Media: Direct Online Database
Coverage: PA, NJ

Name/Desc: Superior Online
Info Provided: Real Estate/Assessor
Media: Direct Online Database
Coverage: NY (NYC), NJ

Statement of Capabilities:
Superior Information Services provides accurate, reliable and comprehensive information to a wide variety of clients including attorneys, investigators, financial institutions, financial underwriters, employment agencies, insurance claims departments, leasing companies, and government agencies. Our proprietary database searches all counties in the following states: NY, NJ, PA, DE, MD, DC, VA and NC. Our search engine uncovers filings under similar/misspelled names. Superior Information Services is the leading supplier of public record information in the Mid-Atlantic region.

Tax Analysts

6830 N Fairfax Dr
Arlington, VA 22213
Telephone: **Fax:**
703-533-4600 703-533-4444
www.tax.org
Applications: Current Events, Litigation, Legal Compliance, Background Info - Business, General Business Information
Proprietary Products:

Name/Desc: Exempt Organization Master List
Info Provided: Corporate/Trade Name Data
Media: CD-ROM and Disk
Coverage: US

Name/Desc: The Tax Directory

Info Provided: Addresses/Telephone Numbers
Media: Publication, CD-ROM and Available on DIALOG & LEXIS
Coverage: US, Itl

Name/Desc: The OneDisc
Info Provided: Legislation/Regulations
Media: CD-ROM
Coverage: US

Name/Desc: TAXBASE
Info Provided: Legislation/Regulations
Media: Internet
Coverage: US, Itl

Statement of Capabilities:
Tax Analysts is a nonprofit organization dedicated to providing timely, comprehensive information to tax professionals at a reasonable cost. They are the leading electronic publisher of tax information. The Exempt Organization Master List contains information about more than 1.1 million not-for-profit organizations registered with the federal government. The Tax Directory contains information about 14,000 federal tax officials, 9000 private tax professionals and 8000 corporate tax professionals. Online databases include daily federal, state and international tax information as well as complete research libraries.

The Search Company Inc

1410-439 University Ave
Toronto, ON M5G 1Y8
Telephone: **Fax:**
800-396-8241 800-396-8219
416-979-5858 416-979-5857

www.thesearchcompany.com
info@thesearchcompany.com
Applications: Asset/Lien Searching/Verification, Background Info - Business, Background Info - Individuals, Government Document Retrieval, Litigation
Proprietary Products:

Name/Desc: Property Ownership & Tenant Data
Info Provided: Real Estate/Assessor
Media: Direct Online to Your Computer, Internet, Printed Report and Software
Coverage: CD

Statement of Capabilities:
The Search Company covers 2 distinct markets: 1) Canada wide public record retrieval; 2) Litigation related asset and corporate background reporting with or without a full narrative report, with analysis and opinion regarding the advisability of litigation.

Thomson & Thomson

500 Victory Rd
North Quincy, MA 02171-3145

Telephone:	Fax:
800-692-8833	800-543-1983
617-479-1600	617-786-8273

www.thomson-thomson.com

Applications: Legal Compliance, Direct Marketing, Competitive Intelligence, Background Info - Business, Background Info - Individuals

Proprietary Products:

Name/Desc: TRADEMARKSCAN
Info Provided: Trademarks and Foreign Country Information
Media: CD-ROM, Direct Online to Your Computer and Internet
Coverage: US, Itl

Name/Desc: Worldwide Domain
Info Provided: Foreign Country Information
Media: Internet
Coverage: US, Itl

Name/Desc: Site Comber
Info Provided: Trademarks/Patents
Media: Internet and Printed Report
Coverage: US

Name/Desc: US Full Trademark Search
Info Provided: Trademarks
Media: Internet and Printed Report
Coverage: US

Name/Desc: US Full Copyright Search
Info Provided: Licenses/Registrations/Permits
Media: Printed Report
Coverage: US

Name/Desc: US Title Availability Search
Info Provided: Vital Records
Media: Printed Report
Coverage: US

Name/Desc: The deForest Report for Script Clearance
Info Provided: Vital Records
Media: Fax-on-Demand

Coverage: US

Statement of Capabilities:
Thomson & Thomson is a world leader in trademark, copyright and script clearance services, with over 75 years of experience and offices in the US, Canada, Europe and Japan. Accessing trademark records from more than 200 countries, T&T analysts provide reports to help clients determine if their proposed trademarks are available for use. Clients can perform their own trademark searches via Thomson & Thomson's TRADEMARKSCAN online databases. Thomson & Thomson also provides a complete offering of equally impressive copyright, title and script clearance services--allowing you to manage and protect your intellectual property assets.

TML Information Services Inc

116-55 Queens Blvd
Forest Hills, NY 11375

Telephone:	Fax:
800-743-7891	718-544-2853
718-793-3737	

www.tml.com

Applications: Insurance Underwriting, Employment Screening, Driver Screening for Auto Rental

Proprietary Products:

Name/Desc: Auto-Search
Info Provided: Driver and/or Vehicle
Media: Online Database, Internet, Call-back, and Fax
Coverage: AL, AZ, CT, DC, FL, ID, IN, KS, KY, LA, MA, MI, MN, MS, NC, ND, NE, NH, NJ, NY, OH, SC, VA, WI, WV

Name/Desc: Title File
Info Provided: Driver and/or Vehicle
Media: Direct Online Database, Call-back and Fax
Coverage: AL, FL, SD

Name/Desc: Driver Check
Info Provided: Driver and/or Vehicle
Media: Direct Online Database and Automated Telephone Lookup
Coverage: AL, AZ, CA, CT, FL, ID, KS, LA, MD, MI, MN, NE, NH, NY, NC, OH, PA, SC, VA, WV

Statement of Capabilities:
TML Information Services specializes in providing access to motor vehicle information

in an online, real-time environment. Their standardization format enables TML to offer several unique automated applications for instant access to multiple states' driver and vehicle information, including a touch-tone fax-on-demand service and a rule-based decision processing service for driver qualification for car rental. TML has online access to more than 200 million driver and vehicle records in more than 30 states and expects to add several more states soon.

Todd Wiegele Research Co Inc

10425 W North Ave #331
Wauwatosa, WI 53226
Telephone: **Fax:**
800-754-7800 414-607-0800
414-607-0700

www.execpc.com/~research

Applications: Real Estate Transactions, Asset/Lien Searching/Verification, Background Info - Individuals, Employment Screening, Litigation

Proprietary Products:

Name/Desc: FASTRACT
Info Provided: Real Estate/Assessor
Media: Disk, Magnetic Tape and Microfiche
Coverage: WI

Statement of Capabilities:
The Todd Wiegele Research Co specializes in Milwaukee County records, but also provides nationwide services utilizing online databases and correspondents. Records specialties include title searches, criminal background checks, asset investigations, civil background checks and database consulting. They offer a database, FASTRACT, to track real estate information in Milwaukee County, WI.

Trans Union

555 W Adams
Chicago, IL 60661-3601
Telephone:
800-899-7132
312-258-1717

www.transunion.com

Applications: Collections, Lending/Leasing, Insurance Underwriting, Real Estate Transactions, General Business Information

Proprietary Products:

Name/Desc: CRONUS
Info Provided: Credit Information, Addresses, Litigation/Judgments/Tax Liens
Media: Direct Online, Paper
Coverage: US

Name/Desc: Real Estate Services
Info Provided: Real Estate/Assessor
Media: Direct Online, Printed Report, Disks
Coverage: US

Name/Desc: Business Information
Info Provided: Credit Information, Corporate/Trade Name Data
Media: Direct Online, Printed Report
Coverage: US

Statement of Capabilities:
Trans Union, best known for its national consumer credit information file, provides a number of information services. Their TRACE product, based on Social Security Numbers, expands searching facilities to locate people who have changed names or moved without a forwarding address.

Tyler-McLennon Inc

707 W 7th St
Austin, TX 78701
Telephone: **Fax:**
512-482-0808 512-482-8727
www.tyler-mclennon.com
tylermclennon@worldnet.att.net

Applications: Asset/Lien Searching/Verification, Employment Screening, Filing/Recording Documents, Insurance Underwriting, Lending/Leasing

Proprietary Products:

Name/Desc: Crimspree
Info Provided: Criminal Information
Media: Call-back Only
Coverage: TX

Name/Desc: Cook County UCCs
Info Provided: Uniform Commercial Code
Media: Call-back Only
Coverage: IL

Statement of Capabilities:
Tyler-McLennon specializes in public records searches in Texas both at the county and federal level. Located in Austin, they have access to all state offices. They perform court record searches, real estate, property

ownership, bankruptcies, asset/lien, UCC searches, also motor vehicle ownership and driving record searches. They utilize database hook-ups with Texas counties and physically do the searches in many. They have employees in Dallas/Ft. Worth, Houston, Austin, Corpus Christi and Tyler, and representatives elsewhere. Larger clients may choose to order and receive records online.

UCC Guide Inc, The
PO Box 338
Ravena, NY 12143
Telephone: **Fax:**
800-345-3822 800-252-0906
www.equides.com
Applications: Legal Compliance,
Lending/Leasing
Proprietary Products:

Name/Desc: Uniform Commercial Code Filing Guide
Info Provided: Uniform Commercial Code Filing Guide
Media: Print, Disk and CD-ROM
Coverage: US

Statement of Capabilities:
The UCC Filing Guide is a unique 5 volume, 6000 page quarterly updated service used by multi-state UCC filers to prepare UCC financing statements accurately. All 4300 UCC filing offices in the US are covered. Monthly newsletter is included with the annual subscription. The service includes UCC searching information. The disk media includes a database for automatic fee determination and address label/cover letter preparation. An affiliated company now publishes the Real Estate Recording Guide, designed to assist real estate documentation specialists.

UCC Retrievals Inc
7288-A Hanover Green Dr
Mechanicsville, VA 23111
Telephone: **Fax:**
804-559-5919 804-559-5920
Applications: Asset/Lien
Searching/Verification, Legal Compliance, Litigation, Filing/Recording Documents

Proprietary Products:

Name/Desc: Federal Tax Liens and UCCs
Info Provided: Litigation/judgments/Tax Liens and Uniform Commercial Code
Media: Printed Reports, Lists or Labels and Online Database
Coverage: VA

Statement of Capabilities:
UCC Retrievals specializes in searching UCC and federal tax liens in Virginia. They also file motor vehicle records, do corporate filings and retrievals, and assist with pending litigation. Their turnaround time is 24-48 hours.

UMI Company
PO Box 1346
Ann Arbor, MI 48106-1346
Telephone: **Fax:**
734-761-4700 734-975-6486
800-521-0600
www.umi.com
info@umi.com
Applications: General Business
Information, Background Info - Business, Competitive Intelligence, Current Events

Statement of Capabilities:
UMI, formerly operated DataTimes, now offers a number of useful electronic and print services with information on business, current events, technology innovations, including graphics, charts, photos. Their products are useful to libraries, researchers, scientists, schools, and competitive intelligence gathering. Products include ProQuest packages (includes newspapers) and IntellX.

Unisearch Inc
PO Box 11940
Olympia, WA 98508-1940
Telephone: **Fax:**
800-722-0708 800-531-1717
360-956-9500 360-956-9504
www.unisearch.com
Applications: Asset/Lien
Searching/Verification, Lending/Leasing, Legal Compliance, Real Estate Transactions, Corporate Registered Agent Service

Proprietary Products:

Name/Desc: WALDO
Info Provided: Uniform Commercial Code
Media: Direct Online to Your Computer,
Internet and Printed Report
Coverage: CA, IL, WA

Statement of Capabilities:

Unisearch is online with over 30 states and
British Columbia, providing instant access to
the most current information available. They
maintain a film library of UCC documents for
WA, OR, AK, UT, CA, IL, MT, NV, WI, MN.
In areas where computer access is not yet
available, Unisearch employs a network of
correspondents to provide service. Additional
branch offices are in; St Paul, MN (800-227-
1256); Reno, NV (800-260-1331); and
lawrence, KS (800-607-4451).

US Corporate Services

200 Minnesota Bldg, 46 E Fourth St
St Paul, MN 55101
Telephone: **Fax:**
800-327-1886   800-603-0266
651-227-7575   651-225-9244

www.uscorpserv.com

info@uscorpserv.com

Applications: Asset/Lien
Searching/Verification, Competitive
Intelligence, Filing/Recording Documents,
Lending/Leasing, Real Estate Transactions

Proprietary Products:

Name/Desc: MN Secretary of State Records
Info Provided: Corporation/Trade Name Data
Media: Direct Online, Print
Coverage: MN

Name/Desc: WI UCCs
Info Provided: Uniform Commerical Code
Media: Direct Online, Print
Coverage: WI

Statement of Capabilities:

US Corporate Services is a full service UCC,
tax lien, judgment, litigation and corporate
search and filing firm. Their optical image
library of Minnesota enables them to provide
custom reports to their clients. They have
nationwide correspondent relationships. Their
turnaround time is 24-72 hours. They will
invoice monthly; projects are generally billed
by the number of names searched.

US Document Services Inc

PO Box 50486
Columbia, SC 29250
Telephone: **Fax:**
803-254-9193   803-771-9905
www.us-doc-services.com

info@us-doc-services.com

Applications: Asset/Lien
Searching/Verification, Background Info -
Business, Filing/Recording Documents,
Government Document Retrieval

Proprietary Products:

Name/Desc: Secretary of State
Info Provided: Corporation/Trade Name Data
Media: Printed Report
Coverage: NC, SC

Statement of Capabilities:

US Document Services is a nationwide public
record search and document retrieval company
specializing in North Carolina and South
Carolina. They offer UCC, tax lien, suit and
judgment, bankruptcy and asset searches, and
provide legal, financial and commercial clients
with a wide variety of services including
formation, qualification and registrations of
corporations, etc. With an in-house South
Carolina and North Carolina microfilm and
online database, they provide up-to-date
results, with 48-hour turnarounds

USADATA.com

292 Madison Ave, 3rd Fl
New York, NY 10017
Telephone: **Fax:**
800-599-5030   212-679-8507
212-326-8760

www.usadata.com

info@usadata.com

Applications: Background Info -
Business, Competitive Intelligence, Direct
Marketing

Proprietary Products:

Name/Desc: Marketing Portal
Info Provided: Corporate/Trade Name Data,
Addresses/Telephone Numbers, Real
Estate/Assessor

Statement of Capabilities:

USADATA.com's Marketing Information
Portal (www.usadata.com) provides fast, easy
access to the information you need to make

critical business decisions. We draw data from the top names in syndicated consumer data on both a local and national level, including Mediamark Research Inc (MRI), Scarborough Research, Arbitron, Acxiom, Competitive Media Reporting (CMR) and National Decision Systems (NDS). Marketers, planners and media buyers can order reports on a pay-per-view basis from our website, or subscribe to unlimited Internet access.

Virginia Information Providers Network

1111 East Main Street
Richmond, VA 23219
Telephone:
804-786-4718
www.vipnet.org
webmaster@vipnet.org

Applications: Employment Screening, Litigation, Insurance Underwriting

Proprietary Products:

Name/Desc: VIPNet
Info Provided: Driver and/or Vehicle
Media: Internet
Coverage: VA

Statement of Capabilities:
The Virginia Information Providers Network was created by the state of Virginia to streamline and enhance the ways in which citizens and businesses access government information. VIPNet premium services includes access to state motor vehicle records.

VISTA Information Solutions

5060 Shoreham Place
San Diego, CA 92122
Telephone: **Fax:**
800-767-0403   619-450-6195
619-450-6100
www.vistainfo.com

Applications: Risk Management, Insurance Underwriting, Legal Compliance, Lending/Leasing

Proprietary Products:

Name/Desc: VISTACheck
Info Provided: Environmental, Corporation/Trade Name Data
Media: Direct Online, Software, Lists
Coverage: US

Statement of Capabilities:
VISTA is a premier provider of environmental risk information software and services and has exclusive endorsements by the American Bankers Association. Their myriad of products provide information to the environmental and insurance underwriting industries to assist with risk management. The VISTA environmental database includes environmental record information from more than 500 state and federal sources, and contains over 10 million records which are geo-coded.

VitalChek Network

4512 Central Pike
Hermitage, TN 37076
Telephone:
800-255-2414
www.vitalchek.com
webcomment@vitalchek.com

Applications: Genealogical Research, Background Info - Individuals

Proprietary Products:

Name/Desc: VitalChek
Info Provided: Vital Records
Coverage: US

Statement of Capabilities:
VitalChek Network has a sophisticated voice and fax network setup to help people get certified copies of birth, death and marriage certificates and other vital records. VitalChek provides a direct access gateway to participating agencies at the state and local level.

West Group

620 Opperman Dr
Eagan, MN 55123
Telephone: **Fax:**
800-328-9352   651-687-7302
651-687-7000

www.westgroup.com

Applications: Legal Compliance, Current Events, General Business Information, Competitive Intelligence, Government Document Retrieval

Proprietary Products:

Name/Desc: West CD-ROM Libraries
Info Provided: Legislation/Regulations
Media: CD-ROM

Coverage: US
Name/Desc: Westlaw
Info Provided: Environmental, Legislation/Regulations
Media: Direct Online Database
Coverage: US

Name/Desc: Westlaw
Info Provided: Corporate/Trade Name Data, Uniform Commercial Code
Media: Direct Online Database
Coverage: US

Statement of Capabilities:
West Group is one of the largest providers of information to US legal professionals. West Group includes renowned names such as Barclays, Bancroft Whitney, Clark Boardman Callaghan, Counterpoint, Lawyers Cooperative Publishing, West Publishing and Westlaw. Westlaw is a computer-assisted research service consisting of more than 9,500 legal, financial and news databases, including Dow Jones News/Retrieval. West Group produces a total of more than 3,800 products including 300 CD-ROMs.

Western Regional Data Inc

PO Box 20520
Reno, NV 89515
Telephone: **Fax:**
775-329-9544 775-324-1652
www.wrdi.com

Applications: Direct Marketing, Asset/Lien Searching/Verification, Legal Compliance, Locating People/Businesses, Real Estate Transactions

Proprietary Products:

Name/Desc: WRDI's Lead Focus
Info Provided: Real Estate/Assessor and Vital Records
Media: Fax-on-Demand, Lists or labels, Disk, Internet and Microfilm/Microfiche
Coverage: NV

Statement of Capabilities:
Western Regional Data (WDRI) gathers public record information from all 17 counties in Nevada and state agencies, making it available in one online system. The information includes property tax data, building permits, business licenses and other less well known types of public records. They have a new program called "Lead Focus" that makes available

targeted mailing list data with more than 35 ways to pinpoint your market.

WinStar Telebase Inc

435 Devon Park Dr #600
Wayne, PA 19087
Telephone: **Fax:**
800-220-4664 610-341-9447
610-254-2420
www.telebase.com

Applications: General Business Information, Background Info - Business, Direct Marketing, Competitive Intelligence, Collections

Proprietary Products:

Name/Desc: Brainwave
Info Provided: SEC/Other Financial, Corporate/Trade Name Data, Trademarks/Patents
Media: Direct Online (www.brainwave.telebase.com)
Coverage: US, Itl

Name/Desc: Iquest
Info Provided: Corporate/Trade Name Data, Addresses/Telephone Numbers, News/Current Events, Credit Information, Trademarks/Patents, SEC/Other Financial
Media: Direct Online via CompuServe and www.request.telebase.com
Coverage: US, Itl

Name/Desc: LEXIS-NEXIS Caselow @AOL
Info Provided: Litigation/Judgments/Tax Liens
Media: Direct Online via America Online - Keyword: LEXIS-NEXIS
Coverage: US

Statement of Capabilities:
Winstar Telebase's Information Services are designed for people with little or no online searching experience and provide easy access to business information for sales prospecting, market analysis, competitive intelligence, product development, and other research. Several thousand sources, from over 450 databases, are available including credit reports, financial reports, company directories, magazines, newspapers, newswires, industry newsletters, etc. For a list of distribution partners visit www.telebase.com..

Useful Web Sites

In this section, you will find profiles of web sites, mostly government-oriented, that many researchers find useful.

Bureau of Economic Analysis in the Commerce Department

www.bea.doc.gov

Statistical analysis and information from the Commerce Department's site for business & investments.

Bureau of Justice Statistics

www.ojp.usdoj.gov/bjs

Justice Department statistics collection, includes crime numbers.

Bureau of Labor Statistics

www.bls.gov

One of the top statistical collections, from the Federal government's Labor Department.

Bureau of Transportation Statistics

www.bts.gov

US Department of Transportation stats, an extensive list.

Campaigns & Elections Magazine

www.camelect.com

Nuts and bolts magazine for campaign strategy from Congressional Quarterly.

Fee-Based Site

Center for Public Integrity

www.publicintegrity.org

Chuck Lewis' excellent site for tracking where money and politics collide.

Center for Responsive Politics

www.opensecrets.org

Excellent advocacy site for tracking campaign information.

CIA World Factbook

www.cia.gov/cia/publications/factbook/index.html

Reference tool for background information on countries.

CNN/Time All Politics

http://cnn.com/ALLPOLITICS

CNN/CQ's combined site – best place for political news online.

Commerce Business Daily

http://cbdnet.gpo.gov

Commerce Business Daily is the government's list of all bids and contracts and announcement awards. Essential reading for anyone wanting to do business with the government. Available free from the government or for pay on many sources.

Commonly Requested Federal Services

www.whitehouse.gov/WH/Services

Central resource for federal sites.

Congressional Quarterly

www.cq.com

News magazine covering US Congress.

CourtLink

www.courtlink.com

Federal court records plus some from NY, OR, TX, WA – includes charges as well as convictions.
Fee-Based Site

DEA Drug Data

www.usdoj.gov/dea/drugdata/
stats.htm

Drug use statistics.

Defense LINK - US Department of Defense (DOD)

www.defenselink.mil

Main Pentagon site.

Defense Technical Information Center (DTIC)

www.dtic.mil

Pentagon's thorough site for technology-related military things.

Department of Education: Topics A to Z

http://ed.gov/topicsaz.html

US Education Department's links to the best starting points on a variety of educational topics.

Documents Center

www.lib.umich.edu/libhome/Docum
ents.center/index.html

University of Michigan's superb document clearinghouse.

EDGAR Database

www.sec.gov/edgarhp.htm

A searchable database of publicly held companies, which are required by law to file information with the SEC.

EDGAR Online People

http://people.edgar-
online.com/people

Allows users to search the SEC filings for information about executives by name. Indexes are free, details cost money. Information is available from the last six months of proxy statements.
Fees for Some Content

Emergency Response Notification System Data & Documentation

www.epa.gov/ERNS/docs/data.html

Environmental Protection Agency Emergency Response reports

Endangered Species Database: US Fish & Wildlife Service

http://endangered.fws.gov/
listdata.html

Lists of endangered species compiled by the US Government.

EPA's Toxic Release Inventory TRI Query Form

www.epa.gov/enviro/html/tris/
tris_query.html

Environmental Protection Agency's database of company toxic filings.

Establishment Search in Occupational Safety & Health Administration (OSHA)

www.osha.gov/cgi-bin/est/est1

Database of health inspection reports.

European Patent Office

www.european-patent-office.org

European patent and trademark information.

FAA Office of System Safety, Safety Data

http://nasdac.faa.gov/
safety_data/

Federal Aviation Administration safety data site, including "Excel" and Bureau of Transportation statistics.

FDIC (Federal Deposit Insurance Corporation) Institutions

www2.fdic.gov/structur/search

US government's database of banks and other institution ownership.

FECInfo

www.tray.com/FECINFO

Former Federal Election Commission staffer Tony Raymond's excellent site for researching political contributions and campaign info.

Federal Court Locator, The

www.law.vill.edu

Federal court locator. Can also be found at http://vls.law.vill.edu/compass/.

Federal Election Commission (FEC)

www.fec.gov

Official site to track campaign-related information.

Federal Judiciary Homepage

www.uscourts.gov/links/html

A great collection of legal cases.

Federal Web Locator, The

www.law.vill.edu

Links to thousands of government agencies and departments. Can also be found at www.infoctr.edu/fwl.

FedLaw

http://fedlaw.gsa.gov

Resource for federal legal and regulatory research. It has more than 1600 links to legal-related information and is operated by the General Services Organization.

Fedstats

www.fedstats.gov

Central clearinghouse for government statistical sites.

FedWorld

www.fedworld.gov

Collection of 14,000 government sites, including bulletin boards so you can reach government employees with expertise on many subjects.

FindLaw

www.findlaw.com

Well-organized directory of Internet legal sites.

FindLaw: Law Crawler

www.lawcrawler.com/index.html

Search engine for legal resources.

Foreign Government Resources on the Web

www.lib.umich.edu/libhome/Docum
ents.center/frames/forfr.html

Excellent list of foreign government resources.

Free Congressional Quarterly Sites: American Voter

http://voter.cq.com

Search for Congressional lawmaker's voting records.

Geneva International Forum

http://geneva.intl.ch/gi/
egimain/edir.htm

International resources for business.

Global Computing

www.globalcomputing.com/states.
html

State-by-state resources.

Global Securities Information's LIVEDGAR

www.gsionline.com

Searches across the entire EDGAR database by key words, SIC (standard industry code) or form type.

Fee-Based Site

GOVBOT - Government Search Engine

http://ciir2.cs.umass.edu/Govbot

Finding agent for government sites.

Governing Magazine

www.governing.com

Congressional Quarterly's magazine for state and local political campaign information.

Fee-Based Site

Government Information Sharing Project

http://govinfo.kerr.orst.edu

Oregon State's resource for regional government information.

Governments on the WWW

www.gksoft.com/govt

A great collection of international and local government related servers.

Healthfinder

www.healthfinder.org

Great starting point for health resources.

Heiros Gamos

http://hg.org

Exhaustive collection of legal and government listings with links to directories of associations, legal vendors and web sites on hundreds of subjects, but its poor design makes it hard to use.

IBM Intellectual Property Network

http://patent.womplex.ibm.com

Searches US Patent and Trademark files.

IGnet: Internet for Federal IG Community

www.ignet.gov

Collection of reports and information from the Inspector General of as many as 60 federal agency departments.

Inter-Parliamentary Union

www.ipu.org

Links to parliamentary web sites around the world – elections information.

International Agencies & Information on the Web

www.lib.umich.edu/libhome/
Documents.center/intl.html

International and inter-governmental web sites lists.

International Documents Task Force (IDTF)

www.indiana.edu/%7Elibgpd/idtf

Documents from international organizations and governments, with links.

Internet Law Library

http://law.house.gov

Congressional resources for lawyers.

Law Guru

www.lawguru.com

An attorney's group launched Law Guru in an effort to become a meta-site for legal information on the web. It's loaded with good legal info.

Law Library of Congress

http://lcweb2.loc.gov/glin/
lawhome.html

Law library of the Library of Congress.

Law.com / Counsel Connect

www.law.com/resources

An excellent legal resource site, but membership is required. Formerly Counsel Connect.

Legal Information Institute

www.law.cornell.edu

One of the best legal libraries online. (Cornell's law school page).

Library of Congress

www.loc.gov

The main site for the Library of Congress.

Litigator's Internet Resource Guide

www.llrx.com/columns/litigat.htm

A tremendous collection of federal, state and local court rules online, from law firm research librarian Genie Tyburski.

Meta-Index for US Legal Research

http://gsulaw.gsu.edu/metaindex

Central clearinghouse for circuit court opinions.

Monthly Estimates of the US Population

www.census.gov/population/
estimates/nation/intfile1-1.txt

Downloadable text files of population estimate information.

NASIRE: National Association of State Information Resource Executives (NASIRE)

www.nasire.org

State-specific information on state government innovations.

National Archives & Records Administration

www.nara.gov

Presidential libraries of all past American presidents.

National Atlas of the United States of America

www-atlas.usgs.gov

Official maps.

National Center for Health Statistics

www.cdc.gov/nchs

Center for Disease Control statistics collection.

National Council of State Legislators

www.ncsl.org/public/sitesleg.htm

Search for state legislation.

National Journal's Cloakroom

www.cloakroom.com

Extensive coverage of congress and politics.

Fee-Based Site

National Science Foundation

www.nsf.gov

This site is focused mainly on the bureaucratic structure of this government agency; but on the interior pages you'll find a wealth of scientific information. Recommended visit: the external links page to National Science Foundation-funded sites – here you'll find the research, supercomputing, and engineering centers that do the work.

National Technical Information Service (NTIS)

www.ntis.gov

Federal government reports related to technology and science.

NTSB (National Traffic Safety Board) Aviation Accident/Incident Database

http://nasdac.faa.gov/asp/
asy_ntsb.asp

Transportation Safety Board's database of aircraft accidents.

NYU EDGAR Development Site

http://edgar.stern.nyu.edu

SEC filings found on EDGAR are also found here,but it allows you to search with some added features like by Zacks Industry Code, which is not available on the SEC site.

Oyez Oyez Oyez

http://oyez.nwu.edu

Information about Supreme Court cases, including some actual proceedings in Real Audio format.

PACER - Directory of Electronic Public Access Services

www.uscourts.gov/PubAccess.html

Federal court's electronic bulletin board of docket numbers, case summaries and opinions.

Regions & Countries Information

www.ita.doc.gov/ita_home/
itacnreg.html

US Dept. of Commerce International Trade Administration's country and regional resource site, good for trade-related issues.

Right Site, The

www.easidemographics.com

This site takes Census data and repackages it into regional information and is a great resource for numbers and info about communities.

Social Law Library

www.socialaw.com

A great legal research site including international law sites.

STAT-USA

www.stat-usa.gov

Comprehensive collection of federal statistics from all agencies.

Fee-Based Site

State & Local Government on the 'Net

www.piperinfo.com/state/
states.html

State government resources as well as local ones.

State Court Locator, The

www.law.vill.edu

State court locator. Can also be found at http://vls.law.vill.edu/compass/.

State Poverty Rates

www.census.gov/hhes/poverty/
poverty96/pv96state.html

HTML tables of US Census information.

State Web Locator, The

www.law.vill.edu

State web locator. Can also be found at www.infoctr.edu/swl.

StateLaw: State & Local Government - Executive, Legislative & Judicial Information

www.washlaw.edu

State Internet resources, legislation, courts, statutes, etc.

Stateline.Org

www.stateline.org

The Pew Center on the States, tracking policy developments on a state-by-state basis.

StateSearch - Sponsored by NASIRE

www.nasire.org/statesearch

The state government search site.

Statistical Abstract of the US

www.census.gov/statab/www

US Government's statistical resource.

Superintendant of Documents Home Page (Government Printing Office)

www.access.gpo.gov/su_docs/
index.html

The Government Printing Office.

System for Electronic Document Analysis & Retrieval (SEDAR)

www.sedar.com

Searches Canada's electronic securities documentation filing system. Also in French.

TaxWeb

www.taxweb.com

Consumer-oriented directory for federal and state information.

Thomas - US Congress on the Internet

http://thomas.loc.gov

Search for federal legislation.

United Nations System

www.unsystem.org

Foreign government resources.

US Census Bureau

www.census.gov

Clearinghouse for statistics, includes the current edition of the Statistical Abstracts, a great reference book. Search by city, state, ZIP Code or specific industries.

US Federal Government Agencies Directory

www.lib.lsu.edu/gov/fedgov.html

Links to hundreds of federal government Internet sites.

US Government Information

www-libraries.colorado.edu/ps/
gov/us/federal.htm

A clearinghouse of government sites

US Postal Service ZIP Code Lookup

www.usps.gov/ncsc/lookups/
lookups.htm

US Postal Services's ZIP Code lookup service.

US Securities & Exchange Commission (SEC)

www.sec.gov

One of the top government sites, let's you track information about publicly held companies.

US State and Local Government Gateway

www.statelocal.gov

Excellent collection of information on state and local resources found on federal government web sites.

US State Department: Regions

www.state.gov/www/regions.html

Information and news from around the world.

USADATA

www.usadata.com/usadata/market

Market data by community and region.

USGS National Mapping Information

http://mapping.usgs.gov

The federal government's site with global land information, online data, and map ordering.

VitalChek - State Map

www.vitalchek.com/states.asp

Vital records by state.

Fee-Based Site

Web sites on National Parliaments

www.soc.umn.edu/~sssmith/
Parliaments.html

Resource of foreign government sites.

Welcome To The White House

www.whitehouse.gov

The White House's site.

White House - Economic Statistics Briefing Room

www.whitehouse.gov/fsbr/esbr.html

White House's statistical clearinghouse.

White House: The Economic Statistics Briefing Room

www.whitehouse.gov/fsbr/esbr.html

Clearinghouses of statistical resources hosted by the White House.

WWW Virtual Library: Law: State Government

www.law.indiana.edu/law/
v-lib/states.html

A collection of state government resources.

Yahoo! Government: Countries

www.yahoo.com/Government/Countries

A collection of foreign government resources reports and information from the Inspector General of as many as 60 federal agency departments.

Yahoo! Government: US Government: US States

www.yahoo.com/Government/U_S__G
overnment/State_Government

A collection of US government resources.

People Finders

Acxiom DataQuick

www.dataquick.com

Commercial service indexing real estate & assessor information.

Ancestry.com

www.ancestry.com

Geneology company; offers SSN's death index free.

Fees for Some Content

Biographical Dictionary

www.s9.com/biography/search.html

Biographies of more than 22,000 notable men and women who have shaped our world from ancient times to present day.

Biographical Dictionary

www.s9.com/biography

For a collection of biographies of well-known people.

Biorgraphy.com

www.biography.com/find/find.html

Searchable database of 20,000 famous people, from the folks who produce the TV show Biography.

Black Book Online

www.crimetime.com/online.html

Robert Scott's excellent site geared to investigators includes links to sites for reverse directories and other phone books, state and federal records online, non-profit sites, verdict and settlement sites, and some pay databases.

BRB Publications

www.brbpub.com

Public records research resources and retrievers.

California Sex Offenders

www.sexoffenders.net

Site that tracks sex offenders who have been released into communities.

Chiefs of State and Cabinet Members

www.odci.gov/cia/publications/chiefs

The CIA maintains an excellent comprehensive database of world leaders, allowing you to find out who's running or ruining what country.

Church Family History Library

www.lds.org/en/2-Family_History/Family_History_Main.html

Good starting place for genealogical research. Find search strategies, forms, and directions to access LDS' reasonably priced Family Searcher and Personal Ancestral File databases, available from the Church or its local Family History Centers..

CompData

http://wcab.net

EDEX data about Workers' Compensation claims.

Deep Data Investigative Sources

www.deepdata.com

Public Record Search Center.

Fee-Based Site

EXPERTCENTRAL

www.expertscentral.com

Find experts in 17 categories including legal, health, medicine and the Internet.

Fees for Some Content

EXPERTCITY

www.expertcity.com

This free site lets you choose from a roster of accredited and rated experts.

Government Records.com

www.governmentrecords.com

Aristotle Industries' new web site with extensive voter records and other public records-oriented databases for sale.

Greek Net

http://greeknet.hypermart.net/links/Directory

Directory from fraternity and sorority resources.

Greek Zone

www.greekzone.com

'Additional Fraternity and sorority resources.

GreekPages University

www.greekpages.com

This collection of resources lets you find folks in sororities and fraternities.

Greekspot.com

www.greekspot.com/directory.htm

A master directory of fraternities and sororities.

Harris County Appraisal District

www.hcad.org

Example of property records on the Web.

INFO-USA

www.infousa.com

Another excellent reverse phone book.

INFOBEL

www.infobel.be

An excellent international phone book from Belgium, especially strong for Europe.

Information & Privacy, The Office of

www.usdoj.gov/oip/oip.html

Various filtering agents and bots.

International Association of Assessing Officers (IAAO)

www.iaao.org

Education and trade arm for tax assessors worldwide; also, web site links.

IQ DATA Systems

www.iqdata.com

Commercial service indexing real estate & assessor information.

Fee-Based Site

KnowX.com

www.knowx.com

Real estate assessor and recorder information.

Montgomery Central Appraisal District

www.mcad-tx.org

Example of property records on the Web.

Nedsite

www.nedsite.nl/search/people.html

An excellent collection of sites and has country-specific phone books.

New York State Education Dept. Online License Verification

www.nysed.gov/dpls.opnme.html

Online database of NY's professional license lists.

Online Athens: Police Blotter

www.onlineathens.com/news/blotter.shtml

Athens (GA) Daily News police blotter.

Public Interest Research Groups (PIRG)

www.pirg.org/reports

Click on Consumer to find consumer protection information, environmental concerns, dangerous toys, tobacco, etc.

Public Interest Research Groups Credit Bureaus

www.pirg.org/reports/consumer/credit

PIRG carries issues about credit bureaus.

Public Record Retriever Network

www.brbpub.com/prrn

Record retrieval companies and public record news.

Superior Information Services LLC

www.superiorinfo.com

Mid-Atlantic states regional provider of public records data .

TELDIR

www.teldir.com

A strong international phonebook, sorted by country.

US Bankruptcy Court for the Western District of North Carolina

www.ncbankruptcy.org

North Carolina bankruptcy court.

Utah Dept. of Commerce Div. of Occupational & Professional Licensing

www.commerce.state.ut.us/web/commerce/DOPL/dopl1.htm

Online database of Utah's professional license listings.

Vital Records Information, United States

http://vitalrec.com/index.html

Vital records for the United States.

VitalChek

www.vitalchek.com

A site that allows you to get copies of actual vital records.

WEBSEARCH

http://websearch.about.com

About.com's Chris Sherman has compiled a great collection of people-finding links.

West Deptford, NJ, Police Blotter Report

www.westdeptford.com/blotter.htm

Sample of a town PD web site.

World Biographical Index

www.biblio.tu%2Dbs.de

Based on the 5th edition of the World Biographical Index, this site containing about 2.4 million short biographical entries of prominent individuals.

Privacy

AIXS.Net

www.aixs.net/aixs

A privacy tool to search anonymously.

Anonymizer

www.anonymizer.com

Tool for anonymous remailing.

Fees for Some Content

CDT - Internet Family Emporwerment White Paper

www.cdt.org/speech/empower.html

A white paper on Internet Parental Empowerment Tools by the Center for Democracy and Technology.

Center for Democracy & Technology

www.cdt.org

Center for Democracy and Technology's excellent privacy site, which allows you to find out what people know about you when you visit their site.

CyberAngels.org Home Page

www.cyberangels.org

Safety and educational programming.

Electronic Privacy Information Center

www.epic.org

Privacy activist group.

Eternity Usenet

www.cyberspace.org/~adam

Anonymizer tool for searching.

HNC Software Inc.

www.hncs.com

Check fraud detection system software and other products.

Fee-Based Site

Junkbusters

www.junkbusters.com/ht/en/cookies.html

Explanation of cookie technology and privacy ramifications.

KidsCom: Play Smart, Stay Safe & Have Fun!

www.kidscom.com

Children's resources and entertainment.

Lucent's Proxymate

www.proxymate.com

An anonymizer-style tool, for free, from Lucent Technologies.

MagusNet Public Proxy Server

http://proxy.magusnet.com/proxy.html

An anonymizer-style searching tool.

National Fraud Information Center (NFIC)

www.fraud.org

Fights telemarketing fraud.

Pretty Good Privacy (PGP)

www.nai.com/asp_set/products/tns/intro.asp

An encryption tool to protect your privacy.

Privacy Rights Clearinghouse

www.privacyrights.org

An activist site with excellent backgrounders on privacy issues.

Privacy Times

www.privacytimes.com

Privacy newsletter.

Fee-Based Site

QSpace Inc

www.qspace.com

An Oakland, CA company, allows you to fill out a form and within minutes you get your credit file on screen.

Fee-Based Site

Rewebber

www.rewebber.de

A Danish anonymizer - free.

Robert Brooks' Cookie Taste Test

www.geocities.com/SoHo/4535/cookie.html

Explanation of "cookies."

The Lucent Personalized Web Assistant: Proxy Home Page

http://lpwa.com:8000

Let's you surf anonymously, protecting your privacy while you are on the Web.

Welcome to Engage Technologies Accipter

www.engagetech.com

A sophisticated marketing technology used by advertisers.

Notes

Notes

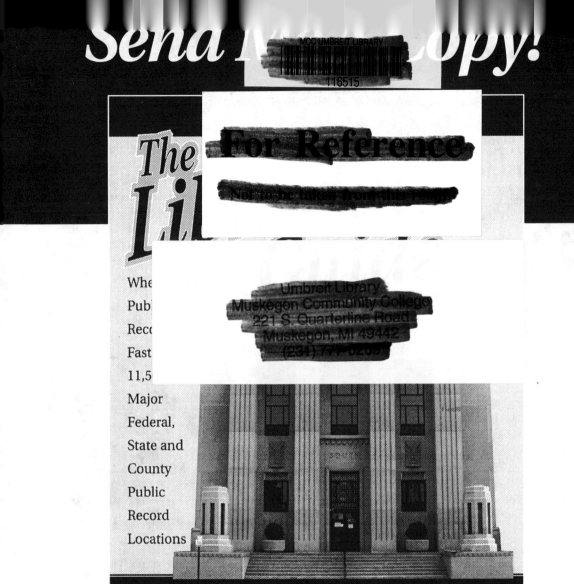